THE YEARS OF EXTERMINATION

Nazi Germany and the Jews, 1939–1945

SAUL FRIEDLÄNDER

HarperCollins*Publishers*

Designed by Joseph Rutt

Library of Congress Cataloging-in-Publication Data

Friedländer, Saul.
The years of extermination : Nazi Germany and the Jews, 1939–1945 /
Saul Friedländer.—1st ed.

p. cm.

Includes bibliographic references and index.

ISBN: 978-0-06-019043-9
ISBN-10: 0-06-019043-4

1. Holocaust, Jewish (1939–1945)—Germany. 2. Jews—Persecutions—Germany—History—20th century. 3. Jews—Germany—History—1933–1945. 4. Germany—Politics and government—1933–1945. 5. Germany—History—1933–1945. 6. Germany—Ethnic relations.

D804.3.F753 2006
940.53'18—dc22 2006048982

07 08 09 10 11 NMSG/RRD 10 9 8 7 6 5

To Yonatan

THE YEARS OF EXTERMINATION

Also by Saul Friedländer

Nazi Germany and the Jews
Pius XII and the Third Reich
Kurt Gerstein
Prelude to Downfall: Hitler and the United States
History and Psychoanalysis
Reflections of Nazism
When Memory Comes
Memory, History, and the Extermination of the Jews

The struggle to save myself is hopeless. . . . But that's not important. Because I am able to bring my account to its end and trust that it will see the light of day when the time is right. . . . And people will know what happened. . . . And they will ask, is this the truth? I reply in advance: No, this is not the truth, this is only a small part, a tiny fraction of the truth. . . . Even the mightiest pen could not depict the whole, real, essential *truth.*

—Stefan Ernest, "The Warsaw Ghetto,"
written in hiding in 1943 on the "Aryan"
side of Warsaw.

Contents

Acknowledgments

This work has greatly benefited from the research funds provided by the "1939 Club" chair at UCLA and, in particular, from an incomparably generous fellowship from the John D. and Catherine T. MacArthur Foundation. To the "1939 Club" and to the MacArthur Foundation I wish to express my deepest gratitude.

I wish, first, to mention in fond memory the friends, all departed now, with whom I shared many thoughts about the history dealt with here: Léon Poliakov, Uriel Tal, Amos Funkenstein, and George Mosse.

Professor Michael Wildt (Hamburg Institut für Sozialforschung) had the kindness to read an almost final version of the manuscript; I feel very grateful for his comments: He drew my attention to recent German research and mainly helped me to avoid some mistakes, as did Dr. Dieter Pohl of the Institute of Contemporary History (Munich) and Professor Eberhard Jäckel (University of Stuttgart). I am equally thankful to Professors Omer Bartov (Brown University), Dan Diner (Hebrew University, Jerusalem, and the Simon Dubnow Institute, Leipzig) and Norbert Frei (Jena University) for having commented on various parts of the text.

Notwithstanding my recurring doubts, I was encouraged over time to complete this project by many colleagues, particularly professors Yehuda Bauer, Dov Kulka, and Steve Aschheim (all from the Hebrew University, Jerusalem), Professor Shulamit Volkov (Tel Aviv University), Professor Philippe Burrin (director of the Graduate Institute of International Studies in Geneva), and the late Dr. Sybil Milton, a wonderful scholar and the most selfless of colleagues, whose untimely passing was a grievous loss.

Of course, as the formula goes, the responsibility for the (certainly many) mistakes remaining in the text is solely mine.

I remained dependent throughout this entire project upon a succession of graduate students. All should be thanked here in the persons of my most recent research assistants: Deborah Brown, Amir Kenan, and Joshua Sternfeld.

Both Susan H. Llewellyn and David Koral of HarperCollins have applied their considerable linguistic skills to the copyediting of this manuscript. I am very grateful to them and, of course, most thankful for the constant attention and encouragement provided by my editor, Hugh Van Dusen. The assistant editor, Rob Crawford, has shown patience beyond the call of duty in dealing with my frequent inquiries. And, to my agents and friends, Georges, Anne, and Valerie Borchardt, I wish to express again my heartfelt thanks. My personal and professional relations with Georges and Anne go back to the publication of my first book in the United States (*Pius XII and the Third Reich*), in 1966.

This work owes more than I can say to Orna Kenan's emotional and intellectual support; she shares my life. The book is dedicated to my newly born fourth grandson.

Introduction

David Moffie was awarded his degree in medicine at the University of Amsterdam on September 18, 1942. In a photograph taken at the event, Professor C. U. Ariens Kappers, Moffie's supervisor, and Professor H. T. Deelman stand on the right of the new MD, and assistant D. Granaat stands on the left. Another faculty member, seen from the back, possibly the dean of the medical school, stands just behind a large desk. In the dim background, the faces of some of the people crowded into the rather cramped hall, family members and friends no doubt, are barely discernible. The faculty members have donned their academic robes, while Moffie and Granaat wear tuxedos and white ties. On the left side of his jacket Moffie displays a palm-size Jewish star with the word *Jood* inscribed on it. Moffie was the last Jewish student at the University of Amsterdam under German occupation.[1]

The usual terms of praise and thanks were certainly uttered according to academic ritual. We do not know whether any other comments were added. Shortly thereafter Moffie was deported to Auschwitz-Birkenau. He survived, as did 20 percent of the Jews of Holland; according to the same statistics, therefore, most of the Jews present at the ceremony did not.

The picture raises some questions. How, for example, could the ceremony have taken place on September 18, 1942, when Jewish students were excluded from Dutch universities as of September 8? The editors of *Photography and the Holocaust* found the answer: The last day of the 1941–42 university year was Friday, September 18, 1942; the 1942–43 semester started on Monday, September 21. The three-day break allowed Moffie to receive his degree before the ban on Jewish students became mandatory.[2]

Actually the break was limited to precisely one weekend (Friday, September 18–Monday, September 21), meaning that the university authorities agreed to use the administrative calendar against the intention of the German decree. This decision signaled an attitude widespread at Dutch universities since the fall of 1940; the photograph documents an act of defiance, on the edge of the occupier's laws and decrees.

There is more. The deportations from Holland started on July 14, 1942. Almost daily Germans and local police arrested Jews on the streets of Dutch cities to fill the weekly quotas. Moffie could not have attended this public academic ceremony without having received one of the seventeen thousand special (and temporary) exemption certificates the Germans allocated to the city's Jewish Council. The picture thus indirectly evokes the controversy surrounding the methods used by the heads of the council to protect—for a time at least—some of the Jews of Amsterdam while abandoning the great majority to their fate.

In the most general terms we are witnessing a common enough ceremony, easy to recognize. Here, in a moderately festive setting, a young man received official confirmation that he was entitled to practice medicine, to take care of the sick, and as far as humanly possible, to use his professional knowledge in order to restore health. But, as we know, the *Jood* pinned to Moffie's coat carried a very different message: Like all members of his "race" throughout the Continent, the new MD was marked for murder.

Faintly seen, the *Jood* does not appear in block letters or in any other commonly used script. The characters were specially designed for this particular purpose (and similarly drawn in the languages of the countries of deportation: *Jude, Juif, Jood,* and so on) in a crooked, repulsive, and vaguely threatening way, intended to evoke the Hebrew alphabet and yet remain easily decipherable. And it is in this inscription and its peculiar design that the situation represented in the photograph reappears in its quintessence: The Germans were bent on exterminating the Jews as individuals, and on erasing what the star and its inscription represented—"the Jew."

Here we perceive but the faintest echo of a furious onslaught aimed at eliminating any trace of "Jewishness," any sign of the "Jewish spirit," any remnant of Jewish presence (real or imaginary) from politics, society, culture, and history. To this end the Nazi campaign deployed, in the Reich and throughout occupied Europe, propaganda, education, research, publications, films, proscriptions, and taboos in all social and cultural domains, in fact every existing method of erasure and stamping out, from the rewriting of religious texts or opera libretti tainted by any speck of Jewishness to the renaming of streets carrying the names of Jews, from the banning of music or literary works written by Jewish artists and authors to the destruction of monuments, from the elimination of "Jewish science" to the "cleansing" of libraries, and, as foretold by Heinrich Heine's famous dictum, from the burning of books to that of human beings.

I

The "history of the Holocaust" cannot be limited only to a recounting of German policies, decisions, and measures that led to this most systematic and sustained of genocides; it must include the reactions (and at times the initiatives) of the surrounding world and the attitudes of the victims, for the fundamental reason that the events we call the Holocaust represent a totality defined by this very convergence of distinct elements.

This history is understandably written as German history in many cases. The Germans, their collaborators, and their auxiliaries were the instigators and prime agents of the policies of persecution and extermination and, mostly, of their implementation. Furthermore, German documents dealing with these policies and measures became widely accessible after the Reich's defeat. These immense troves of material, hardly manageable even before access to former Soviet and Eastern bloc archival holdings, have, since the late 1980s, naturally reinforced still further the focus on the German dimension of this historiography. And, in the eyes of most historians, an inquiry concentrating on the German facet of this history seems more open to conceptualization and to comparative forays, less "parochial" in other words, than whatever can be written from the viewpoint of the victims or even that of the surrounding world.

This German-centered approach is of course legitimate within its limits, but the history of the Holocaust requires, as mentioned, a much wider range. At each step, in occupied Europe, the execution of German measures depended on the submissiveness of political authorities, the assistance of local police forces or other auxiliaries, and the passivity or support of the populations and mainly of the political and spiritual elites. It also depended on the willingness of the victims to follow orders in the hope of alleviating German strictures or gaining time and somehow escaping the inexorable tightening of the German vise. Thus the history of the Holocaust should be both an integrative and an integrated history.

* * *

No single conceptual framework can encompass the diverse and converging strands of such a history. Even its German dimension cannot be interpreted from one single conceptual angle. The historian faces the interaction of very diverse long- or short-term factors that can each be defined and interpreted; their very convergence, however, eludes an overall analytic category. A host of concepts have surfaced over the last six decades, only to be discarded a few years later, then rediscovered, and so on, particularly in regard to Nazi policies per se. The origins of the "Final Solution" have been attributed to a "special course" (*Sonderweg*) of German history, a special brand of German anti-Semitism, racial-biological thinking, bureaucratic politics, totalitarianism, fascism, modernity, a "European civil war" (seen from the Left and from the Right), and the like.

Reviewing these concepts would demand another book.[3] In this introduction I will essentially limit myself to defining the road taken here. Nonetheless, a few remarks regarding two contrary trends in the present historiography of the Third Reich in general and of the "Final Solution" in particular become necessary at this point.

The first trend considers the extermination of the Jews as representing, in and of itself, a major goal of German policies, whose study, however, requires new approaches: the activities of midlevel actors, the detailed analysis of events in limited areas, specific institutional and bureaucratic dynamics—all meant to throw some new light on the workings of the entire system of extermination.[4] This approach has added greatly to our knowledge and understanding: I have integrated many of its findings into my own more globally oriented inquiry.

The other trend is different. It has helped, over the years, to uncover many a new trail. Yet, in regard to the study of the Holocaust, each of these trails eventually branches out from the same starting point: *The persecution and extermination of the Jews of Europe was but a secondary consequence of major German policies pursued toward entirely different goals.* Among these, the ones most often mentioned include a new economic and demographic equilibrium in occupied Europe by murdering surplus populations, ethnic reshuffling and decimation to facilitate German colonization in the East, and the systematic plunder of the Jews in order to facilitate the waging of the war without putting too heavy a material burden on German society or, more precisely, on Hitler's national-racial state (*Hitlers Volksstaat*). Notwithstanding the vistas sporadically opened by such studies, their general thrust is manifestly incompatible with the central postulates underlying my own interpretation.[5]

In this volume, as in *The Years of Persecution*, I have chosen to focus on the centrality of ideological-cultural factors as the prime movers of Nazi policies in regard to the Jewish issue, depending of course on circumstances, institutional dynamics, and essentially, for the period dealt with here, on the evolution of the war.[6]

The history we are dealing with is an integral part of the "age of ideology" and, more precisely and decisively, of its late phase: the crisis of liberalism in continental Europe. Between the late nineteenth century and the end of World War II, liberal society was attacked from the left by revolutionary socialism (which was to become Bolshevism in Russia and communism throughout the world), and by a revolutionary right that, on the morrow of World War I, turned into fascism in Italy and elsewhere, and into Nazism in Germany. Throughout Europe the Jews were identified with liberalism and often with the revolutionary brand of socialism. In that sense antiliberal and antisocialist (or anticommunist) ideologies, those of the revolutionary right in all its guises, targeted the Jews as representatives of the worldviews they fought and, more often than not, tagged them as the instigators and carriers of those worldviews.

In the atmosphere of national resentment following the defeat of 1918 and, later, as a result of the economic upheavals that shook the country (and the world), such an evolution acquired a momentum of its own in Germany. Yet, without the obsessive anti-Semitism and the personal impact of Adolf Hitler, first in the framework of his movement, then on the national scene after January 1933, the widespread German anti-Semitism of those years would probably not have coalesced into anti-Jewish political action and certainly not into its sequels.

The crisis of liberalism and the reaction against communism as ideological sources of anti-Semitism, pushed to their extreme on the German scene, became increasingly virulent throughout Europe, the Nazi message thus garnering a positive response from many Europeans and a considerable phalanx of supporters beyond the shores of the old Continent. Moreover, antiliberalism and anticommunism corresponded to the stances adopted by the major Christian churches, and traditional Christian anti-Semitism easily merged with and bolstered the ideological tenets of various authoritarian regimes, of fascist movements, and partly of some aspects of Nazism.

Finally, this very crisis of liberal society and its ideological underpinnings left the Jews increasingly weak and isolated throughout a continent where the progress of liberalism had allowed and fostered their emancipation and social mobility. Thus the ideological background here defined becomes the indirect link between the three main components of this history: National Socialist Germany, the surrounding European world, and the Jewish communities scattered throughout the Continent. However, notwithstanding the German evolution to which I briefly alluded, these background elements in no way suffice to address the specific course of events in Germany.

II

The peculiar aspects of the National Socialist anti-Jewish course derived from Hitler's own brand of anti-Semitism, from the bond between Hitler and all levels of German society, mainly after the mid-thirties, from the political-institutional instrumentalization of anti-Semitism by the Nazi regime and, of course, after September 1939, from the evolving war situation. In *The Years of Persecution*, I defined Hitler's brand of anti-Jewish hatred as "redemptive anti-Semitism"; in other words, beyond the immediate ideological confrontation with liberalism and communism, which in the Nazi leader's eyes were worldviews invented by Jews and for Jewish interests, Hitler perceived his mission as a kind of crusade to redeem the world by eliminating the Jews. The Nazi leader saw "the Jew" as the principle of evil in Western history and society. Without a victorious redeeming struggle, the Jew would ultimately dominate the world. This overall metahistorical axiom led to Hitler's more concrete ideological-political corollaries.

On a biological, political, and cultural level, the Jew strove to destroy the nations by spreading racial pollution, undermining the structures of the state, and, more generally, by heading the main ideological scourges of the nineteenth and twentieth centuries: Bolshevism, plutocracy, democracy, internationalism, pacifism, and sundry other dangers. By using this vast array of means and methods, the Jew aimed at achieving the disintegration of the vital core of all nations in which he lived—and particularly that of the German *Volk*—in order to accede to world domination. Since the establishment of the National Socialist regime in Germany, the Jew, aware of the danger represented by the awakening Reich, was ready to unleash a new world war to destroy this challenge to his own progress toward his ultimate aim.

These different levels of anti-Jewish ideology could be formulated and summed up in the tersest way: *The Jew was a lethal and active threat to all nations, to the Aryan race and to the German Volk.* The emphasis is not only on "lethal" but also—and mainly—on "active." While all other groups targeted by the Nazi regime (the mentally ill, "asocials" and homosexuals, "inferior" racial groups including Gypsies and Slavs) were essentially *passive* threats (as long as the Slavs, for example, were not led by the Jews), the Jews were the only group that, since its appearance in history, relentlessly plotted and maneuvered to subdue all of humanity.

This anti-Jewish frenzy at the top of the Nazi system was not hurled into a void. From the fall of 1941, Hitler often designated the Jew as the "world arsonist." In fact the flames that the Nazi leader set alight and fanned burned as widely and intensely as they did only because, throughout Europe and beyond, for the reasons previously mentioned, a dense underbrush of ideological and cultural elements was ready to catch fire. Without the arsonist the fire would not have started; without the underbrush it would not have spread as far as it did and destroyed an entire world. It is this constant interaction between Hitler and the system within which he ranted and acted that will be analyzed and interpreted, as it was in *The Years of Persecution*. Here, however, the system is not limited to its German components but penetrates all the nooks and crannies of European space.

For the Nazi regime the anti-Jewish crusade also offered a number of pragmatic benefits at a political-institutional level. *For a regime dependent on constant mobilization, the Jew served as the constant mobilizing myth.* The anti-Jewish drive became ever more extreme along with the radicalization of the regime's goals and then with the extension of the war. It is in this context that we shall be able to locate the emergence of the "Final Solution." As we shall see, Hitler himself modulated the campaign against the Jew according to tactical goals; but once the first intimations of defeat appeared, the Jew became the core of the regime's propaganda to sustain the *Volk* in what soon appeared as a desperate struggle.

As a result of the mobilizing function of the Jew, the behavior of many ordinary German soldiers, policemen, or civilians toward the Jews they encountered, mistreated, and murdered was not necessarily the result of a deeply ingrained and historically unique German anti-Jewish passion, as has been argued by Daniel Jonah Goldhagen;[7] nor was it mainly the result of a whole range of common social-psychological reinforcements, constraints, and group dynamical processes, independent of ideological motivations, as suggested by Christopher R. Browning.[8]

The Nazi system as a whole had produced an "anti-Jewish culture," partly rooted in historical German and European Christian anti-Semitism but also fostered by all the means at the disposal of the regime and propelled to a unique level of incandescence, with a direct impact on collective and individual behavior. "Ordinary Germans" may have been vaguely aware of the process or, more plausibly, they may have internalized anti-Jewish images and beliefs without recognizing them as an ideology systematically exacerbated by state propaganda and all the means at its disposal.

Whereas the essential mobilizing function of the Jew was manipulated by the regime and its agencies, a second function—no less crucial—was more intuitively furthered. Hitler's leadership has often been defined as "charismatic," as based on that quasiprovidential role attributed to charismatic leaders by the populations that follow them. We shall return throughout the following chapters to the bond between the Nazi leader, the party, and the *Volk*. Suffice it to mention here that Hitler's personal hold on the vast majority of Germans stemmed from and expressed, as far as the content of his message went, three different and suprahistorical salvation creeds: The ultimate purity of the racial community, the ultimate crushing of Bolshevism and plutocracy, and the ultimate millennial redemption (borrowed from Christian themes known to all). In each of these traditions the Jew represented evil per se. In that sense Hitler's struggle turned him into a providential leader as, on all three fronts, he was fighting against the same metahistorical enemy: the Jew.

Within the German and European context (dominated by Germany), institutional struggles for power, generalized scrambling for spoils, and the impact of socially embedded vested interests mediated the ideological fervor. The first two elements have often been described and interpreted in any number of studies, and they will be thoroughly integrated in the forthcoming chapters; the third, however, less frequently mentioned, appears to me to be an essential aspect of this history.

In the highly developed German society and at least in part of occupied Europe, even Hitler's authority and that of the party leadership had, in the implementation of any policy, to take into account the demands of massive vested interests, whether those of party fiefdoms, industry, the churches, peasantry, small businesses, and the like. In other words the imperatives of anti-Jewish ideology had also to be attuned to a multiplicity of structural hurdles deriving from the very nature and dynamics of modern societies as such.

Nobody would dispute such an obvious point; its significance derives from an essential fact. Not one social group, not one religious community, not one scholarly institution or professional association in Germany and throughout Europe declared its solidarity with the Jews (some of the Christian churches declared that converted Jews were part of the flock, up to a point); to the contrary, many social constituencies, many power groups were directly involved in the expropriation of the Jews and eager, be it out of greed, for their wholesale disappearance. Thus *Nazi and related anti-Jewish policies could unfold to their most extreme levels without the interference of any major countervailing interests.*

III

On June 27, 1945, the world-renowned Jewish Austrian chemist Lise Meitner, who in 1939 had emigrated from Germany to Sweden, wrote to her former colleague and friend Otto Hahn, who had continued to work in the Reich. After mentioning that he and the scientific community in Germany had known much about the worsening persecution of the Jews, Meitner went on: "All of you have worked for Nazi Germany and never tried even some passive resistance. Certainly, to assuage your conscience, here and there you helped some person in need of assistance but you allowed the murder of millions of innocent people, and no protest was ever heard."[9] Meitner's cri de coeur, addressed through Hahn to Germany's most prominent scientists, none of them active party members, none of them involved in criminal activities, could have applied as well to the entire intellectual and spiritual elite of the Reich (with some exceptions, of course) and to wide segments of the elites in occupied or satellite Europe. And what applied to the elites applied more easily (again, with exceptions) to the populations. In this domain, as already mentioned, the Nazi system and the European context were tightly linked.

Regarding the attitudes and reactions of bystanders, the answers to some fundamental issues still remain partly unclear due either to the very nature of the questions or to the lack of essential documents. The perception of the events among the various populations of bystanders, for example, still remains elusive in part. Yet a vast amount of documentary material will show that while in Western Europe, in Scandinavia, and in the Balkans perceptions concerning the fate of the deported Jews may have been hazy until late 1943 or even early 1944, this was not the case in Germany itself and of course not in Eastern Europe either. Without preempting the forthcoming interpretations, there can be little doubt that by the end of 1942 or early 1943 at the latest, it became amply clear to vast numbers of Germans, Poles, Belorussians, Ukrainians, and Balts that the Jews were destined for complete extermination.

More difficult to grasp is the sequel of such information. As the war, the persecution, and the deportations moved into their ultimate phase, and as knowledge of the extermination spread ever more widely, anti-Semitism also grew throughout the Continent. Contemporaries noted this paradoxical trend, and its interpretation will become a dominant issue in part 3 of this volume.

Notwithstanding all the problems of interpretation, the attitudes and reactions of bystanders are amply documented. Confidential SD reports (by the Security Service, or *Sicherheitsdienst*, of the SS about the state of public opinion in the Reich) and reports of other state or party agencies offer an altogether reliable picture of German attitudes. Goebbels's diaries, one of the main sources concerning Hitler's constant obsession with the Jews, also deal systematically with German reactions to the Jewish issue as seen from the top of the regime, while soldiers' letters give a sample of the attitudes expressed at the bottom, so to speak. In most occupied or satellite countries, German diplomatic reports offered regular surveys concerning the state of mind of the populations in the face of the deportations, for example, as did official sources from the local administrations, such as the *rapports des préfets* in France. Individual reactions of bystanders, also as noted by Jewish diarists, will be part of the overall picture, and at times local diaries, followed throughout an entire period, as in the case of the Polish physician Zygmunt Klukowski, offer a vivid picture of an individual's insights into the changing overall scene.

Among the questions about the bystanders that continue to elude us as a result of the unavailability of essential documents, the attitude of the Vatican and, more specifically, that of Pope Pius XII remain to this day at the top of the list. Despite a vast secondary literature and the availability of some new documents, historians' inability to get access to the Vatican archives represents a major constraint. I shall deal with the pope's attitude as thoroughly as present documentation allows, but historians face an obstacle that could have been yet has not been eliminated.

In its own framework, separate from the detailed history of German policies and measures or from a recounting of the attitudes and reactions of bystanders, the history of the victims has been painstakingly recorded, first during the war years and, of course, since the end of the war. Though it did include surveys of the policies of domination and murder, it did so only sketchily. The emphasis from the outset aimed at the thorough collecting of documentary traces and testimonies regarding the life and death of the Jews: the attitudes and strategies of Jewish leadership, the enslavement and destruction of Jewish labor, the activities of various Jewish parties and political youth movements, the daily life in the ghettos, the deportations, armed resistance, and mass death in any one of the hundreds of killing sites spread throughout occupied Europe. Although soon after the war contentious debates and systematic interpretations became, together with the ongoing collection of traces, an integral part of this historiography, the history of the Jews has remained a self-contained world, mostly the domain of Jewish historians. Of course the history of the Jews during the Holocaust cannot be the history of the Holocaust; without it, however, the general history of these events cannot be written.[10]

In her highly controversial *Eichmann in Jerusalem*, Hannah Arendt put part of the responsibility for the extermination of the Jews of Europe squarely on the shoulders of the various Jewish leadership groups: the Jewish Councils, or *Judenräte*.[11] This largely unsubstantiated thesis turned Jews into collaborators in their own destruction. In fact any influence the victims could have on the course of their own victimization was marginal, but some interventions did take place (for better or worse) in a few national contexts. Thus, in several such settings, Jewish leaders had a limited yet not entirely insignificant influence (positive or negative) on the course of decisions taken by national authorities. This was noticeable, as we shall see, in Vichy; in Budapest, Bucharest, and Sofia; possibly in Bratislava; and of course in the relations between Jewish representatives and the Allied and neutral governments. Moreover, in a particularly tragic way, Jewish armed resistance (at times Jewish communist resistance groups, such as the small Baum group in Berlin), be it in Warsaw or Treblinka and then in Sobibor, may have brought about an accelerated extermination of the remaining Jewish slave labor force (at least until mid-1944) despite the acute need for workers in the increasingly embattled Reich.

In terms of its basic historical significance, the interaction between the Jews of occupied and satellite Europe, the Germans, and the surrounding populations took place at a more fundamental level. From the moment the extermination policy was launched, any steps taken by Jews in order to hamper the Nazi effort to eradicate every single one of them represented a direct countermove, be it on the tiniest individual scale: Bribing officials, policemen, or denouncers; paying families in order to hide children or adults; fleeing to woods or mountains; disappearing into small villages; converting; joining resistance movements; stealing food—anything that came to mind and led to survival meant setting an obstacle in the path of the German goal. It is at this microlevel that the most basic and ongoing Jewish interaction with the forces acting in the implementation of the "Final Solution" took place; it is at this microlevel that it mostly needs to be studied. And it is at this microlevel that documents abound.

The history of the destruction of the European Jews at the individual level can be reconstructed from the perspective of the victims not only on the basis of postwar testimonies (court depositions, interviews, and memoirs) but also owing to the unusually large number of diaries (and letters) written during the events and recovered over the following decades. These diaries and letters were written by Jews of all European countries, all walks of life, all age groups, either living under direct German domination or within the wider sphere of persecution. Of course the diaries have to be used with the same critical attention as any other document, especially if they were published after the war by the surviving author or by surviving family members. Yet, as a source for the history of Jewish life during the years of persecution and extermination, they remain crucial and invaluable testimonies.[12]

It is difficult to know whether during the early stages of the war most Jewish diarists started (or went on) writing in order to keep a record of the events for the sake of future history; but as the persecution turned harsher, most of them became aware of their role as chroniclers and memorialists of their epoch, as well as interpreters of and commentators on their personal destiny. Soon hundreds, probably thousands, of witnesses confided their observations to the secrecy of their private writings. Major events and much of the daily incidents, attitudes, and reactions of the surrounding world—which these diarists recorded—merged into an increasingly comprehensive albeit at times contradictory picture. They offer glimpses into attitudes at the highest political levels (in Vichy France and Romania, for example); they describe in great detail the initiatives and daily brutality of the perpetrators, the reactions of populations, and the life and destruction of their own communities, but they also record their own everyday world: Intense expressions of hope and illusions surface; the wildest rumors, the most fantastic interpretations of the events are considered plausible, at least for a while. For many the catastrophic events also become a test of their former beliefs, of the depth and significance of their ideological or religious commitments, of the values that guided their lives.

Beyond their general historical importance, such personal chronicles are like lightning flashes that illuminate parts of a landscape: They confirm intuitions; they warn us against the ease of vague generalizations. Sometimes they just repeat the known with an unmatched forcefulness. In the words of Walter Laqueur: "There are certain situations which are so extreme that an extraordinary effort is needed to grasp their enormity, unless one happened to be present."[13]

Up to this point the individual voice has been mainly perceived as a trace, a trace left by the Jews that bears witness to and confirms and illustrates their fate. But in the following chapters the voices of diarists will have a further role as well. By its very nature, by dint of its humanness and freedom, an individual voice suddenly arising in the course of an ordinary historical narrative of events such as those presented here can tear through seamless interpretation and pierce the (mostly involuntary) smugness of scholarly detachment and "objectivity." Such a disruptive function would hardly be necessary in a history of the price of wheat on the eve of the French Revolution, but it is essential to the historical representation of mass extermination and other sequences of mass suffering that "business as usual historiography" necessarily domesticates and "flattens."[14]

Each of us perceives the impact of the individual voice differently, and each person is differently challenged by the unexpected "cries and whispers" that time and again compel us to stop in our tracks. A few incidental reflections about already well-known events may suffice, either due to their powerful eloquence or their helpless clumsiness; often the immediacy of a witness's cry of terror, of despair, or of unfounded hope may trigger our own emotional reaction and shake our prior and well-protected representation of extreme historical events.

Let us return to Moffie's photograph, to the star sewed to his coat, with its repulsive inscription, and to its meaning: The new MD, like all the carriers of this sign, was to be wiped off the face of the earth. Once its portent is understood this photograph triggers disbelief. Such disbelief is a quasivisceral reaction, one that occurs before knowledge rushes in to smother it. "Disbelief" here means something that arises from the depth of one's immediate perception of the world, of what is ordinary and what remains "unbelievable." The goal of historical knowledge is to domesticate disbelief, to explain it away. In this book I wish to offer a thorough historical study of the extermination of the Jews of Europe, without eliminating or domesticating that initial sense of disbelief.

PART I

Terror

Fall 1939–Summer 1941

The sadistic machine simply rolls over us.

—Victor Klemperer,
December 9, 1939

CHAPTER I

September 1939–May 1940

"On Friday morning, September 1, the young butcher's lad came and told us: There has been a radio announcement, we already held Danzig and the Corridor, the war with Poland was under way, England and France remained neutral," Victor Klemperer wrote in his diary on September 3. "I said to Eva [that] a morphine injection or something similar was the best thing for us; our life was over."[1]

Klemperer was of Jewish origin; in his youth he converted to Protestantism and later on married a Protestant "Aryan." In 1935 he was dismissed from the Technical University in Dresden, where he taught Romance languages and literature; yet he went on living in the city, painstakingly recording what happened to him and around him. The British and French responses to the German attack remained uncertain for two days. "Annemarie brought two bottles of sparkling wine for Eva's birthday," Klemperer reported on September 4. "We drank one and decided to save the other for the day of the English declaration of war. So today it's the turn of the second one."[2]

In Warsaw, Chaim Kaplan, the director of a Hebrew school, was confident that this time Britain and France would not betray their ally as they had betrayed Czechoslovakia in 1938. On the first day of the war Kaplan sensed the apocalyptic nature of the new conflict: "We are witnessing the dawn of a new era in the history of the world. This war will indeed bring destruction upon human civilization. But this is a civilization that merits annihilation and destruction."[3] Kaplan was convinced that ultimately Nazism would be defeated but that the struggle would entail enormous losses for all.

The Hebrew school director also grasped the peculiar threat that the outbreak of the war represented for the Jews. In that same September 1 entry, he added, "As for the Jews, their danger is seven times greater. Wherever Hitler's foot treads there is no hope for the Jewish people." Kaplan quoted Hitler's notorious speech of January 30, 1939, in which the Nazi leader threatened the Jews with extermination in case of world war. The Jews were thus more eager than most to take a hand at common defense: "When the order was issued that all the inhabitants of the city must dig shelter trenches for protection from air raids, the Jews came in numbers. I, too, was among them."[4]

On September 8 the Wehrmacht occupied Lodz, the second largest Polish city: "All of a sudden the terrifying news: Lodz has been surrendered!" Dawid Sierakowiak, a Jewish youngster, barely fifteen, recorded. "All conversation stops; the streets grow deserted; faces and hearts are covered with gloom, cold severity and hostility. Mr. Grabinski comes back from downtown and tells how the local Germans greeted their countrymen. The Grand Hotel where the General Staff is expected to stay is bedecked with garlands of flowers: [Ethnic German] civilians—boys, girls—jump into the passing military cars with happy cries of *Heil Hitler*! Loud German conversations in the streets. Everything patriotically and nationalistically [German] that was hidden in the past now shows its true face."[5]

And in Warsaw again, Adam Czerniaków, an employee of the Polish foreign trade clearinghouse and an active member of the Jewish community, was organizing a Jewish Citizens Committee to work with the Polish authorities: "The Jewish Citizens Committee of the capital city of Warsaw," he wrote on September 13, "received legal recognition and was established in the Community building."[6] On September 23 he further noted: "Mayor Starzynski named me Chairman of the Jewish Community in Warsaw. A historic role in a besieged city. I will try to live up to it."[7] Four days later Poland surrendered.

I

The voices of many Jewish chroniclers will be heard in this volume, and yet all of them, as different as they may be, offer but a faint glimpse of the extraordinary diversity that was the world of European Jewry on the edge of destruction. After a steady decline of religious observance and an increase in the uncertainties of cultural-ethnic Jewishness, no obvious common denominator fitted the maze of parties, associations, groups, and some nine million individuals, spread all over the Continent, who nonetheless considered themselves Jews (or were considered as such). This diversity resulted from the impact of distinct national histories, the dynamics of large-scale migrations, a predominantly urban-centered life, a constant economic and social mobility driven by any number of individual strategies in the face of surrounding hostility and prejudice or, obversely, by the opportunities offered in liberal surroundings. These constant changes contributed to ever-greater fragmentation within the Diaspora, mainly during the chaotic decades that separated the late nineteenth century from the eve of World War II.

Where, for example, should one locate young Sierakowiak, the Lodz diarist? In his diary entries, started just before the beginning of the war, we discover an artisan family steeped in Jewish tradition, Dawid's own easy familiarity with this tradition and yet, at the same time, a strong commitment to communism ("The most important things are school work and studying Marxist theory," he wrote somewhat later).[8] Sierakowiak's divided world was not untypical of the multiple and at times contradictory allegiances coexisting in various segments in Jewish society on the eve of the war: Liberals of various nuances, Social Democrats, Bundists, Trotskyites, Stalinists, Zionists of all possible stripes and factions, religious Jews sparring in endless dogmatic or "tribal" feuds, and, until the end of 1938, a few thousand members of fascist parties, particularly in Mussolini's Italy.[9] Yet for many Jews, mainly in Western Europe, the main goal was social and cultural assimilation into surrounding society, while maintaining some elements of "Jewish identity," whatever that meant.

All these trends and movements should be multiplied by any number of national or regional idiosyncrasies and internecine struggles, and, of course, by a high count of sometimes notorious individual oddities. Thus the old and terminally ill Sigmund Freud, who had fled from Vienna to London after the Anschluss (the German annexation of Austria), still managed, shortly before the outbreak of the war, to witness the publication of his last work, *Moses and Monotheism*. On the eve of uncommon dangers sensed by all, the founder of psychoanalysis, who often had emphasized his own Jewishness, was depriving his people of a cherished belief: For him Moses was not a Jew.

Notwithstanding graver threats, Jews in many countries reacted with bitterness: "I read in the local press your statement that Moses was not a Jew," an anonymous writer thundered from Boston. "It is to be regretted that you would not go to your grave without disgracing yourself, you old nitwit. . . . It is to be regretted that the gangsters in Germany did not put you into a concentration camp, that's where you belong."[10]

Some basic distinctions nonetheless structured the European Jewish scene between the two world wars. The main dividing line ran between Eastern European and Western Jewries; though geographic to a point, its manifest expression was cultural. Eastern European Jewry (excluding after 1918 the Jews of Soviet Russia, who were developing according to the rules and opportunities offered by the new regime) encompassed in principle the communities of the Baltic countries, Poland, the eastern part of Czechoslovakia, Hungary (except for the large cities), and the eastern provinces of post-1918 Romania. The largely "Spanish" (Sephardi) Jews of Bulgaria, Greece, and parts of Yugoslavia represented a distinct world of their own. East European Jewry was less integrated into surrounding society, more religiously observant—at times still strictly Orthodox—often Yiddish-speaking, occasionally fluent in Hebrew. In short, it was more traditionally "Jewish" than its Western counterpart (although many Jews in Vilna, Warsaw, Lodz, and Iasi were no less "Western" than the Jews of Vienna, Berlin, Prague, and Paris). Economically the majority of Eastern Jewry often hovered on the edge of poverty, but nonetheless it nurtured a distinct, vibrant, and multifaceted Jewish life.[11]

In spite of such specific aspects, the Jews of Eastern Europe also underwent an accelerated process of acculturation and secularization during the interwar period. Yet, as historian Ezra Mendelsohn noted, "The process of acculturation did not contribute to the improvement of Jewish-gentile relations, thus giving the lie to the old accusation that the cultural separateness of East European Jewry was largely responsible for anti-semitism. . . . Such prejudices were particularly strong in Hungary, whose Jewish community was the most acculturated in East Central

Europe, and they were relatively weak in Lithuania, where the Jewish community was the most unacculturated."[12] This perplexing situation may in fact be explained in a wider context.

In Poland, Romania, and Hungary the Jews were numerically important minorities whose collective rights had been ensured, in principle, by the peace treaties following World War I and the "minority treaties" that, again in principle, had to be enforced by the League of Nations. International guarantees meant little to the exacerbated nationalism of the Poles, the Romanians, and the Hungarians, however: The Jews, like other minorities, were seen as obstacles to the full and unbridled national self-expression of the native population. Moreover, as the Jews represented a high percentage of the urban middle class, particularly in business and in the liberal professions but also among small artisans, the indigenous economic and social aspirations to middle-class status and professions forced a growing number of Jews out of these sectors of the economy, often with the help of various state measures. This trend, in turn, brought about a growing pauperization of these Jewish communities and created, mainly in Poland, a "surplus Jewish population" without any major outlets as the world economic crisis spread and most immigration doors closed.[13] Such negative evolution for the Jews as such and in terms of their relations with the environment was of course more intense in countries (or areas) of Eastern and East Central Europe undergoing rapid economic modernization (Poland, Romania, Hungary) than in those still deeply ensconced in a rural economy and traditional social structure (the Baltic countries, among others)—a distinction that may in fact explain the apparently paradoxical impact of acculturation on anti-Jewish feelings.[14]

Despite growing difficulties, however, mainly from the early 1930s onward, Jewish emigration from Eastern and Central Europe to the West went on. By dint of deep-seated cultural and social differences, estrangement between Western and Eastern Jews grew in both directions. For Eastern Jews the Westerners lacked *Yiddishkeit* (Jewishness), while for the Westerners, some idealization of an "authentic" Jewish life notwithstanding, the Eastern European Jews appeared "backward," "primitive," and increasingly a source of embarrassment and shame.[15]

The migration from Eastern Europe in the 1930s was compounded, mainly for the French, British, or Dutch communities, by the arrival of

Jewish refugees from Central Europe following Hitler's rise to power, first from Germany, then from Austria, and finally, after 1938, from the so-called German Protectorate of Bohemia and Moravia. Cultural antagonism was reinforced by the stark difference in economic status: The new immigrants and the refugees were usually bereft of financial means and economically marginalized in countries that had not yet recovered from the Depression. Native Jews, on the other hand, belonged, for the most part, to the middle class and even, not insignificantly, to the haute bourgeoisie; furthermore, increasingly frequent intermarriage had brought them closer to complete assimilation. As a result, throughout Western Europe many native Jews were ready to defend their own position in the face of growing anti-Semitism by sacrificing the interests of their newly arrived "brethren." The widespread urge was to send the immigrants on their way to some other country.

Whatever the degree of estrangement between Western and Eastern Jews on the eve of the war, there is little doubt that the stream of Jewish immigrants and refugees contributed to the surge of anti-Semitism in various Western European countries. But, as we shall see in the next chapters, Jewish immigration—those "hordes of *Ashkenazim*," as Jean Giraudoux, the well-known French playwright and minister of information at the outset of the war, dubbed the Jewish newcomers in his notorious *Pleins Pouvoirs*—was but one aspect of the darkening scene. In the most general terms the crisis of Jewry in the Western world was the direct outcome and expression of the crisis of liberal society as such and the rise of antidemocratic forces throughout the West. Needless to say, Nazi propaganda had found an ideal terrain for its anti-Semitic invective: The Jews were profiteers, plutocrats, and basically warmongers intent on dragging the European nations into another world conflict to further their own interests and eventually achieve world domination.

Actually, at the very time it was accused of the most heinous plots and political maneuvers, European Jewry—Jews wherever they lived, in fact—whatever the political, economic, or cultural achievement of some individuals, was without any significant collective political influence. This powerlessness was not recognized by the environment, and individual success was often interpreted as symptomatic of a collective Jewish drive to undermine and dominate surrounding society.

German Jewry, for example, financially significant, politically sophisticated, with some of its members wielding considerable influence on the mainstream liberal and the left-wing press, was effortlessly swept aside, together with its natural political allies—liberalism and social democracy—by the rise of Nazism.[16] In France, where a Jew, the Socialist Léon Blum, was elected prime minister in 1936, the anti-Semitic backlash had a far greater impact on the existence of the community than did Blum's short-term presence at the national helm. In stable democracies such as Great Britain and the United States, some Jews had access to centers of power; however, aware of the rise of anti-Semitism in their own countries and of the very limited scope of what could be achieved, they became reluctant to intervene in favor of the threatened communities of continental Europe, particularly in matters of immigration.

No less blatant than their powerlessness was the inability of most European Jews to assess the seriousness of the threats that they faced. During the first five years of Hitler's regime, barely one-third of German Jewry emigrated, even with the persecution and the indignities that descended on it month after month, year after year, starting in January 1933. The massive violence unleashed by the Nazis during the pogrom of November 9 and 10, 1938 (the so-called Night of Broken Glass, or Kristallnacht), became the very late moment of real awakening and led to desperate attempts to flee. Tens of thousands of Jews still managed to leave; for many, however, obtaining a visa or scraping together the necessary financial means for departure had become impossible. Hardly any Jews left Austria before the Anschluss in March 1938; nor did the Jews of Bohemia and Moravia before the German occupation in March 1939. Again, notwithstanding all starkly visible warning signals, notwithstanding Hitler's furious anti-Jewish threats and the steep increase of local hostility, the trickle of Jewish emigration from East Central Europe did not grow significantly, nor did almost any Jews leave Western Europe, before the German onslaught.

This apparent passivity in the face of mounting danger seems hard to understand in retrospect, although, as mentioned, the growing difficulties faced by Jewish emigrants explain it in part; a deeper reason may have come into play during the immediate prewar period and also in the weeks and months that followed. In the East, and mainly in the West (apart from Germany), most Jews entirely misjudged the degree of support they could expect from surrounding society and from national or local authorities in the face of a common enemy. In Warsaw in September 1939, let us recall, Kaplan and Czerniaków were proud participants in the common struggle.

In the West the misperception was more extreme, as we shall see. Moreover, mainly in Western Europe, the Jews believed in the validity of abstract principles and universal values, "in a world inhabited by civilized Cartesian phantoms";[17] in other words they believed in the rule of law, even in the rule of German law. Law offered a stable framework for facing ordeals and planning everyday life and long-term survival, in other words—the future. Thus the Jews were unaware that "the Jew" was outside the domain of natural and contractual ties and obligations, a situation that the German Jewish philosopher Hannah Arendt defined in her wartime essay "The Jew as Pariah" by borrowing a sentence from Franz Kafka's *The Castle*: "You are not of the castle, you are not of the village, you are nothing."[18]

Zionism, although growing in strength in the wake of German and European anti-Semitism, still remained a comparatively minor factor on the Jewish scene on the eve of the war. In May 1939, after the failure of the St. James Conference among the British, the Arabs, and the Zionists, London published a white paper that limited Jewish immigration to Palestine to 75,000 immigrants over the next five years and practically put an end to Zionist efforts to buy land in Eretz Israel. Zionist policy had never seemed so far from achieving its goals since the Balfour Declaration.

On August 16, 1939, the Twenty-first Zionist Congress convened in Geneva but was cut short by the impending outbreak of war. In his concluding address to the assembled delegates, on August 22, Chaim Weizmann, the president of the World Zionist Organization, spoke simply, in Yiddish: "There is darkness all around us, and we cannot see through the clouds. It is with a heavy heart that I take my leave. . . . If, as I hope, we are spared in life and our work continues, who knows—perhaps a new light will shine upon us from the thick black gloom. . . . We shall meet again. We shall meet again in common labor for our land and people. . . . There are some things that cannot fail to come to pass, things without which the world cannot be imagined. The remnant shall work on, fight on, live on until the dawn of better days. Toward that dawn I greet you. May we meet again in peace."[19]

II

Hitler's views about the newly conquered populations and territories in the East were tentatively outlined on September 29, in a conversation with one of his earliest companions, party chief ideologue Alfred Rosenberg: "The Poles" the Nazi leader declared "a thin Germanic layer, underneath frightful material. The Jews, the most appalling people one can imagine. The towns thick with dirt. He [Hitler] had learnt a lot in these past weeks. . . . What was needed now was a determined and masterful hand to rule. He wanted to split the territory into three strips: (1) Between the Vistula and the Bug: this would be for the whole of Jewry (including the Reich) as well as all other unreliable elements. Build an insuperable wall on the Vistula—even stronger than the one in the West [the Siegfried Line, which faced France]. (2) Create a broad cordon of territory along the previous frontier to be Germanized and colonized. This would be a major task for the nation: to create a German granary, a strong peasantry, to resettle good Germans from all over the world. (3) In between, a form of Polish state. The future would show whether after a few decades the cordon of settlement would have to be pushed farther forward."[20]

At this stage Hitler's plans included only half of former Poland, up to the Vistula and the Bug Rivers; the eastern part of the country had been invaded by the Soviet Union on September 17 in accordance with one of the main provisions of the secret protocol added to the German-Soviet pact of August 23, 1939. Moreover, the Germans had recognized Soviet "special interests" in the Baltic countries, Finland, and Bulgaria, and with regard to two Romanian provinces. For both sides the August treaty and a further secret arrangement signed on September 27 were tactical moves. Both Hitler and Stalin knew that a confrontation would ultimately come.[21] How long, though, the "truce" between National Socialism and Bolshevism would last was something that in September 1939 nobody could tell.

In a so-called peace offer during a festive Reichstag speech on October 6, Hitler indeed spoke of a territorial reorganization of those areas of Eastern Europe lying between the German border and the Soviet-German demarcation line. His settlement idea was to be based on the principle of nationalities and solve the problem of national minorities, including "in this context, the attempt to solve the Jewish problem."[22]

Reestablishing a Polish state was mentioned as a possibility. By then, however, Great Britain and France had become familiar with Hitler's tactics; the "peace offer" was rejected. The idea of some form of Polish sovereignty disappeared, and German-occupied Poland was further divided. The Reich annexed several areas along its eastern borders: a large region along the river Warthe (Reichsgau Wartheland, or Warthegau[23]), Eastern Upper Silesia (eventually part of Gau Upper Silesia), the Polish corridor with the city of Danzig (Gau Danzig–West Prussia) and a small stretch of territory south of East Prussia. A population of 16 million people was thus added to Germany, around 7.5 million of whom were Germans. After a brief interim plan to establish an autonomous "*Rest-Polen*" (rump Poland), the remaining Polish territory, which included the cities of Warsaw, Kraków, and Lublin, became the "General Government," an administrative unit of around 12 million people, governed by German officials and occupied by German troops. The General Government itself was subdivided into four districts: Warsaw, Radom, Kraków, and Lublin. The district of Galicia would be added in August 1941, after the German attack on the Soviet Union.

On October 17, freed from the peace proposal gimmick, the Nazi leader was back on track. One of the officers present at a meeting between Hitler and a group of military commanders and some high-ranking party members recorded his remarks about what was to be achieved in Poland: "The hard struggle of nationalities (*Volkstumskampf*) does not allow for any legal constraints. The methods will be incompatible with our principles. . . . Prevent Polish intelligentsia from becoming a leadership group . . . the old and the new territory should be cleansed of Jews, Polacks and rabble."[24]

The core notion was that of *Volkstumskampf*, the ethnic-racial struggle. It would be unhampered by "legal constraints," and the methods used would be "incompatible with our principles." On that essential point Hitler's policy departed radically from the goals of pan-German expansionism, widely accepted during the later years of the Wilhelmine empire. *Volkstumskampf* did not mean mere military victory and political domination; it aimed at the destruction of the vital sinews of the enemy national-racial community; in other words it implied mass murder.[25] Murder of well-defined groups for the sake of the racial supremacy of

Germandom became a legitimate instrument of policy. In occupied Poland two groups in particular would be targeted: Jews and "Polish elites": The murder of Jews was haphazard at this stage, that of Polish elites more systematic.

Some sixty thousand Poles whose names had been collected over the prewar years were to be eliminated;[26] the operation was partly camouflaged under directives for ensuring the security of the troops and, more generally, of the occupied territory. SS chief Heinrich Himmler chose the code name Tannenberg for the terror campaign; it evoked the victory of the German armies over the Russian forces at Tannenberg in East Prussia in 1914, and represented a symbolic retaliation against the Poles for the resounding defeat they had inflicted upon the Teutonic Knights at that same place in the early fifteenth century.[27]

Of course the basic order stemmed from Hitler. In July 1940 Reinhard Heydrich, since mid-September 1939 chief of the SS Main Office for the Security of the Reich (Reichssicherheitshauptamt, or RSHA), wrote to his SS colleague Kurt Daluege, the chief of the Order Police (Ordnungspolizei, or ORPO), that at the onset of the Polish campaign Hitler had given him an "extraordinarily radical . . . order for the liquidation of various circles of the Polish leadership, [killings] that ran into the thousands."[28] The same order was well known to the supreme command of the Wehrmacht (Oberkommando der Wehrmacht, or OKW), as confirmed by its chief, Gen. Wilhelm Keitel, to the head of military intelligence, Adm. Wilhelm Canaris, on September 12: "The matter [of the executions of Polish elites] had already been decided by the Führer; the commander of the Army [meant as "ground force"] had been informed that if the Wehrmacht refused to be involved, it had to accept the pressure of the SS and the Gestapo. Therefore, in each military district, civilian commanders would be appointed who would carry the responsibility for ethnic extermination" [added in pencil: political cleansing].[29]

In concrete terms Heydrich was in charge of Tannenberg, although several SS "Death's Head" units, under the command of the inspector of concentration camps, Theodor Eicke, independently took part in the "antiterror" campaign. Initially Heydrich had set up five "operational groups" (*Einsatzgruppen*) and one "special purpose operational group" for the murder campaign; ultimately seven *Einsatzgruppen* were involved. Some basic briefings took place on the eve of the attack. Then, on two occasions following the beginning of the campaign, Heydrich clearly defined the goals of the operation. "The leading strata of the population should be rendered harmless," he declared to his unit commanders, on September 7.[30] In another meeting, on September 27, he stated that merely 3 percent of the Polish elite still remained and that "they too should be rendered harmless."[31] Sometimes authorization for specific murder operations was requested in Berlin. Thus, at the end of 1939, for example, SS Brigadeführer Dr. Dr. Otto Rasch, commander of the Security Police and Security Service in Königsberg, inquired whether the Poles concentrated in the East Prussian camp of Soldau—mainly academics, businesspeople, teachers, and priests—could be "liquidated" on the spot instead of being deported. Heydrich agreed.[32]

On-the-spot executions were the most common practice, in retaliation against Polish civilians for attacks against German troops and as a revenge for Polish murders of *Volksdeutsche* (ethnic Germans) in the initial stages of the war—in Bromberg, for example; for the elimination of the local elites, however, other methods were also used. Thus, on November 3, 1939, 183 faculty members of the Jagellonian University in Kraków were summoned by the Gestapo, arrested, and deported to the Sachsenhausen concentration camp near Berlin. A few months later the older scholars were released and the younger ones sent to Dachau. By that time 13 of the imprisoned scholars had already died; none of the Jews was set free.[33]

III

Victory in the *Volkstumskampf* would be achieved by unbridled ruthlessness against non-Germanic races mainly in the East, and simultaneously, by an equally ruthless cleansing of the *Volksgemeinschaft* (racial community) inside the Germanic space. In line for eradication were the mentally ill, the Gypsies, and various other "racially foreign" elements still mingling with the *Volk*, although many of them had already been shipped to concentration camps.

Thousands of mental patients from asylums in Pomerania, East Prussia, and the Posen region in the Warthegau were eliminated soon after the German attack on Poland.[34] They were murdered without any medical coverup, independent of the "euthanasia" operation. On orders from

Himmler these patients were to be killed so that the buildings they lived in could be used for billeting Waffen SS soldiers and accommodating military casualties, possibly also in order to help in the resettlement of ethnic Germans from neighboring Eastern countries.[35]

Brought by train to Danzig-Neustadt, the Pomeranian patients were delivered to the Eimann SS Commando (named after its chief, Kurt Eimann), led to the surrounding woods, and shot. The bodies were thrown into graves previously dug by prisoners from the Stutthof concentration camp. Day in, day out, one batch of victims followed another; by midafternoon the "work" was over and the trucks that had brought the patients returned empty to the train station, except for the victims' clothes. Soon thereafter the concentration camp inmates who had dug the graves were themselves liquidated. The number of patients killed by Kurt Eimann's unit is not known precisely but in January 1941 its own report mentioned more than three thousand victims.[36]

Newborn children with serious defects had already been targeted by the eve of the war. The "euthanasia" program as such (identified by its code name, T4, in fact an acronym of Tiergartenstrasse 4, the address of the operation's headquarters in Berlin), which also extended to the adult population, secretly started in October 1939 on Hitler's order. It was established under the direct authority of "the Chancellory of the Führer of the National Socialist Party" (*Kanzlei des Führers der NSDAP*, or KdF), headed by Philipp Bouhler. Bouhler appointed the chief of Office II in the KdF, Viktor Brack, to be directly in charge of the killing operations. Under T4, some seventy thousand mental patients were assembled and murdered in six mental institutions between the beginning of the war and August 1941, when the framework of the extermination system changed.

From the end of the nineteenth century, eugenics had preached racial improvement by ways of various social and medical measures meant to bolster the biological health of the national community. Such theories and measures were as fashionable in the Anglo-Saxon and Scandinavian countries as they were in Germany. After the end of World War I, the view increasingly held in Weimar Germany argued that the biological depletion incurred by the Reich as a result of the war, and the economic difficulties that precluded any large-scale social policies to foster "positive" eugenic measures, reinforced the need for excluding the weak, the nonadapted, and diseased individuals from the biological pool of the *Volk*. Such notions became tenets of Nazi ideology during the "years of struggle."

Within months of his accession to the chancellorship, Hitler initiated a new law that ordered *compulsory* sterilization of individuals suffering from certain hereditary diseases. Yet, as late as September 1935, the Nazi leader refused to take the next "logical" step: murdering those individuals "unworthy of living." Negative reactions from the population and the churches could have been expected—a risk that Hitler was not yet prepared to take. At the end of 1938 and mainly in 1939, the Nazi leader's readiness to move ahead in this domain—as in that of foreign aggression—grew and, once the war started, the final authorization was given;[37] the crucial move from sterilization to straightforward group extermination was made.

In each of the medical institutions turned into killing centers, physicians and police officers were jointly in charge. The exterminations followed a standardized routine: The chief physician checked the paperwork; photos of the victims were taken; the inmates were then led to a gas chamber fed by containers of carbon monoxide and asphyxiated. Gold teeth were torn out and the bodies cremated.[38]

The killing of Jewish patients started in June 1940; they had previously been moved to a few institutions designated only for them.[39] They were killed without any formalities; their medical records were of no interest. Their death was camouflaged nonetheless: The Reichsvereinigung (the representative body of Jews in Germany) had to pay the costs of the victims' hospitalization in a fictitious institution: the "Cholm State Hospital," near Lublin. In August 1940 identical letters were sent from Cholm to the families of the patients, informing them of the sudden death of their relatives, all on the same date. The cause of death was left unspecified.[40]

IV

As we saw in the introduction, in Hitler's view the Jews were first and foremost an *active* (eventually deadly) threat. Yet, in the wake of the Polish campaign, the first German reactions to the sight of the *Ostjuden* (Eastern Jews) were more immediately dominated by disgust and utter contempt. On September 10 Hitler toured the Jewish quarter of Kielce; his press chief (*Reichspressechef*), Otto Dietrich, described the impression of the visit in a pamphlet published at the end of that year: "If we had once believed we knew the Jews, we were quickly taught otherwise here.... The appearance of these human beings is unimaginable.... Physical repulsion hindered us from carrying out our journalistic research.... The Jews in Poland are in no way poor, but they live in such inconceivable dirt, in huts in which no vagrant in Germany would spend the night."[41]

On October 7, referring to Hitler's description of his impressions from Poland, Joseph Goebbels, the propaganda minister, added: "The Jewish problem will be the most difficult to solve. These Jews are not human beings anymore. [They are] predators equipped with a cold intellect which have to be rendered harmless."[42] On November 2 Goebbels reported to Hitler about his own trip to Poland. "Above all," Goebbels recorded in his diary, "my description of the Jewish problem gets his [Hitler's] full approval. The Jew is a waste product. It is a clinical issue more than a social one."[43]

In Nazi parlance "to render harmless" meant killing. There was no such concrete plan in the fall of 1939, but murderous thoughts regarding the Jews were certainly swirling around. The harshest measures were not necessarily backed by all members of the Nazi elite, however: "Frick [the minister of the interior] reports about the Jewish question in Poland," Goebbels recorded on November 8. "He is in favor of somewhat milder methods. I protest and so does Ley" [Robert Ley, the labor minister and head of the "German Labor Front"].[44] At times Hitler's musings about Jewry took off, as they did from the outset of his career, into loftier spheres: "We touch again upon religious issues," Goebbels noted on December 29. "The Führer is profoundly religious but totally antichristian. He considers Christianity as a symptom of decline. Rightly so. It is a deposit [*Ablagerung*] of the Jewish race. One also notices it in the similarity of religious rituals. Both have no relation to animals and this will destroy them in the end."[45]

While Hitler's anti-Semitic harangues went on unabated in his conversations with Goebbels, Rosenberg, and other party subordinates, his only *public* anti-Jewish outbursts throughout a period of several months came at the beginning of the war, on the day Great Britain and France joined the conflict. On September 3, in the afternoon, German radio broadcast four proclamations by Adolf Hitler: the first to the German people, the second and third to the armed forces on the Eastern and Western Fronts, the last and most important one to the National Socialist Party. In the first proclamation the Nazi leader lashed out at those who had initiated this war; it was not the British people who were responsible, but "that Jewish-plutocratic and democratic ruling class that wanted to turn all the nations of the earth into its obedient slaves."[46] Whereas in the proclamation to the German people the attack against "Jewish plutocracy" came only in the middle of the address, it opened the proclamation to the party: "Our Jewish-democratic world enemy has succeeded in pulling the English people into a state of war with Germany."[47] The real "world enemy" was clearly identified once again: party and state would have to act. "This time," Hitler warned darkly, "those who hoped to sabotage the common effort would be exterminated without any pity."[48]

Whether these dire threats were signals of steps to come or, at this point, merely ritualized outbursts remains an open question. Hitler's subsequent public restraint derived from obvious political reasons (first the hope of an arrangement with France and Great Britain, then with Great Britain alone). Nothing was said about the Jews either in the annual address to the party "Old Fighters" on November 8, 1939, or in the official announcement that followed an attempt by a single assassin on Hitler's life that same evening.

In his 1940 New Year's message to the party, Hitler merely hinted that the Jews had not been forgotten: "Jewish-international capitalism, in alliance with reactionary forces, incited the democracies against Germany"; the same "Jewish-capitalist world enemy" had only one goal, "to destroy the German people," but, Hitler announced, "the Jewish capitalist world would not survive the twentieth century."[49] And, in the annual speech commemorating the *Machtergreifung*, on January 30, that restraint would be even more noticeable. A year earlier, on the same occasion, Hitler had proclaimed that a world war would bring about the extermination of the Jews of Europe, and a year later, on January 30, 1941, he would renew his threat. On January 30, 1940, however, the Jews were not mentioned at all.

Possibly no less significant was the fact that in his speech of February 24, 1940, the twentieth anniversary of the proclamation of the party program (a program in which the "Jewish question" had loomed large), Hitler referred specifically to the Jews only once, telling the party members assembled in the Hofbraühaus in Munich that when the Jews insulted him, he considered it an honor. Furthermore, in the same speech, he alluded to the people whom everyone knew, the people who had lived among them up to the last eight years, a group whose jargon no German could understand and whose presence no German could bear, a people who knew only how to lie. Even the dumbest party member understood whom Hitler meant, but, contrary to the Nazi leader's rhetorical habits, the word "Jews" was not mentioned.[50]

V

Although at this stage most Nazi anti-Jewish propaganda was aimed at the German public, Goebbels never forgot its potential impact beyond the Reich's borders, mainly among Germany's enemies. By endlessly repeating that the war was a "Jewish war," prepared and instigated by the Jews for their own profit and their ultimate goal, world domination, Goebbels hoped to weaken enemy resolve and foster a growing demand for an arrangement with Germany.

On November 2, during the conversation in which the propaganda minister told Hitler of his Polish trip and described the Jews as a "waste product," as a "clinical issue more than a social one," both concluded that anti-Jewish propaganda aimed toward the outside world ought to be substantially reinforced: "We consider," the minister noted, "whether we shouldn't stress the Zionist Protocols [*sic*] (*The Protocols of the Elders of Zion*) in our propaganda in France."[51] The use of the "Protocols" was to reappear in Goebbels's plans throughout the war, mainly toward the end. More than once he would discuss the issue with his Führer. Incidentally, the dual and contradictory aspect of the Nazi myth of the Jew was strikingly illustrated on this occasion: the Jews were "a waste product" and "a clinical issue" on the one hand and, on the other, Aryan humanity faced the mortal danger of a Jewish domination of the world. . . .

Immediately after the beginning of the war, Goebbels ordered the production of three major anti-Jewish films: *Die Rothschilds* (*The Rothschilds*), *Jud Süss* (*Jew Süss*) and *Der Ewige Jude* (*The Eternal Jew*). The Rothschild project was submitted to the minister by the board of UFA film studios in September 1939; he gave his permission to go ahead with the production.[52] *Der Ewige Jude* was Goebbels's own idea and between October 1939 and September 1940, it became his most consuming anti-Jewish propaganda project. In October, Fritz Hippler, the head of the film section of the propaganda Ministry, was put in charge of the film; in November, Veit Harlan was chosen as director of *Jud Süss*.

The three Nazi film projects had a strange prehistory. All three topics—all three titles, in fact—had probably been chosen by Goebbels to offer violently anti-Semitic versions of identically named films produced in 1933 and 1934 in Great Britain and in the United States, each of which carried a message stigmatizing the persecution of the Jews through history. Of course in the three films of the early 1930s the Jewish figures were presented in a highly favorable light.[53] *The House of Rothschild* was produced by Twentieth-Century Pictures in 1933; *The Eternal Jew* came from the studios of Gaumont-Twickenham in 1934 and, in the same year Gaumont-British produced *Jew Süss* with the German refugee actor Conrad Veidt in the main role (Veidt had left Germany in 1933; his wife was half Jewish).[54] Both *The House of Rothschild* and *Jew Süss* were relatively successful in the United States, in Great Britain, and in several European countries. Needless to say, neither film was shown in Germany, and *Jew Süss* was banned in Austria after a brief run in Vienna.[55] In Britain itself *Jew Süss* received mostly positive reviews, although it garnered some strongly anti-Semitic articles as well. *Punch*, for example, warned the Tivoli theater (where the film had opened): "It must begin to Aryanize itself or it will be too much thought of as the abode of Hebraic eminence and idiosyncrasy. . . . A little Gentile leaven in the Tivoli pogroms—I mean programme—would not be unwelcome."[56] I will return to Goebbels's *Jud Süss*.

In its 1934 British version, *The Eternal Jew* denounced the persecution of the Jews during the Inquisition. At approximately the same time, a first Nazi version of a film carrying the same title was put together by one Walter Böttcher for the Munich anti-Jewish exhibition (also titled *Der Ewige Jude*), which opened in the fall of 1937. Goebbels, who had nothing to do with this party production, disliked it and even mentioned, on November 5, 1937, that it had been done against his instructions.[57] And yet *Juden ohne Maske* (Jews Unmasked), as the 1937 film was titled, already used the method that would be applied with much greater skill in the Goebbels production: images of Jews "as they outwardly appeared" juxtaposed with images of Jews "as they really were."[58]

The second source of *Der Ewige Jude* was the material for an anti-Semitic documentary that was being shot in Poland, literally days after the end of the campaign. On October 6, Goebbels noted: "Discussed a ghetto film with Hippler and Taubert; the material for it is now being shot in Poland. It should become a first-rate propaganda film. . . . In 3–4 weeks it must be ready."[59] Little did Goebbels know that it would take another year before the release of this quintessential anti-Jewish production.

Throughout the end of 1939 and the beginning of 1940, the minister devoted constant attention to the *"Judenfilm"*—the "Jew film," as he called *Der Ewige Jude.*[60] On October 16 he mentioned it to Hitler, who "showed great interest."[61] The next day he returned to the topic in his diary: "Film tests. . . . Pictures from the ghetto film. Never existed before. Descriptions so dreadful and brutal in their details that one's blood freezes. One pulls back in horror at so much brutality. This Jewry must be exterminated."[62] October 24: "Further tests for our Jew film. Pictures of synagogue scenes of extraordinary significance. At this time we work on this, in order to make a propaganda masterpiece of all of it."[63] October 28: "Shot tests for our Jew film. Shocking. This film will be our big hit."[64]

On November 2 Goebbels flew to Poland, first to Lodz: "We travel through the ghetto. We get out and observe everything in detail. It cannot be described. These are no longer human beings, these are animals. Therefore, it is no humanitarian task, but a surgical one. One must cut here, in a radical way. Otherwise Europe will perish of the Jewish disease."[65] November 19: "I tell the Führer about our Jew film. He makes a few suggestions."[66] And so it went through the end of 1939.

The "pictures of synagogue scenes" had been filmed at the Vilker shul in Lodz. The Germans assembled the congregation, ordered it to put on *taleysim* and *tefillin* and to stage a full-scale service. Shimon Huberband later recorded the details of the event for the underground historical archives kept in Warsaw (to which we will return). "A large number of high-ranking German officers came," Huberband noted, "and filmed the entire course of the service, immortalizing it on film!!" Then the order was given to take out the Torah scroll and read from it: "The Torah scroll was filmed in various poses—with the mantle covering it, with its belt on and off, open and closed. The Torah reader, a clever Jew, called out in

Hebrew before beginning to read the scroll: 'Today is Tuesday.' This was meant as a statement for posterity that they were forced to read the Torah, since the Torah is usually not read on Tuesday."[67]

The Germans repeated the operation at the Jewish slaughterhouse: "The kosher meat slaughterers, dressed in *yarmulkes* [skullcaps] and *gartlekh* [sashes], were ordered to slaughter a number of cattle and recite the blessings, while squeezing their eyes shut and rocking with religious fervor. They were also required to examine the animals' lungs and remove the adhesions to the lungs."[68] Incidentally, over the following days the Germans burned down one synagogue and then another, announcing that it was Polish revenge for the destruction by the Jews of the monument to the national hero and anti-Russian freedom fighter Kosciuszko.[69]

The delays in the completion of *Der Ewige Jude* did not mean that the German population was kept waiting for visual material about "the Jew." From the outset of the Polish campaign, the Wehrmacht propaganda units (*Propagandakompanien*, or PK), under the jurisdiction of the OKW but often staffed by personnel chosen from the Propaganda Ministry, started filming Jews for the weekly UFA newsreels. On October 2, the PKs received urgent instructions from Goebbels's ministry: "Of high priority is film footage showing all sorts of Jewish types. We need more than before, from Warsaw and all the occupied territories. What we want are portraits and images of Jews at work. This material is to be used to reinforce our anti-Semitic propaganda at home and abroad."[70] Footage about Jews was shown in newsreels as early as September 14, then on October 4 and 18.[71] Some of this material was later incorporated into *Der Ewige Jude*.

Instructions to newspapers were mostly under Goebbels's control, although there was some competition from Rosenberg, and from the Reich press chief Otto Dietrich. A state secretary in Goebbels's ministry, Dietrich was also Hitler's press officer and a *Reichsleiter* (party equivalent of "minister"); thus he was both Goebbels's subordinate and his equal. In January 1940 Dietrich gave confidential instructions to his charges. "It is to be observed," he complained, "that, with few exceptions, the press did not yet understand how to underscore in their daily journalistic work the propagandistic *'Parole'* [theme] of the Führer's New Year's message, that addressed the battle against the Jewish and reactionary war mongers in the capitalist democracies. Anti-Semitic themes are a part of the daily press material as a clear exposition of the social backwardness of the moneybag democracies who wish to salvage their exploitation methods through this war. . . . Only with closest attention on the part of the editors to stressing Jewish-capitalist themes, will the necessary long-term propagandistic effect be achieved."[72]

At times the Propaganda Ministry guidelines reprimanded newspapers for not respecting the most elementary rules of the profession: painstakingly checking all details to keep as close as possible to the truth. (Such admonishments turned, of course, into an unintended caricature of fact-finding, that would, in another context, be quite comical.) Thus, instruction number 53 of January 9, 1940, "deplored" the major space given by the *Völkischer Beobachter* to the Jewish origins of British statesmen: "The details provided are mostly false. The claim that after the dismissal of [the Jew] Hore-Belisha, [the Jew] Sir Philip Sassoun [*sic*] remained the head of war industries is false. Sassoun has died. Duff Cooper's wife is not Jewish, contrarily to what the *VB* asserts. She is the most Aryan (*das arischste*) that can be found among Scottish aristocracy. Also the claim that Mrs. Daladier is Jewish is false. For a long time now Daladier is widowed. The Propaganda ministry will probably have to publish new material about the Jewish origins of some British statesmen."[73] Incidentally the *Völkischer Beobachter*'s chief editor was Goebbels's archenemy, Alfred Rosenberg.

In fact, whatever the motives for Hitler's own tactical restraint during this early phase of the war, "the Jew" was omnipresent in the flood of publications, speeches, orders and prohibitions that permeated everyday life in Germany. Any party leader of some standing had his own individual style in handling the "Jewish question," and any such leader had a vast constituency that was the instant target and the willing or captive audience of these tirades. Take Robert Ley, for example; his speeches and publications reached millions of workers, as well as the future leadership of the party trained in the centers, which he established and controlled since 1934. Thus, in 1940, when Ley published *Unser Sozialismus: Der Hass der Welt* (*Our Socialism: The Hate of the World*), his voice echoed in many German minds. For him plutocracy was, in the words of his biographer, "one tentacle of the Jewish enemy," and Jewish plutocracy was "the dominance of money and gold, the repression and enslavement of people, the reversal of all natural values and exclusion of reason and insight, the mystical darkness of superstition. . . . The meanness of human carnality and brutality." No common ground existed between this evil and the good that was the National Socialist *Volksgemeinschaft*: Between the two worlds "there is no compromise and no settlement. Whoever wants one, must hate the other. Who gives himself to one, must destroy the other."[74]

On occasion, however, it was necessary not to push the "logical" follow-up of anti-Jewish incitement beyond a given limit, as some measures could lead to negative reactions among the population. Thus, on March 6, 1940, Goebbels, Rosenberg, and their Führer reached the conclusion that some parts of church liturgy should not be forbidden, even if they praised the Jews: "We can't push this matter now."[75] In Dresden, for example, the Church of Zion—which also gave its name to the surrounding area, "the Zion Colony"—was not renamed throughout the war.[76]

VI

Only a small fraction of the approximately 2.2 million Polish Jews who fell into German hands by the end of September 1939 belonged to the bourgeoisie. The great majority, whether living in cities or in small towns, belonged to the lower middle class of shopkeepers and artisans; as mentioned, they were increasingly pauperized due to the persistent economic crisis and growing ambient hostility. In Lodz, for example, in the early 1930s, 70 percent of Jewish working-class families (comprising on average five to eight persons) lived in a single room; almost 20 percent of these rooms were either in attics or in cellars; part were both workshops and living quarters. The Jews of Warsaw, Vilna, and Białystok were not much better off than those of Lodz.[77] More than a quarter of the entire Jewish population of Poland was in need of assistance in 1934, and the trend was on the rise in the late thirties.[78] In Ezra Mendelsohn's words, Polish Jewry, on the eve of the war, "was an impoverished community with no hope of reversing its rapid economic decline."[79]

An important—albeit decreasing—part of this population, let us recall, had been and remained self-consciously Jewish in terms of culture—including language (Yiddish or Hebrew)—and various degrees of religious practice.[80] During the interwar period the cultural separatism of the Jews—not different from that of other minorities living in the new Polish state—exacerbated the already deep-rooted native anti-Semitism. This hostile attitude was nurtured by traditional Catholic anti-Judaism, by an increasingly fierce Polish economic drive to force the Jews out of their trades and professions, as well as by mythical stories of Jewish subversive activities against Polish national claims and rights.[81]

In this fervently Catholic country, the role of the church was decisive. A study of the Catholic press between the wars opened with a resolutely unambiguous statement: "All Catholic journalists agreed . . . that there was indeed a 'Jewish question' and that the Jewish minority in Poland posed a threat to the identity of the Polish nation and the independence of the Polish state." The general tenor of the articles published in the Catholic press was that all attempts to ease the conflict between Poles and Jews were unrealistic. There were even proposals to abandon the existing policy that recognized Jews as equal citizens, with the same rights as Poles. The Catholic press warned against treating the situation lightly: "There could not be two masters (*gospodarze*) on Polish soil, especially since the Jewish community contributed to the demoralization of the Poles, took jobs and income away from Poles, and was destroying the national culture."[82] Once such a premise was accepted, the only diverging views dealt with the methods to be used in the anti-Jewish struggle. While part of the Catholic press (and hierarchy) advocated fighting "Jewish ideas," rather than the Jews as human beings, others went further and advocated "self-defense" even if it resulted in Jewish loss of life.[83]

The press incitement was but the reflection of the church hierarchy's attitudes during the interwar period (and before). Even if one disregards the most extreme anti-Jewish attacks stemming from the Polish clergy, those of one Father Stanisław Trzeciak, for example, the episcopate's voice was threatening enough. Thus, in 1920, during the Polish-Soviet war, a group of Polish bishops issued the following statement in regard to the Jewish role in world events: "The race which has the leadership of Bolshevism in its hands has already in the past subjugated the whole world by means of gold and the banks, and now, driven by the everlasting imperialist greed that flows in its veins, is already aiming at the final subjugation of the nations under the yoke of its rule."[84]

In a pastoral letter issued on February 29, 1936, Cardinal August Hlond, the highest authority in the Catholic Church in Poland, tried to restrain the growing wave of anti-Jewish violence: "It is a fact," the cardinal stated, "that Jews are waging war against the Catholic Church, that they are steeped in free-thinking and constitute the vanguard of atheism, the Bolshevik movement and revolutionary activity. It is a fact that the Jews have a corrupting influence on morals, and that their publishing houses are spreading pornography. It is true that the Jews are perpetrating fraud, practicing usury, and dealing in prostitution. . . . But let us be fair. Not all Jews are this way. . . . One may love one's nation more, but one may not hate anyone. Not even Jews. . . . One should stay away from the harmful moral influence of Jews, keep away from their anti-Christian culture, and especially boycott the Jewish press and demoralizing Jewish publications. But it is forbidden to assault, beat up, maim, or slander Jews."[85]

The most extreme and militant Polish anti-Jewish political organization, the National Democratic Party (the Endeks), established in the 1890s by Roman Dmowski (who led it until the late 1930s), first and foremost demanded the exclusion of Jews from key positions in Polish political, cultural, and economic life. It rejected the possibility of Jewish assimilation (arguing that such assimilation was not real or "in depth"); it identified Jews with communism (coining the term *Zydokomuna*—Jewish communism) and, eventually came to consider mass emigration (or expulsion) of the Jews from Poland as the only solution of the Jewish question.[86]

During the 1920s, apart from pogroms in the immediate postwar period, anti-Jewish attacks were kept under control first by the postwar democratic governments and then by Marshal Józef Piłsudski's autocratic regime.[87] But, after Piłsudski's death, mainly from 1936 on, anti-Jewish aggression grew in all domains. Widespread physical violence, economic boycott, numerous clashes in the universities, and church incitement were encouraged by successive right-wing governments. Thus, as the war started, the largest Jewish community in Europe, already badly bruised by surrounding hostility, was caught in the Nazi net.[88]

The SS *Einsatzgruppen* I, IV, V, and mainly Obergruppenführer Udo von Woyrsch's "Special Purpose Operational Group" were in charge of terrorizing the Jewish populations. The wanton murder and destruction campaign launched against the Jews did not have the systematic goal of liquidating a specific segment of the Jewish population, as was the case with the Polish elites, but it was both a manifestation of generalized Nazi anti-Jewish hatred and a show of violence that would incite the Jewish populations to flee from some of the regions about to be incorporated into the Reich, such as eastern Upper Silesia.[89] More generally the *Einsatzgruppen* had probably received instructions to drive as many Jews as possible beyond the San River to what was to become the Soviet-occupied area of Poland.[90]

The men of Woyrsch's mixed *Einsatzgruppe* of SD and Order Police excelled. In Dynow, near the San, Order Police detachments belonging to the group burned a dozen Jews in the local synagogue, then shot another sixty of them in the nearby forest. Such murder operations were repeated in several neighboring villages and towns (on September 19, more than one hundred Jewish men were killed in Przekopana). Overall, the unit had murdered some five hundred to six hundred Jews by September 20.[91]

For the Wehrmacht, Woyrsch had transgressed all tolerable limits. Fourteenth Army commanding officers demanded the withdrawal of the *Einsatzgruppe* and, atypically, Gestapo headquarters immediately complied. On September 22 the group was pulled back to Katowice.[92] Woyrsch's case, however, was extreme, and more generally the tension between the Wehrmacht and the SS did not lead to any measures against the SS units as such but rather to army complaints about the lack of discipline of Heydrich's men: "An SS artillery unit of the armored corps has herded Jews into a church and massacred them," Gen. Franz Halder, chief of the Army (OKH) General Staff, noted in his service diary. "The court-martial has sentenced them to one year in jail. Küchler [Gen. Georg von, commander in chief of Armies Three and Eighteen] has not confirmed the sentence, because *more severe punishment is due*."[93] Again, on October 10: "Massacres of Jews—discipline!"[94]

The Wehrmacht may have considered massacring Jews as something demanding disciplinary action, but torturing them offered welcome enjoyment to both soldiers and SS personnel. The choice victims were Orthodox Jews, given their distinctive looks and attire. They were shot at; they were compelled to smear feces on each other; they had to jump, crawl, sing, clean excrement with prayer shawls, dance around the bonfires of burning Torah scrolls. They were whipped, forced to eat pork, or had Jewish stars carved on their foreheads. The "beard game" was the most popular entertainment of all: Beards and sidelocks were shorn, plucked, torn, set afire, hacked off with or without parts of skin, cheeks, or jaws, to the amusement of a usually large audience of cheering soldiers. On Yom Kippur 1939 such entertainment for the troops was particularly lively.

Part of the invasion army was strongly ideologized, even at that early stage of the war. In a "Leaflet for the Conduct of German Soldiers in the Occupied Territory of Poland," issued by the commander-in-chief of the army, General Walther von Brauchitsch, on September 19, 1939, the soldiers were warned of the "inner enmity" of "all civilians that were not 'members of the German race.'" Furthermore, Brauchitsch's "leaflet" stated: "The behavior toward Jews needs no special mention for the soldiers of the National-Socialist Reich."[95] It was therefore within the range of accepted thinking that a soldier noted in his diary, during these same days: "Here we recognize the necessity for a radical solution to the Jewish question. Here one sees houses occupied by beasts in human form. In their beards and kaftans, with their devilishly grotesque faces, they make a dreadful impression. Anyone who was not yet a radical opponent of the Jews must become one here."[96]

More commonly soldiers and officers, like their Führer, regarded the Jews with bottomless disgust and contempt: "When you see such people," Pvt. FP wrote to his wife on September 21, "you can't believe that this is still possible in the 20th century. The Jews want to kiss our hands, but—we grab our pistol and hear 'God protect me,'—and they run as fast as they can."[97] Back in Vienna First Cpl. JE recorded some of his impressions from the campaign in a letter of December 30: "And the Jews—I rarely saw such neglected people walking around, covered in tatters, dirty, greasy. To us they looked like a pest. The mean appearances, the cunning questions and behavior have often led us to draw our pistols in order . . . to remind them of reality."[98] Such impressions and reactions constantly recurred, and the line separating this sort of visceral hatred from brutality and murder was very faint.

Looting, however, did not demand any ideological passion: "They knock at eleven in the morning," Sierakowiak noted on October 22, ". . . a German army officer, two policemen and the superintendent come in. The officer asks how many persons are in the apartment, looks at the beds, asks about the bedbugs, and if we have a radio. He doesn't find anything worthy of taking and finally leaves disappointed. At the neighbors' (naturally they go only to Jews), he took away radios, mattresses, comforters, carpets, etc. They took away the Grabinskis' only down quilt."[99]

On October 13, 1939, the Polish physician and longtime director of the hospital in Szczebrzeszyn, near Zamość, Dr. Zygmunt Klukowski, recorded in his diary: "The Germans posted several new regulations. I am noting only a few: 'All men of Jewish religion between the ages of fifteen and sixty must report at 8 a.m. on the morning of October 14, at city hall with brooms, shovels, and buckets. They will be cleaning city streets." On the next day he added: "The Germans are treating the Jews very brutally. They cut their beards; sometimes they pull the hair out."[100] On the fifteenth the Germans added more of the same, yet with a slightly different—and certainly inventive—slant: "A German major, now town commandant, told the new 'police' [an auxiliary Polish police unit, organized by the Germans] that all brutalities against Jews have to be tolerated since it is in line with German anti-Semitic policies and that this brutality has been ordered from above. The Germans are always trying to find new work for the Jews. They order the Jews to take at least a half hour of exhausting gymnastics before any work, which can be fatal, particularly for older people. When the Jews are marched to any assignment, they must loudly sing Polish national songs."[101] And, on the next day, Klukowski's entry encapsulated it all: "Persecution of Jews is increasing. The Germans are beating the Jews without any reason, just for fun. Several Jews were brought to the hospital with their buttocks beaten into raw flesh. I was able to administer only first aid, because the hospital has been instructed not to admit Jews."[102] (The same, of course, was happening everywhere else.) "In the afternoon," Sierakowiak wrote on December 3, "I went outside for a while and visited Ela Waldman. She had been chucked out of school, as they do to all the Jews. They also beat Jews terribly in the streets of the city. They usually come up to the Jews who walk by and slap them in the face, kick, spit, etc." And at that point the young diarist added a puzzling question: "Is this evidence that the end for the Germans will probably come soon?"[103]

Such brutal behavior by the Wehrmacht demonstrates a measure of continuity between the attitudes and actions of German troops at the very outset of the war and their murderous behavior after the attack on the Soviet Union.[104] Yet, during the Polish campaign, at top echelons of the army the inroads of Hitler's exhortations were still neutralized in part by traditional rules of military behavior and discipline, as well as, in some cases, by moral qualms. Thus, Gen. Johannes Blaskowitz, the army commander in Poland (*Oberbefehlshaber Ost*), addressed a protest directly to Hitler. Blaskowitz was shocked by the behavior of Heydrich's units and by the brutalization of the army. "It is wholly misguided," he wrote on February 6, 1940, "to slaughter some 10,000 Jews and Poles, as it is happening at the moment; such methods will eradicate neither Polish nationalism, nor the Jews from the mass of the population."[105] Hitler shrugged off the complaint. By mid-October the Wehrmacht was divested of its authority over civilian matters in occupied Poland.

Heydrich had grasped the thrust of the changes taking place within the Wehrmacht. In his already mentioned letter to Daluege of July 1940, he alluded to his difficulties with "the upper-level commanders of the army" but indicated that "cooperation with troops below staff level, and in many cases with the different staffs of the army themselves, was generally good." He added: "If one compares [the number of] physical assaults, incidents of looting, and atrocities committed by the army and the SS, the SS and police do not come away looking bad."[106]

VII

On September 21, 1939, Heydrich had issued the following guidelines to the commanders of the *Einsatzgruppen*: Their tasks included (1) the rounding up and concentration of Jews in large communities in cities close to railway lines, "in view of the end goal"; (2) the establishment of Jewish Councils in each Jewish community to serve as administrative links between the German authorities and the Jewish population; and (3) cooperation with the military command and the civil administration in all matters relating to the Jewish population.[107]

The "end goal" in this context probably meant the deportation of the Jewish population of the Warthegau and later of the western and central parts of former Poland to the easternmost area of the General Government, the Lublin district, along the lines of Hitler's vague indications at that same time. A few days later, on September 27, in a conference with heads of the RSHA departments and the *Einsatzgruppen* chiefs, Heydrich added an element unmentioned until then: the expulsion of Jews over the demarcation line [between German occupied Poland and the Soviet occupation area] had been authorized by the Führer (*"Abschiebung über die Demarkationslinie ist vom Führer genehmigt"*).[108] Such an authorization meant that at this early stage the Germans had no clear plans. Their policy regarding the Jews of former Poland seemed to be in line with the measures they had elaborated before the war, mainly from 1938 on, regarding the Jews of the Reich—now applied with much greater violence, of course: identification, segregation, expropriation, concentration, and emigration or expulsion (emigration was allowed until early 1940, as far as the Jews of Poland were concerned).

In this context the significance of a September 29 letter from Heydrich to Daluege seems as hazy as the "end goal" he had mentioned a few days before. "Finally," Heydrich wrote, "the Jewish problem will, as you already know, be settled in a special way (*Schliesslich, soll das Judenproblem, wie Du ja schon weisst, einer besonderen Regelung unterworfen werden*)."[109]

By then, however, a new element had become part of the picture and considerably influenced the measures taken against Jews and Poles (particularly in the areas annexed to the Reich): the mass ingathering of ethnic Germans from Eastern and Southeastern Europe. Jews and Poles would be expelled and *Volksdeutsche* would move in. On October 7 Himmler was appointed head of the new agency in charge of these population transfers, the Reichskommissariat für die Festigung des deutschen Volkstums, or RKFDV (Reich Commissariat for the Strengthening of Germandom).

This ethnic-racial reshuffling of vast populations in Eastern Europe after September 1939 was but one further step in the initiatives already launched before the war to bring "home into the Reich" the Germans of Austria, the Sudetenland, Memel, Danzig, and the like. In Nazi phantasms the reshuffling planned at the end of 1939 would eventually lead to entirely new and far-flung Germanic colonization much farther east, if a new political and military situation were to allow it.

Over recent years many historians have sought a link between these plans and the onset of the "Final Solution." Yet, as we shall see further on, these operations appear to have been distinct and to have stemmed from separate motives and plans. Nonetheless, between 1939 and 1942, Himmler's population transfers led directly to the expulsions and deportations of hundreds of thousands of Poles and Jews, mainly from the Warthegau into the General Government.

German projects for the East did not originate in academic research, but German academia volunteered historical justification and professional advice to enhance the exalting new vistas for the expansion of the *Volk*. In fact some of these expansion plans had been part and parcel of ongoing "research on the East" (*Ostforschung*) since the late 1920s. In other words this *Ostforschung* was a major nationalist, *völkisch*, and increasingly Nazi-tainted but self-initiated scholarly effort to bolster German expansion plans and, eventually, to suggest various practical options.[110] A particularly influential role in terms of the historical legitimation of this endeavor was played by a Jewish luminary at the University of Königsberg, the historian Hans Rothfels; of course none of his vocal nationalism protected him from dismissal and forced emigration in the late thirties.[111]

Two of Rothfels's students, the already well-established Werner Conze and his colleagueTheodor Schieder (both destined to become pillars of the historians' guild in West Germany after 1945), came to play an important advisory role after the beginning of the war—with drastic anti-Jewish steps added for good measure. In a paper he had prepared for the International Congress of Sociology, scheduled to open on August 29, 1939, in Bucharest, Conze dwelled at length on the overpopulation problem in Eastern Europe; it could be alleviated, he suggested, by the "de-Judaization (*Entjudung*) of cities and marketplaces, to allow the integration of peasant offspring in commerce and crafts."[112] Schieder's proposals became more immediately applicable once Poland fell into German hands.

In the fall of 1939 Schieder, then a member of the "Königsberg Circle" affiliated with the North and East German Research Association (*Nord- und Ostdeutsche Forschungsgemeinschaft*, or NODFG), was asked by his colleagues in the association to draft a memorandum about "the German national and racial border in the East" for the benefit of the political and administrative authorities in the newly occupied territories. The text was submitted to Himmler on October 7.

In the memorandum Schieder recommended the confiscation of the land and the transfer of parts of the Polish population from the annexed territories to the eastern part of the country in order to open the way to German settlement. And in order to facilitate the transfer of the Poles, the young Königsberg scholar pleaded for the evacuation of the Jews from Polish cities (*die Herauslösung des Judentums aus polnischen Städten*) and, as a further step, even more radically than Conze, the "total de-Judaization of remaining Poland." The evicted Jewish population could be sent overseas. Thus, whereas Hitler, Himmler, and Heydrich were still considering the deportation of the Jews of Poland into a reservation in the Lublin area or even their expulsion over the demarcation line into Soviet-occupied territory, Schieder and his colleagues were already suggesting an overseas territorial solution that would indeed become the next Nazi territorial plan a few months later.[113]

The NODFG was functionally linked to the older Berlin *Publikationsstelle* (PuSte), whose own leading specialists volunteered from day one: "We must make use of our experience, which we have developed over many long years of effort," Hermann Aubin wrote to Alfred Brackmann, the director of PuSte, on September 18, 1939. "Scholarship cannot simply wait until it is called upon, but must make itself heard."[114] Aubin had no reason to worry. On September 23 Brackmann wrote to his colleague Metz: "It is in fact a great satisfaction for us to see that the NODFG with its PuSte offices has now become the central institution for scientific advice to the Foreign Ministry, the Ministry of the Interior, the OKH, and partly also the Propaganda Ministry and a series of SS agencies. We are certain now that we shall be thoroughly consulted on the future drawing of borders."[115]

From the outset PuSte and NOFDG scholars worked on various aspects of the Jewish question in occupied Poland. Statistician Klostermann, for example, calculated the proportion of Jews in Polish towns with populations of ten thousand inhabitants or more; this study was prepared for the Gestapo.[116] Professor Otto Reche prepared a detailed memorandum titled "Main Theses for a Population Policy Aimed at Securing the German East." The study was transmitted by Brackmann to high SS officials, who, it seems, passed it on to Himmler.[117] The main ideas were not fundamentally different from those submitted by Schieder, except that they delved into details that the Königsberg historian had not emphasized. In matters of mass expulsion of Poles and Jews, for example, Reche suggested that the Poles be allowed to take their belongings: "With the Jews however one may act with less generosity" (*bei Juden wird man weniger weitherzig verfahren dürfen*).[118] And, beyond these early studies, another scholar—a specialist in planning the demographic organization of large-scale space—Professor Konrad Meyer-Hetling, was launching his own research for Himmler's colonization projects; it was to become "General Plan East."

Schematically the Germanization of the annexed eastern territories (and later colonization of further space in the East) demanded the liquidation of the Polish elites, the transfer of ethnic Germans or the migration of Reich Germans to the new territories, and of course the expulsion of the local racially alien inhabitants: the Poles and the Jews. The Poles who could not be expelled would be strictly separated from the German colonists, and a "happy few," mainly children, would be mustered as belonging to Germanic stock, included in the *Volksliste*, and integrated into the *Volksgemeinschaft*.

Himmler's RKFdV and the RSHA were in charge of the operations, as we saw, and the general expulsion plan regarding the ex-Polish areas was subdivided by Heydrich in a series of short-term plans (*Nahpläne*) mainly to be launched from the end of 1939 on. There was, however, one exception to the expulsion plans regarding Jews. In heavily industrialized Upper Silesia, the Jews living east of the "police line," which divided the Kattowitz district into two separate administrative regions, were to stay. They would be moved, in the course of 1940, into forced-labor camps and employed in local industries or building projects. The SS officer whom Himmler put in charge of this forced-labor operation, which within a few months was to employ some seventeen thousand Jewish workers, was the former police chief of Breslau, SS Oberführer Albrecht Schmelt.[119]

Except for "Schmelt Jews," the expulsion plans included not only Jewish populations from the annexed Polish territories but also Jews from the Reich and the Protectorate of Bohemia and Moravia. These deportations, which took place between the fall of 1939 and the spring of 1940, ended in failure.

In October 1939 the deportations of Jews from Vienna, Mährisch Ostrau, and Kattowitz to Nisko (a small town on the San River, near Lublin) started. These deportations, agreed to by Hitler, had been demanded by local *Gauleiter* mainly to seize Jewish homes. Moreover, as far as Vienna was concerned, the city would thus recover its pristine

Aryan nature.[120] A few thousand Jews were deported, but within days the operation came to a halt, as the Wehrmacht needed the railway lines for transferring troops from Poland to the West.[121]

The two other transfers were simultaneous and identical in their goals. One, small in scale (by Nazi standards), was the deportation in February 1940 of some eighteen hundred Jews from the German towns Stettin and Schneidemühl on the coast of the Baltic to Lublin. The second operation was a formidable exercise in utter brutality: It aimed at the expulsion of hundreds of thousands of Jews and Poles from the annexed Warthegau into the General Government, over a period of several months. The abandoned homes and farms of the deportees were meant to be distributed to ethnic Germans from the Baltic countries and Volhynia, and Bukovina, whose departure and "ingathering into the Reich" the Germans had negotiated with the USSR.

Nothing was ready for the Jews of Stettin and Schneidemühl in the snow-covered Lublin area, and they were either housed in temporary barracks or taken in by local Jewish communities. For the newly appointed SS and police leader (SSPF) of the Lublin District, Odilo Globocnik, there was no particular problem. On February 16, 1940, he declared that "the evacuated Jews should feed themselves and be supported by their countrymen, as these Jews had enough [food]. If this did not succeed, one should let them starve."[122]

The deportations from the Warthegau soon became mired in total chaos, with overfilled trains stalled for days in freezing weather or maneuvering aimlessly to and fro. The ruthlessness of these deportations, organized mainly by Adolf Eichmann, the RSHA specialist on the emigration and evacuation of Jews, in coordination with the newly established RKFDV, did not compensate for the complete lack of planning and of even minimal preparation of reception areas for the deportees.

During the first weeks of the transfers the governor-general, Hans Frank, who had barely settled down in his capital, Kraków, in the castle of the centuries-old Jagellonian dynasty, seemed rather unconcerned about the sudden influx. Regarding the Jews he even displayed high spirits in a speech given in Radom on November 25, 1939: "It is a pleasure to finally have a chance to get physically at the Jewish race. The more of them die, the better; to hit him [*sic*] is a victory for our Reich. The Jews should feel that we are here. We want to have about one-half to three-quarters of all the Jews east of the Vistula . . . the Jews from the Reich, from Vienna, from everywhere; we have no use for the Jews in the Reich. Probably the Vistula line; behind this line, no more."[123]

But Frank's elation did not last. In early February 1940, after some two hundred thousand new arrivals into the General Government had been counted, he traveled to Berlin and extracted from Göring an order to halt the transfers.[124] Encouraged by this success, Frank took an initiative of his own: On April 12, 1940, he announced his intention to empty Kraków of most of its 66,000 Jews. The governor-general was eloquent: "If we want to maintain the authority of the National Socialist Reich, the representatives of this Reich cannot have to encounter Jews when they enter or leave their houses, they cannot be endangered by contagious diseases." The city would be freed of most of its Jews by November 1, 1940, except for some five thousand to ten thousand "urgently necessary artisans. . . . Cracow must become the city in the General Government that is the most cleansed of Jews. Only thus does it make sense to build it as the German capital." He was ready to allow Jews who would have left voluntarily by August 15 to take along all their possessions, of course "with the exception of those objects they had stolen." The ghetto would then be cleaned, and it would become possible to set up clean German living quarters, where one would breathe German air.[125]

By the beginning of 1941, some 45,000 Jewish inhabitants of the city had left voluntarily or been expelled, and those who remained were concentrated in the district of Podgorce, the ghetto. As for the Jews that had been ousted, they could not go very far. They settled mostly in the surroundings of Frank's capital, to the law of the local German administrators.[126] At least the governor-general and the German civil and military administration in Kraków had chased most of the Jews out of their sight. More or less at the same time, the Jews of Radom and Lublin suffered the same fate as those of Kraków.[127]

After the establishment of the General Government on October 12, 1939, and the appointment of Hans Frank as governor-general fourteen days later, a German administrative apparatus was set up in the heart of Poland, to lord it, as mentioned, over 12 million inhabitants before June 1941 and 17 million after the attack on the USSR and the incorporation of eastern Galicia.

Although Frank was directly subordinate only to Hitler himself, his own authority and that of his administration were constantly undermined by Himmler and his appointees. The SS Reichsführer was of course in charge of all internal security matters in the General Government, as concretely demonstrated by the terror campaign unleashed from day one of the German onslaught. As his delegate Himmler appointed Higher SS and Police Leader [*Höhere SS und Polizeiführer,* or *HSSPF*] Friedrich Wilhelm Krüger, who consulted with Frank but was under the Reichsführer's sole authority. On a regional level, in each of the four districts of the General Government, SS and police leaders followed Krüger's—that is, Himmler's—orders. Moreover, Himmler as chief of the RKFDV took over the dumping of Poles and Jews into the General Government until the operation was temporarily stopped, as we saw. Thus the local SS commanders represented Himmler both in security and in deportation and/or "resettlement" matters. A de facto dual administration was being put in place as 1940 began: Frank's civilian administration and Himmler's security and population transfer SS administration. The tension between the two grew rapidly, mainly at district level and particularly in the Lublin district, where Himmler's appointee and protégé, the notorious Globocnik, established a quasi-independent domain in direct defiance of the authority of District Governor Ernst Zörner.[128]

Unexpectedly the first round in this ongoing power struggle was won by Frank. Not only did the governor-general succeed in halting the deportations into his domain, but, in the Lublin District, he compelled Globocnik to disband his private police, recruited among local ethnic Germans: the *Selbstschutz* (self-protection). Within weeks Globocnik's units had displayed a level of lawlessness that even Krüger and Himmler could then not countenance. The *Selbstschutz* disappeared, and Frank took its recruits into his own new police, the *Sonderdienst* (special service). This, however, was but round one, and soon enough Globocnik would resume his terror activities on a far wider scale.[129]

VIII

"In the morning, I proceeded through the streets with an armband," Czerniaków, the newly appointed chairman of the Warsaw Jewish Council, noted on December 3, 1939. "In view of the rumors about the postponement of the wearing of armbands such a demonstration is necessary."[130] As of December 1 all Jews in the General Government above age ten had to wear a white armband with a blue Star of David on their right arm. And although the definition of "Jew" was applied de facto according to the Nuremberg laws with the German occupation of Poland, it was formally so decreed first in the Warthegau at the end of 1939, and then in Frank's kingdom, on July 27, 1940.[131]

The armband was rapidly followed by a prohibition from changing residence, the exclusion from a long list of professions, being banned from the use of public transportation and barred from restaurants, parks, and the like. But, although the Jews were increasingly concentrated in specific areas of cities and towns, neither Heydrich nor Frank gave an overall order to establish closed ghettos. The ghettoization stemmed from different circumstances from place to place. It extended from October 1939 (Piotrkow Trybunalski) to March 1941 (Lublin and Kraków) to 1942, even 1943 (Upper Silesia), and in some cases, no ghettos were established before the beginning of deportations to the extermination camps. The Lodz ghetto was established in April 1940 and the Warsaw ghetto in November 1940. Whereas in Warsaw the pretext for sealing the ghetto was mainly sanitary (the Germans' fear of epidemics), in Lodz it was linked to the resettlement of ethnic Germans from the Baltic countries in the homes vacated by Jews.[132]

From the outset the ghettos were considered temporary means of segregating the Jewish population before its expulsion. Once they acquired a measure of permanence, however, one of their functions became the ruthless and systematic exploitation of part of the imprisoned Jewish population for the benefit of the Reich (mainly for the needs of the Wehrmacht) at as low a cost as possible. Moreover, by squeezing the food supply and, in Lodz, by replacing regular money with a special ghetto currency, the Germans put their hands on most of the cash and valuables the Jews had taken along when driven into their miserable quarters.[133]

The ghettos also fulfilled a useful psychological and "educational" function in the Nazi order of things: They rapidly became the showplace of Jewish misery and destitution, offering German viewers newsreel sequences that fed existing repulsion and hatred; a constant procession of

German tourists (soldiers and some civilians) were presented with the same heady mix.

"What you see," Fräulein Greiser, the Warthegau *Gauleiter*'s daughter, wrote after touring the Lodz ghetto in mid-April 1940, "is mainly rabble, all of which is just hanging around. . . . Epidemics are spreading and the air smells disgustingly, as everything is poured into the drainpipes. There is no water either, and the Jews have to buy it for 10 Pfennigs the bucket; they surely wash themselves even less than usually. . . . You know, one can really feel no pity for these people; I think that their feelings are completely different from ours and therefore they do not feel this humiliation and everything else. . . . They surely also hate us, although for other reasons." In the evening the young lady was back in the city, where she attended a big rally. "This contrast, in the afternoon the ghetto and in the evening the rally, which could not have been more German anywhere else, in one and the same city, that was absolutely unreal. . . . You know, I was again really happy and terribly proud of being a German."[134]

Eduard Koenekamp, an official of the Stuttgart *Auslandsinstitut*, had visited several Jewish quarters in December 1939. In a letter to a friend, Koenekamp showed less restraint than Fraulein Greiser: "The extermination of this subhumanity would be in the interest of the whole world. However, such an extermination is one of the most difficult problems. Shooting would not suffice [*Mit Erschiessung kommt man nicht durch*]. Also, one cannot allow the shooting of women and children. Here and there, one expects losses during the deportations; thus in a transport of 1,000 Jews from Lublin, 450 perished [Koenekamp probably meant *to* Lublin]. All agencies which deal with the Jewish Question are aware of the insufficiency of all these measures. A solution of this complicated problem has not yet been found."[135]

The Jewish Council (*Judenrat*) was the most effective instrument of German control of the Jewish population. The English term "Jewish Council" is a misnomer, however. Heydrich's order of September 21, 1939, demanded the creation of "Jewish Elders' Councils" (*Jüdische Ältestenräte*), which rapidly became, in most places, the contemptuous *Judenrat*, or "Jews' Council," in line with the appellation introduced on November 28 by Hans Frank's decree. These councils were soon established in all Jewish population centers, large and small.[136]

Of course the councils were established by the Germans for their own purposes, but even during the early days of the war, communal activities were organized by the Jews themselves according to various patterns, to cater to the basic needs of the population. Thus, as pointed out by historian Aharon Weiss, "This combination of German pressure and interest in the establishment of a Jewish representation, on the one hand, and the need and wish of the Jews for a representative body of their own, forms one of the major aspects of the convoluted question of the *Judenräte*.[137]

As far as German policies were concerned, the two sets of founding decrees (Heydrich and Frank) indicated that from the outset both the Security Police and the General Government's civil administration fought for control over the councils. In May 1940, Heydrich's delegate in Kraków, SS Brigadeführer Bruno Streckenbach, openly argued for the Security Police's primacy.[138] Frank did not give in, but in fact, whether formally or not, the SS apparatus increasingly dominated the appointments and the structure of the councils while Frank's appointees were mostly involved in the administrative and economic life of the ghettos, until the beginning of the deportations.[139] Then the SS apparatus would completely take over.

In principle the twelve or twenty-four council members (according to the size of the community) were to be chosen from the traditional Jewish elites, the recognized community leadership.[140] Heydrich's orders, issued as the decimation of the Polish elites was taking place, were probably based on two assumptions: first, that Jewish elites would not be instigators and leaders of rebellion and self-affirmation but rather agents of compliance; and additionally that the Jewish elites—as represented in the councils—would be accepted and, all in all, obeyed by the population. In other words the Polish elites were murdered because they could incite against the Germans; the Jewish elites were kept because they would submit and ensure submission.

In fact in many instances the council members did not belong to the foremost leadership of their communities, but many had previously been active in public life.[141] The *Judenrat* as such was a replica—distorted of course, but a replica nonetheless—of self-government within the framework of the traditional *kehilla*, the centuries-old communal organization of the Jews. And many of those who joined the councils did believe that their participation would benefit the community.[142]

Some of the councils' earliest German-ordered tasks took on an ominous significance only when considered in hindsight; the potentially most fateful one was the census. The entries in Czerniaków's diary show that the census ordered by Heydrich looked like any other administrative measure, fraught with difficulties but not particularly threatening. "From 12 until 2, in the Statistical Office," the chairman recorded on October 21. "Between 3 and 6 p.m., at the SS. . . . I point out that the first [of November] is "All Saints Day" and the second "All Souls Day"; hence the Jewish census should be postponed until the 3rd. . . . A long and difficult conference. It is decided that the census will take place on [October] 28th. . . . The census forms were discussed and approved. I have to see to it that this German announcement is posted on the walls throughout the city."[143]

Actually the *Judenrat* itself needed the census for identifying the pool of laborers at its disposal and for housing, welfare, food distribution, and the like; the immediate needs seemed by far more demanding and urgent than any long-term consequences. Nonetheless Kaplan, usually more far-sighted than any other diarist and suspicious on principle of German intentions, sensed that the registration carried threatening possibilities: "Today, notices inform the Jewish population of Warsaw," he wrote on October 25, "that next Saturday [October 29] there will be a census of the Jewish inhabitants. The *Judenrat* under the leadership of Engineer Czerniaków is required to carry it out. Our hearts tell us evil—some catastrophe for the Jews of Warsaw lies in this census. Otherwise there would be no need for it."[144]

On January 24, 1940, Jewish enterprises in the General Government were placed under "trusteeship"; they could also be confiscated if "public interest" demanded it. On the same day Frank ordered the registration of all Jewish property: Nonregistered property would be confiscated as "ownerless." Further expropriation measures followed, and finally, on September 17, 1940, Göring ordered the confiscation of *all* Jewish property and assets except for personal belongings and one thousand reichsmarks in cash.[145]

The expropriation decrees opened the way to profiteering and enrichment on an enormous scale at all levels of the German administration in the annexed Polish provinces and within the General Government. The corruption that had spread throughout all segments of society in the Reich, in annexed Austria, and in the Protectorate was reaching new proportions in occupied Poland and would keep growing throughout the war.[146] On January 1, 1940, diarist Emanuel Ringelblum—to whom we will return at length—noted: "The Lords and Masters not too bad. If you grease the right palms, you can get along."[147] Throughout the second half of November 1939, Czerniaków spent days trying to raise three hundred thousand złotys to ransom a group of hostages from the Warsaw SS.[148]

Bribery became an integral part of the relations between the Germans and their victims. "The Councils constantly had to satisfy all kinds of demands to remodel and equip German office premises, casinos, and private apartments for various functionaries, as well as to provide expensive gifts, etc. In dealing with a ghetto, each functionary considered himself entitled to be rewarded by its Council. On the other hand, the Councils themselves implemented an intricate system of bribes in an effort to try and 'soften the hearts' of the ghetto bosses or to win favors for the ghetto inmates from the 'good Germans.' This in turn enhanced the pauperization of the Jews."[149] The bribes may have delayed briefly some threats or saved some individuals; but, as the coming months would show, they never changed German policies or, in most cases, major implementation steps. In addition, bribing the Germans or their auxiliaries led to the spreading of corruption among the victims: A "new class" of Jewish profiteers and black marketeers was rising above the miserable majority of the population.

One of the immediate advantages that money could buy was exemption from forced labor. From mid-October 1939 on, the councils, mainly in Warsaw and Lodz, took it upon themselves to deliver the required numbers of laborers to the Germans in order to put an end to the brutal manhunt and the constant roundups that had been the usual procedure. As could have been expected, the poorest part of the population bore the brunt of the new arrangement; the wealthier segments of the community either paid the councils or bribed the Germans. In Warsaw in April

1940, according to statistics found in the Ringelblum archives, "some 107,000 men were forced laborers while during the six months that followed, 33,000 persons payed for the exemption."[150]

How did the "Jewish masses" respond to the hail of physical and psychological blows that descended on them from day one of the German occupation? Of course each individual response was different, but if we look for a common denominator among a substantial majority, the prevalent reaction was a belief in rumors, even the most absurd, as long as they offered hope: Germany had suffered grievous losses at the hands of the French, Hamburg had been occupied by British forces, Hitler was dead, German soldiers were abandoning their units at a growing rate, and so on and on. Bottomless despair gave way to frantic expectations, sometimes in recurring sequences on one and the same day. "The Jews have reached the stage of messianic prophecies," Sierakowiak noted on December 9, 1939. "A rabbi from Gora Kalwarii supposedly announced that a liberation miracle will happen on the sixth day of Chanukah. My uncle says that very few soldiers and Germans can be seen in the streets. This tendency to take comfort from nothing irritates me. It's better not to say anything. In the evening a rumor spread about an armistice," and so it went.[151]

IX

While the German grip on the Jewish population of the Warthegau and the General Government was tightening, in the Soviet-occupied zone of Poland, the 1.2 million local Jews and the approximately 300,000 to 350,000 Jewish refugees from the western part of the country were getting acquainted with the heavy hand of Stalinism. A muddled Polish military announcement calling on men to reassemble in the east of the country, broadcast on September 7, had triggered an eastward exodus, accelerated by the rapid German advance. On the seventeenth, both the refugees and the local population suddenly discovered that they were under Soviet rule. Jews, albeit in much smaller numbers, continued to escape to the Soviet zone until early December, and a trickle of refugees managed to cross the new border until June 1941.[152] The elite of Polish Jewry—intellectuals, religious leaders, Zionists, and Bundists among others—fled the Germans but did not feel safe from communist persecution either: They moved on from eastern Poland to independent Lithuania, particularly to Vilna.

There is little doubt that many local and refugee Jews in eastern Poland, threatened by the Germans and long-suffering victims of the Poles, welcomed the Soviet troops. So did many Ukrainians. Moshe Kleinbaum (later known as Moshe Sneh, a commander of the Jewish underground army in Palestine [the Haganah] and ultimately, although he had started as right-of-center liberal, the leader of the Israeli Communist Party) reported on March 12, 1940, that the Jewish population of Luck, where he was at the time, watched the rolling in of the Red Army with curiosity, like everybody else. The young Jewish communists, not particularly numerous, represented the unpleasant exception: "Their behavior on that day was conspicuous for its vociferousness, which was greater than that of other groups. In this fashion it was possible to obtain the erroneous impression that the Jews were the most festive guests at this celebration."[153]

The sense of relief among Jews was certainly more widespread than Kleinbaum admitted, and their initial attitude to Soviet presence more enthusiastic than he reported. We shall see further on how the Poles perceived the issue. In the late 1970s historian Isaiah Trunk went further than Kleinbaum in his severe assessment of Jewish communists. According to Trunk, these Jewish communists were both tactless and treacherous: Their enthusiasm had a triumphant tinge; they penetrated the local Soviet apparatus and did not hesitate to denounce Poles and Jews ("bourgeois" or "socialist") to the NKVD [the Soviet secret police, precursor of the KGB].[154] Trunk's harsh judgment was probably influenced by his own Bundist hatred for communism and thus may also be in need of some revision.

The difficulty in assessing Jewish reactions to Soviet occupation, at least during the first weeks and months, derives in part from the temporary convergence of gut feelings of relief probably felt by all Jews who came under Soviet rule and the quite differently motivated enthusiasm of Jewish communists. When, for example, the news spread among the Warsaw Jews that they would possibly be in the Soviet zone, their enthusiasm knew no bounds, according to a somewhat later entry in Kaplan's diary. Kaplan was politically conservative and an Orthodox Jew who detested the Soviet regime. Nonetheless, his description of Jewish reactions, on October 13, 1939, is telling: "There are no signs of Jewishness at all in Russia. Yet nevertheless, when the news reached us that the Bolsheviks were coming closer to Warsaw, our joy was limitless. We dreamed about it; we thought ourselves lucky. Thousands of young people went to Bolshevik Russia on foot; that is to say, to the areas conquered by Russia. They looked upon the Bolsheviks as redeeming Messiahs. Even the wealthy, who would become poor under Bolshevism, preferred the Russians to the Germans. There is plunder on the one hand and plunder on the other, but the Russians plunder one as a citizen and a man, while the Nazis plunder one as a Jew. The former Polish government never spoiled us, but at the same time never overtly singled us for torture. The Nazi is a sadist, however. His hatred of the Jews is a psychosis. He flogs and derives pleasure from it. The torment of the victim is a balm to his soul, especially if the victim is a Jew."[155]

Kaplan touched on the most fundamental motivations of the Jewish populace. The role of Jewish communists is more complex; the degree of their participation in the Soviet repression system has been variously assessed. According to historian Jan T. Gross, questionnaires filled by Polish refugees from the formerly Soviet-occupied zone, who fled after the German attack of June 1941, do not seem to confirm this common accusation. "Among other things," Gross writes, "we know scores of names of members of village committees and personnel of rural militias that served all over the area—*and Jews are only infrequently mentioned among them* [emphasis in the original]. We know also that higher echelons of the local Soviet administration—on county, or city level—were staffed by functionaries brought in from the east and while there were Jews among them, of course, they were not any more numerous than in the administration apparatus in the Soviet interior."[156] On the other hand Alexander B. Rossino, quoting research by Yitzhak Arad and Dov Levin, as well as an earlier study by Jan T. Gross and mainly Evgeny Rozenblat's research about the Pinsk district, near Białystok, offers a different picture: "In his examination of various sectors of local society, Rozenblat found that, despite the fact that Jews made up only 10 percent of the regional population, they held 49.5 percent of the leading administrative positions in the Pinsk *oblast* [district], including 41.2 percent of those in the judicial and police administration."[157]

Very soon, however, many Jews became disenchanted with the new rulers: Economic hardship spread; Jewish religious, educational, and political institutions were disbanded; NKVD surveillance became all-intrusive; and in the spring of 1940, mass deportations, which had already targeted other so-called hostile groups, began to include segments of the Jewish population, such as the wealthier Jews, those who hesitated to accept Soviet citizenship, and those who declared that after the war they wanted to return home.[158] In view of these worsening conditions in the Soviet zone, thousands of Jews even attempted—and managed—to return to the German-occupied areas. "It is strange," Hans Frank commented on May 10, 1940, "that also many Jews prefer to come into the Reich [the Reich-controlled territories] than to stay in Russia."[159] Moshe Grossman's memoirs tell of a train filled with Jews going east, which, at a border station, met a train moving west. When the Jews coming from Brisk [the Soviet zone] saw Jews going there, they shouted: "You are mad, where are you going?" Those coming from Warsaw answered with equal astonishment: "You are mad, where are you going?"[160] The story is obviously apocryphal, but it vividly illustrates the plight and the confusion of the Jews in both zones of Poland and, beyond it, the disarray spreading among the Jews of Europe. In the meantime the NKVD, in the new climate of cooperation with the Gestapo, was handing over members of the former German Communist Party (KPD) who had been held in Soviet prisons, including Jews.[161]

In its great majority, the Polish population under German occupation remained hostile toward the Jews in the German-controlled areas and expressed fury at "Jewish behavior" in the Soviet-occupied part of the country, according to a comprehensive report written for the government-in-exile in February 1940 by a young courier from Poland, Jan Karski.[162] The report pointed out that the Germans were striving to gain submission and collaboration from the Polish masses by exploiting anti-Semitism. "And," Karski added, "it must be admitted that they are succeeding in this. The Jews pay and pay and pay . . ., and the Polish peasant, laborer, and half-educated, unintelligent, demoralized wretch loudly proclaim, 'Now, then, they are finally teaching them a lesson.'—'We should learn from them.'—'The end has come for the Jews.'—

'Whatever happens, we should thank God that the Germans came and took hold of the Jews,'—etc."[163]

Karski's comments were unusually forthright: "Although the nation loathes them [the Germans] mortally, this question [the Jewish question] is creating something akin to a narrow bridge upon which the Germans and a large portion of Polish society are finding agreement. . . . The present situation is creating a twofold schism among the Poles, with one group despising and resenting the Germans' barbaric methods . . . and the other regarding them (and thus the Germans, too!) with curiosity and often fascination, and condemning the first group for its 'indifference toward such an important question.' "[164]

Even more disturbing was the part of Karski's report that described Polish perceptions of how the Jews reacted to the Soviet occupation of the eastern part of the country: "It is generally believed that the Jews betrayed Poland and the Poles, that they are basically communists, that they crossed over to the Bolsheviks with flags unfurled. . . . Certainly it is so that Jewish communists adopted an enthusiastic stance towards the Bolsheviks, regardless of the social class from which they came." Karski did, however, venture the explanation that the widespread satisfaction notable among working-class Jews resulted from the persecution they had suffered at the hands of the Poles. What he found shocking was the lack of loyalty of many Jews, their readiness to denounce Poles to the Soviet police and the like. Karski did not include the Jewish intelligentsia among the disloyal majority: The intellectuals and the wealthier Jews, he stated, would much prefer an independent Poland again.

The concluding lines of his report were ominous: "In principle, however, and in their mass, the Jews have created here a situation in which the Poles regard them as devoted to the Bolsheviks and—one can safely say—wait for the moment when they will be able simply to take revenge upon the Jews. Virtually all Poles are bitter and disappointed in relation to the Jews; the overwhelming majority (first among them of course the youth) literally look forward to an opportunity for 'repayment in blood.' "[165]

The Polish government-in-exile was certainly aware of the anti-Jewish attitude of the population even before receiving Karski's report; it was thus facing a quandary that was to grow with time. On the one hand,

Prime Minister Władysław Sikorski's group knew that it could not denounce anti-Semitism in the home country without losing its influence on the population; on the other hand, abetting Polish hatred of the Jews meant incurring criticism in Paris, London, and particularly in the United States where, the Polish government believed, the Jews were all-powerful. As for the future of Polish-Jewish relations, it seems that in 1940 Sikorski's men were giving up the hope that the Jews would help them reclaim the territories occupied by the Soviets. Some of them, moreover, hardly rejected the attitudes reported in the Karski memorandum.

In a report sent on December 8, 1939, to the government-in-exile about the situation in eastern Poland, a local member of the underground wrote: "Jews are so horribly persecuting Poles and everything that is connected to Polishness under the Soviet partition . . . that at the first opportunity all the Poles here, from the elderly to the women and children, will take such a horrible revenge on the Jews as no anti-Semite has ever imagined possible."[166] Sikorski's government soon appointed the former Polish ambassador in Berlin, Roman Knoll, to a senior position in its political delegation to the underground. Knoll did not hide his own views about the desirable fate of the Jews in Poland: "No longer do we face a choice between Zionism and the former state of affairs; the choice is rather—*Zionism or extermination*."[167]

X

The approximately 250,000 Jews still living in Germany and annexed Austria at the outbreak of the war were an impoverished, predominantly middle-aged or elderly community.[168] Part of the male population had been drafted into compulsory labor, and a growing number of families depended on welfare (mainly handed out by the Reichsvereinigung). Throughout the country the number of "Jews' houses" [houses inhabited only by Jews, on order of the authorities] was growing, as were the areas off-limits for Jews. The Jews of the Greater Reich were entirely segregated pariahs among some 80 million Germans and Austrians. Emigrating was their ever-present but rapidly dwindling hope.

On the first day of the war the Jews of Germany were forbidden to leave their homes after eight o'clock in the evening.[169] "All police authorities in the Reich have taken this measure," a confidential instruction to the press explained, "because it has frequently happened that the Jews used the blackout to harass Aryan women."[170]

Yom Kippur, duly remembered by the *Einsatzgruppen* in Poland, had not been forgotten in the Reich, either. On that day (September 23), the Jews had to hand in their radios.[171] On September 12, throughout the Reich, the Jews were ordered to shop only in special stores belonging to "reliable Aryans."[172] Some of the store owners refused to cater to Jews, the SD reported from Cologne on September 29, until they were informed that they would not suffer any disadvantages from doing so.[173] In that same city Jews could shop only from 8 to 9:30 a.m.[174] "The mere presence of Jews in queues was felt as a provocation," the Bielefeld Gestapo explained on September 13: "One could not demand of any German to stand in front of a shop together with a Jew."[175] Five days later the Jews were ordered to build their own air raid shelters.[176]

In October, anyone volunteering to serve as a firefighter had to be instructed "about the notion of the Jew," and declare that he was not one.[177] In November, after it occurred to the RSHA that Jews whose radios were confiscated could simply buy new ones, the names and addresses of all purchasers of new radios had to be registered.[178] The radio issue was in and of itself the source of intense bureaucratic turmoil: How did the ruling apply to the non-Jewish spouses in a mixed marriage? What should be done about radios in a house still inhabited by both Jews and non-Jews? And what about the rights of Jewish wives whose Aryan husbands were fighting for the fatherland: Should they keep their radios or not? Finally, in a detailed list of instructions issued on July 1, 1940, Heydrich tried to give definitive answers to the intractable problems created by Jews listening to radios; it is not recorded whether this put everybody's mind at rest.[179] As for the distribution of the confiscated radios, elaborate hierarchies and priorities were established that had to take into account the rights of army units, party authorities, local grandees, and so on. (On October 4, 1939, for example, 1,000 radios were allocated to Army Group C, stationed in Wiesbaden.)[180]

Equally intricate were the issues raised by shopping restrictions or even by the curfew imposed upon the Jews. In regard to the latter, Heydrich also decided on July 1, 1940, that Jewish women whose husbands or sons were serving in the Wehrmacht were exempted from the curfew, "insofar as there were no negative indications against them, particularly no reasons to believe that they would use the exemption to provoke the German population."[181]

Jewish pediatric nurses who still kept an office had to indicate on their doorplates that they were nurses for Jewish infants and children.[182] From mid-December 1939 to mid-January 1940, Jews were deprived of the special food allocations for the holidays, receiving less meat and butter and no cocoa or rice.[183] On January 3 they were forbidden to buy any meat or vegetables at all until February 4.[184] A few weeks beforehand, the Württemberg minister of food and agriculture, soon followed by the food and agriculture ministers of all the other regions, decreed that the Jews were not allowed to purchase any chocolate products or gingerbread.[185]

Some anti-Jewish measures (or rather safeguards) showed genuine creative thinking. Thus the Reich Ministry of Education and Science announced on October 20, 1939, that, "in doctoral dissertations, Jewish authors may be quoted only when such quoting is unavoidable on scientific grounds; in such a case, however, the fact that the author is Jewish must be mentioned. In the bibliographies, Jewish and German authors are to be listed separately."[186] Yet this major initiative for the cleansing of German science encountered serious obstacles. According to "university sources" alluded to in a SD report of April 10, 1940, students writing their dissertations often did not know whether the author quoted was Jewish or not, and racial identification was at times very difficult. "University sources" therefore suggested that the Ministry of Science should prepare "administrative identification criteria of Jewish scientists which would be used not only for dissertations, but for all other scientific work."[187] On February 17, 1940, a decree of the Ministry of the Interior authorized the training of Jewish female medical technicians or assistants, but only for Jewish institutions. However, they were not allowed to deal with [laboratory] cultures of living bacteria.[188]

On February 23, 1940, a supplementary decree to the "Law for the Protection of German Blood and Honor" reasserted a provision that actually was already implicit in the law of September 15, 1935: In cases of *Rassenschande* ("racial disgrace"—that is, sexual relations between an Aryan and a Jew) only the man was held responsible and would be punished. If the woman was Jewish and the man Aryan—which had happened in several prior instances—the woman received a short prison sentence or was sent to a "retraining camp"—that is, to a concentration camp. Thus the immunity was for Aryan women only.

In forwarding the text of the decree to Washington, the American chargé d'affaires in Berlin, Alexander Kirk, probably revealed a major purpose of the decree: "It has also been observed that the absolute immunity granted [German] women in this respect enhances the opportunities for denunciation and extortion which are known to have already been utilized in connection with this anti-Jewish law in particular."[189] For the Gestapo denunciations were of the essence. Otherwise, of course, the notion that, in most cases, Jewish men seduced guileless Aryan women provided the phantasmal basis of the decree.[190]

Full Jews according to the Nuremberg racial laws of September 1935 were the prime targets of the regime's persecution policies. More complex was the situation of spouses and children in mixed marriages; as for the array of problems encountered in the case of mixed-breeds, it challenged Nazi ingenuity to the very end. In the "mixed" categories, in fact, the number of potential variations was practically endless. Consider the case of the German writer and pious Protestant, Jochen Klepper. Klepper's Jewish wife, Johanna Stein, was previously married to a Jew; thus "Hanni's" two daughters from her first marriage, Brigitte and Renate, were Jewish. The older daughter, Brigitte, had left for England before the war, but Renate (Renerle or Reni) was still living in Berlin with her parents. In principle, while the Aryan Klepper was personally protected from deportation or worse, nothing could ensure Hanni's or Renerle's safety.

From the beginning of the war the Kleppers' main goal was to find a way for Renerle to leave the Reich. "For Hanni and for me," Klepper wrote in his diary on November 28, 1939, "the recent emigration plan [for their daughters] no longer pains us in any meaningful way, as every single month we are in distress as a result of the government's Poland project [after the deportations from Vienna in October 1939, rumors spread among Jews in the Reich that the entire Jewish population would be deported to Poland]; and at every distribution of food or *Bezugsschein* tickets, we worry that Renerle will no longer be included."[191]

Once the war started, the guidelines regarding mixed breeds (*Mischlinge*) of the first and second degrees (half and quarter Jews) became more confusing than ever: These *Mischlinge* were allowed to serve in the Wehrmacht and could even be decorated for bravery, but they were not allowed to fill positions of authority. As for the Jewish members of their families, they were spared none of the usual indignities, "My sons [three soldiers] are *Mischlinge* because of me," Clara von Mettenheim, a converted Jewish woman married into the military aristocracy, wrote in December 1939 to the commander in chief of the army, General Brauchitsch. "During the war, when my sons were fighting in Poland, we were tortured here on the home front as if there were no more important tasks to be done during the war.... Please stop [this mistreatment of half-Jewish soldiers and their parents]." And she added: "I beg you to use your influence to make sure that the party leaves those [*Mischlinge*] alone.... These men already have it bad enough being treated as second-class soldiers, they shouldn't also have to worry about their families at home while they are fighting a war."[192]

Much less frequent, of course, but intrinsically not entirely different, were the decisions that confronted the already overtaxed SS Reichsführer regarding some of his men. Take the sad case of SS Untersturmführer Küchlin, for example. One of his maternal ancestors, sometime after the Thirty Years' War, proved to be a Jew, Abraham Reinau. On April 3, 1940, Himmler had to inform Küchlin that such a racial blemish precluded him from staying in the SS.[193] There was some hope, however, that further inquiry could allow Küchlin's reintegration: Reinau's daughter had married an innkeeper, one Johan Hermann, the owner of At the Wild Man's (*Zum wilden Mann*). According to the Reichsführer the inn's appellation pointed to membership in a secret pagan (old Germanic) and racially aware association. Maybe Reinau had not been a Jew after all.[194]

Hitler's constant presence in the shadows of the harassment campaign was unmistakable. In a memorandum of December 6, 1939, one Dr. Hanssen conveyed to a *Parteigenosse* (party member) called Friedrichs (probably a member of the party chancellery) that regarding several new anti-Jewish steps planned by Goebbels and by the RSHA, "the SS Reichsführer would discuss all measures against the Jews directly with the Führer" (*dass der Reichsführer SS alle Massnahmen gegen die Juden direkt mit dem Führer besprechen würde*).[195]

XI

Did the majority of Germans pay much attention to the persecution of the Jews in the Reich and in Poland during the early months of the war? In Germany the anti-Jewish measures were public and "official"; the fate of the Jews in Poland was not kept secret either, and apart from the press reports or the newsreels watched in the home country, a stream of Germans, soldiers and civilians, visited the ghettos as mentioned and photographed any worthy sight or scene: begging children, emaciated Jews with beards and sidelocks, humble Jewish men doffing their caps to their German masters, and, in Warsaw at least, the Jewish graveyard and the shed in which corpses awaiting burial were piled up.[196]

Various confidential opinion reports (either from the SD or from local authorities) give the impression that, overall, the population was becoming increasingly more hostile toward the Jews, but they also mention occasional acts of kindness or, at times, popular fear of retribution. According to a report of September 6, 1939, from the region of Münster, people were demanding the jailing of Jews or even the shooting of ten Jews for every fallen German.[197] In Worms a report from mid-September indicated that the population was upset that Jews had access to food stores on equal footing with Germans.[198]

In Lahr, on the other hand, during heavily attended church services in early October 1939, older people often interpreted the war as [God's] punishment for the persecution of the Jews.[199] Near Marburg a farmer was arrested at the end of December 1939 for showing friendliness to a Jew who worked for him and for inviting him as well as Polish prisoners to share his meals.[200] The same happened in April 1940 to two Germans who expressed a friendly attitude regarding Jews in the region of Würzburg.[201] In Potsdam, obversely again, a June 1940 court decision to allow a Jewish woman to be the sole inheritor of a deceased Aryan (according to that person's will) caused outrage: It went against "healthy popular instinct."[202]

For many *Volksgenossen*, outright greed or the sense of some material injustice (mainly in regard to housing) was the fuel of ongoing anti-Jewish resentment, as shown for example by a vast trove of letters addressed by citizens of Eisenach, the town where Luther grew up, to the local district leader (*Kreisleiter*), Hermann Köhler. Thus in October 1939, when the Aryan Mrs. Fink was evicted from her apartment, while her neighbor, an eighty-two-year-old Jewish woman named Grünberger, was allowed to remain in hers for three more months [an apartment in which she had lived all her life and in which she was legally allowed to stay to the end of her days], all hell broke loose: "How is it possible," Fink wrote to Köhler, "that in the Third Reich a Jewess is protected by law while I as a German enjoy no protection? . . . As a German in the German Reich I should at least be able to lay claim to the same rights as a Jewess!" The owner of the house, Paul Mies, who acquired it from its former Jewish owners in the 1930s, was also eager to evict Grünberger; his lawyer's argument was "dominant public opinion" (*herrschende Volksmeinung*):

"Ever since the plaintiff [Mies] became a member of the NSDAP in May 1937, his obligation to get rid of the Jewess has become more urgent. . . . According to dominant public opinion, which forbids the living in the same house of Aryans and especially party members with Jews, the plaintiffs are no longer obliged to provide asylum to the Jewess. The age of the Jewess and the length of her residence cannot be factors of consideration. Such questions will not be resolved by feelings. . . ."[203] It does not seem that Eisenach was an exceptionally anti-Semitic town.

Personal relations between ordinary Jews and Germans often appeared contradictory. In the spring of 1940 the Klemperers had to sell the house they had built in the village of Dölzschen for much less than its real value. "Berger, the shopkeeper who will get our house," Klemperer wrote on May 8, 1940, ". . . is here at least once a day. An altogether good-natured man, helps us with ersatz honey, etc., is completely anti-Hitlerist, but is of course pleased at the good exchange."[204]

According to a report of the mayor of P., dated November 21, 1939, "Julius Israel Bernheim was the last Jew to own a house on the Adolf-Hitler-Platz. The inhabitants often went on about why the Jew did not leave. The street in front of the house was covered with inscriptions and, at night, the windows were smashed. . . . B. sold the house, and on October 2, 1939, he moved to a Jewish old people's home."[205]

Details about the murderous violence against Poles and Jews came up frequently in diary entries of opposition members during the first months of the war. Information often stemmed from the highest levels of the Wehrmacht and also from military intelligence officers, some of whom were uncompromising enemies of the regime.[206] Plotting against Hitler was active, as several army commanders believed that an immediate attack in the West, as ordered by the Nazi leader on the morrow of the Polish campaign, would end in a military disaster. Thus details about the crimes committed in Poland fell on fertile ground and confirmed the moral abjection of Nazism. "The disastrous character of the regime, mainly in ethical terms, becomes increasingly clear," Ulrich von Hassell, the former German ambassador to Italy, recorded in his diary on February 17, 1940, on hearing a report from Carl Goerdeler, the former mayor of Leipzig and a major opposition figure, about a trip to Poland. Goerdeler mentioned that "some 1,500 Jews, among them women and children, were moved to and fro in open freight cars [in January or February 1940] until they were all dead. Some two hundred peasants were ordered to dig a mass grave [for the Jews] and were themselves shot afterwards."[207] Hassell mentioned in the same entry that a German widow, whose husband was an officer killed by the Poles, nevertheless protested to Göring about the atrocities against Jews and Poles; Hassell believed that Göring was duly impressed.[208]

None of this genuine hostility to National Socialism, however, excluded the continued existence of various shades of anti-Semitism. Thus, while, as mentioned, plans for a military coup that would bring down Hitler and his regime were swirling among top echelons of the Wehrmacht during the last months of 1939 and in early 1940, while Goerdeler and other opposition members discussed a constitution for post-Nazi Germany, the conservative enemies of the regime generally agreed that in this future Germany citizenship would be granted only to Jews who could claim a long-established ancestry in the country; the more recent arrivals would have to leave.[209] Goerdeler's anti-Semitism did not change to the end of his life.[210]

The role of the Christian churches was of course decisive in the permanence and pervasiveness of anti-Jewish beliefs and attitudes in Germany and throughout the Western world. In Germany some 95 percent of the *Volksgenossen* remained churchgoers in the 1930s and 1940s.[211] Although the party elite was generally hostile to Christian beliefs and inimical to organized (political) church activities, religious anti-Judaism remained a useful background for Nazi anti-Semitic propaganda and measures.

Among German Protestants, who generally shared the strong anti-

Jewish slant of Lutheranism, the "German Christians," who aimed at a synthesis between Nazism and their own brand of "Aryan (or Germanic) Christianity," received two-thirds of the votes in the church elections of 1932.[212] In the autumn of 1933 the grip of the German Christians was challenged by the establishment and growth of the oppositional "Confessing Church." Yet, although the Confessing Church rejected the racial anti-Semitism of the German Christians, and fought to keep the Old Testament (which it often presented, however, as a source of anti-Jewish teaching), it was not exempt from the traditional Lutheran anti-Jewish hostility.

Many German Protestants did not belong to either of the opposing groups, and it is this "neutral" middle ground that came closest to some of the positions of "German Christianity," also in regard to converted Jews.[213] The Confessing Church did, at times, attempt to defend the rights of converts (but not those of Jews as such), except, as we shall see, for some prudent steps at the height of the extermination.

The omnipresence of anti-Semitism in most of the Evangelical Lutheran Church found a telling illustration in the notorious "Godesberg Declaration." This declaration, intended to establish a common basis for German Christians and the "neutral" majority of the Evangelical Church was officially published on April 4, 1939, and greeted with widespread support by most of the regional churches (*Landeskirchen*) in the Reich. Point no. 3 (of 5) stated: "The National Socialist worldview has relentlessly fought against the political and spiritual influence of the Jewish race, on our national [*völkisch*] life. In full obedience to the divine rules of creation, the Evangelical Church affirms its responsibility for the purity of our people [*Volkstum*]. Over and above that, in the domain of faith there is no sharper opposition than the one existing between the message of Jesus Christ and that of the Jewish religion of laws and political messianic expectations."[214]

The Confessing Church issued a response in May 1939, a telling example of its own equivocations: "In the realm of faith, there is a sharp opposition between the message of Jesus Christ and his apostles and the Jewish religion of legalism and political messianic hope, already emphatically criticized in the Old Testament. In the realm of [*völkisch*] life, the preservation of the purity of our people demands an earnest and responsible racial policy."[215]

The Godesberg Declaration was followed in May of that year by the foundation of the "Institute for the Study and Elimination of the Jewish Influence on German Church Life" (*Institut zur Erforschung und Beseitigung des jüdischen Einflusses auf das deutsche kirchliche Leben*) and the appointment as its scientific director of the professor for New Testament and *Völkisch* Theology at the University of Jena, Walter Grundmann.[216] The Institute attracted a wide membership of theologians and other scholars, and already during the first year of the war it published a de-Judaized New Testament, *Die Botschaft Gottes* (250,000 copies sold), a de-Judaized hymnal, and, in 1941, a de-Judaized catechism.[217] We shall return to the positions taken by a majority of German Protestants and to the later productions of Grundmann's institute.

A report sent on November 22, 1940, by the association of communal administrators to the Evangelical Church Board in Breslau addressed the burial of converted Jews: "During the burial of the urns of baptized Jews in the Johannes cemetery in Breslau, the indignation of visitors was unpleasantly expressed on several occasions. In two cases, due to the reactions of families of ["Aryans" buried in] neighboring graves, the urns of the non-Aryans had to be dug up and reburied in a distant corner. . . . A Jew from the Paulus congregation who had been baptized decades ago could not be buried in the Lohbrück congregation's cemetery, due to the opposition of its Aryan members."[218]

It is against such a background that individual support for Jews (even if expressed in an indirect way), usually among ordinary pastors and some members of theological faculties, takes on a particular significance. Thus Assistant Preacher Riedesel of Königsberg did not hesitate, in a sermon in October 1939, to tell the story of the Good Samaritan and to choose a Jew as the only passerby ready to offer help to a wounded person lying on the side of the road. The informant's report added that "the State Police was notified."[219] On December 1, 1939, Pastor Eberle of the Confessing Church in Hundsbach declared in a sermon: "The God of our Church is the God of the Jews, the God of Jacob to whom I profess my faith." According to the report, there were signs of unrest among soldiers who attended the service.[220] Indirectly pro-Jewish statements were also reported at the Theological Faculty of Kiel University, in March 1940, leading to sanctions being put in place by the rector.[221]

The Catholic Church in Germany was more immune to Nazi theories than its Evangelical counterpart. Nonetheless, like the Protestant churches, the German Catholic community and its clergy were in their vast majority open to traditional religious anti-Judaism.[222] Moreover, despite the increasingly hostile stand taken by Pope Pius XI against Hitler's regime during the last years of his pontificate, the church in Germany remained wary of any major confrontation with the authorities, mindful as it was of its minority position and its political vulnerability since the days of the Kulturkampf, under Bismarck, and constantly on the alert as a result of frequent harassment by party and state.

Sometimes, however, German Catholics took daring initiatives, albeit in a paradoxical way. Throughout the 1930s and up to 1942, radical Nazi enemies of the Catholic Church (of the Rosenberg ilk) abundantly used a well-known nineteenth-century anti-Catholic pamphlet, Otto von Corvin's *Der Pfaffenspiegel.* To counter this anticlerical propaganda a host of Catholic writers, theologians, priests, and even bishops argued strenuously over the years that Corvin was Jewish, or part Jewish, or a friend of Jews. As one of these Catholic writers put it, Corvin could well have been of Jewish descent, even if he was not. For the Nazis of course, Corvin was a Protestant Aryan of unimpeachable lineage.[223]

The election of Pius XII on March 2, 1939, inaugurated a new phase of Catholic appeasement of Hitler's regime. Thus, although in the Reich and in occupied Europe, the Catholic hierarchy attempted to offer assistance to converted Jews, it did not venture beyond this strict limit.[224] A Catholic organization established to help emigrants, Sankt Raphaelsverein, took care of the departures of some "Catholic non-aryans," while the Paulus Bund, created in the 1930s, catered to their needs in the Reich.[225]

Old cardinal Adolf Bertram of Breslau, who throughout the war stood at the helm of German Catholicism, displayed unwavering loyalty toward both Führer and fatherland and, as we shall see, kept cordial personal relations with Hitler to the very end. His political stand was that of the majority of the German hierarchy, and, in general terms, it received Pius XII's approval. Facing Bertram, in increasingly starker opposition, stood Bishop Konrad Count Preysing and, depending on the issues, a small group of bishops and other influential members of the clergy. An internal confrontation about the Jewish question would come, very late; it did not change the passive attitude of the majority or lead to any public stand.[226]

XII

The leadership chosen by the Jewish community in Germany in the fall of 1933 remained in place as the war started. The Reichsvereinigung der Juden in Deutschland (Reich Association of Jews in Germany), which in early 1939 came to replace the loosely federated Reichsvertretung, was a centralized body established on the initiative of the Jewish leadership itself for the sake of greater efficiency.[227] From the outset, though, the activities of the association were entirely controlled by the Gestapo, particularly by Eichmann's Jewish section. For all intents and purposes it was a Jewish Council on a national scale. It was the Reichsvereinigung that had to inform Jewish communities of all Gestapo instructions, usually by way of the only authorized Jewish newspaper, the *Jüdisches Nachrichtenblatt*.[228]

In most parts of the Reich, except for Berlin, as the local Jewish community offices and services lost growing numbers of members, they were integrated into the local Reichsvereinigung branches; these branches followed instructions from the main office in Berlin, which in turn had to report every step to the RSHA. In the capital the "Jewish community" was allowed to keep its independent offices and activities, a situation that often created tense relations between the two Jewish organizations.[229]

Until October 1941 the prime function of the association was to foster and organize the emigration of Jews from Germany. But from the outset it was no less involved in welfare and education. Its Berlin offices in Oranienburgstrasse and the board of the association, presided over (as he had the previous Reichsvertretung since 1933) by the elderly rabbi Leo Baeck, as well as the local offices in all major German cities, were the main lifeline for the remaining Jewish population.

Direct material assistance became a major concern. After the beginning of the war, state welfare allocations for needy Jews dropped sharply, and most of the assistance had to be raised by the Reichsvereinigung.[230] The pitiful "wages" paid to the tens of thousands of Jewish forced laborers could not alleviate the growing material distress. At times even the RSHA had to intervene in favor of the Reichsvereinigung against the ruthless exploitation of the laboring Jews by local authorities.[231] Furthermore, because Jewish students had been definitively excluded from all German schools since November 1938, the Reichsvereinigung was solely in charge of the education of some 9,500 children and teenagers in the Old Reich.[232]

While it was facing growing daily burdens, the Reichsvereinigung did not remain immune to bitter internal confrontations with Jewish individuals or groups, sometimes with potentially grievous consequences. In the fall of 1939, approximately 11,500 Polish Jews still lived in the Reich. Some of them had escaped the deportations of October 1938, others had been allowed to return temporarily to wrap up their businesses. On September 8, 1939, the Gestapo ordered their arrest as enemy aliens and their internment in Buchenwald, Oranienburg, and later Sachsenhausen. The Sachsenhausen inmates were soon dying at an alarming rate. It is in this context that an official of the Jewish Agency [the representation of the Jewish community in Palestine] in Berlin, Recha Freier, a woman in charge of youth emigration, tried to save some of the threatened Polish Jews by putting them on priority lists for transports to Palestine. The Reichsvereinigung officials—in particular Otto Hirsch, its administrative director—were determined to keep all emigration slots for German Jews only and insisted that the Polish Jews be sent to the General Government.[233] Apparently Hirsch even threatened Freier with the Gestapo. She escaped and managed to send one transport on its way to Palestine (using forged documents in the process) but never forgave the Berlin Jewish establishment. Leo Baeck was not spared Freier's wrath: she longed for the day, she wrote after the war, "when this man celebrated as a hero has his halo removed."[234]

On December 9, 1939, Klemperer recorded: "I was in the Jewish Community House [the Dresden office of the Reichsvereinigung], 3 Zeughausstrasse, beside the burned down and leveled synagogue, to pay my tax and Winter Aid. Considerable activity: the coupons for gingerbread and chocolate were being cut from the food ration cards.... The clothing cards had to be surrendered as well: Jews receive clothing only on special application to the community. Those were the kind of small unpleasantnesses that no longer count. Then the Party official present wanted to talk to me:... You must leave your house by April 1; you can sell it, rent it out, leave it empty: that's your business, only you have to be out; you are entitled to a room. Since your wife is Aryan, you will be allocated two rooms if possible. The man was not at all uncivil, he also completely appreciated the difficulties we shall face, without anyone at all benefiting as a result—the sadistic machine simply rolls over us."[235]

While in Germany there was a continuity of Jewish leadership, in former Poland much of the prewar leadership was replaced, as we saw, when the Germans occupied the country and many Jewish community leaders fled. Both Adam Czerniaków in Warsaw and Chaim Rumkowski in Lodz were new to top leadership positions, and both were now appointed chairmen of the councils of their cities.

On the face of it Czerniaków's ordinariness was his most notable characteristic. Yet his diary shows him to have been anything but an ordinary person. Czerniaków's basic decency is striking in a time of unbridled ruthlessness. Not only did he devote every single day to his community, but he particularly cared for the humblest and the weakest among his four hundred thousand wards: the children, the beggars, the insane.

An engineer by training (he had studied in Warsaw and in Dresden), Czerniaków filled a variety of rather obscure positions and, over the years, also dabbled in city politics and in the Jewish politics of Warsaw. He was a member of the Warsaw city council and of the Jewish community city council, and when Maurycy Mayzel, the chairman of the community, fled at the outbreak of the war, Mayor Stefan Starzynski nominated Czerniaków in his stead. On October 4, 1939, *Einsatzgruppe* IV appointed the fifty-nine-year-old Czerniaków head of Warsaw Jewish Council.[236]

It seems that Czerniaków did some maneuvering to secure this latest appointment.[237] Was it sheer ambition? If so, he soon understood the nature of his role and the overwhelming challenge that confronted him. He knew the Germans; soon he also lost many illusions about the Poles: "In the cemetery, not one tree," he noted on April 28, 1940. "All uprooted. The tombstones shattered. A fence together with its oak posts pillaged. Nearby at Powaski [Christian cemetery] the trees are intact."[238] He reserved some of his harshest comments for his fellow Jews, though never forgetting the growing horror of their common situation.

Czerniaków could have left, but he stayed. In October 1939 he obviously could not foresee what was about to happen less than three years later, yet some of his witticisms have a premonitory tone: "Expulsions from Krakow," he writes on May 22, 1940. "The optimists, the pessimists and the sophists."[239] In Hebrew *soph* means "end." A witness, Apolinary Hartglas, relates that when the council convened for the first time, Czerniaków showed several members a drawer in his desk where he had put "a small bottle with 24 cyanide tablets, one for each of us, and he showed us where the key to the drawer could be found, should the need arise."[240]

Czerniaków had his foibles of course, as we shall see, but foibles that bring a smile, nothing more. And yet, during his tenure as enslaved mayor of the largest Jewish urban concentration in the world after New York, this mild administrator was mostly reviled and hated for evil measures that were none of his doing and that he had no way of mitigating.

It is in stark contrast to Czerniaków's mostly posthumous image of decency and self-sacrifice that any number of diarists, memoirists, and not a few later historians describe the leader of the second largest Jewish community in former Poland: Mordechai Chaim Rumkowski, the "Elder" of Lodz. Rumkowski's life to age sixty-two was undistinguished: in business he apparently failed several times, in the Zionist politics of Lodz he did not leave much of an impact and even his stewardship of several orphanages was criticized by some contemporaries.

As in Warsaw, the head of the prewar Lodz community, Leon Minzberg, fled; he was replaced by his deputy, and Rumkowski was elevated to the vice-presidency of the community. It was Rumkowski, however, whom the Germans chose to lead the Jews of Lodz. The new "Elder" appointed a council of thirty-one members. Within less than a month these council members were arrested by the Gestapo and shot. The hatred Rumkowski inspired years after his death finds a telling expression in the ambiguous comments of one of the earliest and most distinguished historians of the Holocaust, Philip Friedman, regarding this episode: "What was Rumkowski's part in the fate of the original council? Had he complained to the Germans about the intransigence of the council members? If so, did he know what was in store for them? These are grave questions, which we cannot answer on the basis of the evidence at our disposal."[241] A second council was put in place in February 1940.

Czerniaków had no great respect for his Lodz counterpart: "It seems that Rumkowski in Lodz issued his own currency 'Chaimki'; he has been nicknamed 'Chaim the Terrible,' " the Warsaw chairman noted on

August 29, 1940.[242] And on September 7 Ringelblum recorded Rumkowski's visit to Warsaw: "Today there arrived from Lodz, Chaim, or, as he is called, 'King Chaim,' Rumkowski, an old man of seventy, extraordinarily ambitious and pretty nutty. He recited the marvels of his ghetto. He has a Jewish kingdom there with 400 policemen, three jails. He has a foreign ministry and all other ministries too. When asked why, if things were so good there, the mortality is so high, he did not answer. He considers himself God anointed."[243]

Most contemporaries agree about Rumkowski's ambition, his despotic behavior toward his fellow Jews, and his weird megalomania. Yet a keen observer who lived in the Lodz ghetto (and died just before the mass deportations of early 1942), Jacob Szulman, while recognizing and listing some glaringly repulsive aspects of the Elder's personality, in a memoir written sometime in 1941, nonetheless compared his stewardship favorably to that of his opposite number, Czerniaków.[244] Actually the comparison between the Jewish leaders in Lodz and Warsaw should be pushed even further. Rumkowski, historian Yisrael Gutman argues, created a situation of social equality in the ghetto "where a rich man was the one who still had a piece of bread. . . . Czerniaków, who on the other hand was indisputably a decent man, came to terms with scandalous incidents in the Warsaw ghetto."[245]

Jewish diarists—their chronicles, their reflections, their witnessing—will take center stage in this volume. These diarists were a very heterogenous lot. Klemperer was the son of a Reform rabbi. His conversion to Protestantism, his marriage to a Christian wife, clearly demonstrated his goal: total assimilation. Entirely different was Kaplan's relation to his Jewishness: A Talmudic education at the Yeshiva of Mir (and later, specialized training at the Pedagogical Institute in Vilna) prepared him for his lifelong commitment: Hebrew education. For forty years Kaplan was the principal of the Hebrew elementary school he had established in Warsaw in 1902.[246] Whereas Klemperer's prose had the light ironic touch of his revered Voltaire, Kaplan's diary writing—which had already begun in 1933—carried something of the emphatic style of biblical Hebrew. Kaplan was a Zionist who, like Czerniaków, refused to leave his Warsaw community when offered a visa to Palestine. Klemperer, on the other hand, fervently hated Zionism and in some of his outbursts compared it to Nazism. Yet this self-centered neurotic scholar wrote with total honesty about others and about himself.

Ringelblum was the only professionally trained historian among these Jewish witnesses. The dissertation that earned him a doctorate from Warsaw University dealt with "The History of the Jews in Warsaw up to the Expulsion of 1527."[247] From 1927 to 1939 he taught history in a Warsaw gymnasium, and during the years before the war he helped to set up the Warsaw branch of the Vilna Yiddish Scientific Institute (YIVO) and a circle of young historians. Ringelblum was an active socialist and a committed left-wing Zionist. From the outset, in line with his political leanings, he was hostile to the Jewish Council—the corrupt "establishment" in his eyes—and a devoted spokesman of the "Jewish masses."

Jochen Klepper's diary is different: Suffused with intense Christian religiosity, it should not be read in the same way as the Jewish chroniclers' recordings. Because of his Jewish wife, Klepper had been dismissed from his job at German radio, then from the Ullstein publishing house. However, the bureaucracy did hesitate for a time about the category to which he belonged, the more so because he was the author of successful novels, even of a nationalist bestseller, *Der Vater* (The Father), a biography of King Friedrich Wilhelm I of Prussia. Thus Klepper's tortured life turned him into a witness of an unusual kind, one who shared the fate of the victims yet perceived them from outside the pale in a way, as a German and a Christian.

Many more Jewish diarists will add their voices to those encountered so far, from West and East, from diverse walks of life, of different ages. Dawid Sierakowiak, the high school diarist from Lodz, will soon be joined by the youngest chronicler of all, twelve-year-old Dawid Rubinowicz from the neighborhood of Kielce in the General Government; by the high school chronicler Itzhok Rudashevski in Vilna; the adolescent Moshe Flinker in Brussels, and the thirteen-year-old Anne Frank, in Amsterdam. Other adolescents will be heard, more briefly. None of them survived; very few of the adult chroniclers survived either, but hundreds of hidden diaries were found. Tragically the chroniclers had achieved their aim.

CHAPTER II

May 1940–December 1940

On October 22, 1940, the 6,500 Jews of the German provinces of Baden and the Saar-Palatinate were suddenly deported into nonoccupied France. According to a report from the prosecutor's office in Mannheim, on the morning of that day, eight local Jews committed suicide: Gustav Israel Lefo (age seventy-four) and his wife Sara Lefo (sixty-five), gas; Klara Sara Schorff (sixty-four) and her brother Otto Israel Strauss (fifty-four), gas; Olga Sara Strauss (sixty-one), sleeping pills; Jenny Sara Dreyfuss (forty-seven), sleeping pills; Nanette Sara Feitler (seventy-three), by hanging herself on the door of her bathroom; Alfred Israel Bodenheimer (sixty-nine), sleeping pills.[1]

Registration of the property left behind by the deportees was thorough. Thus the gendarmerie station of Walldorf, in the district of Heidelberg, reported on October 23 that nine hens, four roosters, and one goose were found at Blanca Salomon's; Sara Mayer owned ten hens and three roosters; Albert Israel Vogel was the possessor of four hens and Sara Weil, of three hens and one rooster. As for Moritz Mayer, he owned a German shepherd who responded to the name "Baldo."[2] On December 7, 1940, the gendarmerie of Graben opened and searched the apartment previously shared by four deportees: two Jewish widows, Sophie Herz and Caroline Ott, and a couple named Prager. The officials registered a golden medal—Paris Eiffel Tower—1889, a golden medal—Paris—1878, a gilded wristwatch bracelet, a gilded brooch, three golden rings, seven foreign copper coins, six silver kitchen knives, seven silver coffee spoons in their *étuis*, and so on.[3]

I

No major military operations had taken place from the end of the Polish campaign to early April 1940. The "winter war," which started with the Soviet attack against Finland in December 1939, ended in March 1940 after the Finns gave in to Soviet territorial demands in the province of Karelia. This conflict in northern Europe had no direct impact on the major confrontation except, possibly, by strengthening Hitler's low opinion of the Red Army. During these same months of military inaction on the Western Front (the "phony war") optimism was rife in London and in Paris, and consequently among Jewish officials who kept in touch with Western governments. On November 4, 1939, Nahum Goldmann, the representative of the World Jewish Congress in Geneva, reported to Stephen Wise, president of the World Jewish Congress in New York, that both in London and Paris people in the know had the highest expectations. Goldmann himself was slightly more prudent: "I would not go as far as some do to say that the breakdown of Hitler is already sealed, but it seems indeed that the Reich is in a terrible position. Italy is definitely no more on the Axis' side. . . . Next spring the Allies will have twice or three times as many aeroplanes as Germany, whose aeroplanes, by the way, seem to be inferior to those of the Allies. . . . Most of those who still a month ago in France and Britain believed in a very long war, do not believe in it anymore and very important people hold the view that by next spring or summer the war may be over. The internal situation of Germany seems to be very bad. It is Germany at the end of 1917."[4]

On April 9, in a sudden swoop, German troops occupied Denmark and landed in Norway. On May 10 the Wehrmacht attacked in the West. On the fifteenth, the Dutch surrendered; on the eighteenth, Belgium followed. On May 13 the Germans had crossed the Meuse River, and on the twentieth they were in sight of the Channel Coast near Dunkirk. Some 340,000 British and French soldiers were evacuated back to England, thanks in part to Hitler's order to stop for three days before attacking and taking Dunkirk. At the time the decision appeared of "secondary importance," in German terms.[5] In hindsight it may have been one of the turning points of the war.

In early June the Wehrmacht moved south. On the tenth Mussolini joined the war on Hitler's side. On the fourteenth German troops entered Paris. On the seventeenth French prime minister Paul Reynaud resigned and was replaced by his deputy, the elderly hero of World War I, Marshal Henri-Philippe Pétain. Without consulting France's British ally, Pétain asked for an armistice. The German and Italian conditions were accepted, and on June 25, shortly after midnight, the armistice took effect. In the meantime the British government had been reshuffled. On May 10, the day of the German attack on the Western Front, Neville Chamberlain had been forced to resign; the new prime minister was Winston Churchill.

On July 19, in a triumphal address to the Reichstag, Hitler taunted England with a "peace offer." In a radio broadcast three days later, British foreign secretary Lord Halifax (who, a month earlier, had still been the supporter of a "peace of compromise"), rejected the German proposal and vowed that his country would continue to fight, whatever the cost. Did England have the military resources, and did its population and its leadership have the resolve, to pursue the war alone? None of this was obvious in the early summer of 1940. The appeasement camp, although it had lost one of its champions in Lord Halifax, remained vocal, and some highly visible personalities, the Duke of Windsor in particular, did not hide their desire to come to terms with Hitler's Germany.

Stalin, who within days of the French collapse had occupied the Baltic countries and wrung Bessarabia and northern Bukovina from Romania, snubbed Churchill's carefully worded query about a possible rapprochement. The American scene was contradictory. Roosevelt, an uncompromising "interventionist" if there ever was one, had been nominated again as Democratic candidate at the Chicago convention on July 19; his opponent, the Republican Wendell Willkie, was no less a determined interventionist, which augured well for Great Britain. But in Congress and among the American population, isolationism remained strong; soon the America First Committee would give it a firm political basis and a framework for militant propaganda. At this stage, however, even Roosevelt's reelection would be no guarantee that the United States would move closer to war.

Throughout Europe, in occupied countries and among neutrals, a majority of the political elite and possibly a majority of the populations did not doubt in the summer of 1940 that Germany would soon prevail. Many were those who aspired to a "new order" and were open to the "temptation of fascism." The sources of this surge of antiliberalism were deeper than the immediate impact of German military might; as alluded to in the introduction, they were the outcome of a gradual evolution that had unfolded throughout the previous five or six decades.

A vast literature has described and analyzed all the twists and turns of antiliberalism and the rise of a new "revolutionary Right" (and Left), mainly on the European scene, from the end of the nineteenth century onward. In terms of this "New Right," as opposed to the traditional, essentially conservative Right, it is generally accepted by now that the wide array of movements that came under this rubric did not spring only from a narrow social background (the lower middle classes), inspired mainly by fear of the mounting force of the organized Left on the one hand and of the brutal and unaccountable ups and downs of unrestrained capitalism on the other. The social background of the New Right was wider and extended to parts of a disenchanted working class as well as to the upper middle classes and elements of the former aristocracy. It expressed violent opposition to liberalism and to "the ideas of 1789," to social democracy and mainly to Marxism (later communism or Bolshevism), as well as to conservative policies of compromise with the democratic status quo; it searched for a "third way" that would overcome both the threat of proletarian revolution and capitalist takeover. Such a "third way" had to be authoritarian in the eyes of the new revolutionaries; it carried a mystique of its own, usually an extreme brand of nationalism and a vague aspiration for an antimaterialist regeneration of society.[6]

Whereas the antimaterialist, antibourgeois spirit surfaced both on the Right and among segments of the Left in pre–World War I Europe and found strong support among Catholics and Protestants alike, its fusion with exacerbated nationalism, and the related cult of camaraderie, heroism, and death in the aftermath of the war, became standard fare of the New Right and of early fascism. Following the revolution of 1917 the fear of Bolshevism added an apocalyptic dimension to the sense of looming catastrophe. It is in this context that the attraction of a "new order" (as the political expression of the "third way"), under the leadership of a political savior who could rescue a world adrift from the weak and corrupt paralysis of liberal democracy, grew in the minds of many.

The world economic crisis of the thirties merely brought the fears and the urges of earlier decades to a head: the fascist regime in Italy, inaugurated by Benito Mussolini's so-called march on Rome in October 1922, was outdistanced by the considerably more powerful and impressive Nazi phenomenon: The "new order" was becoming a formidable political and military reality. The defeat of France seemed to confirm the superiority of the new order over the old, of the new values over those that had so utterly failed.

The Danish government, kept in place by the Germans, issued a statement in July 1940 expressing its "admiration" for the "great German victories" [that] "have brought about a new era in Europe, which will result in a new order in a political and economic sense, under the leadership of Germany."[7] For several months the Belgian government, which had taken refuge in London, considered the possibility of rejoining King Leopold III (who had stayed) and accepting German domination; in October 1940 it finally chose opposition and exile. By then Marshal Pétain's government had openly chosen the path of collaboration with the Reich. As for the populations in most of Western Europe, they soon accommodated to the presence of an occupation army widely praised for its correct, even polite behavior.

Intellectual accommodation to the new order and intellectual collaboration with it will be a recurring theme in this book. Suffice it to mention here that not only the far right of the European intellectual scene welcomed the German triumph. A strong contingent of Christian thinkers hailed the demise of materialism and modernity and acclaimed the rise of the "new spirit." Thus, in a letter from Peking, the Jesuit paleontologist and a philosophical luminary of post-1945 Paris, Pierre Teilhard de Chardin, showed an impressive understanding of the new times: "Personally, I stick to my idea that we are watching the birth, more than the death of a world.... Peace cannot mean anything but a higher process of conquest.... The world is bound to belong to its most active elements.... Just now, the Germans deserve to win because, however bad or mixed is their spirit, they have more spirit than the rest of the world."[8]

Teilhard's voice was one among many, even on the Catholic left.

"Europe divided against itself is giving birth to a new order, not only perhaps for Europe but for the whole world," the French left-wing Catholic thinker, Emmanuel Mounier, wrote in October 1940. "Only a spiritual revolution and an institutional rebirth of the same scope as the fascist revolution could perhaps have saved France from destruction. . . . Germany against the West is Sparta against Athens, the hard life against the pleasant life." And Mounier foresaw the birth of a Europe that "will be an authoritarian Europe, because too long it was a libertarian Europe."[9]

More significant for the ready acceptance of a "new order" than the enthusiasm of some Christian thinkers was the coalition between the carriers of this new order and most of the right-wing authoritarian regimes on the Continent. As the nationalist Right in Germany had become the natural ally of National Socialism during the crucial period preceding and immediately following the "seizure of power," and then went along as a submissive partner with the policies of the new Reich, so did the European Right during the thirties and, with even greater enthusiasm, after Hitler's early victories. As in Germany—and in Italy—common enemies, mainly Bolshevism and liberal democracy, superseded the social (and ideological) antagonisms between the traditional elites and the extremism inherent in Nazism or even Italian fascism. And, in order to accommodate its conservative partners, mainly in east central Europe, Hitler at times sided with the authoritarian-conservative governments against their internal fascist opposition; thus, for example, the Nazi leader supported Romanian marshal Ion Antonescu's regime against Horia Sima's fascist "Iron Guard" during the guard's attempted putsch of January 1941.

The ideological ambitions of a "new order" and the Nazi-fascist-authoritarian power coalition were undermined from the outset by contrary forces, weak at first but growing in strength as time went by. When it became clear that Great Britain would not give in and that the United States would mobilize its industrial power to support the British war effort, doubts about a final German victory surfaced here and there. Hatred of the Germans spread, intensely in Poland, then in the Balkans, more slowly yet persistently in the West. Generally speaking, during the early years of the war, before the German attack against the Soviet Union, the majority of the European populations was neither psychologically nor practically ready for some form of anti-German resistance (despite armed attacks against the Wehrmacht in Poland and later in Serbia). In the West in particular the population concentrated on overcoming everyday difficulties and opted for various strategies of "accommodation."[10]

One of the major factors that bolstered accommodation with the existing power coalition on the European continent was the conciliatory attitude of the traditionally conservative Christian churches, and particularly—in terms of its influence—that of the Catholic Church. During the rise of Nazism to power in Germany, and during the 1930s, the tension between Hitler's movement and then between his regime and the Catholic Church had been considerable, as already alluded to; yet, as we shall see, Pius XII's accession to the pontificate signaled a resolute quest on the part of the Vatican for an arrangement with the Reich. Catholicism would not give in on matters of dogma (the sanctity of baptism and its precedence over the notion of race) or on issues of canon law. Yet political considerations outweighed any thought of adopting a strong stand against the fascist-authoritarian front.

And, during these same years, Antonio de Salazar's Portugal, Francisco Franco's Spain, the post-Piłsudski Polish governments, Miklos Horthy's Hungary, and, from March 1939 on, Jozef Tiso's Slovakia, displayed various shades of a not-unnatural political-religious alliance against communism, liberalism, and "materialism," the common enemies of both the Christian churches and authoritarian right-wing regimes. Soon Antonescu's Romania would march down the same path, and, even more violently and viciously, so would Ante Pavelić's Croatia. As for Vichy France, its authoritarianism and Catholicism epitomized a strangely stunted return of the "ancien régime"—without the monarchy.

The alliance against communism, liberalism, and "materialism" included to various degrees, as we have seen, some of the main ingredients of modern anti-Jewish hostility. One should add to this brew the themes spread by Nazi propaganda and a variety of national anti-Semitic rantings: those of the Endeks in Poland, the Arrow Cross in Hungary, the Hlinka Guard in Slovakia, the Croatian Ustasha, the Iron Guard in Romania, the Action Française—and, for good measure—those of the still-exiled Ukrainian OUN and the underground nationalist militants in the Baltic countries in the summer of 1940. The "new order" thus also became an intrinsically anti-Jewish new order. In 1940, however, the ultimate consequences of this tide of hatred could not yet be perceived; the common aim was exclusion and segregation.

* * *

Against the background of this momentous ideological evolution and in the midst of an expanding war and a heightening political and moral crisis throughout much of the Western world, the influence of the pope came to play a major role. A few months before his death, Pius XI, whose growing hostility to the Nazi regime we already mentioned, had demanded the preparation of an encyclical against Nazi racism and anti-Semitism. He received a draft of *Humani Generis Unitas* as he lay dying. His successor must of course have known of the existence of the document and probably decided to shelve it.[11]

Pius XII's attitude toward Germany and mainly toward the Jews has often been contrasted with that of his predecessor, thus creating the impression that, in many ways, Pius XII's policy was unusual, even aberrant.[12] In fact Pius XI, as legate nuncio to Poland in the immediate aftermath of World War I, and during most of his pontificate, openly expressed unconcealed anti-Jewish attitudes, as had been the case among most of his predecessors in the modern era. The change that led to *Humani Generis Unitas* occurred during the last years of Pius XI's life and created a growing rift with the Curia, the Roman Jesuits of the periodical *Civiltà Cattolica*; the Vatican daily, *Osservatore Romano*; and possibly his secretary of state, Eugenio Pacelli, the future Pius XII.[13] Thus it can safely be said that Pacelli himself, as secretary of state and later as pope, merely followed a well-established path, even though he may have perceived that the world around him was changing radically. The new pontiff, however, added a personal imprint and initiatives of his own to a well-honed tradition.[14]

Distant, autocratic, and imbued with a sense of his own intellectual and spiritual superiority, Pacelli was as fiercely conservative in politics as in church matters. Nonetheless he was considered an able diplomat during his tenure as nuncio in Munich (1916–20) and then in Berlin in the 1920s. His drive for centralization and for the control of the Vatican bureaucracy over the national churches led him to strive for a concordat with Germany, even at the cost of sacrificing the German Catholic Party, the Zentrum, in the process. The Concordat was signed in July 1933 and ratified that September. The German signature was Adolf Hitler's. In return, on March 23, 1933, the Zentrum had voted full powers for the

Nazi leader, which, for the Catholic Party, meant its own demise and the final demise of the German Republic.

The appearance of good relations between Pius XI and Nazi Germany did not last. From 1936 on, as the danger Nazi racial tenets posed to Catholic dogma grew clearer, as important aspects of the Concordat regarding Catholic institutions (youth movements and religious orders) and church property were disregarded by Berlin, and as trumped-up charges against priests and nuns signaled the possibility of direct persecution of the Catholic Church, Pius XI became increasingly hostile to the new Reich. The pope's 1937 encyclical *Mit brennender Sorge* ("With Deepest Concern") heightened the existing tension. There can be little doubt that Secretary of State Pacelli was involved in the preparation of the encyclical and shared Pius XI's outrage at Nazi measures. It was most probably in this context that, in April 1938, Pacelli handed a confidential memorandum to the U.S. ambassador to London, Joseph P. Kennedy, during a meeting in Rome. Compromise with the Nazis, it stated, was out of the question. At approximately the same time, in a conversation with the U.S. consul general in Berlin, Alfred W. Klieforth, Pacelli supposedly said "that he [Pacelli] unalterably opposed every compromise with National Socialism. He regarded Hitler not only as an untrustworthy scoundrel, but as a fundamentally wicked person. He did not believe Hitler capable of moderation."[15]

Once Pacelli was elected pope, however, some of his first initiatives (apart from the shelving of *Humani Generis Unitas*) confirmed the persistence of an ultraconservative stance and showed an unmistakable desire to placate Germany. Thus, in mid-April 1939, in a radio broadcast, the pontiff congratulated the Spanish people on the return of peace and the achievement of victory (Franco's, of course), adding that Spain "had once again given the prophets of materialist atheism a noble proof of its indestructible Catholic faith."[16] A few months later Pius XII rescinded his predecessor's excommunication of the French antirepublican, monarchist, furiously nationalist, and anti-Semitic Action Française. The Holy Office lifted the condemnation on July 7, 1939, but the decision was announced in the *Osservatore Romano* on July 15, that is, on the morrow of Bastille Day: The choice of date may have been sheer coincidence.[17]

On March 6, the new pontiff had announced his election to Hitler (as was the custom) in a particularly long letter originally written in Latin, the German version of which he had manifestly reworked himself and signed (as wasn't the custom).

The Nazi-Soviet pact, on the other hand, must have reinforced Pius XII's personal lack of confidence in the Nazi leader; it may explain why the pontiff maintained brief contacts with German opposition groups planning an anti-Hitler coup in the fall of 1939. From the outset, however, the pope was faced with a very different and no less pressing issue: What should both his diplomatic and public reaction be in the face of ever more massive Nazi crimes?

Pius XII made it clear to his entourage that he would be personally in charge of relations with Hitler's Germany. Intentionally, no doubt, the pro-Nazi and anti-Semitic Cesare Orsenigo was kept as nuncio in Berlin.[19] Regarding the entire gamut of Nazi crimes, Pius's policy, during the first phase of the war, may be defined as an exercise in selective appeasement. The pope did not take a public stand regarding the murder of the mentally ill, but he made a plea for the "beloved Polish people" in his encyclical *Summi Pontificatus* of October 20, 1939 (although this appeared insufficient to the Polish episcopate and the Polish minister to the Vatican).[20] Concerning both euthanasia and the fate of the Catholics in Poland, the Vatican also appealed to Berlin either via the nuncio (mainly about Poland) or in urgent pleas to the German bishops. In letters of December 1940 to both Cardinal Bertram of Breslau and Bishop Preysing of Berlin, Pius XII expressed his shock about the killing of the mentally ill.[21] In both cases and otherwise, however, nothing was said about the persecution of the Jews.

On June 11, 1940, the French cardinal Eugène Tisserant sent a letter from the Vatican, where he was residing, to his Paris colleague, Cardinal Emmanuel Suhard. Although the letter should be read in its 1940 context, as France was collapsing and the day after Mussolini's joining the war, it had an uncannily wider significance: "Our governments [the democracies] refuse to understand the true nature of the conflict and persist in imagining that this is a war like the wars of times gone by. But Fascist ideology and Hitlerism have transformed the consciences of the young, and those under thirty-five are willing to commit any crime for any purpose ordered by their leader. Since the beginning of November, I have persistently requested the Holy See to issue an encyclical on the duty of the individual to obey the dictates of conscience, because this is the vital point of Christianity. . . . I fear that history may have reason to reproach the Holy See with having pursued a policy of convenience to itself and very little else. This is sad in the extreme, particularly when one has lived under Pius XI."[22]

II

German occupation differed from country to country. While Denmark kept a semblance of freedom until the summer of 1943, Norway and Holland—although countries of "related racial stock"—were governed by Nazi Party appointees, *Reichskommissare*, who were both satraps and ideological envoys. Belgium and northern France (north of the Loire River and along the Atlantic coast) remained under the authority of the Wehrmacht, and two French departments along the Belgian border were put under the authority of the military command in Brussels. The central and southern parts of France, on the other hand, were granted a measure of autonomy under Marshal Pétain's leadership, becoming "Vichy France." Germany de facto annexed Luxembourg and the French provinces of Alsace and Lorraine. A southeastern part of France was occupied by the Italian army, as a reward for Mussolini.

Occupied Europe was dominated by a whole array of German agencies and appointees, independent of one another but fully subservient to the single central authority of the Führer. In a maze of institutional power attributions, no agency was solely in charge of the Jewish question either in 1940 or later. And, as in all domains since early 1938, state agencies were increasingly shunted aside to subordinate positions by the party and its organizations. The dominance of party old-timers (from Germany or former Austria) in all matters related to occupation or anti-Jewish policies was all-pervasive. Only the military, by dint of wartime circumstances, kept a somewhat undefined position. Whereas in Poland, as we saw, the Wehrmacht had been divested of its control over civilian matters soon after the end of the campaign, it nonetheless remained the dominant authority for imposing anti-Jewish measures in several occupied Western European countries. It would also actively participate in the oppression and mass killings in the occupied Soviet Union and the Balkans.

Otherwise, in *territorial as well as in functional terms*, the party and its organizations had almost all power in its hands. Hans Frank held sway in the General Government; Arthur Greiser in the Warthegau; Arthur Seyss-Inquart in Holland; Konstantin von Neurath (the only initial exception), then Reinhard Heydrich, and finally Hermann Frank in the Protectorate; Josef Terboven in Norway; later Hinrich Lohse in the "Ostland," and Erich Koch in the Ukraine. All of them were party stalwarts. In *functional terms* Hermann Göring oversaw economic exploitation and expropriation, Fritz Sauckel and Albert Speer would handle foreign labor; Alfred Rosenberg looted art and cultural assets (he later would be in charge of the civilian administration of the "occupied eastern territories"); Joseph Goebbels, of course, orchestrated propaganda and its multiple ramifications; Joachim von Ribbentrop dealt with foreign governments, while Heinrich Himmler and his minions controlled population transfers and "colonization" as well as arrests, executions, deportations, and extermination.[23]

Throughout the Continent German domination could rely on a collaboration that was in part determined by "rational" calculations but often was also a willing or even an enthusiastic embrace of Germany's supremacy on assorted ideological and power-political grounds. Such a collaboration involved national and regional agencies and institutions, auxiliaries of all hues, political support groups, and independent agents, ranging from politicians to civil servants, from intellectuals to police forces and railway administrations, from journalists to industrialists; from youth movements to peasant leagues, from clergy to universities, from organized to spontaneous killer gangs. And, as the war became fiercer and resistance movements more active, the dyed-in-the-wool collaborators turned more savage in their hunting down of Germany's enemies and of Germany's victims.

At the time of Hitler's triumph in the West, the Nazi terror system controlled directly (or with the assistance of its satellites) around 250,000 to 280,000 Jews remaining in the Greater Reich, 90,000 in the Protectorate, 90,000 in Slovakia, 2.2 million in the German-occupied or -annexed parts of ex-Poland, 140,000 in Holland, 65,000 in Belgium, about 330,000 in both French zones, between 7,000 and 8,000 in Denmark, and 1,700 in Norway. Thus, at the beginning of the summer of 1940, a total population of almost 3,200,000 Jews was, to all intents and purposes, already caught in Hitler's clutches.[24]

Among the Jews of Europe, Hitler's new victories triggered a wave of fear. "On the Eiffel Tower, the swastika," the Romanian Jewish writer Mihail Sebastian noted in his diary two days after the fall of Paris. "At Versailles, German sentries. At the Arc de Triomphe, the 'Unknown Soldier' with a German 'guard of honor.' But the terrible things are not the trophies or the acts of provocation: they could even arouse and maintain a will to survive among the French population. What scares me more is the 'harmony' operation that is about to follow. There will be newspapers, declarations and political parties that present Hitler as a friend and sincere protector of France. When that time comes, all the panic and all the resentments will find release in one long pogrom. Where can Poldy [Sebastian's brother, who lived in Paris] be? What will he do? What will become of him? And what of us here?"[25]

In 1940 the thirty-three-year-old Sebastian was already a well-known novelist and playwright on the Romanian literary scene. He lived in Bucharest, in close touch with the local intellectual elite—some of whose members, such as E. M. Cioran and Mircea Eliade, were to achieve world fame in the postwar years—an elite massively drawn to fascism in a Romanian garb and to the most vulgar and violent anti-Semitism. Yet Sebastian, strangely enough, tried to find excuses and rationalizations for the behavior and insulting spewings of his former friends and, in fact, ongoing acquaintances. Whatever the peculiarity of Sebastian's forgiveness, his diary offers a faithful portrait of a regime that was to impose Nazi-like measures and participate in mass murder, and of a society widely supporting it.[26]

In Warsaw, Czerniaków noted the rapidly changing situation without adding comments.[27] While Ringelblum and Sierakowiak did not leave any notes for those months, Kaplan moved from wrath to despair and from despair to very short-lived hope. Wrath at Mussolini's move, on June 11: "The second hooligan has dared, as well! Whether voluntarily or by compulsion it is difficult to say, but the fact remains that Benito Mussolini, the classic traitor, the Führer's minion, the monkey-leader of the Italian nation, has gone to war against England and France." The illusions about France were quickly waning, as the same entry indicated: "The French are fighting like lions with the last of their strength. But there is a limit to acts of valor, too. It is dubious that the military strength still remaining to France will suffice to resist the Nazi military might."[28] Then came the dreadful news of Paris's fall and of the French demand for armistice: "Even the most extreme pessimists," Kaplan noted on June 17, "among whom I include myself, never expected such terrible tidings." The unavoidable question followed: "Will England keep fighting?"[29] Kaplan was doubtful at first, then again, three days later, filled with intense hope: "The war is not over yet! England is continuing to fight, and even France will henceforth carry on her battle from the soil of her empire, her colonies in all parts of the world." Thereupon Kaplan added an astute insight: "The Germans are, of course, the heroes of the war, but they require a short war; as they say in their language, a *Blitzkrieg*. They could not survive a long war. Time is their greatest enemy."[30]

Once again, as it had during the previous months, catastrophe bred messianic dreams. "Some people see mystical proof of the imminent coming of salvation," Kaplan noted on June 28, 1940: "This year is *Tav-Shin* [5700 in the Hebrew calendar]. It is known that the redemption of Israel will come at the end of the sixth millennium. Thus, according to this calculation, three hundred years are lacking. But that can be explained! Some of those who calculate the date of the Messianic age have already been disappointed. But this will not prevent people from finding more proofs, nor other people from believing them. They want the Messiah, and someone will yet come forth who will bring him."[31]

After alluding to the despondence among Jews and the certainty of final victory "before the end of the summer" among the German populace, Klemperer noted an incident on July 7 that possibly showed the complex individual feelings of many a German toward the persecuted Jews in their midst: "Yesterday Frau Haeselbarth came to see us in the late morning, in black: her husband fallen near St. Quentin. . . . She brought me socks and shirts and briefs. 'You need it, it's of no use to me anymore.' We really did accept the things. Sympathy? Very great . . . (but) limited to the woman. The husband whom I had not known, had first been a lawyer on his own account, and then for the Regional Farmers' Association, in direct service of the Party therefore."[32]

As with Jews everywhere, Klemperer's mood switched from hope to despair and from despair to hope again with every bit of news, every rumor, even every chance remark. After England's rejection of Hitler's "peace offer," there was widespread belief among Germans—and among many Jews—that England was doomed: "In the Jews' House," Klemperer noted on July 24, "I always play the role of the optimist. But I am not quite sure of my position at all. The language of the charlatan certainly [a reference to Hitler's July 19 Reichstag speech], but so far every charlatanlike announcement has been realized. Even Natscheff [a friend] is now in very low spirits and says: 'I cannot imagine how he can succeed—but so far he has succeeded with everything.' "[33]

In the same July 24 entry, Klemperer went on, significantly: "Peculiarity of the Jews' House that each one of us wants to fathom the mood of the people and is dependent on the last remark picked from the barber or butcher, etc. (*I am too!*) Yesterday a philosophical piano tuner was here doing his job: It will last a long time, England is a world empire—even if there were to be a landing . . . immediately my heart felt lighter."[34]

The most unexpected reaction to Hitler's victories came from the Kleppers: They welcomed them: "We tell ourselves," Jochen Klepper noted on July 4, 1940 (alluding to the opinion he shared with his wife, Hanni), "that for us, in our special situation, nothing could have been as dangerous, in fact as awful, as a lost war the outbreak of which was attributed to world Jewry. We would have had to pay for it. It may well be that we also won't escape paying for a victorious war, but not so terribly."[35]

III

Throughout 1940 the Nazi leader maintained the public restraint regarding the Jews that had already been noticeable since the beginning of the war. Although during the victory speech of July 19, 1940, the Jews were mentioned, it was only in terms of standard Nazi rhetoric: "Jewish capitalists" and "international Jewish world poison" were lumped together with the Freemasons, the armaments industrialists, the war profiteers, and the like.[36] The same almost haphazard mention of the Jews among Germany's enemies surfaced in the September 4 speech for the launching of the annual winter relief campaign, public collections for the poor at the onset of winter.[37] And on December 10, in a speech to the workers of a Berlin munitions factory, Hitler again listed the enemies of the Reich, yet this time the Jews were nothing more than "this people which always believes that it can exterminate nations with the trumpets of Jericho."[38] In other words, at the height of his victory euphoria, in his repeated addresses to the German nation and to the world, Hitler put but minimal emphasis on the Jewish issue. The issue, however, was not forgotten.

On April 13 Hitler declared to Wiljam Hagelin, the Norwegian minister of commerce in the collaborationist government of Vidkun Quisling, that in Sweden the Jews were "taking a large part" in anti-German propaganda.[39] On July 26 the Nazi leader tried to assuage Romanian fears about a collapse of their economy if the Jews were eliminated too rapidly by declaring to the newly appointed prime minister, Ion Gigurta, that "on the basis of numerous examples from the evolution in Germany, despite all talk to the contrary the Jews were proved to be absolutely dispensable."[40]

Of course Hitler's exhortations were not restricted to the sharing of theoretical insights about the role of Jews in the economy. On July 28 he and his foreign minister, Ribbentrop, met with the Slovaks in Salzburg. On the same day Ribbentrop imposed a reorganization of the Slovak government on President Jozef Tiso: Ferdinand Durčansky, who had been both minister of the interior and of foreign affairs, was replaced by two fanatically pro-Nazi politicians, Alexander Mach at the Interior Ministry and Vojtech Tuka at Foreign Affairs. Simultaneously a former SA leader, Manfred von Killinger, was appointed minister to Bratislava. Finally, SS Hauptsturmführer Dieter Wisliceny, one of Eichmann's men at section IVB4 (and, earlier, in charge of the Jewish desk at the SD) became, on September 1, 1940, "the adviser on Jewish affairs" to the Slovak government.[41]

The conversation between Hitler, Tiso, Tuka, and Mach was most urbane: The Nazi leader recommended to his Slovak guests that they align their internal policies with those of the Reich; he explained that Germany was intent on building an economic bloc that would be "independent of international Jewish swindle." Later Hitler imparted to the Slovaks that there were forces in Europe that would try to prevent the cooperation between their two countries (Jews, Freemasons, and similar elements), to which Tiso agreed, adding his own comments about Jews, Magyars, and Czechs.[42]

* * *

During these same months the Nazi leader prohibited the use of individual Jews as laborers in German territories or even among German workers.[43] At the same time, though, as Himmler was busying himself with resettlement plans, Hitler acquiesced to his henchman's memorandum of May 27, 1940, "Some Thoughts on the Treatment of the Alien Populations in the East." The "ethnic mush" under German control would be deported to the General Government and the Jews—worse in Himmler's eyes than just "ethnic mush"—would be shipped off to some colony "in Africa or elsewhere." According to the SS Reichsführer, physical extermination, a "Bolshevik method," would be "un-German."[44]

Thus, on the face of it, Hitler accepted Himmler's ideas, and in several meetings during the second half of June, he backed the project to ship the Jews of Europe to some African colony. To his own ambassador to Paris, Otto Abetz, he disclosed, on August 3, "that he intended to evacuate all Jews from Europe after the war."[45] The island of Madagascar, which belonged to defeated France, seemed an obvious destination; such a deportation had for decades been a pet plan of anti-Semites of all hues.[46]

Mussolini had apparently received the happy tidings from the master of the Reich himself during their discussion of the armistice with France.[47] A few months later, on November 20, the Hungarian prime minister shared the same privilege;[48] this somewhat belated announcement—and even some later ones—show that Hitler used the Madagascar idea as a vague metaphor for the expulsion of the Jews of Europe from the Continent.

For a short while preparations moved into high gear both at the Wilhelmstrasse and at the RSHA, at least on paper.[49] One of the main "planners" at "Department Germany" (*Abteilung Deutschland*) was the fanatical anti-Semite Franz Rademacher, second-in-command to Martin Luther (in charge of Jewish affairs). One sentence in Rademacher's lengthy memorandum of July 3 should be kept in mind: "The Jews [in Madagascar] will remain in German hands as a pledge for the future good conduct of the members of their race in America."[50]

At the beginning of July, Eichmann informed delegates of the Reichsvereinigung and of the Vienna and Prague Jewish communities that the transfer of some four million Jews to an unspecified country was envisioned.[51] In Warsaw it was Gestapo sergeant Gerhard Mende who passed on the good news to Czerniaków: "Mende," Czerniaków noted in his diary on July 1, "declared that the war would be over in a month and that we would all leave for Madagascar. In this way the Zionist dream is to come true."[52]

On July 12 Frank had conveyed the news to the heads of his administration: The entire "Jewish tribe" would soon be on its way to Madagascar.[53] A few days later, in an address in Lublin, the governor-general even showed some unexpected talents as an entertainer when he described how the Jews would be transported "piece by piece, man by man, woman by woman, girl by girl." The audience roared with laughter.[54] And as the governor also had a practical side, he ordered all ghetto construction in his kingdom to be stopped.[55] Greiser had been skeptical from the outset: He doubted that the Jews could be evacuated before the onset of the winter, and for him their transfer from the Warthegau to the General Government was the only immediate and concrete option.[56] Greiser and Frank met in Kraków at the end of July to find a compromise, but to no avail.[57]

The Madagascar fiction was abandoned over the next months, as the defeat of Great Britain was nowhere in sight.[58]

IV

Jewish emigration from the Reich and from occupied countries continued after the beginning of the war. On January 24, 1939, as mentioned, Göring had put Heydrich in charge of Jewish emigration. Gestapo Chief Heinrich Müller became head of the Berlin "Central Emigration Agency," under Heydrich's command. The day-to-day operations were left in Eichmann's hands: For all practical purposes he became the "chief of operations," both for the deportations and for the emigration of Jews (in Nazi eyes both were identical at this stage). It is in line with the overall policy of expulsion—and with Hitler's explicit agreement—that, mainly in the fall of 1939, Jews deported to the Lublin area were often driven by the SS over the Soviet demarcation line or were allowed to flee into Soviet-occupied territory, as mentioned in the previous chapter. By mid-October 1939, however, this possibility tapered off, mainly due to a change in Soviet asylum policy. There also was a semiclandestine route out of Poland over the border into Hungary; it allowed for the flight of several thousand Jews but, as we shall see, not to lasting safety.

During the first few months of the war, Jews from Poland or Polish areas annexed to the Reich could also leave by applying for visas as was the case in the Reich and the Protectorate. Thus, the Jewish Council of the town of Auschwitz, part of annexed eastern Upper Silesia, complained to the office of the Jewish relief organization the American Joint Distribution Committee in Amsterdam on January 4, 1940, for not sending the funds necessary for emigration: "As you might probably know," the Ältestenrat's letter stated, "a central emigration bureau has been established at Auschwitz for the whole district of Kattowitz based on the approval of the competent authorities. To this emigration office belongs also a department for emigration to overseas countries and a Palestine office. . . . In order to release people from various camps, emigration possibilities have to be provided. . . . A considerable number of unused Palestine certificates and several holders of affidavits for America have to be dealt with." Money was needed, urgently.[59]

The Germans soon established their priorities. In April 1940, as departures and border crossings became increasingly difficult, Heydrich issued a first set of guidelines: intensification of Jewish emigration from the Reich, except for men of military age; limitation and control of emigration to Palestine; no emigration of Polish or ex-Polish Jews in concentration camps; no further deportation ("or free emigration") of Jews into the General Government.[60]

On October 25, 1940, Jewish emigration from the General Government was forbidden, mainly to keep the emigration possibilities from the Reich as open as possible. Yet Heydrich added some comments that sound genuine—and true to type: "The migration of the Eastern Jews means a continuous spiritual regeneration of world Jewry, as these Eastern Jews, due to their orthodox religious attitudes, represent a large part of the rabbis, Talmudic teachers, etc., who are much in demand, particularly in Jewish organizations active in the United States. For these American-Jewish organizations, each orthodox Jew also represents an additional element in their constant effort to effect both a spiritual rejuvenation and further cohesion of American Jewry. American Jewry also aims, with the particular help of those Jews newly arrived from Eastern Europe, to create a new basis from which to pursue its struggle, especially against Germany, with ever greater energy."[61] In fact, for Jews trapped in former Poland, the chances of reaching the United States were slim at best, except for the lucky ones who had managed to flee to the Soviet-occupied zone and on.

With the beginning of the war, the number of American visas issued to refugees from Germany or German-occupied countries declined precipitously, well below the already limited possibilities offered by the U.S. quota system. A special committee, the Emergency Rescue Committee, or ERC, was set up on June 25, 1940, to facilitate the immigration (from southern France, where many had found a temporary refuge), of a select group of refugees deemed particularly valuable to the United States or in danger of being delivered to the Gestapo, according to article 19 of the Franco-German armistice agreement.[62]

At first ERC headquarters in New York, in complying with the regulations imposed by the Vichy authorities and in establishing new screening procedures to exclude all politically unwanted immigrants, created as many difficulties as it solved. In August 1940, however, the ERC decided to send a member of the Foreign Policy Association, Varian Fry, on a brief fact-finding mission to France. Instead of returning to the United States, Fry set up the Centre Américain de Secours in Marseilles and started helping the most endangered individuals to leave the country. In the face of the massive obstacles put in place by the French and also the Spaniards and the Portuguese, Fry took it upon himself to cut many a legal corner, in fact to initiate blatantly illegal steps (forged exit and transit visas and the like). Hundreds of refugees—Jews and non-Jews—owed him their move to safety. In August 1941 Fry was briefly arrested by the French and recalled.[63]

At times well-known individuals intervened on their own. Thus, on July 9, 1940, the world-renowned novelist Stefan Zweig wrote (from New York) to a Mr. Adolphe Held at the New York Amalgamated Bank to ask for his help in saving "Frederike Maria Zweig, my former wife and her two daughters; Mr. Hugo Simon, who has been active in a number of anti-Nazi efforts; Theodor Wolff, the former editor-in-chief of the *Berliner Tageblatt* and his family; and Mr. Alfred Polgar, the well-known Austrian writer." All these people were stranded in Montauban, a small town in southwest France.[64]

In most cases, in the summer of 1940, immigration to the United States became a hopeless quest. It seems that the fear of enemy agents infiltrating the country as refugees had a significant influence on American decisions: The fact that among those attempting to flee many were Jews did not alleviate the suspicion.[65] No clash of policies existed between the bureaucratic level (the State Department) and the political level (the president). Roosevelt's advisers believed in the "fifth column" threat as intensely as did the majority of the population, swayed by a hysterical press campaign.[66] In the course of one day in May 1940, 2,900 allegations of espionage were received at the FBI.[67]

One of the most active restrictionists was the head of the State Department's "Special Problems Division," Assistant Secretary of State Breckinridge Long. His attitude, openly expressed in his diary, derived from an unmistakable hostility to Jews. Long's anti-Semitism was neither shrill nor rabid; yet there is little doubt that the assistant secretary of state spared no effort to limit Jewish immigration to the utmost while it was still possible, and to scuttle any rescue projects during the crucial 1942–43 period.[68]

The situation grew worse over time. The Bloom–Van Nuys Bill, signed by Roosevelt on June 20, 1941, authorized the refusal of any type of visa to an applicant whom a U.S. [consular] official would deem liable to "endanger public safety."[69] In real terms the possibility of Nazi agents entering the United States as Jewish refugees and becoming a "threat to public safety," although existent, was minimal.[70] On the eve of crucial elections, Roosevelt's own considerations in this matter were probably political first and foremost. Some American Jewish leaders seemed aware of the president's reasoning (which they described as that of his friends) and were willing to go along with it. Such in any case was the gist of a letter sent by Rabbi Stephen Wise, president of the World Jewish Congress, to Otto Nathan, one of Roosevelt's Jewish economic advisers, in September 1940: "With regard to the political refugees, we are in the midst of the most difficult situation, an almost unmanageable quandary. On the one hand, the State Department makes all sorts of promises and takes all our lists and then we hear that the Consuls do nothing. A few people slip through, but we are afraid, this in strictest confidence, that the Consuls have private instructions from the Department to do nothing, which would be infamous beyond words. What I am afraid lies back of the whole thing is the fear of the Skipper's [Roosevelt] friends in the State Department that any large admission of radicals to the United

States might be used effectively against him in the campaign. Cruel as I may seem, as I have said to you before, his re-election is much more important for everything that is worthwhile and that counts than the admission of a few people, however imminent their peril."[71]

The stringent restrictions on entry to the United States had ripple effects on the policies of other states in the hemisphere. Jews intent on fleeing Germany after the beginning of the war often tried to obtain visas for Latin American countries, such as Chile, Brazil, Mexico, and Cuba. The end result was usually a matter of bribes and sheer luck. But in 1940, Chile and Brazil closed their doors, in part as a result of internal political pressures; also, however, because the United States had warned both governments that German agents could enter in the guise of Jewish refugees. The desperate candidates for emigration now helplessly watched the Western Hemisphere turn increasingly off-limits, except for a happy few.[72]

A special chapter in the saga of Jewish refugees' attempts to reach Latin America is that of the Brazilian visas for "Catholic non-aryans." In the spring of 1939, after repeated requests from the Sankt Raphaelsverein (the German Catholic organization helping Catholic emigrants and particularly converted Jews), Pius XII obtained from Brazil the granting of three thousand visas for the converts. Soon, however, the Brazilian authorities did add new conditions and it does not seem that the Vatican made strenuous efforts to compel Getúlio Vargas's government to keep its promises. Fewer than one thousand of these visas were finally used. The Holy See helped the refugees finance their passage to freedom—with money deposited for that purpose by American Jewish organizations. As we shall see, during the war the pope did not hesitate to mention the efforts he had made and the money he had spent to help Jewish emigrants. After the war the three thousand visas and the financing of the entire Brazilian operation were grandly attributed to the pope's care and generosity.[73]

Three routes remained available: illegal immigration to Palestine, semilegal transit via Spain and Portugal or via Lithuania, the USSR, Japan or Manchukuo, and Shanghai (in very small numbers by then) to overseas destinations, with the United States or some other countries of the Western Hemisphere still remaining the ultimate goal.[74]

On January 23, 1941, the American Jewish Joint Distribution Committee headquarters in New York informed the "Committee for the Assistance of European Jewish Refugees in Shanghai" that five hundred Jewish refugees were en route from Lithuania to Japan without valid visas. The "Joint" assured the Shanghai committee that many of these refugees would ultimately receive U.S. visas, and asked it to do everything possible to get them temporary entry permits to Shanghai, in order to avoid serious difficulties with Japan. The committee's reply, on February 7, casts a glaring light on the situation of the thousands of Jews trying to flee Europe in all possible directions. "We transmitted your message to our friends in Yokohama," the Shanghai committee wrote, "and received telephonic information to the effect that there were already about 300 refugees from Poland and Lithuania in Japan with visas from Curaçao and South American Republican States. . . . There can be no doubt that this is placing our friends in Japan in a very serious predicament, as the South American Republics have since forbidden the entry of further Jewish emigrants.

"As you are no doubt aware, one vessel carrying about 500 emigrants for Haiti is still floating around somewhere trying to land its human freight. . . . Should this vessel not be able to land these unfortunate people, the Shipping Company will be compelled to bring them back to the port of embarkation in Japan. . . . With the further arrival of 500 or more refugees and the 300 that there are already, plus the 500 that were unable to land in South America, we shall be facing a very serious problem in Japan, more so as the Japanese visas are only valid for 14 days. As practically every port is closed to our refugees and in view of the restrictions now in force in Shanghai, we fail to see what can be done in regard to an ultimate destination for the unfortunate beings who are at present roaming the world without an atom of hope."[75]

The unsavory but necessary cooperation between the leaders of the Yishuv [the Jewish community in Palestine], who wanted to draw Jewish emigration to Eretz Israel, and the Nazis, who wished to oust the Jews from the Reich, had started as early as 1933. It went through different phases but was reconfirmed by Hitler himself in 1938. This common venture took an unusual turn in early 1939, after Great Britain closed the doors of Palestine to mass Jewish emigration for fear of pushing the Arab world toward the Axis: Heydrich and emissaries from the Yishuv joined forces to organize the illegal departure of Jews from Europe to Eretz Israel. On the German side Eichmann was in charge of the practical aspects of the operation.

Immediately after the beginning of the war, grandiose plans were concocted on the assumption that the harbors of neutral Holland could be used as departure bases. The so-called Dutch plan failed.[76] Italy was then considered as an alternative outlet, without success.[77] There remained the possibility of reaching a Romanian harbor by sailing down the Danube; from Romania the voyage would lead across the Black Sea, through the Bosporus into the Mediterranean, and—after avoiding British surveillance—to the coast of Palestine. In most of these operations Eichmann used an Austrian Jew born in Bukovina, Berthold Storfer, as agent—and informer—in the negotiations with Jewish organizations: the Mossad L'Aliyah Beth (the agency for illegal immigration set up by the Jewish authorities in Palestine), the right-wing Revisionist Zionists, or the Joint Distribution Committee, which financed a major part of the rescue effort.[78]

For the Mossad activists and for the political leadership in Palestine, the outbreak of the war created an insoluble dilemma: How to help Jews to flee Europe to Eretz Israel in direct opposition to the British and help the British in their struggle against Germany and Italy. No clear priorities were set, and more often than not, the Mossad's operations were ill prepared almost to the point of recklessness.[79] The Kladovo episode was but one such case. In the summer of 1939, the Mossad envoy in Vienna, Ehud Ueberall (later Avriel) insisted on the rapid departure of a group of twelve hundred candidates for immigration (mainly belonging to Zionist youth movements) without previously acquiring a ship for the journey from Romania to Palestine. After being stalled in Bratislava, the group reached a location on the Yugoslav shore of the Danube but then could not proceed any farther. The Romanians would not allow entry if no ship was ready for the Black Sea and Mediterranean crossing. All attempts to acquire ships failed, and when the Mossad finally got hold of one, it planned for months to use it in a covert British operation in the Balkans. In the meantime the Kladovo group lived on unheated river barges on the frozen Danube, and as the thaw came, no solution had been found. A small group of around 110 children was transferred to Palestine; the remaining one thousand Jews were caught by the Germans after the conquest of Yugoslavia and, soon thereafter, murdered.[80] All in all, after the beginning of the war, fewer than thirteen thousand Jews managed to leave the Reich and the Protectorate for Palestine, and only part reached their destination. In March 1941 the Germans put an end to the common venture.

From the outset the British authorities in Palestine, the Colonial Office, and the Foreign Office were determined to foil any such illegal immigration attempts, in view of potential Arab reactions. That a number of high officials, particularly in the Colonial Office, were far from being philo-Semitic added an element of harshness to British policy in the face of a rapidly worsening human tragedy. An April 1940 memorandum by the deputy Undersecretary at the Colonial Office, Sir John Schuckburgh, about the Jews of Palestine illustrated this convergence of anti-Semitism and straightforward national interest: "I am convinced that in their hearts they hate us and have always hated us; they hate all Gentiles. . . . So little do they care for Great Britain as compared with Zionism that they cannot even keep their hands off illegal immigration, which they must realize is a very serious embarrassment to us at a time when we are fighting for our very existence."[81]

Not everybody in the British administration—and even less so at Cabinet level—was as vehemently hostile to the Jews and their attempts to flee Nazi Europe as was the bureaucracy of the Colonial Office, some of whose members even outdid Schuckburgh and saw the Jews as plotting the destruction of the British Empire and as worse enemies than the Germans.[82]

Yet whatever sympathy for the Jewish plight still may have existed in London, measures aimed to deter refugee ships from running the navy's blockade off the coast of Palestine became even more determined once Britain stood alone. In the fall of 1940, the Colonial Office decided that the illegal immigrants who succeeded in reaching Palestine would be deported to the island of Mauritius in the Indian Ocean and put in barrack camps surrounded by barbed wire.[83]

In response the Yishuv leadership hoped to arouse public opinion, mainly in the United States, by an act of defiance. In November 1940 explosives were afixed to the hull of the *Patria* (about to sail to Mauritius with its cargo of illegal immigrants) to disable it and prevent its departure. The ship sank, and 267 refugees drowned.[84] The remaining passengers of the *Patria* were allowed to stay in Palestine, as the only exception to the deportation policy.

Finally there was the route over the Pyrenees. During the days just preceding or following the armistice it was the easiest way to leave France; the main crossing point was Hendaye. Alfred Fabre-Luce, a French journalist and author who in many ways echoed attitudes widespread among his countrymen, commented on "the Hendaye road": "One discovers," he noted, "that the Israelite world is much vaster than one would have thought. It doesn't include only Jews but also all those whom they corrupted or seduced. This painter has a Jewish mistress, this financier would be ruined by racism, this international journalist does not dare to quarrel with the Jews of America. They all find good reasons to take the road of Hendaye. Don't listen to their declarations; rather look at them: you will find somewhere in their body the stamp of Israel. In these days of panic, the most basic passions lead the world and none is stronger than the fear of a pogrom or the urge for it."[85]

Approximately twenty-five to fifty refugees per day were allowed to cross the Spanish border if they carried valid passports and a visa to a country of final destination. Soon, however, passage through Spain became conditional on French exit visas that, as we saw, could take months to obtain, due to a peculiar twist of French administrative sadism. Other restrictions followed: From November 1940 each Spanish transit visa needed permission from Madrid; authorization from the American consulate in Marseilles, for example, was no longer sufficient. These Spanish regulations lasted throughout the war, despite new difficulties in 1942, and did not discriminate between Jews and non-Jews. Ultimately, however, passage through Spain meant salvation for tens of thousands of Jews.[86]

Spain, however, allowed only brief transit; Portugal was even more restrictive. But while the Portuguese dictator, Salazar, ordered stringent anti-immigration measures and strict control of transit visas, from fear of an influx of "ideologically dangerous" individuals, Portugal's consuls in several European countries nonetheless delivered thousands of visas, in the face of Lisbon's explicit instructions.[87] Some, like the consul general in Bordeaux, Aristides de Sousa Mendes, were to pay for their courage with their careers.[88]

Even the limited generosity shown by the fascistlike regimes in Spain and Portugal was not replicated by two other neutral countries, Switzerland and Sweden, model democracies by any standard. The Swiss authorities clamped down on Jewish immigration immediately after the 1938 Anschluss, demanding that a distinctive sign be stamped on the passports of Jews from the Greater Reich. The Germans acquiesced and, from the fall of 1938 onward, every Jewish passport which they issued was stamped with an indelible red *J* (the Swiss made sure that it could not be effaced).[89] For all practical purposes, therefore, Switzerland was closed to the legal entry of Jews, precisely as their need for transit authorizations or asylum became overwhelming. Sweden also wanted a *J* stamp on Jewish passports and was about to demand it from Germany when the Swiss took the initiative. In fact, until the late fall of 1942, Swedish immigration policy regarding Jewish refugees was as restrictive as that of the Swiss. In late 1942, as we shall see, a change occurred in Stockholm.[90]

From the beginning of the war, one may remember, the Kleppers wanted their daughter Reni to leave for Switzerland. Jochen's wife, Hanni, had converted to Protestantism, and Reni was about to take the same step. A Zurich family, also deeply religious, it seems, the Tappolets, were ready to open their home to the young girl and let her stay as long as necessary. A member of the Swiss embassy in Berlin had promised to help and, on January 20, 1940, Klepper recorded that this official was in touch with a relative who worked as secretary at the Bundesrat [the Swiss government]. But he [the secretary] "wishes above anything else to protect Switzerland from being overrun by foreigners" [*Überfremdung*].[91]

In February, after the deportation from Stettin, the rumor spread in Berlin that all Jews would be sent to Lublin. Reni's departure seemed more urgent than ever. The Tappolets wrote daily about the difficulties they encountered with the local authorities.[92] On March 17 Klepper met the well-known Swiss historian and diplomat, Carl Burckhardt, the ex–high commissioner of the League of Nations in Danzig, who promised to intervene. He apparently mentioned the matter to the Swiss minister in Berlin, Fröhlicher, who seemed ready to assist.[93] On March 27 the Swiss legation sent forms and questionnaires.[94]

On April 25 the Tappolets forwarded a letter just received from Carl

Burckhardt: "Unfortunately, I have the feeling that Miss Stein's matter is being dealt with in a very dilatory way. I have myself been asked to help in so many entry and residence requests that my credit is somewhat spent for the time being."[95] On April 28 Klepper was advised that Reni's application had reached Bern. On May 15, as German victories in the West followed one another, the Tappolets wrote that the request had been rejected: "Any further attempt would be hopeless. . . . Due to the critical war situation, the aim is now to expel foreigners who are in possession of residence authorizations. Even somebody like Professor Burckhardt could not help anymore."[96]

At some stage Klepper asked Pastor Grüber's office for assistance in arranging Reni's departure, but to no avail. Set up shortly before the war by the Confessing Church administration to help "non-Aryan" Protestants emigrate, to provide relief for them or cater to their religious and educational needs, Grüber's office cooperated with Bishop Wilhelm Berning's *Raphaelsverein* for assistance to "non-Aryan" Catholics and with the Reichsvereinigung. The Gestapo tolerated these activities for a while. In December 1940 Grüber was arrested and sent to Sachsenhausen and then to Dachau on the charge of using forged passports in his operations. Limited activities continued under the direction of Grüber's colleague, Werner Sylten, a converted *Mischling*. In February 1941 Sylten was also arrested and sent to Dachau: The office was closed. Grüber survived the war; Sylten was murdered.[97]

Eichmann closely followed the dwindling emigration. In an internal memorandum of December 4, 1940, prepared as background material for an address that Himmler was to give on December 10 at the annual meeting of *Gauleiter* and *Reichsleiter* in Berlin, he estimated the total number of Jews who had left the Reich, Austria, and the Protectorate at 501,711. The surplus of deaths over births reduced the remaining Jewish population by 57,036 persons. Thus, according to Eichmann's computation, 315,642 Jews, as defined by the Nuremberg laws, remained in the Greater Reich (including the Protectorate). The head of the Jewish desk at the RSHA then turned to the second section of his report; titled "The Final Solution of the Jewish Question," it was very brief: "It will be achieved by way of transfer of the Jews out of the European economic space of the German people to a still-to-be-determined territory; the numbers that come into consideration in this project are approximately *5.8 million Jews.*"[98]

While Jews from the Reich and Western Europe were desperately trying to leave the Continent, an unexpected and sudden deportation of Jews from two German provinces was ordered by Hitler, as we saw at the beginning of the chapter. In October 1940 the Nazi leader gave the go-ahead for the deportation of the Jews from Baden and the Saar-Palatinate. The operation, led by *Gauleiter* Josef Bürckel and Robert Wagner, was organized by the RSHA;[99] it ran smoothly and was hardly noticed by the population.

Assembly points had been designated in the main towns of the two provinces; buses were ready; a criminal police commissar was assigned to each bus, and, just in case, police units were on standby. The Jews boarded the buses according to names lists: They were allowed to take one suitcase per person, weighing up to fifty kilograms (or thirty kilograms for a child), a blanket, food for several days, tableware, and one hundred reichsmarks in cash, as well as the necessary identification documents. Valuables had to be left behind; food was turned over to the NSV representatives; apartments were closed and sealed after water, gas, and electricity had been disconnected. Pets were delivered to party representatives "against a receipt." Finally, it was forbidden to mistreat the deportees.[100]

Without any consultation with Vichy, the RSHA shipped the deportees to the nonoccupied zone; the French sent them on to camps, mainly to Gurs, Rivesaltes, Le Vernet, and Les Milles; there the cold weather, the lack of food, and the absence of the most elementary hygienic conditions took a growing toll. According to a report of the Swiss *Basler Nachrichten* of February 14, 1941, even without any major epidemics, half of the population of Gurs would be wiped out within two years.[101] The Germans explained to the French authorities that these Jews would be sent to Madagascar in the near future.[102]

It seems that Hitler had decided to take advantage of a clause in the armistice agreement with France that foresaw the expulsion of the Jews of Alsace-Lorraine into the unoccupied zone. The October 1940 expulsion was an "extension" of that clause as Baden, the Palatinate, and the Saar, adjacent to the two French provinces, were meant to become part of two new *Gaue*. The Jews of Alsace-Lorraine had themselves already been expelled on July 16, 1940. Thus, the two new *Gaue* would be entirely *"Judenrein."*[103]

On April 4, 1941, on Himmler's order, the property and assets belonging to the Jews deported from the two provinces and from Pomerania (Stettin and Schneidemühl) were impounded. The Reichsführer based his decision on the decree issued on the morrow of the Reichstag fire, on February 28, 1933, granting extraordinary executive powers to the Reich chancellor for the protection of the *Volk* and the state. On May 29, 1941, Hitler ordered local authorities to turn over all such confiscated property to the Reich.[104]

Two days after the beginning of the deportations, Conrad Gröber, the archbishop of Freiburg, wrote to the papal nuncio in Berlin, Cesare Orsenigo: "Your Excellency will have heard of the events of the last days concerning the Jews. What pained me most as Catholic bishop is that a great number of Catholic Jews were compelled to abandon home and work and to face an uncertain future far away, with only 50 pounds of movable property and 100 RM. In most cases, these are praiseworthy Catholics who appeal by way of my letter to the Holy Father to ask him, as far as is possible for him, to change their lot or at least to improve it. . . . I urgently ask your Excellency to inform the Holy See of the fate of these Catholic Christians [*sic*]. I also ask your Excellency to use your personal diplomatic influence."[105] No answer is on record, either from the nuncio or from the pope.

V

While considering the deportation of all European Jews to Madagascar and ordering the expulsion of Jews from two German provinces to Vichy France, the supreme leader of the German Reich did not miss any detail regarding the fate of the Jews living in his own backyard. On April 8, 1940, Hitler ordered that half Jews—even "Aryan" men married to Jewish or half-Jewish spouses—be transferred from active service to Wehrmacht reserve units. Quarter Jews could be maintained in active service and even promoted. Yet the order had barely been issued when the Western campaign transformed the situation: many of these partly Jewish soldiers received citations for bravery. Without a choice, in October 1940, the Nazi leader had them turned into "full-blooded Germans," on a par with their fellow German soldiers. The status of their Jewish relatives, however, would remain unchanged.[106]

During the same weeks and months, most German state and party agencies were competing to make life ever harder for the Jews of the Reich. On July 7, 1940, the Reich minister of postal services and communications forbade Jews to keep telephones, "with the exception of 'consultants' (the title given to Jewish lawyers after 1938), 'caretakers of the sick' (the appellation of Jewish doctors from the same year), and persons belonging to privileged mixed marriages."[107] On October 4, the remaining rights of Jews as creditors in judicial proceedings were cancelled.[108] On October 7 Göring, as commander of the Luftwaffe, ordered that in air raid shelters "the separation [of the Jews] from the other inhabitants be ensured either by setting aside a special area, or by a separation within the same area."[109] Actually the separation was already being enforced in many shelters, as William Shirer, the CBS correspondent in Berlin, noted in his diary on September 24, 1940: "If Hitler has the best air raid cellar in Berlin, the Jews have the worst. In many cases they have none at all. Where facilities permit, the Jews have their own special *Luftschutzkeller*, usually a small basement room next to the main part of the cellar, where the "Aryans" gather. But in many Berlin cellars, there is only one room. It is for the "Aryans." The Jews must take refuge on the ground floor. . . . This is fairly safe if a bomb hits the roof. . . . But it is the most dangerous place in the entire building if a bomb lands in the street outside."[110] In the fall of 1940 English bombings were not yet a major problem in Berlin; later, when the Allied air attacks became a major threat to German cities, very few Jews were left to worry about shelters.

On November 13, 1940, Jewish shoemakers were allowed to work again in order to take some of the pressure off German shoemakers, but they could cater only to Jewish clients. As for German shoemakers who belonged to the party or affiliated organizations, they were not allowed to repair the shoes of Jews. Those who were not party members "were to decide according to their conscience."[111] In matters of clothing and shoes Jews of all ages, young and old, were actually compelled to engage in complex strategic planning. Thus, in Hamburg, a few months before the war, a Jewish mother received a winter coat for her adolescent son from the Jewish community. In May 1940 the community gave him a pair of shoes and bartered his coat for a used one; he was allowed to have his shoes repaired one last time in January 1941. "By 1942," according to historian Marion Kaplan, "needy Jews sometimes received hand-me-downs of neighbors who had committed suicide or had been summoned for deportation. Receiving such clothing was patently illegal, since the government confiscated all Jewish property."[112]

On November 15, 1940, Himmler instructed all members of the German police to see *Jud Süss* during the winter.[113] On December 12 the minister of the interior ordered that all mentally ill Jewish patients should henceforth be confined to only one institution, Bendorf-Sayn, in the Koblenz district, which belonged to the Reichsvereinigung.[114] This was becoming technically possible because since June of that year a great number of Jewish mental patients were being sent to their death.[115]

On July 4, 1940, the police president of Berlin issued an order limiting the shopping time for Jews to one hour per day, from four to five p.m. "In regard to this police order," the decree indicated, "Jews are persons whose food cards are marked with a 'J' or with the word 'Jew.' "[116] In Dresden the shopping hours for Jews were not yet restricted at the beginning of the summer of 1940, but the *J* card was a constant problem. On July 6 Klemperer noted: "But it is always horrible for me to show the J card. There are shops . . . that refuse to accept the cards. There are always people standing beside me who see the J. If possible I use Eva's "Aryan" card. . . . We go for short walks after our evening meal and utilize every minute until exactly 9 p.m. [the summer curfew hour for Jews]. How anxious I was, in case we got home too late! Katz maintains that we should not eat at the station either. No one knows exactly what is allowed, one feels threatened everywhere. Every animal is more free and has more protection from the law."[117]

Of course all major decrees were uniformly applied throughout the Reich, but nonetheless local variations allowed for the expression of the bountiful production of all imaginable forms of anti-Jewish harassment. Thus, according to the diary of Willy Cohn, a Breslau high school history teacher, his city's officials did not lack imagination. "January 30, 1940: Jews need travel permits; March 27, 1940: Barber service is only available until nine o'clock in the morning; June 14, 1940: Overseas mail must be taken to the post office personally; June 20, 1940: Jews are forbidden to sit on all public benches. [Only three months earlier, on

April 1, Cohn had remarked that along the waterfront there were still some benches where Jews could rest.] July 29, 1940: No fruit available for Jews; November 2, 1940: A storekeeper is summoned by the police after being denounced for selling fruit to Cohn's wife."[118]

With the help of her non-Jewish ex-husband, Hertha Feiner had succeeded in sending their two teenage daughters, Marion and Inge, to a boarding school in Switzerland, immediately after Kristallnacht. Her own chances of leaving were practically nil (registration number 77,454 for an American visa, sometime in the spring of 1940).[119] Her daily life and chores as a teacher in a Jewish school in Berlin were becoming increasingly difficult: The schoolrooms remained unheated during the bitter cold months of early 1940; soon her telephone would be taken away. In Hertha's desolate condition, one essential lifeline remained: the regular exchange of letters with her daughters. It was to them that over the next two years she would, at times openly, but mostly in veiled allusions, describe her path to an as-yet-unimagined end.

"First I want to tell you," she wrote on October 16, 1940, "that we are not in our beautiful school anymore. Yesterday we moved into an old house, which we have to leave again. Yes, yes, comments are superfluous. We do not know yet where we shall teach. I have 46 children in my class."[120] A few weeks later she wrote to her daughters that on the following day she was starting millinery courses (a milliner probably had a better chance of getting an American visa than did a schoolteacher): "Shall we open a fashion shop together?" she asked.[121]

Under the hail of new regulations, issued at all levels of the system, no Jew in the Reich knew exactly what was allowed and what was forbidden. Even the "Jewish Cultural Association," the Kulturbund, now a section of the Reichsvereinigung, was often at a loss regarding what could be included in its programs. Thus, in mid-September 1939, after his first meeting with the immediate overseer of the Kulturbund's activities, Erich Kochanowski from the Propaganda Ministry, the new artistic director of the association, Fritz Wisten, wrote in mock confusion about the contradictory and absurd instructions given him. The performance of Ferenc Molnar's play *The Pastry Chef's Wife* was forbidden, as were all plays with an "assimilatory" tendency ("assimilatory" meaning encouragement for Jews to stay in Germany and assimilate to its society and culture). "I cannot see," Wisten wrote, "any assimilatory aims in 'The Pastry Chef's Wife.' "[122]

On January 5, 1940, Wisten received new instructions. All German composers were banned from the Kulturbund's musical repertory, including Handel (who mostly lived in England), except for German Jews. All foreign composers were allowed. The same principle applied to theater except, it seems, for the contemporary English repertory: "There are no reservations about Shakespeare. All authors of German descent or those who belong to the Reich Theater Chamber are excluded from consideration."[123] Six months later Kochanowski authorized the performance of Liszt and Sibelius, which immediately encouraged Wisten to submit other Hungarian and Nordic composers.[124] Some of Wilde's plays were acceptable, but this demanded much explanation, as Wisten noted on January 3, 1941: "I ask for permission to submit Wilde's 'Bunburry' [the German title of *The Importance of Being Earnest*]. At the same time, I stress that Wilde is Irish and belongs to a past epoch so removed from us that the English atmosphere should not be able to cause offense."[125]

Kochanowski's directives stemmed from the highest reaches of the Propaganda Ministry, possibly from Goebbels himself. Jews had been forbidden to perform for German audiences, and from the very beginnings of the regime Jewish composers and authors had been banned, due to their intrinsic absence of quality and mainly to their potentially dangerous impact on German hearts and minds. Later, Jews were forbidden to attend theater performances or concerts to spare the sensitivity of Aryan audiences to their presence. Thus the Kulturbund catered to the cultural needs of Jews, with works performed by Jews. Why, under these segregated circumstances, would Jews not be allowed to listen to German music or to perform German plays? Clearly the ban meant that a Jew listening to German music was desecrating it in some mysterious way, or, to put it differently, the music, the play, and the poem would be desecrated by Jewish performance or reading. In fact the threshold of magical thinking had been crossed: Any contact between the German spirit and a Jew, even if the Jew was merely a segregated and passive recipient, soiled and endangered the source itself.

Although the ubiquitous propaganda minister was probably the source of the changing directives given to the Kulturbund, throughout the first half of 1940 Goebbels's attention seems to have been strongly focused, as it had been since October 1939, on the production of his three anti-Semitic films. As we saw in the previous chapter, Hitler was regularly consulted and regularly demanded changes, particularly in regard to *Der Ewige Jude.*

On April 4, 1940, the minister noted once again: "New version of the Jew film. Now it is good. As is, it can be shown to the Führer."[126] Something must have gone wrong nonetheless, as Goebbels's June 9 entry indicated: "Reworked once more the text of the Jew film."[127] At least the minister could be pleased by *Jud Süss*: "An anti-Semitic film of the kind we could only wish for. I am happy about it," he noted on August 18.[128] In the meantime the premiere of Erich Waschneck's *Die Rothschilds* had taken place in July. Within two weeks, however, it became clear that the film had to be reworked and better focused. When it reappeared a year later, it had finally received its full title: *Die Rothschilds: Aktien auf Waterloo* (*The Rothschilds: Shares in Waterloo*). It was a story of Jewish worldwide financial power and profiteering by the exploitation of misery and war: "We can make much money only with much blood."[129]

Germany's best actors, as well as 120 Jewish extras, participated in the most effective of all Nazi anti-Jewish productions, *Jud Süss.* In the film Süss (the character's actual name was Joseph Ben Yssachar Suesskind Oppenheimer) befriended a Hapsburg military hero, Prince Karl Alexander, who became Duke of Württemberg in 1772; he appointed Süss as his financial adviser.[130] Some of the most basic Nazi anti-Semitic themes were the leitmotifs of the brilliantly directed and performed "historical" fabrication. Süss, played by Ferdinand Marian—a highly successful Iago on stage—opens the gates of Stuttgart to hordes of Jews, extorts money from Karl Alexander's subjects by the most devious means, seduces any number of beautiful German maidens, particularly the exquisite Maria Dorothea Sturm, who gives in to save the life of her husband, the young notary Darius Faber, threatened by Süss. After submitting to the Jew, Maria Dorothea commits suicide. When Karl Alexander suddenly dies of a stroke, Süss is arrested, put on trial, sentenced to death, and hanged in a cage. The Jews are expelled from Württemberg. To make the Jews appear even more malevolent, Harlan introduced the figure of a mysterious kabbalist, Rabbi Loew, who hovers in the background as the occult and deadly force behind Süss's criminal dealings.

According to excerpts from Harlan's unpublished memoirs, in a notorious synagogue scene, "The Hassidic religious service had a demonic effect. . . . The alien [spectacle] performed with great vitality, was highly suggestive . . . like an exorcism." For this scene and for the arrival of the Jews in Stuttgart and their later expulsion, the director chose "racially pure Jewish extras." These Jews did not come from the Lublin ghetto (although that had been the initial intention) but rather from the Prague community.[131] For the anti-Semitic Harlan and mainly for the enthusiastic viewers, the effect was ultimately the same.

Jud Süss was launched at the Venice Film Festival, in September 1940, to extraordinary acclaim; it received the "Golden Lion" award and garnered rave reviews. "We have no hesitation in saying that if this is propaganda, then we welcome propaganda," wrote Michelangelo Antonioni. "It is a powerful, incisive, extremely effective film. . . . There is not a single moment when the film slows, not one episode in disharmony with another: it is a film of complete unity and balance. . . . The episode in which Süss violates the young girl is done with astonishing skill."[132] On September 24 Goebbels attended the Berlin opening at the Ufa-Palast: "A very large public, almost the entire Reich Cabinet. The film is a wild success. One hears only enthusiastic comments. The audience is in a frenzy. That is what I had wished for."[133] And the next day, the propaganda minister was even prouder: "The Führer is very taken by the success of 'Jud Süss.'" Everybody praises the film to the skies; it deserves it."[134]

The film's popular success was overwhelming: "Although last week the [attendance] of 'Jud Süss' could already be considered excellent," the Bielefeld SD reported on October 15, 1940, "now it surpasses all expectations. No film has yet succeeded in having such an impact on wide segments of the public. Even people who to this day rarely went to the cinema or never went at all do not want to miss the film."[135] The effect of Harlan's production can be judged from a previous report from Bielefeld: "The Jew is shown here as he really is," a worker declared. "I would have loved to wring his neck."[136] On September 30, 1940, as mentioned, Himmler ordered all SS and police members to see the film during the coming winter.[137] By 1943 the number of viewers had reached 20.3 million.[138]

Ten days after the Reichsführer SS had recognized the outstanding educational value of Harlan's film, the third major screen production of the anti-Jewish campaign was completed: " 'The Eternal Jew' finally ready. Now it can confidently be shown. We have worked on it for long enough," Goebbels noted on October 11.[139] On November 29 this ultimate anti-Jewish propaganda product opened throughout the Reich. Two different versions of the film had been prepared: an original version as well as another that deleted the gory scenes of ritual slaughtering. In Berlin alone the film started simultaneously in sixty-six theaters. The posters advertising the opening night in the capital carried the following warning: "As in the 6.30 p.m. presentation original images of Jewish animal slaughtering are shown, a shortened version presented at 4.00 p.m. is recommended to sensitive natures. Women are allowed only to the 4.00 p.m. presentation."[140]

Each city had its own posters. In Betzdorf, in the Altenkirchen district, *Der Ewige Jude* was described as "a documentary film about world Jewry": "It is unique," the description continued, "because it is no fantasy, but undiluted interesting reality." Then came the usual warning, but in its local version: "Only in the evening presentations, to which there is no entry for youngsters, not even when accompanied by adults, the film shows the original images of the slaughtering of animals by Polish Jews. It shows their true face—sadistic and horrible."[141] The singsong of Jewish prayers and a synagogue cantor's modulations were contrasted with Bach's Toccata and Fugue whenever scenes of Aryan Christian beauty appeared. The chiseled faces of princes, knights, and saints were juxtaposed with the most unattractive Jewish physiognomies caught by Nazi cameras in the ghettos.

In a particularly horrendous sequence, swarms of rats scurry through cellars and sewers, and, in rapid alternation, hordes of Jews move from Palestine to the most remote corners of the world. The text was on par: "Where rats turn up, they spread diseases and carry extermination into the land. They are cunning, cowardly and cruel; they mostly move in large packs, exactly as the Jews among the people."[142] Even worse was the ritual slaughter scene depicting the slow death throes of cattle and sheep, bathing in their own blood, heads partly severed, throats slit while the laughing faces of the Jewish ritual slaughterers were set in repeated contrast to the pitiful stares of the dying animals.

Although "racially ideal" Aryans became the ultimate counterpoint to the most revolting portrayals of Jews, no random scenes from the streets of Berlin filled the screen, but rather carefully chosen shots from *Triumph of the Will*, Leni Riefenstahl's 1934 propaganda film about that year's Nuremberg rally. The narrator stressed the first commandment: to maintain the purity of the race. The film closed on Hitler's January 30, 1939, speech to the Reichstag, announcing that in the case of another world war, the European nations would not be destroyed, but the Jewish race would be exterminated.

After the Berlin opening the *Deutsche Allgemeine Zeitung* of November 29 commented: "When the film ends, the viewer can breathe again. . . . From the deepest submersion [*Niederung*], he comes back to the light again."[143] For the *Illustrierte Film-Kurier*, "In shining contrast to this [the swarming rats], the film ends after the most horrifying scenes [probably the scenes of ritual slaughter] with images of German people and German order, which fill the public with the deepest sense of gratitude for having the privilege of belonging to this people, whose leader is fundamentally solving the Jewish problem."[144]

Despite such dutifully positive press reviews, in terms of public response *Der Ewige Jude* was a commercial failure. The SD reports from many regions of Germany and from Austria were unanimous: The horror scenes disgusted viewers; the documentary was considered nerve-racking; having seen *Jud Süss* shortly beforehand, most people were saturated with "Jewish filth," and so on.[145]

Yet the commercial success of *Jud Süss* and the limited commercial appeal of *Der Ewige Jude* should not be viewed as contrary results in terms of Goebbels's intentions. Images from both films were endlessly replicated in Nazi anti-Semitic posters or publications, all over the Reich and occupied Europe. The scurrying rats of *Der Ewige Jude* or its hideously twisted Jewish faces may have ultimately settled in the collective imaginary of European audiences at greater depth than the plot of *Jud Süss*. In both cases the goal was the same: to elicit fear, disgust, and hatred. At this straightforward level both films can be considered two different facets of an endlessly renewed stream of anti-Jewish horror stories, images, and arguments.

The campaign against "the Jew" raged on many fronts; on the home front, Goebbels and Rosenberg confronted each other more often than not. The ongoing feud between the two main architects of the anti-Jewish ideological war and the two guardians of Nazi ideological purity antedated the accession of Hitler to the chancellorship, ran wild throughout the 1930s and, as we saw, did not subside with the beginning of the war.[146] While Goebbels held the political high ground and was vastly savvier than his adversary, Rosenberg managed nonetheless to impose the stricter ideological line in a host of issues. Thus, while in the early 1930s the propaganda minister opposed changing original choir texts to expurgate their Jewish content, particularly in the works of Handel, Rosenberg got his way: In 1939 *Der Feldherr* (military leader), a "cleansed" version of *Judas Maccabeus* reworked by Hermann Stephani (a Rosenberg protégé), premiered throughout Germany.[147] In May 1940 Goebbels changed his initial stance and decided to establish his own organization for the reworking of libretti, choir texts, and the like, as an extension of the music division of his ministry. Obviously Handel's oratorio got another, more radical, reworking and became *Wilhelm von Nassauen*; it opened in Hamburg in 1941.[148] In the meantime, Stephani was busy with Mozart's *Requiem*: "God of Zion" and "Sabaoth" disappeared. Handel's *Jephtha* followed: The struggle went on.[149]

The Jews of Germany were powerless against the blows that hit them ever harder and the constant vilification to which they were subjected. Usually the attitude of the Reichsvereinigung was meek and submissive; in hindsight its compliance was sometimes excessive, even under the existing circumstances. Thus, during the discussions of the Madagascar plan, the RSHA ordered the German Jewish leadership to cooperate in planning the mass transfer of its communities. In compliance, executive director Otto Hirsch came up with a detailed memorandum—apparently discussed at length among the representatives of all the political and religious groups on the executive board—about the education to be given to the Jews deported to their island. . . . The last tenet of the program, as drafted by Hirsch, read: "The aim of this education is to prepare for life in the Jewish settlement. It is our wish that [this settlement] be realized in the Jewish land of Palestine. However, these principles are valid for educational preparation toward life in any Jewish settlement, wherever it may be."[150] There were exceptions to such subservience, however.

The Reichsvereinigung had already protested against the deportations from Stettin and Schneidemühl. After the sudden deportation of the Jews of Baden and the Saar-Palatinate to Vichy France, the association sent a circular to all communities in the Reich, warning the Jews of the two provinces who had been absent from their homes at the time of the roundup not to return.[151] In addresses at synagogues, the leading members of the Vereinigung raised their voices publicly against the new deportations. A fast day was declared, and all cultural events were canceled for a week. Otto Hirsch even lodged a complaint with the RSHA. The Nazi reaction was foreseeable: One of the leading members of the association, the lawyer Julius Seligsohn, was arrested and sent to the Sachsenhausen concentration camp. Shortly thereafter he was dead.[152] As for Otto Hirsch, the Gestapo waited a few more months: He was arrested in February 1941 and transferred to Mauthausen in May. His death was registered as having occurred on June 19, 1941, due to "Colitis ulcerosa."[153]

VI

On May 1, 1940, the Germans hermetically sealed the shabbiest area of Lodz, the Baluty district; the 163,000 Jewish inhabitants of the city who had been ordered to move there were cut off from the outside world.[154] The no-man's land that surrounded the ghetto made escape practically impossible. The city of Lodz as such, increasingly Germanized by a growing influx of Reich Germans and *Volksdeutsche*, most of whom were known to be enthusiastic Nazis, would certainly not have offered any hideout to a Jew. Thus, even more than in Warsaw, the Lodz ghetto would become a vast urban concentration and labor camp of sorts, without clandestine political or economic links to its surroundings, mostly deprived of information about the fate of Jews living and dying outside its own barbed-wire fence.[155] As for the housing conditions in the ghetto, the numbers are telling: apartments with drains, 613; with water pipes and drains, 382; with a toilet, 294; with toilet, drain, and bath, 49; lacking these comforts, 30,624.[156]

In the General Government, Frank, as will be remembered, had stopped the building of ghetto walls in the summer of 1940 in the belief that the Madagascar plan would become concrete; by September he knew better. In a meeting with the heads of his administration on the twelfth, he announced his decision regarding Warsaw: "As far as our handling of the Jews is concerned, I have agreed to close the ghetto in Warsaw, mainly because . . . the danger represented by these 500,000 Jews is so great that we have to eliminate any possibility of their causing mischief."[157]

On October 2, the eve of Rosh Hashanah, the governor of the Warsaw district, Ludwig Fischer, ordered the establishment of an exclusively Jewish quarter in the city. "Today began the removal of Poles from certain streets in the south of Warsaw," Ringelblum recorded. "The Jewish populace is terribly uneasy; no one knows whether he will be sleeping in his own bed tomorrow. People in the south of town sit at home all day waiting for the hour when they will come and drive the Jews out."[158] The next day the Jews were optimistic again: "The fear of the ghetto has passed . . . a rumor is widespread that the matter has been postponed," Kaplan noted; but he also added "The very thought of a ghetto has left an impression on our nerves. It is hard to live in a time when you are not sure of tomorrow, and there is no greater torture than waiting. It is the torture of those condemned to die."[159]

On October 12, Yom Kippur, Czerniaków was informed of the final decision. The chairman was ushered into the presence of several German officials: "It was thereupon proclaimed that in the name of humanity and at the behest of the Governor [the governor-general] and in conformity with higher authority, a ghetto is to be established. I was given a map of the ghetto. It turns out that the ghetto border streets have been allocated to the Poles. . . . Until October 31, the resettlement will be voluntary, after that compulsory. All furniture must remain where it is."[160]

The ghetto was officially sealed on November 16. The wall that surrounded it was built over a period of several months and paid for by the Jewish Council. The Poles who had lived in the area left; the Jews moved in. Some 380,000 Jews were now cut off from the world (their number, inflated by further arrivals from smaller towns or from the Warthegau, would peak at 445,000 in May 1941, even with a catastrophic mortality rate).[161] The ghetto area was divided into a larger section and a smaller one, linked by a wooden bridge built over the "Aryan" Chlodna Street. The entire area comprised only 4.5 percent of the city; even this area was later reduced. According to Trunk, "In March 1941, the population density of the Warsaw ghetto reached 1,309 persons per hundred square meters, with an average of 7.2 persons sharing one room, compared to

3.2 persons sharing one room in the "Aryan" sections of the city. These were average figures, for as many as 25 or even 30 people sometimes shared one room 6 by 4 meters."[162]

By all accounts the Warsaw ghetto was a deathtrap in the most concrete, physical sense. But cutting Warsaw off from the world also meant destroying the cultural and spiritual center of Polish Jewry and of Jewish life well beyond. In his memorandum of March 12, 1940, some six months before the closing of the ghetto gates, Kleinbaum had grasped the situation in its general terms: "With the destruction of the Polish Jewish community, the basis upon which all of world Jewry found support was severely damaged, for both the Jews of the United States and the Jewish community in Palestine obtained spiritual sustenance from Polish Jewry, including national Jewish culture and especially popular culture. . . . During recent times Polish Jewry had fulfilled the same task in the life of the Jewish people that Russian Jewry fulfilled earlier. Now that these two communities have been destroyed, the role of the Eastern [European] Jewry remains vacant."[163]

In October 1939 Ringelblum had begun to document systematically the fate befalling the Jews of Poland. Others soon joined, and the group adopted the code name Oneg Shabat (Sabbath rejoicing), as its meetings usually took place on Saturday afternoons. In May 1940, the structure of the group was finalized and a secretary, Hersch Wasser, appointed to coordinate the effort. Paradoxically, once the ghetto was closed, the activities of Oneg Shabat expanded: "We reached the conclusion," Ringelblum noted, "that the Germans took very little interest in what the Jews were doing amongst themselves. . . . The Jewish Gestapo agents were busy looking for the rich Jews with hoarded goods, smugglers, etc. Politics interested them little. . . . In conditions of such "freedom" among the slaves of the ghetto it was not surprising that the work of Oneg Shabat could develop successfully."[164]

Like so many other Jewish chroniclers of those days, the members of Oneg Shabat—whether they sensed it during this early phase of their work or not—were assembling the materials for the history of their own end.

The small voice of twelve-year-old Dawid Rubinowicz, the youngest of the diarists, had none of the widely shared sense of urgency nor did his notes aim at systematic chronicling. And yet in their simple, unassuming, and straightforward entries, Rubinowicz's five school exercise books reveal an unusual facet of Jewish life in the General Government between March 1940 and June 1942, that of a quasipeasant family of five (Dawid had a brother and sister) living in Krajno, a village near Bodzentyn, in the Kielce district. The father had bought a piece of land, then a dairy. When Dawid started writing, the Rubinowiczes still owned one cow (it is not clear from the text whether they ever owned more than one).[165] Dawid's first entry, on March 21, 1940, mentioned a new decree: "Early in the morning I went through the village in which we live. From a distance I saw a notice on the shop wall. I quickly went up to read it. The new notice said that Jews may under no circumstances travel on vehicles" [the railway had long been forbidden].[166] It was thus on foot that, on April 4, the boy went to Kielce: "I got up earlier today because I had to go to Kielce. I left after breakfast. It was sad following the paths across the fields all by myself. After four hours I was in Kielce. When I went into Uncle's house I saw them all sitting so sad, and I learned that Jews from various streets are being deported [into a ghetto] and I also grew sad. In the evening I went out into the street to get something."[167]

In his matter-of-fact way Dawid noted the small events of his daily life and other occurrences whose significance he may or may not have understood. On August 5, 1940, he wrote: "Yesterday the local government officer came to the mayor of our village and said all Jews with families must go and register at the rural district offices. By 7 o'clock in the morning we were at the village offices. We were there for several hours because the grown-ups were electing the Council of Jewish elders. Then we went home."[168] On September 1, the first anniversary of the outbreak of the war, Dawid mused about suffering and the widespread unemployment: "Take us," he wrote. "We used to have a dairy and now we're utterly unemployed. There is only very little stock left from before the war; we're still using it up, but it's already running out, and then we don't know what we'll do."[169]

"Wherever one looks there is filth, and the Jews themselves are full of filth," Wehrmacht private E, stationed somewhere in former Poland, informed his family on November 17, 1940. "It is really comical: The Jews all salute us, although we don't respond and aren't allowed to. They swing their caps down to the ground. In fact, the greeting is not compulsory, but is a remnant from SS times; that's how they trained the Jews. When one looks at these people, one gets the impression, that they really have no justification for living on God's earth. You must have seen this with your own eyes, otherwise you cannot believe it."[170] In August 1940 Cpl. WW was been stationed near the demarcation line with the Soviet Union; he too had something to write home about the Jews: "Here, in this town (Siedlce), there are 40,000 inhabitants, of whom 30,000 are Jews. Half the houses have been destroyed by the Russians. The Jews lie on the street like pigs, as becomes a 'chosen people.' . . . Wherever we serve our Great German fatherland, we are proud to be able to help the Führer. Only in many generations will the greatness of these times be recognized. But we all want to stand before History, full of pride, as having also done our duty."[171] In March 1941 Cpl. LB summed up the situation of the Jewish population in his own area of Poland: "Here, one deals with the Jews and [you should see] how the SS takes care of these swine. . . . They would like to take off their armbands, not to be recognized as Jews. But then they receive quite a reminder from the SS and become very small, these Jew-pigs."[172]

VII

A month after signing the armistice, seven days after the demise of the Third Republic, Marshal Pétain's new regime, on its own initiative, introduced its first anti-Jewish measure. One hundred fifty years after the emancipation of the Jews of France, the rollback had started.

Of the approximately 330,000 Jews in prewar France almost half were either foreigners or born of foreign parents. And among the foreigners 55,000 had arrived between 1933 and 1939 (40,000 since 1935).[173] While anti-Semitism had been part of the French ideological landscape throughout the nineteenth century, first on the left, then—increasingly so—on the conservative and the radical right, it was the Dreyfus affair that turned it into a central issue of French politics in the 1890s and throughout the turn of the century. Yet World War I brought a significant decrease in anti-Jewish incitement (contrary to what occurred in Germany), and the immediate postwar years seemed to herald a new stage in the assimilation of native French Jewry into surrounding society. The "*Israélites français*" had found their rightful place as one of the *familles spirituelles* that were part and parcel of France.[174]

The resurgence of a vociferous anti-Semitism from the early 1930s on was due to the presence of a deep-rooted anti-Jewish tradition (even if dormant for a few years), to a series of financial-political scandals in which some Jews were conspicuously implicated (the Stavisky affair, among others), to the rising "threat" of the Popular Front (a coalition of Left and Center Left parties) led by the Jewish socialist Léon Blum—and to Blum's brief government—to the influence of Nazi agitation *and* to the massive immigration of foreign Jews. A new sense of unease among the native Jews turned them against their non-French "brethren," whom they accused of endangering their own position. From then on, more forcefully than ever before, the native Jews—although they did set up an assistance organization for the refugees—insisted on establishing a clear dividing line between themselves and the newcomers.

During the months that preceded the war, the French government seriously considered the possibility of integrating Jewish and other refugees into that most sacred of national institutions, the army, by creating special foreigners' units (distinct from the Foreign Legion) to fight in the French ranks. Most of the foreigners were more than ready to join the campaign against Hitler's Germany. But almost as soon as the Hitler-Stalin pact was signed, a sharp reversal took place: Refugees, whether communists or not, Jews or not, were suddenly suspects; the hysterical fear of a "fifth column" turned eager anti-Nazis into potential enemies. Their place wasn't in the army but in internment camps.[175]

A law of November 18, 1939, ordered the internment of people "dangerous to national defense." At the end of the same month some twenty thousand foreigners, among whom were many Jewish German (or Austrian) male refugees, were sent to camps or camplike facilities. Over the following weeks most of the internees were released, once their anti-Nazi credentials had been checked.[176] Their freedom was cut short, however, by the German attack in the west. As described by the Jewish German writer Lion Feuchtwanger, the new government order was read over the radio: "All German nationals residing in the precincts of Paris, men and women alike, and all persons between the ages of seventeen and fifty-five who were born in Germany but who are without German citizenship, are to report for internment."[177] In fact the measure applied to the whole country, and thus, once more, thousands of Jewish and other refugees from Hitler were assembled at Le Vernet, Les Milles, Gurs, Rivesaltes,

Compiègne, and other camps at the very moment when the Germans shattered the French defenses. Some of the internees managed to escape the trap. Others never did: For them the road to death began in the French camps in the spring of 1940.

As France disintegrated, about 100,000 Jews joined the 8 to 10 million people fleeing southward in the utter chaos and panic of *"la débâcle."* They had been preceded by some 15,000 Jews from Alsace-Lorraine and about 40,000 Jews from Belgium, Holland, and Luxembourg.[178] Overall the catastrophe was perceived in national terms; its specific Jewish aspect was as yet no more than a vague anxiety about the possibility of dire changes.

On July 10 the French Republic scuttled itself; a massive vote of both the Chamber of Deputies and the Senate granted Pétain full executive powers. In the nonoccupied zone of the country, the eighty-three-year-old marshal became the leader of an authoritarian regime in which he was both head of state and head of government. Vichy, a small spa city in the Allier department, at the geographical center of the country, was chosen as the capital of the new state. The motto of the État Français, *Travail, Famille, Patrie* (Work, Family, Fatherland) replaced that of the republic: *Liberté, Egalité, Fraternité.*

Most of the hard-core French admirers of Nazism and militant anti-Semites stayed in Paris. Vichy was too conservative for them, too clerical, too timid, too hesitant in its subservience to Germany and its struggle against the Jews. This extremist fringe did not recognize any limits. The writer Louis-Ferdinand Céline demanded an alliance with Germany, in his view a racially kindred country: "France," he proclaimed, "is Latin only by chance, through a fluke, through defeat . . . it is Celtic, three-quarters Germanic. . . . Are we afraid of absorption? We shall never be more absorbed than we are right now. Are we to remain slaves of Jews, or shall we become Germanic once more?"[179] Though Céline's anarcho-nazism, like his anti-Semitic style, was *sui generis* in many ways, his hatred of Jews was shared by a noisy phalanx of writers, journalists, and public figures of all ilks; it was spewed day in, day out, week after week, by an astonishingly high number of newspapers and periodicals with anti-Semitism as their core message. (On the eve of the war forty-seven such publications systematically spread anti-Jewish propaganda.)[180] "Finish with the Jews!" Lucien Rebatet titled an article in *Le Cri du peuple* on December 6, 1940: The Jews were bugs, rats, "but much more harmful"; yet, as they were human bipeds, "we do not demand their extermination." They should be driven out of Europe, punished, and so on.[181] Worse was to come. Anti-Jewish rage found organized political expression in a series of collaborationist parties such as Jacques Doriot's Parti Populaire Français (PPF), Marcel Déat's Rassemblement National Populaire (RNP), and Charles Maurras' Action Française.[182]

Strident collaborationism was rarely heard in Vichy during the summer of 1940, but traditional native anti-Semitism was rife from the very first days. After reporting on August 16, 1940, about an expulsion campaign from Vichy, on orders of the new government, the American chargé d'affaires in Pétain's capital, Robert Murphy, added: "There is no question that one of its objectives [of the campaign] is to cause the departure of Jews. These, Laval [the deputy prime minister] told me recently, were congregating in Vichy to an alarming extent. He believed they would foment trouble and give the place a bad name. He said he would get rid of them."[183]

Vichy's first anti-Jewish decree was issued on July 17. The new law limited civil service appointments to citizens born of a French father. On July 22 a commission, chaired by Justice Minister Raphael Alibert, started checking all post-1927 naturalizations.[184] On August 27, Vichy repealed the Marchandeau Law of April 21, 1939, which forbade incitement on racial or religious grounds: The floodgates of anti-Semitic propaganda reopened. On August 16 a National Association of Physicians was established, whose members had to be born of French fathers. On September 10 the same limitation was applied to the legal profession.[185] And, on October 3, 1940, Vichy, again of its own initiative, issued its *Statut des Juifs* (Jewish Statute.)

In the opening paragraph of the statute, a Jew was defined as any person descending from at least three grandparents of the "Jewish race," or of two grandparents of the "Jewish race" if the spouse too was Jewish (the German definition referred to the grandparents' religion; the French, to their race). The next paragraphs listed all the public functions from which Jews were barred. Paragraph 5 excluded Jews from all positions of ownership or responsibility in the press, theater, and film. The statute, drafted under Alibert's supervision, was signed by Pétain and by all the members of his cabinet. The next day, October 4, a law allowed the internment of foreign Jews in special camps, if the administration of their department so decided. A commission responsible for these camps was established. The same regional administration could also compel foreign Jews to reside in places defined by the authorities.[186]

The October 1940 statute was approved by all members of the French government, with some individual nuances. Neither before nor later did Pétain publicly attack the Jews as such, yet he alluded to an "anti-France" that in common ideological parlance also meant "the Jews"; moreover he strongly supported the new measures during the cabinet discussions.[187] It seems that Laval, arguably the most influential member of the cabinet, although not a declared anti-Semite either, mainly thought of the benefits to be reaped in exchange from Germany; Adm. François Darlan, on the other hand, displayed open anti-Semitism in the French Catholic conservative tradition; as for Alibert, his hatred of Jews was closer to the Paris collaborationist brand than to the traditional Vichy mold.[188]

In a cable sent on October 18 to Gaston Henry-Haye, Vichy's ambassador in Washington, the secretary general of Vichy's Foreign Ministry presented the arguments that could be used to explain the new statute to the Americans. The responsibility was of course that of the Jews themselves. A Léon Blum or a Jean Zay (the minister of education in Blum's government) was accused of having propagated antinational or amoral principles; moreover they helped "hundreds of thousands of their own" to enter the country, and the like. The new legislation, it was said, neither targeted the basic rights of individuals nor threatened their private property. "The new legislation merely aims at solving definitively and without passion a problem that had become critical and to allow the peaceful existence in France of elements whom the characteristics of their race turn into a danger when they are too intimately present in the political and administrative life of the country."[189]

Vichy's anti-Jewish legislation was generally well received by a majority of the population in the nonoccupied zone. As will become increasingly apparent in the coming chapters, French popular anti-Semitism grew as a result of the defeat and during the following years. On October 9, 1940, the Central Agency for the Control of Telephone Communications (Commission centrale de contrôle téléphonique)—a listening service, in other words—reported that "hostility against the Jews remains";

on November 2 it indicated that the statute had been widely approved and even that for some it did not go far enough.[190] Although only fourteen *préfets* (district governors appointed by the state) out of forty-two reported on public reactions to the statute nine indicated positive responses and one reported mixed ones.[191] In the midst of such a dire general situation, public opinion would of course tend to follow the measures taken by the savior and protector, the old *maréchal.* Moreover, a large segment of the population remained attentive to the spiritual guidance offered, now more than ever, by the Catholic Church.

In the 1930s, alongside the resurgence of a vocal Catholic anti-Semitism in France, prestigious thinkers such as Jacques Maritain, Emmanuel Mounier, or the bestselling Catholic novelist François Mauriac, and an influential daily *La Croix*, opposed traditional Catholic anti-Jewish attitudes.[192] Yet even among these liberal Catholic opponents of anti-Semitism, insidious anti-Jewish themes remained close to the surface during the prewar years. Thus, in 1937, when Mauriac joined *La Juste Parole*, a periodical devoted to the struggle against the growing anti-Jewish hatred, he saw fit to send an explanatory letter to the editor of the journal, Oscar de Ferenzy. "For a Catholic," Mauriac stated, "anti-Semitism is not only an offense against charity. We are bound to Israel, we are tied to it, whether we wish it or not." This said, Mauriac turned to the responsibility the Jews carried for the resentment surrounding them: Jewish "clannishness," of course, was brought up, but there was more: "They cannot corner international finance without giving people the feeling of being dominated by them. They cannot swarm everywhere into a place where one of them has insinuated himself [the Blum ministry], without arousing hatred, because they themselves indulge in reprisals. Some German Jews acknowledged in my presence that there existed in Germany a Jewish problem which had to be resolved. I am afraid that in the end one will also exist in France."[193] As for Mounier, he wrote an article on the Jews and had it published on March 1, 1939, in *Le Voltigeur*; it was also meant to defend the Jews against the growing attacks from the Right. It did so to a point, but added that in some respects the Jews bore part of the responsibility for their predicament, along the lines taken by Mauriac; both shared the same hateful stereotypes.[194]

What counted in the end was the official position adopted by the church. During the summer of 1940 the Catholic hierarchy had been informed of the forthcoming statute. When the assembly of cardinals and archbishops met in Lyon, on August 31, 1940, the "Jewish question" was on the agenda. Émile Guerry, adjunct bishop of Cambrai, summed up the assembly's official stand: "In political terms, the problem is caused by a community [the Jews] that has resisted all assimilation, dispersion and the national integration of its members taken individually. The State has the right and the duty to remain actively vigilant in order to make sure that the persistence of this unity [of the Jews] does not cause any harm to the common good of the nation, as one would do in regard to an ethnic minority or an international cartel. Here, we are not mentioning the foreign Jews, but if the State considers it necessary to take measures of vigilance, it is nonetheless its duty to respect the principles of justice in regard to those Jews who are citizens like others: they have the same rights as other citizens as long as they haven't proven that they are unworthy of them. The statute that the State prepares has, in this case, to be inspired by the rules of justice and charity."[195] In other words the assembled leaders of the French Catholic Church gave their agreement to the statute that, a month later, would be announced by the government. Of course when the official announcement came, no Catholic prelate protested. Some bishops even openly supported the anti-Jewish measures.[196]

The most immediate reason for the French Church's attitude stemmed from the unmitigated support granted by Pétain and the new État français to the reinsertion of Catholicism into French public life, particularly in education. Whereas the republic had established the separation of church and state and thus banned the use of state funds for the support of religious schools, Vichy canceled the separation and all its practical sequels: In many ways Catholicism had become the official religion of the new regime.[197] There was more, however.

Since the French Revolution a segment of French Catholicism had remained obdurately hostile to the "ideas of 1789," which they considered to be a Judeo-Masonic plot intent upon the destruction of Christianity. Such militant Catholicism found its modern political voice during the Dreyfus affair in the ultranationalist and anti-Semitic party then created by Charles Maurras: the Action Française. The Action Française had been excommunicated in the 1920s, but many Catholics remained strongly attached to it, and the ban was lifted by Pius XII on the eve of the war. It was the Action Française that inspired Vichy's *Statut des Juifs*, and it was the same anti-Semitism that belonged to the ideological profile of an influential part of the French church in 1940.

Finally, some of the most fundamental tenets of Christian religious anti-Semitism resurfaced among French Catholics, in a less vituperative form than in Poland of course, but resurfaced nonetheless. Thus the newspaper *La Croix*, which during the 1920s and 1930s had abandoned its violent anti-Jewish diatribes of the turn of the century (mainly during the Dreyfus affair), could not resist the temptation offered by the new circumstances. "Are the Jews Cursed by God?" was the title of an article published on November 30, 1940. Having justified the new statute, the author, who wrote under the pseudonym C. Martel, reminded his readers that since the Jews themselves had called Jesus' blood "upon their heads and those of their children," a curse indeed existed. There was only one way of escaping it: conversion.[198]

The small French Reformed (Calvinist) Church was influenced by the general cultural-ideological stance shared by most of the country, although Pastor Marc Boegner, its leader, was to become an outspoken critic of Vichy's anti-Jewish laws. Yet, in the summer of 1941, Boegner himself would emphasize on several occasions that his support was granted to *French* Jews only and that, in his opinion, the influx of Jewish immigrants had created a major problem.[199]

In the occupied zone, the Germans didn't remain idle either. The first anti-Jewish initiatives did not stem from the "delegate of the Security Police and the SD," Helmut Knochen, or from the military command, but from the embassy in Paris. On August 17, after a meeting with Hitler, Ambassador Otto Abetz demanded that Werner Best, the head of the civil administration branch at military headquarters, prepare an initial set of anti-Jewish measures. Best was surprised by Abetz's initiative, but the following instructions were drafted nonetheless: "(a) with immediate enforcement, Jews who had fled southward should no longer be allowed back into the occupied zone; (b) preparations should begin for the removal of all Jews from the occupied zone; (c) the possibility of confiscating Jewish property should be examined."[200] On August 26 Abetz was informed by Ribbentrop that Hitler had agreed to these "immediate measures."[201] Everybody fell into line.

By mid-September 1940, the commander of the army, General Brauchitsch, gave the formal go-ahead, and on the twenty-seventh, the "First Jewish Decree," defining as Jewish anybody with more than two grandparents of the Jewish religion or with two such grandparents and belonging to the Jewish faith or married to a Jewish spouse, was issued. The decree forbade Jews who had fled to the Vichy zone to return into the occupied zone; it instructed the French prefects to start a full registration of all Jews in the occupied zone (in order to prepare their removal), as well as to identify Jewish businesses and register Jewish assets (for later confiscation).[202] On October 16 a "Second Jewish Decree" ordered the Jews to register their enterprises before October 31.[203] From that day on, Jewish stores carried a yellow sign reading *Jüdisches Geschäft/Entreprise Juive* [Jewish business].[204]

The registration of all Jews in the occupied zone started on October 3, Rosh Hashanah. It proceeded in alphabetical order and was to be completed on October 19. In Paris the Jews registered at the police stations of their districts; outside Paris, at the *sous-préfectures*. The vast majority (over 90 percent) of Jews, whether French or foreign, obeyed the orders without much hesitation. Some even turned the registration into a statement. The terminally ill philosopher Henri Bergson, although exempted from the registration and for years far closer to Catholicism than to Judaism, dragged himself in slippers and dressing gown to the Passy police station in Paris to be inscribed as Jew; a Col. Pierre Brissac went in full military uniform.[205]

At the end of October 1940, 149,734 Jews had been listed. Late registration of an additional few thousand Jews continued sporadically during the following weeks and months: 86,664 were French, 65,707 were foreigners.[206] Pierre Masse, a former minister and senator of the Hérault department wrote to Pétain on October 20: "I obey the laws of my country even if they are imposed by the invader." In his letter he asked the *maréchal* whether he should take away the officer stripes that several generations of his ancestors had earned in serving their country since the Napoleonic Wars.[207]

* * *

The identification of "ordinary Jews" as such depended on their readiness to register. No such hurdle existed regarding Jewish writers, alive or dead. It had always been a specialty of anti-Semites to uncover the identity of writers, artists, intellectuals who at first glance were not identifiable as Jews; this was common practice in France as everywhere else. Thus a list of names was readily available when, in September 1940, the association of French publishers promised the German embassy in Paris that no Jewish authors, among other excluded groups, would be published or reprinted any longer: The publishers would, from then on, exercise strict self-censorship. Within days, a first list of banned books, the "liste Bernhard," was made public, soon followed by a "liste Otto." It was preceded by a short declaration from the association: "These are the books which by their lying and tendentious spirit have systematically poisoned French public opinion; particularly the publications of political refugees or of Jewish writers who, having betrayed the hospitality that France had granted to them, unscrupulously agitated in favor of a war from which they hoped to take advantage for their own egoistic aims."[208]

Some French publishers came up with new initiatives. Whereas at Mercure de France, a French translation of the autobiographical part of *Mein Kampf* was being planned, Bernard Grasset, afraid that he would not be allowed to reopen his publishing house in Paris, informed the Germans, by way of intermediaries, that "as far back you go in both branches of my family, you will find neither a Jew or a Jewess."[209]

Possibly more than any other Western European capital, Paris soon became a hotbed of intellectual and artistic collaboration. In the earliest period of German occupation, some initiatives appear as a mixture of abjection and comedy. Thus, the star of the French dance scene, Serge Lifar, much impressed by Goebbels during the latter's visit to Paris in July 1940, started pressing the German embassy for another meeting with the Nazi propaganda chief. In historian Philippe Burrin's words, "Lifar fancied his chances as the führer of European dance." In the meantime, the Germans were worrying about Lifar's Aryan ancestry. After the dancer was cleared of any Jewish stigma, he was invited to perform at the Embassy—not for Goebbels, alas—but at least in honor of Brauchitsch.[210]

* * *

As a result of the Vichy laws of the summer and fall of 1940, 140 faculty members of Jewish origin, around 10 percent of the teaching body nationwide, were banned from the universities. Fourteen particularly eminent Jewish scholars were exempted from the ban on condition that they continue teaching in the Vichy zone only. The French academic community acquiesced.[211] At the Collège de France, the most prestigious academic institution in the country, its four Jewish professors were dismissed, according to the new regulations.

The director of the Collège, Edmond Faral, had not waited for the new laws. In a January 1941 report to Vichy's delegation in occupied France, Faral eagerly mentioned his own initiative: "The Jewish question: no Jew has taught at the Collège de France since the beginning of the academic year. That decision was taken even before the law of October 3, 1940." In the draft of the report, the last sentence, later deleted, read as follows: "The administration had taken that decision."[212] When the Jews were no longer allowed to teach at the Collège, none of their "Aryan" colleagues protested.[213] The same happened in all French institutions of higher learning. At the prestigious Ecole Libre des Sciences Politiques, the assistant director, Roger Seydoux, expelled all Jewish professors when asked to do so by Karl Epting, the head of the cultural section of the German embassy in Paris. No attempts were made to obtain exemptions.[214]

The two main figures of the community, the head of the Consistoire Central, French Jewry's traditional representative body, and the head of the Consistoire de Paris, Édouard and Robert de Rothschild, fled the country in June 1940.[215] They left a Jewry in complete disarray in the feeble hands of the newly elected chief rabbi of France, Isaie Schwartz, and the remaining members of the Consistoire, most of whom had sought refuge in the nonoccupied part of the country.

Even before the armistice became effective, the chief rabbi received a first intimation of things to come: On June 20 the archbishop of Bordeaux broadcast an address to the Catholics of France: on the twenty-third Pastor Boegner spoke to the Protestant community. Schwartz should have been next, but no invitation came; in response to his query he was told that from then on the Jewish religious program would be taken off the air.[216]

Vague forebodings spread among native French Jews and, even more so, among the foreign Jews, whether they lived in the occupied or the nonoccupied zone. In fact nobody knew, in the summer of 1940, what to expect and what to fear. Two very different chroniclers recorded the events from "opposite" perspectives. The first, Raymond-Raoul Lambert, was a native French Jew belonging to an old Alsatian Jewish family; the other, Jacques Biélinky, was born in Vitebsk and, after having experienced the Kishinev pogrom of 1903 and then being jailed in Russia for clandestine socialist activities, he arrived in France in 1909 as a political refugee. For the Germans and for Vichy—both were first and foremost Jews. Lambert was French to the core: French schools, decorated front-line officer during World War I, briefly appointed to the Foreign Ministry, yet also consciously Jewish, even actively so: He organized the assistance to German Jews after 1933 and simultaneously was appointed editor in chief of *L'Univers Israélite*, the main periodical of the Consistoire. When the war broke out, Lambert donned the uniform once again, this time as a reserve officer.

Biélinky had been naturalized in 1927, and thus, belonged to his adoptive France as much as Lambert. During the coming events, however, Biélinky's voice would be that of a foreign Jew, of an *Ostjude*, to a point. He had worked as a journalist for various Jewish newspapers, and although his formal education had stopped with the *cheder* [the traditional Jewish religious elementary school], he acquired a solid knowledge of painting, and it was as a reporter dealing with the Parisian artistic scene that he signed many of his articles. Between 1940 and 1943 Lambert's path would not be the same as Biélinky's; their fates would, however, be identical in the end.[217]

"French Jewry lives in a particular state of anxiety," Lambert, still in the army, recorded on July 14, 1940. "It accepts the suffering shared by all, but fears the possibility that the enemy will demand further discrimination. This anxiety makes my future and that of my sons appear especially threatened, but I am still confident. France cannot accept everything, and it is not for nothing that for more than a century my ancestors have been buried in its soil, that I fought two wars. I cannot imagine for myself, my wife and my sons, the possibility of life under another sky, an uprooting that would be worse than an amputation."[218]

In fact during the summer and fall of 1940, Jewish life seemed at first to return to a measure of normalcy, even in Paris under direct German occupation. As early as October 1940, all communal welfare offices had resumed their activities and, at this stage, they were able to face the needs of a substantial part of the immigrant community. The French Jews turned to the Consistoire, and, in August, Paris's chief rabbi, Julien Weill, returned to the French capital. Among French Jews anxiety about the future seemed to be on the wane. The respite was short-lived.

On October 2, 1940, Lambert got an inkling of the forthcoming *Statut* from early indications in the newspapers. "It is one of the saddest memories of my life," he noted in his diary. "Thus it can be that in a few days I shall be a second-class citizen, that my sons, French by birth, culture, and faith will be brutally rejected from the French community. . . . Is it possible? I can't believe it. France is not France anymore."[219] A few weeks later, the pain was no less intense but saving formulas were emerging: "A friend writes to me: One does not judge one's mother when she is unjust. One suffers and one waits. Thus we Jews of France have to bend our heads and suffer," Lambert noted on November 6 and added: "I agree!"[220]

Biélinky, who continued to live in Paris, noted the announcement of the *Statut* almost laconically. Two days later, on October 4, after attending the Rosh Hashanah prayers, he mentioned the large number of worshippers and the presence of police forces around the synagogue; as for troublemakers, there weren't any. After the service he entered a coffee shop. The owner, "a Catholic one hundred percent, loudly expressed his indignation against the persecution of the Jews. He [the owner] declared that the local population, very French and very Parisian, is indifferent to the fate of the Rothschilds, but otherwise it would openly support the Jewish population of modest condition."[221]

Among the official leaders of French Jewry, the first to respond to the statute was Chief Rabbi Schwartz. In a letter to Pétain on October 22, 1940, he reminded the chief of state that the French Jews, now excluded from all public office, had always been "the faithful servants of the fatherland [*la Patrie*]. . . . We always called in our prayers for the glory and greatness of France . . . Frenchmen, who do not separate the religion of our fathers from the love of our homeland [*sol natal*], we will continue to obey the laws of the State. . . . To a law of exclusion [*loi d'exception*], we will answer with unfailing devotion to our fatherland." Pétain's curt answer praised "obedience to the law."[222]

In the meantime Eichmann's envoy in Paris, the SD officer in charge of Jewish affairs, Theodor Dannecker, was taking the first steps to establish a nationwide Jewish Council. Rather than impose the council by a simple *Diktat*, the sly German used a roundabout way: He persuaded both the Consistoire and the organizations of foreign Jews to coordinate their welfare agencies in a single framework that (so he promised) would not be interfered with by the Germans. They agreed.

On January 30, 1941, the Comité de Coordination was established. Most Jews did not yet understand Dannecker's tactics. However, even those credulous enough to believe Dannecker's promises of nonintervention felt an imminent threat when Eichmann's delegate brought in two former members of the Vienna *Judenrat*, Israel Israelowitz and Wilhelm Bieberstein, and imposed them as "advisers" to the committee. In April 1941 the first issue of *Informations Juives*, written almost entirely by the two Austrian Jews—"in poor French" according to Biélinky—was published.[223] It was becoming increasingly clear that Dannecker's Jewish agents were in Paris to take charge of the new organization.[224]

VIII

As the Wehrmacht broke through the Dutch lines, a wave of panic engulfed the country's 140,000 Jews: On May 13 and 14, thousands rushed to the North Sea coast in the hope of finding some way to reach England:[225] their fear found its hateful echo in the letters of German soldiers. Cpl. HZ described, in a letter of June 2, 1940, an incident that must have taken place in Belgium or in northern France: "You should have seen the Jews, as the Germans were advancing. I saw a Jew with luggage standing by a taxi and offering the driver 6,000 Frs (600 RM) if he could take him to the coast, so that he still could catch a boat to England. Just then, a second Jew arrived and offered 7,000 Frs for the same ride; then came a third one, completely distraught, with trembling knees: please, please, take me along, I shall give you 10,000 Frs."[226] In Amsterdam the number of suicides increased threefold from 1939 to 1940: Most of those who killed themselves were probably Jews. According to various estimates, some two hundred Jews committed suicide during the week starting May 15.[227]

In two ways the situation of Dutch Jewry was different from that of other Western countries at the onset of the German occupation. Whereas the Jews of Belgium were predominantly foreign and one-half of the French community was not native, in the Netherlands the twenty thousand foreign Jews represented only one-seventh of the Jewish population in May 1940. Moreover, even if some measure of traditionally religious anti-Semitism lingered in the rural areas of Holland, in Amsterdam—where half the Jews of the country were concentrated—and in larger cities in general—anti-Jewish feelings did not lead to public intolerance, although traditional religious anti-Judaism persisted among a majority of Dutch Protestants and Catholics. Even Anton Mussert's Dutch Nazi Party counted some Jewish members (about one hundred) before the Germans arrived.[228]

During the first months of the occupation, German domination seemed relatively mild. The Dutch were considered a kindred race and, ultimately, they would be integrated in the greater community of Nordic nations. The two top Nazi envoys to Holland, both Austrians, Reichskommissar Arthur Seyss-Inquart and Higher SS and Police Leader Hanns Albin Rauter (Himmler's delegate in The Hague), did not foresee any major difficulties in handling the Dutch population and its Jews. Queen Wilhelmina and the government had fled to London, but current affairs were impeccably run by a model bureaucracy under the guidance of the so-called College of the Secretaries-General (the highest-ranking officials in every ministry), with the help of an obedient and zealous civil service, an efficient police force, and the full cooperation of all local authorities. The Germans became the supervisors of a smoothly working administrative system.[229]

The Dutch political scene was not unfavorable to the occupiers either. Mussert's party (NSB) never became a significant political force; it was vocal, it supplied henchmen to the Germans, but all in all it remained peripheral, somewhat like the collaborationist parties in occupied France. Yet, soon after the defeat, a new party, the Dutch Union (Nederlandse Unie), gained wide support among the population received tentative acceptance from the Germans and initiated a policy of moderate collaboration not very different from the Vichy line.

It was in this "conciliatory" climate that the first anti-Jewish measures were imposed by the Germans throughout the summer of 1940. They did not seem ominous: air raid protection teams would no longer include Jews: Jews were forbidden to work in Germany; Jews in the civil service could not be promoted, and no new appointments of Jews were allowed. But in October the first standard German steps were taken: By the middle of the month all civil servants had to fill out forms about their racial origin. On October 22, 1940, the edict defining Jews was proclaimed.[230]

The definition of who was a Jew was essentially identical to that of the Nuremberg laws, except in regard to the cut-off date for mixed breeds: A person was considered Jewish if descending from three or more grandparents of the Jewish religion. A person descending from two Jewish grandparents was considered a mixed breed of the first degree if not married to a Jewish spouse or belonging to the Jewish faith on May 9, 1940 (the eve of the German attack in the West); otherwise that person was Jewish.

From this early stage the secretaries-general and the civil service as a whole displayed the compliance that would later have fateful consequences. Although some civil servants had qualms about the anticonstitutional aspect of the forms regarding their racial origin, the highest officials of the land decided to accept them. The secretary-general of the Department of the Interior, K. J. Fredericks, led the way: Out of some 240,000 civil servants, apparently fewer than 20 refused to fill out the questionnaire.[231] By mid-November all Jewish civil servants had been dismissed, and the Dutch Supreme Court voted by a majority of 12 to 5 to dismiss its own president, the Jew Lodewijk E. Visser.[232]

On October 21, 1940, the registration of Jewish businesses began. It was followed on January 10, 1941, by the compulsory registration of the Jews themselves; nearly everyone complied. In the Netherlands, moreover, personal identification had become an unusually precise and foolproof system, "improved" even further regarding Jews (after the German registration order) due to the zeal and talent of the head of the "State Inspectorate of Population Registers," Jacob Lentz. The forging of identity papers became almost impossible until the very last year of the war.[233]

In Amsterdam the city council and the municipal personnel at first went beyond the call of duty in obeying German demands: Although Dutch law did not compel them to fill out declarations of Aryan descent, all volunteered to do so in January 1941.[234] Yet when the Germans mentioned the possibility of establishing a ghetto in the city, the council expressed its opposition. In the meantime, however, a situation was developing that in principle should have helped the German plans. Mussert's

Dutch Nazis, encouraged by the Germans, particularly by Seyss-Inquart's delegate in Amsterdam, Dr. H. Böhmcker, initiated scuffles in the Jewish area of the city. On February 19, 1941, the owners of the Koco (Kohn and Cahn) ice-cream parlor in south Amsterdam mistook a German police unit for Dutch Nazis and sprayed them with ammonium gas.[235] Three days later the Germans sealed off the Jewish quarter of the city and arrested 389 young Jewish men, whom they deported to Buchenwald and then to Mauthausen: One survived.

On November 26, 1940, shortly after the dismissal of all Jewish civil servants, Professor R. P. Cleveringa, the dean of the Law School at the University of Leiden, the oldest Dutch university, addressed a meeting in the main auditorium, so packed with faculty and students that the speech had to be transmitted by loudspeaker to an adjacent hall. He spoke in honor of his Jewish colleague, Professor E. M. Meijers, who, like all other Jewish civil servants, had been dismissed on German orders on November 15. "Their [the Germans'] actions are beneath contempt," Cleveringa declared. "All I ask is that we may dismiss them from our sight and gaze instead at the heights, up to that radiant figure in whose honor we are assembled here. . . . This noble son of our people, this man, this father to his students, this scholar, whom usurpers have suspended from his duties. . . . A man who, as all of us know, belongs here and, God willing, shall return to us."[236] On the afternoon of that day the students in Leiden and Delft started a strike. Both universities were closed on German orders on November 29, 1940, and some of the protesters, including Dean Cleveringa, were arrested.[237]

The Germans had their own way of explaining the situation. In a report of January 16, 1941, on the situation in the Netherlands, the representative of the Foreign Ministry in The Hague, Otto Bene, sent a description of the events in the universities to the Wilhelmstrasse: "Introduction of the anti-Jewish laws has provoked considerable unrest, owing to the strong influences of the Jews on the intellectual life of the Netherlands, especially in the university cities of Leiden and Delft, where students under the leadership of Jewish students and probably, as a result of behind-the-scenes manipulations of the Jewish professors affected, allowed themselves to be carried away to stage demonstrations which resulted in the closing of the two universities."[238]

But protest was not limited to the academic elites. A month before the manifestations in Leiden, the Dutch Protestant Churches (Reformed Churches) and the Mennonites—with the telling exception of the small Lutheran Church of the Netherlands (that is, the same denomination as that of the vast majority of German Protestants) and the Dutch Catholic Church—addressed a jointly signed letter to Seyss-Inquart. After evoking Christian charity and the issue of converted Jews, the letter continued: "Finally, this issue [the statute about the Jews and the expulsion of Jews from public service] has also brought profound dismay because it applies to the people from which the Savior is born, the object of the prayers of all Christians and the one they recognize [as] their Master and King. For all these reasons, we turn to your Excellency, with the urgent request to take the necessary steps to cancel the aforementioned measures."

The last sentence may have been particularly galling for the Reichskommissar: "Besides, we wish to recall the solemn promise given by your Excellency to respect our national identity and not to impose on us a way of thinking that is foreign to us."

The text of the letter was read from the pulpits of all Reformed temples on the following Sunday.[239] Simultaneously the first protest articles appeared in the Dutch clandestine press. Thus a December 1940 issue of the pro-Communist *De Waarheid* (Truth) did not mince words: "Dutch workers and all freedom-loving Dutchmen should fight this imported poison of hate against the Jews."[240] A few months later, in February 1941, *Het Parool* joined the protest and so, one after another, did all major clandestine publications in Holland.[241] And, as we shall see in the next chapter, in February 1941 Dutch workers would go on strike in Amsterdam and other cities to protest German anti-Jewish brutality.

Historically puzzling is the fact that almost *none* of this occurred in France. From the reports sent by the directors of *lycées* (high schools) to the Ministry of Education it appears that all Jewish professors left "without incident"—that is, without any public manifestation of sympathy or open protest by either colleagues or students.[242] French academic institutions of higher learning preempted both Vichy and the Germans in expelling their Jewish faculty members, as we saw; publishers and publications vied for German or Vichy authorizations to resume their activities and showed open readiness for "self-censorship." And, as we also noted, the assembly of French cardinals and archbishops favored the limitation of Jewish rights even before Vichy introduced its statute. The French student unions did organize a pro–de Gaulle rally in Paris, on November 11, 1940, but in the leaflets distributed during the demonstration, not a word appeared regarding the measures taken against the Jews in both zones of the country.[243]

IX

When, in May 1940, the Klemperers were forced to move into a "Jews' house," Victor commented: "It is still quite impossible to know whether a tolerable existence can be established here."[244]

In that summer of 1940, "tolerable" had a very different meaning for the inhabitants of the Jewish quarters or ghettos in former Poland; it had a different meaning for various categories of Jews in the Reich—and, for those among them who, although having been identified as full Jews, lived in "privileged mixed marriages,"[245] or again for mixed breeds of the first or second degree; it had a different meaning for the Jews in Western countries who lived under direct German control and for those who lived in Vichy France, or, for the most favored of all, those who had managed to settle in the Italian-occupied zone in southeastern France. For all, however, growing isolation, anxiety regarding ever-darker prospects, and complete uncertainty about what the future held in store seeped into everyday life.

Increasingly the Jews of occupied Eastern Europe would be convinced that nobody cared about their fate. Thus, in a letter sent from Warsaw in December 1940 to members of her movement in Eretz Israel, Zivia Lubetkin—who some two years later was to become one of the organizers of the Warsaw ghetto uprising—expressed her growing despair about this abandonment: "More than once, I have decided not to write to you anymore. . . . I will not describe here what I am going through, but I want you to know that even one word of comfort from you would have sufficed. . . . To my regret, however, I have to accept your silence, but I will never forgive it."[246]

The same uncertainty, the same dread about what the future held in store, the same feeling that the closest friends living peacefully in the free world were not doing enough, if anything at all, recurred as a constant yet restrained leitmotif in the letters that the German philosopher and literary scholar Walter Benjamin was sending from France. After the Germans occupied Paris, he had found a temporary refuge in the small pilgrimage town of Lourdes, near the Spanish border.

"My dear Teddy," he wrote on August 2, 1940, to his longtime friend, the philosopher Theodor Adorno, who had emigrated from Germany to New York via Paris, "The total uncertainty about what the next day, the next hour is about to bring has dominated my existence for several weeks. I am condemned to read each newspaper (they are published on one single page) as a notification addressed directly to me and to perceive in each radio broadcast the voice of a messenger of misfortune. For some time now it has been impossible for a foreigner to obtain permission to change location. Therefore, I entirely depend on what you will be able to achieve from the outside. . . . My fear is that the time at our disposal could be much more limited than we supposed."[247]

Benjamin received an American visa from the consulate in Marseilles, probably within the nonquota category established by the Emergency Rescue Committee. He also had possession of a transit visa through Spain to Portugal. Normally he would have had no difficulty in crossing the French-Spanish border, notwithstanding the refusal of French authorities to grant exit visas. But by sheer bad luck, on September 26, 1940, the day on which Benjamin and his group arrived at the border, at Port Bou, the Spanish guards refused to recognize visas issued by the American consulate in Marseilles.

In January 1940 a still-defiant Benjamin was urging his friend, the historian of Jewish mysticism Gershom Scholem, to publish the lectures he was giving at the time in New York: "Every line that we publish nowadays—as uncertain as the future to which we transmit it may be—is a victory forced upon the powers of darkness.[248] At the Spanish border, carrying an unpublished manuscript in a briefcase that was never found, too ill, too exhausted, and mainly too desperate to try and cross the border once again, Benjamin killed himself.[249]

CHAPTER III

December 1940–June 1941

On June 15, 1941, in the afternoon, a week before the beginning of the German assault against the Soviet Union, Goebbels was summoned to the Reich Chancellery: Hitler, it seems, wished to get the right support from his most fanatically devoted underling.

The Nazi leader's ruminations were first and foremost an exercise in self-reassurance: "The most powerful attack that history had ever seen," the minister recorded. "What happened to Napoleon would not repeat itself . . . the Führer estimated that the entire campaign would take approximately 4 months; I think it will be much less. We stand on the eve of an unparalleled victory." In Goebbels's view, the attack was a vital necessity for global strategic reasons and no less so on ideological grounds: "It is not Czarism that will be brought back to Russia; an authentic socialism will rcplace Judeo-bolshevism. Every old Nazi will rejoice at the opportunity of witnessing these events. The pact with Russia was in fact a stain on our shield . . . what we have fought against throughout our life, we shall now exterminate. I say this to the Führer and he completely agrees with me."[1]

Suddenly Hitler added a comment as unexpected as it was atypical: "The Führer says," Goebbels recorded, "whether we are right or wrong, we must win. This is the only way. And it is right, moral and necessary. And once we have won, who will ask us about the methods. In any case, we have so much to account for that we must win; otherwise our whole people—and we in the first place, and all that we love—would be erased"

[*Wir haben sowieso soviel auf dem Kerbholz, dass wir siegen müssen, weil sonst unser ganzes Volk, wir an der Spitze mit allem was uns lieb ist, ausradiert würde.*][2] From that point on, in other words, there was no way back.

I

Whether in the summer of 1940 Hitler had ever seriously considered the invasion of the British Isles (Operation Sea Lion) remains a moot question. Throughout those same months the onslaught of the Luftwaffe against Britain's coastal defenses did not achieve the essential precondition for a landing: control of the skies over southern England. The massive bombing of cities that followed, mainly the raids on London (the Blitz), did not break the population's morale, and in the fall the Battle of Britain was turning to the advantage of the Royal Air Force.

At the same time Hitler was considering his alternative strategy. After the defeat of France and the British rejection of his "peace proposal," the Nazi leader mentioned the global strategic impact of an attack against the Soviet Union on several occasions, particularly in the course of the military conference at the Berghof, on July 31, 1940. According to Halder's notes, Hitler's argument ran as follows: "England's hope is Russia and America. If hope in Russia is eliminated, America also is eliminated, because enormous increase in the importance of Japan in the Far East will result from the elimination of Russia."[3]

The overall strategic framework was of course indissolubly linked, as we shall see, to Hitler's unchanged ideological hatred of Bolshevism (of Judeo-Bolshevism, as he would mostly perceive it) and to the more traditional German aspiration to dominate the spaces of the East and their boundless reserves of raw materials. Only control of this economic potential would turn the Reich into an unassailable power, poised to dominate the world.

The Tripartite Pact, signed on September 27, 1940, between Germany, Italy, and Japan, was meant as a warning to the United States no less than to the Soviet Union.[4] But when, in mid-November 1940, the Soviet foreign minister, Vyacheslav Molotov, arrived in Berlin for negotiations and Hitler suggested a common front against Great Britain and the United States by turning the Tripartite Pact into a "Quadripartite" one, the Nazi leader had probably already made up his mind. In any case Molotov steadily brought the discussions back to concrete issues: the full implementation of the 1939 agreement about the Soviet "sphere of interest," mainly in the Balkans (Bulgaria) and regarding Finland.

Molotov's adamant stand reflected Stalin's belief in the possibility of a German attack and thus in the necessity of a westward expansion of Soviet strategic defenses, particularly after the unforeseen collapse of France. Soviet determination could but confirm Hitler in his own decision to eliminate the Eastern colossus. On December 18, 1940, the Nazi leader signed directive no. 21 and changed the previous code name of the attack on the Soviet Union from Fritz to Barbarossa. The assault was to start on May 15, 1941.

There was, in Berlin, another reason for acting rapidly. In November Roosevelt had been reelected for a third term. On December 14, in a press conference, the president used the garden hose metaphor: If a neighbor's house is on fire, the man who owns a hose does not say: "My garden hose costs fifteen dollars and you must pay me this sum before you can have it." He simply lends his hose, helps to put out the fire, and then takes the hose back. America, Roosevelt said, would in the future lend some nations the equipment they needed for defending their lives and their freedom.[5] On December 17, on the eve of signing directive no. 21, Hitler told Gen. Alfred Jodl, deputy chief of staff of the OKW, that Germany should solve all continental problems in 1941, "because in 1942 the United States will be ready to intervene."[6] And, more than ever, in the Nazi leader's view, the policy of the American president was dictated by the Jews.

Unexpected events modified the schedule set for the eastern campaign. On March 27, 1941, two days after Yugoslavia had adhered to the Tripartite Pact, a military coup unseated the pro-German government in Belgrade. Hitler ordered immediate retaliation: Belgrade was bombed to rubble, and the Wehrmacht rolled south. Yugoslavia and Greece were occupied, Bulgaria joined the Axis, and the British forces that had landed in Greece were driven from the Continent and from the island of Crete. However, the attack against the Soviet Union had to be postponed by several weeks. The date now set was June 22, the longest day of the year.

Murderous steps were planned against the Jews on Soviet territory during the preparatory stage of the campaign, yet these steps appear at first as additional ways of destroying Soviet resistance and accelerating the collapse of the Soviet system as a whole, in line with the Nazi identification of Bolshevism, its elites, and its structures with the omnipresence of Jews in power positions. Otherwise Hitler's public declarations during the first half of 1941 do not indicate that the anti-Jewish dimension of the campaign was a goal in itself.

In his annual Reichstag speech of January 30, 1941, the Nazi leader had returned to his dire prophecy of January 1939 regarding the ultimate fate of the Jews of Europe. But this time—whether the change of vocabulary was intentional or not—instead of explicitly mentioning extermination, he prophesied that the war would "put an end to Jewry's role in Europe."[7] His words could have meant complete segregation, deportation—or indeed total extermination. In Hitler's meetings with foreign statesmen or in speeches made throughout the last months of 1940 and during the military buildup period preceding June 22, 1941, his allusions to the Jews appeared to be rather perfunctory and generally remained very brief.

Nonetheless, on March 3, 1941, Hitler sent back a first draft of the campaign guidelines prepared by the OKW, adding, among other points, that "the Jewish Bolshevik intelligentsia, as the oppressor of the past, had to be liquidated."[8] The gist of the Nazi leader's notorious speech to his most senior generals, on March 30, was basically identical, but the Jews were not mentioned as such. "*Struggle of two worldviews*" [emphasis in original], Halder, the chief of staff of the army, summed up: "Devastating judgment about Bolshevism: Nothing else but asocial criminality. Communism, enormous danger for the future. We have to abandon the notion of soldiery camaraderie. The Communist is no comrade before [the battle] and no comrade afterward. This is a war of extermination. If we don't consider it as such, we will achieve victory over the enemy now, but in thirty years the Communist enemy will again stand against us. We do not wage the war to spare the enemy. . . . The Bolshevik commissars and the Bolshevik intelligentsia have to be exterminated. . . . The struggle must be aimed at the poison of disintegration. It is not a matter for military courts. The officers must know what is at stake. . . . The soldiers must defend themselves with the means utilized to attack them. . . . The fighting will be very different from that in the West."[9]

Hitler's address demonstrated to anyone who had been fooled by the 1939 treaty with the Soviet Union that his anti-Bolshevik fervor remained uncompromising. In its scale and ruthlessness, the forthcoming "war of extermination" represented, above and beyond its strategic goals, an ideological crusade and a "*Volkstumskampf*," unprecedented in the annals of modern Europe. Moreover, for Hitler the destruction of Soviet power could not but mean the destruction of Jewish power; the struggle was one and the same.

In 1923 Dietrich Eckart, Hitler's ideological mentor in many ways, had stressed the inherent link between Bolshevism (in its various guises) and the Jews in a pamphlet titled "Bolshevism from Moses to Lenin: A Dialogue Between Hitler and Myself."[10] In *Mein Kampf*, in his "Second Book" (an untitled Hitler manuscript, written in the late 1920s and published only after the war), and in countless speeches, Hitler had rehashed the same theme: The Slav populations of the Soviet Union were an inferior mass that, before the revolution, had been led by a Germanic elite; Jewish Bolsheviks exterminated this traditional ruling class and became the masters of the huge country as a first stage on the road to world revolution and domination.[11] For the Nazi leader the murder of the "Soviet intelligentsia" and of the political commissars meant the extermination of this Jewish ruling elite; without its grip the Soviet system would unravel and collapse.[12]

Hitler's anti-Bolshevik creed quite naturally merged, let us recall, with a no less cardinal theme inherited from pan-Germanism: the need for the *Volk* to control as vast an eastern *Lebensraum* (vital space) as racially and strategically necessary, possibly all the way to the Urals. The conquered space would be open to Germanic colonization and would supply the Reich with all the raw materials and food it needed. As for native populations, they would be enslaved, partly decimated, or deported into Siberia (this was the *Volkstumskampf* part of the campaign). With victory over the Soviet Union, huge eastern colonization projects could be launched.

Hitler, as we saw, decided to change the code name of the campaign from Fritz (presumably referring to the king of Prussia, Frederick the Great) to Barbarossa (the common appellation of the twelfth-century Emperor Frederick I of the Hohenstaufen dynasty); the Nazi leader probably wished to evoke Barbarossa's history and legend.[13] The Hohenstaufen emperor had embarked on a crusade in the East against the infidels; and, over time, the Germans had turned Barbarossa into a mythic figure: He was the secret savior, asleep in the Kyffhäuser mountain range in Thuringia, who would arise at the time of his people's greatest need and lead them to victory and redemption.

Thus, the change of code name pointed to the quasi-mythic dimension of the forthcoming campaign in Hitler's mind, and to his own saviorlike role at this dramatic juncture in the history of Germany. Why Hitler chose the name of an emperor whose crusade failed when he drowned in the Saleph River in Asia Minor is as mysterious as his predilection for Wagner's opera *Rienzi*, telling the story of a late-medieval Roman tribune whose rebellion in the name of the people was crushed and who died a violent death in a fire set to his palace.

On March 26, 1941, at Hitler's command, Heydrich and the quartermaster general of the armed forces, Gen. Eduard Wagner, drafted an agreement (issued as an order by Keitel on April 28), granting the SS full autonomy for maintaining the security behind the front, in the newly occupied territories.[14] On May 13 Keitel signed the order limiting the jurisdiction of military courts over means used by the troops in their fight against the enemy. The execution of suspects thereafter depended on decisions taken by units in the field.[15] On May 19 the OKW chief issued guidelines regarding the behavior of the troops in Russia [*sic*] that ordered officers and soldiers to take "ruthless action" against the carriers of Judeo-Bolshevik ideology.[16] The Jews were twice mentioned in the guidelines as political targets of these "ruthless" measures; the instructions were distributed to divisional level on June 4 and to all units as the attack started.[17] Finally, on June 6, "the guidelines for the treatment of political commissars" (the "commissar order") were issued under the signature of General Alfred Jodl, the Deputy Chief of Staff of the OKW: The commissars were to be shot.[18]

To these guidelines the army added high doses of propaganda that left nothing to the soldiers' imagination. In the June 1941 issue of *Mitteilungen für die Truppe* (Information for the Troops), for example, the soldiers were told: "What the Bolsheviks are must be clear to anybody who ever set sight upon the face of a Red Commissar. Here no theoretical explanations are necessary anymore. To call beastly the traits of these people, a high percentage of whom are Jews, would be an insult to animals. . . . In these Commissars we see the uprising of subhumans against noble blood."[19] These *Mitteilungen* were produced by the propaganda section of the OKW; they were part of standard troop indoctrination in preparation for the war of extermination.[20]

All the terror operations and the ideologically dictated tasks would be in the hands of Hitler's chief party henchmen: Himmler, Göring, and, to a certain degree, Rosenberg. By granting the responsibility for the security of the occupied Soviet territories behind the front to the SS Reichsführer, Hitler was putting him in charge of the complete subjugation of the local populations, the struggle against ideological and partisanlike enemies, and the implementation of whatever decisions would be taken in regard to the Jews. But, as already indicated, not much is recorded about what Hitler may have eventually mentioned concerning specific anti-Jewish measures.

The orders regarding the Jews that we know of were issued by Heydrich to the *Einsatzgruppen* during these same weeks, on two different occasions: at a meeting in Berlin with the unit commanders, probably on June 17, and at another meeting, shortly thereafter, in the small town of Pretzsch, the staging area of the *Einsatzgruppen*. Here again we do not know exactly what was said. For a long time it remained unclear whether Heydrich had given the order to exterminate the Jewish population of the USSR or whether the initial orders were more restrictive. As we shall see in the next chapter, Heydrich himself summed up the orders he had given to the *Einsatzgruppen* in a message of July 2 to the Höhere SS und Polizeiführer (Higher SS and Police leaders); further orders were directly conveyed to the SS units on July 17. These various instructions indeed seem to have targeted only specific categories of Jewish *men*, but they were also open-ended enough in their formulation to have allowed for a rapid expansion of the murder campaign.[21]

Simultaneously, as preparations for the attack went ahead full force, a new "territorial plan" regarding the Jews surfaced as a potential outcome. In his address to the *Gauleiter* and *Reichsleiter* on December 10, 1940 (alluded to in the previous chapter), Himmler had remained vague about the final destination of the two million Jews who, according to him, would be evacuated from the General Government.[22] In the meantime, however, Nazi plans in this regard had become more concrete. On March 26, 1941, Heydrich met with Göring (immediately after signing the agreement with Wagner): "In regard to the solution of the Jewish Question," Heydrich noted on that same day, "I briefly reported to the Reichsmarschall [Göring] and submitted my proposal to him; he agreed after making a change regarding Rosenberg's responsibilities and ordered its [the proposal's] resubmission."[23]

By the end of March 1941 Rosenberg had already been chosen as "special adviser" for the occupied territories in the East. Thus, in view of Göring's mention of Rosenberg, the RSHA chief's proposal was clearly related to Russia and meant the deportation of the Jews of Europe to the conquered Soviet territories, probably to the Russian Far North, instead of Madagascar. Rosenberg himself mentioned as much in a speech on March 28, in which he alluded to the deportation of the Jews of Europe "under police surveillance" to a territory outside Europe "that could not be mentioned for the time being."[24]

On June 20, two days before the attack, an entry in Goebbels's diary confirmed these plans in a somewhat cryptic way. The propaganda minister reported a meeting with Hitler regarding the coming campaign, also attended by Hans Frank: "Dr. Franck [*sic*] tells about the General Government. One already rejoices there that the Jews will be packed off. Polish Jewry will gradually disintegrate [*Das Judentum in Polen verkommt allmählich*]." For Goebbels it was a just punishment for Jewish warmongering; the Führer had prophesied that this would be Jewry's fate.[25]

After the beginning of the campaign, Hitler repeatedly mentioned the new territorial plan.[26] Yet beforehand, on June 2, 1941, during a meeting with Mussolini at the Brenner Pass, the Nazi leader, after excluding the possibility of a Lublin reservation ("they [the Jews] could not remain there for hygienic reasons, as, due to their dirtiness, they became a source of disease") again mentioned Madagascar as a concrete option.[27] It appears almost certain that Hitler was awaiting the completion of the eastern campaign before making a final decision. In the meantime emigration of Jews from the Reich was still allowed, but, on May 20, 1941, the RSHA, following an order from Göring, forbade any such emigration from Belgium and France "in view of the undoubtedly forthcoming final solution of the Jewish question."[28]

* * *

Rosenberg was Hitler's candidate for heading the civilian administration of the newly conquered areas. In April and May the *Reichsleiter* produced a series of "plans" regarding the future of the eastern territories. In the latest of these outlines, on May 7, 1941, the chief ideologue stated that "after the customary removal of Jews from all public offices, the Jewish question will have to undergo a decisive solution through the institution of ghettos or labor battalions. Forced labor is to be introduced."[29]

The future minister for the occupied eastern territories may have believed for a while that as Hitler had decisively taken up the anti-Bolshevik policy he, Rosenberg, had preached from the earliest days of the party, he would now come into his own. However, the chief ideologue was underestimating Hitler's craftiness or overestimating the Führer's assessment of his own (Rosenberg's) ability. In a letter to Martin Bormann, dated May 25, 1941, Himmler informed the *Reichsleiter* that before departing for his headquarters, Hitler had confirmed to him that, regarding his tasks, he would not be subordinated to Rosenberg. The SS chief added: "Working with or under Rosenberg was certainly the most difficult thing there was in the NSDAP."[30]

Himmler's sarcastic comment to Bormann points to the tacit alliance between two masters of intrigue (who were both highly capable organizers) in their quest for ever greater power. Bormann had just been appointed head of the party chancellery, following Rudolf Hess's flight to Scotland, and a Himmler-Bormann front could withstand any possible interference from state agencies or from the military. Both Himmler and Bormann were subservient only to one higher authority, that of Adolf Hitler.

Apart from the authority of the military commanders over the future combat zones and the millions of men who would soon be moving eastward, that of the SS Reichsführer over his own SS and police units (including local auxiliary forces), and that of Rosenberg's civilian administration, a fourth agency would come to play an essential role in the intricate and increasingly chaotic system established to dominate the conquered territories: Economic Staff East. Although subject to Göring's supreme authority, the Economic Staff East was de facto headed by Gen. Georg Thomas, chief of the War Economy and Armaments Bureau (*Wehrwirtschafts-und Rüstungsamt*, or WiRüAmt), whose function would be the seizure and exploitation of Soviet war industries and raw materials. Strongly supported by Hitler, whose own strategic conception did put particular emphasis on the control of economic resources, Thomas planned his economic exploitation and looting campaign in cooperation with Quartermaster General Wagner and State Secretary Herbert Backe, the strongman in the Ministry for Food Supply.[31] It was Backe who added the final touch to economic planning of Barbarossa: the "hunger plans."

The hunger plans (drafted by Backe), intended to facilitate the food supply for the *Ostheer* (Eastern Army) and even for the German population, had been endorsed by Hitler and Göring as early as January 1941; they were then elaborated by the Wehrmacht from February 1941 on. These plans envisioned the possibility of starving the urban population of the western Soviet Union and the Ukraine, including first and foremost the Jews.[32]

The mass starvation idea was also leisurely discussed among Himmler and his top lieutenants during the Reichsführer's stay at his castle in Saxony, the Wewelsburg, between June 12 and 15.[33] On this occasion Himmler hosted SS lieutenant generals Kurt Daluege, Bach (Erich von dem Bach-Zalewski), Karl Wolff, Heydrich, Rudolf Brandt, Werner Lorenz, Friedrich Jeckeln, Hans Adolf Prützmann, and probably also the writer Hanns Johst. In the evenings, they sat by the fireside (*am Kamin gesessen*) and, according to Bach's Nuremberg testimony, the Reichsführer held forth about his vision of the future. The Russian campaign would determine Germany's fate: a great power for all time or annihilation. A leader of Hitler's stature appeared in history only once in a thousand years; the challenge had to be met by this generation. After the conquest of the European part of the Soviet Union, all the Jews of the Continent would be in German hands: They would be removed from Europe. As for the Slav population, it would have to be reduced by some twenty to thirty million people.[34]

II

While at the center of the regime, long-range anti-Jewish plans had not yet been finalized in the spring of 1941, more limited initiatives kept swirling. In January 1941 Heydrich again took up formerly stalled projects and informed Hans Frank that about one million Poles and Jews would have to be moved from the annexed territories into the General

Government, in order to resettle ethnic Germans and vacate training areas for the Wehrmacht.[35]

It is probably during a conversation with Hitler on March 17 that Frank managed once more to deflect the new deportation plans. On the same occasion the Nazi leader fantasized about the germanization of the General Government within the next fifteen to twenty years and promised that after the end of the war Frank's kingdom would be the first occupied area to be emptied of its Jewish population.[36]

Yet, "small-scale" deportations into the General Government could not, in the meantime, be avoided. The Nazi leadership in Vienna had repeatedly tried to get hold of as many remaining Jewish homes as possible (some 12,000 to 14,000 out of 70,000 in March 1938), either by systematically forcing their inhabitants to move into Jews' houses or by having most of the 60,000 elderly and impoverished Jews still living in the city deported. On October 2, 1940, Vienna's *Gauleiter, Reichsleiter* Baldur von Schirach, personally presented the request to Hitler.[37]

Three months later, Hans-Heinrich Lammers, the chief of the Reich Chancellery, informed Schirach of the decision: "The Führer decided that the deportation of the 60,000 Jews still living in Vienna into the General Government should be accelerated and take place even during the war, because of the housing crisis. I have informed the General Governor in Kraków, as well as the SS Reichsführer, of the Führer's decision, and I hereby wish to inform you about it as well."[38] The deportations started at the beginning of February 1941, and within two months some 7,000 Viennese Jews were shipped off to the General Government, mainly to the Lublin district. By mid-March 1941, however, growing military traffic linked to the buildup for Barbarossa put an end to these deportations, as had already been the case in October 1939.

A simpler method of confiscating Jewish homes was developed in the Bavarian capital; it originated in the Munich *Gauleiter*'s "Aryanization office," in coordination with the municipal authorities. In the spring of 1941 a barracks camp was built by the city's Jews, at their own expense, in the Milbertshofen suburb. Some eleven hundred Jews were relocated to the camp, where, from then until their deportation to the East in November of that year, they lived under the guard of the local police. Their former houses were allocated to party members and other "deserving" Germans.[39]

* * *

In February 1941 the Klemperers were ordered to sell the car they had managed to acquire in the midthirties, although they had not been permitted to drive it since the end of 1938 (in December of that year the drivers' licenses of Jews had been revoked). "The next blow to be expected," Klemperer wrote, "is the confiscation of the typewriter. There is one way of safeguarding it. It would have to be lent to me by an Aryan owner." There were some possible "lenders," but they were afraid. "Everyone is afraid of arousing the least suspicion of being friendly to Jews, the fear seems to grow all the time."[40]

At all levels of the system the stream of deliberations, meetings, and decisions regarding the Jews never stopped. While several ministries were involved in an endless debate about which categories of foreign Jews should be reimbursed for war related damages, while, at the same level, an eleventh ordinance to the citizenship law was being drafted and redrafted, some more down-to-earth measures were decided upon without too many hesitations: In Berlin in January 1941, Jews were excluded from the clients' lists of all shoemakers, with the exception of one company and its local branches: *Alsi-Schuhreparaturen* (Alsi-Cobblers).[41] In February and March, 1,000 out of 2,700 employees belonging to the Berlin Jewish community and to the Reichsvereinigung were transferred to compulsory labor.[42] At the end of March, on orders of General Construction Inspector Albert Speer, Jewish tenants had to vacate their homes to be replaced by Aryans whose own homes were being torn down as a result of the major construction projects started in the capital.[43] In April the Jewish community of Berlin had to change its name to "Jewish Religious Association in Berlin."[44]

A decree ordered all Aryanized firms and businesses to de-Judaize their names (*Entjudung von Firmennamen*). Usually such a measure caused no problems. However, in the case of the world-famous Rosenthal-Porzellan, the new Aryan owners demurred: A lengthy exchange ensued involving the company, the Ministry of Justice, the Ministry of Propaganda, and the Party Chancellery. On June 7, 1941, the company could prove that the number of Jews on its board had steadily diminished (in 1931 there had been three Jews on a seven-members board; in 1932, two out of five; in 1933, one out of eight). The Propaganda Ministry saw the importance of keeping the name "Rosenthal," the Justice Ministry concurred, and so did the Party Chancellery: In August 1941 the matter was settled.[45]

The most intricate issues remained those regarding mixed breeds, and not only in the Wehrmacht. Frequently Hitler intervened. At times, however, he gave instructions that he later postponed for reasons that remain unclear. Thus, on May 7, Hans Pfundtner, state secretary at the Ministry of the Interior, informed various agencies that the Führer wished to forbid sexual intercourse (*aussereehelicher Verkehr*) between *Mischlinge* of the first degree and full Germans, or among *Mischlinge* of the first degree themselves. But on September 25, 1941, Lammers advised Frick that Hitler wanted the matter to be deferred.[46] No explanation was offered.

Some of the mixed-breeds issues that the Nazi leader had to decide about, on the eve of the campaign in the East, were straightforward: In April 1941, Lammers informed the minister of Agriculture, Walther Darré, that Hitler did not object to *Mischlinge* of the second degree owning racehorses or stud farms; therefore the stud belonging to the quarter-Jewish Oppenheim brothers, a horse called Schlenderhan, could be sold to the Reich studs' administration.[47]

The most frequent issues relating to mixed breeds of the first degree were petitions for admission to universities, usually after army service followed by discharge (as mixed breeds). Those decorated for bravery were mostly accepted—in line with a Hitler decree of October 1940—the others mostly rejected—even if they boasted of particularly famous ancestry. On February 1, 1941, the Office of the Führer's Deputy had to decide on the petition of one Jürgen von Schwerin, whose ancestors on his father's side belonged to the foremost Prussian aristocracy. The trouble came from the mother's side: Schwerin's maternal grandfather was a Mendelssohn-Bartholdy, a banker who had worked closely with Bismarck. Of course the name also indicated some relation to the famous Jewish composer, and although his grandparents had converted, Schwerin carried the burden of the name Mendelssohn. He was accepted only after lengthy efforts.[48]

Mendelssohn-Bartholdy's descendant was a relatively easy case compared with that of a professor at the University of Munich, Dr. Karl Ritter von Frisch, a *Mischling* of the second degree (his maternal grandmother was "fully Jewish"). According to paragraph 72 of the Civil Service Law, Frisch had to retire and on March 8, 1941; the Minister of Education informed his colleague Interior Minister Wilhelm Frick and the ubiquitous Martin Bormann of his decision to implement the law. Frisch, it should be added, was the head of the zoological institute of the university and a world-renowned bee specialist. Not only were bees essential for food production, but according to a newspaper article included in the file, in the spring of 1941 a disease decimated hundreds of thousands of bees in the Reich and the specialist who was supposed to devise the appropriate countermeasure was none other than Frisch.

For Bormann there was no problem. On July 11, 1941, he informed the education minister that Frisch was to retire, according to paragraph 72, the more imperatively so because even after 1933 he was known to have maintained many contacts with Jews, to have declared that German science was harmed by the departure of Jews, and to have attempted to remove from his institute scientists who were known for their anti-Semitic views. In a further letter, on January 31, 1942, Bormann added that Frisch could continue his research even in retirement.[49] It remains unclear what compelled the all-powerful chief of the party chancellery to change his mind. On April 27, 1942, however, after lamely referring to new information indicating that retirement would harm Frisch's research, Bormann instructed the minister of education to postpone it until after the end of the war.[50]

No matter of any importance in the ongoing anti-Jewish harassment could be settled without Hitler's consent. In August 1940, as we saw, it was Hitler who gave the green light for implementing the anti-Jewish measures in occupied France. During the same month the Nazi leader authorized *Gauleiter* Gustav Simon to introduce anti-Jewish legislation in occupied Luxembourg.[51] In October he ordered the deportation of the Jews of Baden and the Saar-Palatinate into the Vichy zone, and in January 1941, he agreed to the deportations from Vienna. At approximately the same time Hitler authorized the beginning of the "Aryanizations" in Holland: "Following a presentation by the Reich Commissar" (Seyss-Inquart), the head of the Economic Department of the Wilhelmstrasse wrote on March 1, "the Führer had in principle decided three months ago that the Aryanization plan could be carried out. Reichsleiter Bormann is aware of the current status of the matter."[52] Even more telling in this respect was an issue discussed at lower levels since 1938 and brought up again in 1940: the marking of the Jews living in the Reich with a special sign.

In April and May 1941 the matter resurfaced (probably in view of the forthcoming campaign in the East) on Heydrich and Goebbels's initiative. Both turned to Göring for an answer, to no avail.[53] A few days after the onset of the attack, the Reichsmarschall informed the minister and the chief of the RSHA that the matter had to be submitted to Hitler, whereupon Heydrich asked Bormann for a meeting with the Nazi leader to present the case. Goebbels, on his part, sent a message to the *Reichsleiter*, emphasizing that he considered the matter "exceptionally urgent and necessary [*ausserordentlich dringlich und notwendig*]." After expostulating on the manifold difficulties in implementing the anti-Jewish measures as long as the Jews were not outwardly identified, the memorandum, which sums up Goebbels's view, continued: "As a departure of the Jews [from the Reich] is not to be expected in the near future [*da eine baldige Abwanderung der Juden nicht zu erwarten ist*] it is essential to mark the Jews . . . in order to avoid their attempts to influence the morale of the Volksgenossen."[54] As we shall see, in August Hitler agreed to Goebbels's entreaty—and soon thereafter ordered the "departure" of the Jews.

Throughout the Reich the Jews cowered under the increasing incitement surrounding them and the relentless drive of the authorities to harm and humiliate them by an endless accumulation of new measures. "We live here in such troubled times," Hertha Feiner wrote to her daughters on March 11, 1941, "that notwithstanding all my longing, I am glad that you have escaped this and can quietly work. . . . Many teachers have been dismissed: of the 230 teachers, only 100 remain and as many of these have a permanent position [they had worked for the community before 1928]; you can imagine how limited my prospects are [to continue teaching]. It will be decided by April 1. These worries and many more don't leave me the peace of mind to read."[55]

For the time being she was allowed to stay. "Work at the school is very tiring," she reported on June 1, 1941, "as, due to the dismissal of teachers, the number of our students increases while our salaries decrease. But, the community is in bad shape and nothing can be done about it."[56] A week later Feiner continued to describe the everyday life unfolding around her: "I am glad when nothing special happens, because it's rarely something good. Aunt Irma works in a factory. She likes it, even if she earns little, because she and her mother have to live somehow. . . . They have received an affidavit from 'Amerika' and hope to emigrate, possibly in half a year. I spoke with the Goldsteins . . . their daughter is in Palestine but they hear nothing from her."[57]

In December 1940 Jochen Klepper had been drafted into the Wehrmacht; his diary was interrupted for the next ten months.

III

Although the creation of ghettos was an uneven process in the General Government, the concentration of Jews in separate town areas progressed apace throughout early 1941. "At ten o'clock a Jew dropped in from Kielce," Dawid Rubinowicz noted on April 1. "The same day Jews who have relatives outside the Jewish quarter already left Kielce to go to their families. . . . Uncle came from Kielce to consider what he should do. Papa told him he should join us for the time being; he'll do as we do. So he went to order a cart for tomorrow."[58] The first uncle arrived at the Rubinowiczes' in the early hours of April 3; then, during the day, another uncle arrived: "I wondered where on earth they could find room to stay in our house," Dawid noted on the third.[59] But, to everbody's surprise the second uncle "thought things over and drove back to the Jewish quarter. We were worried because we know very well he would get nothing to eat there."[60]

Indeed, during these same months, hundreds of thousands of Jews lived on the edge of starvation, mainly in the largest ghettos of the Warthegau and the General Government. Among German officials two contrary approaches to the crisis were envisioned. On the one hand the new chief administrator of the Lodz ghetto, Hans Biebow, favored a level of economic activity that would grant at least minimum subsistence to its population; on the other Biebow's own deputy did not mind letting the Jews starve to death. Greiser opted for Biebow's policy; Biebow's deputy, Alexander Palfinger, was transferred to Warsaw.[61]

The path of reorganization was not clear, however, even after the

Gauleiter's decision to support a "productionist" policy, in Christopher Browning's terms. Greiser himself displayed an unusual talent for extortion: He levied a 65 percent tax on all Jewish wages. Moreover, local German agencies and businesses withheld raw materials or food from the ghetto (or delivered substandard products and pocketed the difference). It was only in the late spring of 1941 that Biebow was able to impose the regulations he had been demanding: "For working Jews, 'Polish rations' were to be a minimum; non-working Jews were to receive the long-promised 'prison fare.' "[62]

Rumkowski's mistakes sometimes added to the chronic starvation. According to a ghetto survivor interviewed immediately after the war, the population was particularly incensed by the potato affair. "A lot of potatoes were brought into the ghetto," Israel U. told the American psychologist David Boder in a 1946 interview. "When Rumkowski was asked why he didn't distribute them, he answered: 'you have no business to meddle in my affairs. I will distribute the potatoes when I want.' Frosts came and the potatoes became rotten and they had to be thrown away. They were buried. And afterwards for three years people still searched for potatoes at this spot where they lay buried. Moreover, the people talked themselves into believing that they tasted better that way, because the water had evaporated from the potatoes."[63]

Yet the witness also recognized that over time some order was introduced into the food distribution system by the same dictatorial chairman: "In the beginning a committee was organized in every [apartment] house; it received the allotment for the entire house, and distributed it to all the people. This was very bad. They stole. But Rumkowski remedied this. There were forty-three district warehouses arranged according to streets. And everybody had a card for bread, a card for vegetables, and so forth. Today, for instance, bread comes out for such and such numbers. One went to the warehouse, the card was clipped, [and the transaction was] entered in the book."[64]

Rumkowski's "rationalization" of the ghetto food distribution system was effective only insofar as supply from the outside was authorized by the Germans; yet, despite a wave of strikes and protests by ghetto workers in the spring of 1941, the chairman did impose a measure of equality among the inhabitants that, as already mentioned, contrasted with the situation in Warsaw. Even the "Elder's" most adamant ideological opponents noted his initiatives with a derision tempered by acquiescence: "Rumkowski is leaving for Warsaw to bring doctors, and is reorganizing the food-distribution system in the ghetto," Sierakowiak wrote down on May 13. "The number of food cooperatives is increasing; separate vegetable units are being created, while the bread and other food units are being combined. Creation of new squares, lawns, and even cobblestone and construction works completes the "Spring Program" in the ghetto, marching in 'glory on the road of ascent and highest achievement.'"[65]

Even with all the "productivization" efforts—which in Lodz reached a significant scale—the food supply situation never improved beyond chronic starvation for much of the population. We have some knowledge of everyday life from individual records but mainly from the detailed "Chronicle" in which, from January 1941 to July 1944, a group of "official" diarists (in other works, diarists appointed by Rumkowski) regularly wrote down what they considered of significance for "future historians." At first the writers were Lodz Jews; then, after the deportation from the Reich and the Protectorate in late 1941, Jews from Vienna and Prague were added to the initial group. The chroniclers reported the events of everyday life and used documents assembled in the ghetto archives, a vast and ongoing collection of all available information pertinent to the ghetto, and to the life and work of the megalomaniac Rumkowski. Although they avoided comments on the material they thus kept for history, the chroniclers—by their very presentation of the evidence—told a story whose implications the reader could not miss.[66]

In the first entry of the "Chronicle," on January 12, 1941, the authors noted two minor but telling incidents: "Appearing at one of the precincts of the Order Service, an eight-year-old boy filed a report against his own parents, whom he charged with not giving him the bread ration due to him. The boy demanded that an investigation be conducted and that the guilty parties be punished." And immediately following this entry, the chroniclers recorded another strange occurrence: "The residents of a building found themselves in a very disconcerting situation when, after waking up, they discovered that in the course of the night unknown culprits had stolen . . . their stairs as well as their handrail and banister."[67]

In Warsaw the lack of food also became catastrophic in March 1941. Like his counterpart in the Warthegau, Frank had to make a decision;

and he made the same choice as Greiser. A decree of April 19 reorganized the German administration of the ghetto: District Governor Ludwig Fischer appointed the young attorney Heinz Auerswald (a former official in the Department of Internal Affairs of the General Government) as "Commissar for the Jewish district of Warsaw," directly under his own orders. Moreover, a "*Transferstelle* for overseeing the ghetto's economic relations to the exterior" was set up as an independent institution under the management of the banker Max Bischoff.[68] Needless to say the new authorities had very little control over the demands and initiatives of the ever-present Security Police and SD.[69]

It was in this administrative context that Bischoff launched his new economic policy, with some measure of success. According to Raul Hilberg and Stanislaw Staron, the value of exports from the ghetto increased from 400,000 zlotys in June 1941 to 15 million in July 1942, when the deportations started. Most of this production came from Jewish firms and not from German firms in the ghetto employing Jews. The same computation indicates that the number of productively employed Jews in the ghetto rose from 34,000 in September 1941 to more than 95,000 in July 1942.

Yet, despite this "economic upswing," as in Lodz the minimum food level for the entire ghetto population was never assured.[70] The *Information Bulletin* of the Polish underground published a leading article, on May 23, 1941, that seems to give a faithful description of the situation as seen from the "outside." "Further crowding has resulted in conditions of ill-health, hunger and monstrous poverty that defy description. Groups of pale and emaciated people wander aimlessly through the overcrowded streets. Beggars sit and lie along the walls and the sight of people collapsing from starvation is common. The refuge for abandoned children takes in a dozen infants every day; every day a few more people die on the street. Contagious diseases are spreading, particularly tuberculosis. Meanwhile the Germans continue to plunder the wealthy Jews. Their treatment of the Jews is always exceptionally inhuman. They torment them and subject them constantly to their wild and bestial amusements."[71]

Under such circumstances the natural reaction of most individual members of a group on the scale of a large ghetto would be to concentrate solely on personal survival and that of family members or close friends. This indeed was the common behavior of the average ghetto inhabitant in Warsaw (and anywhere else in Jewish communities under the occupation), according to a keen observer, the Bund leader and ghetto fighter Marek Edelman, among many others.[72] Yet these basic reactions were countered by considerable efforts at assistance from the outside, self-help in various guises, the indirectly useful effects of self-interest, and mainly collective attempts to withstand the challenge for the sake of the weakest members of the group, children and youngsters, or for those closest in ideological (political or religious) terms.

Outside help, massively provided by the Joint Distribution Committee (or JDC) allowed for the internal organization of welfare on a significant scale.[73] Thus the "Jewish Social Self-Help"—*Jüdische Soziale Selbsthilfe*, or JSS—started coordinating the efforts of previously independent Jewish welfare agencies throughout Poland. The task of the JSS was overwhelming, although it tried to set priorities, beginning with the neediest: children and the elderly; in its first year of activity it helped some 160,000 people in Warsaw alone by distributing food and other basic necessities.

Tension soon arose between the council and the Warsaw JSS; the latter had to fight every inch of the way to avoid coming under the authority of the *Judenrat*. Whereas the JSS dealt with ghetto populations in general, the "House Committees," as their name indicates, organized self-help at the tenement level.[74] While the "Joint" was the main funding source of the JSS, the House Committees' activities were supported by both the JSS and the dues of those tenants who could afford it.[75] Moreover some welfare organizations established before the war, such as CENTOS, assisting orphanages, and ORT, concentrating on vocational training, maintained their own activities. In Warsaw none of this, however, would have sufficed without large-scale smuggling as an essential part of "self-help."

"Heard marvelous stories of the smuggling that goes on via the Jewish graveyard. In one night they transported twenty-six cows by that route," Ringelblum noted on January 11, 1941.[76] A few weeks later Kaplan added his observations: "Smuggling was carried out through all the holes and cracks in the walls, through connecting tunnels in the cellars of buildings on the border, and through all the hidden places unfamiliar to the conqueror's foreign eyes. The conductors on the Aryan trolleys in particular made fortunes.... Aryan trolleys make no stops inside the ghetto, but that's not a handicap. The smuggled sack is thrown out at an appointed spot and caught by trustworthy hands. This is the way they smuggle in pork fat, in particular, which the religious leaders have permitted us to use in this time of destruction."[77] The smugglers, or rather the ringleaders, were the first to benefit from these operations. German and Polish guards pocketed substantial bribes—and so, on a lesser scale, did members of the Jewish ghetto police.

On the face of it the German administration fought the smuggling and the ghetto commissar took some measures to make the illegal traffic more difficult.[78] Yet "for the most part, smuggling was tolerated, and the measures taken against it were meant only to restrict its magnitude."[79] As for the Jewish Council, it understood perfectly that given the food supply situation, smuggling could not and should not be stopped.[80]

The smuggling and profiteering of all sorts created a new class: Warsaw's nouveaux riches thrived—for a while. They had their restaurants and cabarets where, sheltered from the surrounding misery, they enjoyed their ephemeral wealth and mixed with Poles and Germans, often their associates. "At Number 2, Leszno Street," the Bundist Jacob Celemenski reminisced, "there was now a cabaret called *Sztuka* [Art].... When we reached the nightclub the street was dark. My escort suddenly said to me: 'Be careful not to step on a corpse.' When I opened the door the light blinded me. Gas lamps were burning in every corner of the crowded cabaret. Every table was covered by a white tablecloth. Fat characters sat at them eating chicken, duck, or fowl. All these foods would be drowned in wine and liquor. The orchestra, in the middle of the nightclub, sat on a small platform. Next to it, a singer performed. These were people who once played before Polish crowds.... The audience crowding the tables was made up of the aristocracy of the ghetto—big-time smugglers, high Polish officers, and all sorts of big shots. Germans who had business dealings with the Jews also came here, dressed in civilian clothes.... The audience ate, drank, and laughed as if it had no worries."[81]

Of course the ghetto's "new class" represented just a minute segment of the population. The majority went hungry, despite smuggling, self-help, House Committees, and packages which—until June 1941—mostly arrived from the Soviet Union or Soviet-occupied Poland, and the like.

Increasingly so, potatoes became the basic staple, as in Lodz. "It seems to me," Hersch Wasser, the secretary and coordinator of Oneg Shabat, recorded on January 3, 1941, "there's a sound economic basis underlying the plethora of new latke-shops [*latkes* are potato pancakes, usually prepared for Chanukah] . . . the public eats one or two latkes instead of breakfast, lunch or supper, and thereby stills its hunger. Bread is becoming a dream, and a hot lunch belongs to the world of fantasy. Things are certainly grave if potato latkes are becoming a national dish."[82]

Starvation spread, mainly among refugees from the provinces. The number of deaths from starvation and disease between the closing of the ghetto in November 1940 and the beginning of the deportations in July 1942 may have been as high as 100,000 (at the same time the population was "replenished" by waves of refugees from the provinces and, in the spring of 1942, also by deportees from the Reich). Yet despite the overall misery, maintaining education for children and youngsters remained a constant and partly successful endeavor.

Until 1941 Jewish schools were forbidden in the General Government. After Frank's agreement to the resumption of Jewish education, schooling became official, and the councils took over, bit by bit, according to local German orders. In Lodz schools reopened in the spring of 1941; in Warsaw, only in November 1941. During the two years or so in which schooling had been prohibited in Warsaw, clandestine schools, run by teachers belonging to all prewar educational institutions, working in common, spread throughout the ghetto.

With younger children the educational and play-center activities faced the formidable obstacle of hunger. The Ringelblum archives include abundant material sent in by teachers and social workers confronted with this insoluble problem. "How do you make an apathetic, hungry child, who is all the time thinking about a piece of bread, interested in something else?" asked one; another wrote that a meal "was a point of departure for any activities in which we would like the children to participate."[83] Yet another volunteer teacher stated after the war: "I tried to give tuition to children living in the same courtyard as myself but my attempt failed because they were hungry."[84]

Nonetheless high school and even grade school activity was intense and clandestine libraries in the three languages of the ghetto attracted a vast readership. Children and youngsters had their preferences: Frances

Hodgson Burnett's *Little Lord Fauntleroy* and Edmondo De Amici's *The Heart*.[85] To many of these children, though, much of the "normal" world was unknown. According to a survivor's testimony, "Children confined to the ghetto did not know anything about animals and plants. They didn't even know what a cow looked like."[86]

It seems that one of the favorite books of the adult ghetto population was Franz Werfel's *The Forty Days of Musa Dagh*, a novel set during the genocide of the Armenians by the Turks in World War I, telling of the heroism and endurance of a group of Armenians—and of their ultimate rescue.[87] In more general terms cultural activities, ideological debates, and any expression of the "life of the mind" became both an instinctive and a willed reaction in the face of daily degradation and an ephemeral refuge from utter misery.

Music played a special role in the larger ghettos, mainly in Warsaw and Lodz. Orchestras were established, and a relatively rich and intense musical life developed. Thus in Warsaw, the initiative of setting up a symphony orchestra came from a few musicians; but, was it their intention "to serve the noble art," in Marcel Reich-Ranicki's words, "or to provide joy and pleasure to others? Nothing of the sort—they wanted to earn some money in order to assuage their hunger."[88] An additional reminder of what counted most in ghetto life.

Reich-Ranicki, who enthusiastically and expertly went on to describe the accomplishments of the ghetto musicians, did, at the time, try his hand at occasional pieces of criticism for the German-licensed *Gazeta Zydowska*, under the pen name Wiktor Hart.[89] Twenty-one years old in 1941, he came from a Jewish family from Włocławek but had attended high school in Berlin before being sent back to Poland, in the fall of 1938, during the Nazi expulsion of Polish Jews from the Reich. The family moved to Warsaw, where, after the setting up of the council, Reich-Ranicki, fluent in German, soon found a position as chief of the "Translation and Correspondence Bureau."[90]

His comments regarding the avid attendance at the symphony concerts shed further light on what could be surmised about cultural life in the ghetto in general. "It was not defiance that brought the hungry and the wretched into the concert halls, but a longing for solace and elevation—however hackneyed these words, they are appropriate. Those who were ceaselessly fearing for their lives, those who were vegetating in the ghetto, were seeking shelter and refuge for an hour or two, searching for some form of security and perhaps even happiness. They needed a counter-world."[91]

In Lodz, too, musical life was intense. During the first three weeks of March 1941, for example, the ghetto "Chronicle" mentions concerts on the first, the fifth, the eighth, the eleventh and the thirteenth: "On the 13th, which was Purim," the "Chronicle" recorded, "there was a violin performance by Miss Bronislawa Rotsztat, as well as a symphony concert conducted by Dawid Bajgelman in which Hazomir ["the nightingale," in Hebrew] chorus participated. On Saturday, March 15, that program was repeated in a performance for invited guests, the chairman chief among them. This performance had a special ceremonial quality and lasted until ten o'clock in the evening. On March 17, the School Department organized a performance of music and vocals for schoolchildren. On the 18th, the 20th and the 22nd of March there were symphony concerts for factory workers and, finally, on the 22nd, there was a symphony concert dedicated to classical music and conducted by Theodor Ryder."[92]

Grassroots intellectual (ideological) activity was probably even more intense than public cultural manifestations. On May 8, 1941, Sierakowiak recorded his intention to meet on that same day with three other high school members of the [communist] "all youth unit of lecturers" to "discuss Lenin's famous work, *State and Revolution*, and then . . . lecture on it to all other active youth units in the ghetto."[93] On May 10, "Comrade Ziula Krengiel lectured on the significance of the first of May holiday. . . . In the afternoon," Sierakowiak added, "we had a meeting with girls, during which our most active members (Niutek, Jerzyk and I) had a difficult time explaining the concept of surplus value."[94]

Among the young Lodz ghetto Marxists, intellectual instruction went along with organized action and action itself was induced by misery: "A student from the same grade as ours died from hunger and exhaustion yesterday," Sierakowiak recorded on May 13. "He is the third victim of the class."[95] Sierakowiak led the action against his school's authorities to get additional food. He won, in principle at least.[96] On the sixteenth he was examined by the school doctor: "She was terrified at how thin I am. She immediately gave me a referral for X-rays. Perhaps I will now be able to get a double portion of soup in school. In fact, five such soups would be even better, but the two will do me some good, too. In any case, one soup is nothing."[97]

* * *

It was among the politically organized "youth movements" that ideological and general educational activities naturally were the most widespread and systematic. From the beginning of the occupation to the end of 1941, these activities were hardly interfered with; they were of no interest to the Germans. And thus, in the larger ghettos, the youth movements created a distinct subculture: The anti-Zionist Bund youth movement Zukunft (Future), the Zionist-Revisionist Betar, and the Center-Left and mainly left-wing "pioneering" Zionist youth, each created a world of its own.[98]

Organized Jewish youth had been left to its own devices following the hasty departure of the envoys from Eretz Israel and of much of the senior political or communal leadership, at the beginning of the war. Whereas Bundist youth stayed in close contact with a senior leadership that remained in occupied Poland (or, for a while, in the Soviet Union), the Zionist youth movements gradually lost touch with party headquarters in Palestine, despite their own entreaties that they keep in contact and receive help. The ideological fervor of this Zionist youth did not falter—it was possibly even heightened by the surrounding circumstances; the response from Eretz Israel, however, soon dwindled to increasingly unrealistic and perfunctory advice and instructions, and often, as we already saw from Zivia Lubetkin's letter, it lapsed into silence.[99] Such indifference created a growing rift and soon turned into a desperate sense of independence among the local youth leaders, the oldest of whom were in their early twenties at most.[100]

While the ongoing and intense debates that divided movements sharing, for example, the same Zionist-socialist outlook (like Hashomer Hatzair, Gordonia, or Dror) appear incomprehensible from hindsight, the considerable effort invested in these ideological-cultural activities and the publication of a large number of underground newspapers and periodicals (also geared toward the general Jewish population)—either in Polish, Yiddish, or Hebrew—became a form of resistance and, possibly, a psychologically necessary preparation for the armed resistance of later days.[101]

The council remained at the center of ghetto life. By mid-1941, the Warsaw *Judenrat*, for example, had become a tentacular bureaucracy employing some 6,000 people in a whole array of departments (almost thirty at some point); its achievements were real given the dearth of means, and yet, as already mentioned, it encountered intense hostility among most of the Jewish population, a hostility that grew as time went by. "The Community Council is an abomination in the eyes of the Warsaw community," the acerbic Kaplan noted on April 23, 1941. "When the Council is so much as mentioned, everyone's blood begins to boil. If it were not for fear of the Authorities there would be bloodshed. . . . According to rumor, the President is a decent man. But the people around him are the dregs of humanity. There are two or three exceptions who have no influence. . . . All the rest are the scum of the [Jewish] public. . . . They are known as scoundrels and corrupt persons, who did not avoid ugly dealings even in the period before the war. . . . Everything is done in the name of the President. But in truth, everything is done without his knowledge and even without his consent, and perhaps also against his decisions and wishes."[102] A ghetto joke noted by Shimon Huberband expressed the gist of the populace's attitude: "A contemporary Jewish prayer—O Lord, help me become a chairman or a vice-chairman, so that I can allocate funds to myself."[103] Above and beyond the anger triggered by widespread corruption, popular resentment focused particularly on forced-labor conscription, taxation, and the brutality of the Jewish police.

While Jewish workers were increasingly employed by ghetto workshops, "labor battalions," set up by the councils, were daily marched to work. Moreover, let us remember, in Upper Silesia tens of thousands of local Jews were toiling in the special labor camps of "Organization Schmelt," and Jewish slave laborers were ruthlessly driven by the SS in the eastern part of the General Government, mainly in Globocnik's Lublin district. There the laborers were kept digging antitank trenches and constructing a defense line for no clear military purpose. The OKH had agreed to the enterprise, but its implementation was left entirely in the hands of Himmler's henchmen.[104]

The forced laborers in eastern Poland, like the others, had at first been snatched off the streets of the Jewish quarters or ghettos, then subjected to compulsory draft by Frank's decree of October 26, 1939, and, as we saw, later recruited by the councils. Many would be shipped off to the Lublin labor camps for periods that could stretch for weeks or even months. According to the report of a medical commission that visited the Belzec work camp in the Lublin district in September 1940, "The barracks are totally unfit to hold so many people. They are dark, filthy and overrun with lice. About thirty percent of the workers have no shoes, pants, or shirts. All of them sleep on the ground, without straw. The roofs leak everywhere, and the windows have no panes. Space is terribly lacking: for example, within a space of five by six meters, some seventy-five people sleep on the ground on top of each other. . . . Soap is lacking, and even water is hard to get. The sick lie and sleep together with the healthy. At night, it is forbidden to leave the barracks so that all needs have to be fulfilled on the spot. Thus, it is no wonder that sickness spreads. Yet it is extremely difficult to be excused from work, even for a day. Everybody, including the sick, has to report for work."[105]

Czerniaków was well aware of the situation in the labor camps. The Lublin district was the worst, but conditions in the Warsaw area were not much better. On May 10, 1941, after receiving a report from two council members who had just been allowed a short visit, he noted: "The camp huts have spoiled straw to sleep on and the wind is blowing through the walls. The workers are shivering at night. There are no showers and restrooms. The workers' boots were ruined in wet sand and clay. There are no drugs or bandages. Treatment of the workers by the *Lagerschutz* [camp guards] in many localities is bad. Meissner [the commander of the camp guards in the area in which the visit took place—the Kampinos barracks] did issue orders forbidding the beatings of the workers." And yet, the ghetto poor kept volunteering, in the hope of receiving some money and some food. In the same entry, Czerniaków added: "Wages are not paid. . . . Everything depends on nutrition." Barely a fraction of the promised food was distributed.[106]

Money would protect you from the labor camps. "If you have not appeared before the [mustering] commission yet," Wasser noted on April 28, 1941, "you can go to one of the doctors, pay down 150 zl. [zlotys] on the fee, and he will find some medical reason for requesting your release. . . . And for an additional 200 zl., a work card is miraculously whisked into your home without toil or trouble. And if, God forbid, you have already undergone the medical examination and—o, woe!—been found '*tauglich*' [capable], the procedure costs around 500 zl. for a certificate of being immune, inviolable."[107]

As for taxes, particularly in Warsaw, they were blatantly unjust. The council had opted for indirect taxation of the ghetto's most basic commodities and services, instead of direct taxation of the wealthy inhabitants; it meant that the poorest segments of the population (the immense majority) were carrying most of the tax burden. The wealthy inhabitants, the big smugglers, the profiteers of various ilks, practically avoided all direct levies on their assets.[108]

Possibly the most common target of popular anger was the Jewish police, the Jewish uniformed "order service," which in principle was under the orders of the council and of the Germans. In Warsaw, the ghetto police was some 2,000 men strong and headed by a convert, a former lieutenant colonel in the Polish police, Józef Szerynski.

The policemen were mainly young men from the "better" class, from the "intelligentsia" at times. They had the necessary connections to get the coveted jobs, and once in uniform, they did not hesitate to enforce the most unpopular orders issued by the councils (tax collection, escorting men to forced labor, guarding the inner fence of the ghetto, confiscations of property and the like) or by the Germans, often brutally so. Although, the policemen argued at the time—and after the war—that things would have been much worse if their jobs had been solely implemented by Germans or Poles, there is no doubt that "considerable segments of the ghetto police were morally and materially corrupt, that they enriched themselves on account of the oppressed and persecuted inmates when carrying out their assignments."[109]

Nothing of this stigma is apparent in the memoir that Calel Perechodnik, a Jewish policeman from Ottwock, near Warsaw, wrote in 1944, shortly before his death on the "Aryan" side of the city. More precisely, nothing is apparent as long as the memoir deals with the predeportation period (before the summer of 1942). "In February 1941," Perechodnik recorded, "seeing that the war was not coming to an end and in order to be free from the roundup for labor camps, I entered the ranks of the Ghetto Polizei."[110] The Ottwock Jewish policeman had little to report about his daily activities: "And what did I do during this time? Truthfully speaking, nothing. I didn't go out to seize people because I found it unbecoming. I was afraid of what people would say. In any case, I did not have the 'sporting instinct' for that . . . I collected the bread quota at the Jewish bakery and . . . distributed it at the command post or for the functionaries of the Ghetto Polizei."[111] Too tame to be entirely trustworthy? Probably.

For the Germans, Jewish policemen were as contemptible as any other Jews. Mary Berg, a Jewish girl who lived in the ghetto with her American mother (and was allowed to emigrate in 1941), noted on January 4, 1941: "Yesterday, I myself saw a Nazi gendarme 'exercise' a Jewish policeman near the passage from the little to the big ghetto on Chlodna street. The young man finally lost his breath but the Nazi still forced him to fall and rise until he collapsed in a pool of blood."[112]

The Germans also bypassed the Warsaw council and the Jewish police, and supported their own Jewish agents, variously involved with the Gestapo. Such, for example, were the "Thirteen" (the name derived from the address of their headquarters on 13 Leszno Street), a group of some three hundred shady characters, under the command of one Abraham Ganzweich, whose official job was to fight price hiking and other forms of corruption. Ganzweich was an informer, and so were the owners of the horse-drawn tram service, Kohn and Heller. Although Ganzweich did attempt to achieve some legitimacy in the community by supporting "social work" and "cultural activities,"[113] he was considered with much suspicion by Czerniaków and many others.[114] Most informers, big or small, did not report on political life in the ghetto; they denounced the inhabitants who had hidden some jewelry or cash and usually received a "compensation" from the Germans for their services.[115]

The threat of disease and starvation never disappeared. Two reports on the food and health situation in the Warsaw ghetto, one German and the other Jewish, were written at approximately the same time, in September 1941. The German report, signed by Commissar Auerswald, covered the first eight months of the year and tallied almost exactly with the figures established by the ghetto statisticians.[116] The monthly number of deaths grew approximately sixfold from January (898) to August 1941 (5,560). In both reports stabilization was noted in August and September.

The Jewish statisticians meant essentially to compare the mortality of children under fifteen with that of adults. According to the results collected from January to September 1941, while the death of children grew at a slower rate at first, it overtook that of the general population in the last four months. According to the ghetto statisticians' interpretation, at the outset parents were still able to protect their children from starvation; soon, however, the worsening overall food situation made any such efforts impossible.[117]

The dramatic deterioration of the children's situation at the beginning of the summer of 1941 found an immediate expression in the diarists' entries. "A special class of beggars," Ringelblum recorded on July 11, 1941, "consists of those who beg after nine o'clock at night. You stand at your window, and suddenly see new faces, beggars you haven't seen all day. They walk out right in the middle of the street, begging for bread. Most of them are children. In the surrounding silence of night, the cries of hungry beggar children are terribly insistent and, however hard your heart, eventually you have to throw a piece of bread down to them—or else leave the house. Those beggars are completely unconcerned about curfews and you can hear their voices late at night at eleven or even at twelve. They are afraid of nothing and of no one. . . . It is a common thing for beggar children like these to die on the sidewalk at night. I was told about such a horrible scene . . . where a six-year-old beggar boy lay gasping all night, too weak to roll over to the piece of bread that had been thrown down to him from the balcony."[118]

Given the conditions prevailing in the Warsaw ghetto during the summer of 1941, however, death—of children or of adults—was increasingly becoming a matter of indifference. Typhus was spreading, and there was little the hospitals—"places of execution" according to the director of the ghetto health department—could do: Either the patients died from the epidemics or from the lack of food at the hospital.[119]

"In front of 16 Krochmalna Street," Czerniaków recorded on July 24, 1941, "I was stopped by a commander of a military sanitary column and shown the corpse of a child in an advanced stage of decay. According to information obtained on the site, the corpse, already decomposed, was abandoned there yesterday. On the basis of subsequent investigation it was established that the body was left behind by its own mother, Chudesa Borensztajn . . . and that the child's name was Moszek, age 6. In the same apartment there was the body of Molka Ruda, age 43, in which rigor mortis had not yet set in, and in the courtyard of the same house lay the body of Chindel Gersztenzang. . . . The sanitary column stopped a passing funeral cart belonging to the funeral firm 'Eternity' and ordered the removal of the remains."[120]

* * *

Because increasing numbers of Wehrmacht units were once again moving to Poland in the early stages of *Aufbau Ost* from the summer of 1940 onward, soldiers' descriptions of their encounters with the Jewish population streamed steadily back to the Reich. On September 11 Private HN described, in the usual terms, the "disgusting look" of the thousands of Jews he was encountering. The mostly Orthodox Jews he described apparently provided quite a show for the amusement of throngs of soldiers standing around (*zum Gaudium der Zuschauer*), mainly when these Jews had to perform some heavy work.[121] For Private E his observation of the Jews led to some radical conclusions: "When one looks at these people," he wrote on November 17, "one gets the impression that they really have no justification for living on God's earth" (*dass die wirklich keine Berechtigung haben, überhaupt auf Gottes Erdboden zu leben*).[122] The more extreme opinions were apparently quite widespread, as indicated in a letter written by Cpl. WH, on May 28, 1941: "As I was still having dinner, the conversation moved to the Jewish question in the General Government and in the world; for me, listening to such conversations is very interesting. To my amazement, everybody agreed in the end that the Jews have to disappear completely from the world" (*Zu meinem Erstaunen waren sich schliesslich doch alle einig, dass die Juden ganz von der Welt verschwinden müssen*).[123]

On September 9, 1940, Dr. Zygmunt Klukowski recorded an event that took place in front of his hospital. An elderly Jew was standing across the street, talking to some Jewish women. A group of German soldiers came by: "Suddenly one of the soldiers grabbed the old man and threw him headfirst into the cellar [of a burned-out house in front of which the Jews were standing]. . . . The soldiers calmly walked away. I was puzzled by this incident, but a few minutes later the man was brought to me for treatment. I was told that he forgot to take his hat off when the Germans passed by. . . . During the last few days the Germans have again begun beating Jews on the streets."[124]

The situation in the large ghettos was not different from that in the "provinces." On February 14, 1941, Kaplan noted an incident on Karmelicka Street. Suddenly the street was empty of the crowds that had filled it throughout the day. Two Germans had appeared, one of them with a whip in hand: They discovered a peddler who had not managed to flee in time. "The unfortunate peddler became a target for the blows of the murdering beasts. He fell to the ground at once, and one of them left him and went away. But not so his companion. The very physical weakness of his victim inflamed the soldier. As soon as the peddler fell, he began stamping on him and beating him mercilessly with his whip. . . . The beaten man lay flat, without a breath of life. But the tormentor would not let him alone. It would be no exaggeration to say that he beat him without stopping, without pity, for about twenty minutes. It was hard to comprehend the secret of this sadistic phenomenon."[125]

In an unrelated entry on May 10, 1941, Ringelblum described, as already alluded to, how dead Jews were becoming a sight not to be missed by German tourists: "The dead are buried at night between 1 and 5 a.m., without shrouds—in white paper which is later removed—and in mass graves," Ringelblum recorded on May 10, 1941. "Various groups of [German] excursionists—military men, private citizens—keep visiting the graveyard. Most of them show no sympathy at all for the Jews. On the contrary some of them maintain that the mortality among the Jews is too low. Others take all kinds of photographs. The shed where dozens of corpses lie during the day awaiting burial at night is particularly popular."[126]

IV

While the Germans were still searching for some way of expelling the Jews from the Continent, the struggle against "the Jew" developed apace. Anti-Semitic propaganda and major channels of anti-Jewish political agitation were mainly in Goebbels's hands, although, as we saw, Rosenberg, Himmler, and Ribbentrop never abandoned the field to the tireless propaganda minister. Apart from his major anti-Semitic films, it may be remembered that one of Goebbels's most effective channels for reaching millions of Germans were the weekly UFA newsreels. During the first half of 1941, as the onslaught against the Soviet Union was approaching, the OKW propaganda units were particularly active in gathering material throughout occupied Poland (the Lodz ghetto seems to have been a favorite of PK film crews). The material would be of major use after the beginning of the campaign.[127] It is altogether hard to assess whether the deluge of press attacks against the Jews was more or less effective than the ongoing barrage of sickening images, and whether both had the same effect as the constant anti-Jewish radio propaganda, but—directly or indirectly—the overall orchestration of the campaign followed the instructions of the Propaganda Ministry.

At times, of course, the propaganda minister had to assert his presence. Thus, when *Das Reich* was launched in May 1940, as Germany's highbrow, even modestly independent political-cultural weekly, Goebbels had no direct say regarding the decisions of Editor in Chief Rolf Reinhardt. Before long, though, the minister was signing a weekly editorial in the most successful of the regime's publications and these editorials carried his major written anti-Jewish attacks (usually read on the same day on the radio).[128] Not that *Das Reich* suffered from a paucity of its own independent contributions to anti-Jewish incitement. In the spring of 1941 a journalist, Elisabeth Noelle, published an article on the Jewish-dominated American press, and her colleague Erich-Peter Neumann, offered a very "evocative" description of the Warsaw ghetto;[129] the two, connected by many bonds, were to become the luminaries of public opinion research in postwar West Germany. The average tone of these in-depth studies of the ghetto Jews can be surmised from a report by Hubert Neun about scenes from the Warsaw ghetto published in *Das Reich* on March 9, 1941: "There surely cannot be a place on the continent," Neun told his German readers, "that offers such a graphic cross-section of the chaos and degeneracy of the Semitic mass. At a glance one can take in the enormous, repellent variety of all the Jewish types of the East: a gathering of the asocial, it floods out of dirty houses and greasy shops, up and down the streets, and behind the windows the series of bearded, spectacled rabbinical faces continues—a dreadful panorama."[130]

Actually Goebbels's tentacles extended well beyond his obvious sphere of activity. Among other forays into domains not his, the minister supported Grundmann's institute in its campaign to "de-Judaize" Christian teaching. While the propaganda chief was vilifying the Jews in the political sphere, another luminary of the Jena theological faculty and a colleague of Grundmann's at the institute, Wolf Meyer-Erlach, was touring occupied Europe to demonstrate that Judaism had poisoned England by way of the English Reformation: It explained the English war against Germany. The lectures were published by Goebbels's ministry.[131]

Of course the regime's ongoing struggle against "the Jew" demanded constant research about its object—and research there was. It encompassed every imaginable domain, from physics and mathematics to musicology, from theology to history, from genetics and anthropology to philosophy and literature. It drew on a formidable amount of "scholarship" accumulated mainly since the late nineteenth century, which grew into a torrent during the Weimar period and a boundless flood in the prewar years of Hitler's regime.[132] Part of this work became affiliated with one of two major and mutually hostile institutions: Each had its party patronage, its bureaucratic supporters, and its foreign ties.

The establishment of Walter Frank's "Reich Institute for the History of the New Germany" in 1935 in Berlin, under the aegis of the education minister, did not initially create any problem, nor did that of its Munich branch, which was entirely devoted to the Jewish question and led by the young and ambitious Dr. Wilhelm Grau. In 1938 however, Frank, probably annoyed by Grau's self-importance and growing independence, dismissed him. Grau soon found his way to a new center that was about to start its activities in Frankfurt, Rosenberg's "Institute for the Study of the Jewish Question," actively supported by the city's mayor, Fritz Krebs.[133] The Frankfurt institute was to be the first unit of the "*Hohe Schule*," the party university, Rosenberg's pet project.

The institute was inaugurated on March 25, 1941, and its acting director was none other than Wilhelm Grau. On the opening evening a veritable who's who of European anti-Semitism (Alexander Cuza from Romania, Sano Mach from Slovakia, Vidkun Quisling from Norway, and Anton Mussert from Holland, among others) and party dignitaries, albeit no first-rank figure, congregated in the Römersaal to listen to Rosenberg's diatribe against the "Jewish poison," which was now being rigorously analyzed by German science. Rosenberg stressed that the victories of the Wehrmacht had allowed the establishment in Frankfurt of the "largest library on Jewish matters in the world." In his closing address, two days later, the Reichsleiter described the political goal sought by Germany in regard to the Jews: their complete expulsion from Europe. The scientific part of the inauguration ceremonies took place on March 26 and 27.[134]

Together with Heinz-Peter Seraphim, the main Nazi specialist on Eastern European Jewry, Grau had taken over a party periodical specializing in the "anti-Jewish struggle," *Weltkampf* [The World Struggle], and made it into the official publication of the new institute. The periodical, which had undergone a series of changes since its founding in 1924, now became "academic"; but its subtitle, *Die Judenfrage in Geschichte und Gegenwart* (The Jewish Question in History and in the Present), indicated that its guidelines remained the same. "Weltkampf," Grau wrote in his first editorial, "is going to be the mouthpiece of German and European scholarship. . . . Scholarship, too, today more than at any other time, looks upon this [anti-Jewish] work as a 'world struggle', a war that is inevitable for the peoples that are aware of their own unique characteristics."[135]

In his speech at the inaugural conference, Seraphim did not leave any doubts in the minds of his audience: Neither ghettoization nor a Jewish "reservation" in the East could be considered a solution: The city ghetto could not supply itself with either manufactured goods, raw materials, fuel, or food. Consequently the entire supply would have to be imported. These imports could be small per capita and not exceed the subsistence minimum, and yet in their totality they represented a major burden; the Jews, in short, would be fed and supported by the non-Jews.

Such difficulties might be met by assigning a larger territory to the Jews; the Lublin reservation, for example. "This plan," Seraphim conceded, "looked fascinating at first glance, but there were also difficulties to be reckoned with. The territory could not become self-supporting. Furthermore, 5,000,000 Jews would have to be moved into this reservation and 2,700,000 non-Jews would have to be removed. But in Europe, there is no place for them. This means," he exclaimed indignantly, "that non-Jews would have to be compelled to emigrate from Europe in order to settle Jews in Europe." Moreover, guarding the frontiers of such a giant ghetto would involve colossal expenditures. Seraphim finally emphasized: "*Through legislation and administrative measures, the Jews in the cities are to be replaced by non-Jews to the degree in which qualified non-Jews are available for this substitution . . . the Jew must yield wherever an equally qualified non-Jew is available.*"[136]

The other speakers were more explicit. "The dangerous Jewish influence in Europe," Walter Gross, head of the racial policy office of the NSDAP, explained, "could be fought only by way of total geographical removal."[137] And, for Wilhelm Grau, "The twentieth century, which at its beginning saw the Jew at the summit of his power, will at its end not see Israel anymore because the Jews will have disappeared from Europe."[138]

From the outset the Frankfurt institute looked for alliances with other kindred institutions beyond the Reich's borders. Thus Grau openly welcomed the development of research about Eastern European Jewry at the Institute for German Study of the East (Institut für Deutsche Ostarbeit) in Krakow, set up in one of the buildings of the Jagellonian University under the direction of Fritz Arlt and Heinrich Gottong.[139]

In the face of the massive Rosenberg offensive, Walter Frank did not concede defeat easily. Volumes 5 and 6 of the Reich institute's *Forschungen zur Judenfrage* (*Research Studies on the Jewish Question*) were hastily readied and publicly presented to Keitel just ahead of the official inauguration of Rosenberg's institute.[140] Rosenberg tried to have Frank boycotted by the German press; in the meantime, however, Goebbels had opened the pages of *Das Reich* to Frank for an article on "The Jews and the War."[141]

In December 1940 Frankfurt mayor Krebs, Rosenberg's ally, sent two of his main museum directors to Paris on a scouting expedition. The envoys were given clear instructions: They had to make sure that art "which belonged to Frankfurt should not get into other hands."[142] With money allocated by the city, the Frankfurt emissaries started buying in France, Belgium, and Holland; they knew that in Germany this art would fetch five- or sixfold higher prices.

In the spring of 1941 the potential benefits became even greater, and Krebs's delegates were back in Paris in February, March, and April.[143] The mayor explained the buying spree to the city council on March 31: "In my visits to France and Belgium, I heard from various agencies that art dealers make pilgrimages to Paris in droves and buy whatever can be bought. What is cheap for the dealers is right for the city administrations. That is why we have also gone for these art treasures. Such favorable conditions must be taken advantage of by Frankfurt. . . . I know that other city administrations are buying whatever they can get . . . the acquisitions we made up to now have been a profitable business for us. These are unique occasions. One has to be clever and be the first on the market."[144] The mayor did not need to explain the circumstances that facilitated such easy cleverness: The market was replete with art objects sold by Jews, fleeing for their lives.

Krebs was following in the steps of much greater collectors than German city administrations. On June 30, 1940, five days after the armistice with France, General Keitel had informed the military commander of Paris that "the Führer ordered the safe-keeping of all art objects and historical documents belonging to individuals, and Jews in particular."[145] Such an order had indeed been given by Hitler to Ribbentrop, who conveyed it to the newly appointed German ambassador to France, Otto Abetz. Within weeks Abetz's men pounced on art collections (which the French had moved to Loire castles to protect them) and confiscated whatever belonged to Jewish owners, particularly the Rothschilds. Before the summer was over, some 1,500 Jewish-owned paintings had been transferred to a depot belonging to the embassy and a curator arrived from Berlin to start the inventory of the booty.[146] On September 17, 1940, the authority to impound "ownerless property" was delegated by Hitler to Rosenberg and his "Kommando."[147]

By March 1941, Rosenberg could report to his master that a special train put at his disposal by Göring and carrying art objects having belonged to Jews in France had arrived at Neuschwanstein (in Bavaria). The twenty-five freight cars contained some four thousand pieces "of the highest artistic value." Moreover, the Reichsmarschall had already sent two "special freight cars" to Munich with some of the main pieces that had belonged to the Rothschilds.[148] Some of Hitler's acquisitions were earmarked for the supermuseum he planned to set up in Linz; others were handed out as gifts to his German and foreign devotees; some of the best pieces he kept for himself.

The plunder was unconcealed. On May 18, 1941, Ulrich von Hassell mentioned that Elsa Bruckmann (one of Hitler's earliest supporters) noticed that sizable amounts of French antique furniture were being loaded onto trucks in front of the Prinz-Karl Palast in Munich. The owner of the moving company, whom she knew, told her that the furniture was being sent to Obersalzberg (Hitler's mountain retreat). Had it been bought? she asked; "So to say bought," he replied, "but if you were to give me 100RM for this Louis XVI desk, it would be a good price.[149]

For ordinary Wehrmacht members the booty may have been less grand, yet being an occupier had its advantages: "We live here in a house that had belonged to a Jewish emigrant," Sgt. HH wrote from France on

August 13, 1940. A great amount of silver tableware will no doubt find a new owner. I think that, slowly, the pieces will reach the homeland. That's war."[150]

The SS Reichsführer did not collect art or silverware. His looting was more directly related to his professional activities: At the end of 1940 he had the entire skull collection of eighteenth-century scientist Franz Joseph Gall transferred from Paris to the racial-biological institute of Tübingen University.[151]

V

In his January 30, 1941, speech, Hitler concluded his prophecy of anti-Jewish retribution by expressing the hope that an increasing number of Europeans would follow the German anti-Semitic lead: "Already now," he declared, "our racial awareness penetrates one people after the other and I hope that also those who today stand in enmity against us, will recognize one day their greater internal enemy and then join in a common front with us: the front against the international Jewish exploitation and corruption of nations."[152] As he mentioned the growth of anti-Semitism, the Nazi leader probably had in mind the events that had occurred in Bucharest just a few days beforehand.

On January 21, 1941, the Romanian capital had been shaken by a brief and abortive attempt by the SS-supported Iron Guard to wrest power from its ally, the dictatorial head of state, Marshal Ion Antonescu. During their three-day rampage, Horia Sima's "legionnaries" first and foremost vented their rage upon the Jews of the city. "The stunning thing about the Bucharest bloodbath," Mihail Sebastian recorded a few days after the events, "is the quite bestial ferocity of it, apparent even in the dry official statement that ninety-three persons (person being the latest euphemism for Jew) were killed on the night of Tuesday the 21st in Jilava forest. But what people say is much more devastating. It is now considered absolutely certain that the Jews butchered at Straulesti abattoir were hanged by the neck on hooks normally used for beef carcasses. A sheet of paper was stuck to each corpse: 'Kosher Meat.' As for those killed in Jilava Forest, they were first undressed (it would have been a pity for clothes to remain there), then shot and thrown on top of one another."[153]

The guard was crushed, and its leaders fled to Germany, but their anti-Jewish rage was deeply anchored in Romanian society.

In great part Romanian anti-Semitism shared the basic aspects of anti-Jewish agitation throughout the eastern part of the Continent (except for the USSR), with, as mentioned, some differences between countries or areas of growing modernization and those that remained essentially traditional peasant societies. Whereas in Romania the "Old Kingdom" (the *Regat*) belonged to the first category, the "lost provinces" of Bukovina and Bessarabia belonged to the second. In that sense Romanian anti-Semitism reached some of its most vitriolic manifestations and expressions in the more developed parts of the country, among the incipient native middle class, among students and intellectuals, and in the ultranationalist military establishment.

It was widely believed that the 375,000 Jews living in Romania in early 1941 were guilty of the loss of Bessarabia and Bukovina to the Soviet Union in July 1940 and of northern Transylvania to Hungary. These territorial changes, needless to say, had been arranged by Germany in its secret agreement with the USSR and in its arbitration between Hungary and Romania in the summer of 1940. In any case, these latest accusations were but the tip of the iceberg of Romanian anti-Jewish hatred.

As in other East European countries, the very foundation of Romanian attitudes toward the Jews was nurtured by virulent religious anti-Judaism, spewed, in this case, by the Romanian Orthodox Church. This brand of religious hostility had first flourished among the peasantry before spreading to the new urban middle classes, where it acquired its economic and mainly nationalist dimensions.[154] "Romanianism" mainly targeted ethnic and cultural minorities in its struggle for domination of the borderland provinces, which were considered as rightfully belonging to Greater Romania: The Jews were deemed foreign and hostile both ethnically and culturally, and in the struggle for Romanianism they were accused of siding with the Hungarians or the Russians.

Even before World War I the National Christian Party of Alexander Cuza and Nicolae Jorga, both highly respected intellectuals, demanded the exclusion of Jews from Romanian society. On the morrow of the war, after the Bolshevik Revolution in Russia and Béla Kun's short-lived Communist regime in Hungary, Judeo-communism was added as a major element to the already explosive anti-Jewish mix. In the words of Andrei Petre, a Romanian sociologist writing in 1928: "Our young people confine nationalism particularly to anti-Semitism, . . . they attribute more of a destructive than a creative, constructive note to it. . . . They demand the settlement of the Jewish question even by violent means and put forward as immediate legal measures the removal of Jews from the army and administration . . . and the *numerus clausus* in order to limit the number of Jews in the universities, where the country's ruling class is being trained."[155]

Shortly before Petre wrote his analysis, a movement born among the most extreme anti-Semitic students and baptized by its leader, Corneliu Zelea Codreanu, the "Legion of the Archangel Michael," gave a new and radical political framework to the most extreme expression of anti-Jewish hatred. The "Iron Guard," as the legionary movement became known, soon expanded its constituency to wide segments of Rumanian society, from the peasantry to the urban intelligentsia. One of the peculiar characteristics of Iron Guard ideology was its fanatical, quasimystical identification with Romanian Orthodox Christianity, including of course the most virulent Christian hatred of Jews. Thus, in September 1941, the journalist Mihai Mirescu wrote an editorial significantly titled "The Student Church," in which he emphasized: "The anti-Semitism of the young generation was not only racial struggle. It asserted the necessity of spiritual war, the Jews representing in their spirit amoral materialism, and the only salvation being embodied in Christianity."[156]

The accession of the Nazis to power had buoyed Codreanu's troops. The appointment by the Romanian monarch, King Carol II, of an openly anti-Semitic right-wing government (the Goga-Cuza government, headed by Alexander Cuza and Octavian Goga) in the mid-thirties did not outmaneuver the "legionnaries," notwithstanding a spate of anti-Jewish decrees. The king then decided to crush his radical opponents: Codreanu was assassinated at the end of 1938 and mass executions of guardists followed.[157]

The turn to dictatorial measures did not save Carol's regime. The loss of Bessarabia and Bukovina to the Soviet Union in July 1940 accelerated the monarch's downfall, and his use of anti-Semitic measures to placate his right-wing enemies also petered out: "There is reason to believe," the U.S. minister in Bucharest, Franklin Mott Gunther, commented on

July 2, 1940, that regarding measures against the Jews "more serious leaders are counseling calm and caution . . . while other Government officials are pursuing the traditional policy in Southeastern Europe of using anti-Semitic agitation to cloak from the people at large Government inefficiency and ineptitude. Very strict instructions are being issued by the Government however, to avoid provocative acts."[158]

On September 6, 1940, a coup engineered by the army and by the Iron Guard expelled the King and put the commander in chief of the army, Ion Antonescu, and the Iron Guard's new leader, Horia Sima, in power in a so-called legionary regime. On October 1 Gunther reported about a conversation with the Iron Guard chief, now vice president of the Council of Ministers: "Our conversation turned briefly to the subject of the Jews. After asserting, to my surprise, that the legionaries had swung to the support of the Axis because it is anti-Jewish, he went on to say that he personally was anti-Jewish because the Jews had succeeded in obtaining a strangle-hold upon every branch of Rumanian life. He warned me that they probably were trying to do the same thing in America and would not be convinced that a serious Jewish problem does not exist in the United States." Horia Sima assured Gunther that any anti-Jewish measures would be carried out by "pacific means."[159]

After the January 1941 massacres, Gunther could not help to vent his indignation, even in an official dispatch: "It makes one sick at heart," he wrote to the secretary of state on January 30, "to be accredited to a country where such things can happen even though the real faults of inspiration and encouragement lie elsewhere" [Germany].[160]

The anti-Semitic violence in Romania in early 1941 was but an indication of what was about to happen on *local initiative* in much of Eastern Europe and the Balkans with the beginning of the war against the Soviet Union. In various stages and diverse political and strategic circumstances, local hatred of Jews and German murder policies were soon to mix in a particularly lethal brew.

VI

A Hitler-Pétain meeting took place in the little town of Montoire, on October 24, 1940: "Collaboration" between Vichy France and the Reich was officially proclaimed. Yet on December 13 Laval was dismissed by the elderly marshal. The turmoil was brief. German pressure and internal constraints set Vichy back on track: In early 1941, Darlan replaced the moderate Pierre-Étienne Flandin as the head of government, and the collaboration with Germany tightened. Anti-Jewish measures spread.

In February 1941, out of the 47,000 foreigners imprisoned in French concentration camps, 40,000 were Jews.[161] Aryanization progressed apace. Jewish businesses were increasingly put under the control of "French" supervisors (*commissaires-gérants*) who had, in fact, full power to decide the businesses' fate. Once the *commissaires-gérants* had taken over, yellow signs were replaced by red ones. This, of course, encouraged scoundrels of all hues to buy all remaining wares (or the businesses themselves) from the Jewish owners at a fraction of the price. Simultaneously the largest French banks took steps on their own to interpret German ordinances as extensively as possible. Thus, in the occupied zone, the Germans allowed for the cancellation of agreements dealing with Jewish property (paragraph 4 of the ordinance of October 18, 1940) but did not allude to bank accounts held by Jews. Crédit Lyonnais made sure that the silence of the ordinance would not allow unwanted freedom of action to Jewish depositors. On November 21, 1940, a first internal directive was issued:

"On the basis of the order [of October 18, 1940], assets held by Israelites, which have not been frozen, may be governed by special measures and thus must lead us to exercise caution in our relations with them. We do not believe that withdrawals of French securities or capital as such will be affected by paragraph 4 of the order, but it should be ensured that accounts do not show debit balances if we have not received a regular security before 23 May 1940. However, other operations, such as discounts, advances, security sales, appointments of representatives, etc., should be examined very carefully before being implemented."

In February 1941 Crédit Lyonnais tightened the vise: "As far as cash is concerned, Israelite assets are in principle not restricted. However, large sums should not be withdrawn. . . . Other operations . . . must in principle be refused if they involve significant amounts and may therefore constitute flight of fortune unless, of course, they are authorized by the German authorities."[162]

Aryanization proceeded apace, but not without some strange twists. Thus, one of the largest French perfume enterprises belonged to François Coty. In the 1920s Coty financed a fascist movement, Solidarité Française, and its periodical, *L'Ami du Peuple,* which preached militant anti-Semitism. In 1929 Coty divorced, but when he died, in 1934, his estate still owed a substantial sum to his ex-wife; it was paid in "Coty" shares. The former Mrs. Coty thus became the main shareholder and owner of the company. She married again, this time a converted Romanian Jew, León Cotnareanu. For the Aryanization bureaucracy Parfums Coty was under Jewish influence, the more so because two Jews sat on the board of directors. Complicated transactions and transfers of ownership started, involving subsidiaries in several European countries and the United States, in order to eliminate any trace of Jewish participation. In August 1941 the Germans agreed that Parfums Coty had undergone the necessary purification and in October it officially became an Aryan enterprise again.[163] François Coty could rest in peace.

In April 1941 the Jews were forbidden to fill any position—from selling lottery tickets to any form of teaching—that would put them in contact with the public. Only a few "particularly deserving intellectuals" were exempted from this total professional segregation. As for the vast majority of the French population, it did not react. Anti-Jewish propaganda intensified, as did the number of acts of anti-Jewish violence. Individual expressions of sympathy were not rare, but they were volunteered in private, far from any public notice.

Protecting the French population by eliminating any professional contact with Jews belonged to Vichy. Protecting members of the Wehrmacht in the occupied zone from Jewish presence in the bars they patronized turned into a problem on New Year's Eve 1940. At the Boeuf sur le Toit and at Carrère, Jews were present as German warriors toasted the coming year. Worse, at the Trois Valses, a favorite Wehrmacht hangout, a German song taken up by the band was booed by the French revelers, among whom there were Jews. The informers' reports about these mishaps suggested that all bars patronized by the Wehrmacht should put up signs excluding Jews.[164] Whether the recommendation was followed at the time is not known.

At the beginning of 1941 the Germans decided that further coordination of the anti-Jewish measures throughout both French zones was necessary. In a January 30 meeting at military headquarters in Paris under the chairmanship of Werner Best, Kurt Lischka, Knochen's representative and Theodor Dannecker informed the participants that a central office for Jewish affairs had to be set up in France to implement the measures decided on to solve the Jewish problem in Europe. The functions of the office would be to deal with all police matters regarding the arrest, surveillance, and registration of Jews; to exercise economic control (exclusion of Jews from economic life and participation in the "restitution" of Jewish businesses into Aryan hands); to organize propaganda activities (dissemination of anti-Jewish propaganda among the French population), and to set up an anti-Jewish research institute. In the meantime the Paris Préfecture de Police was ready to assume these functions. The establishment of the new office should be left to the French authorities to avoid opposition to a German initiative; the Germans should limit themselves to "suggestions." Everyone agreed.[165]

The Germans were confident that even if the new office turned out to be less forceful than they wished (mainly in its dealings with native Jews), they would be able in due time to ensnare it in the full scope of their own policies. In reporting to Berlin on March 6, 1941, about a conversation with Darlan regarding the new office and Pétain's wish to protect native Jews, Abetz indicated how any French reservations would be overcome: "It would be advisable," the ambassador wrote, "to have the French Government establish this office. . . . It would thus have a valid legal foundation and its activity could then be stimulated through German influence in the occupied territory to such an extent that the unoccupied territory would be forced to join in the measures taken."[166]

On March 29, 1941, the Vichy government established the Central Office for Jewish Affairs (Commissariat Général aux Questions Juives, or CGQJ); its first chief was Xavier Vallat.[167] Vallat belonged to the nationalist anti-Jewish tradition of the Action Française, and did not share the racial anti-Semitism of the Nazis. Nonetheless the CGQJ soon became the hub of rapidly expanding anti-Jewish activity.[168] Its main immediate "achievement" was the reworking of the Jewish statute of October 3, 1940. The new Statut des Juifs was accepted by the government and became law on June 2, 1941.[169] Strangely enough, for the staunchly Catholic Vallat, baptism seemed inconsequential and, implicitly, inherited cultural-racial elements were at the core of his conception of the Jew.

The new statute aimed at filling the many gaps discovered in the October 1940 edict. In the case of French "mixed breeds," for example, with two Jewish grandparents who had converted to another religion, the cut-off date validating the conversion in terms of the decree was June 25, 1940, the official date of the armistice between Germany and France. Moreover, conversion was considered valid only if the convert had chosen to join a denomination recognized before the separation of church and state of December 1905. Only the CGQJ would be entitled to issue certificates of nonmembership of the Jewish race.[170]

Like the statute of October 1940, that of June 1941 did not establish any distinction between native and foreign Jews. When Vallat called on Abetz on April 3, the ambassador did in fact suggest that in the forthcoming legislation those long-established Jews "who would have acted contrary to the social and natural interests of the French nation" should also be declared "foreign." Such a law, which would have meant the cancellation of citizenship of segments of French Jewry or the denaturalization of recently naturalized French Jews, was not included in the batch of new decrees. On the other hand, loopholes favoring French Jews, about which Abetz was concerned, did not appear either.[171]

While the French authorities were issuing their new decrees, Dannecker decided, in early 1941, to use a small group of rabid French anti-Semites, La Communauté Française, to establish an "Institute for the Study of the Jewish Questions" (Institut d'Étude des Questions Juives), under the direction of a capitaine Paul Sézille. The so-called institute, whose main aim was to spread Nazi-type anti-Semitic propaganda under the cover of a French identity, was not affiliated with Vallat's CGQJ and remained throughout an instrument of Dannecker's agency and of the German embassy in Paris.[172]

Either as a result of the institute's activities or upon an initiative of the German embassy, in the spring of 1941 anti-Jewish posters decorated the streets of Paris: One portrayed the Unknown Soldier surging from his tomb to slit the throats of Jewry and Freemasonry: another displayed a crooked hand stretched out to snatch the scepter and the crown, a direct reference to *Jud Süss,* then playing at two of the largest movie theaters in the city.[173]

It seems that French film critics tended to emphasize the artistic quality of Harlan's production and to downplay its ideological significance.[174] Of course, in the collaborationist press, the film's message got its share of enthusiastic comments: "This is a film full of true statements that it would be infinitely useful to disseminate after all the lies that were fed to us over the years," Rebatet (under the pseudonym Vinneuil) wrote in *Le Petit Parisien* on March 2. "Everyone can draw lessons from its message for the study of a question the solution of which had become not only France's concern, but that of all of Europe."[175]

Left-wing Catholics, particularly those linked to Mounier's *Esprit,* reacted differently. We have seen Mounier's previous hesitations. By mid-1941 his position had become clear; his own review of the film, in the July issue of *Esprit,* concluded as follows: "The prewar French production has accustomed us to less heaviness, to a sounder judgment, less unhealthy . . . more specifically French.[176] In French provincial towns the film even provoked some protests and incidents.[177]

On May 14, 1941, on Dannecker's orders, French police arrested 3,733 Jewish immigrants. The raid was probably meant to bring more pressure on the Coordination Committee to establish an Executive Council in which French and foreign Jews would be equally represented, a move the native French Jews stubbornly opposed.[178] The next day the collaborationist paper *Paris Midi* hailed the disappearance of "five thousand parasites from greater Paris." No other paper (apart from the Jewish press) deemed the event worth mentioning.[179]

Jean Guéhenno, a voice from the Left, reacted in his diary: "Yesterday," he noted, "in the name of the French law, five thousand Jews have been taken to concentration camps. Poor Jews that came from Poland, Austria, Czechoslovakia, penniless people living from lowly trades that must have greatly threatened the State. This is called 'cleansing.' In rue Compans, several men were taken away. Their wives, their children begged the policemen, shouted, wept. . . . The ordinary Parisians [*le petit peuple parisien*] who were witnessing these heart-rending scenes were filled with disgust and shame."[180] Yet despite the reactions mentioned by Guéhenno, no protest was openly voiced, and the commissariat received only a single outraged letter.[181]

Perhaps the *petit peuple parisien* expressed the compassion described by Guéhenno. Biélinky, standing in a food line, received much the same impression, according to a diary entry of June 17: "You know, Célestine," one housewife was telling another, "the little Pole who is my son's friend, they were together at school, so he is very sad to-day—Why is that?—

Because his brother was arrested and apparently sent to a concentration camp. Though they are all so nice and honest. But what did he do, the poor one? . . . —Nothing at all, it's because he is a Jew . . . —Poor people [*les pauvres*], says the other one, melancholically, and the line moves slowly toward the potatoes stall."[182]

It has occasionally been argued that Vichy's anti-Jewish measures and its ready cooperation with the Germans were a "rational" maneuver within the general framework of collaboration in order to maintain as much control as possible over developments in the occupied zone and to obtain a favorable bargaining position for the future status of France in Hitler's new Europe. In other words, Vichy supposedly displayed a nonideological acceptance of Nazi goals (a "*collaboration d'État*" as opposed to some wild "collaborationism") in the hope of harvesting some tangible benefits in return.[183]

Political calculation was undoubtedly part of the overall picture, but Vichy's policy was also determined by the right-wing anti-Semitic tradition that was part and parcel of the "Révolution nationale." Moreover, *collaboration d'État* does not account for the fact that, as we saw, the French episcopate welcomed the exclusion of Jews from public life as early as August 1940, and that mainly among the rural population and the provincial Catholic middle classes, anti-Semitism was not limited to a tiny minority but widespread. Thus, although the Vichy legislation was not dictated by the passions of French "collaborationists," it was nonetheless a calculated response both to a public mood and to ideological-institutional interests, such as those of the church.

In general anti-Semitism may well have been outweighed by sheer indifference, but not to the point of forgoing tangible advantages. As Helmut Knochen put it in January 1941, "It is almost impossible to cultivate among the French an anti-Jewish sentiment that rests on an ideological foundation, while the offer of economic advantages much more easily excites sympathy for the anti-Jewish struggle."[184]

There was a striking (yet possibly unperceived at the time) relation between French attitudes toward the Jews and the behavior of representatives of native Jewry toward the foreign or recently naturalized Jews living in the country. While native Jews affiliated to the community were represented by the Consistoire and its local branches, foreign Jews—and the recently naturalized ones—were loosely affiliated to an umbrella organization, the Fédération des Sociétés Juives de France, comprising various political associations and their related network of welfare organizations. Part of the umbrella organization came to be known as "Rue Amelot" (the Paris address of the main office of its leading committee).

After the Rothschilds had fled the country. Jacques Helbronner, the acting vice-president of the Consistoire, became the de facto leader of native French Jewry (Rue Amelot was more collectively run by the heads of its various associations). In many ways Helbronner was a typical representative of the old-stock French Jewish elite: a brilliant officer during World War I, a sharp legal mind who at a young age was appointed to the Conseil d'État (the highest civil service institution in France), Helbronner married into old (and substantial) French Jewish money. He belonged, quintessentially, to the French Jewish haute bourgeoisie, a group considered almost French by its non-Jewish surroundings. And despite his own genuine interest in Jewish matters—which led him to become active in the Consistoire—Helbronner, like all his peers, saw himself first and foremost as French. Typically enough he was close to Philippe Pétain, since the day during World War I when, as head of the personal staff (*chef de cabinet*) of the minister of war, he was sent to inform Pétain of his appointment as *généralissime* (commander in chief of all French forces). Another friend of Helbronner's was Jules-Marie Cardinal Gerlier, cardinal-archbishop of Lyon and head of the French episcopate. In March 1941 Helbronner was appointed president of the Consistoire.[185]

Few native French Jews achieved the exalted status of a Helbronner, but the great majority felt as deeply integrated in French society as he did and were to share the positions he adopted: France was their only conceivable national and cultural home, notwithstanding the injustice of the new laws. The growing anti-Semitism of the thirties and its most violent outbursts following the defeat were, in their opinion, caused in large part by the influx of foreign Jews; the situation thus created could be mitigated by a strict distinction between native French "separation" Jews and the foreign Jews living in the country. The Vichy authorities had to be convinced of this basic tenet.

It was precisely this difference that Helbronner attempted to convey to Pétain in a memorandum he sent him in November 1940, after the first statute and its corollaries had sunk in. In this statement, titled *Note sur la question juive*, the future president of the Consistoire argued that the Jews were not a race and did not descend from the Jews who had lived in Palestine two thousand years before. Rather, they were a community composed of many races and, as far as France was concerned, a community entirely integrated in its homeland. The problems began with the arrival of foreign Jews "who started to invade our soil." The open-door policies of the postwar governments had been a mistake, and they resulted "in a normal anti-Semitism the victims of which were now the old French Israelite families." Helbronner then suggested a series of measures that would free the native Jews from the limitations of the statute *but not the foreign or recently naturalized Jews* . . . [186] Helbronner's message went unanswered.

Over the following months the head of the Consistoire and a number of his colleagues pursued their futile and demeaning entreaties. The messages and visits to Vichy pointedly continued to ignore the fate of the foreign Jews and to plead for the French Israelites only. The epitome of this course of action was probably the solemn petition sent to the *maréchal* by the entire leadership of the Consistoire, including the chief rabbi of France. The closing paragraph was unambiguous in its omission of any reference to the non-French Jews:

"Jewish Frenchmen still wish to believe that the persecutions of which they are the object are entirely imposed on the French State by the occupying authorities and that the representatives of France have tried their best to attenuate their rigors . . . Jewish Frenchmen, if they cannot safeguard the future and perhaps even the life of their children and grandchildren, but seeking above all to leave them honorable names, demand of the head of state who, as a great soldier and a fervent Christian, incarnates in their eyes the fatherland in all its purity, that he should recognize this solemn protest, which is their only weapon in their weakness. Jewish Frenchmen, more than ever attached to their faith, keep intact their hope and their confidence in France and its destiny."[187] The second Jewish statute was to be Vichy's answer to the petitions.

Time and again some of the most prestigious names of French Jewry confirmed that, in their view, the fate of the foreign Jews was none of their concern. Thus, when, during the spring of 1941, Dannecker started using pressure for the establishment of a unified Jewish Council, René Mayer, also a prominent member of the Consistoire (he would become a postwar French prime minister), asked Vallat to encourage the foreign Jews to emigrate.[188] So did Marc Bloch, one of the most eminent historians of his time.

In April 1941, in response to a project promoted by the Consistoire envisioning the establishment of a center for Jewish studies, Bloch demanded that all trends within *French* Jewry be taken into account: but regarding the foreign Jews living in France, his stand was clear: "Their cause is not exactly our own." Though unable to participate actively in the planning of the center, Bloch suggested that one of the main aims should be to counter the dangerous notion that "all Jews formed a solid homogeneous mass, endowed with identical traits, and subject to the same destiny." In Bloch's view the planners of the center should recognize two distinct Jewish communities, the assimilated (French) and the nonassimilated (foreign). While the fate of the former depended on its complete integration and the preservation of its legal guarantees, the survival of the latter might well depend on "some form of emigration."[189]

VII

In Holland the population staged a small-scale rebellion in reaction to the German treatment of the hundreds of Jewish men arrested in the streets of Amsterdam on February 22, 1941, after the Koco incident. The communists called for a general strike: On February 25 Amsterdam was paralyzed, and soon the strike spread to nearby cities. The Germans reacted with extreme violence against the demonstrators, using both firearms and hand grenades: Several people were killed, scores wounded, and a number of demonstrators arrested.[190] The strike was quashed. The Dutch had learned that the Germans would not hesitate to pursue their anti-Jewish policies with utter ruthlessness; the Germans realized that converting the Dutch to National Socialism would not be an easy task.

During the weeks and months that followed the Amsterdam events, two distinct series of developments reshaped the policies regarding Dutch Jewry, in terms of the German local apparatus and the Dutch enforcers. The nonmilitary German apparatus in Holland was divided in two competing camps, somewhat along the lines that had been noticeable in the General Government. On the one hand *Reichskommissar* Seyss-Inquart, his main delegate in Amsterdam, D. H. Böhmcker, and General Commissars Friedrich Wimmer (administration and justice), Hans Fischboek (finances and economy), and Fritz Schmidt (party affairs) were intent on keeping full control of Jewish matters; the SS on the other hand, led by Higher SS and Police Leader Albin Rauter and his second in command, the head of the Security Police, Dr. Wilhelm Harster, were eager to take over a domain they considered specifically their own.[191]

Whether as a result of the Amsterdam events—which could be seen as a failure of Böhmcker's policy of pushing for the establishment of a ghetto and using the Dutch Nazis as provokers—or as the outcome of prior planning—Heydrich (and Rauter) decided to establish a Central Office for Jewish Emigration in Amsterdam, on the model of the offices set up in Vienna in 1938 and in Berlin and in Prague, in 1939. Usually such offices, controlled by the RSHA and more closely by Eichmann's section IV B4, took over the registration of the Jewish population, of its property, and of course of its departure (and thus of the impounding of the abandoned property). The setting up of a similar agency in Amsterdam should have allowed Rauter, Harster, and eventually their man in Amsterdam, Willi Lages, to control all significant aspects of Jewish affairs in Holland.

In April 1941 the Zentralstelle was indeed established, but its functions were limited at first. Moreover, Seyss-Inquart did not give in. In early May, at a meeting convened by the Reichskommissar, who in the meantime had received Hitler's confirmation of his overall authority, all those involved had to agree that he would keep general supervision over Jewish affairs. De facto the situation was to change again in early 1942, when Harster would bring in his school friend Willy Zöpf to establish a IV B4 section in The Hague, and mainly with the beginning of the deportations, in July 1942.[192]

Aryanization of Jewish property had started. It was fostered by Fischboek's services and by a large number of German firms intent on acquiring shares in major Dutch companies by acquiring first those that belonged to Jews. Several German banks became prominent intermediaries in these operations, particularly Handelstrust West, a local subsidiary of the Dresdner Bank.[193] In order to speed up operations the Zentralstelle would allow for the departure of Jewish owners of *major* businesses, who would sell their enterprises to the German bidders. Thus the German companies, as legal owners, could claim rights to related foreign assets and avoid any lawsuits, particularly in the United States. The deals ensured unhindered emigration for the lucky few (around thirty families) within weeks of the time of the property transfer. Later on the same racketeering would be applied to Jews in several countries in exchange for large sums in foreign currency.[194] Ultimately it would be applied in 1944 to the Manfred Weiss conglomerate in Hungary.

Eventually the German takeover of Jewish property would be much more systematic in Holland than in occupied France, in line with the Nazi master plan for a European economic "new order." The Dutch economy was destined for complete integration into the German system, whether the Dutch wished it or not. Once more ideological creed and economic greed converged. In August 1941 the Jews of Holland were ordered to register all their assets with the formerly Jewish Lippman-Rosenthal bank; on September 15 real estate was included in the registration.[195]

Regarding the Dutch "enforcers," the February 1941 events led to the dismissal of the Amsterdam city council and its replacement by an adequately subservient new group. Mainly a new chief of the Amsterdam police force, a former officer in the colonial army in the Dutch East Indies, Sybren Tulp, was put in command. Tulp could hardly have been shocked by racial discrimination; as a member of Mussert's NSB, he had the appropriate ideological leanings, the more so that he was a great admirer of German National Socialism and particularly of Adolf Hitler.[196]

In the meantime, before the Koco incident, the German roundup and the rebellion, as Böhmcker was considering the establishment of a ghetto in the Jewish quarter of Amsterdam, he conveyed to a few Jewish personalities, including Abraham Asscher, that he required the creation of a unified representation of the Jews of the city.[197] It remains unclear whether Seyss-Inquart's representative mentioned a "Jewish Council" or whether the term was first used by Asscher. The fact is that Asscher volunteered to preside over the new organization and asked for the appointment of David Cohen as copresident. Both Asscher and Cohen then chose the other members, mostly from their own social milieu, Amsterdam's small and wealthy Jewish haute bourgeoisie. On February 12 the council held its first meeting. On the next day, at Böhmcker's demand, Asscher spoke to an assembly of Jewish workers requesting the delivery of any weapons in their possession. As historian Bob Moore pointed out, "in effect, the first steps toward Jewish collaboration with the Germans had begun, with the self-appointed elite of the Jewish Council acting as a conduit for Nazi demands."[198]

Whatever the assessment of the Dutch council's early behavior may be, the Germans did not ask for its approval when it came to dispatching the four hundred young Jewish men arrested after the Amsterdam rebellion to their death. At first they were deported to Buchenwald, then to Mauthausen. They arrived in Mauthausen on June 17, 1941. A batch of fifty was immediately killed: "They were chased naked from the bathhouse to the electrified fence." The others were murdered in the main quarry of the camp, the "Vienna Ditch." According to the German witness Eugen Kogon, these Jews were not allowed to use the steps leading to the bottom of the quarry. "They had to slide down the loose stones at the side, and even here many died or were severely injured. The survivors then had to shoulder hods, and two prisoners were compelled to load each Jew with an excessively heavy rock. The Jews then had to run up the 186 steps. In some instances the rocks immediately rolled downhill, crushing the feet of those that came behind. Every Jew who lost his rock in that fashion was brutally beaten, and the rock was hoisted onto his shoulders again. Many of the Jews were driven to despair the very first day and committed suicide by jumping into the pit. On the third day the SS opened the so-called 'death gate,' and with a fearful barrage of blows drove the Jews across the guard line, the guards on the watchtowers shooting them down in heaps with their machine guns. The next day the Jews no longer jumped into the pit individually. They joined hands and one man would pull nine or twelve of his comrades over the lip with him into a gruesome death. The barracks were 'cleared' of Jews, not in six but in barely three weeks. Every one of the 348 prisoners perished by suicide, or by shooting, beating, and other forms of torture."[199] When asked by the local *Landrat* how the Dutch Jews had adapted to the hard work, Commandant Ziereis answered: "Ah, hardly a one is still alive."[200]

As the news of the death of this first group of Amsterdam Jews was trickling back to Holland, an attack on the Luftwaffe telephone exchange at Schiphol Airport on June 3, 1941, seriously wounded one of the soldiers. In retaliation the Germans tricked council members Cohen and Gertrud van Tijn into giving them the addresses of two hundred young German Jewish refugees. These were arrested together with other young Amsterdam Jews, sent to Mauthausen, and murdered.[201]

What should the council do? In a crisis meeting on June 12 Asscher proposed collective resignation; Cohen, fearing further German reprisals, demurred. If the council resigned, he argued, who would be left to help the community?[202] Was there any possibility that behaving differently—disbanding the council, for example—would have hampered the Germans or helped the Jews?

Etty (Esther) Hillesum was still a young woman student in Slavic languages at Amsterdam University during these spring months of 1941. For years Etty's father had been the headmaster of the municipal gymnasium in Deventer (a midsize city in eastern Holland); her mother, it seems, introduced a tempestuous Russian Jewish personality into the staid Dutch bourgeois environment. Etty's two brothers were unusually gifted: the older, Mischa, as a brilliant concert pianist from age six, and the younger, Jaap, as a budding biochemist who discovered a new vitamin at age seventeen. As for Etty, she was a born writer and a free spirit. In the Amsterdam house that she rented with several other Jewish friends, she launched into a complicated love life, branching out into several simultaneous directions, and started on an idiosyncratic spiritual path tinged with Christianity and some esoteric and mystical components. And she began keeping a diary.[203]

"Sometimes when I read the papers or hear reports of what is happening all around," Etty noted on March 15, 1941, "I am suddenly beside myself with anger, cursing and swearing at the Germans. And I know that I do it deliberately in order to hurt Käthe [the German cook who lived in the house], to work off my anger as best I can. . . . And all this when I know perfectly well that she finds the new order as dreadful as I do, and is just as bowed down by the excesses of her people. But deep down she is of course one of her people, and while I understand, I sometimes cannot bear it. The whole nation must be destroyed root and branch. And now and then I say nastily, 'They are all scum,' and at the same time I feel terribly ashamed and deeply unhappy but cannot stop even though I know that it's all wrong."[204]

The peace of mind that Etty was arduously trying to acquire in the midst of the growing turmoil was badly shaken by the new arrests: "More arrests, more terror, concentration camps, the arbitrary dragging off of fathers, sisters, brothers," she noted on June 14, "Everything seems so menacing and ominous, and always that feeling of total impotence."[205]

The setting up of the Jewish Council, the Aryanization drive, and the two waves of arrests were but one aspect of the German terror campaign; the other aimed, steadily and systematically, at cutting off the Jews from the surrounding Dutch population—at increasingly isolating them—even if publicly marking them was still a year away. At the end of May 1941, as the hot weather was starting, the Germans not only barred all Jews from parks, spas, and hotels but also from public beaches and swimming pools. Shortly afterward Jewish elementary and high school students were ordered to fill out special registration forms. Soon they were excluded from Dutch schools and allowed to attend only Jewish schools.

After fleeing with his parents from The Hague to Brussels, fifteen-year-old Moshe Flinker reminisced, in the opening pages of his diary, about his last term of the school year in Holland: "During the last year I attended [the Jewish school in The Hague] the number of restrictions on us rose greatly. Several months before the end of the school year we had to turn in our bicycles to the police. From that time on, I rode to school by streetcar, but a day or two before vacations started Jews were forbidden to ride on streetcars. I then had to walk to school, which took about an hour and a half. I continued going to school during those last days," Flinker added, "because I wanted to get my report card and find out whether I had been promoted to the next class. At that time I still thought I would be able to return to school after vacations; but I was wrong. Even so, I must mention that I did get my promotion."[206]

Anne Frank; her sister, Margot; her father, Otto; and her mother, Edith, had emigrated from Frankfurt to Amsterdam during the second half of 1933. The father had the franchise for a jelling agent, pectin, from the Pomosin-Werke in Frankfurt. Over time Frank's modest dealership at 263 Prinsengracht reached a measure of stability, thanks to a small group of devoted Dutch employees.

Commenting on the prohibition to use swimming pools, twelve-year-old Anne Frank wrote to her grandmother, who lived in Basel: "We're not likely to get sunburned because we can't go to the swimming pool . . . too bad, but there is nothing to be done."[207]

VIII

The official positions of the national Catholic churches throughout the Continent and those of the Vatican were not essentially different regarding the increasingly harsh anti-Jewish measures. In France, as we saw, in August 1940 the assembly of cardinals and bishops welcomed the limitations imposed on the country's Jews, and no members of the Catholic hierarchy expressed any protest regarding the statutes of October 1940 and June 1941. In neighboring Belgium, Cardinal Joseph-Ernest van Roey, archbishop of Malines, remained equally silent about the anti-Jewish edicts of 1940 and 1941 (in fact van Roey did not speak up until 1943); in so doing the cardinal was in step with the upper echelons of his church and neither able nor willing to oppose the militant Catholic-nationalist anti-Semitism of the Flemish radical Right, mainly active in Antwerp.[208]

In east central Europe, pride of place has to be granted to the Polish Catholic Church. The anti-Semitism of the great majority of Polish Catholics had been notorious before the war, as we saw; it grew fiercer under German occupation. During the preextermination period, the Polish clergy, more often than not, stoked the anti-Jewish fires.

A report originating with the Polish church itself, covering the six-week period between June 1 and July 15, 1941, was transmitted to the government-in-exile in London by the *delegatura.* In its own extremism the report did not represent the general attitude of Polish Catholics toward the Jews, yet its quasiofficial nature indicated some measure of concurrence among underground leadership in the opinions expressed: "The need to solve the Jewish Question is urgent," the report stated. "Nowhere else in the world has that question reached such a climax, because no fewer than four million [*sic*] of these highly noxious and by all standards dangerous elements live in Poland, or to be more precise, off Poland."

As quoted and translated by Gutman and Krakowski, the report continued in the same vein: "As far as the Jewish Question is concerned, it must be seen as a singular dispensation of Divine Providence that the Germans have already made a good start, quite irrespective of all the wrongs they have done and continue to do to our country. They have shown that the liberation of Polish society from the Jewish plague is possible. They have blazed the trail for us which now must be followed: With less cruelty and brutality, to be sure, but no flagging, consistently. Clearly, one can see the hand of God in the contribution to the solution of this urgent question being made by the occupiers." The report then expanded upon the harm done by the Jews to Polish and Christian society. After a lengthy litany of horrendous Jewish deeds, the report turned to the future. First it encouraged the departure of the Jews from the country, but "as long as this cannot be achieved, a far-reaching isolation of the Jews from our society will be mandatory." Segregation measures were enumerated, yet the authors did not underestimate the difficulty of this challenge: "All this will be very difficult. Friction can be expected on this score between the government-in-exile, which is rather exposed to Freemason and Jewish influence and the people in the country who already today are organizing themselves. But the health of our Fatherland, restored with God's help, depends to a very great extent on such measures."[209]

If one disregards its specific expression of extreme anti-Jewish hatred, the Polish church report had a common denominator with Western Catholicism and with what seems to have been the attitude of the Vatican: The Jews were once more to be partly segregated from Christian society, according to each country's regulations.

Two documents belonging to the first half of 1941 may add some insight regarding the pope's own attitude at that time and regarding the views apparently shared by some of the Vatican's most authoritative personalities about the anti-Jewish measures. "Your Holiness is certainly informed about the situation of the Jews in Germany and in the neighboring countries," Bishop Preysing of Berlin wrote to Pius XII on January 17, 1941. "Merely wishing to report," the bishop went on, "I would like to mention that I have been asked by Catholics as well as by Protestants whether the Holy See couldn't do something in this matter, issue an appeal in favor of these unfortunate people?" [*Ob nicht der Heilige*

Stuhl in dieser Sache etwas tun könnte, einen Appell zugunsten der Unglücklichen erlassen?][210]

On March 19 the pope answered several of Preysing's letters and particularly praised the Berlin bishop for his denunciation of euthanasia in a March 6 sermon at Saint Hedwig Cathedral. The pontiff also commented at some length about two conversions to Catholicism that Preysing had written about: The church opened its arms to converts. Not a word, however, alluded to Preysing's unmistakable plea for a papal reaction to the persecution of the Jews.[211]

The second document was no less telling in many ways; it confirmed that the Vatican and national episcopal assemblies, particularly the French assembly of cardinals and bishops, shared a similar view of the ongoing measures taken against the Jews. In response to an inquiry ordered by Pétain in August 1941, Leon Bérard, Vichy's ambassador to the Vatican, provided an exhaustive answer on September 2. First the French diplomat informed the maréchal that although there existed a fundamental conflict between racial theories and church doctrine, it did not follow that the church necessarily repudiated every measure taken by particular countries against the Jews. The fundamental principle, Bérard indicated, was that once a Jew was baptized, he ceased to be a Jew. However, the ambassador added, the church recognized that religion was not the only special characteristic of Jews and that there were also certain ethnic—not racial—factors that set them apart. Historically the church's practice and feeling over the centuries had been that Jews should not have authority over Christians. It was legitimate, therefore, to exclude them from certain public offices and to restrict their access to universities and the professions. He recalled also that ecclesiastical law had required the Jews to wear distinctive garb.

One of the major problems, the ambassador continued, was that of marriages. The new racial legislation in Italy and elsewhere prohibited marriages between Christians and Jews. The church felt that it had the authority to perform such marriages if the Jewish partner had been baptized or if an ecclesiastical dispensation had been obtained. In France, Bérard believed, there would not be similar problems because the circumstances were different (marriages between Jews and non-Jews had not been prohibited on racial grounds). For Pétain, Bérard's report must have been reassuring.[212]

* * *

In its main points Bérard's report was probably reliable. In other words, a few months before the onset of the "Final Solution," the exclusionary postulates of a conservative tradition dominated the attitudes of European Catholicism toward the Jews, while the rights of converted Jews were to be defended. The decisive issue, however, still lay ahead: How would the Holy See respond to and eventually influence the various national churches and tens of millions of church-going Catholics in the face of the extraordinary challenges that were about to arise?

IX

The violence unleashed by the Germans on the Jews under their domination, mainly in former Poland, may appear, in hindsight, as the beginning of a seamless process leading from the first days of the war to the "Final Solution." The murderous forays of the *Einsatzgruppen* at the outset of the Polish campaign and the ongoing terror that followed appear to underscore this sense of continuity.[213] Yet simultaneously, as we saw, no clear plan indicating the fate that would befall the Jews under German domination had been outlined, let alone elaborated in its details. In his instructions to the *Einsatzgruppen,* on September 21, 1939, Heydrich had mentioned a "final goal" but left it undetermined. Almost two years later that final goal still remained elusive, although Hitler made amply clear that the Jews had "to disappear from Europe."

The first "territorial plans" (Lublin and Madagascar) were too obviously unrealistic to have been considered for any length of time. The third plan—the deportation of the Jews of Europe to northern Russia—seemed more concrete but depended upon the outcome of the campaign in the East. No go-ahead that we know of was given before June 1941, but the "territorial plans" were undoubtedly meant to bring about the extinction of the Jewish populations expelled from European space, after victory.

This absence of any precise plan and the somewhat dampened perception of the Jewish world threat are indirectly reflected in Hitler's merely sporadic rhetorical outbursts regarding the "Jewish question" during this first phase of the war. It also appears in the concrete measures taken in the occupied and satellite countries. These measures replicated (with somewhat lesser brutality in the West, with utter brutality in the East) the entire gamut of anti-Jewish steps developed in the Reich between the first days of the new regime and the early phase of the war. In other words the "holding pattern" of Nazi anti-Jewish policy throughout the occupied countries did not initiate radically new steps but led, in the meantime, to the extension of the "Reich model" on a European scale.

One of the indications that no precise plan (dealing with all of European Jewry) was already being systematically pursued can be found in the expulsion-emigration policies of these first two years of the war. Emigration and expulsion from the Reich, then from the Greater Reich and the Protectorate, were applied with the same explicit goals to the newly annexed areas of Poland (the Warthegau, and Upper Silesia in particular), to Alsace and Lorraine, and Baden, Westphalia, and the Saar.

Further steps indicating the extension of the "Reich model" included replicating identification measures; registration of the Jews; Aryanization; setting up "councils" either centrally or locally; concentration of Jews in limited urban areas; forced labor and "productivization" in Poland and less brutally so in the Reich, in exchange for some minimal food supply. In and of itself the "productivization" policy indicated that, during this early phase, extermination plans were not yet the obvious and immediate solution: Otherwise induced mass starvation would have eased the way.

As for the murderous operations that were planned for the Soviet campaign, they targeted specific categories of Jewish men. They were meant, as suggested, to hasten the collapse of the Red Army and of the entire Soviet system. No order for the mass extermination of the Jewish population on Soviet territory seems to have been issued to the *Einsatzgruppen* before the attack, notwithstanding the contrary postwar testimony of some unit commanders, as we shall see in greater detail in the next chapter. Thus, in terms of policy decisions, of administrative measures, and of selective murder plans for the new campaign in the East, the outlines of the "Final Solution of the Jewish question in Europe" were not yet apparent by early June 1941. Jews did still leave the Reich and the Continent, even with some assistance from the RSHA at first, then with its authorization, albeit in ever-smaller numbers.

Yet, in considering the general thrust of the anti-Jewish policies between September 1939 and June 1941, we recognize that the ongoing violence in occupied Poland created a blurred area of murderous permissiveness that, unplanned as it was, would facilitate the transition to more systematic murder policies. The same could be said of the anti-Jewish propaganda campaign and its impact on German and European opinion. An anti-Semitic culture, deeply rooted in Christian and Western civilization, fostered in Germany from the beginnings of the Nazi regime, was increasingly taking hold in the Reich and beyond. In Goebbels's *Der Ewige Jude*, let us recall, Jews were turned into pestilence-carrying vermin; in the propaganda minister's conversations with Hitler, the Jewish cancer demanded radical surgery—imperatively so—to save Aryan humanity from a mortal peril. And, as we saw, Hitler was uncommonly attentive to the production of the 1940 film and aware of the images chosen by Hippler, including his own January 1939 speech prophesying the extermination of the Jews in case of world war. An intimation of deadly anti-Jewish hatred and a wish for mass murder were unmistakable and unmistakably fed into the public sphere. Finally and essentially, even if, as just stated, the outlines of the "Final Solution" were not yet apparent on the eve of Barbarossa, Hitler had "clearly defined" the thrust of the campaign in March 1941: It was to be a war of extermination, and by definition mass murder would expand as long as the enemy was fighting, as long as enemies were still within reach. In other words, the Reich was now set on a path that, at some point, under specific circumstances, within a particular context, would lead to the decision to exterminate all the Jews of Europe.

German policies regarding the Jews did not depend on the level of anti-Semitism in German and European opinion. Yet the very attention given to propaganda (in all domains), the systematic reporting on attitudes of the population, the ongoing attempts—specifically regarding the Jewish issue—to find the "right way" of handling mixed breeds, mixed marriages, or even Jewish soldiers decorated for bravery in frontline fighting, shows that the regime was not indifferent to potential public reactions (this would soon be proved in regard to euthanasia).

It was important, therefore, to reinforce preexisting anti-Semitism and to mobilize it as relentlessly as possible in order to bolster the myth of the archenemy needed by the regime, and to facilitate any further steps, if and when decided. The anti-Jewish fanaticism of ordinary Wehrmacht soldiers, even at the beginning of the war, was sufficient proof of the efficiency of the barrage of words and images endlessly molding the monstrous image of "the Jew."

In many ways the same strategy applied to occupied or satellite Europe. In Poland, as we saw, native anti-Semitism was exploited by the Germans, and at the outset at least, it created a narrow common ground between masters and slaves. In Holland the earliest anti-Jewish steps were carefully planned to avoid a confrontation with the population. When this confrontation occurred nonetheless, in February 1941, the Germans retaliated brutally and forged ahead. In other words, measures against the Jews would be introduced and expanded wherever German presence or influence played a role. However, at this early stage, potential reactions in the occupied countries were not disregarded *if* they did not turn into mass opposition (as in Holland). Generally a measure of popular acceptance of anti-Jewish steps could be expected. And such acceptance also extended to Holland after the initial riots were put down. No such qualms existed in France, where the Vichy government had preempted the German measures without any public reaction.

Seen from the vantage point of local authorities and populations in Western Europe, the common denominator of all anti-Jewish measures was probably perceived as the end of equal rights for Jews in all major domains of public life, or, to put it another way, as a process of resegregation. In Germany resegregation was already complete when the war started; the ongoing measures pointed quite openly to the future disappearance of all Jews from the Reich; in former Poland the perception was one of growing exploitation and ruthless violence that could lead to mass death. *In other words, nowhere was the situation considered static but rather as a process leading to an ever more ominous outcome.* Yet no open protest arose (again with the initial exception of Holland). In fact the opposite became rapidly clear: The anti-Jewish measures were accepted, even approved, by the populations and the spiritual and intellectual elites, most blatantly so by the Christian churches. What was tacitly approved by the French church was explicitly welcomed by the Polish clergy, enthusiastically supported by part of German Protestantism, and more prudently so by the remainder of Christian churches in the Reich. Such religious support for or acceptance of various degrees of anti-Jewish persecution helped of course to still any doubts, particularly at a time when among most Europeans the influence of the churches remained considerable and their guidance was eagerly sought.

The widespread acceptance of resegregation would have an obvious impact on the events to come. If the isolation of the Jews did not provoke any significant protests—and was even welcomed by many—their territorial segregation outside Europe or in some distant part of the Continent would appear as a mere technicality. Some rules would have to be respected: Families, for example, were to be kept together, and undoubtedly the Jews would have to be put to work.

Much attention has been given since the war to the role played by Jewish leadership in the unfolding of the events. It has been argued that Jewish leadership groups on a national or local level did not recognize the total novelty of Nazi persecution, and therefore, as the argument goes, they kept to traditional modes of response instead of adopting entirely new strategies. Yet if one accepts that, *during the early phase of the war* (the period dealt with here), no radically new Nazi policy had been formulated, and resegregation appeared to the Jews themselves as a historically familiar situation, the councils and similar Jewish leadership groups could respond to the ongoing crisis only by means that were familiar in such apparently similar situations and seemed to be the only rational choices within the existing context.

Moreover, as we saw, in the Reich, the Protectorate, and occupied Western countries, native Jews and long-established immigrants were used to obeying the authorities and "the law," even if they perceived that the decrees targeting them were totally unjust and meant only to harm them. As already mentioned, most of these Jews believed that the proliferation of laws and ordinances that weighed on their daily existence nonetheless represented a stable system that would allow them to survive. Within this system they interceded with their oppressors, sometimes successfully. Usually they persevered, day in and day out, in the hope that an emigration possibility would materialize somehow or, in the East, that physical survival would remain a possibility for most if Jewish workers produced enough goods for the German war economy.

In the meantime the same councils or their equivalents distributed available assistance to the growing number of Jews reduced to utter poverty. Although under constant control of the Gestapo, these Jewish leaders were not hampered at this stage in their welfare activities, as almost all the assistance they extended came from Jewish funds. Otherwise, as we saw, they dealt with emigration when still allowed to do so and with education where and when public schools were closed to Jewish children.

The disbanding of the councils was not a viable option at that point. It would have meant not only the disruption of all welfare activities, but also German reprisals against any number of hostages and, in no time, the appointment of a new group of Jews to head the community. Of course the constraints limiting the options of the leadership did not apply to individual Jews, at least in the West. They could avoid registration and opt for living illegally from late 1940 or early 1941 on. With hindsight these would have been the right decisions to take, but at the time the risks appeared to the immense majority as disproportionate in comparison to the immediate hardships.

One of the striking aspects of the dramatically changing Jewish condition appears to be the ongoing disintegration of overall Jewish solidarity—insofar as it ever existed. In late 1939 and early 1940, in order to keep all emigration openings for German Jews only, German Jewish leadership attempted to bar endangered Polish Jews from emigrating from the Reich to Palestine; French Jewish leadership never ceased to demand a clear-cut distinction between the status and treatment of native and of foreign Jews. The councils in Poland—particularly in Warsaw—were allowing a whole array of privileges to whomever could pay a bribe, while the poor, the refugees from the provinces, and the mass of those devoid of any influence or resources were increasingly compelled to do slave labor or suffer starvation, eventually leading to the death of the weakest.

Obversely, a strengthening of bonds appeared within small groups sharing a specific political or religious background. Such was typically the case in political youth groups in the ghettos, among Jewish scouts in France, and, of course, among this or that group of orthodox Jews. Such developments should not lead to disregarding the widespread welfare efforts, or the education or cultural activities open to all; yet a trend was becoming apparent: It would greatly intensify with the growth of the external threat.

X

Given the absence of any significant assistance from the major Christian churches to nonconverted Jews, the role of private institutions and of (sometimes unlikely) individuals grew in importance. The role of Jewish organizations was preeminent, particularly of the JDC, the Organization for Rehabilitation and Training (ORT), and the Oeuvre de Secours aux Enfants (OSE), as well as organizations belonging more directly to Jewish political parties (Zionists, Orthodox, Bundists, Communists) or to various Jewish immigrant associations in Western Europe.[214] Non-Jewish charitable organizations also extended generous help: the American Friends Service Committee, the YMCA, the Protestant CIMADE, and others.

The initiatives of individuals carried a particular moral significance. Even during this early period, and even outside the Reich, the risks incurred were often considerable, albeit mainly in professional and social terms. The qualified stand taken by the head of the French Protestant community, Pastor Marc Boegner, against Vichy's anti-Jewish policies could, for example, have endangered his position within his own flock; the smuggling of Jews across the Swiss border, on the eve of the war, put an end to Paul Grüninger's career in Sankt Gallen's border police; several Swiss consular officers, mainly in Italy, were reprimanded for disregarding the rules about Jewish immigration. As already mentioned, after the defeat of France, the Portuguese consul general in Bordeaux, Aristides de Sousa Mendes, started issuing entry visas to Jews, despite contrary instructions from Lisbon; he was recalled and dismissed from the foreign service. Like Grüninger, he was rehabilitated only several decades after the end of the war. Varian Fry's smuggling of specially endangered and "valuable" Jews out of Vichy France carried, as we saw, all the risks of illegality and led to his recall and dismissal after one year of activity. One of the most unlikely cases in many ways, however, was that of Chiune Sugihara, the Japanese consul in the Lithuanian capital, Kovno.[215]

Sugihara had been transferred from Helsinki to Kovno in October 1939. When Lithuania was annexed by the Soviet Union, the Japanese consulate had to close down and, on August 31, 1940, Sugihara was posted in Berlin, then Prague, later in Königsberg. From the outset Sugihara's real mission had been to observe troop movements and related military developments. But, in order to keep up the appearances of his official cover, he performed all the regular functions of a genuine consul; mainly, he issued visas. On August 10, 1940, against instructions of the Foreign Ministry in Tokyo (or, at best, without any clear instructions whatsoever), Sugihara started issuing Japanese transit visas to all the Jews who reached his consulate. Almost none of them had an entrance permit to a country of final destination; many didn't even have valid passports of any sort.

Within days admonishments from Tokyo reached the wayward consul: "Recently we discovered Lithuanians who possess our transit visas which you issued," a cable of August 16 read. "They were traveling to America and Canada. Among them there are several people who do not possess enough money and who have not finished their procedure to receive their entry visas to the terminal countries. We cannot give them permission to land. And in regard to these cases, there were several instances that left us confused and we do not know what to do. . . . You must make sure that they have finished their procedure for their entry visas and also they must posses the travel money or the money that they need during their stay in Japan. Otherwise, you should not give them the transit visa."[216]

Sugihara remained undeterred: He continued signing visas even from the window of an already moving train as he and his family were leaving for Berlin. He issued more visas in Prague and possibly in Königsberg. The Germans were certainly not adverse to the illegal departure of Jews from the territory of the Reich.[217] Sugihara may have issued up to ten thousand visas, and possibly half the number of Jews who received them managed to survive.[218] There is no concrete clue about his thoughts and motives: "I did not pay any attention [to consequences]," he wrote in a postwar memoir, "and just acted according to my sense of human justice, out of love for mankind."[219]

PART II

Mass Murder

Summer 1941–Summer 1942

The proportions of life and death have radically changed. Times were, when life occupied the primary place, when it was the main and central concern, while death was a side phenomenon, secondary to life, its termination. Nowadays, death rules in all its majesty; while life hardly glows under a thick layer of ashes. Even this faint glow of life is feeble, miserable and weak, poor, devoid of any free breath, deprived of any spark of spiritual content. The very soul, both in the individual and in the community, seems to have starved and perished, to have dulled and atrophied. There remain only the needs of the body; and it leads merely an organic-physiological existence.

—Abraham Lewin,
eulogy in honor of Yitshak Meir Weissenberg,
September 31, 1941

CHAPTER IV

June 1941–September 1941

On September 29, 1941, the Germans shot 33,700 Kiev Jews in the Babi Yar ravine near the city. As the rumors about the massacre spread, some Ukrainians initially expressed doubts. "I only know one thing," Iryna Khoroshunova inscribed in her diary on that same day, "there is something terrible, horrible going on, something inconceivable, which cannot be understood, grasped or explained." A few days later, her uncertainty had disappeared: "A Russian girl accompanied her girlfriend to the cemetery [at the entrance of the ravine], but crawled through the fence from the other side. She saw how naked people were taken toward Babi Yar and heard shots from a machine gun. There are more and more such rumors and accounts. They are too monstrous to believe. But we are forced to believe them, for the shooting of the Jews is a fact. A fact which is starting to drive us insane. It is impossible to live with this knowledge. The women around us are crying. And we? We also cried on September 29, when we thought they were taken to a concentration camp. But now? Can we really cry? I am writing, but my hair is standing on end."[1] In the meantime, the war in the East was entering its fourth month.

For Dawid Rubinowicz the unleashing of the German attack was merely a noisy event at first: "It was still dark," he noted on June 22, "when father woke us all up and told us to listen to that terrible din coming from the north-east. It was such a din the earth quaked. The whole day thundering could be heard. Toward evening Jews dropped in from Kielce and said Soviet Russia was at war with the Germans, and only then did it dawn on me why there had been that din all day."[2]

Of necessity the Lodz chronicles had to keep to the barest facts: "In connection with the war against the Soviets, in the last ten days of June there has been a sudden increase in the price of packaged goods, which the ghetto had received mostly from the USSR," they recorded in their entry of June 20–30, 1941. The mention of the German attack in the East elicited no further comment.[3] The restraint imposed on the official ghetto recorders was not shared by the individual diarists, however. Young Sierakowiak was elated: "Incredible, wonderful news!" he wrote on the twenty-second, though he was not yet entirely sure that the "free, beloved, great Soviets" were not being attacked by a German-British coalition.[4] On the twenty-third he triumphantly confirmed: "It is all true! . . . The entire ghetto is buzzing like one big beehive. Everybody feels that a chance for liberation is finally possible."[5]

Not all Jewish diarists shared Sierakowiak's high spirits. In Romania—which had joined the anti-Bolshevik crusade—fear spread: "In the evening, we gather early at the house," Sebastian noted on June 22. "With the shutters drawn and the telephone out of service, we have a growing sense of unease and anguish. What will happen to us? I hardly dare ask. You are afraid to imagine what you will be like in another day, another week, another month."[6] Two days later Sebastian described a poster put up in the streets with the text 'Who are the masters of Bolshevism?', showing "a Jew in a red gown, with side curls, skullcap, and beard, holding a hammer in one hand and a sickle in the other. Concealed beneath his coat are three Soviet soldiers. I have heard that the posters were put up by police sergeants."[7]

In Vilna, Hermann Kruk did not partake of Sierakowiak's enthusiasm either. Kruk had fled from Warsaw to Lithuania a few days after the beginning of the war. In the Polish capital he had been active in Yiddish cultural circles and was in charge of the cultural activities of the Bund's youth movement, Zukunft, and of the central Yiddish library.[8] On June 22, 1941, he thought of fleeing again but did not succeed. Fatalistically he resigned himself to staying and recording the oncoming events: "I make a firm decision," he noted on June 23, 1941. "I leave myself to the mercy of God; I am staying. And, right away, I make another decision: if I am staying anyway and if I am going to be a victim of fascism, I shall take pen in hand and write a chronicle of a city. Clearly, Vilna may also be captured. The Germans will turn the city fascist. Jews will go into the ghetto—I shall record it all. My chronicle must see, must hear, and must become the mirror and the conscience of the great catastrophe and of the hard times."[9]

In the Warsaw ghetto, as in Lodz, the immediate everyday consequences of the new war seemed to be the main concern. "A newspaper special on the war with the Soviets," Czerniaków noted on June 22. "It will be necessary to work all day, and perhaps they will not let one sleep at night."[10] For days on end the Warsaw chairman hardly mentioned the war in Russia; he had other, more urgent worries. "In the streets the workers are being impressed for labor outside the ghetto, since there are few volunteers for a job which pays only 2.80 zlotys and provides no food," he noted on July 8. I went to [Ferdinand von] Kamlah to obtain food for them. So far, no results. Considering their dire predicament, the Jewish masses are quiet and composed."[11]

Among the Germans, as far as Klemperer could observe, the news of the campaign in the East was well received: "Cheerful faces everywhere," he noted on June 22. "A new entertainment, a prospect of new sensations, the Russian war is a source of new pride for people, their grumbling of yesterday is forgotten."[12] In fact, most observers would not have agreed with Klemperer: the news of the attack, although not unexpected, caused surprise and, at times, consternation.[13]

I

During the first days and weeks of the campaign, the German onslaught seemed, once again, irresistible. Despite repeated warnings from the most diverse sources (including several Soviet-controlled spy rings), Stalin and the Red Army had been caught by surprise. "We will still have some heavy battles to fight," Hitler told Goebbels on July 8, "but the Bolshevik armed forces will not be able to recover from the present series of defeats."[14] Unperceived and unimagined by any observer at the time, Germany's descent to defeat had begun.

Optimism pervaded the high-level meeting convened at Hitler's headquarters on July 16 and attended by Göring, Bormann, Lammers, Keitel, and Rosenberg. In a memorable formula, the "greatest military leader of all times" [*Grösste Feldherr aller Zeiten*, according to Keitel] set the guidelines for German policy in the occupied Soviet Union: "Basically we have to divide this enormous cake in the right way in order, first to rule it, second to administer it, third to exploit it." In this context the Nazi chief considered Stalin's July 3 appeal to Red Army soldiers to start partisan warfare behind the German lines as one more favorable development: "This partisan warfare gives us an advantage by enabling us to destroy everything in our path . . . in this vast area, peace must be imposed as quickly as possible, and to achieve this it is necessary to execute even anyone who doesn't give us a straight look."[15]

It was at the same meeting that Alfred Rosenberg was officially appointed Reich minister for the occupied eastern territories; yet Himmler's responsibility for the internal security of the territories was reaffirmed. According to the formal arrangement confirmed by Hitler on the next day, Rosenberg's appointees, the *Reichskommissare,* would have jurisdiction over Himmler's delegates in their areas, but de facto the HSSPF got their operational orders from the Reichsführer. The arrangement, which was meant to safeguard both Himmler's and Rosenberg's authority, was of course a recipe for constant infighting. Although the tension between both systems of domination has often been highlighted—a tension that also pervaded the control over the General Government—in fact the "results" prove that cooperation in implementing the tasks on hand, particularly in regard to mass murder, usually overcame competition.[16] After all, Rosenberg's appointees, headed by *Reichskommissar* Hinrich Lohse, former *Gauleiter* of Schleswig-Holstein, in the Ostland, and *Reichskommissar* Erich Koch, *Gauleiter* of East Prussia, in the Ukraine, as well as their district chiefs, were drawn from the party's inner core: These local governors and the Reichsführer's delegates—HSSPF Hans-Adolf Prützmann (Russia North), Erich von dem Bach-Zalewski (Russia Center), Friedrich Jeckeln (Russia South), and Gert Korsemann (Extreme South and "Caucasia")—shared the same beliefs and the same goals; together with the Wehrmacht they were intent, beyond anything else, on imposing German domination, exploitation, and terror in the newly conquered territories.

As weeks went by neither the Red Army nor Stalin's regime collapsed; the progress of the Wehrmacht slowed down, and German casualties steadily mounted. In mid-August, following tense discussions with his top military commanders, Hitler—against his generals' advice to concentrate all available forces for an attack on Moscow—decided that although Army Group Center had already made considerable progress in its own part of the front, it would now turn southward to conquer the Ukraine before turning northward again for the final assault on the Soviet capital. Kiev surrendered on September 19, and more than 600,000 Russian soldiers—and their equipment—fell into German hands. Hitler was again in an ebullient mood; yet time was running dangerously short for the attack on the center of Soviet power.

In the meantime the international situation was becoming more ominous for Germany, given the policy systematically pursued by President Roosevelt. After his reelection and his use of the "garden hose" metaphor at the press conference of December 17, 1940, the American president had declared during his December 29 "fireside chat" radio broadcast that the United States would become "the great arsenal of democracy." On March 11, 1941, Roosevelt signed the Lend-Lease Bill: It would take effect on March 26. Within days British ships were carrying "lent" American weapons and supplies across the Atlantic. In the early summer American assistance to the Soviet Union started. The major problem for Washington was not whether to supply the Communist victim of German aggression but to get the American supplies to their destination in the face of increasingly successful German submarine operations.

In April 1941, invoking the Monroe Doctrine and the need to defend the Western Hemisphere, Roosevelt sent American troops to Greenland; two months later U.S. forces established bases in Iceland. Then, in mid-August, Roosevelt and Churchill met off the coast of Newfoundland, and at the end of their talks proclaimed the rather hazy principles of what became known as the Atlantic Charter. In Berlin, as elsewhere, the meeting was interpreted as signaling a de facto alliance between the United States and Great Britain. Secretly Roosevelt had indeed promised Churchill that the U.S. Navy would escort British convoys at least halfway across the Atlantic. By September major incidents between American naval units and German submarines had become unavoidable.

By midsummer 1941 the German population showed some signs of unease. The war in the East was not progressing as rapidly as expected, casualties were growing, and regular food supply became a source of mounting concern.[17] It was under these circumstances that a major incident rattled the Nazi leadership.

On Sunday, August 3, Bishop Clemens Count von Galen defied Hitler's regime. In a sermon at the Münster cathedral, the prelate forcefully attacked the authorities for the systematic murder of the mentally ill and the handicapped. The sermon came four weeks after the German episcopate had issued a pastoral letter, read from every pulpit in the country, denouncing the taking of "innocent lives." Protestant voices, including that of Bishop Theophil Wurm of Württemberg, among others, also rose. Hitler had to respond.[18]

The Nazi leader decided not to retaliate against Galen at this crucial stage of the war. Accounts with the church would be settled later, he declared. Officially operation T4 was discontinued, but in fact the extinction of "lives unworthy of living" continued nonetheless, in less visible ways. Thereafter the victims were mainly chosen from prisoners of concentration camps: Poles, Jews, "criminals against the race," "asocials," cripples. Under the code name 14f13, Himmler had already launched these killings in April 1941 in Sachsenhausen; after mid-August 1941 it became a modified euthanasia operation. Morever, in mental institutions "wild euthanasia" took the lives of thousands of resident inmates. Yet despite the roundabout pursuit of the killings, it was the only time in the history of the Third Reich that prominent representatives of the Christian churches in Germany voiced public condemnation of the crimes committed by the regime.[19]

II

It seems that during the early months of the new campaign Hitler had decided to leave the fate of the Jews of Europe in abeyance until final victory in the East. Between June and October 1941, the Nazi leader's mention of the Jewish enemy remained almost as perfunctory in his public addresses as it had been since the beginning of the war.

Of course the Jewish menace had not been forgotten. During Hitler's broadcast to the German people on June 22, the Jews headed the enumeration of the Reich's enemies; they were mentioned along with democrats, Bolsheviks, and reactionaries.[20] The Jews surfaced again close to the end of the address, as Hitler explained and justified the attack that had just begun: "Now the hour has struck for the necessary counteraction against this plot of Jewish-Anglo-Saxon instigators of the war and the Jewish leaders of Bolshevik headquarters in Moscow."[21] By Hitler's standards this sounded almost trite.

To the Croatian marshal Slavko Kvaternik the Nazi leader declared during a July 21 meeting that after the completion of the eastern campaign, the Jews of Europe would be sent to Madagascar or possibly to Siberia.[22] Manifestly Hitler was using "Madagascar" as a standard illustration of the end goal of his policy: the expulsion of the Jews from Europe. On August 12 the departing Spanish ambassador Eugenio Espinosa was treated to Hitler's usual diatribe against "Roosevelt, his freemasons, his Jews and the whole Jewish bolshevism."[23] A few days later, on August 25, in a meeting with Mussolini, Hitler came back to the same topic: "The Führer gave a detailed analysis of the Jewish clique surrounding Roosevelt and exploiting the American people. He stated that for anything in the world he would not live in a country like the United States, which had a concept of life inspired by the most vulgar commercialism and had no feeling for any of the most sublime expressions of the human spirit."[24]

Similarly, in haranguing the guests and habitués who assembled in his apartments at headquarters near Rastenburg, East Prussia (then at Vinnytsa in the Ukraine, and later at Rastenburg again), the Nazi leader did not dwell at any length on the Jewish topic during the summer of 1941. On July 10 he compared himself to Robert Koch who had discovered the tuberculosis bacillus; he, Hitler, had uncovered the Jews as the element of all social disintegration. He had demonstrated that a state [Germany] could live without Jews.[25] The next day the Nazi leader brought up his theory about religion and world history: "The worst blow to have hit humankind is Christianity; Bolshevism is a bastard child of Christianity; both are the monstrous product of the Jews."[26] In early September, Hitler mentioned the Germans' "extreme sensitivity": the expulsion of six hundred thousand Jews from the territory of the Reich was considered utmost brutality, he argued, while nobody had paid any attention to the expulsion [by the Poles] of eight hundred thousand Germans from East Prussia (at the end of World War I).[27] That was it for the summer.

The Nazi leader possibly wished to maintain the public posture of supreme statesman and strategist who at the time of his greatest historical achievement left the talking to his subordinates. Only once Soviet resistance became a formidable obstacle and when, simultaneously, Roosevelt's initiatives brought the United States closer to a confrontation with Germany, did the Führer's aloofness disappear. The underlings, however, were pushed into action. When Goebbels met Hitler at headquarters on July 8, he was instructed to intensify anti-Bolshevik propaganda to the utmost. "Our propaganda line is clear," the minister recorded the next day. "We must continue to expose the cooperation between Bolshevism and plutocracy and now increasingly stress the Jewish aspect of this common front. In a few days, starting slowly, the anti-Semitic campaign will begin; I am convinced that also in this direction, we can increasingly bring world opinion to our side."[28]

In fact, as early as the very first day of the war in the East, on June 22, Reich Press Chief Dietrich, in his "theme of the day" (*Tagesparole*) for the German press, insisted on the Jewish dimension of the Bolshevik enemy: "It has to be pointed out that the Jews pulling the strings behind the Soviet scene have remained the same, and so have their methods and their system. . . . Plutocracy and Bolshevism have an identical starting point: the Jewish striving for world domination."[29] On July 5 the *Reichspressechef* conveyed once more the daily message: "The greatest Jewish swindle of all time is now uncovered and exposed: the "workers' paradise" turns out to be a gigantic fraud and exploitation system, in the face of the entire world." After describing the horror of existence in the Soviet Union, Dietrich returned to his main theme: "The Jew pushed the peoples of the Soviet Union into this undescribable misery by way of his devilish Bolshevik system."[30]

The tone was set. It would be sustained, with innumerable variations, to the very end. Goebbels's first personal contribution came on July 20, in a massive anti-Jewish attack published in *Das Reich* under the title "Mimicry." Under the minister's pen the Jews became quintessential mimics: "It is difficult to detect their sly and slippery ways. . . . Moscow's Jews invent lies and atrocities, the London Jews cite them and blend them into stories suitable for the innocent bourgeois." The argument was clear: Jews camouflage their presence and move to the background in order to maneuver behind the scenes. The conclusion of Goebbels's tirade was foreseeable: The nations that had been deceived would see the light. "From every corner of the earth the cry would rise: 'The Jews are guilty! The Jews are guilty!' The punishment will be terrible. We need not do anything to bring it about," the minister prophesied. "It will come of itself, because it has to come. As the fist of awakening Germany smashed this racial filth, so one day the fist of awakening Europe will smash it too."[31] From then on and throughout the summer, the minister returned repeatedly to the same theme, on every available occasion.[32]

In those same days Goebbels discovered two "sensational" documents: Roosevelt's picture in Masonic attire and the American president as initiator of the criminal anti-German ideas of the Jew Kaufman. The first document, found in a Norwegian archive, "proves beyond any doubt that the warmonger Roosevelt is under Jewish-Masonic domination," read the instructions to the press.[33] On July 23, the *Völkischer Beobachter* published a full-page article titled "High-Ranking Mason Roosevelt, the Main Instrument of World Jewry."[34] All major German papers toed the line.

The Jewish-Masonic sensation was a minor matter compared to the unearthing of Theodor N. Kaufman.[35] The thirty-one-year-old Kaufman (the middle N. stood for "Newman," but it became "Nathan" for the Nazis), a native of New Jersey, had a small advertising business in Newark, selling mainly theater tickets. In early 1941 he set up the Argyle Press solely in order to publish a pamphlet he had authored: "Germany Must Perish." He demanded the sterilization of all German men and the division of the country into five parts to be annexed by the Reich's neighbors. After printing his pamphlet Kaufman personally wrapped the copies and sent them to the press. The pamphlet found no echo except for a write-up in the March 24, 1941, issue of *Time* magazine under the ironic heading "A Modest Proposal," which also included a few details about the author and his one-man enterprise. Thereafter Kaufman faded back into obscurity in the United States—but not in Germany.[36]

On July 24, 1941, the *Völkischer Beobachter* ran a front-page story with the bloodcurdling title: "Roosevelt demands the sterilization of the German people" and the shocking subtitle: "A Monstrous Jewish Extermination Plan. Roosevelt's Guidelines." Theodor Nathan Kaufman was turned into a close friend of Roosevelt's main speechwriter—the Jew Samuel Rosenman—and was himself a leading personality of American Jewry. According to the story the president was the real initiator of Kaufman's ideas; he "had even personally dictated parts of the shameful work. The leading interventionists make no secret of the fact that the devilish plan of the Jew Kaufman represents the political credo of the President of the United States."[37]

The German press and radio carried the Kaufman story in endless variations and presented it as the hidden agenda of the mid-August Churchill-Roosevelt meeting. In September one of Goebbels's main assistants—the head of the broadcasting division of the ministry, Wolfgang Diewerge—published a pamphlet including translated and commented excerpts from Kaufman's text; it was launched in millions of copies, precisely when the Jews of the Reich were compelled to wear the star.[38] And while the Kaufman story was being relentlessly spread, reports of Bolshevik atrocities were regularly carried by all of Goebbels's channels; of course they were attributed to Jewish executioners.[39]

According to an SD report of July 31, 1941, "The situation in the United States was being followed with the greatest attention [by the population]. Increasingly, the view spreads that this war would turn into a real world war. . . . The excerpts from the book of the Jew Kaufmann [*sic*] and the comments show that this war is really a life-and-death struggle. The Kaufmann plans have deeply impressed even the most obdurate skeptics."[40]

To counter Roosevelt's course, the subtle Ribbentrop decided to directly influence American, even Jewish American, opinion. On July 19, 1941, he expounded to his chargé d'affaires in Washington, Hans Thomsen, that "of all parts of the population in the United States, the Jews, surely, have the greatest interest in America's not entering the war. . . . People will soon recall that the Jews were the principal warmongers and they will be made responsible for the losses that occur. The end of the story will be that one day all the Jews in America will be beaten to death."[41]

According to an SD report of July 24, newsreel scenes showing "the jailing of Jews responsible for the murders" [in the East] triggered audience reactions claiming that "they were being dealt with much too fairly." The scenes showing Jews clearing rubble "elicited great satisfaction" even in the annexed French province Lorraine (particularly in its main city, Metz). . . . Images of "lynch justice meted out by the population in Riga against its [Jewish] tormentors were greeted with shouts of encouragement."[42]

As had been usual over the years, denunciations of political and other known personalities for being Jewish or influenced by Jews demanded exacting research. On June 18, 1941, Streicher's *Der Stürmer* sent an inquiry to the *Reichsschrifttumskammer* (the Reich's Writers Chamber) to check on the Jewishness of some German writers and that of fifteen well-known authors including, among others, Upton Sinclair, Lewis Sinclair [*sic*], Romain Rolland, H. G. Wells, Colette, Charles Dickens, Émil [*sic*] Zola, Viktor [*sic*] Hugo, Theodor [*sic*] Dreiser, and Denis Diderot. On July 3, Meyer of the *Reichsschrifttumskammer* dutifully answered. Of the German writers (Frank Thiess and Ernst Gläser), one was a member of the *Kammer*, the other worked for the Propaganda Ministry. . . . As far as the foreign writers were concerned, none was Jewish, the *Kammer* confirmed, but the three Americans "wrote in accordance with a typical American mentality." The others, except for one Wilhelm Speyer, were not known to have Jewish origins.[43]

III

Several documents signed by Heydrich in June and July 1941 outlined the measures to be taken against the Jews living in the newly occupied areas. In a message sent on June 29 to the *Einsatzgruppen* commanders, the RSHA chief referred to the meeting held in Berlin on the seventeenth and emphasized the need for secretly encouraging local pogroms (Heydrich called it *Selbstbereinigung* (self-cleansing). Simultaneously the SS units were to get ready to take over from the local "avengers."[44] Then, in a July 2 message to Himmler's personal delegates to various countries or major areas, the Higher SS and Police Leaders, Heydrich summed up the instructions previously given to the *Einsatzgruppen*: All Jewish party and state officials were to be executed and local pogroms had to be encouraged.[45] Finally, on July 17, Heydrich ordered the execution of all Jewish prisoners of war.[46]

And so it was. During the first weeks mostly Jewish men were killed, then all Jews without distinction were murdered by SS *Einsatzgruppen* and other SS units, by the much more numerous Order Police battalions, all of which were assisted from the outset by local gangs, then by local auxiliary units organized by the Germans, and often by regular Wehrmacht troops.[47]

Contrary to what had long been assumed, Himmler did not give the order for the general extermination of all Jews in Soviet territory during his August 15 visit to Minsk, when, at his request, he attended a mass execution of Jews on the outskirts of the city.[48] The move from selective to mass murder had started earlier, probably as a result of Hitler's remarks during the July 16 conference regarding the "possibilities" offered by "antipartisan" operations. All Jews may not have been partisans in German eyes, but why not assume that they would offer assistance to partisans if they could?

The change had already become noticeable at the very beginning of August, for example in Himmler's order to eliminate the Jewish population of Pinsk in Belorussia. On August 2 or 3 the Reichsführer sent the appropriate instructions to Franz Magill, commander of the SS second cavalry brigade operating near Pinsk and the Pripet Marshes: "All Jews age 14 or over who are found in the area being combed shall be shot to death; Jewish women and children shall be driven into the marshes [where they would drown]. The Jews are the partisans' reserve force; they support them. . . . In the city of Pinsk the killing by shooting shall be carried out by cavalry companies 1 and 4. . . . The 'Aktion' is to begin at once. A report on the implementation shall be submitted."[49] The women and children of Pinsk escaped death for a time as the marshes were too shallow; but the order clearly meant that they were to die. The reference to "partisans" once again indicated the link between the July 16 conference and the expanding massacres. Women and children would not yet be shot as men were (presumably to spare the feelings of the units involved), but they would nonetheless be murdered. Such distinctions would rapidly disappear.

It is likely that some of the killings were directly linked to the planned reduction of food supply to Soviet POWs, Jews, and wider Slav populations in order to feed the *Ostheer*. This "murder for food supply" strategy may have been applied systematically regarding the POWs, but it did not appear as a decisive factor in the murder of Jews during the summer of 1941. Had it been otherwise, the killing would not have been selective from the outset, and some trace of such plans would have surfaced in Heydrich's directives or in the reports of the *Einsatzgruppen* and the police batallions.[50]

The Soviet annexations in Eastern Europe had added some 2 million Jews to the 3 million already living within the borders of the USSR proper. Approximately 4 million lived in areas that were occupied by the

Germans; of these 1.5 million managed to flee; those who remained were a relatively easy prey, also as a result of their urban concentration.[51]

During this "first sweep" (from June 1941 to the end of the year), part of the Jewish populations survived. The intensity of the massacres differed from area to area according to local circumstances, as did the very uneven ghettoization process, particularly in pre-1939 Soviet territory. The ghettos set up in bigger cities, such as Minsk and Rovno, were liquidated in a few large killing operations over the coming eighteen months or so; the smaller ghettos were often destroyed within weeks, and part of the population was not ghettoized at all but killed on the spot during the first or the second sweep (throughout 1942). We shall return to the exterminations in ex-Soviet territory. Suffice it to mention here that by the end of 1941, about 600,000 Jews had been murdered in the newly conquered eastern regions.

Among the nonghettoized Jewish population, the occupiers could use whomever they chose as household slaves. "We took over an apartment that belonged to Jews," a member of Order Police Reserve Batallion 105, Hermann G., wrote home on July 7, 1941. "The Jews of this place were woken up very early on Sunday morning by a *Vorkommando* and had, in their great majority, to leave their houses and apartments, and make them available to us. The first thing was to clean these places thoroughly. All Jewish women and girls were put to work: It was a great Sunday morning cleaning. Every morning at 7 o'clock, the chosen people must be present and do all the work for us. . . . We don't need to do anything anymore. H.F. and I have a Jew and, each of us, a Jewess, one of whom is 15 and the other 19; one is called Eide, the other Chawah. They do for us everything we want and are at our service. . . . They have a permit, so that they should not be grabbed by somebody else when they depart. The Jews are fair game [*Die Juden sind Freiwild*]. Everybody can snatch any of them on the street and keep them. I wouldn't want to be in a Jew's skin. No store, insofar as any are open, sells anything to them. What they live on, I don't know. We give them some of our bread and also some other things. I cannot be so hard. One can only give well-meant advice to the Jews: Do not bring children into the world; they have no future anymore."[52]

The author of the letter does not read like a born murderer or dyed-in-the-wool anti-Semite, but rather like someone who just went along and enjoyed his newly acquired power. This was probably the case of most soldiers of the *Ostheer*. Yet beyond the involvement of ordinary soldiers, the crimes of the Wehrmacht against local populations and Jews can no longer be denied, although their extent remains the object of intense debate.

The protests of some senior officers regarding the murders committed by the SS during the Polish campaign did not reappear at the outset of the war against the Soviet Union. Even among the small group of officers, mostly belonging to the Prussian aristocracy, who congregated at Army Group Center around Lt. Col. Henning von Tresckow and who, to varying degrees, were hostile to Nazism, the need to overthrow the Bolshevik regime seems to have been fully accepted, and none of the orders issued in the spring of 1941 was seriously questioned.[53] It appears, moreover, that several of these officers were well informed, from the very beginning of the Russian campaign, about the criminal activities of Arthur Nebe's *Einsatzgruppe* B, which operated in their own area, without however admitting to that knowledge.[54] Only several months later, after the October 20–21 extermination of the Jews of Borisov, did this nucleus of the military opposition to Hitler explicitly recognize the mass murder surrounding them and start drawing conclusions.

Whereas acknowledgment of criminal operations was but slowly admitted by a small military group, the participation of the Wehrmacht in such operations was widespread, as we shall see, and indirectly encouraged by some of the most senior commanders of the *Ostheer*. Thus, in a notorious order of the day, on October 10, 1941, Field Marshal Walter von Reichenau, an outright Nazi, set the tone for several of the highest-ranking commanders: "The soldier must have complete understanding for the necessity of the harsh but just atonement of Jewish subhumanity. This has the further goal of nipping in the bud rebellions in the rear of the Wehrmacht which, as experience shows, are always plotted by the Jews."[55] Hitler praised Reichenau's proclamation and demanded its distribution to all frontline units in the East.[56] Within a few weeks, the Nazi field marshal was imitated by Generals Erich von Manstein, Stülpnagel, and the commander of the seventeenth Army, Gen. Hermann Hoth.[57] As for Field Marshal Wilhelm Ritter von Leeb, the commander of Army Group North, he did not believe that the Jewish question could be solved by mass executions: "It would most reliably be solved by sterilizing all males."[58]

Some commanders were more reticent. Thus, on September 24, 1941, Field Marshal Gerd von Rundstedt, commander of Army Group South, made it clear that operations against foes such as communists and Jews were solely the task of the *Einsatzgruppen*. "Independent participation of Wehrmacht members or participation of Wehrmacht members in the excesses of the Ukrainian population against the Jews" were forbidden. Members of the Wehrmacht were also forbidden "to watch or take pictures during the measures taken by the *Sonderkommandos*."[59] The order was only very partially followed.

In the meantime Wehrmacht propaganda units were hard at work promoting anti-Jewish rage in the ranks of the Red Army and among the Soviet populations. In early July 1941, the first major drops of millions of German leaflets over Soviet territory started. The "Jewish criminals," their murderous deeds, their treacherous plots, and the like were the mainstays in an endless litany of hatred.[60] And, more virulently so than during the Polish campaign, soldiers' letters demonstrate the growing impact of the anti-Jewish slogans.

On the eve of the attack, Pvt. Richard M, stationed somewhere in the General Government, described the Jews he encountered there in a letter to his girlfriend: "This nation of bandits and gypsies (here this expression applies exactly without any exaggeration) hangs about in the streets and alleys and refuses to do any work voluntarily. . . . They show greater skill at stealing and haggling. . . . Moreover these creatures are covered with dirty tatters and infected with all kinds of diseases. . . . They live in wooden huts with thatched roofs. A brief look through the window makes it clear that vice is at home here."[61] On the second day of the campaign, Sgt. A.N. wrote home: "Now Jewry has declared war on us along the whole line, from one extreme to the other, from the London and New York plutocrats to the Bolsheviks." And he added: "All that is under Jewish domination stands in one common front against us."[62]

On July 3 Cpl. F marched through an eastern Galician town (probably Lutsk): "Here, one witnesses Jewish and Bolshevik cruelty of a kind that I hardly thought possible." After describing the discovery of the massacres that had taken place in local jails before the Soviets departed, he commented: "This kind of thing calls for vengeance, and it is being meted out."[63] In the same area Cpl. WH described the houses in the Jewish quarter as "robber dens" and the Jews he encountered as the most sinister beings. His comrade Helmut expressed their feelings: "How was it possible that this race claimed for itself the right to rule all other nations."[64]

On August 4 Pvt. Karl Fuchs was convinced that "the battle against these subhumans, who have been whipped into a frenzy by the Jews, was not only necessary but came in the nick of time. Our Führer has saved Europe from certain chaos."[65] A mid-July letter sent by an NCO was equally blunt: "The German people owes a great debt to our Führer, for had these beasts, who are our enemies here, come to Germany, such murders would have taken place as the world has never seen before. . . . And when one reads the 'Stürmer' and looks at the pictures, this is only a weak illustration of what we see here and the crimes committed here by the Jews."[66] While ordinary soldiers probably garnered their views from the common font of anti-Jewish propaganda and popular wisdom, killer units underwent regular indoctrination courses in order to be up to the difficulties of their tasks.[67]

IV

Before retreating from eastern Galicia, the Soviet Secret Police, the NKVD, unable to deport all the jailed Ukrainian nationalists (and also some Poles and Jews), decided to murder them on the spot. The victims, in the hundreds—possibly in the thousands—were found inside the jails and mainly in hastily dug mass graves when the Germans, accompanied by Ukrainian units, marched into the main towns of the area: Lwov, Zloczow, Tarnopol, Brody. As a matter of course the Ukrainians accused the local Jews of having sided with the Soviet occupation regime in general, and particularly of having helped the NKVD in its murderous onslaught against the Ukrainian elite.

This was but the latest phase of a history reaching back several centuries and punctuated by massive and particularly murderous pogroms: the killings led by Bogdan Chmielnicki in the seventeenth century, by the Haidamaks in the eighteenth century, and by Semyon Petlura on the morrow of World War I.[68] The traditional hatreds between Ukrainians and Poles, Ukrainians and Russians, and Poles and Russians added their own exacerbating elements to the attitudes of these groups toward the Jews, particularly in areas such as eastern Galicia, where Ukrainians, Poles, and Jews lived side by side in large communities, first under Hapsburg rule, then under Polish domination after World War I, and finally under the Soviets between 1939 and 1941, until the German occupation.

Traditional Christian anti-Jewish hostility was reinforced in the Ukraine by the frequent employment of Jews as estate stewards for Polish nobility, thus as the representatives (and enforcers) of Polish domination over the Ukrainian peasantry. Drawing on such hostility, modern Ukrainian nationalists accused Jews of siding with the Poles after World War I in fought-over areas such as eastern Galicia (while as we saw, the Poles accused the Jews of siding with the Ukrainians), and throughout the interwar period as being part and parcel either of Bolshevik oppression or of Polish measures against the Ukrainian minority, according to region. Such intense nationalist anti-Semitism was further exacerbated when a Ukrainian Jew named Sholem Schwarzbart assassinated the much-admired Petlura in Paris on May 25, 1926, in retaliation for the postwar pogroms.[69]

Within the Ukrainian nationalist movement itself, the extremists led by Stepan Bandera and supported by the Germans gained the upper hand against more moderate groups.[70] Bandera's men led the OUN–B (Organization of Ukrainian Nationalists–Bandera) auxiliary units that marched into eastern Galicia in June 1941 together with the Wehrmacht.

In Lwov the Ukrainians herded local Jews together and forced them to dig up the corpses of the NKVD's victims from their mass graves or retrieve them from the jails. The Jews then had to align the bodies of those recently murdered and also of already badly decomposed corpses along the open graves, before being themselves shot into the pits—or being killed in the jails and the fortress, or on the streets and squares of the main east Galician town.[71]

In Zloczow the killers belonged first and foremost to the OUN and to the Waffen SS "Viking" Division, while *Sonderkommando 4b* of *Einsatzgruppe C* kept to the relatively passive role of encouraging the Ukrainians (the Waffen SS did not need any prodding). The murders took place under the watchful eye of the 295th Infantry Division, and it was finally as a result of the protests of the first general staff officer of the division, who sent a complaint to Seventeenth Army headquarters, that the killings of Jews stopped—temporarily.[72]

In his first diary entry, on July 7, 1943, Aryeh Klonicki, a Jew from Kovel, described the events of June 1941 in Tarnopol: "I came one day before the outbreak of the war [with the Soviet Union] as a guest of my wife's sister who lives there. On the third day of the [German] invasion a massacre lasting three consecutive days was carried out in the following manner. The Germans, joined by Ukrainians, would go from house to house in order to look for Jews. The Ukrainians would take the Jews out of the houses where the waiting Germans would kill them, either right by the house or they would transport the victims to a particular site where all would be put to death. This is how some five thousand people found their death, mostly men. As for women and children they were murdered only in exceptional cases. I myself and my wife were saved at the time only because we were living in a street inhabited by Christians who declared that there were no Jews living in our house."[73]

On July 6 Pvt. Franzl also recorded the events at Tarnopol, for the enjoyment of his parents in Vienna. The discovery of the mutilated corpses of *Volksdeutsche* and Ukrainians led to vengeance against the local Jews: They were forced to carry the corpses from the cellars and line them up by newly dug graves; afterward the Jews were beaten to death with truncheons and spades. "Up to now," Franzl went on, "we have sent approximately 1,000 Jews to the other world, but this is by far too little for what they have done." After asking his parents to spread the news, Franzl ended his letter with a promise: "If there are doubts, we will bring photos. Then, no more doubts."[74]

In smaller towns in eastern Galicia most of the murderous anti-Jewish outbreaks during these early days of occupation took place without apparent German intervention. Witnesses from Brzezany, a town to the south of Zloczow, described, decades later, the sequence of events: As the Germans entered the town, "the Ukrainians were ecstatic. Throngs of Ukrainian peasants, mostly young people, carrying yellow-and-blue flags adorned with the Ukrainian trident, filled the . . . streets. They came from the villages, dressed in Ukrainian national costumes, singing their Ukrainian songs." In the prisons and outside, the corpses of Ukrainian activists killed by the NKVD were uncovered: "The sights were indescribable, [so was] the stench from the corpses. They were spread out on the prison cellar floor. Other corpses were floating in the river, the Zlota Lipa. People blamed the NKVD and the Jews." What followed was to be expected: "Most of the Jews who perished in Brzezany on that day were murdered with broomsticks with nails attached to them. . . . There were two rows of Ukrainian bandits, holding big sticks. They forced those people, the Jews, in between the two rows and murdered them in cold blood with those sticks."[75] Farther east the attitude of the populations was somewhat different.

On August 1, 1941, eastern Galicia was annexed to the General Government and became part of the district of Galicia with Lwov as its main administrative center. Some 24,000 Jews had been massacred before the annexation; afterward the fate of the Jews in the new district differed for some time from the situation prevailing in other parts of the General Government. For several months Frank forbade the setting up of ghettos in order to keep the option of transferring these additional Jewish populations "to the East," eventually to the Pripet Marshes area.

In Lwov, for example, ghettoization started only in November 1941. The Governor-general's desire to get rid of his newly acquired Jews was so intense that little was done to hinder thousands of them from fleeing to Romania and Hungary. Otherwise tens of thousands of Jewish men from Galicia were soon herded into labor camps, mainly along the new strategic road that would link Lwov to the southern Ukraine and eventually to the Black Sea. This notorious *Durchgangstrasse IV* (transit road IV) would be useful both to the Wehrmacht and to Himmler's colonization plans. It is this project that, in the later summer of 1941, inaugurated de facto the systematic annihilation of Jews by way of slave labor.[76]

In early August 1941, the small town of Bjelaja Zerkow, south of Kiev, was occupied by the 295th Infantry Division of Army Group South; the Wehrmacht area commander, Colonel Riedl, ordered the registration of all Jewish inhabitants and asked SS *Sonderkommando 4a*, a subunit of *Einsatzgruppe C*—which in the meantime had moved from eastern Galicia to pre-1939 Soviet Ukraine—to murder them.

On August 8 a section of the *Sonderkommando*, led by SS Obersturmführer August Häfner, arrived in the town.[77] Between August 8 and August 19 a company of Waffen SS attached to the *Kommando* shot all of the 800 to 900 local Jews, with the exception of a group of children under the age of five.[78] These children were abandoned without food or water in a building on the outskirts of the town near the army barracks. On August 19 many were taken away in three trucks and shot at a nearby rifle range; ninety remained in the building, guarded by a few Ukrainians.[79]

Soon the screams of these ninety children became so unbearable that the soldiers called in two field chaplains, a Protestant and a Catholic, to take some "remedial action."[80] The chaplains found the children half naked, covered with flies, and lying in their own excrement. Some of the older ones were eating mortar off the walls; the infants were mostly comatose. The divisional chaplains were alerted and, after an inspection, they reported the matter to the first staff officer of the division, Lt. Col. Helmuth Groscurth.

Groscurth went to inspect the building. There he met Oberscharführer Jäger, the commander of the Waffen SS unit who had murdered the other Jews of the town; Jäger informed him that the remaining children were to be "eliminated." Colonel Riedl, the field commander, confirmed the information and added that the matter was in the hands of the SD and that the *Einsatzkommando* had received its orders from the highest authorities.

At this point Groscurth took it upon himself to order the postponement of the killings by one day, notwithstanding Häfner's threat to lodge a complaint. Groscurth even positioned armed soldiers around a truck already filled with children and prevented it from leaving. He communicated all this to the staff officer of Army Group South. The matter was referred to the Sixth Army, probably because *Einsatzkommando 4a* operated in its area. That same evening, the commander of the Sixth Army, Field Marshal Reichenau, personally decided that "the operation . . . had to be completed in a suitable way."[81]

The next morning, August 21, Groscurth was summoned to a meeting at local headquarters in the presence of Colonel Riedl, Captain Luley, a counterintelligence officer who had reported to Reichenau on the course of the events, Obersturmführer Häfner, and the chief of *Einsatzkommando 4a*, the former architect SS Standartenführer Paul Blobel. Luley declared that, although he was a Protestant, he thought that the "chaplains should limit themselves to the welfare of the soldiers"; with the full support of the field commander, Luley accused the chaplains of "stirring up trouble."

According to Groscurth's report, Riedl then "attempted to draw the discussion into the ideological domain . . . The elimination of the Jewish women and children," he explained, "was a matter of urgent necessity, whatever form it took." Riedl complained that the division's initiative had delayed the execution by twenty-four hours. At that point, as Groscurth later described it, Blobel, who had been silent up until then, intervened: He supported Riedl's complaint and "added that it would be best if those troops who were nosing around carried out the executions themselves and the commanders who were stopping the measures took command of these troops." "I quietly rejected this view," Groscurth wrote, "without taking any position as I wished to avoid any personal acrimony." Finally Groscurth mentioned Reichenau's attitude: "When we discussed what further measures should be taken, the Standartenführer declared that the commander in chief [Reichenau] recognized the necessity of eliminating the children and wished to be informed once this had been carried out."[82]

On August 22 the children were executed. The final sequence of the events was described by Häfner at his trial: "I went out to the woods alone. The Wehrmacht had already dug a grave. The children were brought along in a tractor. The Ukrainians were standing around trembling. The children were taken down from the tractor. They were lined up along the top of the grave and shot so that they fell into it. The Ukrainians did not aim at any particular part of the body. . . . The wailing was indescribable. . . . I particularly remember a small fair-haired girl who took me by the hand. She too was shot later."[83] The following day Captain Luley reported on the completion of the task to Sixth Army headquarters and was recommended for a promotion.[84]

The first Germans with any authority to be confronted with the fate of the ninety Jewish children were the chaplains. The field chaplains were compassionate, the divisional ones somewhat less so. In any case, after sending in their reports the chaplains were not heard from again.

The killing of the Jewish adults and children was public. In postwar court testimony, a cadet officer who had been stationed in Bjelaja Zerkow at the time of the events, after describing in gruesome detail the execution of a batch of approximately 150 to 160 Jewish adults, made the following comments: "The soldiers knew about these executions and I remember one of my men saying that he had been permitted to take part. . . . All the soldiers who were in Bjelaja Zerkow knew what was happening. Every evening, the entire time I was there, rifle fire could be heard, although there was no enemy in the vicinity."[85] The same cadet added, however: "It was not curiosity which drove me to watch this, but disbelief that something of this type could happen. My comrades were also horrified by the executions.[86]

The central personality in the Bjelaja Zerkow events was in many ways Lt. Col. Helmuth Groscurth. A deeply religious Protestant, a conservative nationalist, he did not entirely reject some of the tenets of Nazism and yet became hostile to the regime and close to the opposition groups gathered around Adm. Wilhelm Canaris and Gen. Ludwig Beck. He despised the SS and in his diary referred to Heydrich as "a criminal."[87] His decision to postpone the execution of the children in Bjelaja Zerkow by one day, notwithstanding Häfner's threat, and then to use soldiers to prevent an already loaded truck from leaving, is certainly proof of courage.

Moreover Groscurth did not hesitate to express his criticism of the killings in the conclusion of his report: "Measures," he wrote, "against women and children were undertaken which in no way differed from atrocities carried out by the enemy about which the troops are continually being informed. It is unavoidable that these events will be reported back home where they will be compared to the Lemberg atrocities." [This is probably an allusion to executions perpetrated by the NKVD.][88] For these comments Groscurth was reprimanded by Reichenau a few days later. Yet his overall attitude is open to many questions.

After mentioning Reichenau's order to execute the children, Groscurth added: "We then settled the details of how the executions were to be carried out. They are to take place during the evening of August 22. I did not involve myself in the details of the discussion."[89] The most troubling part of the report appears at the very end: "The execution could have been carried out without any uproar if the field and local headquarters had taken the necessary steps to keep the troops away. . . . Following the execution of all the Jews in the town it became necessary to eliminate the Jewish children, particularly the infants. Both infants and children should have been eliminated immediately in order to avoid this inhuman agony."[90]

Groscurth was captured by the Russians at Stalingrad, together with the remaining soldiers and officers of the Sixth Army. He died in Soviet captivity shortly afterward, in April 1943.

V

In Lithuania the first victims of the Germans were the 201 mostly Jewish men (and one woman) of the small border town Gargždai (Garsden), executed on June 24 by an *Einsatzkommando* from Tilsit and a Schutzpolizei (SCHUPO) unit from Memel under the overall command of SS Brigadeführer Franz Walter Stahlecker, the commander of *Einsatzgruppe A* (the Tilsit unit received its orders directly from Gestapo chief Müller).[91] The Jewish women and children (approximately 300), spared at the outset, were locked up in barns and shot in mid-September.[92]

A few days later the killings started in the main cities, Vilna and Kovno, and went on in several waves, during the summer and the fall; at the same time the Jewish populations of small towns and villages were entirely exterminated. The destruction of the Jews of Lithuania had begun. Next to Warsaw, Vilna—the "Jerusalem of Lithuania"—a city inhabited on the eve of the German occupation by some 60,000 Jews, was for centuries one of the most important centers of Jewish life in Eastern Europe. In the eighteenth century, Rabbi Elijah ben Solomon, the "Vilna Gaon," carried religious scholarship to rarely equaled heights; albeit in a tradition of strict intellectual orthodoxy that fiercely opposed Hasidism, the emotional and popular Jewish revivalism born at the same time in the Ukrainian borderlands. It was also in Vilna that the Jewish workers' party, the Bund, was created at the end of the nineteenth century. As we saw, the Bund was a fervent protagonist of the international proletarian struggle, but it was decidedly anti-Bolshevist; it advocated Jewish cultural (Yiddish) and political (socialist) autonomy in Eastern Europe and thus opposed the Zionist brand of Jewish nationalism. It was possibly the most original and numerically important Jewish political movement of the interwar period—and the most unrealistic.

On the morrow of World War I, the Baltic countries became independent, but Lithuania lost Vilna to Poland. At that stage the hatred of Lithuanian nationalists and of their fascist fringe, the Iron Wolf movement, was essentially directed against the Poles, much less so against the Jews. In fact, for a short period, Jewish existence in the new state thrived (the government even established a Ministry of Jewish Affairs) and the community, 150,000 strong, could shape its own educational system and, more generally, its own cultural life with a great measure of autonomy. In 1923, however, the Ministry of Jewish Affairs was abolished, and soon Jewish educational and cultural institutions were denied government support. Stepwise, from 1926 on, Lithuania moved to the right, first under the government of Antanas Smetona and Augustin Voldemaras, then under Smetona alone. Yet the Lithuanian strongman did not initiate any anti-Semitic laws or measures.

During those same years the Jewish minority in Polish-controlled Vilna also energetically developed its cultural and internal political life. Apart from a vast school system in Yiddish, Hebrew, and Polish, the Vilna community boasted a Yiddish theater, a wealth of newspapers and periodicals, clubs, libraries, and other cultural and social institutions. The city became home to major Yiddish writers and artists, as well as to the YIVO research center in the Jewish humanities and social sciences founded in 1925—a Jewish university in the making.[93]

The political scene changed radically with the Soviet annexation of the Baltic countries in July 1940: Jewish religious institutions and political parties such as the Bund or the Zionist-Revisionist Betar soon became targets of the NKVD. As we saw in regard to eastern Poland, any kind of balanced assessment of Jewish involvement in the new political system is rendered quasi impossible by contrary aspects in various domains: Jews were highly represented in officer schools, midrank police appointments, higher education, and various administrative positions. The situation was not different in the two other Baltic countries. Thus, it was not too difficult for extremist Lithuanian right-wing émigrés who had fled to Berlin and who, together with the Germans, were fostering anti-Soviet operations in the home country, to pretend—by exaggerating and twisting numbers that the Jews collaborated with the Bolsheviks. Elimination of the Jews from Lithuania became a goal of the underground "Lithuanian Activists' Front" (LAF). When, a week before the German invasion, the NKVD deported some 35,000 Lithuanians to the Soviet interior, the Jews were widely accused of being both agents and informers.[94]

* * *

The Wehrmacht occupied Vilna in the early morning hours of June 24. The systematic killings in the city started on July 4, two days after the arrival of *Einsatzkommando 9*. Lithuanian gangs (self-styled "partisans") had started rounding up hundreds of male Jews whom they either slaughtered on the spot or in the woods of Ponar, close to the city. Once the Germans openly stepped in, they extended and organized the anti-Jewish operations, and the Lithuanians became willing auxiliaries in the German murder campaign. According to report no. 21 of July 13 about the activities of *Einsatzgruppe A:* "In Vilna . . . the Lithuanian Ordnungspolizei, which was placed under the command of the Einsatzkommando . . . received instructions to take part in the Jewish extermination actions. Consequently, 150 Lithuanians are engaged in arresting and taking Jews to the concentration camp, where after one day they were given 'special treatment' (*Sonderbehandlung*)."[95]

The massacre of some 5,000 Vilna Jewish men in Ponar during July inaugurated a series of mass killings that lasted throughout the summer and the fall. Women and children were included from August onwards; the German aim seems to have been the extermination of Jews unable to work, while workers and their families were left alive. Itzhak Rudashevski, a Vilna schoolboy, not yet fourteen in the summer of 1941, described in the diary he had probably started in June the Yom Kippur round-up (as the Jews were already in the ghetto): "Today the ghetto is full of storm troopers. They thought Jews would not go to work today, so they came to the ghetto to take them. At night things suddenly became turbulent. The people get up. The gate opens. An uproar develops. Lithuanians have arrived. I look at the courtyard and see them leading away people with bundles. I hear boots pounding on the stairs. Soon, however, things calmed down. The Lithuanians were given money and they left. In this way the defenseless Jews attempted to rescue themselves. In the morning the terrible news spread. Several thousand people were uprooted from the ghetto at night. These people never came back again."[96] Rudashevski's last sentence indicates that his entry was written later, from memory; it shows clearly nonetheless that neither he nor the Jews being taken away had any idea of what was going on and where they were headed. By the end of these successive *Aktionen*, in December 1941, some 33,000 Jewish inhabitants of Vilna had been murdered.[97]

For many Lithuanians the prospect of easy looting became a major incentive. A Pole who lived near Ponar and observed the traffic in Jewish possessions shrewdly noted: "To the Germans, 300 Jews means 300 enemies of humanity. To the Lithuanians it means 300 pairs of pants, 300 pairs of boots."[98] This Polish observer probably did not know at the time that before murdering them the Germans robbed the "enemies of humanity" much more systematically than the Lithuanians did. According to the same *Einsatzgruppe* report of July 13, "about 500 Jews . . . are liquidated daily. About 460,000 rubles in cash, as well as many valuables belonging to Jews who were subject to special treatment, were confiscated as property belonging to enemies of the Reich."[99]

In Kovno, Lithuanian murder squads [the "partisans"] ran wild during the early days of the occupation. In a postwar statement a German soldier in the 562nd Bakers' Company (which moved to Kovno at the time and witnessed the killings) volunteered a remark that expressed much more than it was meant to convey: "From where I was standing I saw Lithuanian civilians beating a number of civilians with different types of weapons until they showed no signs of life. Not knowing why these people were being beaten to death in such a cruel manner, I asked a medical-corps sergeant standing next to me. . . . He told me that the people being beaten to death were all Jews. . . . Why these Jews were being beaten to death I did not find out."[100] Other reports describe the enthusiastic attendance of the Lithuanian population (many women with children settling in "front rows" for the day) and of throngs of German soldiers, all of them goading the killers with shouts and applause. Over the following days groups of Jews were shoved off to the forts surrounding the city (Forts VII and IX in particular) and shot.

While some German soldiers did not grasp what exactly was going on with the Jews, many Jews themselves didn't understand either. Thus on July 2, a Jewish woman from Kovno, Mira Scher, wrote to the chief of the Security Police to ask why, on June 26, Lithuanian "partisans" had arrested most of her family, including her granddaughters Mala (thirteen), Frida (eight) and her grandson Benjamin (four). As "all the people mentioned are entirely innocent," Mrs. Scher added, "I ask, with all courtesy, to free them." On the same day a similar letter was sent to the same authorities by Berkus Friedmann, whose wife, Isa (forty-two), daughter, Ester (sixteen), and son, Eliahu (two and a half), were also arrested by the "partisans." Friedmann assured the chief of the SIPO [Sicherheitspolizei] that his family had never belonged to any party and that they all were legal citizens."[101]

Whereas in eastern Galicia the OUN squads had started on their own to murder Jews from day one, in the Baltic countries some German prompting may have been necessary at times. In a notorious October 15, 1941, report about the activities of *Einsatzgruppe A* in the Baltic countries, Stahlecker repeatedly insisted on this point. "Native anti-Semitic forces were induced to start pogroms against Jews during the first hours after capture [occupation]," Stahlecker wrote in the introductory part of the report, "*though this inducement proved to be very difficult* [emphasis added]." Further on Stahlecker returned to this point in his description of the events in Lithuania: "This [local involvement in the killings] was achieved for the first time by partisan activities in Kovno. *To our surprise it was not easy at first to set in motion an extensive pogrom against Jews* [emphasis added]. Klimatis, the leader of the partisan unit . . . who was primarily used for this purpose, succeeded in starting a pogrom on the basis of advice given to him by a small advanced detachment acting in Kovno, and in such a way that no German order or German instigation was noticed from the outside."

Stahlecker may of course have emphasized these initial difficulties to underscore his own talents of persuasion; Lithuanian reticence did not last long in any case, as, according to Stahlecker himself, in Kovno the local gangs murdered some fifteen hundred Jews during the first night of the occupation.[102]

The extermination frenzy that engulfed the immense majority of the Jews of Lithuania raged throughout the other two Baltic countries as well. By the end of 1941 the quasi totality of the 2,000 Jews of Estonia had been killed. A year later the approximately 66,000 Jews of Latvia had been almost entirely exterminated (some 12,000 Jews remained on Latvian territory, 8,000 of whom were deportees from the Reich).[103]

The massacres spread throughout the occupied eastern territories. Even the Reich's downtrodden victims, the Poles, took a hand in the mass killing of Jews. The best-known massacres occurred in the Bialystók district, in Radzilow and in Jedwabne, on July 10. After the Wehrmacht occupied the area, the inhabitants of these small towns exterminated most of their Jewish neighbors by beating them, shooting them, and burning scores of them alive in local barns. These basic facts seem indisputable, but some related issues demand further investigation. Apparently, a high humber of fiercely anti-Semitic priests indoctrinated their flock in the Jedwabne region.[104] Was this high pitch of anti-Jewish hatred exacerbated by German incitement or even by direct German intervention, but also by the role of Jewish Communist officials in the Białystok district during the Soviet occupation?[105] Most helpful throughout, as far as incitement and killing went, were the ethnic Germans; they greatly facilitated the task of their new masters.[106]

At times, however, local populations refused to participate in the anti-Jewish violence. In Brest Litovsk, for example, both the White Russians and the Poles expressed quite openly their pity for the Jewish victims and their disgust for the "barbaric" methods of the Germans, the "hangmen of the Jews."[107] The same reluctance to initiate pogroms was noticed in the Ukraine, in the Zhytomyr region for example. According to an *Einsatzgruppe C* report from August and early September 1941, "almost nowhere could the population be induced to take active steps against the Jews." The Germans and the Ukrainian militia had to take the initiative and to instigate the violence in various ways.[108] Similar attitudes were indirectly confirmed in Wehrmacht reports dealing with the impact of anti-Semitic propaganda operations on the Russian population. "After examining the reasons behind the relatively small impact of German propaganda to date," an Army Group Center report indicated in August 1941, "it appears that German propaganda basically deals with matters of no real interest to the average Russian. This is particularly true of anti-Semitic propaganda. Attempts to spark pogroms against the Jews have come to naught. The reason is that in the eyes of the average Russian, Jews live a proletarian life and thus do not represent a target for attack."[109]

As weeks and months went by a basic fact became obvious to the populations of the occupied eastern territories: No law, no rule, no measure protected a Jew. Even children understood as much. On October 21, 1941, a Polish schoolboy, Georg Marsonas, wrote to the *Gebietskommissar* (district commissar) in Pinsk: "I am thirteen years old and I want to help my mother because she is having a difficult time making a living. I cannot work because I have to go to school but I can earn some money as a member of the municipal band because it plays in the evenings. Unfortunately, I do not have an accordion, which I know how to play. I know a Jew who has an accordion, so I very much ask your permission to have the instrument given or lent to the municipal band. That way I'll have a chance to fulfill my wish—to be useful to my family."[110]

VI

While the Germans and their local auxiliaries actively pursued their killing campaign in the north, center, and south of the Eastern Front, the Romanian army and gendarmerie were outperforming Otto Ohlendorf's *Einsatzgruppe D.*[111] Over a one-year period the Romanians were to massacre between 280,000 and 380,000 Jews.[112] They could not compete with the Germans in the total number of victims, but like the Latvians, the Lithuanians, the Ukrainians, and the Croats, they were ingenious tormentors and murderers.

The earliest large-scale massacre of Romanian Jews took place, in Romania proper, before the reoccupation of the "lost provinces" (Bessarabia and northern Bukovina), particularly in Iasi, the capital of Moldavia. On June 26, 1941, in "retaliation" for two Soviet air raids and "to quell a Jewish uprising," the killings started, organized by Romanian and German army intelligence officers and local police forces. After thousands of Jews had been massacred in the city, several thousand more were packed into the hermetically sealed cars of two freight trains and sent on an aimless journey, lasting several days. In the first train 1,400 Jews suffocated to death or died of thirst; 1,194 bodies were recovered from the second one. The exact number of the victims of the Iasi pogrom remains in dispute, but it may have exceeded 10,000.[113]

The decimation of the Jews of Bessarabia and Bukovina, which began as a local initiative (mainly in the countryside), then continued on orders from Bucharest. On July 8 Ion Antonescu harangued his ministers: "I beg you, be implacable. Saccharine and vaporous humanitarianism has no place here. At the risk of being misunderstood by some traditionalists who may still be among you, I am for the forced migration of the entire Jewish element from Bessarabia and Bukovina, which must be thrown over the border." After ordering similar measures against Ukrainians and other unreliable elements, Antonescu turned to historical precedents and national imperatives as supreme justifications: "The Roman Empire performed a series of barbarous acts against its contemporaries and yet it was the greatest political establishment. There are no other more favorable moments in our history. If need be, shoot with machine guns, and I say that there is no law. . . . I take full legal responsibility and I tell you, there is no law!"[114] And, while the supreme leader invoked history, the head of the government, Mihai Antonescu (not related to Ion Antonescu), turned again, in the Iron Guard's steps, to the rhetoric of Christian anti-Jewish hatred: "Our Army has been humiliated [by the Soviet occupation]—forced to pass under the Caudine Forks of its barbaric enemies—accompanied solely by the treacherous scorn of the accomplices of Bolshevism, who added to our Christian crucifixion their Judaic offense." The crusade was now launched against those "who had desecrated the altar in the land of our ancestors, against the Yids and Bolsheviks [who] have emptied the house of the Redeemer, crucifying the faith on their vilainous [*sic*] cross."[115]

The massacre of Jews became an everyday occurrence; tens of thousands were herded into ghettos (the most important being in Kishinev, the main city of Bessarabia) until, in the autumn, they were driven over the river Dniester into "Transnistria," the area of southern Ukraine that was Romanian-occupied and was to remain under Romanian control.[116]

On October 16, 1941, the Romanian army entered Odessa; a few days later, on October 22, its headquarters were destroyed by an explosion set up by the NKVD. The murderous fury of the occupiers of course turned against the Jews of the city. After killing some 19,000 Jews (according to German estimates) in the Odessa harbor area, the Romanians drove a further 25,000 to 30,000 to neighboring Dalnic, where they exterminated them by shooting, explosives, or by burning them alive.[117]

On several occasions in October 1941 the president of the Union of Jewish Communities in Romania, Wilhelm Filderman, and Chief Rabbi Alexander Safran interceded with Antonescu to stop the deportations to Transnistria and ease the fate of the Jews of Bessarabia and Bukovina. On October 19, in a violent answer released to the press, Antonescu accused the Jews of Romania of treachery toward their country and of responsibility for the supposed mutilations of Romanian officers captured by Soviet Jews, their "brethren": "In keeping with tradition," Antonescu went on, "you wish now to transform yourselves from accused into accusers, acting as if you have forgotten the reasons which caused the situation of which you complain. . . . From the cellars of Chisinau [Kishinev] our martyrs are removed daily, terribly mutilated cadavers thus rewarded for the friendly hand which, for twenty years, they stretched out to those ungrateful beasts. . . . Do not pity, if you really have a soul, those who do not merit it."[118]

As public as Antonescu's letter had been, so was information about the massacres, from the outset. "Lunch at Alice's with Hillard, a cavalry lieutenant who returned yesterday from the Ukrainian front," Sebastian recorded on August 21, 1941. "A lot about the massacre of the Jews on both sides of the Dniester. Tens, hundreds, thousands of Jews were shot. He, a simple lieutenant, could have killed or ordered the killing of any number of Jews. The driver who took them to Iasi had himself shot four."[119]

Over time, ever more details about the killings kept reaching Bucharest: "The roads of Bessarabia and Bukovina are filled with corpses of Jews driven from their homes toward Ukraine." Sebastian noted on October 20: "It is an anti-Semitic delirium that nothing can stop. There are no breaks, no rhyme or reason . . . This is sheer uncontrolled bestiality without shame or conscience, without goal or purpose. Anything, absolutely anything, is possible."[120]

Sebastian's perception of the events was confirmed by the American minister in the Romanian capital who, however, set greater emphasis upon Ion Antonescu's crucial role: "It is becoming more and more evident," Gunther wrote on November 4, "that the Romanians, obviously with the moral support of the Germans, are utilizing the present period for handling the Jewish problem in their own way. I have it on good authority that Marshal Antonescu has stated . . . that 'this is wartime, and a good time to settle the Jewish problem once and for all.' "[121]

After the German victory in the Balkans, Yugoslavia had been divided: The Germans occupied Serbia and the Italians large stretches of the Dalmatian Coast; the Hungarians were given the Backa and Baranya regions, and the Bulgarians received Macedonia. An independent Croatian state was established under the leadership of Ante Pavelić and his Ustasha movement. While the Dalmatian coast of Croatia remained partly under Italian control, some German troops also stayed on Croatian territory.

In Serbia the Germans set up a collaborationist government under Prime Minister Milan Nedić, a fervent anticommunist. Nedić hardly mattered, though, and even before the German attack against the Soviet Union, armed resistance started mainly in the countryside. Throughout the summer relatively small and untrained Wehrmacht forces fought a losing battle against the spreading insurrection by Communist and Serbian nationalist guerrillas belonging to Tito (Josip Broz) and Draža Mihajlovic, respectively. Notwithstanding the widespread shooting of hostages (Serbs and mainly Jews) by the Germans, the destruction of villages, and the killing of their inhabitants, the rebellion spread. In September, on the recommendation of Field Marshal List, the commander in chief of the Wehrmacht in the Balkans, Hitler appointed the Austrian general Franz Boehme, a notorious Serb hater, as commanding general of the forces stationed in Serbia and gave him a free hand to use "severe methods" to regain control of the situation. Boehme complied, enthusiastically.[122]

In Croatia, no sooner did Pavelić return from Italian exile and establish his new regime–a mixture of fascism and devout Catholicism—then, as the German envoy to Zagreb, Edmund von Glaise Horstenau, reported "the Ustasha went raging mad."[123] The *poglavnik* ("leader," in Serbo-Croat) launched a genocidal crusade against the 2.2 million Christian Orthodox Serbs (out of a total population of 6.7 million) living on Croatian territory, and against the country's 45,000 Jews, particularly in ethnically mixed Bosnia. The Catholic Ustasha did not mind the continuous presence of Muslims or Protestants, but Serbs and Jews had to convert, to leave or to die. According to historian Jonathan Steinberg, "Serbian and Jewish men, women and children were literally hacked to death. Whole villages were razed to the ground and the people driven to barns to which the Ustasha set fire. There is in the Italian Foreign Ministry archive a collection of photographs of the butcher knives, hooks and axes used to chop up Serbian victims. There are photographs of Serb women with breasts hacked off by pocket knives, men with eyes gouged out, emasculated and mutilated."[124]

While Archbishop Alois Stepinac, the head of the Catholic Church in Croatia, waited for months to denounce the savage murder campaign publicly, some local bishops rejoiced at the extermination of the schismatics and the Jews, or at their forced conversion. In the words of the

Catholic bishop of Mostar, "There was never such a good occasion as now for us to help Croatia to save the countless souls."[125] And while bishops blessed the unique occasion to save souls, some Franciscan monks took a leading role in the most vicious murder operations and in the decimation of Serbs and Jews in the uniquely Croat Jasenovac extermination camp.[126]

The Vatican was well informed, of course, of the unfolding atrocities perpetrated by the new Catholic state. Yet, not everything appeared in a negative light either to the Curia or to the Holy See's apostolic visitor to Zagreb, the Benedictine abbot Giuseppe Ramiro Marcone. In May 1941 anti-Semitic laws and the wearing of the star inscribed with the letter *Z* (for *Zidov*, or Jews) had been introduced throughout Pavelić's state. On August 23, shortly after his arrival, Marcone reported to the Vatican secretary of state, Luigi Maglione: "The badly tolerated badge and the hatred of the Croats toward them [the Jews], as well as the economic disadvantages to which they are subjected, often brings about in the minds of the Jews the desire to convert to the Catholic Church. Supernatural motives and the silent action of divine grace cannot be *a priori* excluded from this. Our clergy facilitates their conversion, thinking that at least their children will be educated in Catholic schools and therefore will be more sincerely Christian."[127]

In his answer of September 3, 1941, Maglione did not comment on the role of God's hand in the conversions, nor did he instruct his delegate *to protest* against the treatment of Serbs or Jews: "If your Eminence [Marcone] can find a suitable occasion, he should recommend in a discreet manner that would not be interpreted as an official appeal, that moderation be employed with regard to Jews on Croatian territory. Your Eminence should see to it that activities of a political nature engaged in by the clergy should not cause friction between the parties, and that the impression of loyal cooperation with the civil authorities be always preserved."[128] Throughout 1941 and early 1942 the Croats exterminated some 300,000 to 400,000 Serbs and most of the 45,000 Jews (either directly or by delivering them to the Germans). Throughout the entire period not a word about the Ustasha murders was heard from the pope himself.[129]

In the meantime Serbs and Jews were seeking refuge in the Italian zone in ever greater numbers, and the Croats were increasingly treated as enemies by Mussolini's army. Soon the Italians went one step further and, to put an end to Ustasha crimes, they moved forces farther into Croatian territory.[130] On September 7, 1941, the commander of the Italian Second Army, General Vittorio Ambrosio, issued a proclamation that established Italian authority over the new occupation area; its final lines read: "All those who for various motives have abandoned their country are herewith invited to return to it. The Italian armed forces are the guarantors of their safety, their liberty and their property." The Germans were outraged; Italian protection of Serbs and Jews had become open, and Italian declarations were hardly disguised expressions of scorn and disgust at Croatian behavior and even more so at that of their German masters.[131]

In their mixture of Christian beliefs, fascist policies, and savage murderousness, the Croat Ustasha and the Romanian Iron Guard, or even Antonescu's regime, had much in common; the same extremist ingredients characterized the Ukrainian nationalists, mainly Bandera's faction in the OUN, and the sundry groups of Lithuanian and Latvian "partisans." For all these radical killer groups, local Jews were a prime target, as we saw. Similar ideological components also characterized the Slovak People's Party—created before World War I by a Catholic priest, Father Andrej Hlinka—and its armed militants, the Hlinka Guard. Hlinka, who died in 1938, had fought for Slovak autonomy and the defense of church interests. From the outset the People's Party was divided between traditional conservatives and a militant quasifascist wing led by Vojtech Tuka (a former law professor at the University of Bratislava), a fierce nationalist and no less fierce anti-Semite. After Hlinka's death, Dr. Jozef Tiso, a conservative priest, became the chief of the party and the president of independent Slovakia in March 1939, while Tuka drifted ever closer to National Socialism and was soon appointed prime minister of the new state.[132] Of course the new Slovak regime did not forfeit the confidence of its Berlin masters—nor could it; its anti-Semitism was inherent in a religious tradition and open to direct German influence.[133]

The great majority of the largely rural Slovak population of approximately 2.6 million was devoutly Catholic; the Evangelical community counted around 15 percent of the population, and at the end of 1940, the Jews (after the transfer to Hungary of a south Slovak province) represented some 80,000 people—that is, around 3.3 percent of the population.[134]

It may be remembered that when Tiso, Tuka, and Interior Minister Sano Mach were received by Hitler on July 28, 1940, the Nazi leader demanded of his Slovak partners that they coordinate their anti-Jewish legislation.[135] Soon thereafter SS Hauptsturmführer Dieter Wisliceny arrived in Bratislava as "adviser for Jewish affairs." A Central Office for the Economy (UHU) was established to oversee the Aryanization of Jewish property and expel the Jews from any significant functions in business life; a Jewish Council (UŽ) was set up, and in September 1941 the "Jewish Codex," a whole array of anti-Jewish laws, was promulgated. The new decrees included the wearing of the Jewish star (just then being introduced in the Reich and in the Protectorate), and compulsory labor; the measures closely copied the basic anti-Jewish legislation in existence in Germany.[136] The stage was set for further steps that would lead Catholic Slovakia to be the first country—after the Reich—to start the deportation of its Jews.

Hungary remained relatively calm; in 1941 some 825,000 Jews lived in the country (according to the census of that year, which included provinces annexed since the fall of 1938, with German support: a part of southern Slovakia, Subcarpathian Russia (also previously a part of Czechoslovakia), northern Transylvania (transferred to Hungary by Romania as a result of German "arbitration," and finally the Banat, previously a Yugoslav province, acquired after the April 1941 campaign. Thus around 400,000 Jews of these new provinces were added to the 400,000 Jews who lived in pre-1938, so-called Trianon Hungary. In the larger cities of pre-1938 Hungary—and mainly in Budapest—most Jews were a highly assimilated community that had thrived in a quasi symbiosis with the country's social elite until the end of World War I.[137]

In 1918 the political situation changed radically. A defeated and "dismembered" Hungary was engulfed by revolution. Although Béla Kun's communist dictatorship lasted only 133 days, his own Jewish origins and the massive presence of Jews in his government triggered a violent anti-Semitic reaction and a "white terror" that left thousands of Jewish victims in its wake. Moreover, the presence of a substantial minority of nonassimilated, mainly Polish Jews added to growing anti-Jewish hostility, fueled over the following years by nationalist revisionism, militant anticommunism, and increasingly so by the ever stronger pull of Nazism.

Yet through the interwar period, the regent, Adm. Miklós Horthy, succeeded in keeping conservative governments in power and in staving off Ferenc Szalasi's Arrow Cross fascist and rabidly antisemitic movement. One of the methods chosen by Horthy and the traditional conservatives to stem the rise of the Arrow Cross was to enact anti-Jewish discriminatory laws. An early law of 1920 introducing an anti-Jewish quota in the universities—the first anti-Semitic law in postwar Europe—was adopted but not applied very stringently. The laws of 1938 and 1939, however, concretely limited Jewish participation in the political and economic life of the country, at least as far as the Jewish middle class was concerned (the Jewish banking and industrial elites generally remained untouched). The "third law," that of August 1941—was a replica of the Nuremberg racial legislation. In most of these policies Horthy was backed by the Hungarian Catholic Church and by the Protestant churches. The Hungarian episcopate readily accepted the anti-Jewish decrees of 1938 and 1939 but, as could be expected, balked at the law of August 1941 because of its openly racial dimension, a threat to Jewish converts.[138]

Thousands of foreign Jews who lived in Hungary had to pay for the regent's appeasement tactics. In the course of August 1941, 18,000 of these foreign Jews (almost all Polish, some of whom had barely escaped from occupied eastern Galicia) were rounded up by the Hungarian police and turned over to the SS in the western Ukraine, in the area of Kolomea and Kamenets-Podolsky. On August 27–28 the expellees and a few thousand local Jews (around 23,600 in all) were exterminated.[139] When the news of the massacre seeped back to Hungary, the minister of the interior ordered an end to the deportation. In the meantime, however, first thousands, then tens of thousands of Jewish men were being drafted for forced-labor in the occupied Ukraine. By the end of 1941 some 50,000 Jews had been conscripted; some 40,000 of the first lot would not return. It became apparent, however, that Horthy was not ready to go beyond a certain limit in his anti-Jewish measures, despite repeated German prodding. A stabilization of sorts would last from March 1942, when the relatively liberal Miklós Kallay replaced the pro-German Laszlo Bardossy as the head of government, until the German occupation of the country in March 1944.

VII

For the SS Reichsführer the conquest of immense expanses in the East meant first and foremost the sudden possibility of implementing his colonization dreams: SS strongholds of racially perfect warrior-farmers would become the infrastructure of German domination from the Lublin district in the General Government to the Ural Mountains. Hostile population groups (Russians and Ukrainians) would be subdued, deported (part of the Polish population), or annihilated by expulsion to the polar wastes of northern Russia or by mass-murder operations (the Jews). Such extraordinary prospects demanded immediate action.

After Hitler's decision of July 16 about the division of authority between the SS chief and Rosenberg, Himmler finalized the administrative technicalities in a conversation with Lammers and Brautigam on the seventeenth.[140] On July 20, he was in Lublin. It was probably there, in a meeting with Globocnik and Oswald Pohl (the chief of the SS Main Office for Economy and Administration) that the first measures required by the new projects were decided upon.[141] Existing workshops on Lipowa Street in Lublin (with Jewish forced laborers) would be expanded; a new and much larger slave labor camp would be set up in the city (Lublin-Majdanek) for Jews, Poles, and Russians, and the first settlement plans for *Volksdeutsche* in the Zamość area of the district were discussed.[142]

Of course the complementary aspect to the grandiose colonization plans had to be implemented simultaneously: The group considered as most hostile and dangerous for the security of the newly conquered territories, the Jews, had to be eliminated. Himmler's plans fitted perfectly with the killings that had started immediately after the beginning of the campaign, and with Hitler's new directives regarding "partisans." In this sense the rapid expansion of the murder operations from Jewish men only to that of entire Jewish communities was determined by a convergence of policies; these new dimensions in the scope of the killings in turn demanded the most efficient mass murder methods. The execution of women and children seemed to Himmler to be too stressful for his commando members; toxic gas was more promising.

In the euthanasia program the gassing of mental patients had been used alongside other killing methods. Carbon monoxide was released from bottles into stationary gas chambers or into vans (first adopted for this purpose in the Warthegau in the summer of 1940). In September 1941 a technical modification in the euthanasia gas vans, developed at the Criminal Technical Institute of the RSHA, opened new possibilities. The redesigned vans (Saurer models equipped with powerful engines) would become mobile suffocating machines for batches of around forty people per van and per operation: A metal pipe connected to the exhaust gas hose would be inserted into a hermetically sealed van. Running the engine sufficed to asphyxiate its human cargo. The van was first tested on Soviet prisoners in Sachsenhausen, and the first units were activated in Poltava, in the Southern Ukraine, in November 1941, under the direct command of Paul Blobel's *Einsatzkommando 4a*, which itself belonged to Max Thomas's *Einsatzgruppe C*.

In his postwar testimony, commando member Lauer described the process: "Two vans were in service [in Poltava]. . . . They drove into the prison yard, and the Jews—men, women and children—had to get straight into the vans from their cells. . . . The exhaust fumes were piped into the interior of the vans. I can still hear the hammering and the screaming of the Jews—'Dear Germans, let us out!' . . . As soon as the doors were shut, the driver started the engine. He drove to a spot outside Poltava. I was there when the van arrived. As the doors were opened, dense smoke emerged, followed by a tangle of crumpled bodies. It was a frightful sight."[143] Within a few months some thirty gas vans were to become operational in the Baltic countries, in Belorussia, in the Ukraine, in the Warthegau, and in Serbia.

It was but a short step from the gas van to the stationary gas chamber, which functioned on the same technical principles: the use of carbon monoxide produced by attached engines. As we shall see, while several gas vans were used at the Chelmno extermination site in the Warthegau from early December 1941 on, the construction of gas chambers—activated by the exhaust gas from various engines—began in November on the site of the future Belzec extermination camp. Somewhat earlier, in September 1941, a different set of murder experiments by gas had started at Auschwitz.

* * *

Auschwitz had undergone several stages of development since opening its gates in June 1940 as a concentration camp for Polish political prisoners. Situated near the eastern Upper Silesian town of the same name (half of whose fourteen thousand inhabitants were Jewish), it was conveniently located between the rivers Vistula and Sola and close to a railway junction of some importance. On April 27, 1940, Himmler had decided on the setting up of the camp and, on May 4, Rudolf Höss, formerly on the staff of Dachau, was put in charge. On June 14, as the Wehrmacht marched into Paris, the first transport of 728 Polish political prisoners from Tarnów in Galicia arrived at the new camp.[144]

In September 1940, Pohl, who, during a visit, had grasped the possibilities offered by the camp's location at the rim of sand and gravel pits, ordered Höss to add a second story to each of the existing barracks; new batches of inmates would become slave laborers in the production of building materials, a cost-effective addition to the usual fare of torture and executions.

Pohl's project was soon overshadowed by plans of a totally different scale. In March 1941 it was Himmler's turn to visit the Upper Silesian camp, in the company of representatives of the chemical industry giant, I.G. Farben. This visit had been preceded by arduous negotiations between I.G. Farben, officials of Göring's four-year-plan administration and the SS. The continuation of the war with England and the planned attack on the Soviet Union had convinced Hitler and Göring that the production of synthetic rubber and gasoline should be given the highest priority. I.G. Farben, the German pioneer in this domain, was ordered to expand its production capability considerably. A new plant had to be built as rapidly as possible.

Otto Ambros, the head of the Commission for Rubber and Plastics at I.G. Farben, had been aware for some time of the favorable conditions for a new plant in the Auschwitz area (abundant water supply, flat land, a nearby railway junction). Yet the firm's directorate hesitated to send its workers and engineers to the rundown Polish town.[145] In March and April 1941 Himmler finalized the deal by promising the supply of cheap slave labor (from Auschwitz and other concentration camps) and the construction of adequate housing for the German personnel. Höss was ordered to expand the capacity of the camp from 11,000 to 30,000 inmates. The Jews from the town of Auschwitz were expelled and their homes taken over while Poles were rounded up for construction work both at the camp and at I.G. Farben's future Buna plant site at Dwory.[146]

As these vast expansion plans were set in motion and as, in the meantime, the new campaign in the East had started, the function of the camp as a mass murder center was also taking shape. By sheer coincidence, just after the beginning of the Russian campaign, an Auschwitz disinfection team "discovered" that the powerful pesticide Zyklon B—used for the decontamination of ship hulls and military barracks and thus also regularly utilized in Auschwitz—could kill animals and, therefore, human beings.[147] Testing on a small group of Soviet prisoners of war successfully took place in early September 1941 in the cellar of Block 11, in the main camp. According to the camp chronicler, Danuta Czech, a major test then followed: This time the victims were first selected from the camp infirmary (some were brought on stretchers) and packed into the basement of Block 11, where all windows had been filled with earth. "Then," Czech reported, "some 600 Russian war prisoners, officers and commissars who had been selected by the special units of the Gestapo in war prisoners' camps, are pushed in. As soon as the prisoners have been pushed into the cells and the SS men have thrown in the Zyklon B gas, the doors are closed and isolated. The action takes place during the evening roll-call in the camp; after that, curfew is imposed: it means that the inmates are forbidden to leave their barracks and to move around in the camp."[148] As some of the prisoners were still alive on the next day, the operation was repeated.[149]

Even when the gas vans and gas chambers were used at full capacity, the Germans never abandoned mass executions by shooting or starvation, mainly in the occupied territories of the Soviet Union but also in Poland, even close to extermination camps. Their victims were not only Jews. Three and a half million Russian POWs were starved to death by the Wehrmacht, under the expert guidance of Quartermaster General Edward Wagner.[150] Hundreds of thousands of Russian civilians were executed by the Army or by the *Einsatzgruppen* for any reason whatsoever. Further west, the execution of Polish civilians did not reach the same scope but became, from the outset, a matter of routine within the context of "anti-resistance operations." In that context the diaries of anatomist Hermann Voss, a professor at the Reich University in Posen, leave very little to the imagination. On June 15, 1941, Voss noted: "Yesterday I viewed the cellar for corpses and the cremation oven that is also located in the cellar. This oven was built to eliminate parts of bodies left over from dissection exercises. Now it serves to incinerate executed Poles. The gray car with the gray men—that is, SS men from the Gestapo—comes almost daily with material for the oven."[151] On September 30 Voss had good news: "Today I had a very interesting discussion with the chief prosecutor, Dr. Heise, about obtaining corpses for the anatomical institute. Königsberg and Breslau also get corpses from here. So many people are executed here that there are enough for all three institutes."[152]

VIII

While technical improvements in the murder methods were progressing apace, alongside common mass executions, at the top of the Nazi hierarchy hesitation between several possible "solutions" of the Jewish question did persist throughout the summer of 1941. On occupied Soviet territory, as we saw, the extermination was first aimed at Jews as carriers of the Soviet system, then at Jews as potential partisans and finally as hostile elements living in territories ultimately destined for German colonization: The three categories merged of course into one but did not apply, at least during the summer and the fall of 1941, to the entire European continent. In terms of mass murder the first phase of what was to become the "Final Solution of the Jewish Question in Europe" had started on Soviet territory, but it was probably not yet seen as part of an overall extermination plan of all European Jews. How, then, should we interpret the letter addressed by Göring to Heydrich on July 31, 1941?

"In completion of the task which was entrusted to you in the edict dated January 24, 1939, of solving the Jewish question by means of emigration or evacuation in the most convenient way possible, given the present conditions," Göring wrote, "I herewith charge you with making all the necessary preparations with regard to the organizational, practical and financial aspects for an overall solution [*Gesamtlösung*] of the Jewish question in the German sphere of influence in Europe." The letter went on: "Insofar as the competencies of other central organizations are affected, they are to cooperate with you. I further charge you with submitting to me promptly an overall plan of the preliminary organizational, practical and financial measures for the execution of the intended final solution (*Endlösung*) of the Jewish question."[153]

Göring's letter had been drafted by Heydrich and submitted to the Reichsmarschall for his signature; this much we know from Eichmann's deposition at his 1961 trial in Jerusalem.[154] Manifestly the document was meant to ensure Himmler's (and thus Heydrich's) authority on all matters pertaining to the fate of the Jews, either in regard to all ongoing operations on Russian territory or in regard to the expected deportations after victory in the East. It seems probable that, contrary to what had happened in March 1941 (as we saw in the previous chapter), this time Göring did not demand the inclusion of Rosenberg's name, *precisely in order to limit the new minister's ambitions.* The letter was meant to inform all those concerned that, in practical terms, the solution of the Jewish question was Himmler's domain (subject, of course, to Hitler's instructions.)

Göring's letter was also appropriately vague concerning any particular time frame, as it seems that Hitler still held to the view that the general evacuation of the Jews to northern Russia would take place only after the end of the campaign. This was confirmed by Eichmann in early August 1941, at a conference of high officials of the Propaganda Ministry convened to prepare Goebbels's forthcoming visit to his leader. "The Führer," Eichmann declared, "had rejected Obergruppenführer Heydrich's official request regarding evacuations [of Jews] during the war." Consequently Heydrich drew up a proposal for a partial evacuation of Jews from the main cities.[155] It was an idea submitted to Hitler when Goebbels met him at the Rastenburg headquarters on August 18, and—as we shall presently see—was also rejected.

According to Goebbels's diary entry of August 19 (in which he recorded the events of the previous day), Hitler agreed to the marking of the Jews in the Reich "with a large and clearly visible sign," but in regard to the deportations he merely indicated that the Jews would be evacuated from Berlin to the East, once the first means of transportation were available. "There [in the East], under a hard climate, they would be worked over."[156] On the next day (August 20), Goebbels again referred to his discussion with Hitler on the eighteenth and, this time, quoted him as promising that the Jews of Berlin would be evacuated "after the end of the Eastern campaign."[157] The two time frames were in fact two complementary elements of one conversation: The Jews would be deported after the victory in the East, when the first transportation means were to become available. According to Hitler's assessment of the military situation, this meant approximately mid-October 1941.

During the August 18 conversation, the Nazi leader again mentioned his "prophecy" regarding the price the Jews would pay for unleashing the war. "The Führer is convinced," Goebbels recorded, "that the prophecy he made in the Reichstag, namely that if Jewry succeeded once again in unleashing a world war, it would end with the extermination of the Jews, is being fulfilled. It [the prophecy] is being confirmed during these last weeks and months with what appears to be an almost uncanny certainty. In the East, the Jews are paying the bill; in Germany, they have already paid it in part and will have to pay more in the future. Their last refuge is North America; and there, either in the long or the short run, they will have to pay as well. Jewry is a foreign body among the cultured nations and its activity over the last three decades has been so devastating that the reaction of the peoples is absolutely understandable, necessary, and one could almost say naturally compelling. In any case, in the world that is coming, the Jews will not have many grounds for laughing. Today, in Europe, there is already in good part a united front against the Jews."[158]

Significantly, immediately after this tirade Hitler made mention of the eight points of the Roosevelt-Churchill declaration (the Atlantic Charter). Next, he once again returned to the Jewish issue: "And, regarding the Jewish Question one can ascertain today that somebody like Antonescu for example goes ahead in this matter even more radically than we did up to now. But, in this matter, I shall not rest until we too have exacted the ultimate consequences in regard to Jewry (*Aber ich werde nicht ruhen und nicht rasten, bis auch wir dem Judentum gegenüber die letzten Konsequenzen gezogen haben*)."[159]

Hitler's declarations to Goebbels were indeed highly threatening; still, it is notable that these threats remained vague. The Jews of Germany "will have to pay more in the future" could mean that after victory was achieved in the East, the Jews of Germany would be deported to northern Russia and there "under a hard climate, they would be worked over."

Mass death was implicit in Hitler's words; however, it is unlikely that at this stage the Nazi leader's declaration meant *organized, generalized, and immediate extermination.*[160]

IX

There is something at once profoundly disturbing yet rapidly numbing in the narration of the anti-Jewish campaign that developed in the territories newly occupied by the Germans or their allies. History seems to turn into a succession of mass killing operations and, on the face of it, little else. The chief of *Einsatzkommando 3* (belonging to *Einsatzgruppe A*), the notorious SS colonel Karl Jäger, reported, by September 10, 1941, the massacre of 76,355 persons, almost all Jews; by December 1, 1941 the number of the Jews murdered had reached 137,346. Two months later Stahlecker, the commander of *Einsatzgruppe A*, reported the results achieved by his unit (excluding mass executions in Riga): 218,050 Jews killed by February 1, 1942.[161] All there is to report, it seems, is a rising curve of murder statistics, in the North, the Center, the South, and the Extreme South. And yet another history unfolds, over short or longer periods from prewar years and decades to the last moment, literally to the edge of the execution pits.

For long periods before the beginning of the war, notwithstanding the political and social tensions to which we alluded, there were also close relations on an individual basis between the Jews and their gentile neighbors; at times, after the German conquest, some of these relations included the occupiers. Thus, in the smaller communities, the killers, whether local auxiliaries or Germans, often knew their victims, adding a further layer of horror to the massacres. In any case, each community, large or small, had an existence of its own, as did each *Judenrat*, each resistance organization, or, for that matter, every Jewish inhabitant. In some cases the "meeting of East and West" (Jews deported from central Europe and local Jews) in Lodz or in Minsk, for example, would create difficult problems and add yet another dimension to the history of the victims. As for the extermination of the ghetto populations, it took place at different sites, at different times, under different circumstances, all of importance and significance for historians—but it inexorably took place, before the arrival of any liberating force, even during the very last months of the war.

* * *

In Vilna a first *Judenrat* was established in July; most of its members were among the Jews murdered in early September. A second council was appointed under the chairmanship of Anatol Fried; the real authority, however, was increasingly in the hands of Jacob Gens, the Jewish police chief, who was to become the head of the council in July 1942. On September 6, 1941, the remaining Jews were ordered to move into the ghetto.

"They came before dawn today," Kruk recorded, "and gave half an hour to pack and take whatever you can. Flocks of wagons drove in and, right in front of the inhabitants who were already gathered in the courtyard, the last pieces of furniture were dragged out of their abandoned homes. . . . The mournful track of being driven out of your home into the ghetto lasts for hours."[162] Rudashevski also recorded the miserable exodus from the city into the ghetto: "The small number of Jews of our courtyard begin to drag the bundles to the gate. Gentiles are standing and taking part in our sorrow. . . . People are harnessed to bundles which they drag across the pavement. People fall, bundles scatter. Before me a woman bends under her bundle. From the bundle a thin string of rice keeps pouring over the street."[163]

The young diarist then went on to describe the first hours of ghetto life: "The newcomers begin to settle down, each in his tiny bit of space, on his bundles. Additional Jews keep streaming in constantly. We settle down in our place. Besides the four of us there are eleven persons in the room. The room is a dirty and stuffy one. It is crowded. The first ghetto night. We lay three together on two doors. . . . I hear the restless breathing of people with whom I have been suddenly thrown together, people who have just like us suddenly been uprooted from their homes."[164] The ghetto area, previously inhabited by some 4,000 people, was now home to 29,000 Jews.

In Kovno, after the first wave of killings, the remaining 30,000 Jews were expelled into the old Jewish suburb of Slobodka, across the river, where on July 10, 1941, a ghetto was officially established. The ghettoization was of course a German measure, but in Kovno, as in most cities and towns of Eastern Europe, it was fully supported by local authorities and populations. Abraham Tory, a former law office clerk and, from June 22, 1941, the chronicler of Kovno Jewry, noted a conversation between the newly appointed Lithuanian finance minister, Jonas Matulionis, and a Kovno Jewish personality, Jacob Goldberg: "The Lithuanians are divided on the Jewish question," Matulionis explained. "There are three main views: according to the most extreme view all the Jews in Lithuania must be exterminated; a more moderate view demands setting up a concentration camp where Jews will atone with blood and sweat for their crimes against the Lithuanian people. As for the third view? I am a practicing Roman Catholic; I—and other believers like me—believe that man cannot take the life of a human being like himself . . . but during the period of Soviet rule I and my friends realized that we did not have a common path with the Jews and never will. In our view, the Lithuanians and the Jews should be separated from each other and the sooner the better. For that purpose the Ghetto is essential. There you will be separated and no longer able to harm us. This is a Christian position."[165]

In late July the Germans ordered the appointment of a "chief Jew" (*Oberjude*). On August 4 delegates of the Jewish community met to choose their main representative. According to Tory, "There was one candidate nobody was prepared to let go, Dr. Elchanan Elkes." Elkes, a physician, argued that he lacked experience for the position. It was then that a member of the assembly, Rabbi Shmukler, rose and delivered a memorable speech: The Kovno Jewish community stands on the brink of disaster. . . . The German authorities insist that we appoint an *Oberjude,* but what we need is a "head of the community," a trustworthy public servant. The man most fitting for this position at this tragic moment is Dr. Elkes. We therefore turn to you and say: Dr. Elkes, you may be our *Oberjude* for whoever wants to regard you as such, but for us you will be our community leader. We all know that your path will be fraught with hardship and danger, but we will go with you all the way and may God come to our aid."[166]

Elkes accepted, but there was little he could do to fend off or mutigate the German decrees that from the outset descended on the ghetto inhabitants, mainly by way of SA captain Fritz Jordan, the spokesman of the town commander. One of the first edicts, issued on August 10, forbade Jews "to walk on the shores of the Viliga River" and also "to walk in the streets with their hands in their pockets."[167]

During these same days, at the end of August 1941, Klukowski took a week off and traveled to Warsaw. "I passed through the Jewish ghetto a few times," he noted in his diary. "It is almost impossible to figure out how something like this can happen. All points of entry are guarded by Germans. High brick walls around the perimeter divide the Jewish ghetto from the rest of the city. Traffic on the streets is rather heavy; many stores are open. That's how it looks from the streetcar. From a friend of mine I learned that the mortality rate in the ghetto is very high, especially among the poor Jews, who are living in terrible conditions."[168]

Nothing out of the ordinary daily misery happened on the other side of the walls that Klukowski saw from his streetcar. In August 1941, as may be recalled, the monthly death rate in the ghetto was stabilizing at around 5,500 persons. Thus, if the Germans had been aiming at a slow death of the population, tighter controls and some patience would have sufficed. Auerswald told Czerniaków as much on July 8: "The Jews should show good will by volunteering for labor. Otherwise the ghetto would be surrounded by barbed wire. There is plenty of it, the spoils of war captured in Russia. The ring will be tightened more and more and the whole population will slowly die out."[169] Outbreaks of typhus added their toll, and nobody was immune from the danger, not even the chairman himself: "Last night," he noted on July 10, "I spotted a louse on my nightshirt. A white, many-footed, revolting louse."[170]

And, against this background of desolation, none of the ongoing power struggles, none of the distrust, none of the hatreds of old lost any of their virulence—quite the contrary. Converted Jews whom the Germans had herded together with their "racial brethren" supposedly got the better positions in the ghetto hierarchy. In some cases they did (commander of the Jewish police, chairman of the health council, director of the ghetto hospital), as a result of their former training and professional ability. Such reasoning did not assuage the more militantly "Jewish" members of the community: "The rabbis are in an uproar," Czerniaków noted on July 2, "because Ettinger [Dr. Adam Ettinger, a former professor of criminology at Warsaw Free University], who was engaged as criminal counsel, is a baptized Jew."[171]

As for the converts themselves—1,761 ghetto inhabitants were registered as such, on January 1, 1941[172]—whether belonging to the prewar Christian community, the elite, or to the newly converted Jews usually less educated and of lower social background—most wished to distance themselves as much as possibly from the Jewish population.[173] Each of the two groups of converts congregated around its own church, led by its own priest (All Saints' Church and Father Godlewski for the old converts, Birth of the Holy Virgin Mary Church and Father Poplawski for the newly converted). Both Godlewski and Poplawski were themselves converted Jews and both were long-standing anti-Semites. The converts garnered a few advantages from their special situation (better organized and more systematic welfare assistance, some respite, during services and Christian holidays, from the pressure of everyday ghetto life, their own support group, and the right to be buried in a Christian cemetery outside the ghetto walls). But they could not escape the basic fact that for the Germans, they were full-fledged Jews and treated as such.[174] As one of the ghetto underground newspapers put it: "As a foreign entity, they were thrust into a dual exile in the ghetto. A decisive majority of the Jewish population maintains no contact with these 'Jews.' Foreign to the Jewish masses in their culture, hopes and yearnings, they share the Jews' suffering as uninvited partners in misfortune."[175]

The anti-Semitism displayed by some of the baptized Jews was virulent and unabashed: "I returned a visit to Reverend Poplawski who called on me at one time on the subject of assistance to the Christians of Jewish origins," Czerniaków recorded on July 24, 1941. He proceeded to tell me that he sees God's hand in being placed in the ghetto, that after the war he would leave as much of an anti-Semite as he was when he arrived there, and that the Jewish beggars (children) have considerable acting talents, even playing dead in the streets."[176]

For some of the Jewish children, the detestation was not reciprocal, and if it existed at all, it didn't preclude the wish to enjoy the peace and quiet of the All Saints' gardens. Thus a few children from Dr. Janusz Korczak's orphanage addressed a letter to Father Godlewski.

"To the Reverend Father, the Vicar of All Saints':

We kindly request the Rev. Father to grant us permission to come a few times to the church garden on Saturday, in the morning hours, early if possibly (6:30–10:00).

We long for a little air and greenery. It is stuffy and crowded where we are. We want to become acquainted and make friends with nature. We shall not damage the plants. Please don't refuse us. Signed: Zygmus, Sami, Hanka, Aronek."

The reply—if any—is not known.[177]

On June 6, 1941, Himmler had visited the Lodz ghetto. Accompanied by Rumkowski, the Reichsführer inspected the large tailoring workshop on Jakuba Street and was apparently satisfied with the work done there for the Wehrmacht. The following day the administration promised to raise the food supply for the inhabitants, but the promise was not kept.[178] On August 4 the Lodz chroniclers recorded "an extremely characteristic" court case. The "culprits" admitted having cut off part of a dead horse's hindquarters, as the carcass was already on a rubbish heap and doused with chloride before being buried.[179]

Since Lodz was part of the Reich, euthanasia in its old or new guise applied to the mental institution of the ghetto. In March 1940 some forty inmates had already been removed and murdered in a nearby forest.[180] In May 1941 a German medical commission made the rounds again, and on July 29 another removal took place. A German doctor was on hand for a last check. According to the chroniclers, Rumkowski was also present and pleaded that the twelve patients out of seventy considered as cured be released. The German physician, however, had decided that one of these patients [about to be evacuated] a Mr. Ilsberg, clearly an acquaintance of Rumkowski's, should be kept among those destined for death. No entreaties helped. "In spite of their mental confusion," the chroniclers recorded, "the patients realized what fate was in store for them. They understood, for example, why they had been injected with tranquilizers during the night.... They resisted in many cases.... A covered pick-up with a squad of five uniformed escorts came for the patients. Thanks to the selfless work done by the hospital staff, the loading of the tragic transport took place with exemplary order."[181]

Three days later the chroniclers added a postscript of sorts to this episode, which in many ways was a telling comment: "In spite of being aware of the sad fate which might be in store for mental patients, the families of people qualified for the hospital for the mentally ill are demanding that they be accepted. Since space is at such a painful premium and conditions are so deplorable in the ghetto, it is a form of deliverance for the families to have their mentally ill relatives in the hospital. Apparently the first patient since the most recent purge has already been admitted."[182]

In the larger ghettos the councils assumed that productivity was the only path to survival; if at all possible the ghetto should work for the Wehrmacht. Several council leaders, Ephraïm Barash in Białystok for example (or later Jacob Gens in Vilna), succeeded for a time to steer their ghetto along the work strategy, as Rumkowski did in Lodz. The acquisition of raw materials was one of the major hurdles. In Białystok the problem was solved by local ingenuity: Teams of organized ghetto ragpickers and scrap collectors filled part of the needs; rags were also smuggled in from the surrounding areas. Mostly, however, the Germans themselves were ready to supply the bulk of the materials to the factories working for the army. According to one of the speakers at a Białystok council meeting on August 28, 1941, "All that is necessary for industrial output is gladly furnished by the authorities."[183]

In the Białystok facilities working for the Wehrmacht, employment grew from 1,730 workers in March 1942 to 8,600 in July of that year. After the deportations of April 1943 to Treblinka, "productivization" was pushed to extremes, and approximately 43 percent of the total remaining ghetto population of 28,000 was employed in local industries.[184]

The German onslaught caught the forty-nine-year-old Jewish Polish novelist Bruno Schulz in Drohobycz in eastern Galicia, the town in which he was born and where he had spent his life.[184] Schulz, whose international fame spread only belatedly (after World War II), had been recognized on the Polish literary scene in the mid-1930s following the publication of two volumes of short stories, *Cinnamon Shops*, and soon thereafter, *Sanatorium under the Sign of the Hourglass*. The deeply unsettling dreamlike world of this pathologically shy and modest high school teacher found further expression in his drawings and paintings; there fairy tales mixed with representations of grotesque and distorted male figures groveling at the feet of splendid women who showed only sexual superiority, domination, and contempt for their "suitors."

It was Schulz the painter who, soon after the German occupation, caught the attention of SS Hauptscharführer Felix Landau, "coordinator of Jewish affairs" in Drohobycz.[186] Landau was the father of a young child who lived with him and with his mother, Landau's girlfriend. The SS Scharführer was a man of taste and apart from his well-known hobby—taking aim at Jewish workers from his window and, according to witnesses, rarely missing—he wanted Schulz to cover his walls with fairy-tale paintings for the child, and the walls of Gestapo offices with "frescoes." Schulz was paid in food and so it went, "peacefully," from July 1941 to the beginning of 1942.

Farther north, in Riga, it was one of the most eminent Jewish historians of his day, Simon Dubnow, who fell into German hands.[187] When the Germans occupied Latvia, in early July 1941, Dubnow was turning eighty-one. His multivolume *History of the Jews* and his *History of the Jews in Russia and Poland* had brought him worldwide fame and admiration. Dubnow had been a steady proponent of Jewish cultural autonomy in the Diaspora and thus was close to the Bund in many ways. Yet in the 1930s, in the face of the mounting dangers, he became increasingly critical of the radical anti-Zionist stance of the Bund. An article published in *Zukunft*, in June 1938, is indicative of Dubnow's position and mirrors the internal squabbling in so-called Jewish politics, despite the increasingly threatening world situation: "The Bund's greatest sin is its tendency toward isolation. . . . The indisputable failings of Zionism . . . should not prevent some joint actions. We have seen 'popular fronts,' coalitions of all progressive forces in a society, emerge in several European countries. Jewry also needs a 'popular front' to fight growing anti-Semitism and worldwide reaction."[188]

Soon after German occupation, the Jews of Riga were moved into a ghetto. The well-known Dubnow was tracked by the Gestapo: He tried to hide but was caught and jailed, released, and jailed again. Finally, physically broken, he was also moved to the ghetto.[189] In 1934 Dubnow had written a short article for the bulletin of the World Jewish Congress about the growing tragedy of European Jewry. The *Völkischer Beobachter* quoted Dubnow's words: "The house of Israel is in flames," adding: "That is just what we wanted!"[190]

X

The Jewish population of the USSR was quite well informed about the anti-Jewish persecutions in the Reich and, after September 1939, in

German-occupied Poland. Before the Hitler-Stalin pact the Soviet press reported abundantly about the Nazi anti-Semitic policies and atrocities. Then, from the end of August 1939 to June 22, 1941, official reporting stopped, but the stream of Jewish refugees who reached eastern Poland or the Baltic countries spread information about German behavior wherever they went.[191]

Within days following the German attack, the Soviet media resumed their description of the aggressors' anti-Jewish drive. Leaflets dropped by the Luftwaffe, and German broadcasts beamed at the Soviet Union, left no doubt, as we saw, about the centrality of the Jewish enemy within the Bolshevik system as the Germans perceived it, which, in their own words, they were intent on destroying. Yet it seems that not a few Jews, mainly "the little Jewish people," did not believe that their life under German occupation would be worse than before. Some allegedly even hoped that their existence would improve. Many stayed because family members were unable to join them in their flight or because they were loath to abandon a house and property usually acquired at great and lengthy effort.[192] When the Wehrmacht marched in, all such hopes and hesitations quickly disappeared; by then, however, it was too late.

Soon all Jews of the Soviet Union understood that their own survival now depended on the survival of their country. For many, identification with the Soviet regime was natural, unquestioned, often enthusiastic. From the outset the regime born from the 1917 revolution had appeared as a liberating force that freed the Jewish population from czarist oppression and territorial segregation in the Pale of Settlement, banned anti-Semitism, and offered equal opportunity to all. While the initial Soviet plans to foster the administrative autonomy and cultural identity of the country's national groups—and, within that framework, to encourage Yiddish culture and Jewish autonomy in Birobidzan—petered out in the early thirties, the country's stupendous modernization drive opened vast possibilities for the comparatively well educated Jewish citizens. By 1939 the Jews, who had become an increasingly urban population, although accounting for less than 2.0 percent of the general population, numbered around 7.5 percent of the middle-class professionals (engineers, accountants, physicians) and 13 percent of the student body, mainly in scientific fields. On the eve of World War II, Soviet Jews "constituted the best-educated ethnic group of the roughly 100 nationalities in the USSR."[193]

Simultaneously many Jews, mostly of the younger generation, abandoned their religious ties and enthusiastically embraced a system that allowed for complete assimilation and considerable social improvement.

Undoubtedly the percentage of Jews among the social and cultural elites of the Soviet Union was many times higher than their share of the country's population. This predominance was no less striking in the most sensitive areas of the state apparatus. According to historian Yuri Slezkine, "By 1934, when OGPU was transformed into the NKVD, Jews 'by nationality' constituted the largest single group among the 'leading cadres' of the Soviet secret police (37 Jews, 30 Russians, 7 Latvians, 5 Ukrainians, 4 Poles, 3 Georgians, 3 Belorussians, 2 Germans, and 5 assorted others)."[194] As for the high number of Bolshevik leaders of Jewish background (mainly among the first generation), it constituted an obvious fact that of course fueled anti-Semitic propaganda not only in the Reich but throughout the West. Even Lenin—and this was kept a state secret on Stalin's orders—had a Jewish grandfather.[195] The crucial point that anti-Semites missed, however, was the simple fact that Soviet Jews, at all levels of the system, were first and foremost Soviet citizens, devoted to the ideas and goals of the Soviet Union and oblivious of their own origins—until the German invasion. June 22, 1941, transformed many of these "non-Jewish Jews" (according to Isaac Deutscher's notorious formulation) into Soviet Jews suddenly aware of their origins—and proud of being Jewish:

"I grew up in a Russian city," the writer and journalist Ilya Ehrenburg proclaimed in a speech in August 1941: "My native language is Russian. I am a Russian writer. Now, like all Russians, I am defending my homeland. But the Nazis have reminded me of something else: my mother's name was Hannah. I am a Jew. I say this with pride. Hitler hates us more than anyone else. And that does us credit."[196]

In all areas of Soviet society, the Jews mobilized to the utmost to participate in the anti-Nazi struggle. Whatever one may think of Ehrenburg's twisted path in Stalin's Russia, his stream of articles, mainly in the Red Army's newspaper, *Krasnaya Zvezda*, galvanized the soldiers and the population.[197] One hundred sixty thousand Jewish members of the Red Army were decorated for bravery (half a million Jewish soldiers fought in the Soviet forces and two hundred thousand were killed or reported missing); fifty Jewish officers were elevated to the rank of general, and

123 received the highest military distinction: "Hero of the Soviet Union."[198] And yet Stalin dismissively told the Polish general Władysław Anders: "Jews are poor warriors."[199]

Soon, in the ghettos and forests of occupied Soviet territory, the first Jewish resistance groups would be organized. A few months later (mainly in the summer of 1942), some of these units, such as the group led by the Bielski brothers, acquired legendary fame.[200] And, in Minsk, on October 26, 1941, possibly one of the earliest and certainly one of the most famous Soviet resistance fighters, eighteen-year-old Masha Bruskina, was publicly hanged with two comrades; her Jewish origins, however, were unknown to the Germans and never mentioned in Soviet publications, either during the war or later.[201]

Stalin—whose postwar anti-Semitism had possibly started to show in the late thirties, and who, after 1945, launched his own massive anti-Jewish campaign—considered the Soviet Jews as useful intermediaries to the West, particularly to the United States, as long as the German threat was real. In his own mythic world the Soviet leader (like Hitler) vastly overrated the influence of American Jews. However, he did not overrate the tireless energy Jewish personalities called to meet in August 1941 (and who subsequently established the Jewish Antifascist Committee) would devote to mobilizing Western public support for the USSR from the second half of 1941 onward.[202] More than anything else, however, this political effort demonstrated, as did several other initiatives during these years, that the Jews as Jews, East and West, were essentially defenseless instruments, even in the hands of leaders belonging to the anti-Nazi coalition. The Erlich-Alter case was typical.

In the fall of 1939 the NKVD had arrested the two most prominent leaders of the *Bund*, Henryk Erlich [Dubnow's son-in-law] and Wiktor Alter, who had fled to the Soviet-occupied area of Poland. They were dragged from cell to cell, from interrogation to interrogation, and both were condemned to death shortly after the German attack of June 1941. In mid-September, however, they were released from prison. The Soviet change of attitude probably had several aims: to use both Bundist leaders in the anti-Nazi propaganda campaign; to impress the West, mainly British and American trade unionists, with Soviet liberalization; to reinforce the socialist wing of the Polish government-in-exile, which showed some readiness to come to an agreement with the USSR, notwithstanding continuing Soviet claims to the territories of eastern Poland.

Erlich and Alter remained in the Soviet Union but rapidly became involved in what could appear in Stalinist eyes as independent, Jewish-socialist political activity on an international scale. Thus, as the Soviet military situation improved, the two Bundist leaders were arrested again in December 1941. The British, obviously unwilling to put any strain on their relations with Moscow, declared the issue to be an internal Soviet matter. The Polish government-in-exile made only feeble attempts to intervene, as it hoped to use the anger of American Jewish labor organizations to bolster its own position in the territorial controversy with Stalin. And the American entry into the war overshadowed any "divisive" issues that could have been raised on the U.S. public scene. Erlich committed suicide in his Soviet jail in May 1942; Alter was executed in February 1943.[203]

XI

A few days after Goebbels received Hitler's authorization, the marking of the Reich's Jews with a "distinctive and clearly visible sign" was launched. A decree of September 1, 1941, issued by the Ministry of the Interior, ordered that from the nineteenth of that month all Jews of the Greater Reich and the Protectorate aged six and above should wear a yellow six-pointed star with the word *Jude* inscribed on it in (twisted) black letters. The palm-size star had to be sewed to the clothes, on the left side of the breast, at the height of the heart, so as to be fully visible when a Jew was in a public place (defined as any place where people not belonging to the family circle could be encountered).[204] From the same date (September 19), it was forbidden to Jews to leave their area or residence without police authorization, as well as to carry medals, honorary decorations, and any other kind of badge.[205]

The Jews had to obtain the stars at their community offices. On delivery they usually signed a receipt that also included an acknowledgment of the related ordinances: "I certify hereby the receipt of 1 Jewish Star," Gustav Israel Hamel from Baden Baden certified on September 20. "I am informed of the legal regulations regarding the display of the Jewish Star and of the prohibition to carry decorations, medals and any badges.

I also know that I am not allowed to leave my domicile without carrying a written authorization from the local police authorities. I undertake to handle the identification sign with attention and care and to ensure that when sewing it on clothing, the fabric that surrounds the sign will be turned over."[206]

In Goebbels's mind the star allowed for total control over the Jews once they left their home and thus protected Germans from dangerous contact, mainly from the spreading of rumors and defeatist talk. But, as in the case of most anti-Jewish measures, the additional intent was the humiliation and degradation of the victims, and, of course, a further opening for the ongoing anti-Jewish propaganda campaign. Dietrich's *Tagesparole* of September 26 was explicit: "On the occasion of the identification of the Jews there are possibilities to deal with the theme in the most diverse ways, to explain to the German people the necessity of these measures and mainly to point to the harmfulness of the Jews. From tomorrow on the information service will publish material that offers proof of the harm the Jews inflicted on Germany and the fate they planned and still plan for it" [the obvious reference here is to the Kaufman story and to the Diewerge pamphlet, which, as we saw, included commentary on excerpts of Kaufman's book].[207]

"Today, the Jew's star," Klemperer wrote on September 19: "Frau Voss has already sewn it on, intends to turn her coat back over it. Allowed? I reproach myself with cowardice. Yesterday Eva wore out her feet on the pavements and must now go shopping in town and cook afterwards. Why? Because I am ashamed. Of what? From Monday I intend to go shopping again. By then we shall certainly have heard what effect *it* has" (Klemperer's wife, Eva, not being Jewish, did not have to wear the star).[208] How did the German population react?

As we saw, the opinion summaries of the SD for the early summer indicated widespread anti-Jewish hostility. Newsreels showing the arrest of Jews, their toil as forced laborers, and even lynch scenes from Riga, apparently received loud approval from movie audiences.[209] As such footage regularly emphasized the Jewish "racial traits," audiences expressed their disgust and often wondered aloud what should be done with these "hordes."[210]

Did the introduction of the star change these attitudes? According to a September 26 SD report from Westphalia, the new measure was often greeted with satisfaction; criticism was directed, rather, at the existence of exceptions. Why were the Jewish spouses of Aryans exempted from wearing the tag? As the saying went, there were now "Aryan Jews" and "non-Aryan Jews."[211] An SD report from the previous day (from the same area) mentioned the general opinion that the Jews should also wear the star on the back of their clothes for better visibility: It would compel those still remaining in Germany to "disappear."[212]

And yet, many witnesses also recorded different reactions. On September 20 Klemperer described what happened to Frau Kronheim: "The latter took the tram yesterday—front platform. The driver: Why was she not sitting in the car? Frau Kronheim is small, slight, stooped, her hair completely white. As a Jewess she was forbidden to do so. The driver struck the panel with his fist: 'What a mean thing!' Poor comfort."[213] The most extraordinary expression of sympathy was recorded on November 25: "Frau Reichenbach . . . told us a gentleman had greeted her in a shop doorway. Had he not mistaken her for someone else?—'No, I do not know you, but you will now be greeted frequently. We are a group 'who greet the Jew's star.' "[214] Yet, exactly a month beforehand, on October 25, Klemperer had written: "I always ask myself: Who among the 'Aryan' Germans is really untouched by National Socialism? The contagion rages in all of them, perhaps it is not contagion, but basic German nature."[215]

It seems indeed that such expressions of sympathy were not infrequent: "The population in its majority disapproves of this defamation," Elisabeth Freund, a Jewish woman from Berlin, wrote in her memoir.[214] She noted incidents very similar to those mentioned by the Dresden diarist: "I am greeted on the street with special politeness by complete strangers, and in the streetcar ostentatiously a seat is freed for me, although those wearing a star are allowed to sit only if no Aryan is still standing. But sometimes guttersnipes call out abusive words after me. And occasionally Jews are said to have been beaten up. Someone tells me of an experience in the city train. A mother saw that her little girl was sitting beside a Jew: 'Lieschen, sit down on the other bench, you don't need to sit beside a Jew.' At that an Aryan worker stood up, saying: 'And I don't need to sit next to Lieschen.' "[217]

A report sent by the United States consul general in Berlin Leland Morris, to the State Department, on September 30, confirmed the information described by Klemperer and Freund. "It may be noted that a very large proportion of Berliners have shown embarrassment and even sympathy rather than satisfaction at the display of Jewish badges under the recent decree. This may be due to the fact that the Jewish Question as a domestic issue has been deliberately kept out of the public notice since before the war and most ordinary people had willingly tried to forget it. Disapproval of this measure is so general that one of the justifications advanced for it . . . by those responsible is that Germans in the United States are obliged to wear a swastika with the letter 'G.' This preposterous lie is passed from mouth to mouth but finds little credence."[218]

In fact the most diverse sources confirmed the disapproval of the badge among part of the German population.[219] In David Bankier's nuanced assessment, it was the visibility of the persecution that caused so many Germans to react as they did, at least for a while: "As long as anonymous Jews were persecuted, the population could remain emotionally distant from the moral consequences of the affliction they had helped to cause, easily coming to terms with persecution since shame and guilt were not involved. Labeling the victim, however, made him an accusing public witness who testified to the cost of conformity and adjustment in a murderous system. . . . These disturbing feelings obviously did not last long. As had happened with other measures, the penalties exacted from those who sympathized with Jews plus mounting insensibility to what became a common sight, produced increasing apathy and insensitivity."[220]

Yet we also have to accept the possibility of an ongoing dissonance in attitudes and reactions, as was bluntly stated in a detailed report sent to the Foreign Ministry in Stockholm by Arvid Richert, the Swedish minister in Berlin, on October 31, 1941. After mentioning the "noteworthy courtesy" of the German population in its attitude to the Jews who had received their "decoration," he expressed a warning: "In order to avoid any misunderstanding, I would like to add that even if many Germans dislike the draconian measures against the Jews, anti-Semitism appears to be deeply rooted in the people."[221]

Oral history confirms both the negative reaction of part of the population to the star and the approval of other Germans; it also confirms that, once the star was introduced, many Germans were astonished at the number of Jews still living in their midst, thus confirming a finding of the SD. According to Eric Johnson's and Karl-Heinz Reuband's study, it seems that "older people disapproved of the star much more than younger people, and that Catholics and women were more opposed to the measures than Protestants and men, as were people from urban than rural areas and midsize towns. . . . In general, . . . the pattern we found in this regard closely resembles that of Nazi supporters [analyzed in another part of the study.] Those who were least supportive of National Socialism were least positively disposed to the introduction of the Jew's star." The authors confirm that among critics of the measure, indifference took over after a while: "For a couple of days, one swallowed hard," as a respondent put it, and then one accepted it. After all, "There wasn't any changing it."[222]

In fact all interpretations seem to confirm the fact that the negative reactions to the introduction of the star among part of the German population were ephemeral and did nothing to change overall acceptance and passivity. As for the Jews, not all felt unmixed gratitude at the early shows of compassion. Ruth Kluger, a Jewish girl of twelve in the late fall of 1941, born and living in Vienna, was given an orange by a stranger, as the subway they were riding entered a tunnel (for the gesture to pass unnoticed). "By the time we were back in the daylight, I had stowed it in my bag," she wrote in her memoirs, "and gratefully looked at the stranger, who looked down on me with a benevolent smile. But my feelings were mixed. . . . I didn't like the role of the passive victim who could be comforted with a small demonstration of kindness. . . . An orange, no matter what it stood for, was no help as my life became progressively more restricted and impoverished. It was a sentimental gesture, and I was a prop for the donor's good intentions."[223] The memory of such mixed feelings in a twelve-year-old, may of course have been influenced by the events that followed: A year later, in September 1942, Ruth and her mother, a nurse and a physical therapist, were on their way to Theresienstadt; later on they would be sent to Auschwitz. The father, a physician, had performed an abortion on an Aryan woman; he had to flee to Italy, then to France, where he was arrested, deported to the Baltic countries, and murdered.

Whether as an afterthought in the wake of the star decree or as an early sign of decisions to come, on September 11, 1941, the Gestapo disbanded the Kulturbund. Most of its cultural activities had already been forbidden beforehand. Thus in July, the association's musicians met for the last time to celebrate Verdi; then, their instruments were confiscated and handed out to SA and SS units, the pianos were sent to Nazi welfare organizations and Wehrmacht sanatoriums, and their records were recycled by the German record industry.[224] In Germany the last remains of authorized Jewish cultural activity had been snuffed out.

XII

After the proclamation of the new statute of June 1941, the Vichy government forged ahead: On July 22, "Aryanization" was introduced in the nonoccupied zone according to the same criteria and methods used in the north. Businesses were liquidated or put under "French" control, assets were seized, and the proceeds were deposited in a special government bank, the Caisse des Dépôts et Consignations.[225]

For Darlan and Vallat this did not suffice. On the day the June statute was published, the registration of all Jews (according to the new definition) in the Vichy zone was mandated. According to Vallat's estimate, approximately 140,000 Jews had been registered by the spring of 1942, although the head of the national office of statistics, René Carmille, had reached the much lower total of 109,000.[226] The exact number of Jews living in the Vichy zone at that time is not clear.[227] More immediately ominous was Darlan's order of December 1941, to register all Jews who had entered France after January 1, 1936 (even those who had in the meantime acquired French citizenship); this identification was to become an essential element of the Franco-German agreements concerning the round-ups and deportations that were to come.[228]

On the morrow of the June statute, Lambert noted that Pétain had met Helbronner and told him that all the measures had been ordered by the Germans. The marshal supposedly commented: "These are horrible people!" (*Ce sont des gens épouvantables!*)[229] After some further remarks about the new measures, Lambert naively added: "One gets the feeling that even the details of the law have been inspired or dictated by the German authorities—as the Reich now considers the way France will solve the Jewish question as a test of its sincerity in the policies of collaboration."[230] Lambert did not yet dare to acknowledge that the initiative was French and the anti-Jewish decrees were indeed meant as a proof—but one volunteered by Vichy—of its will to collaborate.

And while, during the summer and fall of 1941, the situation of the Jews in France looked more precarious by the month, the Germans made further attempts to convince the French population that the struggle against Jewry was a vital necessity. On September 5 a major anti-Semitic exhibition opened its doors in Paris. Officially it was organized by Sézille's "Institute for the Study of Jewish Questions": Thus, it appeared as a French exhibition organized by a purely French institution. On the seventh Biélinky commented: "An anti-semitic exhibition has just opened at the Palais Berlitz, on the Boulevards; a blustering advertisement campaign promotes it in the newspapers and on the walls. A Jewish female friend who does not look semitic went to the opening and heard in the crowd: 'here at least, one is sure not to meet any Jews.' "[231] The exhibition remained open through January 3, 1942, and drew more than three hundred thousand visitors (most of whom had to buy tickets), with indeed a few Jews among them. Apparently some of the Jewish visitors even dared to express open criticism.[232]

The Germans however, did not keep at propaganda campaigns. On August 20, 1941, on German instructions, the Paris police arrested a further 4,230 Jews, mainly in the eleventh arrondissement; they were sent to Drancy, the newly established concentration camp near the French capital. This second roundup was probably undertaken in reprisal for the anti-German demonstrations organized in the city on August 13 by communist youth organizations; the police had supposedly noticed a substantial number of Jews among the demonstrators (the French police had ready lists of these Jews, as many had served in the French army in 1939–40). This time some French Jews, mainly communists, were also arrested.[233]

In the autumn further attacks against German military personnel drew reprisals, but mainly against communists (Jewish or not) at first. Even the execution of fifty hostages after the killing of the field commander of Nantes, Lt. Col. Karl Holtz, on October 20, 1941, did not specifically target Jews.[234] For Heydrich, Stülpnagel's anti-Jewish reprisals were too mild, and it is against this background that French pro-Nazi militants perpetrated bomb attacks against three Paris synagogues on October 3, on Knochen's instigation.[235] Stülpnagel, soon informed of the origin of the attacks, lodged a complaint with the OKH against Heydrich, but to no avail. The commander in chief had no choice but to escalate his own anti-Jewish reprisals.

On November 28, 1941, another attack against German soldiers took place. This time Stülpnagel proposed to the OKH that, henceforth, the reaction should be the mass arrest of French Jews and their deportation to the East. On December 12, 743 Jewish men, mainly French and mostly belonging to the middle classes, were seized by the German police and sent to Compiègne, a camp under direct German command. Their deportation was scheduled for the following weeks; it was delayed until March 1942, when this group and additional Jewish prisoners (1,112 in all) were deported to Auschwitz.[236] Thus, in France, it was the Army High Command that put into effect increasingly drastic anti-Jewish measures. While the execution of French hostages caused qualms, the deportation of Jews to their death (a fate increasingly known by the upper echelons of the Wehrmacht in Paris)[237] was taken in stride and implemented by the largely non-Nazi military elite.

Simultaneously with the multiplication of anti-Jewish measures, with the arrests and the early deportations, Dannecker exercised growing pressure on the Jewish organizations to transform the "coordination committee" into a full-fledged Jewish Council. The Germans expected Vichy to take the initiative of imposing the new institution.[238] In the fall of 1941 it became obvious to the Jewish leaders, natives and foreigners alike, that they would have to accept the *Diktat*. Yet, the common fate imposed upon all did not heal the rift between the two communities.[239] Against this background of internecine squabbles, a group of French Jewish personalities—among whom Lambert came to play an increasingly important role—decided to go along with Vichy's decisions and to participate in repeated consultations with Vallat, against the will of the Consistoire and that of the more activist elements of the "Federation."[240] On November 29, 1941, Vallat signed the decree establishing the Union Générale des Israélites de France. On January 9, 1942, the executive boards of the UGIF-North (occupied zone) and UGIF-South (Vichy zone) were officially appointed. De facto, Lambert became the dominant personality of UGIF-South.

It has been argued that anti-Jewish measures were less readily applied in the countries and areas of Western Europe under direct German military authority than in those under civilian Nazi rule. While this was not the case in occupied France, it seems that in Belgium the commander in chief of the Wehrmacht, Gen. Alexander von Falkenhausen, was indeed reticent in regard to measures that could create unrest in the population. Yet the usual anti-Jewish measures enacted in Holland and in France were imposed in Belgium at approximately the same time.

Thus, on October 28, 1940, the military administration imposed a "Statut des juifs," similar to the French and Dutch ones, on the 65,000 to 75,000 Jews living in Belgium at the time.[241] Registration was ordered, identity cards marked, Jewish businesses listed, Jewish officials dismissed, Jews expelled from the legal professions and from journalism, as elsewhere in the West. In the spring of 1941 the registration of all Jewish property followed, as well as further segregation measures as implemented in neighboring Holland, and approximately at the same time. In the fall of that same year a Jewish Council, the Association des Juifs en Belgique (AJB), was imposed; a few days later the UGIF was established in France.[242]

There were some differences, however, between the situation of the Jews of Belgium and those of Holland and France. Whereas two-thirds of the Jews of Holland and half of the Jews of France were native or naturalized citizens in 1940, only 6 percent of the Jews of Belgium were Belgian citizens. Whereas in the three Western countries, small pro-Nazi movements had damaged Jewish property and attacked individual Jews once German presence eased the way, only in Belgium did large-scale pogromlike riots take place, on April 14 and 17, 1941. In Antwerp, several hundred militants of the VNV [Vlaamsch National Verbond] set fire to synagogues and to the chief rabbi's house on Easter Monday after attending the screening of *Jud Süss*. And, as 1941 was coming to an end, neither the Belgian church dignitaries nor the resistance movements took a strong stand against the German anti-Jewish measures or against the violence of the Belgian (mostly Flemish) extreme Right. A liberal underground publication did protest against the Antwerp riots, concluding: "Dear readers—Do not think that we Belgians are pro-Jewish. No, far from it. Yet, even a Jew is a human being."[243]

After the end of the Babi Yar massacre, a few elderly Jews (witnesses mention that there were nine of them) returned to Kiev and sat by the

Old Synagogue. Nobody dared to approach or leave food or water for them, as this could mean immediate execution. One after another the Jews died until only two remained. A passerby went to the German sentry standing at the corner of the street and suggested shooting the two old Jews instead of letting them also starve to death. "The guard thought for a moment and did it."[244]

CHAPTER V

September 1941–December 1941

On November 12, 1941, Himmler ordered Friedrich Jeckeln, the HSSPF Ostland, to murder the approximately 30,000 Jews of the Riga ghetto.

On the eve of the operation, on November 29, the able-bodied Jews were separated from the bulk of the ghetto population.[1] On November 30, in the early-morning hours, the trek from the ghetto to the nearby Rumbula forest began. Some 1,700 guards were ready, including around 1,000 Latvian auxiliaries. In the meantime several hundred Soviet prisoners had dug six huge pits in the sandy terrain of Rumbula.[2]

Jews trying to escape the evacuation were killed on the spot—inside houses, on stairways, in the streets. As, group after group, the ghetto inhabitants reached the forest, a tightening gauntlet of guards drove them toward the pits. Shortly before approaching the execution site, the Jews were forced to dispose of their suitcases and bags, take off their coats, and finally remove their clothes. Then the naked victims descended into the pit by means of an earthen ramp, lay facedown on the ground, or over the bodies of the dying and the dead, and were shot in the back of the head with a single bullet from a distance of about two meters.

Jeckeln stood on the edge of the pits surrounded by a throng of SD, police, and civilian guests. *Reichskomissar* Lohse paid a short visit, and some police commanders were brought from as far away as the Leningrad front.[3] Twelve marksmen working in shifts shot the Jews throughout the entire day. The killing stopped sometime between five p.m. and seven p.m.; by then about fifteen thousand Jews had been murdered.[4]

A week later, on December 7 and 8, the Germans murdered almost the entire remaining half of the ghetto population. The RSHA's report no. 155 of January 14, 1942, summed up the overall outcome: "The number of Jews who remained in Riga—29,500—was reduced to 2,500 as a result of the *Aktion* carried out by the Higher SS and Police leader Ostland."[5]

The historian Simon Dubnow, who lay ill, had been overlooked during the first massacre. The second time he was caught in the dragnet. The sick and feeble ghetto inhabitants were brought to the execution area in buses; as Dubnow could not board the bus fast enough, one of the Latvian guards shot him in the back of the head. The next day he was buried in a mass grave in the ghetto. According to rumor—fast turning into legend—on his way to the bus, Dubnow repeated: "People, do not forget; speak of this, people; record it all."[6] A few months later, on June 26, 1942, SS Obersturmführer Heinz Ballensiefen, head of the Jewish Section of Amt VII (research) in the RSHA, informed his colleagues that in Riga his men had "secured" (*sichergestellt*) "about 45 boxes containing the archive and library of the Jewish historian Dubnow."[7]

Himmler continued to worry about the heavy stress that these mass killings imposed upon his men. On December 12, 1941, he once again issued secret instructions in this regard: "It is the sacred obligation of the higher SS leaders and commanders to see to it personally that none of our men who have to fulfill this heavy duty, become brutalized. . . . This will be achieved by keeping the strictest discipline in the performance of the official duties and by comradely evening gatherings after days filled with these difficult obligations. However, these comradely gatherings should never end with abuse of alcohol. During such evenings, as far as conditions allow, one should sit together around the table and eat in the best German domestic tradition; moreover, these evenings should be devoted to music, to lectures and to introducing our men into the beautiful domains of German spiritual and emotional life."[8]

On the day of the first massacre of the Riga Jews, in the early-morning hours, a transport of 1,000 Jews from Berlin had arrived at a suburban railway station. Jeckeln did not deem it appropriate to send these new arrivals into a ghetto in full upheaval, from where the trek to Rumbula would be starting at any moment. The solution was at hand: The Berlin

Jews were transported straight from the station to the forest and killed on the spot.

The deportees transported from the Reich to Riga were but one group among others who, since October 15, following a sudden decision taken by Hitler, were being sent off from cities in Germany and the Protectorate to ghettos in former Poland or the Ostland. Just a month earlier, Hitler had told Goebbels that the deportation of the Jews of Germany (and, implicitly, of all European Jews) would take place after the victory in Russia and would be directed to the Russian Far North. What could have triggered the Nazi leader's sudden initiative?

I

The precise date of Hitler's decision about the deportation of the Jews from Germany remains undetermined. Some historians have argued that Hitler reached his decision on September 17. The following day, in a letter to Greiser, with copies to Heydrich and to Wilhelm Koppe, the HSSPF in the Warthegau, Himmler summed up the "Führer's wish": "The Führer wishes the Altreich and the Protectorate to be cleared of and freed from Jews from west to east as soon as possible. Consequently, I shall endeavor, this year if possible and initially as a first stage, to transport the Jews from the Altreich and the Protectorate to those eastern territories that became part of the Reich two years ago and then deport them even farther eastward next spring. My intention is to take approximately 60,000 Jews of the Altreich and the Protectorate to spend the winter in the Litzmannstadt ghetto, which, I have heard, still has available capacity. I ask you not only to understand this step, which will certainly impose difficulties and burdens on your Gau, but to do everything in your power to support it in the interest of the Reich. SS Gruppenführer Heydrich, whose task is to carry out the transfer of the Jews, will contact you in good time, directly or through SS Gruppenführer Koppe."[9]

Himmler's letter to Greiser demonstrates that Hitler's decision was sudden and that nothing was ready for its implementation. To deport 60,000 to 80,000 Jews to the overcrowded Lodz ghetto was manifestly impossible. The promise that these Jews would be sent farther eastward in the spring was clearly an improvised commitment, devoid of practical significance, meant only to preempt any protests from Greiser or from the Lodz authorities. Thus the immediate context of the Nazi leader's decision becomes even more puzzling.

Starting the evacuation in the West of the Reich points to one of Hitler's possible motives: persistent demands from the *Gauleiter* of western and northwestern Germany for housing, as a result of the damages inflicted by British bombings. A particularly pressing request was addressed directly to Hitler by Hamburg Gauleiter Karl Kaufmann on September 16 after a heavy British raid on the city, on the previous day.[10] Such demands were reinforced by Goebbels's constant insistence upon "cleansing Berlin of its Jews."

Hitler's sudden decision has mainly been attributed to information about Stalin's order to deport the entire population of Volga Germans to Siberia.[11] Rosenberg's adjutant, Otto Bräutigam, who brought the news to Hitler's headquarters on September 14, was told that the Führer attached the greatest importance to this information.[12] After consulting with Ribbentrop on September 16, Hitler—according to this interpretation—made up his mind on the seventeenth. Yet we know that six days beforehand Goebbels had already mentioned Stalin's order in his diary, and, on the following day, the propaganda chief recorded the worldwide echo stirred by the deportation.[13] Thus Hitler could hardly have been impressed on September 14 by information he undoubtedly received nearly a week earlier and to which, until then, he had not reacted. Moreover, he certainly knew that deporting the Jews of Germany to avenge the Volga Germans would hardly impress somebody of Stalin's ilk. The Volga Germans could, of course, have been a convenient pretext for a decision taken earlier for an entirely different reason: Roosevelt's steady efforts to involve the United States in the war.

The Nazi leader had more than enough information concerning the direct assistance Roosevelt was providing Great Britain; the Churchill-Roosevelt meeting in August 1941 underscored the foundations of what had virtually become an alliance. And Berlin was following with no less concern Roosevelt's determination to keep Stalin willing and capable to fight on. The Germans knew of Roosevelt's unofficial envoy Harry Hopkins's mission to Moscow and of Roosevelt's decision to send planes and tanks directly from American assembly lines to the Soviet forces, even before filling the U.S. Army's immediate needs.[14] All this unquestionably tallied with Hitler's belief that the Jews were the threatening force behind

Roosevelt. How else could one explain the readiness of the leader of world capitalism to rush aid and assistance to the threatened fortress of Bolshevism?

In January 1939 Hitler had threatened the Jewish "warmongers" in Paris, London, and mainly Washington with his notorious "prophecy" in order to dissuade the democracies from intervening in the incipient Polish crisis. In January 1941 the Nazi leader took up his prophecy again (albeit in slightly different terms), possibly as a reaction to Roosevelt's reelection and mainly to his fireside chat about the United States becoming "the great arsenal of democracy." As speeches and threats did not seem to deflect the American president from his course, the Nazi leader may have thought that direct and highly menacing steps against a closely scrutinized Jewish community, the Jews of Germany (with any number of American correspondents posted in Berlin), would have some effect on Roosevelt's "Jewish entourage." The German Jews became, concretely and visibly, hostages on the brink of a dire fate if the United States moved further toward war.

In July 1940 Fritz Rademacher of the Foreign Ministry had expressed the same idea regarding the Madagascar plan: "The Jews [in Madagascar] will remain in German hands as a pledge of the future good conduct of the members of their race in America."[15] In March 1941, the Foreign Ministry once again linked measures against Jews in Germany to American policy; it demanded that a new decree (then in preparation) about the loss of citizenship and expropriation of Jews leaving the Reich be announced on March 26, the day the Lend-Lease Bill was to take effect.[16]

The need to put pressure on Roosevelt may have seemed increasingly urgent to Hitler during the first days of September 1941. On September 4, a German submarine, *U-652*, dangerously trailed by the U.S. destroyer *Greer*—and attacked by British aircraft guided by the *Greer*—attempted to torpedo the American vessel. Both the *Greer* and *U-652* escaped unharmed, but a week later, on September 11, Roosevelt gave a distorted account of the incident and announced the "shoot-on-sight" policy, a major American step on the path to war with Germany.[17] "The time for active defense has come," the president declared in a radio speech, and two days later American naval forces received the order to shoot on sight at all Axis ships encountered within the American "neutrality zone" (unilaterally defined by the United States and extending to the mid-Atlantic).[18]

One may assume that, in Hitler's mind, the counterthreat could work both ways: Either the fate menacing the Jews of Germany would eventually stop Roosevelt in his tracks (due to Jewish pressure) *or*, if Roosevelt and the Jews were bent on war with the Reich—that is, if total war was in the offing—the most dangerous internal enemy would already have been expelled from German territory.

Hitler's decision may, in fact, have been taken in the early days of September. On September 2, Himmler was the Nazi leader's guest for lunch. Other issues were on the agenda, but later that same day, the Reichsführer met his delegate in the General Government, Krüger, and discussed with him the deportation of Jews from the Reich ("*Judenfrage-Aussiedlung aus dem Reich*"). Two days later, as the *Greer* incident was unfolding, the Reichsführer again met with Hitler and, later in the evening, had a discussion with Koppe, his man in the Warthegau.[19] The main practical obstacles were Frank's uncompromising opposition to further transports of Poles and Jews into the General Government, and the overcrowding of the Lodz ghetto.[20]

Hitler hesitated for some three additional weeks, as the attack against Moscow unfolded, probably in order to assess the difficulties that the deportation trains could be adding to the already overburdened supply routes from the Reich to the East. In early October, after the German victories in Vyasma and Briansk, the decision was finalized: The deportations could begin.[21] When the president of the Lodz district, Friedrich Uebelhoer, prodded by the city mayor, Werner Ventzki, dared to protest to Himmler against the forthcoming influx of Jews and even accused Eichmann of providing false information about the situation in the ghetto, Himmler sent him a sharp rebuff.[22]

On October 15, the first transport left Vienna for Lodz; it was followed by transports from Prague and Luxembourg on the sixteenth, and from Berlin, on the eighteenth. By November 5 twenty transports carrying 19,593 Jews completed the first phase.[23] In the meantime, on October 23, Eichmann and his men reviewed the reports about the first deportations and added some administrative steps and practical measures to the existing procedures.[24] Then, on November 8, the second phase started and lasted until mid-January 1942. This time twenty-two transports with some 22,000 Jews in all were headed further east, to the Ostland, to Riga, Kovno, and Minsk (upon Heydrich's suggestion, as we shall see further on).[25] Of the transports destined for Riga, five were rerouted to Kovno; none of these 5,000 deportees ever set foot in the ghetto: Upon their arrival, they were immediately transferred to fort IX and shot in two batches on November 25 and 29.[26] A month beforehand, on October 28, approximately 10,000 inhabitants of the Kovno ghetto had been murdered. In Minsk 13,000 local Jews were exterminated on November 7, and a further group of 7,000 on November 20. Clearly the mass slaughters of October and November 1941 were intended to make space for the new arrivals from the Reich. And, as we saw, at times some of the new arrivals were killed on reaching their destination.

Soon the Reichsführer was receiving a growing number of complaints about the inclusion of *Mischlinge* and decorated war veterans in the transports. And, as information about the Kovno massacres spread, Himmler precipitously ordered, on Sunday, November 30, that "no liquidation" of the Jews deported from Berlin to Riga "should take place."[27] The order reached Riga too late, and an irate SS chief threatened Jeckeln with "punishment" for acting on his own.[28] During the following months mass executions of Jews deported from Germany stopped. It was but a brief respite.

II

Typhoon, the Wehrmacht's offensive against Moscow, was launched on October 2; it was Germany's last chance to win the war in the East before the onset of the winter. For a few days victory again seemed within reach. As in July, Hitler's euphoric state of mind was shared by the OKW and also by Fedor von Bock, the commander of Army Group Center, the main force advancing on the Soviet capital. On October 4, when the Nazi chief returned to Berlin for a major speech at the Sportpalast, Goebbels noted: "He looks at his best and is in an exuberantly optimistic frame of mind. He literally exudes optimism. . . . The Führer is convinced that if the weather remains halfway favorable, the Soviet army will be essentially demolished in fourteen days." And, on October 7: "It goes well on the front. The Führer continues to be extraordinarily optimistic."[29]

Hitler's mood during those days was indeed so exuberant, his declarations about the collapse of the Red Army and of the Soviet Union so peremptory, that on October 13 press chief Dietrich could announce the momentous news: "Militarily, this war has been decided. What still remains to be done is essentially of a political nature, both internally and externally. At some stage, the German armies in the East will stop their advance and a border determined by us will be drawn; it will protect the greater Europe and the European bloc community of interests led by Germany, against the East."[30] Dietrich was in fact merely repeating his Führer's assessment and, so it seems, that of the army itself.

All over Europe, Jews were following the military news like an anxious choir, in despair at first, with hope somewhat later, then with exaltation at the end of the year. "Hitler is reported to have given a speech in which he said that he has begun a gigantic offensive in the east," Sierakowiak noted on October 3. "I wonder how it will develop. It looks like this one will be as victorious as all the previous ones."[31] And on October 10: "The Germans have supposedly broken the Russian front with their 3 million-man army and are marching on Moscow. Hitler has personally taken command on the front. So it's to be another successful offensive. The Germans are really invincible. We'll rot in this ghetto for sure."[32] A few days later Kaplan became the voice of despair: "The Nazis continue to advance on the Eastern front," he recorded on October 18, "and have reached the gates of Moscow. The city is still fighting desperately but its fate has been decided—it will surely be captured by the Nazis. . . . And when Moscow falls, all the capitals of Europe will be under the Nazi rule. . . . A Nazi victory means complete annihilation, morally and materially, for all the Jews of Europe. The latest news has left even the most hopeful among us dejected. It seems this war will go on for years."[33] On October 25, Klemperer just mentioned laconically: "German advance continues in Russia, even though the winter has begun."[34]

Other diarists were somewhat less pessimistic. Thus, Willy Cohn, the former high school teacher from Breslau, noted, on October 11, that all the special victory announcements of the previous day looked like "advance laurels" (*Vorschusslorbeeren*) and added: "After all, the whole world belongs to the others!"[35] On October 20, Cohn mentioned the repeal of the "Neutrality Law" by Congress, and concluded, "This means, in the short as the long run, the entry of the United States in the war."[36]

As for Sebastian, he noticed slight nuances in the German communiqués; after recording the news of victory in the East, as trumpeted by German and Romanian newspapers on October 10, he noted on the next day: "A slight, almost imperceptible lowering of the tone in today's papers. 'The Hour of Collapse Is Near,' said one headline in *Universal.* Yesterday the collapse was already an established fact. But the fact is that fighting is still taking place."[37] Among Jews farther west, opinions may have been more starkly divided: "The events in Russia divide the Jews into two groups," Biélinky noted on October 14. "There are those who consider Russia as already defeated and who hope for some generous gesture on the part of the victor. The others keep a robust faith in Russian resistance."[38]

Strangely enough the misperception of the military situation on the German side went on, particularly at army headquarters, until early November. Halder, the cool planner, envisioned an advance of 200 kilometers east of Moscow, the conquest of Stalingrad, and the capture of the Maykop oil fields, no less. It was actually Hitler who brought his generals' fantasies down to earth and back to the more modest goal of taking Moscow.[39] On November 1, the Nazi leader ordered the resumption of the offensive against the Soviet capital.[40] By then, however, stiffening Soviet resistance, lack of winter equipment, subzero temperatures, and sheer exhaustion of the troops brought the Wehrmacht to a halt. By the end of November the Red Army had recaptured Rostov-on-Don, which the Germans had occupied a few days earlier; it was the first major Soviet military success since the beginning of the campaign. On December 1, the German offensive was definitively halted. On December 4, fresh Soviet divisions transferred from the Far East counterattacked before Moscow: The first German retreat of the war started.

Goebbels's diary reflected growing pessimism: "A detailed OKW report about the communications and food supply situation in the East reveals considerable difficulties," he wrote on November 16. "The weather conditions compel us to take constantly new and unplanned measures. And, as the weather situation is so exceptionally unstable, the measures sometimes have to be changed from one day to the next. Our troops are confronted with unprecedented difficulties."[41]

While the Wehrmacht faced a perilous situation on the Eastern Front, the United States further inched toward war. On October 17 a German submarine attacked the US destroyer *Kearney*, killing eleven sailors; an American merchant ship, the *Lehigh*, was torpedoed off the African coast a few days later; and on October 31, the destroyer *Reuben James* was sunk, and more than one hundred American sailors perished. In the midst of this undeclared naval war (in which, apparently, German submarines did not identify the nationality of the vessels in time),[42] the American president announced, on October 27, that he was in possession of documents showing Hitler's intention to abolish all religions, and of maps indicating German plans to divide Latin America into five Nazi-controlled states.[43] Roosevelt's allegations were false, but his intentions were clear enough. Congress—and public opinion—did not remain indifferent: On November 13, the Neutrality Act, which considerably hampered the delivery of American aid to Britain and the Soviet Union, was repealed. On November 16 Goebbels commented: "The political situation is essentially determined by the course of events in the United States. The American press makes no secret anymore of what Roosevelt's aims are. He wants to join the war at the end of next year at the latest."[44]

For Berlin, Roosevelt's moves were of course the result of a Jewish plot. "Roosevelt's speech [of October 27] made a big impression," Italian foreign minister Galeazzo Ciano noted in his diary on the twenty-ninth. "The Germans have firmly decided to do nothing that will accelerate or cause America's entry into the war. Ribbentrop, during a long lunch, attacked Roosevelt. 'I have given orders to the press to always write: "Roosevelt, the Jew"; I wish to make a prophecy: that man will be stoned in the Capitol by his own people.' I personally believe that Roosevelt will die of old age, because experience teaches me not to give much credit to Ribbentrop's prophecies."[45]

Besides the pressure Hitler may have hoped to put on "the Jewish clique" around Roosevelt by deporting the Jews of Germany, the best chance of avoiding the American entry into the war rested on the success of the isolationist campaign. The antiwar agitation was led, at this stage, by the America First Committee and its star speaker, Charles A. Lindbergh, the world-famous pilot and tragic father of a kidnapped and murdered son.

On September 11, following Roosevelt's "active defense" speech, Lindbergh delivered his most aggressive address yet, entitled "Who Are the War Agitators?" before some eight thousand Iowans packed into the Des Moines Coliseum. Lindbergh indicted the administration, the British, and the Jews.[46] Regarding the Jews, he began by expressing compassion for and understanding of their plight and for their reasons to wish the overthrow of the regime in Germany. "But no person of honesty and vision," he added, "can look on their pro-war policy here today without seeing the dangers involved in such a policy, both for us and for them."

Lindbergh's second point in no way mitigated the impact of the first: "Instead of agitating for war, the Jewish groups in this country should be opposing it in every possible way, for they will be among the first to feel its consequences. Tolerance is a virtue that depends upon peace and strength." After mentioning that a few Jews understood the threat that war could mean for them, Lindbergh continued: "But the majority still do not. Their greatest danger to this country lies in their large ownership and influence in our motion pictures, our press, our radio and our Government." Probably without sensing it, Lindbergh had sunk at that stage to the level of a notorious American anti-Semitic rabble-rouser, the radio preacher Father Charles Coughlin, or, for that matter, to the level of Goebbels's arguments.

The third and final part regarding the Jews was, implicitly, the most provocative of all: "I am not attacking either the Jewish or British people," he declared. "Both races, I admire. But I am saying that the leaders of both the British and Jewish races, for reasons which are understandable from their viewpoint as they are inadvisable from ours, for reasons which are not American, wish to involve us in the war. We cannot blame them for looking out for what they believe to be their own interests, but we must also look out for ours. We cannot allow the natural passions and prejudices of other peoples to lead our country to destruction."[47]

"Lindbergh," one of his biographers commented, "had bent over backward to be kind about the Jews; but in suggesting the American Jews were 'other' people and that their interests were 'not American,' he implied exclusion, thus undermining the very foundation of the United States."[48] The widespread outrage raised by his speech not only put an end to Lindbergh's political activity but also demonstrated that, despite strong anti-Semitic feelings among segments of American society, the great majority would not admit any exclusionary talk, even if presented in "reasonable terms." Goebbels missed neither the speech nor the reactions to it.

"During the day," the minister recorded on September 14, "the original text of Colonel Lindbergh's speech arrives. He has launched a sharp attack against the Jews but of course was caught as a result in a wasps' nest. The New York press howls as if stung by a tarantula. One cannot but admire Lindbergh: relying just on himself he has dared to face this association of business manipulators, Jews, plutocrats and capitalists."[49]

On December 7, the Japanese attacked Pearl Harbor. On December 11, preempting the inevitable, the Nazi leader declared war on the United States.

III

Hitler's prolonged low-key rhetorical stance regarding the Jews came to an abrupt end in the fall of 1941: The restraint of the previous months gave way to an explosion of the vilest anti-Jewish invectives and threats. This sharp reversal closely followed the decision to deport the Jews of Germany; it was inaugurated by what must have been the most bizarre "order of the day" in modern times.

On the eve of Typhoon, on October 2, addressing the millions of soldiers poised for what was to be "the last of the great decisive battles of the year . . . the last powerful blow that will shatter this enemy before the onset of the winter," Hitler left no doubt about the true identity of the "horrendous, beast-like" foe that had been about to "annihilate not only Germany, but the whole of Europe." Those who upheld the system in which Bolshevism was but the other face of the vilest capitalism, he proclaimed, were in both cases the same: "Jews and only Jews!" (*Juden und nur Juden*!).[50] The next day, in his Sportpalast speech to mark the opening of the annual Winter-Relief campaign, Hitler designated the Jews as "the world enemy."[51] From then on his anti-Jewish diatribes became torrential.

On October 13, the Nazi leader attributed the catastrophic state of U.S. economic policies to "Jewish thinking."[52] The next day he again attacked Jewish business thinking and practices.[53] On the seventeenth the Jews came up twice in conversation, at noon and in the evening. During lunch Hitler discussed the situation of Romania and its notoriously corrupt officials: "The precondition [for change] is the elimination of the Jews; otherwise a state cannot be freed [of corruption]."[54] After dinner, in the presence of Fritz Sauckel and Fritz Todt, the discussion turned to the future German settlement of Belorussia and the Ukraine: The "destructive Jews" would be gone, the Nazi leader promised.[55] On the eighteenth Hitler's anti-Jewish obsession turned to the Jews' role in England's path to war.[56] On the nineteenth he brought up the Christian "pre-Bolshevik" mobilization of the slaves in the Roman Empire, manipulated by the Jews to destroy the structure of the state.[57] Two days later, on October 21, Hitler unleashed a more extensive attack: Jesus was not a Jew; the Jew Paul falsified Jesus' teaching in order to undermine the Roman Empire. The Jews' aim was to destroy the nations by undermining their racial core. In Russia, the Nazi leader declared, the Jews deported hundreds of thousands of men in order to leave the abandoned women to males imported from other regions. They organized miscegenation on a grand scale. The Jews continued to torture people in the name of Bolshevism, just as Christianity, the offshoot of Judaism, had tortured its opponents in the Middle Ages. "Saul became Saint Paul; Mordechai became Karl Marx." Then came the notorious finale: *"By exterminating this pest, we shall do humanity a service of which our soldiers can have no idea."*[58] The most rabid themes of the early speeches, of the dialogue with Dietrich Eckart, and especially of *Mein Kampf*, were back, sometimes in almost identical words.

In the meantime the Nazi leader did not miss the opportunity to vent his fury on an individual Jew. On October 20, the *Berliner Illustrierte Nachtausgabe* reported that a seventy-four-year-old Hamburg Jew, Markus Luftgas, had been condemned to two years in jail for blackmarketeering in eggs. When Hitler read about it, he demanded that Luftgas be condemned to death. On October 23, the Justice Ministry informed the Reich Chancellery that Luftgas had been delivered to the Gestapo for execution.[59]

On October 25, Hitler reminded his guests, Himmler and Heydrich—as if they needed to be reminded—of his notorious "prophecy": "I prophesied to Jewry: The Jew would disappear from Europe if the war could not be avoided. This race of criminals carries the guilt of the two millions of dead of the World War and now already that of hundreds of thousands. Nobody should come and tell me that one cannot drive them into the marshes in the East! Who thinks of our men? It is not bad, moreover, that public rumor attributes to us the intention of exterminating the Jews. Terror is a salutary thing."[60] And, he added, in an unrelated statement: "The attempt to establish a Jewish State will fail."[61] The remark about "public rumor" could apply to the German population; more likely, it referred to rumors circulating abroad, particularly in the United States. . . . That same day the Nazi leader lectured Ciano about the influence of Jewish propaganda in Latin America. During the same conversation, the ironic foreign minister informed his host that "Jewish propaganda" was depicting the internal situation of Italy in the bleakest colors; of course, Ciano added, none of this was true.[62]

At the beginning of November, Hitler served another long historical-political tirade against the Jews to his dentist, SS Standartenführer Prof. Dr. Hugo Blaschke, and Blaschke's assistant, one Dr. Richter. Once the Europeans discovered the nature of the Jew, Hitler told his guests, they would also understand the solidarity that tied them together. The Jew was the obstacle to this solidarity; he only survived because European solidarity did not exist: "Now he lives to destroy it." At the outset of his disquisition Hitler had prophesized that the end of the war would witness the fall (*Himmelssturz*) of the Jews. They had no spiritual or artistic understanding, he went on; they were essentially inveterate liars and cheaters.[63]

The first of Hitler's two major public anti-Jewish speeches of those weeks was the annual address to the party "Old Fighters" on November 8, 1941. The previous year, on the same occasion, the Jews had not been mentioned at all. This time the Nazi leader launched into a vicious and massive anti-Jewish tirade. Many of his themes were merely a repetition of his former rants, those of 1936 and 1937 in particular, but also of the outpourings of the previous three or four weeks. He knew, Hitler told his audience, that behind this war "one ultimately had to look for the 'arsonist' who had always lived off the trading of nations: the international Jew. I wouldn't be a National Socialist anymore," he yelled, "if I distanced myself from this finding." The Nazi leader then recalled the saying of "a great Jew" [Disraeli] that "race was the key to world history." Indeed the Jewish race was behind the present events, using straw men for its bloody deals. At this point, once again, Hitler exclaimed: "I have come to know these Jews as world arsonists" [*Ich habe diese Juden als die Weltbrandstifter kennengelernt*].[64] This was only the prologue.

The Nazi leader went on to describe all the methods used by the Jews to poison the nations (press, radio, film, theater), and to push them into a war in which capitalists and democratic politicians would make money from their stocks in the armaments industries. This kind of coalition headed by the Jews had been eradicated from Germany; now the same enemy was standing on the outside, against the German *Volk* and the German Reich. After pushing a series of nations to the forefront of the battle, the Jew turned to his most trusted instrument: "What was more understandable," Hitler exclaimed, "than the fact that one day the Power where the Jewish spirit is the most clearly in control, would move against us: the Soviet Union, now the greatest servant of Jewry [*Die Sowjetunion, die nun einmal der grösste Diener des Judentums ist*]. After describing the horrors of a regime in which the "organization of Jewish commissars"—in fact "slave-drivers"—ruled over subhuman masses, Hitler rejected the idea that a Russian nationalism could have taken over: "The carriers of such a [nationalist] trend do not exist anymore and the man who is for the time being the ruler of this state is nothing else but an instrument in the hands of this all powerful Jewry. . . . When Stalin is on scene, in front of the curtain, Kaganowitsch [Lazar Kaganowitsch was Stalin's Jewish acolyte] stands behind him with all these Jews who . . . lead this huge empire." Between these anti-Jewish insults and threats, the Nazi leader gave clear expression to the apocalyptic dimension of the ongoing struggle: "This struggle, my old party comrades, has really become not only a struggle for Germany, but for the whole of Europe, a struggle [that will decide] between existence and annihilation!"[65] In this same speech Hitler again reminded his audience that he had often been a prophet in his life. This time, however, the prophecy did not refer to the extermination of the Jews (implicit in his entire speech), but rather to a closely related theme: November 1918, when Germany was stabbed in the back, would never occur again. "Everything is imaginable," he exclaimed, "except one thing, that Germany will ever capitulate!"[66]

On November 10, the Jews were mentioned, albeit briefly, in a letter Hitler addressed to Pétain. The Jewish theme had never before come up in an exchange between the Nazi leader and the head of the Vichy state. "If I had not decided at the last minute, on June 22, to move against the Bolshevist menace," Hitler wrote, "then it could have happened only too easily that with the collapse of Germany the French Jews would have triumphed, but the French people would likewise have been plunged into a horrible catastrophe."[67]

On November 12, Hitler again took up his anti-Jewish tirades at headquarters: By excluding the Jews from Prussia, King Friedrich II had opted for an "exemplary" policy.[68] On the nineteenth the Nazi leader warned against compassion for the Jews "who had to emigrate"; according to him, these Jews had enough relatives throughout the world, whereas the Germans who had been forced to leave their country had nobody and were compelled to rely entirely on themselves.[69] Hardly anybody in Hitler's circle (or, for that matter, throughout Germany) did not know that the Jews were no longer emigrating but being deported to places where no relatives would help them to start a new life.

In *Das Reich* of November 16, under the title "The Jews Are Guilty!" Goebbels echoed his master's voice. He reminded his readers of Hitler's prophecy that the Jews would be exterminated in case of war: "We are now witnessing the fulfillment of this prophecy; the fate befalling the Jews is harsh, but more than deserved. Pity or regret is completely out of place in this case. In triggering this war," the minister went on, "world Jewry completely miscalculated the forces it could muster. It is now gradually being engulfed by the same extermination process that it had intended for us and that it would have allowed to happen without any scruples, had it had the power to do so. But now it undergoes destruction according to its own law: 'An eye for an eye, a tooth for a tooth!' "[70] On December 1, the minister brandished the same threats in a lecture at the Friedrich Wilhelm University in Berlin, in front of a highly select audience. Thoughout his speech, the propaganda chief openly alluded to what could be understood only as a murderous solution of the "Jewish question." Whether the ominous diatribe referred to an ongoing and systematic extermination of all the Jews of Europe is not clear, however.[71]

On November 21, Hitler was back in Berlin for the funeral of Luftwaffe hero Gen. Ernst Udet (who had committed suicide after being held responsible by Göring—and by Hitler—for the failure of the Battle of Britain). In a discussion with Goebbels, the Nazi leader expressed his intention to pursue an "energetic policy" in regard to the Jews but not one "that could create difficulties." The Jews would be evacuated from the Reich city after city, but Hitler could not tell when Berlin's turn would come. He demanded that his minister show restraint regarding mixed marriages, mainly in artists' circles. In his opinion "these marriages would die out and one should not get any gray hair about it."[72]

On November 27 the Nazi leader harangued the Finnish foreign minister, Rolf Witting: "One should be clear about the fact that the entire world Jewry stood on the side of Bolshevism. An objective political point of view was not possible in any country in which public opinion was controlled and molded by those forces which in the last analysis had brought about Bolshevism. . . . The entire national intelligentsia of England should be *against* the war, as even victory could not achieve anything for England. It was the Bolshevist and Jewish forces which kept the English from pursuing a reasonable policy."[73]

Hitler received the Grand Mufti of Jerusalem on the following day. The Palestinian Arab leader, Haj Amin al-Husseini, had fled to the German capital after the collapse of Rashid 'Ali al-Gaylani's anti-British government in Iraq. Hitler made clear to his Arab visitor that Germany's struggle against the Jews was "uncompromising" and that it included the Jewish settlement in Palestine. "Germany was determined to demand, systematically, from one European nation after another, to solve the Jewish problem; in due time, it would also address the same call to nations outside of Europe."[74] That same day, the Nazi leader could not abstain from a further anti-Jewish tirade in his conversation with the Romanian vice–prime minister, Mihai Antonescu; this time, however, a new theme appeared: "Speaking at length," the official record stated, "the Führer gave a survey of the current situation. World Jewry in combination with the Slavs and unfortunately also the Anglo-Saxons was carrying on the fight with embitterment. Germany and her allies confronted real colossi in terms of space, which possessed all raw materials and fertile land in copious measure. In addition, Jews had a certain destructive tendency, which found expression in the fight of Bolshevism and Pan-Slavism."[75]

Pan-Slavism was unexpected. It surfaced briefly following the "discovery" first by the Belgian and then the German press, of the "will of Czar Peter the Great," urging the Russia's expansion to the West. Hitler, soon informed that the testament was a forgery, ordered its use nonetheless, as if it were authentic. "[The Führer] ordered the widest possible discussion in the German press with the theme: the imperialist policy of Czar Peter the Great had been the guideline of Russian prewar policy and of the policy of Stalin. Bolshevist world hegemony and Slav imperialism have joined hands in the policy of Stalin. . . . It didn't matter what some professor or other had discovered with regard to this Testament of Peter the

Great. What mattered rather was that history had demonstrated that Russian policy was conducted according to these principles as they were laid down in the testament of Peter the Great." The press thereupon "took up the subject in a big way and treated it to the satisfaction of the Führer."[76]

In his circle of intimates, Hitler briefly returned to his favorite topic on the evening of November 30, as he reminisced about a fight with Jews at the Nuremberg railway station during the early days of the party.[77] More was said on the night of December 1. Prodded about the issue of racial instinct, Hitler declared that some Jews did not necessarily intend to harm Germany, but even so they would never distance themselves from the long-term interests of their own race. Why were Jews destroying other nations? The Nazi leader admitted that he did not know the fundamental natural-historical laws of this phenomenon. But, as a result of their destructive activity, the Jews created the necessary defense mechanisms among the nations. Hitler added that Dietrich Eckart had once mentioned that he knew of one single upright Jew, Otto Weininger, who took his own life after he discovered the destructive nature of his race. Strangely, Hitler concluded, second- or third-generation Jewish mixed breeds would often come together again with Jews. But, he added, ultimately nature eliminated the destructive elements: In the seventh, eighth, or ninth generation the Jewish part would be "out-Mendeled" (*ausgemendelt*—a pun on the name of the Czech monk, Gregor Mendel, who discovered the laws of heredity) and "racial purity, reestablished."[78]

On December 11, four days after Pearl Harbor, Hitler announced to the Reichstag that Germany was declaring war on the United States. From the outset the messianic theme was present: "If Providence wanted that the German people not be spared this struggle, then I am grateful to it [Providence] for having entrusted me with the leadership of this historical confrontation, a confrontation that will decisively mold not only the history of our Germany but that of Europe, actually that of the entire world for the next 500 or 1,000 years."[79] A first overview of the coming confrontation followed, which, after mention of the attack that the Soviet Union had been preparing against "Europe," led to historical comparisons: The Romans and the Germans had saved Western civilization from the Huns; now as then Germany was not fighting just for its own sake but for the defense of the whole continent.[80]

Another lengthy sequence followed about responsibility for the war; it brought Hitler somewhat closer to the object of the Reichstag meeting. Two American presidents had caused untold misery during the past decades: Wilson and Roosevelt. Wilson, the "paralytic professor," was merely the forerunner of Roosevelt's policies; but to understand fully Roosevelt and his hatred of Germany, one crucial element had to be kept in mind: The American politician acceded to the presidency at precisely the time Hitler took over the leadership of Germany. A comparison between both personalities and the achievements of both regimes would inevitably demonstrate the Nazi leader's manifest superiority. Moreover, Hitler continued: "The forces that supported Mr. Roosevelt were the forces against which I struggled, given the fate of my people and from my own innermost and holiest conviction. The 'brain trust' the American president relied upon included the members of the same people that we fought in Germany as a parasitical manifestation and that we started excluding from public life." Then, after once more demonstrating how catastrophic Roosevelt's leadership had been, Hitler reached the core of his argument: "The evolution of the United States should not be surprising once one remembered that the spirits on whom this man had called to help him or, better said, the spirits that called him, belonged to those elements who, as *Jews* [underlined in the original printed text] could only be interested in destruction and never in order." What followed was unavoidable: To deflect attention from his failures, Roosevelt—and the Jews behind him—needed a foreign diversion.[81]

At this point Hitler was ready for a full-scale anti-Jewish tirade of hate: "He [Roosevelt] was strengthened in this [political diversion] by the circle of Jews surrounding him, who, with Old Testament–like fanaticism, believe that the United States can be the instrument for preparing another Purim for the European nations that are becoming increasingly anti-Semitic. It was the Jew, in his full satanic vileness, who rallied around this man [Roosevelt], but to whom this man also reached out."[82] By formally declaring war on the United States, in accordance with the Tripartite Pact, Hitler had closed the circle of his enemies in a world war of yet-unknown fury.

On the following day, December 12, Hitler addressed the *Reichsleiter* and *Gauleiter* in a secret speech summed up by Goebbels: "In regard to the Jewish question the Führer is determined to wipe the slate clean [*reinen Tisch zu machen*]. He prophesied to the Jews that if they once more brought about a world war, they would be annihilated. These were not mere words. The world war is here, the extermination of the Jews must be its necessary consequence. This matter has to be envisaged without any sentimentality. We are not here to have compassion for the Jews, but to have compassion for our German people. As the German people has once again sacrificed some 160,000 dead in the eastern campaign, those responsible for this bloody conflict will have to pay for it with their lives."[83]

Then, according to an entry in Himmler's appointment calendar dated December 18, in a meeting that same day, the Nazi leader instructed him: "Jewish question | exterminate as partisans."[84] The vertical line remains unexplained. The identification of the Jews as "partisans" obviously did not refer to the Jews on Soviet territory who were being exterminated for six months already. It referred to the deadly internal enemy, the enemy fighting within the borders of one's own territory, who, by plotting and treachery could, as in 1917–1918, stab the Reich in the back, now that a new "world war," on all fronts, rekindled all the dangers of the previous one. Moreover, "partisans" associated maybe with the most general connotation used by Hitler in his declaration at the conference of July 16, 1941: All *potential enemies* within Germany's reach; it was understood, as we saw, to include any civilians and entire communities at will. Thus the order was clear: Extermination without any limitation here applied to the Jews.

On December 17, on the eve of the meeting with the SS Reichsführer, Hitler once more raised the Jewish issue with Goebbels. "The Führer is determined to proceed consistently in this matter [the 'Jewish question']," the propaganda minister recorded, "and not be stopped by bourgeois sentimentality." Hitler and his minister discussed the evacuation of the Jews from the Reich, but it seems that subsequently the Jewish issue in general was addressed: "All the Jews have to be transferred to the East. What happens to them there cannot be of great interest to us. They have asked for this fate; they brought about the war, now they must also foot the bill." Then Goebbels added: "It is comforting that despite the burden of military responsibility the Führer still finds the time . . . for these matters and mainly has a clear view about them. He alone is in the position to solve this problem definitively, with the necessary toughness."[85]

* * *

In the course of two months the Nazi leader had explicitly mentioned *the extermination of the Jews* on October 19, October 25, December 12, December 17, and December 18, and was indirectly quoted to that effect by Goebbels, Rosenberg, and Frank between December 12 and 16. Nothing of the kind had ever happened before in Hitler's declarations. Indeed, the fact that five out of seven of these exterminatory statements were made within a few days of December 11, could be seen as a thinly veiled message conveying that a final decision had been made as a result of American entry into the war. On the night of December 28–29, Hitler came to speak of the arch-anti-Semite, Julius Streicher: "What Streicher did in *Der Stürmer*: He drew an idealized portrait of the Jews. The Jew is much meaner, much more bloodthirsty than Streicher described him."[86]

For good measure the Nazi leader added a strong dose of anti-Jewish threats and insults in his last public message of the year. According to Goebbels, he dictated it on December 31 to have it read by his minister on the radio that same evening.[87] The general tone of the address was unusually defensive and insecure—understandably so. Those who forced the war on the Reich, the German chief declared, carried the responsibility for having deflected Hitler from forging ahead with the grand internal changes he had launched. But victory would be achieved with the help of Providence (invoked any number of times in this short message). The archvillains, the Jews, were mentioned no fewer than four times. At first they were merely designated as an element, though prime one, in the foes' "Jewish-capitalist-Bolshevik world conspiracy"; they reappeared shortly thereafter, when the Nazi leader told his people—and all of Europe—what a horrendous fate would have befallen them if "Jewish Bolshevism in alliance with Roosevelt and Churchill had achieved victory"; then part of the notorious prophecy surfaced: "The Jew will not eradicate the European nations, but will be the victim of his own attack" [*Der Jude aber wird nicht die europäischen Völker ausrotten, sondern er wird das Opfer seines eigenen Anschlages sein*]; finally, in the closing part of the exhortation, after the savior of Germany and of Europe had once more invoked "the Almighty," he brought in the Jews for the fourth time as the very root of evil: "If all of us together faithfully accomplish our duty, our fate will fulfill itself as Providence willed it. Those who fight for the life of their people, for its daily bread and for its future will win! But those who, in their Jewish hatred, attempt to exterminate the peoples in this war will be hurled down!" A further appeal to God ended the message.[88] Thus the year 1941 closed: It should have been, in Hitler's own words, the year of "the greatest victory in world history."

IV

As the deadly threats spewed by "the highest authority" became one continuous rant, the ever more murderous campaign developed apace. From midsummer 1941 on, the massacres of Jews throughout the German- and Romanian-occupied Soviet territories had reached colossal proportions. In Kamenets-Podolsky, Kiev, Kovno, Minsk, Riga, the towns of eastern Galicia—now part of the General Government—and in Odessa, among other killing fields, the Jews were murdered by the thousands, sometimes by the *tens of thousands*, in each *Aktion*. Some of the local commanders excelled at their task.

In Stanisławów, for example, in southern Galicia, the local Security Police commander, Hans Krüger, resolutely took things in hand after Friedrich Katzmann, the SSPF in Galicia, and Karl Eberhard Schöngarth, head of the Security Police in the General Government, had given him free rein.[89] On the morning of October 12, 1941, the Jews of the town were driven in groups to the local cemetery. The first batch of 1,000 Jews was then led through the gates, ordered to undress, and the shooting into the open pits started. Next to the mass graves, Krüger had had tables set with food and vodka for the killing commandos (German police units, Ukrainian auxiliaries, and groups of ethnic German volunteers). Krüger himself oversaw the increasingly chaotic murder scene as the line of Jews moved from the town to the cemetery; at times the SD chief made the rounds of his men with a salami sandwich in one hand and a bottle of schnapps in the other. Panic drove entire families to jump together into the pits, where they were either shot or buried alive; others tried to climb the walls of the cemetery until they were mowed down. With the onset of darkness, Krüger announced to the remaining Jews that the Führer had granted them a reprieve; the stampede toward the gates left further victims on the grounds: 10,000 to 12,000 of the Jews of Stanisławów had been murdered that day.[90] The remnant was driven into a ghetto.

Three months later a young female diarist, Elisheva, to whom we shall return, commented on the death of two women friends, Tamarczyk and

Esterka, during the killings in the cemetery on October 12. "I hope," Elisheva wrote, "that death was kind to [Tamarczyk] and took her right away. And that she didn't have to suffer like her companion, Esterka, who was seen being strangled."[91]

Even before the departure of the first transport from the Reich, Heydrich convened a meeting in Prague on October 10, attended by the highest local SS commanders and by Eichmann. Fifty thousand deportees, the RSHA chief told his acolytes, would be sent to the Ostland (Riga, Minsk); Kovno was added somewhat later.[92] Regarding the Jews of the Protectorate, Heydrich planned the establishment of two transit camps (he spoke of "assembly camps"), one in Moravia and one in Bohemia, from which the Jews would leave eastward after being already "heavily decimated." The "decimation" was not further explained; it may have been an improvised statement (like the identically worded forecast Heydrich would make at the Wannsee conference in January 1942 regarding the fate of Jewish slave labor building roads on Soviet territory).

Heydrich's final sentence, according to the protocol of the meeting, echoed Himmler's opening statement in his September 18 letter to Greiser: "The Führer wishes," the Reichsführer had written, "the Altreich and the Protectorate to be cleared and freed of Jews." Heydrich closed the October 10 meeting by reminding those present of the Führer's wish: "As the Führer wishes that possibly even by the end of this year the Jews should be evacuated from German space, all outstanding issues have to be solved immediately. The transportation problem should not create any difficulty either."[93]

On October 13 the Reichsführer met Globocnik and Krüger. It was probably at this meeting that the SS chief ordered Globocnik to start building the Belzec extermination camp.[94] We do not know with any certainty whether the camp was being set up "only" to exterminate Jews of the Lublin district in order to make space for Jewish deportees from the Reich or whether the killing of all Jews in the district was also linked to colonization plans in the area (particularly in the Zamość region), as a first step of the constantly reworked "General Plan East."[95] It may have been intended for both objectives.[96]

On the other hand we may surmise that it was essentially in order to deal with the influx of deportees from the Reich to Lodz that preparations for mass murder were initiated in the Warthegau. A euthanasia specialist, Herbert Lange, began searching for an appropriate killing site sometime in mid-October 1941. The extermination sites planned for the Ostland (Riga, Mogilev) were most probably also part of the same immediate murder projects regarding the local ghetto populations.

With Himmler's agreement a few euthanasia experts had already been sent to Lublin in early September. If Hitler's order about the deportation from the Reich had been conveyed to the Reichsführer at the beginning of September, the arrival of euthanasia experts at that time meant that the elimination of part of the ghetto populations was considered from the outset as the best solution to the overcrowding issue. A visit by Brack, and then by Bouhler himself, followed, and on November 1 the construction of Belzec started.[97] The killing installation Lange set up in Chelmno near Lodz was much simpler: Three gas vans were delivered by the RSHA sometime in November, and by early December everything was ready for the first batch of victims.

In regard to this sequence of events, Eichmann's testimony at his Jerusalem trial was confusing. According to Eichmann, Heydrich sent him on an inspection visit to Lublin after telling him that Hitler had decided to exterminate all the Jews of Europe. When he arrived in Lublin the trees still had their autumn foliage, and at Belzec (Eichmann did not remember the name) he saw only two small huts being prepared for the gassing. This does not fit, of course, with the fact that the construction of Belzec started only in early November (when the trees would already have lost their autumn colors) and that the first barracks were ready in December. It seems that Eichmann did not remember precisely when Heydrich told him about the "final order" and which inspection tour took place in early autumn in the Lublin area.[98]

Additional indications pointing to the initially "local" function of Belzec and Chelmno include the technically "limited capacity" of the Belzec gassing installations (before their "upgrading" in the late spring of 1942), and the letter Greiser sent Himmler in May 1942, indicating that Chelmno was meant to exterminate part of the Jewish population of the Warthegau, including Lodz (about 100,000 Jews, according to Greiser).[99]

A few days after his meeting with Krüger and Globocnik, Himmler ordered the cessation of all Jewish emigration from the Reich (and thus, from the entire Continent). The Reichsführer's order, issued on October 18, was conveyed by Müller to all Gestapo stations on the twenty-third, "in view of the forthcoming 'Final Solution' of the Jewish question."

Furthermore, on the eve of Himmler's order, a step, puzzling at first glance, had been taken by Heydrich. The chief of the RSHA asked Luther to reject an offer from the Spanish government to evacuate to Morocco two thousand Jews of Spanish nationality arrested over the previous months in Paris. Heydrich argued that the Spaniards would be unwilling and unable to guard the Jews in Morocco and that, moreover, "these Jews would also be too far out of the direct reach of measures for a basic solution to the Jewish question to be enacted after the war."[100] Heydrich demanded that this explanation be conveyed to the Spaniards.

In fact, to allow any exception would have considerably reduced the ominous significance of the deportations from the Reich that had just started and of Himmler's end-of-all-emigration decree. Moreover, had the transfer of Spanish Jews been agreed to, wouldn't the Hungarian, Romanian, or Turkish governments, for example, ask for custody of their own Jews living in France or elsewhere in Western Europe?

A teletype sent to the Wilhelmstrasse on October 30, 1941 (barely a few days after Heydrich's decision), by Rudolf Schleier, the councillor in charge of Jewish affairs at the German embassy in Paris, confirmed that fear of setting a precedent may have been on Heydrich's mind when he turned down the Spanish request: "Military Commander France has arrested a considerable number of Jews including foreign nationals, in the course of the big roundup on August 20, 1941, of French and foreign Jews involved in communist and de Gaullist activities and in attempts against members of the Wehrmacht in the occupied zone of France. Foreign consuls in Paris have requested assistance of the embassy for the release of Jewish nationals of their respective countries. Military commander and Security Service take the view that the fact that arrested Jews are foreign nationals can in no way influence the measures taken. *Release of individual Jews would create precedents.*"[101] As for the last part of Heydrich's comment—"these Jews would be too much out of reach of measures for a basic solution to the Jewish question to be enacted after the war"—the reference to the forthcoming "Final Solution" in forbidding emigration had become a standard Nazi formula; as may be remembered, it was also used by Göring on

May 20, 1941, when he forbade further emigration of Jews from France and Belgium.

While Heydrich was dealing with the Spaniards, one of Rosenberg's acolytes in the ministry for the Occupied Eastern Territories, Eberhard Wetzel, ventured to issue instructions of his own: He had no objections that those Jews from the Ostland ghettos who were unable to work *and* Reich Jews of the same category should be "removed by Brack's device" [gas vans].[102] Wetzel's *nihil obstat* of October 25 would have been a first direct allusion to a general extermination plan, except for the fact that neither Wetzel nor Rosenberg had any say in the matter. Moreover, it should be kept in mind that Rosenberg *may have been* informed of a general extermination plan in mid-November at the earliest (if such a plan existed at the time), and otherwise only in December.

A number of other documents, mostly of less intrinsic significance, have been adduced to argue that Hitler's final decision to exterminate the Jews of Europe was made sometime in late September or early October 1941; others, obversely, have been introduced to demonstrate that it was made after the American entry into the war.[103] Either way the decision was taken sometime during the last three months of 1941.

If the decision for total extermination had already been made in October, the apparently local killings deriving from the deportations from Germany would turn out to be part and parcel of that overall plan; if the final decision was taken later, the "local measures" seamlessly became part of the generalized "Final Solution" from December 1941 on. Moreover, one could plausibly argue that from October to December, Hitler mulled over the decision, as shown by his obsessive daily attacks on the Jews: The Nazi leader had to convince himself that systematically murdering millions of people was indeed the right decision. In that case the decision may first have been considered in October or even before, to become final once the United States joined the war, the Soviet forces counterattacked, and the dreaded "World War," in the East and in the West, became a reality.

Hitler's acolytes and their underlings may have interpreted his anti-Jewish harangues from October 1941 on as implicit encouragement to forge ahead with local murderous initiatives to solve the problems caused by the deportations from the Reich; they could not, however, have interpreted them as an order to start the complete extermination of all European Jews. Crossing the line from local murder operations to overall extermination required a go-ahead signal from the supreme authority.

We do not know, of course, at what point Hitler started harboring the project of immediate extermination; this much, however, is certain: The timing of Hitler's decisions was a matter of circumstances; the decisions as such were not. And the timing regarding the "Final Solution" was in part determined by the "prophecy" of January 1939. This prophecy, although politically motivated (as a deterrent), was nonetheless solemnly uttered again in January 1941 (despite its more open-ended wording). A prophet could not afford to hesitate when the circumstances heralding the fulfillment of the prophecy occurred; a savior could not, at that crucial moment, shy away from implementing an open and repeated threat. Thus, beyond his belief in the Jewish danger in case of world war, Hitler had to make good on what he had prophesied, once the circumstances that would lead to extermination of the Jews were becoming reality. The Jews could have been deported to northern Russia and decimated there; this, however, was no longer an option in the late fall of 1941. They would have to be murdered in areas closer to the heart of the Nazi empire and that of the "new Europe."

And, what was generally true in regard to the whole *Volk* was particularly valid about Hitler's bond with his old guard. As we saw, the Nazi leader delivered the most threatening indication regarding the pending annihilation of the Jews to the assembled *Gauleiter* and *Reichsleiter* on December 12. He was addressing the innermost circle, the most fanatical party faithful, men who in their immense majority were as radical as he was in regard to "the Jewish question," and possibly as ready as he was to move from massacre to total extermination. Withholding the go-ahead at this stage would have meant that the supreme and providential leader did not believe in the most basic tenet of the common faith. Procrastination could have undermined the Führer's grip on the hearts and minds of his most devoted followers, those who would be ready to stand by him in this struggle to the very last. A process that had started months earlier had reached the point of no return.

Furthermore, now that a rapid and victorious campaign in the East was receding out of sight, now that the dangers of a prolonged and difficult war had become concrete—the mobilization of all national energies was essential. For Nazism the Jews, the Jewish peril, and the uncompromising struggle against "the Jew" were, as we have seen, *the mobilizing myth of the regime.* The time had come not only to brandish Goebbels's slogan "The Jews Are Guilty!" but to take the steps that would galvanize the *Volksgenossen* into fighting this mortal threat with all available strength and would offer the hard-core party members an increasingly necessary taste of retribution.

Finally Hitler's unusual declaration to Goebbels on the eve of the attack on the Soviet Union had become more real than ever before. If, before the attack, the Reich had no choice but to win in order to escape eradication, how vastly more compelling the argument must have appeared after six months of mass murder on an unprecedented scale. The increasing number of Germans from all segments of society involved in all aspects of the extermination campaign knew perfectly well, as did the party elite, that they were now accomplices in crimes of previously unimagined scope; victory or fighting to the end were the only options left to their leader, their party, their country—and themselves.

V

Throughout the weeks and months of the fall of 1941, as the deportations from the Reich started and the signal for the extermination of all the Jews of Europe was given, "ordinary" persecution of Jews in the Reich did not abate. Moreover, legislation dealing with the practical sequels of the deportations was finalized mainly to allow a smooth takeover of all assets and property left behind.

On September 18, 1941, the Reich Transportation Ministry issued a decree barring Jews from using sleeping and dining cars of the Reichsbahn; they were also forbidden to use excursion buses or excursion ships (outside their usual domicile area). Jews were allowed to use all other means of public transportation only when available seats remained, never at times of heavy traffic when seats were unavailable to non-Jews. Jews were allowed to travel only in the lowest class (at the time third class was the lowest passenger class on railways), and they could be seated "only when no other passengers were standing."[104] On September 24 the Reich Ministry of the Economy forbade Jews to use checks.[105] On that same day, the Ministry of Justice excluded them from any benefit (property or asset) received from a full German. "Such benefits," the decree stated, "are in sharp contradiction with healthy German popular feelings."[106]

A month later an RSHA circular ordered the arrest of any German publicly showing friendly relations with a Jew; in serious cases the Aryan offender would be sent to a concentration camp for at least three months; in each case the Jew was to be sent to a concentration camp.[107] On November 13 Jews had to register their electric appliances; that same day they had to turn in typewriters, bicycles, cameras, and binoculars; on November 14 Jews were forbidden to sell their books.[108]

The main laws and decrees were of course aimed at canceling any remaining legal rights of Jews still living in the Reich and also of those who had emigrated or were being deported. The RSHA got involved in the deliberations, and so did the Führer's Chancellery. At times Hitler himself would intervene.

Three issues were at the top of the agenda: The judicial status of Poles and Jews, the legal situation of Jewish laborers, and finally the status of Jews who were still German nationals but were no longer living in the Reich. . . . By mid-October 1941 the first law was ready: Almost any offense committed by a Pole or a Jew was punishable by death; the law was signed on December 4.[109]

The new "Labor Law" for Jews was published on November 4. Like the one covering judicial status, it had been discussed for more than a year. The result was no less clear-cut: A Jewish laborer had no rights whatsoever and could be dismissed from one day to the next. Apart from a minimal daily salary, a Jew could not claim any social benefit or compensation.[110] Nonetheless Jewish laborers had to forgo nearly half of their meager salary in income tax and social benefits payments.[111]

The citizenship decree brought Hitler's intervention. The Ministries of Justice and the Interior, the Finance Ministry, and the RSHA were working out complex formulas that would have enabled the state to impound any remaining assets and possessions of Jews who left the Reich.[112] Hitler decided on a simpler solution. German Jews residing outside the Reich would lose their citizenship and all their assets would become the property of the state. On November 25, 1941, the new regulation was promulgated as the Eleventh Ordinance to the Reich Citizenship Law.[113] This ordinance brought into the open an ongoing tug-of-war between the Reich Finance Ministry and the RSHA regarding the ultimate fate of the assets and property of the Jewish deportees from Germany.

As we saw, the property of the Jews deported from the Reich in 1940 was confiscated by an order issued by Himmler on April 4, 1941, and turned into law by Hitler, on May 29, 1941. While the SS impounded this property for its own operations, the Finance Ministry claimed its own right of receivership. During the summer of 1941 the Finance Ministry had demanded that all banks prepare a list of Jewish accounts, while the Reichsvereinigung—under instructions from the RSHA—informed all the country's Jews of the obligation to establish a precise inventory of their homes, apartments, and property; thereafter any nonauthorized transfer would be punishable by arrest. Thus both the Finance Ministry and the RSHA (via the Reichsvereinigung) were poised for the beginning of the deportations (to the Russian Far North or elsewhere).

On November 4, the finance minister established the mandatory administrative channels for the takeover of the deportees' property by the ministry's local, regional, and central authorities. "It is especially necessary," the minister stressed, "to make sure that there are no appropriation orders for these properties by other offices."[114] A few days later, however, the Reichsvereinigung conveyed an order from the RSHA demanding that all Jews about to be deported to settle any outstanding amounts owed to the association (which would transfer them to the RSHA). They were told not to include these amounts on the forms they had to present at the assembly points (to avoid their transfer to the Reich Finance Ministry) in fact, they were prodded to settle these financial matters before reaching the assembly points.[115]

The Eleventh Ordinance to the Reich Citizenship Law seemed to settle the competition in favor of the state authorities. Jews whose "usual place of residence was abroad" lost their German citizenship. The law applied with immediate effect to Jews who resided abroad on the date of its publication and to those who were to reside abroad thereafter. The loss of citizenship entailed the forfeiture of all property and assets to the benefit of the Reich.[116] To avoid any misunderstanding about the significance of "abroad," the finance minister issued a circular on December 3 indicating that this notion also included "the territories occupied by German troops . . . especially the General Government and the Reichskommissariate Ostland and the Ukraine.[117]

Ultimately, however, the RSHA had its way in regard to the funds owed to the Reichsvereinigung by arguing among other things that these funds were the financial basis for implementing all measures regarding the Jews. And to increase these amounts, Heydrich's men figured out various schemes to further delude and despoil the unsuspecting victims. Thus elderly Jews could buy homes in the "old people's ghetto" by signing off to the Reichsvereinigung the necessary funds, which would then be transferred to the RSHA. Some of these homes, the deportees were told, had a lake view and others faced a park. In one way or another, the victims were financing their own deportation and, ultimately, their extermination.[118]

The homes abandoned by the deportees generated a measure of local cooperation between Gestapo and party officials, as had already been the case in Vienna and in Munich. In the Frankfurt area, for example, in order to avoid tension and competition, the *Gauleiter* of Hesse-Nassau, Jakob Sprenger, appointed the Frankfurt *Kreisleiter* as the sole representative of the *Gau* entitled to negotiate with the Gestapo about the fate of Jewish homes and apartments.[119]

Sometimes, however, unexpected difficulties arose. The Jews who over the first two years of the war (or even beforehand) had been compelled to leave their apartments or homes to congregate in a "Jews' house" were mostly renting apartments in buildings where they alone were allowed to live but which nonetheless belonged to "Aryan" landlords. When the deportations started, some of the apartments were vacated by the deportees, while others remained temporarily inhabited by their Jewish tenants. According to a letter of complaint sent to the Düsseldorf Gestapo on August 25, 1942, by one August Stiewe to (the landlord of such a house), the deportation of some of his Jewish tenants entailed a significant loss of income from unpaid rents, since Aryan tenants could not be asked to move into a house still partly occupied by Jews. The Gestapo did not deny the existence of the financial loss but told Stiewe to address his grievance to the local branch of the Finance Ministry, as it was pocketing the Jewish assets.[120]

By the fall of 1941 the status and fate of mixed-breeds remained as confused as ever. On the eve of the deportations from the Reich, in a conversation with Lammers, Walter Gross, head of the racial policy office of the party, pointed to two major *desiderata*, from "a purely biological viewpoint": "1. No reappearance of persons of mixed blood of the second degree—that is, the necessity of sterilizing persons of mixed blood of the first degree where exceptions [having to do with marriage] are necessary for political reasons. 2. The maintenance of some kind of clear distinction between persons of mixed blood of the second degree and Germans, so that a certain stigma could still be attached to the term 'Mischling.' Only by clearly keeping persons of mixed blood beyond the pale can racial consciousness be kept alive and the birth of children of mixed blood . . . be prevented in the future. We must reckon with such births in view of the extensive contacts between peoples and races in the future. Reichsminister Lammers listened attentively to both ideas and *declared himself in favor of the sterilization of persons of mixed blood of the first degree, if they were allowed to remain on the territory of the Reich* (emphasis added). Furthermore, he himself suggested that a marriage permit be compulsary for persons of mixed blood of the second degree, in order to keep control in every case over their choice of partners. The aim of such a measure would be to prevent, under all circumstances, the marriage of mixed-breeds of the second degree among themselves, because of the danger of transmitting Jewish characteristics in accordance with Mendel's [heredity] laws. I answered," Gross added, "that . . . one should thoroughly examine whether it was more advantageous to spread Jewish traits throughout the entire Volk rather than isolating them among a limited section of the community from which, now and than, persons possessing an accumulation of Jewish characteristics would appear, who in turn could be eradicated in some way."[121] The issue was left pending.

Finding a solution was becoming urgent, however, first and foremost in view of the deportations, but also in regard to the continuing service of at least some categories of *Mischlinge* in the Wehrmacht or in regard to their admission to universities. In principle Hitler's decisions of 1940 regarding *Mischlinge* serving in the Wehrmacht remained valid, and were actually imposed more rigorously after the end of the French campaign and maintained despite the growing difficulties on the Eastern Front: Half Jews had to be discharged; quarter Jews could stay in the army but were not to be promoted, even to NCO ranks.

In reality, though, confusion persisted. It seems that in Rommel's Afrika Korps these rules were entirely disregarded; in the navy their implementation was postponed, whereas in the army and the Luftwaffe, they were applied only if and when the racial identity of the soldier or officer was declared or discovered.[122] Hitler usually kept for himself the right to promote quarter Jews to NCO or officer ranks. And, in addition to the existing confusion, the Nazi leader decreed that if a *Mischling* (even a half Jew) fell on the battlefield, the family should be protected from anti-Jewish measures.[123] It seems, in other words, that in 1941 the Wehrmacht was still drafting half Jewish *Mischlinge* for active service.[124]

As could be expected, some *Mischlinge* were mistreated by commanding officers or fellow soldiers when their identity was uncovered. Many later testified, however, that they encountered humane, even friendly, attitudes from members of their units. Some *Mischlinge* felt deeply deprived at having to leave the army; others were relieved not to have to serve Hitler any longer. Most of the mixed-breeds found civilian work, at times in highly sensitive positions, such as scientific research in missile construction plants at Peenemünde, among other places.[125]

Access to universities remained extremely difficult for *Mischlinge* of the first degree, although, as we saw, the Reich Ministry of Education accepted candidates with distinguished military credentials. As beforehand, however, the Party Chancellery and the rectors represented the hard line and used every possible argument (including the observation by some of the rectors of negative racial traits of the candidates) to close the doors of the universities to part Jews.[126]

Generally, part Jews were spared from deportation, as were the Jewish spouses in mixed marriages with children, although as time went by and defeat appeared more certain, the radicalization and extension of the persecution increased.

VI

In the Reich information about massacres perpetrated in the East was first and foremost spread by soldiers who often wrote home quite openly about what they witnessed—and quite approvingly as well. "In Kiev," Cpl. LB wrote on September 28, "mines explode one after the other. For eight days now the city is on fire and all of it is the Jews' doing. Therefore all Jews aged 14 to 60 have been shot and the Jewish women will also be shot, otherwise there will be no end to it."[127] On November 2 Pvt. XM described a former synagogue, built in 1664, that was in use up to the war. Now, only the walls remained. "It won't ever be used in the previous function," XM added. "I believe that in this country [the Soviet Union] the Jews will soon not be in need of any prayer house. I already described to you why it is so. For these dreadful creatures it remains after all the only right redemption."[128]

An SD report of October 2 from Münster conveyed a conversation between two officials of the mayor's office about soldiers' letters recently received from the Russian front. The extraordinary brutality of the fighting stemmed, for example, from "the intentional destruction of all religious and moral feelings by the Jews. The Russians were solely driven by their blind fear of the Jewish commissars. The Russian defends himself and bites like an animal. This is what Jewry has done to the Aryan peoples of Russia. . . . Already in peacetime, a substantial part of the Russian soldier hordes were purely Mongols. The Jews have mobilized Asia against Europe."[129] The letters these officials received in Münster must have represented a random opinion sample of the *Ostheer*.

The information about the gigantic exterminations of Jews in the East was of course not conveyed only by soldiers' letters. As early as in July 1941, Swiss diplomatic and consular representatives in the Reich and in satellite countries were filling detailed reports about the mass atrocities; all their information stemmed from German or related sources.[130] Senior and even midlevel officials in various German ministries had access to the communications of the *Einsatzgruppen* and to their computations of the staggering number of Jews they had murdered. Such information was mentioned in internal Foreign Ministry correspondence in October 1941 and not even ranked top secret.[131]

In a letter addressed to his wife, Freya, Helmuth von Moltke displayed a clear understanding of what was going on: "The news from the East is terrible again. Our losses are obviously very, very heavy. But that could be borne if we were not burdened with a hecatombe of corpses. Again and again one hears reports that in transports of prisoners or Jews only 20 percent arrive . . . What will happen when the nation as a whole realizes that this war is lost, and lost differently from the last one? With a blood guilt that cannot be atoned for in our lifetime and can never be forgotten."[132] These lines were written at the end of August 1941.

Later that year, in October and November, Moltke commented on the deportations: "Since Saturday," he wrote to Freya on October 21, "the Berlin Jews are being rounded up. They are picked up at 9:15 in the evening and locked into a synagogue overnight. Then they are sent off, with what they can carry to Litzmannstadt and Smolensk. We are to be spared the sight of them being simply left to perish in hunger and cold, and that is why it is done in Litzmannstadt and Smolensk."[133] And, on November 13: "I find it hard to remember these two days. Russian prisoners, evacuated Jews, evacuated Jews, Russian prisoners. . . . That was the world of these two days. Yesterday, I said goodbye to a once famous Jewish lawyer who has the Iron Cross First and Second Class, the Order of the House of Hohenzollern, the Golden Badge for the Wounded, and who will kill himself with his wife today because he is to be picked up tonight."[134]

Regarding the killings in occupied Soviet territories, Hassell received much of his information from Gen. Georg Thomas, chief of the Economic and Armaments Division of the Wehrmacht (who played a strange role as enforcer of looting in the occupied Soviet territories on the one hand, and source of information for the opposition to the regime on the other). "Conversations with Frida [Dohnanyi], among others and particularly a report from Auerley [Thomas], who again arrived from the front," Hassell recorded on October 4, "confirm the continuation of the most disgusting atrocities mainly against the Jews who are executed row after row without the least shame. . . . A headquarters commanding medical officer . . . reported that he tested Russian dum-dum bullets in the execution of Jews and achieved such and such results; he was ready to go on and write a report that could be used in [anti-Soviet] propaganda about this ammunition!"[135]

German populations were also quite well informed about the goings-on in the concentration camps, even the most deadly ones. Thus, people living in the vicinity of Mauthausen, for example, could watch what was happening in the camp. On September 27, 1941, Eleanore Gusenbauer sent a letter of complaint to the Mauthausen police station: "In the concentration camp Mauthausen at the work site in Vienna Ditch inmates are being shot repeatedly; those badly struck live for yet some time, and so remain lying next to the dead for hours or even half a day long. My property lies upon an elevation next to the Vienna Ditch, and one is often an unwilling witness to such outrages. I am anyway sickly and such a sight makes a demand on my nerves that in the long run I cannot bear. I request that it be arranged that such inhuman deeds be discontinued, or else done where one does not see it."[136]

As for the fate of Jewish deportees from the Reich, some information seeped back from the very outset. Thus, on December 12, 1941, the SD reported comments from the inhabitants of Minden, near Bielefeld in Westphalia, on the fate of the Jews from their own town, deported to the East a few days beforehand. "Until Warsaw," people were saying, "the deportation takes place in passenger trains. From there on, in cattle cars. . . . In Russia, the Jews were to be put to work in former Soviet factories, while older Jews, or those who were ill, were to be shot."[137]

The killers themselves were not shy about describing their deeds, even regarding mass executions in the supposedly secret operation 14f13. During the last months of 1941, Dr. Friedrich Mennecke, one of the SS physicians directly involved in the operation, left a few notorious letters to his wife—and to posterity. On November 19, 1941, he reported to his "dearest Mummy" from the Ravensbrück women's concentration camp that on that day he had filled out ninety-five forms [of inmates to be murdered], that after completing the task he had supper ("3 sorts of sausages, butter, bread, beer"), that he slept "marvelously" in his bed and felt "perfect."[138] Seven days later he wrote from Buchenwald: The first "portion" of victims was Aryan. "A second portion of some 1200 Jews followed, who need not be 'examined,' but for whom it suffices to take the incarceration reasons (often considerable!) from the file and transfer them to the form. Thus it is a purely theoretical task."[139] A few days later the Jews were transported to Bernburg and gassed.

The German population's reactions to the deportations and the fate of the Jews sent from the Reich to the East, remained diverse as already mentioned. While some of the inhabitants of Minden, for example, welcomed the deportations,[140] others expressed their compassion ("the Jews are also God's creatures").[141] Yet others simply remained hostile to the Jews, whatever may have been happening to them. Thus, in the same area, many housewives were infuriated by a change in the hours allocated to Jews for their food purchase. The change either compelled German housewives to shop at an inconvenient time or to do so together with Jews.[142]

Knowledge about the exterminations also spread to German academics in the East and created panic among some "field researchers." Take the dire straits in which the Viennese Dr. Elfriede Fliethmann from the Race and Folklore (*Volkstumskunde*) section of the Krakow Institute for

Research on the East found herself in October 1941: "We do not know what measures are being planned for the evacuation of the Jewish population in the next few months," Fliethmann wrote on October 22 to her close friend and colleague in the Anthropology Department of the University of Vienna, Dr. Dora Maria Kahlich. "It could possibly happen that if we wait too long, valuable material could escape us; mainly our material could be torn out of its family background and of its habitual environment, whereby the shots would have to be taken under difficult conditions and the very possibilities for photographing would have considerably changed."[143]

Fliethmann and Kahlich were soon on their way to Tarnów in Galicia to take pictures and measurements of various Jewish family members, "so that we could save at least something of the material, in case measures were to be taken."[144] As the "objects" resisted, the snapshots and measurements had to be taken with the "kind" help of the Security Police. Tarnów Orthodox families with many children were the main material; they were considered as "typical representatives of the original Galician Jewry."[145] Both researchers forged energetically ahead as their correspondence of the following weeks showed: They did not hide their enthusiasm about the racial-anthropological "wonders" which they were discovering. Thus Kahlich, who, back in Vienna, was interpreting the material informed Fliethmann of the first results but with all the scientific caution necessary: "I must immediately set something right. I only established that the Jews of Tarnów can be included in the Near eastern-oriental racial mixture, which does not mean that they will not also show some other racial trace."[146]

The importance of Fliethmann's and Kahlich's research led to further inquiries at the SD in Lemberg: Couldn't the Tarnów Jewish community be left in place somewhat longer?[147] We can only surmise what the answer from Lemberg may have been. Nonetheless the preliminary results of Fliethmann's endeavor were not lost. They can still be found in the "Preliminary Report about the Anthropological Photographs of Jewish Families in Tarnów" published in volume 2 of *Deutsche Forschung im Osten* in 1942.[148]

And, at the very time when the Kahlichs and the Fliethmanns of German academe were increasingly worried about the disappearance of their "material," at the end of 1941 and in January 1942, historian Schieder—

whose advice on the handling of Poland's Jews we already encountered in October 1939—was writing a "confidential" survey about ethnic relations in the newly annexed Białystok region. Contrary to the two female anthropologists, the eager historian from Königsberg prided himself on an "extraordinarily good" collaboration with the authorities. Schieder strongly encouraged the same authorities to pursue their policies in regard to the Jewish inhabitants of Białystok; the ghettoization had put an end to the economic primacy acquired by the Jews under the czars and reestablished by other means during the 1939–41 Soviet occupation period when "the Bolshevik organization of the Jewish-Russian bureaucracy soon controlled the entire economic life of the Bialystok district." Schieder uncovered the roots of this Jewish ability to dominate its economic environment in pre-1917 Russian history: Jewish assimilation to Russian society was sheer "whitewash" (*Tünche*) that, in his eyes, "did not deter these Jews from tenaciously keeping the racial characteristics which had allowed them in the past to occupy all key economic positions." Now, however, "Anti-Semitism was becoming understandable to the Belorussians from their everyday experience."[149]

VII

The two most extreme measures taken against the Jews of the Reich from mid-September 1941 on, the introduction of the star and the beginning of the deportations, confronted the German churches with challenges they could no longer disregard. Even more immediately than other segments of German society, the Christian churches had to take a stand, as at least some of the victims were converted Jews.

On September 17, two days before the enforcement of the star decree, Cardinal Theodor Innitzer of Vienna sent out a pastoral letter commending respect and love toward the Catholic Jews; on September 18, the cardinal's message was withdrawn and replaced by a short text from which any mention of love and respect had disappeared; it merely allowed non-Aryan Christians to continue to participate in church life as previously.[150]

Also on September 17, Breslau's Cardinal Bertram set the guidelines for the Church in the Reich. He reminded the Bishops of the equal standing of all Catholics, Aryans or non-Aryans, and demanded that discriminatory measures in church services be avoided "as long as possible." But, if asked by (non-Aryan) Catholics, priests should recommend "attendance of early morning services." If disturbances were to occur, then—and only then—a statement reminding the faithful that the church did not recognize any differences among its members, whatever their background, should be read, but separate church attendance should also be considered.[151] A month later, however, Bertram wrote to Munich's Cardinal Michael von Faulhaber that the church had more urgent issues to deal with than the problem of the converted Jews.[152] As for the Jews as such, they were not even mentioned.

For some Catholic institutions, keeping converts was too much of a burden. In her memoirs Cordelia Edvardson, at the time a young Jewish convert to whose story we shall return, describes a telling episode. Shortly after the introduction of the star, the headmistress of the Berlin branch of the Catholic Girls Association to which Cordelia belonged informed her that "if it became known that one kept members who wore the Jewish star, the authorities would disband the association; it would be better therefore if the girl did not come to their meetings anymore." And, unaware of the irony, the director added: "You know our slogan: one for all and all for one."[153]

Among Protestants stark differences of course appeared between the Confessing congregations and the "German Christians." Some members of the Confessing Church demonstrated outright courage. Thus, in September 1941, Katerine Staritz, a church official in Breslau, published a circular letter in support of the star bearers, calling on her congregation to show an especially welcoming attitude toward them.[154] The SD reported on the circular;[155] the *Schwarze Korps* commented on it, and officials of the church dismissed Staritz from her position as "city curate." A few months later she was shipped to Ravensbrück for a year. Upon her return she was not allowed to perform any significant duties in the church and had to report twice a week to the Gestapo.[156]

As could be expected, the German Christians reacted to the new measure with glee. A few weeks beforehand, they had published a manifesto praising the anti-Bolshevik campaign in the East: "We are opposed," they declared in their message, "to a form of Christianity which allies itself with Bolshevism, which regards the Jews as the Chosen People, and which denies that our Volk and our Race are God-given."[157] For them the introduction of the star allowed barring "Jewish Christians from attending services, entering church buildings, or being buried in Christian cemeteries."[158]

When the deportations from the Reich started, the controversies within both the Protestant and the Catholic churches sharpened. In November 1941 the most prominent personality of the Confessing Church, Bishop Theophil Wurm, tried to convince Goebbels that the measures taken against the non-Aryans could only be grist to the mill of Germany's worst enemies, particularly "Roosevelt and his accomplices."[159] The propaganda minister noted that Wurm probably aspired to play among the Protestants the role held by Galen for the Catholics: "His letter goes to the wastebasket."[160] On December 10 Wurm, in the name of the assembly of church leaders [of the Confessing Church], handed a memorandum addressed to Hitler to State Secretary Friedrich Wilhelm Kritzinger; a short paragraph also alluded to the fate of the Jews: "Much has happened that can help enemy propaganda: we include in this the measures taken to eliminate the mentally ill and the growing hardness in dealing with the non-Aryans, also those who adhere to the Christian faith."[161] There is no known answer.

Thereupon, on December 17, the German Christian church leaders of Saxony, Nassau-Hesse, Mecklenburg, Schleswig-Holstein, Anhalt, Thuringia, and Lübeck announced their position regarding Jews in general and converted Jews more specifically: "The severest measures were to be taken against the Jews," who were "to be expelled from German territories. . . . Racially Jewish Christians have no place and no right in the church." The undersigned church leaders had "discontinued every kind of communion with Jewish Christians."[162]

The German Christian manifesto demanded a response; it came from the highest authority of the Evangelical Church—the Church Chancellery, the mouthpiece of mainstream German Protestantism. An open letter addressed to all provincial churches, published two days before Christmas 1941 and signed by the deputy director, Dr. Günther Fürle, in the name of the chancellery and its spiritual advisory board of three bishops, took an uncompromisingly anti-Semitic stand: "The breakthrough of racial consciousness in our people, intensified by the experience of the war and the corresponding measures taken by the political leadership, has brought about the elimination of Jews from the community of us Germans. This is an incontestable fact, which the German Evangelical

Churches, which serve the one eternal Gospel within the German people and live within the legal domain of this people as corporations under public law, cannot heedlessly ignore. Therefore, in agreement with the Spiritual Council of the German Evangelical Church, we request the highest authorities to take suitable measures so that baptized non-Aryans remain separate from the ecclesiastical life of the German congregations. The baptized non-Aryans will have to find the ways and means to create their own facilities to serve their particular worship and pastoral needs. We will make every effort to help obtain permission for such facilities from the responsible authorities."[163]

Bishop Wurm responded in the name of the Confessing Church. He remained very prudent in his criticism of the chancellery's stand, adding a fair amount of anti-Semitism to his reservations about the discrimination between Aryan and non-Aryan Christians.[164] The Provisional Church (the Confessing Church) Administration was more forthright: "Together with all the Christians in Germany who stand on the ground of the Scripture and the Confession, we are compelled to declare that this request from the Church Chancellery is incompatible with the confession of the church. . . . By what right do we desire to exclude, for racial reasons, Christian non-Aryans from our worship services? Do we want to be like the Pharisees, who renounced communion with the "tax collectors and sinners" in the worship service and, because of this, reaped Christ's judgment?"

To be consistent, the Provisional Church Administration noted, the chancellery would have to "expel . . . all the Apostles and, not least of all, Jesus Christ himself, the Lord of the church, because of their racial membership in the Jewish people." The Provisional Church Administration did not contest, however, that the state could take measures against the Jews and, as in Wurm's case, its statement was not devoid of anti-Jewish comments.[165] The controversy persisted for several months, while an increasing number of regional churches adopted the chancellery's attitude.[166]

Klepper, who in the meantime had been dismissed from the Wehrmacht on account of his Jewish wife, had resumed his diary recordings. On Christmas Day 1941, he noted: "No solution has yet been found [in K.'s church] for the carriers of the star [his wife and daughter, although both Protestants by then, had to display the star, of course]. . . . Today no

Jew with the star was present at the Christmas service" [*Heute war kein Jude mit dem Stern in der Weihnachtskirche*].[167]

The lack of *public* response of the German Catholic church to the deportations and to the growing awareness of the mass exterminations in the East was calculated. A small group of bishops (Gröber, Berning, and Preysing) had drafted a pastoral letter that bore the date November 15, 1941; it listed and denounced in clear and courageous terms the hostile measures taken by the state and party authorities against the church and its institutions, as well as against the basic rights of Germans to life, freedom, and property; the Jewish issue was not included in the text.[168] The reason adduced for this omission is to be found in an unsigned memorandum dated November 25 found in Cardinal Faulhaber's archives; in setting the guidelines for the publication of the pastoral message, it indicates the reason for this omission: "(2) Simultaneously with the reading [of the message], the Reich government will be informed of its content; it will be told that this public way had to be chosen, as none of the petitions or memoranda [addressed to the authorities] were adequately answered. Moreover, some further issues are to be presented to the government that could not be dealt with in the pastoral letter without hurting the reputation of the people and the government (Jewish question, treatment of Russian prisoners, atrocities of the SS in Russia, etc.)."[169]

There may have been several reasons for avoiding the "Jewish question": a tactical show of moderation despite what could have appeared as a public confrontation with the regime, or the avoidance of issues that may have found little echo among the churchgoing part of the population. Whatever the reasons may have been, Cardinal Bertram opposed the publication of the letter "in principle and for practical reasons."[170]

The exclusion of the "Jewish question" from the draft letter was of particular significance given that it was decided by two out of the three bishops who usually showed the greatest concern for the fate of converts and even of Jews as such (Preysing and Berning). It was even more significant in light of the declaration of these same bishops that the success or failure of the letter was not the essential issue, and that all that mattered was: "What is our duty in the present moment? What does conscience require? What does God, what do German believers expect of their bishops?"[171] Finally, as the letter was still being debated in early 1942, the exclusion takes on an even more ominous significance in light of what was becoming known about the fate of the deportees.

Margarete Sommer, in charge of relief work at the Berlin archdiocese, was informed in early 1942 by Lithuanian Catholics and also, it seems, by Hans Globke, a high official of the Ministry of the Interior, of the mass killings in the Baltic countries of Jews deported from the Reich.[172] After meeting with Sommer, Bishop Berning of Osnabrück noted on February 5, 1942: "For months no news arrived from Litzmannstadt. All postcards are returned. . . . Transports from Berlin arrive in Kovno, but it is doubtful whether anybody is still alive. No exact news from Minsk and Riga. Many have been shot. The intention is to exterminate the Jews entirely" [*Es besteht wohl der Plan die Juden ganz auszurotten*].[173]

At the Paderborn conference of November 24 and 25, 1941, the German episcopate dealt with one further "Jewish" issue: separation from the spouses of mixed marriages on the demand of the Aryan partner. The bishops decided to deal with each case individually, according to "pastoral wisdom."[174]

Two months before the debates about the pastoral letter, an anonymous German Jew addressed a letter to Bishop Galen. He expressed his admiration for the bishop's stand on euthanasia and reminded him of what was happening to the Jews in Germany, even to deeply patriotic Jews like himself who were no longer allowed to be Germans. "Only the senseless wish, the mad hope," the letter ended, "that somewhere a helper will stand up for us incited me to address this letter to you. May God bless you!"[175] Galen went on preaching throughout the war and his patriotic and anti-Bolshevik exhortations carried no less fervor than his defense of the mentally ill.[176] About the persecution of the Jews, however, even in private letters he never uttered one single word.

Bernhard Lichtenberg, prior of Saint Hedwig's Cathedral in Berlin, was a lone exception. Like Pastor Grüber on the Protestant side, Lichtenberg was helping non-Aryan Catholics. And from November 1938 on, during every evening service he prayed aloud for the Jews. On August 29, 1941, two women parishioners denounced him to the Gestapo. He was arrested on October 23, 1941, interrogated, and sentenced to prison on May 29, 1942. He died on his way to Dachau on November 3, 1943.[177]

VIII

In late 1941, as details about the fate of the Jews in the East were seeping back into the Reich, British high officials were also becoming aware of the mass murders on Soviet territory, from decoded German messages. However, any such information remained strictly secret to protect the most precious trump card of the war: the possession of a German "Enigma" encoding machine that gave access to a large number of enemy radio communications.[178]

In the meantime the leadership of American Jewry and that of the Jewish community in Palestine seemed rather unconcerned about the European situation, both because of inadequate information and more pressing and immediate challenges. For American Jews their veneration of Roosevelt and their fear of anti-Semitism added to the reticence regarding any interventions that might have displeased "the Chief" and the higher levels of the administration. At times, however, these Jewish leaders may have overstepped the limits of subservience by taking measures that, unwittingly no doubt, added to the hardship of ghetto inhabitants.

In the spring of 1941 Rabbi Wise had decided to impose a complete embargo on all aid sent to Jews in occupied countries, in compliance with the U.S. government's economic boycott of the Axis powers (whereby every food package was seen as direct or indirect assistance to the enemy). The "patriotic" surrender to the boycott also stemmed from political considerations regarding postwar relations of the American Jewish leadership with Britain, mainly on the question of Palestine.[179] Strict orders were given to World Jewish Congress representatives in Europe to halt forthwith any shipment of packages to the ghettos, despite the fact that these packages did usually reach their destination, the Jewish Self-Help Association in Warsaw. "All these operations with and through Poland must cease at once," Wise cabled to Congress delegates in London and in Geneva, "and at once in English means AT ONCE, not in the future."[180]

The display of unconditional Americanism became particularly loud after Lindbergh's anti-Jewish attack in Des Moines, in September 1941. "We will not put even what he [Lindbergh] considers our 'interests' before those of our country," the American Jewish Committee responded, "since our interests and those of our country are one and indivisible." The American Jewish Congress was no less decisive in tone and content: "Surely it is needless to state that we [Jews] are of and for America as truly as any other group within the nation. . . . We have no view or attitude in relation to foreign affairs that is not determined solely by American interests, the needs and interests of our own free country."[181] Official American Jewry was paralyzed.

More perplexing in many ways was the attitude of the Jewish leadership in Palestine. At the beginning of the war, the Jewish Agency Executive had established a four-member committee to monitor the situation of European Jewry. The head of the committee, Itzhak Gruenbaum, himself a former member of the Polish parliament, did not instill much energy or sense of purpose into the activities of his group. Nobody, it must be added, seems to have prodded him on or questioned his ability to fulfill the (undefined) task. In the first months of 1941 for example, the Committee of Four published an overview of the situation in Europe that defined the German policy in Poland as aiming at the destruction of Jewish economic life in that country; "the Jews," it added, "were fighting for their dignity with all their strength, refusing to give up."[182]

At the time the strongest political party of the Yishuv was Mapai ("Party of the Workers of Eretz Israel," in other words the "Labor Party"); it was the major political force in all the central institutions of the Jewish community in the country and particularly in the most important of them—its highest executive body, The Jewish Agency. The one political leader who, in turn, held a dominant position in Mapai in general and on the Jewish Agency Executive in particular (although he had formally resigned as its chairman at that time), was David Ben-Gurion.

In February 1941 Ben-Gurion returned to Palestine after a lengthy stay in Great Britain and in the United States. His comments at a meeting with his Mapai colleagues offer an indication of what had been and would be his approach to the events in Europe: a uniquely Zionist perspective. After mentioning that the Yishuv was not fully aware of the scope of the war, he 'turned to the situation of the Jews: "No one can estimate the enormity of the destruction of the Jewish people ["destruction" was not meant as physical extermination.] . . . Of course there is information available on all this, but people here are not living out these matters. . . . What we must do now, more than anything, above all and before anything, for ourselves and for the Diaspora, that same small Diaspora still left to us . . . is [create] Zionist commitment."[183] In other words, for Ben-Gurion there was but one way of helping European Jewry: achieving the goals of Zionism. And simultaneously such help would eventually allow a Jewish state in Palestine to survive.

Notwithstanding Ben-Gurion's exhortations, no concrete plans emerged from the Yishuv throughout most of 1941. The Jewish Agency hardly dealt with the situation in Europe, and the common opinion was that nothing much could be done to alleviate whatever suffering there was.[184] Between August and December 1941, the Mapai Central Committee did not address the plight of European Jewry even once.[185]

Richard Lichtheim, the delegate of the Jewish Agency in Geneva, whose reports had been a steady series of warnings about the looming catastrophe, himself seemed to hesitate about possible developments in view of the first German setbacks on the Eastern Front. In the final lines of a report sent to Jerusalem on December 22, 1941, about the fate of German Jews, he considered two contrary yet possible developments: "The turn of the tide on the Eastern Front may have the effect that the expulsions of the Jews from the Reich will cease, at least temporarily, owing to transport difficulties and to the necessity of employing all available labor in the German factories; it may also lead—and that is a tragic probability—to further persecutions and pogroms in Germany and in the occupied territories if the wounded beast of prey feels that the end is near."[186]

IX

Throughout the Reich and the Protectorate, the local Jewish community offices were informed well in advance of the date of deportations from their area. The local Gestapo station received the lists of names from the district office of the Reichsvereinigung and decided whom to include in the upcoming transport. Those designated for departure were given a serial number and informed by the Reichsvereinigung or by the Gestapo about the procedures regarding assets, homes, outstanding bills, the amount of cash allowed, the authorized weight of the luggage (usually fifty kilograms), the amount of food for the journey (three to five days, and so on), as well as the date by which they had to be ready. From then on they were forbidden to leave their homes—even briefly—without permission from the authorities.[187] For some Jews, the summons seems to have come more suddenly; thus, in Breslau, Willy Cohn interrupted his diary in midsentence. On November 17, he started to describe his visit to the community offices and his conversation with the chairman, Dr. Kohn: "First, he told me, that at the Secret State Police [Gestapo] there was no possibility. . . ."[188]

On the departure day these Jews were assembled by the Schutzpolizei and marched or driven in trucks to a waiting area where they would be kept, sometimes for several days, before being marched again or driven to the railway station, often in broad daylight and in full view of the population. According to Herta Rosenthal, then sixteen years old, deported from Leipzig to Riga in January 1942, when the Jews were taken by truck from the school where they had been assembled to the railway station, "Everybody saw it, and they were screaming bloody murder. All the Jews were leaving Leipzig and they [the Germans] were happy, a lot of them. They were standing there laughing. . . . They brought us up during the day, not at night. There were both SA and ordinary citizens there."[189] Rosenthal's testimony is confirmed by various contemporary reports. As the twelve Jews of Forchheim were taken from the *Paradeplatz* ("parade square") to the railway station on their way to Bamberg, Nuremberg, and Riga, on November 27, 1941, "a great number of inhabitants gathered [in the square] and followed the evacuation [*Abtransport*] with interest and great satisfaction."[190] A minority reacted differently, and in Bremen, for example, ten members of the Confessing Church were briefly arrested in early December of that year as they were taking up a collection for the Jews about to be evacuated.[191]

In exceptional cases some Jews were taken off the deportation list, even at the very last moment: Marianne Ellenbogen (at that time, Strauss) and her parents were among them. It all took place in their hometown, Essen, on October 26, 1941. The house was sealed and, luggage in hand, the family set off for the assembly point. There many of the city's Jews were already waiting. Boarding of the streetcar that was to take them to the railway station had started when two Gestapo officials arrived and told the Strausses to go back home. "We were sent back home," Marianne reminisced, "and that was the most dreadful experience anybody had, to hear this animal howl go up [from the crowd of fellow Jews]."

The wealthy Strausses had apparently promised the director of the Deutsche Bank in Essen, Friedrich Wilhelm Hammacher, an old business acquaintance of Strauss senior, to sell him their house at a very advantageous price. Hammacher, it seems, got in touch with high-ranking Abwehr (military intelligence) officers who used some Jews, allowed to emigrate, as agents, mainly in North and South America. The Abwehr was interested in the Strausses; its Bremen headquarters informed the Düsseldorf Gestapo, which in turn instructed the Essen Gestapo to set the family free. Nothing came of the project in the end.[192] In 1943 the Strausses were deported to the East and perished with their fellow Jews. Marianne escaped and went into hiding in Germany.[193]

Other Jews also avoided deportation, but differently. "Nineteen Jews who should have gone with the first transport from Vienna to Lodz on October 15 took their own lives, either by jumping from windows or by gassing themselves, by hanging, with sleeping tablets, by drowning, or by means unknown. Within the space of three weeks, the Gestapo reported 84 suicides and 87 suicide attempts in Vienna."[194] According to statistics of the Berlin police, 243 Jews took their lives during the last three months of 1941 (from the beginning of the deportations to the end of the year).[195] The quota was filled with other Jews, of course.

"In the evening," Goebbels recorded in his diary, on November 7, 1941, "the unpleasant news that the [non-Jewish] actor [Joachim] Gottschalk, who was married to a Jewish wife, committed suicide with wife and child . . . I take all measures so that this humanly regrettable but concretely almost unavoidable case should not lead to the spreading of alarming rumors."[196]

The first transport of Jews from Munich left the Bavarian capital on November 20; its original destination had been Riga but since the Riga ghetto was overfilled, the train was redirected to Kovno. All the deportees were inmates of the barracks camp in Milbertshofen. The young Erwin Weil was ordered to help those unable to board the train on their own: "At the merchandise station stood a long train with the locomotive already under steam. The people were pushed into the wagons under a hail of the wildest curses. At daybreak we were yelled at to throw out the luggage, so that the people would be pushed in faster. Then a bus arrived with armed SS and the (small) children from the Antonienstrasse. We had to put them on the train. We tried to calm their panic; it was horrible."[197] On November 23 the transport arrived in Kovno. There too the ghetto was overfilled; the deportees never even came close to it, as we know. They were directly transported to fort IX. For two days they remained in the ditches surrounding the fort. On November 25 they were murdered.[198]

During the journey to the East, the transports were guarded by members of the *Schutzpolizei* (SCHUPO). "On the way from the *Schlachthof* [slaughterhouse] to the loading ramp a Jewish male tried to commit suicide by jumping under a tramway," SCHUPO captain Salitter wrote in his reported about the December 11 transport of 1,007 Jews from Düsseldorf to Riga, for which he was responsible. "Also," he went on, "an elderly Jewess moved stealthily away from the loading ramp, taking advantage of the fact that it was very dark and rainy. She dashed into a nearby house, where she quickly undressed and went to a public bath. But a cleaning woman spotted her and she was brought back to the transport."

Salitter then described the journey, via Berlin and eastward. In Konitz he got into a squabble with the stationmaster. For better surveillance Salitter demanded that one of the carriages transporting the Jews be switched with that of the *Schutzpolizei*; the stationmaster refused and offered to move the passengers: "It seems necessary for the train authorities to explain to this employee that members of the German police must be treated differently from Jews. I was under the impression that he was one of those Germans who still thought of them as 'poor Jews' and for whom the concept 'Jew' was totally unknown."

Finally, on December 13, around midnight, the train arrived in the vicinity of Riga. The outside temperature had dropped to minus 10 degrees Celsius. The Germans were brought to the city and replaced by Latvian guards; the Jews were left in the unheated train until the following morning. In Riga, Salitter met with Latvians who told him about the attitude of the population: "They especially hate the Jews, this being the reason they took such an intensive part in the annihilation of these parasites since the liberation [from Soviet rule]. Through my contacts . . . I heard that some of the people wonder why Germany bothers to transport the Jews to Latvia instead of annihilating them right there."[199]

A deportee from Berlin, Haim Baram (Heinz Bernhardt at the time), described the arrival of his transport in Minsk. The train had left Berlin on December 14, 1941; it arrived in Minsk on the eighteenth at 10 a.m. Latvian SS auxiliaries chased everybody out of the cars; the elderly and the children were driven away in trucks, while the bulk of the deportees were marched to a neighborhood of wooden huts (without water or electricity) whose inhabitants had disappeared. "The wrecked houses looked as if a pogrom had taken place there. Pillow feathers everywhere. Hanukah lamps and candlesticks laying around in every corner. . . . Later we were informed that this was the Russian ghetto whose Jewish residents were shot in early November 1941." An SD officer confirmed what had happened. Most of the inhabitants of the ghetto had been massacred to make space for the transports from Germany. [The officer] "pointed and said: 'There, in front of you, a heap of bodies.' And in fact we saw a hillock with parts of human bodies sticking out."[200]

Oskar Rosenfeld was deported from Prague to Lodz on November 4, 1941, in the last of the transports that had carried some 5,000 Jews from the Protectorate to Lodz before the end of the year. From then on most Jews from Bohemia and Moravia would be deported to Theresienstadt, a "transit camp" on the way to the killing sites for part of the inmates (but a camp whose function in the general extermination system was a peculiar one, as we shall see).

Born in Moravia, Rosenfeld grew up in Vienna, where he became a journalist and a writer, somewhat in the expressionist vein of his time. His major interest, however, seems to have been theater. In 1909 he established the first Jewish theater in the Austrian capital; later on he encouraged visits to Vienna by Yiddish and Hebrew theater companies. In many ways an intellectual like Klemperer, Rosenfeld was his opposite in terms of Jewish outlook and politics—he was a staunch "anti-assimilationist" and a right-wing (revisionist) Zionist to boot. After the Anschluss, Oskar and his wife, Henriette, fled to Prague. Henriette managed to leave for England in the summer of 1939; he was to follow. The war put an end to his emigration plans.[201] In early November 1941, after the usual summons, Rosenfeld had to report to the assembly point at the Messepalast (The Fair Palace).

"The Messepalast was a warehouse," Rosenfeld recorded in his Notebook A, "where, instead of goods and wares, people were exhibited, closely pressed together in bunks, resting on backpacks and mattresses, with bundles, suitcases, packages, stuffed to bursting, and cots that served as sleeping places. Three days and three nights they lingered here, in this filthy warehouse, slowly consuming their stores of food since the provisions from the Jewish community were inadequate."[202]

Rosenfeld went on, describing the days and nights at the Messepalast and the last expropriation measures before departure. The trek to the railway station took place without any secrecy: "Along the way, behind the windows of the houses, the faces of the Czechs were visible, here and there Czech passersby, without exception serious faces, some sad, pensive, disturbed. A train was waiting. Doors were pulled open, they entered the cars by numbers, which each one had to display clearly visible on clothing and luggage."[203]

The deportees were not informed of their destination, and it was only in the course of the journey, once they saw "the desolate Polish landscape," that they guessed it would be Lodz. In a strange improvisation, the officers in charge of the transport ordered, in the middle of the night, that the men shave their faces and polish their shoes: "Hungover, hungry, sleepy, hundreds of men began to polish their shoes in the dark coupé and to shave with a shaver, [using] water from the toilet. From time to time a Gestapo man with a flashlight appeared and had some of them line up, cursing when an evacuee didn't seem elegant enough for him."[204] The transport stopped on the outskirts of the ghetto, and one thousand Jews were marched to a school building, their temporary quarters. Within days hunger set in, weakness increased, and some died of "enfeeblement" in their temporary abode.

At the beginning of December the deportees from the Reich and the Protectorate to Lodz were still living in separate encampments, although they could move around in the ghetto in search of some work, of possible deals to enhance the weekly ration of bread (a single loaf) or of the daily cabbage soup (whose very odor usually brought nausea): "At the beginning of winter, the price of a loaf of bread on the bread exchange, on the black market, is already 20 marks. From autumn to the beginning of winter it rose from 8 to 20. But the selling prices for textiles, clothing, shoes, leather bags, did not keep up with the bread prices, so the owners of the wares they had brought along sank daily into greater poverty."[205]

On September 23, Rumkowski had been informed by the Germans of coming deportations into the ghetto. Statistics gathered by the "Elder" regarding overcrowding obviously had no effect whatsoever. For the 143,000 inhabitants of the ghetto in the fall of 1941, first the arrivals of Jews from the surrounding small towns and then of the 20,000 Jews from the Reich and the Protectorate and of 5,000 Gypsies meant a sudden 20 percent increase in the population. Seen from the perspective of the new arrivals it meant sleeping in evacuated school buildings and halls of all types, often on the floor and without heating or running water; for most, toilets were located a few buildings away. For the ghetto inhabitants it meant greater overcrowding, less food, and other unpleasant consequences, as we shall see. Tension between the newcomers and the ghetto population became unavoidable.[206]

During the first two weeks of October 1941, everyday life in the ghetto had followed its "normal" course, notwithstanding the arrival of the approximately 2,000 Jews from Włocławek and the surrounding small towns. The chroniclers reported "beautiful" autumn weather, 277 deaths, and eighteen births ("October 9 marked the lowest daily death rate since the inception of the ghetto: scarcely 11 people died that day"). They also counted five suicide attempts and one murder.[207] Then came the dumping of the 20,000 new deportees.

The "Chronicle" entries for the second half of October are lost and with them the first semi-official reactions to the new situation. Sierakowiak, however, kept his own recordings of the events. "October 16: The first transport of deportees from Vienna arrived . . . in the afternoon. There are thousands of them, pastors and doctors among them, and some have sons on the front. They have brought a carload of bread with them and excellent luggage, and are dressed splendidly. Every day the same number is supposed to arrive, up to 20,000. They will probably overwhelm us completely."[208]

The next day Sierakowiak witnessed the arrival of a transport from Prague; again he noticed the cartloads of bread, the luggage, the clothes: "I have heard," he added, "that they have been inquiring whether it's possible to get a two-room apartment with running water. Interesting types."[209] On October 18 the young diarist brought up the same theme again. On October 19, however, the first practical consequences of the influx of the new deportees were recorded: "More Luxembourg Jews arrived today. They are beginning to crowd the ghetto. They have only one patch on the left breast with the inscription *Jude*. They are dressed splendidly (you can tell they haven't lived in Poland). They are buying up all they can in the ghetto, and all the prices have doubled. Bread is 12 to 13RM; socks which cost 70pf. before, are now 2RM. Although they have been here only a few days, they already complain about hunger. So what can we say, we who haven't had our stomach full for more than a year? You can apparently get used to everything."[210]

The economic disruption soon worsened: "Since the transports arrived from Germany," the "Chronicle" reported in November 1941, "all the restaurants and pastry shops in the ghetto, half-empty until then, have truly been besieged by newcomers. . . . From the moment they arrived the newcomers began selling their personal property and, with the cash they received, began to buy up literally everything available on the private food market. In the course of time, this caused a shortage in the food supply, and prices rose horrendously with indescribable speed. On the other hand, the availability of all sorts of items which had been lacking in the ghetto for quite a while has caused trade to become brisk, and a few of the ghetto's stores have shelves filled with goods that have not been seen in the ghetto for a long time. Because of the newcomers who are popularly known as *Yekes*, stores never really closed their doors in the month of November. They sold their clothing, shoes, linen, cosmetics, traveling accessories, and so forth. For a short while this caused a decline in prices for the most varied items; however, to match the price increase on the food market, the newcomers began to raise the prices of the items they were selling. From the point of view of the ghetto's previous inhabitants, this relatively large increase in private commerce has caused undesired disturbances and difficulties and, what is worse, the newcomers have, in a short span of time, caused a devaluation of the [ghetto] currency. That phenomenon is particularly painful for the mass of working people, the most important segment of ghetto society, who only possess the money they draw from the coffers of the Elder of the Jews."[211]

Immediately after the war some of the surviving deportees to Lodz confirmed the unexpected effects of their arrival upon business transactions within the ghetto—and with the Germans: "I had a new suit of clothes," Jacob M. recalled, "for which I had paid 350 marks in Hamburg . . . I got 1 kilo [2.2 pounds] of flour for it. You could purchase a pair of shoes for 100 grams of margarine. . . . Germans who would at times come into the ghetto with 1 pound of bread or margarine would leave with a trunkful of new things."[212]

X

As transports of deportees were arriving in Lodz from the Reich and Protectorate, the Germans started murdering part of the ghetto's inhabitants. On December 6 the Chelmno gas vans had become operational and that same day Rumkowski was ordered to have 20,000 of "his" Jews [the local Jews] ready for "labor deployment outside the ghetto." The number was finally reduced to 10,000. Shortly afterward the *Chronicle* recorded a sudden interruption of all mail services between the ghetto and the outside world. On the face of it the chroniclers could not make any sense of the order: "There have been various stories concerning the suspension of mail service, and a question of fundamental interest has been whether this was a purely local event or whether there have been nationwide restrictions. There are, in addition, conjectures about the reasons behind this latest restriction."[213] Obviously the chroniclers could not write that these conjectures pointed to the forthcoming deportation.[214]

As rumors continued to spread, Rumkowski decided to address the issue in a speech at the House of Culture on January 3, 1942: "I don't like to waste words," the Elder began that part of the speech, according to the "Chronicle" record: "The stories circulating today are one hundred percent false. I have recently agreed to accept twenty thousand Jews from the smaller centers, setting as a condition that the territory of the ghetto must be enlarged. At the present time, only those who are in my opinion deserving of such fate will be resettled elsewhere. The authorities are full of admiration for the work which has been performed in the ghetto and it is due to that work that they have confidence in me. Their approval of my motion to reduce the number of deportees from 20,000 to 10,000 is a sign of that confidence. I have complete confidence in the Resettlement Commission. Obviously it too is capable of making mistakes from time to time. . . . Bear in mind that at the center of all my projects is the aspiration that honest people may sleep in peace. Nothing bad will happen to people of goodwill." (Thunderous applause.)[215]

We do not have Sierakowiak's notes for the period of the January deportations, but Rosenfeld described some of the ghetto scenes of these same days, albeit not in precisely dated entries: "The [Jewish] police stormed the lodgings of the Jews marked for evacuation. Not infrequently they found the corpses of children who had starved to death or of old people who had frozen to death. . . . Only 12½ kg of luggage and 10 marks of money were allowed to be taken away. . . . The bundles of the evacuees contained slices of bread, potatoes, margarine. . . . They had better not be sick. No doctor accompanied them, no medications."[216]

From Rosenfeld's notes it appears that he did not yet know where the transports were headed. Between January 12 and 29, 10,103 Jews were deported from Lodz to Chelmno and gassed.

The deportations continued in February and March: By April 2, a further 34,073 ghetto Jews had been deported and murdered. "Nobody was safe anymore from being deported," Rosenfeld noted; "at least eight hundred people had to be delivered every day. Some thought they would be able to save themselves: chronically ill old people and those with frozen limbs—not even that helped. The surgeons in the hospital were very busy. They amputated hands and feet of the poor 'patients' and discharged them as cripples. The cripples too were taken away. On March 7 nine people froze to death at the railway station where they had to wait nine hours for the departure of the train."[217]

Rosenfeld's comments about the deporation of cripples find a poignant echo in a diary fragment written by an anonymous young girl from the ghetto, covering merely three weeks, from the end of February to mid-March 1942. The diarist tells about her friend, Hania Huberman [mostly HH in the diary], "extremely intelligent and wise. She knows life. A third-year gymnasium student, a very good girl." The diarist and HH herself were both convinced that HH would not be deported because she had a crippled father who could not walk. Then, on March 3 the news arrived: "Hania H. was leaving." The diarist could not imagine how her friend and her father would face the future: "Where will she go with her sick, helpless father, without a shirt for him and with nothing for herself? Hungry, exhausted, without money and food. My mom immediately found some shirts for her and her father. My sister and I ran upstairs. When I came back, I couldn't stop crying. I couldn't stay there longer because I had to finish the laundry. . . . I promised to visit her."[218]

Rumors spread among some of the Germans working in the Chelmno area—and probably among the local Poles. Heinz May was forest inspector (*Forstmeister*) in Kolo County, near Lodz. In the fall of 1941 May was informed by Forest Constable Stagemeir that some commandos had arrived in the vicinity. In reporting this "Stagemeier was strangely serious," a detail to which May did not pay attention at the moment. Somewhat later, as May was traveling through the forest with *Kreisleiter* Becht, the district chief pointed to Precinct 77 and declared: "The trees will be growing better soon"; by way of explanation, Becht added: "Jews make good fertilizer." Nothing else.

Strange events occurred in May's precinct over the following weeks: A closed truck about four meters in length and two meters high, with iron bolt and padlock in the rear, was being pulled out of a ditch by another truck among a group of policemen: "A definitely unpleasant smell came from the truck and from the men standing around it." May and his son, who arrived on the scene, were quickly chased away. A succession of further incidents and some rumors induced May to drive to Stagemeier's home for more information.

"Stagemeier explained to me," May reported in 1945 testimony, "that a large detachment of military police was stationed in Chelmno. The palace [castle] on the western side of Chelmno had been enclosed by a high wooden fence. Military police sentries armed with rifles were standing by the entrance. . . . I passed by there on the way back to my forest district and confirmed that what Stagemeier had said concerning the wooden fence and the sentries was true. There were row upon row of trucks with improvised canvas tops in Chelmno. Women, men, and even children had been crammed into those trucks. . . . During the short time I was there I saw the first truck drive up to the wooden fence. The sentries opened the gates. The truck vanished into the palace courtyard and immediately afterwards another closed truck came out of the courtyard and headed for the forest. And then both sentries closed the gates. There was no longer the slightest doubt that terrible things, things never before known in human history, were being played out there."[219]

The killing capacity of Chelmno was approximately 1,000 people a day (around fifty people could be crammed into each of the three vans). The first victims were the Jews from villages and small towns in the Lodz area. Then, before the deportation of the Jews from the Lodz ghetto started, came the turn of the Gypsies herded into a special area of the ghetto (the Gypsy camp). "For the last ten days the Gypsies have been taken away in trucks, according to people who live in the immediate vicinity of the [Gypsy] camp,"[220] the entry for the first week of January 1942 in the ghetto "Chronicle" indicates. Approximately 4,400 Gypsies were killed in Chelmno but there were few witnesses. After the war some Poles who lived in the area mentioned the Gypsies, as did both the driver of one of the gas vans and another SS member of Lange's unit. None of the Gypsies survived.[221]

As mentioned, the vast majority of the Lodz ghetto inhabitants remained unaware of Chelmno, although over the weeks and months information reached them in diverse ways. Strangely enough some information was even sent by mail. Thus on December 31, 1941, three weeks after the beginning of the exterminations, an unknown Jew sent a card later forwarded to Lodz to an acquaintance in Posbebice: "Dear cousin Mote Altszul, as you know from Kolo, Dabie, and other places Jews have been sent to Chelmno to a castle. Two weeks have already passed and it is not known how several thousands have perished. They are gone and you should know, there will be no addresses for them. They were sent to the forest and they were buried. . . . Do not look upon this as a small matter, they have decided to wipe out, to kill, to destroy. Pass this letter on to learned people to read."[222]

Two weeks later a letter based on an eyewitness account was sent by the rabbi of Grabów to his brother-in-law in Lodz: "Until now I have not replied to your letters because I did not know exactly about all the things people have been talking about. Unfortunately, for our great tragedy, now we know it all. I have been visited by an eyewitness who survived only by accident, he managed to escape from hell. . . . I found out about everything from him. The place where all perish is called Chelmno, not far from Dabie, and all are hidden in the neighboring forest of Lochów. People are killed in two different ways: By firing squad or by poison gas. This is what happened to the cities Dabie, Isbicza, Kujawska, Klodawa, and others. Lately thousands of Gypsies have been brought there from the so-called Gypsy camps of Lodz, and for the past several days, Jews have been brought there from Lodz and the same is done to them. Do not think that I am mad. Alas, this is the tragic cruel truth. . . . O Creator of the world, help us! Jakob Schulman."[223]

The eyewitness was probably the man called the "gravedigger from Chelmno," Yakov Groyanowski from Izbica, a member of the Jewish commando that dug the pits into which the corpses were thrown in the forest. The gravedigger's story reached both Ringelblum and Yitzhak Zuckerman, a Zionist youth leader in Warsaw.[224] He told of people undressing in the castle for showering and disinfection, then being pushed into the vans and suffocated by the exhaust gas pumped in during the ride to the forest, some sixteen kilometers away. "Many of the people they [the gravediggers] dealt with had suffocated to death in the truck. But there were a few exceptions, including babies who were still alive; this was because mothers held the children in blankets and covered them with their hands so the gas would not get to them. In these cases, the Germans would split the heads of the babies on trees, killing them on the spot." Groyanowski managed to flee, and hid in small communities (probably also in Grabów) until he reached Warsaw, in early January 1942.

XI

In Western Europe, in the meantime, life—a kind of life—was going on. In Paris the bombing of the synagogues didn't cause any panic among the Jewish population. Although the round-ups of hostages, the executions, and the sending of thousands of Jews to Compiègne and Drancy signaled a worsening situation, Biélinky's diary entries did not indicate a sense of upheaval.[225] On October 9 it was registration time again, and Biélinky noted the long line of " 'B's. . . . It is interesting to notice," he added, "that in this crowd of Jews, thoroughly Jewish types are rare; all look physically like ordinary Parisians . . . no trace of a ghetto."[226] Most of his entries in these days dealt with the ongoing difficulties in getting enough food.

For Lambert, in October, the new German victories in the East did not mean the end of the war. "But, what will become of France and what will become of us, the Jews, in the meantime?"[227] Lambert's question was somewhat rhetorical as he immediately added in the same October 12 entry: "Of course, in this immense blaze, Jewish worry is but one element of the universal anxiety and expectation. This quietens me, at least in regard to the future of my sons, as a Pole, a Belgian or a Dutch are not more assured of the next day than I am myself."[228] A few weeks later, at the end of December, one thing at least had become clear: The outcome of the war was no longer in question. "Victory is certain; it could even take place in 1942."[229]

In Bucharest in these same days, Sebastian certainly did not feel that his fate as a Jew was like that of other Romanians. He wanted to flee: "Never have I thought so intensely about leaving," he wrote on October 16. "I know it's absurd, I know it's impossible, I know it's pointless, I know it's too late—but I can't help it. . . . In the last few days I have read a number of American magazines . . . and I suddenly saw in detail another world, another milieu, other cities, another time."[230] He wished to sail on the *Struma* that was taking some seven hundred "illegal" emigrants to Palestine.[231] Maybe he could join.

Sebastian, like most Jews in Romania, knew what was happening to the Jews in Bessarabia, Bukovina, and—Transnistria. "It is an anti-Jewish delirium that nothing can stop," he wrote on October 20. "There are no brakes, no rhyme or reason. It would be something if there were an anti-Semitic program; you'd know the limits to which it might go. But this is sheer uncontrolled bestiality, without shame or conscience, without goal or purpose. Anything, absolutely anything, is possible. I see the pallor of fear on Jewish faces."[232]

In the diary entries that followed from mid-October to mid-December, Sebastian reacted to the daily indignities and threats that targeted Romanian Jewry (before and after Antonescu's public letter to Filderman) which, in Sebastian's eyes, was an intentional call for violence.[233] Well-intentioned Romanian friends tried to convince the Jewish writer to convert to Catholicism: "The Pope will defend you!" they argued.[234] "I don't need arguments to answer them, nor do I search for any," he noted on December 17. . . . Even if it were not so stupid and pointless, I would still need no arguments. Somewhere on an island with sun and shade, in the midst of peace, security, and happiness, I would in the end be indifferent to whether I was or was not Jewish. But here and now, I cannot be anything else. Nor do I think I want to be."[235]

In the Reich the Jews not included in the first wave of deportations desperately attempted to understand the new measures and their personal fate. "Even more shocking reports about deportations of Jews to Poland," Klemperer noted on October 25. "They have to leave almost literally naked and penniless. Thousands from Berlin to Lodz. . . . Will Dresden be affected and when? It hangs over us all the time."[236] November 1: "Today urgent warning card from Sussman, he must have read something alarming about the deportations, I should immediately renew my USA application. . . . I wrote back immediately, every route was now blocked. In fact, we heard from several sources that a complete ban on all emigration has just been decreed on the German side."[237] November 28: "The alarm abroad about the deportations must be very great: Without having asked for them, Lissy Meyerhof and Caroli Stern received, by telegram, from relatives in the USA visa and passage to Cuba. But it doesn't help them; the German side is not issuing any passports . . . cf. also Sussman's card to me. We weighed matters up again. Result as always: stay. If we go, then we save our lives and are dependents and beggars for the rest of our lives. If we remain, then our lives are in danger, but we retain the possibility of afterward leading a life worth living. Consolation in spite of it all: going hardly depends on us anymore. Everything is fate, one could be rushing to one's doom. If, e.g., we had moved to Berlin in the spring, then by now I would probably be in Poland."[238]

Klemperer's rationalizations (ultimately borne out in his case, albeit by pure chance), were common among those who did not immediately board the trains. Hertha Feiner assumed that her status as former wife of an Aryan would save her: "We have serious worries and are living through a very grave time," she wrote to her daughters on October 16. "I can't and won't burden you with details; I am fortunate in being better off than many others. You don't have to worry about me. Because of my special status, I hope to be able to go on living here as before. Should there be any change, I would notify you immediately, but I don't think there will be."[239]

The only aspects of everyday life shared in various degrees by most Jews living throughout the German-dominated continent at the end of 1941 were the daily struggles for material survival, the sense of complete lack of any control over their own fate, and the passionate hope that, somehow, liberation was on its way. Even in Rubinowicz's remote hamlet, in the Kielce district, the total uncertainty about the fate of Jews, day in, day out, was inescapable in those winter days. "Yesterday afternoon I went to Bodzentyn to get my tooth filled," young Dawid noted on December 12. "Early this morning the militia came. As they were driving along the highway, they met a Jew who was going out of town, and they immediately shot him for no reason, then they drove on and shot a Jewess, again for no reason. So two victims have perished for absolutely no reason. All the way home I was frightened I might run across them but didn't run across anybody."[240] The next day, another Jew was killed, again for no reason.[241]

A few days later the order came, as in most occupied countries and in the Reich, that the Jews had to deliver all furs to the authorities: "Father said," Dawid noted on December 26, "an order had come that Jews were to hand over all furs, down to the smallest scrap. And 5 Jews were to be made responsible for those who didn't hand them over. And whoever they found with any furs would receive the death-penalty—that's how harsh the regulation was. The militia men gave till 4 p.m. for all furs to be handed over. After a short while the Jews began bringing in small remnants and whole furs. Mother unpicked three furs right away and took the fur collars off all the coats. At 4 o'clock the militia man himself came to our house for the furs and ordered the Polish policeman to make out a list of the furs that the Jews had handed over. Then we put them into 2 sacks, and 2 Jews took them to a peasant who was to take them to the local police at Bieliny."[242]

Dawid knew little about the course of the war and about the immediate reasons for the fur collection. But elsewhere, East and West, the portents were not missed. In Stanisławów, the town in eastern Galicia where, on October 12, 1941, Hans Krüger had presided over the massacre in the local cemetery, a young woman in her early twenties, Elisheva (Elsa Binder), whom we already briefly met, had started recording her observations in the newly set-up ghetto.[243] "Yesterday's newspaper," Elisheva noted on December 24, "said that the Great Leader [Hitler] assumed command of the army. Jews are therefore drawing the most optimistic and far-reaching conclusions. . . . The Reds are marching ahead, slowly but steadily. It is rumored that they took Kharkov (where they didn't see a single Jew), Kiev and Zhitomir. Some people claim to have 'heard' our radio broadcast from Kiev. I wish I could believe it, although I am trying to look into the future with hope and optimism."[244]

The lines that follow in the same entry are indicative of the intense doubts that nonetheless assailed some Jews when it came to portents of liberation: "I have to admit," Elisheva went on, "that I personally don't believe in early liberation. I want it and I fear it. From today's perspective a free tomorrow seems to be extremely bright. In my dreams I expect so much from it. But in reality? I am young, I have a right to fight and to demand everything from life. But desiring it so much, I fear it. I realize that under the circumstances such thoughts are irrational, but. . . . Never mind. What really matters is liberation."[245]

"When death strikes," Kaplan noted in Warsaw on October 9, "the mourner turns the 'merchandise' over to the burial office, which then attends to everything. So the black wagon proceeds—sometimes drawn by a horse and sometimes pulled rickshe fashion by the employees of the burial office—from corpse to corpse, loading as many bodies as it can hold and transporting them wholesale to the cemetery. Usually the expedition to 'the other world' begins at noon. A long line of horse-drawn and rickshe-drawn wagons then stretches along the length of Gesia Street. This death traffic makes no impression on anyone. Death has become a tangible matter, like the Joint's Soup Kitchen, the bread card, or the raising of one's hat to the Germans. At times it is difficult to distinguish who is pushing whom, the living the dead or vice versa. The dead have lost their traditional importance and sanctity. The sanctity of the cemetery is also being profaned; it has been turned into a marketplace. It now resembles a 'fair' of the dead."[246]

Yet the shift in the war situation sufficed to dispel the gloom, at least for a while. "A firm conviction burns within us," Kaplan recorded on December 19, "that the beginning of the end has begun for the Nazis. What basis have I for such optimism? A 'communiqué' from the battlefield was published yesterday, December 18, which reads as follows: 'Because of the approach of the Russian winter . . . the front line must be shortened. . . .' This is disaster veiled in rhetoric." News secretly heard on the BBC confirmed the conclusion reached from the German announcement. The ghetto was abuzz with rumors eagerly peddled and amplified: "A wit comes along and reports bona fide information to the effect that Churchill sent a cable to the ghetto saying, 'let the Jews not run after the Nazis so fast because he has not the strength to follow them.' " And in part melancholy, part hopeful tone, as was his wont, Kaplan added: "This is the way our people are—the bitter reality does not constrain their glowing imaginations: 'On the very day the Temple was destroyed, Messiah was born.' "[247]

In Lublin, during these same weeks, the ghetto in the General Government targeted by the worst German brutality and one that, a few months later, would be the first destined for total extermination, the council debated mundane issues, including the sloppy and downright dishonest management of the hospital and various plans for its reorganization.[248] Farther north, in Białystok, the council under Barash's leadership could even claim some "achievements" at its meeting of November 2, 1941: "As much as possible, mitigation of the [German] demands was achieved; instead of 25 kg of gold—6 kg, instead of 5 million [rubles]—2.5 million. Instead of a ghetto in the quarter of Chanajkes—today's ghetto. The order for 10 million was annulled. No more than 4,500 persons were evacuated to Pružana. The order to submit lists of the intelligentsia was revoked. All this succeeded after much effort, thanks to our good relations with the authorities." However, the Germans were demanding ransom money once again: "The Judenrat must pay 700,000–800,000 rubles every three days, starting Thursday the 6th of this month. If a deadline is missed, we will be liable to the 'ruthless means of the Gestapo . . .' If we comply with the demands for work and taxes," Barash concluded, "we will be sure of our life—otherwise, we are not responsible for the life of the ghetto. God grant that we will meet again and that none of us will be missing."[249]

In the Ostland, as we saw, mass killings had followed one another throughout October and November 1941, to make space for the deportees from the Reich. In Kovno in early October, some sporadic *Aktions* targeted the hospital and the orphanage, which the Germans burned with their inmates.[250] Then, on October 25, the council was informed by SS Master Sgt. Helmut Rauca, the man in charge of the Jewish desk at the Kovno Gestapo, that all the inhabitants—that is all 27,000 of them, had to assemble on October 28 at six a.m. at Demokratu Square—"to allow a reallocation of food rations to those who did labor for the Germans as one category and to the nonworkers on the other; the nonworkers would be transferred to the "small ghetto." The council was ordered to announce the general roll call to the inhabitants.[251]

Unable to get any information about the Germans' real intentions, the members of the council asked for another meeting with Rauca; he agreed. Dr. Elkes attempted, in vain, to persuade him to offer some explanation, even implying that if the war turned badly for the Reich, the council would vouch for the Gestapo man's readiness to help.[252] At a loss about whether they should publish the decree or not, the ghetto leaders turned for advice to the old chief rabbi, Abraham Shapiro. After several postponements the rabbi finally told them to publish the decree in the hope that it would eventually save at least part of the population. Thus, on October 27, the decree was posted, in both Yiddish and in German.[253]

On the morning of the twenty-eighth, the whole population assembled at the square; each and every adult Jew who did not possess a working permit carried some document—a "school certificate," a "commendation from the Lithuanian army," and the like: Maybe these would help. At the square Rauca was in charge of the selection: The good side was the left. Those sent to the right were counted and pushed to an assembly point in the small ghetto. From time to time Rauca was informed of the number of Jews that had been moved to the right. After nightfall the quota of 10,000 people had been reached: The selection was over; 17,000 Jews were returning home.[254]

Throughout the entire day Elkes had been at the square; in some rare cases he could appeal to Rauca and achieve a change of decision. When he reached home that evening of the twenty-eighth, a crowd besieged him, and each Jew implored him to save somebody. The next day, as the first column of Jews started the trek from the small ghetto to Fort IX, Elkes, with a list of names in hand, tried once more to intervene. Rauca granted him 100 people. But when Elkes tried to remove these 100 from the columns, he was hit by the Lithuanian guards and collapsed. According to Tory, who was among those who carried the chairman away, days went by before Elkes's wounds healed and he could stand on his feet again. In the meantime, from dawn to noon on the twenty-ninth, the 10,000 Jews from the small ghetto marched to Fort IX where, batch after batch, they were shot.[255] Days beforehand, pits had been dug behind the fort: They were not for the Lithuanian Jews, however, but as we saw, for the Jews from the Reich and the Protectorate who arrived in November and disappeared without ever reaching the ghetto.

In a longer-than-usual description of several weeks in the life of the Vilna ghetto, probably written sometime in December 1941 (as it mentions, at the end, the Soviet counterattack before Moscow), Rudashevski noted at some point: "I feel we are like sheep. We are being slaughtered in the thousands and we are helpless. The enemy is strong, crafty, he is exterminating us according to a plan and we are discouraged."[256] For the fourteen-year-old diarist there was little that the ghetto inhabitants could do other than hope for quick liberation from the outside: "The only consolation has now become the latest news at the front. We suffer here, but there, far in the East, the Red Army has started an offensive. The Soviets have occupied Rostov, have dealt a blow from Moscow and are marching forward. And it always seems that any moment freedom will follow it."[257]

Other Vilna Jews also drew conclusions from the events, yet without any such hopefulness. In the eyes of some members of the Zionist youth movements, the systematic manner in which the Germans carried out the killings indicated the existence of a plan, of an extermination project that would ultimately extend to all the Jews of the Continent. It was a chance intuition and could not be anything else; it was the right intuition.

One of the first to grasp the significance of the Vilna massacres was the twenty-three-year-old poet and member of Hashomer Hatzair, Abba Kovner, who was hiding in a monastery close to the city. He found the words and the arguments that convinced an increasing number of his fellow youth movement members.[258] And, if his interpretation was correct, if sooner or later death was unavoidable, only one conclusion remained possible: The Jews had to "die with dignity"; the only path was armed resistance.

Kovner was asked to write a proclamation that would be read at a gathering of members from all youth movements in the ghetto.[259] The meeting, which took place under the guise of a New Year's celebration, brought together some 150 young men and women at the "Pioneers' Public Kitchen," 2 Straszun Street, on December 31, 1941. There Kovner read the manifesto that was to become the first call for a Jewish armed resistance.[260] "Jewish Youth," Kovner proclaimed, "do not believe those that are trying to deceive you. . . . Of those taken through the gates of the ghetto not a single one has returned. All the Gestapo roads lead to Ponar, and Ponar means death.

"Ponar is not a concentration camp. They have all been shot there. Hitler plans to destroy all the Jews of Europe, and the Jews of Lithuania have been chosen as the first in line.

"We will not be led like sheep to the slaughter. True, we are weak and helpless, but the only response to the murderer is revolt! Brothers! It is better to die fighting like free men than to live at the mercy of the murderers. Arise! Arise with your last breath!"[261]

Within a short time Kovner's appeal led to the creation of the first Jewish resistance organization in occupied Europe, the FPO (Fereynegte Partizaner Organizatsye [United Partisans Organization]). It brought together young Jews from the most diverse political frameworks, from the communists to the right-wing zionists of Betar.[262] Yet, precisely in Vilna, the situation seemed to change again: A relative stability that was to last for more than two years settled on the remaining 24,000 Jews of the ghetto—most of whom worked for the Germans—and on the members of their immediate families.

When the Vilna massacres of the summer and fall of 1941 became known in Warsaw, they were generally interpreted as German retribution for the support given by the Jews of Lithuania to the Soviet occupation. It was only among a minority within the youth movements that, there too, a different assessment was taking shape. Zuckerman explained the change of perception that was emerging in his group: "My comrades [from Dror] and the members of Hashomer Hatzair had already heard the story of Vilna [the massacres of Jews in Ponar]. We took the information to the Movement leadership, to the political activists in Warsaw. The responses were different. The youth absorbed not only the information but also accepted the interpretation that this was the beginning of the end. A total death sentence for the Jews. We didn't accept the interpretation . . . that this was all because of Communism. . . . Why did I reject it? Because if it had been German revenge against Jewish Communists, it would have been done right after the occupation. But these were planned and organized acts, not immediately after the occupation, but premeditated actions. . . . That was even before the news about Chelmno, which came in December-January."[263]

A few weeks later, in early 1942, "Antek" would grasp from the comments of a Dror female emissary, Lonka, that his own family in Vilna had perished: "Among other things, she said, but not explicitly, that she [Lonka] and Frumka [another female Dror courier] had decided to save my sister's only son, but hadn't managed to do it. Then it was clear to me that my family was no longer alive. My family—my father and mother, my sister, her husband, and the child Ben-Zion whom the girls had decided to rescue, only him, because they couldn't save any more and, ultimately, they couldn't save him either. . . . Uncles, aunts, a big tribe of the Kleinstein and Zuckerman families, a big widespread clan, in Vilna."[264]

As the fateful year 1941 reached its last day and the course of the war seemed to be turning, the mood of a vast majority of European Jews differed starkly for a short while from that of a tiny minority. In Bucharest, Sebastian had overcome his worst fears: "The Russians have landed in eastern Crimea," he noted on December 31, "recapturing Kerch and Fedosiya. The last day of the year. . . . I carry inside myself the 364 terrible days of the dreadful year we are closing tonight. But we are alive. We can still wait for something. There is still time; we still have some time left."[265] Klemperer, for once, was even more ebuliant than Sebastian. At a small New Year's Eve gathering at his downstairs neighbors, the Kreidls, he made a speech for the occasion: "It was our most dreadful year, dreadful because of our own real experience, more dreadful because of the constant state of threat, most dreadful of all because of what we saw others suffering (deportations, murder), but . . . at the end it brought optimism. . . . My adhortatio was: Head held high for the difficult last five minutes!"[266]

Of course Klemperer's optimism had been fueled by the news from the Eastern Front. Herman Kruk, less emphatically so, also sought solace in the "latest information." The gathering of friends at his home was suffused with sadness: "In sad silence we assembled, and in sad silence we wished each other to hold out, survive, and be able to tell about all this! Meanwhile we consoled ourselves with the latest information: Kerch has fallen. Kaluga has fallen. An Italian regiment surrendered and promised to fight against the Germans. On the front 2,000 [Germans] are found frozen."[267] As for Elisheva, in her Stanisławów ghetto, she expressed both the hope and the dread ultimately shared by all: "I welcome you, 1942, may you bring salvation and defeat. I welcome you, my longed-for year. Maybe you will be more propitious for our ancient, miserable race whose fate lies in the hands of the unjust one. And one more thing. Whatever you are bringing for me, life or death, bring it fast."[268]

On that last day of the year, incidentally, the freezing weather was celebrated by many an inhabitant of occupied Europe, and not only by the small community of Jews: "We watch as military ambulances and trains go west," Klukowski noted on December 31, "loaded with wounded and frostbitten soldiers. Most frostbite occurs on hands, feet, ears, noses, and genitals. You can judge the desperation of the German military situation by the fact that Hitler has taken direct responsibility for all military action in Russia."[269] Klukowski's entry for the last day of 1941 ended with words that, again, must have become increasingly common throughout Europe: "Many people are dying, but everyone still alive feels sure that our time of revenge and victory will come."[270]

In the same entry Klukowski also mentioned that all Jews had been ordered to deliver any furs or parts of furs in their possession within three days, under threat of the death penalty. "Some people," he wrote, "are boiling mad, but some are happy because this fur business shows that the Germans are suffering. The temperature is very low. We lack fuel and people are freezing, but everyone hopes for an even colder winter, because it will help defeat the Germans."[271]

For some young Jews like Kovner in Vilna or Zuckerman in Warsaw, the closing days of 1941 also meant a profound change, but a different one. "Antek" defined this psychological turning point: "A new chapter began in our lives. . . . One of its first signs was a sense of the end."[272]

CHAPTER VI

December 1941–July 1942

On December 15, 1941, the SS *Struma*, with 769 Jewish refugees from Romania on board, was towed into Istanbul harbor and put under quarantine. The ship, a rickety schooner originally built in the 1830s, patched up over the decades and equipped with a small engine that hardly enabled it to sail on the Danube, had left Constanta, on the Black Sea, a week beforehand and somehow made it to Turkish waters, after several mechanical failures.[1]

Five days later the British ambassador in Ankara, Sir Hughe Knatchbull-Hugessen, gave a wrong impression of British policy to a Turkish Foreign Ministry official: "His Majesty's Government did not want these people in Palestine," the ambassador declared, "they have no permission to go there, but . . . from the humanitarian point of view, I did not like his [the Turkish official's] proposal to send the ship back into the Black Sea. If the Turkish government must interfere with the ship on the ground that they could not keep the distressed Jews in Turkey, let her rather go towards the Dardanelles [on the way into the Mediterranean]. It might be that if they reached Palestine, they might, despite their illegality, receive humane treatment."[2]

The ambassador's message provoked outrage in official circles in London. The sharpest rebuff came from the colonial secretary, Lord Moyne, in a letter sent on December 24 to the parliamentary undersecretary at the Foreign Office, Richard Law: "The landing [in Palestine] of seven hundred more immigrants will not only be a formidable addition to the difficulties of the High Commissioner . . . but it will also have a deplorable effect throughout the Balkans in encouraging further Jews to embark on a traffic which has now been condoned by His Majesty's Ambassador. . . . I find it difficult to write with moderation about this occurrence which is in flat contradiction of established Government policy, and I should be very glad if you could perhaps even now do something to retrieve the position, and to urge that [the] Turkish authorities should be asked to send the ship back to the Black Sea, as they originally proposed." The Colonial Office's argument was and would remain throughout that Nazi agents could infiltrate Palestine under the guise of Jewish refugees.[3]

As weeks went by the British decided to grant visas to Palestine to the seventy children on board. The Turks however, remained adamant: None of the refugees would be allowed to disembark. On February 23 they towed the boat back into the Black Sea. Soon thereafter a torpedo, almost certainly fired by mistake from a Soviet submarine, hit the ship: The *Struma* sank with all its passengers, except for one survivor.[4]

"Yesterday evening," Sebastian noted on February 26, "a Rador dispatch reported that the *Struma* had sunk with all on board in the Black Sea. This morning brought a correction in the sense that most of the passengers—perhaps all of them—have been saved and are now ashore. But before I heard what had really happened, I went through several hours of depression. It seemed that the whole of our fate was in this shipwreck."[5]

During the first half of 1942, the Germans rapidly expanded and organized the murder campaign. Apart from the setting up of the deportation, selection, extermination, and slave labor systems as such (or expanding already existing operations), the "Final Solution" also implied major political-administrative decisions: establishing a clear line of command regarding the responsibility for and the implementing of the extermination, as well as determining the criteria for the identification of the victims. It also demanded negotiated arrangements with various national or local authorities in the occupied countries and with the Reich's allies. Throughout these six months (once again a time of German military successes), no major interference with the increasingly more obvious aims of the German operation took place either in the Reich, in occupied

Europe, or beyond. And, during the same period, the Jews, under tight control, segregated from their environment and often physically debilitated, waited passively, in the hope of somehow escaping a fate that looked increasingly ominous but that, as before, the immense majority was unable to surmise.

I

On December 19, 1941, Hitler dismissed Brauchitsch and personally took over the command of the army. During the following weeks the Nazi leader stabilized the Eastern Front. But despite the hard-earned respite and despite his own rhetorical posturing, Hitler probably knew that 1942 would be the year of "last chance." Only a breakthrough in the East would turn the tide in favor of Germany.

On May 8, 1942, the first stage of the German offensive started in the southern sector of the Russian front. After Army Group South withstood a Soviet counteroffensive near Kharkov and inflicted heavy losses on Marshal Semyon Timoshenko's divisions, the German forces rolled on. Once again the Wehrmacht reached the Donets. Farther south Manstein recaptured the Crimea, and by mid-June, Sebastopol was surrounded. On June 28 the full-scale German onslaught (Operation Blue) began. Voronezh was taken, and while the bulk of the German forces moved southward toward the oil fields and the Caucasus foothills, Friedrich Paulus's Sixth Army advanced along the Don in the direction of Stalingrad. In North Africa, Bir Hakeim and Tobruk fell into Rommel's hands, and the Afrika Korps crossed the Egyptian border: Alexandria was threatened. On all fronts—and in the Atlantic—the Germans heaped success on success; so did their Japanese allies in the Pacific and in Southeast Asia. Would the strategic balance tip to Hitler's side?

In the meantime the Nazi leader's anti-Jewish exhortations continued relentlessly, broadly hinting at the extermination that was unfolding and endlessly repeating the arguments which, in his eyes, justified it. Raging anti-Jewish assaults surfaced in literally all Hitler's major speeches and utterances. The overwhelming fury that had burst out in October 1941 did not abate. In most cases the "prophecy" reappeared, with some particularly vile accusations added for good measure. The Führer's harangues could sound to some Germans, other Europeans, and Americans like undiluted madness; obversely, though, they may have convinced others that the pitiful groups of Jews marching to the "assembly points" with their suitcases and bundles throughout the streets of European towns, were but the deceitful incarnations of a hidden satanic force—"the Jew"—ruling over a secret empire extending from Washington to London and from London to Moscow, threatening to destroy the very sinews of the Reich and the "new Europe."

The prophecy had been present, let us recall, as 1942 started and Hitler addressed his New Year's message to the nation.[6] On January 25 historical "insights" and unusually open remarks about the fate of the Jews were volunteered for the benefit of two cognoscenti, Lammers and Himmler: "It must be done quickly," Hitler told them. "The Jew must be ousted from Europe. If not, we shall get no European cooperation. He incites everywhere. In the end I don't know: I am so immensely humane [*Ich bin so kolossal human*]. At the time of papal rule in Rome, the Jews were mistreated. Until 1830 every year eight Jews were driven through the city on donkeys. I only say: he [the Jew] must go. If he is destroyed in the process, I can't help it. I see only one thing: total extermination, if they do not leave voluntarily. Why should I look at a Jew any differently from a Russian prisoner? In the prisoners' camps many die, because we have been pushed into this situation by the Jews. But what can I do? Why did the Jews start this war?"[7]

On January 30, 1942, in the ritual yearly address to the Reichstag, this time delivered at the Berlin Sportpalast, Hitler reverted in full force to his seer's rhetoric: "We should be in no doubt that this war can only end either with the extermination of the Aryan peoples or with the disappearance of Jewry from Europe." And, after again reminding the audience of his prophecy, Hitler went on: "For the first time, the ancient Jewish rule will now be applied: 'An eye for an eye, a tooth for a tooth!' " Thereupon messianic ardor took hold of the Nazi leader: "World Jewry should know that the more the war spreads, the more anti-Semitism will also spread. It will grow in every prisoner-of-war camp, in every family that will understand the reasons for which it has, ultimately, to make its sacrifices. And, the hour will strike when *the most evil world enemy of all times* will have ended his role at least for a thousand years."[8] The millennial vision of a final redemption capped off the litany of hatred.

The *Volk*'s intuition was unerring. A general SD opinion report of

February 2 showed how well the January 30 speech had been understood. The population interpreted Hitler's use of "an eye for an eye, a tooth for a tooth" as proof that their Führer was "pursuing his campaign against Jewry with inexorable single-mindedness to its very end and that soon the last Jew would be expelled from European soil."[9] According to a February 21 report from Minden, people were saying: "When one speaks to soldiers about the East, one recognizes that here, in Germany, the Jews are treated much too humanely. The right thing would be to exterminate the entire brood" [*Es wäre das richtige, die ganze Brut müsste vernichtet werden*].[10]

In Warsaw, Kaplan also understood the main thrust of Hitler's speech: "The day before yesterday," he noted on February 2, "we read the speech the Führer delivered celebrating January 30, 1933, when he boasted that his prophecy was beginning to come true. Had he not stated that if war erupted in Europe, the Jewish race would be annihilated? This process has begun and will continue until the end is achieved. For us the speech serves as proof that what we thought were rumors are in effect reports of actual occurrences. The Judenrat and the Joint have documents which confirm the new direction of Nazi policy toward the Jews in the conquered territories: death by extermination for entire Jewish communities."[11]

Hitler's apocalyptic vision surfaced once again in his February 24 message to the "Old Fighters" assembled in Munich for the annual gathering celebrating the proclamation of the party program. The Nazi leader bandied his prophecy once more. They had been a small group of "believers," the leader told the party inner core, who as early as in 1919 "had not only recognized the international enemy of humankind, but also fought him." Much had changed since those heroic beginnings, and now their ideas were embraced by powerful states. The messianic incantation followed: "Whatever the present struggle may bring or whatever its duration may be, this will be its final outcome [the extermination of the Jews]. And only then, after the elimination of these parasites, the suffering world will attain a long period of understanding among nations and thus achieve true peace."[12] On the March 15, "Memorial Day for Fallen Soldiers" (*Heldengedenktag*), Hitler's furious anti-Jewish campaign went on, as threatening as ever.

Again and again the Nazi leader announced the extermination of the Jews, and each time many Germans understood perfectly well that he meant it. Thus, after reading the February 24 speech in the next day's *Niedersächsische Tages Zeitung (NTZ)*, Karl Dürkefälden, an employee in an industrial enterprise near Hannover, noted Hitler's threats in his diary; in his view the threats had to be taken seriously, and he quoted the title given to the Nazi leader's speech in the *NTZ*: "The Jew will be exterminated" (*Der Jude wird ausgerottet*).[13] A few days beforehand Dürkefälden had listened to a speech by Thomas Mann, broadcast on the BBC, in which the writer had mentioned the gassing of 400 young Dutch Jews. Dürkefälden commented that such gassings were entirely credible given Hitler's constant harangues against the Jews.[14] In other words, as early as during the first months of 1942, even "ordinary Germans" knew that the Jews were being pitilessly murdered.

As usual Goebbels was his master's voice, but he was also the scribe of his master's private tirades and, at times, a keen observer on his own. On January 13, for example, he noted that a people was defenseless against the Jewish threat if it lacked the right "anti-Semitic instinct": "That," he added, "cannot be said of the German people."[15] At each of his meetings with Hitler, the minister was invariably told that the Jews had to be eradicated: "Together with Bolshevism," Hitler declared to his minister on February 14, "Jewry will undoubtedly experience its great catastrophe. The Führer declares once again that he has decided to do away ruthlessly with the Jews in Europe. In this matter one should not have any sentimental impulses. The Jews have deserved the catastrophe that they are now experiencing. We must accelerate this process with cold determination, as in so doing we render a priceless service to humanity, which for millennia was tortured by Jewry. This clear-cut anti-Jewish position must also be impressed upon one's own people against all willfully opposed groups. The Führer repeated this explicitly, somewhat later, to a gathering of officers."[16]

On March 7 the minister alluded for the first time to the Wannsee conference. Twenty days later he recorded the sequence of the extermination process: "Starting with Lublin, the Jews are now being deported from the General Government to the East. The procedure used is quite barbaric and should not be described in any further detail. Not much remains anymore of the Jews themselves. In general terms one has to admit that some 60 percent have to be liquidated, whereas only 40 percent can be used for work. The former Gauleiter of Vienna [Globocnik], who is in charge of this operation, proceeds quite cautiously and in a way that does not draw much attention. The Jews are being subjected to a sentence that is barbaric, but they have fully deserved it. The prophecy that the Führer made to them for provoking a new world war starts to come true in the most terrible way. In these things no sentimentality should be allowed. If we didn't defend ourselves, the Jews would exterminate us. It is a life-or-death struggle between the Aryan race and the Jewish microbe. No other government and no other regime would have been able to muster the strength to find a general solution to this issue. Here too the Führer is the unswerving pioneer and spokesman of a radical solution, which the state of things requires and which appears, therefore, as unavoidable. Thank God, during the war we now have a whole range of possibilities that we couldn't use in peacetime; we have to exploit them. The ghettos of the General Government that are being liberated will now be filled with Jews deported from the Reich and, after a certain time, the same process will take place again. Jewry has nothing to laugh about and the fact that its representatives in England and America organize and propagate the war against Germany must be paid for very dearly by its representatives in Europe; this also is justified."[17]

In the crescendo of anti-Jewish abuse and threats that Hitler unceasingly spewed, his most "encompassing" speech was his Reichstag address of April 26, 1942. In a meeting with Goebbels the morning of that day, the Nazi leader once again launched into the Jewish question. "His position regarding this problem is inexorable" Goebbels noted. "The Jews have brought so much suffering to our part of the world that the hardest punishment would still remain too mild. Himmler now organizes the vast transfer of the Jews from the German cities to the eastern ghettos. I ordered that many films should record it. We will urgently need this material for the future education of our people."[18]

The "Great German Reichstag" convened at the Kroll Opera House at three p.m.; it was to be its last meeting.[19] Right from the beginning of his speech, Hitler set the "historical framework" of his entire address. This war, he proclaimed, was not an ordinary one in which nations fight each other in the pursuit of their specific interests. This was a fundamental confrontation "the like of which shakes the world once in a thousand years and ushers a new millenium." As for the pitiless enemy confronted in this apocalyptic struggle, it had, of course, to be the Jews. Hitler reminded his audience of the Jews' evil role in World War I and since: They pushed America into the conflict, they were behind Wilson's "Fourteen Points" in 1918, and they brought Bolshevism to "the heart of Europe."

But no paraphrase can render the fury of the original: "We know the theoretical principles and the horrible reality of the aims of this world plague. It is called the dictatorship of the proletariat but it is the dictatorship of Jewry! . . . If Bolshevik Russia is the visible product of this Jewish infection, one should not forget that democratic capitalism creates the preconditions for it," Hitler thundered on. "Here the Jews prepare what the same Jews complete in the second act of this process. In the first phase they turned the masses in their millions into helpless slaves or—as they say themselves—into a despoiled proletariat. Afterward they incite this fanaticized mass to destroy the very foundations of its own state. The extermination of the national elites follows and, finally, so does the liquidation of all the cultural creations that, over the millennia, molded the traditions of these peoples. . . . What remains after all of this is the beast in humanity and a Jewish layer that reached leadership but that in the end, as the parasite, destroys the ground which nurtured it. It is against this process, which Mommsen called the decomposition of states by the Jews, that the awakening new Europe has declared war."[20]

A major surprise followed the end of the speech. Göring introduced the text of a resolution granting the Führer extraordinary new powers, particularly in the judicial domain. Hitler was to be the supreme judge, the supreme source of the law and of its implementation. Why the Nazi leader felt the need for this repeat performance of the so-called *Ermächtigungsgesetz* [the Enabling Act of 1933] seemed unclear at the time, as his power was unchallenged in any case. Goebbels, like many other commentators, dwelled on this particular aspect of the meeting. "The new law," the propaganda minister commented, "is accepted by the Reichstag with jubilant unanimity. Now the Führer has the full powers to do whatever he considers right. It has been confirmed once again by the representatives elected by the people. Thus, no judge and no general will dare to question the Führer's full powers any longer.[21] Goebbels knew as well as Hitler did that the winter crisis that had barely been overcome, was the portent of increasingly difficult times . . . Klemperer, for one, noticed the other part of the speech, writing: "The concentration of hatred has this time turned into utter madness. Not England or the USA or Russia—*only*, in everything, nothing but *the Jew*."[22] Both aspects of the speech may in fact have been linked.

It could be that, as full-scale mass extermination was now starting, Hitler wanted to avoid the slightest possibility of another threat of criminal charges (as the one brandished by Bishop Galen in his sermon against the murder of the mentally ill in August 1941). The German Jews, let us remember, remained subjects of the Reich as long as they had not left German territory: Lodz and Chelmno were in newly annexed German territory—and so was Auschwitz. On May 4, just a few days after the Reichstag meeting, 10,000 Jews from the Reich and the Protectorate were transported from the Lodz ghetto to the Chelmno gas vans.

"A proper understanding of Jews and Judaism cannot but demand their total annihilation," *Volk und Rasse* proclaimed in May 1942.[23] In *Der Angriff* of that same month, Ley's threats competed with his master's prophecies: "The war will end," the labor minister announced to the 300,000 readers of the weekly magazine, "with the extermination of the Jewish race."[24] A few days later the same minister spelled out his threats once more: "The Jews will pay with the extermination of their race in Europe," he clamored in *Das Reich* of June 6, 1942.[25]

The Kaufman story seems to have kept its hold on the *Volk*'s imagination. Thus a March 15, 1942, SD report from Bielefeld about the general attitude of the population to the war emphasized that "thanks in particular to the extraordinarily effective influence of propaganda, it has become clear to all that the Jew is the instigator of this war and bears the responsibility for the endless misery that it causes to so many Volksgenossen. The acceptance of this view by such wide parts of the population is due in no small measure to the propagation of the text of the American Jew Kaufmann [*sic*]."[26]

The upsurge in anti-Jewish hatred noted in Bielefeld probably explains why the *Völkischer Beobachter* of April 30, 1942, could, without qualms, carry a detailed article (thinly veiled as rumor) by its war correspondent Schaal about SD operations in the East: "The rumor has spread among the population that it is the task of the Security Police to exterminate the Jews in the occupied territories. The Jews were assembled in the thousands and shot; beforehand they had to dig their own graves. At times the execution of the Jews reached such proportions that even members of the Einsatzkommandos suffered nervous breakdowns."[27]

On May 8 School Councillor Dr. Borchers lectured to an assembly of school directors in Erfurt; the topic: "What do we need to know about bolshevism to be able to teach it to the children?" The lecture on bolshevism dealt with the Jews, starting with Abraham, continuing with Moses, and onward with the penetration of Jewry into all civilized nations, infecting them with its pestilential breath. Step by step the lecturer moved from one deadly Jewish conspiracy to the next until he reached bolshevism, the ultimate means to subvert all states. Borchers's finale was of course a hymn to the Führer, who had been the first to recognize the spiritual link between Jewry and bolshevism, who exposed it ruthlessly, and who knew in time how to adapt his policy to these findings.[28] This was the message that school directors were asked to impart to their students.

The all-pervasive anti-Jewish hate campaign found a typical expression in the letter addressed on January 20, 1942, by one Karl Gross, party district chief of the small town of Immenhausen, to his boss in Hofgeismar (near Kassel): "Further to your communication dated January 17, 1942, regarding privileged mixed marriages, I hereby inform you that the local inhabitants have taken great exception to the fact that the local woman doctor (a full-blooded Jewess) is not required to wear a Jewish star. The Jewess takes full advantage of this in that she often goes to Kassel by train, second class, and can travel free from interference without the star. The entire population would welcome it if this state of affairs could be remedied in some way. I inform you at the same time that consideration might be given to deporting the local Jewess because her husband (a doctor) is having an affair with an Aryan woman doctor, who is expecting a child by him in the next few weeks. If the Jewess were deported, the Aryan woman doctor could continue to run Dr. Jahn's household. It might be appropriate to discuss the said circumstances [with him] in person. This could bring about the disappearance of the only Jewess still resident here."[29]

We shall come back to the story of Lilly Jahn, born Schlüchterer, to a well-to-do Jewish family from Cologne, herself a successful practicing physician, married to an Aryan colleague, Ernst Jahn. The couple had five children, which indeed put them in the category of a privileged mixed marriage and exempted Lilli from wearing the star. As Gross correctly indicated, at that time Ernst Jahn was openly having an affair with a German woman physician, Rita Schmidt, and the marriage was about to fall apart.

II

Initially scheduled for December 9, 1941, the high-level meeting convened by Heydrich in Berlin, at the guesthouse of the Security Police, 56-58, Strasse Am Grossen Wannsee, opened at noon on January 20, 1942. It assembled fourteen people: several state secretaries or other high-ranking officials and a few SS officers, including Adolf Eichmann, who had sent the invitations (in Heydrich's name) and who drew up the minutes of the meeting.[30] Some of the invitations pointed to the main purpose of the conference even before it started.

A December 1, 1941, exchange between HSSPF Krüger and the chief of the RSHA had indicated that Hans Frank was manuevering for control of Jewish matters in the General Government.[31] As for Rosenberg's ambition to lord over the Jews in the newly conquered eastern territories, it was notorious, as we saw. Thus the invitations extended to Frank's second-in-command, Secretary of State Josef Bühler and to Rosenberg's own number two, Secretary of State Alfred Meyer, were clearly meant to convey to them who would be in charge of the 'Final Solution.' To a lesser degree, a similar affirmation of authority may have been intended for State Secretaries Wilhelm Stuckart and Roland Freisler from the Interior and Justice Ministries, whose institutions had an important say in the fate of mixed breeds and mixed marriages and did not automatically follow suggestions from the RSHA.[32]

Heydrich opened the meeting by reminding the participants of the task Göring had delegated to him in July 1941 and of the ultimate authority of the SS Reichsführer in this matter. The RSHA chief then presented a brief historical survey of the measures already taken to segregate the Jews of the Reich and force them to emigrate. After further emigration had been forbidden in October 1941, given the danger it represented during wartime, Heydrich went on, another solution had been authorized by the Führer: the evacuation of the Jews of Europe to the East. Some 11 million persons would be included, and Heydrich listed this Jewish population, country by country, including all Jews living in the enemy and neutral countries of Europe (Great Britain, the Soviet Union, Spain, Portugal, Switzerland, and Sweden).

The evacuated Jews would be assigned to heavy forced labor (like the building of roads) which naturally would greatly reduce their numbers. The remnants, "the strongest elements of the race and the nucleus of its revival," would have to be "treated accordingly." To implement the operation Europe would be "combed from West to East," whereby the Reich would be given priority "because of the housing problem and other sociopolitical considerations." Jews over sixty-five, war invalids, or Jews decorated with the Iron Cross would be evacuated to the newly established "old people's ghetto," Theresienstadt: "This adequate solution would put an end in one stroke to the many interventions." The beginning of major evacuations would greatly depend on the evolution of the military situation.

The statement regarding the latter was strange and has to be understood in relation to the formula "evacuation to the East," used from then on to mean extermination. To maintain the linguistic fiction, a general comment about the war was necessary given the impossibility of actual deportations "to the East" in January 1942.

In regard to the extension of the "Final Solution" to occupied or satellite countries, the Foreign Ministry, in cooperation with the representatives of the Security Police and the SD, would negotiate with the appropriate local authorities. Heydrich did not foresee any difficulties in Slovakia or Croatia, where preparations had already begun; an adviser on Jewish affairs needed to be sent to Hungary; as for Italy the RSHA chief deemed it necessary to get in touch with the head of the Italian police. Regarding France, Heydrich, in his initial listing, had mentioned 700,000 Jews from the Vichy zone, which probably meant the inclusion of the Jews of French North Africa. Heydrich expected considerable problems in getting hold of this Jewish population. Undersecretary Martin Luther, the Foreign Ministry delegate, set him straight: No problems were foreseen in Vichy France. On the other hand Luther pointed out (quite correctly) that difficulties would be encountered in the Nordic states; thus, given the small number of Jews involved, the deportations there should be left for a later phase. No potential reaction of any of the Christian churches or of public opinion in general (except, as we shall see, in the neighborhood of the camps) was mentioned.

Up to that point Heydrich's survey presented both an overly detailed statement on one issue and an obvious gap regarding another. The country-by-country listing of the Jews who would be targeted in the "Final Solution," including the Jews of Great Britain, the Soviet Union, Switzerland, and so on, was of course unnecessary in itself; yet the enumeration had a purpose, nonetheless: It conveyed that every Jew in Europe, wherever that Jew might be living, would eventually be caught. None would escape or be allowed to survive. Moreover, all Jews, everywhere, even in countries or areas still outside Germany's reach, were and would be subjected to Himmler and Heydrich's authority.

As for the gap, it was ominous and clear: Able-bodied Jews would be assigned to heavy forced labor and thus decimated; decorated war veterans, invalids, and elderly Jews (from Germany and possibly some Western or Scandinavian countries) would be deported to the "old people's ghetto" in Theresienstadt (where they would die off). But what of all the others, the unmentioned vast majority of European Jewry? Heydrich's silence about their fate stated loudly that these nonworking Jews would be exterminated. The discussion that followed the RSHA chief's address clearly showed that he was well understood.

Heydrich then moved to the issue of mixed breeds and mixed marriages.[33] He systematically attempted to include some groups of *Mischlinge* and some of the partners in mixed marriages in the deportations, in line with the steady endeavors of party radicals since 1933 to extend the reach of the anti-Jewish measures. In 1935, during the discussions that immediately preceded and followed the proclamation of the Nuremberg laws, the aim of party radicals had been to identify *Mischlinge* with full Jews as widely as possible; in January 1942 Heydrich's aim was the same; also, the larger the array of victims, the greater his own power would be.

During the discussion that followed, State Secretary Stuckart of the Ministry of the Interior warned of the considerable amount of bureaucratic work that the *Mischlinge* and mixed marriage issues would create, and strongly recommended the generalized sterilization of mixed breeds of the first degree as an alternative policy. Moreover, Stuckart favored the possibility of annulling mixed marriages by law. State Secretary Erich Neumann of the Four-Year Plan did not wish Jews working in essential war industries to be included in the evacuations; Heydrich answered that currently this was not the case.

State Secretary Bühler pleaded for starting the evacuations in the General Government where transport was a minor issue, the Jews were mostly not part of the workforce and where, moreover, they were a source of epidemics and of economic instability as black marketeers: The 2.5 million Jews of the General Government should be the first to go. Bühler's request demonstrates that he perfectly understood what Heydrich had omitted to spell out: The nonworking Jews were to be exterminated in the first phase of the overall plan. Thereupon Frank's delegate felt the need to add a "loyalty declaration": The executive authority for the solution of the Jewish question in the General Government was in the hands of the chief of the Security Police and the SD; he was getting full support from all General Government authorities. Bühler demanded once again that in Frank's kingdom the Jewish question be solved as rapidly as possible.

In the final part of the discussion both Meyer and Bühler stressed that despite the need for preparatory measures in the designated territories, unrest among the local population had to be carefully avoided. The conference ended with Heydrich's renewed appeal to all the participants to extend the necessary help for implementing the solution.[34] Whether during the discussion of the "practicalities" Heydrich volunteered information about Chelmno or about Globocnik's construction of the first extermination camp in the General Government is not known.

Heydrich's reference to the decimation of the Jews by way of forced labor, particularly in road building in the East, has for years been regarded as code language designating mass murder. It is likely, however, that at this stage (and of course only in regard to Jews capable of working) the RSHA chief meant what he said: Able-bodied Jews would first be exploited as slave labor given the escalating manpower needs of the German war economy. "Road building" was probably an example of slave labor in general; it may also have been a reference to the building of Durchgangstrasse IV, in which, as we saw, Jewish slave laborers were already used en masse and where they also perished en masse.[39] Moreover, either at the end of 1941 or in early January 1942, Hitler ordered the use of Jewish slave labor for the building of roads in the northern part of the occupied Soviet Union.[40] This interpretation seems (very indirectly) confirmed by Heydrich's comments on February 2, 1942, to an assembly of German officials and party representatives in the Protectorate: "We could perhaps [use] those Czechs who cannot yet be Germanized when we further open up the area of the Arctic Sea (*Eismer*), where we will take over the concentration camps of the Russians, which according to our present knowledge hold some 15–20 million deported inmates and which could become the ideal homeland for the 11 million European Jews. Perhaps there the Czechs who cannot be Germanized—and that would be a positive contribution—could fulfill pro-German tasks as supervisors, foremen, etc."[37] In any case, as Heydrich made amply clear at Wannsee, none of the working Jews would eventually survive.

Did the RSHA chief ensure at the January 20 conference, the exclusive authority of the SS in the implementation of the "Final Solution"? Regarding mixed-breeds and mixed marriages, the Ministry of the Interior and, later, the Ministry of Justice, would continue to push ideas of their own. As a rule however, these ideas applied to a limited number of persons living in the Reich, not to the millions included in the continent-wide scope of the "Final Solution." In general terms, even if discussions about the fate of mixed-breeds and mixed marriages went on, there is no doubt that, at Wannsee, Himmler's and Heydrich's overall authority in the implementation of the "Final Solution" throughout Europe was generally recognized. On the morrow of the conference, Heydrich reported to his chief.[38]

On January 25, 1942, Himmler informed the inspector of concentration camps, Richard Glücks, that "as no more Russian prisoners of war are expected in the near future," he would send to the camps "a large number of Jews and Jewesses from Germany (. . . Make the necessary arrangements for the reception of 100,000 male Jews and up to 50,000 Jewesses into the concentration camps during the next four weeks . . .)."[39] Nothing came of this immediate deportation order. In fact, Himmler's message to Glücks appears to have been an improvised step, an immediate follow-up to the Wannsee conference. The Reichsführer probably wanted to show that he was firmly in charge and ready to order the next concrete measures. In concrete terms, Himmler's teletype demonstrated—as did the Wannsee conference as such—that apart from ensuring the cooperation and subordination of all concerned to the SS chief and his delegates, very little had been prepared regarding the continent-wide deportation of the Jews, and very little had been planned ahead of time.

On January 31, Eichmann informed the main Gestapo offices throughout Germany that "the evacuations of Jews that took place recently from several areas of the Reich to the East represented the beginning of the 'Final Solution' of the Jewish Question in the Old Reich, in Austria, and in the Protectorate." Yet, Eichmann stressed, "the evacuation measures were initially restricted to especially urgent plans. . . . New reception sites are presently being arranged with the aim of deporting additional contingents of Jews. Clearly, these preparations would take some time."[40]

The fate of mixed-breeds and mixed marriages was discussed again at a meeting that took place on March 6, 1942, in Berlin, at the RSHA headquarters; it was later dubbed "the second 'Final Solution' conference." The meeting was attended by representatives of a large number of agencies; it did not lead to any definitive agreement. Following suggestions made by Stuckart in a circular of February 16, sterilization of mixed-breeds of the first degree and compulsory dissolution of mixed marriages after the Aryan spouse had been given sufficient time to opt freely for divorce were decided, in principle.[41] Yet barely were these measures agreed on that they were called into question by the acting minister of justice (since Franz Gürtner's death in January 1941), Franz Schlegelberger.[42] Schlegelberger's proposals were no more conclusive than Stuckart's guidelines. In fact both issues were never fully resolved. On the one hand, various exemptions were granted by Hitler himself, whereas on the other, some chance remarks by the Nazi leader about Jewish traits among second-, third-, and fourth-degree *Mischlinge* led to further exclusions from the Wehrmacht and to even harsher treatment of the mixed-breeds in general. A third conference, convened by the RSHA on October 27, 1942, did not proceed much beyond the March 6 proposals.[43] Ultimately, most mixed-breeds were not deported.

* * *

On the same March 6, and in the same building of the RSHA, Eichmann convened a meeting of Gestapo delegates from all over the Reich to discuss the further deportation of 55,000 Jews from Germany and the Protectorate. This time the majority of deportees would come from Prague (20,000), from Vienna (18,000), and the remainder from various German cities. It was imperative, Eichmann stressed, that local Gestapo authorities be extremely attentive not to include elderly deportees to avoid a recurrence of previous complaints. A special camp was being established for this category of Jews in Theresienstadt, "in order to save face in regard to the outside world" (*Um nach aussen das Gesicht zu währen*). Moreover, Eichmann admonished, the Jews should not be informed of the deportations ahead of time. The local Gestapo office would be informed of the departure date only six days in advance, possibly to limit the spreading of rumors and any attempts by Jews to avoid deportation.

After instructing his acolytes how to keep the deportees' assets for the RSHA as far as possible, despite the Eleventh Ordinance (which transferred their assets to the state), Eichmann dwelled on the transportation difficulties: The only available trains were *Russenzüge*, which brought workers from the East and returned empty. These trains were set for 700 Russians, but should be filled with 1,000 Jews each.[44]

III

Aside from the evolution of the war and of its overall impact, the major factors influencing the course of the "Final Solution" from early 1942 on, were the need for Jewish slave labor in an increasingly overextended war economy on the one hand, and the "security risk" the same Jews represented in Nazi eyes on the other. These issues applied only to a small minority of the Jewish population of Europe but regarding this minority, policies would change several times.

The reorganization and "rationalization" of the German economy (and that of the occupied countries) from a *Blitzkrieg* economy to an effort adapted to a total and prolonged war became an urgent necessity in view of the global strategic changes during the winter of 1941–42. In February 1942, following the death of Fritz Todt, Hitler appointed Albert Speer as overlord of armaments production, despite Göring's ambitions in this domain. And on March 31, Hitler named the *Gauleiter* of Thuringia,

Fritz Sauckel, as general plenipotentiary for labor (*Generalbevollmächtigter für den Arbeitseinsatz*, or *GBA*). The ruthless deportation to the Reich of millions of forced laborers from all over Europe began (2.7 million by the end of 1942, 8 million by the end of the war).[45]

The new "rationalization process" also led to changes within the SS system. During the same month of February 1942, the "SS Main Office for Administration and Economy" and the "Main Office for Budget and Construction," both led by Pohl, were unified and became, under Pohl's command throughout, the "SS Main Office for Economic Administration" (*SS Wirtschaftsverwaltungs-Hauptamt*, WVHA). A month later, the WVHA took over the Inspectorate of the Concentration Camps: Section D of Pohl's Main Office, under Richard Glücks, now administered the entire *concentration camp* system. However, the "Aktion Reinhardt" camps (Belzec, Sobibor, Treblinka, and Majdanek at a later stage) remained Globocnik's domain, and Globocnik himself received his orders from Himmler. Otherwise, as far as the extermination camps were concerned, the WVHA managed the hybrid centers of slave labor *and* extermination, mainly Auschwitz, but RSHA kept its control over the "political section" of the Upper Silesian camp and thus over all decisions concerning the rate of extermination of the growing number of Jewish inmates. Chelmno stayed in the hands of the *Gauleiter* of the Wartheland, under Himmler's direct authority.

In a memorandum submitted to Himmler on April 30, 1942, Pohl stressed the need for a change of policy as a result of the new constraints imposed by the total war economy: "The detention of prisoners for reasons of security, correction and prevention is no longer the first priority. The center of gravity has shifted to the economic side. The mobilization of the labor power of all internees primarily for war tasks (increase of armaments) must take absolute precedence, until such time as it can be used for peacetime assignments. Such being the case, all necessary measures must be taken to transform the concentration camp from an exclusive political organization into one fitted for its economic mission."[46]

In that same memorandum Pohl informed Himmler that all instructions about the change of course had been transmitted to the camp commanders and the heads of SS enterprises: In each camp and in each SS plant the work force had from now on to be utilized to the utter limit (on the assumption that there would a sufficient supply of new inmates to replace those who would succumb to the truly exhausting pace). The political section would ensure that the policies regarding Jews be adhered to.[47] Thus Heydrich's scheme was basically intact.

The same policy was increasingly applied to the large ghettos. In Lodz, Sierakowiak had been assigned to a saddler's workshop. "The ghetto population," he recorded on March 22, 1942, "has been divided into three categories: "A," "B," and "C." "A": workshop workers and clerks; "B": clerks and ordinary laborers; "C": the rest of the population.[48] Wave after wave, the "rest of the population" was shipped to Chelmno.

In the General Government a "substitution" policy developed, at least for a short while: Jewish labor gradually replaced Polish workers sent to the Reich. This policy started around March 1942 and grew in scope over the following months, with the support of the "Armaments Inspectorate" of the Wehrmacht and even of Globocnik's main deportation and extermination expert, Hermann Höfle.[49] It became standard procedure to stop deportation trains from the Reich and Slovakia in Lublin in order to select the able-bodied Jews for work in the General Government; the others were sent on to their death in Belzec. Hans Frank himself seemed more than ready to move from the ideological stand to the pragmatic one: "If I want to win the war, I must be an ice-cold technician. The question what will be done from an ideological-ethnic point of view I must postpone to a time after the war."[50]

As Christopher Browning has shown, the new policy led to some improvement in the food supply for the working Jews in the ghettos—and to the rapid extermination of the nonworking population. On May 5, 1942, Bühler declared to the heads of his administration: "According to the latest information, there are plans to dissolve the Jewish ghettos, keep the Jews capable of work, and deport the rest farther east. The Jews capable of work are to be lodged in numerous large concentration camps that are now in the process of being constructed." Actually Bühler was concerned about the effect of such a reorganization on the working-capacity of the Jews and so did other high-ranking officials of the General Government administration.[51]

In other words, at the beginning of the summer of 1942, the presence of Jewish labor in the General Government seemed assured; HSSPF Krüger went so far as to promise, in June, "that not only would Jewish workers in the armaments industry be retained but their families would also be."[52] Yet, precisely as Krüger was outlining these new perspectives, German policy regarding Jewish workers was modified once again: The security risk represented by Jewish workers and other able-bodied Jews had become a major issue.

There is no straightforward documentary proof that two unrelated events that followed each other during the second half of May 1942 led to the general acceleration and radicalization of the "Final Solution." Yet this connection, mentioned in discussions, speeches, and orders, is likely.

On May 18 an incendiary device exploded on the site of the anti-Soviet exhibition, "The Soviet Paradise," in Berlin's *Lustgarten*. Within days the Gestapo caught most members of the small pro-communist "Herbert Baum group," which had organized the attack. As Goebbels wrote on May 24, "characteristically five [of the members of the group] are Jews, three half-Jews and four Aryans."[53] The propaganda minister then recorded Hitler's reaction: "He is extraordinarily outraged and orders me to see to it as soon as possible that the Jews of Berlin be evacuated. Speer objects to the inclusion of those Jews who work in the armaments industry; we must find a way to get replacements. It is incidentally quite funny that nowadays we consider the Jews as irreplaceable high-quality workers, whereas not too long ago we constantly declared that Jews did not work at all and understood nothing about work. . . . Moreover the Führer allows me to arrest 500 Jewish hostages and to react with executions to any new attempts."[54]

That same afternoon (May 23) Hitler spoke to the *Reichsleiter* and *Gauleiter* assembled at the Reich Chancellery. "The Jews," the Nazi leader declared, "were determined to achieve victory in this war, under any circumstances, as they know that defeat would mean their personal liquidation. . . . Now we clearly see what Stalin, in fact as front man for the Jews, had prepared for this war against the Reich."[55]

Goebbels remained agitated. On May 28, he recorded that he did not want "to be shot by some 22-year-old Ostjude like one of those types who are among the perpetrators of the attack against the anti-soviet exhibition."[56] After being tortured Baum committed suicide. All the other members of the group were executed. Moreover, 250 Jewish men were shot at Sachsenhausen in reprisal, and a further 250 Berlin Jews were sent to the camp.[57]

On May 29 the Nazi leader and his propaganda minister once more discussed the attack and its wider implications. "I again present to the Führer my plan to completely evacuate the Jews from Berlin," Goebbels recorded on the next day. "He is in total agreement and gives the order to Speer to replace the Jews employed in the armament industries with foreign workers as soon as possible. That 40,000 Jews who have nothing to lose can still freely roam around Berlin represents a great danger. It is a challenge and an invitation to assassinations. If this ever starts, then one's life is not safe anymore. In the most recent fire-bomb attacks, even 22-year-old Eastern Jews participated; this speaks volumes. I plead once again for a more radical policy against the Jews, whereby I encounter the Führer's complete agreement. The Führer thinks that for us personally the danger will grow if the war situation becomes more critical."[58]

After both Hitler and his minister agreed that the situation of the Reich was much better than it had been in 1917 and that, this time no uprisings or strikes threatened in any way, Hitler added that "the Germans participated in subversive movements only when incited by the Jews."[59] Hitler then launched into one of his usual diatribes, stressing the brutality of the Jews and their thirst for vengeance; therefore sending the Jews to Siberia could be dangerous, as under difficult living conditions they could regain their vitality. The best course of action, in his view, would be to send them to Central Africa: "There they would live in a climate that would certainly not make them strong and resistant."[60]

The reference to 1917 and the uprisings and strikes was indeed telling: In Hitler's mind the elimination of the Jews ensured that no repeat performance of the revolutionary activities of 1917–18 would occur; the Baum attempt was a warning: The extermination of the Jews had to be completed as rapidly as possible.

A second event may also have accelerated the extermination process, albeit indirectly. On May 27 Heydrich was fatally wounded by Czech commandos parachuted by the British into the Protectorate; he died on June 4. Five days later, on the day of the state funeral, Hitler ordered the murder of most of the population of Lidice (a village near Prague, where the Germans thought Heydrich's assailants had hidden). All men aged fifteen to ninety were shot; all women sent to concentration camps, where most of them perished; some children were "germanized" and brought up in German families under new identities; the great majority of the children who did not show Germanic traits were sent to Chelmno and gassed. As for the village, it was leveled to the ground.[61] After an interim period during which Himmler himself took over the leadership of the RSHA, he appointed the Austrian Ernst Kaltenbrunner as Heydrich's successor, in January 1943.[62]

Himmler met Hitler on June 3, 4, and 5.[63] Whether it was during these meetings that the Nazi leader and his henchman decided to accelerate the extermination process and set a deadline for the completion of the "Final Solution" is not known, but seems plausible in light of the Baum attempt and Heydrich's death. More than ever, the Jews were an internal threat. On June 9, in the course of a lengthy memorial address for the RSHA chief, delivered to a gathering of SS generals, Himmler declared, as if incidentally: "We will certainly complete the migration of the Jews within a year; after that, none of them will wander anymore. It is time now to wipe the slate clean."[64] Then, on July 19, after a two-day visit to Auschwitz, the Reichsführer sent Krüger the following order: The resettlement of the entire Jewish population of the General Government should be implemented and completed by December 31, 1942. On December 31, 1942, no persons of Jewish origin are allowed to stay in the General Government, except if they are in assembly camps in Warsaw, Kraków, Czestochowa, Radom, and Lublin. All projects that employ Jewish labor have to be completed by that date or transferred to the assembly camps."

The Reichsführer could not leave it at that; he had to adduce some ideological elements to explain this sudden acceleration of the murder process: "These measures are necessary for the separation of races and peoples demanded by the new organization of Europe and for the security and cleanness of the German Reich and of its sphere of interest. Every infraction of these regulations represents a danger for the calm and order in the overall German sphere of interest, a starting point for the resistance movement and a source of moral and physical infection. For all these reasons, the total cleansing is necessary and has to be implemented. Any foreseeable delays have to be reported to me, to allow a timely search for assistance. Any attempt by other agencies to change [these instructions] or seek exceptions have to be submitted personally to me."[65] Himmler was probably alluding to potential demands from the Wehrmacht.

IV

The majority of the Jews of Europe were exterminated after being held for different periods of time (between several months and several years) in camps or assembly areas in the West (Drancy, Westerbork, Malines [Mechlen]) or in ghettos in the East. Most of these concentration or assembly areas were established before general extermination was decided on, but some were set up as part ghettos, part holding pens at the very outset of the "Final Solution": Theresienstadt, for example, or Izbica, near Lublin.

Theresienstadt (Terezín in Czech), which was to become an assembly camp and the Jewish "model camp" of the concentration and extermination system, was a small fortified town in northern Bohemia that, by the end of 1941, housed some 7,000 German soldiers and Czech civilians; an annex (the small fortress) was already the central Gestapo prison in the Protectorate. At the end of 1941 (November and December) Jewish labor details started preparing Terezín for its new function, and at the very beginning of January 1942, the first transports arrived with around 10,000 Jews.[66]

An "elder of the Jews" and a council of thirteen members were appointed. The first "elder" was the widely respected Jakob Edelstein. A native of Horodenka in eastern Galicia, Edelstein moved to Czechoslovakia and settled in Teplitz, in the Sudetenland. Politically he turned to socialism, but mainly to Zionism. Although quite unremarkable in appearance and in his professional life as a salesman, Edelstein soon proved to be an able public speaker, much in demand at Zionist meetings.[67] Shortly after the Nazi accession to power in Germany, Edelstein was called to head the "Palestine office" in Prague, in other words to assist the growing flow of refugees ready to emigrate to Eretz Israel.

The German occupation of Bohemia and Moravia and the establishment of the Protectorate led, as we saw, to the setting up of a Central Office for Jewish Emigration in Prague, along the pattern already honed in Vienna, then in Berlin. While the Vienna center was left in the hands of Rolf Günther and Alois Brunner, Eichmann himself took over emigration from the Protectorate together with another Günther brother, Hans.

Edelstein's common sense—and his courage—made him, de facto, the central personality of Czech Jewry in its contacts with the Germans. In October 1939, he was ordered to head the groups of Jews evacuated from Ostrava to Nisko; the deportees from Austria were shepherded by Storfer, the emigration specialist, and by Rabbi Benjamin Murmelstein who, in 1942, would become Edelstein's problematic colleague in Theresienstadt. The failure of the Nisko attempt brought Edelstein back to Prague.[68] Soon thereafter, in March 1941, Eichmann dispatched him together with another member of the Prague community, Richard Friedmann, to advise Asscher and Cohen in Amsterdam on the setting up of their Council. Edelstein tried to warn his Dutch counterparts about the dangers that awaited them, including the possibility of deportations to the East, but to no avail.[69]

When in the fall of that same year, Heydrich decided to deport the Jews of the Protectorate to an assembly camp on Bohemian territory, Edelstein was naturally chosen to head the "model ghetto." In mid-December 1941, a few days after Edelstein's arrival in Theresienstadt, Hans Günther came on an inspection tour: "Now, Jews," the SS officer declared, "when you are *im Dreck* [in shit] let's see what you can do." The Jews thought that this was a challenge they could handle.[70]

At the outset the camp leadership was criticized for its Zionist slant; yet the growing number of inmates and the increasing harshness of everyday life soon dampened ideological confrontations, and the Zionist commitment of the majority of the leadership remained unchanged. Thus a twenty-three-year-old teacher in a Jewish school in Prague, Egon "Gonda" Redlich, became head of the Youth Welfare Department. Redlich and his associate Fredy Hirsch (mainly responsible for sports and physical education) created a quasi-autonomous domain of the young for the young (that over time comprised on average three to four thousand youngsters); there in particular a strongly Zionist-inspired youth culture developed.

Nothing, however, could protect either the young or the old from deportation to killing areas or sites. "I heard a terrible piece of news," Redlich noted in his diary on January 6, 1942, "a transport will go from Terezin to Riga. We argued for a long while if the time had not yet come to say 'enough.'" Redlich's next-day entry continued in the same vein: "Our mood is very bad. We prepared for the transport. We worked practically all night. With Fredy's help, we managed to spare the children from the transport." And on January 7: "We were not able to work because we were locked in the barracks. I asked the authorities to remove children from the transport and was told that the children will not be traveling. . . . Our work is like that of the Youth Aliyah [the organized emigration of children and youngsters to Palestine]. There we brought children to freedom. Here we attempt to save the children from death."[71]

Saving children from the transports soon became impossible; when Redlich spoke of "death," he actually did not know what the fate of deportees "to the East" would be. The "counselors" debated whether they should volunteer for the transports, to continue providing assistance and education to their charges. But, in historian Ruth Bondy's words, "The arguments remained theoretical: in the end, family considerations, and the will to cling to Theresienstadt for as long as possible, prevailed."[72] On January 10 Redlich noted: "Yesterday we read in the orders of the day that another ten transports will go. There is reason to believe that an additional four will also depart." He added: "An order of the day: nine men were hanged. The reason for the order: they insulted German honor."[73]

As the summer of 1942 began, tens of transports of elderly Jews from the Reich and the Protectorate were sent on their way to the Czech "ghetto." "In June," Redlich recorded, "twenty-four transports arrived and four left. Of those entering, fifteen thousand came from Germany proper [*Altreich*], most of them very old."[74] On June 30: "I helped Viennese Jews yesterday. They are old, lice-ridden, and they have a few insane people among them."[75]

Among its "insane" passengers the transport from Vienna included Trude Herzl-Neumann, the younger daughter of the founder of political Zionism, Theodor Herzl.[76] Edelstein was not impressed and refused to come and greet the new inmate. But Trude Herzl was not to be dismissed so easily: "I, the younger daughter of the deceased Zionist leader, Dr. Theodor Herzl," she wrote to the ghetto leaders and to the "Zionist branch" in Theresienstadt, "take the liberty of informing the local Zionists of my arrival and asking them for help and support during the present difficult times. With Zionist and faithful greetings, T. Neumann-Herzl."[77] Her many messages reflected her mental state, and six months after her arrival, she died.

A small ceremony took place at the camp's mortuary, after which, as usual, the corpse was carried on a farm cart to the crematorium, outside the walls. There the ashes of all the dead were kept in numbered cardboard boxes. The residents hoped that once the ordeal was over, they would find the ashes of their loved ones and bury them in a decent grave. In late 1944, to erase evidence, the Germans ordered all the ashes to be thrown into the nearby Eger River.[78]

The number of incoming transports kept growing throughout July. "People arrive by the thousands," Redlich wrote on August 1, "the aged that do not have the strength to get the food. Fifty die daily."[79] Indeed the mortality rate in the "old people's ghetto" shot up, and in September 1942 alone, some 3,900 people from a total population of 58,000 died. At approximately the same time transports of the elderly inmates from Theresienstadt to Treblinka started. By then, as we shall see, the waves of deportations from Warsaw were subsiding and the gas chambers of Treblinka could take in the 18,000 new arrivals from the Protectorate ghetto.

It was in one of the September transports from Vienna, the "hospital transport," that Ruth Kluger (the young girl who had received an orange in the subway after the star was introduced in the Reich) and her mother arrived in Theresienstadt. Ruth was sent to one of the youth barracks that were under Redlich and Hirsch's supervision. There, as she writes, she became a Jew: The lectures, the all-pervading Zionist atmosphere, the sense of belonging to a community of *haverim* and *haveroth* (male and female comrades, in Hebrew) where one didn't say *gute Nacht* but *Laila tov* ("good night," in Hebrew), gave the young girl a new feeling of belonging. And yet, even in Theresienstadt, even among the young, some of the inmates kept feeling superior to the other and showed it: "The Czechs in L410 [the children's barracks] looked down on us because we spoke the enemy's language. Besides, they really were the elite, because they were in their own country. . . . So even here we were disdained for something that wasn't in our power to change: our mother tongue."[80]

Throughout its existence Theresienstadt offered a dual face: On the one hand, transports were departing to Auschwitz and Treblinka, on the other, the Germans set up a "Potemkin village" meant to fool the world. "Will money be introduced?" Redlich asked in an entry on November 7, 1942. "Of course it could be. The thing could be an interesting experiment in national economics. Anyway, a coffee house has been opened (they say there will even be music there, a bank, a reading room). Two days later: "They are making a film. Jewish actors, satisfied, happy faces in the film, only in the film." This was to be the first of two Nazi films about Theresienstadt.[81]

Whereas Theresienstadt, designated a ghetto, was part assembly camp and part concentration camp, the nondescript Izbica, in the Lublin district, was in fact a ghetto without walls. Two-thirds of Izbica's initial Jewish population had been deported to Belzec and, from March 1942 on, transports of Jews from the Protectorate, then from any deportation center in the Reich, filled the town with its new inhabitants. A remarkable "report from Izbica," offers a detailed description of daily life in this waiting room to Belzec or Sobibor.[82] This eighteen-page letter was written in August 1942 by a deportee from Essen, Ernst Krombach, to his fiancée, Marianne Ellenbogen, whom we encountered in the previous chapter, and delivered to her by an SS employee from Essen whom the couple knew.

Krombach's letter, studded with all the prejudices against Polish and Czech Jews common among German Jews, is one more expression of the absence of overall solidarity, the tensions among inmates, and the *sauve qui peut* mentality (his own words) that prevailed in Izbica, as everywhere else.[83] Whether Izbica's Jews knew the destination of the outgoing transports is unclear from the letter, as he certainly wished to shield Ellenbogen from further anguish. "In the meantime [since his arrival in April]," he writes, "many transports have left here. Of the approximately 14,000 Jews who arrived, only 2–3,000 are still here. They go off in cattle trucks, subject to the most brutal treatment, with even fewer possessions, i.e. only the clothes they are wearing. That is one rung farther down the ladder. We have heard nothing more of these people (Austerlitz, Bärs, etc.). After the last transport, the men who were working outside the village returned to find neither their wives, nor children, nor their possessions.[84]

After indicating that in the recent transports the men had been taken off the trains in Lublin—which confirms what we know of the selection process introduced there—Krombach admits that, although he refused to join the Jewish police, he was compelled to take part in the deportation of "Polish Jews": "You have to suppress every human feeling and, under the supervision of the SS, drive the people out with a whip, just as they are—barefoot, with infants in their arms. There are scenes which I cannot and will not describe but which will take me long to forget."[85] It remains puzzling that somebody who did not belong to the Jewish police would have been compelled to chase the Polish Jews "with a whip" out of their homes and into the cattle cars.

In a second part of his report, Krombach seems to know more or be ready to tell more: "Recently on one morning alone more than 20 Polish Jews were shot for baking bread. . . . Our lives consist of uncertainty and insecurity. There could be another evacuation tomorrow, even though the officials concerned say that there won't be any more. It becomes more and more difficult to hide given how few people are here now—particularly as there is always a given target [a quota of deportees] to be met."[86] Then, almost paradoxically, he uses a metaphor from his youthful readings: "The Wild West was nothing compared to this!"[87] Could it be that, after all, he had no clear understanding of his situation?

In the fall of 1942 all contact with Ernst Krombach was lost. According to some reports, at about that time he had been blinded either in an accident or by the SS. In April 1943 the last Jews of Izbica were shipped to Sobibor.[88]

V

While the killings in Chelmno ran smoothly on, the building of Belzec, which had started on November 1, 1941, progressed apace, and in early March, the first transports of Jews reached the Lublin district, close to the camp. Assistance from the local authorities was necessary at first. On March 16, 1942, an official from the Population and Social Welfare Bureau of the district, Fritz Rauter, discussed the situation with Hauptsturmführer Hermann Höfle, Globocnik's main deportations expert, who volunteered some explanations. A camp was being built in Belzec, along the railway line Deblin-Trawniki; Höfle was ready to take in four or five transports daily. These Jews, he explained to Rauter, "were crossing the border [of the General Government] and would never return." The next day the gassings started.[89]

At first, some 30,000 out of the 37,000 Jews of the Lublin ghetto were exterminated. Simultaneously another 13,500 Jews arrived from various areas of the district (Zamość, Piaski, and Izbica), and from the Lwov area;

in early June deportees from Krakow followed. Within four weeks some 75,000 Jews had been murdered in this first of the three "Aktion Reinhardt" camps (named in Heydrich's memory),[90] by the end of 1942 about 434,000 Jews would be exterminated in Belzec alone.[91] Two survived the war.

Sometime in late March or April 1942, the former Austrian police officer and euthanasia expert Franz Stangl traveled to Belzec to meet its commandant, SS Hauptsturmführer Christian Wirth. Forty years later, in his Düsseldorf jail, Stangl described his arrival in Belzec: "I went there by car," he told the British journalist Gitta Sereny. " 'As one arrived, one first reached Belzec railway station, on the left side of the road. It was a one-story building. The smell . . .' he said. 'Oh God, the smell. It was everywhere. Wirth wasn't in his office. I remember, they took me to him. . . . He was standing on a hill, next to the pits . . . the pits . . . full . . . they were full. I can't tell you; not hundreds, thousands, thousands of corpses. . . . Oh God. That's where Wirth told me—he said that was what Sobibor was for. And that he was putting me officially in charge.' "[92] Some two months later Sobibor—whose construction began at the end of March 1942—was in operation and Stangl, its attentive commandant, usually toured the camp in white riding attire.[93]

About 90,000 to 100,000 Jews were murdered in Sobibor during its first three months of operation; they came from the Lublin district and, either directly or via ghettos of the Lublin area, from Austria, the Protectorate, and the *Altreich*.[94] And, while the exterminations were launched in Sobibor, the construction of Treblinka began.

Extermination in the "Aktion Reinhardt" camps followed standard procedures. Ukrainian auxiliaries, usually armed with whips, chased the Jews out of the trains. As in Chelmno, the next step was "disinfection"; the victims had to undress and leave all their belongings in the assembly room. Then the throng of naked and terrified people was pushed through a narrow hallway or passage into one of the gas chambers. The doors were hermetically sealed; the gassing started. At the beginning bottles of carbon monoxide were still used in Belzec; later they were replaced by various engines. Death was slow to come in these early gas chambers (ten minutes or more): Sometimes the agony of the victims could be watched through peepholes. When all was finished, the emptying of the gas chambers was left, again as in Chelmno, to Jewish "special commandos," who would themselves be liquidated later on.

* * *

Around Belzec and throughout the Lublin district, rumors spread. On April 8, 1942, Klukowski, the Polish hospital director, noted: "The Jews are upset [probably "in despair" in the original]. We know for sure that every day two trains, consisting of twenty cars each, come to Belzec, one from Lublin, the other from Lwow. After being unloaded on separate tracks, all Jews are forced behind the barbed-wire enclosure. Some are killed with electricity, some with poison gases, and the bodies are burned." Klukowski went on: "On the way to Belzec the Jews experience many terrible things. They are aware of what will happen to them. Some try to fight back. At the railroad station in Szczebrzeszyn a young woman gave away a gold ring in exchange for a glass of water for her dying child. In Lublin, people witnessed small children being thrown through the windows of speeding trains. Many people are shot before reaching Belzec."[95]

On April 12, having mentioned on the previous day that the deportation of Jews from Zamość was about to start, Klukowski noted: "The information from Zamość is horrifying. Almost 2,500 Jews were evacuated. A few hundred were shot on the streets. Some men fought back. I do not have any details. Here in Szczebrzeszyn there is panic. Old Jewish women spent the night in the Jewish cemetery, saying they would rather die here among the graves of their own families than be killed and buried in the concentration camps." And the following day: "Many Jews have left town already or hidden. . . . In town a mob started assembling, waiting for the right moment to start removing everything from the Jewish homes. I have information that some people are already stealing whatever can be carried out from homes where the owners have been forced to move out."[96]

By April 1942 gassings had reached their full scale in Chelmno, Belzec, and Sobibor; they were just starting in Auschwitz, and would soon begin in Treblinka. Simultaneously, within a few weeks, huge extermination operations by shooting or in gas vans would engulf further hundreds of thousands of Jews in Belorussia and in the Ukraine (the second sweep), while "standard" on-the-spot killings remained common fare throughout the winter in the occupied areas of the USSR, in Galicia, in the Lublin district, and several areas of eastern Poland. At the same time again, slave labor camps were operating throughout the East and in Upper Silesia; some camps in this last category were a mix of transit areas, slave labor, and killing centers: Majdanek near Lublin or Janowska Road, on the outskirts of Lwov, for example. And, next to this jumble of slave labor and extermination operations, tens of thousands of Jews toiled in ordinary factories and workshops, in work camps, ghettos, or towns, and hundreds of thousands were still alive in former Poland, in the Baltic countries, and further eastward. While the Jewish population in the Reich was rapidly declining as deportations had resumed in full force, in the West, most Jews were leading their restricted lives without a sense of immediate danger. Yet the German vise was closing rapidly, and within two or three months, even minimal everyday normality would have disappeared for most Jews in occupied Europe.

In Auschwitz the gassing of the Jews began with small groups. In mid-February 1942, some 400 older Jews from the Upper Silesian labor camps of "Organization Schmelt," deemed unfit for work, arrived from Beuthen.[97]

On this occasion, as during the previous killing of Soviet prisoners in the Zyklon B experiments, the reconverted morgue of the main camp (Auschwitz I) crematorium was turned into a gas chamber. The proximity of the camp administration building complicated matters: The personnel had to be evacuated when the Jews marched by and a truck engine was run to cover the death cries of the victims.[98] Shortly thereafter the head of the construction division of the WVHA, Hans Kammler, visited the camp and ordered a series of rapid improvements. A new crematorium with five incinerators, previously ordered for Auschwitz I, was transferred to Auschwitz II–Birkenau—and set in the northwest corner of the new camp, next to an abandoned Polish cottage. This cottage, "Bunker I," soon housed two gas chambers. On March 20 it became operational; its first victims were another group of elderly "Schmelt Jews."[99]

VI

In the occupied territories of the Soviet Union, the "second sweep" of the killing units was launched on an even larger scale than the first, at the end of 1941; it lasted throughout 1942.[100] In some areas, such as the Reichskommissariat Ukraine (RKU), according to a report from the Wehrmacht Armaments Inspectorate, mass executions had never stopped and were going on without interruption apart from brief organizational slowdowns, from mid-1941 to mid-1942.

The Wehrmacht report indicated that barely a few weeks after the end of the military operations, the systematic execution of the Jewish population had started. The units involved belonged mainly to the Order Police: they were assisted by Ukrainian auxiliaries and "often, unfortunately, by the voluntary participation of members of the Wehrmacht." The report described the massacres as "horrible"; they included indiscriminately men, women, old people and children of all ages. The scope of the mass murders was yet unequaled on occupied Soviet territory. According to the report, approximately 150,000 to 200,000 Jews of the Reichskommissariat were exterminated (it would ultimately be around 360,000). Only in the last phase of the operation a tiny "useful" segment of the population (specialized artisans) was not killed. Previously economic considerations had not been taken into account.[101]

At the outset, as we saw, the intensity of the massacres differed from one area to another; at the end, of course, in late 1942 and early 1943, the outcome would be the same: almost complete extermination. During the "first sweep," as *Einsatzkommandos*, police battalions, and Ukrainian auxiliaries were moving along with the Werhmacht, the killings in the western part of the Ukraine—Generalbezirk Volhyn-Podolia (General district Volhynia-Podolia)—encompassed approximately 20 percent of the Jewish population. In Rovno, however, the capital of the Reichskommissariat, some 18,000 people—that is, 80 percent of the Jewish inhabitants, were murdered.[102]

From September 1941 to May 1942, the Security Police (*Einsatzgruppe C* and *Einsatzkommando 5*), headquartered in Kiev, organized its hold on the RKU. The HSSPF in the Ukraine, SS General Prützmann and his civilian counterpart, *Reichskomissar* Koch, cooperated without any difficulty, as both came from Königsberg. Koch delegated all "Jewish matters" to Prützmann, who in turn passed them on to the chief of the Security Police. But, as emphasized by historian Dieter Pohl, "the civilian authorities and the Security Police reached harmonious cooperation in the mass murder: The initiatives came from both sides."[103]

Given the immense territories they had under their control and the variety of languages or dialects of the local populations, the Germans relied from the outset on the help of local militias that, over the months, became regular auxiliary forces, the *Schutzmannschaften*. The Order Police units and the Gendarmerie were German; the *Schutzmannschaften* soon widely outnumbered them and participated in all activities, including the killings of Jews in some major operations such as the extermination of part of the Jewish population of Minsk in the late fall of 1941. There the Lithuanian *Schutzmannschaften* distinguished themselves.[104]

The auxiliary units included Ukrainians, Poles, Lithuanians, and Belorussians. A Polish underground report about the liquidation of the Brest Litovsk ghetto in late 1942 is telling: "The liquidation of the Jews has been continuing since 15 October. During the first three days about 12,000 people were shot. The place of execution is Bronna Góra. At present the rest of those in hiding are being liquidated. The liquidation was being organized by a mobile squad of SD and local police. At present, the 'finishing off' is being done by the local police, in which Poles represent a large percentage. They are often more zealous than the Germans. Some Jewish possessions go to furnish German homes and offices, some are sold at auction. Despite the fact that during the liquidation large quantities of weapons were found, the Jews behaved passively."[105]

Once Hitler decided to move his forward headquarters to Vinnytsa (in the Ukraine), the Jews of the area had to disappear. Thus, in the first days of 1942, 227 Jews who lived in the immediate neighborhood of the planned headquarters were delivered by "Organization Todt" to the "Secret Military Police" and shot on January 10. A second batch of approximately 8,000 Jews who lived in nearby Chmelnik were shot around the same time. Then came the turn of the Jews of Vinnytsa. Here the operation was delayed by a few weeks, but in mid-April the Secret Military Police reported that the 4,800 Jews of the town had been executed (*umgelegt*). Finally approximately 1,000 Jewish artisans who worked for the Germans in the same area were murdered in July, on orders of the local commander of the Security Police.[106]

The two *Reichskommissare*, Lohse and Koch, enthusiastically supported mass murder operations. Koch in particular requested that in the Ukraine *all* Jews be annihilated in order to reduce local food consumption and fill the growing food demands from the Reich. As a result the district commissars, at their meeting in August 1942, agreed with the head of the Security Police, Karl Pütz, that all the Jews of Reichskommissariat

Ukraine, with the exception of 500 specialized craftsmen, would be exterminated: This was defined as the "hundred percent solution."[107]

In the Baltic countries—in Lohse's domain—particularly in Lithuania, Jäger could always be relied on as far as mass murder was concerned. On February 6, 1942, Stahlecker asked him to urgently report the total number of executions of his *Einsatzkommando 3*, according to the following categories: Jews, communists, partisans, mentally ill, others; furthermore, Jäger had to indicate the number of women and children. According to the report, sent three days later, by February 1, 1942, *Einsatzkommando 3* had executed 136,421 Jews, 1,064 communists, 56 partisans, 653 mentally ill, 78 others. Total: 138,272 (of whom 55,556 were women and 34,464 were children).[108]

At times Jäger went too far. Thus, on May 18, 1942, following an army complaint about the liquidation of 630 Jewish craftsmen in Minsk, contrary to prior agreements, Gestapo chief Müller had to remind him of several orders issued by Himmler: "Jews and Jewesses capable of working, between ages 16 and 32, should be exempt from special measures, for the time being."[109]

On several occasions the extermination campaign led to difficulties between one of Rosenberg's appointees, the *Generalkommissar* for Weissruthenien (Belorussia), *Gauleiter* Wilhelm Kube, and the SD. At the end of 1941, Kube had been shocked to discover that *Mischlinge* and decorated war veterans had been included among the deportees from the Reich to Minsk. But, it is at the beginning of 1942 that the General Kommissar launched his main assault against the SS and their local commander, chief of the Security Police, Dr. Eduard Strauch. Kube did not object to the extermination of the Jews as such but rather to the methods used in the process: gold teeth and bridges were pulled out of the mouths of victims awaiting their death; many Jews, merely wounded in the executions, were buried alive, and the like. This, in Kube's terms, was "*bodenlose Schweinerei*" [utterly disgusting] and Strauch was the chief culprit, denounced to Lohse, to Rosenberg, possibly to Hitler.

Kube's complaints drew a sharp response from Heydrich on March 21. As for Strauch, he started compiling a hefty file of accusations against the *Generalkommissar* whose leadership he considered worse than nil, whose entourage was corrupt and dissolute and who, on various occasions, had shown friendliness to Jews.[110] Neither Kube nor Strauch was recalled, and, as we shall see, the confrontation was to culminate in 1943. In the meantime, however, Strauch had approximately half of the remaining Minsk ghetto population of 19,000 Jews massacred in late July 1942.[111]

At times technical difficulties hampered the killings. On June 15, 1942, for example, the commander of the Security Police and the SD in the Ostland urgently requested an additional gas van, as the three vans operating in Belorussia did not suffice to deal with all the Jews arriving at an accelerated rate. Furthermore, he demanded twenty new gas hoses [carrying the carbon monoxide from the engines back into the vans], as those in use were no longer airtight.[112] In fact the functioning of the vans occasioned a series of complaints that, in turn, led to a spirited response from "Referat IID3" of the RSHA, on June 5, 1942.

The author of the lengthy report reminded his critics that three of the vans [in Chelmno] "had processed 97,000 since December 1941, without any visible defects." Nonetheless he suggested a series of six major technical improvements to deal more efficiently with the "number of pieces" (*Stückzahl*) usually loaded in each van.[113] Regarding the "97,000," the expert had probably deemed it safer to avoid any further identification. In the second section of the report he referred to "pieces" and in the sixth section, he changed the identification once more: "It has been noted from experience that upon the shutting of the back door [of the van] the load [*Ladung*] presses against the door [when the lights are turned off]. This stems from the fact that once darkness sets in, the load pushes itself towards light."[114]

Apparently the single van sent from Berlin to Belgrade to kill the 8,000 Jewish women and children of the Sajmište concentration camp gave no reason for any complaints. After the Wehrmacht had shot most of the men as hostages in the "antipartisan" warfare during the summer and fall of 1941, the women and children were moved to a makeshift camp—a few dilapidated buildings—near Belgrade until their fate was decided. It remains unclear who in the German administration in Belgrade, whether SS Gruppenführer Harald Turner, head of the civilian administration, or SS Standartenführer Emanuel Schäfer, the chief of the security police in Belgrade, asked the RSHA to send the van.[115] Whatever the case may be, the van reached Belgrade at the end of February 1942. In early March the killings started, and by May 9, 1942, the Jewish women and children of Sajmište, as well as the patients and staff of the Jewish hospital in Belgrade and Jewish prisoners from a nearby camp had all been asphyxiated. On June 9 Schäfer informed the head of the carpool at the RSHA: "Subject: Special Saurer type van. The drivers . . . Götz and Meier finished their special assignment. They are returning with the van. Because of damage to the rear part of the van . . . I ordered its transportation by train."[116]

In August 1942 Turner reported: "Serbia is the only country in Europe where the Jewish problem has been solved."[117]

Killings could not be extended at will, however, to other groups than the designated Jews even when a high-ranking party official deemed them necessary. Thus, on May 1, 1942, in a message to Himmler, Greiser expressed his confidence that within two to three months the "special treatment" of some 100,000 Jews in Chelmno would be completed. He asked for the authorization to murder some 35,000 Poles suffering from open tuberculosis.[118] The authorization was granted at first but then canceled by Hitler; the Nazi leader wished to avoid any rumors about the resumption of euthanasia.

* * *

Calls for Jewish armed resistance, such as Kovner's manifesto in Vilna, arose from the ranks of politically motivated Jewish youth movements, and the first Jews to fight the Germans as "partisans," in the East or in the West, usually belonged to non-Jewish underground political-military organizations. In western Belorussia, however, a uniquely Jewish unit, without any political allegiance except for its aim of saving Jews sprung up in early 1942: the already briefly mentioned Bielski brothers' group. The Bielskis were villagers who had lived for more than six decades in Stankiewicze, between Lida and Novogrodek, two midsize Belorussian towns.[119] Like their peasant neighbors they were poor, notwithstanding the mill and the land they owned. The only Jews in their village, they fully belonged to it in most ways. They knew the people and the environment, particularly the nearby forests. The younger generation included four brothers: Tuvia, Asael, Zus, and Arczik.

In December 1941 the Germans murdered 4,000 inhabitants of the

Novogrodek ghetto, among them the Bielski parents, Tuvia's first wife, and Zus's wife. In two successive groups, the one led by Asael, the second by Tuvia, the brothers moved to the forests, in March and then in May 1942. Soon all deferred to Tuvia's leadership: An even larger number of family members and other Jews fleeing the surrounding ghettos joined the "Otriad" (a partisan detachment); weapons were acquired and food was secured. By the end of the German occupation, the Bielski brothers had assembled some 1,500 Jews in their forest camp, notwithstanding almost insuperable odds.[120]

While the Bielski group was one of its kind, other Jewish resistance movements organized within the ghettos of the occupied Soviet Union did often receive support from the council leadership. In Minsk, for example, the noncommunist Ilya Moshkin, an engineer who knew some German and was probably appointed head of the *Judenrat* precisely for that reason, was in regular (weekly) contact with the commander of the communist underground in the ghetto and the city, Hersh Smolar. Such regular cooperation—for which Moshkin ultimately paid with his life—was entirely atypical farther west, in the Baltic countries and in former Poland, be it from fear of German repraisals against the ghetto population.[121] The only partly comparable situation to that in Minsk was, for a time at least, that of the Białystok ghetto, where Ephraïm Barash's *Judenrat* did keep in touch for more than a year with Mordechai Tenenbaum's underground organization, a case to which we shall return.

VII

In mid-March 1942, the sixty-seven-year-old former owner of a shoe business and chairman of the Nuremberg Jewish community, Leo Israel Katzenberger, was interrogated by the criminal police, then put on trial for *Rassenschande,* race defilement. The codefendant was the thirty-two-year-old "full-German" woman, Irene Seiler (born Scheffler), owner of a photo business, also in Nuremberg; she was accused of race defilement and perjury. The presiding judge, regional court director and head of the special court, Dr. Oswald Rothaug, had been handed a choice case: He rose to the occasion, the more so because the trial attracted wide public interest. "The courtroom was filled to capacity with leading jurists, Party members, and military personnel."[122]

During the interrogation the defendants readily confirmed that for many years they had been acquainted and on affectionate terms (Seiler had been introduced to Katzenberger by her own father, a friend of his), that Katzenberger had at times helped Seiler financially and advised her in her business. Moreover, they lived in the same housing complex and thus were in close and frequent contact. Yet both strenuously denied, also under oath, that their mutual affection, which at times had led her to kiss him as a natural expression of her feelings, ever led to any sexual relations. At times Katzenberger brought Seiler some chocolates, cigarettes, or flowers and also occasionally gave her shoes. Seiler married on the eve of the war, and according to her testimony, her husband had met Katzenberger and knew of their longtime friendship. In 1941 and early 1942, as Katzenberger and Seiler were arrested and prosecuted, Seiler's husband was at the front.

"Rothaug," Seiler testified after the war, "reproached me that as a German woman whose husband was on the front, I had forgotten myself to the point of having an affair with the little syphilitic Jew. . . . He told me that from Katzenberger's point of view it [the affair with me] would not have constituted race pollution since the Talmud permitted it."[123] The witnesses for the prosecution, whose testimonies Seiler reported in detail, were sworn in by the judge whenever the accusations against the defendants appeared sufficiently incriminating. The examination of the witness Paul Kleylein was typical: "Rothaug asked the witness to describe his observations. He began by stating that Katzenberger's conduct had been unbearable and that both he and his wife had been profoundly shocked by my immoral behavior, particularly since my husband was a soldier. Asked to furnish further details, Kleylein stated that the tenant Oesterleicher had said to me, in the presence of other persons in an air-raid shelter: 'You Jewish bitch, I am going to give it to you.' Yet, I had not replied to this, and I had also not done anything about it later. He therefore had concluded that I had not undertaken anything out of shame and because of a guilty conscience."[124]

Witnesses for the defense, such as Ilse Graentzel, an employee in Seiler's photo business, were also called. Rothaug asked Graentzel "whether Jews had not been photographed in my photo-studio up to the end. Mrs. Graentzel said yes, and I also confirmed it. Rothaug accepted this as a new proof of my attachment to the Jews."[125]

Seiler was condemned to two years in a penitentiary for perjury. As for

Katzenberger, there was no doubt about the outcome. As Rothaug put it: "It is enough for me that this swine said that a German girl was sitting on his lap."[126] On June 3, 1942, the Jew was condemned to death.[127] Nobody was surprised.

On January 6, 1942, on his way home after shopping at Chemnitzer Platz, Klemperer was arrested on the tram and brought to Gestapo headquarters. The official in charge yelled at him: "Take your filth (briefcase and hat) off the table. Put the hat on. Isn't that what you do? Where you stand, that's holy ground."—"I'm Protestant."—"What are you? Baptized? That's just a cover-up. As a professor you must know the book by . . . by somebody Levysohn, it's all in there. Are you circumcised? It's not true that it's a hygienic prescription. It's all in the book." And so it went. Klemperer was forced to empty his briefcase, to have every item checked. Then: "Who is going to win the war? You or us?"—"What do you mean?"—"Well, you pray for our defeat every day, don't you?—To Yahweh, or whatever it's called. It is the Jewish War, isn't it. Adolf Hitler said so—(shouting theatrically) and what Adolf Hitler says is true!"[128]

In early 1942 Goebbels had prohibited the sale of any media items (newspapers, journals, periodicals) to Jews.[129] Some two weeks earlier the use of public phones had also been forbidden.[130] Private telephones and radios had already been confiscated long ago; the new instructions would close another gap. Moreover, the growing scarcity of paper seemed to add greater urgency to curtailing the distribution of newsprint. The minister of posts and communications was ready to adopt the new measure, despite some technical difficulties. Unexpected opposition arose, however, from the RSHA. In a February 4 letter to Goebbels, Heydrich argued that it would be impossible to inform the Jews, particularly their representatives both nationally and locally, of all the measures they had to heed, only by way of the *Jewish News Bulletin* (*Jüdisches Nachrichtenblatt*). Moreover, professional periodicals were essential for Jewish "caretakers of the sick" or "consultants." "As I have to keep the Jews firmly in hand," Heydrich added, "I must ask to ease these instructions, the more so since they were issued without the essential consultation with my office."[131] By March, Goebbels's regulations had been partly abandoned.

The prohibition of Jewish emigration led to the closing, on February 14, 1942, of the Reichsvereinigung offices, which advised and helped the emigrants.[132] As for the public identification of Jews, the individual star did not suffice; on March 13, the RSHA ordered the fixing of a white paper star to the entrance door of every apartment inhabited by Jews or to the entrance of any Jewish institution.[133]

The display of signs and badges favored by the RSHA was in turn questioned by the propaganda minister. Thus on March 11 Goebbels rejected an SD proposal that Jews allowed to use public transportation should display a special badge. The minister, who wanted to avoid further public discussion of the star issue, suggested that these Jews be given a special permit to be presented to the ticket taker or, on demand, to army officers and party officials.[134] On March 24 Heydrich forbade the use of public transportation to Jews, except for holders of the special police permit.[135]

Random Gestapo raids on Jews' houses were particularly feared. At the Klemperers', the first of these "house visits" took place on May 22, 1942, a Friday afternoon, while Victor K. was not at home: the house was left upside down, its inhabitants had been slapped, beaten, spat on, but, as Klemperer noted, "we got away not too badly this time."[136]

On May 15, Jews were forbidden to keep pets. "Jews with the star," Klemperer recorded, "and anyone who lives with them, are, effective immediately, forbidden to keep pets (dogs, cats, birds); it is also forbidden to give the animals away to be looked after. This is the death sentence for [their cat] Muschel, whom we have had for more than eleven years and to whom Eva is very attached. Tomorrow he is to be taken to the vet."[137]

In mid-June, as already mentioned, Jews had to give up all electrical appliances, including any electric cooking and household appliances, as well as cameras, binoculars, and bicycles.[138] On June 20, the Reichsvereinigung was informed that by the end of the month, all Jewish schools would be closed: No further schooling was available for Jews in Germany.[139] A few days later, an order that apparently originated with the Propaganda Ministry, but was issued by the Reich Transportation Ministry on June 27, forbade the use of freight cars for the transportation of the corpses of Jews. "In doubtful cases evidence had to be produced that the corpse belonged to an Aryan."[140] On September 2, upon decree from the Ministry of Agriculture and Food Supply, Jews would no longer receive meat, milk, white bread, or smoking wares or any scarce commodities; no exceptions were made for pregnant women and sick people.[141]

While the rhythm of deportations from the Reich accelerated, the availability of Jewish homes nonetheless declined well below the demand for them, due to the housing shortage created, among other things, by the Allied bombings. Some painful situations led to interventions from the highest authority. Thus the newly appointed general director of the Munich State Opera Orchestra and Hitler protégé, Clemens Krauss, could not find suitable apartments for the musicians he brought to the Bavarian capital. On April 1, 1942, Martin Bormann, who had been apprised of the difficulties, wrote to the Munich lord mayor, Karl Fiehler: "Today I reported to the Führer about the correspondence from general director Krauss. The Führer wished you to check one more time to see whether a few more Jewish apartments could be made available for the newly contracted members of the Bavarian State Opera." Fiehler answered right away that no Jewish apartments were left as he had distributed some to members of the party office (Bormann's agency) and—according to Krauss's own wishes—the last six had been given to three choir singers, two orchestra musicians and one lead dancer.[142]

On the eve of the assembly date for the Jews slated for deportation, neighbors in the Jews' house would try to extend a helping hand. "Yesterday with the Kreidls," Klemperer recorded on January 20, 1942, "downstairs until midnight. Eva helped sew straps for Paul Kreidl, so that he can carry his suitcase on his back. Then a feather bed was stuffed, which one has to hand over (and apparently one does not always see again). Today Paul Kreidl carted it to the prescribed forwarding agent on a little handcart."[143] The next day Klemperer added: "Before a deportee goes, the Gestapo seals up everything he leaves behind. Everything is forfeit. Yesterday evening, Paul Kreidl brought me a pair of shoes that fit me exactly and are most welcome given the terrible condition of my own. Also a little tobacco which Eva mixes with blackberry tea and rolls in cigarettes. . . . The transport now includes 240 persons; there are said to be people among them who are so old, weak and sick that it is unlikely that everyone will still be alive on arrival."[144]

The information available about the trains' destinations was scant, often disbelieved, mixed with fantastic rumors, and yet sometimes astonishingly close to reality. "In the last few days," Klemperer noted on March 16, "I heard Auschwitz (or something like it), near Königshütte in Upper Silesia, mentioned as the most dreadful concentration camp. Work in a mine, death within a few days. Kornblum, the father of Frau Seligsohn, died there, likewise—not known to me—Stern and Müller."[145] In March 1942 Auschwitz was just becoming an extermination center, as we saw. Yet, through channels hard to trace, rumors seeped back to the Reich.

At the end of November 1941, Hertha Feiner had been dismissed from her teaching position and was employed at the Berlin community offices. In veiled words she informed her daughters of the worsening situation, in a letter on January 11, 1942: "We are in a very serious time. Now it has been Walter Matzoff's turn and that of many of my girl students. I have to be very much involved and I try to assist as many people as possible."[146]

Feiner was only a recent employee, and although she apparently worked in the community office that established the lists of Berlin Jews she hardly could have an overview of the process or any knowledge of its outcome. But, in and of itself, the updating of these lists and mainly of the addresses of the remaining Jews was of help to the Gestapo. Of course, to keep the deportation trains rolling, the Germans also had lists of their own. Nonetheless, in this domain in particular, the Reichsvereinigung and the Berlin community leadership became involved in the same kind of collaboration as most Jewish Councils throughout occupied Western and Central Europe.[147]

The registration efforts of the Berlin community may have been questionable; but the assistance offered to those summoned for deportation by the Reichsvereinigung or by community employees, in Berlin or in various parts of the Reich, cannot be considered in the same way, despite the severe interpretation of some historians.[148] Although local employees of the Jewish organizations informed the Jews of the decision, the procedure, the time, and the assembly place, there is no indication that the victims followed instructions just because they trusted their coreligionists. All knew that the orders were issued by the Gestapo and that the Jewish representatives had no influence whatsoever on the process as such.

On March 29, 1942, for example, the main office of the association in Baden-Westphalia [located in Karlsruhe] wrote to its Mannheim branch concerning the 125 Jews of Baden whom they had to inform "on instructions from the authorities" that they were to get ready for deportation. The list of those to be sent away was attached. "We ask you," the main office wrote to the Mannheim employees, "that you visit the persons who are going to take part in the journey as soon as possible and extend to them advice and assistance." Given the number of those involved, Karlsruhe suggested finding "tactful" volunteers to assist the deportees. The volunteers did not have to be members of the Reichsvereinigung, but, obviously, they had to belong to "the Jewish race." As time was very short, employees and volunteers had to be available "in the coming days" to stand by those to be evacuated. The Karlsruhe office added that if one of the persons designated was totally unable to travel for health reasons, a medical certificate should immediately be sent to them and they would submit it to "the authorities." "However," the letter ended, "we cannot foresee how far the authorities will be ready to change their orders in these cases."[149]

It was probably in regard to the same transport that, on April 4, Frau Henny Wertheimer, an employee of the Reichsvereinigung in Offenburg, wrote to Dr. Eisenmann, head of the Karlsruhe office. She informed him first that Joseph Greilsheimer from Friesenheim, one of the people designated for deportation, had hanged himself. "It is naturally difficult for the wife who must now move away [*abwandern*] alone. It is good that the mother is with her." More difficulties in Schmieheim: "Old Frau Grumbacher is in bed with some sort of flu; if I only knew what to do with the old lady and with paralyzed Bella and how I could transport the sick from Schmieheim." Frau Wertheimer inquired at the Gestapo and was told to use an ambulance to bring the sick to the local railway station and from there by train to Mannheim [the ambulance had to be paid by the Reichsvereinigung]. She added a postscript: "I also have to ask for a few more stars to sew on the clothes."[150]

Eisenmann had more problems on his hands: what, he asked the local Gestapo, was to be done with the seventy inmates of the sick ward of the Jewish old people's home in Mannheim, as the staff of the institution was being deported and as the mayor had rejected a demand to transfer these elderly invalids to a municipal institution.[151] We can surmise the Karlsruhe Gestapo's answer to Eisenmann's query.

* * *

While the deportations from the Reich were engulfing all segments of the Jewish population, a few small groups of Germans, mainly in Berlin, offered their help; they hid Jews on the run, they produced forged identity papers, fake draft deferrals, food ration cards, and the like. And, beyond the immediate practical help, they offered humaneness and some hope. Of course there was only so much that two or three dozen anti-Nazis determined to help Jews could do, mainly in 1942 or 1943. In her diary Ruth Andreas-Friedrich, a journalist, bestselling writer, and the driving force behind the "Uncle Emil" group, admits to many a tragic failure in this first half of 1942.

Margot Rosenthal, one of the Jewish women whom the group was hiding, was denounced by her concierge as she briefly slipped back into her apartment. On April 30, 1942, Ruth and her friends received a piece of tissue paper: Margot and 450 other Jews were about to be sent away: "knapsack, blanket roll, and as much baggage as one can carry. I can't carry anything, and so shall simply leave everything by the roadside. This is farewell to life. I weep and weep. God be with you forever, and think of me!"[152] One after another most of Ruth's Jewish friends were caught: "Heinrich Muehsam, Mother Lehmann, Peter Tarnowsky, Dr. Jakob, his little Evelyn, his wife and the Bernsteins, his father- and mother-in-law."[153] Some other hiding strategies would have to be devised, for the few and by the few.

VIII

The first transport of Jewish deportees from Slovakia left for Auschwitz on March 26, 1942. It carried 999 young women. Tiso's country thereby acquired the doubtful distinction of immediately following the Reich and the Protectorate in delivering its Jews to the camps. The deportation was not the result of German pressure but of a Slovak request. The Slovak initiative had its own rationality. Once the Aryanization measures had despoiled most Jews of their property, getting rid of this impoverished population followed strict economic logic. In early 1942 the Germans had demanded 20,000 Slovak workers for their armament factories; Tuka's government offered 20,000 able-bodied Jews. After some hesitation Eichmann accepted; he could use young Jewish workers to accelerate the building of Birkenau after Soviet prisoners had almost all died, as we saw; he could even take their families along. The Slovaks would pay 500 reichsmarks per deported Jew (to cover German expenses), and in exchange the Reich allowed them to keep the deportees' property. Moreover, they received the assurance that the deported Jews would not return. This was the "Slovak model" Eichmann hoped to apply elsewhere over time.

By the end of June 1942, some 52,000 Slovak Jews had been deported, mainly to Auschwitz and to their death. Then, however, the deportations slowed to a standstill.[154] Tuka insisted on forging ahead, but Tiso hesitated. The intervention of the Vatican, followed by the bribing of Slovak officials on the initiative of a group of local Jews, did eventually play a role.

Vatican Secretary of State Luigi Maglione twice summoned the Slovak minister between April and July 1942. However, as the second intervention took place in April, while the deportations went on until July (to be briefly resumed in September), it is doubtful that a mere diplomatic query—and Maglione worded his protest as such—unknown to the Slovak public and to the world—did suffice.[155] Moreover, the attitude of the Slovak church remained ambiguous at first. A pastoral letter issued in April 1942 demanded that the treatment of Jews remain within the limits of civil and natural law but deemed it necessary to berate them for rejecting Christ and for having prepared an "ignominious death for Him on the cross."[156] There were however dissenting attitudes, such as that of Bishop Pavol Jantausch of Trnava and also of the small Slovak Lutheran Church, which issued a courageous plea in favor of the Jews "as human beings."[157] Once the devoutly Catholic populations became fully aware of the mistreatment of the Jews by the Hlinka guard and by Slovak ethnic Germans, on hand to help the guard in loading the deportees into cattle cars, the atmosphere started to change; even the local church would modify its stance, as we shall see.[158]

On June 26, 1942, the German minister to Bratislava, Hans Ludin, informed the Wilhelmstrasse: "Evacuation of Jews from Slovakia has reached deadlock. Because of clerical influence and the corruption of individual officials, 35,000 Jews have received special consideration on the basis of which they need not be evacuated. . . . Prime Minister Tuka wishes to continue the deportations, however, and requests strong support by diplomatic pressure on the part of the Reich."[159] On June 30, Ernst von Weizsäcker, state secretary of the Foreign Ministry, responded: "You can render the diplomatic assistance requested by Prime Minister Tuka by stating that stopping the deportation of the Jews and excluding

35,000 Jews would cause surprise [the initial formulation "would leave a very bad impression" was crossed out and replaced by "would cause surprise"] in Germany, particularly since the previous cooperation of Slovakia in the Jewish question has been much appreciated here."[160]

The "corruption of individual officials" referred to by Ludin was almost certainly the bribing operation initiated by the "Working Group," led by the ultra-Orthodox rabbi Michael Dov Ber Weissmandel, a Zionist female activist, Gisi Fleischmann, and other individuals representing the main segments of Slovak Jewry. The "Working Group," thoroughly researched by historian Yehuda Bauer, also made substantial payments to Eichmann's representative in Bratislava, Dieter Wisliceny.[161] That bribing the Slovaks contributed to a halt in the deportations for two years is most likely; whether the sums transferred to the SS had any influence remains an open question. Completing the deportations from Slovakia was not a German priority, as we shall see; this may have allowed the SS to trick the "Working Group" into paying much needed foreign currency in the belief that they were helping postpone the dispatch of the remaining Slovak Jews, and possibly of other European Jews, to their death.

The major operational decision regarding the deportations from France, Holland, and Belgium was taken after Heydrich's death, at a meeting convened by Eichmann at the RSHA on June 11. Present were the heads of the Jewish sections of the SD in Paris, Brussels, and The Hague. According to Dannecker's summary of the meeting, Himmler had demanded the increase of deportations either from Romania or from the West, due to the impossibility—for military reasons—of continuing deportations from Germany during the summer. The deportees, both men and women, were to be between ages sixteen and forty, with an additional number (10 percent of Jews unable to work. The plan was to deport 15,000 Jews from Holland, 10,000 from Belgium, and a total of 100,000 from both French zones. Eichmann suggested that, in France, a law similar to the Eleventh Ordinance be passed; thereby French citizenship of any Jew having left French territory would be abolished, and all Jewish property would be transferred to the French state. In the same way as in Slovakia, the Reich would be paid approximately 700 reichsmarks per deported Jew.[162]

Clearly Himmler wanted a regular inflow of Jewish slave labor during the summer months, while masses of Polish Jews unfit for work would fill the extermination centers to capacity. The Reichsführer's instructions predated the radical change of policy that was about to take place regarding Jewish workers. During the second half of June it became obvious to the Germans that they would not be able to arrest and transport more than 40,000 Jews from France during a first three-month phase; to make up for the loss, the number of deportees from Holland, where direct German domination simplified matters, was raised from 15,000 to 40,000.[163]

The Germans could rely upon the subservience of the Dutch police and of the civil service; the grip on the country's Jews progressively tightened. On October 31, 1941, the Germans appointed the Amsterdam Jewish Council as the sole council for the whole country.[164] Soon thereafter the deportation of Jewish workers to special labor camps started.[165] On January 7, 1942, the council called on the first contingent of workers: unemployed men on public welfare. Over the following weeks the German demands for laborers steadily increased, and the array of those being called up grew.[166] Although the council operated in coordination with the Amsterdam and The Hague labor offices, the admonishments to report originated essentially from Jewish leaders. Historian Jacob Presser, no admirer of the council, emphasized the role of Asscher, Cohen, and Meijer de Vries in their relentless recruitment campaign.[167] What the alternative might have been, apart from disbanding the council, remains unclear.

The labor camps—in fact concentration camps using Jewish and non-Jewish forced labor, such as, over time, Amersfoort, Vught (near 's-Hertogenbosch), as well as smaller camps—were mainly staffed by Dutch Nazis who often outdid the Germans in sheer sadism. Westerbork (from July 1942 on, the main transit camp to Auschwitz, Sobibor, Bergen Belsen, and Theresienstadt) had been a camp for a few hundred German Jewish refugees since the beginning of the war; by 1942 they had become "old-timers" and de facto ruled the camp under the supervision of a German commandant. In early 1942 transports of foreign Jews were increasingly sent to Westerbork, while Dutch Jews from the provinces were being concentrated in Amsterdam. Dutch police supervised the transfer operations and access to vacated Jewish homes. The Germans dutifully registered furniture and household objects, which *Ein-*

satzstab Rosenberg then carted off to the Reich. During the same months a Dutch equivalent of the Nuremberg laws, prohibiting marriage between Jews and non-Jews (among other things), became mandatory.

All of this still remained less important for Etty Hillesum than her intense love affair with a German Jewish refugee, Hans Spier, a spiritual guide of sorts and a highly idiosyncratic psychotherapist. The German measures did not spare her, of course. "Yesterday Lippmann and Rosenthal [to hand over assets]," she noted on April 15, 1942, "Robbed and hunted."[168] Yet she perceived most of the measures through the prism of her emotions: "I am so glad that he [Spier] is a Jew and I am a Jewess," she wrote on April 29. "And I shall do what I can to remain with him so that we get through these times together. And I shall tell him this evening: I am not really frightened of anything, I feel so strong; it matters little whether you have to sleep on a hard floor, or whether you are only allowed to walk through certain specified streets, and so on—these are only minor vexations, so insignificant compared with the infinite riches and possibilities we carry within us."[169]

On June 12 Etty's notes dealt again with the everyday persecution: "And now Jews may no longer visit greengrocers' shops, they will soon have to hand in their bicycles, they may no longer travel by train and they must be off the streets by 8 o'clock at night."[170] On Saturday, June 20, less than a month before the beginning of the deportations from Amsterdam to Westerbork and from Westerbork to Auschwitz, Etty directed her thoughts to Jewish attitudes and responses: "Humiliation always involves two. The one who does the humiliating and the one who allows himself to be humiliated. If the second is missing, that is if the passive party is immune to humiliation, then the humiliation vanishes into thin air. . . . We Jews should remember that . . . they can't do anything to us, they really can't. They can harass us, they can rob us of our material goods, of our freedom of movement, but we ourselves forfeit our greatest assets by our misguided compliance. By our feelings of being persecuted, humiliated and oppressed. . . . Our greatest injury is one we inflict upon ourselves."[171]

IX

A day after the departure of the first transport from Slovakia to Auschwitz, a transport with 1,000 Jews detained in Compiègne left France for the Upper Silesian camp. On March 1 Eichmann received the Wilhelmstrasse's authorization to start this first deportation from France; on the twelfth, the head of IVB4 informed Dannecker that, in response to a request of the French authorities, a further batch of 5,000 Jews could be deported.

The early deportations from France did not encounter any difficulties, either in the occupied zone or in Vichy. In the occupied zone French authorities were far more worried about the increasing number of attacks on Wehrmacht personnel. The execution of hostages did not have the desired effect (in December 1941, ninety-five hostages had been shot, among them fifty-eight Jews). In early 1942 the commander in chief, Otto von Stülpnagel, deemed too lenient, was replaced by his cousin, Karl-Heinrich von Stülpnagel, a brutal anti-Semite who showed his colors on the Eastern front; on June 1, SS general Karl Oberg, previously posted in Radom, in the General Government, arrived in France as higher SS and police leader.

Before taking office Oberg had paid a visit to the French capital on May 7, in the company of Heydrich. The atmosphere was favorable for closer collaboration between France and the Reich, as, since the end of April, Laval was back at the head of the Vichy government. Vallat had been replaced at the head of the CGQJ by a much fiercer Jew hater, Louis Darquier de Pellepoix, and the French police in the occupied zone were now headed by a brilliant and ambitious newcomer, René Bousquet, all too ready to play his part in the German-French rapprochement.

During Heydrich's visit Bousquet again requested the further deportation of some 5,000 Jews from Drancy to the East. Although Heydrich made his agreement conditional on the availability of transportation, four trains with approximately 1,000 Jews each left for Auschwitz in the course of June.[172]

Two major points of contention between the Germans and Vichy remained unresolved at the end of spring: the inclusion of French Jews in the deportations, and the use of French police in the roundups. As Vichy did not appear ready to agree to either German demand, a serious crisis loomed during the last week of June; it brought Eichmann to Paris on June 30 for a reassessment. Finally, in a July 2 meeting with Oberg and his acolytes, Bousquet gave in to the Germans, and, on the fourth he conveyed Vichy's official stand. According to Dannecker's notes, "Bousquet declared that, at the recent cabinet meeting, Marshal Pétain, the head of the state, and Pierre Laval, the head of the government, agreed to the deportation, *as a first step* [*dans un premier temps*], of all stateless Jews from the Occupied and Unoccupied zones."[173] French police forces would arrest the Jews in both zones.

Moreover, as Dannecker reported on July 6, in a conversation with Eichmann, while all "stateless" Jews (that is, formerly German, Polish, Czechoslovak, Russian, Lithuanian, Latvian, or Estonian Jews) were to be deported, Laval had also suggested, on his own initiative, the deportation of children under age sixteen from the unoccupied zone. As for children in the occupied zone, Laval declared that their fate was of no interest to him. Dannecker added that in a second phase, Jews naturalized after 1919 or after 1927 would be included in the deportations.[174]

In this deal each party had its own agenda. The Germans were intent in achieving complete success both in Holland and in France, the first mass deportations from the West. They did not have sufficient police forces of their own on hand and had to rely on the full participation of each national police. For Laval full collaboration had become his unquestioned policy in the hope of extracting a peace treaty from Germany and ensuring a rightful place for France within the new German-led Europe. And, in the late spring of 1942, as the head of the French government was maneuvering to deliver enough foreign Jews to postpone any decision regarding the fate of French Jews (whose deportation, he thought, French opinion would not readily accept), Hitler seemed, once more, to march on the road to victory.

In early May the Jewish star was introduced in Holland and, a month later, in France.[175] In both countries the measure caused momentary indignation in part of the population and expressions of sympathy for the "decorated" Jews, as had been the case in Germany. Yet individual gestures of support for the victims did not derail German policy in the least. The Germans had given the council exactly three days to implement the measure. A prolongation was grudgingly granted by Ferdinand Aus der Fünten (de facto in charge of the "Emigration Office" and increasingly so of Jewish affairs in Amsterdam) when it became clear that the distribution of stars on such short notice was impossible; after May 4, the newly set date, measures against Jews not wearing the star were rigorously enforced.[176] On June 8, 1942, the head of IVB4 in Holland gave a somewhat mixed report about public reactions. Zöpf first described at some length manifestations of solidarity with the Jews, but nonetheless concluded on an upbeat note: "The members of the Jewish race who at first wore the star with pride, have since climbed down, afraid as they are of further legislation by the Occupying Power."[177]

On June 7 the star became mandatory in the occupied zone of France. Vichy refused to enforce the decree on its territory, in order to avoid the accusation that a French government stigmatized Jews of French citizenship (the more so because Jewish nationals of countries allied with Germany, as well as of neutral or even enemy countries, were exempted from the star decree by the Germans). There was some irony and much embarrassment in the fact that Vichy had to beg the Germans to exempt the Jewish spouses of some of its highest officials in the occupied zone. Thus, Pétain's delegate in Paris, the anti-Semitic and actively collaborationist Fernand de Brinon, had to ask the favor for his wife, née Frank.[178] Among Catholic intellectuals, communists, and many students, reactions to the German measure were particularly negative.[179] The Jews themselves quickly recognized the mood of part of the population and, at the outset at least, the star was worn with a measure of pride and defiance.[180]

In fact indications about French attitudes were contradictory: "Lazare Lévy, professor at the Conservatory, has been dismissed," Biélinky noted on February 20. "If his non-Jewish colleagues had expressed the wish to keep him, he would have remained as professor, as he was the only Jew at the Conservatory. But they did not make the move; cowardice has become a civic virtue."[181] On May 16 Biélinky noted some strange inconsistencies in Parisian cultural life: "The Jews are eliminated from everywhere and yet René Julliard published a new book by Elian J. Finbert, *La Vie Pastorale*. Finbert is a Jew of Russian origin raised in Egypt. He is even young enough to inhabit a concentration camp. . . . Although Jews are not allowed to exhibit their work anywhere, one finds Jewish artists at the Salon [the largest biannual painting exhibition in Paris]. They had to sign that they did not belong to the 'Jewish race'. . . . A concert by Boris Zadri, a Romanian Jew, is announced for May 18, at the Salle Gaveau [a well-known Paris concert hall]."[182] And on May 19 Biélinky recorded the opinion voiced by a concierge: "What is done to the Jews is really disgusting. . . . If one didn't want them, one should not have let them enter France; if they have been accepted for many years, one has to let them live as everybody else.... Moreover, they are no worse than we Catholics."[183] And, from early June on, Biélinky's diary indeed recorded numerous expressions of sympathy addressed to him and to other Jews tagged with the star, in various everyday encounters.[184]

Yet individual manifestations of sympathy were not indicative of any basic shifts in public opinion regarding the anti-Jewish measures. Despite the negative response to the introduction of the star and soon thereafter to the deportations, an undercurrent of traditional anti-Semitism persisted in both zones. However, both the Germans and Vichy recognized that the population reacted differently to foreign and to French Jews. Thus in a survey that Abetz sent to Berlin on July 2, 1942, he emphasized "the surge of anti-Semitism" due to the influx of foreign Jews and recommended, along the lines of the agreement reached on the same day between Oberg and Bousquet, that the deportations should start with the foreign Jews in order to achieve "the right psychological effect" among the population.[185]

"I hate the Jews," the writer Pierre Drieu la Rochelle was to confide to his diary on November 8, 1942. "I always knew that I hated them."[186] In this case at least, Drieu's outburst remained hidden in his diary. On the eve of the war, however, he had been less discreet (but far less extreme) in *Gilles,* an autobiographical novel that became a classic of French literature. Compared to some of his literary peers, Drieu was in fact relatively moderate. In *Les Décombres,* published in the spring of 1942, Lucien Rebatet showed a more Nazi-like anti-Jewish rage: "Jewish spirit is in the intellectual life of France a poisonous weed that must be pulled out right to its most minuscule roots.... Auto-da-fés will be ordered for the greatest number of Jewish or Judaic works of literature, paintings, or musical compositions that have worked toward the decadence of our people."[187] Rebatet's stand regarding the Jews was part and parcel of an unconditional allegiance to Hitler's Reich: "I wish for the the victory of Germany because the war it is waging is my war, our war.... I don't admire Germany for being Germany but for having produced Hitler. I praise it for having known how... to create for itself the political leader in whom I recognize my desires. I think that Hitler has conceived of a magnificent future for our continent, and I passionately want him to realize it."[188]

Céline, possibly the most significant writer (in terms of literary importance) of this anti-Semitic phalanx, took up the same themes in an even more vitriolic form; however, his manic style and his insane outbursts marginalized him to a point. In December 1941 the German novelist Ernst Jünger encountered Céline at the German Institute in Paris: "He says," Jünger noted, "how surprised and stupefied he is that we soldiers do not shoot, hang, exterminate the Jews—he is stupefied that someone availed of a bayonet should not make unrestricted use of it." Jünger, no Nazi himself but nonetheless quite a connoisseur in matters of violence, strikingly defined Céline and—undoubtedly—also a vast category of his own compatriots: "Such men hear only one melody, but that is singularly insistent. They're like those machines that go about their business until somebody smashes them. It is curious to hear such minds speak of science—of biology, for instance. They use it the way the Stone Age man would; for them, it is exclusively a means of killing others."[189]

Robert Brasillach was outwardly more polished, but his anti-Jewish hatred was no less extreme and persistent than that of Céline or Rebatet. His anti-Jewish tirades in *Je Suis Partout* had started in the 1930s, and for him the ecstatic admiration of German victories and German dominance had a clearly erotic dimension: "The French of different persuasions have all more or less been sleeping with the Germans during these last years," he wrote in 1944, "and the memory will remain sweet."[190] As for the French and German policies regarding the Jews, Brasillach applauded at each step but, as far as the French measures went, they appeared to him at times too incomplete: "Families should be kept together and Jewish children deported with their parents," he demanded in a notorious *Je Suis Partout* article on September 25, 1942.[191]

How far the virulent anti-Semitism spewed by the Paris collaborationists influenced public opinion beyond the rather limited segment of French society that supported them politically is hard to assess. Be that as it may, Rebatet's *Les Décombres* became a runaway bestseller and could have sold about 200,000 copies (given the orders for the book) despite its very high price, had the publisher been able to receive a sufficient allocation of paper. It was the greatest publishing success in occupied France.[192]

Les Décombres was published by the notoriously collaborationist Denoël. More-respected publishers found other ways to make some profit under the circumstances. Thus on January 20, 1942, Gaston Gallimard made a bid for the acquisition of the previously Jewish-owned publishing house Calmann-Lévy. In a registered letter sent that day to the provisional administrator of Calmann-Lévy, with a copy to the CGQJ, Gallimard stated: "We herewith confirm our offer to buy the publishing and bookselling firm known under the name of Calmann-Lévy.... This offer is based on a price of two million five hundred thousand francs payable in cash. It is understood that the Librairie Gallimard (Éditions de la Nouvelle Revue Française) will not absorb the Calmann-Lévy company, which will remain autonomous and have its editorial board, of which Mssrs Drieu la Rochelle and Paul Morand [also a notorious anti-Semite] will no doubt agree to be members. We wish to inform you at this time that the Librairie Gallimard... is an Aryan firm backed by Aryan capital."[193]

Neither UGIF-North nor UGIF-South played much of a role during the first six months of 1942. In the occupied zone the council, which had been fined one billion francs by the Germans, was mainly trying to find ways of repaying the loans taken from French banks without imposing heavy new taxes on the impoverished community. The situation was quieter in the South but for both councils, apart from dealing with the growing welfare needs, much time was spent in fending off demands of all sorts from the Germans or from the CGQJ, and dealing with difficulties created by the Consistoire and with the Fédération's warring leaders.[194] "The very rich Jews, the majority of the Consistoire," Lambert noted on March 29, 1942, "are afraid that the Union (the UGIF) will compel them to pay too much for the poor; and, look at the scandal: at the instigation of two or three young Turks, they prefer to give money to the "*Amitiés Chrétiennes*" than to leave it to the welfare organizations that are part of the Union."[195]

X

After most of the Jewish population of Vilna had been murdered in the summer and fall of 1941, a "quiet" period (that was to last for some eighteen months) set in at the beginning of 1942. Now more than ever, Kruk and Rudashevski tried to record the "everyday." And the everyday offered its ordinary lot of misery but also quite unexpected dilemmas: For example, should one allow a theater in the ghetto? Kruk, a moralist in the

Bundist-socialist tradition, was appalled: "Today," he recorded on January 17, "I received a formal invitation from a founding group of Jewish artists in the ghetto announcing that the first evening of the local artistic circle will be held on Sunday, January 18, in the auditorium of the Real Gymnasium at Rudnicka 6. . . . I felt offended, personally offended about the whole thing, let alone the festive evening. In every ghetto you can amuse yourself, cultivating art is certainly a good deed. But here, in the doleful situation of the Vilna Ghetto, in the shadow of Ponar, where of the 76,000 Vilna Jews, only 15,000 remain—here, at this moment, this is a disgrace. An offense to all our feelings. But, as we know, the real initiators of the evening are the Jewish police. Furthermore, important guests, Germans, will come to the concert. Lyuba Bewicka, the brilliant German singer, is even trying to have some Jewish songs 'on hand.' In case, God forbid, a German will ask for them! . . . You don't make a theater in a graveyard.

"The organized Jewish labor movement [the Bund] has decided to respond to the invitation with a boycott. Not one of them will go to the 'crows' concert.' But the streets of the ghetto are to be strewn with leaflets: 'About today's concert. You don't make theater in a graveyard!' The police and the artists will amuse themselves, and the Vilna ghetto will mourn."[196]

Notwithstanding the Bund's initial qualms, intense cultural activity developed in the ghetto throughout 1942 and early 1943: "The number of cultural events in March [1942]," a contemporary record indicated, "was exceptionally high, because all existing suitable premises in the ghetto, like the theater, gymnasium, youth club and school quarters, were used. Every Sunday, six to seven events took place with over two thousand participants." However, lack of space soon became a problem: "At the end of the month the Culture Department had to give up to the incoming out-of-town Jews a number of premises like the gymnasium, School No. 2, Kindergarten No. 2, and a part of School No. 1. This will greatly affect the work of the schools, the sports division, and also the theater, which had to take into its building the sports division and the workers' assemblies." The section of the report dealing with the activity of the lending library indicated that as of April 1 the library had 2,592 [subscribing] readers. "An average of 206 persons visited the reading room daily (155 in February). . . . During the month the Archives collected 101 documents. Besides that, 124 folklore items were assembled.[197]

In Kovno, the German presence was more direct than in Vilna, even during the respite period. On January 13, 1942, a German Ghetto Guard was established inside the Jewish area.[198] Moreover, the local Germans seem to have been more inventive: "An order," Tory noted on January 14, "to bring all dogs and cats to the small synagogue in Veliounos Street, where they were shot [the bodies of the cats and dogs remained in the synagogue for several months; the Jews were forbidden to remove them]."[199] On February 28 Tory recorded: "Today is the deadline for handing over all the books in the ghetto, without exception, as ordered by the representative of the Rosenberg organization, Dr. Benker." (Benker had threatened anybody failing to hand in books with the death penalty.)[200]

XI

From the beginning of 1942 mass killings of Jews were spreading throughout the Warthegau and the General Government, as the days of total annihilation were rapidly approaching. One may wonder whether the exceptional and exceptionally visible German bestiality had any impact upon the traditional attitudes of the majority of Poles toward their Jewish countrymen. The answer seems negative. "Only in Poland," Alexander Smolar wrote in the 1980s, "was anti-Semitism compatible with patriotism (a correlation considerably strengthened under the Soviet occupation in 1939–1941) and also with democracy. The anti-Semitic National Democratic Party was represented both in the Polish government in London and in the structures of the underground within Poland. Precisely because Polish anti-Semitism was not tainted by any trace of collaboration with the Germans, it could prosper—not only in the street but also in the underground press, in political parties, and in the armed forces."[201]

Polonsky, who quoted Smolar, rephrased the argument by pointing out that "whereas the socialist and democratic organizations continued to advocate full equality for the Jews in a future liberated Poland, pre-war antisemitic parties did not abandon their hostility to the Jews merely because the Nazis were also anti-semites."[202] The socialist and democratic organizations represented a minority in relation to the anti-Semitic camp. And among the anti-Semites themselves there were nuances. Thus in January 1942, *Narod*, the paper of the Christian Democratic Party of Labor, a party that belonged to the government-in-exile coalition, phrased its stance as clearly as could be: "The Jewish question is now a burning issue. We insist that the Jews cannot regain their political rights and the property they have lost. Moreover, in the future they must entirely leave the territories of our country. The matter is complicated by the fact that once we demand that the Jews leave Poland, we will not be able to tolerate them on the territories of the future federation of Slavic nations [which the journal advocated.] This means that we will have to cleanse all of Central and Southern Europe of the Jewish element, which amounts to removing some 8 to 9 million Jews."[203]

Is there much difference between the views expressed in *Narod*, considered moderately anti-Semitic, and those carried in these same days of January 1942 by *Szaniec*, the organ of prewar Polish fascists? *Szaniec* put it thus: "Jews were, are and will be against us, always and everywhere. . . . And now the question arises, how are the Poles to treat the Jews. . . . We, and certainly 90 percent of Poles, have only one answer to this question: like enemies."[204]

Szaniec's emphatic statement seems indeed to have expressed widely held views. Even German anti-Jewish propaganda was manifestly well accepted and internalized by many Poles. On January 16, 1942, Dawid Rubinowicz, the young diarist from the Kielce area, noted that on that evening the mayor of nearby Bieliny visited his family's home: "Father fetched some vodka and they finished it off together because he [the mayor] was a bit chilled. . . . The mayor said all Jews would have to be shot because they were enemies. If I could only write down just a part of all he said at our house, but I simply can't."[205] German anti-Jewish posters adorned the walls of the smallest villages and the populace enjoyed it. On February 12 Dawid described one of the posters put up by the "village constable": "A Jew is shown mincing meat and putting a rat into the mincer. Another is pouring water from a bucket into milk. In the third picture a Jew is shown stamping dough with his feet and worms are crawling over him and the dough. The heading of the notice reads: 'The Jew is a Cheat, Your only Enemy.' A ditty followed commenting on each caricature; The last two lines rendered the tone of the entire 'poem': 'Worms infest their home-made bread/Because the dough with feet they tread.' When the village constable had put it up," Dawid added, "some people came along, and their laughter gave me a headache from the shame that the Jews suffer nowadays."[206]

During the weeks and months that followed, Dawid's diary repeatedly evoked the killing spree that engulfed his region. On June 1, the diary entry started untypically: "A happy day." Dawid's father, who had been arrested, was back. Then, however, the tone changed: "I have forgotten to write down the most important and most terrible news of all. This morning, a mother and a daughter had gone out into the country. Unfortunately the Germans were driving from Rudki to Bodzentyn. . . . When the two women caught sight of the Germans they began to flee, but were overtaken and arrested. They intended shooting them on the spot in the village, but the mayor wouldn't allow it. They then went into the woods and shot them there. The Jewish police immediately went there to bury them in the cemetery. When the cart returned it was full of blood. Who—"[207] There, in midsentence, Dawid Rubinowicz's diary ended.

In his straightforward way Dawid described events as they happened before his eyes. Some of the other Jewish diarists in the Polish provinces, more "sophisticated" and older by a few years, were more reflective. But for most of them, be they in the neighborhood of Kielce or a few hundred miles away, the writing would also suddenly end, in the same month of June 1942. In the early spring Elisheva from Stanisławów had inserted the notes of an anonymous friend in her own chronicle: "We are utterly exhausted," the "guest diarist" recorded on March 13, 1942. "We only have illusions that something will change; this hope keeps us alive. But how long can we live on the power of the spirit that is also fading? Sometimes there are rumors in the ghetto that graves are being dug. Seemingly strong people, both young and old, submit to the gossip. It is a terrible feeling. You feel that you have a halter on your neck and the guards are watching you very carefully, and on the other hand you are aware that you could live longer since you are healthy and strong but without any human rights. . . . Yesterday, Elsa [Elisheva] told me that a man who had died of starvation couldn't fit into the coffin, so his legs had to be broken. Unbelievable!"[208]

On May 14 Elisheva reminisced that the situation in Stanisławów had suddenly changed at the end of March: "It started in March. All the handicapped on the Aryan side were killed. It was a signal that something ominous was coming. And it was a disaster. On March 31, they started searching for the handicapped and old people, and later several thousand young and healthy people were taken. We were hiding in the attic and through the window I saw the transports of Hungarian Jews [who had been expelled from Hungary to Galicia in the late summer of 1941] leaving Rudolfsmühle [an improvised German prison]. I saw children from the orphanage wrapped in bed sheets. The houses around the ghetto were on fire. I heard some shooting, children crying, mothers calling, and Germans breaking into the neighboring houses. We survived."[209]

On June 9 Elisheva recognized that her own survival had been but a short reprieve: "Well, this whole scribbling does not make any sense. It is a fact we are not going to survive. The world will know about everything even without my wise notes. The members of the Jewish Council have been imprisoned. The hell with them, the thieves. But what does it mean to us? Rudolfsmühle has finally been liquidated. Eight hundred people have been taken to the cemetery [the killing site of Stanisławów]. . . . The situation is hopeless but some people say it is going to be better. Let us hope so! Is being alive after the war worth so much suffering and pain? I doubt it. But I don't want to die like an animal."[210] Ten days later Elisheva's diary ended. The circumstances of Elisheva's death are not known. Her diary was discovered in a ditch along the road leading to the Stanisławów cemetery.[211]

In Lodz, Sierakowiak's chronicling resumed in mid-March. In his saddler's workshop, the food, it seems, was sufficient for "workshop workers" like him (category A). "The deportations are in progress, while the workshops are receiving huge orders, and there is enough work for several months," he noted on March 26.[212] The deportations were temporarily halted on April 3. On that day the diarist recorded: "The deportations have been halted again, but nobody knows for how long. Meanwhile winter has returned with thick snow. Rumkowski has posted an announcement that there will be a cleaning of the ghetto on Monday. From eight in the morning to three in the afternoon, all inhabitants from the ages of fifteen to fifty will have to clean apartments and courtyards. There won't be any other work anywhere. All I care about, however, is that there is soup in my workshop."[213]

By mid-May 1942 the number of deportees from Lodz had reached 55,000.[214] The last wave, between May 4 and 15, included exclusively 10,600 "Western Jews" from a total of 17,000 of these Jews still alive in the ghetto at that time.[215] It remains unclear why none of the "Western Jews" were included in the earlier deportations and why at the beginning of May they were the only deportees. After considering various possibilities, historian Avraham Barkai interpreted the earlier reprieve as the probable result of German orders: To secure the orderly pace of deportations from the Reich, it was imperative to avoid the spreading of any rumors about Lodz.[216] As we saw, Hitler's new judicial powers could also offer an explanation, as the German Jews deported to Chelmno from Lodz were still German subjects who were deported to an extermination site located within the borders of the Greater Reich. In any case, once the impediments were dealt with, it is probable that the Germans decided to dispose of Jews who were elderly, the majority of whom could not be integrated into the work force. Whether Rumkowski was involved in the decision is not known, although he did not hide his growing hostility to the "newcomers."[217]

The forthcoming "resettlement" of the "Western Jews" had been announced during the last days of April. Immediately frantic attempts began to trade whatever remaining possessions could not be taken along, all the more so since luggage was forbidden. The deportees were a particularly pitiful crowd in the eyes of the chroniclers: "Schooled by the experience of recent days, some people have struck on the old idea of putting on a few suits, a few changes of underwear and, quite frequently, two overcoats. They tie the first coat with a belt from which they hang an extra pair of shoes and other small items. And so their faces, cadaverously white or waxy yellow, swollen, and despairing, sway disjointedly on top of disproportionately wide bodies that bend and droop under their own weight. They are possessed by a single thought: To save the little that remains of what they own, even at the expense of the last of their strength. Some people have been overcome by utter helplessness, whereas some still believe in something."[218]

At the same time Jews from small towns in the Warthegau (mainly Pabianice and Breziny) moved into the ghetto. On May 21 one of the "official" chroniclers (Bernard Ostrowsky) visited and described a refugee asylum where more than a thousand women from Pabianice had been quartered. "In every room, in every corner, one sees mothers, sisters, grandmothers, shaken by sobs, quietly lamenting for their little children. All children up to the age of ten have been sent off to parts unknown [Chelmno]. Some have lost three, four, even six children."[219] Two days later Ostrowsky added: "The Jews from Pabianice who were recently settled in the ghetto saw that in the village of Dobrowa, located about three kilometers from Pabianice, in the direction of Lodz, warehouses for old clothes have recently been set up.. . . . Every day trucks deliver mountains of packages, knapsacks, and parcels of every sort to Dobrowa . . . each day, thirty or so Jews from the Pabianice ghetto are sent to sort the goods. Among other things they have noticed that, among the waste papers, there were some of our Rumkis [money used in the Lodz ghetto, also called chaimki], which had fallen out of billfolds. The obvious conclusion is that some of the clothing belongs to people deported from this ghetto."[220] No comment was added.

The department of statistics of the ghetto indicated that during the month of May 1942, the total population (110,806 persons at the beginning of the month) had increased by 7,122, practically all of whom were new arrivals. During that same month there were fifty-eight births and 1,779 deaths; moreover, 10,914 persons were 'resettled.' "[221]

On July 2 the Lodz Gestapo wrote its own monthly report. At the outset the report mentioned that the population had not given the Gestapo any reason for intervention, although "the evacuations have caused a certain measure of disquiet." The total interruption of all postal links with the ghetto, "introduced in order to facilitate the evacuations," ensured that the Jews "have no way to communicate with the outside world."[222]

XII

During the first half of 1942, the rapidly expanding deportations to the extermination centers had yet to reach the Jews of Warsaw. In the largest ghetto, death remained ordinary: starving, freezing, disease. As before, the refugees from the provinces were the worst off: "The plight of the refugees is simply intolerable," Ringelblum noted in January 1942. "They are freezing to death for lack of coal. During the month, 22 percent of over a thousand refugees died in the center at 9 Stawki Street. . . . The number of those who have frozen to death grows daily; it is literally a commonplace matter." Ringelblum also noted: "There is no coal to be had for the refugee centers, but there is plenty for the coffee houses."[223] Kaplan recorded on January 18: "All along the sidewalks, on days of cold so fierce as to be unendurable, entire families bundled up in rags wander about, not begging but merely moaning with heartrending voices. A father and mother with their sick little children, crying and wailing, fill the street with the sound of their sobs. No one turns to them, no one offers them a penny, because the number of panhandlers has hardened our hearts."[224] In January 1942, 5,123 inhabitants died in the Warsaw ghetto.[225]

On February 20 Czerniaków noted a case of cannibalism: a mother had cut off a piece of the buttock of her twelve-year-old son who had died on the previous day.[226] But there was also inventiveness in the ghetto in those early weeks of 1942: "contraceptives made of baby pacifiers, carbide lamps made from the metal 'Mewa' cigarette boxes."[227] On March 22 Czerniaków gave some indications about the situation in the Jewish prison: "Every day two detainees die in the Jewish prison. Corpses lie there for eight or more days because of unsettled formalities. On March 10, 1942, there were 1,261 prisoners and 22 corpses in the detention facility. The capacity of these two buildings is 350 persons."[228] April 1: "(The Seder night) tomorrow Passover. News from Lublin. Ninety percent of the Jews are to leave Lublin within the next few days. The 16 Council members together with the chairman, Becker, were reportedly arrested. Relatives of the older councilors, aside from their wives and children, must also leave Lublin. The Kommissar [Auerswald] telephoned to say that a transport of 1,000–2,000 Jews from Berlin will arrive at 11:30 p.m. . . . In the morning hours about 1,000 expellees from Hannover, Gelsenkirchen, etc were sent over. They were put in the quarantine . . . at 10 a.m. I witnessed the distribution of food. The expellees had brought only small packages with them . . . Older people, many women, small children."[229] April 11: "The Kommissar sent me a letter yesterday suspending performances of the orchestra for two months for having played the works of Aryan composers. When I tried to explain, I was told that the Propaganda and Culture Department has a list of the Jewish composers."[230]

Further information about the systematic extermination campaign was spreading in the ghetto, mainly among activists of the various clandestine political movements. In mid-March, Zuckerman as representative of Hechalutz and other members of left-wing Zionist parties invited leaders of the Bund to attend a meeting to discuss the setting up of a common defense organization. Previous attempts to contact the Bund had not been successful: The ideological differences were too extreme, mainly in the eyes of the Bundists. The Bund, let us remember, was socialist-internationalist and hence opposed to the Zionist kind of separatist nationalism. Historically allied to the Polish Socialist Party, the PPS, the Bund strove for a common struggle with Eastern European Socialist parties to establish a new social order, within which the Jewish people would have the right to an autonomous life and a cultural identity rooted in a secular Yiddish culture.

The clandestine meeting took place at the Workers' Kitchen on Orla Street sometime in mid-March 1942 (none of the reports on the meeting gives an exact date).[231] After summing up the available information about the expanding extermination, Zuckerman came up with his proposal for a common Jewish defense organization that would also act in common with the Polish military underground and reading the acquisition of weapons outside the ghetto.[232] These suggestions were rejected by the two Bund representatives, dogmatically by one (Mauricy Orzech), more diplomatically by the other (Abrasza Blum). Orzech's main argument seems to have been that the Bund was bound by its relations with the PPS and that, as far as the Polish Socialist Party was concerned, the time for rebellion had not yet come.[233]

Once the Bund had stated his position, the representative of the Poalei Zion left, Hersch Berlinski, defended Zuckerman's position, but his party decided that given the situation (the Bund's refusal), they would not participate either.[234] The Zionists, although recognizing the sufferings of the Poles, were increasingly convinced that the Germans were planning a special fate for the Jews: total extermination. Even on the brink of annihilation, the traditional hostility between Bundists and Zionists exacerbated their contrary interpretations of the events.[235]

The importance of the Bund in the setting up of a common fighting underground derived of course from its relations with the PPS; in principle, the Polish Socialists could be willing to provide at least some weapons. Moreover, the Bund had better channels to the outside world than its Zionist counterparts. Cooperation would ultimately be established some seven months later—in radically changed circumstances.

Incidentally, the Bund's contacts with the outside world came to play an important role in May 1942, when one of its leading members in Warsaw, Leon Feiner, sent a lengthy report to London. The information was precise; it mentioned the extermination of approximately 1,000 victims per day in the Chelmno gas vans and the estimate that some 700,000 Polish Jews had already been murdered. The Bund report was given significant publicity in the British press and on the BBC.[236] In the United States, however, the echo of the horrendous details was relatively weak. The *New York Times,* generally considered the most reliable source about the international scene and the events in Europe in particular, published a brief story on page 5 of the June 27 issue, at the bottom of a column including several short items. The information was attributed to the Polish government in London; it reported the number of 700,000 Jewish victims.[237] The attribution of the information and its modest display could in fact convey serious doubts about its reliability.

On April 17 Czerniaków recorded a sudden and bloody upheaval: "In the afternoon panic erupted in the ghetto. Stores are being closed. People are crowding in the streets in front of their apartment buildings. To calm the population I took a stroll through several streets. The Order Service detachment was to report at 9:30 p.m. in front of the Pawiak (prison). It is now 10:30 and I am waiting for a report from the Order Service headquarters on what has transpired. It arrived at 7 a.m. Fifty-one persons had been shot."[238] Fifty-one or fifty-two Jews, some members of the Bund, some of those working for the underground press, and some just Jews in the Gestapo's path were pulled out of their apartments and shot in the back of the neck, on the streets.[239]

To this day the reasons for the massacre of April 17–18 are not entirely clear. The Germans were probably becoming aware of the first attempts to organize a Jewish underground in the Polish capital and mainly of the growing influence of the clandestine press (such as *Yedies,* launched by Zuckerman and his group). According to Zuckerman's memoirs, the Gestapo had his name and usual address (he did not stay there on the night of April 17), but otherwise it did not have much precise information.[240] The main aim of the executions was therefore, as Zuckerman surmised, "to instill terror."[241] An additional aim may have been to paralyze any underground plans ahead of the forthcoming *Aktion*. And indeed, as a result of the April massacres, the council attempted to convince the clandestine groups to put an end to their meetings. In fact the underground movements did not manage to establish any coordinated plan of action before the fateful days of July.[242]

With hindsight, the silencing of Rubinstein the ghetto jester, could be considered as an indication of the end: "Rubinstein is finished," Wasser noted on May 10, 1942. "The most popular philosopher of 'Oh boy, keep your head,' renowned throughout the Warsaw ghetto is expiring. In rags and tatters, he wallows in the streets . . . taking the sun, almost naked. Thus expires an idea, a symbol that dazzled everyone with its truth and lie of 'All Men Are Equal.' "[243] In fact, the sentence was *Alle Glaich*, all equal before death. Within weeks, what had already been almost true in the ghetto was to become an absolute reality that no jester—or anybody else—could imagine. The new reality was about to obliterate the jest, the jester, and the population that, notwithstanding all misery—or because of it—needed a jester and loved his sayings and antics.[244]

On July 15, 1942, a week before the beginning of the deportations, Janusz Korczak invited the ghetto's who's who to a performance of Rabindranath Tagore's *The Post Office* staged and acted by the staff and the children of his orphanage. Korczak (Dr. Henryk Goldszmit) was a widely known educator and writer—mainly of highly prized children's books; for three decades he had been the director of the most important Jewish orphanage in Warsaw. After the establishment of the ghetto, the "old doctor," as he was affectionately nicknamed, had to move his two hundred small charges within the walls. As we saw, a few of these children addressed a petition to the curate of All Saints to be allowed a visit to the church's gardens.

The play, the story of a sick boy confined to his dark room in a hut, expressed the same yearning as the children's letter: to wander among trees and flowers, to hear the birds singing. . . . In the play a supernatural being enables Amal (the hero's name) to walk an invisible path to the paradise he dreamed about.[245] "Perhaps illusions would be a good subject for the Wednesday dormitory talk," Korczak wrote in his diary on July 18. "Illusions, their role in the life of mankind.[246]

* * *

The Germans wanted to keep a "record" of it all—"for the education of future generations," in Goebbels's words. Film was the medium of choice. "The filming that the Germans have been carrying out in the ghetto continues," Abraham Lewin noted in his diary on May 19, 1942. Lewin, both a deeply religious Jew and a fervent Zionist, was a teacher and administrator at the Yehudia School, a private high school for girls. He was a member of Oneg Shabbat, and his diary was probably linked to Ringelblum's collective historical enterprise.[247]

"Today," Lewin went on, "they set up a film session in Szulc's restaurant. . . . They brought in Jews they had rounded up, ordinary Jews and well-dressed Jews, and also women who were respectably dressed, sat them down at the tables and ordered that they be served with all kinds of food and drinks at the expense of the Jewish community: meat, fish, liqueurs, white pastries and other delicacies. The Jews ate and the Germans filmed. It is not hard to imagine the motivation behind this. Let the world see the kind of paradise the Jews are living in. They stuff themselves with fish and goose and drink liqueur and wine."

On the same day Lewin recorded another such scene. "The Germans set up an original film set at the corner of Nowolipie and Smocza Streets. It involved the finest funeral wagon in the possession of the Jewish community. Around it gathered all the cantors of Warsaw, ten in number. . . . It seems that they want to show that Jews not only live a cheerful decent existence, but that they also die with dignity and even get a luxury burial.[248]

Although members of the Warsaw ghetto underground had understood that the mass murder of the Jews in Lithuania, in the Warthegau, and in Lublin were indications of an overall German extermination plan, it remains unclear whether they fully grasped what the rapid construction of a second camp in Treblinka, next to the labor camp, meant before the onset of the deportations. Messages did reach them from outside the ghetto during June 1942, as the construction of Treblinka II was entering its final stage. Thus, in early June, an unknown survivor of the extermination in Włodawa sent an easily decipherable code letter into the ghetto: "Uncle has the intention to celebrate the wedding of his children also at your place; he has rented a house close to you, very close to you. You probably don't know a thing about it. We write to you, so that you may be informed and do find a house outside of the city, for yourself and also for all our brethren and children, as the uncle has already prepared a new house for all, the same as in our case." The Jews of Włodawa had been exterminated in Sobibor.[249]

On July 8 Czerniaków noted in his diary: "Many people hold a grudge against us for organizing play activities for the children, for arranging festive openings of playgrounds, for the music, etc. I am reminded of a film: a ship is sinking and the captain, to raise the spirits of the passengers, orders the orchestra to play a jazz piece. I have made up my mind to emulate the captain."[250]

PART III

Shoah

Summer 1942–Spring 1945

"It is like being in a great hall where many people are joyful and dancing and also where there are a few people who are not happy and who are not dancing. And from time to time a few people of this latter kind are taken away, led to another room and strangled. The happy dancing people in the hall do not feel this at all. Rather, it seems as if this adds to their joy and doubles their happiness. . . ."

—Moshe Flinker (sixteen years old),
Brussels, January 21, 1943

CHAPTER VII

July 1942–March 1943

Wilhelm Cornides, a Wehrmacht noncommissioned officer, was stationed in Galicia in the summer of 1942. According to his diary entry of August 31, while he was waiting for a train at the railway station in Rava Ruska, another train entered the station: It carried Jews in some thirty-eight cattle cars. Cornides asked a policeman where the Jews came from. " 'Those are probably the last ones from Lvov,' the policeman answered. 'That has been going on now for five weeks uninterruptedly. In Jaroslav, they let only eight remain, no one knows why.' I asked: 'How far are they going?' Then he replied, 'To Belzec.' 'And then?' 'Poison.' I asked: 'Gas?' He shrugged his shoulders. Then he said only: 'At the beginning, they always shot them, I believe.' "

Later, in his compartment, Cornides struck up a conversation with a woman passenger, a railway policeman's wife, who told him that such transports "were passing through daily, sometimes also with German Jews. I asked: 'Do the Jews know then what is happening with them?' The woman answered: 'Those who come from far won't know anything, but here in the vicinity they know already.' . . . Camp Belzec is supposed to be located right on the railway line and the woman promised to show it to me when we pass it."

"At 6:20 p.m.," Cornides recorded, "the train passed Belzec: Before then, we had traveled for some time through a tall pine forest. When the woman called, 'Now it comes,' one could see a high hedge of fir trees. A strong sweetish odor could be made out distinctly. 'But they are stinking already,' says the woman. 'Oh nonsense, that is only the gas,' the railway policeman [who had joined them] said, laughing. Meanwhile we had gone on about 200 yards—the sweetish odor was transformed into a strong smell of something burning. 'That is from the crematory,' says the policeman. A short distance further the fence stopped. In front of it, one could see a guard-house with an SS post."[1]

I

By late August 1942 the German armies on the Eastern Front had reached the oil fields and the (destroyed) refineries of Maikop and, farther south, the slopes of the Caucasus; soon the German army flag would be hoisted on Mount El'brus, Europe's highest peak. At the same time, Paulus's Sixth Army was approaching Stalingrad's outer defenses; it reached the Volga, north of the city, on August 23. In the north a new attack to break through the defenses of Leningrad was planned for early September.

Yet, in the late summer of 1942, despite such impressive advances, the German military situation on the Eastern Front was becoming increasingly precarious. In the center and the south, the armies were spread over considerable distances and their supply lines were dangerously overstretched. But, instead of heeding the warnings of his generals, Hitler obstinately insisted on forging ahead.

The confrontations at headquarters led to a series of dismissals, that of Army chief of staff Halder, among others (Halder was replaced by Kurt Zeitzler) and to the breakdown of all personal relations between Hitler and his top commanders. On Hitler's orders the daily military conferences were thereafter stenographically recorded so that his words could no longer be twisted.[2] According to Hassell's diary entry of September 26, Ferdinand Sauerbruch, the director of the Charité hospital in Berlin, a world-renowned surgeon and probably the most eminent medical authority in Germany at the time, told him—after meeting Hitler during those same days—that "he was now unquestionably mad" (*Er sei jetzt unzweifelhaft verrückt*).[3]

The fateful turn about came suddenly, in the course of a few weeks. On October 23, 1942, Montgomery's Eighth Army attacked at El Alamein; within days Rommel was in full retreat. The Germans were ousted from Egypt, then from Libya. The debacle of the "Afrika Korps" would halt, albeit for a short time, only at the Tunisian border. On November 7, American and British forces landed in Morocco and Algeria. On November 11, in response to the Allied landings, the Germans occupied the Vichy zone and sent forces to Tunisia, while the Italians slightly enlarged their own occupation area in the Southeast of France. The major drama, however, unfolded on the Eastern Front.

The battle for Stalingrad had started in the last days of August, after a devastating German bombing of the city that left some 40,000 civilians dead. To face the mediocre Paulus, Stalin had sent his most brilliant strategist, Marshal Georgy Zhukov, to command the Stalingrad front and the unflappable Vasily Chuikov to organize the defense of the city itself. By October the battle had turned into house-to-house combat among the hulks of buildings, the ruins of factories, the remnants of grain silos, carrying names that resonated as so many symbols, "Stalingrad" itself, "Red October," and the like. And as, under Hitler's relentless pressure, Paulus was desperately attempting to take the city center and reach the Volga, Soviet divisions were gathering undetected on both flanks of the Sixth Army.

On November 19 the Red Army counterattacked, and soon the Soviet pincer movement shattered the German rearguard at its weakest point, the area held by Romanian forces. Paulus's army was cut off. A second Soviet offensive destroyed a mixture of Italian and Hungarian units: The encirclement was complete.

While ordering a hasty retreat from the Caucasus, Hitler adamantly refused to abandon Stalingrad. The battle for the city soon became, in the eyes of millions the world over, a portent of ultimate victory or defeat. Hoth's attempt to break through the Soviet ring failed, as did the airlift of supplies to the beleaguered German forces. By the end of the year the Sixth Army was doomed. Nonetheless the Nazi leader rejected Paulus's entreaty to allow him to surrender: Soldiers and commanders, the newly promoted field marshal was told, had to resist to the last and die a heroic death. On February 2, 1943, the Sixth Army stopped fighting. It had lost 200,000 men; 90,000 soldiers, including Paulus and his generals, were led into captivity.

The German defeats in North Africa and on the Eastern Front were compounded by the rapid expansion of the Anglo-American bombing campaign: German industrial production did not slow down, but the toll in lives, homes, and entire city areas began to undermine the population's faith in victory.

Simultaneously partisan warfare turned into a growing threat in the occupied territories of Eastern Europe and the Balkans, while resistance networks multiplied and grew bolder in the West. And, in order to demonstrate their common resolve (mainly for the benefit of their suspicious Soviet ally), Roosevelt and Churchill announced, at their meeting in Casablanca, on January 24, 1943, that the sole option left to Germany and its allies was "unconditional surrender."

In the meantime, Hitler's diatribes against the Jews went on with the same fanatical obsessiveness. The themes, either in his public speeches or in his private disquisitions, were the same as before. The "prophecy" resurfaced again and again as a mantra announcing to all and sundry that the fate of the Jews was sealed and soon none would remain alive. Yet minute nuances surfaced here and there. Thus, in his Sportpalast speech of September 30 for the launching of the "winter relief" campaign, Hitler bandied his extermination threat with a particularly sadistic twist. Once more he reminded his audience that in his September 1, 1939, Reichstag speech he had stated: "If Jewry instigated an international world war for the elimination of the Aryan peoples of Europe, then not the Aryan peoples would be exterminated but Jewry would be. The wire-pullers of the madman in the White House (*des Geisteskranken im Weissen Haus*) succeeded in dragging one nation after another into the world war. But, in the same measure, a wave of anti-Semitism engulfed one people after the other and it will further expand and include one state after the next, that joins this war, and each one will turn into an anti-Semitic state over time. The Jews have once laughed at my prophecies, also in Germany. I don't know whether they are still laughing today, or if they have stopped laughing. But I can assure now as well: Everywhere they will stop laughing (*Es wird Ihnen das Lachen überall vergehen*). And I shall also be vindicated in this prophecy."[4]

Some Jews understood what the crazed German messiah was proclaiming. " 'The Jews will be exterminated,' Hitler said in his speech yesterday [at the Sportpalast]. He hardly said anything else," Sebastian commented on October 1.[5] The next day, Klemperer recorded: "Hitler's speech at the beginning of the Winter Aid campaign. The same old song mercilessly exaggerated.... Merciless threats against England, against the Jews in all the world, who wanted to exterminate the Aryan nations of Europe and whom he is exterminating.... The shocking thing is not that a crazy man raves in ever greater frenzy, but that Germany accepts it, for the tenth year now and in the fourth year of the war, and that it [Germany] continues to allow itself to be bled ..."[6]

Of course the party grandees were now following the extermination stage by stage. After mentioning protest meetings that had taken place in London, Goebbels noted on December 14: "All this won't help the Jews. The Jewish race has prepared this war, it is the spiritual instigator of all this misfortune which came upon the world. Jewry must pay for its crimes, as the Führer prophesied at the time in his Reichstag speech; it means the wiping out [*Auslöschung*] of the Jewish race in Europe and possibly in the entire world."[7]

Goebbels was well informed: "The higher SS and police leader who is in charge [probably Krüger] informs me about the situation in the [Warsaw] ghetto," the minister had recorded on August 21, 1942. At this time the Jews are being evacuated in vast numbers and pushed to the East. All this is happening on quite a significant scale. Here the Jewish question is handled in the right way, without sentimentality and without much consideration. That is the only way to solve the Jewish problem.[8]

No dissenting voices arose among the party faithful or anywhere else. At most, some suggestions from the regime's elite pointed to possible adaptations of the killing program to the needs of the hour. Thus, on June 23, 1942, Viktor Brack, in a letter to Himmler, had suggested that some two to three million of the "ten million" Jews designated for extermination should be sterilized instead by using X-rays. These Jewish men and women were, according to Brack, "in very good condition to perform work."[9] In response Himmler encouraged Brack to start the sterilization experiments in one camp, not more.[10]

A few months later, on October 10, 1942, "a long conversation regarding the Jewish question" took place between Göring and Bormann. According to the head of the Party Chancellery, Göring declared that he considered Himmler's measures "entirely correct" but emphasized that exceptions were necessary in special cases and that he [Göring] would discuss the matter with Hitler.[11] What these exceptions were and whether this discussion with Hitler ever took place remains unclear. In the meantime, at various administrative levels, a flurry of activity surrounded the exclusion of Jews from any recourse to the Reich's judiciary system. In fact, by then the problem was losing its relevance, except for the implications of the "Thirteenth Ordinance" of July 1, 1943, to which we shall return.[12]

It also seems that, in the fall of 1942, keeping the extermination at least formally hidden from the population was still considered important, although the information was widely available, also from the bloodthirsty speeches of the "highest authority." In any case the constant flood of propaganda depicting the Jews as the enemies of humanity, as the leaders of the hordes of *Untermenschen*, beastly creatures who had only the semblance of human beings (according to the SS propaganda pamphlet *Der Untermensch*, distributed in a score of languages throughout the Continent), led logically to only one possible solution. Thus not too many soldiers could have misunderstood Bormann when, in October 1942, in answering the questions most frequently asked by the troops, he addressed question number 9—"How will the Jewish question be solved?"—in the tersest yet clearest way: "Very simply!"[13]

II

During his visit to Auschwitz, on July 17, 1942, after touring some of his pet agricultural projects, Himmler watched the extermination of a transport of Jews from Holland. According to Höss, the SS chief remained silent throughout. While the gassing took place, "he unobtrusively observed the officers and junior officers engaged in the proceedings, including myself."[14] A few days later, an order came from the Reichsführer: "All mass graves were to be opened and the corpses burned. In addition the ashes were to be disposed of in such a way that it would be impossible at some future time to calculate the number of corpses burned."[15]

In the evening Himmler attended a dinner party organized in his honor by *Gauleiter* Fritz Bracht. Höss, invited with his wife, found the guest a changed man, "in the best of spirits" . . . he talked on every possible subject which came up in the conversation. He discussed the education of children and new buildings and books and pictures. . . . It was fairly late before the guests departed. Very little was drunk during the evening. Himmler, who scarcely ever touched alcohol, drank a few glasses of red wine and smoked, which was also something he did not usually do. Everyone was under the spell of his good humor and lively conversation. I had never known him like that before."[16]

During these same days of July 1942, the German onslaught against the Jews of Europe reached its full scale. Throughout the spring and early summer, the extermination process—after decimating part of the Jewish population of the Warthegau, of Lodz, and of the occupied territories of the Soviet Union—had expanded to Jews from the Reich, from Slovakia, and, district after district, from the General Government, except for Warsaw. In the second half of July the deportations from Holland and France began, followed by Warsaw, all within days of one another. In August the Jews of Belgium were included. In the General Government, while the Warsaw Jews were being killed, a large part of the Jewish population of Lwów was carted away. In the first days of September major roundups struck again at the Jews of Lodz, and throughout, deportations from the West continued.

The steady expansion of deportations and killings from the early summer of 1942 on was enabled by the activation of further extermination facilities: "Bunker 2" at Auschwitz-Birkenau; and Belzec, Sobibor as previously, and also at Treblinka. Thus while most of the Jewish populations from the General Government were deported to Belzec and Sobibor, the first victims of Treblinka would be the Warsaw Jews. Simultaneously the deportees from the Reich, Slovakia and the West would increasingly be directed to Auschwitz-Birkenau (and, for a time, from Holland to Sobibor, due to a typhus epidemic in Auschwitz).

Although Himmler's supervision of the entire system remained necessary and his interventions regarding transportation and slave labor allocation (or extermination) guided the rhythm and implementation of the killings, Hitler himself kept regularly abreast. As we shall see, within a few months he would be given the most updated progress report and would intervene personally to push for or decide on the deportations, which had not yet started (Hungary, Denmark, Italy, and again Hungary). Otherwise the "Final Solution," despite all unforeseen political, technical, and logistic problems, had turned into a smoothly running mass-murder organization on an extraordinary scale. In regard to control over various aspects of the extermination whatever the feuds between various agencies and individuals within the SS or between the SS and party officials may have been, nothing indicates that these tensions had any impact on the overall progress of the campaign, on its unfolding, or on the ultimate distribution of the spoils.

As for the attitude of the surrounding populations and their social, political, or spiritual elites, throughout the Continent, although some small groups were ready to help Jews once the deportations started, in general only very rare gestures of solidarity with the victims occurred on a collective scale. And, in their vast majority, the Jews did not understand the fate that awaited them.

The Jews whose murder Himmler had watched were probably the deportees of the first transport that had left the Netherlands for Auschwitz, on July 14. The meticulous registration work accomplished by the Dutch census office, the German Central Emigration Office (*Zentralstelle*), and the Jewish Council allowed for summons to be sent on July 4 to 4,000 (mainly refugee) Jews chosen from the updated lists. To fill the quota the Germans organized a sudden police raid in Amsterdam on July 14; it netted 700 more Jews.[17]

The Dutch police outdid German expectations: "The new Dutch police squadrons are performing splendidly as regards the Jewish question and are arresting Jews in the hundreds, day and night," an obviously elated Rauter reported to Himmler on September 24.[18] Indeed the Amsterdam police performed magnificently; and Sybren Tulp personally participated in every roundup.[19] Secretary-General of the Interior Fredericks feebly tried to shield the municipal police from participating in the roundups, but in vain. Rauter insisted on the involvement of all Dutch police forces, and all took part.[20] Dutch detectives were attached to the German Security Police. Moreover, in May 1942, a unit of "Voluntary Auxiliary Police" had been created, comprising some 2,000 men belonging either to the NSB "storm detachments" or to the Dutch SS.[21] These local police collaborators vied with the Germans in sheer sadism and brutality; most of the spies who obtained handsome profits from denouncing Jews in hiding came from their ranks.[22]

The German staff in charge of the "Final Solution" in Holland was small. According to Harster's testimony in 1966, "Some 200 employees worked for Section IV [the Security Police] in the whole country." The

Jewish section at The Hague headquarters, under the command of Willi Zöpf, employed no more than thirty-six officials.[23] In his computation Harster did not include the Amsterdam "annex" of Zöpf's IVB4 office. This "annex," the *Zentralstelle*, headed by Willi Lages and Aus der Fünten, steadily grew in importance until, in July 1942, it was put in charge of organizing all the deportations from Amsterdam to Westerbork. By then its staff, partly German but mainly Dutch, had grown to about one hundred employees.[24]

According to historian Louis de Jong, the Germans had informed the Jewish Council as early as March 1942 that Jews would be sent to labor camps in the East. The council believed that the deportees would be German Jews only and thus "took no action; it even refrained from warning those representatives of the German Jews with whom it was in touch."[25] It was shocked in late June when informed that Dutch Jews would be included in the deportations.[26] Lages and Aus der Fünten then chose the usual method: Some Dutch Jews would not be sent away (for the time being), and the council was allowed to distribute exemption certificates that, quite naturally, offered the hope of reprieve. The Germans knew they could rely on the docility of the people not immediately threatened.

The general secretary of the council, M. H. Bolle, established several categories of Jews (identified by numbers) and compiled the list of the 17,500 privileged ones whom the council could exempt: These Jews had special stamps affixed to their identity cards, the "Bolle stamps." According to a member of the council, Gertrud van Tijn, when the first exemption stamps were issued, the scenes at the Jewish Council were quite indescribable. Doors were broken, the staff of the council was attacked, and the police had often to be called in. . . . The stamps quickly became an obsession with every Jew."[27] More often than not the decisions of the "exemptions' committee" were influenced by favoritism and corruption.[28]

"The Jews here are telling each other lovely stories: They say that the Germans are burying us alive or exterminating us with gas. But what is the point of repeating such things, even if they should be true?"[29] This July 11 entry in Etty Hillesum's diary shows that ominous rumors about "Poland" were circulating in Amsterdam as the deportations started; it also shows that neither Hillesum nor most of the other Jews really believed them. Etty had been advised to seek a job with the council as a possible way of escaping immediate danger. "My letter of application to the Jewish Council . . . has upset my cheerful yet deadly serious equilibrium," she noted on July 14, 1942, "as if I had done something underhanded. Like crowding onto a small piece of wood adrift on an endless ocean after a shipwreck and then saving oneself by pushing others into the water and watching them drown. It is all so ugly. And I don't think much of this particular crowd either [the council]."[30] The next day she was hired as a typist at the Cultural Affairs department of the council; she became (briefly) one of the privileged Amsterdam Jews.

A few days later Etty wrote the most concise and damning two sentences about what she perceived as the council's overall behavior: "Nothing can ever atone for the fact, of course, that one section of the Jewish population is helping to transport the majority out of the country. History will pass judgment in due course."[31] On July 29, shortly after her guru and lover, Hans Spier, suddenly fell ill and died, Etty volunteered to work for the council at Westerbork.[32]

Immediate deportation threatened foreign refugees such as the Franks. On July 5, Margot, Anne's elder sister, received a summons to report to the assembly center. On the next day, assisted by the faithful Dutch couple Miep and Jan Gies, the Franks were on their way to a carefully prepared hiding place, an attic in the building where Otto Frank's office was located. Margot and Miep left first, on bicycles. Anne made sure that her cat would be taken in by neighbors, and on July 6, at seven-thirty in the morning, the Franks left their home. "So there we were," Anne noted on July 9, "Father, Mother, and I, walking in the pouring rain, each of us with a schoolbag and a shopping bag filled to the brim with the most varied assortment of items. The people on their way to work at that early hour gave us sympathetic looks; you could tell by their faces that they were sorry they couldn't offer us some kind of transportation; the conspicuous yellow star spoke for itself."[33]

The relations between council members and Aus der Fünten seem to have been almost cordial at times, and the Hauptsturmführer did apparently convince David Cohen, council official Leo de Wolff, and others that he was fulfilling his task against his will.[34] Jacob Presser believed that the SS officer's protests were genuine, and yet, in his postwar history of the destruction of Dutch Jewry, he described an event in which he was involved, when Aus der Fünten—obsequiously attended by de Wolff—displayed prime sadism.

On August 5, 1942, a hapless crowd of some 2,000 Jews had been kept overnight in the yard of the *Zentralstelle.* The following day, after a short interview, individuals would be waved to the left (reprieve) or to the right (Westerbork). Aus der Fünten intentionally kept the majority waiting almost to the end of the selection (five p.m.). Those who had not been interrogated by then were automatically sent to Westerbork: "The tension became unbearable in the afternoon," Presser wrote. "There we were, hundreds of us, anxiously watching the clock." At ten to five, at what turned out to be the last muster, the writer and his wife came face-to-face with Aus der Fünten, who looked at their papers, waved him to the left and then, turning to de Wolff, said: 'She's still very young.' What de Wolff replied, I cannot say, but my wife was waved to the left as well. A moment later we were in the street with ordinary people and children playing. . . . Some 600 were sent to Westerbork and on."[35]

On September 18, 1942, at a special meeting of the council, both Cohen and Asscher expressed their belief that cooperation with the authorities was necessary. According to the minutes of the meeting, David Cohen affirmed that, "in his opinion, it was the bounden duty of community leaders to stay at their post; indeed it would be criminal to abandon the community in the hour of its greatest need. Moreover, it was imperative to keep at least the most important men back [in Amsterdam] for as long as possible."[36] At the end of that same meeting Cohen made a terse announcement: "Finally, the first report of a case of death in Auswitz [*sic*] is received by the meeting."[37]

While transports of Jews were leaving Amsterdam for Westerbork, Jews from the provinces were steadily being moved to Amsterdam. The Wessels family, who lived in the village of Oostvoorne, was transported to Amsterdam in October 1942 (the eldest son had already been deported to Westerbork, then to Auschwitz, in August); they remained in the city for almost a year. The younger son, Ben—whose letters to Oostvoorne friends have been saved—was sixteen in October 1942: He was first employed as a "courier" for the Jewish Council, then as an elevator boy in the building of the German police.

One of Ben's initial letters from Amsterdam indicates how thoroughly the Wehrmacht officer and the soldiers who arrested him in Oostvoorne took care of every small detail. "I guess you mustn't mind the pencil writing," Ben informed his friends on October 15, 1942. "My fountain pen was taken away. . . . My entire equipment with backpack and six woolen blankets is gone. . . . That pocket flashlight, the one with the battery they also took from us, there, opposite the bandstand in Oostvoorne. We were frisked completely, and whatever they could use, money, in fact everything, they took from us. That day, Mother had already been picked up in the afternoon. That night was frightful. . . . The family van Dijk [the only other Jewish family in Oostvoorne], we were with them, they are going on to Poland. . . ."[38]

Much of the outrage expressed by the Dutch population at the German persecution of the Jews during the first year of the occupation had turned into passivity by 1942. The Dutch government-in-exile did not exhort its countrymen to help the Jews when the deportations started, although on two occasions, at the end of June and in July 1942, "Radio Oranje" did broadcast information previously aired by the BBC about the exterminations in Poland. These reports did not make any deep impression on either the population or even the Jews. The fate of Polish Jews was one thing; the fate of the Jews of Holland quite another; this was common belief even among the leaders of the council.[39]

Two young Dutch political prisoners who had witnessed the earliest gassings in Auschwitz (those of Russian prisoners and small groups of Jews) were released from the camp and, on their return to Holland, attempted to convince the leadership of the Dutch churches of what they saw: to no avail.[40] Letters sent home by members of the Dutch Waffen SS described in detail and with pride their participation in the massacre of Jews in the Ukraine, but the information was either taken in stride or, as one of the authors intimated, considered as a portent of things to come once men like himself returned to the home country.[41]

Some protests against the deportations nonetheless did take place. On July 11 all major church leaders signed a letter addressed to Seyss-Inquart. The Germans tried conciliation first: They promised exemptions for some baptized Jews (but not for the Jews baptized after the occupation of the country). At first the churches did not give in: The main Protestant church (Herformde Kerk) proposed having the letter publicly read on Sunday, July 26. The Catholic and Calvinist church leaders agreed. When the Germans threatened retaliation, the Protestant leadership wavered; the Catholic bishops, led by the archbishop of Utrecht, Jan de Jong, decided to proceed nonetheless, and they did. In retaliation, during the night of August 1–2, the Germans arrested most Catholic Jews and sent them to Westerbork. According to Harster's postwar testimony, Seyss-Inquart's retaliation stemmed from the fact that the bishops had protested against the deportation of all Jews, not that of converted Jews only. Ninety-two Catholic Jews were ultimately deported to Auschwitz, among them the philosopher, Carmelite nun, and future Catholic saint, Edith Stein.[42]

As months went by, the Germans had every reason to be satisfied. On November 16, Bene, Ribbentrop's representative in The Hague, sent a general report to the Wilhelmstrasse: "The deportation has been going on without difficulties and incidents. . . . The Dutch population has gotten used to the deportation of the Jews. They are making no trouble whatsoever. Reports from Rauschwitz [*sic*] camp sound favorable. Therefore the Jews have abandoned their doubts and more or less voluntarily come to the collecting points."[43]

Generally speaking Bene wasn't wrong, as we know, although some details of the overall picture manifestly escaped him, as they escaped Harster's and Tulp's men. Soon after the beginning of the deportations, children were moved from the main assembly and processing hall, the Hollandsche Schouwburg (renamed Joodsche Schouwburg), to an annex on the opposite side of the same street (the Crèche), a child-care center mainly for working-class families. At that point two members of the Jewish Council, Walter Süskind and Felix Halvestad succeeded in gaining access to some of the children's files and destroying them.[44] Thus bereft of administrative identity, children were sporadically smuggled out of the Crèche with the help of the Dutch woman director, Henriette Rodriguez-Pimental; they were passed on to various clandestine networks that usually succeeded in finding safe places with Dutch families.[45] Hundreds of children—possibly up to one thousand—were saved in this way.[46]

Jewish adults encountered much greater difficulties in hiding among the population. The refusals (or the inaction) they encountered could have resulted from fear, distaste for Jews, traditional anti-Semitism and "civic obedience," although—regarding the last—when in the spring of

1943, the Germans used utter brutality against any assistance to Dutch men hiding from work in the Reich, the readiness for illegal initiatives grew all around. From the outset, however, small networks of people who knew and trusted one another and mostly shared a common religious background (Calvinist and Catholic) did actively help Jews, notwithstanding the risks. The limited scope of the grassroots actions has been attributed to the absence of hands-on leadership from the hierarchy of all Dutch Christian churches, despite some of the courageous protests, particularly of Archbishop de Jong.[47]

At the beginning of 1943 the Germans started rounding up the approximately eight thousand Jewish patients in various hospitals, and among them the psychiatric inmates of Het Apeldoornse Bos. The raid on this largest Jewish mental institution was conducted on the night of January 21 by a Schutzpolizei unit under the personal command of Aus der Fünten. The patients were ferociously beaten and pushed into trucks. "I saw them place a row of patients," an eyewitness declared, "many of them older women, on mattresses at the bottom of one lorry, and then load another load of human bodies on top of them. So crammed were these trucks that the Germans had a hard job to put up the tail-boards."[48] The trucks carried the patients to the cordoned-off Apeldoorn railway station.

According to the station master's report, when he tried to activate the ventilation system in the wagons, the Germans closed them. The report then continued: "I remember the case of a girl of twenty to twenty-five, whose arms were pinioned [in a straightjacket] but who was otherwise stark naked. . . . Blinded by the light that was flashed in her face, the girl ran, fell on her face and could not, of course, use her arms to break the fall. She crashed down with a thud. . . . In general, the loading was done without *great* violence. The ghastly thing was that when the wagons had to be closed, the patients refused to take their fingers away. They simply would not listen to us and in the end the Germans lost patience. The result was a brutal and inhuman spectacle."[49] Some fifty (Jewish) nurses accompanied the transport.

A Dutch Jew described the arrival of the transport in Auschwitz: "It was one of the most horrible transports from Holland that I saw. Many of the patients tried to break through the barrier and were shot dead. The remainder were gassed immediately."[50] There are diverging accounts of the fate of the nurses, none of whom survived. Some declare that they were sent to the camp; others that they were gassed; according to another witness "some of them were thrown into a pit, doused with gasoline, and burned alive."[51] Aus der Fünten had promised them that they could return immediately after the trip or work in the East in a thoroughly modern mental institution.[52]

In early 1943 the Germans established the Vught labor camp, which supposedly would allow Jews to remain as forced laborers in Holland. It was a sophisticated "legal" option to avoid deportation; the council strongly encouraged it, and the obedient Dutch Jews went along. Of course it was one further German scam, and the Vught inmates were systematically transferred to Westerbork or, on several occasions, deported directly to the East.[53]

Between July 1942 and February 1943, fifty-two transports carrying 46,455 Jews left Westerbork for Auschwitz. Some 3,500 able-bodied men were redirected to the hydrogenation plant in Blechhammer (later Auschwitz III–Monowitz and Gross Rosen). Of the workers' group, 181 men survived the war; of the remaining 42,915 from the 1942 and early 1943 transports, 85 remained alive.[54] The deportations went on.

III

"The papers announce new measures against the Jews," Jacques Biélinky recorded on July 15, 1942: "They are forbidden access to restaurants, coffeehouses, movie theaters, theaters, concert halls, music halls, pools, beaches, museums, libraries, exhibitions, castles, historical monuments, sports events, races, parks, camping sites and even phone booths, fairs, etc. Rumor has it that Jewish men and women between ages eighteen and forty-five will be sent to forced labor in Germany."[55] That same day the roundups of "stateless" Jews started in the provinces of the occupied zone, on the eve of the operation in Paris.

According to a July 15 report from the police chief of the Loire-Inférieure, French gendarmes were accompanying German soldiers on their way to arrest Jews in the department; according to another report of the same day, the French authorities were providing police officers to guard fifty-four Jews on the request of the SS chief of Saint-Nazaire.

Jews arrested throughout the west of the country—among them some two hundred arrested in Tours, again on July 15—were taken to an assembly point in Angers (some were selected from French camps in the region) and, a few days later, a train carried 824 of them directly from Angers to Auschwitz.[56]

On July 16, at 4:00 a.m., the Germano-French roundup of 27,000 "stateless" Jews living in the capital and its suburbs began. The index cards prepared by the French police had become essential: 25,334 cards were ready for Paris, and 2,027 for the immediate suburbs.[57] Every technical detail had been jointly prepared by French and German officials in their meetings on July 7 and 11. On the sixteenth fifty municipal buses were ready, and so were 4,500 French policemen.[58] No German units participated in the arrests. The manhunt received a code name: *Vent printanier* (Spring Wind).

As rumors about the forthcoming raids had spread, many potential victims (mostly men) had gone into hiding.[59] The origins of these rumors? To this day they remain uncertain, but as historian André Kaspi noted, "a roundup such as had never taken place in France, could not remain secret for long."[60] UGIF employees, resistance groups, police personnel must all have been involved in some way in spreading warnings.

Nine hundred groups, each including three police officials and volunteers, were in charge of the arrests. "Suddenly, I heard terrible banging on the front door . . . ," Annette Müller, then nine years old, recalled. "Two men entered the room; they were tall and wore beige raincoats. 'Hurry up, get dressed,' they ordered, 'we are taking you with us.' I saw my mother get on her knees and embrace their legs, crying, begging: 'Take me but, I beseech you, don't take the children.' They pulled her up. 'Come on, madam, don't make it more difficult and all will be well.' My mother spread a large sheet on the floor, and threw in clothes, underwear. . . . She worked in a panic, throwing in things, then taking them out. 'Hurry up!' the policemen shouted. She wanted to take dried vegetables. 'No, you don't need that,' the men said, 'just take food for two days; there, you will get food.' "[61]

By the afternoon of July 17, 3,031 Jewish men, 5,802 women, and 4,051 children had been arrested; the number of Jews finally caught in *Vent printanier* totaled 13,152.[62] Unmarried people or childless couples were sent directly to Drancy; the others, 8,160 men, women, and children, were assembled in a large indoor sports arena known mainly for its bicycle races, the Vélodrome d'Hiver (Vel d'Hiv).[63]

At the Vel d'Hiv, nothing was ready—neither food, water, toilets, nor beds or bedding of any sort. For three to six days, thousands of hapless beings received one to two portions of soup per day. Two Jewish physicians and one Red Cross physician were in attendance. The temperature never fell below one hundred degrees Fahrenheit. Finally, group after group, the Vel d'Hiv Jews were temporarily sent to Pithiviers and Beaune-la-Rolande camps just vacated by the inmates deported in June.[64]

Vent printanier had not achieved the expected results. In order to keep Drancy stacked with Jews ready for deportation, the arrests of stateless Jews had to extend to the Vichy zone, as agreed by the French government. The major operation, again exclusively implemented by French forces (police, gendarmes, firemen, and soldiers), took place from August 26 to 28; some 7,100 Jews were seized.[65] Although Laval had promised in early September to cancel the naturalization of Jews who had entered the country after January 1933, the roundups in the Vichy zone were aimed at filling the German quotas without having to start denaturalizing French citizens.[66] By the end of the year 42,500 Jews had been deported from France to Auschwitz.[67] On July 22 Biélinky noted: "My shoemaker of the rue Broca, a Polish Jew, has been arrested with his wife. The pair of shoes that I left with him for repair remained at his home. And, his house is closed as he had neither children nor parents."[68]

Until mid-1943 Drancy remained under French authority. The main goal for the camp administration remained filling the quotas imposed by the Germans for each departing transport. "Under our current obligation to come up with one thousand deportees on Monday," a French police officer noted on September 12, 1942, "we must include in these departures, at least in reserve, the parents of sick [children] and advise them that they could be deported without their children remaining in the infirmary."[69]

On August 11 Untersturmführer Horst Ahnert, from Dannecker's office, informed the RSHA that due to the temporary halt in the roundups, he planned to send the children assembled in the camps Beaune-la-

Rolande and Pithiviers to Drancy, and asked for Berlin's authorization.[70] On the thirteenth, Günther gave his approval but warned Ahnert not to send transports filled with children only.[71]

It was probably the arrival of these children, aged two to twelve, that Drancy inmate George Wellers described after the war: "They were disembarked from the buses in the midst of the courtyard like small animals. . . . The elder children held the younger ones and did not let go of them until they reached their allocated places. On the stairs the bigger children carried the smaller ones, panting, to the fourth floor. There, they remained fearfully huddled together. . . . Once the luggage had been unloaded the children returned to the courtyard, but most of the younger ones could not find their belongings; when, after their unsuccessful search they wished to get back to their rooms, they could not remember where they had been assigned."[72]

On August 24, transport number 23 left Drancy for Auschwitz with its load of 1,000 Jews, including 553 children under age seventeen (288 boys and 265 girls). Among the children, 465 were under twelve, of whom 131 were under six. On arrival in Auschwitz, 92 men aged from twenty to forty-five were selected for work. All the other deportees were immediately gassed. Three Jews from this transport survived the war.[73]

As a result of the only petition sent to Vichy by UGIF-North shortly after the Paris roundup, some relatives of war veterans and some "French children of foreign parents" (these were the words used in the petition) were released. André Baur, the president of UGIF-North, thanked Laval for his gesture.[74]

On August 2 Lambert met Helbronner. Despite the ongoing roundups and deportations, the head of the Consistoire was not ready to share his contacts at Vichy with any member of UGIF nor to tell Lambert that in fact Laval was refusing to see him. In the course of the conversation, Helbronner declared to a stupefied Lambert that on August 8 he was going on vacation and that "nothing in the world would bring me back."[75] This declaration, quoted by Lambert only, has to be taken guardedly given the tense relations between the author of the *Carnet* and the Consistoire. "The president of the Consistoire seems to me to be more deaf, more pompous and older than ever. The fate of the foreign Jews does not touch him at all," Lambert added on September 6, describing another meeting with Helbronner, on July 30.[76] The remark about Helbronner's attitude toward *les juifs étrangers* was probably on target.

In August the Consistoire prepared two drafts of a protest letter. The milder version, not alluding to "extermination" (mentioned in the other draft) or to the participation of the French police or to that of the Germans, was delivered in Vichy on August 25, not to Laval to whom it was addressed and who once again refused to meet with the delegate of French Jewry, but to some low-ranking official.[77] That was all.

UGIF-North was embroiled in endless debates with officials of the Commissariat about the payment of the one-billion-franc fine, and its regular budget was collapsing under the growing burden of welfare assistance, mainly for destitute foreign Jews. UGIF-South attempted, with the help of the Consistoire and of foreign, mainly American organizations (the Quakers, the Nîmes committee, among others, and of course the Joint) to convince the Vichy authorities to allow the emigration of one thousand Jewish children to the United States. After weeks of negotiation and slow bureaucratic moves on both the French and the American sides, an agreement was almost wrapped up. Then, however, as the Allied forces landed in North Africa, the Germans occupied the southern zone, Vichy broke off diplomatic relations with Washington, and the project came to naught.[78]

The cooperation of UGIF-South with the Consistoire in the rescue attempt of the Jewish children indicated that the relations between the two organizations (and their leaders) were changing from sharp antagonism to growing and unavoidable cooperation. The German occupation of the southern zone and the common fate threatening all Jews living in France contributed to the change in relations. The leaders of French Jewry were losing faith in their privileged status and in the protection French Jewry could expect from Vichy. Major roundups in Marseilles and Lyons in early 1943 would confirm their suspicions and reinforce the links with UGIF-South during the months to come.[79]

In both Rivesaltes and Drancy the Germans tried to persuade inmates that family members in hiding should be persuaded to report in order to avoid separation. In Rivesaltes the German enticements were mainly addressed to parents of hidden children. Jewish social workers, aware of the trap, either had to inform the parents that deportation meant death for them and their children or shield them from what was in store. Some detainees understood the indirect warnings; others did not: More than a hundred additional children joined their parents.[80]

Then, as in early 1943 the number of foreign Jews in France was rapidly dwindling and the weekly quotas of deportees were no longer met, the Germans decided to move to the next step: Pétain and Laval were now prodded to cancel the naturalizations of Jews that had taken place after 1927. It was at this point, as we shall see, that unexpectedly, after first agreeing, Laval changed his mind.

The immediate reaction of the majority of ordinary French people to the roundups was unmistakably negative in both zones.[81] Although it did not lead to any organized protest, it did enhance readiness to help Jews on the run. Feelings of pity at the sight of the unfortunate victims, particularly women and children, spread, albeit briefly; but, as already mentioned, basic prejudice towards the Jews did not disappear.

"The persecution of the Jews," a February 1943 report from a Resistance agent stated, "has profoundly wounded the French in their humane principles; it has even, at times, made the Jews almost sympathetic. One cannot deny, however, that there is a Jewish question: the present circumstances have even helped plant it firmly. The Blum ministry, which was overflowing with Jewish elements, and the penetration of tens of thousands of foreign Jews into France, provoked a defensive mechanism in France. People would pay any price not to see a similar invasion repeated."[82] A March report from another agent was almost identical in its main assessment. "The persecutions directed against the Jews have not stopped stirring and angering the population. Public opinion is nevertheless somewhat suspicious of them. It is feared that after the war some leading professions (banking, broadcasting, journalism, cinema) will be invaded again and in some fashion controlled by the Jews. Certainly, no one wants the Jews to be victimized and even less that they be molested. People sincerely want them to be as free as possible, in possession of their rights and property. But no one wants them to be supreme in any domain."[83]

Within the Resistance itself, the same kind of low-key anti-Semitism was present, even explicitly so. In June 1942 the first issue of *Cahiers*, published by the central body of the French underground, the OCM (Organisation Civile et Militaire), carried a study on ethnic minorities in France. The author, Maxime Blocq-Mascart, singled out the Jews as the group that caused "ongoing controversies": "Antisemitism in its moderate form was quasi universal, even in the most liberal societies. This indicates that its foundation is not imaginary." Blocq-Mascart 's analysis brought up the usual repertory of anti-Jewish arguments and suggested the usual measures: "stopping Jewish immigration, avoiding the concentration of Jews in a small number of cities, encouraging complete assimilation." The article was widely debated and denounced by some high-ranking members of the underground; it nonetheless represented the opinion of a great majority of the French people.[84]

The Assembly of French cardinals and archbishops met in Paris on July 21, 1942, less than a week after the raid. A minority was in favor of some form of protest, but the majority, headed by Archbishop Achille Liénart of Lille and Cardinal Emmanuel Suhard of Paris, opposed it. Unsigned notes, drafted after the assembly, most probably by Liénart, indicate the main points of the discussion and the views of the majority. "Fated to disappear from the Continent. Those who support them are against us. The expulsions have been ordered. The answers: some belong to us; we keep them; the others, foreigners—we give them back. No, all have to leave by the action of our agencies, in both zones. Individualist project. Letter to our government out of sense of humanity. Help of social services to children in centers. They themselves ask only for charity from us. Letter addressed in name of humanity and religion."[85]

In other words the notes indicated that the French episcopate knew (probably on information received from the government or the Vatican) the Jews were fated to disappear from the Continent; whether this disappearance was understood as extermination is unclear. Support for the Jews, the note further mentioned, came mainly from segments of the population that were hostile to the church (communists? Gaullists?). The deportations have been ordered by the Germans; Vichy wants to keep the French Jews and have the foreigners expelled; the Germans insist on generalized deportation from both zones and demand the help of French agencies (mainly the police). The meaning of the words "individualist project" (*Projet individualiste*) are unclear but it could be that assistance to individuals was discussed. The bishops apparently believed that the caretaking of children would be implemented by French welfare agencies. The Jews, according to the notes, did not ask for anything else but charitable help (not for political intervention or public protest). A letter would be sent to the government in the spirit of the declaration issued by the assembly.[86]

On July 22 Cardinal Suhard, in the name of the assembly, sent the letter to the maréchal. It was the first official protest of the Catholic church of France regarding the persecution of the Jews: "Deeply moved by the information reaching us about the massive arrests of Israelites that took place last week and by the harsh treatment inflicted upon them, particularly at the Vélodrome d'Hiver, we cannot suppress the call of our conscience. It is in the name of humanity and of Christian principles that our voice is raised to protest in favor of the unalienable rights of human beings. It is also an anguished call for pity for this immense suffering, mainly for that of mothers and children. We ask you, Monsieur le Maréchal, to accept to take [our call] into account, so that the demand of justice and the right to charity be respected."[87]

The papal nuncio in Vichy, Monsignor Valeri, considered the letter as rather "platonic."[88] Helbronner thought so as well and beseeched his friend Gerlier to intervene personally with Pétain. After obfuscating for a while, the cardinal of Lyons (also prodded by Pastor Boegner) agreed to send a letter to the maréchal, and did so on August 19. But, like Suhard before him, Gerlier wrote in convoluted terms that could only indicate to Pétain and Laval that the French church would ultimately abstain from any forceful confrontation. Despite his promise to Helbronner, the cardinal did not ask for a meeting with Pétain.[89] A few months beforehand, however, Gerlier had allowed the establishment in his diocese of an association to help Jews (Amitiés Judéo-Chrétiennes), led by Abbé Alexandre Glasberg and the Jesuit priest Pierre Chaillet; in August 1942 he intervened in favor of the same Father Chaillet, arrested for having hidden eighty-four Jewish children.[90]

It is in this context that, on August 30, 1942, Jules-Gérard Saliège, archbishop of Toulouse, had a pastoral letter denouncing the roundups and deportations read in the churches of his diocese: "It has been reserved to our time to witness the sad spectacle of children, of women, of fathers and mothers being treated like a herd of animals; to see members of the same family separated from one another and shipped away to an unknown destination. . . . In our diocese, scenes of horror have taken place in the camps at Noé and Récébédou. Jews are men. Jewesses are women. Foreigners are men, foreign women are women. They cannot be mistreated at will, these men, these women, these fathers and mothers of families. They are part of the human race. . . ."[91]

Saliège's pastoral letter found an echo well beyond the Southwest of France, but as suggested by historian Michèle Cointet, it has to be set in its context. The letter was not only, so it seems, the expression of an impetuous and immediate moral reaction to the roundups of foreign Jews in the Vichy zone. It was apparently suggested to the Toulouse prelate by emissaries from Lyons. In other terms, as the Assembly of French Cardinals and Archbishops was paralyzed, Saliège became its voice, as shortly afterward, did Bishop Pierre-Marie Théas of Montauban. The Episcopal Assembly probably knew that these individual protests would be considered too marginal to cause official retaliation, yet they would allow to save face: The church of France had not remained silent.[92]

Saliège's protest may have been partly tactical, but it must also have expressed his feelings, as demonstrated by the very tone of the appeal and, more concretely, by the help he extended to various Jewish rescue operations in the Southwest of France. The same practical help was offered by a number of other prelates, including Bishop Paul Rémond in Nice or, indirectly, Gerlier himself. Throughout the Continent—and we shall return to this issue—Christian institutions did hide Jewish children and, at times, Jewish adults. Occasionally assistance was collective, remarkable in its scope, and no less so in the absence of any proselytizing aims, such as in the French Protestant community Le Chambon-sur-Lignon, a village in the mountainous Cévennes region, guided by its pastor, André Trocmé and his family. The entire village took part in this extraordinary venture and ultimately did hide hundreds, possibly thousands, of Jews at one moment or another throughout the entire period.[93] It took a Protestant police officer sent by Vichy to uncover part of the hiding operation and to ensure the deportation of all the young Jewish charges of the children's home, Maison des Roches, and that of its director the pastor's cousin Daniel Trocmé, gassed at Majdanek.[94]

The usual German decrees had been applied in Belgium as they had in France and in Holland, and approximately at the same time. Yet the commander in chief, General Falkenhausen, and the all-important head of the military administration, Eggert Reeder, were concerned lest the deportations, also scheduled for July, cause unrest among the population. Reeder took the matter directly to Himmler.

A report sent to the Wilhelmstrasse on July 9, by Werner von Bargen, the Foreign Ministry representative with the military high command in Brussels, gave a faithful picture of the situation: "The military administration intends to implement the requested deportation of 10,000 Jews. The head of the military administration is presently at [Hitler's] headquarters to discuss the matter with the SS Reichsführer. Considerations against the measure could stem, first, from the fact that understanding of the Jewish question is not yet very widespread here and that Jews of Belgian nationality are considered by the population as Belgians. Therefore the measure could be interpreted as the beginning of general forced evacuations [for labor in Germany]. Moreover the Jews here are integrated in economic life, so that one could be worried about difficulties in the labor market. The military administration expects, however, to overcome these considerations, if the deportation of Belgian Jews is avoided. Thus, to start with, Polish, Czech, Russian and other Jews will be chosen, which should allow, theoretically, reaching the target number" [*das Soll*].[95]

Himmler had no qualms in agreeing to postpone the deportation of Belgian Jewish nationals, as he knew that they represented barely 6 percent of the 57,000 Jews registered by the Security Police. On August 4, 1942, the first transport of foreign Jews left Malines (Mechelen, in Flemish) for Auschwitz. Yet the events in Belgium would, paradoxically, take a somewhat different course from those in neighboring Holland, for example.

The beginning of the German onslaught caught both Jews and non-Jews by surprise, and it was during the first two months of the operation that one-third of Belgian Jewry was sent to its death. However, while approximately 15,000 Jews were deported until November 1942, the German roundups became rapidly less successful during the following months: Some further 10,000 Jews were deported before the liberation of the country. Approximately half the Jewish population survived the war.

Despite strong prejudice against Jews and particularly against the vast number of foreign Jews, two factors led to a far higher rescue percentage in Belgium than in neighboring, relatively non-anti-Semitic Holland, home to a vast majority of native Dutch Jews: The spontaneous reaction of the population and the involvement of Belgian resistance organizations.

There is no question that large-scale rescue operations initiated by "ordinary Belgians" took place at all levels of society. The issue that remains unresolved—and probably unresolvable—is the degree of influence of the Catholic Church and its institutions on this surge of compassion and charity. That Catholic institutions did hide Jews, particularly Jewish children, is well documented; whether these institutions, and mainly the rank-and-file Catholic population, responded to the encouragements and instructions of the church hierarchy or merely to their own feelings remains unclear, as does the degree of the memory of German brutality in World War I.[96]

Active cooperation between a rapidly established Jewish underground (Comité de Défense des Juifs, or CDJ) and Belgian resistance organizations led to the hiding of about 25,000 Jews.[97] This cooperation was facilitated by the fact that, from the outset, a significant number of foreign Jewish refugees were affiliated, one way or another, with the Belgian Communist Party or with left-wing Zionist organizations—particularly with the Communist organization for foreign workers, MOI (Main d'Oeuvre Immigrée, or "Immigrant Labor Organization");[98] the communists were highly influential moreover in the Belgian Resistance.

IV

While Jews were rapidly disappearing from the Reich, the "Jewish question" remained as present as ever not only in official propaganda but also in everyday life. In early December 1942, for example, as the issue was about to reach the courts, "Katag A.G.," a textile firm in Bielefeld, decided to consult the Reich Justice Ministry. "Katag," the firm's petition read, "was 'aryanized' in the years 1937–38. The name "Katag," an abbreviation for Katz & Michel Textil A.G., was changed in the course of the 'aryanization' insofar as we registered it as fantasy identification and added 'A.G.' [Aktien Gesellschaft], so that now the business registry in Bielefeld carries the name 'Katag A.G.' Recently, however, the German Labor Front objected to the identification of our company as 'Katag' because it still carries a syllable of the Jewish name Katz. We hold to the point of view that in the name 'Katag A.G.' the first two letters *Ka* cannot in any way be recognized as the components of a Jewish name." . . .[99]

There was no easy resolution to the problem; the Justice Ministry asked for the opinion of the Party Chancellery, and after much debate, on March 23, 1943, Bormann's office reached a Solomonic decision, if one dare say: "Katag A.G." would be allowed to keep its name temporarily for the duration of the war.[100]

During the same fateful days of December 1942, the Reich Ministry of Education decided that *Mischlinge* of the second degree could, under certain conditions, enroll as students of medicine, dentistry, and pharmacy, but not veterinary medicine. The decision was based on the assumption that mixed breeds of the second degree did not have the slightest chance of finding employment as veterinarians on completion of their studies.[101] In other words *Mischlinge* of the second degree could eventually take care of sick people, but no good German would wish them to attend to sick animals.

Completing the deportations from Germany was, of course, only a matter of logistics and of time. As we previously saw, from the early summer of 1942 onward, probably as a consequence of the attempt by the "Baum group" to set fire to the "Soviet Paradise" exhibition, no Jewish laborers were to be kept in the Reich, even in war-essential jobs. A letter sent by Sauckel on November 26, 1942, to the heads of labor exchanges stated this in the clearest terms: "In agreement with the Chief of the Security Police and the Security Service, Jews still employed will now be evacuated from the territory of the Reich and replaced by Poles, who are being deported from the General Government.... Poles ... if fit for labor, will be transported without their families to the Reich, particularly to Berlin; there they will be put at the disposal of the labor exchange offices to serve as replacements for Jews to be eliminated from armament factories. The Jews who will become available as a result of the employment of Polish labor will be deported *at once.* This will apply first to Jews engaged in unskilled labor since they can be exchanged most easily. The remaining so-called qualified Jewish laborers will be left in the industries until their Polish replacements become sufficiently familiar with the work process after a period of apprenticeship to be determined for each case individually. Loss of production in individual industries will thus be reduced to the absolute minimum."[102] As we shall see further on, this was the exact expression of Himmler's policy as stated in a letter of October 1942 to the OKW.

On February 27, 1943, the deportation of the "Jews employed in industry" (the *Fabrikaktion*) began. It had a double aim: to seize and deport all full Jews working in industry in the Old Reich and to expel any Jewish partners of mixed marriages from these workplaces.[103] In fact the roundups included not only the Jewish laborers but also their families and, more generally, any full Jews still remaining anywhere in the Reich.[104] In Berlin, where more than 10,000 Jewish forced laborers had still been employed, the operation lasted almost one full week. On March 1, the first transport departed for Auschwitz. Within a few days some 7,000 Jews were deported from the capital, and 10,948 from all over the Reich.[105]

Some 1,500 to 2,000 Berlin Jews who had been seized but excluded from deportation (mainly mixed-marriage partners) were assembled in a building on 2-4 Rosenstrasse, for identification and work selection in remaining Jewish institutions (such as the one remaining Jewish hospital). Most of these internees were released by March 8.[106] During these few days scores of spouses, other relatives, and friends did gather on the opposite sidewalk and at times called for the prisoners; they mainly waited for information or tried to get food parcels into the building. Such unusual gatherings certainly demanded a measure of courage, but they were relatively modest and completely nonaggressive. They did not bring about the release of the detainees, as deportation had not been planned at any time for these Jews. The event turned into legend, however: A demonstration of thousands of German women brought about the liberation of their Jewish husbands. It is an uplifting legend, yet a legend nonetheless.[107]

The *Fabrikaktion* had been preceded, in late 1942, by the deportation of Jewish concentration camp inmates from camps in the Reich to camps in the East;[108] on October 20, 1942, the *Gemeindeaktion* (the "community operation") had led to the deportation of most of the staff of the Reichsvereinigung and of the Berlin community.[109] Several transports followed at the end of 1942 and in early 1943. After the *Fabrikaktion* another transport carried half of the remaining Berlin Jewish hospital staff to Auschwitz;[110] in May and June transports of bedridden patients followed from the Jewish hospital to Theresienstadt.[111] In the meantime, however, 10,000 elderly inmates were deported from Theresienstadt to Treblinka. According to a report from Müller to Himmler, it would ease the overpopulation in the "ghetto." . . .[112]

Leo Baeck and other leaders of the Reichsvereinigung were deported to Theresienstadt in January 1943, and in June the Reich association de facto ceased to exist. The one-thousand-year-old history of the Jews in Germany was coming to an end.

Hertha Feiner was among the last employees of the Berlin community to be deported. She did not wait for the Gestapo in her apartment but, warned by neighbors, moved to the community building; there she was arrested on March 9, 1943. A non-Jewish acquaintance tried without success to have her released, as mother to two *Mischling* daughters. On March 12 she was put on the transport to Auschwitz. She poisoned herself in the train.[113]

A few months earlier, it seemed that the Kleppers would be able to escape the worst. On December 5, 1942, the Swedish legation informed them that their daughter Renate had been granted a visa.[114] Would Hanni be able to join her daughter? On the eighth Jochen Klepper was in the office of his protector, Interior Minister Frick. The minister, apparently quite distressed, informed Klepper that he couldn't do a thing to facilitate the mother's departure: "Such matters cannot be kept secret; the Führer hears of them and a terrible outburst takes place."[115] Frick arranged for Klepper to meet Eichmann. The head of IVB4 didn't even promise that Reni would be allowed to leave; in any case the mother would not be authorized to follow.[116] The next day, December 10, Eichmann definitively rejected Hanni's departure. Jochen, Hanni, and Renerle did not hesitate: They would die together. That same night all three committed suicide.[117]

V

On June 18, 1942, Wehrmacht private HK wrote home from Brest-Litowsk: "In Bereza-Kartuska, where I stopped for lunch, 1,300 Jews had just been shot on the previous day. They had been brought to a pit outside of the town. Men, women and children had to undress completely and were then liquidated with a shot in the back of the neck. The clothes were disinfected and used again. I am convinced that if the war goes on much longer, the Jews will be turned into sausage and served to Russian war prisoners and to the Jewish specialized workers. . . ."[118]

That same day a meeting of district governors and SS commanders in the General Government reviewed the progress of the extermination: "*Oberregierungsrat* Engler: The Jewish question has been solved in the city of

Lublin. What was the Jewish quarter has been evacuated. . . . SS and Police Leader Katzmann presented the security situation in the *district of Galicia*. . . . Jews have already been evacuated in rather large numbers. . . . In the next few weeks further Jews are to be resettled. . . . *Amtschef* Dr. Hummel reports on conditions in the *Warsaw District*. . . . He hopes that the city of Warsaw will be freed of the burden of Jews unable to work in a reasonable period of time. . . . To the question of State Secretary Dr. Bühler whether there was a chance of decreasing the ghetto population more quickly, State Secretary Krüger responded that a better overview would be possible in the course of August. . . . Deputy *Amtschef* Oswald spoke about the current situation in the *Radom District*: The Radom District had fallen behind in resettling the Jews. . . . This resettlement of the Jews now depended only on the problem of transport. . . . State Secretary Krüger indicated that as far as the police were concerned, the Jewish operation had been prepared down to the last detail and that implementation was only dependent on transport."[119]

In mid-July, Höfle arrived in Warsaw from Lublin with a group of "specialists." SS units in the city would in due time be reinforced by Polish "police," and by Ukrainian, Latvian, and Lithuanian auxiliaries. On July 20 Czerniaków, aware of widespread rumors about pending deportations, decided to get some information from his longtime German "interlocutors": "In the morning at 7:30 at the Gestapo. I asked Mende how much truth there was in the rumors. He replied that he had heard nothing. I turned to Brandt; he also knew nothing." And so it went. Czerniaków continued his tour of German officials and was repeatedly told that the rumors were *Quatsch* and *Unsinn* [utter nonsense]. "I ordered Lejkin [the acting Jewish police chief] to make the public announcement through the precinct police stations." The chairman then proceeded to Auerswald to discuss the fate of children held in detention centers: "He [Auerswald] ordered me to write him a letter for their release, on condition that they be placed in reformatories and that a guarantee would be given that they would not escape. . . . It appears that about 2,000 children will qualify for reformatories."[120]

On July 21 several members of the council were arrested as hostages and so were other prominent Jews in the ghetto administration and beyond (Czerniaków's wife was also on the list but managed to remain with him in his office).[121] The next morning, July 22, the entrance to the council building was blocked by a few SS cars; the council members and the heads of all departments assembled in Czerniaków's office, and Höfle arrived with a small retinue. Reich-Ranicki was called in to take down the minutes of the meeting in the conference room. The windows were wide open on that sunny day, and in the street the SS were playing Strauss waltzes on a portable phonograph.[122]

Höfle announced that the deportations would start within a few hours, and, according to Reich-Ranicki, read out the German instructions, "awkwardly and with some difficulty," as if he had hardly glanced at the text beforehand: "There was a strained silence in the room, made even more tense by the rattle of my typewriter, the clicking of the cameras of some SS officers, who kept taking pictures, and the gentle melody of the 'Blue Danube Waltz' wafting in from the street. . . . From time to time Höfle looked at me to make sure I was keeping up. Yes, I was keeping up all right. . . . The final section of the 'Instructions and Tasks' set out the penalties for those who attempted to evade or disrupt the resettlement measures! There was but one punishment and it was repeated at the end of each sentence like a refrain: '. . . will be shot.' "[123]

Czerniaków tried to negotiate some exemptions (he was particularly worried about the fate of many orphans) but received no assurances whatsoever. On the twenty-third, he noted in his diary: "In the morning at the Community. SS 1st Leut. [Lt.] Worthoff from the deportation staff came and we discussed several problems. He exempted the vocational school students from deportation. The husbands of working women as well. He told me to take up the matter of the orphans with Höfle. The same about craftsmen. When I asked for the number of days per week in which the operation would be carried on, the answer was seven days a week. Throughout the town a great rush to start new workshops. A sewing machine can save a life. It is 3 o'clock. So far 4,000 are ready to go. The orders are that there must be 9,000 [at the *Umschlagplatz*, the assembly square] by 4 o'clock."[124] In the afternoon of the twenty-third, as the Jewish police were unable to fill the quota, the auxiliary police units launched their own roundup without taking any exemptions into account. Czerniaków's "negotiations" had been in vain.

That same evening the SS called Czerniaków back from home; he was told that the next day 10,000 Jews had to be sent to the *Umschlagplatz*. The chairman returned to his office, closed the door, wrote one farewell note to the council informing it of the new German demands, another to his wife, and took poison.[125] Kaplan, no friend of Czerniaków, noted on July 26: "The first victim of the deportation decree was the President, Adam Czerniaków, who committed suicide by poison in the Judenrat building. . . . There are those who earn immortality in a single hour. The President, Adam Czerniaków, earned his immortality in a single instant."[126]

On July 22 Treblinka had opened its gates. Every day thousands of terrified ghetto inhabitants were driven to the assembly point and from there, a freight train carried five thousand of them to Treblinka.[127] At first most of the Jews of Warsaw did not know what fate awaited them. On July 30 Kaplan mentioned "expulsion" and "exile": "The seventh day of the expulsion. Living funerals pass before the windows of my apartment—cattle trucks or coal wagons full of candidates for expulsion and exile, carrying small bundles under their arms . . . rosters promising 3 kgs of bread and 1 kg of marmalade drew many a famished Jew to the assembly square."[128]

On August 5 the deportations engulfed all institutions for children, including all orphanages. Since May of that year, Korczak had been keeping his "ghetto diary"—a record of thoughts, reminiscences, even dreams, more than actual events. Yet every line reflected, to varying degrees, the anxiety that the "old doctor" felt about the fate of his charges and that of the ghetto. His imprisonment by the Gestapo in the dreaded Pawiak jail, at the end of 1940 and in early 1941 (following his insistence on transporting potatoes for his orphanage during the transfer to the ghetto, his wearing a Polish officer's uniform—he had been an officer in the Polish army, but such a display was of course forbidden—and his steady refusal to wear the mandatory armband with the Jewish star), left him shaken and ill. Vodka soothed his anxiety but not sufficiently to keep his mind off macabre ruminations, even when he joked.[129] Thus sometime in late May or early June of 1942, he wrote:

"All is fine, I say, and it's my wish to be merry. An amusing reminiscence: Five decagrams of so-called smoked sausage now costs 1 zloty 20. It used to cost only 80 grosze (and bread a bit more). I said to a saleswoman: 'Tell me, dear lady, isn't that sausage by chance made of human flesh? It's rather too cheap for horsemeat.' And she replied: 'How should I know? I wasn't there when it was being made.'" Leaving his peculiar sense of humor at that, Korczak turned again to his single overwhelming concern: the orphans. "The day began with weighing the children," he noted in the same entry. "The month of May has brought a marked decline [in their weight]. The previous months of this year were not too bad and even May is not yet alarming. But we still have two months or more before the harvest. No getting away from that. And the restrictions imposed by official regulations, new additional interpretations and overcrowding are expected to make the situation still worse."[130]

During these same days, Korczak noted a street scene: "The body of a dead boy lies on the sidewalk. Nearby, three boys are playing horses and drivers. At one point they notice the body, move a few steps to the side, go on playing."[131]

On August 4 Korczak described another minute episode: In the early-morning light he was watering the flowers on his windowsill while in the street an armed German soldier stood watching him. "I am watering the flowers. My bald head in the window—What a splendid target. He has a rifle. Why is he standing and looking on calmly? He has no orders to shoot. And perhaps he was a village teacher in civilian life, or a notary, a street sweeper in Leipzig, a waiter in Cologne? What would he do if I nodded to him? Waved my hand in a friendly gesture? Perhaps he doesn't even know that things are as they are? He may have arrived only yesterday, from far away."[132]

The following day the whole orphanage, like all Jewish orphanages in the ghetto, was ordered to proceed to the *Umschlagplatz*. Korczak walked at the head of the column of children marching to their death. On August 6 Lewin noted: "They emptied Dr. Korczak's orphanage with the doctor at the head. Two hundred orphans."[133] Kaplan was no longer alive to describe the deportation of Korczak's children. His ultimate diary entry had been written on August 4; the last line read: "If my life ends—what will become of my diary."[134]

By September 21 the great *Aktion* was over: 10,380 Jews had been killed in the ghetto during the deportations; 265,040 had been deported to Treblinka and gassed.[135]

Capt. Wilm Hosenfeld, head of sports facilities for Wehrmacht officers in Warsaw, knew quite a lot about what was happening to the Jews—although he refused to believe in systematic murder—as his diary throughout the *Aktion* indicates. "If what they are saying in the city is true," he noted on July 25, 1942, "and it does come from reliable sources—then it is no honor to be a German officer, and no one could go along with what is happening. But I can't believe it. The rumors say that thirty thousand Jews are to be taken from the ghetto this week and sent east somewhere. In spite of all the secrecy people say they know what happens then: Somewhere near Lublin, buildings have been constructed with rooms that can be electrically heated with strong current, like the electricity in a crematorium. Unfortunate people are driven into these heated rooms and burned alive, and thousands can be killed like that in a day, saving all the trouble of shooting them, digging mass graves and then filling them in. The guillotine of the French revolution can't compete, and even in the cellars of the Russian secret police they hadn't devised such virtuoso methods of mass slaughter. But surely this is madness. It can't be possible. You wonder why the Jews don't defend themselves. However, many, indeed most of them, are so weak from starvation and misery that they couldn't offer any resistance."[136]

In brief notes jotted down at the end of 1942, Ringelblum established a clear distinction between the previous period and the one that had started during the last few months: "The latest period. The time of atrocities. Impossible to write a monographic study because—the shadows of Ponar, 9,000 from Slonim, expulsions—the tragedy of Lublin . . . Chelmno—gas. Treblinki [*sic*]. . . . Time of persecutions, and now the time of atrocities."[137]

Treblinka, the last and deadliest of the "Aktion Reinhardt" camps, had been built to the northeast of Warsaw, close to the Warsaw-Białystok railway line, on sandy terrain stretching to a bend in the river Bug. The closest station was Malkinia, from which a single-track line led to the camp. The "lower" or first camp extended over the larger area; it included the assembly and undressing squares and, farther on, workshops and barracks. The second or "upper" camp was isolated from the first by barbed wire and thick foliage fences that hindered unwelcome observation. A heavy brick building concealed the three gas chambers linked to a diesel engine by a system of pipes (a larger building with ten gas chambers would be added in October 1942). As in Chelmno, Belzec, or Sobibor, on arrival the deportees had to undress and leave all clothes or valuables for the sorting squads. From the "undressing square" the victims were driven to the gas chambers along "the road to heaven" (*Himmelstrasse*), a narrow corridor also hidden from the surroundings by thick branches. A sign pointed "to the showers."[138]

SS Obersturmführer Richard Thomalla had been in charge of the construction of the camp. Euthanasia physician Dr. Irmfried Eberl was appointed first commandant, and on July 23, 1942, the exterminations began. According to SS Unterscharführer Hans Hingst's testimony, "Dr. Eberl's ambition was to reach the highest possible numbers and exceed all the other camps. So many transports arrived that the disembarkation and gassing of the people could no longer be handled."[139] Within days Eberl completely lost control of the situation. By the end of August some 312,000 Jews, mainly from Warsaw but also from the districts of Radom and Lublin, had been gassed at the new camp.[140]

Eberl's "incompetence" was compounded by widespread corruption: The money and valuables carried by the victims found their way into the camp staff's pockets and also into those of the commandant's euthanasia colleagues in Berlin.[141] When Globocnik became aware of the situation in Treblinka in August, he traveled to the camp with Wirth and Josef Oberhauser. Eberl was relieved of his position then and there, and Wirth was ordered to move in and tidy up the chaos so that Stangl, the Sobibor commandant, could take over, which he did in early September.[142]

In his prison interviews with Sereny, Stangl described his first visit to Treblinka while Eberl was still in charge: "I drove there, with an SS driver. . . . We could smell it kilometers away. The road ran alongside the railway. When we were about fifteen, twenty minutes' drive from Treblinka we began to see corpses by the [railway] line, first just two or three, then more, and as we drove into Treblinka station, there were what looked hundreds of them—just lying there—they'd obviously been there for days, in the heat. In the station was a train full of Jews, some dead, some still alive . . . that too, looked as if it had been there for days. . . . When I entered the camp and got out of the car on the square I stepped knee-deep into money; I didn't know which way to turn, where to go. I waded in notes, currency, precious stones, jewelry, clothes. . . . The smell was indescribable; the hundreds, no, the thousands of bodies everywhere, decomposing, putrefying. Across the square, in the woods, just a few hundred yards away on the other side of the barbed-wire fence and all around the perimeter of the camp, there were tents and open fires with groups of Ukrainian guards and girls—whores, I found out later, from all over the countryside—weaving drunk, dancing, singing, playing music."[143]

VI

In Lodz in the fall of 1942, as had been the case in Warsaw, the Germans established priority rules of their own. On September 1 the deportations started. The patients of the ghetto's five hospitals were "evacuated" within two hours; whoever protested was shot on the spot. In all 2,000 patients, including 400 children, were carted away. Once the Germans had arrested most of the patients, they checked the hospital registry, and if anybody was missing, most of the time family members were taken instead.

According to Josef Zelkowicz, one of the ghetto chroniclers and a Yiddish writer of some renown, who apart from his "official" contributions to the "Chronicle" also kept a private diary, the procedure was in fact more tortuous: "The authorities insisted that all patients who escaped from the hospitals be turned in," he recorded on September 3. "However, since some were missing and many others could not be handed over because they had 'backing' and connections in the ghetto, it was agreed with the authorities that the *kehilla* would transfer two hundred other people in their stead. Those to be sacrificed would be sought not only among the escapees but among people who had been hospitalized at some other time, for any illness and had long since been discharged but lacked [protectors]. Even those who had never been hospitalized but who had applied for hospitalization on the basis of a doctor's recommendation would be included."[144]

The deportation of the sick was immediately followed by an order to evacuate some further 20,000 Jews, including all children under ten and all the elderly above sixty-five. As these categories totaled only 17,000 people, 3,000 unemployed or unemployable inhabitants were added.[145] "In the evening," Sierakowiak recorded on September 3, "disturbing news spread that the Germans had allegedly demanded that all children up to the age of ten must be delivered for deportation and, supposedly, extermination."[146]

On September 5 Sierakowiak's mother was taken away. "My most sacred, beloved, worn-out, blessed, cherished Mother has fallen victim to the bloodthirsty German Nazi beast!!! Two doctors, Czech Jews, suddenly arrived in the Sierakowiaks' apartment and declared the mother unfit for work; throughout the doctors' visit, the father continued to eat the soup left by relatives in hiding and was also "taking sugar out of their bag." The mother left, with some bread in her bag and some potatoes. "I couldn't muster the willpower to look through the windows after her or to cry," Sierakowiak went on. "I walked around, talked and finally sat as though I had turned to stone. . . . I thought my heart was breaking. . . . It didn't break, though, and it let me eat, think, speak and go to sleep."[147]

On September 4 Rumkowski addressed a crowd of some 1,500 terrified inhabitants assembled on "Fireman's Square": "The ghetto has been dealt a grievous blow. They ask that we give them that which is most precious—the children and old people. I was never privileged to have a child of my own and therefore I devoted my best years to children. . . . In my old age I am compelled to stretch out my hand and beg: 'My brothers and my sisters, give them to me! Fathers and mothers, give me your children!' . . . I must carry out the grim bloody surgery, I must amputate limbs to save the body! I must take away children and if I do not, others too may be taken. . . . I wanted at least to save one age group—from age nine to ten. But they would not relent. . . . We have in the ghetto many tuberculosis patients; their days or perhaps weeks are numbered. I do not know—maybe it is a satanic plot, maybe it is not—but I cannot refrain from presenting it: Give me these patients and it may be possible to save healthy people in their stead."[148] "The President cries like a little boy," Zelkowicz added.[149]

After describing the deportations, the chroniclers added a highly significant postscript conveying, as Sierakowiak had confessed about himself, the prevailing emotional numbness of the ghetto population: "The populace's strange reaction to the recent events is noteworthy. There is not the slightest doubt that this was a profound and terrible shock, and yet one must wonder at the indifference shown by those . . . from whom loved ones had been taken. It would seem that the events of recent days would have immersed the entire population of the ghetto in mourning for a long time to come, and yet, right after the incidents, and even during the resettlement action, the populace was obsessed with everyday concerns—getting bread, rations and so forth—and often went from immediate personal tragedy right back into daily life.[150]

Zelkowicz, who had written the chronicle entry about emotional numbness, offered some explanation for it in his private diary on September 3; it could have been called "the psychology of starvation." While mentioning how death had become "a daily event that surprised and frightened no one," the diarist noted that a distribution of potatoes had been announced on that same day; that had become the real event. "As long as a ghetto inhabitant lives, he wants at least once, if only for the last time, to experience the sense of satisfaction, to gorge himself. Afterward, whatever will be, will be. . . . So whenever there is talk about handing out potatoes, everything that has happened till now is shunted aside. . . . Yes, potatoes will be given out; it's a fact. Starting tomorrow, Friday, September 4. . . . The crowd is elated. . . . The people can only wish one another: may we be the privileged to eat these potatoes while we are still alive."[151]

Between August 10 and 23, 1942, many of the Jews of Lwov were deported to the Janowska Road slave labor camp and, after a further selection, from there to Belzec. Some 40,000 of the victims arrested during the August roundup were exterminated.[152] The remaining Jews of the city were driven into a ghetto, soon surrounded by a wooden fence. The *Judenrat* office was relocated to the ghetto area, but the *Judenrat* officials and among them the chairman, Henryk Landesberg, were not to resume their functions. According to the Germans, Landesberg had been in touch with the Polish underground.[153] The chairman and twelve other Jewish officials were to be publicly hanged from the roof of the building and from lampposts.

The executions took some time, as the ropes used for the hangings broke; the victims who fell to the pavement were compelled to climb the stairs leading to the roof and were hanged again. The highest spot was kept for Landesberg, as chairman. He fell to the pavement three times and three times was brought back to his balcony. The bodies were left on display for two days. A survivor from the ghetto described the scene. "I went with my mother to the office of the Jewish community regarding an apartment and there in the light breeze, dangled the corpses of the hanged, their faces blue, their heads tilted backward, their tongues blackened and stretched out. Luxury cars raced in from the center of the city, German civilians with their wives and children came to see the sensational spectacle, and, as was their custom, the visitors enthusiastically photographed the scene. Afterward the Ukrainians and Poles arrived by with greater modesty."[154] The Germans sent the bill for the ropes to the new *Judenrat*.[155] As for the Jews of the Lwov ghetto, they did not survive long: Most were liquidated in sporadic *Aktionen* and the remnant transferred to the Janowski camp in early 1943. When Lwov was liberated at the end of July 1944, out of a community of some 160,000 Jews in June 1941, some 3,400 were still alive.[156]

In nearby Drohobycz, the writer Bruno Schulz, who, as will be remembered, was painting the walls of SS Felix Landau's mansion and of the local Gestapo offices, was still alive in the autumn of 1942, protected by his "patron." In the meantime he had had to move into the ghetto and was by then mainly employed in cataloging the approximately 100,000 books seized by the Germans in the town and assembled at the old-age home.[157]

Schulz sensed that his end was near. "They are supposed to liquidate us by November [1942]," he told a Polish ex–fellow teacher of the local gymnasium.[158] And indeed on November 19 a shooting incident in the ghetto triggered wild reprisals against the population. Landau was away; the Gestapo man's personal enemy, SS Scharführer Karl Günther, seized the occasion of the "wild action," tracked Schulz on one of the ghetto streets, and killed him. About one hundred Jews were murdered in the action: On the next day their bodies were still lying on the streets.[159]

In July 1942 the chief of the Vilna Jewish police, Jacob Gens, became the sole head of the Vilna ghetto. Among community leaders he was in many ways atypical. Born in Kovno, he fought as a volunteer in the Lithuanian war of independence in the aftermath of World War I and was promoted to officer rank. He married a Christian and was well regarded by Lithuanian nationalists (he himself was a right-wing Zionist, a member of Wladimir Jabotinski's Revisionist Party). In Philip Friedman's words "it remains something of a mystery why Gens had accepted the position [of chief of the ghetto police]."[160] His wife and daughter remained on the Aryan side of the city. He possibly felt a moral obligation to take the position offered by the Germans. In the first letter Gens sent his wife from the ghetto, he wrote. "This is the first time in my life that I have to engage in such duties. My heart is broken. But I shall always do what is necessary for the sake of the Jews in the ghetto."[161]

During the selections of late November 1941, Gens succeeded in saving some lives in particularly difficult circumstances; his standing among the inhabitants grew and the Germans also kept adding to his tasks. But in mid-October 1942 the almost legendary "kommandant" was confronted with a grim challenge: the order to kill Jews.

Gens and his policemen were sent to a nearby town, Oszmiana, where about 1,400 Jews had been assembled for extermination. The police chief negotiated with the Germans, who finally agreed that only 400 Jews were to be murdered. Gens's men and some Lithuanians carried out the executions. Somehow news of the approaching operation had spread in the ghetto as the policemen got on their way. Rudashevski was outraged by the very idea of such participation: ". . . Jews will dip their hands in the dirtiest and bloodiest work. They wish simply to replace the Lithuanians. . . . The entire ghetto is in uproar about this departure [of the Jewish policemen to Oszmiana]," he recorded on October 19. "How great is our shame, our humiliation! Jews help the Germans in their organized, terrible work of extermination."[162]

In fact the ghetto was not in an uproar, contrary to what Rudashevski intensely hoped for and reported. It seems rather that the inhabitants accepted Gens's reasoning and his justifications: Saving some by sacrificing others. "The tragedy is that the . . . public mostly approves of Gens's attitude," Kruk wrote on October 28. "The public figures that perhaps this may really help."[163]

It was not only the ordinary population of the ghetto that supported Gens's decision; on October 27 the highly respected YIVO founder and linguist Zelig Kalmanovitch noted in his diary. "The rabbi [of Oszmiana] ruled that the old ones should be handed over. Old ones who asked that they should be taken. . . . If outsiders [the Lithuanians or the Germans] had done the job—there would have been more victims and all the property would have been stolen."[164] These lines do not reveal if Kalmanovitch was merely recording Gens's arguments or expressing his own agreement. But he did so at length a few days later when Gens was again ordered to participate with his policemen in an *Aktion* in Święciany: "In truth," Kalmanovitch wrote in November 1942, "we are in any case not innocent. . . . We have bought our lives and our future with the death of tens of thousands. If we have decided that we must continue with this life despite everything, then we must go on to the end. May the merciful Lord forgive us. . . . That is the situation and it is not in our hands to change it. Of course delicate souls cannot bear such acts, but the protest of the soul has no more than psychological value, and there is no moral value to it. Everybody is guilty or, more correctly, all are innocent and holy, and most of all those who take real action, who must overcome their spirit, who must overcome the torture of the soul, who free others of this task, and save their souls from pain."[165]

A few weeks later a briefly oblivious community celebrated a significant achievement: "100,000 books in the ghetto." Kruk was in charge: "In November the ghetto library went beyond the figure of a hundred thousand books distributed to readers. Because of this, the library is organizing a big cultural morning event, which will take place in the Ghetto Theater on Sunday, the 13th of this month [December], at noon. On the program: Opening by G. Yashunski, welcome from the ghetto chief [Gens], writers, scientific circles, teachers and the Youth Club. Dr. Ts. Feldstein will speak on "The Book and Martyrdom," then a lecture by H. Kruk "100,000 Books in the Ghetto." The second part will be a concert of words and music. The finale: distribution of gift books to the first reader in the ghetto and the youngest reader of the library."[166]

VII

During the last months of 1942 a small minority of European Jews understood their common fate; the vast majority remained tossed to and fro among momentary insight, disbelief, despair, and, as we saw, ever new hope.

Hidden in her Amsterdam attic, Anne Frank seemed to know what was happening to the Jews of the outside world. "Our many Jewish friends and acquaintances are being taken away in droves," she noted on October 9, 1942. "The Gestapo is treating them very roughly and transporting them in cattle cars to Westerbork, the big camp in Drenthe to which they are sending all the Jews." After adding some horrible details about Westerbork, apparently based on rumors that had reached Miep Gies, Anne went on. "If it's that bad in Holland, what must it be like in those faraway and uncivilized places to which the Germans are sending them? We assume that most of them are being murdered. The English radio says they're being gassed. Perhaps that's the quickest way to die."[167]

A few weeks later Anne described the arrests in Amsterdam as reported to the inhabitants of the attic by a new tenant, Mr. Dussel, and again she seemed to reach the same conclusion: "Countless friends and acquaintances have been taken off to a dreadful fate. Night after night, green and gray military vehicles cruise the streets. They knock on every door, asking whether any Jews live there. . . . No one is spared. The sick, the elderly, children and babies and pregnant women—all are marched to their death."[168]

During those very same days Rudashevski was recording events and incidents of everyday life in the ghetto. In Vilna, as we saw, the end of 1942 was a relatively quiet period. On October 7, 1942, Rudashevski's voice was almost that of a happy and carefree youngster. "The club work has begun. We have groups for literature and natural science. After leaving class at 7:30, I go immediately to the club. It is gay there, we have a good time and return home evenings in a large crowd. The days are short, it is dark in the street when our bunch leaves the club. [Jewish] policemen shout at us but we do not listen to them."[169]

Did Anne, in her faraway hiding place, understand the situation more thoroughly than Rudashevski in his decimated Vilna ghetto? It is doubtful. At times both recorded the most ominous information, then appeared to forget about it while turning their minds to the more immediate issues of their teenage lives.

Etty Hillesum, as an employee of the Jewish Council, had already stayed briefly in Westerbork. On her return to Amsterdam in December 1942, she tried to describe the camp and the ultimate fate of the deportees in a letter to two Dutch friends: "Finding something to say about Westerbork is difficult . . . it is a camp for a people in transit . . . to be deported a few days later to their unknown destiny . . . deep within Europe, from where only a few indistinct sounds have come back to the rest of us. But the quota must be filled; so must the train, which comes to fetch its load with mathematical regularity."[170]

How could Etty have known the exact meaning of the deportations when Gonda Redlich in Theresienstadt, so intent on saving children and youngsters from the transports to the East, and so often alluding to the fact that the deportees were being carried to their death, was making plans for the postwar years? In one and the same diary entry, on June 14–15, 1942, for example, Redlich recorded both his fears about the transports and his plans for the future: "I fear that the transports will not stay in one place in the East. What will happen when we go to our land after the war? What will our position be toward the others? I already feel that for me Aliyah [emigration to the land of Israel] will be an escape, an escape from people here in Europe, an escape because of life here in the Goluth [exile], an escape when you compare the old life to the new."[171]

The total confusion about what was happening to the deportees, from whom nothing was heard directly once they had boarded the transports, reappears in Paris at the end of 1942. Although on August 18 Biélinky had emphasized that "one never had news from the deportees,"[172] on December 2 he reported: "It is said that the Jews deported from France, Belgium, etc. have been found—about 35,000 of them—in a town in Russia, where they have been well received by the population."[173] December 17 Biélinky recorded his last diary entry. He was arrested on the night of February 10, 1943, by the French police and deported from Drancy to Sobibor on March 23.[174]

On December 9, 1942, Lambert was ordered by the Commissariat Général to dismiss all foreign Jews still working for the UGIF (approximately one-quarter of the staff) and told that—at that price—the French employees would be spared from deportation. Did he believe it? Even when he heard the Allied governments' declaration about the extermination of the Jews of Europe later the same month, he wrote that he still believed in his "star."[175]

Thus in almost all the diaries written by Jews in Western Europe, in Germany, and even in Theresienstadt, the entries during the second half of 1942 indicate both sporadic intimations about Nazi intention to exterminate all of them and, often simultaneously, contrary information and personal plans for the postwar period. Lambert, like Redlich, dreamed of the future: He hoped to own "a house on a hill" in his old age, although he immediately added that he knew this to be impossible.[176]

As for Klemperer, after noting on October 23, 1942, how the German military situation was worsening, he added: "But all conversations among

Jews again and again lead to the same reflection: 'If they have the time, they will kill us first.' One said to Frau Ziegler yesterday: He felt like a calf at the slaughterhouse, looking on, as the other calves are slaughtered, and waiting for his turn. The man is right."[177] And yet, a day later, as though what he had just written was meaningless, Klemperer mused about his future projects "after Hitler's fall:" "With what shall I start? I very certainly do not have so much more time [Klemperer had a heart condition]. The *18ème* [a book project on eighteenth-century literature] has slipped into the background for me. Tackle a supplement of my Modern Prose? Continue with the Curriculum?"[178] and the like.

Even close to the killing sites, Jews at times did not know what happened to the deportees, nor did they believe the information that reached them. Jews in Warsaw and in London knew the details about Chelmno, while the inhabitants of Lodz dismissed them. Thus a little-known Lodz ghetto diarist, Menachem Oppenheim, a native of the city and apparently an Orthodox Jew, recorded his reaction after the great deportations of September 1942. Oppenheim, like everybody else, was wondering about the use of small children, the elderly, and hospital patients in labor camps in places unknown, and yet he recorded—probably on October 16, 1942: "People say that they were taken to Chelmno near Kolo and there is a gasworks where they are gassed. But I believe that something else happened with the Jews of Warsaw and Kielce Cracow. For when I remember my beloved wife child mother sister brother brothers-in-law with their children I hope that they are alive and that soon I'll rejoice with them. . . . If not then why am I tormenting myself."[179]

By mid-August 1942, on the other hand, Abraham Lewin was no longer fooled about what was happening to the deportees from Warsaw: "When people get out of the train, they are beaten viciously. Then they are driven into huge barracks. For five minutes heart-rending screams are heard, then silence. The bodies that are taken out are swollen horribly. . . . Young men from among the prisoners are the gravediggers, the next day they too are killed."[180] On August 28, the information was brought by a Jew who escaped from Treblinka and returned to the ghetto: "His words confirm once again and leave no room for doubt that all deportees, both those who have been seized and those who reported voluntarily, are taken to be killed and no one is saved," Lewin wrote. "In the last weeks at least

300,000 Jews have been exterminated, from Warsaw and other towns. . . . God! Now it is certain that all those deported from Warsaw have been killed."[181] Very soon Lewin's turn would come.

In Western Europe the situation of the Flinkers was not an unusual one in the summer of 1942. At the beginning of the deportations from Holland, Eliezer Flinker, a Polish-born Orthodox Jew and a successful businessman residing in The Hague with his wife and seven children (six girls and a boy), paid what it took and the family crossed the border to Belgium. In Brussels further payments to the right intermediaries ensured an Aryan residence permit. The son, Moshe, whom we already encountered as a high school student in Holland, was sixteen years old when the Flinkers settled in the Belgian capital.

Moshe's diary, started on November 24, 1942, not only provides insight into the daily life of a Jewish family hiding in the open, so to speak, in a Western European city, but also gives us a glimpse of the inner turmoil of a profoundly religious Jewish boy in the face of the extraordinary persecution befalling his people. "Our sufferings have by far exceeded our wrongdoings," Moshe wrote on November 26, 1942. "What other purpose could the Lord have in allowing such things to befall us? I feel certain that further troubles will not bring any Jew back to the paths of righteousness; on the contrary, I think that upon experiencing such great anguish they will think that there is no God at all . . . and indeed what can God intend by all these calamities that are happening to us in this terrible period? It seems to me that the time has come for our redemption, or rather, that we are more or less worthy of being redeemed."[182] On December 3, however, he was uncertain. "Today is the eve of Hanukkah, but I have the feeling that this Hanukkah will pass, as have so many others, without a miracle or anything resembling one."[183]

More often than not the Flinkers quarreled: The mother wanted the father to find some work; she wanted them to move on to Switzerland, despite the fact than an acquaintance who had attempted to cross the Swiss border had been betrayed by the guides and had barely escaped with his life.[184] The father was wary: Both looking for work and attempting the journey and passage to Switzerland were too dangerous; better to stay where they were and remain as unobtrusive as possible. Yet, when it was not school time [during which children out on the street would have looked suspicious], Moshe could venture out of the house, even go to see a film, although cinemas were forbidden to Jews.

On December 13 Moshe saw *Jud Süss.* "What I saw there," he recorded on the following day, "made my blood boil. I was red in the face when I came out. I realized the wicked objectives of these evil people—how they want to inject the poison of anti-Semitism in the blood of the gentiles. While I was watching the film I suddenly remembered what the evil one [Hitler] had said in one of his speeches: Whichever side wins the war, anti-Semitism will spread and spread until the Jews are no more" [Moshe was probably paraphrasing Hitler's speech of April 1942]. "In that film I saw the means he is using to achieve his aim. . . . The way in which jealousy, hatred and loathing are aroused is simply indescribable. . . . The Jews are being made so hateful to the world that nothing that anyone can do will be able to undo his work."[185]

The smallest incident triggered the worst fears. "Last night my parents and I were sitting around the table," Moshe noted on January 7, 1943. "It was almost midnight. Suddenly we heard the bell: we all shuddered. We thought that the moment had come for us to be deported. . . . My mother had already put her shoes on to go to the door, but my father said to wait until they ring once more. But the bell did not ring again. Thank heaven it passed quietly. Only the fear remained, and all day long my parents have been very nervous. They can't stand the slightest noise, and the smallest thing bothers them."[186]

Deportation from Brussels, as halting as it was, continued nonetheless. On January 21, 1943, Moshe was sent to the [former] synagogue beadle to buy some clothing and bread coupons. The beadle was gone; his door had been sealed with a swastika sign: "When I stood in the street, I saw that the shutters were closed. I thought: This man [the beadle] took so much trouble in hiding from the Germans, and now, despite all his labor, he is taken away—he, his wife, and his two children. The younger child was a four-year-old girl."[187]

At the end of that fearsome day, Moshe wanted to pray: "I do not know in whose name to pray. Our forefathers are too far from us. Our people? It looks as though they have no merit at all, otherwise so many troubles could not have befallen them. Maybe the prayer that will be most effective will be about the magnitude of our pain. As great as our sins have been, our troubles have already surpassed them. A little more and we shall perish."[188]

VIII

It was in this atmosphere of total uncertainty that, on September 20 and 21, 1942, the Jews of Europe had tried—as much as each community could or each individual wished—to observe Yom Kippur, the Day of Atonement. There were places where the "Kol Nidre" service, on the eve of Yom Kippur, could not take place at all. In Paris, for example, the Germans had imposed a curfew from three p.m. on that day (a Sunday) in response to renewed attacks on members of the Wehrmacht. But according to Bielinky, there were many people in the synagogues on the twenty-first.[189] Sebastian's diary entry of September 22 was laconic: "Yesterday was Yom Kippur. A day of fasting—and of trying to believe and hope."[190] The key word was "trying," trying against all odds, in spite of the events of the past months, and in the face of "God's silence."

Klemperer's entry on the twenty-first was, formally speaking, that of a converted Jew. Much had changed, however, in terms of self-perception, for this "Protestant" who, as we saw, had explicitly declared at the outset of the war that he did not want to have anything to do with the Jewish community. "Today is Yom Kippur," he noted, "and this very day the last 26 'old people' are sitting in the Community house, from where they will be transported early tomorrow." The Klemperers went on "farewell visits" to the friends slated for deportation. Victor mentioned, among others, the reaction of the Neumanns, "who were defiantly merry: 'Yes and no.' On the one hand the corpses themselves were there. On the other hand they were really going into a beyond, from which, as yet there had been no reliable news. Because what had been reported was no more than supposition. He gave me a prayer book with Hebrew and German text. I: 'How was it possible to forgive one's enemies on the Day of Atonement?' He: 'The Jewish religion does not require it. The relevant prayer says Atonement for all Israelites and for the stranger in our midst, that is only for the peaceful guest among us. Judaism nowhere requires love of one's enemy.' I: 'Love of one's enemy is moral softening of the brain.' " . . . At the end of his visits, Klemperer summed up his impression: "The mood of all Jewry here is without exception the same: The terrible end is imminent. *They* will perish, but perhaps, probably, they will have time to annihilate us first."[191]

In Theresienstadt, on the eve of Yom Kippur, Redlich recorded an extraordinary scene: "The attics. A blind woman has been registered for a transport. She has been sitting without help for many hours. They are bringing her to the attic. A small child, ten years old, helps her. A spectacle not to be believed."... On the Day of Atonement, the usual was recorded: "A transport from Berlin arrived. They traveled all day Yom Kippur. Nevertheless, some women fasted all day."[192]

In Warsaw the *Aktion* went on until September 21. That day the last transport left for Treblinka with 2,196 Jews.[193] A member of Globocnik's staff must have scrutinized the Jewish calendar: The day the deportations began, July 22, was the eve of the Ninth of Av, the commemoration of the destruction of the Temple, and the last day of the *Aktion* was Yom Kippur.

Not much, of course, was recorded by the Warsaw diarists about Yom Kippur as such, but the coincidence was not missed by some. "The SS men—as is their wont—had prepared a surprise for the Jews on the Day of Atonement," Peretz Opoczynski, whose fragmentary diaries were found in the Oneg Shabbat archives, noted on September 21.... "In honor of the Day of Atonement the factories were not working, to make believe that the Jewish religion was tolerated. In return, however, new sorrow was being added to the Jewish cup of woe. The SS men are alleged to have finally left Warsaw yesterday. The fact that today's action has been carried out by the 'shop-commissars,' Jewish policemen and 'shop guards' [*Werkschutz*], and not by the German soldiers, seems to fully confirm the rumor. The Day of Atonement has brought us plenty of fear and shattered nerves."[194] And yet, on September 21, Lewin noted: "In our courtyard Jews are praying, pouring out their cares to the Creator."[195]

In Kovno, Rabbi Shapiro did inform the inhabitants that workers had to go to work and he allowed those in poor health to eat, according to Tory's diary entry of September 20. "Despite the ban on praying in public," Tory further recorded, "many *minyanim* [prayer quorums of ten Jewish men] assembled in the ghetto. The wording of '*Hazkarat neshamot*' [remembrance of souls] had been printed on a typewriter by the council because of the shortage of prayer books ... for the Holy Days." The next day Tory recorded that many workers fasted at their workplaces. Two [German] officials were inspecting the ghetto on that day: "They went in the direction of the hospital where a prayer meeting was taking place.

The praying Jews were warned only at the last moment, but succeeded in dispersing before the Germans came."[196]

None of this secretiveness was necessary in Vilna. Apart from smaller services, an official prayer service was organized in the hall of the ghetto theater, with a cantor and a choir. Gens attended, and so did all the Jewish officials of the ghetto. "After Kol Nidre," Kruk noted, "[Tsemakh] Feldstein announces that Mr. Gens will speak. Gens says: let us begin with a kaddish [prayer for the dead] for those who are gone. We have gone through a hard year; let us pray to God that next year will be easier. We must be hard, disciplined, and industrious. At the beginning of Gens's speech, a great lament broke out. It was the wind of Ponar, of death of the children, women, and men who were torn away. Even Gens was strongly moved."[197]

There was of course no place for young Rudashevski at the main prayer meeting. "It is Yom Kippur eve," he noted on the twentieth. "A sad mood suffuses the ghetto. People have had such a sad Holy Day feeling. I am as far from religion now as before the ghetto. Nevertheless, this holiday, drenched in blood and sorrow, which is solemnized in the ghetto, now penetrates my heart. . . . People sit at home and weep. They remind themselves of the past. . . . The hearts which have turned to stone in the grip of the ghetto woes and did not have time to weep their fill have now on this evening of lamentation poured out all their bitterness."[198]

In Kovno and Vilna the memory of the massacres of the previous year rekindled the sorrow in the September days of 1942. In Lodz, as in Warsaw, the inhabitants were barely reaching the end of a period of unequaled extermination and, of course, the chroniclers abstained from any comment. Yom Kippur was a workday like any other. Yet it was not an entirely ordinary day: "Great appreciation and gratitude were felt for the especially good and substantial midday meal—a potato and pea dish cooked with bones—that was served to mark the holiday. The midday meal was the sole evidence of the holiday, which is normally celebrated so solemnly. Only a few private stores were closed."[199]

Such lack of loftier feelings angered Rosenfeld, although he could not have forgotten the events of the past weeks and, more generally, the utter misery of the ghetto population. Yet, on September 23, he did not restrain his feelings: "In shirts, gloves—in the ghetto workshops, hundreds of Eastern Jews were shopping on YK [Yom Kippur], no Western Jew was to be seen. Hardening of the human spirit, deafness to the heart, alienation. Basest mentality doesn't matter. What kind of human beings are these? Terrible, downcast, melancholy, sobering."[200]

IX

While, during the second half of 1942, the hunting down of Jews and their wholesale murder had spread to every country and territory in Germany's direct grip, for some segments of European Jewry the attitudes of a few governments, either allied with the Reich or neutral, were becoming a matter of life and death.

Crossing the Spanish border was relatively easy following the defeat of France, as we saw, provided the (mainly Jewish) refugees had visas for a further destination. Once the deportations from France started, escape via Spain became a chance of survival. By then, however, Spanish border guards were sending the fleeing Jews back to France. A few months later, after the Allied landing in North Africa and the occupation of the whole of France by the Germans, refugees—Jewish and others—also tried to cross into Spain in order to join the Allied forces in North Africa. The Spaniards soon found themselves caught between the contrary pressures of Germany and of the Anglo-Saxon powers. It took a direct threat from Churchill, in April 1943, to convince Franco that, at that stage of the war, Spain's frontiers could not be fully closed.[201]

No such problems arose between Germany and Switzerland. Authority over the foreigners living in Switzerland and over immigration was in the hands of the Federal Department of Justice and Police (headed since 1940 by Federal Councillor Eduard von Steiger) and, more specifically, in the hands of Heinrich Rothmund's Police Division. During 1942 Swiss border police and customs officials were steadily reinforced by army units whose main task became to hunt down Jewish refugees. On the other side of the border, well remunerated but often unreliable guides (including at times outright criminals who defrauded their hapless charges and in some cases even murdered them for their money and valuables) tried to slip through the blockade.

On July 16, 1942 (the day the mass roundups started in Paris), the Intelligence and Security Division of the Swiss army warned Rothmund's deputy, Robert Jezler. "We have noticed that for some time now the number of Jewish, Dutch and Belgian civilian refugees, as well as that of Polish refugees living in these countries, had been increasing in an alarming manner. All of them leave their own country for the same reason: to avoid the work camps to which they are sent by the occupying power. . . . Urgent measures would seem to be needed to prevent whole groups of refugees from entering our country, as has been the case recently. . . . In our opinion certain elements should be turned back; the relevant organizations would then no doubt hear about the measures taken, and this would put an end to their activities."[202] Identifying these "certain elements" did not demand much imagination.

The Police Division faced a decision whose full consequences it knew: "We have not been able recently to decide about sending these people back," Jezler wrote on July 30. "Reports confirming each other and entirely reliable about the way the deportations are taking place and about the situation in the Jewish areas in the East are so horrible that one has to understand the desperate attempts of the refugees to escape such a fate; one cannot anymore take the responsibility of sending them back."[203]

Rothmund thought otherwise. A decree of October 17, 1939, ordered the sending back of refugees who entered Switzerland illegally. Until the summer of 1942 it had not been strictly applied by all cantonal authorities (which often sent the refugees to internment camps); from then on it was to be enforced. On August 4, Steiger signed the directive. In a circular sent on August 13 to all relevant civilian and military authorities, the police division, after indicating that the number of refugees, "mainly Jews of various nationalities," arriving at the border had grown to an average of twenty-one persons a day over the previous two weeks, explained that both for security and economic reasons, these refugees had to be sent back. *Political refugees were not to be sent back but "persons who have fled purely on racial grounds, for example Jews, cannot be considered political refugees"* (emphasis in original).[204] At the first attempt to cross the border the refugee was to be sent back; if a further attempt took place, the refugee was to be delivered to the army or the relevant authorities on the other side despite all the risks involved."[205]

From the minutes of a police directors' conference that took place on August 28, 1942, it becomes amply clear that everyone knew that excluding Jews from the status of political refugees was "a farce" in Rothmund's own words. Even Steiger admitted as much: "Political Refugees. Theory is no good," the federal councillor declared. "Jews are also in a way political refugees."[206] Notwithstanding some exceptions, Swiss policy of sending Jews back remained unchanged until late 1943 and, more selectively, even beyond that date.

Throughout the first years of the war Sweden had been no less restrictive than Switzerland. Yet, as information about the exterminations accumulated in Stockholm (as it did in Bern), and once the deportations reached Scandinavia, the attitude of the Swedish Foreign Ministry, and particularly of the undersecretary in charge of immigration, Gösta Engzell, changed. When, in November 1942, the deportations from Norway started, the Swedes reacted: Jews from Norway—and not only those who were Norwegian citizens—who managed to flee to Sweden were given asylum. From then on Swedish help to Jews was extended not only to the whole of Scandinavia but also in other rescue operations on the Continent.[207] Whether Sweden's about-face was induced by humanitarian feelings or by a more prosaic assessment of the course of the war is a moot question. Both incentives were probably at work in Engzell's mind and in those of his colleagues from the Foreign Ministry.[208]

Himmler's attempt, during his visit to Helsinki in July 1942, to persuade the Finns to deliver the foreign Jews living in the country (about 150 to 200 people at that time) to Germany offers a telling example of the relentlessness of the Nazi anti-Jewish campaign.[209] No colonization in the East was at stake, or any economic benefit for the *Volksgemeinschaft,* or any other political or economic advantage so often adduced to explain the Nazi anti-Jewish drive—nothing except mere ideological fury.

Although we do not know Prime Minister Johan Rangell's answer to Himmler's request, we know of the Reichsführer's demand as such.[210] The Finnish secret police started drawing lists of foreign Jews who could be deported (thirty-five persons according to some estimates) and delivered to the Germans in Estonia.[211] The rumor spread; protests erupted in the government and in public opinion. Finally the number of deportees was reduced to eight. On November 6, 1942, they were deported to Tallinn: One survived the war.[212]

The Jewish communities of Romania, Hungary, and Bulgaria represented a prize of quite different magnitude. No sooner had the Germans launched their major extermination campaign in the General Government and in Western Europe than pressure to deliver the Jews of southeastern Europe started. On September 24, 1942, Luther noted that Ribbentrop had asked him "to accelerate as much as possible the evacuation of Jews from the most diverse European countries, "as it is proven that everywhere the Jews incite against us and have to be considered responsible for sabotage acts and assassination attempts."[213]

The Germans did score an initial success in Romania when Antonescu authorized the deportation of Romanian Jews living in Germany or in German-occupied countries.[214] In principle Bucharest had promised that the deportation of the approximately three hundred thousand Jews still living in Romania as such would follow. At the end of July 1942 Eichmann had no doubts whatsoever: "From September 10, 1942, the Jews of Romania could foreseeably be transferred to the Lublin district in ongoing transports; there, those able to work will be allocated for labor while the remaining part will be subjected to special treatment."[215] What followed came as a complete surprise: The Romanians changed their mind.

The reasons for the turnabout in Bucharest have been attributed to the whole array of reasons: repeated interventions by Jewish personalities, by the papal nuncio, Monsignor Andrea Cassulo, and the Swiss minister, René de Weck; the bribing of officials and of Ion Antonescu's family by wealthy Romanian Jews and, also, Antonescu's resentment of German interference in an essentially internal matter.[216] By October it became clear that the Romanians were stalling. On October 11 Antonescu ordered the postponement of the deportations until the spring, and on November 11 Mihai Antonescu told Himmler's delegate in Bucharest, Gustav Richter, to his face that the Germans were behaving barbarically toward the Jews.[217]

Although by the end of 1942, the Romanian Jewish policy had obviously shifted and although there were even rumors that Bucharest would allow Jews from Transnistria to leave for Palestine (for adequate per capita remuneration)—a move the Germans tried to stop by all means—Luther, increasingly spurned by Ribbentrop and in dire need of proving commitment for all to see, hurled another desperate exhortation at Ambassador Manfred von Killinger on January 23, 1943. The ambassador was ordered to inform the Romanians that the Italians would be brought to heel regarding the deportations from Western Europe. All

European states were being made aware of the principles announced by the Führer in his latest speech [presumably the speech of November 8, 1942, in which Hitler again dwelled on his prophecy and its ongoing vindication]. "Please inform Romanian government," Luther went on "that Jews are elements of disintegration, that they perpetrate sabotage and help enemy intelligence activities. The German government has many proofs of the above. The evacuation of the Jews from Europe is therefore a compelling necessity for the security of the continent. The positive attitude adopted until now by the Romanian government regarding the Jewish question justified our hope that it would continue to offer its exemplary support to the common cause."[218]

Luther's rhetoric did not help. And at the end of January, Himmler ordered Richter back to Berlin.[219] In the meantime, it should be kept in mind, the Romanian forces near Stalingrad had been destroyed, the German Sixth Army was on the brink of surrender, and in North Africa, the Allies were gaining control of much of the area stretching from the Atlantic to the Egyptian border.

In Hungary events would ultimately take a different course, but, in early 1943, the situation still looked similar to that in Romania. A year before, in March 1942, as we saw, the ultraconservative and pro-German prime minister Laszlo Bardossy had been dismissed by Horthy and replaced by the more moderate Miklós Kallay. During the first six months of Kallay's premiership, however—that is, during the phase of German military successes—no change occurred in Hungarian policies. In the spring of 1942, in response to German pressure, one-third of the Hungarian armed forces, the Second Hungarian Army, was sent to the Eastern front and positioned along the Don River. At the same time Horthy and Kallay allowed widespread volunteering of German Hungarians (mostly belonging to the pro-Nazi *Volksbund*) for the SS, although the volunteers had to give up their Hungarian citizenship. A new law ordered the nationalization of land belonging to Jews. The treatment of Jews conscripted into labor battalions on the Eastern Front was so harsh that thousands died.

More ominously, radical anti-Jewish initiatives were planned at the same time by the Hungarian military, apparently with the knowledge and even support of Kallay's staff: The deportation of Hungarian Jews, first of one hundred thousand of them, was discussed with the Germans.

It remains unclear to this day whether Horthy or even Kallay himself knew of these contacts. As historian Yehuda Bauer has pointed out, the entire episode remains something of a mystery.[220]

In the fall of 1942 the change in policy started, obviously as a result of the shift in the global strategic balance. In October, when the Germans demanded that the Jews of Hungary be compelled to wear the yellow star as a first step toward their deportation, Kallay refused. At the same time efforts were undertaken by the defense minister to alleviate the fate of the Jewish conscripts in the labor battalion.[221] The change found its expression on October 5, when Luther met the Hungarian ambassador in Berlin, Döme Sztójay, and demanded that the deportation of Hungary's eight hundred thousand Jews should start. The ambassador mentioned rumors about the fate of deported Jews: Prime Minister Kallay did not want to reproach himself later with having delivered Hungarian Jews to misery or possibly even worse. Luther replied that the Jews were employed in road building and that later they would be settled in a reservation.[222] The Hungarians were not convinced. The German demand was rejected. In April 1943, as we shall see, Hitler would personally intervene with Horthy, to no immediate avail. In January 1943 the Second Hungarian Army had been completely destroyed near Voronezh.

In Bulgaria, Jewish policy also moved from cooperation with Germany to an increasingly independent stance. In June 1942 the Bulgarian parliament had authorized the government "to implement a solution of the Jewish problem:" A notorious anti-Semite, Alexander Beleff, was appointed commissar for Jewish affairs in the Ministry of the Interior. The first victims of King Boris's policies of collaboration were the Jews of Thracia (a former Greek province) and Macedonia (a formerly Yugoslav province), areas Bulgaria had received as a reward for joining the German campaign against its two neighbors, in April 1941. These eleven thousand foreign Jews (from Sofia's standpoint), were rounded up by the Bulgarian police, delivered to the Germans, and shipped to their death in Treblinka, in March and April 1943. The deportation of native Bulgarian Jews would, as we shall see, become a different matter altogether.

Italy was certainly not setting the right example for these countries of Southeastern Europe. Of course Mussolini was not fooled by Himmler's account about the fate of the Jews during the Reichsführer's visit to the *Duce* on

October 11, 1942. The SS chief admitted that in the eastern territories the Germans had to shoot a "not unmeaningful number" of Jews, including women and youngsters as even these were messengers of the partisans; according to Himmler, Mussolini's response was that "this represented the only possible solution." Otherwise Himmler spoke of labor camps, of road work, of Theresienstadt—and of the many Jews shot by the Russians whenever the Germans tried to chase them to the Soviet side through gaps in the front lines.[223] The Italians had their own sources of information.

As indicated by historian Jonathan Steinberg, the head of the occupied territories division at the Italian Ministry of Foreign Affairs recorded at the end of November 1942: "The Germans continue imperturbably to massacre Jews." He further mentioned foreign radio reports according to which six to seven thousand Warsaw Jews were deported each day and exterminated. The Germans, according to him, had already murdered one million Jews. King Vittorio Emmanuele III, it seems, knew as well. Thus with the implicit support of the highest levels of the state, wherever it could, in Croatia, in Greece, and in France, Italy was protecting the Jews. The Germans, as Goebbels's diaries show, were fuming but there was little they could do.[224]

In Croatia, as the Germans were busy deporting the very last Jews under their control, the Italians, despite Hitler's promise to Pavelic and an order from Mussolini to arrest the 5,000 Jews of their zone, did not act. In France matters came to a head. Not only did the Italian consul general in Nice, Alberto Calisse, refuse to have the identity papers of Jews marked, but during the last days of December 1942 he forbade the transfer of Jews from the Italian zone to the German-occupied areas, in the face of an order from Vichy (which, in principle, had jurisdiction over Jewish affairs on all of French territory). Calisse's stand was backed within days by the Foreign Ministry in Rome.[225]

There was true refinement in the Italian response: The French were told that the Italians would agree to the transfer of French Jews but not to that of foreign Jews; Vichy was paralyzed.[226] When, in January 1943, the German ambassador in Rome, Hans Georg von Mackensen, demanded of Ciano that these decisions be rescinded, Mussolini's minister put the Germans on the spot: As the matter was complex, Ciano argued, Berlin had to formulate its demands in a detailed written memorandum that would be duly studied.[227]

In early 1943 Ciano was appointed ambassador to the Vatican and the *Duce* himself took over foreign affairs. A few days beforehand Mussolini and Ciano had seen the cable sent on January 3 by the Italian ambassador in Berlin, Dino Alfieri: "Regarding the fate of [deported German Jews], like that of Polish, Russian, Dutch and even French Jews, there cannot be much doubt. . . . Even the SS talk about the mass executions. . . . A person who was there recalled with horror some scenes of executions by machine guns of nude women and children lined up at the mouth of a common ditch. About the tales of torture running the gamut I will limit myself to the one told to my colleague by an SS official who confided that he hurled babies of six months against a wall, shattering them, to give an example to his men, tired and shaken by an execution that was particularly horrible because of the number of victims."[228]

Italian obstruction of German anti-Jewish measures would continue, as we shall see, during the spring and summer of 1943, until the German occupation of the country.

At the other end of the Continent, in Norway, the German anti-Jewish campaign had started in the fall of 1942. The usual decrees turned the small Jewish population into a group of pariahs. On November 20 the deportations began by ship from Oslo to Stettin, then by train on to Auschwitz. By the end of February 1943 the Jewish community of Norway had ceased to exist: More than 700 Jews had been murdered and some 900 had fled to Sweden.[229]

X

Whereas during the summer and autumn of 1942, information about the "Final Solution" was accumulating in the Allied capitals, hesitations about its publication came from some unexpected quarters, such as the Polish government-in-exile. Within days of the beginning of the deportations to Treblinka, the Polish underground was informed of details about the camp and the fate of its victims by a member of the Home Army working at the Treblinka railway station. Although the information was immediately transmitted to London, the government-in-exile kept it to itself until mid-September.[230]

The government-in-exile comprised representatives of the main political parties in the homeland; thus as far as possible it remained attuned to the attitudes of its constituency. And, as beforehand, the constituency itself may well have found the right expression of its feelings in the article published on August 15, 1942, at the peak of the exterminations in Treblinka, in the already mentioned *Narod*, the periodical of the mainstream Christian Democratic Party of Labor.

"At this moment," *Narod* wrote, "from behind the ghetto walls, we can hear the inhuman moans and screams of the Jews who are being murdered. Ruthless cunning is falling victim to ruthless brutal power and no Cross is visible on this battlefield, since these scenes go back to pre-Christian times. If this continues, then it will not be long before Warsaw will say farewell to its last Jew. If it were possible to conduct a funeral, it would be interesting to see the reaction. Would the coffin evoke sorrow, weeping or perhaps joy? . . . For hundreds of years, an alien, malevolent entity has inhabited the northern sections of our city. Malevolent and alien from the point of view of our interests, as well as our psyche and our hearts. So let us not strike false attitudes like professional weepers at funerals—let us be serious and honest. . . . We pity the individual Jew, the human being and, as far as possible, should he be lost or trying to hide, we will extend a helping hand. We must condemn those who denounce him. It is our duty to demand from those who allow themselves to sneer and mock to show dignity and respect in the face of death. But we are not going to pretend to be grief-stricken about a vanishing nation which, after all, was never close to our hearts."[231]

Finally the Polish Directorate of the Civilian Struggle (the *delegatura*) published a declaration on September 19, 1942, in agreement with the government-in-exile: "Without being able to actively oppose what is being done," the directorate declared, "the leadership of the Civilian Struggle in the name of the entire Polish people protests against the crimes being committed against the Jews. All the political and social organizations in Poland are united in this protest."[232] No help was promised, however, nor was any encouragement given to the Jews to flee Warsaw and hide among the Polish population.

The same policy of delayed and reluctant sharing of information was noticeable in the "mission to the West," undertaken in the fall of 1942 by the Polish courier and underground militant Jan Karski (who, it will be recalled, reported on the anti-Jewish attitude of the Polish population at the beginning of the war).[233] The underground sent Karski to the West to report on the situation in Poland but without any importance being given to the fate of the Jews. It was only after two leaders of Jewish clandestine organizations became aware of Karski's impending mission that he was allowed to meet with them, to enter the Warsaw ghetto and probably the Belzec slave labor camp. Moreover, the names of two Polish Jewish political individuals in London (Ignacy Schwarzbart and Szmuel Zygielbojm) were added to the list of people the envoy had to contact, but only as a last priority. At that stage Karski followed the line dictated to him and, acting on instructions, waited for several weeks before meeting his Jewish contacts in the British capital.[234] Yet he was apparently taken aback by the minimal importance given to the Jewish issue by both the *delegatura* and the government-in-exile.[235] He finally met Zygielbojm at the end of December 1942.[236]

The government-in-exile's position was shaped, in fact, by an array of considerations.[237] First, any emphasis put on the Jewish tragedy could deflect Western attention from the Polish tragedy per se. Thus declarations about German war crimes in Poland usually conveyed the impression that the victims were Poles in general and that there was no specificity to the fate of the Jews. In the fall, as ever-more-precise news reached Great Britain and the United States, the Polish government (hesitantly) revised its policy, in order to draw sympathy for the Polish plight, in view of what the Germans were capable of perpetrating on Jews—and on Poles.

The Polish struggle to mobilize Western public opinion was itself dominated by a major political goal: support of Poland against Soviet demands regarding the postwar eastern borders of the country. Stalin insisted on returning to the "Curzon line" of 1920, which was almost identical to the Ribbentrop-Molotov line of September 1939, whereas the Poles were adamantly demanding a return to the international border that had been recognized until the beginning of World War II.[238] In the desperate Polish campaign for political support, the Jews played an important role, and not only as competitors in the struggle for sympathy.

For the Polish leadership, Jewish influence in London and Washington was axiomatic; moreover the Poles assumed that in the conflict over the postwar borders, the Jews would be readier to side with the Soviet Union than with Poland: Hadn't their pro-Soviet sympathies been amply demonstrated during the occupation of eastern Poland between September 1939 and June 1941? In the late fall of 1942, Stanislaw Kot, a former minister of the interior and ambassador to the Soviet Union, as well as a close political ally of Prime Minister Sikorski, arrived for an extended visit to Palestine.

Given the contrary agendas of the Polish government-in-exile and the Jewish leadership in Palestine, their negotiations did not turn into helpful exchanges between the victims of a common enemy. Kot accused the Jews of Poland of lacking loyalty to their homeland and at some point threatened that if the issue of Polish anti-Semitism was not dropped, the Poles would publicize the brutal behavior of the Jewish police and possibly the callousness of the councils toward their fellow Jews.[239]

The fundamental issues remained unresolved. Although they asked Kot for a stronger Polish commitment to help the hounded Jews, the Yishuv leaders were not ready for a clear quid pro quo in support of Poland's position regarding its postwar borders. Presumably, as the Poles had surmised, their assessment of Soviet influence in the postwar world, and of the importance of Soviet political support for Zionist demands, played a major role. Morever Ben-Gurion and his companions hoped that Moscow would allow the emigration to Eretz Israel of hundreds of thousands of Jews from the USSR, particularly the refugees from Poland.[240] Finally the leaders of the Yishuv might have been skeptical about concrete Polish readiness to rescue Jews or about the Poles' ability to do so.

In the meantime the Zionist leadership itself did not demonstrate any major commitment to alleviating the fate of the Jews in Europe, nor did it seem to devote much attention to the unfolding of the ever-more-manifest catastrophe. During the historic conference that took place at the Biltmore Hotel in New York in May 1942, which led to a resolution demanding the establishment of a Jewish state in Palestine, the assumption, voiced by several of the main speakers, was that two to three million European Jews would no longer be alive at the end of the war; it did not cause any particular stir. In the months that followed, Ben-Gurion's main political agenda kept his attention away from the events in Europe and focused on the local political scene: He needed to convince part of Mapai to support the Biltmore program (which implied the partition of Palestine). He failed, and on October 25, 1942, at a meeting in Kfar Vitkin, the "B faction," opposed to partition, left the party. In the words of Tuvia Friling, the historian most supportive of Ben-Gurion's role in those years, when addressing the assembly about the situation in Europe, the Mapai leader found nothing better than the terminology commonly used until then: "Everything is at risk. The liberty of mankind, the physical existence of our people, the beginnings of our new homeland, the soul of our own movement—it is all at risk."[241] Or, as Ben-Gurion put it on several occasions in 1942 and 1943: "There has never yet been a time like today when we have all been threatened with destruction. . . . The destruction of the Jews of Europe is ruinous for Zionism for there will be no one left to build the state of Israel."[242]

On November 16, 1942, a group of Polish Jews who carried passports of the British mandate and were exchanged for German citizens living in Palestine brought firsthand information about the fate of the local Jews and about deportations from Western Europe to the killing sites in the General Government. The news shocked the Yishuv and would soon be confirmed by official Polish and Allied announcements.

In the summer of 1942 three German sources also confirmed the most horrendous information available until then about the systematic and all-encompassing aspect of the exterminations. The impact of the first two reports remained limited, as their addressees did not forward them to London or Washington; the third report, however, would have major consequences within a few months.

Kurt Gerstein, a deeply religious Protestant, was a disinfection expert in the hygiene service of the Waffen SS when, in late July 1942, he was ordered by "SS Officer Günther of the RSHA," as he later wrote, to obtain about 100 kg (220 pounds) of prussic acid (Zyklon B) and deliver it to Lublin.[243] After meeting with Globocnik, Gerstein proceeded to Belzec on August 2, possibly in the company of Globocnik and certainly in that of SS Obersturmbannführer Otto Pfannenstiel, professor of hygiene at the University of Marburg, who had accompanied him on his trip.

In the camp Gerstein witnessed the arrival of a transport from Lwov. He saw how Ukrainian auxiliaries drove the Jews out of the freight cars, how the deportees were forced to strip naked, and how, told they would undergo disinfection, they were pushed into the gas chambers. Gerstein timed the asphyxiation: The engine did not work at first. The Jews cried and wailed: "like in a synagogue," said Pfannenstiel, his eye glued to the peephole. After two and a half hours, the engine started; thirty-two minutes later all the Jews were dead.[244] In June 1950 Pfannenstiel's deposition confirmed the gist of Gerstein's report.[245]

On the train journey from Warsaw to Berlin, Gerstein, without any SS travel companion this time, started a conversation with a Swedish diplomat, Göran von Otter, attaché at the embassy in Berlin. Gerstein identified himself, gave references (among them, the Evangelical bishop in Berlin, Otto Dibelius), and told Otter what he had witnessed. Back in the capital, the diplomat checked the SS officer's credentials and, convinced of his reliability, sent a report to Stockholm. The Swedish Foreign Ministry did not respond and did not inform the Allies. After the war Otter repeatedly confirmed his conversation with Gerstein, and the Swedish Ministry of Foreign Affairs admitted having received the report and having kept it undisclosed till the end of the war.[246]

During the weeks that followed his return to Berlin, Gerstein attempted to inform the nuncio and the Swiss legation. He also informed Preysing's coadjutor, one Dr. Winter, as well as Bishop Dibelius and others: to no avail.[247] Gerstein continued to play his double role to the end. He delivered Zyklon B shipments to the camps and unsuccessfully attempted to arouse German and foreign awareness of the events. At the end of the war he wrote three reports on what he had seen and otherwise knew, and handed them to the Americans to whom he had given himself up. He was transferred to the French occupying forces and jailed in Paris as a potential war criminal. On July 25, 1945, he hanged himself in his cell.[248]

Almost exactly at the date on which Otter's report reached Stockholm, a similar report was forwarded by the Swedish consul in Stettin, Karl Ingve Vendel.[249] Vendel was in fact a Swedish intelligence agent monitoring German troop movements under the guise of consular activities and thus was also secretly in touch with some members of the German military opposition to the regime. After visiting a friend on an estate in East Prussia, Vendel, on August 9, 1942, filed a lengthy report on the situation in the General Government, which included a section on the extermination of the Jews:

"In a city, all the Jews were assembled for what was officially announced as 'delousing.' At the entrance they were forced to take off their clothes; the delousing procedure, however, consisted of gassing and, afterward, all of them would be stuffed into a mass grave. The source from which I obtained all this information on the conditions in the General Government is such that not the slightest shade of disbelief exists concerning the truthfulness of my informant's descriptions."[250]

According to historian Jozef Lewandowski's inquiry, Vendel was given the information by his friend, Count Heinrich von Lehndorff, a reserve lieutenant at Army Group Center, and by a guest who joined them at Lehndorff's estate, "Gross Steinort," in East Prussia. The guest was probably Lt. Col. Henning von Tresckow, whom we already encountered, the most active organizer of the military conspiracy against Hitler.[251] Vendel's report wasn't forwarded to the Allies either.

Again at approximately the same time, a third German source conveyed information that, in due time, put an end to Allied disbelief. In the last days of July 1942, a German industrialist, Eduard Schulte, well connected to high Nazi officials, traveled to Zurich and informed a Jewish business friend of a plan "prepared at Hitler's headquarters" for the total extermination of the Jews of Europe by the end of the year. The information was conveyed to Benjamin Sagalowitz, the press attaché of the Jewish community in Switzerland, who, in turn, alerted Gerhart Riegner, the director of the Geneva office of the World Jewish Congress. Riegner asked to send a cable to World Jewish Congress headquarters in New York and London via the American and British legations in Bern. Both the American and the British diplomats agreed.

The identically worded text sent to Washington and to London read as follows. "Received alarming report that in Führer's headquarters plan discussed and under consideration according to which all Jews in countries occupied or controlled by Germany numbering three and a half four million should after deportation and concentration in East be exterminated at one blow to resolve once and for all the Jewish question in Europe stop Action reported planned for autumn methods under discussion including prussic acid stop We transmit information with all necessary reservation as exactitude cannot be confirmed stop Informant stated to have close connections with highest German authorities and his reports generally speaking reliable."

The State Department and the Foreign Office remained skeptical, and Washington did not forward the cable to Stephen Wise, its main addressee. However, as the same cable had been received by the head of the British section of the World Jewish Congress, it was transmitted to Stephen Wise from London, notwithstanding some initial difficulties. On September 2 U.S. Undersecretary of State Sumner Welles phoned

Wise and asked him to avoid publicizing the contents of the report before it could be independently confirmed. Wise accepted.[252]

The International Committee of the Red Cross (ICRC), with headquarters in Geneva, included Swiss members only, and the Bern government's directives regarding major decisions went generally unchallenged. According to Jean-Claude Favez, the foremost historian of the ICRC and the Holocaust, Riegner insisted [in 1998] that in August or September 1942 he had informed three key members of the committee, Carl J. Burckhardt, Susanne Ferrière, and Lucie Odier, of the information that had been imparted to him. Burckhardt confirmed the facts reported by Riegner to the American consul in Geneva, Paul C. Squire, and to Riegner's colleague, Paul Guggenheim, from his own sources, sometime at the end of October 1942 and again to Riegner himself in November.[253]

Despite the information at his disposal, Burckhardt was opposed to any form of public ICRC protest, even very mildly formulated. This was also the position of the Swiss government, which had appointed Federal Councillor Philippe Etter to sit on the committee. And although at a plenary meeting on October 14, 1942, a majority of the members was in favor of a public declaration, Burckhardt and Etter blocked the initiative. Yet Burckhardt's confirmation to the American consul in Geneva of the information sent by Riegner probably contributed to the steps that followed in Washington and in London.

By November 1942, as further information about the German extermination campaign was accumulating in Washington, Welles had no choice but to tell Wise: "The reports received from Europe confirm and justify your deepest fears."[254] Within days the news became public in the United States, in England, in neutral countries, and in Palestine.

In fact, since October 1942 information about the extermination had been spreading in Great Britain, and on October 29 a protest meeting chaired by the Archbishop of Canterbury, with the participation of British, Jewish, and Polish representatives took place at the Royal Albert Hall. A month later, on November 27, the Polish government-in-exile officially recognized the murder of the country's Jews "along with Jews from other occupied countries who had been brought to Poland for this purpose."

On December 10 a detailed report about the mass exterminations in Poland was submitted to the Foreign Office by the Polish ambassador to London, Count Edward Raczynski. The total and systematic eradication of the Jewish population of Poland was once again confirmed. The information reached Churchill, who demanded additional details. At this point the diplomatic obfuscations both in London and in Washington finally stopped, and on December 14 Foreign Secretary Anthony Eden informed the cabinet of what was known about the fate of the Jews of Europe.[255]

A few days beforehand, on December 8, Roosevelt had received a delegation of Jewish leaders. Although the half hour conversation was in and of itself of a rather perfunctory nature, Roosevelt clearly indicated that he knew what was happening: "The government of the United States," he is quoted as saying, "is very well acquainted with most of the facts you are now bringing to our attention. Unfortunately, we have received confirmation from many sources. . . . Representatives of the United States government in Switzerland and other neutral countries have given us proof that confirms the horrors discussed by you."[256] Roosevelt also readily agreed to a public declaration.[257] On December 17 all the Allied governments and the "Free French National Committee" solemnly announced that the Jews of Europe were being exterminated, vowing that "those responsible for these crimes would not escape retribution."[258]

In his diaries Goebbels dismissed the significance of the protests arising in London and Washington, but his instructions to the press demanded a sharp counterattack describing atrocities perpetrated by the Allies, "in order to get away from the unpleasant topic of the Jews."[259] Thus, for representatives of the German newspapers, the extermination was no longer denied but had to be downplayed as quickly as possible.

In that respect Himmler had some problems of his own. On November 20 he passed on to Müller "a memorandum" written by Stephen Wise two months beforehand. Although the memorandum attached to Himmler's letter has not been found, its date as such, what we know of Wise's communications at the time, and Himmler's response all imply that the president of the World Jewish Congress had used the information sent by the representative of the Association of Orthodox Rabbis in Switzerland, Isaac Sternbuch, to the president of Agudath Israel in New York, Jacob

Rosenheim. According to this information, "the corpses of the murdered victims are used for the manufacture of soap and artificial fertilizer."[260] The Reichsführer was indignant about such calumny. He wanted Müller "to guarantee" that everywhere the corpses were either burned or buried and that "nowhere can something else happen with the bodies."[261]

XI

On March 17, 1942, Gerhard Riegner and Richard Lichtheim were received by Monsignor Filippe Bernardini, the apostolic nuncio in Bern. Following the meeting, a lengthy memorandum about the fate of the European Jews in the countries under German rule or control was submitted to the Nuncio and, undoubtedly, sent by him to the Vatican. The report listed camps, ghettos and mass executions in considerable detail.[262]

In fact, since the beginning of 1942, news about the extermination of the Jews were reaching the Vatican from the most diverse sources. As previously mentioned, in February 1942 German prelates were already informed about the mass murder of Jews in the Baltic countries. On March 9 Giuseppe Burzio, the Vatican's chargé d'affaires in Bratislava, sent a particularly ominous report. After having previously warned of the imminent beginning of the deportation from Slovakia to Poland and after stating in his March 9 telegram that the intervention with Tuka to have deportations postponed had failed, Burzio ended his communication with a sentence that has become an indelible part of the events: "The deportation of 80,000 people to Poland, at the mercy of the Germans, is equivalent to the condemnation of a majority to a certain death" [*La deportazione di 80,000 persone in Polania alla merce' dei tedeschi equivale condannare la gran parte a una morte sicura*].[263]

In May the Italian abbot Piero Scavizzi, who frequently traveled to Poland, officially with a hospital train but possibly on secret missions for the Vatican, sent the following report directly to Pius XII: "The struggle against the Jews is implacable and constantly intensifying, with deportations and mass executions. The massacre of the Jews in the Ukraine is by now nearly complete. In Poland and Germany they want to complete it also, with a system of murders."[264]

Among the messages that continued to arrive at the Vatican during the following months, one carried particular weight due to the standing of its author and his direct witnessing of the events: It was the letter sent on August 31, 1942, by the spiritual leader of the Uniate Catholic Church in Lwov, Metropolitan Andrei Sheptyskyi. The letter's importance could not have escaped the pope or Sheptyskyi's friend at the Vatican, the French cardinal Eugène Tisserant. The metropolitan, although known for his personal friendship for Jews, did repeatedly condemn "Judeo-Bolshevism" in letters to the Vatican during the Soviet occupation of eastern Galicia and, like most nationalist Ukrainians, enthusiastically greeted the Germans when they entered eastern Poland.[265] Thus the author's credentials were impeccable. His letter was written after the deportation of some 50,000 Jews from Lwov.

"Liberated by the German army from the Bolshevik yoke," the metropolitan wrote, "we felt a certain relief. . . . [However], gradually the German [government] instituted a regime of truly unbelievable terror and corruption. . . . Now everybody agrees that the German regime is perhaps more evil and diabolic than the Bolshevik. For more than a year, not a day has passed without the most horrible crimes being committed. The Jews are the primary victims. In time, they began to kill Jews openly in the streets, in full view of the public. The number of Jews killed in our region has certainly surpassed 200,000."[266] Although the pope answered the metropolitan's letter, not a single word addressed the Jewish issue. In the meantime the liquidation of the Warsaw ghetto was known to all, and week after week the deportations from the West were carrying their loads of Jews to "unknown destinations," by then well known to the Vatican.

On September 26, 1942, the American minister to the Holy See, Myron C. Taylor, delivered a detailed note to Secretary of State Maglione: "The following was received from the Geneva Office of the Jewish Agency for Palestine in a letter dated August 30, 1942. The office received the report from two reliable eyewitnesses (Aryans), one of whom came on August 14 from Poland. (1) Liquidation of the Warsaw ghetto is taking place. Without any distinction all Jews, irrespective of age or sex, are being removed from the Ghetto in groups and shot. . . . (2) These mass executions take place, not in Warsaw, but in especially prepared camps for the purpose, one of which is stated to be in Belzek. . . . (3) Jews deported from Germany, Belgium, Holland, France and Slovakia are sent to be butchered, while Aryans deported to the East from Holland and France are genuinely used for work." Taylor's note ended as follows. "I should much appreciate it if Your Eminence could inform me whether the Vatican has any information that would tend to confirm the reports contained in this memorandum. If so, I should like to know whether the Holy Father has any suggestion as to any practical manner in which the forces of civilized public opinion could be utilized in order to prevent a continuation of these barbarities."[267]

The cardinal secretary of state's answer was handed to the American chargé d'áffaires, Harold Tittman, who, on October 10, cabled the gist of it to Washington: "Holy See replied today to Mr. Taylor's letter regarding the predicament of the Jews in Poland in an informal and unsigned statement handed me by the Cardinal Secretary of State. After thanking Ambassador Taylor for bringing the matter to the attention of the Holy See the statement says that reports of severe measures taken against non-Aryans have also reached the Holy See from other sources but that up to the present time it has not been possible to verify the accuracy thereof. However, the statement adds, it is well known that the Holy See is taking advantage of every opportunity offered in order to mitigate the suffering of non-Aryans."[268]

The British minister to the Vatican, Francis d'Arcy Osborne, confided his bitterness about the pope's obstinate silence in private letters and in his diary: "The more I think of it," he wrote in his diary on December 13, "the more I am revolted by Hitler's massacre of the Jewish race on the one hand and, on the other, by the Vatican's apparently exclusive preoccupation with the . . . possibilities of the bombardment of Rome." A few days later Osborne wrote to the cardinal secretary of state that "instead of thinking of nothing but the bombing of Rome, the Vatican should consider its duties in respect of the unprecedented crime against humanity of Hitler's campaign of extermination of the Jews."[269] The Vatican's answer, as conveyed by Maglione, was brutal: "The pope could not condemn 'particular atrocities' or verify the numbers of Jews killed that had been reported by the Allies."[270]

In the Vatican's view the pope did speak up in his Christmas Eve message of 1942. On page 24 of the twenty-six-page text, broadcast on "Radio Vatican," the pontiff declared: "Humanity owes this vow to lead humanity back to divine law to hundreds of thousands of people who, through no fault of their own and solely because of their nation or their race, have been condemned to death or progressive extinction." And Pius XII then added: "Humanity owes this vow to the thousands upon thousands of noncombatants—women, children, the sick and the aged; those whom the air war—and we have, from the outset, often denounced its horrors—has deprived, without distinction of life, possessions, health, homes, refuges and places of worship."[271]

Mussolini scoffed at the speech's platitudes; Tittman and the Polish ambassador both expressed their disappointment to the pope; even the French ambassador was apparently perplexed.[272] It seems that most German officials also missed the portent of the papal address: Ambassador Bergen, who, at the Vatican, followed every detail of Pius's policy, did not refer to the speech at all. As for Goebbels, the master interpreter of any propaganda move, his opinion of the papal speech was entirely dismissive: "The Christmas speech of the pope is without any deep significance," he noted on December 26. "It carries on in generalities that are received with complete lack of interest among the countries at war."[273] The only German document that interpreted the speech as an attack on the basic principles of National Socialist Germany and also on its persecution of Jews and Poles was an anonymous RSHA report, whose date is unclear, although it must have been drafted between December 25, 1942, and January 15, 1943, when it was addressed to the Foreign Ministry.[274]

The pope was convinced that he had been well understood. According to Osborne's January 5, 1943, report to London, the pontiff believed that his message "had satisfied all demands recently made on him to speak out."[275]

In early July 1942 Henry Montor, the president of the United Palestine Appeal in the United States, asked Lichtheim to send him a 1,500-word article reviewing "the position of Jews in Europe." "I feel at present quite unable to write a 'report,'" Lichtheim answered Montor on August 13, "a survey, something cool and clear and reasonable.... So I wrote not a survey but something more personal—an article, if you like—or an essay, not of 1,500 words, but of 4,000, giving more of my own feelings than of the 'facts.'" The letter concluded with "all good wishes for the New Year to you and the happier Jews of 'God's own country.'" Lichtheim titled his essay "What Is Happening to the Jews of Europe":

"A letter has reached me from the United States, asking me 'to review the position of Jews in Europe.' This I cannot do because the Jews are today no more in a 'position' than the waters of a rapid rushing down into some canyon, or the dust of the desert lifted by a tornado and blown in all directions.

"I cannot even tell you how many Jews there are at present in this or that town, in this or that country, because at the very moment of writing thousands of them are fleeing hither and thither, from Belgium and Holland to France (hoping to escape to Switzerland), from Germany—because deportation to Poland was imminent—to France and Belgium, where the same orders for deportation had just been issued. Trapped mice running in circles. They are fleeing from Slovakia to Hungary, from Croatia to Italy. At the same time, thousands are being shifted under Nazi supervision to forced labor camps in the country further east, while other thousands just arrived from Germany or Austria are thrown into the ghettos of Riga or Lublin."

As Lichtheim was writing his "essay," information was reaching Allied and neutral countries from increasingly reliable sources about what was really happening to the European Jews, as we saw. And yet, even without indications about the extermination, Lichtheim's letter conveyed his anguish in sentences that, decades later, can sear the reader's mind: "I am bursting with facts," he went on, "but I cannot tell them in an article of a few thousand words. I would have to write for years and years. . . . That means I really cannot tell you what has happened and is happening to five million persecuted Jews in Hitler's Europe. Nobody will ever tell the story—a story of five million personal tragedies every one of which would fill a volume."[276]

CHAPTER VIII

March 1943–October 1943

"My dear little Daddy, bad news: After my aunt, it's my turn to leave." Thus began the hasty pencil-written card sent on February 12, 1943, from Drancy by seventeen-year-old Louise Jacobson to her father in Paris. Both Louise's parents—divorced in 1939—were French Jews who had emigrated from Russia to Paris before World War I. Louise and her siblings were born in France and all were French citizens. Louise's father was a master cabinetmaker; his small business had been "Aryanized," and, like all French Jews (naturalized or not), he was waiting.

Louise and her mother had been arrested in the fall of 1942, following an anonymous denunciation: They were not wearing their stars and supposedly were active communists. On a demand from the SD, French police officers searched their home and indeed discovered communist pamphlets (belonging in fact to Louise's brother and brother-in-law, both prisoners of war). A neighbor must have seen Louise's sister hiding the subversive literature under a stack of coal, in the cellar. While her mother remained in a Paris jail, Louise was transferred to Drancy in late 1942 and in February 1943, slated for deportation.

"Never mind," Louise went on. "I am in excellent spirits, like everybody else. You should not worry, Daddy. First, I am leaving in very good shape. This last week I have eaten very, very well. I got two packages by proxy, one from a friend who was just deported, the other from my aunt. Now your package arrived, exactly at the right moment.

"I can see your face, my dear Daddy, and, that's precisely why I would like you to have as much courage as I do. . . . You should send the news to the Vichy zone [to her sister, among others] but carefully. As for Mother, it would probably be better if she knew nothing. It is entirely unnecessary that she be worried, mainly as I may well be back before she gets out of jail.

"We leave tomorrow morning. I am with my friends, as many are leaving. I entrusted my watch and all my other belongings to decent people from my room. My daddy, I kiss you a hundred thousand times with all my strength. Be courageous and see you soon [*Courage et à bientôt*], your daughter Louise."[1]

On February 13, 1943, Louise left for Auschwitz in transport number 48 with one thousand other French Jews. A surviving female friend, a chemical engineer, went through the selection with her. "Tell them that you are a chemist," Irma had whispered. When her turn arrived and she was asked about her profession, Louise declared: "Student"; she was sent to the left, to the gas chamber.[2]

I

Five months after Stalingrad, the last German attempt to regain the military initiative failed at the decisive battles of Kursk and Orel. From July 1943, the Soviet offensives determined the evolution of the war on the Eastern Front.[3] Kiev was liberated on November 6, and in mid-January 1944 the German siege of Leningrad was definitively broken.

In the meantime the remnants of the Afrika Korps had surrendered in Tunisia, and in July 1943, while the Germans were being battered on the Eastern Front, British and American forces landed in Sicily. Before the month was over the military disasters swept the *Duce* away. On July 24, 1943, a majority of the Fascist Grand Council voted a motion of no confidence in their own leader. On the twenty-fifth, the king briefly received Mussolini and informed him of his dismissal and his replacement by Marshal Pietro Badoglio as the new head of the Italian government. As he left the king's residence the Italian dictator was arrested. Without a single shot being fired, the fascist regime had collapsed. The former *Duce* was moved from Rome to the island of Ponza and finally imprisoned at Gran Sasso, in the Appenines. Although German paratroopers succeeded in liberating Hitler's ally on September 12, and the Führer appointed him the head of a fascist puppet state in northern Italy (the

"Italian Social Republic"), a broken and sick Mussolini regained neither popular acceptance nor power.

English and American troops landed in southern Italy on September 3, and on the eighth the Allies announced the armistice secretly signed by Badoglio the day of the landing. The German reaction was immediate: On the ninth and the tenth the Wehrmacht, which had been moving troops to Italy for several weeks (also from the Eastern Front), occupied the northern and central parts of the country and seized all Italian-controlled areas in the Balkans and in France. The Allies remained entrenched in the south of the peninsula; over the coming months their northward advance would be slow.

The Allied successes on land were compounded by the steadily fiercer bombing campaign against both German military targets and cities. The July 1943 British bombing of Hamburg and the resulting "firestorm" caused the death of some thirty to forty thousand civilians. The nighttime raids were British, the daytime operations American.

Despite the uninterrupted series of military disasters and the increasing vacillation of "allies" such as Hungary and Finland, Hitler was far from considering the war lost in the fall of 1943. New fighter planes would put an end to the Anglo-American bombing campaign, long-range rockets would destroy London and play havoc with any Allied invasion plans, newly formed divisions equipped with the heaviest tanks ever built (just rolling out of the factories) would stem the Soviet advance. And if a military stalemate was achieved for some time, the Grand Alliance would crumble, due to its inherent political-military tensions.

However, such optimistic forecasts could not alter the unmistakable sense of crisis that had been spreading both in the German population and among the Reich leadership since the outset of 1943. Though Hitler's authority was not in question, and no major step could be taken without his approval, the Nazi leader's increasing obsession with every detail of the military situation (due in part to his endemic lack of confidence in his generals) interfered with the rational running of operations. His growing reluctance to speak in public created further uncertainty among the population and may have weakened the quasi-religious confidence that, until then, had set him beyond any criticism.

In early 1943 Hitler appointed a "Committee of Three"—Lammers,

Bormann, Keitel—to achieve some coordination among the overlapping and competing state, party, and military agencies. Yet within a few months the committee's authority dwindled, as ministers intent on defending their own power positions steadily undermined its initiatives. Only Bormann's influence kept growing: Above and beyond his control of the party, he had become the "Führer's secretary," and Hitler increasingly relied on him. Independently Himmler's power reached new heights when, in August 1943, he replaced Frick as minister of the interior. Goebbels, on the other hand, as clever an intriguer as he was, reaped no added power from preaching the "total war" effort, at least not in the immediate future; nor did he succeed, despite Speer's support, in reviving Göring's authority as head of the ministerial committee for the defense of the Reich (established at the beginning of the war) to counter the Committee of Three, due to Hitler's fury at the repeated failures of the Luftwaffe.[4]

Whipping up anti-Jewish frenzy was, in Hitler's imagination, one of the best ways to hasten the falling apart of the enemy alliance. If the Jews were the hidden link that held capitalism and Bolshevism together, a deluge of anti-Jewish attacks endlessly repeating that the war was a Jewish war launched only for the sake of Jewish interests, could influence foreign opinion and add momentum to the antagonism between the West and the Soviet Union. Moreover, at this time of peril for Fortress Europe, stamping out all remnants of the internal foe remained of the highest importance. Jews were—and Hitler kept harping on it—the subterranean communication line between all enemy groups; they spread defeatist rumors and hostile propaganda, and they were the ferment of treason in countries that Germany had not yet set under its heel. The renewed ferocity of the anti-Jewish campaign after Stalingrad had its inner logic.

A few days after the surrender of the Sixth Army, Goebbels opened the floodgates of German rage: The minister's "total war" speech, delivered at the Sportpalast on February 18, was in many ways the epitome of the regime's propaganda style: the unleashing of demented passion controlled by the most careful staging and orchestration. The huge crowd packing the hall had been carefully selected to represent all parts of the

Volk, to be ideologically reliable, and thus ready to deliver the expected response. The event was broadcast on all German radio stations to the nation and the world. And, as Goebbels's speech was meant to mobilize every last spark of energy, it had to brandish *the* mobilizing myth of the regime:

"Behind the onrushing Soviet divisions we can see the Jewish liquidation squads—behind which loom terror, the spectre of mass starvation and unbridled anarchy in Europe. Here once more international Jewry has been the diabolical ferment of decomposition, cynically gratified at the idea of throwing the world into the deepest disorder and thus engineering the ruin of cultures thousands of years old, cultures with which it never felt anything in common. . . . We have never been afraid of the Jews and today we are less afraid of them than ever. We have unmasked Jewry's rapid and infamous maneuvers to deceive the world in fourteen years of struggle before the accession to power and in a ten years' struggle afterwards. The aim of Bolshevism is the world revolution of the Jews. . . . Germany in any case has no intention of bowing to this threat, but means to counter it in time and if necessary with the most complete and radical extermi—[correcting himself]—elimination" [*Ausrott—Ausschaltung*] [Applause. Shouts of "Out with the Jews." Laughter].

The lengthy speech reached its climactic finale in the paraphrase of a verse written by poet Theodor Körner at the time of the national uprising against Napoleon, in 1814: "Und jetzt Volk, steh auf! Und Sturm brich los!" ("And now people, stand up and storm, break loose!").[5] Wild cheering greeted the apocalyptic outburst, with its litany of Sieg Heils and the singing of the anthem. Tens of millions of Germans, glued to their radios, were engulfed in a rhetoric of rage and vengeance. Most of them probably caught the "*Ausrott—Ausschaltung*." In the hall, as we saw, it was greeted with applause and laughter. Simply put, the extermination of the Jews was no secret unveiled amid shock and stony silence.

"A few hours ago," Moshe Flinker recorded, "I heard a speech made by Propaganda Minister Goebbels. I shall try to describe the impression this speech made on me and the thoughts it aroused in me. First of all I heard what I could have heard any number of times—unlimited anti-Semitism. One whole section of his speech he addressed to the great hatred he and nearly all Germans have for our people, the reasons for which to this day

I cannot understand. A thousand times I have heard from the German leaders angry words against the Jews, accompanied by the epithets 'capitalist' or 'communist,' but I doubt very much if they themselves believe their own words. On the other hand, however, they pronounce these words with so much excitement that I can almost believe they are sincere. Apart from their excitement and emotion, there is other evidence for their sincerity. It should be remembered that now, when Germany is receiving blow after blow from all sides and when she is compelled to abandon one Russian city after another, they never forget the people they have already so tortured and crushed, nor do they let the slightest opportunity pass to shame or humiliate them. In these very days, which are times of trouble for Germany, the Propaganda Minister considers it to be the right moment to abuse us and blaspheme our people even more violently. Maybe it is that the wild, primitive hatred which exists in almost all peoples appears in the Germans more clearly and openly and with more consequence for us.... But from their actions we see that this war must end in the solution of the Jewish problem (speaking from the Orthodox Jewish point of view, I would say in the redemption of the Jews) because, as far as I know, the hatred of the Jews has never been as widespread or poisonous as it is now."[6]

In Bucharest, Sebastian had also heard the Goebbels speech: "Goebbels' speech last night," he noted, "sounded unexpectedly dramatic.... The Jews are once more threatened with extermination."[7] The next day Klemperer got the text of the speech at the Jewish cemetery where he was working: "The speech contains a threat to proceed against the Jews, who are guilty of everything, 'with the most draconian and radical measures' if the foreign powers do not stop threatening the Hitler government because of the Jews."[8]

In his two-hour-long address to the *Reichsleiter* and *Gauleiter* assembled at Rastenburg on February 7, 1943, Hitler repeated once again that Jewry had to be eliminated from the Reich and all of Europe.[9] On the Memorial Day for Fallen Soldiers, March 21, the same threat reappeared with the extermination prophecy added for good measure. And, as constant repetition was of the essence, Hitler unleashed the traditional anti-Jewish torrent of invectives: "The driving force [behind capitalism and Bolshevism] is anyway the eternal hatred of that accursed race which for thousands of years punishes the nations like a true scourge of God, until the time comes when these nations will get back to their senses and arise against their tormentors."[10] The order of the day was anti-Jewish propaganda and ever more anti-Jewish propaganda. "The Führer issues instructions to set the Jewish question once more at the forefront of our propaganda, in the strongest possible way," Goebbels noted on April 17.[11]

The propaganda minister did not miss the benefits of linking "Katyn" (the discovery of a mass grave in the eastern Polish Katyn Forest with the bodies of more than four thousand Polish officers shot by the NKVD about a year before the German attack against the USSR) and the "Jewish question."[12] In other words the Jews, always held responsible for all Soviet crimes, could now be denounced as the instigators and perpetrators of this major Bolshevik atrocity.

Back in Berlin on May 7, for the funeral of SA chief Viktor Lutze, Hitler exhorted the assembled *Gauleiter* to "set anti-Semitism again at the core of the ideological struggle, as we fostered and propagated it in the party in earlier days" [*dass der Antisemitismus, wie wir ihn früher in der Partei gepflegt und propagiert haben, auch jetzt wieder das Kernstück unserer geistiger Auseinandersetzung sein muss*].[13]

Goebbels recorded further Hitler promptings on May 9. "The Führer attaches great importance to hard-hitting anti-Semitic propaganda. Success will be achieved by constant repetition. He is extremely pleased with our sharper anti-Semitic campaign in the press and on the radio. I tell him how important the place of anti-Semitic propaganda is in our foreign broadcasts. It amounts at times to 70 or 80 percent of our entire foreign broadcasts. The anti-Semitic bacteria are naturally present in the entire European public; we need only to make them virulent" [*Die antisemitischen Bazillen sind natürlich in der ganzen europaischen Öffentlichkeit vorhanden; wir müssen sie nur virulent machen*].[14]

To "make the bacteria virulent," the minister turned to some basic recipes: "Once more I thoroughly study the Zionist Protocols" [*sic; The Protocols of the Elders of Zion*], he noted in his diary entry of May 13, 1943.[15] "The Zionist Protocols are as modern today as when they were published for the first time. It is amazing to see the extraordinary consistency that characterizes the Jewish striving for world domination. If the Zionist Protocols are not authentic, then they have been invented by a genius interpreter of our epoch. At noon I broach the topic with the Führer. The Führer thinks that the Zionist Protocols can be considered as absolutely authentic. Nobody would have had such an extraordinary ability to describe the Jewish striving for world domination, as the Jews themselves perceive it. The Führer is of the opinion," Goebbels went on, "that the Jews do not need at all to follow a pre-established plan; they work according to their race instinct; it will always drive them to act as one, as they have demonstrated in the course of their entire history."[16]

The discussion of the Jewish race instinct allowed the German leader to roam far and wide. He pointed to the similarity of Jewish characteristics all over the world and to the natural causes that explained the very existence of the Jews: "The modern peoples have no option left but to eliminate the Jews," the obsessed Führer went on. "They use all available means to defend themselves against this oncoming extermination process. One of these means is war. Thus we have to know that in this conflict between Aryan humanity and the Jewish race we still have to withstand hard battles, as Jewry has been able, consciously or unconsciously, to use large national groups of the Aryan race at its own command."[17] And so it continued, on and on.

In the course of his monologue Hitler repeated his belief that the Jews were not, as they thought, on the eve of a "world triumph" but on the eve of a "world catastrophe." "The peoples who were the first to recognize the Jew and the first to fight him would raise to world domination in his [the Jew's] stead."[18] The themes of these anti-Jewish tirades were not new, but this was no speech to the masses: Hitler was discussing the Jews with his propaganda minister, the minister who had just rediscovered the "Protocols." The conversation had a ring of demented authenticity. And for the first time, it seems, Hitler revealed his ultimate goal: world domination.

In the meantime, of course, Goebbels was furiously mobilizing all German media outlets for the most systematic anti-Jewish campaign ever. On May 3, 1943, the minister issued a highly detailed circular (labeled confidential) to the press. After berating papers and journals for still lagging in this domain, the minister offered his own suggestions: "For example, countless sensational stories can be used, in which the Jew is the culprit. Above all, American domestic politics offers an inexhaustible reservoir. If those journals, in particular, which are geared to commenting on current affairs, apply their staff to this issue, they will be able to show the true face, the true attitude and the true aims of the Jews in a varied manner. Apart from that, of course, the Jews must now be used in the German press as a political target: the Jews are to blame; the Jews wanted the war; the Jews are making the war worse; and, again and again, the Jews are to blame."[19]

Klemperer soon became aware of the systematic aspect of the new propaganda frenzy, and his diary entries show that Goebbels's directives were being faithfully applied: "The last few days have been dominated by the river dam business," he recorded on May 21, 1943. "First the English have 'criminally' bombed two dams (location not stated); very many civilian casualties. Then: It has been proven, proven by an English newspaper article, that the criminal plan was hatched by a Jew. . . . The river dam business—it has superseded the 10,000 officers' corpses at Katyn—is reinforced by the American child murder in Italy: There the Americans dropped toys filled with explosives (also similarly prepared ladies' gloves). A 'Serbian newspaper' writes, this murder of children is a Jewish invention. No news-hour without such reports."[20] On May 29 Klemperer noted that one of his coworkers at the Zeiss factory brought a newspaper article from the *Freiheitskampf,* "The Jew is to blame" by Professor Dr. Johann von Leers: . . . 'If the Jews are victorious our whole nation will be slaughtered like the Polish officers in the forest of Katyn. . . . The Jewish question became the core and central question of our nation once it had let the Jews loose.' "[21]

A few days later Klemperer once again turned to the unceasing anti-Jewish blasts: "On the radio, on Friday evening, Goebbels's editorial from *Das Reich* on the dissolution of the Comintern [the Communist International had been dissolved by Stalin]. The Jewish *race* always master of camouflage. They adopt every political position that can benefit them, according to country and circumstance. Bolshevism, plutocracy—behind Roosevelt, behind Stalin there are Jews, their goal, the goal of this war is Jewish world dominion. But our propaganda is gradually having an effect, even in the enemy camp. The victory of our ideas is certain."[22]

"Katyn" had some effect on anti-Bolshevik hatred and fear among the German population; yet comparison of these Soviet atrocities with German atrocities against the Poles and Jews came up quite frequently, according to SD reports. A typical reaction of this kind was overheard in mid-April: "If I did not know that in our people's struggle for existence every method is right, the hypocrisy shown in the pity for the murdered Polish officers would be unbearable."[23] The report drew the conclusion that even among "positively attuned Volksgenossen, superficial comparisons were made which allowed for easy exploitation by hostile circles."[24]

Yet almost a year later, in March 1944, Klemperer recorded that the relentless anti-Jewish propaganda had its effect. He mentioned a conversation with a good-natured foreman at the Zeiss factory. They came to speak of cities both of them knew, also about Hamburg; this led to a discussion of the bombing, and, for this mild fellow, the Americans, whom Europe had never threatened, were in the war because "a few billionaires" pushed them into it. "Behind the couple of billionaires," Klemperer noted, "I heard 'a couple of Jews' and felt the belief in Nazi propaganda. This man, who is undoubtedly not a Nazi, most certainly believes that Germany is acting in self-defense, is completely in the right, and that the war was forced upon it; most certainly he believes, at least in large part, in the guilt of 'world Jewry' etc., etc. The National Socialists may have miscalculated in the conduct of the war, but certainly not in their propaganda. I always have to remind myself of Hitler's words, that he is not making speeches for professors."[25]

From mid-1942 on the continent-wide murder campaign ran as an administrative bureaucratic system in all its basic operations. However, had these operations unfolded only according to bureaucratic norms of instrumental rationality, they would increasingly have adapted, mainly after Stalingrad and Kursk, to the worsening military situation. A whole array of activities of no use to the war effort, such as transporting the Jews to their death despite growing logistic problems or exterminating Jewish workers—although, of course, the argument of the Jewish threat could always be brandished—would have probably slowed down. Yet the contrary was happening: Anti-Jewish propaganda became more pervasive than ever and the danger represented by every single Jew turned into a generalized ideological obsession.

In order to be effective, however, the ideological impetus had to emanate not only from the top but also be fanatically adopted and enforced at intermediate levels of the system by the technocrats, organizers, and direct implementers of the extermination—by those, in short, who made the system work, several levels below the main political leadership. Key figures in the agencies involved—particularly some of the best organizers and technocrats among them—were motivated by anti-Jewish fanaticism.[26]

In the face of such ruthless German determination, the absence of major opposition or protest from the surrounding world did not change significantly. As before, hundreds of thousands (possibly millions) of Germans and other Europeans continued tacitly to support the extermination campaign, both for profit and on ideological grounds (that, in occupied countries, did not exclude the simultaneous hatred of Germans, particularly among many Poles). The determining factors in the passivity of most remained fear, of course, the absence of any sense of identification with Jews, and the lack of decided and sustained encouragement to help the victims from the leaders of Christian churches or the political leadership of resistance movements.

Among the Jews—the majority of whom had already been murdered by mid-1943—the two contrary trends that have already been mentioned became ever more noticeable: increasing passivity and lack of solidarity with fellow sufferers among the mass of terrorized and physically weakened victims (mainly in the camps) on the one hand, and on the other the tightening bonds within small, usually politically homogeneous groups that, as we shall see, would rise in some places in desperate armed revolts.

II

On January 11, 1943, Hermann Höfle sent a radiogram from Lublin to SS Obersturmbannführer Franz Heim, the deputy commander of the Security Police and the SD in the General Government; a few minutes later he sent a second, most probably identical one to Eichmann. Whereas the radiogram from Höfle to Heim was partially decoded by the British and distributed on January 15 (to the small group of recipients of these decodes), the second message was either not fully intercepted or not decoded except for the indication of the source and of the addressee.[27]

Höfle's message to Heim was, in its main part, a computation of the number of Jews exterminated in the camps of "Aktion Reinhardt" up to

December 31, 1942. After listing the number of Jews who had arrived in the four camps during the third and fourth weeks of December, Höfle gave the following overall results of the extermination for each camp:

L [Lublin-Majdanek]: 24,733.
B [Belzec]: 434,508.
S [Sobibor]: 101,370.
T [Treblinka]: 71,355 (read: 713,555).
TOTAL: 1,274,166.[28]

Höfle's report was probably related to a more encompassing set of results being put together at the same time. According to his postwar declarations, Eichmann had given Himmler a first progress report at the SS leader's headquarters near Zhitomir, on August 11, 1942 (although Himmler's calendar indicates that the meeting dealt essentially with the planned deportations from Romania).[29] A second report, this time a written one, was prepared by Eichmann's IV B 4 department and sent to Himmler on December 15, 1942, under the title "Operations and Situation Report 1942 on the Final Solution of the European Jewish Question."[30] Though the report is considered lost, it is known to have displeased the SS chief intensely.

In a letter of January 18, 1943, addressed to Müller, the irate Reichsführer did not mince words: "The Reich Main Security Office is hereby relieved of its statistical responsibilities in this area, since the statistical materials submitted to date have consistently fallen short of professional standards of precision."[31] On the same day the Reichsführer put the SS chief statistician, Richard Korherr, in charge of the report: "The Reich Security Main Office," Himmler wrote Korherr, "is to put at your disposal whatever materials you request or need for this purpose."[32]

An initial Korherr report, sixteen pages long, establishing the total of Jews killed by December 31, 1942, was submitted to Himmler on March 23, 1943: The number of Jews "evacuated" was estimated at 1,873,539. On Himmler's demand an abridged estimate, updated to March 31, 1943, was prepared for Hitler; it was six and a half pages long. In this second version, Korherr was ordered to replace the words "special treatment" (of the Jews) by "transport of Jews from the eastern provinces to the Russian East: passed through camps in the General Government . . . through camps in the Warthegau.[33] We do not know the total number that could have been alluded to or deduced from the second version, but it must have been close to 2.5 million. Korherr titled his report "The Final Solution of the European Jewish Question."[34]

According to some interpretations, Himmler needed the report to defend himself against criticism coming from Speer and from the commander of the Reserve Army, Gen. Friedrich Fromm, in regard to the extermination of potential workers or even soldiers.[35] This seems unlikely, as, on Hitler's orders, thousands of Jews working in German industries were seized and deported in February 1943 and further tens of thousands of Jewish slave laborers would be systematically murdered throughout the year. Moreover, on December 29, 1942, Himmler had reported to Hitler about the extermination of Jews in the Ukraine, in southern Russia, and in the Białystok district during the summer of 1942; as we saw, in the Ukraine no distinctions were made between working and nonworking Jews. According to the Reichsführer, 363,211 Jews had been exterminated in these operations.[36] Had Hitler criticized such indiscriminate annihilation, some hint of it would most probably have been mentioned.

The Korherr report was an overall progress report that, let us remember, Himmler had been trying to obtain since midsummer 1942. Was it pure chance that the Nazi leader received it on the eve of his fifty-fourth birthday, after Germany had suffered its worst military defeats yet? Here at least was a war that Hitler was winning. The document was eventually returned to Eichmann's office with Himmler's remark: "The Führer has taken note: destroy. H.H."[37]

During these same days Rosenberg forwarded his own general survey of Jewish spoils, explicitly for his leader's birthday: "My Führer," the minister wrote on April 16, 1943, "with the wish to make you happy for your birthday, I allow myself to submit to you a folder with photos of some of the most valuable paintings from Jewish ownerless property secured by my Commando in the occupied western countries. . . . This folder gives but a weak impression of the extraordinary value and quantity of the art objects seized by my agency in France and put in security in the Reich." Rosenberg attached a written summary of all the treasures his commando had seized in the West. Until April 7, 1943, the "recovery locations" in the Reich had received 2,775 boxes of art objects in ninety-two freight cars; of these objects, 9,455 had already been inventoried, while "at least" 10,000 further objects had yet to be processed.[38]

While Rosenberg's fawning birthday offering definitively stamps National Socialism's foremost thinker not only a criminal but also a grotesque figure, even by Nazi standards, the significance of the other gift, Korherr's report, whether meant for Hitler's birthday nor not, is quite different in several ways. First, Korherr's wording of one sentence was corrected on Himmler's order to avoid associating the Führer with an expression openly used as a reference to mass murder. Yet strangely enough the new phrasing—"Transport to the Russian East . . . passed through the camps"—was as easily identifiable with mass murder as the previous euphemism. Moreover, as historian Gerald Fleming quite cogently noted, no mistake could be made about the meaning of these words, as another part of the same document alluded to "the collapse of the Jewish masses . . . since the evacuation measures of 1942."[39]

Mainly, whatever the intent of Himmler's linguistic exercises may have been, Korherr's report is not merely a statistical survey to be tucked away in the history of the "Final Solution" in a section dealing with the number of victims. Of course, it *is* that, but also much more. Himmler sent the report to Hitler (or presented it to him) either because the Nazi leader had asked for it or the SS chief knew that his Führer would be pleased to see it. Be that as it may, we have to imagine Hitler reading the six pages of the report (typed on his special typewriter) outlining for him the interim results of the mass murder operation that he had ordered. Two and a half million Jews had already been killed, and the campaign was rapidly unfolding. We do not know whether the Nazi leader showed satisfaction as he read, or impatience about the slow pace of the killings. The killing in and of itself, but also the perusal of the report by its initiator, the leader of one of the most advanced nations in the world, remains of the essence. The scene thus imagined—which necessarily took place—tells more about the regime and its "messiah" than many an abstract treatise.

Another aspect of this ghoulish occurrence comes to mind. We do not know of any other equally elaborate and detailed statistical report about a specific group of people whom Hitler ordered to murder; we know merely of general estimates and aggregates. It is only in regard to the number of murdered Jews that Himmler gave full vent to his anger, in view of the unprofessional statistical work of Eichmann's office. And Korherr offered the precision Himmler requested: 1,873,539 Jews by December 31, 1942. To Kaltenbrunner, Himmler wrote: "In the brief monthly reports of the Security Police, I only want figures on how many Jews have been shipped off and and how many are currently left."[40] In other words, *every* Jew still alive remained a danger, and *every* Jew still alive had to be caught and murdered in the end.

III

To keep the extermination progressing at full pace, the Germans had to impose their will on increasingly reluctant allies. In the case of Romania, Hitler gave up. He did not want to confront Antonescu, whom he considered a trustworthy ally, although he continued to prod him. In Hungary the situation was different. The Nazi leader believed that Horthy and Kallay were under Jewish influence, and he (rightly) suspected them of aspiring to switch sides. Moreover, for Hitler the 800,000 Jews of Hungary were a huge prize, almost within his grasp. On April 17 and 18, 1943, the Nazi leader met with Horthy at Klessheim Castle, near Salzburg, Austria, and berated him about the mildness of Hungary's anti-Jewish measures. German policies, the Nazi leader explained, were different. In Poland, for example, "if the Jews did not want to work, they were shot; if they could not work, they had to perish. They were to be dealt with like tuberculosis microbes that could infect a healthy body. This was not cruel if one considered that even innocent beings such as deer or hares had to be killed to avoid damages. Why should one spare the beasts that wanted to bring us bolshevism?" At this point in his exhortation, the Nazi leader felt the need to add a historical proof to his arguments: "People who did not defend themselves against the Jew," he went on, "perished. One of the best-known examples was the downfall of the once so proud Persian people, who now lived a miserable life as Armenians."[41]

Whether the regent was impressed by the German leader's erudition is hard to tell, but he certainly understood that Hitler was set on the speedy extermination of all of European Jewry. Just in case German aims had not been sufficiently hammered home at Klessheim, a cable from Ambassador Sztójay to Kallay, sent on April 25, left no further doubt:

"National Socialism," the ambassador reported, "despises and deeply hates the Jews whom it considers as its greatest and most relentless enemy with which it is engaged in a life and death struggle. . . . The Reich Chancellor is determined to rid Europe of the Jews. . . . He has decreed that until the summer of 1943 all the Jews of Germany and of the countries occupied by Germany will be moved to the Eastern territories that is to the Russian territories. . . . The German Government has expressed the wish that its allies should participate in the action mentioned."[42]

Neither Hitler's exhortations nor Sztójay's report sufficed to change Horthy's policies—increasingly aimed at an understanding with the Allies. In fact Kallay made a point of stating openly that, in regard to the Jews, Hungary would not budge. In a speech delivered at the end of May 1943, the Hungarian prime minister was explicit: "In Hungary," he declared, "live more Jews than in all of Western Europe. . . . It is self-explanatory that we must attempt to solve this problem; hence the necessity for temporary measures and an appropriate regulation. The final solution, however, can be none other than the complete resettlement of Jewry. But I cannot bring myself to keep this problem on the agenda so long as the basic prerequisite of the solution, namely the answer to the question where the Jews are to be resettled, is not given. Hungary will never deviate from those precepts of humanity, which, in the course of history, it has always maintained in racial and religious questions."[43] Given Hitler's declarations to the regent a few weeks before, Kallay's speech was nothing less than a slap in the Nazi leader's face. Clearly the moment of confrontation with Germany was rapidly approaching; it did not bode well for Hungary—mainly, not for its large Jewish community.

In the meantime the Bulgarian attitude regarding the country's further deportations of Jews still looked promising to Berlin. As we saw, in March and April 1943, Sofia had given all necessary assistance to Dannecker and his men in deporting the Jews of occupied Thracia and Macedonia to Treblinka. Simultaneously, in March 1943, thousands of Bulgarian Jews had already been concentrated at assembly points, and the transports from the "Old Kingdom" were about to start. King Boris had promised this to the Germans. When it came to the deportation of native Bulgarian Jews, however, public protest erupted. The opposition found its strongest expression in parliament and among the leaders of the Bulgarian Orthodox Church. The monarch backed down: Any further such deportations were definitively canceled.[44]

The king, slightly embarrassed, it seems, had some explaining to do to his German ally. On April 2, during a visit to Germany, the Bulgarian monarch informed Ribbentrop that "he had had given his agreement to the deportation to Eastern Europe only in regard to the Jews of Thracia and Macedonia. As for the Jews of Bulgaria as such, he was merely ready to allow for the deportation of a small number of Bolshevik-communist elements, while the other 25,000 Jews would be put into concentration camps, as he needed them for road construction." The protocol of the conversation indicates that Ribbentrop did not address Boris's remarks in detail but merely told him: "According to our view on the Jewish question, the most radical solution is the only right one."[45]

A few days after the meeting, a general overview of the events in Bulgaria, sent by the Foreign Ministry to the RSHA, indicated that, there as in other countries of southeastern Europe, "distancing from harsh anti-Jewish measures was noticeable."[46]

Even in Slovakia, hesitation about further deportations persisted. It may be remembered that merely 20,000 mostly baptized Jews remained in the country after the last three transports to Auschwitz had departed in September 1942 following a three-month lull. In the meantime rumors about the fate of the deportees had seeped back. Thus when Tuka mentioned the possibility of resuming the deportations in early April 1943, protests from Slovak clergy, and also from the population, put an end to his initiative.[47] On March 21, a pastoral letter condemning any further deportations had been read in most churches.

The growing turmoil led to a meeting between Ludin and Tuka, as reported by the German envoy to Berlin on April 13. After minimizing the significance of the pastoral letter, Tuka mentioned that information about atrocities perpetrated by the Germans against the Jews had reached the Slovak bishops. "Prime Minister Dr. Tuka let me know," Ludin went on, "that the 'naïve Slovak clergy' was prone to believe such atrocity fairy tales and he [Tuka] would be grateful if they were countered from the German side by a description of conditions in the Jewish camps. He considers that from a propaganda viewpoint it might be especially valuable if a Slovak delegation, which should appropriately comprise a legislator, a journalist, and perhaps also a Catholic clergyman, could visit a German camp for Jews. If such an inspection might be organized," Ludin concluded, "I would certainly welcome it.[48]

On April 22, 1943, Hitler met Tiso at Klessheim. Essentially the Nazi leader held forth against the protection that Horthy granted to the Jews of Hungary; Ribbentrop, who attended the meeting, added a few comments of his own to his Führer's declarations.[49] Tiso, in other words, was being indirectly encouraged to complete the job on his own turf by delivering his remaining Jews. On this occasion, the Slovak president did not make any promise.

As by the early summer of 1943 the deportations from Slovakia had not yet been resumed, Eichmann added a heavy dose of what could only be defined as comic relief to the messages sent to Bratislava. In a memorandum dated June 7, 1943, that the Wilhelmstrasse passed on to Ludin, Tuka, and Tiso, the head of IVB4 demanded that the Slovaks be informed of the favorable reports published about the "conditions in Jewish camps" by a series of newspapers in Eastern Europe (and even one in Paris), with "numerous photographs." "For the rest," Eichmann added, "to counteract the fantastic rumors circulating in Slovakia about the fate of the evacuated Jews, attention should be drawn to the postal communications of these Jews with Slovakia, which are forwarded directly through the advisor on Jewish affairs with the German legation in Bratislava [Wisliceny] and which for instance amounted to more than 1,000 letters and postcards for February-March this year. Concerning the information apparently desired by Prime Minister Dr. Tuka about the conditions in Jewish camps, no objections would be raised by this office against any possible scrutinizing of the correspondence before it is forwarded to the addressees."[50]

The German pressure on the Slovaks was relatively mild, possibly due to a bottleneck at Auschwitz resulting from the ongoing deportations from the West, the final transports from the Reich and the General Government, and the transports from Salonika, followed by the typhus epidemic in the camp that diverted transports to Sobibor. The fate of the remnants of Slovak Jewry would be sealed on the very eve of Germany's collapse.

* * *

There was a measure of coordination between the deportations from Slovakia and from Croatia (or, more precisely put, from "Greater Croatia"). As we saw, the 40,000 Jews in Pavelic's state, together with the Serbs and the Gypsies, were hunted down by the Croats, despite Italian efforts to protect as many of them as they could, in their own zone. The Germans, probably unimpressed by the thoroughness of the Ustasha butchering operations and worried from early 1943 on about the psychological impact of Stalingrad, took direct control of the final phase of the liquidation. A first wave of deportations had already substantially decimated the Jewish population in August 1942. The second wave followed in the early summer of 1943, after a visit by Himmler to Zagreb, on May 5. The mopping-up operations that took place after the end of Italian control of the Dalmatian coastal regions were only partly successful, as groups of Jews succeeded in joining Tito's partisans.[51] Throughout the entire period the local Catholic church played a major role in accepting or stemming the Ustasha persecutions and massacres, as already mentioned; we shall return to this issue in the next chapter.

During the first days of 1943 (possibly even at the end of 1942), while Dannecker was about to start the deportations from neighboring Thracia and Macedonia, Rolf Günther arrived in Greece to coordinate the deportations from Salonika. In early February, Dieter Wisliceny and Alois Brunner followed.[52] Within a month everything was ready. The first train, with some 2,800 Jews, left the northern Greek city for Auschwitz on March 15, 1943; the second train departed two days later. Within a few weeks 45,000 out of the 50,000 Jews of Salonika had been deported and mostly killed on arrival.[53] Simultaneously deportee trains were leaving Thracia and Macedonia for Treblinka.

A host of factors have been adduced to explain the flawless implementation of the German assault upon the Jews of Salonika while the same operation encountered serious obstacles, a year later, when the deportation of the Jews of Athens started. The arrival in Salonika of Eichmann's top men certainly played an important role, as did the eager collaboration of Vassilis Simonides, the German-appointed governor-general of Macedonia, and the "determination" of the Wilhelmstrasse delegate to Greece, Günther Altenburg.[54] Other elements of course reinforced the efficiency of the German officials and the role of Simonides and like-minded Salonikans. Historian Mark Mazower mentions the periodic tension between the Greek inhabitants of the city and the still incompletely assimilated post–World War I Jewish refugees (and thus the lack of active solidarity of the population), the immediate compliance of Chief Rabbi Zwi Koretz, the spiritual head of the community, with all German orders, the absence of any information among the local Jews about the fate that awaited them once they boarded the trains and, also, the absence of a Greek resistance movement that would play a major role a year later, during the deportation of the remaining Jews of the country.[55]

It has been argued that the total incomprehension of local Jews regarding German policies stemmed—as in Thracia and Macedonia—from the intrinsically different historical memory of these mainly Sephardi communities. They had direct experience or detailed knowledge of Turkish atrocities, of expulsions from Asia Minor, in short of the misery, discrimination, massacres, and resettlements of the World War I years and their immediate aftermath.[56] Many of these Jews probably imagined their fate at the hands of the Germans in somewhat similar terms. Whether this was a significant factor in their attitudes is less certain, however: No Jew in occupied Europe imagined what the German measures would be.

During the two years that had elapsed between the German occupation of Greece and the beginning of the deportations, the Jewish community of Salonika had undergone the usual persecutions: looting of libraries and synagogues by the Einsatzstab Rosenberg, conscription of thousands of men to forced labor for the Wehrmacht, involvement of Greek collaborators and sundry prewar fascist groups in anti-Jewish propaganda, and, of course, the usual expropriations.[57]

By February 1943 the Jews of the city had been marked with the star, segregated in a run-down area, and robbed by Germans and Greeks of whatever remained of their possessions. The Jewish police participated in the *razzias* and the extortions in a particularly vicious way, while the head of the community, Rabbi Koretz, was spreading soothing comments.[58] A camp set up near the railway station, in a tightly enclosed part of the Jewish quarter, became the assembly and transit site from which batch after batch of the Salonikan Jews boarded the trains.[59]

As the first Jews were on their way to Auschwitz, a strange diplomatic imbroglio caused some annoyance in Berlin, without influencing, however, the speedy implementation of the deportations. First, the acting Greek prime minister, Constantine Logothetopoulos, protested against the German measures and had to be reassured by the combined persuasive talents of Altenburg and Wisliceny. The ICRC delegate in Athens, René Burckhardt, was more troublesome, as he insisted that the Jews of Salonika be sent to Palestine instead of Auschwitz.[60] The exasperated Germans finally demanded his removal from Greece.[61] The most concrete interference, as usual, came from the Italians.

There had been some dispute about the role of the Italian consul in Salonika as the deportations started. It seems proved now that, from the outset, Consul Guelfo Zamboni did not spare any effort to protect as many Jews as possible: "It should be recalled that protection was granted not only to Jews of Italian nationality, but also to those who claimed a right to such nationality, or raised some forgotten, real or fabricated, familial relationship to Italian Jews, or even in some cases to Jews who in fact did not have any such relationship but who, in the consul's opinion, had clearly contributed to the cultural or economic interests of Italy in the city or the region."[62]

The Italian minister plenipotentiary in Athens, Pellegrino Ghigi strongly supported Zamboni's interventions, as did the Foreign Ministry in Rome. It seems that the Italians even appealed to the Wilhelmstrasse to obtain the release of some of the protected Jews who had already been deported—to no avail, of course.[63] All in all the Germans tried to block the Italian initiative. "Inland IIg," which succeeded the former "department Germany," recommended the rejection of Rome's demands for reasons that illustrate the changing context of the German operations. The Swedes were also demanding exemptions for their newly minted nationals. A positive response to the Italians, Inland II argued, could only strengthen such demands. Moreover, accepting the Italian request would bolster the increasingly hostile attitude of Balkan states regarding German anti-Jewish policies. Finally "the Reich's reputation" in the whole of Greece would suffer if Italy succeeded in its intervention.[64] The Italians nonetheless managed to transfer some 320 protected Jews to Athens.[65] As for the pliant Rabbi Koretz and a few other privileged Jews, they were sent to Bergen-Belsen, where Koretz died of typhus on the eve of liberation.[66]

The old Jewish cemetery of Salonika, with its hundreds of thousands of graves, some of which dated back to the fifteenth century, was destroyed: The Germans used the tombstones for paving roads and building a swimming pool for the troops; the city used the space for developing its vast new university campus.[67] What happened to the remnants of generations of Salonikan Jews is nowhere told.

IV

For the Germans carrying the Jews to their death remained a logistic headache to the very end; for some of the Jews the transports as such became death traps, there and then.

In Holland, Belgium, and France the Jews were mostly assembled in Westerbork, Malines, or Drancy (where a sufficient supply of inmates to fill the transports remained the main priority); in these national assembly centers, special trains arrived at regular weekly intervals. In the Reich itself, however, where no such central assembly camp existed, a *Russenzug* ("Russian train") arriving from the East with laborers had to be readied at one of the main departure cities and scheduled so as to allow for the timely arrival of connecting trains from smaller towns with their own loads of Jews. This demanded complex scheduling in and of itself, also due to the irregular arrivals of the trains from the East.

As the *Russenzug* from Brest-Litovsk to Cologne, programmed to carry 1,000 Jews from Düsseldorf to Izbica, had not yet left Brest, a Düsseldorf police official reported in March 1942, it was to be replaced by *Russenzug* RU7340 from Russia to Hemer, in Westphalia. The train was to be ready to leave Düsseldorf on April 22, 1942, at 11:06 (it should have arrived in Düsseldorf on the twentieth or twenty-first, after thorough cleaning and delousing); it included twenty cars of unspecified type. Since most trains for the East comprised diverse types of cars, loading at the cattle station was not possible.

For the transport of seventy Jews from Wuppertal to Derendorf, one four-axle car or two two-axle cars would be added to passenger train Pz286 leaving Steinbeck at 14:39, arriving at Düsseldorf Main Station at 15:20. The one hundred Jews from Mönchen-Gladbach would be transported in two cars added to passenger train Pz2303 leaving Mönchen-Gladbach at 14:39 and arriving at Düsseldorf at 15:29. For the 145 Jews from Krefeld, the passenger train leaving Krefeld at 15:46, arriving at Düsseldorf at 17:19, would get two additional four-axle passenger cars and one freight car. The freight car had to be ordered from the merchandise station in Krefeld with the destination Izbica.

The railway administration in Essen allocated a special train, Da152, with passenger cars to which two merchandise cars would be attached for baggage. The cars had to be ordered in Essen with the destination Izbica. The merchandise cars would be directed to the slaughterhouse station, whereas special train Da152 and the cars from Wuppertal, Krefeld, and Mönchen-Gladbach would be directed to the Tussmannstadt platform.[68] Of course, in the Reich such problems rapidly dwindled in 1943.

Periodically the Reichsbahn had to be paid for its services. Although most of the transports were easily funded by the RSHA from the victims' assets, at times the payments were not readily available or the moving of the trains through several currency zones created complex accounting problems for all involved.[69]

The major challenge, however, was the availability of trains as such. Thus in early June 1942, Himmler's adjutant, SS Obergruppenführer Karl Wolff, demanded the personal intervention of the secretary of state at the Transportation Ministry, Dr. Theodor Ganzenmüller, to ensure the daily deportations from Warsaw. On July 27 Ganzenmüller reported to Wolff: "Since 22.7. a train with 5,000 Jews travels daily from Warsaw over Malkinia to Treblinka. Moreover, twice a week a train with 5,000 Jews travels from Przemysl to Belzec. Gedob [the "General Directorate of the Ostbahn"] stays in ongoing contact with the Security Service in Cracow."[70] Wolff's notorious answer of August 13 remains engraved in history: "Hearty thanks in the name of the Reichsführer SS for your letter of July 28, 1942. With great joy I learned from your announcement that, for the past fourteen days, a train has gone daily to Treblinka with 5,000 members of the chosen people."[71]

Wolff's plea to Ganzenmüller—and Himmler's own repeated demands for help—are perplexing in regard to deportations within the General Government, given the short distances between any of the ghettos and the "Aktion Reinhardt" camps. The matter looks even more perplexing if we take into account that in the overall daily traffic of 30,000 trains operated by the Reichsbahn in 1942, only two *Sonderzüge* ("special trains") per day carried Jews to their death during that same period.[72] Yet Wolff's and Himmler's nervousness was partly justified. The Reichsbahn gave very low priority to the "special trains" in its planning: "[They] were put into unoccupied slots intended for through freight trains or were run as freight extras. The result was that they were allowed onto the main line only after all other traffic had passed. Wehrmacht trains, military supply trains carrying armaments and coal trains all moved before the *Sonderzüge*. This explains the long stops in sidings and yards recorded in the anecdotal evidence of survivors and guards. Moreover, the trains were assigned old, worn-out locomotives and old cars, explaining their slow speed and frequent stops for repairs."[73]

Yet, as the "special trains" represented such a minute fraction of the overall traffic, timely planning ultimately allowed almost any problem to be solved. From September 26 to 28, 1942, a conference of Transportation Ministry officials attended either by Eichmann or by Rolf Günther rose to the challenge in a highly positive spirit. After a listing of the number of trains required for the district-by-district deportation of the Jewish population of the General Government to the extermination camps, the protocol expressed the overall confidence of the participants: "With the reduction of the transport of potatoes, it is expected that it will be possible for the special train service to be able to place at the disposal of the Directorate of the German Railways in Cracow the necessary number of freight cars. Thus the train transportation required will be available in accordance with the above proposals and the plan completed this year."[74]

Notwithstanding such goodwill, the Reichsführer had to plead again with Ganzenmüller on January 20, 1943, and explain that in order to ensure internal security East and West, the accelerated deportation of the Jews was essential: "I must receive more transport trains, if I want to complete this rapidly," Himmler wrote. "I know very well the overstretched situation of the railways and what constant demands are made upon you. Nonetheless, I must address my request to you: Help me and get me more trains."[75]

As for the "cargo" itself, it did not cause any major problems. Of course there were the usual suicides and some attempts to flee before boarding the trains and others during the transports. Thus, on April 23, 1942, the Krefeld Gestapo informed Düsseldorf that among the Jews scheduled for deportation on April 22, Julius Israel Meier, Augusta Sara Meier, Else Sara Frankenberg, and Elisabeth Sara Frank could not be evacuated as the first three had committed suicide, and the fourth had disappeared.[76]

Throughout the deportation period there are no records of any fights breaking out on the trains between the deportees and the guards. Deaths during the transports were frequent, from exhaustion, thirst, suffocation, and the like. They were duly accounted for and reported. On April 13, 1943, for example, a police lieutenant Karl reported about a transport from Skopje (Macedonia) to Treblinka: "On March 29, at 6:00, the loading of 2,404 Jews into freight cars commenced at the former tobacco sheds. Loading was completed at 12:00 and at 12:30 the train departed. The train passed through Albanian territory. The final destination, Treblinka (the camp), was reached on April 5, 1943, at 7:00. . . . The train was unloaded that same day between the hours of 09:00 and 11:00. Incidents: Five Jews died en route. On the night of March 30—an elderly woman of seventy, on the night of March 31—an elderly man aged eighty-five; on April 3 an elderly woman aged ninety-four and a six-month-old child. On April 4 an elderly woman aged ninety-nine died. Transport roster: received 2,404—less 5—total delivered at Treblinka: 2,399."[77]

Oskar Rosenfeld's journey from Prague to Lodz had been relatively easy at the end of 1941.[78] Generally the travel from Western Europe, Italy, or even from Germany, appears to have been less lethal than the transports within Eastern Europe or from the Balkans to Auschwitz or Treblinka. The Italian writer Primo Levi, to whom we will return, briefly described his journey from the assembly camp at Fossoli di Carpi, near Modena, to Auschwitz in early 1944:

"Our restless sleep was often interrupted by noisy and futile disputes, by curses, by kicks and blows blindly delivered to ward off some encroaching and inevitable contact. Then someone would light a candle, and its mournful flicker would reveal an obscure agitation, a human mass, extended across the floor, confused and continuous, sluggish and aching, rising here and there in sudden convulsions and immediately collapsing again in exhaustion."[79] Levi evokes the changing landscape, the successive names of cities, Austrian first, then Czech, and finally Polish: "The convoy stopped for the last time, in the dead of night, in the middle of a dark silent plain."[80] They had arrived.

Most deportees would have considered Levi's journey a luxury trip. Usually freight cars had insufficient openings for fresh air and an entirely insufficient supply of water. Even the relatively privileged transport from

Theresienstadt to Auschwitz in June 1944, described by Ruth Kluger, gives an intimation of the more common traveling conditions: "The doors were sealed, and air came through a small rectangle that served as window. Maybe there was a second rectangle at the back of the car, but that was the place for the luggage. . . . Only one person could stand in this privileged spot [the small rectangle for air], and he was not likely to give it up. Rather he was apt to be someone who knew how to use his elbows. There were simply too many of us. . . . Soon the wagon reeked with the various smells that humans produce if they have to stay where they are. . . . The train stood around, it was summer, the temperature rose. The still air smelled of sweat, urine, excrement. A whiff of panic trembled in the air."[81]

All of this was still peaceful. With a few more deportees per car, everything changed. Barely some weeks later, in July 1944, the very short trip (140 miles) from the Starachowice labor camp to Auschwitz unfolded differently. According to surviving deportees, the train was brutally overloaded on orders of the Starachowice police chief, as the Red Army was approaching. Around 75 women were packed per freight car, and separately 100 to 150 men were crammed into each wagon.[82] The journey lasted thirty-six hours. The struggle for water and mainly for air soon started in the men's cars. "Nineteen-year-old Ruben Z. was 'very lucky' to find a place beside the small window for fresh air at the beginning of the trip. He got several beatings from people who were desperate to get near the window, and was finally pushed away and lost his place. He became so dizzy and weak that he could not remember what happened thereafter, other than that fifteen people had died in his car by the time they reached Birkenau."[83] In one car 27 men died; in another, 30 out of 120 men.[84]

Not all the men who died on the train suffocated. About twenty members of the Starachowice Jewish Council and the Jewish police, among them the head of the camp police, Wilczek, and a man called Rubenstein, were strangled by a group of inmates recently transferred from Majdanek.[85] Henry G. and many others in the same car saw it all: The fighting for air turned into a life-and-death struggle between the "Lubliners," mostly young and strong, and the Starachowice *Prominenten.* Henry G. arrived in Birkenau sitting on the pile of corpses.[86]

* * *

If transportation of the deportees was the backbone of the "Final Solution" for the Germans and one further deadly trap for the Jews, the growing demands for slave labor represented a fundamental dilemma for the killers. The wholesale murder of the vast majority of Jews in the General Government was of course not in question, and the continent-wide annihilation progressed apace. The contentions chiefly arose from the use of Jewish skilled labor both for the needs of the Wehrmacht and in the ambitious industrial projects of the SS themselves, mainly in the Lublin district. Obversely, however, both for Hitler and Himmler, the security risks involved in the survival of Jewish workers would remain the overriding imperative, also in 1943.

The Wehrmacht forcefully expressed its views in a memorandum presented on September 18, 1942, by Gen. Kurt von Gienanth, the commander of the German forces in the General Government. Gienanth spelled out in great detail the essential function of Jewish specialized workers and the damage that would result from their elimination. His conclusion was clear: "Unless work of military importance is to suffer, Jews cannot be released until replacements have been trained, and then only step by step.... The general policy will be to eliminate the Jews from work as quickly as possible without harming work of military importance."[87]

Himmler replied on October 9. The Reichsführer's letter was uncompromising, even threatening. To bolster its overall thrust, it did not offer any detailed answers to Gienanth's point-by-point argumentation but invoked Hitler's decision: "I have given orders," Himmler wrote, "that all so-called armament workers who are actually employed solely in tailoring, furrier and shoe-making workshops be collected in concentration camps on the spot.... The Wehrmacht will send its orders to us, and we guarantee the continuous delivery of the items of clothing required. I have issued instructions, however, that ruthless steps be taken against all those who consider they should oppose this move in the alleged interest of armament needs, but who in reality only seek to support the Jews and their own businesses.

"Jews in real war industries, i.e., armament workshops, etc are to be withdrawn step by step. As a first stage they are to be concentrated in separate halls in the factories. In a second stage in this procedure the work teams in these separate halls will be combined ... so that we will then have simply a few closed concentration camp industries in the Government-General.

"Our endeavor will be to replace this Jewish labor force with Poles and to consolidate most of these Jewish concentration camp enterprises—in the Eastern part of the Government-General, if possible. But there, too, in accordance with the Führer's wish, the Jews are some day to disappear."[88]

In his answer Himmler did not hide his ambition to control the specialized Jewish work force that would be slaving in "concentration camps enterprises—in the Eastern part of the General Government, if possible." There, in the existing overall framework of SS enterprises (*Deutsche Wirtschaftsbetriebe*, or DWB), a new company, *Ostindustrie* Gmbh (or OSTI) had been set up by Globocnik according to Pohl's (and Himmler's) directives. Jewish slave labor would toil in the previously existing and the newly established SS workshops, and the entire endeavor would be financed by the assets of the victims murdered in the "Aktion Reinhardt" camps.[89]

Very soon, however, these plans would be put in abeyance, and OSTI would be scuttled in view of ominous portents in Himmler's eyes: the Warsaw ghetto uprising of April 1943, followed a few months later by the uprisings in Treblinka and Sobibor, and the rapid progress of the Red Army toward former Poland. Thus immediately after the ghetto revolt the Reichsführer was back at his "full extermination" policy to preempt any further Jewish threat. In a meeting held on May 10, 1943, he restated his immediate goals: "I shall not stop the evacuation of the approximately 300,000 Jews remaining in the General Government but rather implement it in the greatest haste. Notwithstanding the unrest that the evacuation of the Jews creates at the time of its implementation [an obvious reference to the Warsaw uprising], once accomplished it will be the main condition for a total calming down of the territory."[90] Two days later SS Obergruffenführer Ulrich Greifelt, chief of staff of the RKFdV, probably alluded to the same meeting when he noted: "A priority task in the General Government remains the evacuation of the still remaining 300,000 to 400,000 Jews."[91]

Himmler's fears about Jewish armed actions in the General Government, possibly in coordination with Soviet partisans or with the Polish underground, were apparently not taken as seriously by a local administration more immediately worried by the needs of the armaments industry. The divergence of views became blatant at a high-level meeting, held in Kraków on May 31. Krüger, the HSSPF elevated to the rank of secretary of state in Frank's domain, took a rather unexpected stand: "The elimination of the Jews," he declared, "did undoubtedly bring about a calming down of the overall situation. For the police, this had been one of the most difficult and unpleasant tasks, but it was in the European interest. . . . Recently he [Krüger] had again received the order to complete the elimination of the Jews in a very short time [*Er habe neulich erst wieder den Befehl erhalten in ganz kurzer Zeit die Entjudung durchzuführen*]. One has been compelled to pull out the Jews from the armaments industry and from enterprises working for the war economy. . . . The Reichsführer wished that the employment of these Jews should stop. He [Krüger] discussed the matter with Lieutnant General Schindler [head of the armaments inspectorate of the OKW, under the command of General Gienanth] and thought that in the end the Reichsführer's wish could not be fulfilled. The Jewish workers included specialists, precision mechanics, and other qualified artisans, that could not be simply replaced by Poles at the present time." After further mentioning the qualities and physical endurance of these Jewish workers, Krüger told the meeting that he would ask Kaltenbrunner to describe the situation to Himmler and persuade him to keep these workers.[92] Yet none of these arguments would ultimately help, as we shall see.

V

Throughout the twelve years of the Third Reich, looting of Jewish property was of the essence. It was the most easily understood and most widely adhered-to aspect of the anti-Jewish campaign, rationalized, if necessary, by the simplest ideological tenets. But even looting encountered unexpected problems at every step, particularly during the extermination years. Thus notwithstanding dire threats, theft and corruption eluded all controls to the very end, although the Reich finance agencies and the SS bureaucracy attempted to keep a handle on all operations, large and small.[93]

On the spot, at local murder sites, the procedure was simple. The victims, for example groups of Vilna Jews about to be killed in Ponar, would hand over any valuables to the SD man in command of the operation; after the killing their belongings would be searched again by members of the commando and any object of value had to be handed over to the officer in charge, under penalty of death.[94] Denunciation of Jews in hiding or of other related offenses was rewarded in kind. Such a stroke of good fortune befell a Frau Meyer in Riga: Having turned in a neighbor for keeping Jewish property, she was allowed to buy a gold chain bracelet at a dirt-cheap price.[95]

Of course major operations were centralized in the Reich capital. In Berlin all gold (including gold dental crowns torn from corpses' mouths) was usually smelted right away by Degussa and, often mixed with gold from other provenances, turned into ingots for the Reichsbank.[96] Other metals were mostly smelted as well, except if the value of the item as such was greater than its value as smelted metal. According to historian Michael MacQueen the most valuable items were turned over to a few jewelers trusted by the Finance Ministry or the SS, and were exchanged in occupied or neutral countries for industrial diamonds essential to the German war industry. The activities of one such longtime intermediary working mainly with Swiss dealers have been pieced together, and it seems that the authorities in Bern were well aware of the ongoing transactions and of the steady supply of industrial diamonds to the Reich, despite Allied economic warfare measures.[97]

From mid-1942 on, most of the victims' belongings piled up in the major killing centers of "Aktion Reinhardt" and in Auschwitz-Birkenau, as the exterminations reached a high point. In early August 1942 negotiations among WVHA and all central Reich finance and economic agencies led to an agreement according to which Pohl's main office would centralize and itemize the booty. Himmler informed the HSSPFs of the decision and officially appointed Pohl to his new function. Within a few weeks, on September 26, Pohl's deputy, SS Brigadeführer August Frank, issued a first set of guidelines, regulating all use and distribution of Jewish spoils from the camps, from precious stones to "blankets, umbrellas, baby carriages," to "glasses with gold frames," to "women's underwear," to "shaving utensils, pocket knives, scissors," and the like. Prices were set by the WVHA: "a pair of used pants—3 marks; a woolen blanket—6 marks." The final admonition was essential: "Check that all Jewish stars have been removed from all clothing before transfer. Carefully check whether all hidden and sewn-in valuables have been removed from all articles to be transferred."[98]

Regarding any items to be transfered to the Reichsbank, Pohl appointed SS Hauptsturmführer Bruno Melmer to be directly in charge of the operation. While the first deliveries of valuables from the camps were deposited in the "Melmer account" on August 26, all precious metals, foreign currency, jewelry, and so on, were further turned over to Albert Thoms's precious metals section of the Reichsbank for further use.[99]

Throughout the Continent Jewish furniture and household goods were, as we saw, the domain of Rosenberg's agency. An undated note from Rosenberg's office, probably written in the late fall of 1942 or in early 1943, gave a succinct overview of the distribution process. While part of the furniture was allocated to Rosenberg ministry's offices in the eastern territories, most of the spoils were handed out or auctioned off to the Reich population. "On 31 October 1942, the Führer agreed with the proposal of Reich Minister Alfred Rosenberg to give primary consideration to persons suffering from bomb damage in the Reich and ordered that, in the execution of the project, all assistance be given to Office-West and that transports are to be dispatched as Wehrmacht goods.

"Up to now, by using free freight space, 144,809 cubic meters of household goods have been removed from occupied Western Territories . . . Parts of the material were delivered to the following German cities: Oberhausen, Bottrop, Recklinghausen, Münster, Düsseldorf, Cologne, Osnabrück, Hamburg, Lübeck, Rostock, and Karlsruhe.[100]

Vast amounts of goods, coming mainly from the camps (Pohl's, Globocnik's and Greiser's territories), had to be mended before being shipped on to German agencies or markets; clothing was processed with particular care: Stars had to be taken off, as we saw; blood and other bodily stains washed away; and the usual wear and tear dealt with as thoroughly as possible in SS clothing workshops. Who decided what items could or could not be repaired or who had the authority to assess degrees of damage remains unclear. One could not send tens of thousands of torn socks to the outlets in the Reich. The issue arose—but received no answer—in an incident described by Filip Müller, sometime in the late spring of 1942, in one of the Auschwitz crematoriums.

Müller, himself a Slovak Jew, arrived in Auschwitz in April 1942. He had just been transferred to the *Sonderkommando* (which will be discussed further on): This was his initiation, so to speak, under the supervision of SS Unterscharführer Stark. As was still common during these months, a group of Slovak Jews had been gassed with their clothes on. "Strip the stiffs!" Stark yelled and gave Müller a blow. "Before me," Müller remembered, "lay the corpse of a woman. With trembling hands and shaking all over I began to remove her stockings. It was the first time in my life that I touched a dead body. She was not yet quite cold. As I pulled the stocking down her leg, it tore. Stark, who had been watching, struck me again, bellowing: 'What the hell d'you think you're doing? Mind out, and get a move on! These things are to be used again!' To show us the correct way he began to remove the stockings from another female corpse. But he, too, did not manage to take them off without at least a small tear."[101]

Hamburg has been thoroughly studied. In 1942, in Hamburg alone forty-five shiploads of goods looted from Dutch Jews arrived; they represented a net weight of 27,227 tons. Approximately 100,000 inhabitants acquired some of the stolen belongings at harbor auctions. According to a female witness, "Simple housewives . . . were suddenly wearing fur coats, dealt in coffee and jewelry, had antique furniture and carpets from the harbor, from Holland, from France."[102]

Throughout 1943 assessments and inventories of looted Jewish property became frequent at all levels of the system. The total value of "Jewish belongings" secured during "Aktion Reinhardt" up to December 15, 1943, was estimated at the operation's headquarters in Lublin as amounting to 178,745,960.59 reichsmarks. This official estimate, signed by SS Sturmbannführer Georg Wippern, was forwarded to the WVHA on January 5, 1944, from Trieste, the headquarters of Globocnik's new assignment.[103] It seems to have been the late sequel to a January 15, 1943, message from Himmler to both Krüger and Pohl: "On my visit to Warsaw," the Reichsführer's admonition ran, "I also inspected the warehouses containing the material and the goods taken over from the Jews, that is, at the emigration of the Jews.

"I again request SS Obergruppenführer Pohl to arrange a written agreement with the Minister of Economics," Himmler went on, "regarding each individual category; whether it is a question of watch crystals, of which hundreds of thousands—perhaps even millions—are lying there, and which, for practical purposes could be distributed to the German watchmakers; or whether it is a question of turning lathes." After adding some further examples, Himmler warned: "I believe, on the whole, we cannot be too precise." And, following more instructions, he added: "I request SS Obergruppenführer Pohl to clear up and arrange these matters to the last detail, as the strictest accuracy now will spare us much vexation later." Three weeks later Pohl sent in a detailed account of the textile items collected from Lublin and Auschwitz: They filled 825 railway freight cars.[104]

There can be no precise overview of the plunder and expropriation of Europe's Jewish victims. Orchestrated and implemented throughout the Continent first and foremost by the Germans, it spread to local officials, police, neighbors, or just any passerby in Amsterdam or Kovno, in Warsaw or Paris. It included "feeding" extortionists, distributing bribes, or paying "fines," individually but mainly on a huge collective scale. It comprised the grabbing of homes, the looting of household objects, furniture, art collections, libraries, clothes, underclothes, bedding; it meant the impounding of bank accounts and of insurance policies, the stealing of stores, or of industrial or commercial enterprises, the plundering of corpses (women's hair, gold teeth, earrings, wedding rings, watches, artificial limbs, fountain pens, glasses), in short pouncing on anything usable, exchangeable, or salable. It comprised slave labor, deadly medical experiments, enforced prostitution, loss of salaries, pensions, any imaginable income—and, for millions—loss of life. And of socks torn in stripping the corpses.

On July 1, 1943, the Thirteenth Ordinance to the Reich Citizenship Law was signed by the ministers of the interior, finance, and of justice. Article 2, paragraph 1 read: "The property of a Jew shall be confiscated by the Reich after his death."[105]

VI

From the early summer of 1942, Auschwitz II–Birkenau gradually changed from a slave labor camp where sporadic exterminations had taken place to an extermination center where the regular flow of deportees allowed for the selection of constantly expendable slave laborers. Throughout 1943 the Auschwitz complex of main and satellite camps grew vastly: The number of inmates rose from 30,000 to about 80,000 in early 1944, and simultaneously tens of satellite camps (about fifty in

1944) were established next to plants and mines, even on the site of agricultural stations. In Birkenau a women's camp, a Gypsies' "family camp" and a "family camp" for Jews from Theresienstadt were set up in 1943 (the inmates of both "family camps" were later exterminated). On September 15, 1942, Speer authorized the allocation of 13.7 million reichsmarks for the rapid development of buildings and killing facilities.[106]

As we saw, the first gassing had taken place at Auschwitz Main Camp (Auschwitz I), in the reconverted morgue. Then provisional gas chambers were set up in Birkenau, first at the "red house" (Bunker I), then at the "white house" (Bunker II). After some delay a technically much improved Crematorium II, which had initially been ordered for the main camp, was set up in Birkenau. Crematoriums III, IV, and V followed. After the shutting down of the gas chamber in the main camp, the installations were renumbered I to IV, all in Birkenau.[107] These gas chambers became operational in the course of 1943.[108] Crematoriums VI and VII were apparently planned but never built. They would certainly have been of help in the late spring of 1944, as hundreds of thousands of Hungarian Jews were gassed within a few weeks and the murdering capacity of the system was stretched to its utmost limits, even after Bunker II had been reactivated as an auxiliary killing installation.

The man who, more than anyone else, orchestrated the transformation of Auschwitz into *the* central extermination camp of the Nazi system by overseeing the building of the new gassing installations in Birkenau was Pohl's construction chief, Hans Kammler. "In Kammler," historian Michael Thad Allen wrote, "technological competence and extreme Nazi fanaticism coexisted. . . . For his intensity, his mastery of engineering, his organizational genius, and his passion for National Socialism, SS men esteemed Kammler as a paragon."[109] In Speer's words, "nobody would have dreamed that some day he would be one of Himmler's most brutal and most ruthless henchmen."[110] The Kammlers of the Third Reich were the technological managers of the "Final Solution" during its mid- and late phases. As previously emphasized, their ideological fanaticism was essential to keep the system working in spite of increasing difficulties.

On January 29, 1943, Max Bischoff, the head of Auschwitz Zentrale Bauleitung (Central Building Management) reported to Kammler: "Crematorium II has been completed—save for some minor construction work—using all the forces available, in spite of unspeakable difficulties and severe cold, in twenty-four-hour shifts. The fires were started in the ovens in the presence of Oberingenieur Kurt Prüfer, representative of the contractors of the firm Topf and Sons, Erfurt, and they are working most satisfactorily. The planks from the concrete ceiling of the cellar used as a mortuary have not yet been removed, on account of the frost. This is not very important, however, as the gassing cellar can be used for that purpose. The firm Topf and Sons was not able to start deliveries of the aeration and ventilation equipment according to the timetable requested by Central Building Management because of restrictions in the use of railroad cars. As soon as the aeration and ventilation equipment arrives, the installing will start."[111]

Crematorium II was activated in March 1943. The gas chamber was built mainly underground and accessed by way of the underground disrobing hall. But its roof was slightly elevated above ground level to allow the pouring in of the Zyklon B pellets from the canisters, through four openings protected by small brick chimneys built around and over them. In the gas chambers of Crematoriums II and III, the Zyklon pellets were not thrown from the vents to the floor of the chamber but lowered in containers that descended into "wire mesh introduction devices [*Drahtnetzeinschiebvorrichtungen*]," or wire mesh columns. The columns allowed for the full release of the gas into the chamber—once the adequate temperature was reached—and the retrieval of the pellets at the end of the operation to avoid further release of gas while the corpses were being pulled from the chamber (which had no other openings but the single access door.)[112]

Apart from the hall for disrobing and the gas chamber (or gas chambers), the basements of crematoriums built on two levels included a hall for the handling of the corpses (for the pulling out of gold teeth, cutting women's hair, detaching prosthetic limbs, collecting any valuables such as wedding rings, glasses, and the like) by the Jewish *Sonderkommando* members after they had dragged the bodies out of the gas chamber. Then elevators carried the corpses to the ground floor, where several ovens reduced them to ashes. After the grinding of bones in special mills, the ashes were used as fertilizer in the nearby fields, dumped in local forests, or tossed into the river, nearby. As for the members of the *Sonderkommandos,* they were periodically killed and replaced by a new batch.

Prüfer was so proud of his installation that he had it patented.[113] Besides Topf, a dozen other firms were involved in the construction of the four crematoriums.[114] Despite the slow process of setting up the new units, their frequent malfunctioning, and the insufficient burning capacity of the ovens during peak activity (which compelled the camp authorities to revert to open-pit burning), the Auschwitz murder machinery did fulfill its task.

Primo Levi, whose journey to Auschwitz we described, was a twenty-four-year-old chemist from Turin who had joined a small group of Jews hiding in the mountains above the city, within the loose framework of the Resistance organization Giustizia e Libertà (Justice and Liberty). On December 13, 1943, Levi and his companions were arrested by the Fascist militia and, a few weeks later, transported to the Fossoli assembly camp. By the end of February 1944 the Germans took over. On February 22 the 650 Jews of the camp were deported northward.

"The climax [of the four-day journey] came suddenly," Levi later wrote: "The door opened with a crash, and the dark echoed with outlandish orders in that curt, barbaric barking of Germans in command which seems to give vent to millennial anger. . . . In less than ten minutes all the fit men had been collected together in a group. What happened to the others, to the women, to the children, to the old men, we could establish neither then nor later: The night swallowed them up, purely and simply. Today, however, we know . . . that of our convoy no more than ninety-six men and twenty-nine women entered the respective camps of Monowitz-Buna and Birkenau, and that of all the others, more than five hundred in number, not one was living two days later."[115]

About her arrival in Birkenau at the age of twelve, Ruth Kluger remembered that when the doors of the freight car were unsealed, unaware that one had to jump, she fell on the ramp: "I got up and wanted to cry," she reminisced, "or at least sniffle, but the tears didn't come. They dried up in the palpable creepiness of the place. We should have been relieved . . . to be breathing fresh air at last. But the air wasn't fresh. It smelled like nothing on earth, and I knew instinctively and immediately that this was no place for crying, that the last thing I needed was to attract attention." Kluger then noted the same welcoming party as Levi: "We were surrounded by the odious, bullying noise of the men who had hauled us out of the train with the monosyllables '*raus, raus*' (get out), and who simply didn't stop shouting as they were driving us along, like mad, barking dogs. I was glad to be walking safely in the middle of our heap of humanity."[116]

In the din of human barking, some inmates later remembered the *Raus,* others the *Schneller*: The effect was the same. Greta Salus, who also arrived from Theresienstadt, described her first impression: "*Schneller, schneller, schneller* (faster, faster, faster)—it still rings in my ears, this word that from now on hounded us day and night, whipped us on, and never gave us any rest. On the double—that was the watch word; eat, sleep, work, die on the double. . . . I often asked people with the same experiences what their impressions were on their arrival in Auschwitz. Most of them weren't able to tell me much about it, and almost all of them said they were utterly addled and half-dazed, as though they had been hit on the head. They all perceived the floodlights as torturous and the noise as unbearable."[117]

The first selection took place on arrival, on the spot. As SS physician Friedrich Entress explained in his postwar statement, "The young people under sixteen, all the mothers in charge of children, and all the sick or frail people were loaded into trucks and taken to the gas chambers. The others were handed over to the head of the labor allocation and taken to the camp."[118]

In fact Entress should have remembered one more category of Jews selected on arrival: interesting specimens for some of the medical or anthropological experiments. Thus Entress's notorious colleague, Joseph Mengele, who very often took part in the initial selections, was also present at arrivals to search for his special material. "Scouting incoming transports for twins with the order *Zwillinge heraus!* (Twins forward!), he also looked for individuals with physical abnormalities who might be used for interesting postmortems. Their measurements were taken, they were shot by an SS noncom, and their bodies dissected. Sometimes their cleaned bones were sent to Verschuer's research institute in Berlin-Dahlem."[119] (Prof. Dr. Otmar von Verschuer was Mengele's mentor and the Director of the Institute for Biological-Racial Research at the Kaiser Wilhelm Institute in Berlin-Dahlem.)

The deportees selected for slave labor were usually identified with a serial number, tattooed on their lower left arm; the category to which they belonged was indicated on their striped inmate "uniform" by a colored triangle (with different colors for politicals, criminals, homosexuals, Gypsies) which, for all Jews was turned into a six-pointed star by the addition of a reversed yellow triangle.[120] The results of the initial selections aimed at filling the ranks of the labor pool were at times truly disappointing. For example, in a transport from Theresienstadt at the end of January 1943, fewer than 1,000 out of some 5,000 deportees could be of some use at the I. G. Farben works. The others were immediately gassed.[121] It was even worse in March, although the transports from Berlin were filled with deportees seized during the *Fabrikaktion.* As family members had been taken along with the deported men, in the transport of March 3, out of a total 1,750 Jews, 1,118 were women and children. Only two hundred of these women and children were not immediately subjected to "special treatment." And so it went with the four transports that followed.[122]

The march, or transportation to the crematoriums, of those selected for immediate gassing usually took place without incidents, as, according to a well-honed routine, the victims were told they would undergo disinfection. At the entrance of the crematorium, the new arrivals were taken in charge by a few SS men and by Jewish *Sonderkommando* members. These *Sonderkomanndo* men mixed with the unsuspecting victims in the undressing hall and, if need be, like the SS guards, they offered a few soothing comments. Once the undressing was completed and the belongings carefully hung on numbered hooks (shoes tied together), to prove that there was no ground for fear, the party of SS men and *Sonderkommando* inmates accompanied the throng of candidates for "disinfection" into the gas chamber, fitted with the shower contraptions. A member of the *Sonderkommando* usually stayed until the very last moment; often an SS man also remained standing at the doorsill until the last victim had crossed it. Then, the door was hermetically sealed and the gas pellets poured in.[123]

A physician was on duty to ensure that gassing had been completed and no sign of life remained. Dr. Johann Paul Kremer, professor of medicine at the University of Münster and an SS Hauptsturmführer, kept a diary about his daily activities at Auschwitz between August 30 and November 20, 1942: "2 September 1942. For the first time, at three this morning, present at a special operation (*Sonderaktion*) . . . 5 September

1942. . . . In the evening around 8 o'clock again attended a *Sonderaktion* from Holland. The men [the *Sonderkommando* inmates] push themselves to participate in these operations, because special provisions are passed out, including a fifth of liquor, 5 cigarettes, 100 grams of baloney [bologna], and bread. . . . 6 September: Today, Sunday, excellent lunch: tomato soup, one-half chicken with potatoes and red cabbage (20 grams fat). Sweets and fantastic vanilla ice cream. . . . Evening at 8 o'clock outside again for a *Sonderaktion*."[124]

Incidentally, there could be a weird association between Kremer's obsessive attention to his daily food intake, which reappears throughout the diary, and his research in Auschwitz on the medical aspects of starvation. His specimens would be put on a dissection table, interrogated about their weight loss, then killed and dissected. The effects of starvation could then be studied at leisure. According to Robert Jay Lifton, Kremer was expecting to pursue his research after the war.[125]

On September 5 Kremer attended a selection of *Muselmannen* [Muslims], in this case of women slave laborers no longer fit for work; it did not proceed as easily as the selection of new arrivals; the victims knew what awaited them. "The gassing of exhausted women in the concentration camp, cachectics generally known by the term 'Muslims' was especially unpleasant," Kremer declared in his deposition in a postwar trial. "I remember that I once took part in the gassing of a group of women. I couldn't say now how many there were. When I arrived near the bunker, they were sitting on the ground, still dressed. Because their camp clothes were in rags, they were not admitted into the undressing barracks; they had to undress in the open air. From their behavior I deduced that they knew what was in store for them, for they were crying and pleading with the SS men for their lives. But all were chased into the gas chambers and gassed. . . . It was under the impressions that I felt at the time that I wrote in my diary on 5 September 1942: 'The most horrible of horrors. Hauptscharführer Thilo was quite right when he said to me today that we had reached the anus of the world.' I used that expression because I couldn't imagine anything more frightful or more monstrous."[126]

Much has been written about the members of the *Sonderkommando*, those few hundreds of inmates, almost all Jews, who lived at the very bottom of hell, so to speak, before being killed and replaced by others. As we just saw, at times they helped the SS in soothing the fears of the prisoners entering the gas chambers, they pulled out the bodies, plundered the corpses, burned the remains, and disposed of the ashes; sorted and dispatched the belongings of the victims to "Kanada" (the derisive appellation of the hall where the belongings were stored and processed). An inmate of the women's camp that adjoined the crematoriums, Krystina Zywulska, asked one of the *Sonderkommando* members how he could bear to do this work, day in and day out. His explanations—the will to live, witnessing, revenge—ended with what probably was the gist of it all: "You think that those working in Sonderkommandos are monsters? I'm telling you, they're like the rest, just much more unhappy."[127]

In many ways Auschwitz illustrated the difference between the Nazi concentration camp system in general and the extermination system in its specific anti-Jewish dimension. In this multipurpose camp with a mixed population of inmates, the non-Jewish inmates soon became aware of the fundamental difference between their own fate and that of the Jews. The non-Jewish inmate could survive, given some luck and some support from his national or political group. The Jew, on the other hand, had ultimately no recourse against death and, as a norm, remained utterly defenseless. For many a Polish or Ukrainian inmate, or for many a German "criminal" inmate, this was but one more opportunity to exercise their own anti-Jewish terror within the generalized system of terror or just to assert their own power against this entirely powerless group.[128]

Alluding to the status of Jews in the camp system in general and in Auschwitz particularly, where he himself had been an inmate, Yisrael Gutman put it this way: "The Jews were pariahs in the concentration camps and were regarded as such by the other internees. Anti-Semitism was perceptible in the camps and assumed the most violent forms. Attacks against Jews were encouraged by the Nazis. Even those who were not anti-Jewish and were in a position to oppose the tide of hatred which flooded the camp acceded to the accepted norms and regarded the Jews as abandoned, miserable creatures who were best avoided." There were also many examples of help extended to Jews, but for Gutman, "These were of sporadic, individual nature, while anti-Semitic attitudes and attacks on Jews were the rule in the majority of camps."[129]

Among Jews themselves the constant threat of death at any sign of weakness exacerbated tensions, including the prejudices of each national group against some others: "Instead of displaying solidarity [the Jews in Auschwitz] felt enmity toward one another," Benedikt Kautsky wrote, with somewhat exaggerated harshness. . . . "The 'Poles' now stood opposed to the 'Germans,' the 'Dutch' to the 'French,' and the 'Greeks' to the 'Hungarians.' It was by no means unusual for one Jew to use arguments against another Jew that were not very different from those of the anti-Semites."[130] As for those Jews who had been granted some power over their brethren, as "kapos," for example, they often clung to the illusion of saving their own skin by brutalizing other Jews. Not all of them followed this path, but many did.[131]

As Auschwitz was turning into the main murdering center of the regime, the Jewish inmates soon considerably outnumbered all the other groups added together. According to historian Peter Hayes, "From the opening of the camp in May 1940 to its evacuation in January 1945, some 1.3 million people were transported to the site, of whom only about 200,000 ever left alive, only 125,000 of these surviving the Third Reich. Of these captives, 1.1 million were Jews, about eighty percent of whom succumbed upon arrival or shortly thereafter."[132]

"The Jews arrive here, that is, to Auschwitz, at a weekly rate of 7 to 8,000," Pvt. SM wrote home on December 7, 1942, on his way to the front. "Shortly thereafter they die a 'hero's death.'" And he added: "It is really good to see the world."[133]

SM was not alone in enjoying Auschwitz. For the approximately 7,000 members of the SS who at one time or another were assigned to the camp and served there first under Höss until November 1943, then under Arthur Liebehenschel and Richard Baer, life was definitely not unpleasant.[134] All the usual amenities were available: decent housing, good food (as we saw from Kremer's diary), medical care, long stays for spouses or companions, and regular furloughs to the *Heimat* or to special vacation spots.[135] In the camp itself, to relieve the stress generated by their work, the SS could enjoy music played specially for them by the female inmates' orchestra, which performed from April 1943 to October 1944.[136] And outside the camp, cultural life comprised an array of performances, once every two or three weeks at least, with a preference for comedies, *A Bride in Flight*, *Interrupted Wedding Night*, or *Merry Varieties,* and soirées under the motto "Attack of the Comics." There was no shortage of classics either: In February 1943 the Dresden State Theater presented *Goethe Then and Now.*[137]

VII

Details about the extermination spread through any number of channels in the Reich and beyond. Thus, for example, every summer hundreds of women visited their husbands who were guards in Auschwitz and other camps, as just mentioned; they often stayed for long periods of time. As for the German population of the town of Auschwitz, it complained about the odor produced by the overloaded crematories.[138] This particular problem was confirmed by Höss: "It became apparent during the first cremations in the open air that in the long run it would not be possible to continue in that manner. During bad weather or when a strong wind was blowing, the stench of burning flesh was carried for many miles and caused the whole neighborhood to talk about the burning of Jews, despite official counter-propaganda. It is true that all members of the SS detailed for the extermination were bound to strict secrecy over the whole operation, but as later SS legal proceedings showed, this was not always observed. Even the most severe punishment was not able to stop their love of gossip."[139]

What German civilians living in eastern Upper Silesia gathered about Auschwitz, what railwaymen, policemen, soldiers, and anybody traveling through the eastern reaches of the Reich could easily hear or witness, Reich Germans visiting the Warthegau or settled there learned simply by comparing what they had seen on their earlier visits, in 1940 or 1941, and what could not be missed one or two years later. "I saw nothing more of the Jewish population of what had been Poland," Annelies Regenstein reminisced in an interview. "In 1940, I traveled on one occasion through the ghetto in Litzmannstadt, a dark area of the city fenced off with barbed wire in which thousands of Jews were herded together and left to vegetate. *Something of the terrible fate of these people probably seeped into the population* (emphasis in original). But anti-Semitic propaganda and a hostile attitude on the part of the resettled Germans towards the Jews made them indifferent." As historian Elisabeth Harvey put it: "She [Regenstein] did not spell out her own reactions at the time to the knowledge that was 'probably seeping' into German consciousness."[140]

Another former woman settler, Elisabeth Grabe, spoke more explicitly of her own experience, also in the Warthegau: "The Jews who had lived in the ghetto in Zychlin and Kutno disappeared one day (I can't remember when that was, perhaps 1942). People whispered to each other that they had been loaded into lorries and gassed [*Sie wären in Autos geladen und vergast, wurde genuschelt*]. These rumors affected me even more painfully than the notion that I was using confiscated [Polish] furniture."[141] Of course the information thus whispered around described quite precisely the killings in Chelmno.

By early 1943 the information about mass extermination of the Jews was so widespread in the Reich (even if the "technical details" were mostly not precise) as to have probably reached a majority of the population. A recurring rumor mentioned the gassing of Jews in tunnels somewhere on the way to the East.[142] This kind of information didn't seem to soften anti-Jewish hatred and brutality. Thus the Spanish Consul in Berlin reported that, in April 1943, trucks with deportees were stopped on their way to the railway station by bombed-out people, who attempted to seize the luggage of the victims.[143] Generally speaking, recent historical research increasingly turns German ignorance of the fate of the Jews into a mythical postwar construct.

The Party Chancellery deemed it necessary to issue appropriate guidelines in response to the spreading knowledge. The opening sentences of the confidential document sent out on October 9, 1942, were telling: "In the context of work on the final solution of the Jewish question there has recently been some discussion by people in various parts of the Reich about 'very harsh measures' against the Jews, particularly in the eastern territories. It has been established that such statements—usually distorted and exaggerated—are passed on by people on leave from the various units engaged in the East, who have themselves had the opportunities to observe such measures."[144]

Opposition leaders were particularly well informed. Historian Hans Mommsen has shown that in 1942 the gassing of Jews was known to the Jesuit priest Alfred Delp, to the Prussian finance minister Johannes Popitz, and to Helmuth von Moltke, among others.[145] On October 10, 1942, Moltke wrote to his wife: "Yesterday's lunch was interesting in that the man I ate with had just come from the [General] Government and gave an authentic report on the 'SS blast-furnace.' So far I had not believed it, but he assured me that it was true: 6,000 people a day are 'processed' in that furnace. He was in a prison camp 6 km away, and the officers there reported it to him as absolute fact."[146]

At about the same time members of the clandestine "Freiburg Circle" were putting the final touch to the "Great Memorandum," the outcome of the group's discussions about the social, political, and moral bases of a post–National Socialist Germany. The Freiburg economics professor Konstantin von Dietze authored the fifth and last appendix to the memorandum, "Proposals for the Solution of the Jewish Question in Germany." The document was discussed in November 1942 at Dietze's home by several leaders of the political opposition (among them Karl Goerdeler), key members of the Confessing Church, and others. Although the "Final Solution" as such was not mentioned in the fifth appendix, the mass extermination of Jews was recognized: "These persecutions [of the Jews] have unmistakably been at the will of the central authorities. They led not only to innumerable forced evacuations, during which many Jews died; hundreds of thousands of human beings have been killed systematically merely because of their Jewish ancestry. . . . The full extent of such infamous deeds is hardly imaginable; in any case it cannot be portrayed fully in objective facts or figures, since no agency has openly assumed responsibility for them."[147]

Recognition of the mass extermination did not, however, induce the Freiburg group to consider the Jews in post-Nazi Germany as individuals and citizens like all others. "The existence of a numerically significant body of Jews within a people," the memorandum emphasized, "constitutes a problem that must lead to recurrent difficulties, if it is not subjected to a fundamental and large-scale arrangement."[148] A series of contemplated measures for dealing with this "Jewish problem," both in Germany and on the international level, followed: The traditional anti-Semitism of German conservatives and of the German churches found full expression, with an additional touch of notions garnered from Nazism: "All who belong to the Jewish confession, as well as those who belonged to this confession earlier but have not joined another religious affiliation, are considered Jews. If Jews convert to Christianity then they remain members of the body of Jews, as long as they have not been naturalized by the state in their homeland." And, beforehand, the authors declared: "The state, after revoking the Nuremberg Laws, renounces all special regulations for the Jews, since the number of surviving Jews and those returning to Germany will not be so large that they still could be considered a danger for the German Volkstum."[149]

Another illustration of the mixture of knowledge regarding the exterminations and the permanence of anti-Semitism among German opposition groups and in much of the population appeared in the second clandestine leaflet distributed in early July 1942 by the essentially Catholic "White Rose" resistance group based at the University of Munich. In this leaflet the murder of Jews in Poland was mentioned. Yet the Munich students presented the issue in a strangely convoluted way and added an immediate disclaimer:

"We do not intend to say anything about the Jewish question in the broadsheet; nor do we want to enter a plea in their defense. No, we simply want to cite as an example the fact that since the conquest of Poland 300,000 Jews have been murdered in that country in the most bestial fashion. In this we see the most fearful crime against human dignity, a crime with which no other in the whole history of mankind can be compared. For whatever one thinks of the Jewish question, the Jews too are human beings and this has been done to human beings. Perhaps someone may say the Jews deserved such a fate; this statement would be an incredible presumption. But assuming somebody did say this, how would he deal with the fact that the whole of the younger generation of Polish nobility has been annihilated?"[150]

In other words these militant enemies of the regime were well aware that the mass killing of Jews would not impress most readers of the leaflet and that crimes committed against Polish Catholics had to be added. Whether this addition also expressed the attitude of the "White Rose" group is hard to tell, but it certainly indicates their own assessment of Catholic middle-class public opinion in Germany sometime in mid-1942.

Notwithstanding such spreading knowledge, the regime's propaganda was, as we saw, penetrating the minds of the *Volksgenossen*, activating preexisting layers of anti-Jewish hostility. A report of July 7, 1942, from the SD in Detmold to the SD main office in Bielefeld emphasized again a point already previously made. "The population has no understanding for the fact that Jews married to an Aryan are not obligated by law to display the star of David [This probably applied to the Jewish partners in mixed marriages with children]. . . .It is being asked with increasing frequency on what ground full-blooded Jews still run around without the star. Precisely this exception—so people say—is especially dangerous as the non-tagged Jew may nowadays be much more easily mistaken for an Aryan than before and may thus, without being suspected, eavesdrop and spy, as one encounters only marked Jews on the streets." The report went on to describe a scandalous incident that had taken place on a local train, when a former SS man (now political leader) made space for an untagged Jew on his bank. Another passenger drew the attention of the former SS man to what he had just done, which led to embarrassment and anger all around.[151]

There were exceptions, of course. The same SD office sent a different report to Bielefeld on July 31 about the deportation of the last Jews from neighboring Lemgo. According to the agent, many of the older inhabitants (even party members) criticized the deportations "for all kinds of reasons." People related to the Catholic Church often expressed the fear that the Germans would be punished by God for these acts. In discussions with supporters of the deportations, some people went so far as to argue that Jews would not harm a fly and that many had done much good. In neighboring Sabbenhausen, the wife of the teacher Heumann tried to bring sausage and other sorts of food to the Jews being deported: She was arrested.[152]

Whether as God's punishment or as retaliation by the Jews, for many Germans the original sin that would cause the retribution was the pogrom of November 9 and 10, 1938, when all synagogues in the Reich were set on fire;[153] and of course the deportations added to the burden of guilt. Thus an SD report of August 3, 1943, from Ochsenfurt, near Würzburg, alluded to the widespread rumor "that Würzburg would not be attacked by enemy planes because in Würzburg no synagogue had been set on fire. However, others say that now the planes would come to Würzburg, as a short while ago the last Jew had left Würzburg. Before his deportation he predicted that now Würzburg would be bombed."[154]

At times, however, the reactions were mixed with political comments that squarely put the blame upon the regime. In mid-August a local party official in Wiegolshausen (in *Gau* Mainfranken) reported on an hour-long conversation with a "very religious" peasant whose views "clearly expressed various trends that are dominant in this part [the religious one] of the population": "Without Hitler—no war—our fight against the Jews has brought about the present developments of the war; Bolshevism, not as dangerous as is described—Doubts about victory—and if something changes regarding religious matters, there will be an uprising in the country."[155]

In many ways the SD reports show the resilience of religious feelings and beliefs and thus point to the important role that guidance from religious authorities could have played. As we saw, both Protestant and Catholic prelates and many ordinary priests knew that the trains transporting the Jews from the Reich and from all over Europe to "Poland" were not carrying them to labor camps but to their death. Clergymen who after the war claimed lack of knowledge, the likes of Cardinal Bertram or Bishop Gröber, for example, simply lied. They did not know, in historian Michael Phayer's words, because they did not want to know.[156] Typically Bertram refused to receive briefings about the situation of the Jews from Margarete Sommer, the extremely well informed assistant to Bishop Preysing (whom we already encountered). Bertram demanded that any report from Sommer be put in writing and undersigned by Preysing to guarantee its authenticity; otherwise, he threatened, "I will not schedule anymore appointments for her."[157] Bertram could not have ignored that writing down the reports was tantamount to severe punishment.

As beforehand Catholic dignitaries remained divided about the appropriate way to react: The leading advocates of a public protest were Preysing and a group of Munich Jesuits, while the majority wished to avoid any confrontation with the authorities and favored various degrees of accommodation. Not unexpectedly the most "accommodating" prelate of all was Bertram. Matters came to a head when, in August 1943, upon Preysing's request, Sommer prepared the "Draft for a Petition Favoring the Jews," that would be signed by all the country's bishops and sent to Hitler and to other members of the party elite.

The opening paragraph represented a courageous statement regarding *all* Jews: "With deepest sorrow—yes, even with holy indignation—have we German bishops learned of the deportation of non-Aryans in a manner that is scornful of all human rights. It is our holy duty to defend the unalienable rights of all men guaranteed by natural law. . . . The world would not understand if we failed to raise our voice loudly against the deprivation of rights of these innocent people. We would stand guilty before God and man because of our silence. The burden of our responsibility grows correspondingly more pressing as . . . shocking reports reach us regarding the awful, gruesome fate of the deported who have already been subjected in frightfully high numbers to really inhumane conditions of existence." A series of demands that would have alleviated the fate of the deportees followed, but throughout the petition avoided any direct reference to extermination.[158] The bishops' conference rejected the idea of submitting the petition and merely issued a pastoral letter admonishing German Catholics to respect the right of others to life, also that of "human beings of alien races and origin."[159]

Preysing still hoped to sway his fellow bishops by trying to muster encouragement and guidance from the Vatican. No encouragement was provided by Orsenigo: "Charity is well and good," the nuncio told the bishop, "but the greatest charity is not to make problems for the Church."[160] Preysing's repeated pleas to Pius XII himself elicited no guidance from the pontiff except, as we shall see in the next chapter, for the statement that bishops throughout the Continent were free to respond to the situation according to their own best judgment, an implicit support for Bertram's passivity. The pope knew of the attitude prevalent among the German bishops and almost certainly understood that Preysing hoped for clear support from Rome, precisely in order to overcome their faintheartedness.[161] In fact Pius XII further bolstered the abstentionist course of the majority by praising the choice made in 1942—and restated in the pastoral letter of 1943—the choice of private help instead of public protest.[162]

The only *private* letter of protest addressed to Hitler by a church dignitary was sent on July 16, 1943, once again by Bishop Theophil Wurm, the leading figure of the Confessing Church. The bishop first mentioned the absence of any response to letters already addressed to various state and party dignitaries about matters of concern to all Christians. After affirming his own love of the fatherland and alluding to the heavy sacrifices that had become his own lot (he had lost his son and his son-in-law on the Eastern Front) and that of countless Evangelical Christians, Wurm, writing as "the most senior Evangelical bishop," declared himself to be "assured of the understanding and support of wide circles within the Evangelical Church." At this point he turned to the core issue of the letter:

"In the name of God and for the sake of the German people we give expression to the urgent request that the responsible leadership of the Reich will check the persecution and annihilation to which many men and women under German domination are being subjected, and without judicial trial. Now that the non-Aryans who have been the victims of the German onslaught have been largely eliminated, it is to be feared . . . that the so-called 'privileged' non-Aryans who have so far been spared are in renewed danger of being subjected to the same treatment." Wurm then protested against the threat that mixed marriages would be dissolved. Indirectly he returned to the measures that had been taken against the Jews as such: "Such intentions like the measures taken against the other non-Aryans are in the sharpest contrast to Divine Law and an outrage against the very foundation of Western thought and life and against the very God-given right of human existence and human dignity."[163]

Wurm's letter received no response, and although it was not a declaration *ex cathedra*, as Galen's sermon against euthanasia had been, it was widely circulated. A few months later, on December 20, 1943, Wurm sent a letter to Lammers, pleading again for the safety of *Mischlinge*. This time he received a handwritten warning from the head of Hitler's chancellery: "I hereby warn you emphatically," Lammers wrote, "and request that in the future you scrupulously stay within the boundaries established by your profession and abstain from statements on general political matters. I urgently advise you further to show the greatest restraint in your personal and professional conduct. I ask you to refrain from replying to this letter."[164] This warning of dire retribution silenced Wurm and the Confessing Church.

VII

In October 1942 Dr. Ernst Jahn, the general practitioner from Immenhausen, divorced his Jewish wife, Lilli, notwithstanding the fact that four of their five children were adolescents and one even younger. As we saw, Ernst had been involved with one Rita Schmidt, a colleague who had borne him a child. He may have believed (as he declared after the war) that the very existence of the five mixed-breed children would protect Lilli from any serious danger, even if she was separated from her Aryan husband. He could not ignore, however, that Lilli's situation would in any case become more precarious than beforehand. The slightest infringement of any of the regulations and decrees impinging on every move of the last Jews living in the Reich could be fatal.

Lilli herself did not seem aware of what her new status implied. Hadn't her eldest child, her son Gerhardt, become an enthusiastic auxiliary in an antiaircraft unit based near Kassel? Of course she could not know what had happened to other Jewish women in her situation—to a Hertha Feiner for example. Was Lilli trying to taunt fate? The business card she put on the door of the Kassel apartment merely indicated: "Dr. Med. Lilli Jahn." She had forgotten—or maybe not?—that Jewish physicians were forbidden to use their professional title, that she had to add "Sara" to her name, and, in any case, was not allowed to cater to Aryan patients. Somebody denounced her; she was summoned to the Gestapo and, on August 30, 1943, she was arrested.[165]

By mid-1943 the remnants of German Jewry, bereft of any institutional framework, had become a scattering of individuals, defined on Gestapo lists as so many specific "cases"; in the logic of the system, they would have to disappear. The Klemperers, although they were a childless mixed marriage, had not yet received a summons. But how long could they hope to remain in limbo? Their daily existence was becoming harder. At the end of 1943 they were ordered to move again, to yet another "Jews' house," even more overcrowded than the previous one. "The worst thing here," Victor Klemperer noted on December 14, "is the *promiscuity.* The doors of three households open into a single hallway [on the third floor]: the Cohns, the Stühlers, and ourselves. Shared bathroom and lavatory. Kitchen shared with the Stühlers, only partly separated—*one* source of water for all three—a small adjoining kitchen space for the Cohns."[166] The fear of informers had grown with time, even in conversations with Jews whom one did not know well; Klemperer heard rumors about one of the inhabitants in his own house, and he noted a telling joke: "A star-wearing Jew is abused on the street, a small crowd gathers, some people take the Jew's side. After a while, the Jew shows the Gestapo badge on the reverse of his jacket lapel, and the names of his supporters are noted."[167] In one form or another, this was part of everyday reality in the Reich, in the remaining ghettos, in every occupied country.

To Klemperer the attitudes of the population appeared as contradictory as ever, even in this last phase of the war. Frequently he encountered expressions of sympathy and encouragement ("it can't last much longer") or just unremarked acts of kindness; nonetheless anti-Semitism was never far away. "On my way to Katz," he noted on February 7, 1944, "an elderly man in passing: 'Judas!' In the corridor of the health insurance office. The only wearer of the star, I walk back and forth in front of an occupied bench. I hear a worker talking: 'They should give them an injection. Then that would be the end of them!' Does he mean me? Wearers of the star? The man is called a few minutes later. I sit down in his place. An elderly woman beside me, whispering: "That was nasty! Perhaps one day what he wished upon you will happen to him. One can never know. God judges!"[168]

The reader may remember young Cordelia, the Jewish girl who grew up as a Catholic and, in September 1941, was expelled from the Berlin Catholic Girls Association by her headmistress who didn't want to keep "girls carrying a Jewish star." Cordelia's mother, Elisabeth Langgässer, a convert herself and already a well-known writer, was half Jewish, but the girl's father, who did not live with Langgässer anymore, was a full Jew. Thus, Cordelia, who turned fourteen in 1943, was a "three-quarter Jewess."

Sometime in late 1942 or early 1943, Langgässer succeeded in getting a Spanish passport for her daughter and even an entry visa to Spain. Cordelia Langgässer became Cordelia Garcia-Scouvart and stopped wearing the star. Before long both daughter and mother were summoned to Gestapo headquarters in Berlin. In the presence of her mother, who remained silent throughout, Cordelia was given the choice of signing a declaration that she agreed to keep her German citizenship and was ready to submit to all laws and decrees applying to her status as a Jew, or to have her mother prosecuted for getting the Spanish passport under false pretenses and thus committing a treasonable act. Cordelia signed. "And now," the Gestapo official volunteered, "you may go to the office across the hall and purchase a new Jewish star; it costs 50 Pfennig."[169]

In Berlin in 1943 the Gestapo used *Mischlinge* to arrest any remaining Jews slated for deportation. Two such half-Jewish auxiliaries took Cordelia to the Jewish hospital that had become an assembly and administrative center for all Jews, after the disbanding of the Reichsvereinigung. The hospital (first using its buildings on Iranischestrasse, then on Schulstrasse), was of course under complete Gestapo control; Eichmann had dispatched SS Hauptsturmführer Fritz Woehrn to supervise it, while an obscure Jewish physician, albeit a very able and energetic one, Dr. Walter Lustig, a "one-man Reichsvereinigung," was in charge of everyday matters. A number of Jewish patients continued to stay on the premises, mostly protected by some special status; Jews rounded up in other German cities temporarily landed there, as did Jews caught in hiding. At the end of the war some 370 patients and around one thousand inmates in all still lived at the hospital; this number included ninety-three children and seventy-six Gestapo prisoners.[170]

At the hospital any male with some power could share any woman's bed; Lustig had an array of eager nurses at his disposal, as he promised to one or another an exemption from deportation. Cordelia, the young newcomer, was shared by two *Mischling* twins from Cologne, Hans and Heinz, although, at fourteen, she had not even menstruated.[171] But Hans and Heinz could not protect her in any way: Toward the end of 1943, she was transferred from the children's section to that of the mentally ill, all gathered for deportation. Before the end of the year she boarded the train for Theresienstadt.[172]

Cordelia's mother had come to visit once, just before her daughter's departure. She conveyed her impressions in a letter to a friend: "We [Elisabeth Langgässer and her Aryan husband] found her entirely calm, even cheerful and confident, as first, it was really only Theresienstadt and not Poland and, second, because she traveled as accompanying nursing personnel. She had to take care of two children and of an infant and wore a nurse's uniform; she even had a small bonnet and that, I think, filled her with pride."[173]

After a brief stay in Theresienstadt, Cordelia Maria Sara was shipped to Auschwitz.

VIII

Following the failed attempts to establish a unified resistance group in the spring of 1942, the Jewish Fighting Organization (Zydowska Organizacia Bojowa, or ZOB) was created in Warsaw on July 28, 1942, a few days after the beginning of the *Aktion.* The initial group of some two hundred members mostly succeeded in dodging the deportations, but beyond that there was little the ZOB could do. In August some pistols and hand grenades were purchased from the Polish communist underground. A first and minor operation—an attempt to kill the chief of the Jewish police, Józef Szerynski—failed. Much worse occurred a few days later: The Germans arrested a group of ZOB members on their way from Warsaw to Hrubieszow and tortured and killed them; soon afterward, on September 3, the Gestapo caught some leading members of the organization in Warsaw and murdered them as well: The weapons were discovered and seized. This catastrophic series of events seemed, at first, to put an end to a courageous venture that had hardly begun.[174]

An eerie period of apparent respite and complete uncertainty descended on the surviving inhabitants of the ghetto after mid-September. The approximately 40,000 Jews left in an area of drastically reduced size either worked in the remaining workshops or in sorting the mounds of belongings abandoned by the victims. The German administrators had been replaced by Gestapo officials, mainly of low rank.[175]

None of the remaining Jews knew when the next German move would take place. By then much had transpired about Treblinka: "The women go naked into the bath house to their death," Abraham Lewin quoted the report of an escapee on September 27: "The condition of the dead bodies. What are they killing them with? With simple vapour (steam). Death comes after seven or eight minutes. On their arrival they take away the shoes of the unfortunates. The proclamation in the square: 'Emigrants from Warsaw.' "[176] On October 5 he noted: "No one knows what tomorrow will bring and we live in perpetual fear and terror."[177] News seeped in from the outside world. On November 10 the diarist recorded news of the Anglo-American landings in North Africa and the British offensive in Egypt; he also reported about Hitler's speech to the "Old Fighters" on the previous day: "As yet we have not received a copy of this speech in print, but the Jews already *know* that it is steeped in venomous hatred and full of terrible threats against the Jews, that he talked of the total annihilation of the Jews of Europe, from the youngest to the very old."[178] On November 17 Lewin mentioned the final liquidation of all the Jews of Lublin.[179] News reports about mass exterminations in the Polish provinces soon replaced a spate of reports about protests in England and in the United States regarding the murder of the Jews: "Departing this life is a matter of 10 or 15 minutes in Treblinka or in Oswiecim (Auschwitz)."[180] On January 15, 1943, Lewin wrote of renewed anxiety as the ghetto expected a forthcoming *Aktion*.[181] The following day he recorded his last entry.[182]

In the meantime the ZOB had overcome the crisis triggered by the events of September 1942. Yet, even under the dire new circumstances, unification of all political forces in support of armed resistance occurred only stagewise and not in full. The lengthy negotiations proved once more how deeply divisive ideological issues remained even among the younger generation of ghetto Jews. A Jewish National Committee was first established in October 1942, uniting all left-wing and centrist Zionist youth movements with the communists. The Bund, however, again refused to join, and only after further—and lengthy—discussions did it agree to "coordinate" its activities with the national committee. A Jewish Coordinating Committee was set up.[183] As for the right-wing Zionists (the Revisionists and their youth movement, Betar), they had already established an independent armed organization, the Jewish Military Union (Zydowski Zwiazek Wojskowski, or ZZW), prior to (and without any link with) the Jewish Coordinating Committee.[184] Whether the Revisionists did not want to cooperate with the "leftists" of the ZOB or whether the ZOB kept them at arm's length remains unclear. Ideological divisiveness persisted to the end.

On January 18, 1943, following a brief visit by Himmler, the Germans launched a new *Aktion* (albeit a limited one at this stage); their plan was partly foiled. Resistance members—Mordechai Anielewicz, the commander of the ZOB, among them—attacked the German escort of the front column and the Jews dispersed. Some 5,000 to 6,000 Jews were ultimately caught during the January operation. Lewin and his daughter were among them; they were deported to Treblinka and murdered.[185] This first sign of armed resistance probably led Himmler to issue an order to Krüger on February 16 to liquidate the ghetto entirely, "for security reasons."[186]

The January events considerably bolstered the authority of the fighting organization among the ghetto population and garnered praise from various Polish circles. During the weeks that followed, the ZOB executed a few Jewish traitors (Jacob Lejkin, the second-in-command of the Jewish police; Alfred Nossig, a shady eccentric who apparently worked for the Gestapo; and some others); it collected—at times "extorted"—money from some wealthy ghetto inhabitants, acquired a few weapons from the communist Gwardia Ludowa and also from private dealers, and mainly organized its "combat groups" in expectation of the forthcoming German operation. In the meantime the inhabitants, increasingly ready to face an armed struggle in the ghetto, were hoarding whatever food they could get and preparing underground shelters for a lengthy standoff. The council, now chaired by a nonentity, Marc Lichtenbaum, and reduced to utter passivity, nonetheless contacted Polish resistance groups, mainly the Home Army (Armeia Krajowa, or AK), to denounce the ZOB as a group of reckless adventurers without any backing in the ghetto.[187]

The council's denunciations were not the source of the AK's reticence to provide help for the ZOB, although after the January events it accepted to sell some weapons. Gen. Stefan Rowecki, the commander in chief of the Home Army remained evasive when asked for stronger support. The traditional anti-Semitism of nationalist conservative Poles may have played a role but there was more to this basically negative stand. The Armeia Krajowa was suspicious of the leftist and pro-Soviet leanings of part of the ZOB (while it was ready to supply some weapons to the Revisionists); furthermore, and mainly so it seems, the Polish command was worried that fighting could spread from the ghetto to the city while its own plans for an uprising and its own forces were not yet ready. As a result AK even offered its help to transfer the Jewish fighters from the ghetto to partisan groups in the forests. The offer was turned down.[188]

The Germans did not expect major difficulties in the final "evacuation" of the ghetto, notwithstanding the January events and other signs indicating that some ghetto Jews throughout the General Government were opting for armed action (such as the attack, on December 22, 1942, by a Jewish group in Kraków on a coffeehouse popular with Wehrmacht personnel, the Cyganeria).[189] Nor were the Germans attaching any significance to the failure of the campaign organized by their largest entrepreneurs in the ghetto, Toebbens and Schultz, to transfer Jewish workers to workshops in the Lublin area.

As for the leaders and members of the ZOB, they had no illusions about the outcome of the approaching struggle. "I remember a conversation I had with Mordechai Anielewicz," Ringelblum wrote. "He gave an accurate appraisal of the uneven struggle, he foresaw the destruction of the ghetto and he was sure that neither he nor his combatants would survive the liquidation of the ghetto. He was sure that they would die like stray dogs and no one would even know their last resting place."[190]

When the final liquidation of the Warsaw ghetto started on April 19, 1943, the eve of Passover, the Jews were not caught by surprise: The streets were empty, and as soon as German units entered the area, firing started. The early street battles took place mainly in three distinct and unconnected areas: parts of what had been the Central Ghetto, the Brushmakers Workshop surroundings, and the Toebbers-Schultz Workshop surroundings.[191] The ideological opposition that precluded some arrangement between the Revisionists and ZOB before the uprising apparently persisted during the fighting and in the later historiography. According to Moshe Arens's painstaking reconstruction of the combat, the role of the ZZW in the bitter street battle around Muranowski Square and their hoisting of a Polish and a Zionist flag on the tallest building in the area are generally left unmentioned in later renditions of the uprising. And the names of the ZZW commanders, Pawel Frenkel, Leon Rodal, and David Apfelbaum, are rarely mentioned; all three fell in battle.[192]

Fighting in the open lasted for several days (mainly from April 19 to April 28) until the Jewish combattants were compelled to retreat into the underground bunkers. Each bunker became a small fortress, and only the systematic burning down of the buildings and the massive use of flame throwers, tear gas, and hand grenades finally drove the remaining fighters and inhabitants into the streets. On May 8 Anielewicz was killed in the command bunker at Mila Street 18. Combat continued sporadically while some groups of fighters succeeded in reaching the Aryan side of the city by way of the sewers. Days later some of the fighters, "Kazik" for example, took again to the sewers and returned to the ghetto ruins to try and save some remnants: They found nobody alive.

On May 16 SS general Jürgen Stroop proclaimed the end of the *Grossaktion*: "The Jewish quarter in Warsaw exists no more." Symbolically the Germans concluded the operations by blowing up the Warsaw [Great] Synagogue at 20:15 hours.[193] According to Stroop, fifteen Germans and auxiliaries had been killed and some ninety wounded during the fighting. "Of the total of 56,065 Jews caught," the SS general reported further, "about 7,000 were exterminated within the former Ghetto in the course of the action, and 6,929 by transporting them to T.II [Treblinka], which means 14,000 Jews were exterminated altogether. Beyond the number of 56,065 Jews, an estimated number of 5,000 to 6,000 were killed by explosions or in fires."[194]

Posters informed the Polish population that anybody hiding a Jew would be executed. Moreover, according to Stroop, "permission was granted to the Polish police to pay one-third of the cash seized, to any of its men who arrested a Jew in the Aryan part of Warsaw. This measure already produced results," he wrote. Finally the SS general reported, "for the most part the Polish population approved the measures taken against the Jews. Shortly before the end of the large-scale operation, the governor issued a special proclamation . . . to the Polish population; in it he informed them of the reasons for destroying the former Jewish Ghetto by mentioning the assassinations carried out lately in the Warsaw area and the mass graves found in Catyn [Katyn]; at the same time they were asked to assist us in our fight against Communist agents and Jews."[195]

On May 1 the uprising found its first echo in Goebbels's diary: "Reports from the occupied territories do not bring anything sensationally new. Noteworthy though is the exceptionally sharp fighting in Warsaw between our police and even Wehrmacht units and the rebelling Jews. The Jews have managed to organize the defense of the ghetto. The fighting there is very hard; it goes so far that the Jewish command issues daily military reports. This whole fun will probably not last long. One sees though what one may expect from the Jews when they manage to set their hands on weapons. Unfortunately they have in part also good German weapons, mainly machine guns. God knows how they got them."[196]

During the following days and weeks the minister regularly mentioned the ghetto uprising. According to him the Jews had bought their weapons from Germany's allies returning home via Warsaw; the Jews fought with such desperation because they knew what was awaiting them and so on. On May 22 he noted: "The fighting for the Warsaw ghetto continues. The Jews are still resisting. But, all in all, it can be considered as not dangerous and overcome."[197]

The desperate Jewish resistance further came up on May 31, 1943, at a high-level meeting in the General Government convened to discuss the worsening security situation, in the presence of RSHA chief Kaltenbrunner, a representative of the Führer Chancellery and senior Wehrmacht officers. Frank's second-in-command, President Ludwig Losacker, reported on the ghetto uprising: "[The liquidation of the ghetto] was, by the way, very difficult. The police forces lost 15 dead and suffered 88 wounded. One noticed that . . . armed Jewish women fought to the last against the Waffen-SS and policemen."[198]

German opposition circles were also informed, although details were at times strangely off the mark. In a letter to his wife dated May 4, 1943, Helmuth von Moltke described a brief stay in Warsaw during these same days. "A big cloud of smoke stood above the city and could still be seen a good half hour after my departure by the express train, that means about 30 km. It was caused by a fight which had been raging for some days in the ghetto. The remaining Jews—30,000—reinforced by airborne Russians, German deserters, and Polish communists, had turned part of it into an underground fortress. It is said that they have made passages between the cellars of houses while the Germans were patrolling the streets, and reinforced the ceilings of the cellars; exits are said to lead by underground passages from the ghetto to other houses. I was told that cows and pigs had been kept in those catacombs and large food depots and wells had been installed. In any case it was said that something like partisan fighting in the town had been directed from these headquarters, so that it was decided to clear out the ghetto: but the resistance was so strong that a real assault with guns and flamethrowers was needed. And that is why the ghetto is still burning. It had already been going on for several days when I got there and was still burning on my return journey yesterday."[199]

German or Polish sources must have supplied Moltke with some of the fantastic stories about "airborne Russians, German deserters, and Polish communists"; such tales may have stemmed from the generally shared belief that Jews would not be able to put up a fight on their own. In Hassell's diary the ghetto uprising appeared a few days later, preceded by a few lines about the gassing of hundreds of thousands of Jews "in specially built halls." Then: "In the meantime the hopeless Jewish remnant in the ghetto defended itself; there has been heavy fighting which will end in total extermination by the SS."[200]

Some sixteen months later, on September 1, 1944, during a military conference dealing, among other issues, with the Polish uprising in Warsaw, Hitler was told by Gen. Walter Wenck that the center of the city had been the area of the ghetto. "Has that been eliminated now?" Hitler asked. The (incompletely transmitted) answer came of course from Himmler's representative at the military conferences, SS general Hermann Fegelein (the hero of the drowning attempt of Jewish women and children in the Pripet Marshes at the end of July 1941): "As such already everything."[201] In fact, on June 11, 1943, Himmler had to order again "that the city area of the former ghetto be totally flattened, every cellar and every sewer be filled up. After completion of this work, topsoil will be placed over the area and a large park will be laid out."[202] In one year, between July 1943 and July 1944 (when the Red Army approached the city), the full destruction of the ghetto ruins was the only completed part of Himmler's project.[203]

The news of the ghetto uprising rapidly spread among Jews in Germany and in most occupied countries: "On Sunday [May 30]," Klemperer recorded on June 1, "Lewinsky related as an entirely vouched for and widespread rumor (originating with soldiers): there had been a bloodbath in Warsaw, revolt by Poles and Jews, German tanks had been destroyed by mines at the entrance of the Jewish town, whereupon the Germans had shot the whole ghetto to pieces—fires burning for days and many thousands of dead. Yesterday I asked several people about it. Whispered reply: yes, they too had heard the same or similar, but not dared to pass it on. Eva, coming from the dentist, reported that Simon stated with certainty, 3,000 German deserters had also taken part in this revolt, and that battles lasting weeks (!) had taken place before the Germans had mastered the situation. Simon's credibility is limited. Nevertheless: *that* such rumors are in circulation is symptomatic." Simon had added that there was also unrest in other occupied countries.[204]

In Lodz, Kovno, Vilna, and most probably all throughout occupied Eastern Europe, people knew. Rosenfeld wrote of it in his diary;[205] so did Tory, who reported that the news had spread among the Lithuanian population, throughout Kovno.[206]

By April 22 the news had reached Herman Kruk in Vilna and, so it seems, the entire population of the ghetto.[207] On April 30, under the title

"Warszawskie Getto Kona!" [The Warsaw Ghetto Is Dying], Kruk returned to the uprising: "Yesterday *Swit* [British broadcasts camouflaged as originating in Poland] once again sounded the alarm to the world, and once again the radio announcer repeated, as if he wanted the world to remember, the Warsaw Ghetto is bleeding to death. The Warsaw Ghetto is dying! Warsaw Jews are defending themselves like heroes. For thirteen days now, the Germans have had to fight with the ghetto for every threshold. Jews do not let themselves be taken and are fighting like lions. . . . The Warsaw Ghetto is dying! . . . My brother-in-law has a wife and two children there—he is silent. My neighbor has a mother and a sister—she is silent. And my own sister and children? . . . I am ashamed of my silence."[208]

In October 1942 the well-known Yiddish novelist Yehoshua Perle completed his chronicle of the deportation of the Warsaw Jews for the "Oneg Shabbat" archive; he called it *Khurbm Varshe* (the destruction of Warsaw.) Three sentences in this record "shocked the surviving Yiddish world," in the words of historian David Roskies: "Three times 100,000 people," wrote Perle, "lacked the courage to say: No. Each one of them was out to save his own skin. Each one was ready to sacrifice even his own father, his own mother, his own wife and children."[209] These harsh words were written several months before the uprising.

The events of April 1943 introduced a new perspective. Of course the Warsaw fighters did not seek even a minimal success in military terms. Whether they wanted to redeem the image of Jews facing death, and to erase, so to speak, Perle's terrible verdict, is not certain, either. They knew that most of a leaderless, hungry, and utterly desperate mass could not but submit passively to unbridled violence, before the uprising and no less so in its wake. Not all of them meant to send a message to their own political movements in Eretz Israel or to the socialist community: For a long time already, many had given up on the active solidarity of their comrades outside Europe. They just wanted, as they had proclaimed, to die with dignity.

In June 1943, one Herbert Habermalz, a sergeant in the Luftwaffe who belonged to a flight crew, wrote to his former colleagues at the Rudolf Sack machine engineering firm, where he had been employed as a clerk in the sales department. He described a flight from Kraków to Warsaw: "We flew several circles about the city [Warsaw]. And with great satisfaction we could recognize the complete extermination of the Jewish ghetto. There our folks did really a fantastic job. There is no house that has not been totally destroyed. This we saw the day before yesterday. And yesterday we took off for Odessa. We received special food, extra cookies, additional milk and butter, and, above all, a very big bar of bittersweet chocolate."[210]

IX

The life of Jews in former Poland was coming to an end. On March 31, 1943, the Kraków ghetto was liquidated and those of its inhabitants who were selected for work were sent to the Plaszow slave labor camp, commanded by the notoriously sadistic Austrian Amon Goeth; their liquidation was to follow later on. And so it went, from ghetto to ghetto, then from work camp to work camp.

Yet in some ghettos, the situation appeared different at times, for a short while of course. Thus, the 40,000 Jews who, in the fall of 1942, were still alive in Białystok, had good reasons for hope. Like in Lodz, the ghetto was particularly active in manufacturing goods and performing services for the Wehrmacht. Barash's relations with the military and even with some of the civilian authorities seemed good. A local resistance movement was getting organized under the leadership of Tenenbaum-Tamaroff, although the German threat did not appear immediate.[211]

The first warning signals came in late 1942–early 1943 with the deportation of all Jews from the Białystok district to Treblinka. During the first days of February 1943, the Germans struck again, but as had previously happened in Lodz, only part of the population (10,000 Jews) was deported and approximately 30,000 inhabitants remained. Moreover, in a meeting on February 19, a representative of the Białystok security police commander promised Barash that no further resettlement of Jews was expected for the time being. The continued presence of 30,000 Jews in the ghetto was likely to last until "the end of the war."[212]

Life returned to "normal" for the remaining population of the ghetto: Barash was confident that the new stability would last; Tenenbaum, however, was convinced that the liquidation of the ghetto was approaching.[213] As we saw, in May Himmler had restated his full extermination policy, with the exception of essential workers who for the time being would be transferred to the slave labor camps in the Lublin area; the remaining Jews of Białystok would be sent to Treblinka.[214]

Under Globocnik's personal command, the Germans prepared the liquidation in utter secrecy to avoid a repeat performance of the Warsaw events. On August 16, 1943, when the operation started, Barash and Tenenbaum (who had broken off all relations by that time) were both taken completely by surprise. While the mass of the population followed the orders and moved helplessly to the assembly sites, sporadic fighting flared up in various parts of the ghetto, with only minimal impact on the "evacuation" operation. Within days the ghetto was emptied and the fighters had either been killed or had committed suicide. Barash was deported to Treblinka; Tenenbaum probably took his life.[215]

In July 1943 the Germans massacred 26,000 inhabitants of the Minsk ghetto; some 9,000 Jewish laborers remained alive for a few months but, at the end of 1943, no Jews were mentioned any longer in the Reichskommissar's report about the capital of Belorussia.[216] One after the other, the ghettos of "Weissruthenien" were liquidated, like those of the General Government. Small groups of Jews fled to nearby forests to join partisan units. A number of armed rebellions took place but were easily quelled as the Germans now expected some sporadic resistance. In some ghettos, on the other hand, where determined resistance could have been expected, as in Vilna, events took an unexpected turn.

"Here in the ghetto, the mood is cheerful," Kruk recorded on June 16, 1943. "All rumors about liquidation have disappeared for the time being. A rapid building and expansion of the ghetto industry has been going on in recent weeks. . . . Yesterday, District Commissar Hingst and [Hingst's deputy] Murer visited the ghetto. Both left very satisfied and "amused" themselves with the ghetto representatives. The ghetto breathed in relief. We ask—for how long?"[217]

At the beginning of 1943 the situation in Vilna had indeed been relatively peaceful. On January 15 Gens gave an indirect expression to this state of things in an address celebrating the first anniversary of the ghetto theater: "How did the idea come up?" Gens said, "Simply to give people the opportunity to escape from the reality of the ghetto for a few hours. This we achieved. These are dark and hard days. Our body is in the ghetto but our spirit has not been enslaved.... Before the first concert they said that a concert must not be held in a graveyard. That is true, but the whole of life is now a graveyard. Heaven forbid that we should let our spirit collapse. We must be strong in spirit and in body.... I am convinced that the Jewish [life] that is developing here and the Jewish [faith] that burns in our hearts will be our reward. I am certain that the day of the phrase. 'Why hast Thou deserted us?' will pass and that we shall still live to see better days. I would like to hope that those days will come soon and in our lifetime."[218]

In April, though, Gens's optimism and that of the ghetto population were sharply challenged. During the first days of the month, the Germans assembled several thousands of Jews from the smaller ghettos of the Vilna district under the pretext of sending them to Kovno. Instead of Kovno they were dispatched to Ponar and massacred. The killings instilled terror in the ghetto. "Today," Rudashevski recorded on April 5, "the terrible news reached us: 85 railroad cars of Jews, around 5,000 persons, were not taken to Kovno as promised but transported by train to Ponar where they were shot to death. 5,000 new bloody victims. The ghetto was deeply shaken, as though struck by thunder. The atmosphere of slaughter has gripped the people. It has begun again.... People sit caged as in a box. On the other side lurks the enemy, which is preparing to destroy us in a sophisticated manner according to a plan, as today's slaughter has proved."[219] Yet, like so often beforehand, the fear was soon dispelled as nothing seemed to happen in Vilna as such; the cheerfulness that Kruk had noted returned.

On June 21, 1943, Himmler ordered the liquidation of all ghettos in the Ostland. Working Jews were to be kept in concentration camps and "the unnecessary inhabitants of the Jewish ghettos were to be evacuated to the East."[220]

Of course the members of the FPO were not aware of the liquidation decision but, nonetheless, perceived the April killings as an omen. For them the question now arose: Should armed resistance be organized in the ghetto, or should the FPO leave for the forests and eventually join Soviet partisan units before the Germans struck? Gens himself, aware of the debate, was determined to have the FPO stay in the ghetto, together with the population that it would help to defend and, eventually, allow to flee.[221] Yet by the end of June, as the Germans were systematically liquidating the remaining small communities in the Vilna region, an increasing number of FPO members moved to the forests against Gens's will: A confrontation within the ghetto was barely avoided.[222]

It seems that at this point (June–July 1943), the communist members of the FPO were hiding from Kovner and his left-wing Zionist comrades (Hashomer Hatzair) that they were actually under the orders of a far larger communist organization and that their "delegate," Itzik Wittenberg, had been elected head of the FPO without Kovner and his people being aware of the dimension and secretive nature of the communist penetration.[223]

Gens had apparently decided that Wittenberg represented a danger to his own plans, and on July 15, late at night, as the communist leader was conferring with the ghetto chief (at Gens's invitation), police forces (probably Lithuanians) arrested him. Freed by FPO members, Wittenberg went into hiding. The German reaction was foreseeable: If Wittenberg was not delivered, the ghetto population would be exterminated. Whether under pressure from his underground comrades (his communist fellow militants were the first to suggest that the step be taken) or because he sensed the fear of the ghetto populace and its increasingly threatening attitude toward the FPO, Wittenberg agreed to give himself up; once in German hands, instead of submitting to torture and certain death, he committed suicide.[224]

Kruk's Vilna diary was interrupted on the eve of "Wittenberg Day." It is not unlikely that the pages dealing with it were hidden or destroyed when Soviet forces reentered the city: "Wittenberg's betrayal" by his comrades could have been of interest to the NKVD. That part of the chronicle never resurfaced.[225] Kalmanovitch described the events in some detail in his own diary, apparently on the basis of rumors rather than precise knowledge. Throughout, the YIVO scholar was hostile to the FPO and to attempts at armed resistance that endangered the population. In this particular case he (wrongly) attributed all responsibility to the Revisionists, whereas he praised the communist Wittenberg for giving himself up and committing suicide.[226]

On September 14 the Germans ordered Gens to report to the headquarters of the Security Police. Although he had been warned of danger and told to flee, the ghetto chief went nonetheless, to avoid reprisals against the population. At six o'clock that same afternoon the Germans shot him.[227]

Part of the remaining 20,000 inhabitants were murdered in Ponar, part were deported to Sobibor, while able-bodied men (including Kruk and Kalmanovitch) were shipped to labor camps in Estonia. The Jews left in the ghetto were murdered just before the arrival of the Red Army.[228]

The FPO was unable to organize any significant resistance inside the ghetto, possibly due to Gens's hostility, mainly because the majority of the population was opposed to an armed uprising and believed that the labor camps in Estonia offered a safer option, and possibly also as a result of Kovner's hesitant leadership. Thus, after some minor skirmishes with the Germans, some eighty members of the FPO slipped out of the city in several groups and joined the partisans.[229]

On April 6, 1943, on the day he had recorded the massacre in Ponar, Rudashevski's diary ended. The last line read: "We may be fated for the worst."[230] Itzhok and his family were murdered in Ponar a few months later.[231] In Lodz, Sierakowiak broke off his own diary entries a week or so after Rudashevski; the last line was recorded on April 15: "There is really no way out of this for us."[232] In the summer he died of tuberculosis and starvation.[233]

X

Just before the uprising of the Warsaw ghetto, a merry-go-round was set up on Krasínski Square, on the Aryan side, close to the ghetto walls. As the desperate struggle unfolded, the merry-go-round did not stop, and joyful crowds besieged it day in, day out, while the Jews were dying on the other side of the wall:

Sometimes the wind from burning houses
Would bring the kites along
And people on the merry-go-round
Caught the flying charred bits.
This wind from the burning houses
Blew open the girls' skirts
And the happy throngs laughed
On a beautiful Warsaw Sunday.

It was during the uprising that Czesław Miłosz wrote "Campo di Fiori," his best-known poem, "as an ordinary human gesture."[234] The poet compares the burning at the stake of the Italian philosopher Giordano Bruno on the Campo di Fiori, while busy and indifferent Roman crowds are milling around, to the indifference of the Polish masses during the agony of the ghetto Jews. And so it was. There is nothing unlikely, therefore, about the assessment sent in August 1943, a few months after the uprising, by a representative of the Polish underground to the government-in-exile regarding the "Jewish question" in postwar Poland:

"In the Homeland as a whole—independently of the general psychological situation at any given moment—the position is such that the return of the Jews to their jobs and workshops is completely out of the question, even if the number of Jews were greatly reduced. The non-Jewish population has filled the places of the Jews in the towns and cities; in a large part of Poland this is a fundamental change, final in character. The return of masses of Jews would be experienced by the population not as a restitution but as an invasion against which they would defend themselves, even with physical means."[235]

In the meantime, in Poland as in much of occupied Europe, money did help. Marcel Reich-Ranicki, whom we encountered in the Warsaw ghetto as music critic, then as typist during the fateful meeting of the council at which Höfle announced the beginning of the deportations, had escaped the main *Aktion* and that of January 1943, as employee of the Council. Tosia, Marcel's wife, was left alive; his parents were shipped to Treblinka. In February 1943, Marcel and Tosia fled the ghetto. The underground had given him some money for his assistance in getting hold of a large sum from the council's safe.

Marcel bribed a Jewish guard, then two Polish policemen, and the couple reached the Aryan side of the city. But as they were moving from one hiding place to another, like most fleeing Jews they were confronted with the same constantly recurring pattern: "Extortion and escape. . . . Thousands of Poles, often unemployed adolescents . . . spent their days suspiciously watching all passers-by. They were everywhere, especially near the ghetto boundary, looking for Jews, hunting down Jews. This pastime was their profession and probably also their passion. It was said that, even if there were no other signs, they were able to identify Jews by the sadness in their eyes."[236] These "Schmaltsovniks," as they were commonly called, did not aim at delivering Jews to the

Germans; they wanted money or anything of value, "at least a jacket or a winter coat."[237]

And yet some Poles offered help, at great danger to themselves and their families. Thus Marcel and Tosia were hidden and saved by a Polish couple living in the Warsaw suburbs, "by Bolek, the typesetter, and by Genia, his wife."[238] It happened in the capital, and it happened in the provinces. In the words of a survivor: "These people helped us and risked their lives because they had to fear every neighbor, every passerby, every child, who might inform on them."[239] This, however, is precisely the point made by historian Jan Gross: "*Because* the Poles were not ready to assist the Jews and by and large refrained from doing so, the death punishment for harboring Jews was meted out by the Germans systematically and without reprieve and the task of helping was so difficult."[240]

The diary kept by a Polish teacher, Franciszka Reizer, living in a village in the Rszezow province, starkly illustrates these various outcomes: "20 November 1942. The Germans drove many peasants and firemen from the villages and, with their help, arranged a hunt for Jews. . . . In the course of this action seven Jews were captured, old, young and children. These Jews were taken to the firemen's station and shot the next day." November 21: "On the fields belonging to Augustyn Bator Jews arranged themselves an earth bunker. . . . They were caught by the gendarmes who were hunting after Jews. All of them were shot on the spot." On November 30, Reizer mentioned the death of a Jewish woman who tried to find shelter in the village. A year later, on October 2, 1943: "These days the last Jews in the vicinity were tracked down and murdered. They were shot near the tannery which belonged to the Jew Blank. Here, 48 Jews were buried."[241] A year later again, the diary mentions that the Germans murdered a Polish family who had hidden Jews.

In the vast rural areas of eastern Poland (or western Ukraine) there was no difference of attitude between Polish and Ukrainian peasants: traditional hatred, isolated instances of courage, and mostly, almost everywhere, the insatiable greed for money or other spoils.

Aryeh Klonicki (Klonymus) had, as may be remembered, described in his diary the fate of Jews in Tarnopol, eastern Galicia, during the first days of the German invasion. Together with his wife, Malwina (Hertzmann), Aryeh returned to Buczacz, where he had lived and been a high school teacher for many years. In July 1942 their son Adam was born. In

July 1943 Aryeh and Malwina fled to the neighboring villages desperately trying to save their son and themselves. The Klonickis' bitterness emerges in the very first entry (July 7) of Aryeh's short diary: "A new period has begun here since the end of 1943: it is the era of liquidation. A Jew is no longer allowed to remain alive. . . . If it weren't for the hatred of local inhabitants one could still find a way of hiding. But, as things are, it is difficult. Every shepherd or Christian child who sees a Jew immediately reports him to the authorities, who lose no time following up these reports. There are some Christians who are ostensibly prepared to hide Jews for full payment. But actually no sooner have they robbed their victims of all their belongings than they hand them over to the authorities. There are some local Christians who have gained distinction in the discovery of Jewish hideouts. There is an eight-year-old boy (a Christian one, of course) who loiters all day long in Jewish houses and has uncovered many a hideout."[242]

The Klonickis tried one hideout after another and each time were cheated out of their money or possessions. Their former maid, Franka was ready to help save the child, while they hid in nearby fields. "Franka is really displaying considerable devotion towards us and very much wants to help us. But she is afraid. Posters throughout town announce the death penalty for anyone hiding Jews. This is the reason for our being out in the field rather than at her home. We gave Franka all our money amounting to 2,000 zloty and 15 'lokschen' (i.e., dollars). Should we succeed in finding a place for our child we could stay here for some time—as long as our presence is not discovered in the village."[243]

The child, Adam, was finally taken in by nuns. Aryeh and Malwina had to leave him at night in the entrance of the convent: "On a dark night as the rain was coming down in torrents my wife and I took our boy with a sackful of belongings. . . . We left him together with the sack in the corridor of the convent and hurriedly ran off. We are overjoyed at having succeeded in arranging for our child's keep under such favorable conditions. I was not bothered by the fact that they would baptize the child."[244]

As the days went by, the Klonickis survived precariously, fleeing from one place to another. On July 27 Aryeh started his last diary entry; it was never completed: "The situation is very bad. All through the night it was raining and in the morning too. . . . At midday Samen once again looked us up in the company of someone called Vaitek and they took from us another three hundred zloty. What can we do! It is impossible to stay here any longer."[245] According to Franka's brother, Aryeh and Malvina were killed by the Germans in a forest near Buczacz, in January 1944. As for their son, Adam, baptized Taras, all traces of him disappeared.

Farther east the Ukrainian populations of Volhynia and of "Dnieper Ukraine" displayed generally the same mix of anti-Jewish attitudes as their western brethren. Jewish dominance in the local Soviet institutions replaced the argument of Jewish collaboration. Here too greed, envy, religious hatred, and some form of Ukrainian nationalism and anti-Bolshevism contributed in various degrees to the same brew. Yet, as the careful assessment by historian Karel C. Berkhoff's has shown, a clear picture is hard to establish.[246]

Hostility toward Jews was widespread, but for many ordinary Ukrainians there clearly existed a distinction between anti-Jewish hostility, even hatred, and outright mass murder. Many Kiev inhabitants had expressed disbelief and then horror when faced with the Babi Yar massacres. According to *Einsatzgruppen* reports of the summer and fall of 1941, in the Ukraine as such, local anti-Jewish violence was not easily triggered: "To persecute Jews using the Ukrainian population is not feasible because the leaders and the spiritual drive are lacking; all still remember the harsh penalties which Bolshevism imposed on everyone who proceeded against the Jews," one report stated. Another report repeated the same complaint: "The careful efforts once undertaken to bring about Jewish pogroms unfortunately have not produced the hoped-for success."[247]

Yet paradoxically, once the Red Army reconquered the Ukraine, local anti-Semitism became more virulent. In the eastern Ukraine pogroms erupted in the summer of 1944, followed by fierce anti-Jewish riots in Kiev in September 1945. The reaction of the local authorities was hesitant; some of the key leaders of the restored Ukrainian Communist Party were themselves outspoken anti-Semites.[248]

It is in this overall Eastern European context that an outstanding initiative was taken in 1942 by a group of Polish Catholics, under the impulse of a well-known female writer, Zofia Kossak-Szezucka. A declaration ("Protest"), written by Kossak in August 1942, during the deportation of the ghetto inhabitants to Treblinka, stated that, despite the fact that the

Jews were and remained the enemies of Poland, the general silence in the face of the murder of millions of innocent people was unacceptable and Polish Catholics had the obligation to raise their voices: "We are unable to do anything against the murderous German action, we are unable to take action to save one person, but we protest from the depth of our hearts, full of compassion, anger and dread. This protest is demanded by the Almighty God who forbade killing. It is demanded by Christian conscience."[249] At the end of September, a Provisional Committee for Aid to Jews was established. Its first meetings took place in October, and in December it was reorganized and became the Council to Aid Jews, or Zegota, recognized and supported by the Delegatura.[250]

Over the ensuing months and until the occupation of Poland by the Soviet army, Zegota saved and assisted thousands of hidden Jews mainly on the Aryan side of Warsaw. The political-ideological composition of the leadership changed, however, over time. The right-wing Catholic movement, which had initiated the establishment of the council, left it in July 1943; its anti-Semitic ideology could not, at length, countenance the assistance given to the Jews.[251] The withdrawal of these conservative Catholics from the rescue operations tallied with the positions taken by much of the Polish Catholic Church, and of course with those of the majority of the population and of the underground movements.

On March 2, 1943, following a lengthy conversation with Göring, Goebbels noted in his diary: "Goering is completely aware of what would threaten us all, if we were to weaken in this war. He has no illusions in this regard. In the Jewish question in particular, we are so fully committed that for us there is no escape anymore. And it is good that way. Experience shows us that a movement and a people which have burnt their bridges fight by far more unconditionally than those who still have a way back.[252]

CHAPTER IX

October 1943–March 1944

"I am taking advantage of a lonely Sunday evening to write you a letter that I have owed you for a long time." Thus began the plea that Kurt Gerstein—the deeply religious Protestant, Waffen SS officer, and haunted witness of extermination who, in vain, had tried to inform the world—addressed on March 5, 1944, to his father, a retired judge and a firm supporter of the regime. "I do not know what goes inside you, and would not presume to claim the smallest right to know. But when a man has spent his professional life in the service of the law, something must have happened inside him during these last few years. I was deeply perturbed by one thing you said to me, or rather wrote to me.... You said: Hard times demand tough methods!—No, no maxim of that kind is adequate to justify what has happened.

"I cannot believe that this is the last word my father has to say on such unparalleled happenings: my old father cannot depart from this place with such words and thoughts. It seems to me that all of us with some time left to live have more than enough cause to reflect on the practical possibilities and limits, as well as on the consequences of this casting away of all restraint.... However tight the limitations on a man may be and however much, in many things, he may follow the principle that discretion is the better part of valor, he must never lose his standards or his ideas. He must never exonerate himself before his conscience and before the higher order of things to which he is subject by saying: that is not my business, I can do nothing to change things.... He keeps silent but he thinks: that *is* my business. I am involved in this responsibility and guilt, having knowledge of what is happening and a corresponding measure of blame.

"Dear father, there are situations in which a son is obliged to offer advice to the very father who laid the foundations and formed the ideas in him. The time will come when you, along with others, will have to stand up and be called to account for the age in which you live and for what is happening in it. There would be no understanding left between us . . . if it were not possible or permissible for me to ask you not to underestimate this responsibility, this obligation on your part to answer for yourself. The call may come sooner than we think. I am aware of this obligation and, admittedly, it is devouring me (*consumor in ea*). But that is immaterial."[1]

The father did not understand. Gerstein added in a further and last letter: "If you look around you, you will find that this is a rift that is cutting through many families and friendships that were once close."[2] Gerstein was exceptional and lonely in his ways as a morally tormented and "treasonous" member of the extermination system; however, the religious source of his attitude of course also played a role for other Germans and Europeans, some of whom we mentioned and thousands of whom we know nothing about. Their oppositional stand, whatever form it may have taken, albeit of limited impact, should be part of any reflections on the role of Christianity in the years of extermination. Generally speaking, however, their path was not the one chosen by the Christian churches as major institutions in the Western world and even less so, as we shall primarily see in this chapter, by their most exalted leaders.

I

In strictly military terms, the last months of 1943 and early 1944 were dominated by steady Soviet progress in all sectors of the Eastern Front, whereas the Western Allies edged only very slowly up the Italian peninsula and actually stalled at the German "Gustav Line." Yet in terms of the Grand Alliance, the defining event of these months took place at the Roosevelt-Churchill-Stalin meeting in Tehran, from November 28 to December 1. Notwithstanding British fears and hesitations, the American strategy was accepted: American and British forces would land on the coast of Normandy sometime in May 1944. Simultaneously the

Soviet Union would launch a major offensive, thus precluding the shift of any German forces to the West.

Hitler anticipated the Allied landing with much confidence. The German defenses along the Atlantic and North Sea coasts, and the Wehrmacht forces in the West, would turn the Anglo-American operation into a catastrophic defeat for the invaders. Then, immune for a long time to the further threat of a landing, the Nazi leader would turn the entire German might against the Soviet army, recapture the lost territories, and eventually force Stalin to sue for peace.[3] In the meantime, unable to effectively counter the allied bombing offensive, the Führer was, in Speer's words, "in the habit of raging against the British government and the Jews, who were to blame for the air raids."[4] And, indeed, the bombings added an element of blind fury and even stronger thirst for murderous vengeance to Hitler's anti-Jewish obsession: The Jews were guilty!

In his deluge of anti-Jewish tirades, Hitler donned all garbs: prophet, statesman, rabble-rouser; Goebbels was mostly the latter—an extraordinarily effective rabble-rouser who, as Moshe Flinker had sensed, totally believed in his message. And, in unison with the leading tenors, the Rosenbergs, the Darrés, the Leys, sundry *Gauleiter*, *Kreisleiter*, *Ortsleiter*, *Blockleiter*, clergymen, academics, high school teachers, Hitler Youth, and BdM leaders all spewed the same invectives. Amid this tremendous howling, another voice, on a par with that of Goebbels but different and more ominous, regularly explained and threatened: the voice of Heinrich Himmler. The Reichsführer did not address the mass audiences of grassroot party rallies; he usually kept the presentation of his murderous activities, his admonishments suffused with "moral health" principles, and the lessons he drew from his far-flung "research" for the elite: SS officers or the highest levels of party and Wehrmacht. While Hitler never missed an occasion to let his audience know that, in prophesing and ordering the disappearance of the Jews, he was fulfilling a quasi-divine mission, a task dictated by Providence, fate, history—that in other words he was the exceptional leader chosen for this mission by higher powers and thus beyond doubts and qualms—Himmler's approach was different.

The Reichsführer regularly presented the extermination of the Jews as a heavy responsibility delegated to him by the Führer and thus not open to discussion; it demanded, from him and from his men, a steady devotion to their task and a steady spirit of self-sacrifice. When, on July 26, 1942, the SS chief rebuffed Rosenberg's attempts to come up with a definition of "Jew" in the eastern occupied territories, he typically added: "The eastern occupied territories will be freed of Jews: The Führer has laid on my shoulders the implementation of this very difficult order. Nobody can take this responsibility from me in any case. Hence, I strongly resent all intervening" [*Also verbiete ich mir alles mitreden*].[5]

At times, aside from fulfilling his "difficult orders," the Reichsführer conceived of grandiose anti-Jewish propaganda operations of his own. The *Untermensch* pamphlet, for example, published by the SS, was circulated throughout the Continent in fifteen languages.[6] In early 1943, another such large-scale project took shape. Impressed by a book on *Jewish Ritual Murders*, Himmler informed Kaltenbrunner on May 19 that he was having it distributed to SS officers up to the rank of Standartenführer; he was sending him one hundred copies for distribution to the *Einsatzkommandos* and "particularly to the men who have to deal with the Jewish question." Moreover, the Reichsführer ordered inquiries into ritual murders among those Jews who had not yet been "evacuated" in order to stage some public trials; these inquiries had to be particularly intensive in Romania, Hungary, and Bulgaria to allow the Nazi press to publicize the results and thus enhance the effort to deport Jews from these countries.

Finally the SS chief suggested the creation, together with the Foreign Ministry, of a special radio program aimed at England and the United States, and exclusively focused on anti-Semitic material, of the kind Streicher's *Der Stürmer* had used during "the years of struggle." The English press and English police announcements should be combed through for any report about a missing child; Himmler's program would then broadcast that the child had probably been victim of Jewish ritual murder. "In conclusion," the Reichsführer suggested," I believe that by launching a vast anti-Jewish propaganda action in English, possibly even in Russian, centered on ritual murder, we could enormously increase worldwide anti-Semitism."[7]

When he addressed the higher SS echelons or other prominent audiences, Himmler often adopted a matter-of-fact, poised, and rational tone. He confidentially reported about the fate of the Jews, and indicated why what was done had to be done. In 1943 and 1944 the Reichsführer discussed the "Final Solution" with audiences which were well informed and involved in its implementation in one form or another; each time, Himmler offered encouragement and justification. It was in this vein that he addressed SS generals on October 4, 1943, and *Gauleiter* on October 6, in both cases in Posen (the address to the SS generals is the better known of the two very similar speeches). Once more, on October 6, Himmler described the extermination of the Jews as "the task which became the most difficult of my life."[8]

"The question has been asked of us," the Reichsführer declared in his October 6, 1943, address, "how is it with the women and children? I have taken the decision to achieve a clear solution also in this matter. I did not consider that I had the right to eliminate the men—that is to kill them or have them killed—and to let their children grow up to become the avengers against our own sons and grandsons. The difficult decision had to be taken to have this people disappear from the face of the earth."[9] Himmler was to repeat the same arguments to an assembly of Wehrmacht generals in May 1944, and on several further occasions throughout that year.[10]

Goebbels attended the daylong *Gauleiters*' conference on October 6: "As far as the Jewish question is concerned," the propaganda minister recorded on October 9, "he [Himmler] gives a very unvarnished and frank presentation. He is convinced that we can solve the Jewish question throughout Europe by the end of this year. He proposes the harshest and most radical solution: to exterminate the Jews root and branch [*Kind und Kegel*]. It is certainly a logical solution, even if it is a brutal one. We have to take the responsibility of completely solving this issue in our time. Later generations will certainly not handle this problem with the courage and the ardor that are ours."[11]

Himmler adorned his speech to the SS generals, on October 4, with some flights of rhetoric: "The evacuation of the Jews . . . is a never-written-down and never-to-be-written page of glory of our history." The explanation that followed closely toed the line of Hitler's ever-repeated argument: "We know," Himmler went on, "how difficult it would be if today, given the bombings, the burdens, and the privations of the war, we still had, in every city, the Jews as secret saboteurs, agitators and inciters. We would probably have now reached the 1916–1917 stage, when the

Jews were still part of the German national body." The Reichsführer found it necessary to sustain the sense of a grim, hard, but glorious and vital task among his highest-ranking officers at a time when the threat of defeat was becoming more concrete and, with it, the danger of retribution. There may also have been another aim to Himmler's praise: to soften but nonetheless convey the message that followed the praise, threatening with death those who used the extermination for their own profit ("even one fur, even one watch, even one Mark or cigarette").[12]

In fact, while the Reichsführer was both praising and threatening, an inquiry commission, headed by SS investigating judge Konrad Morgen, had uncovered widespread corruption and unauthorized killings of political prisoners (mainly Poles and Russians) at the very center of the extermination system, in Auschwitz. Rudolf Höss was relieved of his command (but transferred to a more elevated position in Berlin);[13] others also had to leave: the head of the political section, Maximilian Grabner; the head of the Kattowitz Gestapo, Rudolf Mildner; even one of the chief physicians whom we already met, Friedrich Entress (who also specialized in phenol injections into the hearts of inmates in the infirmary of the main camp), and smaller fry.[14]

Himmler was of course confronted with an ongoing and intractable issue: How to stem wanton murder in an organization set up for mass murder; how to stem widespread corruption in an organization set up for huge-scale looting. Relatively speaking, however, such internal problems of discipline were minor and the Reichsführer's authority was never in question. Simultaneously his power within the overall structure of the regime was steadily growing.

The Waffen SS had become an army within the Wehrmacht, and in 1944 it comprised some thirty-eight divisions (approximately 600,000 men).[15] As we saw, under Pohl's leadership both the camp system and the SS industrial enterprises were growing apace; so did the number of their slave laborers. In August 1943 the Reichsführer replaced Frick as minister of the interior. After a brief clash with Bormann over the autonomy of the *Gauleiter*, Himmler did not further insist on imposing his authority over the party stalwarts, and he soon joined forces with Hitler's all-powerful "secretary" in an alliance that could crush any competing force.[16] Finally, in early 1944, military intelligence (the Abwehr) was liquidated after accusations of plotting against the regime; its chief, Admiral Canaris, arrested; and the entire organization taken over by the RSHA.[17]

In terms of the Reich's history and that of the extermination of the Jews, the crucial question is not only that of the Reichsführer's power within the system but of how subservient he still was to his Führer. Mainly, was Himmler extending feelers for potential contacts with the Western Allies, without Hitler's knowledge? This issue has exercised historians for decades, as no documents allow for any conclusive answer, and as postwar testimonies and memoirs are only partly reliable and lead in different directions; circumstantial evidence is no more conclusive. The "Final Solution" is at the very core of this debate. Is there any indication that, in order to become an acceptable partner to the West Himmler attempted to slow down the rhythm of the extermination or allowed German offers secretly to free Jews to be made? Despite arguments to the contrary, nothing of the kind appears convincing in late 1943 or early 1944. The situation will become more confusing after the German occupation of Hungary, in March 1944, as we shall see in the last chapter.

II

While the deportation and extermination of the tens of thousands of Jews from Salonika, in the spring of 1943, demanded German planning at every stage, including the availability of trains and of sufficient space in the barracks and gas chambers of Birkenau, deporting the eight thousand Jews of Denmark depended essentially on the right political circumstances in the framework of a unique arrangement.

The Germans had allowed a semiautonomous Danish government to stay in place, and their own presence as occupiers was hardly felt. Hitler had decided on this peculiar course to avoid unnecessary difficulties in a country strategically important (the passage to Norway and Sweden and the proximity of the English coast), "racially related" to the community of Nordic peoples, and mainly an essential supplier of agricultural products (more than 15 percent of Germany's needs by 1941).[18] Until September 1942, a professional diplomat, Cecil von Renthe-Fink, ably represented this policy in Copenhagen. At that point, however, Hitler, irked by King Christian X's laconic response to the birthday congratulations he had sent him, ordered Renthe-Fink's recall and, more generally, demanded a harsher policy against the Danes.[19] Werner Best, who had left his position in Paris a few months beforehand and had been attached to the Foreign Ministry, was appointed to Copenhagen in late October, 1942. Hitler's orders to Best, whom he summoned to Vinnytsa were by then somewhat more moderate than those he had imparted a few weeks earlier to the new military commander in Denmark, Gen. Hermann von Hanneken.[20] In fact, during the first nine months of his tenure as Reich plenipotentiary (*Reichsbevollmächtigter*), Best pursued his predecessor's policy.

From April 1940 to the late summer of 1943, the persecution of the Jews of Denmark had remained minimal; even Best urged caution, notwithstanding some pressure from the RSHA. The leaders of the Jewish community went along, so to speak, and agreed to the minor discriminations imposed by Prime Minister Eric Scavenius's government.[21]

In late July 1943, the situation began to change. Mussolini's fall, the Allied landing in Sicily, and the massive bombing of Hamburg convinced most Danes that Germany's defeat was approaching. Sabotage, limited until then, grew; strikes erupted in several cities. The Scavenius government was losing its grip. For Best a change of policy appeared unavoidable, as he wrote to Himmler on August 22. Indeed, two days later Hitler ordered sharp countermeasures, and on the twenty-ninth the Germans imposed martial law. It was then, on September 8, as martial law was in force and anti-German demonstrations could be quelled immediately, that in a cable to Berlin, Best demanded that the "Jewish question" be solved. On September 17 Hitler gave his authorization.[22] That same day Best ordered the seizure of the membership lists from the Jewish community office.[23]

On September 22 Ribbentrop asked Hitler about the advisability of the deportations of the Danish Jews in view of the troubles that could follow: the Nazi leader confirmed his previous decision.[24] The date of the operation was set for October 2, although both the army and the navy commanders made it clear that their units would not participate. In fact in Best's entourage skepticism about the planned round-up was widely shared. Sometime at the end of September, the embassy adviser on shipping matters, Georg F. Duckwitz, disclosed the date of the *razzia* to one of his Danish friends.[25] Thereupon the Swedish government, informed of the forthcoming operation by its ambassador in Copenhagen, made an offer to Berlin to take in all of Denmark's Jews. Moreover, Stockholm broadcast its offer, thus informing the endangered Jews that they could find asylum in Sweden.[26]

There is no basis to the widespread interpretation that Best himself, after initiating the deportations, actively engineered their failure by letting Duckwitz inform his Danish counterparts. Still, most likely the *Reichsbevollmächtigter* was not unhappy that, on the eve of the German move, around 7,000 Jews were ferried over to Sweden in a coordinated operation supported by the vast majority of the Danish population. Some 485 Jews were seized and, after Best's intervention with Eichmann, deported to Theresienstadt, where most of them survived the war.[27]

III

By September 29, 1943, Amsterdam was "Jew free."[28] In the previous months, as we saw, some 35,000 Jews from Holland had been rerouted from Auschwitz to Sobibor, as the Auschwitz gas chambers were out of service for a while due to a typhus epidemic in the camp. Nineteen of these Dutch deportees survived. In the meantime deportations from France and Belgium had been temporarily discontinued.[29]

During the last months of their anti-Jewish campaign in Holland, the Germans went beyond the call of duty. When the hundreds of Jews of Portuguese descent claimed that due to centuries of intermarriage with the local population, they could not be regarded as Jews, the Germans launched a systematic investigation of their racial background; it went on, as we shall see, until early 1944. Mixed marriages represented another difficult problem. Seyss-Inquart suggested sterilization of the Jewish partners as a reprieve from deportation, thereby preempting steps that had been merely discussed but not implemented in the Reich. Some 2,500 Jews (men and women) were ultimately sterilized as a result of the Reichskommissar's initiative.[30]

"The partners of mixed marriages have been told that they could postpone their decision about sterilization until next Thursday," Philip Mechanicus, a Dutch Jewish journalist and inmate of Westerbork from May 1943 to March 1944, noted in his diary on Tuesday, June 15, 1943. "Before then two Jewish doctors will explain to them the significance and consequences of sterilization. Yesterday a typed notice to that effect was put up in the vestibule of the Registration Hall."[31] The next day, according to Mechanicus's entry, the debate became quite heated: "A storm of criticism and indignation descended this morning after breakfast upon the young man who had decided to let himself be sterilized. 'You are a coward!' 'You've no strength of character.' 'No proper man would do that.' 'I am doing it for my wife.' 'Your wife wouldn't want that. . . . What a joke—a sterilized man!' 'Do you know for sure that you won't be sterilized as soon as you get to Poland? I don't. Better have it done right away here. And stay with my wife.'"[32]

And as these futile debates were going on and the daily hurdles of the Westerbork routine filled the inmates' lives, transports were bringing in more Jews from all parts of Holland and from the labor camps. Then, with absolute regularity, every Tuesday, another transport loaded its cargo of between 1,000 and 3,000 Jews and departed for "Poland." By the end of the war, more than 100,000 Jews had transited through Westerbork alone, mostly on their way to extermination.

In the camp, as already mentioned, the old-timers were the German Jews, and under the control of the German commandant and his small staff, they lorded it over the mass of Dutch Jews. Mechanicus was an acerbic observer, somewhat in Kaplan's style, or maybe in the Klemperer vein: "The German Jews have undeniably abused their position of supremacy and continue to do so," he noted on June 3, 1943. "They form, as it were, an almost exclusive association for the protection of the interests of German Jews. As individuals and acting together they do their best to save all German Jews brought here from being deported and endeavor to keep them here. They have done this from the time that Dutch Jews began arriving at Westerbork. In this way they have, in point of fact, handed over the Dutch Jews to the Germans to suit their own convenience. Wherever possible they have pushed the Germans into jobs and have kept the Germans here. The Registration Department with Kurt Schlesinger at its head has been able to do this. For example, during the seven months that I have been in the hospital, it has *nearly* always been Dutch Jews that have been deported."[33]

Mechanicus explained part of the existing supremacy of German Jews by the simple fact that the Germans in command preferred to work with German rather than with Dutch Jews: "They are closer together and understand one another better, both psychologically and as far as language and ways of behavior are concerned. . . . The last commandant mentioned [Commandant Albert Gemmeker] even has a Jewish adjutant in the person of Herr Todtmann who forms the link between the commandant and the Registration Department. The adjutant wears a service uniform. He, Gemmeker, has awarded the now famous red stamps to German Jews" [stamps that, in principle, protected one from deportation—for a while].[34]

Mechanicus reserved his sharpest barbs for the former members of the Jewish Council. The council was officially disbanded on July 5, but, on that same day, its former members were granted various privileges for themselves and their families, including the "red stamp." "It is in reality a fiendish tribute," Mechanicus commented, "from the representatives of a regime which used Jews to catch Jews and hand over Jews and guard Jews. It was the desire to have a safe stamp, the longing to save their own skins that induced these Jews to perform the grisly services that their tormentors demanded and exacted from them. . . . Now that they have a respite from the breathless chase and the evil frenzy, they should dig down into their consciences, if they have a conscience at all."[35]

Nothing changed the German routine in the end. Even a few hundred privileged Jews who had been sent from Amsterdam to a castle at Barneveld with full assurance that they would stay there to the end of the war were suddenly moved to Westerbork in the summer of 1943, albeit with Theresienstadt as their final destination. For the immense majority, however, the ripples on the surface of Westerbork life did not make any difference in regard to the final outcome.

"It will be my parents' turn to leave soon," Etty Hillesum recorded on July 10, 1943. "If by some miracle not this week, then certainly one of the next. Mischa [Etty's brother] insists on going along with them, and it seems to me that he probably should; if he had to watch our parents leave this place, it [would] totally unhinge him. I shan't go. I just can't. It is easier to pray for someone from a distance than to see him suffer by your side. It is not fear of Poland that keeps me from going along with my parents, but fear of seeing them suffer. And that, too, is cowardice."[36]

A month earlier, on June 8, Etty had described the departure of the weekly transport. "The people have already been loaded into the freight cars; the doors are closed. . . . The quota of people who must go is not yet [filled]. Just now I met the matron of the orphanage, carrying a small child in her arms who has also to go, alone. I climbed on a box lying among the bushes here to count the freight cars. There were thirty-five, with some second-class cars at the front for the escorts. The freight cars had been completely sealed, but a plank had been left out, here and there, and people put their hands through the gaps and waved as if they were drowning."[37]

While Etty, still manifestly uncertain about the fate of the deportees, was watching the transports leaving Westerbork, for Anne, life in hiding was replete with small miseries, but nonetheless it was also increasingly dominated by her first teenage love. The Annex sheltered the Franks, the van Daans, and a Mr. Dussel. Anne would turn fifteen in 1944, and Peter van Daan seventeen. On February 16 Anne recorded some of the topics they had been discussing: "He [Peter] talked about the war, saying that Russia and England were bound to go to war against each other, and about the Jews. He said life would have been much easier if he'd been a Christian or could become one after the war. I asked if he wanted to be baptized, but that wasn't what he meant either. He said he would never be able to feel like a Christian, but that after the war he would make sure nobody would know he was Jewish. I felt a momentary pang. It's such a shame he still has a touch of dishonesty in him."[38]

In the meantime Rosenberg's looting agency was sending the furniture stolen from Dutch Jewish homes to the Reich but also, as we saw, to German officials and agencies in the East. On April 30, 1943, the Jews of Holland unexpectedly surfaced in Kruk's diary: "We have already written about the packing up of 130,000 Jews from Holland and their transport to the East. We have also mentioned that carloads filled with goods from the Dutch Jews are in the Vilna railroad station. Now an issue that clears it all up—beautiful old furniture has been brought here, to our joiners' workshop, to be repaired. In the drawers people find Dutch documents, including documents from December 1942, which means that ostensibly, the Dutch were not taken to the East before January or February. Thus the Jews [there] . . . did not know they were going to be exterminated. . . . In our area, dozens of railroad cars are scattered filled with Jewish junk, remnants of the former Dutch Jewry."[39]

In order to increase the number of deportees from France, the Germans were now pushing Vichy to adopt a law revoking the citizenship of Jews naturalized since 1927. But, after seemingly going along with the German scheme in the early summer of 1943, Laval rejected the new demand in August. Reports from the prefects had convinced the head of the Vichy government that public opinion would resent the handing over of French citizens (even recently naturalized ones) to the Germans.[40]

Due to the importance of the issue, Laval informed Eichmann's men, the decision would have to be taken by the head of state himself. Pétain was of course aware of the possible reactions of the population. Moreover, he had been warned by the delegate of the Assembly of Cardinals and Archbishops, Henri Chappoulie, that the church would react negatively to any collective cancellation of the naturalization of Jews who had become French citizens after 1927.[41] Finally it is likely that by August 1943, when Pétain and Laval rejected the German demand, both—like everybody else beyond the borders of the Reich—simply perceived that the Germans were undoubtedly losing the war.

It is hard to assess which of these elements played a decisive role in determining Vichy's decision. A public opinion poll completed by the CGQJ in the spring of 1943 on the demand of the government pointed to the existence of an absolute majority (more than 50 percent) of anti-Semites in the country.[42] These results, which may have been manipulated by the Commissariat, have of course to be regarded cautiously; they did, however, confirm trends previously mentioned, although they did not tally with the prefects' reports about potential reactions to the cancellation of naturalizations.

The Germans were not deterred: They would start the deportation of French Jews. To that effect, Dannecker's successor, Obersturmbannführer Heinz Röthke, got reinforcement: Eichmann's special delegate, Aloïs Brunner, arrived directly from Salonika, where, as we saw, the deportation of almost the entire Jewish population had just been successfully completed. Accompanied by a special group of some twenty-five SS officers, Brunner would be in direct contact with Berlin. He immediately replaced the French officials in charge of Drancy with his own men and ordered UGIF-North to take over the internal administration of the camp.[43]

In the face of the unremitting German determination, both UGIF-North and South were helpless. André Baur, the head of UGIF-North, refused to go along with Brunner's plan to entice Jews who had not been arrested to join their families in Drancy (the "Missionary Plan"). When, in desperation in the face of Brunner's relentless pressure, Baur demanded a meeting with Laval, Eichmann's delegate had him arrested (on the pretext that two Drancy detainees, one of them Baur's cousin, had escaped).[44]

Brunner's intention to decapitate UGIF-North in order to have an entirely submissive Jewish leadership in hand became even clearer when, after Baur's arrest, the Germans raided various UGIF offices and, using the flimsiest pretexts, sent other UGIF leaders to Drancy. Within a few months the Gestapo envoy had achieved this particular aim: UGIF-North continued to exist (which was all to German advantage as long as tens of thousands of Jews were still residing in the northern zone and children's homes remained under the control of the organization), but its new leaders were now the subservient Georges Edinger and somebody later never entirely cleared of the suspicion of having played a dubious role, Juliette Stern.[45]

In the meantime, however, still under Baur's stewardship and more actively so later on, UGIF-North was ready to cooperate in a German scheme whose intention must have been obvious from the start. Some Jewish children would be released from Drancy and, together with others already in UGIF's care, they would be kept out of the camp on condition that all be sent to designated homes, under the responsibility of the organization. It meant, in other words, that the children were a captive group whom the Germans could seize whenever they wished. In the meantime UGIF would have to take care of them. Foiling the German plan became an increasingly urgent task for some members of UGIF itself, the semi-clandestine Children's Relief Committee (OSE), the officially disbanded Jewish Scouts organization, and the communist "Solidarity" welfare association. All attempted to transfer children from the UGIF homes to foster families, Christian institutions, and OSE safe havens. Yet, as we shall see, when, shortly before the liberation of Paris, the Germans pounced on the UGIF homes, many of the young charges were still there.[46]

In the southern zone the German-French roundups continued to encounter Italian obstruction during the last months of the Mussolini regime and during Badoglio's brief rule. On February 25, 1943, Ribbentrop had traveled to Rome to confront Mussolini personally. The *Duce* tried to avoid a clash by declaring that his men were arresting the Jews in their zone, a statement that both he and Ribbentrop knew to be false. In fact, in early March, the Italian military commander in France ordered the local French authorities to release immediately the Jews they had arrested in some of the cities under Italian control.[47] As news about the Italian attitude spread, Jews fled in ever-greater numbers to this paradoxical safe haven and, by March 1943, some 30,000 of them lived under "fascist" protection in southeast France.

To assuage the Germans, Mussolini announced new measures. The inspector general of the Italian police, Guido Lospinoso, was sent to France to implement the *Duce*'s decision to cooperate with his Axis partner. With the help of the army and some advice from the Italian Jew Angelo Donati, Lospinoso started the transfer of Jews from the Côte d'Azur to hotels in the alpine resorts of the Haute-Savoie.[48]

In these rescue efforts the somewhat mysterious Donati played a crucial role. No less essential was the assistance he received from a French Capuchin priest, Father Pierre Marie-Benoît, who on his own had already actively helped Jews in the southern zone for two years, mainly by providing them with false identity papers and by finding hiding places in religious institutions. During the summer of 1943, under the Badoglio government, Donati and Marie-Benoît went one step further and planned the transfer of thousands of Jews from the Italian zone via Italy to North Africa. Four ships had even been leased with the financial support of the Italian (Jewish) association for helping refugees, Delasem, and groups of Jews were being moved toward the French-Italian border when the Italian armistice was announced and the peninsula occupied by the Wehrmacht.[49]

No sooner had the Germans moved into Rome, and into Nice and its surroundings, than Brunner and Röthke arrived on the Côte d'Azur: The hunt for the Jews residing in the former Italian zone started. The Germans were ready to pay 100, 1,000, and at times 5,000 francs per individual to professional denouncers who specialized in identifying Jews on the streets.[50] They also received other well-remunerated help, that of a "society lady," for example, who delivered seventeen of her clients to the Gestapo.[51] The overall results were disappointing nonetheless. By mid-December 1943, when Brunner returned to Drancy, barely 1,819 Jews had been caught and deported. The partial German failure may have been the result of the nonparticipation of the French police in the operations, and of the greater readiness now shown by the population and by religious institutions to hide the mostly French Jews. And, as the Wehrmacht also refused to take part in the roundups, the Gestapo was essentially left to its own devices.[52]

In other regions of France the German anti-Jewish drive also ended in mixed results during the last months of 1943, despite the ultra collaborationists' rise to greater power. In early 1944, the chief of Vichy's anti-Resistance squads, the Milice, Joseph Darnand, the Gestapo's man, replaced Bousquet at the head of the French police. And, at the head of the Commissariat Général, Darquier, incompetent and corrupt, was succeeded by the even more incompetent Charles du Paty de Clam, and, shortly thereafter, by yet another outright accomplice of the Germans, Joseph Antignac.

Brunner's growing frustration led to repeated shows of Gestapo strength in the liquidation of the leadership of French Jewry. As we saw, Baur and several other leaders of UGIF-North had been arrested with their families in the early summer of 1943. In the meantime, in the South, Lambert seemed impervious to the growing threat. "Days go by," he noted on July 9, "without the events we hoped for having happened. . . . However, everybody believes that the war will end before the winter. I aspire to it with all my strength, as I doubt whether I shall be able to escape enslavement for more than six months. . . . Nonetheless some instinct tells me to be confident. I remember how calm I was as a soldier in 1916, during the terrible offensive of April when I underwent my baptism of fire.[53]

Despite some nervousness, Lambert kept to his routine: much traveling, even some short vacations (two days with his family), and extensive reading (as usual, he noted all titles and wrote some comments about most of the books.) When, on August 17, he was informed of the "huge Russian offensive," he added: "I believe that we will be in Paris for Christmas."[54] Lambert recorded his last diary entry on August 20, 1943; there he summed up the sharp criticism of the Consistoire people that he had meant to write in 1941: "They preferred their own well-being to uncertainty and to the heroism of fighting. . . . We [UGIF] chose the heroism of doubt and action, the reality of striving."[55] It sounded strangely like an epitaph.

On August 21 Lambert, his wife, and their four children were arrested and sent to Drancy; on December 7 they were deported to Auschwitz and murdered. Helbronner's turn followed. On October 28 the Gestapo arrested the president of the Consistoire, Petain's and Gerlier's friend, the most thoroughly French of all French Jews. Vichy was immediately informed, and so was Cardinal Gerlier. Helbronner and his wife were deported from Drancy to Auschwitz in transport number 62 that left French territory on November 20, 1943; they were gassed on arrival. Between October 28 and November 20, neither the Vichy authorities nor the head of the French Catholic Church intervened in any way.[56] That Pétain did not intervene isn't astonishing; that Gerlier abstained demonstrates that to the very end the leaders of the French church maintained their ambiguous attitude even toward those French Jews who were the closest to them.

Leo Baeck, Paul Eppstein, David Cohen, and Abraham Asscher, Zwi Koretz, and other Jewish leaders had been deported to Theresienstadt or Bergen Belsen, and most of them survived the war. Why Baur, Lambert, and Helbronner were sent to immediate death in Auschwitz remains unexplained.

As the leaders of French Jewry were being murdered, none of the council heads appointed by the Germans (or by Vichy) at the outset of the war or in the course of the expanding occupation were in office any longer, with the exception of Rumkowski. In a study dealing with former Poland, and comparing a first wave of 146 heads of councils and a second or third one of 101 appointees, historian Aharon Weiss concluded: "Most of the first chairmen managed to defend the interests of their communities. The majority of these [chairmen] were liquidated or removed. The patterns of behavior in the later terms changed greatly. The most striking fact emerging from this summary is the steep rise in submissiveness and yielding of the *Judenräte* to German pressure in the last period. Responsible leaders were replaced, often with German support, by people less attuned to the interests of the community; during the stages of mass extermination and brutal terror they carried out the Nazi orders."[57]

Although it is difficult to compare the Jewish leadership in occupied Poland with Jewish leaders in the Reich, the West, the Baltic countries, the Balkans, and the more ephemeral ghettos of the occupied Soviet

Union, the correlation between the passage of time and growing submissiveness is substantiated, but not only, so it seems, for the reasons adduced by Weiss. The passage of time meant moving from the predeportation phase to that of systematic deportations and extermination. In other words, while during the earlier phase Jewish leaders were faced with the practical difficulties of survival, albeit under dire circumstances, in the later period they were faced with mass murder. Such would also be the case in 1944 regarding remnants of all Western communities and mainly regarding Hungarian Jewry. There was no Jewish Council in Budapest before March 1944, but no leadership would be more submissive than this first and only batch of appointees.

In fact from the beginning of systematic mass murder, even the Jewish leaders appointed at the outset of the occupation discovered no other way of facing the German demands (except by committing suicide) than delivering the weakest segments of the community (including, of course, the foreigners) *in order to "gain time" and attempt to safeguard the "most valuable" elements* (emphasis added). In Cohen and Asscher's views, the most valuable Jews were a small group of middle-class Amsterdam Jews; for Helbronner, the most valuable elements were the *French* Jews (the Consistoire should be included in the leadership groups, on par with the UGIF); for Rumkowski, only working—mostly local—Jews would eventually be saved. Once the deportations started, Helbronner and Lambert were as compliant as Cohen and Asscher. Rumkowski, for all practical purposes the first major ghetto leader and the last to stay in office, was possibly more compliant than any of the other leaders, east and west, and the remnants of the Lodz ghetto would "almost" be saved, as we shall see.

In other words compliance was not a function of the time spent as head of council, but rather of the phase during which the head of council negotiated with the Germans. During the extermination phase none of the strategies devised by the councils or any other Jewish leader to counter the German drive did work; larger or smaller numbers of Jews remained alive by pure chance and as a result of entirely independent circumstances: the readiness of local authorities, populations or resistance movements to help, or not. Armed Jewish resistance, as important as it was in symbolic terms, did not save lives but accelerated the rhythm of extermination. The council's interference with armed resistance, as in Vilna, did not save the community either.

Historian Dan Diner has assumed that the Jewish Councils' frantic search for a strategy to save their communities from extermination, given their attempts to understand the various "rational interests" of the Germans they were facing (the Wehrmacht as well as the SD), offers a starting point for inquiry into the "counterrational" world of extermination policies.[58] Such an indirect approach may not be necessary if we recognize that the policy ordered by Hitler and implemented by Himmler and the entire murder system stemmed from a single postulate: The Jews were an *active threat*, for all of Aryan humanity in the long run, and in the immediate future for a Reich embroiled in a world war. Thus the Jews had to be exterminated before they could harm "Fortress Europe" from within or join forces with the enemy coalition they had themselves set against the Reich.

Whether or not they recognized the exact nature of German reasoning during the extermination phase, Jewish leaders could not know that dilatory tactics were hopeless in the end and that, at the last moment, the Germans would attempt to exterminate everyone without taking any "interests" into account. Whatever choice they made, Jewish leaders during the extermination phase were confronted with insuperable dilemmas; neither their organizational and diplomatic talents nor their moral "red lines" and political allegiances had any impact whatsoever on the ultimate fate of their communities.

When no hope of survival remained and no German promise sounded believable anymore, psychological conditions were ready for an uprising: Such was the situation in Warsaw after the January 1943 *Aktion,* and such it was, in the summer and fall of 1943, for the Jewish workers' teams left alive in Treblinka and Sobibor. As the deportations to both camps were winding down, these Jews understood that their own liquidation could not be far off.

According to Shmuel Wilenberg, one of the survivors of the Treblinka uprising, by May 1943, after the extermination of the remaining Warsaw ghetto population, not much doubt remained about the outcome: "The workload in the camp was dwindling. . . . For some time we had been receiving better and more satisfying portions of food. We got the impression that the Germans wanted to kill us all and were trying to dull our senses and deceive us with their behavior."[59]

In late July 1943, as the exhuming and burning of corpses that had been going on in the upper camp (the extermination area) was coming to an end, the decision was finalized: The uprising had to take place as soon as possible in order to allow as many inmates as possible to flee before the final liquidation of the camp. The date and time were set for August 2, at four-thirty in the afternoon. The head of the main organizing committee in the lower camp, Marceli Galewski, an engineer from Lodz and a former camp elder, could in principle coordinate the exact time for the beginning of the operation with the upper camp, given the fact that master carpenter Jacob Wiernik was allowed by the Germans to move freely throughout both areas.[60] At the decisive moment, however, nothing went according to plan.

The first shot was fired half an hour ahead of the time set for the beginning of the revolt, due to unforeseen circumstances and, soon, coordination between the different combat teams broke down. Nonetheless, as chaos was spreading and part of the camp was set on fire, hundreds of inmates, either in groups or on their own, succeeded in breaking through the fences and escaping.[61]

In his prison conversations with Gitta Sereny, camp commander Stangl described the scene: "Looking out of my window I could see some Jews on the other side of the inner fence—they must have jumped down from the roof of the SS billets and they were shooting. . . . In an emergency like this my first duty was to inform the chief of the external security police. By the time I had done that our petrol station blew up. . . . Next thing the whole ghetto camp was burning and then, Matthess, the German in charge of the *Totenlager* [upper camp] arrived at a run and said everything was burning up there too."[62]

According to various estimates, of the 850 inmates living in the camp on the day of the uprising, 100 were caught at the outset, 350 to 400 perished during the fighting, and some 400 fled but half of them were caught within hours; of the remaining 200, approximately 100 succeeded in escaping the German dragnet and the hostile population; the number of those who ultimately survived is unknown.[63] After fleeing the immediate surroundings of the camp, Galewski was unable to go on and poisoned himself.[64] Wiernik survived and became an essential witness.[65]

The immediate reason for the uprising in Sobibor was the same as in Treblinka, and from early 1943 on, a small group of the camp's working Jews started planning the operation. Yet only in late September, when a young Jewish Red Army lieutenant, Alexander Pechersky, who had arrived from Minsk with a group of Soviet POWs, joined the planning group, were concrete steps rapidly taken.[66] The date of the uprising was set for October 14. The plan foresaw the luring of key SS members to various workshops under some fictitious pretext, and killing them. The first phase of the plan, the liquidation of the SS personnel, succeeded almost without a hitch; although the second phase, the collective moving through the main gate, soon turned into uncontrolled fleeing, more than three hundred inmates succeeded in escaping to the surrounding forests.[67] Pechersky and his group crossed the Bug River and joined the partisans.

The cooperation of Jewish inmates and Soviet POWs in the breakout was a unique aspect of the Sobibor uprising. Yet it added a further dimension to the security scare in Berlin. Coming after the Warsaw rebellion, the uprisings in Treblinka and Sobibor convinced Himmler that the murder of most Jewish workers, even in the Lublin district, should be completed as rapidly as possible. On November 3, 1943, the SS killed 18,400 inmates in Majdanek while music was played over loudspeakers to cover the sounds of shooting and the cries of the dying prisoners. In July 1942 the roundup of Jews in Paris had been baptized "Spring Wind"; in November 1943 the mass murder of the Jews of Majdanek received an equally idyllic code name: "Harvest Festival."

IV

Barely two weeks after the German occupation of Rome, the main leaders of the community, Ugo Foà and Dante Almansi, were summoned by SS Obersturmbannführer Herbert Kappler, the SD chief in the Italian capital. They were ordered to deliver fifty kilograms of gold within thirty-six hours. If the ransom was paid on time, no harm would befall the city's Jews. Although Kappler had been secretly instructed by Himmler to prepare the deportation from Rome, it now appears (from declassified OSS documents) that the extortion was Kappler's own idea, meant to avoid the deportation and eventually help instead in sending the Jews of Rome to work at local fortifications.[68] Kappler, who had very few police forces at his disposal, preferred to use them in order to arrest Italian *carabinieri*, a far more real danger in his eyes than the mostly impoverished Jews of the city.[69]

The gold was collected in time from members of the community (a loan offered by the pope proved unnecessary) and shipped to the RSHA on October 7.[70] Foà and Almansi believed Kappler's assurances and, when warned by Chief Rabbi Israel Zolli and by leading officials of Delasem that further German steps could be expected, they chose for a while to ignore the omens: What had happened elsewhere could not happen in Rome. The community itself, mostly the 7,000 poorer Jews living in or near the former ghetto area, also remained unconcerned, like their leaders.[71]

And indeed, during the following days, the Germans appeared more interested in looting than in anything else. The priceless treasures of the Biblioteca della Comunità Israelitica (the Library of the Israelite Community) became a special target. For good reasons. In the words of historian Stanislao G. Pugliese, "among the manuscripts were works of the rabbi and medical doctor Moses Rieti; manuscripts spirited out of Spain and Sicily during the Jewish expulsion in 1492; a Portuguese incunabulum of 1494; a mathematics text of Elia Mizrahi; and an extremely rare edition of a Hebrew-Italian-Arabic vocabulary published in Naples in 1488. There were also twenty-one Talmudic tracts published by Soncino [in the early sixteenth-century] . . . and a rare eight-volume edition of the Talmud by the famous sixteenth-century Venetian printer Daniel Bomberg."[72]

In early October the Rosenberg agency specialists examined the collection. While some precious artifacts belonging to the main synagogue of the ghetto were hidden in the walls of the mikvah [the ritual bath for purification], the library could not be saved: On October 14 Rosenberg's men loaded the books into two railroad cars and shipped them off to Germany.[73] And, although some of the Jews of Rome argued that "crimes against books were not crimes against people," panic started spreading.[74] Frantically Jews looked for hiding places; the richer among them were soon gone.

On October 6 Theodor Dannecker arrived in Rome at the head of a small unit of Waffen SS officers and men. A few days later, on October 11, Kaltenbrunner reminded Kappler of the priorities he seemed to ignore: "It is precisely the immediate and thorough eradication of the Jews in Italy which is the special interest of the present internal political situation and the general security in Italy," the message, decoded and translated by the British, stated. "To postpone the expulsion of the Jews until the Carabinieri and the Italian army officers have been removed can no more be considered than the idea mentioned of calling up the Jews in Italy for what would probably be very unproductive labor under responsible direction by Italian authorities. The longer the delay, the more the Jews who are doubtless reckoning on evacuation measures have an opportunity by moving to the houses of pro-Jewish Italians of disappearing completely. [undecoded] has been instructed in executing the RFSS orders to proceed with the evacuation of the Jews without further delay."[75] Kappler had no choice but to submit.

On October 16 Dannecker's unit, with small Wehrmacht reinforcements, arrested 1,259 Jews in the Italian capital. After *Mischlinge*, partners in mixed marriages, and some foreigners had been released, 1,030 Jews, including a majority of women and some 200 children under the age of ten, remained imprisoned at the Military College. Two days later these Jews were transported to the Tiburtina railway station and from there to Auschwitz. Most of the deportees were gassed immediately, 196 were selected for labor; 15 survived the war.[76]

Throughout the country the roundups continued until the end of 1944: The Jews were usually transferred to an assembly camp at Fossoli (later to Risiera di San Sabba, near Trieste) and, from there, sent to Auschwitz. Thousands managed to hide among a generally friendly population or in religious institutions; some managed to flee across the Swiss border or to the areas liberated by the Allies. Nonetheless, throughout Italy about 7,000 Jews, some 20 percent of the Jewish population, were caught and murdered.[77]

Since the end of the war the arrest and deportation of the Jews of Rome (and of Italy) have been the object of particular scholarly attention and of a number of fictional renditions, given their direct relevance to the attitude of Pope Pius XII. The events as such are known in detail; the reasons for some of the most crucial decisions can only be surmised at best.

By early October 1943, several German officials in the Italian capital, including Eitel Friedrich Möllhausen, embassy councillor with the German diplomatic mission to Mussolini's Salo Republic but himself posted in Rome, Ernst von Weizsäcker, former state secretary at the Wilhelmstrasse and newly appointed Ambassador to the Vatican, as well as Gen. Rainer Stahel, the Wehrmacht commander of the city, became aware of Himmler's deportation order.

For a variety of reasons (fear of unrest among the population, wariness about the possibility of a public protest by Pius XII and its potential consequences), these officials attempted to have the order partly changed: The Jews would be used for labor in and around Rome. Möllhausen went so far as to convey his worries to Ribbentrop, on October 6, in unusually explicit terms: "Obersturmbannführer Kappler has received the order from Berlin to arrest the eight thousand Jews living in Rome and to transport them to northern Italy where they will be liquidated. The city commander of Rome, General Stahel, informs me that he will allow the operation only if the Foreign Minister agrees to it. I am personally of the opinion that it would be a better deal (*besseres Geschäft*) to use the Jews for work on fortifications, like in Tunis, and together with Stahel, I would present the case to Field Marshall Kesselring."[78]

The next day Luther's successor, Eberhard von Thadden, replied: "By order of the Führer, the 8,000 Jews living in Rome have to be taken to Mauthausen as hostages. The Minister asks you to avoid interfering in this matter under any circumstances and leave it to the SS."[79] On October 16, as we saw, the roundup took place.[80]

On the morning of the raid a friend of the pope, Countess Enza Pignatelli, informed him of the events. Immediately Maglione summoned Weizsäcker and mentioned the possibility of a papal protest if the raid went on. Strangely enough, however, after hinting that such a step could trigger a reaction "at the highest level," Weizsäcker asked whether he was allowed *not* to report the conversation, and Maglione agreed. "I observed," Maglione noted, "that I had asked him to intervene appealing to his sentiments of humanity. I was leaving it to his judgment whether or not to mention our conservation, which had been so friendly."[81]

The reason for Weizsäcker's suggestion is unclear. Did he wish to avoid receiving an "official" message that could indeed have led to retaliation against church interests in the Reich? His next step (the letter from

Hudal, which we shall refer to) would be a nonofficial warning and thus probably exclude any violent reaction. But if the pope were to protest, all such precautions would have been in vain. Weizsäcker probably hoped that the threat of papal protest would suffice to stop the roundup; a protest would thus not be necessary. Either Maglione was informed of Weizsäcker's next step and understood his reasoning, or else the cardinal's acceptance of Weizsäcker's suggestion not to report the conversation could only be interpreted as a rather strange signal that the possibility of a papal protest should not be taken too seriously.

Be that as it may, on that same day Weizsäcker and fellow German diplomats in the know approached the rector of the German church in Rome, Bishop Aloïs Hudal, a prelate notorious for his pro-Nazi leanings, and convinced him to write a letter to Stahel in which the strong possibility of the pope's public protest would be mentioned.[82] Hudal accepted.

A few hours later Weizsäcker cabled Hudal's message to Berlin and added his personal comments for Ribbentrop's benefit: "With regard to Bishop Hudal's letter," Weizsäcker informed the minister, "I can confirm that this represents the Vatican's reaction to the deportation of the Jews of Rome. The Curia is especially upset considering that the action took place, so to say, under the Pope's own windows. The reaction could perhaps be dampened if the Jews were to be employed in labor service here in Italy. Hostile circles in Rome are using this event as a means of pressuring the Vatican to drop its reserve. It is being said that when similar incidents took place in French cities, the bishops there took a clear stand. Thus the Pope, as the supreme leader of the Church and as Bishop of Rome, cannot do less. The Pope is also being compared with his predecessor, Pius XI, a man of a greatly more spontaneous temperament. Enemy propaganda abroad will certainly also use this event, in order to disturb the friendly relations between the Curia and ourselves."[83]

The pope kept silent. On October 25, after the deportees' train had left Italy on its way to Auschwitz, an article in the Vatican's official newspaper, *L'Osservatore Romano*, sang the praises of the Holy Father's compassion: "The August Pontiff, as is well known . . . had not desisted for one moment in employing all the means in his powers to alleviate the suffering, which, whatever form it may take, is the consequence of this cruel conflagration. With the intensification of so much evil, the universal and paternal charity of the Pontiff has become, it could be said, ever more active; it knows neither boundaries nor nationality, neither religion nor race. This manifold and ceaseless activity on the part of Pius XII has intensified even more in recent times in regard for the increased suffering of so many unfortunate people."[84]

Weizsäcker sent a translation of the article to the Wilhelmstrasse, with a notorious cover letter: "The Pope, although under intense pressure from various sides, has not allowed himself to be pushed into a demonstrative comment against the deportation of the Jews of Rome. Although he must know that such an attitude will be used against him by our adversaries . . . he has nonetheless done everything possible in this delicate matter in order not to burden relations with the German government and the German authorities in Rome. As there apparently will be no further German action taken on the Jewish question here, it may be expected that this matter, so unpleasant in regard to German-Vatican relations, is liquidated." Referring then to the article in *L'Osservatore Romano*, Weizsäcker added: "No objections need be raised against this statement, insofar as its text . . . will be understood by very few people only as a special allusion to the Jewish question."[85]

In August 1941 Hitler had been sufficiently worried about the impact of Bishop Galen's sermon against euthanasia to alter the course of the operation. Why didn't the Nazi leader make the faintest move to forestall a threat of much greater magnitude—a public declaration by the pope against the deportation and extermination of the Jews? Why, in fact, did Hitler insist on deporting the Jews of Rome, notwithstanding warnings about dire potential consequences? Even if he assumed that German Catholics would not take a stand regarding the Jews as they could have done regarding their own people (the mentally ill), a public condemnation by the pope would have constituted a worldwide propaganda disaster. Only one answer is plausible: *Hitler and his acolytes must have been convinced that the Pope would not protest.* This belief probably derived from the multiple and quasi-identical reports reaching Berlin about the pontiff's political stand.

As early as the beginning of 1943, in a conversation with the German ambassador to the Vatican, Diego von Bergen, Pius XII had expressed his desire to postpone dealing with all outstanding contentions between the Reich and the Holy See (regarding the situation of the church in

Germany) until the end of the war. According to Bergen the pope added that such was his intention except if the Germans took measures that would compel him to speak out "to fulfill the obligations of his office." Given the context the remark referred to the situation of the church in Germany.[86] The pope's readiness to accept, temporarily, the everyday difficulties that party and state created for German Catholics, and to postpone the discussion until after the war, derived, of course, from the ever-increasing worry of the Holy See in the face of gathering "Bolshevik" strength.

A short comment in Goebbels's diary entry of February 8, 1943, confirmed that Hitler was well aware of the Vatican's fears. The propaganda minister was listing the main points of Hitler's address to the *Reichsleiter* and *Gauleiter* at Rastenburg headquarters, on February 7. In the course of his survey of Germany's strategic and international situation after Stalingrad, the Nazi leader came to speak of the Vatican: "Also the Curia has become somewhat more active as it sees that now it has only one choice left: National Socialism or Bolshevism."[87]

Two further Goebbels diary entries of the same weeks have to be viewed with caution, as the minister may have added some wishful thinking to information that was reaching him. Thus on March 3 he noted: "I hear from the most diverse sides, that it could be possible to do something with the present Pope. He is supposed to share, in part, some very reasonable views and not to be as hostile to National Socialism as one could surmise from the declarations of some of his bishops."[88] Two weeks later Goebbels noted the "very sharp declaration against the twisting, in the U.S., of a speech by [New York Cardinal Francis] Spellman [who had just met with the pope]. . . . The Vatican declares that it has nothing to do with the war aims of the enemy. One can see from this, that the Pope is possibly closer to us than is generally assumed."[89]

On July 5, on presenting his credentials as new German ambassador to the Holy See, Weizsäcker had a conversation with the pontiff that seemed to tally entirely with prior German assessments: Pius first mentioned his "gratitude for the years he had spent as Nuncio in Germany and his affection for Germany and the German people." After alluding to the ongoing problems between church and state in Germany, the pope expressed the hope that these issues would later be solved. The conversation then turned to Bolshevism. Weizsäcker emphasized Germany's role in the fight against the Bolshevik threat. According to the ambassador, "the Pope spoke of his own Munich experience with the communists in 1919. He condemned the mindless formula of our enemies that refers to 'unconditional surrender.'" After mentioning Pius's lack of expectations regarding any peace initiatives "at the present time," Weizsäcker indicated in conclusion that although in general the conversation took place without apparent passion, it was "suffused with hidden spiritual ardor which turned into an acknowledgement of common interests with the Reich only when the fight against Bolshevism was evoked." ("*Das Gespräch . . . wurde vom Papst ohne sichtbare Leidenschaft, aber mit einem Unterton von geistlichen Eifer geführt, der nur bei der Behandlung der Bolschewisten-Bekämpfung in eine Annerkenung gemeinsamer Interessen mit dem Reich überging.*")[90]

The Vatican's fear of the communist menace grew after Mussolini's fall and, a few weeks later, in the wake of Italy's surrender. On September 23 Weizsäcker informed Berlin that "by chance" he had had a look at three Vatican documents all dated July 25 (the day of Mussolini's fall). The third—and the most important—of these documents was, so Weizsäcker reported, "an exposition by Cardinal Secretary of State Maglione to the Italian Government of the dangers threatening the world. Maglione says that the fate of Europe depends on the victorious resistance by Germany on the Russian front. The German Army is the only possible bulwark—'*baluardo*'—against Bolshevism. Should this bulwark break, European culture would be finished."[91]

On September 3 Weizsäcker sent an even more explicit report to Berlin regarding the pope's political attitude: "I continually receive proof how very much annoyed Vatican people are over Anglo-American policy, the spokesmen of which are regarded as clearing the path for Bolshevism. Concern in the Vatican about the fate of Italy and of Germany, too, is growing. A diplomat who enjoys special connections with the Vatican assured me yesterday the Pope sternly condemns all plans aimed at weakening the Reich. A bishop working in the Curia told me today that in the Pope's view a powerful German Reich is quite indispensable for the future of the Catholic Church. From confidential transcript of conversation between an Italian political publicist and the Pope, I gather that the Pope, in reply to question as to what he thought of the German people, replied: "They are a great nation who, in their fight against Bolshevism, are bleeding not only for their friends but also for the sake of their present enemies."[92]

Three weeks later Orsenigo paid a visit to the new state secretary at the Wilhelmstrasse, Gustav Adolf Steengracht von Moyland, and, without any prodding, started expostulating about the threat represented by world communism. Only Germany and the Vatican could counter the threat: Germany, in material terms, and the Vatican, spiritually.[93] In all probability Weizsäcker in his reports and Orsenigo in his communications were trying to please Ribbentrop and, beyond him, Hitler himself, in order to alleviate the constant pressure put by the regime on the church in Germany. Nonetheless the authenticity of the constantly repeated political message could not be doubted.

All this must have been known to both Hitler and Goebbels when, on August 7, they discussed the situation in Italy following Mussolini's fall. At some point Goebbels broached the subject of the pope: "Undoubtedly, as the Führer also agreed, the Pope is a Roman and an Italian. His efforts are concentrated upon holding back Bolshevism in Europe, under any circumstances. Also, he can certainly be considered as a friend of the Germans; after all he did spend fourteen years in Germany. Naturally he is no friend of National Socialism; but, all the same, he likes it more than Bolshevism. In any case, during the entire Italian crisis he did not express any hostility against fascism or against Mussolini. The Italian clergy in its majority is favorable to fascism. Admittedly though, the Pope is advised by a wide circle of enemies of National Socialism. His Secretary of State in particular, Maglioni [*sic*], is thoroughly hostile to Germany and National Socialism. I believe however that one can do something with the Pope and that is also Ribbentrop's opinion. The Führer wants to keep him for a favorable occasion. Here too we have a piece on the chessboard. When to move it remains open."[94]

On October 14, as the first anti-Jewish measures had already been taken in the Italian capital, Goebbels noted: "The Cardinal Archbishop of Paris has expressed himself regarding the present situation in a conversation with one of our informants: According to him, the Vatican is absolutely hostile to Bolshevism. It would wish to reach firm agreements with the Reich. The Pope watches with greatest worry the increasingly bolshevist mood in all European countries. There is no doubt that the Catholic Church knows that if Bolshevism were to stand at Germany's borders, it would mean mortal danger for her [the Church]."[95] Closer to home, Mussolini's fall energized the partisans active in the northern and central parts of Italy and, among them, communist units, which particularly worried the Vatican.[96]

The Nazi leader could assume therefore that Pius XII would abstain from any step that would harm Germany and increase the communist danger from outside "Europe," or from inside. The only way that seemed open to the Vatican in order to avoid what it deemed an oncoming catastrophe was to broker a peace agreement between the Western powers and Germany that would establish a common "bulwark" against the advancing Soviets and defend the heart of the Continent. Hence Pius's criticism of the unconditional surrender formula, if indeed he expressed himself in the way Weizsäcker reported on July 5. Both sides were aware of the papal plan and knew it to be the Vatican's first priority. Within such a grand scheme there could be no place, the pontiff probably thought, for a public stand regarding the fate of the Jews, either in general or in relation to the events in Rome and in Italy.

It has been argued that in order to bring about the diplomatic compromise that he considered his mission, the pope had decided, from the very beginning of the war, not to speak up for any group of victims of the Nazi regime—either the Poles, the victims of euthanasia, or the Jews. This, however, was not the case. As we saw, the pope publicly expressed his sympathy for the Poles in his encyclical *Summi Pontificatus* of December 1939. Over the following years Polish bishops and the Polish population felt that Pius did not protest frequently and forcefully enough. This may have been the case until May 31, 1943, when the pontiff expressed a ringing recognition of "the tragic fate of the Polish people," adding warm praise about the "faithful Polish people, heroically silent about their sufferings down the centuries, [who] have contributed to the development and preservation of Christian Europe."[97] Pius spoke again about Polish sufferings in his June 2, 1943, address to the College of Cardinals. Regarding euthanasia the pope most energetically condemned it in letters to the German bishops. Mainly the Holy See addressed numerous protests, demands, and inquiries *via diplomatic channels* both regarding the situation of Catholics in Poland and about the killing of the mentally ill.[98] *Not one such diplomatic intervention dealt with the overall fate of the Jews.*

Was the pope convinced that the Nazis would be impervious to any declaration he would make against their anti-Jewish policies? Did he believe that the bishops should respond according to their assessment of local conditions and not be prompted by Rome? Did he fear retaliation against baptized mixed breeds? Was he afraid of endangering the Jews who had gone into hiding in Italy, or did he believe that concealed assistance to the victims was the only possible way of countering the persecution? Furthermore, was he worried about a Nazi onslaught against German Catholics? Or did he fear the occupation of the Vatican? All these arguments have been made, either during the war or in the debates that followed since, and all, in some minor way, may have influenced Pius's decision to remain silent. The political argument must have played the central role. However, a few of these secondary points demand brief comments.[99]

Was Pius XII referring to the situation of the Jews in the already mentioned address to the College of Cardinals, on June 2, 1943? I thought so in my 1964 interpretation of papal policy, mainly in view of the pope's mention of "the anxious entreaties of all those who, because of their nationality or their race, are being subjected to overwhelming trials and sometimes, through no fault of their own, are doomed to extermination."[100] Yet, according to the Vatican editors of the document themselves, the address dealt essentially with the situation of the Poles.[101] Therefore the pope's remarks could have dealt with the Jews only *incidentally if at all*, and in this context "extermination" may have meant the widespread killing of Poles. The word "sometimes" reinforces this interpretation.

"Every word We address to the competent authority on this subject," Pius went on, "and all Our public utterances, have to be carefully weighed and measured by Us in the interests of the victims themselves, lest, contrary to Our intentions, We make their situation worse and harder to bear. To put the matter in its most basic terms, the ameliorations apparently obtained do not match the scope of the Church's maternal solicitude on behalf of the particular groups that are suffering the most appalling fate. The Vicar of Christ, who asked no more than pity and a sincere return to elementary standards of justice and humanity, faced a door that no key could open."[102]

If this address referred at all to the fate of the Jews, the pope, in mentioning the possibility that his interventions could create an even worse situation, may have had the events in Holland in mind, where, as we saw, the Catholic bishops' protest of July 1942 led to the deportation of ninety-two Catholic Jews. However, by specifically alluding to a "situation . . . even harder to bear," the Pontiff must indeed have rather been pointing only to the sufferings of the Poles; for the deported Jews, there was no situation harder to bear any longer. Moreover, "the ameliorations apparently obtained" also could not refer to the fate of the Jews.

The most important papal document regarding the Jewish issue, during those same months of 1943, is the letter Pius XII addressed to Bishop Preysing on April 30. The bishop of Berlin had informed the pontiff, in a message sent on March 6, 1943, of the new deportations from the Reich (the *Fabrikaktion*, among others): "Even harder [than by the bombings], we are hit here in Berlin by the new wave of deportations of Jews. Many thousands are destined for the probable fate to which your Holiness has alluded in your Christmas [1942] radio message. There are also many Catholics among these deportees. Would it not be possible for your Holiness to try once again to intervene for these many unfortunate innocents? It is the last hope of so many of them and the innermost prayer of all people of goodwill."[103]

The Pope did not avoid answering Preysing's anguished cry: "It was a consolation for Us to learn that Catholics, notably in Berlin, had manifested great Christian charity toward the sufferings of 'non-Aryans.' Let this be the occasion for Us to express Our paternal gratitude and Our profound sympathy to Msgr Lichtenberg who is in prison."[104]

Preysing, however, had implored the Pope to intervene in some way. The answer made clear that the pontiff was not ready to do anything beyond his private message of encouragement. He explained his abstention as follows: "So far as Episcopal declarations are concerned, We leave to pastors on the spot the task of assessing whether, and to what extent, the danger of reprisals and pressures and, perhaps, other circumstances due to the length and the psychological climate of the war, counsel restraint—despite reasons that may exist for intervention—in order to avoid greater evils. *This is one of the motives for the limitations which We impose upon Ourself in Our declarations.*"[105]

In other words the complex circumstances and the dangers of each local situation prescribed utmost prudence lest a move by a Catholic dignitary could result "in reprisals and pressures" and even "greater evils." The pope thus favored a general code of conduct that gave much freedom of decision to the bishops in assessing the advisability of their own interventions in view of local circumstances and, as he explicitly mentioned in the letter, also applied it to his own decisions.

Some historians have suggested that following his Munich "experience" with the local Soviet in 1919, an experience that certainly remained engraved in his memory, as shown by the conversation with Weizsäcker in July 1943, Pius XII's traditional Christian anti-Judaism became straightforward anti-Semitism. Bolshevism was identified with Jewry, as, indeed, some Jewish leaders had played a prominent role during the brief communist takeover of the Bavarian capital.[106] There is no specific indication that the pope was anti-Semitic or that his decisions during the war stemmed, be it in part, from some particular hostility toward Jews. Yet, contrary to his feelings for his "beloved Polish people," and mainly for the German people, it does not seem that Pius XII carried the Jews in his heart.[107] This becomes apparent in the last part of the letter to Preysing, in which Pius addresses the help that he extended to Jews in need:

"To non-Aryan Catholics as well as those of the Jewish faith, the Holy See has acted charitably, within the limits of its responsibilities, on the material and moral plane. This action has necessitated a great deal of patience and disinterestedness on the part of the executive arms of Our relief organizations in meeting the expectations—one might even say demands—of those asking for help, and also in overcoming the diplomatic difficulties that have arisen. Let us not speak of the very large sums in American money, which we have had to disburse on shipping for emigrants. We gave those sums willingly because the people concerned were in distress. The money was given for love of God, and We were right not to expect gratitude on this Earth. Nevertheless, Jewish organizations have warmly thanked the Holy See for these rescue operations."

At this point Pius once more turned to Preysing's entreaty for some public gesture for the Jews who were being deported to their death: "In our Christmas message We said a word about the things that are presently being done to non-Aryans in the territories under German authority. It was short, but it was well understood. It is superfluous to say that Our paternal love and solicitude are greater today toward non-Aryan or semi-Aryan Catholics, children of the Church like the others, when their outward existence is collapsing and they are going through moral distress. Unhappily, in the present circumstances, We cannot offer them effective help other than through Our prayers. We are, however, determined to raise Our voice anew on their behalf as circumstances indicate and permit."[108]

"Moral distress" and the collapse of "outward existence" were not exactly the right terms regarding the fate of non-Aryan Catholics and all other Jews. As for the "circumstances" that would "indicate" another appeal (such as the Christmas 1942 message), one may wonder what in Pius's mind would justify such an appeal above and beyond the deportation of the Jews from the bishop of Rome's own city.

Finally, we mentioned that hundreds, possibly thousands of Jews found hiding places in religious institutions throughout Rome and in all major Italian cities; some even took refuge inside the Vatican. Could it be that the pope chose to abstain from any public challenge in order to facilitate the covert rescue operations by the church in Italy? There is no indication of any connection between the pontiff's silence and the assistance given to Jews. As for the assistance as such, it has been thoroughly researched by historian Susan Zuccotti; her conclusion, regarding Rome and Vatican City in particular, is that the pope must have known of the rescue activities without ever explicitly approving them but not forbidding them either.[109] Personally he was not involved in any of the rescue operations throughout Italy.[110] No trace of any written directive has ever surfaced; moreover, from among the main religious personalities involved in assistance to the victims, in Rome or elsewhere, no indication of an oral directive from the Holy See to help the fleeing Jews has ever been mentioned. The rescue activities were mostly spontaneous, with or without support from the Jewish relief organization Delasem.[111]

When the arguments that would explain Pius's silence are assessed as a whole, it seems plausible that, in the pontiff's opinion, the drawbacks of an intervention far outweighed any beneficial results. The pope may have thought that by intervening he would grievously jeopardize his grand political project, possibly draw fierce retaliation against the church and its interests, first and foremost in Germany and, arguably, endanger converted mixed-breeds who hadn't yet been deported. In his mind such calamitous results would probably not be offset by any tangible advantage; he may also have believed that nothing could change the course of Nazi policy regarding the Jews. According to this line of thinking, the only open course would have been covert assistance to individual Jews and some degree of intervention with predominantly Catholic satellite states (Slovakia, Croatia, and Vichy France to a certain extent). We shall return to the issue of individual assistance. As for diplomatic intervention with satellite states close to the Vatican, no direct appeal by the pope himself is known of. Maglione's remonstrances, whenever they took place, were usually expressed with such diplomatic restraint that they could almost be considered as steps undertaken for the record rather than attempts to effect a change of policy or at least some greater reluctance in collaborating with German measures.[112]

In more general terms, if the Catholic Church is merely considered as a political institution that has to calculate the outcome of its decisions in terms of instrumental rationality, then Pius's choice may be deemed reasonable in view of the risks entailed. If, however, the Catholic Church also represents a moral stand, as it claims, mainly in moments of major crisis, and thus has to move on such occasions from the level of institutional interests to that of moral witnessing, then of course Pius's choice should be assessed differently.[113] What we do not know and have no way of knowing—and there lies the core of the issue—is whether for Pius XII the fate of the Jews of Europe represented a major crisis situation and an anguishing dilemma, or whether it was but a marginal problem that did not challenge Christian conscience.

Whatever Pius's anguish about the deportation from Rome may have been, none of it was even hinted at, when he met the American envoy Harold Tittman, on October 19. That day the deportees' train had reached Vienna: The Vatican was being informed of the transport's progress at each stage of the journey to Auschwitz. According to Tittman's cable to Washington, "The Pope seemed preoccupied that in the absence of sufficient police protection, irresponsible elements (he said it is known that little communist bands are stationed in the environs of Rome at the present time) might commit violence in the city." Tittman added that the pope expressed the wish that "the matter be attended to by the Allies in due time." Finally, the pontiff conveyed to the American diplomat that "the Germans had respected Vatican City and the Holy See's property in Rome, that the German general commanding in Rome seemed well disposed toward the Vatican." According to Tittman, the pope then added that "he was feeling restriction due to the 'abnormal situation.'"[114] Presumably the 'abnormal situation' meant the deportation of the Jews of Rome.

V

Little changed in the attitude of the Christian churches (Catholic and Protestant) in continental Europe from the end of 1943 to the end of the war in regard to the fate of the Jews in their midst. Generalizations may possibly not be warranted in considering such vast and diverse domains, yet some basic facts cannot be dismissed and some comments may at least be ventured at this stage:

- Although sporadic protests by some Catholic bishops or Protestant religious leaders did take place, the vast majority of Catholic and Protestant authorities remained publicly silent in the face of the deportations of the Jews and the growing knowledge of their extermination. Whatever the reasons for it may have been, the pope's silence contributed to the lack of open protest by Catholic prelates in various countries, including Germany. Generally no explicit guidance was given to Christians (both Catholic and Protestant) regarding the duty to help Jews, and almost no obstruction of the roundups and the deportations by religiously motivated groups took place.
- In terms of private interventions and assistance rendered by both Catholic and Protestant personalities or institutions, a clear distinction was systematically established between the tiny minority of converted Jews and the quasi totality of the "ordinary Jews."
- The distinction thus applied to the two categories of Jews derived of course from a fundamental tenet of religious doctrine in both Catholicism and mainstream Protestantism (with the exception of the "German Christians") regarding the radical difference existing between Christians (including converts) on the one hand and Jews on the other, not only in terms of ultimate salvation but also in terms of their status within Christian societies. Thus, as we saw, Catholic and Protestant church leaders generally took no exception to legislation that excluded Jews from positions in public life and from significant economic activities in most con-

tinental European states; in several countries (apart from Nazi Germany) they supported it.

• The be-all and end-all of this doctrine of fundamental inequality between Christians and Jews (both in this world and in the next) naturally created a "gray zone" in terms of individual Christian conscience and in regard to moral obligations; it allowed for a mix of traditional religious mistrust and contempt toward Jews that could easily—and frequently did—offset any urges of compassion and charity, or even fueled aggressive anti-Semitism.

The stigmatizing of Jews intrinsic to Christian dogma or tradition found a vast array of expressions in accepted theological thinking and mainstream public utterances among all the Christian churches of Europe. Some of it was formulated as generously and carefully as possible, some—although avoiding extreme vituperation—could be downright aggressive, even violently so. In Germany all forms and nuances found their way into the minds and hearts of tens of millions of believers, Protestant or Catholic.

Even an outstanding religious personality such as Dietrich Bonhoeffer, the moral beacon of the Confessing Church, could not escape the traditional dogmatic position. Bonhoeffer denounced the persecution and deportation of the Jews and in his *Ethics,* he tried to establish a theological underpinning for his defense of the Jewish people: "Jesus Christ was the promised Messiah of the Israelite-Jewish people, and for that reason the line of our forefathers goes back beyond the appearance of Jesus Christ to the people of Israel. Western history is, by God's will, indissolubly linked with the people of Israel, not only genetically but also in genuine uninterrupted encounter. The Jew keeps open the question of Christ. He is the sign of the free mercy choice and of the repudiating wrath of God. 'Behold therefore the goodness and severity of God.' (Rom.11:22). An expulsion of the Jews from the West must necessarily bring with it the expulsion of Christ. For Jesus Christ was a Jew."[115]

As one of the commentators on this "intriguing passage" indicated, "It contains the characteristic ambivalence of Bonhoeffer's work. The ultimate importance of Jews for Bonhoeffer's Christianity lay in their rejection of Christ, their role as a sign both that belief is a choice and that God punishes unbelievers."[116]

* * *

Archbishop Gröber of Freiburg used a different tone altogether. In a long report on the situation of the church in Germany sent to the pope on February 2, 1944, he took an unambiguous stand against Nazi ideology and against the Nazi cult of the *Volk*. In that sense, the prelate who had once been called "the brown bishop" had decidedly turned against any ideological accommodation with the regime. And yet, a quite unexpected transformation occurred when Gröber came to mention Judaism and repeated for the benefit of the pope the content of his own New Year's message to his archdiocese. "I declared further [after having discussed other themes regarding the *Volk*] that the new concept of Volk entirely misunderstands the essence of Christianity. It [Christianity] is not some Judaism even if it considers the Israelite people [*Volk*] as the carrier and mediator of divine ideas and promises. But how Christ himself stood in regard to contemporary Judaism is shown in his struggle against the Pharisees and the doctors [*Schriftgelehrten*] and it is shown by the cross on Golgotha. The story of the apostles proves that the hatred of the Jews pursued Christians often during early Christianity, that in fact it went on fanatically throughout the history of Christendom."[117] And on May 8, 1945, as Germany surrendered, Gröber again attacked Nazi ideology and again offered the same interpretation of the relation of Judaism to Christianity.[118] In both cases Pius XII avoided comment on Gröber's stand regarding the Jews.

Sermons such as Gröber's, and tens of thousands of more extreme ones, were but a fraction of a religious-cultural domain including teaching, catechism, and, more generally, a complex web of cultural expressions carrying all forms and degrees of everyday anti-Semitism. None of this, of course, was new either in Europe or in other parts of the Christian world, but the question that surfaced and surfaces repeatedly in our context is stark: What was the contribution of such a religious anti-Jewish culture to the passive acceptance, sometimes to the occasional support, of the most extreme policies of persecution, deportation, and mass murder unfolding in the midst of Europe's Christian populations?

Paradoxically, evaluating and interpreting the assistance given by Christian organizations, institutions, and religiously motivated individuals to Jews in need of a hiding place or other forms of help is no less difficult. Such assistance, let us remember, entailed risk, extreme risk in

Eastern Europe, various degrees of risk in the West. On the other hand, proselytism and conversion were major, albeit most elusive elements in granting such help, particularly in the hiding of children. In some places conversion may have been considered essential for better camouflage, but generally it was an aim in itself. This of course changes the historical assessment of Christian assistance, notwithstanding risk, compassion, or charity. It would be pointless to try and disentangle the components of such situations, the more so since, to a degree, all these motivations probably played some role, wherever mere greed was not the sole overriding factor. Actually, from the point of view of the devout Christian, bringing about the conversion of a Jew (or any other nonbeliever), even as a result of dire circumstances, may have been considered a religious obligation and an act of ultimate charity.

It is probably from that strictly religious point of view that one should interpret the pope's decision, at the end of the war, to allow the Holy Office to instruct bishops throughout Europe not to return baptized Jewish children hidden in Catholic institutions to the Jewish fold. The pope also allowed the keeping of such children who had not (yet) been baptized but had no family members who could claim their return.[119]

VI

Cordelia Maria Sara was deported from Theresienstadt to Auschwitz in early 1944, more or less at the time Primo Levi arrived from Fossoli, a few months before the arrival of Ruth Kluger. Levi was dispatched to Auschwitz III Monowitz where he slaved as a laborer first, then as a chemist in the Buna laboratories. Young Cordelia, first mustered by Maria Mandel, the female commandant of the women's camp in Birkenau, then by Mengele himself (or was it possibly another SS officer?), was found fit for work and, temporarily at least, dispatched to the camp's offices.[120]

Ruth Kluger and her mother arrived at Auschwitz from Theresienstadt in May 1944, and for a short while they were shoved into the "family camp" (to which we shall return). Then both were transferred to the women's camp, where the decisive selection took place: Healthy women aged fifteen to forty five would be sent to a labor camp; the others would be gassed. Ruth was twelve. When her turn arrived, she declared her age. Her fate would have been sealed had her mother not taken a daring initiative: In a moment of inattention among the guards, she rushed her daughter to another line. Ruth promised her to say that she was thirteen. "The line moved," Kluger recalled, "towards an SS man who, unlike the first one, was in a good mood. . . . His clerk was perhaps nineteen or twenty. When she saw me, she left her post, and almost within the hearing of her boss, she asked me quickly and quietly and with an unforgettable smile of her irregular teeth: 'How old are you?' 'Thirteen,' I said as planned. Fixing me intently, she whispered, 'Tell him you are fifteen.' Two minutes later it was my turn. . . . When asked for my age I gave the decisive answer . . . 'I am fifteen.' 'She seems small,' the master over life and death remarked. He sounded almost friendly, as if he [were] evaluating cows and calves. 'But she is strong,' the woman said, 'look at the muscles in her legs. She can work.' He agreed—why not? She made a note of my number, and I had won an extension on life."[121]

"Neither psychology nor biology explains it," Kluger later wrote about the young German woman's initiative. "Only free will does. . . . The good is incomparable and inexplicable, because it doesn't have a proper cause outside itself, and because it doesn't reach for anything beyond itself."[122]

While Cordelia and Ruth were still in Theresienstadt, throughout 1943, some changes took place in the ghetto camp. At the beginning of the year the heads of the Reichsvereinigung arrived from Berlin and so did the remaining leaders of Austrian and Czech communities. For reasons not entirely clear, Eichmann decided on a change in the leadership of the camp: Edelstein remained on the council, but a German and an Austrian Jew were put ahead of him in the new hierarchy. Paul Eppstein, the former de facto leader of the Reichsvereinigung, and Benjamin Murmelstein, the Viennese rabbi whom Edelstein had already met in Nisko, took over the (Jewish) reins of the ghetto. In the meantime a German *Mischling* converted to Protestantism, ex-officer in the Imperial Army and Prussian to the marrow of his bones, Karl Löwenstein, had been transferred from the Minsk ghetto, on Wilhelm Kube's request, and appointed chief of the Theresienstadt Jewish police. The changes did not stop at that: For no clear reason again the first commandant, Siegfried Seidl, was replaced by the brutal Austrian SS captain Tony Burger (whose main claim to fame—the deportation of the Jews of Athens—was still a year away).

In August 1943 a mysterious transport of more than one thousand children arrived from Białystok. The rumor had it that they would be exchanged for Germans and possibly sent to Palestine. Two months later, well dressed and without wearing the yellow patch, they were sent on their way, accompanied by a few counselors, including Franz Kafka's sister Ottla, straight to Auschwitz.[123]

Shortly before the departure of the Białystok children, another transport, an unusually massive one, had also left Theresienstadt. In his diary Redlich did not hide his panic: "What has happened? They incarcerated Fredy [Hirsch] and [Leo] Janowitz and put them on a transport. A transport of five thousand people. They sent five thousand in one day."[124] On September 6 the transport was on its way to Auschwitz.

The prehistory of this particular transport started several months earlier when the International Committee of the Red Cross requested a visit to Theresienstadt and also a "Jewish labor camp." By late 1942, as we saw, the Geneva organization was aware of the extermination and, according to Favez, throughout early 1943, information about the mass murder of Europe's Jews kept accumulating at ICRC's headquarters. On April 15, 1943, the Red Cross chief delegate in Berlin, Roland Marti, reported that the Jewish population of the Reich capital had dwindled to fourteen hundred persons and that they, too, were slated for deportation to camps in the East. He then added: "There is no news or trace of the 10,000 Jews who left Berlin between 28.2.43 and 3.3.43 and who are now presumed dead" (if they were presumed dead less than six weeks after deportation they had obviously been murdered). Favez then adds: "The Geneva Secretariat replied thanking Marti for the information and added that it was anxious to discover the deportees' new addresses, for all the world as if they had merely moved."[125]

Before sending his report to Geneva, Marti had inquired at the German Red Cross whether packages could be sent to the deportees; the answer had been negative (as reported by an official of the German Red Cross to the ICRC delegate).[126] Eichmann and his acolytes could have no doubts by then that a request from Geneva to allow ICRC representatives to visit a Jewish camp would be forthcoming. This was precisely the kind of situation Theresienstadt had been established for. But what should be done if the Red Cross delegates insisted on visiting the ultimate reception place for deportees leaving Theresienstadt? As Theresienstadt was meant to be a hoax from the outset, some kind of sham complement had to be set up in Auschwitz, just in case. This was the rationale behind the establishment of a "family camp."

No selection took place on the arrival of the five thousand deportees' transport, and the entire group was settled in a special subcamp, BIIb, in which most of the draconian rules of life and death in Birkenau did not apply. The inmates could wear their civilian clothes, families were kept together, and every day some 500 children were sent to a special area, Block 31, where, under the guidance of Fredy Hirsch, they attended some classes, sang in a choir, played games, were told stories—in short were kept as unaware as possible of what Auschwitz-Birkenau was really all about.[127] In December 1943 another 5,000 Jews from Theresienstadt joined the first batch.

Exactly six months after their arrival, on March 7, 1944, on the eve of the Jewish festival of Purim, the 3,792 survivors of the September transport (the others had died in the meantime, despite their "favorable" living conditions) were sent to Crematorium III and gassed. Hirsch had been warned of the forthcoming gassing by members of the *Sonderkommando* and encouraged to start a rebellion. Unable to decide between passivity or a course of action that meant death for all his charges, he committed suicide.[128] Other transports from Theresienstadt arrived in May 1944.

In July, when it became obvious to Eichmann that the Red Cross commission, led by Dr. Maurice Rossel, which had visited Theresienstadt on June 23, would not ask to see Auschwitz, the entire "family camp," with a few exceptions (such as Ruth Kluger and her mother) was sent to the gas chambers.[129]

The extermination of the first batch of Jews from the "family camp," on March 7, was secretly chronicled in the diary of one of the *Sonderkommando* members. Three such diaries were found after the war, buried near the Birkenau crematoriums: those of Zalman Gradowski, Zalman Leventhal, and Leyb Langfus.[130] Gradowski had been deported to Auschwitz in November 1942 from Lona, near Białystok, together with his entire family: "mother, wife, two sisters, brother-in-law, and father-in-law." The entire family was gassed on December 8, except for Gradowski himself, who was sent to the *Sonderkommando*.[131] Of the four notebooks hidden by Gradowski, the second includes the story of "The Czech Transport":

After the defiant but helpless first load of these Czech Jews had been driven into the gas chamber and suffocated, Gradowski and his companions unbolted the doors: "They lay as they had fallen, contorted, knotted together like a ball of yarn, as though the devil had played a special game with them before their deaths, arranging them in such poses. Here one lay stretched out full length on top of the pile of corpses. Here one held his arms around another as they sat against the wall. Here part of a shoulder emerged, the head and feet intertwined with the other bodies. And here only a hand and a foot protruded into the air, the rest of the body buried in the deep sea of corpses. . . . Here and there heads broke through this sea, clinging to the surface of the naked waves. It seemed that while the bodies were submerged only the heads could peer out from the abyss."[132]

Dealing with the corpses was the *Sonderkommando*'s main task: They dragged them out of the gas chamber into the *Leichenkeller*, where anything of value was put away: "Three prisoners prepare the body of a woman," Gradowski went on with his chronicle. "One probes her mouth with pliers, looking for gold teeth, which, when found, are ripped out together with the flesh. Another cuts the hair, while the third quickly tears off earrings, often drawing blood in the process. And, the rings, which do not come off the fingers easily, must be removed with pliers. Then she is given to the pulley. Two men throw on the bodies like blocks of wood; when the count reaches seven or eight, a signal is given with a stick and the pulley begins its ascent."[133]

The *Sonderkommando* diarists knew of course that they could not be allowed to survive as witnesses nor could they hope to survive the uprising they were preparing. On the eve of the rebellion, in early October 1944, Gradowski, one of its organizers, buried his notebooks. Throughout it seems that he remained a religious Jew: After each of the gassings, he would say Kaddish for the dead.[134]

The last part of the process began once the pulley was sent on its way to the upper floor: "On the upper level, by the pulley, stand four men," the chronicle continued. "The two on one side of the pulley drag corpses to the 'storeroom'; the other two pull them directly to the ovens, where they are laid in pairs at each opening ["mouth" is used in the translation]. The slaughtered children are heaped in a big stack, they are added, thrown onto the pairs of adults. Each corpse is laid out on an iron "burial board"; then the door to the inferno is opened and the board shoved in. . . . The hair is the first to catch fire. The skin, immersed in flames, catches in a few seconds. Now the arms and legs begin to rise—expanding blood vessels cause this movement of the limbs. The entire body is now burning fiercely; the skin has been consumed and fat drips and hisses in the flames. . . . The belly goes. Bowels and entrails are quickly consumed, and within minutes there is no trace of them. The head takes the longest to burn; two little blue flames flicker from the eyeholes—these are burning with the brain. . . . The entire process lasts twenty minutes—and a human being, a world, has been turned to ashes."[135]

Why the Red Cross delegate, Maurice Rossel, did not demand to proceed to Birkenau after the visit to Theresienstadt is not clear. He was told by his SS hosts that the Czech ghetto was the "final camp"; yet Rossel could hardly have believed, in June 1944, that Theresienstadt was all there was to see regarding the deportation of the Jews of Europe. Be that as it may, on July 1, the ICRC representative sent an effusive thank-you note to Thadden, the senior official at the Wilhelmstrasse he dealt with. He even enclosed photos taken by the delegation during the visit of the camp as mementos of the pleasant excursion, and asked Thadden to forward a set to his colleagues in Prague. After expressing his gratitude, also in the name of the ICRC, for all the help extended to the delegation during its visit, Rossel added: "The trip to Prague will remain an excellent memory for us and it pleases us to assure you, once again, that the report about our visit in Theresienstadt will be reassuring for many, as the living conditions [in the camp] are satisfactory."[136]

The German concentration and extermination camp system was geared to send its Jewish victims either to immediate extermination or to slave labor that would end in extermination after a short time. Yet some of the smaller labor camps attached to enterprises working for the armaments industry, whether under control of the SS or not, sometimes kept their Jewish slaves alive for longer stretches of time, either due to essential production imperatives or (and) for the personal benefit of local commanders.[137] There was also Theresienstadt, of course, antechamber to extermination and holding pen for international propaganda. Then, in the course of 1943, another (very limited) series of camps was added to the overall landscape of destruction—and deception: camps for Jews who could be used as trading objects.

The very notion of keeping some Jews either as hostages or as exchange material for Germans in enemy hands, or else as sources of large sums of foreign currency, was nothing new from a Nazi perspective. Both the hostage idea and that of selling Jews predated the war and reappeared, as we saw, from late 1941 onward: it grew in importance as the war became increasingly difficult for the Reich. Some Palestinian Jews who had remained in Poland were exchanged for German nationals living in Palestine in the late fall of 1942, and at the same time a few Dutch Jews managed to bankroll their way to freedom. In December 1942 Hitler allowed Himmler to release individual Jews for hefty sums in foreign currency.

In early 1943 on the initiative of the Wilhelmstrasse, the same ideas became a larger-scale project. On March 2 a memorandum addressed to the RSHA suggested keeping some 30,000 Jews, first and foremost of British and American nationality, but also Belgian, Dutch, French, Norwegian, and Soviet nationals and to barter them for appropriate groups of Germans.[138] Himmler agreed, and in April 1943 a partly empty POW camp, Bergen-Belsen, was transferred by the Wehrmacht to the WVHA. As historian Eberhard Kolb has noted, Himmler's decision not to establish a civilian internees' camp but to include the new setup within the framework of the concentration camps section of the WVHA was in line with his notion that "the 'exchange Jews' could at any time still be transported to extermination camps."[139]

And indeed the earliest groups of "exchange Jews," mainly Polish Jews with Latin American "promesas" (promises to receive passports), who were assembled in Warsaw at the Hotel Polski, arrived in Bergen-Belsen in July 1943; by October of that same year, however, they had been transported to Auschwitz under the pretext that the Latin American papers were not valid.[140] Further categories of Jews arrived in Bergen-Belsen throughout 1944, and although very few of these were exchanged for Germans, their fate has to be considered within wider exchange schemes tossed around by German and Jewish operatives during the last two years of the war. These projects, as we shall see, would take on their momentary significance in late 1944 and early 1945.

VII

At the end of October 1943, the Kovno ghetto became a concentration camp. A few days beforehand, batches of young Jews had been deported to the Estonian labor camps, while the children and the elderly were sent to Auschwitz.[141] In late December the pits at the ninth fort were opened and tens of thousands of corpses, undug: These remnants of most of the Kovno community and of the transports of Jews from the Reich and the Protectorate were then burned on a number of huge pyres, restacked day after day.[142]

Abraham Tory, the Kovno diarist, escaped from the city at the end of March 1944 and survived the war. Three months later, as the Soviet army was approaching, the remaining 8,000 inhabitants of the ghetto-camp were deported (including the members of the council and its chairman, Elchanan Elkes). The men were sent to Dachau, the women to Stutthof, near Danzig. By the end of the war three-quarters of these last Kovno Jews had perished. Elkes himself died in Dachau shortly after his arrival.[143]

On October 19, 1943, Elkes had written a "last testament." It was a letter to his son and daughter who lived in London; it was given to Tory and retrieved with the diary, after the liberation of Kovno. The very last words of the letter were filled with fatherly love, but they could not erase the sense of utter despair carried by the lines that just preceded: "I am writing this in an hour when many desperate souls—widows and orphans, threadbare and hungry—are camping on my doorstep, imploring us [the council] for help. My strength is ebbing. There is a desert inside me. My soul is scorched. I am naked and empty. There are no words in my mouth."[144]

In the fall of 1943 Lodz remained the last large-scale ghetto in German-dominated Europe (except for Theresienstadt). Throughout the preceding months Himmler had reached the decision to turn the Warthegau ghetto into a concentration camp, not on its location, however, but in the Lublin district, within the still existing framework of OSTI, the SS East Industries Company. The advance of the Red Army toward the former

Polish borders put an end to the Lublin project, but Himmler continued to cling to his plans, albeit in some other location.[145] Neither Greiser nor Biebow, nor anybody else in the Warthegau administration, had been consulted. When Himmler's project became known, it triggered fierce opposition at all levels of the *Gau*, and from the Wehrmacht's armaments inspectorate. In February 1944 the Reichsführer visited Posen and, atypically, gave in to Greiser's objections. The *Gauleiter* did not waste any time in informing Pohl of the new agreement. On February 14, 1944, Greiser wrote a rather abrupt letter to the chief of the WVHA:

"The ghetto in Litzmannstadt is not to be transformed into a concentration camp. . . . The decree issued by the Reichsführer on June 11, 1943, will therefore not be carried out. I have arranged the following with the Reichsführer." Greiser went on to inform Pohl that (a) the ghetto's manpower would be reduced to a minimum; (b) the ghetto would not be moved out of the Wartheland; (c) its population would be gradually reduced by Bothmann's *Kommando* [Hans Bothmann was Lange's successor in Chelmno]; (d) the administration of the ghetto would remain in the hands of the officials of the Wartheland; and (e) "After all Jews are removed from the ghetto and it is liquidated, the entire grounds of the ghetto are to go to the town of Litzmannstadt."[146]

As their fate was being sealed, the unsuspecting inhabitants of the ghetto went on with the misery of their daily life plagued by hunger, cold, endless hours spent in workshops, exhaustion, and ongoing despair. And yet the mood also changed on occasion, as on December 25, 1943, for example, the first day of Hanukkah: "There are gatherings in larger apartments. Everyone brings a small appropriate gift: a toy, a piece of *babka* (cake), a hair ribbon, a couple of brightly coloured empty cigarette packages, a plate with a flower pattern, a pair of stockings, a warm cap. Then comes the drawing of lots; and chance decides. After the candles are lighted, the presents are handed out. Ghetto presents are not valuable, but they are received with deep gratitude. Finally, songs are sung in Yiddish, Hebrew, and Polish, as long as they are suitable for enhancing the holiday mood. A few hours of merrymaking, a few hours of forgetting, a few hours of reverie."[147]

A few weeks before Hanukkah the chroniclers noted the same urge for some spiritual or cultural sustenance in its wider expression: "Though life weighs heavily upon people in the ghetto," they recorded on November 24, "they refuse to do without cultural life altogether. The closing of the House of Culture has deprived the ghetto of the last vestiges of public cultural life. But with his tenacity and vitality, the ghetto dweller, hardened by countless misfortunes, always seeks new ways to sate his hunger for something of cultural value. The need for music is especially intense, and small centers for the cultivation of music have sprung up over time; to be sure, only for a certain upper stratum. Sometimes it is professional musicians, sometimes amateurs who perform for an intimate group of invited guests. Chamber music is played, and there is singing. Likewise, small, family-like circles form in order to provide spiritual nourishment on a modest level.[148] Poets and prose writers read from their own works. The classics and more recent works of world literature are recited. Thus does the ghetto salvage something of its former spiritual life."[149]

On March 8, 1944, "by order of the authorities," all musical instruments were confiscated; they would be distributed to the Litzmannstadt municipal orchestra, to the mayor, and to the music school of the Hitler Youth.[150]

VIII

To the very end, research about "the Jew" went on. Notwithstanding the course of the war and the rapid disappearance of their "objects," German "specialists" did not give up; moreover, some local Nazi officials, apparently acting on their own, launched projects meant to document what had been the world of an extinct race. And throughout all these years, Heinrich Himmler himself, whose thirst for knowledge on the Jewish issue was hard to match, often personally encouraged the most promising avenues of investigation.

Thus on May 15, 1942, Himmler's personal assistant, Obersturmbannführer Dr. Rudolf Brandt informed Standartenführer Max Stollmann, head of Lebensborn [the SS institution taking care of racially valuable single mothers and children born out of wedlock, among others], that the Reichsführer demanded the setting up of "a special card index for all mothers and parents [*alle die Mütter und Kindeseltern*] who had a Greek nose, or at least the indication of one."[151] But Greek noses weighed less on Himmler's mind than the indentification of Jewish traits or hidden ancestry, although these matters were indirectly related.

A year after his foray into the domain of nasal shapes, on May 22, 1943, the SS chief wrote to Bormann about the need for researching the racial evolution of mixed breeds, not only those of the second degree but even of a higher degree [one-eighth or one-twelfth Jewish, for example]. "In this matter—strictly between us [*das aber nur unter uns gesprochen*]—we have to proceed like in the breeding of higher races [*Hochzucht*] of animals or the cultivation of better plants. At least during several generations (3 or 4 generations), the descendants of such mixed-breed families will have to be racially tested by independent institutions; in case of racial inferiority, they have to be sterilized and thus excluded from hereditary transmission."[152]

At times the Reichsführer gave vent to justified anger against some incompetent scientist. Thus in the matter of three SS men of part-Jewish ancestry, Himmler agreed to keep them temporarily in the SS, but their children were excluded from joining the order or marrying into it. This unpleasant confusion was the result of a scientific evaluation by Prof. Dr. B. K. Schultz, who had pointed out that in the third generation, it could happen that not even one Jewish chromosome would any longer be present. "Thus," Himmler wrote to SS Obergruppenführer Richard Hildebrandt, on December 17, 1943, "one could argue that the chromosomes of all other ancestors also disappear. Then one should ask: from where does a person get its heredity if after the third generation the ancestors' chromosomes have all disappeared? For me, one thing is certain: Herr Professor Dr. Schultz is not suitable to head the Race office."[153]

Sometimes the Reichsführer ventured into somewhat dangerous territory. In April 1942 Winifred Wagner, the widow of Richard and Cosima Wagner's son Siegfried and herself a much-loving and beloved friend of the Führer, had complained about a lecture allegedly held in Würzburg in an SS institution about "the Jewish ancestry [*Versippung*] of the Wagner family." On December 30, 1942, Himmler assured the "lady of Bayreuth" that no such lecture had taken place, but that the rumor stemmed from a conversation between SS officers. To put all such insinuations to rest the Reichsführer asked Winifred Wagner to send him her family's genealogical chart.[154] It is unknown if this was ever done.

Throughout, collective racial identification remained of the essence, and in this domain some issues stayed unsolved for years, that of the Karaites, for example. On June 13, 1943, Dr. Georg Leibbrandt, head of the political division of Rosenberg's Ministry of the Eastern Occupied Territories, issued the following statement: "The Karaites are religiously and nationally different from the Jews. They are not of Jewish origin, rather they are viewed as being people of Turkic-Tatar origin closely related to the Crimean Tatars. They are essentially a Near Asian–Oriental race possessing Mongolian features, thus they are aliens. The mixing of Karaites and Germans is prohibited. The Karaites should not be treated as Jews, but should be treated in the same fashion as the Turkic-Tatar peoples. Harsh treatment should be avoided in accordance with the goals of our Oriental policies."[155]

At first glance it may seem unusual that, as late as June 1943 (and later), the Germans had to restate a decision that the head of the *Reichstelle für Sippenforschung* (the "Reich Agency for Ancestry Research") had already officially conveyed, in a letter of January 5, 1939, to the representative of the eighteen-member Karaite community in Germany, Serge von Douvan. "The Karaite sect should not be considered a Jewish religious community within the meaning of paragraph 2 point 2 of the First Regulation to the Reich's Citizenship Law," the letter stated. "However, it cannot be established that Karaites in their entirety are of blood-related stock, for the racial categorization of an individual cannot be determined without further ado by his belonging to a particular people, but by his personal ancestry and racial biological characteristics."[156]

The *Reichsstelle*'s decision was dictated by political considerations such as the thoroughly anti-Soviet attitude of the Karaites, many of whom had fought in the White armies during the Russian civil war, and by the racial-cultural research of a well-known German Orientalist, Paul E. Kahle, in the Leningrad archives during the 1930s; it confirmed the position taken by the former czarist regime defining the Karaites as a religious group unrelated to Judaism.[157] Yet, as the war began, and mainly after the attack on the Soviet Union, some hesitation remained.

In Lithuania, Gebietskommissar Adrian von Renteln sent researchers to the heads of the local Karaite community, and in the course of 1942 several Jewish specialists were ordered to participate in the investigation: Kalmanovitch in Vilna, Meir Balaban and Yitzhak Schipper in Warsaw; Philip Friedman in Lwov.[158] In a diary entry of November 15, 1942, Kalmanovitch noted: "I continue to translate the book of the Karaite *hakham* ["sage," in Hebrew]. (How limited is his horizon! He is proud of his

Turkish-Tatar descent. He has a better understanding of horses and arms than of religion, although he is religious in the Christian sense.)"[159]

Friedman was loath to participate in the Nazi-directed project: "At the beginning of 1942," he recollected after the war, "when I was in Lwov, I was asked by Dr. Leib Landau, a well-known lawyer and director of the Jewish Social Self-Help in the Galicia district, to prepare a study of the origins of the Karaites in Poland. The study had been ordered by Colonel Bisanz, a high official of the German administration in Lwov. Both Landau and I saw clearly that a completely objective and scholarly study, indicating the probablility of the Karaites' Jewish origin, might endanger their lives. Besides, everything in me revolted against writing a memorandum for the use of the Nazis and I asked Landau to give the assignment to another historian of Polish Jewry, Jacob Schall. He agreed, and Dr. Schall prepared a memorandum which I went over carefully, together with Landau. The memorandum was so drafted as to indicate that the origin of the Karaites was the object of heated controversy, and great emphasis was laid on those scholars who adhered to the theory of the Karaites' Turko-Mongol extraction."[160]

Additional German research in the Ukraine and elsewhere in the East, objections to the non-Jewish identification of the Karaites that came from the Commissariat Général aux Questions Juives in France, as well as some opposition within Germany itself delayed Leibrandt's decision until June 1943. The decision, however, was final. The Karaites escaped the fate of the Jews, and also that of 8,000 Krymchaks murdered by Ohlendorf's *Einsatzgruppe D* in the Crimea, although in many ways Karaites and Krymchaks were linguistically related and both groups displayed identical Turkic-Mongolian features.[161]

Rosenberg's ministry, his Frankfurt Institute, and the ERR never established exclusive control over research on Jewish matters, as we saw. Thus RSHA Office VII, dealing with "Research about Enemies" (*Gegnerforschung*), under the leadership of Prof. Dr. Franz Alfred Six, displayed an impressive level of activity, even after Six moved to the Wilhelmstrasse in September 1942.[162] He was soon replaced by the no-less-dedicated Prof. Dr. Günther Franz, who, in June 1942, had had the brilliant idea of organizing a conference on the "Jewish question" in which appropriate themes were distributed among talented doctoral students (to prepare the next generation of researchers in this domain). When Franz took over the leadership of Office VII, further series of volumes on Jews in various countries were published by the SS Nordland Verlag in runs of one hundred thousand copies in several cases. The volumes came out through 1943 and 1944.[163] Research on Jews and Jewry was only one aspect of the office's activities (along with the study of Freemasonry, Bolshevism, "Political Churches"—and on Himmler's specific order—"Witches and Witchcraft").

While Rosenberg's men were looting in the Baltic countries, for example, Six's and Franz's envoys were simultaneously emptying Jewish archives and libraries in the very same areas. In Riga, it will be remembered, they got hold of Dubnow's library. In the same operation "80 boxes containing Jewish literature were taken from the community in Dorpat, as well as various materials from the 'Jewish Club' in Reval."[164] Incidentally, until the end of 1941 at least, Jewish "assistants" were working for the various projects of "Amt VII."[165]

Rosenberg's "commando" started operating systematically in Vilna from February 1942 on, following a brief survey of the Jewish libraries in the early summer of 1941. As main delegate of the ERR in the Lithuanian capital, Rosenberg appointed one Dr. Johannes Pohl, a Judaica specialist who had spent two years (1934–36) at the Hebrew University in Jerusalem, had written a book on the Talmud, and contributed articles to *Der Stürmer*.[166] Kruk, put in charge of the team of Jewish scholars and workers employed by the *Einsatzstab*, kept regular contacts with Pohl, whom he called the "Hebraist": "Accidentally I learn from the German *Illustrierter Beobachter*, Munich, April 30, 1942, that Dr. Pohl is one of those doing *Judenforschung ohne Juden* ["the study of Jews without Jews"]. Among other things, he is the director of the Hebrew Department of the library for Research of the Jewish Question" [the library of the Frankfurt institute].[167]

The main targets of the *Einstazstab* were the Strashun Library (Vilna's Jewish communal library), the religious book collections of the city's main synagogues and the YIVO library.[168] The Yiddish poet Abraham Sutzkever (who, together with Kalmanovitch and another Yiddish poet, Shmerke Kaczerginski, were Kruk's colleagues in this enterprise) "noted the parallels between the operations of the Gestapo and the Rosenberg squad. Just as the former raided houses in search of Jews in hiding, the latter conducted aggressive searches for collections of Jewish books."[169]

"In the Rosenberg Task Force in the Yivo building, books rain down again," Kruk noted on November 19, 1942. "This time, Yiddish ones. In the cellars, where the Yivo library once was, on one side they load . . . potatoes, on the other, the books of Kletzkin and Tomor publishers. The whole cellar and several side rooms of the ground floor are crammed with packs of those book treasures. Whole sacks of Peretz and Sholem Aleichem are there, bags of Zinberg's *History of Jewish Literature,* sets of Kropotkin's *Great French Revolution*, Ber Mark's *History of Social Movements of Jews in Poland*, etc., etc. Your heart bursts with pain at the sight. No matter how much we have become used to it, we still don't have enough nerves to look at the destruction calmly. By the way, at my request, they have nevertheless promised to let us take some books for the ghetto library. Meanwhile, we take them on our own. We will, naturally, use the promise."[170] And, indeed, the Jewish team (the "paper brigade") secretly smuggled as many books as they could into the ghetto.[171]

At times the ERR "scholars" came up with truly arcane questions: "Today the head of the Rosenberg task force got a new problem," Kruk noted on June 29, 1943. "He is interested in knowing if there is a connection between the Star of David and the Soviet five-pointed star."[172]

Collecting the skulls of Jewish-Bolshevik commissars to identify the racial-anthropological characteristics of this vilest species of Jewish political criminality was naturally the preserve of Himmler's *Ahnenerbe*. Yet, despite the scientific importance of such a project, it remains unclear who authored the first memorandum addressed to Himmler on February 9, 1942, under the signature of the anatomist Prof. Dr. August Hirt of the Reich University in Strasbourg. On the face of it Hirt must have initiated the project and made the technical suggestions about the safest way of killing the subjects, severing the head from the spine, as well as packing and transporting the precious skulls *without damaging them in the process*.[173] There are indications, however, that, although Hirt was ultimately to be the recipient of the material and the project director, the original idea came from *Ahnenerbe* anthropologist Bruno Beger, a member of the Anthropology Institute of Munich University, led by the world-famous Tibet expert, Ernst Schäfer.[174] Whatever the case may be, during the following months and years, Beger and Hirt cooperated closely. Ultimately the anatomical institute in Strasbourg did not receive the skulls of Jewish-Bolshevik commissars as, by 1942, the Wehrmacht had second thoughts about executing commissars and frightening away those among them who eventually were ready to cross over to the Germans. This difficulty did not derail Hirt's and Beger's project; it merely redirected it.

On November 2, 1942, the acting chief of the *Ahnenerbe*, Wolfram Sievers, wrote to the head of Himmler's chancellery, Rudolf Brandt, that "for anthropological research purposes," 150 skeletons of Jews were necessary, that should be made available at Auschwitz. Brandt forwarded the request to Eichmann who in turn informed the Auschwitz authorities. On June 10, 1943, Beger visited the camp, selected his subjects and performed the necessary measurements.[175] On the twenty-first, Eichmann reported back to Sievers that the Munich anthropologist had "processed" 115 inmates: 79 Jewish men, 30 Jewish women, 2 Poles and 4 men from "inner Asia" (*Innerasiaten*).[176] The selected inmates were transported to the Natzweiler camp in Alsace. In the early days of August 1943, the commandant of the Natzweiler-Struthof camp, Joseph Kramer, personally gassed the first batch of Jewish women with the special chemical agent requested by Hirt.[177] Over the following days the operation was completed. The corpses were all sent to Hirt's anatomy laboratory in Strasbourg: Some were preserved and others macerated so that only the skeleton remained.[178]

The results of Hirt's research have not been preserved, although Beger survived the war and was briefly sent to jail (Hirt committed suicide). Sievers had ordered the destruction of all related documents and photographs. Yet as the Allied occupied Strasbourg, they nonetheless found some evidence that allowed the record to be kept for posterity.[179]

Some projects, such as the setting up of a Jewish Central Museum in Prague, remain puzzling.[180] Whether the idea of establishing such a museum, while the deportations from the Protectorate were putting an end to Jewish life in Bohemia and Moravia, was initiated by officials of the dwindling *Jüdische Kultusgemeinde* (for all practical purposes, the Jewish Council) or by the two senior Eichmann delegates in Prague, Hans Günther and his deputy, Karl

Rahm, is irrelevant. Even if the project was initiated by Jewish officials, it had to be accepted by Günther and Rahm and furthered by them. It was.

The museum project started officially on August 3, 1942, on the site of the prewar Jewish museum; it soon extended to all major synagogue buildings in the Jewish quarter and to tens of warehouses. Artifacts left behind by the disappearing communities of Bohemia and Moravia and pertaining to all aspects of their daily life, to religious rituals and specific customs throughout the centuries, were systematically collected and registered. Whereas the Prague Jewish museum's collection comprised some 1,000 items in 1941, it included 200,000 artifacts by the end of the war.[181]

Goebbels's filming of ghetto life strove to present the most demeaning and repulsive image of Jews to contemporaries and to posterity. All exhibitions dealing with Jewry organized in the Reich during the 1930s or throughout occupied Europe during the war, had a similar aim and so of course, did, full-length films such as *Jud Süss* and *Der Ewige Jude*. As for the two films shot in Theresienstadt in 1942 and in 1944, their aim was propaganda of another kind: to show the world the good life that the Führer granted the Jews.

None of these aims was apparent in the Prague museum project. For example, in preparing the exhibition about Jewish religious customs set up in the spring of 1943, "both sides [the Jewish scholars working at the museum and the SS officers] seem to have had a certain objectivity in mind."[182] Günther and Rahm possibly thought that once the war was (victoriously) over and no Jews were left, the material stored at the museum—not to be shown publicly until then—could easily be molded according to the regime's needs. Whatever the case may be, Rahm soon had to leave his cultural endeavors to become the last commandant of Theresienstadt.

IX

While throughout 1943 and most of 1944, the Germans were trying to complete the deportations from every corner of the Continent, and while, by then, the Allies had publicly recognized the extermination of the Jews, London and Washington obstinately shied away from any concrete rescue steps, even minor plans. In all fairness it remains difficult to this day to assess whether some of the rescue plans initiated by Germany's satellites or by some subordinate German officials were genuinely meant as exchanges of some sort or were extortionist ploys, no more.

Thus in late 1942 and during the first months of 1943, the Romanian authorities informed the Jewish Agency that they were ready to release 70,000 Jews from Transnistria for 200,000 lei (or 200 Palestine pounds) per person. The offer could have been an early Romanian feeler for contacts with the Allies but, in a hardly subtle maneuver to keep in the good graces of both sides, Radu Lecca, general secretary for Jewish affairs in Antonescu's government, who traveled to Istanbul to negotiate with Jewish Agency representatives, soon thereafter informed the German ambassador in Bucharest of the initiative. From that moment on the initiative was doomed.

The Yishuv leadership was divided in its estimate of the proposal and was well aware of the fact that the Allies would not allow the transfer of 70,000 Jews to Palestine. Indeed, the British position, shared by the State Department, was one of adamant rejection. In February 1943 the Romanian offer was reported in Swiss newspapers and in the *New York Times*, leading to some public outcry about the Allied passivity, to no avail. Over the coming weeks the plan was reduced to the transfer of 5,000 Jewish orphans from Transnistria to Palestine. Eichmann agreed to this latter proposal provided the Allies allowed the transfer to Germany of 20,000 able-bodied German prisoners of war, in exchange for the children.

Sporadic negotiations with the Romanians continued nonetheless throughout 1943, and the possibility of bribing whoever had to be bribed in Bucharest seemed to keep the rescue option alive. The operation was definitively scuttled by the obstruction of the U.S. State Department and the British Ministry of Economic Warfare regarding the transfer by the World Jewish Congress of the necessary money to Switzerland. The Treasury Department had given its authorization but to no avail. In December 1943 the Foreign Office delivered a note to the American ambassador in London, John Winant, indicating that the British authorities were "concerned with the difficulty of disposing of any considerable number of Jews should they be rescued from enemy-occupied territories."[183]

From early 1943 on, the angry publicity given to the absence of rescue operations had convinced both the Foreign Office and the State Department that some gesture was necessary: A conference on the "refugee situation" was decided. The conference, attended by high-ranking British and American officials (and by a senator and a congressman) opened in Bermuda on April 19, 1943, under the chairmanship of the president of Princeton University, Harold W. Dodds. After twelve days of deliberations, the meeting ended with the release of a statement to the press declaring that "concrete recommendations" would be submitted to both governments; however, due to the war situation, the nature of these recommendations could not be revealed.

American Jewish leaders were themselves anxious to achieve results and well aware of the demand for more forceful initiatives that arose from growing segments of the country's Jewish population. Moreover, added prodding stemmed not only from the increasingly precise reports about the situation in Europe but also from the relentless campaign for intervention orchestrated by a small but vocal group of right-wing Zionist-Revisionists led by Peter Bergson.[184] Yet for a Stephen Wise, for example, embarrassing the president by public demonstrations against American inaction was unacceptable. Wise's restraint was recognized by the administration. On the eve of a major meeting organized by the "Bergsonites"—the "Emergency Conference to Save the Jewish People in Europe"—scheduled for July 1943, Welles sent a message to Myron C. Taylor, the onetime chairman of the 1938 Evian conference on refugees and later Roosevelt's special envoy to the Vatican: "I have refused this invitation," Welles informed Taylor. "Not only the more conservative Jewish organizations and leaders but also such leaders as Rabbi Wise, who was with me this morning, are strongly opposed to the holding of this conference, have done everything they could to prevent it, and are trying to get Bishop Tucker and one or two others who have accepted this invitation to withdraw their acceptance."[185]

Wise did not hesitate to air his views publicly, however. At the American Jewish Conference held in August 1943, one month after Bergson's "Emergency Conference," he told his audience: "We are Americans, first, last, and at all times. Nothing else that we are, whether by faith or race or fate, qualifies our Americanism. . . . We and our fathers chose to be, and now choose to abide, as Americans. . . . Our first and sternest task, in common with all other citizens of our beloved country . . . is to win the anti-Fascist war. Unless that war be won, all else is lost."[186]

Wise's views were echoed by most of the participants at the conference and, all in all, by most of American Jewish organizations and their publications such as the *National Jewish Monthly* or *New Palestine* (which expressed the positions of American Zionism). Rare were the mainstream leaders who ready to admit that not enough had been or was being done; one of those was Rabbi Israel Goldstein, who, at the same American Jewish Conference of August 1943, did not hide his feelings: "Let us forthrightly admit that we American Jews, as a community of five millions, have not been stirred deeply enough, have not exercised ourselves passionately enough, have not risked enough of our convenience and our social and civic relations, have not been ready enough to shake the bond of so-called amicability in order to lay our troubles upon the conscience of our Christian neighbors and fellow citizens."[187]

To the dismay of the administration and that of mainstream American-Jewish leadership, the Bergsonites did not let go. At the end of 1943, they succeeded in persuading Senator Guy Gillette from Iowa and Rep. Will Rogers from California to introduce a rescue resolution into Congress. During the debates Breckinridge Long demanded he be allowed to testify and presented the House Committee on Foreign Affairs with misleading data about the number of Jewish refugees the State Department had allowed to enter the United States.[188] When Long's testimony became known, officials at the Treasury Department brought up evidence about the State Department's ongoing efforts to hide information about the extermination and hinder rescue efforts. This evidence was submitted to the president by secretary of the Treasury Henry Morgenthau. This time Roosevelt considered it politically wise to react and, in January 1944, he announced the establishment of the War Refugee Board (WRB) to be headed by John Pehle, assistant secretary of the treasury. The (WRB) had the mandate to coordinate and lead any rescue operations that its officials would have examined and recommended.[189]

The confirmation of the news about the ongoing extermination of European Jewry led to mass protests in the streets of Tel Aviv, to the proclamation by the Yishuv's chief rabbis of days of fasting and other manifestations of collective mourning. Soon, however, everyday concerns and even traditional celebrations resurfaced; throughout 1943 major festivals were organized by the kibbutz movement (the Dalia Dance Festival), and Hebrew University students celebrated Purim in the usual carnival procession. In the words of historian Dina Porat, "agony was a part of daily life and when the news was particularly bitter, expressions of pain multiplied. But public attention was not sustained, and life would return to normal for weeks or months, until the next shocking event."[190]

Even so, the Jewish population in Palestine was probably more responsive to the tragedy of European Jewry than the leadership of the Yishuv itself. Of course, among the leadership as among the population, the individual ties to European Jewry were equally intense, and, as the great majority of the Jewish inhabitants of Palestine stemmed from Central or Eastern Europe, many, at all levels, were aware of the possibility (or already knew) of tragic personal loss.

Yet, as strange and even as callous as it may appear with hindsight, in their public declarations from the end of 1942 on, most Zionist leaders, as already mentioned, considered the extermination first and foremost in terms of its impact on the building of a Jewish state. Ben-Gurion's despondency regarding the impact of the European situation upon the Zionist project may have contributed to his lack of involvement in rescue operations; thus it was left to the hesitant and weak Gruenbaum to coordinate activities in which he did not believe.

A meeting of the Zionist Executive Committee in Jerusalem in February 1943 starkly illustrated the prevalent mood at the top of the establishment: "We certainly cannot abstain from any action," Gruenbaum declared. "We should do all we can . . . but our hopes are infinitesimal. . . . I think we have only one hope left—and I would say the same thing in Warsaw—the only action, the only effort that provides us with hope, that is unique, is the effort being made in the Land of Israel."[191] The debate about the 1943 budget better reflected this shared attitude than any declarations: 250,000 Palestine pounds for new settlements, the same amount for agricultural development, vast sums for irrigation and the like, and 15,000 pounds for rescue activities.[192]

Over the following months the debate concerning the allocation of funds for rescue operations continued. While the Jewish Agency maintained its reticence and Gruenbaum continued to show only apathy, the trade union organization (Histadrut) took the initiative of raising funds by way of a public campaign: "Diaspora Month." The initiative, launched in mid-September 1943, failed dismally. The skepticism of the population regarding the commitment of the political leadership to the rescue operations certainly contributed to the meager results of the appeal. It seemed to some that "the Yishuv had fallen into atrophy."[193]

Zygielbojm, it will be recalled, was the Bund's delegate to the Polish National Council in London. As we saw, it is only at the end of December 1942, that Karski was allowed to meet with him and with his colleague Ignacy Schwarzbart. Until the fall of that year, Zygielbojm had not fully understood the information about the total extermination of the Jews of Poland. By November and December, however, he had grasped major aspects of the German murder campaign and was increasingly bitter about the absence of adequate response, particularly from the Polish government-in-exile and the Delegatura, which did not call upon the population to extend help to the hounded Jews. On December 23 he declared at the meeting of the National Council: "War will end and the tragedy of Polish Jewry [Zygielbojm had not yet perceived the total dimension of the events] will weigh upon the conscience of humanity for generations. Unfortunately, it will be associated with the attitude of part of the Polish population. I leave it to you to find the adequate answer."[194]

There wasn't much the Bund delegate could do. When, a few months later, the ghetto uprising started and was abandoned to its fate without any outside support, Zygielbojm knew he had reached the end of the road.[195] On May 11, 1943, he wrote a letter to the president of the Polish republic, Władisław Raczkiewicz, and to the prime minister of the government-in-exile, Władysław Sikorski. "The responsibility for the crime of the murder of the whole Jewish nation in Poland rests first of all on those who are carrying it out, but indirectly it falls also upon the whole of humanity, on the peoples of the Allied nations and on their governments, who up to this day have not taken any real steps to halt this crime. By looking passively upon this murder of defenseless millions . . . they have become partners to the responsibility.

"I am obliged to state that although the Polish Government contributed largely to the arousing of public opinion in the world, it still did not do enough. It did not do anything that was not routine, that might have been appropriate to the dimension of the tragedy taking place in Poland. . . .

"I cannot continue to live and to be silent while the remnants of Polish Jewry, whose representative I am, are being murdered. My comrades in the Warsaw ghetto fell with arms in their hands in the last, heroic battle. I was not permitted to fall like them, together with them, but I belong with them, to their mass grave. By my death I wish to give expression to my most profound protest against the inaction in which the world watches and permits the destruction of the Jewish people."[196]

On May 12 Zygielbojm committed suicide. To his comrades of the Bund in New York he had written: "I hope that with my death I shall succeed in what I failed to achieve during my life: to contribute really in saving at least some of the 300,000 Jews still alive [in Poland] out of a population of over 3 million."[197]

X

Unlike her brother Mischa, Etty Hillesum had decided to stay in Westerbork when her parents' deportation date arrived. But on September 6, 1943, the order came: She was to board the same transport. No interventions helped. In a letter of September 7, a friend, Jopie Vleeschouwer, described the events of that day: "Her parents and Mischa went to the train first. Then I trundled a well-packed rucksack and a small hamper with a bowl and mug dangling from it to the train. And there she stepped on to the platform . . . talking gaily, smiling, a kind word for everyone she met on the way . . . every inch the Etty you all know so well. . . . Then I lost sight of her for a bit and wandered along the platform. . . . I saw Mother, Father H. and Mischa board Wagon No. 1. Etty finished up in wagon No. 12, having first stopped to look for a friend in wagon No. 14 who was pulled out again at the last moment. Then a shrill whistle and the 1000 'transport cases' were moving out. Another flourish from Mischa who waved through a crack in wagon No. 1, a cheerful 'bye' from Etty in No. 12 and they were gone."[198]

On that same September 7 Etty still managed to throw a postcard from the train; it was addressed to a friend in Amsterdam: "Opening the Bible at random I find this: 'The Lord is my high tower.' I am sitting on my rucksack in the middle of a full freight car. Father, Mother, and Mischa are a few cars away. In the end, the departure came without warning. On sudden special orders from the Hague. We left the camp singing, Father and Mother firmly and calmly, Mischa too. We shall be traveling for three days. Thank you for all your kindness and care. . . . Good-bye for now from the four of us."[199]

According to a Red Cross report, Etty was murdered in Auschwitz on November 30, 1943; her parents and her brother Mischa shared the same fate. Her brother Joop survived the camp but died on his way back to Holland, at the end of the war.[200]

CHAPTER X

March 1944–May 1945

On April 6, 1944, Klaus Barbie, chief of the Gestapo in Lyons, informed Röthke of a particularly successful catch:

"This morning, the Jewish children's home 'Colonie d'Enfants' in Izieu (Ain) has been taken away. A total of 41 children, aged 3–13, have been caught. Moreover all the Jewish staff was captured: 10 people, including 5 women. We have not seized any cash or valuables. The transport to Drancy will take place on April 7."[1]

Most of the children and staff of Izieu were deported from Drancy to Auschwitz on April 13 in transport 71; the remaining ones were deported on May 30 and June 30: None survived. The first ten names on the list (in alphabetical order) included children from five countries: Adelsheimer, Sami, age five (Germany); Ament, Hans, age ten (Austria); Aronowicz, Nina, age twelve (Belgium); Balsam, Max-Marcel, age twelve (France); Balsam, Jean-Paul, age ten (France); Benassayag, Esther, age twelve (Algeria); Benessayag, Ellie, age ten (Algeria); Benessayag, Jacob, age eight (Algeria); Benguigui, Jacques, age twelve (Algeria); Benguigui, Richard, age seven (Algeria). The last children on the list were Weltner, Charles, age nine (France); Wertheimer, Otto, age twelve (Germany); Zuckerberg, Émile, age five (Belgium).[2]

The murder of the children and staff of Izieu was but a minute event in the routine of German mass extermination, but it demonstrated, as the war entered its last year, that despite the rapidly deteriorating situation of the Reich, no effort would be spared, no roundup deemed too insignificant in the final drive toward the complete extermination of the European Jews.

Both the evolution of the war and that of the anti-Jewish campaign between March 1944 and May 1945 can be divided into three distinct and yet roughly coinciding phases. The first and longest phase ended approximately at the beginning of 1945, after the failure of Hitler's major offensive in the West and the liberation of Auschwitz. At the end of this phase the Führer's state controlled hardly more territory than the prewar Reich. Yet through the preceding months it had remained a unified political entity capable of conducting large-scale military operations and implementing thoroughly planned measures against the Jews within its reach.

During the second phase, stretching from the beginning of 1945 to early April, Allied forces in the East and the West were closing on Germany's vital centers. The disintegration of the Nazi state and regime had become irreversible, and chaos spread within the shrinking Reich. The murderous anti-Jewish steps taken during those few months resulted in part from the growing anarchy combined with the persistence of raging anti-Semitism among party officials high and low and in wide strata of the population. Nonetheless there was no unified anti-Jewish policy any longer as Himmler in particular started following an independent course.

The last phase (April and early May 1945) was that of the Reich's collapse and surrender, of course, but also that of Hitler's final message to future generations. The Jewish issue dominated the Nazi leader's ultimate ramblings but, in some aspects, it did so in quite a peculiar way, as we shall see.

During this entire final year the Allies did not countenance any major rescue efforts and rejected the main plans submitted to them in regard to Hungarian Jewry (in one case at least, not without plausible reasons). But the liberation of camps and of ever-larger areas in which Jews had survived, as well as the initiatives of individuals and neutral organizations mainly in still-occupied parts of Hungary, saved tens of thousands of lives. The Jewish issue as such, however, was generally speaking nonexistent in terms of Allied decisions.

As for the majority of the surviving Jews themselves, they had become, by early 1944, a motley population of isolated individuals. Those who could joined the partisans or Resistance forces; the vast majority clawed its way through slave labor, starvation, and potential extermination at every step and, finally, survived by pure chance or mostly perished by German design.

I

During the first phase the Wehrmacht stemmed the Allied advance on Rome until early June 1944, and in mid-March it had occupied Hungary. German armaments production did not drastically decrease until the end of the year. Although the Allied landing in Normandy on June 6 succeeded, and although in the summer and autumn Soviet forces occupied Poland and the Baltic countries, toppled the Romanian regime, took over Bulgaria, and established a front line on the outskirts of Budapest, the Germans still launched dangerous counteroffensives in both the east and the west.

By the end of the year, however, after the failure of the military countermoves on all fronts (particularly the offensive in the West, definitively halted on December 27), the Reich's military might was spent: East Prussia had already partly fallen into Soviet hands, and huge Allied forces were poised on the borders of the Reich; by that time, too, the country's industrial capacity was rapidly sinking under the relentless Anglo-American bombing attacks.

At times some minor incident allowed Hitler to give a new and unexpected twist to his anti-Jewish rage, as for example, in the case of the Hungarian general Ferenc Feketehalmy-Czeydner and some fellow officers. Feketehalmy and his associates were responsible for the massacre of about 6,000 Serbs and 4,000 Jews in Novi Sad in March 1943. About to be put on trial by Kallay's government (as a sign of goodwill directed at the Western Allies), the Hungarian officers fled to Germany in early 1944. When the Budapest government asked for their extradition, Hitler granted them political asylum. On January 19 the Nazi leader's adjutant, Walter Hewel, informed Ribbentrop that, in his chief's words, "everyone in Europe should know that a person accused of persecuting Jews who would flee to Germany would be granted asylum. Anybody who fights against the Jewish pest in Europe, stands on our side. We did not yet hear that in Hungary there had been complaints against the Jews who were responsible for the mass murder of women and children in the Anglo-American bombings. It should be clear to everybody that only the Jews could be the agitators behind these horrifying terror-attacks." Hitler asked that Horthy be informed of the message.[3] The Jews as inciters of the "terror attacks" became one of Hitler's most recurrent themes.

On April 27, 1944, the propaganda minister recorded a conversation that must have taken place on the previous day in Berlin. The most recent bombing of Munich had caused heavy damage. Hitler was filled with intense desire for vengeance against England and expected a great deal from the forthcoming "reprisal weapons." Then, without transition, Goebbels noted: "The Führer's hatred against the Jews has intensified even further rather than declined. The Jews must be punished for their crimes against the European nations and in general against the entire cultured world. Wherever we can get hold of them, they should not escape retribution. The advantages of anti-Semitism do offset its disadvantages, as I always said. All in all, a long-term policy in this war is only possible if one considers it from the standpoint of the Jewish question."[4]

Why, in fact, could Hitler's hatred of the Jews have eventually lessened? For the obvious reason that most of the Jews of Europe had already been murdered. Yet as German cities were reduced to rubble and as total defeat loomed ever closer, the Führer's hatred increased.[5] Furthermore Hitler's declaration indicated once again that for him Jewry as an active entity was independent of the concrete fate of the Jews who had been murdered under German domination. The destruction of German cities was the work of "the Jew." Thus the full significance of the war and any long-term policy could not be grasped and formulated without setting the "Jewish question" (the role of the Jew) at center stage.

The same crazed obsession resurfaced in Hitler's address to an assembly of generals and officers of other ranks on May 26, 1944, in Berchtesgaden. This group of several hundred newly minted "National Socialist guidance officers" responsible since December 1943 for ideological indoctrination in the Wehrmacht, had just completed their own special training before returning to the front.[6] Two days before the meeting with Hitler, they had been harangued by Himmler at Sonthofen. As in Posen in October 1943, the Reichsführer did not mince words: The extermination of the Jews, as difficult as it was, had been a necessity for the safety and the future of the *Volk*.[7] Now it was Hitler's turn.

According to historian Hans-Heinrich Wilhelm, who first published the speech in 1976, Hitler's main aim was to inform these officers of the extermination of the Jews (already widely known by then and mentioned to them by Himmler).[8] The Jews, the Nazi leader proclaimed, had been a "foreign body" in the community of the *Volk;* it had been necessary to expel them, although not everybody grasped why it had to be done "so brutally and ruthlessly." "In removing the Jew," Hitler explained, "I eliminated in Germany the possibility of creating some sort of revolutionary core or nucleus. You could naturally say: Yes, but could you not have done it more simply—or not more simply, since everything else would have been more complicated—but more humanely? Gentlemen, we are in a life-or-death struggle. If our opponents are victorious in this struggle, the German people will be eradicated [*ausgerottet*]. Bolshevism would slaughter millions and millions and millions of our intellectuals. Anyone not dying through a shot in the neck would be deported. The children of the upper classes would be taken away and eliminated. This entire bestiality has been organized by the Jews." After evoking the 40,000 women and children killed in Hamburg, he went on, now answering his own initial rhetorical question: "Don't expect anything else from me except the ruthless upholding of the national interest in the way which, in my view, will have the greatest effect and benefit for the German nation." The speech was greeted with frenetic applause.[9]

As was his wont, when haranguing foreign dignitaries, the Nazi leader rarely missed some threatening reference to the Jews. Yet in 1944, the anti-Jewish outbursts turned even shriller than before and their setting, ever more grotesque, as the once-all-powerful Führer was now trying to convince his Balkan and Central European allies that Germany would win in the end and that they should faithfully accept his explanations despite the overwhelming Soviet military tide surging at their very borders.

Thus on March 16 and 17, on the eve of the browbeating of Horthy and the occupation of Hungary, Hitler preached at great length to the Bulgarian regency council set up after King Boris's sudden and mysterious death. The Jews were unavoidably present, of course. Atypically however, the Nazi leader started with defensive remarks: "One had often reproached him that by his ruthless handling of the Jews he had turned them into inexorable enemies." The answer was ready: The Jews would have been his enemies and those of Germany in any case; "by totally excluding them, he had completely eliminated the danger to the internal morale that they represented."[10] Just beforehand, he had mentioned 1917 and 1918 again: The link was clear enough. Whether the Bulgarians were convinced is doubtful. In any case, it would be the last visit of a Bulgarian delegation to the leader of the Great German Reich.

The "*Priesterchen*" Tiso, as the Nazi leader referred to him at times, Antonescu, or the new Hungarian prime minister, Sztójay, remained Hitler's only "politically significant" guests (there were Croats as well and the former *Duce*—still a *Duce* in title—and soon de Brinon would arrive, as spokesman of the French government-in-exile in Germany, probably in the company of his Jewish-born wife).

Hitler had already addressed the Jewish issue at length in his conversation with Tiso on April 22, 1943. On May 12, 1944, the Nazi leader was ready for a repeat performance. Right from the outset he informed his Slovak guest that the military struggle that was unfolding was certainly the mightiest confrontation in Europe since the breakup of the Roman Empire. In such a gigantic battle, crises and difficulties were unavoidable. The greatest difficulty was "that in this battle against world bolshevism we also have to take up the struggle for those who are not bolsheviks but who, by way of the Jewish segment of their society, have an inner connection to bolshevism."[11]

In this case as a year earlier, Hitler brought up the situation in Hungary. Later in his quasi monologue, the Nazi leader told Tiso that "the degree of Judaization of Hungary was astonishing; over a million Jews lived in Hungary. It was great luck for the German nation that its Führer was an Austrian. Yet notwithstanding his familiarity with the issue, the Führer would not have imagined the possibility of such a degree of Jewification."[12] Three days after this conversation the deportations from Hungary to Auschwitz started.

Among the political leaders of central and southeastern Europe, Antonescu was Hitler's most frequent guest and also the one on whom the Nazi chief seemed to rely most. Under the circumstances, however, the strengthening of Romanian resolve was greatly needed. In September

1943 and in February 1944, Hitler had already conferred at length with his Romanian counterpart. The Jews had not been forgotten then nor were they forgotten during the meetings of March 23 and 24, 1944. After the German occupation of Hungary, both leaders agreed about the disastrous political consequences of Jewish influence in Budapest. And, Hitler assured the marshal, the Werhmacht, fully equipped with new weapons, would soon regain its superiority.[13]

II

According to a report sent by Bene to the Wilhelmstrasse, on February 9, 1944, the overall situation regarding the Jews in the Netherlands was by then as follows: 108,000 Jews had "left the country." The roundup of hidden Jews was successfully going on, and not more than 11,000 Jews were still in hiding. Some 8,610 Jewish partners in mixed marriages had not been "concentrated," as these couples were sterile (either after a procedure or due to age); they would be used as laborers; they could possibly all be transferred to Westerbork for that purpose.[14]

It took eight more months to complete the roundups and empty Westerbork. In February, as Bene was sending his report, Mechanicus was still in the camp. On the fifteenth he described the departure of one more weekly transport; obviously, like Etty Hillesum before him he did not know what awaited the deportees: "This train is a decent one, for human beings, but the journey is compulsory and the fate of the travelers is not known."[15] Yet the sentence that followed sounded like an intimation: "We have seen old familiar faces for the last time—we have heard from them for the last time."[16]

A routine not observed in Drancy or Malines followed the departure: "At the camp boundary, in front of the barrier, the train stops. There it is officially handed over to the German military occupation forces who have come on the train to accompany the 'travelers.' The Jews are counted one by one. Not a single Jew must be missing. Before the barrier the Commandant bears the responsibility for the consignment—after the barrier the occupation forces."[17] Was the Dutch police thought insufficiently trustworthy to accompany the deportees to the German border?

Even in Westerbork, albeit rarely so, one could indulge in a laugh at the expense of the Germans. "The Portuguese [Jews]," the diarist recorded on February 16, 1944, "have been notified to appear in hut 9 today with the papers referring to their personal antecedents. There was a rumour that they were to have their craniums measured. Merriment throughout the camp. The place is full of different skull shapes, even among thoroughbred Jews with four grandparents of pure race."[18] A few days later, on February 28, the diary ended.

On March 8 Mechanicus was deported to Bergen-Belsen and from there to Auschwitz, on October 9, together with 120 other Belsen inmates. On October 12, 1944, they were all shot.[19] Young Ben Wessels followed the same path to Belsen. On May 7, 1944, he sent a last postcard from the camp, written in German, to his friend Johan in Oostvoorne: "Fortunately, I can tell you that I am in excellent shape. A food package would please me a great deal and also please some wool for mending." Ben probably died in the typhus epidemic, in March 1945.[20]

Anne Frank's thoughts, in the spring of 1944, took an unusual turn. Her chronicle of everyday life in hiding and of the ebb and flow of intimate feelings became more widely open to reflections on the fate of her people, on religion and history: "Who has inflicted this on us?" she asked on April 11. "Who has set us apart from all the rest? Who has put us through such suffering? It's God who has made us the way we are, but it is also God who will lift us again. In the eyes of the world, we're doomed, but if, after all this suffering, there are still Jews left, the Jewish people will be held up as an example. Who knows, maybe our religion will teach the world and all the people in it about goodness, and that's the reason, the only reason, we have to suffer. We can never be just Dutch, or just English, or whatever, we will always be Jews as well. And we'll have to keep on being Jews, but then, we'll want to be."[21]

Anne exhorted herself: "Be brave! Let's remember our duty and perform it without complaint. There will be a way out. God has never deserted our people. Through the ages Jews have had to suffer, but through the ages they've gone on living, and the centuries of suffering have only made them stronger. The weak shall fall and the strong shall survive and not be defeated!"[22]

Anne's proclamation of faith was followed, in the same entry of April 11, by a declaration of overflowing love for the Dutch nation. After describing a brief alarm, during which she believed that the police had discovered their hiding place, she went on: "But now, now that I have been spared, my first wish after the war is to become a Dutch citizen. I love the Dutch, I love this country, I love the language, and I want to work here. And even if I have to write to the Queen herself, I won't give up until I have reached my goal!"[23]

Barely a month later, however, Anne was less sure about her place in postwar Dutch society: "To our great sorrow and dismay," she noted on May 22, "we have heard that many people have changed their attitude toward us Jews. . . . "We've been told that anti-Semitism has cropped up in circles where once it would have been unthinkable. This fact has affected us all very, very deeply. The reason for the hatred is understandable, maybe even human, but that doesn't make it right. According to the Christians, the Jews are babbling their secrets to the Germans, denouncing their helpers and causing them to suffer the dreadful fate and punishments that have already been meted out to so many. All this is true. But, as with everything, they should look at the matter from both sides: Would Christians act differently if they were in our place? Could anyone, regardless of whether they are Jews or Christians, remain silent in the face of German pressure? Everyone knows it's practically impossible, so why do they ask the impossible from the Jews? . . . Oh, it's sad, very sad that the old adage has been confirmed for the umpteenth time: 'What one Christian does is his own responsibility, what one Jew does reflects on all the Jews.' "[24]

Anti-Semitism did indeed spread in Holland and, as we saw, throughout the Continent. It was as tangible in France as in the Ukraine, as real in Poland as in Germany itself; Klemperer, the keenest of observers, had expressed it precisely: Whatever else the Nazis had miscalculated, they had been right to concentrate their propaganda campaign against the Jew. Anne had also heard that, after the war, foreign Jews would be sent back to the countries they had fled from. Thus, the young girl who, a few weeks earlier, had proclaimed her intense wish to become Dutch now assessed her chances of being accepted with some wariness after she heard about the change in public mood: "I have only one hope": she wrote that same day, "that this anti-Semitism is just a passing thing, that the Dutch will show their true colors, that they will never waver from what they know in their hearts to be just, for this is unjust! And if they ever carry out this terrible threat, the meager handful of Jews still left in Holland will have to go. We too will have to shoulder our bundles and move on, away from this beautiful country, which once so kindly took us in and now turns its back on us. I love Holland. Once I hoped it would become a fatherland to me, since I had lost my own. And I hope so still!"[25]

Somebody denounced the Jews hidden at 263 Prinsengracht. On August 4, 1944, they were arrested, transferred to a prison in Amsterdam, then deported to Auschwitz, probably in the last transport from Holland. Margot and Anne were taken to Bergen-Belsen, where, like Ben Wessels, they both died of typhus a few weeks before the liberation of the camp. They were probably buried in a mass grave. Except for Otto Frank, none of the eight residents of the Annex survived. Miep and Bep found Anne's diary pages scattered all over the hiding place.[26]

In Brussels the Gestapo, led by a Jewish informer, arrived at the Flinkers' home on April 7, 1944, Passover eve. The Flinkers had prepared matzot and all traditional dishes for the seder: They could not deny their identity. All were arrested and deported. Moshe and his parents perished in Auschwitz. Moshe's sisters survived, and among the belongings they retrieved after the war, they discovered three notebooks of his diary.[27]

The German roundups were partly hampered by a lack of sufficient police forces and other personnel, as Müller explained to Thadden in October 1943, after the failure in Denmark.[28] The growing absence of cooperation from regular local police units was only partly compensated by the expansion of diehard militias, including both common criminals and fanatical pro-Nazis. The rise of these extremist militias had elements in common with a wider radicalization process among some segments of Western and Central [Hungary] European societies in the shadow of German defeat.

In France collaborationist extremism surged in early 1944 with Darnand's appointment as secretary-general for the maintenance of order, and, a few months later, as secretary of state for the interior, and that of Philippe Henriot, a militant Catholic and extreme rightist from the prewar years, as secretary of state for propaganda and information; their views and their fanaticism were on par with that of their models and allies, the SS. While Henriot spewed the vilest anti-Semitic propaganda in his twice-daily broadcasts, Darnand's men denounced, arrested, tortured, and killed Resistance fighters and Jews. They killed Victor Basch, the Jewish former chairman of the League of Human Rights and his wife, both in their eighties; they killed Blum's Jewish former minister of Education, Jean Zay; they killed Reynaud's minister of the interior, Georges Mandel, to name only their best-known Jewish victims.[29] An inscription left on Basch's body proclaimed: "Terror for terror: the Jew is always made to pay. This Jew has paid with his life for the assassination of a Frenchman."[30] As for Henriot's rhetoric, it was astonishingly successful even at this late stage of the war: The man was in many ways equal to Goebbels, and the Resistance considered him dangerous enough to execute him at the end of June 1944. His fierce anti-Semitism found at least some echo among wide segments of the population.

On the eve of the liberation, anti-Semitic attitudes in France were not on the decrease; they were even blurted out among the Free French in obviously well-meant declarations. Thus, in alluding in a French BBC broadcast to the assistance given by collaborationist Frenchmen to the murder of Jews, André Gillois, the commentator, put the matter as follows: "The policemen, civil servants, and prison guards should know that in accepting to take part in the massacre of Jews, they have no more excuse than [they have] for lashing out against all other victims of Nazism."[31] It was the same climate of opinion that led André Weill-Curiel, a Jew who had spent the war years with de Gaulle, to advise a "young Jewish friend," in 1945: "Do not display your rights conspicuously, that would be an abuse; do not wear your war medals, that would be a provocation. . . . Act in such a way that the blueblooded French in France who hoped never to see you again forget that you exist."[32]

Undeterred by the landing in Normandy and by the approaching allied forces, the Paris Gestapo forged ahead. On July 20 and 24 the Germans raided the children's homes of UGIF-North, where some 650 children were still kept assembled by the organization's leadership, despite entreaties and pressure to disband the homes. Edinger wavered, procrastinated, and basically opted for the status quo.[33] At first 233 children were taken and transported to Drancy. Edinger's immediate reaction was to order the dispersal of the remaining children, but shortly thereafter he canceled the order. The remaining children were taken away.[34] To the very end the leaders of UGIF-North were afraid of German retaliation—probably against themselves.

On August 17 and 22 the last transports of Jews left France for Auschwitz.[35] On August 25 Gen. Jacques Philippe Leclerc's Free French division, attached to the U.S. forces in the West, liberated Paris.

In Italy and in the formerly Italian-occupied areas the roundups of Jews achieved uneven results. A memorandum dated December 4, 1943, of Inland II of the Wilhelmstrasse confirmed that the measures taken over the previous several weeks had not encountered much success, as the Jews had had the time to find hiding places in small villages. The means at the disposal of the Germans did not allow for thorough searches in small or even in midsize communities. On the other hand the Germans placed some hopes on a new ordinance issued by the fascist government (Police Order Number 5), that all Jews should be sent to concentration camps. It was to be hoped that the fascist police would take matters in hand, the memorandum noted, and allow the small Gestapo task force to spread its men as advisers to the local police units.[36]

In some areas the order issued by Mussolini's government was indeed followed, even without German participation. Thus, in Venice, on December 5–6, 1943, the local police arrested 163 Jews (114 women and girls and 49 men and boys) either in their houses or at the Old People's Home. A repeat performance, this time with German participation, took place at the Old People's Home on August 17, and finally, on October 6, 1944, twenty-nine Jewish patients were seized in three Venetian hospitals. In the old rice mill, La Risiera di San Sabba, which, it will be remembered, replaced Fossoli after August 1944, the oldest and weakest inmates were murdered on the spot and the rest, the majority, were deported to Auschwitz and exterminated (including Venice's chief rabbi, Adolfo Ottolenghi, whom the Swiss police had prevented from crossing the border a few months beforehand).[37]

In Milan a gang of Italian fascists outperformed the Germans in feats of bestiality; this was an uncommon achievement by all accounts, and an atypical one. Pietro Koch's men had established their headquarters in a villa soon known as Villa Triste ("sad villa"), where they tortured and executed their victims, Jews and non-Jews. Koch's thugs were assisted by two famous Italian actors, Luisa Ferida and Osvaldo Valenti, "the Fred Astaire and Ginger Rogers of torture, who lent a macabre, surreal quality to Villa Triste that has made it a symbol of the decadent twilight of fascism."[38]

Simultaneously with the roundups in Italy (and in southeast France) the Germans turned to mainland Greece and to the Greek islands. Wisliceny was ordered back to Athens in September 1943. However, the deportations from the Greek capital were temporarily delayed due to the "kidnapping"—by the Greek Resistance—of the chief rabbi of Athens and the destruction of the community register. Wisliceny was soon replaced by the more brutal Hauptsturmführer Tony Burger, transferred to the Greek capital from Theresienstadt. Two weeks before Passover, on March 23, 1944, some 800 Jews had assembled at the main Athens synagogue for a distribution of matzoth promised by the Germans. All were arrested, driven to the Haidari transit camp, and in early April deported to Auschwitz.[39]

No Jewish community in the Aegean was forgotten, not even the smallest. Most of the Jews of the Greek islands were arrested in the course of July 1944. On July 23 the 1,750 Jews of Rhodes and the 96 Jews of the tiny island of Kos were rounded up, crammed into three barges, on their way to the mainland. Due to bad weather the transport left on the twenty-eighth, sailing in full view of the Turkish coast, within a short flying distance of the British airfields in Cyprus and through an area of the eastern Mediterranean fully controlled by the British navy. On August 1 the convoy reached mainland Greece. There 1,673 Jews from Rhodes and 94 from Kos who had survived the sea voyage and rough treatment on arrival were herded into the usual freight cars, and on August 16 they reached Auschwitz. One hundred fifty-one deportees from Rhodes survived the war, as did twelve Jews from Kos.[40]

III

The Wehrmacht occupied Hungary on March 19, 1944. On the previous day Horthy had met Hitler at Klessheim. Under threat of unilateral military action, the Nazi leader compelled the regent to accept the German occupation and set up a pro-German government.[41] Hitler also demanded that some 100,000 Jews be delivered "for labor" in Germany. Horthy submitted. The train that took the regent back to Budapest carried another prominent passenger: Edmund Veesenmayer, Hitler's special delegate to the new Hungarian government. On that same day, Eichmann also arrived in the Hungarian capital, soon followed by the members of his "special intervention unit Hungary" (*Sondereinsatzkommando Ungarn*).

The appointment of Döme Sztójay, the former ambassador to Berlin, as prime minister did not lead to major changes in the political structure of the cabinet or in the functioning of the existing administration, although in a meeting with Goebbels, on March 3, Hitler told his minister that the occupation of Hungary would be followed by an immediate disarming of the Hungarian military forces, as well as by a rapid move against the country's aristocratic elites—and against the Jews.[42] The anti-Jewish measures were indeed immediately launched.

A Jewish Council was set up on March 12; additional anti-Semitic legislation followed, including the introduction of the star, on April 7. The appointment of two violently anti-Semitic secretaries of state, Laszlo Endre and Laszlo Baky, in Andor Jaross's Ministry of the Interior gave the Germans all the assistance they needed to round up the Jewish population. On April 7 the roundups started in the Hungarian provinces, with the enthusiastic cooperation of the Hungarian gendarmerie. Within less than a month, ghettos or camps for hundreds of thousands of Jews sprang up in Carpatho-Ruthenia, in Transylvania, and later in the southern part of the country.[43]

The furious pace of the German-Hungarian operation ensured the quasi-total success of the concentration phase. One may wonder, however, whether the attitude adopted by the Jewish Council did not, more than in most other places, add to the passivity and subservience of the Jewish masses. The council was well informed, and so were many Hungarian Jews, especially in Budapest. Returning members of the labor batallions, Hungarian soldiers back from the Eastern Front, Jewish refugees from Poland and Slovakia spread the information they had gathered about the mass extermination of Jews, as did the Hungarian services of the BBC. Moreover, on April 7, two Slovak Jews, Rudolf Vrba (Walter Rosenberg) and Alfred Wetzler, escaped from Auschwitz and on the twenty-first reached Slovakia. Within days they had written a detailed report about the extermination process in the Upper Silesian camp and delivered it to the "Working Group" in Bratislava. These "Auschwitz Protocols" reached Switzerland and the Allied countries; large excerpts were soon published in the Swiss and the American press. To this day, however, it isn't exactly clear how long it took for the report to reach the Jewish Council in Budapest.

Vrba himself expressed the view that the "Working Group" did not act rapidly enough and that, once it received the report, the council kept the information to itself; thus the Jews of the Hungarian provinces were not warned against boarding the trains to Auschwitz. Yehuda Bauer has countered Vrba's accusation: The report may have reached Budapest and the council as early as the end of April;[44] but nothing could have been done in any case to stop the masses of Jews in the provinces from following the deportation orders.[45] In fact the Budapest council members admitted after the war to having had precise knowledge of what was happening to the Jews all over occupied Europe and, in that sense, whether they received the "protocols" at the end of April or at a somewhat later date was not of major importance.[46]

The Budapest council, headed by Samu (Samuel) Stern, included representatives of all the major religious and political groups of the community. It may have assumed that any warning to Jews of the provinces would be useless. Possibly for that reason and because the council members were utterly assimilated, law-abiding Magyar citizens, the council made no attempt to inform the heads of communities in the provinces covertly;[47] its announcements were soothing all along, as if the Budapest leaders mainly wanted to avoid panic among the hapless Jewish masses. The council's attitude did not change after two more Jews, Czeslaw Mordowicz and Arnost Rosin, escaped from Auschwitz at the end of April and confirmed the previous information. Some of the council members, such as the Orthodox Fülöp Freudiger, were in close touch with Wisliceny (on Weissmandel's recommendation) and succeeded in saving themselves, members of their family, and some other closely related Orthodox Jews by crossing over to Romania.[48] Others, after being threatened by the Gestapo, went into hiding.[49]

Almost from the outset of the German occupation several thousand Jews, mostly public figures, journalists, known antifascists, and the like, were seized and sent to concentration camps in Austria.[50] On May 14 the full-scale deportations from the Hungarian provinces to Auschwitz started, at the rate of approximately 12,000 to 14,000 deportees a day. Hungarian trains ran to the Slovak border; there the deportees were transferred to German trains that carried them to Auschwitz. The crematoriums of Birkenau could not keep up with the gassing pace, and open-air cremation pits had to be added.

According to SS officer Perry Broad's testimony at the Auschwitz trial in Frankfurt, "a triple track railway line leading to the new crematoria enabled a train to be unloaded while the next one was arriving. The percentage of those who were assigned to 'special accommodation'—the term that had been used for some time in place of 'special treatment'—was particularly high in the case of these transports. . . . All four crematoria operated at full blast. However, soon the ovens were burnt out as a result of the continuous heavy use and only crematorium No. III was still smoking. . . . The special commandos had been increased and worked feverishly to keep emptying the gas chambers. The 'white farmhouse' was brought back into use. . . . It was given the title 'Bunker 5.' . . . The last body had hardly been pulled from the gas chambers and dragged across the yard behind the crematorium, which was covered in corpses, to the burning pit, when the next lot were already undressing in the hall ready for gassing."[51]

Paul Steinberg, a young Jewish deportee from France, described the situation from his perspective, that of a Buna inmate. In the background a discussion was taking place about the advantages of an uprising as against staying put, just after D-day: "And while this strange debate is going on," Steinberg reminisced, "the Hungarians arrive, whole trainloads of them, two or three a day. . . . Almost all transports wind up in the gas chamber: men, women, children. The labor camps are stuffed to bursting; they wouldn't know what to do with more workers. . . . The crematoria are going full bore around the clock. We hear from Birkenau that they've burned 3,000, then 3,500, and last week up to 4,000 bodies a day. The new Sonderkommando had been doubled to keep everything running smoothly between the gas chambers and the ovens, day and night. From the chimneys flames shoot thirty feet into the air, visible for leagues around at night, and the oppressive stench of burnt flesh can be smelt as far as Buna."[52] Höss himself described the cremation in the open pits: "The fires in the pits had to be stoked, the surplus fat drained off, and the mountain of burning corpses constantly turned over so that the draught might fan the flames."[53]

In Buna, Steinberg had merely heard some details of the mass extermination, but a few of the Hungarian Jews did in fact arrive at the I.G. Farben site. One of them, unforgettably evoked by Levi, was called Kraus:

"He is Hungarian, he understands German badly and does not know a word of French. He is tall and thin, wears glasses and has a curious, small, twisted face; when he laughs he looks like a child, and he often laughs."[54] Kraus is clumsy, works too hard, cannot communicate, in short has none of the attributes that may help survival, even in Buna. Levi talks to Kraus very slowly in some pidgin German; he tries to comfort him; he invents a dream about Kraus returning home to his family; Kraus must have understood something of this idyllic fantasy: "What a good boy Kraus must have been as a civilian," Levi muses. "He will not survive very long here, one can see it at a first glance, it is as logical as a theorem. I am sorry I do not know Hungarian, for his emotion has broken the dykes, and he is breaking out in a flood of outlandish Magyar words. . . . Poor silly Kraus. If he only knew that it is not true, that I have really dreamt nothing about him, that he is nothing to me except for a brief moment, nothing like everything is nothing down here, except the hunger inside and the cold and the rain around."[55]

Soon after the beginning of the deportations, pressure from within the country, particularly from Horthy's longtime conservative political allies and from his closest circle of advisers, started building up to bring a halt to cooperation with the German deportations.[56] That in this matter at least the regent wished to extricate Hungary from Hitler's clutches finds an indirect expression in the conversation which took place on June 7 (after the Allied landing in Normandy) between Prime Minister Sztójay and the Nazi leader, at Klessheim.

The Hungarian prime minister started by assuring the Führer of the regent's and the country's will to fight on faithfully alongside the German ally; yet the activities of the German state police in Hungary could give the impression of interference in the country's internal affairs and of a limitation of its sovereignty. Hitler did not need any further explanations. He answered by reminding the prime minister that during the previous year he had already pressed the regent to take steps against the Jews but unfortunately Horthy had not followed his advice; he then reviewed Hungarian attempts to change sides and, implicitly, linked them to the strong presence of the Jews. The regent, Hitler continued, had been warned about the dimensions of the country's "Jewification" but had dismissed the warnings by referring to the important role played by the

Jews in Hungary's economy. The Führer then explained at length that eliminating the Jews would only bring new opportunities that the Hungarians would undoubtedly be able to master. "Moreover," he declared, "even as Horthy tried to stroke the Jews, the Jews nonetheless hated him, as could be daily surmised from the world press." The conclusion was obvious: The Germans were not limiting Hungarian sovereignty but rather defending Hungary against the Jews and the agents of the Jews.

As Sztójay turned to the internal difficulties that had hindered Horthy's intended measures against the Jews, and also mentioned Horthy's age (seventy-five), Hitler did not show any sign of understanding. Horthy, the Führer declared, is a man who shies away from violence; so did he, Hitler, try to avoid the war by offering a compromise about the Polish corridor. But, Hitler reminded Sztójay, the Jewish press clamored for war and he then warned the Jews, in his Reichstag speech: The Nazi leader, needless to say, spelled out his prophecy once again. Then he significantly added: "When, moreover, he had to remember that in Hamburg 46,000 German women and children had been burnt to death, nobody could demand of him to have the least pity for this world pest; he now went by the ancient Jewish proverb: 'an eye for an eye, a tooth for a tooth.' . . . If the Jewish race were to win, at least 30 million Germans would be exterminated and many millions would starve to death."[57]

Toward the end of June international intervention strengthened internal Hungarian opposition to continuing the deportations: the king of Sweden, the pope, the American president—all intervened with the regent. On July 2 a heavy American raid on Budapest emphasized Roosevelt's message.[58] Horthy vacillated, ready to comply with these demands, yet unable for several weeks to impose his will on the pro-Nazi members of his government.[59] Finally, on July 8, the deportations were officially stopped. Nonetheless, Eichmann succeeded in getting two more transports out of country to Auschwitz, the first from the Kistarcsa camp on July 19, the second from Starvar, on July 24.[60]

According to a report sent by Veesenmayer on June 30, a total of 381,661 Jews had been deported to Auschwitz from Zones I to IV in the Hungarian provinces. "Concentration in Zone V (an area so far not included, west of the Danube, not comprising Budapest)," Veesenmayer added, "has started on June 29. Simultaneously small special actions in suburbs of Budapest as preparatory measures have been launched. Furthermore a few small special transports with political Jews, intellectual Jews, Jews with many children and especially skilled Jewish workers are still on the way."[61] When, on July 9, the deportations from the Hungarian provinces finally stopped, 438,000 Jews had been sent to Auschwitz and approximately 394,000 immediately exterminated. Of those selected for work, very few were still alive at the end of the war.[62] In Budapest about 250,000 Jews were still awaiting their fate.

As usual in east-central and eastern (non-Soviet) Europe, the main institutions that to a certain degree could have stemmed the anti-Jewish drive were the churches (the great majority of the population was Catholic; a minority was Lutheran). Pius XII did join other leaders in interceding with Horthy to stop the German operation. This first public intervention of the pope in favor of the Jews was sent on June 25, 1944, after the "Auschwitz Protocols" had reached the Vatican via Switzerland.[63] Despite full knowledge of the ongoing extermination, even this message was worded in rather hazy terms: "Supplications have been addressed to Us from different sources that we should exert all Our influence to shorten and mitigate the sufferings that have, for so long, been peacefully endured on account of their national or racial origin by a great number of unfortunate people belonging to this noble and chivalrous nation. In accordance with Our service of love, which embraces every human being, Our fatherly heart could not remain insensible to these urgent demands. For this reason we apply to your Serene Highness, appealing to your noble feelings, in the full trust that your Serene Highness will do everything in your power to save many unfortunate people from further pain and sorrow."[64] As historian Randolph Braham noted, the word "Jew" did not appear in Pius's message, even in these circumstances.[65] Neither, it should be added, was there any mention of extermination.

Such lack of pontifical forcefulness did not encourage the head of the Hungarian Catholic hierarchy, Cardinal Justinian Seredi, to take any bold step of his own. Seredi was an anti-Semite of the traditional Christian ilk and had voted in favor of the first two anti-Jewish laws of 1938 and 1939.[66] The heads of the Catholic and Protestant churches in Hungary knew what the deportations to Germany meant, and some of their main leaders (including Seredi) had apparently received the "Auschwitz

Protocol." Yet, from March to July 1944, the leading Christian dignitaries could not be swayed to take a public stand against the policies of the Sztójay government. Both Seredi and the heads of the Protestant Churches sought, first and foremost, to obtain exemptions for converted Jews, and in this they were partly successful precisely because they abstained from any public protest against the deportations in general.[67]

Regarding the deportation of the Jews as such, Cardinal Seredi finally drafted a short pastoral note that was read on July 16, a week after Horthy had stopped the transports. In the original pastoral letter—never publicly read—Seredi had stated that one part of Jewry "had had a guilty and subversive influence on the Hungarian economic, social and moral life . . . [while] the others did not stand up against their co-religionists in this respect."[68] In other words, all Jews were guilty, and Seredi's position was very close to that of his deputy, Gyula Czapik, archbishop of Eger, who in May 1944 had argued "not to make public what is happening to the Jews; what is happening to the Jews at the present time is nothing but appropriate punishment for their misdeeds in the past."[69]

The papal nuncio in Budapest, Monsignor Angelo Rotta, was more outspoken than the Holy See itself and tried to sway Seredi toward more active protest; he drew Seredi's ire, and on two different occasions Rotta's interventions showed the cardinal's frustration with the pope's own abstention. On the first occasion, on June 8, Seredi told the nuncio that it was "deceitful for the Apostolic Holy See to maintain diplomatic relations with the German government which carries out these atrocities."[70] The second occasion was a meeting of representatives of the Christian churches to discuss the possibility of a joint intervention. Apparently an angry Seredi burst out: "If His Holiness the Pope does nothing against Hitler, what can I do in my narrower jurisdiction? Damn it."[71]

A few Catholic bishops courageously spoke out in their dioceses but these were lone voices that could not have a major impact on the attitude of the Hungarian population.

IV

As the events in Hungary unfolded with extraordinary speed in the face of the world, two related issues arose that remain highly contentious to this very day: The attempt of some members of the Jewish "Relief and Rescue Committee" (the *Vaadah*—the Committee, in Hebrew) to negotiate with the Germans; and the Allied decision concerning the bombing of the railway line from Budapest to Auschwitz or of the Auschwitz killing installations as such.

The *Vaadah* was established in the Hungarian capital at the beginning of 1943 to help Jewish refugees, mainly from Slovakia and Poland, who had fled to Hungary. Rudolf Kastner, a Zionist journalist from Cluj; Joel Brand, another native from Transylvania and something of an adventurer in politics and otherwise; and an engineer from Budapest, Otto Komoly, became the leading personalities of the *Vaadah*, whose executive committee had been joined by several other Hungarian Jews.

In late March or early April 1944 Kastner and Brand met in Budapest with the ubiquitous Wisliceny, on Weissmandel's recommendation and following contacts established by some SD officers. Eichmann's envoy was offered a substantial amount of money (two million dollars) to avoid the deportation of the Jews of Hungary. But as it became clear that the *Vaadah* could not come up with such an amount, Eichmann summoned Brand sometime in mid or late April, and made several offers that ultimately became the notorious exchange of the lives of 800,000 Hungarian Jews against the delivery by the Western Allies of 10,000 winterized trucks to be used solely on the Eastern Front. The SS would allow Brand to travel to Istanbul, in the company of Bandi Grosz, a multiple agent and a shady figure by all accounts, on whom Himmler's men were relying, at least so it seemed, to establish contacts with the West.[72]

Eichmann's proposal should be interpreted in relation to a cable sent by Veesenmayer to Berlin on April 3. The Reich plenipotentiary advised Ribbentrop that Allied bombings of the Hungarian capital had exacerbated anti-Jewish feelings; the possibility of executing one hundred Jews for each Hungarian killed had been evoked. Veesenmayer was not sure whether such a large-scale retaliation was practical, but before considering any concrete steps, he wanted to know whether another track, apparently suggested to Hitler by Ribbentrop, remained an option; if the answer was in the affirmative, mass executions would of course be excluded: "In reference to the suggestions made by Herr Reichsaussenminister to the Führer about offering the Jews [of Hungary] as a gift to

Roosevelt and Churchill, I would like to be informed whether this idea is still being pursued."[73]

Veesenmayer's cable indicates that the kind of barter suggested by Eichmann had been discussed between Hitler and Ribbentrop, and that its implementation was taken over by Himmler's men, almost certainly with Hitler's agreement. Of course there was no intention to free any substantial number of Hungarian Jews. The unparalleled rapidity and scale of the deportations and of the exterminations is the best indication of what, at that stage, the Germans really meant. The intent behind the contacts with the naive Jewish representatives was grossly simple: If the Allies rejected the German offer, they could be saddled with the responsibility for contributing to the extermination of the Hungarian Jews; as after the Evian conference of July 1938, the Germans could proclaim once again: "Nobody wants them!" If by chance, however, due to Jewish pressure (as seen from Berlin), the Allies were to start any kind of negotiations, Stalin would be apprised of it and the rift in the Grand Alliance, which Hitler impatiently awaited, would follow. The rationale behind Grosz's mission was most probably identical: If the West accepted the idea of separate negotiations, the Soviets would be informed and the end result would be the same.[74]

On May 19, 1944, Brand and Grosz landed in Istanbul. While Grosz went on his separate "mission," Brand conveyed the SS proposal to the Yishuv's delegates in Istanbul. A series of quickly unfolding events followed. One of the Yishuv envoys in Istanbul, Venia Pomeranz, traveled to Jerusalem to inform Ben-Gurion of the German proposal. The Jewish Agency Executive, convened by Ben-Gurion, decided to intervene immediately with the Allies, even if the chances of a deal with the Germans were generally seen as very slim. The British high commissioner in Palestine, informed by Ben-Gurion, agreed that Moshe Shertok, in charge of foreign affairs in the Executive Council of the Jewish Agency, be allowed to travel to Istanbul to meet with Brand. While Shertok's departure was delayed, Brand himself had to leave Turkey. Thus it was in Aleppo (Syria), where he was kept under British arrest, that the envoy from Budapest met with Shertok, on June 11.[75] Brand repeated the gist of the German message to Shertok. The issue became further complicated, at least on the face of it, by a German offer to invite one of the

Jewish Agency delegates in Istanbul, Menachem Bader, to travel to Budapest—even to Berlin—and negotiate directly there. The Germans even seemed ready to relinquish their demand for trucks and return to the initial idea of an adequate financial offer. According to postwar testimony, Eichmann promised to liberate 5,000 to 10,000 Jews, upon reception of the first positive answer from the West and in exchange for German POWs.[76]

Although the leadership of the Yishuv soon understood that Grosz's mission was the main German ploy and Brand's a mere accessory and additional bait, Shertok and Weizmann nonetheless interceded with Eden in London for some gesture that would allow time to be gained and eventually save part of Hungarian Jewry. On July 15 they were told that the German "offer" was rejected. Churchill himself, in a letter to Eden of July 11, estimated that the German proposal was not serious, as it was a "plan broached through the most doubtful channel . . . and is itself of a most doubtful character."[77] In the meantime Brand had been transferred from Aleppo to Cairo, where he remained under British interrogation. At that point his mission came to an abrupt end. It seems that before his death in 1964, Brand himself reached the conclusion that his mission had essentially been a German maneuver meant to undermine the alliance between the Soviets and the West.[78]

For the Yishuv leadership the failure of this rescue attempt, as flimsy as its chances had been, represented a serious setback. The hope of saving hundreds of thousands of Hungarian Jews disappeared. For Ben-Gurion, moreover, the crucial question surfaced once again: Who would build the Jewish state in Eretz Israel? "We are now on the brink of the end of the war," he declared in September 1944, "with most of the Jews destroyed. Everyone wonders: Where will we find the people for Palestine?" Later he wrote: "Hitler harmed more than the Jewish people whom he knew and hated: he caused damage to the Jewish state, whose coming he did not foresee. The state appeared and did not find the nation that awaited it."[79]

On July 10 Ribbentrop informed Veesenmayer that Hitler had agreed to the demands addressed to Horthy by the United States, Sweden, and Switzerland to repatriate their Jewish nationals from Budapest to their home countries. But, Ribbentrop added, "We can agree to this accommodation only under the condition that the deportation of Jews to the Reich, temporarily stopped by the Regent, be immediately resumed and brought to its conclusion."[80] On July 17 the foreign minister demanded that Veesenmayer inform the regent of the following, in Hitler's name: "The Führer expects that now the measures against the Jews of Budapest be taken without any further delay, with the exceptions . . . granted to the Hungarian government. However, no delay in the implementation of the general Jewish measures [*Judenmassnahmen*] should occur as a result of these exceptions. Otherwise, the Führer's acceptance of these exceptions will have to be withdrawn."[81]

As for the Reichsführer, he met Hitler on July 15 for a discussion of the "Jewish question" in Hungary and indicated Hitler's approval of his proposals with a check.[82] A few days later Himmler boasted in a letter to *Gauleiter* Martin Mutschmann about the 450,000 Hungarian Jews he had already sent to Auschwitz and assured him that, despite some difficulties encountered elsewhere—in France, for example—in Hungary the task would be completed. "Be assured," Himmler concluded, "that particularly at this decisive moment of the war, I do possess the necessary hardness, as before."[83]

It remains hard to believe that the shrewd Kastner had high hopes regarding the success of Brand's mission. Whatever the case may be, he must soon have understood that SS officers of Wisliceny's ilk—and the whole Budapest group—were also ready for more limited deals that could be explained away as ransoming operations for the Reich. And such operations could also be highly lucrative for some of the SS participants. Thus, in a series of negotiations that lasted from April to June 1944, Kastner convinced Wisliceny, Eichmann, and Himmler's underling (whose function at the time was supplying horses to the SS), Kurt Becher, to allow a train with (ultimately) 1,684 Jews to leave Budapest for Switzerland, as a sign of German goodwill, in the framework of the wider "exchange negotiations." The price was one thousand dollars per Jew, and Becher, who negotiated the final arrangement, managed to have some of the lucky passengers pay twice.[84] On June 30 the train left, first—and unexpectedly—for Bergen-Belsen: The Kastner Jews nonetheless reached Switzerland in two transports, one in the early fall; the second, several weeks later. Although Kastner was not alone in choosing the passengers, his influence on the selection committee was considerable; it led to postwar accusations of nepotism and to two court cases in Israel; eventually it cost Kastner his life.[85]

When, in mid-August, the Swiss delegation in Budapest informed Bern that a first batch of 600 Hungarian Jews, temporarily sent to Bergen-Belsen, would arrive in Switzerland within days, the information was positively received by head of the police division, Rothmund, but with some hesitation by his chief, Federal Councillor Steiger.[86] As for Carl Burckhardt of the ICRC, he immediately grasped the advantage of letting these unexpected refugees enter Switzerland, as we know from a Swiss official's memorandum of August 14, 1944: "Mr. Burckhardt did not seem at all surprised by the information sent by the delegation in Budapest; he declared he was delighted. It is a very good thing for Switzerland to be able now to do something positive for the Jews. It will make a good impression in foreign countries and could help to dissipate the resentment that could develop against our country from the stories of refugees and foreign [Swiss camp] inmates (mainly intellectuals) who are dissatisfied with the way they are being treated."[87]

Some Jews left Hungary by their own means. The SS negotiated the acquisition of the Manfred Weiss industrial empire belonging to Jewish family and its Jewish and non-Jewish associates. By acquiring major munitions and machine-tool firms, Himmler and Pohl hoped to join the select elite of German industry. They had no difficulty in convincing Hitler of the advantages of this particular extortion. Becher, once again the go-between in Budapest, kept a neat percentage of the benefits. In exchange some fifty members of the Jewish families involved were allowed to leave for Switzerland, Spain, or Portugal with the help of the SS—and were even paid part of the sums that had been agreed upon.[88]

* * *

During the same months another rescue project of a very different kind also collapsed: the Allied bombing of the railway line from Hungary to Auschwitz and, possibly, of the extermination sites in Auschwitz-Birkenau.

On May 25, 1944, the highly competent and motivated representative of the War Refugee Board in Bern, Roswell McClelland, passed on to Washington a message he had received from Isaac Sternbuch, the representative of the American Union of Orthodox Rabbis in Switzerland; the message was addressed to the Union of Orthodox Rabbis in New York: "We received news from Slovakia," Sternbuch wrote, "according to which they ask prompt air raids should be made over the two towns Kaschau (Kosice) as transit place for military transports and also Presov as town junction for deportations coming through Kaschau and also the whole railroad line between them where there is a short bridge of about 30 yards. It is the single near route from Hungary to Poland, whereas all the other small and short lines, going eastwards, can be used only in Hungary, but not for the traffic to Poland being already battlefields. Do the necessary that bombing should be repeated at short intervals to prevent rebuilding. Without named towns just one too long route via Austria remains which is almost impracticable."[89]

The "Working Group" was the source of the information from Slovakia received by Sternbuch. A first letter sent by Weissmandel sometime in early May 1944 had not been acknowledged, so that on May 31 the Slovak rabbi repeated his entreaty and again gave details about the deportations: These details were extraordinarily precise, as was the description of the killing installations (probably based upon the Vrba-Wetzler report). Weissmandel's letter ended with an agonized plea: "Now we ask: how can you eat, sleep, live? How guilty will you feel in your hearts if you fail to move heaven and earth to help us in the only ways that are available to our own people and as quickly as possible? . . . For God's sake, do something now and quickly."[90]

Intense consultations and contacts followed in late June, after Jewish organizations and the WRB in Washington received Sternbuch's message. Pehle transmitted the message to the assistant secretary of war, John J. McCloy, but with reservations: "I saw Assistant Secretary McCloy today on the proposal of the Agudas Israel that arrangements be made to bomb the railroad line between Kassa (Kosice) and Presov being used for the deportation of Jews from Hungary to Poland. I told McCloy that I wanted to mention the matter to him for whatever exploration might be appropriate by the War Department but that I had several doubts about the matter, namely (1) whether it would be appropriate to use military planes and personnel for this purpose, (2) whether it would be difficult to put the railroad line out of commission for a long enough period to do any good; and (3) even assuming that this railroad line were put out of commission for some period of time, whether it would help the Jews in Hungary. I made it very clear to Mr. McCloy that I was not, at this point at least, requesting the War Department to take any action on this proposal other than to appropriately explore it. McCloy understood my position and said that he would check into the matter."[91]

A few days later Leon Kubowitzki, the head of the Rescue Department of the World Jewish Congress, addressed a letter to Pehle, this time suggesting not the bombing of the railway line from Hungary to Auschwitz but rather the destruction of the death installations at the camp by Soviet paratroopers or Polish underground units. The idea of bombing the installations from the air came at the same time from another Jewish representative, Benjamin Akzin.[92]

On July 4, 1944, McCloy dismissed this flurry of projects and entreaties in a letter to Pehle: "I refer to your letter of June 29th, enclosing a cable from your representative in Bern, Switzerland, proposing that certain sections of railway lines between Hungary and Poland be bombed to interrupt the transportation of Jews from Hungary. The War Department is of the opinion that the suggested air operation is impracticable. It could be executed only by the diversion of considerable air support essential to the success of our forces now engaged in decisive operations and would in any case be of such very doubtful efficacy that it would not amount to a practical project. The War Department fully appreciates the humanitarian motives which prompted the suggested operation but for the reasons stated above, the operation suggested does not appear justified."[93]

In the meantime Shertok and Weizmann, despite their failure to sway the British government in regard to the Brand mission, now pleaded for the bombing operations. Although Churchill was briefly involved and appeared to be in favor of some action, by mid-July London was as negative as Washington. At the top of the refusal letter that he received on July 15, 1944, from the Secretary of State for Air, Sir Archibald Sinclair, Eden scribbled: "A characteristically unhelpful letter. Dept. will have to consider what is to be done about this. I think that we should pass the buck to this ardent Zionist in due course, i.e. tell Weizmann that we have approached Sir A. Sinclair and suggest he may like to see him. AE July 16."[94]

Höss had been recalled to Auschwitz to supervise the extermination of the Hungarian Jews. For the flawless implementation of his task, he was awarded the War Merit Cross first and second class. On July 29 he returned to Berlin.[95]

V

In late July 1944 the Red Army liberated Majdanek. In their hasty flight the Germans did not manage to destroy the gas chambers and other traces of the camp's murderous activities: Soon, pictures of killing installations, victims' belongings, mounds of glasses, hair, or prosthetic limbs appeared in newspapers all around the world.

For the Germans, erasing traces of their crimes hence became highest priority. On July 13, the Polish physician Klukowski noted: "Recently, we heard a rumor that the Germans are planning to open the graves of the murdered Jews, remove the bodies, and burn them. . . . Strange things are going on in the Jewish cemetery. No one is allowed to enter. The cemetery is surrounded by military guards armed with rifles. Warning signs stating that anyone entering will be shot were posted. Many cars and trucks come and go. A large group of prisoners was brought from Zamość. The cemetery has been divided into sections; then the Germans built fences covered with tarps, so no one can observe what is taking place."[96] And on July 14 he added: "We learned that the Germans are moving Jewish bodies to be burned at the Rotunda. No bodies were burned at the cemetery."[97]

The next day Klukowski once more took up the same topic: "Sometimes, with heavy wind, you can smell the odor of decomposed bodies from the Jewish cemetery."[98] A day later the Germans left: "Today around 10:00 a.m., the Germans completed their work in the cemetery and left. The roads are all open. The church is open also. The Germans did a lot of digging; they did move something but it is impossible for them to have removed thousands of badly damaged bodies in only a few days."[99] This indeed was the gist of the matter: The Germans had killed too many Jews to be able to move all the corpses and burn them.

On July 26 the Russians entered Szczebrzeszyn.

On August 23 Antonescu's regime collapsed, and on the thirty-first, the Soviet army occupied Bucharest. A few days later it was Bulgaria's turn.

Among the dramatic upheavals in eastern and southeastern Europe, the events in Poland turned into a dismal tragedy: On August 1, after the Soviet forces had reached the Eastern bank of the Vistula in the Warsaw area, the Home Army gave the signal for an uprising in the city. A fierce urban battle unfolded between the insurgents and German reinforcements, while the Soviets at first could not, then did not intervene in any forceful way. On October 2, the remaining Polish forces finally surrendered, while their capital had been reduced to ruins and rubble. Soon thereafter the Soviet army occupied Warsaw. At the outset, Rokossovski's divisions had been pushed back by German counter-attacks along the Vistula; later on, Stalin, in his own way, solved the problem of a nationalist opposition to the communist rule he meant to impose on Poland: He let the Germans decimate it.[100]

In March 1944 Emmanuel Ringelblum and his son were caught by the Germans before the Polish uprising and shot. Many other Jews, who had also found refuge on the Aryan side of the city, such as Calel Perechodnik, perished during the battle for Warsaw.

On May 5, 1944, one more anonymous diarist began recording details of his life in the Lodz ghetto in the margins of a French novel by François Coppée, *Les Vrais Riches* ["The Truly Rich"]. The diarist was an adolescent who at times wrote down his entries in English (to hide some of the comments from his twelve-year-old sister), but also in Polish, Hebrew and mainly in Yiddish. For the approximately 77,000 Jews still living in the ghetto and working for the Wehrmacht, daily life was, as before, dominated by one major obsession: food. The young diarist had every good reason to write his first entry in English, on May 5, 1944:

"I committed this week an act which is best able to illustrate to what degree of dehumanization we have been reduced—namely, I finished my loaf of bread at a space of three days, that is on Sunday, so I had to wait till next Sunday for a new one. I was terribly hungry. I had a prospect of living only from the [factory] soups which consist of three little potato pieces and two decagrams of flower [*sic*]. I was lying on Monday morning quite dejectedly in my bed and there was the half loaf of bread of my darling sister. . . . I could not resist the temptation and ate it up totally. . . . I was overcome by a terrible remorse of conscience and by a still greater care for what my little one would eat for the next few days. I felt a miserably helpless criminal.... I have told people that it was stolen by a supposed reckless and pitiless thief and, for keeping up appearance, I have to utter curses and condemnations on the imaginary thief: 'I would hang him with my own hands had I come across him.' "[101]

By the time the anonymous diarist started writing, the ghetto's end had arrived. In line with Himmler's decision, extracted from him by Greiser, as we saw in the previous chapter, the extermination of the ghetto population started again. Between June 13 and July 14, 1944, more than 7,000 Jews were deported to Chelmno.[102] Within a month, however, the killing site had to be dismantled as the Red Army was approaching: No repetition of the Majdanek fiasco would take place. The brief respite in the deportations triggered hope and joy in the ghetto, as Rosenfeld noted on July 28: "We are facing either apocalypse or redemption. The chest dares breathe more freely already. People look at each other as if to say: 'We understand each other, right!'... There are plenty of skeptics, nigglers, who don't want to believe it and still have doubts about that for which they have been longing and waiting for years. They are being told: 'It has to come sometime, and now that the time is here, you don't want to believe it.' Then they look with a vacuous gaze into empty space and bask in their pessimism. After so much suffering and terror, after so many disappointments, it is hardly surprising that they are not willing to give themselves over to anticipatory rejoicing.... And if at long last, the day of the 'redemption' should be at the doorstep, it is better to let oneself be surprised than to experience yet another disappointment. That's human nature, this is the human mentality of Ghetto Litzmannstadt at the end of July 1944."[103] It was Rosenfeld's last diary entry.

On August 2 the Germans announced "the relocation of the ghetto." Beginning on August 3, 5,000 Jews a day had to assemble at the railway station. Part of the population, which at the outset had been slow in responding, was fooled once again by Biebow's appeals to reason and by his reassurances: "The relocation of the ghetto should proceed with calm, order and benevolence.... I assure you that we will do our very best to continue to achieve the utmost and to save your life through the relocation of the ghetto.... I know you want to live and eat, and that's what you will do.... If you are not reasonable, the ghetto administration will resign and forcible measures will be taken. . . . There's room enough in the railway cars, the machinery is adequately relocated. Come with your families, take your pots, drinking vessels and flatware; we don't have those in Germany since everything has been distributed to bombing victims."[104]

While Rosenfeld's last entry was suffused with hope, the anonymous adolescent's last entry [written in English], dated August 3, was of a very different tone. It may have been the most unconstrained expression of anti-German hatred expressed in a Jewish diary in those days; it was also an outburst of anger at the meekness of the Jews, of intense compassion for his people, of challenge to God. After quoting one of Biebow's arguments ("In order that the German Reich should win, our Führer has ordered the use of every worker"), the diarist commented: "Evidently! The only right which entitles us to live under the same sky with Germans—though to live as the lowest slaves—is the privilege of working for their victory, working much! and eating nothing. Really, they are even more abominable in their diabolical cruelty than any mind could follow. . . . He asked the crowd if they are ready to work faithfully for the Reich and everyone answered *"Jawohl"*—I thought about the abjectedness of such a situation! What sort of people are the Germans that they managed to transform us into such low, crawling creatures, as to say "Jawohl." Is life really so worthy? Is it not better not [to] live in a world where there are 80 millions of Germans? Or, is it not a shame to be a man on the same earth as the Ger-man? . . . What will they do with our sick? With our old? With our young? Oh, God in Heaven, why didst thou create Germans to destroy humanity?" An undated entry followed: "My God, why do you allow them to say that you are neutral? Why will you not punish, with all your wrath, those who are destroying us? Are we the sinners and they the righteous? Is that the truth? Surely you are intelligent enough to understand that it is not so, that we are not the sinners and they are not the Messiah!"[105]

Some of the inhabitants tried to hide. As the Jewish police were unable to deal with the situation, German police and firemen units from the city moved into the ghetto and started dragging out the rapidly dwindling number of Jews. On August 28 the ghetto's end had come. Rumkowski, his wife, the son they had adopted, and his brother with his wife were on the last transport that left that day for Auschwitz-Birkenau.[106] Neither Rumkowski nor any member of his family survived.

The last entry of the "Chronicle," on July 30, 1944, had included the usual indications about the weather, vital statistics ("Deaths: one; Births: none"), and the number of inhabitants (68,561), before recording the "news of the day": "Today, Sunday, also passed very calmly. The Chairman held various meetings. But all in all, the ghetto is peaceful and orderly. Langiewnicka Street now has a different look. Traffic is extraordinarily lively. One can see the war gradually approaching Litzmannstadt. The ghetto dweller peers curiously at the motor vehicles of various service branches as they speed through; for him, though, the crucial question remains: What is there to eat?"

Information about the arrival of potatoes, white cabbage, and kohlrabi followed: "If no flour arrives tomorrow, Monday, then the situation will be extremely critical. It is claimed that flour supplies will suffice for barely two or three more days." No cases of contagious disease were reported. The cause of the single death was suicide.[107] The chroniclers, including Zelkowicz and Rosenfeld, were all deported to Auschwitz and murdered. When the Red Army occupied the city, in January 1945, 877 ghetto Jews were still alive.

Poland was liberated. Over the months and years some Polish Jews who had hidden as Aryans resurfaced; larger groups who had fled in 1939 to the Soviet occupation area and had been evacuated into the Soviet interior, returned. Of the 3.3 million Jews who had lived in Poland in 1939, some 300,000 survived the war; among these some 40,000 at most survived in hiding on Polish territory.[108]

In early July 1944, as the Red Army reached the eastern borders of Lithuania, 33,000 Jews were still alive in the German-occupied Baltic countries, mainly in the Kovno and Shavli ghettos and in the labor camps of Estonia. On July 14 and 15, as we saw, the Kovno ghetto was liquidated: Some 2,000 of its inhabitants were killed on the spot and 7,000 to 8,000, deported to camps in Germany.[109] Between July 15 and 22 some 8,000 Jews were deported from Shavli to the Stutthof camp near Danzig.[110]

Kalmanovitch died in the Narva slave labor camp in Estonia before the end of 1943. Kruk, in the meantime, was an inmate of Klooga, the main Estonian slave labor camp. He had resumed his chronicling, although less systematically than in Vilna. At the end of August 1944, he was transferred again, this time to neighboring Lagedi. "So far I have slept on the bare ground," he wrote on August 29. "Today I built a lair for myself, boarded up the holes in the barrack—an achievement for Lagedi. . . . If possible, I shall continue to record."[111] He did so for a few more days. "Sunday, we had some tension," the entry for September 5 reads. "The chief butcher came, the chief doctor. But everything remained as it was. Today again some anxiety. The commandant came here, the so-called Vaivarchik, the so-called Sortovshchik" [Selectioner].[112] And on September 8: "Again experienced some anxiety: the Vaivarchik, Dr. Botmann, was here, with Schwartzer, the whole "butcher shop," as it is called. Everybody was sure something horrible was imminent, in the best case, transport to Germany. The result is zero—we remain. He orders underwear, clothes, etc., sent; it seems we are staying. Thus we are playing for time."[113]

The last entry in Kruk's diary was dated September 17, 1944. He recorded the hiding of his manuscripts in the presence of witnesses: "Today, the eve of Rosh Hashanah, a year after we arrived in Estonia, I bury the manuscripts in Lagedi, in a barrack of Mrs. Shulma, right across from the guard's house. Six persons are present at the burial. My coexistence with my neighbors [the Germans] is difficult."[114]

"The next day," according to Benjamin Harshav, the editor of the English translation of Kruk's diary, "all Jews from Klooga and Lagedi, including Herman Kruk, were hastily exterminated. The inmates were ordered to carry logs and spread them in a layer, and then they were forced to undress and lie down naked on the logs, where they were shot in the neck. Layer was piled on top of layer, and the entire pyre was burned. The next morning, the first Red Army units reached the area. One of the six witnesses mentioned by Kruk in his final entry, survived. He returned to Lagedi, dug up the diary, and brought it to Vilna."[115]

VI

As Germany was swaying under Allied military pressure on all fronts in the summer of 1944, an event of major importance took place in the Reich itself: the attempt on Hitler's life.

A growing number of officers, many of whom had previously been unquestioning, even enthusiastic devotees of the regime and of its leader, were ready in 1944 to support the small circle of determined opponents of Nazism who were conspiring to kill the Nazi leader and save Germany from total catastrophe. Although several prior attempts had been unsuccessful, the assassination plan meticulously prepared by Claus von Stauffenberg and set for July 20, 1944, seemed foolproof. Once again, though, the plot failed due to sheer bad luck. It brought frightful retribution in its wake. Over the following months and up to the last weeks of the war, reprisals did not stop, not only against the main plotters but against most of the opposition groups and personalities we encountered throughout this history: Moltke was executed and so were Hassell, Goerdeler, Bonhoeffer, Oster, Canaris, and thousands more with them.

Yet, as heroic and significant as July 20, 1944, is for the history of Germany, more immediately fateful was the unwavering loyalty to Hitler and his regime displayed at this crucial juncture—and into 1945—by a majority of Germans, the bulk of the Wehrmacht and of course the party and its organizations. If anything, the attempt on Hitler's life seemed, in historian Stephen G. Fritz's words "to bind more *Landser* [soldiers] to him." Wrote BP indignantly: "Thank God that Providence allowed our Führer to continue his task of the salvation of Europe, and our holiest duty is now to cling to him even more strongly, in order to make good what the few criminals . . . did without regard for [the welfare] of the entire nation." Lt. KN thought it "unspeakably tragic that the enemy nations will see symptoms of disunity, where before they perhaps supposed only unanimous solidarity." "These bandits tried to destroy that for which millions are ready to risk their lives," exclaimed Lt. HWM. "It is a good feeling to know that a November 1918 cannot be repeated."[116]

The Jews were never absent for long. On August 8 Sergeant E lashed out: "We are totally convinced that we shall soon overcome the damage caused by these damned traitors; then the greatest difficulties will be behind us and it means: full speed to victory! You can see how these pigs wanted to deprive us of everything, at the very last moment. We know that all these bandits are Freemasons and therefore in cahoots with international Jewry, or, better said, dominated by it. Too bad that I could not be part of the operation against these criminals. It would have been a pleasure to see the smoke come out of my gun."[117]

The tragic irony of such an identification of the plotters and the Jews stems from the fact that, as repeatedly mentioned, many of these conservative opponents of the regime were themselves anti-Semites to various degrees. This became clear once again during their interrogation by the Gestapo about their political and ideological beliefs. The reports of the interrogations ("The Kaltenbrunner Reports") were forwarded to Bormann by the head of the RSHA. A report of October 16, 1944, dwelled at length on the Jewish question.

The former finance minister of Prussia, Popitz (a friend of Moltke and Preysing), said: "As somebody who was very familiar with conditions in the system period [that is, Weimar] my view of the Jewish question was that the Jews ought to disappear from the life of the state and the economy. However, as far as the *methods* were concerned I repeatedly advocated a somewhat more gradual approach, particularly in the light of diplomatic considerations." Popitz reasserted the same view at greater length in the course of the interrogation. The report then emphasized that: "A number of other persons who were interrogated expressed similar views. Thus Count Yorck von Wartenburg, for example, said that the extermination measures against the Jews, which went beyond law and justice, caused him to break with National Socialism. Count Lehndorff declared 'that although he was hostile to Jews, nevertheless he had never quite approved of the National Socialist view of race, in particular *its practical implementation*.' Count Alexander von Stauffenberg [Alexander and Berthold von Stauffenberg were brothers of Claus] said he 'took the view that the Jewish question should have been dealt with *in a less extreme manner* because then it would have produced less disturbance among the population.' Count Berthold von Stauffenberg took a similar line: 'He and his brother had basically approved of the racial principle of National Socialism but considered it to be *exaggerated* and *excessive*.' "

Further on, Kaltenbrunner's report quoted Goerdeler's memorandum "The Goal": "The *Jewish persecution*, which has taken the *most inhuman, merciless* and deeply shaming forms, for which no compensation can be adequate, is to be halted immediately. Anyone who believed that he could enrich himself with Jewish property will discover that it is a disgrace for any German to seek such dishonestly acquired property. The German people truly want nothing to do with marauders and hyenas among God's creatures."[118]

As the Reich was sliding into total defeat, few Germans remained indifferent to the "Jewish question." Whether influenced by Goebbels's propaganda or partaking of more traditional forms of anti-Semitism, Germans of all walks of life were obsessed with the Jews. The most prevalent attitudes were hatred of course, but also fear, as we saw—the fear of retribution. Many a party member must have shared the feelings of Cpl. KB. In a letter written to his mother, on August 27, 1944, KB asked her to hide his party uniform or, better, to burn it. He admitted that these outward signs of his former commitment to National Socialism did not let him sleep at night; his fear had its good reasons: "You well know that the Jew will take a bloody vengeance, particularly against party members."[119]

On August 5 Hitler had had his last chance to lecture Antonescu on the Jewish question. He explained to the Romanian marshal that Germany's exemplary fight was due to the "pitiless destruction of the inner enemies. The Jews, the accomplices and instigators of revolutions, did not exist in Germany anymore. If somebody believed that by sparing the Jews, one could expect them to become advocates of their host nation in the event of defeat, this was a complete mistake as shown by the events in Bavaria and Hungary after the World War. In those countries the Jews proved to be the absolute organizers of the Bolshevik overthrow."[120] Thus, against all odds, as Antonescu's regime was about to collapse, Hitler was still trying to persuade his ally to resume his anti-Jewish campaign.

VII

Jakob Edelstein had been arrested in the fall of 1943 for having helped some inmates to escape from Theresienstadt by manipulating numbers and names on the registration lists of the camp. He was sent to Auschwitz with his wife, Miriam; his son, Aryeh; and old Mrs. Olliner, Miriam's mother. While Edelstein was kept in block 11 of the main camp, his family members were detained in the "family camp" in Birkenau. On June 20, 1944, they were all reunited in front of Crematorium III and shot. Jakob was shot last, after he had to witness the killing of his son, his wife, and his mother-in-law.[121]

On September 27, 1944, Paul Eppstein was arrested on the trumped-up charge of attempting to escape. He was brought to the small fortress and executed.[122] The inmates of Theresienstadt were now led by the last of the three elders, the Viennese Murmelstein: He remained a controversial figure, notwithstanding his postwar judicial rehabilitation. When he died in Rome in 1989, the chief rabbi of the city did not allow his burial next to his wife, but only at the outer limit of the Jewish graveyard, a symbolic rejection.[123] In the camp Murmelstein's German protagonist was the ex-"curator" of the Prague Jewish museum, SS commandant Karl Rahm.

In the autumn of 1944 a second film was shot in Theresienstadt, this time by Kurt Gerron. Gerron was a well-known Jewish actor, director, and overall Weimar star performer, who had been deported to Theresienstadt from Holland. It presented Theresienstadt as a happy resort town, complete with parks, swimming pools, soccer tournaments, schools, and endless cultural activities (concerts, theater, and so on); it featured "happy faces" all around. Completed in November 1944, this second hoax on a grand scale, titled *Theresienstadt: A Documentary from the Jewish Settlement Area*—and not, as is often mentioned, *The Führer Gives a Town to the Jews* (an ironic title made up by the inmates themselves)—was never shown in public. Gerron left Theresienstadt on the last transport to Auschwitz and was gassed on arrival.[124]

In April 1945, after some further improvement work, a second ICRC delegation visited the camp, once more in the company of a vast SS retinue that included Adolf Eichmann. Once again the Geneva delegates were satisfied: In their report Theresienstadt became a "small Jewish state." Incidentally they were the only audience to see Gerron's film; even they found it "slightly too propagandistic."[125]

There was no armed uprising in Theresienstadt, although it seems that the Germans took such a possibility into account in the fall of 1944, after the events in Treblinka and Sobibor, and the desperate and immediately-beaten-down rebellion of the Auschwitz *Sonderkommando* Jews in October. Thus, mainly young people boarded the transports to Auschwitz during the deportations of those months.[126]

There was no lack of defiance in the ghetto-camp, however, some of it quite open. The performance of Verdi's *Requiem*, with its *Dies Irae* and particularly its *Libera me*, was meant as a powerful message. The conductor, Raphael Schächter, had assembled a very large choir, soloists, and a sizable orchestra. The first performance took place at the end of the summer of 1944. Schächter reworked the *Libera me*, too tame in its original rendition, "giving to those final words the Beethoven victory code: three short notes, one long." Whether or not Eichmann sat in the audience, as he was in the camp to bestow a medal on Rahm in Himmler's name, is unclear. Be that as it may, on September 28, on the morrow of the final performance (during which they already knew of their deportation), the members of the choir, the soloists and the orchestra boarded the transport for Auschwitz.[127]

Throughout October eleven transports followed the September 28 one, leaving 11,077 Jews in the camp, which, in mid-September, still had had a population of 29,481 detainees. As deportees from Slovakia, the Protectorate, and the Reich (mainly *Mischlinge* and mixed couples) trickled in over the following months, the number of inmates grew again to some 30,000 (in the meantime a first transport of some 1,200 detainees was sent to Switzerland following negotiations between Himmler and the former Swiss president, Jean-Marie Musy, which we will discuss further on). In February 1945 Rahm ordered the building of two sites, a vast hall whose doors closed hermetically, and a covered pit of huge proportions: Both sites could have been used to exterminate the entire Jewish population on the spot, had the decision been taken to liquidate the camp before the arrival of the Soviet forces. The detainees were ultimately spared: 141,184 Jews had at one time or another been sent to Theresienstadt; at the end of the war, 16,832 were still alive.[128]

The final entry in Redlich's diary, dated October 6, 1944, was part of the "Diary of Dan" [the name of his newborn son], in which he commented on events by addressing his infant child: "Tomorrow, we travel, my son. We will travel on a transport like thousands before us. As usual, we did not register for this transport. They put us in without a reason. But never mind, my son, it is nothing. All of our family already left in the last weeks. Your uncle went, your aunt, and also your beloved grandmother. . . . Parting with her was especially difficult. We hope to see her there.

"It seems they want to eliminate the ghetto and leave only the elderly and people of mixed origin. In our generation, the enemy is not only cruel but also full of cunning and malice. They promise [something] but do not fulfill their promise. They send small children, and their prams are left here. Separated families. On one transport a father goes. On another, a son. On a third, the mother. "Tomorrow, we go too, my son. Hopefully, the time of our redemption is near."[129]

For Redlich sending the child and leaving the pram behind meant death. On the eve of his deportation he had exchanged food to get a pram for his son. He was authorized to take it along. This, in his mind, allowed for optimism. To his friend Willy Groag, Redlich said: "Why else would they permit us to take a baby carriage with us?"[130] Redlich and his infant son, Dan, were murdered on arrival. Dan's pram, with tens of thousands of other baby carriages, probably found its way to the Reich.

After her arrest in Kassel, in August 1943, Lilli Jahn, the physician from Immenhausen, was sent to a "corrective labor camp" in Breitenau. Such relatively mild treatment (non-Jewish inmates, the majority, were often liberated after a few weeks of detention) may have been due at first to Lilli's five *mischling* children or to the intervention of her former husband's acquaintance, a Gestapo official in Kassel. Yet after six months in Breitenau, Lilli was deported to Auschwitz, in March 1944. By early June, she must have become very weak, as she was barely able to sign her name at the bottom of a letter sent to her sister-in-law and manifestly written by another inmate. The end came soon thereafter.

An official death certificate indicating that Lilli Sara Jahn died on June 19, 1944, was sent to her children's address in Kassel, on September 28; her identity card was returned to the mayor of Immenhausen as "District Police Authority." A short announcement appended to the card indicated that the death had taken place on June 17.[131] Whether Lilli Sara Jahn died on June 17 or 19 was all the same to the Auschwitz administration.

VIII

In Slovakia the uprising of the underground was premature, notwithstanding the rapid advance of the Red Army: The Germans and their Hlinka Guard auxiliaries rapidly overcame the local partisans. The Jews who had joined the armed rebellion were usually shot whenever caught, and so were three of the four parachutists sent by the Yishuv; the remnants of the community were mainly deported to Auschwitz, also to some other camps, including Theresienstadt, during the last months of 1944 and early 1945.[132]

Once again the Vatican tried to intervene to halt the deportations, at least those of converted Jews, but without success. Tiso, who previously had been less extreme than his closest aides, now defended the deportations in a letter to Pius XII: "The rumors about cruelties are but an exaggeration of hostile enemy propaganda. . . . The deportations were undertaken in order to defend the nation from its foe. . . . We owe this as [an expression] of gratitude and loyalty to the Germans for our national sovereignty. . . . This debt is in our Catholic eyes the highest honor. . . . Holy Father, we shall remain faithful to our program:—For God and the Nation Signed: Dr. Josephus Tiso (sacerdos) [priest]."[133] As noted by a Catholic historian, the Reverend John Morley: Tiso was reprimanded on several occasions by the Vatican, but not excommunicated; the Holy See lost the opportunity "for a great humanitarian and moral gesture."[134]

In the meantime the events in neighboring Hungary took again a sharp turn for the worse. On October 15 Horthy announced his country's withdrawal from the war. On the same day the Germans took control of Budapest, arrested the regent and his son, and appointed an Arrow Cross (Niylas) government led by Szalasi and backed by most of the Hungarian army. On October 18 Eichmann returned to Budapest.

Over the following days and weeks the Germans sent some 50,000 Jews on a trek from the Hungarian capital to the Austrian border, under the escort of Hungarian gendarmerie first, then of German guards. The aim was to march these Jews to the vicinity of Vienna, where they would build fortifications to defend the Austrian capital. Thousands of marchers perished from exhaustion and mistreatment or were shot by the guards.

Another 35,000 Jews were organized into labor battalions to build fortifications around Budapest: They became prime targets for Niylas thugs whose fury increased as the Soviet forces approached the capital. When compelled to retreat into the city with the fleeing army units, the members of the Jewish labor battalions were killed on the bridges or on the banks of the Danube and thrown into the river. The carnage took such proportions that "special police units had to be called out to protect the Jews from the raging Niylas."[135]

In fact local Arrow Cross gangs had started murdering Jews in Budapest immediately after the change of government. As Arrow Cross deputy Karoly Marothy put it in a speech in parliament: "We must not allow individual cases to create compassion for them [the Jews]. . . . Something must also be done to stop the death rattle going on in the ditches all day, and the population must not be allowed to see the masses [of Jews] dying. . . . The deaths should not be recorded in the Hungarian death register."[136] National Police Commissioner Pal Hódosy shared Marothy's worries: "The problem is not that Jews are being murdered; the only trouble is the method. The bodies must be made to disappear, not put out in the streets."[137] As in Croatia, some priests excelled in the killings. Thus a Father Kun admitted to having murdered some 500 Jews. Usually he would order: "In the name of Christ—fire!"[138] Women, too, were active participants in the mass murders.[139]

A few days after the Arrow Cross came to power, Ribbentrop advised Veesenmayer that the Hungarians should "be encouraged in every way to continue taking measures that compromise them in the eyes of our enemies. . . . It is particularly in our interest," the minister added, "that the Hungarians should now proceed against the Jews in the most extreme way."[140] It does not seem that the Hungarians were in need of any German prodding.

The Jews who remained in the city for the most part lived in two ghettos. At the end of November, according to Veesenmayer, a minority inhabited a so-called international ghetto or special ghetto; they were protected by various foreign countries, particularly by Sweden and Switzerland. The others, the great majority, had been packed into an ordinary ghetto. A few hundred Jews were granted immunity by the Arrow Cross itself.

In fact Veesenmayer's assessment was off the mark: By the end of November only 32,000 Jews lived in the "ordinary ghetto," while tens of thousands, mostly protected by forged papers, stayed in the international ghetto. The Arrow Cross regularly raided both ghettos, and once the forged papers were discovered, mass deportations from the international to the ordinary ghetto started. Soon, some 60,000 Jews were enclosed in some 4,500 apartments, at times as many as 14 to a room.[141] In January, most of the inhabitants of the international ghetto were marched into the "ordinary ghetto," where daily deaths were reaching ten times the pre-occupation rate.[142]

About 150,000 protection papers, some 50,000 of these genuine and the others forged, were in circulation.[143] The Arrow Cross recognized some 34,800 of these documents, under the pressure of foreign governments. A group of foreign diplomats and delegates of humanitarian organizations spared no effort, sometimes at the risk of their own lives, to help the Jews of Budapest, in the ghettos, in "protected houses," on the trek from Budapest to Vienna. The Swiss diplomats, Carl Lutz, and the delegate of the ICRC, Friedrich Born; the Italian Giorgio Perlasca, impersonating a "Spanish chargé d'affaires"; the Portuguese, Carlos Branquinho; and, of course, the Swede, Raoul Wallenberg, became the tireless rescuers of thousands of Budapest Jews and their main sources of hope.[144]

The Niylas remained undeterred, to the very end. As Soviet troops were already fighting in the city, the killings went on, including mostly Jews but also other "enemies." A Hungarian lieutenant described events that probably occured in mid-January 1945: "I peeped round the corner of the Vigadó Concert Hall and saw victims standing on the track of the number 2 streetcar line in a long row, completely resigned to their fate. Those close to the Danube were already naked; the others were slowly walking down and undressing. It all happened in total silence, with only the occasional sound of a gunshot or machine-gun salvo. In the afternoon, when there was nobody left, we took another look. The dead were lying in their blood on the ice slabs or floating in the Danube. Among them were women, children, Jews, Gentiles, soldiers, and officers."[145] The last word should be left to Ferenc Orsós, a Hungarian professor of medicine who had belonged to the international commission that investigated the Katyn massacre: "Throw the dead Jews into the Danube; we don't want another Katyn."[146]

In February 1945 the Soviet army occupied the whole of Budapest.

While the march of the 50,000 Jews from Budapest to Vienna may be considered as the first large-scale death march, smaller groups of Jewish slave laborers from Hungary had already started their treks at least a month earlier. The well-known Hungarian Jewish poet Miklós Radnoti, then thirty-five, was among the "labor servicemen" who had been dispatched to Serbia, to the neighborhood of the Bor copper mines. On September 15, 1944, Radnoti and his group were ordered back to Bor, and on September 17 their march toward Hungary began.[147]

Attempts by the officers in command of the escort to leave the marches at railway stations failed; the column passed Belgrade and, on the road to Novi Sad, the Hungarian guards were reinforced by *Volksdeutsche*. From then on the number of Jews murdered along the road grew into the hundreds. On October 6 the column reached Cservenka, where it was divided into two groups: some eight hundred men, Radnoti among them, continued on their way; the other group, one thousand strong, was exterminated by SS in the local brickyards. Two days later, in Oszivac, Radnoti's group was surrounded by an SS cavalry unit: The "servicemen" were ordered to lie on the ground and were shot at random. As one of those wounded, a violinist, tried to get up and continue to march, one of the SS men exclaimed: *"Der Springt noch auf!"* ("He is still jumping up!") and shot him. A few days later Radnoti scribbled his last poem on a piece of paper that he probably found on the ground, and placed it in his notebook:

> I fell beside him and his corpse turned over,
> tight already as a snapping string.
> Shot in the neck. "And that's how you'll end too,"
> I whispered to myself; "lie still; no moving.
> Now patience flowers into death." Then I could hear
> "Der springt noch auf," above, and very near.
> Blood mixed with mud was drying on my ear.

About a month later Radnoti and a few other "servicemen" were murdered by their guards.[148]

"For English soldiers." That was the address of a letter left on the kitchen table in a house abandoned by the Germans somewhere on the Italian front in the last days of 1944; its message was unambiguous: "Dear Kamerad, on the Western front German troops are attacking the line of Americans. German tanks have destroyed a great deal of the enemy troops. The new German Luftwaffe is on the West front and she is very,

very good. The war is in a new station, she is over when the Germans are victorious. Germans are fighting for their lives. The English are fighting for the Jews. A GERMAN SOLDIER."[149]

Beyond the anti-Jewish hate outburst, the soldier's message carried faint echoes of Hitler's last major military initiative: the Ardennes offensive (Operation Autumn Mist), launched against mainly American forces on December 16 and stopped less than ten days later. A "new Luftwaffe," flying the first jet planes, did indeed participate in the operations, with no major results, however. The first phase of Germany's collapse was over, sometime in the early days of 1945.

IX

The disintegration of the Reich accelerated as weeks went by and as, between January and March 1945, the command and control systems increasingly broke down. In the West, Belgium and Holland were liberated; the Rhineland and the Ruhr fell into Allied hands and, on March 7, the ninth U.S. Armored Division crossed the Rhine at Remagen. On the Eastern Front in the meantime, after taking control of Budapest, Soviet forces were moving toward Vienna; to the northeast, the Baltic countries were again in Stalin's grip; most East Prussian strongholds fell one after another, and millions of German civilians were fleeing westward in an increasingly chaotic panic as news of Soviet savagery was spreading. In March, Soviet units crossed the river Oder: The road to Berlin was open. A few weeks beforehand Stalin, Roosevelt and Churchill had met at Yalta and redrawn the borders of Eastern Europe—and divided Germany into occupation zones. And, in those same days of February 1945, Dresden, filled with refugees fleeing the Russians, was turned into a burning inferno by two successive air raids: a British and then an American one. During the first days of March, the short-lived and last German offensive of the war unfolded and petered out near Lake Balaton, in a desperate attempt to secure the control of Hungarian oil fields and bauxite mines.[150]

As the Nazi leader lived in an increasingly delusional world, it is not certain that even in early 1945 he recognized that the game was over. Of course in his morbid mind, mulling over the Jewish issue never stopped: "Jesus was certainly not a Jew," he explained to Bormann on November 30,

1944. "The Jews would never have delivered one of their own to the Romans and to a Roman court; they would have convicted him themselves. It seems that many descendants of Roman legionaires lived in Galilee and Jesus was one of them. It could be that his mother was Jewish." The usual themes followed: Jewish materialism, the perversion of Jesus' ideals by Paul, the link between Jews and communism, etc.[151] Nothing seemed to have changed in Hitler's innermost ideological landscape from his earliest forays into political propaganda in 1919 to the last months of his crusade against "the Jew."

In his 1945 New Year's address to the party, the people, and the troops, Hitler brandished once again the omnipresent Jewish threat: Didn't Ilya Ehrenburg and Henry Morgenthau represent the two faces of the identical Jewish will to destroy and exterminate the German nation?[152] On January 30 it was the Jewish-Asiatic-Bolshevik conspiracy to undermine Germany after World War I that resurfaced in the endlessly repeated self-justificatory history of the rise of the party and of Hitler's own providential-political destiny.[153]

On February 24, in his traditional address commemorating the February 1920 proclamation of the party program, Hitler avoided traveling from Berlin to Munich; old-timer Hermann Esser read his address to the assembled Nazi elite. The Führer may have wished to avoid meeting the "old guard," but his message remained the same and the archenemy was the same: "At the time" [of the party's beginnings], Hitler reminded the faithful, "the semblance of an opposition between the forces that acted together was but the expression of the single will of the one inciter and beneficiary. For a long time international Jewry used both forms [capitalism and Bolshevism] to exterminate the freedom and social happiness of nations."[154]

In case such a statement sounded too abstract and too vague, Hitler turned to the ongoing events in the eastern provinces of the Reich that were already in Soviet hands: "What this Jewish pest inflicts there upon our women, children and men is the most horrible fate that a human brain can imagine."[155] The concluding exhortation followed in all "logic": "The life that has been left to us can serve but one commandment: to restore and regain what the international Jewish criminals and their handymen have caused to our people."[156]

Goebbels did not let go of the Jews either: "This afternoon," he recorded on January 7, 1945, "I write an article on the Jewish question. It is again necessary to deal with the Jewish question on the widest scale. This theme cannot be allowed to rest. The Jews all over the world will not rejoice about my arguments."[157] The minister, needless to say, was not bereft of "compelling proofs" to make his anti-Jewish points: "That Bolshevism is essentially inspired by the Jews," he noted on February 6, "is demonstrated in the news coming from Moscow, that Stalin has married for a third time, now the sister of the vice-chairman of the Council of the people's representatives, Kaganowitch, a Jewess through and through. She will see to it that Bolshevism does not follow any wrong path."[158]

Notwithstanding the continuous fury of the anti-Jewish propaganda, which was to reach its ultimate stage (in both meanings of the word) in Hitler's "political testament," German policies regarding the fate of the remaining Jews became increasingly inconsistent. On the one hand Hitler himself and part of the SS apparatus directly involved in the implementation of the "Final Solution" did not waver to the very end in the policy of extermination, although it was delayed at times by last-minute need for slave labor. In fact, in early 1944 already, Hitler had been ready to compromise regarding the presence of Jewish slave laborers on German soil. Speer confirmed, in a memorandum dated April 1944, that the Nazi leader authorized the use of 100,000 Hungarian Jews in urgent building projects for munitions factories to be located in the Protectorate.[159] Soon thereafter Jewish camp inmates would be brought back to the Reich.

Thus in the late summer of 1944, some 40,000 Jews selected in Auschwitz and Stutthof had been shipped to two major satellite camps of Dachau—Kaufering and Mühldorf (in the vicinity of Munich)—where Organization Todt used them to build the heavily protected, semiunderground halls needed for the production of aircraft. Somewhat later, mainly in the wake of the Auschwitz evacuation, other Jewish workers would be marched to the Harz Mountains, to slave in the tunnels of Dora-Mittelbau where, some Germans still believed, the ongoing production of V-2 rockets would save the Reich.[160]

The Jewish workers shipped to the Dachau satellite camps were joined by thousands of Hungarian Jews marched directly from Budapest to the Bavarian construction sites.[161] OT rapidly proved itself equal to the SS in its mistreatment of the slave laborers, and by the fall of 1944, hundreds had been killed or were too weak to continue working. At this point the Dachau commandant decided to send these Jews back to Auschwitz for gassing.[162] Some of these transports left Bavaria at the end of September, others in October 1944.[163]

It is at this point, in late 1944, that Himmler's hesitant search for a way out becomes apparent. It seems that at some stage the Reichsführer countermanded the steps taken by his underlings (and approved by his master) to pursue the "Final Solution" but was unable to sustain this alternative, afraid as he was of Hitler's reaction. Nonetheless, from early 1945 on, in order to find an opening to the West, Himmler was ready to give up *some small groups* of Jews to prove his goodwill.

During his earlier forays into secret diplomacy, the Reichsführer was represented by the head of the Foreign Intelligence Department of the SD, Walter Schellenberg, who in 1944 had taken over the operations and most of the agents of the disbanded Abwehr. Apart from Schellenberg and his outfit, Himmler's main delegate had been and continued to be, until the fall of 1944, the business-savvy Becher and, at times, Becher's colleagues in Budapest, Gerhard Clages, Wisliceny, and Hermann Krumey. Himmler would allow contacts with representatives of Jewish organizations in Switzerland, the War Refugee Board delegates in Bern and various Swiss personalities, without giving any firm commitment about what he was ready to undertake. Simultaneously he would be in touch with Jewish and non-Jewish personalities in Sweden.

According to Becher's postwar testimony, sometime in the fall of 1944, he convinced Himmler to order an end to the deportations, as an opening to further negotiations with representatives of the Joint and, more specifically with its representative in Switzerland, Sally Mayer. The Jewish representatives were asked to transfer money.[164] It seems that in reciprocation, along the lines suggested by Becher, Himmler did indeed issue some order both to Kaltenbrunner and to Pohl; it also appears that in response Mayer, with the agreement of the representative of the War Refugee Board in Switzerland, was ready to set up a blocked account for the Germans in a Swiss bank. But Himmler, who must have sensed that Hitler would not agree to any major compromise in Jewish matters, probably backed down.

Yet, other negotiations went on between the Reichsführer and an old friend of his, the Swiss Federal Councillor Jean-Marie Musy, aiming at the release of tens of thousands of Jews as an opening to negotiations with the Western Powers. As already mentioned, a first train carrying 1,200 Jews from Theresienstadt arrived in Switzerland in January 1945. Informed of the deal, Hitler put an immediate end to it.[165] At that stage a third channel appeared more promising: negotiations by way of Sweden. The Swedes informed Himmler in February 1945 that they were ready to undertake a series of humanitarian missions, which, if agreed to by the Germans, could possibly open the way for wider contacts. To that effect Count Folke Bernadotte was dispatched to Germany.[166]

Bernadotte's mission, ostensibly under the banner of the Swedish Red Cross but, as in Wallenberg's case backed in fact by the Swedish government, aimed first at liberating Scandinavian internees from Neuengamme (near Hamburg) and transfering them to Sweden. Himmler agreed. The Swedes then pushed for the release of Jews from Theresienstadt and Bergen-Belsen, while during the previous months Raoul Wallenberg had extended his activities in Budapest. During March and April 1945 initiatives to save Jews still alive in the camps multiplied, and groups of internees were indeed released as chaos spread throughout Germany.

X

Sometime in January 1945, after preparations had already started several months earlier (including the destruction of crematoriums, the emptying of burial pits, the clearing of ashes, the shipment of hundreds of thousands of items of clothing, and so on), Himmler gave the order for the complete evacuation of all the camps in the East with, according to several testimonies, an ominous warning to the camp commanders: "The Führer holds you personally responsible for . . . making sure that not a single prisoner from the concentration camps falls alive into the hands of the enemy."[167] Other testimonies indicate that the decision about the fate of the inmates was left to the camp commanders.[168] Moreover, in a basic directive that had already been issued in July 1944, Glücks had stated clearly that in an "emergency situation" (evacuation) the camp commanders were to follow the directives of the regional HSSPFs. In other words nobody seemed to know who was in charge of the evacuations. But in the rapidly increasing chaos, the marches westward started.

Not all the 700,000 to 800,000 camp inmates lurching along the roads or stranded in open railroad cars during these last months of the war were Jews. A mixed sample of all of Germany's victims had been herded together; yet, as a reflection of the camps' population, the Jews ultimately represented a majority of these final victims of the monstrous Reich. During the marches approximately 250,000 of these Jewish prisoners perished from exhaustion, freezing, shooting, or being burned alive.

On January 18, columns of Auschwitz detainees—some 56,000 inmates, including those of satellite camps—started on their way westward toward Gleiwitz from where part was to be sent off by rail to camps in the interior of the Reich and others were to be marched farther on to Gross-Rosen and other camps in Upper Silesia. Hundreds of "stragglers" were shot during the earliest phase of the evacuation.[169] In this respect—and regarding the spreading chaos—the rendering of the situation in Höss's memoirs appears credible: "On all the roads and tracks in Upper Silesia west of the Oder, I now met columns of prisoners, struggling through the deep snow. They had no food. Most of the noncommissioned officers in charge of these stumbling columns of corpses had no idea where they were supposed to be going. They only knew that their final destination was Gross-Rosen. But how to get there was a mystery. On their own authority they requisitioned food from the villages through which they passed, rested for a few hours, then trudged on again. There was no question of spending the night in barns or schools, since these were all crammed with refugees. The route taken by these miserable columns was easy to follow, since every few hundred yards lay the bodies of prisoners who had collapsed or been shot. . . . I saw open coal trucks, loaded with frozen corpses, whole trainloads of prisoners who had been shunted on to open sidings and left there without food or shelter."[170]

Not all evacuees ordered to clamber onto the open train cars stayed in or around Gleiwitz. Some trains actually departed with their human load. Paul Steinberg, whom we already met in Buna, was in one of them. While the Jews marching through German villages mostly remembered indifference from the population or additional brutality, Steinberg tells of a different event, "a precise, detailed, overwhelming memory." The train had reached Prague in the early hours of a winter day and was crawling with its open load of "vaguely human creatures" under bridges while the

Czechs were marching overhead on their way to work. "As one man," Steinberg recalls, "the Czechs opened their satchels and tossed their lunches down to us without a moment's hesitation. . . . We were showered with rolls, slices of bread and butter, potatoes." Then on the railroad cars the fighting erupted: "A terrible struggle broke out as everyone fought to grab a morsel, a mouthful. . . . I witnessed a scene of complete degradation. . . . Three or four men died around a crumbled loaf of bread. . . . I waited twelve hours, until night came and my neighbors were only half-conscious, before I ate my bread, silently hiding my face, and my mouth savored my survival. I do not think I would have made it without that bread." A few days later the surviving passengers reached Buchenwald.[171]

While the camp inmates were moving westward on foot or in open railroad cars, SS officers, camp staff members, and guards, were of course traveling in the same direction, but under better conditions. At times, however, the camp evacuations linked staff and detainees in unexpected ways. Thus during the last days of the war, on April 28, 1945, a Red Cross member watched some 5,000 detainees and their male and female SS guards moving westward out of Ravensbrück. At the head of one of the columns, a small cart pulled by six skeletal females carried the wife of one of the SS officers of the camp and her mounds of belongings. The lady, it seems, had to be particularly well attended to, as she was suffering from the consequences of an excessive binge of raisins.[172]

During the marches the guards usually decided on their own to kill the stragglers. However, some notorious decisions to murder the prisoners were taken at higher levels. Thus, during the second half of January between 5,000 and 7,000 Jewish inmates were assembled in Königsberg from various Stutthof satellite camps and sent marching to the northeast along the Baltic coast. Most were women. As the column reached the fishing village of Palmnicken, and could not move on overland, the *Gauleiter* of East Prussia, Erich Koch, together with local SS officers, members of Organization Todt, and the commanders of the satellite camps from which the inmates had arrived, decided to liquidate the entire group.[173] Only two to four hundred of the prisoners survived the massacre on the seashore.

The same murderous conditions surrounded the evacuation of the Buchenwald inmates. Of the 3,000 Jews sent to Theresienstadt, barely a few hundred reached it in early April.[174] As for the 22,000 inmates sent marching to Bavaria at the same time, around 8,000 were murdered, while the others reached Dachau and were liberated by the Americans. From the 45,000 inmates of the satellite camps of Buchenwald, 13,000 to 15,000 lost their lives during the evacuation.[175]

None of the major camps was entirely emptied of inmates in the evacuations. In Auschwitz, for example, sick inmates remained in each of the three camps after the January 19 mass evacuation. And SS units, still sporadically battling the Soviets in the area, also remained for a full week. Although the Breslau HSSPF had given the order to murder all the remaining inmates, the SS units rather concentrated on the destruction of what remained of the gas chambers and the crematoriums and the burning of archives. Yet one such unit murdered 200 female inmates in Birkenau before Himmler's men finally left the camp.

"We all said to each other that the Russians would arrive soon, at once," Primo Levi, who in those days was an inmate in the Monowitz infirmary block, reminisced. "We all proclaimed it, we were all sure of it, but at bottom nobody believed it. Because one loses the habit of hoping in the Lager [the camp], and even of believing in one's own reason. In the Lager it is useless to think, because events happen for the most part in an unforeseeable manner; and it is harmful, because it keeps alive a sensitivity which is a source of pain, and which some providential natural law dulls when suffering passes a limit."[176]

As Levi was waiting for the Soviet troops to liberate the camp—which they did on January 29—Ruth Kluger and Cordelia (Edvardson) had already left Auschwitz for some time. Kluger and her mother had been transferred to the small Christianstadt labor camp, a satellite camp of Gross-Rosen, also in Upper Silesia; Cordelia had been shipped off to a camp near Hamburg (probably Neuengamme). In early 1945 Ruth and her mother started marching in the mass of inmates, but after a few days they escaped from the march and survived by moving from farm to farm, then by blending into the stream of German refugees fleeing westward, until they reached Straubing, in Bavaria. Soon thereafter the Americans arrived.[177] Cordelia was among the sick inmates (mainly children and youngsters) saved by the arrangement between Himmler and the Swedish government; a new life started for her, too, in Sweden.[178]

As for Filip Müller, his chances of survival were slim: Members of the *Sonderkommando* were not to be left alive. He did escape nonetheless, marching, then ferrying, then marching again to Mauthausen, then to Melk, and farther to Gusen 1, and by early April 1945, out of Gusen again. The SS did not give up: All stragglers were shot; yet, instead of leaving the corpses by the roadside, they ordered Müller and some of his companions to load them on a horse-drawn vehicle, take them to a local cemetery, and bury them in a mass grave; traces had to be effaced as thoroughly as possible.[179] Finally the group reached some small camp near Wels: starving prisoners lay there on the floors of the barracks: The guards were gone. Müller settled on a rafter and waited. A few days later shouting inmates spread the news: "We are free!"

"It was, incredibly, a complete anti-climax," Müller reminisced. "The moment, on which all my thoughts and secret wishes had been concentrated for three years, evoked neither gladness nor, for that matter, any other feelings inside me. I let myself drop down from my rafter and crawled on all fours to the door. Outside I struggled along a little further, but then I simply stretched out on a woodland ground and fell fast asleep." The final image, whether precise or not, was a necessary finale to his memoir and, in one form or another, to many individual stories of liberation: "I awoke to the monotonous noise of vehicles rumbling past. Walking across to the nearby road I saw a column of American tanks clanking along in the direction of Wels. As I stared after the convoy of steel giants I realized that the hideous Nazi terror had ended at last."[180]

XI

During the last months of the war, while one German city after another suffered catastrophic damages, while transportation was becoming increasingly chaotic, the Gestapo sent out new deportation summonses. In January 1945 many of the 200 *Mischlinge* or partners in mixed marriages who still lived in Stuttgart were ordered to be ready for deportation to Theresienstadt.[181]

Sent on January 27, 1945, the Stuttgart Gestapo summonses ordered recipients "to report to the Transit Camp Bietigheim (Ludwigsburg

County) on Monday February 12, 1945, for assignment to an external work commando." The usual list of food rations and items to be taken along followed, and so did the usual administrative orders: "You must report your departure as well as relinquish any food ration cards to the police by February 10, 1945. Children [mainly *Mischlinge* of the first degree] under the age of 16 are to be placed in the care of relatives."[182]

Similar summonses were being sent out, approximately at the same time, throughout the entire Reich. On February 13, in the afternoon ("perfect spring weather"), Klemperer recorded: "Today at eight o'clock [in the morning] I was at Neumark's. Frau Jährig came out of his room weeping. Then he told me: Evacuation of those capable of work, it's called outside work duty; as I myself [i.e., Klemperer] am released from duty, I remain here. So, the end is more likely for me than for those who are leaving. He: That is not the case; on the contrary, remaining here is a privilege. . . . The circular to be delivered stated that one had to present oneself at 3 Zeughausstrasse early on Friday morning, wearing working clothes and with hand luggage, which would have to be carried for a considerable distance, and with provisions for two to three days travel. . . . The whole thing is explicitly no more than outside work duty—but is without exception regarded as a death march."[183]

A few hours later the bombing of Dresden started. At first Victor and Eva lost contact with each other in the pandemonium. . . . By chance they met again on the Elbe riverbank. They took off Victor's star and, as non-Jews now, they hid with other refugees at the house of acquaintances outside the burning city, before moving westward.

The last opinion reports of the SD collected in the Reich in early 1945 confirm the generalized obsession with the Jewish issue in the crumbling Reich. They mainly indicate various (fragmentary) aspects of the depth of anti-Jewish hatred both among wide segments of the populace and the elites. The belief in the Jewish responsibility for the war had taken root. According to historian Robert Gellately, during the last two years of the war, letters (including some from academics) were sent to the Ministry of Propaganda suggesting that the Jews remaining in Germany be collected at likely bombing targets. The number of Jews killed would be announced after each raid. One of these letters suggested that even if this measure did not stop Allied bombings, at least many Jews would be exterminated; another proposal was to threaten the Americans and the British that a tenfold number of Jews would be shot for each German civilian killed in a bombing raid.[184] The *Volksgenossen* had forgotten that essentially there were no Jews in the Reich anymore.

During the last weeks of 1944 people in the Stuttgart region criticized the publicity given to Soviet atrocities and argued that the Germans had done much worse in their treatment of the Jews;[185] others believed that whatever was befalling Germany was the result of Jewish vengeance.[186] All in all, it seems that Nazi indoctrination was keeping its hold. On April 12, 1945, the British chief of military intelligence reported: "The Germans . . . caution us against appointment of Jewish burgomeisters which [they say] is a psychological mistake and which militates against cooperation of German civilian population."[187]

The persistence of such deep-rooted anti-Semitism was confirmed by various opinion polls conducted in the Western zones of Germany shortly after the surrender.[188] This in turn indicates that, after a certain point, the decline of Hitler's popularity did not necessarily lead to a fading of anti-Jewish hatred. It has been argued that Hitler still had much popular support at the beginning of 1945.[189] This may have been true in January and February 1945 but was probably changing around March and April, according to the well-informed yet traditionally optimistic entries in Goebbels's diaries.

"Unfortunately," the propaganda minister recorded on March 24, 1945, "Führer, too, is now increasingly mentioned in critical assessments. . . . It seems to me disastrous that now criticism does not stop at the person of the Führer, or at the National Socialist idea or at the movement."[190] And on April 1 Goebbels recorded again (referring mainly to attitudes in the western parts of the country); "Morale has sunk extraordinarily among the soldiers and the population. People are no longer afraid even of sharply criticizing the Führer."[191]

At least he, the Reichsminister, unlike most *Volksgenossen*, kept the faith, but like many, nursed the rage: "The Jews speak up again," he recorded on March 14. "Their spokesman is the well-known and notorious Leopold Schwarzschild who now pleads in the American press against any milder treatment of Germany. These Jews should be killed like rats, whenever one gets the possibility to do it. In Germany, thank god, we already took care of it quite seriously. I hope that the world will adopt this as an example."[192] The raving and ranting went on ever more furiously as the twelve-year Reich was fast approaching its end.

XII

After part of the Reich Chancellery had been destroyed by massive American bombings in early February 1945, Hitler retreated to the vast underground maze of living quarters, offices, conference rooms, and utilities spreading two stories deep under the building and its garden. It was there that, a few weeks later, he decided to stay as the Red Army was closing in on Berlin. Almost to the end the Nazi leader apparently believed in his star and in a last-minute miracle that would turn the utterly hopeless military situation around. It was there in his subterranean abode that he heard extraordinary tidings: On April 12 Roosevelt died.

The enemy coalition would collapse now as, at another time, in another hopeless war, the coalition arrayed against Frederick the Great foundered with Czarina Elizabeth's death. Great expectations surged again and Hitler shared them with the troops on the Eastern front in his April 16 proclamation: "For the last time the Jewish-Bolshevik mortal enemy has attacked. . . . In this hour the entire German nation looks to you, my Eastern Front warriors [*meine Ostkämpfer*] and only hopes that as a result of your steadfastness, your fanaticism, your weapons and your leadership, the Bolshevik assault will suffocate in a bloodbath. At the moment when fate has taken away the greatest war criminal of all times [Roosevelt], the turn of this war will be decided."[193]

On April 20, as somewhat subdued toasts were raised in Hitler's bunker to celebrate the Führer's fifty-sixth birthday, Dr. Alfred Trzebinski, senior physician at the Neuengamme concentration camp, received the order to dispose of twenty Jewish children who had been used as guinea pigs for SS doctor Kurt Heissmeyer's experiments on tuberculosis.[194]

About a year beforehand, Heissmeyer, assistant director of the SS sanatorium at Hohenlychen, had received Himmler's authorization to conduct his experiments on adults and children in secluded barracks at Neuengamme. The twenty Jewish children, ten boys and ten girls, aged five to twelve, had arrived in Birkenau with their families from France, Holland, Poland, and Yugoslavia. The families disappeared in the gas chambers and, in the fall of 1944 the twenty children were sent to Neuengamme.[195]

During the following months, the children, injected with Heissmeyer's preparations, became seriously ill. On April 20, as British forces were approaching the camp, the order came. The killing would not take place in Neuengamme but at the Bullenhuser Damm school in Rothenburgsort, near Hamburg, a subcamp of Neuengamme.

At his postwar trial Trzebinski described the course of the events. The SS personnel arrived at Bullenhuser Damm with six Russian prisoners, two French doctors, two Dutch inmates, and the children. The children were put in a separate room, an air raid shelter: "They had all their things with them—some food, some toys they had made themselves, etc. They sat on the benches and were happy that they had gotten out. They didn't suspect a thing."

Trzebinski gave the children sedatives, while, in the boiler room, all the adult inmates were put to death. "I must say," Trzebinski went on, "that in general the children's condition was very good, except for one twelve-year-old boy who was in bad shape; he therefore fell asleep very quickly. Six or eight of the children were still awake—the others were already sleeping. . . . Frahm [an orderly] lifted the twelve-year-old boy and said to the others that he was taking him to bed. He took him to a room that was maybe six or eight yards away, and there I saw a rope already attached to a hook. Frahm put the sleeping boy into the noose and with all his weight pulled down on the body of the boy so that the noose would tighten."[196] The other children followed, one by one.

One of the most criminal political leaders in history was about to put an end to his life. There is no point in probing once more "the mind of Adolf Hitler" or the twisted emotional sources of his murderous obsessions. It has been attempted many times without much success. However, the significant and unavoidable historical question, the one that we briefly addressed in the introduction and repeatedly throughout the volume, has to be restated and considered again at the end. The major question that challenges all of us is not what personality traits allowed an "unknown corporal" of the Great War to become the all-powerful leader

Adolf Hitler, but rather why tens of millions of Germans blindly followed him to the end, why many still believed in him at the end, and not a few, after the end. It is the nature of *"Führer-Bindung,"* this "bond to the Führer," to use Martin Broszat's expression, that remains historically significant.[197]

Among twentieth-century leaders none but Hitler was surrounded by the frenzied devotion of so many fellow countrymen in one of the most advanced and powerful nations on earth. Roosevelt was divisive, and a large segment of the American people opposed him and at times hated him throughout his four terms in office; many Britons detested Churchill before and during his premiership; fear surrounded Stalin, the statesman most often compared to Hitler. Whereas in the Soviet Union the elite was terrorized and the population lived in a mixed atmosphere of fear and admiration for the worthy disciple of Marx and Lenin, Hitler was surrounded by the hysterical adoration and blind faith of so many, for so long, that well after Stalingrad, as we saw, countless Germans still believed in his promises of victory. Of course nothing of the kind ever applied to Mussolini, and whatever bond had existed between the *Duce* and his people at the onset of his regime fast vanished from the midthirties on.

Previously we indicated how brandishing the threat represented by "the Jew" reinforced Hitler's charismatic appeal. A metahistorical enemy demanded, when the time for the decisive struggle arrived, a metahistorical personality to lead the fight against those forces of evil. Yet we are hard put to identify the importance of charisma in a modern society functioning along the rules of instrumental rationality and bureaucratic procedures. There remains but one plausible interpretation: Modern society does remain open to—possibly in need of—the ongoing presence of religious or pseudoreligious incentives within a system otherwise dominated by thoroughly different dynamics. Above and beyond the "reactionary modernism" evoked by historian Jeffrey Herf, Nazism confronts us with some kind of "sacralized modernism."[198] Propaganda and all the trappings of mass manipulation were an essential part of the emotional-psychological mobilization that took hold of the German population. However, without Hitler's uncanny ability to grasp and magnify the basic urges of such a mass craving for order, authority, greatness, and salvation, the techniques of propaganda alone would not have sufficed. In that sense National Socialism could not have arisen and taken hold without Adolf Hitler on the one hand, and without the Germans' response to Hitler on the other.

Of course, had Hitler only ranted and raved without delivering any tangible results, disenchantment would rapidly have undermined his appeal. But within a few years, despite the mobilization of sundry enemies by the "master of deceit," he did achieve full employment and economic growth, the elimination of humiliating shackles and a new sense of national pride, social mobility for the great number and improvement of the standards of living and the working conditions of the masses, together with hefty rewards—and the promise of much greater ones—for the leaders of business and industry. Above and beyond anything else, Hitler instilled in the majority of Germans a sense of community and purpose. Later extraordinary diplomatic success followed, capped by stunning military victories that drove German national exaltation to the rim of literal collective insanity.

Throughout, Hitler was loath to sacrifice standards of living to the demands of an increasingly total war, and, as was amply shown in the preceding pages, conquered peoples, and mainly the Jews, were indeed defrauded and exploited to sustain, in part, the well-being of the *Volksgemeinschaft* or, at least, to alleviate some of the material burdens of the war. In that sense the arguments mustered by Götz Aly in *Hitlers Volkstaat* cannot be dismissed out of hand. But why should the Jews have been exterminated in the face of the demands of the Wehrmacht for skilled labor and other economic arguments, unless entirely different reasons motivated the master of the Reich and the multitude of his acolytes and supporters? Unavoidably the question leads us back once again to the phantasmal role played by "the Jew" in Hitler's Germany and the surrounding world.

As the struggle reached its critical phase, at the height of the war, to lose faith in Hitler meant only one outcome: the prospect of horrendous retaliation at the hands of "Jewish liquidation squads," in Goebbels's words. Robbing the Jews contributed to the upholding of the *Volkstaat*; murdering them and fanning the fears of retribution became the ultimate bond of Führer and *Volk* in the collapsing *Führerstaat*.

At the very end the "bond" snapped for many Germans. For others, however, pride in the achievements of the regime and belief in its rightful path, marred solely by minor blemishes, remained silently and anonymously alive for decades to come, as did the nostalgia for the *Volksgemeinschaft*.[199]

On April 21, 1945, in the evening, as Soviet shells started falling near the former buildings of the Reich Chancellery, the Nazi leader thanked the *Duce* for his birthday greetings: "My thanks, *Duce*, for your wishes on my birthday. The struggle that we are leading for our sheer existence has reached its high point. With limitless supplies of war material, Bolshevism and the troops of Jewry [*Bolschewismus und die Truppen des Judentums*] set everything in action to unite their destructive forces in Germany and thus push our continent into chaos."[200] For the first time, it seems, the Anglo-American forces were designated as "the troops of Jewry."

The Nazi chief let his entourage know that he would stay in the bunker and kill himself; everybody else could leave if they wished to. Eva Braun, whom Hitler would marry on the eve of their suicide, was determined to die with him. The faithful Goebbels, his wife, Magda, and their six children were also in the bunker: They would share their leader's fate. On April 29 the time had come: The Führer dictated his "Private Testament" and then his message to future generations, his "Political Testament."

In the first half of the document, the Nazi leader addressed the German people, the world, and history. "It is untrue," he declared, "that he or anybody else in Germany had wanted the war in 1939." And, immediately, at the very outset of the message, he turned to his main obsession: "It [the war] was exclusively willed and triggered by the international statesmen, who were either of Jewish descent or worked for Jewish interests." After denying again any responsibility in the outbreak of the war, the Nazi leader, as was his wont, prophesied retribution: "From the ruins of our cities and our monuments hatred will arise again against the people that bears the responsibility in the end, the one to whom we have to thank for all of this: international Jewry and its acolytes!"

After a brief but, as we shall see, essential comment on British responsibility for the outcome of the Polish crisis of September 1939, Hitler could not fail to end this short paragraph without returning to Jewish warmongering. Full-scale raving followed: "I left no doubt that if the peoples of Europe were treated again as bundles of stocks belonging to the international conspiracy of money and finance, then the culprit for this murderous struggle would have to pay: Jewry! Moreover I did not leave anybody unaware of the fact that, this time, not only millions of men would be killed, not only hundreds of thousands of women and children would be burnt and bombed to death in the cities, but those truly responsible would have to pay for his culpability, albeit by more humane methods." The responsibility for the extermination of five to six million Jews was laid squarely upon the victims. The address then turned to Hitler's decision to share the fate of Berlin's inhabitants but, typically, it shifted again: "Moreover, I do not want to fall into the hands of the enemies who need a new show staged by the Jews for their excited masses."

Volk and soldiers got their share of praise: The seeds had been sown, Hitler declared, that would lead to the rebirth of National Socialism. Then he settled accounts with Göring and Himmler, whom he demoted and expelled from the party for their dealings with the Western Powers, nominated Grand Adm. Karl Dönitz as the new head of state ("president," not "Führer," of course) and chief of the armed forces, Goebbels as chancellor, and designated the new ministers. Hitler reached the inevitable final exhortation: "Most of all, I commit the leadership of the nation and its followers to the strictest keeping of the race laws and the merciless struggle against the universal poisoner of all people, international Jewry."[201]

The wording of such a document, dictated in the direst of circumstances, cannot be taken in the same way as if it had been carefully prepared at the height of the Nazi leader's power. And yet isn't it plausible that precisely the historical importance (in Hitler's eyes) of this last message would bring forth only the essentials, the barest tenets, of Hitler's faith?

That "Providence" or "fate"—still invoked less than two weeks earlier—had disappeared from the Nazi leader's rhetoric needs no explanation. That the "Reich" and the "party" also remained unmentioned (except for "Berlin, the capital of the Reich") is not surprising either. The Reich was in ruins and the party replete with traitors. Not only were

Göring and Himmler negotiating with the enemy but, in the West, the *Gauleiter* were surrendering one after another, and SS generals were sending false reports on the military situation. The party, whose members should have been ready to die for the Reich and their leader, had ceased to exist.

All this was in line with Hitler's usual reactions toward anyone daring to wander off the path he alone was allowed to dictate. But besides such foreseeable reactions, one aspect of the testament was utterly unexpected: In Hitler's final message there was no trace of Bolshevism.

Hitler had probably decided to concentrate his entire apologia on demonstrating that neither Germany's catastrophic end nor the murder of the Jews was *his* responsibility. The responsibility was laid squarely upon those who, in September 1939, pushed for war, whereas he sought only compromise: the Western plutocrats and the warmongering Jews. Stalin, his ally at the time, was better left unmentioned as the partition of Poland within days of the invasion showed that the Reich and the Soviet Union had decided to share the Polish spoils in a pact that considerably facilitated the German attack and proved that Hitler was intent on launching the war.

On April 30, shortly after 3:00 p.m., Hitler and Eva Braun committed suicide. On Dönitz's order, German radio broadcast the following announcement on May 1 at 10:26 p.m.: "The Führer's headquarters announce that this afternoon, our Führer, Adolf Hitler, fell at his command post in the Reich Chancellery, in fighting against Bolshevism to his last breath."[202] Seven days later Germany surrendered.

Either on May 1 or 2, as he was informed of Hitler's death, Cardinal Bertram—who in the meantime had left Breslau for safer surroundings—requested, in a handwritten letter addressed to all the parish priests of his diocese, that they "hold a solemn requiem mass in memory of the Führer."[203]

Before continuing their trek to the West the Klemperers, as mentioned, stayed briefly in an acquaintances' house near Dresden. On the night of March 21, all the inhabitants huddled in the corridor during an air raid warning. The Klemperers struck up a conversation with one Fräulein

Dumpier: "She cautiously began to come out of her shell," Victor later noted. "She gradually came out with strong doubts on National Socialist teaching. . . . She turned the conversation toward the Jewish question. I side-stepped carefully. . . . I went through quite a few contortions. The girl's last words were amusing . . . she believed in the rights of nations, she found the arrogance and brutalization in Germany repugnant—'It's only the Jews I hate. I think I have been influenced a bit in that.' I would have liked to ask her how many Jews she knew, but swallowed it down and merely smiled. And noted for myself, how demagogically justified National Socialism was in putting anti-Semitism at the center."[204]

Two weeks later the Klemperers, now ordinary German refugees, reached Upper Bavaria; their identity had not been discovered: They were saved. And so were some other diarists: Mihail Sebastian, in Bucharest (who soon after the Russian takeover was killed in an accident); Abraham Tory, from Kovno; Hersch Wasser, from Warsaw. So also were the dazed survivors who had been left behind in the camps, those who remained alive during the death marches, those who emerged from their hiding places in Christian institutions, in "Aryan" families, in mountains or forests, among partisans or in Resistance movements, those who lived in the open under false identities, those who had fled in time from German-dominated areas, those who kept their new identities, and those, known or unknown, who had betrayed and collaborated for the sake of survival.

Between five and six million Jews had been killed; among them almost a million and a half were under the age of fourteen.[205] They comprised the immense mass of silent victims and also most of the diarists and authors of letters whose voices we heard in these pages. Etty Hillesum, Anne Frank, Ben Wessels, and Philip Mechanicus, from Amsterdam;[206] Raymond-Raoul Lambert, Jacques Biélinky, and Louise Jacobson, from Paris; Moshe Flinker, from The Hague and Brussels; Jochen Klepper and Hertha Feiner, from Berlin; Lilli Jahn, from Cologne; Ernst Krombach from Essen; Gonda Redlich and Oskar Rosenfeld, from Prague; Dawid Sierakowiak, Josef Zelkowicz, the other "chroniclers," and at least three anonymous young diarists, from Lodz; Elisheva (Elsa Binder) and her unknown "guest diarist" from Stanisławów; Adam Czerniaków, Emanuel Ringelblum, Shimon Huberband, Chaim Kaplan, Abraham Lewin, and

Janusz Korczak, from Warsaw; Calel Perechodnik, from Ottwock; Dawid Rubinowicz, from Kielce; Aryeh and Malwina Klonicki, from Kovel and Buczacz; Herman Kruk, Itzhok Rudashevski, and Zelig Kalmanovitch, from Vilna; and the diarist of the Auschwitz *Sonderkommando*, Zalman Gradowski. Many more diarists, of course, were murdered, and another handful remained alive.[207]

From among the few hundreds of thousands of Jews who had stayed in occupied Europe and survived, most struck roots in new surroundings, either by necessity or by choice; they built their lives, resolutely hid their scars, and experienced the common share of joys and sorrows dealt by everyday existence. For several decades, many evoked the past mainly among themselves, behind closed doors, so to speak; some became occasional witnesses, others opted for silence. Yet, whatever the path they chose, for all of them those years remained the most significant period of their lives. They were entrapped in it: Recurrently, it pulled them back into overwhelming terror and, throughout, notwithstanding the passage of time, it carried along with it the indelible memory of the dead.

Notes

Introduction

1. This photograph is reproduced on the cover of "Photography and the Holocaust," ed. Sybil Milton and Genya Markon, special issue, *History of Photography* 23, no. 4 (Winter 1999). All details about the individuals depicted are from the caption of the photograph.

2. Ibid.

3. For some reviews (particularly the devastating assessment of Zygmunt Bauman, *Modernity and the Holocaust* (Cambridge, 1989), see Yehuda Bauer, *Rethinking the Holocaust* (New Haven, 2001), particularly pp. 70ff.

4. For one of the best examples of this approach see the essays collected in Ulrich Herbert, *National Socialist Extermination Policies: Contemporary German Perspectives and Controversies* (New York, 2000).

5. Regarding this approach see in particular Götz Aly, Belinda Cooper, and Allison Brown, *"Final Solution": Nazi Population Policy and the Murder of the European Jews* (London and New York, 1999); Götz Aly, *Hitlers Volksstaat* (Munich, 2005).

6. See Saul Friedländer, *Nazi Germany and the Jews, Volume 1: The Years of Persecution, 1933–1939* (New York, 1997).

7. Daniel Jonah Goldhagen, *Hitler's Willing Executioners: Ordinary Germans and the Holocaust* (New York, 1996).

8. Christopher R. Browning, *Ordinary Men: Reserve Police Battalion 101 and the Final Solution in Poland* (New York, 1992).

9. Quoted in Ute Deichmann, *Biologen unter Hitler: Porträt einer Wissenschaft im NS-Staat* (Frankfurt am Main, 1995), p. 372.

10. For a very thorough analysis of the Jewish historiography of the Holocaust, see Dan Michman, *Holocaust Historiography: A Jewish Perspective* (London and Portland, OR, 2003).

11. Hannah Arendt, *Eichmann in Jerusalem: A Report on the Banality of Evil* (New York, 1963).

12. I do not share Raul Hilberg's skepticism about diaries as valid sources for our understanding of the events. See Raul Hilberg, *Sources of Holocaust Research: An Analysis* (Chicago, 2001), mainly pp. 141–42, 155–59, and 161–62. The problems with some of the diaries are easily recognizable when the case arises.

13. Walter Laqueur, "Three Witnesses: The Legacy of Viktor Klemperer, Willy Cohn and Richard Koch," *Holocaust and Genocide Studies* 10, no. 3 (1996), p. 266.

14. For a very close position, see Tom Laqueur, "The Sound of Voices Intoning Names," *London Review of Books* (1997), pp. 3ff.

Chapter 1: September 1939–May 1940

1. Victor Klemperer, *I Will Bear Witness: A Diary of the Nazi Years, 1933–41* (New York, 1998), p. 306.

2. Ibid.

3. Chaim Aron Kaplan, *Scroll of Agony: The Warsaw Diary of Chaim A. Kaplan*, ed. Abraham I. Katsh (Bloomington, 1999), p. 19.

4. Ibid., p. 20.

5. Dawid Sierakowiak, *The Diary of David Sierakowiak*, ed. Alan Adelson (New York, 1996), p. 36.

6. Adam Czerniaków, *The Warsaw Diary of Adam Czerniaków*, ed. Raul Hilberg, Stanislaw Staron, and Josef Kermisz (New York, 1979), p. 74.

7. Ibid., p. 76.

8. Sierakowiak, *Diary*, p. 93. For details on Sierakowiak's background, see Adelson's "Introduction" to the *Diary*.

9. There were some Jewish members of several European fascist parties—of course not in the Nazi Party—but it seems that in Italy at least one-fifth of the native population of 47,000 Jews was at one stage or another affiliated with Mussolini's party.

10. Peter Gay, *Freud: A Life for Our Time* (New York, 1989), pp. 646–47.

11. For an excellent overview of the political scene, see Ezra Mendelsohn, *The Jews of East Central Europe Between the World Wars* (Bloomington, 1983).

12. Ibid., p. 255.

13. For this analysis see, among many publications, Shmuel Ettinger, "Jews and Non-Jews in Eastern and Central Europe between the World Wars: An Outline," in *Jews and Non-Jews in Eastern Europe, 1918–1945*, ed. Bela Vago and George L. Mosse (New York, 1974), pp. 1ff.

14. William W. Hagen, "Before the 'Final Solution': Toward a Comparative Analysis of Political Anti-Semitism in Interwar Germany and Poland," *Journal of Modern History* 68, no. 2, (1996), pp. 351ff.

15. For the idealizing trend see Steven E. Aschheim, *Brothers and Strangers: The East European Jew in German and German Jewish Consciousness, 1800–1923* (Madison, 1982).

16. For the fate of German Jewry see Friedländer, *Nazi Germany and the Jews, Volume 1*.

17. Primo Levi, *Survival in Auschwitz: The Nazi Assault on Humanity* (New York, 1958; reprint, 1996), p. 13.

18. Hannah Arendt, *The Jew as Pariah: Jewish Identity and Politics in the Modern Age*, ed. Ron H. Feldman (New York, 1978), p. 84.

19. Norman Rose, *Chaim Weizmann: A Biography* (New York, 1986), p. 354.

20. Alfred Rosenberg, *Das politische Tagebuch Alfred Rosenbergs, 1934/35 und 1939/40*, ed. Hans Günther Seraphim (Munich, 1964), p. 81. (For the translation see Jeremy Noakes and Geoffrey Pridham, eds., *Nazism, 1919–1945: A Documentary Reader*, vol. 3, *Foreign Policy, War and Racial Extermination* (Exeter, UK: 1997), p. 319.

21. For an analysis of Stalin's policy at this point see Gabriel Gorodetsky, *Grand Delusion: Stalin and the German Invasion of Russia* (New Haven, 1999), pp. 5ff.

22. Adolf Hitler, *Hitler: Reden und Proklamationen, 1932–1945: Kommentiert von einem deutschen Zeitgenossen*, ed. Max Domarus, vol. 2, part 1 (Munich, 1965), pp. 1377ff, particularly 1391.

23. First called Reichsgau Posen, the area became the Warthegau in January 1940. The region of Lodz, inhabited by some 500,000 Poles and 300,000 Jews, was annexed to the Reichsgau Posen in November 1939, on the assumption that the Poles and the Jews would be transferred to the General Government and that ethnic Germans would occupy the vacated urban area. Cf. Götz Aly, *Endlösung: Völkerverschiebung und der Mord an den europäischen Juden* (Frankfurt am Main, 1995), p. 59.

24. See mainly Franz Halder, *Kriegstagebuch: Tägliche Aufzeichnungen des Chefs des Generalstabes des Heeres, 1939–1942*, ed. Hans Adolf Jacobsen (Stuttgart, 1962–64) vol. 1, p. 107.

25. For an excellent presentation of the *Volkstumskampf* as applied to Poland, see Alexander B. Rossino, *Hitler Strikes Poland: Blitzkrieg, Ideology and Atrocity* (Lawrence, KS, 2003), pp. 1ff.

26. For the preparation of the operation see ibid., pp. 14ff.

27. For the various significations of this code name see Richard Breitman, *The Architect of Genocide: Himmler and the Final Solution* (New York, 1991), p. 68.

28. For Heydrich's letter to Daluege, see Helmut Krausnick, "Hitler und die Morde in Polen," *Vierteljahrshefte für Zeitgeschichte* 11 (1963), pp. 206–9.

29. Martin Broszat, *Nationalsozialistische Polenpolitik 1939–1945* (Frankfurt am Main and Hamburg, 1965), p. 20.

30. Kurt Pätzold, ed., *Verfolgung, Vertreibung, Vernichtung: Dokumente des faschistischen Antisemitismus 1933 bis 1942* (Frankfurt am Main, 1984), p. 234.

31. Ibid., p. 239.

32. Broszat, *Nationalsozialistische Polenpolitik*, p. 42. The double Dr. indicates, according to German academic custom, that Rasch had more than one doctoral degree (he had doctorates in law and in political science).

33. Michael Burleigh, *Germany Turns Eastwards: A Study of Ostforschung in the Third Reich* (Cambridge, UK, 1988). For a more detailed discussion of the German terror measures in Krakow see Czeslaw Madajczyk, *Die Deutsche Besatzungspolitik in Polen (1939–45)* (Wiesbaden, 1967), pp. 13ff. According to Bogdan Musial, the number of victims was 39,500 Poles and 7,000 Jews; see Bogdan Musial, "Das Schlachtfeld zweier totalitären Systems. Polen unter deutscher und sowjetischer Herrschaft 1939–1941," in *Genesis des Genozids: Polen 1939–1941*, ed. Klaus-Michael Mallmann and Bogdan Musial (Darmstadt, 2004), pp. 13ff, particularly 15. Although I disagree with many of Musial's interpretations and with those of some contributors to this volume, the factual details contained in several of the essays are useful.

34. Aly estimates the number of these victims at 10,000 to 15,000. Götz Aly, "Judenumsiedlung," in *Nationalsozialistische Vernichtungspolitik, 1939–1945: Neue Forschungen und Kontroversen*, ed. Ulrich Herbert (Frankfurt am Main, 1998), p. 85.

35. Aly, "Judenumsiedlung," pp. 85–87.

36. Michael Burleigh, *Death and Deliverance: "Euthanasia" in Germany c. 1900–1945* (Cambridge, 1994), pp. 131–32. See also an excerpt of the verdict against Kurt Eimann in Ernst Klee, ed., *Dokumente zur Euthanasie.* (Frankfurt: 1985).

37. Klee, ed., *Dokumente zur Euthanasie.* p. 112.

38. Ibid. pp. 117ff.

39. Henry Friedlander, *Der Weg zum NS-Genozid: Von der Euthanasie zur Endlösung* (Berlin, 1997), pp. 431ff.

40. See Ernst Klee, *"Euthanasie" im NS-Staat: Die "Vernichtung lebensunwerten Lebens"* (Frankfurt am Main, 1983), pp. 260ff; see also Leni Yahil, *The Holocaust: The Fate of European Jewry, 1932–1945* (New York, 1990), p. 310.

41. Otto Dietrich, *Auf den Strassen des Sieges: Erlebnisse mit dem Führer in Polen: Ein Gemeinschaftsbuch* (Munich, 1939), quoted in Breitman, *The Architect of Genocide*, p. 73.

42. Joseph Goebbels, *Die Tagebücher von Joseph Goebbels*, ed. Elke Fröhlich, part 1, vol. 7, (Munich, 1998), p. 141.

43. Ibid., p. 180.

44. Ibid., p. 186.

45. Ibid., p. 250.

46. Hitler, *Reden*, vol. 2, part 1, p. 1340.

47. Ibid., p. 1342.

48. Ibid.

49. Ibid., vol. 3, pp. 1442 and 1443.

50. Ibid., pp. 1465 and 1468.

51. Joseph Goebbels, *Die Tagebücher von Joseph Goebbels: Sämtliche Fragmente*, ed. Elke Fröhlich, part 1, vol. 7, (Munich, 1987), p. 180.

52. Felix Moeller, *Der Filmminister: Goebbels und der Film im Dritten Reich* (Berlin, 1998), p. 240.

53. For indications about the early films and the "coincidence" between the choice of the latter topics with that of the prior ones see Susan Tegel, "The Politics of Censorship: Britain's 'Jew Süss', (1934) in London, New York and Vienna," *Historical Journal of Film, Radio and Television* 15, no. 2 (1995), pp. 219ff.

54. Ibid., p. 221ff.

55. Ibid., p. 230ff.

56. Ibid., p. 227.

57. Goebbels, *Tagebücher* part 1, vol. 7, p. 140. Also Moeller, *Der Filmminister*, p. 239.

58. For the connection between both films see Evelyn Hampicke and Hanno Loewy, "Juden ohne Maske: Vorlüfige Bemerkungen zur Geschichte eines Kompilationsfilms," in *"Beseitigung des jüdischen Einflusses—": Antisemitische Forschung, Eliten und Karrieren im Nationalsozialismus*, ed. Fritz Bauer Institut, *Jahrbuch 1998/99 zur Geschichte und Wirkung des Holocaust* (Frankfurt, 1999), pp. 259–60.

59. Goebbels, *Tagebücher,* part 1, vol. 7, p. 140.

60. For a summary of the literature about *Der Ewige Jude* and the main aspects of its production and distribution, see Yizhak Ahren, Stig Hornshøj-Møller, and Christoph B. Melchers, *Der ewige Jude: Wie Goebbels hetzte: Untersuchungen zum nationalsozialistischen Propagandafilm* (Aachen, 1990).

61. Goebbels, *Tagebücher*, part 1, vol. 7, p. 157.

62. Ibid.

63. Ibid., p. 166.

64. Ibid., p. 172.

65. Ibid., p. 177.

66. Ibid., p. 202.

67. Shimon *Huberband*, "The Destruction of the Synagogues in Lodz," in *Lodz Ghetto: Inside a Community under Siege*, ed. Alan Adelson and Robert Lapides (New York, 1983), p. 70.

68. Ibid.

69. Ibid., 70–71.

70. Daniel Uziel, "Wehrmacht Propaganda Troops and the Jews," *Yad Vashem Studies* 29 (2001), p. 33.

71. Ibid., p. 34.

72. *Trials of War Criminals Before the Nuremberg Military Tribunals*, vol. 13, *U.S. v. von Weizsäcker: The Ministries Case*, (Washington, DC: US GPO., 1952), Nuremberg doc. NG-4699, p. 143. (When quoting original translations from documents presented at the Nuremberg trials, I mostly kept the text as is, despite the poor quality of some of the translations.)

73. Quoted in Josef Wulf, ed., *Presse und Funk im Dritten Reich: Eine Dokumentation*, vol. 5, *Kunst und Kultur im Dritten Reich* (Gütersloh, 1964), p. 102.

74. Quoted in Ronald M. Smelser, *Robert Ley: Hitler's Labor Front Leader* (Oxford and New York, 1988), p. 261.

75. Goebbels, *Tagebücher*, part 1, vol. 7, p. 337.

76. Eberhard Röhm and Jörg Thierfelder, *Juden, Christen, Deutsche, 1933–1945* vol. 3, part 2 (Stuttgart, 1990—), p. 67.

77. David Vital, *A People Apart: A Political History of the Jews in Europe, 1789–1939* (Oxford, 2001), p. 776.

78. Ibid., pp. 776–77.

79. Mendelsohn, *The Jews*, p. 74.

80. One of the most significant indicators of the cultural autonomy of the Jews of Poland can be found in educational statistics. At the primary-school level, a vast number of Jewish children still attended the traditional religious *heder*. Moreover, almost 20 percent of Jewish pupils at that level went to either Yiddish or Hebrew schools; about 50 percent of all Jewish pupils at the secondary-school level went to either Yiddish or Hebrew schools, and so did around 60 percent of the pupils in the vocational schools. For these statistics see Salo Baron's testimony at the Eichmann trial in Jerusalem in 1961. Cf. Adolf Eichmann, *The Trial of Adolf Eichmann: Record of Proceedings in the District Court of Jerusalem*, vol. 1 (Jerusalem, 1992–) pp. 176ff.

81. The contrary interpretations of Polish anti-Semitism before and during the Holocaust on the one hand and of Jewish anti-Polish attitudes on the other by Jewish and Polish historians respectively have not lost their pugnacity with the passage of time. On the overall issue see, among others, Michael R. Marries, *The Holocaust in History* (New York, 1987), pp. 96ff. On a typically mythical rendition of Jewish attitudes see David Engel, "Lwów, 1918: The Transmutation of a Symbol and its Legacy in the Holocaust," in *Contested Memories: Poles and Jews during the Holocaust and Its Aftermath*, ed. Joshua D. Zimmerman (New Brunswick, 2003), pp. 32ff.

82. Anna Landau-Czajka, "The Jewish Question in Poland: Views Expressed in the Catholic Press between the Two World Wars," *Polin: Studies in Polish Jewry* 11 (1998), p. 263.

83. Ibid., p. 265.

84. Quoted in Brian Porter, "Making a Space for Antisemitism: The Catholic Hierarchy and the Jews in the Early Twentieth Century," *Polin: Studies in Polish Jewry* 16 (2003), p. 420. For Hlond's pastoral letter and other such texts, see also Viktoria Pollmann, *Untermieter im Christlichen Haus: Die Kirche und die "jüdische Frage" anhand der Bistumspredigte der Metropolie Krakau 1926–1935* (Wiesbaden, 2001).

85. Porter, "Making a Space for Antisemitism," p. 420.

86. See in particular Yisrael Gutman, "Polish Antisemitism Between the Wars: An Overview," in *The Jews of Poland Between Two World Wars*, ed. Yisrael Gutman et al. (Hanover, NH, 1989), pp. 97ff. See also the somewhat apologetic article by Roman Wapinski, "The Endecja and the Jewish Question," *Polin: Studies in Polish Jewry* 12 (1999), pp. 271ff.

87. See for example the energetic intervention of the Polish government against anti-Semitic rabble-rousing in Lwow, in 1929, in part incited by church authorities and triggered by fictitious Jewish profanation of Catholic rituals. Antony Polonsky, "A Failed Pogrom: The Demonstrations in Lwow, June 1929," in *The Jews of Poland Between Two World Wars*, ed. Yisrael Gutman et al. (Hanover, NH, 1989), pp. 109ff.

88. For a generally much milder view of Polish policies toward its Jewish population and thus a far more positive assessment of the situation of Polish Jewry on the eve of the war, see Norman Davies, *God's Playground: A History of Poland*, vol. 2 (New York, 1984), pp. 259ff and 407ff.

89. Rossino, *Hitler Strikes Poland*, pp. 90ff. See also Mallmann and Musial, *Genesis des Genozids*, and Jochen Böhler, *Auftakt zum Vernichtungskrieg: Die Wehrmacht in Polen 1939* (Frankfurt, 2006).

90. Rossino, *Hitler Strikes Poland*, p. 92.

91. Ibid., p. 99.

92. Ibid., pp. 99–100.

93. Halder, *Kriegstagebuch*, vol. 1, p. 67.

94. Ibid.

95. Quoted in Omer Bartov, *Hitler's Army: Soldiers, Nazis, and War in the Third Reich* (New York, 1991), p. 64.

96. Alexander B. Rossino, "Destructive Impulses: German Soldiers and the Conquest of Poland," *Holocaust and Genocide Studies* 7, no. 3 (1997), p. 356.

97. Walter Manoschek, ed., *"Es gibt nur eines für das Judentum-Vernichtung": Das Judenbild in deutschen Soldatenbriefen 1939–1944.* (Hamburg, 1997), p. 9.

98. Ibid., p. 12.

99. Sierakowiak, *Diary*, p. 54.

100. Zygmunt Klukowski, *Diary from the Years of Occupation, 1939–44*, ed. Andrew Klukowski and Helen Klukowski May (Urbana, IL. 1993), p. 40.

101. Ibid., p. 41.

102. Ibid., p. 42.

103. Sierakowiak, *Diary*, p. 67.

104. Rossino, *Hitler Strikes Poland*, particularly pp. 227ff.

105. For Blaskowitz's memorandum, see Ernst Klee, Willi Dressen, and Volker Riess, eds., *"The Good Old Days": The Holocaust as Seen by Its Perpetrators and Bystanders* (New York: 1991), pp. 4–5.

106. Quoted in Rossino, *Hitler Strikes Poland*, p. 120.

107. Quoted in Pätzold, *Verfolgung*, pp. 236ff.

108. Ibid., p. 239.

109. For the full text of Heydrich's letter see Henry Friedlander and Sybil Milton, eds., *Archives of the Holocaust: An International Collection of Selected Documents.* vol. 11, part 1 (New York, 1992), pp. 132–33.

110. The most encompassing study remains Burleigh, *Germany Turns Eastwards.*

111. For the debate on Rothfels, see Joachim Lerchenmüller, "Die "SD-mässige" Bearbeitung der Geschichtswissenschaft," in *Nachrichtendienst, politische Elite, Mordeinheit: Der Sicherheitsdienst des Reichsführers SS*, ed. Michael Wildt (Hamburg, 2003), pp. 162–63. Two major conferences on Rothfels, one in Berlin and the other in Munich, took place in July 2003. See, among other accounts, Rainer Blasius, "Bis in die Rolle gefärbt: Zwei Tagungen zum EinfluB von Hans Rothfels auf die deutsche Zeitgeschichtsschreibung," *Frankfurter Allgemeine Zeitung*, July 19, 2003. For more comprehensive assessments of Rothfels's intellectual impact, see Jan Eckel, *Hans Rothfels: Eine intellektuelle Biographie im 20.Jahrhundert* (Göttingen, 2005); Johannes Hürter and Hans Woller, *Hans Rothfels und die deutsche Zeitgeschichte* (Munich, 2005).

112. Quoted in Götz Aly and Susanne Heim, *Vordenker der Vernichtung: Auschwitz und die deutschen Pläne für eine neue europäische Ordnung* (Hamburg, 1991), pp. 102–3. See also Ingo Haar, *Historiker im Nationalsozialismus: Deutsche Geschichtswissenschaft und der "Volkstumskampf" im Osten* (Göttingen, 2002); Peter Schöttler, ed., *Geschichtsschreibung als Legitimationswissenschaft 1918–1945* (Frankfurt am Main, 1997); Winfried Schulze and Otto Gerhard Oexle, *Deutsche Historiker im Nationalsozialismus* (Frankfurt am Main, 1999).

113. For Schieder's memorandum, as well as for the suggestions of the "Ostforscher" in the 1930s and after the beginning of the war, see Götz Aly, *Macht-Geist-Wahn: Kontinuitäten deutschen Denkens* (Berlin, 1997), pp. 153ff and particularly pp. 179ff.

114. Burleigh, *Germany Turns Eastwards*, p. 165.

115. Michael Burleigh, "Die Stunde der Experten," in Mechtild Rössler, Sabine Schleiermacher, and Cordula Tollmien, eds., *Der "Generalplan Ost": Hauptlinien der nationalsozialistischen Planungs- und Vernichtungspolitik* (Berlin, 1993), p. 347.

116. Ibid.

117. Ibid., p. 348.

118. Ibid. On the scholars and their ideological commitment, see also Michael Falhlbusch, *Wissenschaft im Dienst nationalsozialistischer Politik: Die "Volksdeutscher Forschungsgemeinschaften" von 1931–1945* (Wiesbaden, 1999).

119. For a thorough study of the "Jewish policies" in East Upper Silesia see Sybille Steinbacher, "In the Shadow of Auschwitz: The Murder of the Jews of East Upper Silesia," in *The Holocaust*, ed. David Cesarani (New York, 2004), vol. 2, pp. 110ff. See also Sybille Steinbacher, *"Musterstadt" Auschwitz: Germanisierungspolitik und Judenmord in Ostoberschlesien* (Munich, 2000) p. 138ff.

120. See mainly Gerhard Botz, *Wohnungspolitik und Judendeportation in Wien 1938 bis 1945: Zur Funktion des Antisemitismus als Ersatz nationalsozialistischer Sozialpolitik* (Vienna, 1975), p. 105. On this operation as such see Seev Goshen, "Eichmann und die Nisko-Aktion im Oktober 1939. Eine Fallstudie zur NS-Judenpolitik in der letzten Epoche vor der 'Endlösung.' " *Vierteljahrshefte fur Zeitgeschichte* 29 (1981); see also Seev Goshen, "Nisko- Ein Ausnahmefall unter der Judenlagern der SS," *Vierteljahrshefte für Zeitgeschichte* 40 (1992); Hans Safrian, *Die Eichmann-Männer* (Vienna, 1992), pp. 76, 78ff.

121. Safrian, *Die Eichmann-Männer*, pp. 76, 78ff.

122. Quoted in Dieter Pohl, *Von der "Judenpolitik" zum Judenmord: Der Distrikt Lublin des Generalgouvernements, 1939–1944* (Frankfurt am Main, 1993), p. 52.

123. Quoted in Tatiana Berenstein, ed., *Faschismus, Getto, Massenmord: Dokumentation über Ausrottung und Widerstand der Juden in Polen während des zweiten Weltkrieges.* (East Berlin, 1961), p. 46.

124. Raul Hilberg, *The Destruction of the European Jews*, vol. 1 (New Haven 2003), p. 208.

125. Hans Frank, *Das Diensttagebuch des deutschen Generalgouverneurs in Polen 1939–1945*, ed. Werner Präg and Wolfgang Jacobmeyer (Stuttgart, 1975), p. 165.

126. On the wrangling surrounding the expulsions from Kraków, see Christopher R. Browning and Jürgen Matthäus, *The Origins of the Final Solution: The Evolution of Nazi Jewish policy, September 1939–March 1942* (Lincoln, Neb., 2004), pp. 131ff.

127. Ibid., pp. 135ff. In Radom and Lublin, the needs for billeting of Wehrmacht units in early 1941, in preparation for the attack against the Soviet Union, added pressure to the expulsion and ghettoization processes. See ibid.

128. For this evolution, with particular emphasis on Lublin, see Pohl, *Judenpolitik*, pp. 33ff.

129. For the *Selbstschutz*, see mainly Peter R. Black, "Rehearsal for 'Reinhard'? Odilo Globocnik and the Lublin *Selbstschutz*," *Central European History* 25, no. 2 (1992) pp. 204ff; see also Christian Jansen and Arno Weckbecker, *Der "Volksdeutsche Selbstschutz" in Polen, 1939/40* (Munich, 1992).

130. Czerniaków, *Warsaw Diary*, p. 96.

131. Berenstein, ed., *Faschismus, Getto, Massenmord*, pp. 55 and 55n.

132. Aly, "Judenumsiedlung," pp. 79–80.

133. For the specific German measures in Lodz, see in particular Florian Freund, Bertrand Perz, and Karl Stuhlpfarrer, "Das Ghetto in Litzmannstadt (Lodz)," in *Unser einziger Weg ist Arbeit [Unzer eyntsiger veg iz arbayt]*, ed. Hanno Loewy and Gerhard Schoenberner (Vienna, 1990), p. 22.

134. Helma Kaden et al., eds., *Dokumente des Verbrechens: Aus Akten des Dritten Reiches, 1933–1945*, vol. 1 (Berlin, 1993), pp. 176–77.

135. Quoted in Aly and Heim, *Vordenker der Vernichtung*, p. 204.

136. See Isaiah Trunk, *Judenrat: The Jewish Councils in Eastern Europe under Nazi Occupation* (New York), pp. 11ff.

137. Aharon Weiss, "Jewish Leadership in Occupied Poland—Postures and Attitudes," *Yad Vashem Studies* 12 (1977), p. 344. The same dual aspect could in fact be noted in the foundation and mainly in the evolution of the representation (then association) of the Jews of Germany (then *in* Germany).

138. Frank, *Diensttagebuch*, pp. 215ff.

139. More generally, tension and rivalry would soon develop throughout the General Government between Frank's administration and the SS apparatus. See Pohl, *Judenpolitik*, pp. 60–62.

140. Trunk, *Judenrat*, pp. 21ff.

141. Weiss, "Jewish Leadership in Occupied Poland—Postures and Attitudes," pp. 355–56.

142. Ibid., p. 353.

143. Czerniaków, *Warsaw Diary*, p. 85.

144. Kaplan, *Scroll of Agony*, p. 57.

145. For these measures, see mainly Bernhard Rosenkötter, *Treuhandpolitik: Die "Haupttreuhandstelle Ost" und der Raub polnischen Vermögens, 1939–1945* (Essen, 2003).

146. The most thorough studies of corruption in Nazi Germany are Frank Bajohr, *"Arisierung" in Hamburg: Die Verdrängung der jüdischen Unternehmer 1933–1945* (Hamburg, 1997), and Frank Bajohr, *Parvenüs und Profiteure: Korruption in der NS-Zeit* (Frankfurt am Main, 2001).

147. Emanuel Ringelblum, *Notes from the Warsaw Ghetto: The Journal of Emmanuel Ringelblum*, ed. Jacob Sloan (New York, 1974), p. 8.

148. Czerniaków, *Warsaw Diary*, pp. 90ff.

149. Trunk, *Judenrat*, p. 244.

150. Joseph Kermish, ed., *To Live with Honor and Die with Honor!: Selected Documents from the Warsaw Ghetto Underground Archives "O.S." ("Oneg Shabbath")*. (Jerusalem, 1986), p. 250.

151. Sierakowiak, *Diary*, p. 69.

152. For most of the details included in this section Antony Polonsky and Norman Davies, eds., *Jews in Eastern Poland and the USSR, 1939–1946* (New York, 1991).

153. Letter of March 12, 1940, from Moshe Kleinbaum to Nahum Goldmann, in

Henry Friedlander and Sybil Milton, eds., *Archives of the Holocaust: An International Collection of Selected Documents*. 22 vols. (New York: Garland, 1989–), vol. 8, 1990, [doc. 34], pp. 112–13.

154. Isaiah Trunk, *Jewish Responses to Nazi Persecution: Collective and Individual Behavior in Extremis* (New York, 1979), p. 44.

155. Kaplan, *Scroll of Agony*, pp. 49–50.

156. Jan T. Gross, "A Tangled Web: Confronting Stereotypes Concerning Relations between Poles, Germans, Jews and Communists," in *The Politics of Retribution*, ed. István Deák, Jan T. Gross, and Tony Judt (Princeton, 2000), pp. 97–98; see also, from a Polish national perspective, Marek Wierzbicki, "Die polnisch-jüdischen Beziehungen unter sowjetischer Herrschaft: Zur Wahrnehmung gesellschaftlicher Realität im Westlichen Weissrussland 1939–1941," in *Genesis des Genozids. Polen 1939–1941*, ed. Klaus-Michael Mallmann and Bogdan Musial (Darmstadt, 2004), pp. 187ff. Wierzbicki repeats the traditional Polish arguments about Jewish disloyalty, and so on.

157. Alexander B. Rossino, "Polish 'Neighbors' and German Invaders: Anti-Jewish Violence in the Bialystok District during the Opening Weeks of Operation Barbarossa," *Polin: Studies in Polish Jewry* 16 (2003), pp. 441–42.

158. Polonsky and Davies, *Jews in Eastern Poland*, p. 28.

159. Frank, *Diensttagebuch*, p. 199:

160. Polonsky and Davies, *Jews in Eastern Poland*, p. 28.

161. Robert C. Tucker, *Stalin in Power: The Revolution from Above, 1928–1941* (New York, 1992), pp. 606–07.

162. The Karski report of February 1940 was first published in David Engel, "An Early Account of Polish Jewry under Nazi and Soviet Occupation Presented to the Polish Government-in-Exile, February 1940," *Jewish Social Studies* 45 (1983), pp. 1–16.

163. Ibid., p. 12.

164. Ibid., pp. 12–13. Karski's comments on the German use of anti-Semitism as a way of gaining support among the Polish population were also confirmed by reports reaching the Foreign Office in London throughout 1940. See Bernard Wasserstein, "Polish Influences on British Policy Regarding Jewish Rescue Efforts in Poland 1939–1945," *Polin: Studies in Polish Jewry* 11 (1998), particularly p. 189.

165. Engel, "Early Account," p. 11.

166. Gross, "A Tangled Web," pp. 103–4.

167. For the attitude of the Polish government-in-exile and Knoll's threats, see David Engel, *In the Shadow of Auschwitz: The Polish Government-in-Exile and the Jews, 1939–1942* (Chapel Hill, NC, 1987), pp. 62ff., particularly 64–65.

168. At the beginning of the war the Jewish population of the "Old Reich" included approximately 190,000 "full Jews"; according to the census of May 1939 there were also 46,928 "half-Jews" and 32,669 "quarter-Jews" living in Germany. Cf. Ino Arndt and Heinz Boberach, "Deutsches Reich," in *Dimension des Völkermords: Die Zahl der jüdischen Opfer des Nationalsozialismus*, ed. Wolfgang Benz, vol. 33, *Quellen und Darstellungen zur Zeitgeschichte* (Munich, 1991), p. 34. In annexed Austria, the "full Jewish" population at the beginning of the war was 66,260 persons (belonging to the Jewish

community) and 8,359 (not belonging to the community). Cf. Jonny Moser in Wolfgang Benz, ed., *Dimension des Völkermords: Die Zahl der jüdischen Opfer des Nationalsozialismus.* (Munich, 1991), p. 69 n. 13.

169. Joseph Walk, ed., *Das Sonderrecht für die Juden im NS-Staat: Eine Sammlung der gesetzlichen Massnahmen und Richtlinien, Inhalt und Bedeutung.* (Heidelberg, 1981), p. 303.

170. Ibid., p. 305.

171. Marion A. Kaplan, *Between Dignity and Despair: Jewish Life in Nazi Germany* (New York, 1998), p. 146.

172. Walk, *Das Sonderrecht*, p. 304.

173. Otto Dov Kulka and Eberhard Jäckel, *Die Juden in den geheimen NS-Stimmungsberichten 1933–1945* (Düsseldorf, 2004), p. 408.

174. Ibid. The shopping time for Jews changed from place to place but was usually limited to a maximum of two hours.

175. Pätzold, *Verfolgung*, p. 235.

176. Walk, *Das Sonderrecht*, p. 306.

177. Ibid., p. 308.

178. Ibid., p. 310.

179. For the issues raised by the initial order see Paul Sauer, ed., *Dokumente über die Verfolgung der jüdischen Bürger in Baden-Württemberg durch das nationalsozialistische Regime 1933–1945*, vol. 2 (Stuttgart, 1966), pp. 179ff.

180. Ibid., p. 181.

181. Ibid., p. 184.

182. Walk, *Das Sonderrecht*, p. 309.

183. Ibid., p. 312.

184. Ibid., p. 314.

185. Pätzold, *Verfolgung*, p. 250.

186. Walk, *Das Sonderrecht*, p. 307.

187. Heinz Boberach, ed., *Meldungen aus dem Reich, 1938–1945: Die geheimen Lageberichte des Sicherheitsdienstes der SS*, vol. 4 (Herrsching, 1984), p. 979.

188. Walk, *Das Sonderrecht*, p. 318.

189. For Kirk's cable of February 28, 1940, see John Mendelsohn and Donald S. Detwiler, eds., *The Holocaust: Selected Documents in Eighteen Volumes* (New York: Garland Publishing, 1982), pp. 120ff.

190. For some of these phantasmal representations, see Patricia Szobar, "Telling Sexual Stories in the Nazi Courts of Law: Race Defilement in Germany, 1933–1945," *Journal of the History of Sexuality* 11, nos. 1–2 (2002), pp. 131–63.

191. Jochen Klepper, *Unter dem Schatten Deiner Flügel: Aus den Tagebüchern der Jahre 1932–1942*, ed. Hildegard Klepper (Stuttgart, 1956), p. 822.

192. Bryan Mark Rigg, *Hitler's Jewish Soldiers: The Untold Story of Nazi Racial Laws and Men of Jewish Descent in the German Military* (Lawrence, 2002), pp. 113–14.

193. Helmut Heiber, *Reichsführer! Briefe an und von Himmler* (Munich, 1970), p. 75.

194. Ibid., p. 76.

195. *Akten der Parteikanzlei der NSDAP*, vol. 2, part 3, abstract No. 33179.

196. Ringelblum, *Notes*, p. 181.

197. Kulka and Jäckel, *Die Juden in den geheimen NS-Stimmungsberichten 1933–1945*, p. 412.

198. Ibid., pp. 407–08.

199. Ibid., p. 411.

200. Boberach, *Meldungen*, vol. 3, p. 541.

201. Kulka and Jäckel, *Die Juden in den geheimen NS-Stimmungsberichten 1933–1945*, p. 427.

202. Boberach, *Meldungen*. Vol. 4, pp. 1317ff.

203. John Connelly, "The Use of Volksgemeinschaft: Letters to the NSDAP Kreisleitung Eisenach 1939–1940," *Journal of Modern History* 68, no. 4 (1996): pp. 924–25.

204. Klemperer, *I Will Bear Witness*, vol. 1, p. 335.

205. Sauer, *Dokumente über die Verfolgung*, vol. 2, p. 186.

206. See in particular the diary and documents in Helmuth Groscurth, *Tagebücher eines Abwehroffiziers 1938–1940: Mit weiteren Dokumenten zur Militäropposition gegen Hitler*, ed. Helmut Krausnick and Harold C. Deutsch (Stuttgart, 1970).

207. Ulrich von Hassell, *Die Hassell-Tagebücher 1938–1944: Aufzeichnungen vom Andern Deutschland*, ed. Klaus Peter Reiss (unter Mitarbeit) and Freiherr Friedrich Hiller von Gaertringen (Berlin, 1988), p. 167.

208. Ibid., p. 168.

209. Joachim C. Fest, *Plotting Hitler's Death: The Story of the German Resistance* (New York, 1996), p. 150.

210. On this issue see Hans Mommsen, "Der Widerstand gegen Hitler und die nationalsozialistische Judenverfolgung," in *Alternative zu Hitler: Studien zur Geschichte des deutschen Widerstandes* (Munich, 2000), pp. 388ff.

211. About the percentage of church members, see John S. Conway, *The Nazi Persecution of the Churches, 1933–45* (New York, 1968), p. 232. Two-thirds of all baptized members of Christian churches in Germany were Protestants, and one third were Catholics. These numbers are mentioned in Doris L. Bergen, "Catholics, Protestants, and Christian Antisemitism in Nazi Germany," in David Cesarani, ed., *Holocaust: Critical Concepts in Historical Studies*. 6 vols. (New York: Routledge, 2004), vol. 1, p. 342.

212. On the "German Christians," see in particular Doris L. Bergen, *Twisted Cross: The German Christian Movement in the Third Reich* (Chapel Hill, N.C., 1996).

213. For these attitudes see in particular *infra*, chapter V, of this book.

214. For this text, see Röhm and Thierfelder, *Juden*, vol. 3, part 2 (1938–1941), pp. 27–28.

215. For this text see Susannah Heschel, *Transforming Jesus from Jew to Aryan: Protestant Theologians in Nazi Germany* (Tucson, 1995), p. 4.

216. Susannah Heschel, "Deutsche Theologen für Hitler. Walter Grundmann und das Eisenacher Institut zur Erforschung und Beseitigung des Jüdischen Einflusses auf das deutsche kirchliche Leben," in *"Beseitigung des jüdischen Einflusses—": Antisemitische*

Forschung, Eliten und Karrieren im Nationalsozialismus, ed. Fritz Bauer Institut, *Jahrbuch 1998/99 zur Geschichte und Wirkung des Holocaust* (Frankfurt am Main, 1999), p. 151.

217. Ibid., p. 153.

218. Quoted in Röhm and Thierfelder, *Juden*, vol. 3, part 2, p. 106.

219. Heinz Boberach, ed., *Berichte des SD und der Gestapo über Kirchen und Kirchenvolk in Deutschland 1934–1944.* (Mainz, 1971), p. 365.

220. Ibid., p. 376.

221. Ibid., p. 406.

222. For manifestations of this traditional Catholic anti-Semitism during the thirties see Friedländer, *Nazi Germany and the Jews,* vol. 1, pp. 42–60.

223. For details on this controversy see Guenter Lewy, *The Catholic Church and Nazi Germany* (New York, 1964), pp. 278–79.

224. Lewy, *The Catholic Church and Nazi Germany*, p. 283. The Paulus Bund was essentially open to Jewish converts who were in line with the "new Germany" (ibid.); it later allowed the SD to find at least one notorious informant among its members. See Wolfgang Benz, *Patriot und Paria: Das Leben des Erwin Goldmann zwischen Judentum und Nationalsozialismus: eine Dokumentation* (Berlin, 1997).

225. Ibid.

226. For the relations between Bertram and Preysing, see Klaus Schölder, *A Requiem for Hitler: And Other New Perspectives on the German Church Struggle* (London, 1989), pp. 157ff.

227. For the transition from Reichsvertretung to Reichsvereinigung see Otto Dov Kulka, "The Reichsvereinigung and the Fate of German Jews, 1938/9–1943," in Arnold Paucker, ed., *Die Juden im Nationalsozialistichen Deutschland* (Tübingen, 1986), pp. 353ff.

228. See Friedländer, *Nazi Germany and the Jews,* vol. 1, p. 284.

229. For the relations between the Reichsvereinigung and the Berlin community see, among others, Beate Meyer, "Gratwanderung zwischen Verantwortung und Verstrickung—Die Reichsvereinigung der Juden in Deutschland und die jüdische Gemeinde zu Berlin 1938–1945," in Beate Meyer and Hermann Simon, eds *Juden in Berlin, 1938–1945* (Berlin, 2000), pp. 291ff.

230. Wolf Gruner, "Public Welfare and the German Jews under National Socialism," in *Probing the Depths of German Antisemitism: German Society and the Persecution of the Jews, 1933–1941*, ed. David Bankier (New York, 2000), pp. 78ff.

231. On these issues see Wolf Gruner, "Poverty and Persecution: The Reichsvereinigung, the Jewish Population, and Anti-Jewish Policy in the Nazi State, 1939–1945," *Yad Vashem Studies* 27 (1999), pp. 23ff.

232. Salomon Adler-Rudel, *Jüdische Selbsthilfe unter dem Naziregime 1933–1939, im Spiegel der Berichte der Reichsvertretung der Juden in Deutschland* (Tübingen, 1974), pp. 31–33.

233. Yfaat Weiss, "The 'Emigration Effort' or 'Repatriation,'" in *Probing the Depths of German Antisemitism: German Society and the Persecution of the Jews, 1933–1941*, ed. David Bankier (New York, 2000), pp. 367–68; See also Arnold Paucker and Konrad Kwiet, "Jewish Leadership and Jewish Resistance," in *Probing the Depths of German*

Antisemitism: German Society and the Persecution of the Jews, 1933–1941, ed. David Bankier (New York, 2000), p. 379.

234. Paucker and Kwiet, "Jewish Leadership and Jewish Resistance," p. 379.

235. Klemperer, *I Will Bear Witness*, p. 321.

236. See mainly Raul Hilberg and Stanislaw Staron, introduction to Czerniaków, *Warsaw Diary*, pp. 29–30.

237. Ibid., p. 27.

238. Ibid., p. 144.

239. Ibid., p. 152.

240. Apolinary Hartglas, "How Did Czerniaków Become Head of the Warsaw Judenrat?" *Yad Vashem Bulletin* 15 (1964), pp. 4–7.

241. Philip Friedman, *Roads to Extinction: Essays on the Holocaust*, ed. Ada June Friedman (New York, 1980), p. 336.

242. Czerniaków, *Warsaw Diary*, p. 191.

243. Ringelblum, *Notes*, pp. 47–48.

244. For Szulman's diary and his remarks on Rumkowski, see Robert Moses Shapiro, "Diaries and Memoirs from the Lodz Ghetto in Yiddish and Hebrew," in *Holocaust Chronicles: Individualizing the Holocaust through Diaries and Other Contemporaneous Personal Accounts*, ed. Robert Moses Shapiro (Hoboken, NJ, 1999), pp. 195ff.

245. Israel Gutman, "Debate," in *Patterns of Jewish Leadership in Nazi Europe, 1933–1945*, ed. Cynthia J. Haft and Yisrael Gutman (Jerusalem, 1979), p. 186.

246. About Kaplan's life, see Abraham I. Katsh's introduction to Kaplan's *Diary*, pp. 9–17.

247. The details of Ringelblum's life are taken from Jacob Sloan's introduction to Ringelblum's *Notes* and from a recent analysis: Samuel David Kassow, "Vilna and Warsaw, Two Ghetto Diaries: Herman Kruk and Emanuel Ringelblum," in *Holocaust Chronicles: Individualizing the Holocaust through Diaries and Other Contemporaneous Personal Accounts*, ed. Robert Moses Shapiro (Hoboken, 1999), pp. 171ff.

Chapter 2: May 1940–December 1940

1. Otto Dov Kulka and Eberhard Jäckel, *Die Juden in den geheimen NS-Stimmungsberichten 1933–1945* (Düsseldorf, 2004), p. 439.

2. Paul Sauer, ed., *Dokumente über die Verfolgung der jüdischen Bürger in Baden-Württemberg durch das nationalsozialistische Regime 1933–1945*, vol. 2, (Stuttgart, 1966), p. 240.

3. Ibid., p. 257.

4. Goldman's letter is reproduced in Abraham J. Peck, ed., *Archives of the Holocaust*, vol. 8 (New York: 1990), pp. 76ff.

5. See most recently Ian Kershaw, *Hitler, 1936–45: Nemesis* (New York, 2000), pp. 294ff. and 296.

6. For this "antimaterialist" dimension see in particular Zeev Sternhell, *La Droite Révolutionnaire 1885–1914: Les Origines françaises du fascisme* (Paris, 1978); Zeev Sternhell, *Neither Right nor Left: Fascist Ideology in France* (Berkeley, 1986).

7. John Lukacs, *The Duel: Hitler vs. Churchill: 10 May–31 July 1940* (Oxford, 1992), pp. 206ff.

8. Ibid.

9. Emmanuel Mounier, "A Letter from France," *The Commonweal*, October 25, 1940, p. 10–11.

10. "Accomodation" was thoroughly described and analyzed in regard to occupied France in Philippe Burrin, *France under the Germans: Collaboration and Compromise* (New York, 1996). See in particular pp. 175ff.

11. For this issue see Georges Passelecq and Bernard Suchecky, *L'Encyclique cachée de Pie XI: Une occasion manquée de l'Église face à l'antisémitisme* (Paris, 1995).

12. I shared this misinterpretation. See Saul Friedländer, *Pius XII and the Third Reich: A Documentation* (New York, 1966).

13. For the most recent publications on the anti-Jewish tradition of the church and the modern papacy, see mainly James Carroll, *Constantine's Sword: The Church and the Jews: A History* (Boston, 2001), and David I. Kertzer, *The Popes Against the Jews: The Vatican's Role in the Rise of Modern Anti-Semitism* (New York, 2001).

14. For Pacelli's personality see in particular John Cornwell, *Hitler's Pope: The Secret History of Pius XII* (New York, 1999).

15. For both documents, uncovered in 2003, see Laurie Goodstein, "New Look at Pius XII's Views of Nazis," *New York Times*, August 31, 2003, p. 17. On the prewar years see Thomas Brechenmacher, "Teufelspakt, Selbsterhaltung, universale Mission? Leitlinien und Spielräume der Diplomatie des Heiligen Stuhls gegenüber dem nationalsozialistischen Deutschland (1933–1939) im Lichte neu zugänglicher vatikanischer Akten," *Historische Zeitschrift* 280, no. 3 (2005), pp. 591ff.

16. See Peter C. Kent, "A Tale of Two Popes: Pius XI, Pius XII and the Rome-Berlin Axis," *Journal of Contemporary History* 23, no. 4 (1988), p. 604.

17. For the decision and its context see Eugen Weber, *Action Française: Royalism and Reaction in Twentieth Century France* (Stanford, 1962), pp. 251–52.

18. Friedländer, *Pius XII*, pp. 10ff.

19. Regarding Pius XII's decision to keep German affairs to himself and for Orsenigo's role, see Michael Phayer, *The Catholic Church and the Holocaust, 1930–1965* (Bloomington, 2000), pp. 44–45.

20. For the Encyclical, see Heinz Boberach, ed., *Berichte des SD und der Gestapo über Kirchen und Kirchenvolk in Deutschland 1934–1944* (Mainz, 1971), p. 382 n. 1; for the Polish demands, see most recently Giovanni Miccoli, *Les Dilemmes et les silences de Pie XII: Vatican, Seconde Guerre Mondiale et Shoah* (Bruxelles, 2005), pp. 52ff.

21. Burkhart Schneider, Pierre Blet, and Angelo Martini, eds., *Die Briefe Pius' XII. an die deutschen Bischöfe 1939–1944* (Mainz, 1966), pp. 104–11.

22. For the full context of this letter see Eberhard Jäckel, "Zur Politik des Heiligen Stuhls im Zweiten Weltkrieg," *Geschichte in Wissenschaft und Unterricht* (Jan. 1964), translated in Friedländer, *Pius XII*, pp. 55–56.

23. Within Himmler's empire the "Main Office for the Security of the Reich" (Reichssicherheitshauptamt, or RSHA), established on September 27, 1939, and placed

under Heydrich's command, created a single institutional framework for the security and police agencies (the SD, the Gestapo, and the criminal police) that had already been coordinated since 1936. Heydrich's (later Kaltenbrunner's) main office became one of the centers of the planning and implementation of the anti-Jewish measures of the regime, within the general policy framework set up by Hitler. New initiatives were often worked out at the RSHA and submitted for Himmler's and ultimately Hitler's approval, although, as we shall see, on many occasions proposals were rejected or sent back for modification, due to political or military constraints. The RSHA delegates, the commanders of the Security Police (*Befelshaber der Sicherheitspolizei*, or *BdS*), operated in each occupied country or area throughout the Continent, and at times their relations with the Wehrmacht or with other Nazi agencies were tense, as a result of their independent initiatives and frequent disregard for the established chain of command. In 1940, the basic structure of the RSHA was finalized. Regarding Jewish matters, two offices were of special importance: Amt (office) IV and Amt V. Amt IV—"Research About and Fighting Against Enemies"—was, in fact, the Gestapo, under the command of Heinrich Müller. Subsection IVB4, the Jewish *Referat* or "desk," under Eichmann's authority, became the hub of the administrative and logistic organization of the anti-Jewish policies decided by the higher echelons. Eichmann had direct access to Heydrich and often to Himmler as well. Amt V, the criminal police central office, in charge of all measures against "asocials," homosexuals, and the "Gypsies" also developed methods, mainly gas installations, for the murder of the mentally ill, later to be adapted to the extermination of the Jews; it worked in close cooperation with the headquarters of the "euthanasia" operation, often identified as T4 (the address of its headquarters, Tiergarten 4). For a thorough study of the RSHA see Michael Wildt, *Generation des Unbedingten: Das Führungskorps des Reichssicherheitshauptamtes* (Hamburg, 2002). Kurt Daluege's Order Police, also under Himmler's command as chief of the German police, soon became an indispensable auxiliary of the Security Police units, mainly in the East. It was from the ranks of the Security Police that most of the commanders of the *Einsatzgruppen* were chosen.

Notwithstanding its crucial role, the RSHA was only one of the agencies within the SS that fulfilled a major function in the terror system. The higher SS and police leaders (*Höhere SS und Polizeiführer*, or *HSSPF*) were Himmler's personal delegates, East and West. They carried the ultimate responsibility for operations against the Jews and the fight against "partisans" or various resistance movements in their country or area. They represented the goals and interests of the SS in any policy debate with local authorities, the Wehrmacht, or party appointees in the occupied countries. The HSSPF commanded a network of district SS and police leaders (SSPF) and were the commanders of the Order Police units in their area. For a thorough study of the HSSPF, see Ruth Bettina Birn, *Die höheren SS und Polizeiführer: Himmlers Vertreter im Reich und in den besetzten Gebieten* (Düsseldorf, 1986).

The concentration camps had been one of the main SS instruments of terror from the outset of the regime: The first of these camps, Dachau, was established at the very beginning of the regime, in March 1933. The camps became a single system, from

1934 onward under the command of the SS Concentration Camps Inspectorate (The first inspector, SS general Theodor Eicke, was followed by Richard Glücks). The camps grew from seven in the 1930s to hundreds of main and satellite camps, spread all over occupied Europe at the height of the war; some of them were almost as deadly as the extermination camps set up from the end of 1941 on. In early 1942, the Concentration Camps Inspectorate was integrated into Oswald Pohl's SS Main Office for Economic Administration (*Wirtschaftsverwaltungs-Hauptamt*, or *WVHA*) in charge of the entire SS economic realm. On the WVHA see Erik Schulte, *Zwangsarbeit und Vernichtung: Das Wirtschaftsimperium Oswald Pohls und das SS-Wirtschafts- und Verwaltungshauptamt* (Paderborn, 2001), and Michael Thad Allen, *The Business of Genocide: SS, Slave Labor and the Concentration Camp* (Chapel Hill, 2002).

New SS organizations such as Himmler's Reich Agency for the Strengthening of Germandom (RKFDV) played a major role after the beginning of the war. The RKFDV ruled over the ethnic reshuffling in Eastern Europe: ingathering, expulsions, deportations. Himmler's chief of staff at the RKFDV was SS Obergruppenführer Ulrich Greifelt and the ongoing contact with the ethnic Germans, their transportation, and resettlement (or their ever longer waiting in transit camps) was more directly in the hands of the *Volksdeutsche Mittelstelle* (VOMI), headed by an old-timer of Nazi propaganda and incitement operations among German communities in foreign countries, SS Gruppenführer Werner Lorenz. Notwithstanding major achievements in the historiography dealing with the SS, one of the best overviews still remains the two-volume study: Hans Buchheim et al., *Anatomie des SS-Staates*, 2 vols. (Olten, 1965).

24. For an assessment of Jewish population statistics in 1940, see the studies in Wolfgang Benz, ed., *Dimension des Völkermords: Die Zahl der jüdischen Opfer des Nationalsozialismus* (Munich, 1991).

25. Mihail Sebastian, *Journal, 1935–1944* (Chicago, 2000), p. 297.

26. For details about Sebastian's life and work see mainly Radu Ioanid, Introduction to Sebastian, *Journal*, pp. viiff.

27. See Adam Czerniaków, *The Warsaw Diary of Adam Czerniaków*, ed. Raul Hilberg, Stanislaw Staron, and Josef Kermisz (New York, 1979), pp. 161ff.

28. Chaim Aron Kaplan, *Scroll of Agony: The Warsaw Diary of Chaim A. Kaplan*, ed. Abraham I. Katsh (Bloomington, 1999), p. 162.

29. Ibid., p. 163.

30. Ibid., p. 164.

31. Ibid., p. 166.

32. Victor Klemperer, *I Will Bear Witness: A Diary of the Nazi Years, 1933–41* (New York, 1998), p. 346.

33. Ibid., p. 349.

34. Ibid.

35. Jochen Klepper, *Unter dem Schatten Deiner Flügel: Aus den Tagebüchern der Jahre 1932–1942*, ed. Hildegard Klepper (Stuttgart, 1956), p. 902.

36. Adolf Hitler, *Hitler: Reden und Proklamationen, 1932–1945: Kommentiert von einem deutschen Zeitgenossen*, ed. Max Domarus, vol. 2, part 1 (Munich, 1965), p. 1541.

37. Ibid., p. 1580.

38. Ibid., p. 1628.

39. *Documents on German Foreign Policy: Series D, 1937–1945*, vol. 9 (Washington, DC, 1956), p. 146. (Hereafter cited as *DGFP: Series D.*)

40. Ibid., vol. 10, (Washington, DC, 1957), p. 316.

41. Tatjana Tönsmeyer, *Das Dritte Reich und die Slowakei 1939–1945: Politischer Alltag zwischen Kooperation und Eigensinn* (Paderborn, 2003), pp. 63 and 137ff.

42. Andreas Hillgruber, *Staatsmänner und Diplomaten bei Hitler: Vertrauliche Aufzeichnungen über Unterredungen mit Vertretern des Auslandes*, vol. 1 (Frankfurt am Main, 1967–70), pp. 187ff.

43. Joseph Goebbels, *Die Tagebücher von Joseph Goebbels*, ed. Elke Fröhlich, vol. 8, part 1 (Munich, 1998), p. 103.

44. Helmut Krausnick, ed., "Einige Gedanken über die Behandlung der Fremdvölkischen im Osten," *Vierteljahrshefte für Zeitgeschichte* 5, no. 2 (1957), pp. 194ff.

45. DGFP, Series D, vol. 10, p. 484.

46. For the exchange of views on this issue between Ribbentrop and Bonnet on December 7, 1938, see Saul Friedländer, *Nazi Germany and the Jews, Volume I: The Years of Persecution, 1933–1939* (New York, 1997), p. 301.

47. Galeazzo Ciano, *Diary 1937–1943: The Complete Unabridged Diaries of Count Galeazzo Ciano, Italian Minister for Foreign Affairs, 1936–1943* (London, 2002), p. 363.

48. *DGFP: Series D*, vol. 11 (Washington, DC, 1960) p. 635.

49. Hans Safrian, *Die Eichmann-Männer* (Vienna, 1992), p. 94.

50. *DGFP: Series D*, vol. 10, p. 113.

51. Ibid., p. 95.

52. Czerniaków, *Warsaw Diary*, p. 169.

53. Hans Frank, *Das Diensttagebuch des deutschen Generalgouverneurs in Polen 1939–1945*, ed. Werner Präg and Wolfgang Jacobmeyer (Stuttgart, 1975), p. 252.

54. Ibid., p. 258.

55. Christopher R. Browning, *The Path to Genocide: Essays on Launching the Final Solution* (Cambridge, 1992), p. 33

56. Safrian, *Die Eichmann-Männer*, p. 94.

57. Greiser opened the discussion by mentioning the new plan [Madagascar], which he welcomed, but as far as his *Gau* was concerned, the Jewish problem had to be solved before the winter. "Obviously this all depended on the duration of the war. If the war were to continue, then one had to find an interim solution" (Frank, *Diensttagebuch*, p. 261). At that point Greiser became more specific: It had been foreseen, he emphasized, that the 250,000 Jews in the Litzmannstadt (Lodz) ghetto would be transported into the General Government. These Jews could not stay in Litzmannstadt throughout the winter due to the lack of food and the danger of epidemics. Frank was adamant: Hitler had promised him that there would be no further deportations into the General Government, and he had "officially" informed Himmler of the Führer's decision (ibid., p. 261).

SS general Friedrich Wilhelm Krüger, Himmler's chief delegate in the General

Government, referred to the Madagascar plan and emphasized that the situation in Litzmannstadt should be given priority in all evacuations of Jews overseas . . . SS general Wilhelm Koppe, Krüger's counterpart in the Warthegau, brought the discussion back to the immediate situation. The establishment of the ghetto in Litzmannstadt, he argued, had been decided only on the assumption that the evacuation of the Jews into the General Government would start "by the middle of the year, at the latest" (ibid., p. 262). Frank held his ground, and when Greiser stated that he understood from the discussion that the General Government could not take in the 250,000 Jews of Litzmannstadt, even on a temporary basis, Frank concurred that Greiser had correctly assessed the situation (ibid., p. 263). Nothing helped the Warthegau delegation, not even a lurid description of the epidemics that threatened the German citizens who had moved to Litzmannstadt, including members of the *Gau* administration themselves. At present, Frank reiterated, he could do nothing (ibid., p. 264).

58. A strange epilogue to the Madagascar plan appeared in internal party correspondence on October 30, 1940. Martin Bormann informed Rosenberg that Hitler deemed the publication of Rosenberg's article "Jews in Madagascar" as inadvisable for the time being, "but it possibly would be so within a few months." Helmut Heiber, ed., *Akten der Partei-Kanzlei der NSDAP: Rekonstruktion eines verlorengegangenen Bestandes. Regesten.*, vol. 1, part 2 (München, 1983), abs. no. 24983.

59. Sybil Milton and Frederick D. Bogin, eds., *Archives of the Holocaust*, vol. 10, part 2 (New York: 1995), pp. 649ff.

60. Joseph Walk, ed., *Das Sonderrecht für die Juden im NS-Staat: Eine Sammlung der gesetzlichen Massnahmen und Richtlinien, Inhalt und Bedeutung* (Heidelberg, 1981), p. 320. The interdiction regarding the deportation of Jews into the General Government was reversed a few days later. John Mendelsohn and Donald S. Detwiler, eds., *The Holocaust: Selected Documents in Eighteen Volumes*, vol. 6, doc. 150 (New York, 1982), pp. 234–38. In May of the same year, the United States chargé d'affaires in Berlin, Alexander Kirk, informed Washington that according to a high-ranking German official, "It was still Germany's policy to encourage emigration of German Austrian and Czech Jews respectively from the Old Reich, Austria, and the Protectorate." In the case of Polish Jews, they would be allowed to leave only if they were not hindering the departure possibilities of Jews from Germany for the Protectorate; mixed areas would be given preference over the General Government.

61. Heydrich's memorandum is quoted verbatim in a circular sent by Hans Frank's office on November 23, 1940, to the district governors in the General Government. Tatiana Berenstein, ed., *Faschismus, Getto, Massenmord: Dokumentation über Ausrottung und Widerstand der Juden in Polen während des zweiten Weltkrieges* (East Berlin, 1961), p. 59.

62. On French acceptance of the German demands on this issue and the consequences it entailed, see Regina M. Delacor, "Auslieferung auf Verlangen: Der deutsch-französische Waffenstillstandsvertrag 1940 und das Schicksal der sozialdemokratischen Exilpolitiker Rudolf Breitscheid und Rudolf Hilferding," *Vierteljahrshefte für Zeitgeschichte* 30 (1999), pp. 217ff.

63. About the activities of the ERC and the role of Varian Fry, see Varian Fry, *Surrender on Demand* (New York, 1945); Anne Klein, "Conscience, Conflict and Politics: The Rescue of Political Refugees from Southern France to the United States, 1940–1942," in *Year Book of the Leo Baeck Institute* (London, 1998), pp. 287ff. See also "The Varian Fry Papers," in *Archives of the Holocaust: An International Collection of Selected Documents*, ed. Henry Friedlander and Sybil Milton, vol. 5 (New York, 1990), pp. 1–76.

64. For Zweig's letter, see Henry Friedlander and Sybil Milton, eds., *Archives of the Holocaust: An International Collection of Selected Documents*, vol. 14 (New York, 1993), p. 111. One of the strangest rescue operations was that of the Lubavitcher Rebbe Joseph Schneersohn, and of his extended family, from Warsaw via Berlin, Riga, and Stockholm, to the United States. At one point or another, it led to the involvement of Secretary of State Cordell Hull; one of the leading officials of the Reich's Four-Year Plan administration, Helmut Wohltat; the chief of the Abwehr, Admiral Canaris; of half-Jewish Abwehr officers; and many others on both sides of the Atlantic. Let it be added, to compound the imbroglio, that the Rebbe created some difficulties of his own: He insisted on the rescue of his forty-thousand-volume library. For this operation see Bryan Mark Rigg, *Rescued from the Reich: How One of Hitler's Soldiers Saved the Lubavitcher Rebbe* (New Haven, 2004).

65. Richard Breitman and Alan M. Kraut, *American Refugee Policy and European Jewry, 1933–1945* (Bloomington, 1987), p. 112.

66. Ibid., pp. 126ff. About public opinion on this issue and the attitude of the press, see Deborah E. Lipstadt, *Beyond Belief: The American Press and the Coming of the Holocaust, 1933–1945* (New York, 1986), pp. 125ff.

67. Klein, "Conscience, Conflict and Politics," p. 292.

68. On Long see in particular Henry L. Feingold, *The Politics of Rescue: The Roosevelt Administration and the Holocaust, 1938–1945* (New Brunswick, 1970), pp. 131ff., and Henry L. Feingold, *Bearing Witness: How America and Its Jews Responded to the Holocaust* (Syracuse, 1995), pp. 86ff.

69. Breitman and Kraut, *American Refugee Policy and European Jewry*, p. 135.

70. In fact, some Jewish refugees became a rather formidable asset to the security of the United States. Albert Einstein was certainly the most famous Jewish emigrant to leave Germany after Hitler's accession to the chancellorship. When the Nazi leader came to power, Einstein was on his way back to Germany from a visit in the United States. He interrupted his trip in Belgium and, after some hesitation, returned to the United States on the invitation of the Princeton Institute for Advanced Studies. Until then Einstein had been a determined pacifist, but he soon understood that in the face of Nazism such an ideological choice was untenable. For him as for other Jewish refugee physicists, the Nazi danger became overwhelming after the takeover of Czechoslovakia. The Germans now controlled the richest uranium mines in Europe; moreover, Otto Hahn and Fritz Strassmann, who had discovered the principle of nuclear fission, continued to work in Germany. Hitler's Reich could eventually build nuclear weapons.

In August 1939 Leo Szilard, Edward Teller, and Eugene Wigner, all three newly arrived Jewish refugees, asked Einstein to approach the president and draw his attention to the looming threat. Einstein prepared a short draft of a letter to the president (in German), Teller wrote the final English version, and Einstein signed it. After describing the main aspects of the nuclear fission of uranium and of its military significance, and after suggesting a series of measures for taking up the challenge, the letter concluded on an ominous note. "I understand," Einstein wrote, "that Germany has actually stopped the sale of uranium from Czechoslovakian mines which she has taken over. That she should have taken such early action might perhaps be understood on the ground that the son of the German Under-Secretary of State, Weizsäcker, is attached to the Kaiser Wilhelm Institute in Berlin, where some of the American work on uranium is now being repeated."

Einstein's letter was delivered to Roosevelt on October 11, 1939; on the nineteenth the president replied and appointed an advisory committee "to thoroughly investigate the possibilities of your suggestions regarding the element of uranium." As the bureaucratic follow-up was slow, Szilard again approached Einstein, and in March 1940 a second letter was sent to Roosevelt. This time more decisive steps were taken: U.S. nuclear weapons research and planning began. Bernard T. Feld, "Einstein and the Politics of Nuclear Weapons," in *Albert Einstein, Historical and Cultural Perspectives*, ed. Gerald James Holton and Yehuda Elkana (Princeton, 1982), pp. 372–74. In Great Britain other Jewish refugees, among them Rudolf Peierls and Maurice Halban, helped their British counterparts to start on a similar track. Soon the American and the British programs were coordinated.

While the first meetings of the new, enlarged advisory committee were taking place, Hitler's victory in Europe seemed plausible and American intervention in the war unlikely. If Hitler alone were to acquire nuclear weapons, Nazi domination of the world would become a nightmarish possibility. About Germany's progress in the field of nuclear physics and its plans to construct nuclear weapons, mainly between 1939 and 1943, see, among a vast literature, Kristie Macrakis, *Surviving the Swastika: Scientific Research in Nazi Germany* (New York, 1993), pp. 164ff.

71. Quoted in Guile Ne'eman Arad, *America, Its Jews, and the Rise of Nazism* (Bloomington, 2000), pp. 211–12.

72. For the unsuccessful attempts of a German Jewish family to reach the United States, then Chile and Brazil, then the United States again, see David Clay Large, *And the World Closed Its Doors: The Story of One Family Abandoned to the Holocaust* (New York, 2003).

73. On this issue see Susan Zuccotti, *Under His Very Windows: The Vatican and the Holocaust in Italy* (New Haven, 2000), pp. 72ff.

74. The Western Hemisphere country possibly most hostile to any Jewish immigration was Canada (despite the favorable attitude of its prime minister, William Mackenzie King), as a result of the (ultra-Catholic) xenophobic and anti-Semitic attitudes of the authorities and the population of Quebec Province. On this subject see Irving M. Abella and Harold Martin Troper, *None Is Too Many: Canada and the Jews of Europe, 1933–1948* (Toronto, 1982).

75. Milton and Bogin, eds., *Archives of the Holocaust*, vol. 10, part 1, pp. 391ff. Ultimately, in 1940 and 1941, 2,178 Polish Jews reached Japan, among them many rabbis of ultra-Orthodox yeshivas: The majority had to move to Shanghai and remain there throughout the war. Cf. Efraim Zuroff, "Rescue Via the Far East: The Attempt to Save Polish Rabbis and Yeshivah Students, 1939–1941," *Simon Wiesenthal Center Yearbook* 1 (1988), pp. 171–72.

76. Yehuda Bauer, *Jews for Sale? Nazi-Jewish Negotiations, 1933–1945* (New Haven, 1994), p. 50.

77. Ibid.

78. Ibid.

79. For a detailed study see Dalia Ofer, *Escaping the Holocaust: Illegal Immigration to the Land of Israel, 1939–1944* (New York, 1990). For the events described here see mainly pp. 42ff.

80. Ibid., pp. 49ff.

81. Quoted in Bernard Wasserstein, *Britain and the Jews of Europe, 1939–1945* (London, 1979), p. 50.

82. Ibid., pp. 50–51.

83. Ibid., p. 63.

84. Ibid., pp. 64ff.

85. Alfred Fabre-Luce, *Journal de la France 1939–1944*, vol. 1 (Geneva, 1946), p. 246. (The first edition of volume 1 was published in Paris in 1940 and in Hamburg in 1941.)

86. Haim Avni, *Spain, the Jews, and Franco* (Philadelphia, 1982), pp. 73ff. Spanish policy was apparently more reticent toward Jews carrying Spanish passports and living in German-occupied countries; on this issue see mainly Bernd Rother, "Franco und die deutsche Judenverfolgung," *Vierteljahrshefte für Zeitgeschichte (VfZ)* 46, no. 2 (1998), pp. 189ff. In more general terms, however, Franco's refusal to go along with Hitler's military plans saved Gibraltar and helped British operations in North Africa and in the Mediterranean. On October 4, 1940, an incensed Hitler told Mussolini that, in a conversation with Franco, he [Hitler] "was almost represented as if he were a little Jew who was haggling about the most sacred possessions of mankind." *DGFP: Series D*, vol. 11 (Washington, D.C., 1960), p. 251.

87. On this subject see Avraham Milgram, "Portugal, the Consuls and the Jewish Refugees, 1938–1941," *Yad Vashem Studies* 37 (1999), pp. 123ff.

88. See in particular Rui Alfonso, "Le 'Wallenberg Portugais': Aristides de Sousa Mendes," *Revue d'Histoire de la Shoah. Le monde juif*, no. 165 (1999), pp. 7ff.

89. For a summary about Swiss policy regarding Jewish refugees in the fall of 1938, see Independent Commission of Experts Switzerland—Second World War, *Switzerland, National Socialism and the Second World War* (Zurich, 2002), pp. 108–9. About the indelible ink to be used for the red J stamp, see Friedländer, *Nazi Germany and the Jews, Volume I: The Years of Persecution, 1933–1939*, p. 265.

90. See in particular Paul A. Levine, *From Indifference to Activism: Swedish Diplomacy and the Holocaust, 1938–1944* (Uppsala, 1996).

91. Klepper, *Unter dem Schatten Deiner Flügel*, p. 845.

92. Ibid., p. 843.

93. Ibid., p. 860.

94. Ibid., p. 866.

95. Ibid., p. 874.

96. Ibid., p. 884.

97. Wolfgang Gerlach, *And the Witnesses Were Silent: The Confessing Church and the Persecution of the Jews*, ed. Victoria Barnett (Lincoln, NE, 2000), pp. 155ff.

98. This document was found in the Bundesarchiv in Koblenz by Dr. Joseph Henke. The initials at the bottom of the document were identified as those of Adolf Eichmann. The document was published in French (with a photocopy of the German original) in Lucien Steinberg, *Un document essentiel qui situe les débuts de la "solution finale de la question juive"* (Paris, 1992). See also Götz Aly, *Endlösung: Völkerverschiebung und der Mord an den europäischen Juden* (Frankfurt am Main, 1995), pp. 124–26.

99. Memorandum of Department Germany of the Foreign Ministry, October 31, 1940, *DGFP: Series D*, vol. 11, p. 444.

100. Instructions for the officials in charge of the deportations of the Jews from the Palatinate, n.d., reproduced in Sauer, *Dokumente über die Verfolgung*, vol. 2, pp. 236–37.

101. Ibid., p. 231.

102. Leni Yahil, *The Holocaust: The Fate of European Jewry, 1932–1945* (New York, 1990), p. 177.

103. Anne Grynberg, *Les Camps de la honte: Les internés juifs des camps français, 1939–1944* (Paris, 1991), p. 142. Tens of thousands of non-Jews considered French nationalists were also expelled from Alsace and Lorraine in the course of the summer and fall of 1940. See Jean-Pierre Azéma, *De Munich à la Libération* (Paris, 1979), p. 116.

104. Both decrees are quoted in Harold James, *Die Deutsche Bank und die "Arisierung"* (Munich, 2001), p. 199.

105. Eberhard Röhm and Jörg Thierfelder, *Juden, Christen, Deutsche, 1933–1945*, vol. 3, part 2, (Stuttgart, 1995), p. 193. On the same day, Gröber asked Prelate Kreutz to intervene with the nuncio, together with Bishop Heinrich Wienken. To the arguments used in his letter to Orsenigo, Gröber added that the deportees for whom he was interceding "were Catholics who had made great sacrifices in separating themselves from the members of their race." Bernhard Stasiewski and Ludwig Volk, eds., *Akten deutscher Bischöfe über die Lage der Kirche, 1933–1945*. Veröffentlichungen der Kommission für Zeitgeschichte bei der Katholischen Akademie in Bayern. Reihe A: Quellen, Bd. 5; v. 2–6: Veröffentlichungen der Kommission für Zeitgeschichte. Reihe A: Quellen, 6 vols. (Mainz, 1968–1985).

106. Jeremy Noakes, "The Development of Nazi Policy Towards the German-Jewish 'Mischlinge' 1933–1945," in *Holocaust*, ed. David Cesarani, vol. 2 (London, 2004), p. 280. See also Beate Meyer, *"Jüdische Mischlinge": Rassenpolitik und Verfolgungserfahrung 1933–1945* (Hamburg, 1999).

107. Walk, *Das Sonderrecht*, p. 325.

108. Heiber, *Akten der Partei-Kanzlei der NSDAP,* vol. 1, Part 2, abs. no. 24935.

109. Walk, *Das Sonderrecht*, p. 327.

110. William L. Shirer, *Berlin Diary: The Journal of a Foreign Correspondent, 1934–1941* (New York, 1941; reprint, Boston, 1988), pp. 520–21.

111. Walk, *Das Sonderrecht*, p. 330.

112. Marion A. Kaplan, *Between Dignity and Despair: Jewish Life in Nazi Germany* (New York, 1998), p. 153.

113. Walk, *Das Sonderrecht*, p. 332.

114. Ibid.

115. See Supra, chapter 1, pp. 15ff.

116. Kurt Pätzold, ed., *Verfolgung, Vertreibung, Vernichtung: Dokumente des faschistischen Antisemitismus 1933 bis 1942.* (Frankfurt am Main, 1984), p. 266; Walk, *Das Sonderrecht*, p. 324.

117. Klemperer, *I Will Bear Witness*, vol. 1, pp. 345–46.

118. Quoted and summed up in Moshe Ayalon, "Jewish Life in Breslau, 1938–1941," *Leo Baeck Institute Yearbook* (1996), pp. 327–28. For a considerably abridged version of Cohn's diary during the year 1941, see Joseph Walk, ed., *Als Jude in Breslau 1941: Aus den Tagebüchern von Studienrat a. D. Dr. Willy Israel Cohn* (Gerlingen: 1984).

119. Hertha Feiner, *Vor der Deportation: Briefe an die Töchter, Januar 1939–Dezember 1942*, ed. Karl Heinz Jahnke (Frankfurt am Main, 1993), p. 16.

120. Ibid., p. 64.

121. Ibid., p. 77.

122. Quoted in " 'Protocols,' Nazi Propaganda Ministry," in Rebecca Rovit and Alvin Goldfarb, eds., *Theatrical Performance during the Holocaust: Texts, Documents, Memoirs* (Baltimore, 1999), p. 76.

123. Ibid., p. 77.

124. Ibid., p. 78.

125. Ibid., p. 79.

126. Joseph Goebbels, *Die Tagebücher von Joseph Goebbels: Sämtliche Fragmente*, ed. Elke Fröhlich (Munich, 1987), part 1, vol. 8, p. 35.

127. Ibid., p. 165.

128. Ibid., p. 279.

129. Juliane Wetzel, "Die Rothschilds," in Wolfgang Benz, Hermann Graml, and Hermann Weiss, eds., *Enzyklopädie des Nationalsozialismus* (Stuttgart, 1997), p. 705.

130. These details about the film were taken from David Culbert, "The Impact of anti-Semitic Film Propaganda on German Audiences: *Jew Süss* and *The Wandering Jew* (1940)," in *Art, Culture, and Media Under the Third Reich*, ed. Richard A. Etlin (Chicago, 2002), pp. 139ff.

131. Susan Tegel, " 'The Demonic Effect': Veit Harlan's Use of Jewish Extras in *Jud Süss*," *Holocaust and Genocide Studies* 14, no. 2 (2000), pp. 215ff. About further aspects of the film, see also, most recently, Alexandra Przyrembel and Jörg Schönert, eds., *Jud Süss: Hofjude, literarische Figur, antisemitisches Zerrbild.* (Frankfurt am Main, 2006).

132. Quoted in Eric Rentschler, *The Ministry of Illusion: Nazi Cinema and its After-*

life (Cambridge, MA, 1996), pp. 153–54. (Antonioni remains better known as director of *L'Avventura* and particularly of *Blow-Up*.)

133. Goebbels, *Tagebücher*, part 1, vol. 8, p. 345.

134. Ibid. p. 346.

135. Kulka and Jäckel, *Die Juden in den geheimen NS-Stimmungsberichten 1933–1945*, p. 435.

136. Ibid., p. 434.

137. Quoted in Josef Wulf, ed., *Theater und Film im Dritten Reich: Eine Dokumentation* (Frankfurt/am Main, 1989), p. 405.

138. Rentschler, *The Ministry of Illusion*, p. 154.

139. Goebbels, *Tagebücher*, part 1, vol. 8, p. 372.

140. Wulf, *Theater und Film*, p. 410.

141. Yizhak Ahren, Stig Hornshøj-Møller, and Christoph B. Melchers, *Der ewige Jude: Wie Goebbels hetzte: Untersuchungen zum nationalsozialistischen Propagandafilm* (Aachen, 1990), p. 23. The film was entirely based on graphic demonstrations and on the mixing of images and sequences taken from different sources: Nazi filming of Jews in Poland (in Lodz, for example, as we saw); sequences from Yiddish films; newsreel footage representing various German Jewish individuals and revolutionary scenes of the postwar period; scenes from a Leni Riefenstahl film and of German everyday working life. A sophisticated intercutting technique was used to show how a repulsive ghetto Jew became an assimilated Western Jew when he exchanged his traditional garb for Western clothes, cut sidelocks and beard, and thereby appeared as an almost unrecognizable and successful member of modern society. Bankers and stock exchange tycoons extended their spiderlike control over the productive potential of the nations, whereas Jewish revolutionaries incited the masses against the ruling order. The Jewish domination of journalism, culture, and the arts all led to the same disintegration. The "Relativitätsjude" (relativity Jew) Albert Einstein and the "Bühnediktator" (stage dictator) Max Reinhardt, were of the same ilk. And every year, on Purim, Jews the world over celebrated their murderous vengeance against their enemies at the Persian court, 75,000 of whom were slaughtered. (The Purim scenes, for instance were lifted from two Yiddish films—Joseph Green's *Der Purim Schpiler* [1937] and *Yidl mitn Fidl* [1936].) Hilmar Hoffmann, *Und die Fahne führt uns in die Ewigkeit: Propaganda im NS-Film* (Frankfurt am Main, 1988), p. 167.

142. Quoted in Hermann Glaser, "Film," in Benz, Graml, and Weiss, eds. *Enzyklopädie des Nationalsozialismus*, p. 175.

143. Hoffmann, *Und die Fahne*, p. 166.

144. Ibid.

145. Dorothea Hollstein, *"Jud Süss" und die Deutschen: Antisemitische Vorurteile im nationalsozialistischen Spielfilm* (1971; reprint, Frankfurt/am Main, 1983), pp. 116–17.

146. For the Goebbels-Rosenberg feud during the 1930s, see Friedländer, *Nazi Germany and the Jews, Volume 1*, pp. 131ff.

147. Erik Levi, *Music in the Third Reich* (New York, 1994), p. 80.

148. Ibid.

149. Ibid., pp. 80ff.

150. O. D. Kulka, "The 'Reichsvereinigung of the Jews in Germany' (1938/9–1943)," in *Patterns of Jewish Leadership in Nazi Europe, 1933–1945*, ed. Cynthia J. Haft and Yisrael Gutman (Jerusalem, 1979), p. 56.

151. The Gestapo had the addresses of all Jews in Baden and the Palatinate, as everywhere else in the Reich, on the basis of the *Judenkartei*, the regularly updated list of all members of the community, established by every local Reichsvereinigung office. See among others, David Martin Luebke and Sybil Milton, "Locating the Victim: An Overview of Census-Taking, Tabulation Technology, and Persecution in Nazi Germany," *IEEE Annals of the History of Computing* 16, no. 3 (1994), pp. 25ff and in particular 33.

152. Yahil, *The Holocaust*, p. 234

153. Paul Sauer, "Otto Hirsch (1885–1941): Director of the Reichsvertretung," in *Yearbook of the Leo Baeck Institute* (1987), p. 367.

154. For an assessment of the ghetto population on May 1, 1940, see Lucjan Dobroszycki, Introduction, in *The Chronicle of the Lódz Ghetto, 1941–1944* (New Haven, 1984), p. xxxix n. 103.

155. For the ghetto's isolation, see ibid., pp. xxxiiiff.

156. For these statistics see Alan Adelson and Robert Lapides, eds., *Lodz Ghetto: Inside a Community Under Siege* (New York: 1989), p. 36.

157. Frank, *Diensttagebuch*, p. 281.

158. Emanuel Ringelblum, *Notes from the Warsaw Ghetto: The Journal of Emmanuel Ringelblum*, ed. Jacob Sloan (New York, 1974), pp. 61–62.

159. Kaplan, *Scroll of Agony: The Warsaw Diary of Chaim A. Kaplan*, p. 203.

160. Czerniaków, *Warsaw Diary*, p. 206.

161. Yisrael Gutman, *The Jews of Warsaw, 1939–1943: Ghetto, Underground, Revolt* (Bloomington, 1982), p. 63.

162. Isaiah Trunk, *Judenrat: The Jewish Councils in Eastern Europe under Nazi Occupation* (New York, 1972), p. 145.

163. Antony Polonsky and Norman Davies, eds., *Jews in Eastern Poland and the USSR, 1939–46* (New York, 1991), p. 288.

164. For Ringelblum's comments see Yitzhak Arad, Yisrael Gutman and Abraham Margaliot, eds., *Documents on the Holocaust: Selected Sources on the Destruction of the Jews of Germany and Austria, Poland, and the Soviet Union* (Lincoln, NE, and Jerusalem, 1999), pp. 235–36.

165. For all biographical details, see Derek Bowman, introduction to Dawid Rubinowicz, *The Diary of Dawid Rubinowicz* (Edmonds, WA, 1982), pp. viiff.

166. Ibid., p. 3.

167. Ibid.

168. Ibid., p. 5.

169. Ibid., p. 6.

170. Walter Manoschek, ed., *"Es gibt nur eines für das Judentum—Vernichtung": Das Judenbild in deutschen Soldatenbriefen 1939–1944* (Hamburg, 1997), p. 18.

171. Ibid., p. 16.

172. Ibid., p. 19.

173. In the fall of 1940 the Jewish population included refugees from Holland and Belgium who did not return to their countries and, from the end of October 1940 on, also the Jews expelled from Baden, the Saar, and the Palatinate. These numbers, all based on post–June 1940 computations, do not include some 10,000 to 15,000 Jewish prisoners of war, nor do they take into account that in the various censuses, a few thousand foreign Jews did not register. See André Kaspi, *Les Juifs pendant l'occupation* (Paris, 1991), pp. 18ff.

174. On this period of harmony see, among others, Paula Hyman, *From Dreyfus to Vichy: The Remaking of French Jewry, 1906–1939* (New York, 1979), pp. 33ff. See also Saul Friedländer, *The Third Reich and the Jews*, vol. 1, chapter 7.

175. About this policy reversal, see Regina M. Delacor, "From Potential Friends to Potential Enemies: The Internment of 'Hostile Foreigners' in France at the Beginning of the Second World War," *Journal of Contemporary History* 35, no. 3 (July 2000), pp. 361ff.

176. For these events see mainly Grynberg, *Les camps de la honte* and Anne Grynberg, "1939–1940: L'Internement en temps de guerre. Les politiques de la France et de la Grande-Bretagne," *Vingtième Siècle: Revue d'Histoire* (1997), pp. 24ff.

177. Lion Feuchtwanger, *The Devil in France: My Encounter with Him in the Summer of 1940* (New York, 1941), p. 8. For another particularly vivid description of incarceration at Le Vernet and of the outbursts of French anti-Semitism during the collapse of the country, see Arthur Koestler, *Scum of the Earth* (New York, 1947), pp. 96ff., 142, 193, 237ff.

178. Renée Poznanski, *Être juif en France pendant la Seconde Guerre mondiale* (Paris, 1994), p. 55.

179. Quoted in Burrin, *France Under the Germans*, p. 56.

180. Kaspi, *Les Juifs pendant l'occupation*, p. 56.

181. Jeannine Verdès-Leroux, *Refus et violences: Politique et littérature à l'extrême droite des années trente aux retombées de la Libération* (Paris, 1996), p. 164.

182. The best analysis of these personalities and parties is in Burrin, *France Under the Germans*, and in Philippe Burrin, *La dérive fasciste: Doriot, Déat, Bergery, 1933–1945* (Paris, 1986).

183. *Foreign Relations of the United States, General and Europe 1940*, vol. 2 (Washington, D.C., 1957), p. 565.

184. A 1927 law had eased the naturalization process. The intention of Alibert's commission was clear: Forty percent of the naturalizations that were cancelled were those of Jews. See Robert O. Paxton, *Vichy France: Old Guard and New Order, 1940–1944* (New York, 2001), p. 171.

185. Michael R. Marrus and Robert O. Paxton, *Vichy et les juifs* (Paris, 1990), pp. 17–18.

186. For the full text of both laws, see ibid., p. 399–401.

187. Pétain's own anti-Semitism was apparently fed by his wife (*La Maréchale*) and

by his physician, Dr. Bernard Ménétrel. See Denis Peschanski, *Vichy, 1940–1944: Contrôle et exclusion* (Bruxelles, 1997), p. 78.

188. Scholarly studies of these issues and of French anti-Jewish policies during the war are very extensive by now. Of necessity, only a few will be mentioned in this volume. On the responsibility regarding the statutes of October 1940 (and June 1941) and various reactions see in particular Denis Peschanski, "The Statutes on Jews, October 3, 1940 and June 2, 1941," *Yad Vashem Studies* 22 (1992), pp. 65ff.; Pierre Laborie, "The Jewish Statutes in Vichy France and Public Opinion," *Yad Vashem Studies* 22 (1992), pp. 89ff; Renée Poznanski, "The Jews of France and the Statutes on Jews, 1940–1941," *Yad Vashem Studies* 22 (1992), pp. 115ff.

189. Quoted in Kaspi, *Les Juifs pendant l'occupation*, pp. 61–62.

190. Peschanski, *Vichy, 1940–1944: Contrôle et exclusion*, p. 180.

191. Marrus and Paxton, *Vichy et les juifs*, p. 28.

192. François Bédarida and Renée Bédarida, "La Persécution des Juifs," in *La France des années noires*, vol. 2, *De l'occupation à la libération*, ed. Jean-Pierre Azéma and François Bédarida (Paris, 1993), pp. 135–36.

193. Quoted in Pierre Birnbaum, *Anti-Semitism in France: A Political History from Léon Blum to the Present* (Oxford, 1992), p. 183.

194. Ibid., p. 185.

195. In a book published in 1947, *L'Église Catholique en France sous l'occupation*, Monsignor Guerry himself reproduced the gist of the declaration, possibly without even perceiving its problematic aspect. For a very mild discussion of this issue see Jean-Marie Mayeur, "Les Églises devant la Persécution des Juifs en France," in *La France et la question juive: 1940–1944*, ed. Georges Wellers, André Kaspi, and Serge Klarsfeld (Paris, 1981), p. 151ff.

196. For example the bishop of Grenoble and the archbishop of Chambéry, ibid., p. 143 n. 11.

197. For a good summary of these attitudes, see François Delpech, "L'Episcopat et la persecution des juifs et des étrangers," in *Églises et chrétiens dans la IIe Guerre mondiale* (Lyon, 1978).

198. Quoted in Michèle Cointet, *L'Église Sous Vichy, 1940–1945. La repentance en question* (Paris, 1998), pp. 187–88.

199. Marrus and Paxton, *Vichy et les juifs*, pp. 203–4.

200. Regarding Abetz's role and his use of anti-Semitism for his own political ambitions, see Barbara Lambauer, "Opportunistischer Antisemitismus: Der deutscher Botschafter Otto Abetz und die Judenverfolgang in Frankreich," *Vierteljahrshefte für Zeitgeschichte* 2 (2005), pp. 241ff and in particular pp. 247ff. See also Ahlrich Meyer, *Täter im Verhör: Die Endlösung der Judenfrage in Frankreich 1940–1944* (Darmstadt, 2005), pp. 23ff. Thus the initial role of the German military administration had to be nuanced. For the traditional interpretation see Ulrich Herbert, "Die deutsche Militärverwaltung in Paris und die Deportation der französischen Juden," in *Von der Aufgabe der Freiheit: Politische Verantwortung und bürgerliche Gesellschaft im 19. und 20. Jahrhundert: Festschrift für Hans Mommsen zum 5. November 1995*, ed. Christian Jansen,

Lutz Niethammer, and Bernd Weisbrod (Berlin, 1995), p. 431; Serge Klarsfeld, *Vichy-Auschwitz: Le rôle de Vichy dans la solution finale de la question juive en France, 1943–1944* (Paris, 1985), p. 356. For Hitler's initial order see Franz Halder, *Kriegstagebuch: Tägliche Aufzeichnungen des Chefs des Generalstabes des Heeres, 1939–1942*, ed. Hans Adolf Jacobsen, vol. 2 (Stuttgart, 1962–64), p. 77.

201. Herbert, "Die deutsche Militärverwaltung in Paris und die Deportation der französischen Juden," p. 432.

202. Ibid., p. 433.

203. Ibid.

204. Poznanski, *Être juif*, p. 67.

205. Ibid., pp. 67ff.

206. Ibid., pp. 68–69.

207. Renée Poznanski, *Jews in France during World War II* (Waltham, MA, 2001), p. 85.

208. Herbert R. Lottman, *La Rive gauche: Du Front populaire à la guerre froide* (Paris, 1981), pp. 303–4. For a sample of the categories of forbidden authors of books, see Verdès-Leroux, *Refus et violences*, p. 149. All Jewish authors were excluded, whereas in many other cases the exclusion targeted only specific books.

209. Burrin, *France under the Germans*, p. 29.

210. Ibid.

211. See Lutz Raphael, "Die Pariser Universität unter deutscher Besatzung 1940–1944," in *Universitäten im nationalsozialistisch beherrschten Europa*, ed. Dieter Langewiesche, *Geschichte und Gesellschaft* 23, no 4. (1997), pp. 511–12, 522. Some protests against the anti-Jewish measures were expressed by a few faculty members, but these were rare exceptions in a climate of indifference and acceptance (ibid., p. 523).

212. Burrin, *France under the Germans*, p. 307.

213. Ibid., p. 308.

214. Ibid.

215. Simon Schwarzfuchs, *Aux prises avec Vichy: Histoire politique des Juifs de France, 1940–1944* (Paris, 1998), p. 73.

216. Ibid.

217. For Lambert's prewar biography see Richard Cohen, introduction in Raymond-Raoul Lambert, *Carnet d'un témoin: 1940–1943*, ed. Richard I. Cohen (Paris, 1985); for Biélinky's prewar life see Renée Poznanski, introduction to Jacques Biélinky, *Journal, 1940–1942: Un journaliste juif à Paris sous l'Occupation*, ed. Renée Poznanski (Paris, 1992).

218. Lambert, *Carnet d'un témoin*, p. 72.

219. Ibid., p. 83.

220. Ibid., pp. 85–86.

221. Biélinky, *Journal*, p. 57.

222. See Pierre Birnbaum, *Prier pour l'État: Les juifs, l'alliance royale et la démocratie* (Paris, 2005), p. 117.

223. Biélinky, *Journal*, p. 106.

224. For the details of the negotiations between Dannecker and the Jewish organizations, see Jacques Adler, *The Jews of Paris and the Final Solution: Communal Response and Internal Conflicts, 1940–1944* (New York, 1987), p. 53ff.

225. Bob Moore, *Victims and Survivors: The Nazi Persecution of the Jews in the Netherlands, 1940–1945* (London, 1997), p. 45.

226. Manoschek, *"Es gibt nur eines für das Judentum,"* p. 13.

227. Moore, *Victims and Survivors,* p. 49.

228. Louis de Jong, "Jews and Non-Jews in Nazi-Occupied Holland," in *The Nazi Holocaust: Historical Articles on the Destruction of European Jews,* ed. Michael R. Marrus (Westport, 1989), vol. 4: *The Final Solution Outside Germany (I),* pp. 130–31.

229. For a general study of the German occupation of Holland and Dutch cooperation see Gerhard Hirschfeld, *Nazi Rule and Dutch Collaboration: The Netherlands under German Occupation, 1940–1945* (Oxford, 1988).

230. Moore, *Victims and Survivors,* p. 57.

231. B. A. Sijes, "The Position of the Jews During the German Occupation of the Netherlands: Some Observations," in *The Nazi Holocaust: Historical Articles on the Destruction of European Jews,* ed. Michael R. Marrus (Westport, CT, 1989) vol. 4, p. 153.

232. Joseph Michman, "The Controversial Stand of the Joodse Raad in the Netherlands: Lodewijk E. Visser's Struggle," *Yad Vashem Studies* 10 (1974), p. 13.

233. Moore, *Victims and Survivors,* pp. 196ff.

234. Guus Meershoek, "The Amsterdam Police and the Persecution of the Jews," in *Holocaust: Critical Concepts in Historical Studies,* vol. 3, ed. David Cesarani (New York, 2004), p. 540.

235. For further details see J. Presser, *Ashes in the Wind: The Destruction of Dutch Jewry* (Detroit, 1988), p. 50.

236. Quoted in ibid., p. 27–28.

237. For a detailed account see Gerhard Hirschfeld, "Die Universität Leyden unter dem Nationalsozialismus," in *Universitäten im nationalsozialistisch beherrschten Europa,* ed. Dieter Langewiesche, *Geschichte und Gesellschaft* 23, vol. 4 (1997) pp. 573ff.

238. *DGFP: Series D,* vol. 11, p. 1120.

239. Quoted in Röhm and Thierfelder, *Juden,* vol. 3, part 2, p. 270.

240. Benjamin Leo Wessels, *Ben's Story: Holocaust Letters with Selections from the Dutch Underground Press,* ed. Kees W. Bolle (Carbondale, IL, 2001), p. 21.

241. Ibid., pp. 21ff.

242. Claude Singer, *Vichy, l'université et les juifs: Les silences et la mémoire* (Paris, 1992), pp. 163ff. There were of course many private expressions of sympathy and one known resignation in protest against the anti-Jewish measures, that of a high official of the education system in Paris, Gustave Monod (ibid., p. 100). For some letters of sympathy see in particular ibid., pp. 379–82.

243. Marcel Baudot, "Les Mouvements de Résistance devant la persécution des juifs," in *La France et la question juive: 1940–1944,* ed. Georges Wellers, André Kaspi, and Serge Klarsfeld (Paris, 1981), p. 279.

244. Klemperer, *I Will Bear Witness,* vol. 1, pp. 340–41.

245. A privileged mixed marriage was one whose children were not raised as Jews; its members were exempted from anti-Jewish measures. A nonprivileged mixed marriage was one whose children were raised as Jews, or a childless union like that of the Klemperers. Usually, even in the case of nonprivileged mixed marriages, deportations were delayed if the Jewish partner was a convert or if the Jewish partner was the wife.

246. Ruth Zariz, ed., *Mikhtave halutsim mi-Polin ha-kevushah, 1940–1944* (Ramat Ef'al, 1994), p. 51.

247. Walter Benjamin, *Correspondence*, vol. 2, p. 861.

248. Walter Benjamin, *Briefe*, ed., Gershom Scholem and Theodor Adorno, vol. 2 (Frankfurt am Main, 1978), p. 846.

249. Hannah Arendt "Introduction" to Walter Benjamin, *Illuminations: Essays and Reflections*, New York, 1968, p. 18.

Chapter 3: December 1940–June 1941

1. Joseph Goebbels, *Die Tagebücher von Joseph Goebbels: Sämtliche Fragmente*, ed. Elke Fröhlich, part 1, vol. 9 (Munich, 1998), pp. 377–78.

2. Ibid., p. 379.

3. Franz Halder, *Kriegstagebuch: Tägliche Aufzeichnungen des Chefs des Generalstabes des Heeres, 1939–1942*, ed. Hans Adolf Jacobsen, vol. 2 (Stuttgart, 1962–64), pp. 21, 31, 32, 34, 36, mainly 49ff.

4. The draft of the treaty indicates that "America" was its main target, at least on paper. *DGFP: Series D*, vol. 11, p. 188.

5. On the president's stand and German reactions, see Saul Friedländer, *Prelude to Downfall: Hitler and the United States, 1939–41* (New York, 1967), pp. 165ff.

6. Ibid., p. 171.

7. Adolf Hitler, *Hitler: Reden und Proklamationen, 1932–1945: Kommentiert von einem deutschen Zeitgenossen*, ed. Max Domarus, part 2 (Leonberg, 1987–88), pp. 1663–64.

8. KTB/OKW (3/3/1941), quoted in Jürgen Förster, "Operation Barbarossa as a War of Conquest and Annihilation," in *The Attack on the Soviet Union*, ed. Horst Boog, *Germany and the Second World War* (Oxford, 1998), p. 185.

9. Halder, *Kriegstagebuch*, vol. 2, pp. 336–37.

10. For a discussion of Eckart's pamphlet see Friedländer, *Nazi Germany and the Jews, Volume I*, pp. 97–98.

11. For Hitler's interpretation of the role played by the Jews in Russia/the Soviet Union, see Adolf Hitler, *Hitler's Second Book: The Unpublished Sequel to Mein Kampf*, ed. Gerhard L. Weinberg (New York, 2003), pp. 144ff., 150ff., and 232ff.

12. Sometimes Hitler's utterances give the impression that, in his view, Stalin had liquidated the "Jewish" part of Judeo-Bolshevism, particularly regarding the political commissars. Thus, on January 7, 1941, he declared to the Bulgarian prime minister, Bogdan Filov, "First, the Bolshevists installed Jewish commissars, who tortured their former opponents to death. Next came the Russian commissars who, in turn, displaced the Jews." (*DGFP: Series D*, vol. 11, p. 1023). Of course it may have been an indirect way of justifying to a foreign leader his arrangement with the Soviet Union: It was no longer Jewish.

13. These interpretations appear in Arno J. Mayer, *Why Did the Heavens Not Darken?: The Final Solution in History* (New York, 1988).

14. The negotiations between SS and army started much earlier than was thought for a long time; discussions were already ongoing in February 1941. See Richard Breitman, *The Architect of Genocide: Himmler and the Final Solution* (New York, 1991), pp. 149–150.

15. For the changing preambles attached to this order that at first pointed specifically to the Jews but then, however, remained limited to security arguments, see Christopher R. Browning and Jürgen Matthäus, *The Origins of the Final Solution: The Evolution of Nazi Jewish policy, September 1939–March 1942* (Lincoln, NE, 2004), pp. 219–20.

16. For the text of the guidelines, see Peter Longerich and Dieter Pohl, eds., *Die Ermordung der europäischen Juden: Eine umfassende Dokumentation des Holocaust 1941–1945* (Munich, 1989), p. 136.

17. Browning and Matthäus, *The Origins of the Final Solution*, pp. 222–23.

18. For discussions and supplementary decrees stemming from the order, see ibid., pp. 220–22.

19. Quoted in Manfred Messerschmidt; *Die Wehrmacht im NS-Staat; Zeit der Indoktrination* (Hamburg, 1969), pp. 326ff.

20. At the end of 1941, 750,000 copies of *Mitteilungen* were printed per issue. See Martin Moll, "Die Abteilung Wehrmachtpropaganda im Oberkommando der Wehrmacht," *Beiträge zur Geschichte des Nationalsozialismus* 17 (2001), p. 130.

21. Peter Longerich, *Politik der Vernichtung: Eine Gesamtdarstellung der nationalsozialistischen Judenverfolgung* (Munich, 1998), pp. 313ff. and 320.

22. Götz Aly, *"Final Solution": Nazi Population Policy and the Murder of the European Jews* (London, 1999), p. 126.

23. Ibid., p. 172.

24. Ibid.; Longerich, *Politik der Vernichtung*, pp. 290–91; Heinrich Himmler, *Der Dienstkalender Heinrich Himmlers 1941/42*, ed. Peter Witte et al. (Hamburg, 1999), p. 139 n. 69.

25. Goebbels, *Tagebücher*, part 1, vol. 9, pp. 389–90.

26. There is no direct evidence regarding the date on which Heydrich received Göring's order (that is, Hitler's order) to prepare a new territorial solution of the "Jewish question" in replacement of the "Madagascar plan." But, on the basis of documents stemming from Eichmann's delegate in Paris, Theodor Dannecker and from Eichmann himself, the order must have been given sometime at the end of 1940. Aly, *"Final Solution,"* pp. 172–73.

27. Andreas Hillgruber, *Staatsmänner und Diplomaten bei Hitler: Vertrauliche Aufzeichnungen über Unterredungen mit Vertretern des Auslandes* vol. 1 (Frankfurt am Main, 1967–70), pp. 573–74.

28. This measure was most probably taken to allow for a maximum of emigration possibilities for Jews from the Reich and the Protectorate. As for the reference to the forthcoming final solution, it was, at this stage, a vague and widely used formula referring to any range of possibilities. For the text of the RSHA's decree, see Kurt Pätzold,

ed., *Verfolgung, Vertreibung, Vernichtung: Dokumente des faschistischen Antisemitismus 1933 bis 1942* (Frankfurt am Main, 1984), p. 289.

29. Nuremberg doc. 1028-PS, U.S. Office of Chief of Counsel for the Prosecution of Axis Criminality and International Military Tribunal, *Nazi Conspiracy and Aggression*, vol. 3 (Washington, DC, 1946), p. 690.

30. Himmler, *Der Dienstkalender*, p. 161 n. 23.

31. For the preparation of the economic exploitation of the eastern territories, see mainly Rolf-Dieter Müller, "From Economic Alliance to a War of Colonial Exploitation," in *Germany and the Second World War*, ed. Horst Boog et al. (Oxford, 1998), pp. 118ff and in particular 136ff.

32. About these plans see mainly Christian Gerlach, *Krieg, Ernährung, Völkermord: Forschungen zur deutschen Vernichtungspolitik im Zweiten Weltkrieg* (Hamburg, 1998), pp. 10ff. and 14ff. For an English summary of Gerlach's argument see Christian Gerlach, "German Economic Interests, Occupation Policy, and the Murder of the Jews in Belorussia 1941/43," in *National Socialist Extermination Policies: Contemporary German Perspectives and Controversies*, ed. Ulrich Herbert, *Studies on War and Genocide*, vol. 2 (New York, 2000), pp. 210ff.

33. See Wulff Breback, "Wewelsburg," in Wolfgang Benz, Hermann Graml, and Hermann Weiss, eds., *Enzyklopädie des Nationalsozialismus* (Stuttgart, 1997), p. 806.

34. Himmler, *Der Dienstkalender*, p. 172; Richard Breitman, *Official Secrets: What the Nazis Planned, What the British and Americans Knew* (New York, 1998), p. 40. There is no necessary connection between Himmler's musings that seem to imply long-term plans (also related to the Reichsführer's colonization projects) and the "hunger plans" discussed at the OKW, whose aim was the immediate easing of the food supply for the *Ostheer*.

35. Hans Frank, *Das Diensttagebuch des deutschen Generalgouverneurs in Polen 1939–1945*, ed. Werner Präg and Wolfgang Jacobmeyer (Stuttgart, 1975), pp. 326ff.

36. Ibid., pp. 335ff.

37. Gerhard Botz, *Wohnungspolitik und Judendeportation in Wien 1938 bis 1945: Zur Funktion des Antisemitismus als Ersatz nationalsozialistischer Sozialpolitik* (Vienna, 1975), p. 108.

38. Kurt Pätzold, ed., *Verfolgung*, p. 279.

39. Stadtarchiv München, ed., "*. . . verzogen, unbekannt wohin*": *Die erste Deportation von Münchner Juden im November 1941* (Zurich: 2000), p. 17.

40. Victor Klemperer, *I Will Bear Witness: A Diary of the Nazi Years, 1933–41* (New York, 1998), vol. 1, p. 374.

41. Wolf Gruner, *Judenverfolgung in Berlin 1933–1945: Eine Chronologie der Behördenmassnahmen in der Reichshauptstadt* (Berlin, 1996), p. 77.

42. Ibid.

43. Ibid.

44. Ibid., p. 78.

45. Peter Longerich, ed., *Akten der Partei-Kanzlei der NSDAP: Rekonstruktion eines verlorengegangenen Bestandes. Regesten*, part 4, vol. 2 (Murich, 1992), abs. no. 41008.

46. For the documents regarding this issue, see John Mendelsohn and Donald S. Detwiler, eds., *The Holocaust: Selected Documents in Eighteen Volumes*, vol. 2 (New York, 1982), pp. 249ff.

47. *Archives of the Holocaust: An International Collection of Selected Documents*, ed. Henry Friedlander and Sybil Milton, vol. 20 (New York, 1993), pp. 32–33.

48. Longerich, *Akten der Partei-Kanzlei der NSDAP,* part 4, vol. 2, abs. no. 40601.

49. Ibid., part 1, vol. 1, abs. no. 14865.

50. Ibid.

51. Nuremberg doc. NG 2297, in Mendelsohn and Detwiler, eds., *The Holocaust*, vol. 2: *Legalizing the Holocaust: The Later Phase, 1939–1943* (New York, 1982), pp. 135ff.

52. *DGFP: Series D*, vol. 12 (Washington, DC, 1962), p. 204.

53. Longerich, *Akten der Partei-Kanzlei der NSDAP*, Part 4, vol. 2, abs. no. 41006.

54. Ibid., abs. no. 41282.

55. Hertha Feiner, *Before Deportation: Letters from a Mother to Her Daughters, January 1939–December 1942*, ed. Karl Heinz Jahnke (Evanston, 1999), pp. 79–80.

56. Ibid., p. 85.

57. Ibid., p. 87.

58. Dawid Rubinowicz, *The Diary of Dawid Rubinowicz* (Edmonds, WA, 1982), p. 11.

59. Ibid., p. 12.

60. Ibid.

61. Christopher R. Browning, *The Path to Genocide: Essays on Launching the Final Solution* (Cambridge, 1992), pp. 35ff.

62. Ibid., pp. 44–46.

63. Donald L. Niewyk, ed., *Fresh Wounds: Early Narratives of Holocaust Survival* (Chapel Hill, NC, 1998), p. 174.

64. Ibid., p. 175.

65. Dawid Sierakowiak, *The Diary of Dawid Sierakowiak* (New York, 1996), p. 89.

66. Lucjan Dobroszycki, ed., *The Chronicle of the Lódz Ghetto, 1941–1944* (New Haven, 1984), p. 6.

67. For the establishment of the archives and the work of the chroniclers see Dobroszycki, introduction, pp. ixff.

68. See indications in Frank, *Diensttagebuch*, pp. 340 and 340 n. 12.

69. Hilberg and Staron, "Introduction," Adam Czerniaków, *The Warsaw Diary of Adam Czerniaków*, ed. Raul Hilberg, Stanislaw Staron, and Josef Kermisz (New York, 1979), p. 48.

70. Ibid., pp. 48ff.

71. Quoted in Wladislaw Bartoszewski, "The Martyrdom and Struggle of the Jews in Warsaw Under German Occupation 1939–1943," in *The Jews in Warsaw. A History*, ed. Wladislaw T. Bartoszewski and Antony Polonsky (Oxford, 1991), p. 314.

72. Quoted in Joanna Michlic-Coren, "Battling Against the Odds: Culture, Edu-

cation and the Jewish Intelligentsia in the Warsaw Ghetto, 1940–1942," *East European Jewish Affairs* 27, no. 2 (1997), p. 80.

73. For the JDC's financial support to Polish Jewry and its institutions during the period 1939–1941 see mainly Yehuda Bauer, *American Jewry and the Holocaust: The American Jewish Joint Distribution Committee, 1939–1945* (Detroit, 1981), pp. 67ff and particularly p. 73.

74. Yosef Kermish, "The Judenrat in Warsaw," in *Patterns of Jewish Leadership in Nazi Europe, 1933–1945*, ed. Israel Gutman and Cynthia J. Haft (Jerusalem, 1979), pp. 78–80.

75. Lucy S. Dawidowicz, *The War Against the Jews, 1933–1945* (Toronto, 1986), pp. 328ff.

76. Emanuel Ringelblum, *Notes from the Warsaw Ghetto: The Journal of Emmanuel Ringelblum*, ed. Jacob Sloah (New York, 1974), p. 121.

77. Chaim Aron Kaplan, *Scroll of Agony: The Warsaw Diary of Chaim A. Kaplan*, ed. Abraham Isaac Katsh (New York, 1965), p. 245. There are many detailed descriptions of the inventiveness of the smugglers and the crucial function of these operations. See for example Yitzhak Zuckerman, *A Surplus of Memory: Chronicle of the Warsaw Ghetto Uprising*, ed. Barbara Harshav (Berkeley, 1993), p. 129.

78. Yisrael Gutman, *The Jews of Warsaw, 1939–1943: Ghetto, Underground, Revolt* (Bloomington, 1982), p. 68.

79. Ibid., p. 71.

80. Ibid.

81. Jacob Celemenski's text is excerpted from his memoirs (in Yiddish) and quoted in Moshe Fass, "Theatrical Activities in the Polish Ghettos during the Years 1939–1942," in *Theatrical Performance during the Holocaust: Texts, Documents, Memoirs*, ed. Rebecca Rovit and Alvin Goldfarb (Baltimore, 1999), pp. 100–101. The pianist Władysław Szpilman performed in such a cabaret. See Władysław Szpilman, *The Pianist: The Extraordinary True Story of One Man's Survival in Warsaw, 1939–1945* (New York, 1999), pp. 83ff.

82. Hersch Wasser, "Daily Entries of Hersch Wasser," in *Yad Vashem Studies*, ed. Joseph Kermish (1983), vol. 15, p. 239.

83. These testimonies are quoted in Michlic-Coren, "Battling Against the Odds," pp. 79–80.

84. Ibid., p. 80.

85. Ibid., p. 91.

86. Ibid.

87. Joanna Michlic-Coren, "Battling Against the Odds: Culture, Education and the Jewish Intelligentsia in the Warsaw Ghetto, 1940–1942." *East European Jewish Affairs*, vol. 27, no. 2, 1997, p. 91.

88. Marcel Reich-Ranicki, *The Author of Himself: The Life of Marcel Reich-Ranicki* (London, 2001), p. 153.

89. Ibid., p. 157.

90. Ibid., p. 141.

91. Ibid., p. 159.

92. Dobroszycki, *The Chronicle*, pp 25ff and 35.

93. Sierakowiak, *Diary*, p. 88.

94. Ibid., p. 89.

95. Ibid., p. 90.

96. Ibid.

97. Ibid., p. 91.

98. Yisrael Gutman, "Zionist Youth," in *Zionist Youth Movements during the Shoah*, ed. Asher Cohen and Yehoyakim Cochavi, *Studies on the Shoah* 4 (New York, 1995), pp. 13–14; Aharon Weiss, "Zionist Youth Movements in Poland during the German Occupation," in *Zionist Youth Movements during the Shoah*, ed. Asher Cohen and Yehoyakim Cochavi, *Studies on the Shoah* 4 (New York, 1995), p. 243.

99. Dina Porat, "Zionist Pioneering Youth Movements in Poland and Their Attitude to Erets Israel during the Holocaust," *Polin: Studies in Polish Jewry* 9 (1996), pp. 195ff.

100. The deep sense of betrayal and the bitterness of the survivors were papered over at the end of the war but reappeared as time went by and found widespread expression in interviews, memoirs, and in new historical research, mainly from the 1980s on.

101. See the notes above, as well as Erica Nadelhaft, "Resistance through Education: Polish Zionist Youth Movements in Warsaw, 1939–1941," *Polin: Studies in Polish Jewry* 9 (1996), pp. 212ff.

102. Quoted in Yitzhak Arad, Yisrael Gutman, and Abraham Margaliot, eds., *Documents on the Holocaust: Selected Sources on the Destruction of the Jews of Germany and Austria, Poland, and the Soviet Union* (Jerusalem, 1981), p. 230.

103. Shimon Huberband, "Kiddush Hashem: Jewish Religious and Cultural Life in Poland during the Holocaust," ed. Jeffrey S. Gurock and Robert S. Hirt (New York, 1987), p. 120.

104. Rolf-Dieter Müller, *Hitlers Ostkrieg und die deutsche Siedlungspolitik: Die Zusammenarbeit von Wehrmacht, Wirtschaft und SS* (Frankfurt am Main, 1991), pp. 21ff. Immediately after the end of the Polish campaign, Himmler had declared that "2.5 million Polish Jews would be used to dig antitank ditches along the demarcation line with the Soviet Union." See Halder, *Kriegstagebuch*, vol. 1, 184n. There was yet another way of sending tens of thousands of Jews into slave labor. In early 1941 Greiser took an ideologically unusual step: He offered some 70,000 Jewish workers from his territory to the Reich labor minister for employment in Germany. Göring, faced with the growing needs of the German war economy as the preparations for the campaign against the Soviet Union were moving into high gear, gave his assent. The Reichsmarschall apparently informed all regional authorities not to hinder the employment of this new and unexpected work force. All these plans came to naught: In April 1941, Hitler forbade any transfer of Jews from the East into the Reich, even for employment in war industries.

105. Tatiana Berenstein, ed., *Faschismus, Getto, Massenmord: Dokumentation über*

Ausrottung und Widerstand der Juden in Polen während des zweiten Weltkrieges (Berlin [East], 1961), p. 221.

106. Czerniaków, *Warsaw Diary*, p. 233.

107. Wasser, "Daily Entries of Hersch Wasser," p. 266.

108. Kermish, "The Judenrat," in Yisrael Gutman and Cynthia J., Haft, *Patterns of Jewish leadership in Nazi Europe, 1933–1945* (Jerusalem, 1979), pp. 80–81.

109. Isaiah Trunk, *Judenrat: The Jewish Councils in Eastern Europe under Nazi Occupation* (New York, 1972), pp. 499–500.

110. Calel Perechodnik, *Am I a Murderer?: Testament of a Jewish Ghetto Policeman*, ed. Frank Fox (Boulder, CO, 1996), p. 9.

111. Ibid., p. 14.

112. Mary Berg, *Warsaw Ghetto, A Diary*, ed. Sh. L. Shnayderman (New York, 1945), pp. 45–46. Berg's diary may well have been thoroughly reworked by the author and the publishers and thus is hardly used in this study.

113. Gutman, *The Jews of Warsaw*, p. 92.

114. Ganzweich's case shows in fact that at times there was possibly more solidarity among the ghetto Jews than met the eye. An inhabitant of the ghetto, Hillel Zeidman, met with Ganzweich in his apartment, probably in early 1941, and was shown some of the reports prepared for the Germans. "Do these reports (I browsed through dozens of them) amount to denunciation?" Zeidman noted in his diary. "One cannot say that. On the contrary, they contain proposals . . . meant to prove to the Germans that it is to their advantage to treat the Jews with lesser severity." Hillel Zeidman, *Diary of the Warsaw Ghetto* [Hebrew] (New York, 1957), pp. 177–78. Ganzweich's reports were found and published in the 1980s: The milder evaluation was confirmed. Much in the reports was intended to convince the Germans "that the ghetto residents should be regarded as a valuable asset." Christopher R. Browning and Yisrael Gutman, eds., "The Reports of a Jewish 'Informer' in the Warsaw Ghetto—Selected Documents," *Yad Vashem Studies* 17 (1986), pp. 247ff. and 255. The case of another notorious informer Alfred Nossig was not fundamentally different. Shmuel Almog, "Alfred Nossig: A Reappraisal," *Studies in Zionism* 7 (1983).

115. See in particular Huberband, "Kiddush Hashem: Jewish Religious and Cultural Life in Poland during the Holocaust," pp. 136ff.

116. Auerswald's report is published in Arad, Gutman, and Margaliot, *Documents on the Holocaust*, pp. 244–46.

117. Berenstein, *Faschismus, Getto, Massenmord*, p. 140.

118. Ringelblum, *Notes*, pp. 204–5. The health condition of the Jewish populations was not the same from one ghetto to another. Thus, in Vilna for example, from the fall of 1941 (after the establishment of the ghetto) mortality rates from disease stabilized at a relatively low level. This unusual situation may have been the result of a series of unconnected factors: The remaining population (after the exterminations of the summer and fall) was mostly young, the food supply was ampler than in Warsaw or Lodz, the number of physicians in the ghetto was relatively high, the main Jewish hospital of the city remained within the ghetto boundaries, and strict rules of hygiene and sanita-

tion were imposed by the health department of the council. On the health situation in the Vilna ghetto see Solon Beinfeld, "Health Care in the Vilna Ghetto," *Holocaust and Genocide Studies* 12, no. 1 (1998), p. 66.

119. Ringelblum, *Notes*, p. 194.

120. Czerniaków, *Warsaw Diary*, p. 261.

121. Walter Manoschek, ed., *"Es gibt nur eines für das Judentum—Vernichtung": Das Judenbild in deutschen Soldatenbriefen 1939–1944* (Hamburg, 1997), p. 17.

122. Ibid., p. 18.

123. Ibid., p. 25.

124. Zygmunt Klukowski, *Diary from the Years of Occupation, 1939–44*, ed. Andrew Klukowski and Helen Klukowski May (Urbana, IL, 1993), p. 115.

125. Kaplan, *Scroll of Agony*, pp. 241–42.

126. Ringelblum, *Notes*, p. 181.

127. Daniel Uziel, "Wehrmacht Propaganda Troops and the Jews," *Yad Vashem Studies* 29 (2001), pp. 36–37.

128. On "Das Reich" see Norbert Frei and Johannes Schmitz, *Journalismus im Dritten Reich* (Munich, 1989), pp. 108ff.

129. Ibid., pp. 114ff. and 118ff.

130. Quoted in Elizabeth Harvey, *Women and the Nazi East: Agents and Witnesses of Germanization* (New Haven, 2003), p. 126.

131. Susannah Heschel, *Transforming Jesus from Jew to Aryan: Protestant Theologians in Nazi Germany* (Tucson, 1995), p. 6.

132. For some aspects of this research during the 1930s see Friedländer, *Nazi Germany and the Jews, Volume 1*, pp. 190ff.

133. For the most detailed study of both Institutes see Helmut Heiber, *Walter Frank und sein Reichsinstitut für Geschichte des neuen Deutschlands* (Stuttgart, 1966). See also Patricia von Papen, "Schützenhilfe nationalsozialistischer Judenpolitik: Die Judenforschung des Reichsinstituts für Geschichte des neuen Deutschlands, 1935–1945," in *"Beseitigung des jüdischen Einflusses—": Antisemitische Forschung, Eliten und Karrieren im Nationalsozialismus*, ed. Fritz Bauer Institut, *Jahrbuch 1998/99 zur Geschichte und Wirkung des Holocaust* (Frankfurt, 1999), p. 17ff; Dieter Schiefelbein, "Das Institut zur Erforschung der Judenfrage Frankfurt am Main," in *"Beseitigung des jüdischen Einflusses . . . ": Antisemitische Forschung, Eliten und Karrieren im Nationalsozialismus*, ed. Fritz Bauer Institut, *Jahrbuch 1998/99 zur Geschichte und Wirkung des Holocaust* (Frankfurt, 1999), pp. 43ff.

134. For the opening ceremony and for Rosenberg's address, see *Völkischer Beobachter*, March 27–30, 1941.

135. Max Weinreich, *Hitler's Professors: The Part of Scholarship in Germany's Crimes against the Jewish People* (New York, 1946), p. 104.

136. Ibid., pp. 107–10. Emphasis in original.

137. Götz Aly and Susanne Heim, *Vordenker der Vernichtung: Auschwitz und die deutschen Pläne für eine neue europäische Ordnung* (Hamburg, 1991), p. 219.

138. Weinreich, *Hitler's Professors*, p. 110.

139. Aly and Heim, *Vordenker der Vernichtung*, pp. 217ff.

140. Papen, "Schützenhilfe," p. 29.

141. Ibid.

142. Monica Kingreen, "Raubzüge einer Stadtverwaltung: Frankfurt am Main und die Aneignung 'Jüdischen Besitzes,'" *Beiträge zur Geschichte des Nationalsozialismus* 17 (2001), pp. 32ff.

143. Ibid.

144. Ibid.

145. Quoted in Hector Feliciano, *The Lost Museum: The Nazi Conspiracy to Steal the World's Greatest Works of Art* (New York, 1997), p. 33.

146. For the details, see mainly Jonathan Petropoulos, *Art as Politics in the Third Reich* (Chapel Hill, 1996), p. 129.

147. Ibid., p. 130.

148. Pätzold, *Verfolgung*, p. 285.

149. Ulrich von Hassell, *Die Hassell-Tagebücher 1938–1944: Aufzeichnungen vom Andern Deutschland*, ed. Klaus Peter Reiss (unter Mitarbeit) and Freiherr Friedrich Hiller von Gaertringen (Berlin, 1988), p. 254.

150. Manoschek, *"Es gibt nur eines für das Judentum—Vernichtung,"* p. 16.

151. Kater, *Das "Ahnenerbe,"* p. 254.

152. Hitler, *Reden*, part 2, pp. 1663–64.

153. Mihail Sebastian, *Journal, 1935–1944* (Chicago, 2000), p. 316. For a more graphic description of the "bestial ferocity," see particularly the report sent by the U.S. minister in Bucharest, Gunther, to the secretary of state, on January 30, 1941. *Foreign Relations of the United States, Europe, 1941*, vol. 2 (Washington, DC, 1959), p. 860. The German minister to Romania, SA leader Manfred von Killinger, mentioned on January 23 Antonescu's description of "unbelievably brutal acts. . . . The 693 Jews who were interned in Jilava dead under the most shameful torture." *DGFP: Series D*, vol. 11, p. 1175.

154. For a general survey of Romanian anti-Semitism see Leon Volovici, *Nationalist Ideology and Antisemitism: The Case of Romanian Intellectuals in the 1930s* (Oxford, 1991); Stephen Fischer-Galati, "The Legacy of Anti-Semitism," in *The Tragedy of Romanian Jewry*, ed. Randolph L. Braham (New York, 1994), mainly p. 10ff.

155. Quoted in Volovici, *Nationalist Ideology*, p. 63.

156. Quoted in Jean Ancel, "The 'Christian' Regimes of Romania and the Jews, 1940–1942," *Holocaust and Genocide Studies* 7, no. 1 (1993), p. 16. Among the young Iron Guard intellectual anti-Semites, the future world-renowned historian of religion Mircea Eliade was probably one of the most rabid. As Warsaw crumbled under the German onslaught, in September 1939, Eliade declared: "The Poles' resistance in Warsaw is a Jewish resistance. Only Yids are capable of the blackmail of putting women and children in the frontline to take advantage of the Germans' sense of scruple . . . What is happening on the frontier of Bukovina is a scandal, because new waves of Jews are flooding into the country. Rather than a Romania again invaded by kikes, it would be better to have a German protectorate." Sebastian, *Journal*, p. 238.

157. Fischer-Galati, "The Legacy of Anti-Semitism," mainly pp. 19ff.

158. *Foreign Relations of the United States Europe, 1940*, vol. 2, p. 764.

159. Ibid., p. 774.

160. Ibid., 1941, vol. 2, p. 860.

161. Anne Grynberg, *Les Camps de la honte: Les internés juifs des camps français, 1939–1944* (Paris, 1991), p. 12. In a meeting at the German embassy on February 2, 1941, Dannecker confirmed these data. See Serge Klarsfeld, ed., *Die Endlösung der Judenfrage in Frankreich: Deutsche Dokumente 1941–1944* (Paris, 1977), p. 17.

162. Matteoli Commission, "Interim Report," p. 181, quoted and translated in Michael J. Bazyler, *Holocaust Justice: The Battle for Restitution in America's Courts* (New York, 2003), p. 175.

163. See Philippe Verheyde, "L'aryanisation economique: Le cas des grandes entreprises," *Revue d'Histoire de la Shoah: Le monde juif* 168 (Jan.–Apr. 2000).

164. Klarsfeld, *Die Endlösung*, p. 13.

165. Pätzold, *Verfolgung*, pp. 281–82.

166. *DGFP: Series D*, vol. 12 (Washington, DC, 1962), p. 228.

167. For details on the establishment of the CGQJ and on Vallat's activities, see Michael R. Marrus and Robert O. Paxton, *Vichy et les juifs* (Paris, 1990), pp. 79ff.

168. The Commissariat Général even established its own police unit (*La Police aux Questions Juives*, or PQJ), but after a year or so, it became obvious to both the Germans and the French that this special police force did not have the means for systematic action. It was finally integrated into the general police as a *Section d'Enquêtes et de Contrôle*, or SEC. See in particular Serge Klarsfeld, *Vichy-Auschwitz: Le rôle de Vichy dans la solution finale de la question juive en France, 1943–1944* (Paris, 1985), pp. 55ff.

169. Marrus and Paxton, *Vichy et les juifs,* pp. 92ff.

170. For the full text of the law summed up here, see ibid., p. 402.

171. *DGFP*, Series D, 1941, vol. 12 (Washington, DC 1962), p. 438.

172. For a thorough study of the "Institute" see Joseph Billig, *L'Institut d'étude des questions juives* (Paris, 1974).

173. For the propaganda posters display, see Reneé Poznanski's note in Biélinky, *Journal*, p. 122 n. 47.

174. See Claude Singer, *Le Juif Süss et la propagande Nazie: L'Histoire confisquée* (Paris, 2003), p. 206.

175. Ibid., p. 211.

176. Ibid., p. 220.

177. Ibid., pp. 221 ff.

178. Jacques Adler, *The Jews of Paris and the Final Solution: Communal Response and Internal Conflicts, 1940–1944* (New York, 1987), p. 70.

179. Renée Poznanski, *Être juif en France pendant la Seconde Guerre mondiale* (Paris, 1994), p. 103.

180. Jean Guéhenno, *Journal des années noires, 1940–1944* (Paris, 1947), p. 111.

181. Poznanski, *Être juif*, p. 104.

182. Biélinky, *Journal*, p. 123.

183. For a definition of this policy see among others Claude Singer, *Vichy, l'université et les juifs: Les silences et la mémoire* (Paris, 1992), pp. 136ff. As for the distinction between "collaboration d'État" and "collaborationism," see Stanley Hoffmann, "Collaborationism in France during World War II," *Journal of Modern History* 40 (Sept. 1968).

184. Marrus and Paxton, *Vichy et les juifs*, p. 209.

185. For Helbronner's career see mainly Simon Schwarzfuchs, *Aux prises avec Vichy: Histoire politique des Juifs de France, 1940–1944* (Paris, 1998), pp. 94ff.

186. Ibid., pp. 90ff.

187. For the full text of the petition see ibid., pp. 107ff. For the (slightly revised) translation of the last paragraph quoted here, see Paula Hyman, *The Jews of Modern France* (Berkeley, 1998), p. 167.

188. Adler, *The Jews of Paris*, p. 84.

189. Carole Fink, *Marc Bloch: A Life in History* (Cambridge, 1989), p. 272.

190. Bob Moore, *Victims and Survivors: The Nazi Persecution of the Jews in the Netherlands, 1940–1945* (London, 1997), pp. 72–73.

191. Ibid., pp. 73ff.

192. For SS bureaucracy in the Netherlands, see Johannes Houwink ten Cate, "Der Befehlshaber der Sipo und des SD in den besetzten niederländischen Gebieten und die Deportation der Juden 1942–1943," in *Die Bürokratie der Okkupation: Strukturen der Herrschaft und Verwaltung im besetzten Europa*, ed. Wolfgang Benz, Johannes Houwink ten Cate, and Gerhard Otto, *Nationalsozialistische Besatzungspolitik in Europa 1939–1945*, vol. 4 (Berlin, 1998), pp. 197ff.

193. See now the following extremely thorough study: Friederike Sattler, "Der Handelstrust West in den Niederlanden," in *Die Expansion der Dresdner Bank in Europa*, ed. Harald Wixforth, in Klaus-Dietmar Henke, ed., *Die Dresdner Bank im Dritten Reich* (Munich, 2006), vol. 3, pp. 682ff.

194. About the ransom deals in Holland, see mainly Bettina Zeugin and Thomas Sandkühler, *Die Schweiz und die deutschen Lösegelderpressungen in den besetzten Niederlanden: Vermögensentziehung, Freikauf, Austausch 1940–1945: Beitrag zur Forschung*, ed. Unabhängigen Expertenkommission Schweiz—Zweiter Weltkrieg (Zurich, 2001), pp. 46ff.

195. Moore, *Victims and Survivors*, p. 83.

196. Guus Meershoek, "The Amsterdam Police and the Persecution of the Jews," in *Holocaust: Critical Concepts in Historical Studies*, ed. David Cesarani (New York, 2004), pp. 541ff.

197. For the details see J. Presser, *Ashes in the Wind: The Destruction of Dutch Jewry* (Detroit, 1988), pp. 47ff; Moore, *Victims and Survivors*, pp. 68ff.

198. Moore, *Victims and Survivors*, p. 70.

199. Quoted in Gordon J. Horwitz, *In the Shadow of Death: Living Outside the Gates of Mauthausen* (New York, 1990), pp. 52–53.

200. Ibid., p. 53.

201. Moore, *Victims and Survivors*, pp. 81–82.

202. Ibid., p. 83.

203. For these biographical details, see J. G. Gaarlandt, Introduction to Etty Hillesum, *An Interrupted Life: The Diaries of Etty Hillesum, 1941–1943* (New York, 1983), pp. viiff.

204. Ibid., p. 9.

205. Ibid., pp. 23–24.

206. Moses Flinker, *Young Moshe's Diary: The Spiritual Torment of a Jewish Boy in Nazi Europe*, ed. Shaul Esh and Geoffrey Wigoder (Jerusalem, 1971), pp. 19–20.

207. Melissa Müller, *Das Mädchen Anne Frank: Die Biographie* (Munich, 1998), p. 174.

208. On van Roey's "flexible attitude" on the Jewish question see Lieven Saerens, "The Attitude of the Belgian Roman Catholic Clergy Towards the Jews Prior to the Occupation" in *Belgium and the Holocaust: Jews, Belgians, Germans*, ed. Dan Michman (Jerusalem, 1998), p. 144–45; Mark Van den Wijngaert, "The Belgian Catholics and the Jews During the German Occupation, 1940–1944," in *Belgium and the Holocaust: Jews, Belgians, Germans*, ed. Dan Michman (Jerusalem, 1998), p. 227.

209. Yisrael Gutman and Shmuel Krakowski, *Unequal Victims: Poles and Jews during World War Two* (New York, 1986), pp. 52–53.

210. Quoted in Burkhart Schneider, Pierre Blet, and Angelo Martini, eds., *Die Briefe Pius' XII. an die deutschen Bischöfe 1939–1944.* (Mainz, 1966), p. 134 n. 4.

211. Ibid., pp. 132–34.

212. John F. Morley, *Vatican Diplomacy and the Jews during the Holocaust, 1939–1943* (New York, 1980), pp. 51–53. The full text of Bérard's report was first published in *Le Monde Juif*, October 1946, pp. 2ff. According to the selected documents published by the Vatican, Pétain mentioned, then showed, Bérard's report to the nuncio, Monsignor Valerio Valeri, to justify his own policies. Valeri protested against what he considered as the marshal's simplistic interpretation but did not state that the report misrepresented the Vatican's position. See Pierre Blet, Angelo Martini, and Burkhart Schneider, eds., *Actes et documents du Saint Siège relatifs à la Seconde Guerre mondiale*, vol. 8, *Le Saint Siège et les Victimes de la Guerre* (1974), pp. 295–97. The report probably expressed the views of Vatican undersecretaries of state, Monsigners Giovanni Battista Montini and Domenico Tardini or those of the superior general of the Dominican order, Father Gillet. In both cases, the report would have been authoritative. See Jean-Marie Mayeur, "Les Églises devant la Persécution des Juifs en France," in *La France et la question juive: 1940–1944*, ed. Georges Wellers, André Kaspi, and Serge Klarsfeld (Paris, 1981), p. 155 n. 17.

213. For the argument of continuity, see in particular Dieter Pohl, *Von der "Judenpolitik" zum Judenmord: Der Distrikt Lublin des Generalgouvernements, 1939–1944* (Frankfurt am Main, 1993), pp. 30ff; see also Dieter Pohl, "The Murder of the Jews in the General Government," in *National Socialist Extermination Policies: Contemporary German Perspectives and Controversies*, ed. Ulrich Herbert (New York, 2000), pp. 84ff.

214. On the activities of the JDC and those of related organizations, see mainly Bauer, *American Jewry and the Holocaust.*

215. For details on Sugihara's story see Hillel Levine, *In Search of Sugihara: The Elusive Japanese Diplomat Who Risked His Life to Rescue 10,000 Jews from the Holocaust* (New York, 1996).

216. Ibid., p. 257.

217. Ibid., p. 5.

218. Ibid.

219. Ibid., p. 253.

220. Quoted on p. 195: "Die Relationen von Leben und Tod": Abraham Lewin, "Eulogy in Honor of Yitshak Meir Weissenberg, September 31, 1941," in *A Cup of Tears: A Diary of the Warsaw Ghetto,* edited by Antony Polonsky (Oxford, 1988), p. 243.

Chapter Four: June 1941–September 1941

1. Quoted in Karel C. Berkhoff, *Harvest of Despair: Life and Death in Ukraine under Nazi Rule* (Cambridge, MA, 2004), pp. 75–76.

2. Dawid Rubinowicz, *The Diary of Dawid Rubinowicz* (Edmonds, WA, 1982), p. 16.

3. Lucjan Dobroszycki, ed., *The Chronicle of the Lódz Ghetto, 1941–1944* (New Haven, 1984), p. 62.

4. Dawid Sierakowiak, *The Diary of Dawid Sierakowiak* (New York, 1996), p. 105.

5. Ibid.

6. Mihail Sebastian, *Journal, 1935–1944* (Chicago, 2000), p. 370.

7. Ibid.

8. Benjamin Harshav, introduction to Herman Kruk, *The Last Days of the Jerusalem of Lithuania: Chronicles from the Vilna Ghetto and the Camps, 1939–1944*, ed. Benjamin Harshav (New Haven, 2002), pp. xlff.

9. Kruk, *The Last Days*, pp. 46–47.

10. Adam Czerniaków, *The Warsaw Diary of Adam Czerniaków*, ed. Raul Hilberg, Stanislaw Staron, and Josef Kermisz (New York, 1979), p. 251.

11. Ibid., p. 256.

12. Victor Klemperer, *I Will Bear Witness: A Diary of the Nazi Years, 1933–41* (New York, 1998), vol. 1, pp. 390–91.

13. See for example the various reports summed up in Marlis G. Steinert, *Hitlers Krieg und die Deutschen: Stimmung und Haltung der deutschen Bevölkerung im Zweiten Weltkrieg* (Düsseldorf, 1970), pp. 206ff.

14. Joseph Goebbels, *Die Tagebücher von Joseph Goebbels: Sämtliche Fragmente*, ed. Elke Fröhlich (Munich, 1998), part 2, vol. 1 (Munich, 1996), pp. 30, 35.

15. Nuremberg Doc. L-221, International Military Tribunal, *Trial of the Major War Criminals Before the International Military Tribunal, Nuremberg, 14 November 1945–1 October 1946*, 42 vols. (New York, 1971), vol. 38, pp. 68–94.

16. Reichskommissariat Ostland included eastern Poland, part of Belorussia (*Weissruthenien* for the Germans), and the Baltic countries (Białystok and its district were annexed to East Prussia. Reichskommissariat Ukraine included part of Belorussia

and the pre–September 1939 Ukraine; Western Ukraine (or Eastern Galicia) was annexed to "Galicia" as a district of the General Government.

17. See for example Goebbels, *Tagebücher*, part 2, vol. 1, pp. 42–43 and 115–16.

18. About the context of Bishop Galen's sermon, see Beth Griech-Polelle, "Image of a Churchman-Resister: Bishop von Galen, the Euthanasia Project and the Sermons of Summer 1941," *Journal of Contemporary History* 36, no. 1 (2001), pp. 41ff.

19. About this second phase of euthanasia, see among others Ernst Klee, *"Euthanasie" im NS-Staat: Die "Vernichtung lebensunwerten Lebens"* (Frankfurt am Main, 1983), pp. 345, and Michael Burleigh, *Death and Deliverance: "Euthanasia" in Germany c. 1900–1945* (Cambridge, 1994), pp. 220ff.

20. Adolf Hitler, *Hitler: Reden und Proklamationen, 1932–1945: Kommentiert von einem deutschen Zeitgenossen*, ed. Max Domarus, 4 vols. (Leonberg, 1987–88), p. 1726.

21. Ibid., p. 1731.

22. Andreas Hillgruber, *Staatsmänner und Diplomaten bei Hitler: Vertrauliche Aufzeichnungen über Unterredungen mit Vertretern des Auslandes* (Frankfurt am Main, 1967–70), vol. 1, p. 614.

23. Ibid., p. 625.

24. *Documents on German Foreign Policy. Series D, 1937–1945*, vol. 13 (Washington, DC, 1964), p. 387.

25. Hewel diary entry, quoted in Peter Longerich and Dieter Pohl, eds., *Die Ermordung der europäischen Juden: Eine umfassende Dokumentation des Holocaust 1941–1945* (Munich, 1989), p. 76.

26. Adolf Hitler, *Monologe im Führer-Hauptquartier 1941–1944*, ed. Werner Jochmann and Heinrich Heim (Hamburg, 1980), p. 41.

27. Henry Picker, ed., *Hitlers Tischgespräche im Führerhauptquartier 1941–1942* (Stuttgart, 1965), p. 144.

28. Goebbels, *Tagebücher*, part 2, vol. 1, p. 35 (*In einigen Tagen wird, langsam beginnend, nun die antisemitische Kampagne anlaufen, und ich bin davon überzeugt, dass wir auch in dieser Richtung mehr und mehr die Weltöffentlichkeit auf unsere Seite bringen können*).

29. For the full text of Dietrich's *Tagesparole* see Bianka Pietrow-Ennker, "Die Sowjetunion in der Propaganda des Dritten Reiches: Das Beispiel der Wochenschau," *Militärgeschichtliche Mitteilungen* 46, no. 2 (1989), pp. 79ff. and 108–9.

30. Ibid., p. 133. See also Willi A. Boelcke, ed., *Wollt Ihr den totalen Krieg? Die geheimen Goebbels Konferenzen 1939–1943* (Herrsching, 1989), p. 183.

31. Joseph Goebbels, *Die Zeit ohne Beispiel: Reden und Aufsätze aus den Jahren 1939/40/41* (Munich, 1941), pp. 526–31. The translation of the opening sentences is taken from German Propaganda Archive (CAS Department—Calvin College, [cited 2004]); available from www.calvin.edu/academic/cas/gpa/goeb18.htm.

32. Goebbels, *Die Zeit ohne Beispiel: Reden und Aufsätze aus den Jahren 1939/40/41*, pp. 533–535, 558, 566, 582–83, 585.

33. Philipp Gassert, *Amerika im Dritten Reich: Ideologie, Propaganda und Volksmeinung 1933–1945* (Stuttgart, 1997), pp. 328–29ff.

34. "Roosevelt, Hauptwerkzeug der jüdischen Freimaurerei" (Roosevelt, the main instrument of Jewish Freemasonry), *Völkischer Beobachter*, July 23, 1941, p. 3.

35. Goebbels, *Tagebücher*, part 2, vol. 1, pp. 116, 168, 225, 271, 312, 328, 334, and 515. On the Kaufman affair, see mainly Wolfgang Benz, "Judenvernichtung aus Notwehr? Die Legenden um Theodore N. Kaufman," *Vierteljahrshefte für Zeitgeschichte*, 29 (1981), pp. 615–626.

36. Ibid.

37. "Das Kriegsziel Roosevelts und der Juden: Völlige Ausrottung des deutschen Volkes. Ungeheuriges jüdisches Vernichtungsprogram nach den Richtlinien Roosevelts," *Völkischer Beobachter*, July 24, 1941, p. 1.

38. Benz, "Judenvernichtung," pp. 620ff.

39. See for example Goebbels, *Tagebücher*, part 2, vol. 1, p. 48.

40. Heinz Boberach, ed., *Meldungen aus dem Reich, 1938–1945: Die geheimen Lageberichte des Sicherheitsdienstes der SS*, 17 vols. (Herrsching, 1984), pp. 2592ff.

41. *DGFP: Series D*, vol. 13, p. 201.

42. Boberach, ed., *Meldungen*, pp. 2563ff; Otto Dov Kulka and Eberhard Jäckel, *Die Juden in den geheimen NS-Stimmungsberichten 1933–1945* (Düsseldorf, 2004), p. 450.

43. For both letters, see Josef Wulf, ed., *Literatur und Dichtung im Dritten Reich: Eine Dokumentation* (Gütersloh, 1963), pp. 431–32.

44. See Peter Klein, ed., *Die Einsatzgruppen in der besetzten Sowjetunion 1941/42.* (Berlin: 1997), pp. 318–19.

45. Ibid., pp. 323ff.

46. Ibid., p. 337. According to the testimony given at Nuremberg by Otto Ohlendorf, head of *Einsatzgruppe D* (the only chief of an *Einsatzgruppe* to be put on trial), an oral order to exterminate all Jews on Soviet territory was transmitted by Heydrich's emissary, Bruno Streckenbach, to the commanders of the *Einsatzgruppen* a few days before the beginning of the campaign. At the time of this testimony (1947), Streckenbach was thought to be dead. However when he returned from a Soviet prisoner-of-war camp in the mid-1950s, he declared that no such order was ever given or transmitted before the beginning of the Russian campaign. Other members of the killing units (heads or members of *Einsatzkommandos*—that is, subunits of the *Einsatzgruppen*) who were put on trial were more or less equally divided in support of either one of these opposing claims; moreover, any number of other versions that could help their own defense were brought forth. See Philippe Burrin, *Hitler and the Jews: The Genesis of the Holocaust* (London, 1994), pp. 94ff. In a masterly analysis of all available documents and testimonies, Burrin confirms the view first presented by Alfred Streim: The initial orders targeted Jewish men only; the killings expanded to entire Jewish communities from August on. For Streim's view, see mainly Alfred Streim, "Zur Eröffnung des allgemeinen Judenvernichtungs befehls gegenüber den Einsatzgruppen," in *Der Mord an den Juden im Zweiten Weltkrieg: Entschlussbildung und Verwirklichung*, ed. Eberhard Jäckel and Jürgen Rohwer (Stuttgart, 1985). See also Klein, ed., *Die Einsatzgruppen in der besetzten Sowjetunion 1941/42*, p. 23.

47. The three thousand members of the four SS *Einsatzgruppen* (A, North; B, Center; C, South; D, Extreme South) were reinforced by Waffen SS units and by special SS units such as *Kommandostab Reichsführer SS*. The *Kommandostab* was a conglomerate of SS units (numbering approximately 25,000 men divided in three SS brigades) directly under Himmler's command. The *Reichsführer* used it for "special tasks": the killing of some 16,000 Jews in the area of the Pripet marshes and of thousands more in Pinsk and Bobruisk, as well as "minor" operations including only a few hundred victims in each case. Mostly, however, the *Kommandostab* brigades were under the command of the HSSPF and occasionally under that of the Wehrmacht (the first SS brigade, for example, was "lent" by Himmler to the HSSPF South, Jeckeln; then to Reichenau's Sixth Army). See Yehoshua Büchler, "Kommandostab Reichsführer SS: Himmler's Personal Murder Brigades in 1941," *Holocaust and Genocide Studies* 1 (1986), pp. 11ff.

48. Heinrich Himmler, *Der Dienstkalender Heinrich Himmlers 1941/42*, ed. Peter Witte et al. (Hamburg, 1999), p. 195 n. 14.

49. Quoted in Tikva Fatal-Knaani, "The Jews of Pinsk, 1939–1943: Through the Prism of New Documentation," *Yad Vashem Studies* 29 (2001), p. 162. At the same time—and most probably as a follow-up to Hitler's July 16 remarks—the SS chief considerably increased the number of SS units and police battalions on Soviet territory; he also ordered the large-scale inclusion of local auxiliaries in the killing process. See Christopher R. Browning, *The Path to Genocide: Essays on Launching the Final Solution* (Cambridge, 1992), p. 106.

50. For the most thorough presentations of the food-supply argument see Christian Gerlach, "Deutsche Wirtschaftsinteressen," in *Nationalsozialistische Vernichtungspolitik, 1939–1945: Neue Forschungen und Kontroversen*, ed. Ulrich Herbert (Frankfurt am Main, 1998), and Christopher Dieckmann, "Ermordung Litauischer Juden," in ibid., pp. 263ff. and 292ff.

51. For the Jewish population statistics, see Raul Hilberg, *The Destruction of the European Jews*, 3 vols. (New Haven, CT, 2003), vol. 1, pp. 295–97.

52. Hermann G.'s letters were first published in Ludwig Eiber, "Ein bischen Wahrheit . . ." *1999: Zeitschrift für Sozialgeschichte des 20. und 21. Jahrhunderts* 6, no. 1 (1991), pp. 58ff. This letter is quoted in Bernhard Chiari, *Alltag hinter der Front: Besatzung, Kollaboration und Widerstand in Weissrussland 1941–1944* (Düsseldorf, 1998), p. 240ff. On September 12, the employment of Jews by soldiers was forbidden by Keitel: "There will be no collaboration between the armed forces and the Jewish population, whose attitude is openly or secretly anti-German, and no employment of individual Jews to render preferential auxiliary services for the armed forces." Nuremberg doc. NOKW-3292.

53. Johannes Hürter, "Auf dem Weg zur Militäropposition: Tresckow, Gersdorff, der Vernichtungskrieg und der Judenmord: Neue Dokumente über das Verhältnis der Heeresgruppe Mitte zur Einsatzgruppe B im Jahr 1941," *Vierteljahrshefte fur Zeitgeschichte* 3 (2004), pp. 527ff.

54. Documents explicitly referring to the widespread murder of Jews were brought

to the knowledge of the future military resisters as early as mid-July 1941. See ibid., pp. 552ff. Hürter's article restarted a controversy that had initially been launched in a series of publications by Christian Gerlach; see, most recently, Christian Gerlach, "Hitlergegner bei der Heeresgruppe Mitte und die 'verbrecherische Befehle,'" in *NS-Verbrechen und der militärische Widerstand gegen Hitler*, ed. Gerd R. Uberschär (Darmstadt, 2000), pp. 62ff.

55. The English translation is quoted in Omer Bartov, *Hitler's Army: Soldiers, Nazis, and War in the Third Reich* (New York, 1991), p. 130.

56. Ibid.

57. Ibid., pp. 130–31.

58. Quoted in Jürgen Förster, "The Wehrmacht and the War of Extermination Against the Soviet Union," *Yad Vashem Studies* 14 (1981), p. 7.

59. Quoted in Helmut Krausnick and Hans-Heinrich Wilhelm, *Die Truppe des Weltanschauungskrieges: Die Einsatzgruppen des Sicherheitspolizei und des SD, 1938–1942* (Stuttgart, 1981), p. 232.

60. Ortwin Buchbender, *Das tönende Erz: Deutsche Propaganda gegen die Rote Armee in Zweiten Weltkrieg* (Stuttgart, 1978), pp. 60ff.

61. Klara Löffler, *Aufgehoben: Soldatenbriefe aus dem Zweiten Weltkrieg* (Bamberg, 1992), p. 115.

62. Walter Manoschek, ed., *"Es gibt nur eines für das Judentum—Vernichtung": Das Judenbild in deutschen Soldatenbriefen 1939–1944* (Hamburg, 1997), p. 28.

63. Ortwin Buchbender and Reinhold Sterz, eds., *Das andere Gesicht des Krieges: Deutsche Feldpostbriefe 1939–1945* (Munich, 1982), p. 73.

64. Manoschek, ed., *"Es gibt nur eines für das Judentum—Vernichtung,"* p. 32.

65. Letters quoted in Stephen G. Fritz, " "We are trying . . . to change the face of the world": Ideology and Motivation in the Wehrmacht on the Eastern Front: The View from Below," *Journal of Military History* 60, no. 4 (1996), p. 693.

66. Quoted in Bartov, *Hitler's Army: Soldiers, Nazis, and War in the Third Reich*, p. 106.

67. For the special anti-Jewish indoctrination of the SS units and order police battalions see in particular Jürgen Matthäus, "Ausbildungsziel Judenmord? Zum Stellenwert der "weltanschaulichen Erziehung" von SS und Polizei im Rahmen der 'Endlösung,'" *Zeitschrift für Geschichtswissenschaft* 47 (1999), pp. 673ff. See also Jürgen Matthäus et al., *Ausbildung Judenmord? "Weltanschauliche Erziehung" von SS, Polizei, und Wassen-SS im Rahmen der "Endlösung"* (Frankfurt, 2003).

68. For a general historical survey see "Ukrainian-Jewish Relations During the Nazi Occupation," in Philip Friedman, *Roads to Extinction: Essays on the Holocaust*, ed. Ada June Friedman (New York, 1980), pp. 176ff.

69. Friedman, *Roads to Extinction*, p. 177. The relations between Ukrainians and Jews throughout the centuries remain a strongly contested history, at least as intensely so as some major aspects of the relations between Jews and Poles (or Ukranians and Poles). For what appears (to a nonspecialist like myself) to be a balanced view, see Robert Magocsi, *A History of the Ukraine* (Seattle, 1996).

70. Friedman, *Roads to Extinction*, pp. 179–80. Very soon, however, the Germans, intent on turning the Ukraine into an area of colonization, would oppose Ukrainian nationalist demands and try to suppress their movements. See in particular Wendy Lower, *Nazi Empire-Building and the Holocaust in Ukraine* (Chapel Hill, NC, 2005), pp. 182ff.

71. Out of a population of approximately 110,000 Jews, some 4,000 were killed by the Germans and the Ukrainians during the early days of the occupation.

72. Bernd Boll, "Zloczow, July 1941: The Wehrmacht and the Beginning of the Holocaust in Galicia: From a Criticism of Photographs to a Revision of the Past," in *Crimes of War: Guilt and Denial in the Twentieth Century*, ed. Omer Bartov, Atina Grossman, and Mary Nolan (New York, 2002), pp. 61ff.

73. Aryeh Klonicki and Malwina Klonicki, *The Diary of Adam's Father: The Diary of Aryeh Klonicki (Klonymus) and His Wife Malwina, With Letters Concerning the Fate of Their Child Adam* (Jerusalem, 1973), pp. 22–23.

74. Manoschek, ed., *"Es gibt nur eines für das Judentum—Vernichtung,"* p. 33.

75. For these testimonies by Jews and Poles from Brzezany, see Shimon Redlich, *Together and Apart in Brzezany: Poles, Jews, and Ukrainians, 1919–1945* (Bloomington, 2002), pp. 114ff.

76. Thomas Sandkühler, "Anti-Jewish Policy and the Murder of the Jews in the District of Galicia 1941/1942," in *National Socialist Extermination Policies: Contemporary German Perspectives and Controversies*, ed. Ulrich Herbert (New York, 2000), pp. 199ff.

77. About the operation of *Sonderkommando 4a* and of its subunits, see among others, Helmut Krausnick, *Hitlers Einsatzgruppen: Die Truppe des Weltanschauungskrieges 1938–1942* (Frankfurt, 1993), p. 163.

78. For the events that followed see mainly Helmuth Groscurth, *Tagebücher eines Abwehroffiziers 1938–1940*, ed. Helmut Krausnick and Harold C. Deutsch (Stuttgart, 1970), pp. 534ff. The main documents relating to these events are available in English translation in Ernst Klee, Willi Dressen, and Volker Riess, eds., *"The Good Old Days": The Holocaust as Seen by Its Perpetrators and Bystanders* (New York, 1991); pp. 137ff. Michael Burleigh, *The Third Reich: A New History* (New York, 2000), pp. 617–19.

79. Klee et al., *"The Good Old Days,"* p. 138.

80. Ibid.

81. Ibid.

82. Ibid., p. 149.

83. Ibid., p. 154.

84. Bernd Boll and Hans Safrian, "Auf dem Weg nach Stalingrad: Die 6. Armee 1941/42," in *Vernichtungskrieg: Verbrechen der Wehrmacht 1941 bis 1944*, ed. Hannes Heer and Klaus Naumann (Hamburg, 1995), p. 277.

85. Klee et al., *"The Good Old Days,"* p. 141.

86. Ibid., p. 141.

87. For more about Groscurth's personality, see the detailed introduction to the *Tagebuch*. For Groscurth's reference to Heydrich, see *Tagebuch*, p. 130.

88. Klee et al., *"The Good Old Days,"* p. 150.

89. Ibid., p. 149.

90. Ibid., pp. 150–51.

91. Christoph Dieckmann, "Der Krieg und die Ermordung der litauischen Juden," in *Nationalsozialistische Vernichtungspolitik, 1939–1945: Neue Forschungen und Kontroversen*, ed. Ulrich Herbert (Frankfurt am Main, 1998), p. 244. For a detailed reconstruction of the orders received by "EK-Tilsit" see Konrad Kwiet, "Rehearsing for Murder: The Beginning of the Final Solution in Lithuania in June 1941," *Holocaust and Genocide Studies* 12, no. 1 (1998), pp. 4ff. For these early stages, see also Jürgen Matthäus, "Jenseits der Grenze: Die ersten Massenerschiessungen von Juden in Litauen (Juni–August 1941)," *Zeitschrift für Geschichtswissenschaft* 2 (1996), pp. 101ff. There are several computations of the total number of Jews exterminated in Lithuania during the German occupation. According to the most recent studies, out of the Jewish population of 250,000, approximately 200,000 (80 percent) were exterminated. See Michael MacQueen, "Massenvernichtung im Kontext: Täter und Voraussetzungen des Holocaust in Litauen," in *Judenmord in Litauen*, ed. Wolfgang Benz and Marion Neiss, *Reihe Dokumente, Texte, Materialien*, Bd. 33 (Berlin, 1999), p. 15.

92. Dieckmann, "Der Krieg und die Ermordung der litauischen Juden," ibid.

93. Harshav, introduction to Kruk, *The Last Days of the Jerusalem of Lithuania*, pp. xxxiii–xxxiv.

94. On these intricate developments, see among others Dov Levin, "The Jews in the Soviet Lithuanian Establishment, 1940–1941," *Soviet Jewish Affairs* 10, n. 2 (May 1980), pp. 21ff; Dov Levin, "The Sovietization of the Baltics and the Jews, 1940–1941," *Soviet Jewish Affairs* 21, no. 1 (Summer 1991), pp. 53ff. See also Michael MacQueen, "The Context of Mass Destruction: Agents and Prerequisites of the Holocaust in Lithuania," *Holocaust and Genocide Studies* 12 (1998), pp. 32–34.

95. For the sequence of events and the quote, see Yitzhak Arad, *Ghetto in Flames: The Struggle and Destruction of the Jews in Vilna in the Holocaust* (Jerusalem, 1980), pp. 66–67. During the second half of July the Ministry for the Occupied Eastern Territories took over the civilian administration of the "Reichskommissariat Ostland."

96. Isaac Rudashevski, *The Diary of the Vilna Ghetto, June 1941–April 1943*, ed. Percy Matenko (Tel Aviv, 1973), pp. 35–36.

97. For a thorough presentation of the exterminations and an assessment of the number of victims, see Arad, *Ghetto in Flames*, pp. 101ff. and pp. 216–17.

98. MacQueen, "The Context of Mass Destruction," p. 36.

99. Quoted in Yitzhak Arad, "Plunder of Jewish Property in the Nazi Occupied Areas of the Soviet Union," *Yad Vashem Studies* 29 (2001), p. 134.

100. Ernst Klee, Willi Dressen, and Volker Riess, eds., *"The Good Old Days,"* p. 32.

101. Both handwritten letters are reproduced in Wolfgang Benz, Konrad Kwiet, and Jürgen Matthäus, *Einsatz im "Reichskommissariat Ostland": Dokumente zum Völkermord im Baltikum und in Weissrussland, 1941–1944* (Berlin, 1998), pp. 177–78.

102. For Stahlecker's report see Nuremberg doc. L-180, U.S. Office of Chief of Counsel for the Prosecution of Axis Criminality and International Military

Tribunal, *Nazi Conspiracy and Aggression*, 8 vols. (Washington, DC, 1946) vol. 7, pp. 978ff.

103. Andrew Ezergailis, *The Holocaust in Latvia, 1941–1944: The Missing Center* (Riga and Washington, DC, 1996), pp. 58 and 72.

104. I am grateful to Omer Bartov for this information based on recent Polish scholarship.

105. The participation of the Poles has been described in Jan T. Gross, *Neighbors: The Destruction of the Jewish Community in Jedwabne, Poland* (Princeton, 2001). Gross's book triggered a fierce controversy whose main aspects are thoroughly documented in Antony Polonsky and Joanna B. Michlic, eds., *The Neighbors Respond: The Controversy over the Jedwabne Massacre in Poland.* (Princeton, 2004), and also, from a different angle, in Alexander B. Rossino, "Polish 'Neighbors' and German Invaders: Anti-Jewish Violence in the Bialystok District during the Opening Weeks of Operation Barbarossa," *Polin: Studies in Polish Jewry* 16 (2003), pp. 431ff.

106. Lower, *Nazi Empire-Building and the Holocaust in Ukraine*, p. 91.

107. Christian Gerlach, *Kalkulierte Morde: Die deutsche Wirtschafts- und Vernichtungspolitik in Weissrussland 1941 bis 1944* (Hamburg, 1999), p. 536.

108. Lower, *Nazi Empire-Building and the Holocaust in Ukraine*, p. 91.

109. Quoted in Daniel Uziel, "Wehrmacht Propaganda Troops and the Jews," *Yad Vashem Studies* 29 (2001), p. 54.

110. Quoted in Fatal-Knaani, "The Jews of Pinsk," p. 149.

111. For a thorough study of the operations of Ohlendorf's unit, see Andrej Angrick, *Besatzungspolitik und Massenmord. Die Einsatzgruppe D in der Südlichen Sowjetunion 1941–1943* (Hamburg, 2003).

112. International Commission on the Holocaust in Romania, *Final Report of the International Commission on the Holocaust in Romania. Presented to Romanian President Ion Iliescu. November 11, 2004*, available from http://www.ushmm.org/research/center/presentations/programs/presentations/2 005-03-10/pdf/english/chapter_03.pdf., p. 2.

113. For the most complete description of the Iasi pogrom and of the Holocaust in Romania more generally, see Radu Ioanid, *The Holocaust in Romania: The Destruction of Jews and Gypsies under the Antonescu Regime, 1940–1944* (Chicago, 2000); about the Iasi pogrom, see particularly pp. 62ff. The report of the International Commission on the Holocaust in Romania states that "at least 15,000 Jews from the Regat (Old Romania) were killed in the Iasi pogrom and as a result of other anti-Jewish measures." International Commission on the Holocaust in Romania, *Final Report*, p. 3.

114. Quoted in Jean Ancel, "The Romanian Way of Solving the Jewish Problem in Bessarabia and Bukovina, June–July 1941," *Yad Vashem Studies* 19 (1988), p. 190.

115. Ancel, "The 'Christian' Regimes of Romania and the Jews," p. 19.

116. About the ghetto in Kishinev, see Paul A. Shapiro, "The Jews of Chisinău (Kishinev): Romanian Reoccupation, Ghettoisation, Deportation," in *The Destruction of Romanian and Ukrainian Jews during the Antonescu Era*, ed. Randolph L. Braham (Boulder, CO, 1997), pp. 135ff.

117. Ioanid, *The Holocaust in Romania*, pp. 177ff.

118. Quoted in Shapiro, "The Jews of Chisinău," p. 167.

119. Sebastian, *Journal*, p. 397.

120. Ibid., pp. 430–31.

121. *Foreign Relations of the United States 1941*, vol. 2 (Washington, DC, 1959), p. 871.

122. For an overview of German policies in Serbia see Walter Manoschek, *"Serbien ist judenfrei": Militärische Besatzungspolitik und Judenvernichtung in Serbien 1941/42* (Munich, 1993); Walter Manoschek, "The Extermination of the Jews in Serbia," in *National Socialist Extermination Policies: Contemporary German Perspectives and Controversies*, ed. Ulrich Herbert (New York, 2000), pp 163ff. Christopher R. Browning, "The Wehrmacht in Serbia Revisited," in *Crimes of War: Guilt and Denial in the Twentieth Century*, ed. Omer Bartov, Atina Grossmann, and Mary Nolan (New York, 2002), pp. 31ff.

123. Jonathan Steinberg, *All or Nothing: The Axis and the Holocaust, 1941–1943* (London, 1990), p. 30.

124. Ibid.

125. Quoted in John Cornwell, *Hitler's Pope: The Secret History of Pius XII* (New York, 1999), p. 255.

126. See Menachem Shelah, "Jasenovac," in Yisrael Gutman, ed., *Encyclopedia of the Holocaust*, New York, 1990, vol. 2, pp. 739–40.

127. Pierre Blet, *Le Saint Siège et les Victimes de la Guerre, Janvier 1941–Décembre 1942.*, vol. 8 (Vatican City, 1974), p. 261. Translated in John F. Morley, *Vatican Diplomacy and the Jews during the Holocaust, 1939–1943* (New York, 1980), p. 150

128. *Actes et Documents* (*ADSS*), vol. 8, p. 261. Translated in Menachem Shelach, "The Catholic Church in Croatia, the Vatican and the Murder of the Croatian Jews," *Holocaust and Genocide Studies* 4, no. 3 (1989), p. 329.

129. Michael Phayer, *The Catholic Church and the Holocaust, 1930–1965* (Bloomington, 2000), pp. 31ff. and 37–38.

130. For this section see Steinberg, *All or Nothing*, pp. 15ff. and particularly pp. 29ff.

131. Ibid., p. 47.

132. On Slovakia, see Jörg K. Hoensch, "Slovakia: "One God, One People, One Party!" The Development, Aim and Failure of Political Catholicism," in *Catholics, the State, and the European Radical Right, 1919–1945*, ed. Richard J. Wolff and Jörg K. Hoensch (Highland Lakes, NJ, 1987), pp. 158ff.

133. For an overview of the anti-Jewish policies of the Slovak state, see Livia Rothkirchen, "The Situation of the Jews in Slovakia between 1939 and 1945," in *Jahrbuch für Antisemitismusforschung* 7 (1998), pp. 46ff.

134. Ibid., p. 49.

135. See Supra, chapter 2, p. 80.

136. Rothkirchen, "The Situation of the Jews in Slovakia between 1939 and 1945," pp. 49–50.

137. For this synthesis I relied mainly on Randolph L. Braham, *The Politics of*

Genocide: The Holocaust in Hungary, abridged edition (Detroit, 2000); Randolph L. Braham, "The Holocaust in Hungary: A Retrospective Analysis," in *Genocide and Rescue: The Holocaust in Hungary 1944*, ed. David Cesarani (Oxford, 1997); Ivan T. Berend, *Decades of Crisis: Central and Eastern Europe before World War II* (Berkeley, 1998); Stanley G. Payne, *A History of Fascism, 1914–1945* (Madison, WI, 1995); Ezra Mendelsohn, *The Jews of East Central Europe Between the World Wars* (Bloomington, 1983); and István Deák, "A Fatal Compromise? The Debate over Collaboration and Resistance in Hungary," in István Deák, Jan T. Gross, and Tony Judt., *The Politics of Retribution in Europe: World War II and its Aftermath* (Princeton, 2000), pp. 39ff.

138. On the attitude of the Hungarian Churches see Randolph L. Braham, "The Christian Churches of Hungary and the Holocaust," *Yad Vashem Studies* 29 (2001), pp. 244ff.

139. Braham, *The Politics of Genocide* (condensed), p. 34. While HSSPF Friedrich Jeckeln volunteered to murder the 18,000 Jews expelled by the Hungarians, more than 27,000 Jews expelled by the Romanians into German-controlled territory were pushed back into the Romanian-controlled area by *Einsatzgruppe D.* These contrary initiatives indicate that no clear overall policy had yet been decided by the end of August 1941 regarding the fate of large Jewish groups of this kind (that is, not local Jewish communities). On this point see Klaus-Michael Mallmann, "Der qualitative Sprung im Vernichtungsprozess: Das Massaker von Kamenetz-Podolsk Ende August 1941," *Jahrbuch für Antisemitismusforschung* 10 (2001), pp. 239ff. and in particular, 255.

140. Himmler, *Der Dienstkalender*, p. 185 n. 15.

141. On July 17, Himmler had appointed Globocnik as "delegate of the Reichsführer-SS for the establishment of the SS and police strongholds in the new Eastern territories." Ibid., n. 14.

142. Ibid.

143. For details about the testing of the van and its use in Poltava, see Eugen Kogon, Hermann Langbein, and Adalbert Rückerl, eds., *Nazi Mass Murder: A Documentary History of the Use of Poison Gas* (New Haven, 1993), pp. 54ff and 60ff.

144. Part of the details on the origins and the early history of Auschwitz are taken from Danuta Czech, "Entstehungsgeschichte des KL Auschwitz, Aufbau und Ausbauperiode," in *Auschwitz: Nationalsozialistisches Vernichtungslager*, ed. Franciszek Piper and Teresa Swiebocka (Oswiecim [Auschwitz], 1997), pp. 30ff. It seems, however, that no Polish caserns were used but rather a workers' and refugees' camp. For these indications see Sybille Steinbacher, *Auschwitz: Geschichte und Nachgeschichte* (Munich, 2004), p. 13.

145. On the successive stages of IG Farben's involvement in the Auschwitz Buna plant, see mainly Peter Hayes, *Industry and Ideology: IG Farben in the Nazi Era* (New York, 1987), pp. 347ff.

146. For details see Debórah Dwork and Robert Jan van Pelt, *Auschwitz* (New York, 2002), pp. 197ff; Himmler, *Der Dienstkalender*, p. 123n.; Danuta Czech, *Kalendarium der Ereignisse im Konzentrationslager Auschwitz-Birkenau 1939–1945* (Reinbek bei Hamburg, 1989), p. 79. Contrarily to Höss's testimony, during this visit Himmler

did not order the construction in Birkenau of a camp for (future) Soviet prisoners. The construction of the Birkenau prisoners' camp started in October 1941, and, as will be seen further on, only several months later would it be turned into an extermination camp. Sybille Steinbacher, *"Musterstadt" Auschwitz: Germanisierungspolitik und Judenmord in Ostoberschlesien* (Munich, 2000), pp. 238ff.

147. Since World War I, prussic acid—as Zyklon B was then called—was increasingly used as a powerful pesticide for major disinfection purposes. In September 1939, at the outset of operation T4, the use of Zyklon B was considered as a possible method for the killing of the mentally ill, yet it was rejected in favor of carbon monoxide, which was deemed more efficient. Although the potential of Zyklon B for killing human beings was underrated at first, it was widely used as a disinfectant. Thus, in early 1940, as the decision to set up a concentration camp in Auschwitz was taken, Zyklon B was utilized to disinfect the first buildings of the new camp. Over the coming year and a half, Auschwitz, like all other concentration camps, regularly used Zyklon B to this end.

In the early summer, smaller, thus much more effective, disinfection rooms for processing clothes, blankets, and the like were introduced after being suggested by the Zyklon producer, DEGESCH (*Deutsche Gesellschaft für Schädlingsbekämpfung*). According to postwar testimony, during one such operation the slave workers in charge and their SS overseer noticed the rapid death of a cat that had remained in one of these rooms. "Why not use it on human beings?" the overseer supposedly commented. An idea too hastily abandoned in 1939 was born again.

There were plenty of inmates on whom the product could be tested. We saw that mainly after August 1941, within the context of the 14f13 killing program, camp detainees in the hundreds were selected and sent to their death in the T4 institutions. Although some of these institutions remained "operational" until the end of the war, it became obvious that the murder on site, in the camps, would be more efficient. Moreover, following the attack on the Soviet Union, the killing of political commissars, other functionaries of the communist party and all Jewish prisoners of war started. The POW camps were searched by the Gestapo, and those destined for execution were either killed on the spot or transferred to nearby concentration camps to be murdered there. The killing procedures differed from one camp to another; the shot in the back of the neck seems to have been the most common method, but much leeway was left for the inventiveness of the executioners. In Auschwitz, Zyklon B was chosen. On these developments see Florent Brayard, *La "Solution finale de la question juive": La Technique, le temps et les catégories de la décision* (Paris, 2004), pp. 262ff.

148. Danuta Czech, *Auschwitz Chronicle, 1939–1945* (New York, 1990), pp. 85–86.

149. Ibid.

150. For Wagner's role in the starving to death of the Soviet POWs see mainly Christian Gerlach, "Militärische 'Versorgungszwänge,' Besatzungspolitik und Massenverbrechen: Die Rolle des Generalquartiermeister des Heeres und seiner Dienststellen im Krieg gegen die Sowjetunion," in *Ausbeutung, Vernichtung, Öffentlichkeit*, ed. Norbert Frei et al. (Munich, 2000), pp. 175ff. The most thorough study concerning the German

treatment of Soviet POWs remains Christian Streit, *Keine Kameraden: Die Wehrmacht und die Sowjetischen Kriegsfangenen 1941–1945* (Stuttgart, 1978).

151. Götz Aly, ed., *Cleansing the Fatherland: Nazi Medicine and Racial Hygiene* (Baltimore: 1994), p. 130.

152. Ibid., p. 135.

153. Nuremberg Doc. PS-710.

154. See Eichmann's memoirs in Adolf Eichmann, *Ich, Adolf Eichmann*, ed. R. Aschenauer (Leoni am Starnberger See, 1980), p. 479.

155. Notes of the meeting were taken by Bernhard Lösener, the adviser on Jewish affairs at the Ministry of the Interior. See Peter Witte, "Two Decisions Concerning the "Final Solution to the Jewish Question": Deportations to Lodz and Mass Murder in Chelmno," *Holocaust and Genocide Studies* 9, no. 3 (1995), p. 322.

156. Goebbels, *Tagebücher*, part 2, vol. 1, pp. 265–66.

157. Ibid., p. 278.

158. Ibid., p. 269.

159. Ibid.

160. Heydrich was ready to start the deportations from the Reich forthwith, but, as we saw, Hitler vetoed any such immediate step as he vetoed the immediate implementation of Goebbels's evacuation plans. It is thus difficult to follow Christopher Browning's interpretation of Göring's letter as "Heydrich's charter" instructing the chief of the RSHA to draw up a "feasibility study" for the mass murder of European Jewry. "Heydrich needed the July 1941 authorization because he now faced a new and awesome task that would dwarf even the systematic murder program emerging on Soviet territory." See Christopher R. Browning and Jürgen Matthäus, *The Origins of the Final Solution: The Evolution of Nazi Jewish Policy, September 1939–March 1942* (Lincoln, NE, 2004), pp. 315–16. Two documents adduced to bolster the "feasibility study" thesis can also be read differently. On August 28, Eichmann rejected a demand from the Wilhelmstrasse to allow Jewish emigration from the occupied countries in the West, "in view of the imminent 'Final Solution,' *now in preparation*." Ibid., p. 322. This formula could, however, be applied either to the preparation of a general deportation of all European Jews to northern Russia or to the preparation for their extermination. However, as there was no preparation that we know of, Eichmann may simiply have used a general formula to explain his refusal.

A second document, a memorandum sent on September 3 by the chief of the Emigration Central Office [*Umwandererzentrale*, or UWZ] of the RKF in Posen, SS Sturmbannführer Rolf-Heinz Höppner, to Eichmann, seems to confirm that the "preparations" were aimed at the deportation of European Jewry to the Russian North. Höppner suggested the expansion of the Berlin Central Office for Emigration to the whole of European Jewry; he also suggested that control over the "reception areas" be granted to the new central agency. But precisely this document indicated that no decision had yet been taken: "I could well imagine," Höppner wrote, "that *large areas of the present Soviet Russia* are being prepared to receive the undesired ethnic elements of the greater German settlement area. . . . To go into further details about the organization of the reception area would be fantasy, because first of all the basic decisions must be made. It is essential in this regard, by the way, that total clarity prevails about what finally shall happen to those undesirable ethnic elements deported from the Greater German settlement area. Is the goal to ensure them a certain level of life in the long run, or shall they be totally eradicated?" Ibid.

In a further section of the September memorandum, Höppner stressed that "his proposals concerning 'reception areas' [Russia] had to remain 'patchwork' for the moment, as he did not yet 'know the intentions' of Hitler, Himmler and Heydrich." Christopher R. Browning, *Nazi Policy, Jewish Workers, German Killers* (Cambridge, MA, 2000), p. 37. Had a "feasibility study" for total extermination been in preparation when Höppner wrote his memorandum, Eichmann would probably have hinted about it and the entire memorandum would not have been so tentative and open-ended.

161. For these numbers see Wolfgang Scheffler, "Die Einsatzgruppe A 1941/2," in Klein, ed., *Die Einsatzgruppen in der besetzen Sowjetunion 1941/42*, pp. 34–35.

162. Kruk, *The Last Days of the Jerusalem of Lithuania*, pp. 96–99.

163. Rudashevski, *The Diary of the Vilna Ghetto, June 1941–April 1943*, pp. 31–32.

164. Ibid., pp. 32–33.

165. Avraham Tory, *Surviving the Holocaust: The Kovno Ghetto Diary*, ed. Martin Gilbert and Dina Porat (Cambridge, UK, 1990), p. 13.

166. Ibid., pp. 26–28.

167. Ibid., p. 32.

168. Zygmunt Klukowski, *Diary from the Years of Occupation, 1939–44*, ed. Andrew Klukowski and Helen Klukowski May (Urbana, IL, 1993), p. 168.

169. Czerniaków, *Warsaw Diary*, p. 256.

170. Ibid., p. 257.

171. Ibid. On January 1, 1941, 1,761 inhabitants of the ghetto belonged to non-Jewish denominations. See Raul Hilberg, *Perpetrators, Victims, Bystanders: The Jewish Catastrophe, 1933–1945* (New York, 1992), pp. 154ff.

172. Ibid.

173. See mainly Havi Ben-Sasson, "Christians in the Ghetto: All Saints' Church, Birth of the Holy Virgin Mary Church, and the Jews of the Warsaw Ghetto," *Yad Vashem Studies* 31 (2003), pp. 153ff.

174. Ibid.

175. Ibid., p. 165.

176. Czerniaków, *Warsaw Diary*, p. 261.

177. Ben-Sasson, "Christians in the Ghetto," pp. 163–64.

178. Himmler, *Der Dienstkalender*, p. 167 n. 7.

179. Dobroszycki, ed., *The Chronicle*, p. 71.

180. Ibid., p. 67n.

181. Ibid., pp. 68–69.

182. Ibid., p. 69. On July 29, the day the patients were removed, Rumkowski's sec-

retary, Szmul Rozensztajn, tersely noted in his diary: "All efforts by the Chairman to save the mentally ill were to no avail. At 11 A.M. today, a van arrived at the hospital on 3 Wesola Street to take 58 persons. They had been given injections of the sedative scopolamine." Quoted in Alan Adelson and Robert Lapides, eds., *Lodz Ghetto: Inside a Community Under Siege* (New York, 1989), p. 156.

183. Isaiah Trunk, *Judenrat: The Jewish Councils in Eastern Europe under Nazi Occupation* (New York, 1972), p. 84.

184. Ibid.

185. All details about Bruno Schulz are taken from Jerzy Ficowski, *Regions of the Great Heresy: Bruno Schulz: A Biographical Portrait* (New York, 2003).

186. Ibid., pp. 164–65.

187. All details about Dubnow's life are taken from Sophie Dubnov-Erlich, *The Life and World of S. M. Dubnov: Diaspora Nationalism and Jewish History* (New York, 1991).

188. Ibid., p. 229.

189. Ibid., pp. 245–46.

190. Ibid., p. 218.

191. For the spreading of information, see Mordechai Altschuler, "Escape and Evacuation of Soviet Jews at the Time of the Nazi Invasion," in Lucjan Dobroszycki and Jeffrey S. Gurock, *The Holocaust in the Soviet Union* (Armonk, NY, 1993), pp. 84ff.

192. For an overview of these attitudes see Berkhoff, *Harvest of Despair*, pp. 61–62.

193. Mordechai Altschuler, *Soviet Jewry on the Eve of the Holocaust: A Social and Demographic Profile* (Jerusalem, 1998), p. 188.

194. Yuri Slezkine, *The Jewish Century* (Princeton, 2004), p. 221.

195. Ibid., p. 245.

196. Quoted in ibid., p. 288.

197. See mainly Joshua Rubenstein, *Tangled Loyalties: The Life and Times of Ilya Ehrenburg* (New York, 1996), pp. 189ff.

198. Jonathan Frankel, "Empire tsariste et Union Sovietique," in *Les juifs et le XXe siècle: Dictionnaire critique*, ed. Elie Barnavi and Saul Friedländer (Paris, 2000), p. 298.

199. David Engel, *In the Shadow of Auschwitz: The Polish Government-in-Exile and the Jews, 1939–1942* (Chapel Hill, NC, 1987), p. 136.

200. See mainly Nechama Tec, *Defiance: The Bielski Partisans* (New York, 1993). See also Peter Duffy, *The Bielski Brothers: The True Story of Three Men Who Defied the Nazis, Saved 1,200 Jews, and Built a Village in the Forest* (New York, 2003).

201. Nechama Tec and Daniel Weiss, "The Heroine of Minsk: Eight Photographs of an Execution," in "Photography and the Holocaust," ed. Sybil Milton and Genya Markon, special issue, *History of Photography* (1999), pp. 322ff. Also in Minsk, another Jewish woman, Yelena Mazanik, planted the bomb that killed Reichskommissar Wilhelm Kube in September 1943. Cf. John Garrard, "Russia and the Soviet Union" in Walter Laqueur and Judith Tydor Baumel, eds., *The Holocaust Encyclopedia.* (New Haven, 2001), p. 590.

202. For a detailed account of the genesis and activities of the committee, see Shimon Redlich, *Propaganda and Nationalism in Wartime Russia: The Jewish Antifascist Committee in the USSR, 1941–1948* (Boulder, CO, 1982).

203. The Erlich-Alter affair has generated an abundant scholarly literature. For the above mentioned rendition of the events, see Daniel Blatman, *Notre liberté et la vôtre: Le mouvement ouvrier juif Bund en Pologne, 1939–1949* (Paris, 2002), pp. 101ff.

204. Joseph Walk, ed., *Das Sonderrecht für die Juden im NS-Staat: Eine Sammlung der gesetzlichen Massnahmen und Richtlinien, Inhalt und Bedeutung* (Heidelberg, 1981), p. 229.

205. Ibid., p. 347.

206. Paul Sauer, ed., *Dokumente über die Verfolgung der jüdischen Bürger in Baden-Württemberg durch das nationalsozialistische Regime 1933–1945*, 2 vols., vol. 2, (Stuttgart, 1966), p. 214.

207. Quoted in Léon Poliakov and Josef Wulf, *Das Dritte Reich und seine Denker: Dokumente* (Berlin, 1959), p. 452.

208. Klemperer, *I Will Bear Witness: A Diary of the Nazi Years, 1933–41*, vol. 1, p. 434.

209. Kulka and Jäckel, *Die Juden in den geheimen NS-Stimmungsberichten 1933–1945*, p. 450.

210. Boberach, ed., *Meldungen*, pp. 2645ff.

211. Kulka and Jäckel, *Die Juden in den geheimen NS-Stimmungsberichten 1933–1945*, p. 458.

212. Ibid., pp. 456–57.

213. Klemperer, *I Will Bear Witness: A Diary of the Nazi Years, 1933–41*, p. 434.

214. Ibid., p. 445.

215. Ibid., p. 441.

216. Elisabeth Freund, "Waiting," in *Hitler's Exiles: Personal Stories of the Flight from Nazi Germany to America*, ed. Mark M. Anderson (New York, 1998), p. 122.

217. Ibid., p. 123.

218. Telegram from Morris to Secretary of State, September 30, 1941, reproduced in John Mendelsohn and Donald S. Detwiler, eds., *The Holocaust: Selected Documents in Eighteen Volumes* (New York: Garland Publishing, 1982), vol. 2, p. 280.

219. For the manifold confirmations of these attitudes see David Bankier, *The Germans and the Final Solution: Public Opinion under Nazism* (Oxford, 1992), pp. 124ff.

220. Ibid., p. 129.

221. Quoted in Paul A. Levine, *From Indifference to Activism: Swedish Diplomacy and the Holocaust, 1938–1944* (Uppsala, 1996), p. 118.

222. Eric A. Johnson and Karl-Heinz Reuband, *What We Knew: Terror, Mass Murder and Everyday Life in Nazi Germany: An Oral History* (Cambridge, MA, 2005), pp. 362–63.

223. Ruth Kluger, *Still Alive: A Holocaust Girlhood Remembered* (New York, 2001), p. 49.

224. Michael H. Kater, *The Twisted Muse: Musicians and Their Music in the Third Reich* (New York, 1997), p. 103.

225. Renée Poznanski, "The Jews of France and the Statutes on Jews, 1940–1941," *Yad Vashem Studies* 22 (1992), pp. 115–16.

226. René Rémond, *Le "Fichier juif"* (Paris, 1996), pp. 67–68.

227. Ibid., p. 68.

228. Ibid., p. 74.

229. Raymond-Raoul Lambert, *Carnet d'un témoin: 1940–1943*, ed. Richard I. Cohen (Paris, 1985), p. 105.

230. Ibid., p. 187.

231. Jacques Biélinky, *Journal, 1940–1942: Un journaliste juif à Paris sous l'Occupation*, ed. Renée Poznanski (Paris, 1992), p. 146.

232. About the exhibition see Joseph Billig, *L'Institut d'étude des questions Juives* (Paris, 1974), pp. 160ff.

233. Lucien Steinberg and Jean Marie Fitère, *Les Allemands en France: 1940–1944* (Paris, 1980), pp. 75–76. Jacques Adler, *The Jews of Paris and the Final Solution: Communal Response and Internal Conflicts, 1940–1944* (New York, 1987), pp. 75ff; Renée Poznanski, *Être juif en France pendant la Seconde Guerre mondiale* (Paris, 1994), p. 311.

234. For a detailed history of local French life in the Nantes region during the war, see Robert Gildea, *Marianne in Chains: Everyday Life in the French Heartland under the German Occupation* (New York, 2003), pp. 229ff.

235. On this issue, see in particular Philippe Burrin, *Hitler und die Juden: Die Entscheidung für den Völkermord* (Frankfurt am Main, 1993), pp. 144–45.

236. Ulrich Herbert, *Best: Biographische Studien über Radikalismus, Weltanschauung und Vernunft, 1903–1989* (Bonn, 1996), p. 312.

237. Ibid.

238. Adler, *The Jews of Paris*, pp. 79–80.

239. Ibid., p. 105–6.

240. See particularly Lambert, *Carnet d'un témoin*, pp. 129ff.

241. Exact statistics are unavailable. See Rudi von Doorslaer, "Jewish Immigration and Communism in Belgium, 1925–1939," in *Belgium and the Holocaust: Jews, Belgians, Germans*, ed. Dan Michman (Jerusalem, 1998), p. 63. For the early measures taken in Belgium, see Maxime Steinberg, *La Persécution des Juifs en Belgique (1940–1945)* (Brussels, 2004), pp. 33ff.

242. Ibid.

243. For the Antwerp events and the text of the "protest" see Lieven Saerens, "Antwerp's Attitude Toward the Jews from 1918 to 1940 and Its Implications for the Period of Occupation," in *Belgium and the Holocaust: Jews, Belgians, Germans*, ed. Dan Michman (Jerusalem, 1998), pp. 192–193.

244. Berkhoff, *Harvest of Despair*, p. 77.

Chapter Five: September 1941–December 1941

1. The general description of the events follows Andrew Ezergailis, *The Holocaust in Latvia, 1941–1944: The Missing Center* (Riga and Washington, DC, 1996), pp. 244–50.

2. It seems that SS architects and other experts were consulted about the disposals of the bodies of the 30,000 Riga Jews. See Konrad Kwiet, "Rehearsing for Murder: The Beginning of the Final Solution in Lithuania in June 1941," *Holocaust and Genocide Studies* 12, no. 1 (1998), p. 7.

3. Ezergailis, *The Holocaust in Latvia, 1941–1944*, p. 253.

4. Ibid., p. 254.

5. Wolfgang Benz, Konrad Kwiet, and Jürgen Matthäus, *Einsatz im "Reichskommissariat Ostland": Dokumente zum Völkermord im Baltikum und in Weissrussland, 1941–1944* (Berlin, 1998), p. 96.

6. Sophie Dubnov-Erlich, *The Life and World of S. M. Dubnov. Diaspora Nationalism and Jewish History* (New York, 1991), pp. 246–47.

7. Jürgen Matthäus, "Weltanschauliche Forschung und Auswärtung. Aus den Akten des Amtes VII im Reichssicherheitshauptamt," *Jahrbuch für Antisemitismusforschung* 5 (1996), p. 316.

8. Quoted in Konrad Kwiet, "Erziehung zum Mord: Zwei Beispiele zur Kontinuität der deutschen 'Endlösung der Judenfrage,'" in *Geschichte und Emanzipation*, ed. Michael Grüttner et al. (Frankfurt, 1999), p. 449.

9. Peter Witte, "Two Decisions Concerning the "Final Solution to the Jewish Question": Deportations to Lodz and Mass Murder in Chelmno," *Holocaust and Genocide Studies* 9, no. 3 (1995), p. 330.

10. Ibid., pp. 324–25.

11. Ibid.

12. Ibid.

13. Joseph Goebbels, *Die Tagebücher von Joseph Goebbels: Sämtliche Fragmente*, ed. Elke Fröhlich part 2, vol. 1 (Munich, 1996), pp. 384, 388.

14. Gerhard L. Weinberg, *A World at Arms: A Global History of World War II* (Cambridge, UK, 1994), pp. 243–44.

15. This had been the pretext for the anti-Jewish boycott of April 1933 and was mentioned time and again as an effective anti-Jewish strategy from the end of 1938 to the war. See Saul Friedländer, *Nazi Germany and the Jews, Volume 1: The Years of Persecution, 1933–1939* (New York, 1997), p. 316.

16. Martin Dean, "The Development and Implementation of Nazi Denaturalization and Confiscation Policy up to the Eleventh Decree to the Reich Citizenship Law," *Holocaust and Genocide Studies* 16, no. 2 (2002), p. 230.

17. Saul Friedländer, *Prelude to Downfall: Hitler and the United States, 1939–41* (New York, 1967), pp. 290ff.

18. Ibid., p. 291.

19. On these discussions and related issues see Heinrich Himmler, *Der Dienst-*

kalender Heinrich Himmlers 1941/42, ed. Peter Witte et al. (Hamburg, 1999), pp. 203, 205.

20. Ibid., p. 205 n. 19.

21. Christopher R. Browning and Jürgen Matthäus, *The Origins of the Final Solution: The Evolution of Nazi Jewish Policy, September 1939–March 1942* (Lincoln, NE, 2004), p. 328.

22. About the exchanges between Himmler and Übelhör, then between Heydrich and Übelhör, see mainly ibid., pp. 331ff. See also, among others, H. G. Adler, *Der verwaltete Mensch: Studien zur Deportation der Juden aus Deutschland* (Tübingen, 1974), pp. 173ff.

23. Henry Friedlander, "The Deportation of the German Jews: Post-War German Trials of Nazi Criminals," in *Year Book of the Leo Baeck Institute* (London, 1984), vol. 29, p. 212.

24. For the additional measures see Yaacov Lozowick, "Malice in Action," *Yad Vashem Bulletin* 27 (1999), pp. 300–301.

25. For the fate of the Reich Jews deported to Kovno see, among other publications, Dina Porat, "The Legend of the Struggle of the Jews from the Third Reich in the Ninth Fort near Kovno, 1941–1942," *Tel Aviver Jahrbuch für deutsche Geschichte* 20 (1991), pp. 363ff. and particularly 375ff.

26. Friedlander, "The Deportation of the German Jews: Post-War German Trials of Nazi Criminals," p. 214.

27. Himmler, *Der Dienstkalender*, p. 278 n. 104.

28. Ibid.

29. Goebbels, *Tagebücher*, part 2, vol. 2, pp. 49–50, 73 (for the translation see Christopher R. Browning, *Nazi Policy, Jewish Workers, German Killers* [Cambridge, 2000], p. 38).

30. Willi A. Boelcke, ed., *Wollt Ihr den totalen Krieg? Die geheimen Goebbels Konferenzen 1939–1943* (Herrsching, 1989), p. 246.

31. Dawid Sierakowiak, *The Diary of Dawid Sierakowiak*, ed. Alan Adelson (New York, 1996), p. 136.

32. Ibid., p. 138.

33. Chaim Aron Kaplan, *Scroll of Agony: The Warsaw Diary of Chaim A. Kaplan*, ed. Abraham I. Katsh (Bloomington, 1999), p. 272.

34. Victor Klemperer, *I Will Bear Witness: A Diary of the Nazi Years, 1933–41* (New York, 1998), p. 440.

35. Willy Cohn, *Als Jude in Breslau 1941*, ed. Joseph Walk (Gerlingen, 1984), p. 106.

36. Ibid., p. 110.

37. Mihail Sebastian, *Journal, 1935–1944* (Chicago, 2000), p. 425.

38. Jacques Biélinky, *Journal, 1940–1942: Un journaliste juif à Paris sous l'Occupation*, ed. Renée Poznánski (Paris, 1992), p. 156.

39. Ian Kershaw, *Hitler, 1936–45: Nemesis* (New York, 2000), p. 440.

40. Ernst Klink, "The Conduct of Operations: 1. The Army and the Navy," in

The Attack on the Soviet Union, ed. Horst Boog (Oxford, 1998), pp. 685ff, 690ff, and 701–2.

41. Goebbels, *Tagebücher*, part 2, vol. 2, p. 296.

42. Friedländer, *Prelude to Downfall: Hitler and the United States, 1939–41*, pp. 292ff.

43. David M. Kennedy, *Freedom from Fear: The American People in Depression and War, 1929–1945* (New York, 1999), p. 499.

44. Goebbels, *Tagebücher*, part 2, vol. 2, p. 297.

45. Galeazzo Ciano, *Diary 1937–1943: The Complete Unabridged Diaries of Count Galeazzo Ciano, Italian Minister for Foreign Affairs, 1936–1943* (London, 2002), p. 459.

46. About the Des Moines speech, see A. Scott Berg, *Lindbergh* (New York, 1998), pp. 324ff.

47. Ibid., p. 426–27.

48. Ibid., p. 427.

49. Goebbels, *Tagebücher*, part 2, vol. 1, p. 417.

50. For the text of Hitler's order of the day of October 2, 1941, see Adolf Hitler, *Hitler: Reden und Proklamationen, 1932–1945: Kommentiert von einem deutschen Zeitgenossen*, ed. Max Domarus, 4 vols. (Leonberg, 1987–88), part 2, vol. 4, pp. 1756–57.

51. Ibid., p. 1759.

52. Adolf Hitler, *Monologe im Führer-Hauptquartier 1941–1944*, ed. Werner Jochmann and Heinrich Heim (Munich, 2000), p. 78.

53. Ibid., p. 88.

54. Ibid., p. 90.

55. Ibid.

56. Ibid., p. 93.

57. Ibid., p. 96.

58. Ibid., pp. 96–99 (for the translation of some of the excerpts, see also Adolf Hitler, *Hitler's Table Talk, 1941–1944*, ed. H. R. Trevor-Roper [London, 1953]), p. 79.

59. Nuremberg doc. NG-287. Quoted in Josef Wulf, ed., *Presse und Funk im Dritten Reich: Eine Dokumentation* (Gütersloh, 1964), p. 254.

60. Hitler, *Monologue*, p. 106.

61. Ibid.

62. Andreas Hillgruber, *Staatsmänner und Diplomaten bei Hitler: Vertrauliche Aufzeichnungen über Unterredungen mit Vertretern des Auslandes* (Frankfurt am Main, 1967–70), vol. 1, pp. 634–35.

63. Hitler, *Monologe*, pp. 130–31.

64. Hitler, *Reden*, vol. 4, p. 1772.

65. Ibid., pp. 1772–73.

66. Ibid., p. 1778.

67. *DGFP: Series D*, vol. 13, (Washington, 1964), p. 767.

68. Hitler, *Monologe*, p. 137.

69. Ibid., p. 143.

70. Joseph Goebbels, "Die Juden sind schuld!" in Joseph Goebbels, *Das eherne Herz: Reden und Aufsätze aus den Jahren 1941/42*, ed. Moritz Augustus Konstantin von Schirmeister (Munich, 1943), pp. 85ff.

71. For an excellent analysis of Goebbels's article in *Das Reich* and his lecture of December 1, see Jeffrey Herf, "The 'Jewish War': Goebbels and the Antisemitic Campaign of the Nazi Propaganda Ministry," *Holocaust and Genocide Studies* 19, no. 1 (2005), pp. 67–68. Now, see mainly Jeffrey Herf, *The Jewish Enemy: Nazi Propaganda during World War II and the Holocaust* (Cambridge, Mass., 2006), pp. 122ff.

72. Goebbels, *Tagebücher*, part 2, vol. 2, pp. 340–41.

73. *DGFP: Series D*, vol. 13, pp. 850–51.

74. Hillgruber, *Staatsmänner*, pp. 664ff.

75. *DGFP: Series D*, vol. 13, p. 893.

76. Memorandum for Ribbentrop from Schmidt, November 30, 1941, ibid., pp. 908–9.

77. Hitler, *Monologe*, p. 144.

78. Ibid., pp. 147–8.

79. Hitler, *Reden*, part 2, vol. 4, p. 1794.

80. Ibid., pp. 1794–97.

81. Ibid., pp. 1800–1804. "The spirits this man has called" was of course a reference to Goethe's *Faust*.

82. Ibid., p. 1804.

83. Goebbels, *Tagebücher*, part 2, vol. 2, pp. 498ff.

84. Himmler, *Der Dienstkalender*, p. 194; Christian Gerlach, "Die Wannsee-Konferenz, das Schiksal der deutschen Juden und Hitlers politische Grundsatzentscheidung, alle Juden Europas zu ermorden," in Christian Gerlach, *Krieg, Ernährung, Völkermord: Forschungen zur deutschen Vernichtungspolitik im Zweiten Weltkrieg* (Hamburg, 1998), pp. 8, 121.

85. Goebbels, *Tagebücher*, part 2, vol. 2, pp. 533–34.

86. Hitler, *Monologe*, p. 158.

87. Goebbels, *Tagebücher*, part 2, vol. 2, p. 614.

88. Hitler, *Reden*, pp. 1820–21.

89. The killing operations in Galicia—including the mass murders in the fall of 1941—have been studied in considerable detail. See in particular Dieter Pohl, *Nationalsozialistische Judenverfolgung in Ostgalizien 1941–1944: Organization und Durchführung eines staatlichen Massenverbrechens* (Munich, 1996); Dieter Pohl, "Hans Krüger and the Murder of the Jews in the Stanislawow Region (Galicia)," *Yad Vashem Studies* 26 (1998); Thomas Sandkühler, *"Endlösung" in Galizien: der Judenmord in Ostpolen und die Rettungsinitiativen von Berthold Beitz, 1941–1944* (Bonn, 1996); Browning and Matthäus, *The Origins of the Final Solution: The Evolution of Nazi Jewish Policy, September 1939–March 1942*, pp. 347ff.

90. For the description of the events at the cemetery, see in particular Sandkühler, *Endlösung in Galizien*, pp. 151–52.

91. Elsa Binder's diary is quoted in Alexandra Zapruder, *Salvaged Pages. Young Writers' Diaries of the Holocaust* (New Haven, 2002), pp. 301ff., particularly 315.

92. The deportations to Minsk also led to mass executions of local Jews; the killing of local Jews to make space for the deportees from the Reich may explain the aborted plans for setting up an extermination site in Mogilev. On this issue see Christian Gerlach, "Failure of Plans for an SS Extermination Camp in Mogilev, Belorussia," *Holocaust and Genocide Studies* 7, no. 1 (1997), pp. 60ff.

93. The full text of Heydrich's statement is quoted in H. G. Adler, *Theresienstadt, 1941–1945: Das Antlitz einer Zwangsgemeinschaft. Geschichte, Soziologie, Psychologie* (Tübingen, 1960), pp. 720ff. The Wannsee conference will be discussed in chapter 6.

94. Himmler, *Der Dienstkalender*, pp. 233–34 n. 35.

95. For the function of the Zamosc region as the first colonization project in the framework of General Plan East, see in particular Bruno Wasser, "Die 'Germanisierung' im Distrikt Lublin als Generalprobe und erste Realisierungsphase des 'Generalplans Ost,'" in Mechtild Rössler, Sabine Schleiermacher, and Cordula Tollmien, eds., *Der "Generalplan Ost": Hauptlinien der nationalsozialistischen Planungs- und Vernichtungspolitik* (Berlin, 1993), pp. 271ff.

96. Hitler, *Monologe*, pp. 78ff. Hans Mommsen's suggestion that the extermination process leading to the full-scale "Final Solution" was triggered by Globocnik's extermination initiatives in Lublin and Katzmann's murder operations in Galicia is hard to sustain. According to this argument it was Globocnik who convinced Himmler to send him T4 personnel to deal with the Jews unfit for work on his road-building projects (*Durchgangstrasse IV*) and also to make space for ethnic Germans from the Zamosc region. Along the lines of the same interpretation, Globocnik's initiative would have led to the construction of the other extermination camps in the General Government and started a murderous chain reaction that ultimately engulfed the whole of European Jewry. For this thesis see Hans Mommsen, *Auschwitz, 17. Juli 1942: Der Weg zur europäischen "Endlösung der Judenfrage"* (Munich, 2002), pp. 134ff. and 138. There is no doubt that the fanaticism and the activism of a Globocnik—or a Jeckeln or a Greiser—were highly valued by Himmler and certainly acknowledged by Hitler; yet nothing indicates that these or any other local initiatives set a course that "die höchste Instanz" then adopted as his own. The Globocniks of the system could act only within the limits set by Himmler, and when it came to the general extermination plan, the Reichsführer himself got his orders from Hitler.

97. Philippe Burrin, *Hitler and the Jews: The Genesis of the Holocaust* (London, 1994), p. 127.

98. To make sense of Eichmann's story, Christopher Browning, who uses the testimony as an indication that Hitler gave the go-ahead for the "Final Solution" sometime in September, when the order to deport the Jews from Germany was issued, has to assume that the head of IVB4 was sent to Lublin before the construction of the camp, and that the use of existing huts was at first considered sufficient for gassing purposes. No documents indicate that this may have been the case. See Browning and Matthäus, *The Origins of the Final Solution*, pp. 362ff.

99. The limited gassing capacity of Belzec at this initial stage has been pointed out in Dieter Pohl, *Von der "Judenpolitik" zum Judenmord: Der District Lublin des Generalgouvernements, 1933–1941*, vol. 3 (Frankfurt am Main, 1993). For Greiser's notorious letter to Himmler, see Tatiana Berenstein, ed., *Faschismus, Getto, Massenmord: Dokumentation über Ausrottung und Widerstand der Juden in Polen während des zweiten Weltkrieges* (East Berlin, 1961), p. 278.

100. For Heydrich's response to the Spanish offer, see Bernd Rother, "Franco und die deutsche Judenverfolgung," *Vierteljahrshefte für Zeitgeschichte* 46, no. 2 (1998), pp. 189ff. and particularly p. 195. See also Bernd Rother, *Spanien und der Holocaust* (Tübingen, 2001).

101. *Trials of war criminals before the Nuremberg Military Tribunals*, 15 vols., vol. 13, *U.S. v. von Weizsaecker: The Ministries Case* (Washington, DC: U.S. GPO, 1952), Nuremberg doc. NG-5095, p. 174 [emphasis added].

102. Quoted in full in Peter Longerich, *Politik der Vernichtung: Eine Gesamtdarstellung der nationalsozialistischen Judenverfolgung* (Munich, 1998), p. 443.

103. On December 12, as mentioned, Hitler told his old-time party companions that the Jews of Europe were to be exterminated. On the sixteenth of that month, Hans Frank, having heard Hitler's address, parroted his Führer in a speech to his top administrators in Kraków. Could not a comparison be made between Frank's reaction to Hitler's speech and a secret Rosenberg address to the German press, on November 18, after a lengthy meeting with Himmler three days beforehand?

According to this interpretation, Rosenberg probably had been told by Himmler of the decision, and he echoed the newly acquired information in his speech to the press, as Frank was to echo Hitler a month later. "This Eastern territory," Rosenberg declared, "is called upon to solve a question which is posed to the peoples of Europe; that is the Jewish Question. In the East, some 6 million Jews still live, and this question can only be solved in the biological eradication of the entire Jewry of Europe. The Jewish Question is only solved for Germany when the last Jew has left German territory, and for Europe when not a single Jew lives on the European continent up to the Urals. That is the task that fate had posed to us. . . . It is necessary to expel them over the Urals or eradicate them in some other way." (Quoted in Browning and Matthäus, *The Origins of the Final Solution: The Evolution of Nazi Jewish policy, September 1939–March 1942*, p. 404.)

Rosenberg's meeting with Himmler was in fact primarily intended to establish some clear rules regarding the division of tasks in the occupied Eastern territories between SS and police leaders on the one hand, and Reich or *Gebietskommissare* on the other. It is in this context that the Jewish issue was discussed, and we do not know whether on that occasion Himmler imparted any further information—if any decision was to be imparted at all—to a rival whom he despised. On the next day, Himmler and Rosenberg were both Hitler's guests at dinner. Were the Jews discussed on that occasion? We do not know either. (For the Himmler-Rosenberg meeting, see Himmler, *Der Dienstkalender*, p. 262, n. 46; for the dinner with Hitler, see Ibid., p. 264.) The "table-talk" records for that day indicate no allusion to the Jewish issue. (Hitler, *Monologe*, p. 140–42.)

As for Rosenberg's speech as such, it is ambiguous. It refers both to biological eradication and to expulsion over the Urals. It could be that Rosenberg meant eradication and not mere expulsion, as later, in the same speech, he stressed the urgency of the issue and the necessity for his generation of Germans to accomplish this historical task. (For the text of the speech see Browning and Matthäus, p. 404). But could not the same urgency apply to the expulsion of all the Jews beyond the Urals, leading eventually to their extinction (like all other territorial plans)?

Other documents of these same November 1941 days are no less ambiguous than Rosenberg's speech. Thus, on November 6, Goebbels recorded that, according to information from the General government, the Jews were setting all their hopes on a Soviet victory. "They don't have much to lose anymore," the minister went on. "In fact, one cannot hold it against them that they look for new glimmers of hope. It can even be of help to us, as it should allow us to deal with them in an even more decisive way in the general government as in the other occupied countries, and first of all also in the Reich." (Joseph Goebbels, *Die Tagebücher von Joseph Goebbels*, ed. Elke Fröhlich [Munich, 1995], part 2, vol. 2, p. 241.)

On November 29, 1941, Heydrich sent invitations to a conference that was to take place on December 9 in Berlin, at the Interpol center on Am Kleinen Wannseestrasse 16. The invitation letter clearly defined the subject of the meeting: "On 31 July 1941 the Reich Marshal of the Greater German Reich commissioned me to make all necessary preparations in organizational, factual, and material respect for the total solution [*Gesamtlösung*] of the Jewish question in Europe with the participation of all central agencies and to present to him a master plan as soon as possible.... Considering the extraordinary importance which has to be conceded to these questions and in the interest of the achievement of the same viewpoint by the central agencies concerned with the remaining work connected with this final solution [*Endlösung*], I suggest to make these problems the subject of a combined conversation, especially since Jews are being evacuated in continuous transports from the Reich territory, including the Protectorate of Bohemia and Moravia, to the East ever since 15 October 1941." [Nuremberg doc. 709-PS, *The Ministries Case*, pp. 192–93.] The conference was postponed as a result of the Japanese attack on the United States and the planned German response ("Unfortunately," Heydrich wrote on January 8, 1942, "I had to call off the conference ... because of events which suddenly became known and of the engrossment with them of some of the invited gentlemen"). (Ibid.); it was reconvened for January 20, 1942.

The way the initial invitation was formulated indicates that no preparations for a "general solution" of the Jewish question had been made since Göring's instructions to Heydrich; had there been some significant overall decisions taken in October, for example, they would have been alluded to, at least indirectly. The only concrete developments mentioned were the deportations from Germany. This very fact, as well as the date on which Heydrich sent the letters, indicate that the "evacuation" from the Reich and the complaints it generated would be a major item on the discussion agenda. (This is Gerlach's argument in Christian Gerlach, "*Die Wannsee-Konferenz, das Schicksal der deutschen Juden und Hitlers politische Grundsatzentscheidung, alle Juden Europas zu ermor-*

den," in *Werkstatt Geschichte* 18 (1997), p. 16. The invitation of Stuckart and Schlegelberger confirmed Heydrich's intention. Whether this was to be the only topic of the December 9 conference cannot be determined.

One could also argue, however, that the inclusion of Luther, the chief of "Division Germany" of the Wilhelmstrasse (dealing with Jewish matters throughout the continent) points to the discussion of plans extending beyond the deportations from the Reich (Hans-Jürgen Döscher, *Das Auswärtige Amt im Dritten Reich: Diplomatie im Schatten der "Endlösung"* [Berlin, 1987], p. 221). Rademacher, Luther's second-in-command, prepared a list of issues to be dealt with, particularly the deportation of Jews from Serbia, of stateless Jews living in territories occupied by Germany, and of Jews of Croat, Slovak, or Romanian nationality living in the Reich. Moreover, Rademacher suggested to inform the governments of Romania, Slovakia, Croatia, Bulgaria, and Hungary that Germany would be ready to deport their Jews to the East. Finally, the representative of the Wilhelmstrasse proposed to ask "all European governments" to introduce anti-Jewish legislation (Döscher, p. 223). Of course, these were suggestions of the Wilhelmstrasse; whether they would have been discussed, we do not know. Moreover, Rademacher's agenda does not indicate anything beyond the deportation plans to the East. Significantly, the countries of western and northern Europe were not mentioned.

On November 18, in a speech at the University of Berlin, Hans Frank unexpectedly praised the Jewish workers toiling in the General Government and forecast that they would be allowed to continue working for Germany in the future (Yitzhak Arad, Yisrael Gutman, and Abraham Margaliot, eds., *Documents on the Holocaust: Selected Sources on the Destruction of the Jews of Germany and Austria, Poland, and the Soviet Union* [Jerusalem, 1981], pp. 246–47). Could it be, if extermination had already been decided in early October, that Frank, in his visit to Berlin in mid-November, would not have been told anything? As we saw, by December 16 the tone had changed, and Frank spoke of only one goal: extermination.

The same change of tone is noticeable in the exchange between the Ostland Reichskommissar Lohse and Rosenberg's chief acolyte, Bräutigam. On November 15, Lohse asked Bräutigam whether the ongoing liquidations in the Baltic countries should also include Jews employed in war production. Bräutigam replied on December 18: "In the Jewish question, recent oral discussions have in the meantime clarified the issue (*In der Judenfrage dürfte inzwischen durch mündliche Besprechungen Klarheit geschaffen sein*). In principle, economic considerations are not to be taken into account in the settlement of the problem" (Ibid., pp. 394–95).

In other words, in mid-November, Rosenberg's delegate to the area, which had been the scene of some of the largest local massacres, was not yet aware of a general policy of extermination. But, as in Frank's case, by mid-December he was told of the guidelines, "recently clarified." (On this specific exchange see also Christian Gerlach, "Die Wannsee-konferenz."

Finally, in a letter sent to Himmler a few months later, on June 23, 1942, Viktor Brack, referring to the extermination camps in the General Government, added: "At one time, you yourself, Reichsführer, indicated to me that for reasons of secrecy we ought to complete the work as quickly as possible." It has been plausibly assumed that "at one time" referred to a personal meeting between Himmler and Brack. Such a meeting took place on December 14, 1941 (Ibid.).

In more general terms, if the deportation of the Jews from Germany had been the starting signal for the "Final Solution," why should the transports from the Reich have been directed to Lodz to begin with? No killing site was yet ready in or near Lodz, whereas choosing Riga, Kovno, or Minsk from the outset would have befitted a killing plan—at least as a possibility. But the *Ostland* destinations were alternatives chosen to ease the burden imposed upon Lodz. The setting up of Chelmno, the building of Belzec, and plans for other camps also appear as "solutions" for the overcrowding of Lodz, of the Lublin district, and of the *Ostland* ghettos, in view of the new arrivals, not necessarily as the first steps of a general extermination plan.

If it was in Hitler's plan to turn the Jews of Germany into hostages, mainly in order to deter the United States from entering the war, murdering the hostages before December 1941 would have been contrary to the very aim of the operation; murdering them once America was at war was true to type.

The Wannsee conference of January 20, 1942, will show, as the conference of December 9 would have shown, that no preparations had been made and that, except for general statements, Heydrich, the convener, had no concrete plans: there was no time schedule, no clear operational plan, no accepted definition of the categories of *Mischlinge* that were to be spared or deported and the like. Hitler probably finalized his decision in December; in January, Heydrich was barely starting to consider various possibilities, apart from the phased deportation to the East.

104. Joseph Walk, ed., *Das Sonderrecht für die Juden im NS-Staat: Eine Sammlung der gesetzlichen Massnahmen und Richtlinien, Inhalt und Bedeutung.* (Heidelberg, 1981), p. 350.

105. Ibid.

106. Ibid., p. 351.

107. Ibid., p. 353.

108. Ibid., p. 355.

109. Uwe Dietrich Adam, *Judenpolitik im Dritten Reich* (Düsseldorf, 1972), p. 284. For an exhaustive discussion of this issue, see ibid., pp. 274ff.

110. Ibid., p. 291.

111. Götz Aly mentions the case of the Jewish laborer Ernst Samuel who worked at Daimler Benz, received a net weekly salary of twenty-eight reichsmarks, after an amount of twenty-four reichsmarks had been paid as income tax, benefits, and so on. Götz Aly, *Im Tunnel: Das kurze Leben der Marion Samuel 1931–1943* (Frankfurt am Main, 2004), p. 64.

112. For this complicated bureaucratic process see Dean, "The Development and Implementation of Nazi Denaturalization and Confiscation Policy," pp. 217ff.

113. Adam, *Judenpolitik im Dritten Reich*, pp. 292ff and 299–301.

114. Avraham Barkai, *From Boycott to Annihilation: The Economic Struggle of German Jews, 1933–1943* (Hanover, NH, 1989), p. 176.

115. Ibid., pp. 179–80.

116. For the full text of the law see Kurt Pätzold, ed., *Verfolgung, Vertreibung, Vernichtung: Dokumente des faschistischen Antisemitismus 1933 bis 1942.* (Frankfurt am Main, 1984), pp. 320–321.

117. Barkai, *From Boycott to Annihilation*, pp. 177ff.

118. Ibid., pp. 177–79. Regarding the H and W accounts one may accept the hypothesis that the Reichsvereinigung was itself cheated at the outset, but for how long? On the policies of the Reichsvereinigung see, among others, Yehoyakim Cochavi, " "The Hostile Alliance": The Relationship Between the Reichsvereinigung of Jews in Germany and the Regime," *Yad Vashem Studies* 22 (1992), pp. 262ff.

119. Pätzold, *Verfolgung*, p. 309.

120. See Henry Friedlander and Sybil Milton, eds., *Archives of the Holocaust: An International Collection of Selected Documents*, 22 vols. (New York, 1990), vol. 20, doc. 17, pp. 32–33.

121. Nuremberg doc. NG-978, reproduced in John Mendelsohn and Donald S. Detwiler, eds., *The Holocaust: Selected Documents in Eighteen Volumes* (New York, 1982), vol. 2, pp. 284–85 (the translation has been slightly revised).

122. For this issue see Beate Meyer, *"Jüdische Mischlinge": Rassenpolitik und Verfolgungserfahrung 1933–1945* (Hamburg, 1999), pp. 230ff; Bryan Mark Rigg, *Hitler's Jewish Soldiers: The Untold Story of Nazi Racial Laws and Men of Jewish Descent in the German Military* (Lawrence, KS, 2002), pp. 116ff.

123. Rigg, *Hitler's Jewish Soldiers*, pp. 128ff.

124. Ibid., pp. 144ff.

125. Ibid., p. 132.

126. Béla Bodo, "The Role of Antisemitism in the Expulsion of Non-Aryan Students, 1933–1945," *Yad Vashem Studies* 30 (2002), pp. 216–17.

127. Walter Manoschek, ed., *"Es gibt nur eines für das Judentum—Vernichtung": Das Judenbild in deutschen Soldatenbriefen 1939–1944.* (Hamburg, 1997), p. 45.

128. Ibid., p. 49.

129. Otto Dov Kulka and Eberhard Jäckel, *Die Juden in den geheimen NS-Stimmungsberichten 1933–1945* (Düsseldorf, 2004), pp. 467–68.

130. For the reports of Swiss diplomatic representatives, see Daniel Bourgeois, *Business helvétique et Troisième Reich: Milieux d'affaires, politique étrangère, antisémitisme* (Lausanne, 1998), pp. 197ff.

131. Walter Laqueur, *The Terrible Secret: An Investigation into the Suppression of Information about Hitler's 'Final Solution'* (London, 1980), p. 26. What German officials knew, British intelligence knew even more precisely by intercepting and decoding the radio messages sent by police battalions operating on Soviet territory to their headquarters in Berlin. However, this information was kept strictly secret to protect the British codebreaking operation. See mainly Richard Breitman, *Official Secrets: What the Nazis Planned, What the British and Americans Knew* (New York, 1998).

132. Helmuth James von Moltke, *Letters to Freya: 1939–1945*, ed. Beate Ruhm von Oppen (New York, 1990), pp. 155–56.

133. Ibid., p. 175.

134. Ibid., p. 183.

135. Ulrich von Hassell, *Die Hassell-Tagebücher 1938–1944: Aufzeichnungen vom Andern Deutschland*, ed. Klaus Peter Reiss and Freiherr Friedrich Hiller von Gaertringen (Berlin, 1988), p. 277.

136. Quoted in Gordon J. Horwitz, *In the Shadow of Death: Living Outside the Gates of Mauthausen* (New York, 1990), p. 35.

137. SD Aussenstelle Minden, 12.12.1941 in Kulka and Jäckel, *Die Juden in den geheimen NS-Stimmungsberichten 1933–1945*, p. 477.

138. Quoted in Jeremy Noakes and Geoffrey Pridham, eds., *Nazism, 1919–1945: A Documentary Reader.* vol. 3: *Foreign Policy, War and Racial Extermination*; (Exeter, UK, 1998), p. 1044.

139. Ernst Klee, *"Euthanasie" im NS-Staat: Die "Vernichtung lebensunwerten Lebens"* (Frankfurt am Main, 1983), p. 349.

140. Kulka and Jäckel, *Die Juden in den geheimen NS-Stimmungsberichten 1933–1945*, pp. 476ff.

141. Ibid. p. 478.

142. Ibid., pp. 483–84.

143. Quoted in Götz Aly and Susanne Heim, *Vordenker der Vernichtung: Auschwitz und die deutschen Pläne für eine neue europäische Ordnung* (Hamburg, 1991), p. 199.

144. Ibid.

145. Ibid.

146. Ibid., p. 200.

147. Ibid., pp. 200–201.

148. Ibid., p. 199 n. 22.

149. For all the details regarding Schieder's confidential survey and for the quotations, see Götz Aly, "Theodor Schieder, Werner Conze oder die Vorstufen der physischen Vernichtung," in *Deutsche Historiker im Nationalsozialismus*, ed. Winfried Schulze and Otto Gerhard Oexle (Frankfurt, 1999), p. 167.

150. Quoted in Ludwig Volk, ed., *Akten deutscher Bischöfe über die Lage der Kirche, 1933–1945.* 6 vols., vol. 5: *1940–1942* (Mainz, 1983), p. 555 n.

151. For Cardinal Bertram's pastoral letter, see ibid., p. 555ff.

152. Bertram to Faulhaber, 17.11.1941, quoted in Ernst Klee, *Die SA Jesu Christi: Die Kirchen im Banne Hitlers* (Frankfurt am Main, 1989), p. 144.

153. Cordelia Edvardson, *Gebranntes Kind sucht das Feuer* (Munich, 1989), pp. 54–55.

154. Richard Gutteridge, *Open Thy Mouth for the Dumb! The German Evangelical Church and the Jews 1879–1950* (Oxford, 1976), pp. 229–30.

155. Kulka and Jäckel, *Die Juden*, pp. 468–69.

156. Gutteridge, *Open Thy Mouth for the Dumb! The German Evangelical Church and the Jews 1879–1950*, p. 230.

157. Ibid., p 231.

158. Ursula Büttner, " 'The Jewish Problem Becomes a Christian Problem': German Protestants and the Persecution of the Jews in the Third Reich," in *Probing the*

Depths of German Antisemitism: German Society and the Persecution of the Jews, 1933–1941, ed. David Bankier (New York, 2000), pp. 454ff.

159. Quoted in Klee, *Die SA Jesu Christi*, p. 148.

160. Goebbels, *Tagebücher*, part 2, vol. 2, pp. 362–63.

161. Klee, *Die SA Jesu Christi*, p. 148.

162. Gutteridge, *Open Thy Mouth for the Dumb! The German Evangelical Church and the Jews 1879–1950*, pp. 231–32.

163. Quoted and translated in Wolfgang Gerlach, *And the Witnesses Were Silent: The Confessing Church and the Persecution of the Jews*, ed. Victoria Barnett (Lincoln, NE, 2000), p. 194.

164. Ibid., pp. 194–96.

165. Ibid., p. 196.

166. Ibid., p. 197.

167. Jochen Klepper, *Unter dem Schatten Deiner Flügel: Aus den Tagebüchern der Jahre 1932–1942*, ed. Hildegard Klepper (Stuttgart, 1956), p. 1009.

168. For the text of the draft pastoral letter, see Ludwig Volk, ed., *Akten Kardinal Michael von Faulhaber*, vol. 2, *1935–1945* (Mainz, 1978), pp. 827ff.

169. Ibid., p. 853.

170. Klaus Schölder, *A Requiem for Hitler: and Other New Perspectives on the German Church Struggle* (London, 1989), p. 163.

171. Ibid.

172. Volk, *Akten deutscher Bischöfe*, vol. 5, Mainz, 1983, p. 675n.

173. Ibid.

174. Ibid., p. 636.

175. Bischof Clemens August Graf von Galen, *Akten, Briefe und Predigten*, ed. Peter Löffler, vol. 2, *1939–1946* (Mainz, 1988), pp. 910–11.

176. Ibid., pp. 910 ff.

177. Raul Hilberg, *Perpetrators, Victims, Bystanders: The Jewish Catastrophe, 1933–1945* (New York, 1992), p. 268.

178. Breitman, *Official Secrets*, pp. 68 and 106, among others.

179. Raya Cohen, "The Lost Honor of Bystanders? The Case of Jewish Emmissaries in Switzerland," in *Bystanders to the Holocaust: A Re-Evaluation*, ed. David Cesarani and Paul A. Levine (London, 2002), p. 162.

180. Riegner protested but had to accept Wise's decision. On the other hand, Alfred Silberschein, the man in charge of the Relief Committee (RELICO) set up to help the starving Jewish populations, continued to organize the sending of food against Wise's instructions. See ibid., pp. 162ff.

181. For both quotes see Gulie Ne'eman Arad, *America, Its Jews, and the Rise of Nazism* (Bloomington, 2000), p. 212.

182. Dina Porat, *The Blue and the Yellow Stars of David: The Zionist Leadership in Palestine and the Holocaust, 1939–1945* (Cambridge, MA, 1990), p. 18.

183. Quoted in Tuvia Friling, *Arrow in the Dark: David Ben-Gurion, the Yishuv's Leadership and Rescue Efforts during the Holocaust* (Tel Aviv, 1998), 2 vols., vol. 1, p. 45.

184. Yoav Gelber, "Zionist Policy and the Fate of European Jewry (1939–1942)," *Yad Vashem Studies* 13 (1979), pp. 191–92.

185. Porat, *The Blue and the Yellow Stars of David*, p. 22.

186. Friedlander and Milton, eds., *Archives of the Holocaust*, vol. 4, *Central Zionist Archives*, p. 40. It was in this context of utter misperception regarding the fate of European Jewry under German rule that a splinter of the Revisionist clandestine group Irgun, the "Stern group" (or *Lehi*), offered the Reich, in late 1940 (via a German diplomat in Beirut), to fight on the Axis side of against the British, in exchange for German help in the establishment of a Jewish state in Palestine. The *Lehi* offer never received an answer.

187. Adler, *Der verwaltete Mensch*, pp. 380ff.

188. Cohn, *Als Jude in Breslau 1941*, p. 122.

189. Eric A. Johnson and Karl-Heinz Reuband, *What We Knew: Terror, Mass Murder and Everyday Life in Nazi Germany: An Oral History* (Cambridge, MA, 2005), p. 306.

190. Kulka and Jäckel, *Die Juden in den geheimen NS-Stimmungsberichten 1933–1945*, p. 474.

191. Ibid., p. 472.

192. It seems that in most such cases the Jews were not utilized as agents; the Abwehr used the pretext to help some selected (and wealthy) individuals to leave the Reich. See for example Winfried Meyer, *Unternehmen Sieben: eine Rettungsaktion für vom Holocaust Bedrohte aus dem Amt Ausland/Abwehr im Oberkommando der Wehrmacht* (Frankfurt am Main, 1993). However, notwithstanding the opposition of some senior Abwehr officers to the regime, other members and particularly the secret military police (Geheime Feldpolizei) units and their commanders were deeply involved in the mass murder of Jews and other groups, in the eastern territories. Even later participants in the military conspiracy against Hitler were implicated. See Christian Gerlach, "Männer des 20 Juli und der Krieg gegen die Sowjetunion," in *Vernichtungskrieg: Verbrechen der Wehrmacht 1941–1944*, ed. Hannes Heer and Klaus Naumann (Hamburg, 1995), pp. 434ff.

193. Mark Roseman, *A Past in Hiding: Memory and Survival in Nazi Germany* (New York, 2001), pp. 125ff, 130ff, and 133ff.

194. Konrad Kwiet, "The Ultimate Refuge: Suicide in the Jewish Community under the Nazis," in *Year Book of the Leo Baeck Institute* (London), p. 151.

195. Ursula Baumann, "Suizid im 'Dritten Reich'—Facetten eines Themas," in *Geschichte und Emanzipation*, ed. Reinhard Rürup et al. (Frankfurt am Main, 1999), p. 500.

196. Goebbels, *Tagebücher*, part 2, vol. 2, p. 247.

197. Stadtarchiv Müchen, ed., "*. . . verzogen, unbekannt wohin": Die erste Deportation von Müchner Juden im November 1941.* (Zürich: Pendo, 2000), doc. 14 [the document section is unpaginated].

198. Ibid., p. 20; Porat, "The Legend of the Struggle of the Jews from the Third Reich in the Ninth Fort near Kovno, 1941–1942," pp. 363 and 370.

199. Yaacov Lozowick, "Documentation: "Judenspediteur," Deportation Train," *Holocaust and Genocide Studies* 6, no. 3 (1991), pp. 286ff.

200. Shalom Cholavsky, "The German Jews in the Minsk Ghetto," *Yad Vashem Studies* 17 (1986), pp. 223–25.

201. For the details about Rosenfeld's life see the editor's introduction to Oskar Rosenfeld, *In the Beginning Was the Ghetto: Notebooks from Lódz*, ed. Hanno Loewy (Evanston, IL, 2002), pp. xiii–xviii.

202. Ibid., pp. 8–9.

203. Ibid., p. 11.

204. Ibid.

205. Ibid., p. 21.

206. For an excellent survey and analysis see Avraham Barkai, "Between East and West: Jews from Germany in the Lodz Ghetto," in *The Nazi Holocaust: Historical Articles on the Destruction of European Jews*, ed. Michael R. Marrus (Westport, 1989), vol. 6, pt. 1, pp. 378ff, and, specifically, pp. 394–395.

207. Lucjan Dobroszycki, ed., *The Chronicle of the Lódz Ghetto, 1941–1944* (New Haven, 1984), p. 79.

208. Sierakowiak, *Diary*, p. 141.

209. Ibid., p. 144.

210. Ibid., p. 142.

211. Dobroszycki, *The Chronicle*, pp. 80–81.

212. Donald L. Niewyk, ed., *Fresh Wounds: Early Narratives of Holocaust Survival* (Chapel Hill, NC, 1998), p. 303.

213. Dobroszycki, *The Chronicle*, p. 109.

214. Ibid., pp. 109 and 109n3.

215. Ibid., p. 113.

216. Rosenfeld, *In the Beginning Was the Ghetto*, pp. 31–32.

217. Ibid., p. 32.

218. Zapruder, *Salvaged Pages*, p. 233.

219. May's postwar memoir is quoted in Dobroszycki's "Introduction" to Dobroszycki, ed., *The Chronicle*, pp. lv–lvi.

220. Ibid., p. 108.

221. Guenter Lewy, *The Nazi Persecution of the Gypsies* (New York, 2000), p. 115.

222. Translated from the original and quoted in Laqueur, *The Terrible Secret*, p. 130.

223. Ibid., p. 131.

224. David Graber, "Some Impressions and Memories," in Joseph Kermish, ed., *To Live with Honor and Die with Honor! . . . : Selected Documents from the Warsaw Ghetto Underground Archives* "O.S." ("Oneg Shabbath"). (Jerusalem: Yad Vashem, 1986), p. 61.; Yitzhak Zuckerman, *A Surplus of Memory: Chronicle of the Warsaw Ghetto Uprising* (Berkeley, 1993), p. 156ff.

225. Biélinky, *Journal*, pp. 153ff.

226. Ibid., p. 155.

227. Raymond-Raoul Lambert, *Carnet d'un témoin: 1940–1943*, ed. Richard I. Cohen (Paris, 1985), p. 132.

228. Ibid.

229. Ibid., p. 163.

230. Sebastian, *Journal*, p. 427.

231. Ibid.

232. Ibid., pp. 428–29.

233. Ibid., p. 434.

234. Ibid., p. 452.

235. Ibid.

236. Klemperer, *I Will Bear Witness: A Diary of the Nazi Years, 1933–41*, p. 440.

237. Ibid., p. 442.

238. Ibid., p. 446.

239. Hertha Feiner, *Before Deportation: Letters from a Mother to Her Daughters, January 1939–December 1942*, ed. Karl Heinz Jahnke (Evanston, IL, 1999), p. 53.

240. Dawid Rubinowicz, *The Diary of Dawid Rubinowicz* (Edmonds, WA, 1982), p. 26.

241. Ibid.

242. Ibid., p. 27.

243. For details about Elsa Binder, see Alexandra Zapruder's "Introduction" to the diary in Zapruder, *Salvaged Pages: Young Writers' Diaries of the Holocaust*, pp. 301ff.

244. Ibid., pp. 306–7.

245. Ibid.

246. Kaplan, *Scroll of Agony*, p. 267.

247. Chaim Aron Kaplan, *Scroll of Agony: The Warsaw Diary of Chaim A. Kaplan*, ed. Abraham Isaac Katsh (New York, 1973) p. 285.

248. Lucy S. Dawidowicz, ed., *A Holocaust Reader* (New York, 1976), p. 264ff.

249. Ibid., pp. 273–74.

250. Martin Gilbert, introduction to Avraham Tory, *Surviving the Holocaust: The Kovno Ghetto Diary*, ed. Martin Gilbert and Dina Porat (Cambridge, OK, 1990), p. xiv.

251. Tory, *Surviving*, p. 44.

252. Ibid., p. 46.

253. Ibid., p. 47.

254. Ibid., pp. 49–55.

255. Ibid., pp. 55–59.

256. Isaac Rudashevski, *The Diary of the Vilna Ghetto, June 1941–April 1943*, ed. Percy Matenko (Tel Aviv, 1973), p. 46.

257. Ibid., p. 48.

258. Dina Porat, "The Vilna Proclamation of January 1, 1942 in Historical Perspective," *Yad Vashem Studies* 24 (1996), pp. 106ff.

259. Ibid., pp. 108ff.

260. Ibid., pp. 111ff.

261. Yisrael Gutman, *Resistance: The Warsaw Ghetto Uprising* (Boston, 1994), p. 103.

262. Ibid., pp. 104–5.

263. Zuckerman, *A Surplus of Memory*, pp. 153–54.

264. Ibid., p. 156.

265. Sebastian, *Journal*, p. 458.

266. Klemperer, *I Will Bear Witness: A Diary of the Nazi Years, 1933–41*, p. 456.

267. Herman Kruk, *The Last Days of the Jerusalem of Lithuania: Chronicles from the Vilna Ghetto and the Camps, 1939–1944*, ed. Benjamin Harshav (New Haven, 2002), p. 149.

268. Zapruder, *Salvaged Pages*, p. 311.

269. Zygmunt Klukowski, *Diary from the Years of Occupation, 1939–44*, ed. Andrew Klukowski and Helen Klukowski May (Urbana, IL), 1993), p. 179.

270. Ibid., p. 180.

271. Ibid., p. 179.

272. Zuckerman, *A Surplus of Memory*, p. 153.

Chapter Six: December 1941–July 1942

1. For a detailed narration of the *Struma* tragedy, see Douglas Frantz and Catherine Collins, *Death on the Black Sea: The Untold Story of the Struma and World War II's Holocaust at Sea* (New York, 2004).

2. Quoted in Dalia Ofer, *Escaping the Holocaust: Illegal Immigration to the Land of Israel, 1939–1944* (New York, 1990), p. 158.

3. Quoted in Bernard Wasserstein, *Britain and the Jews of Europe, 1939–1945* (London, 1979), pp. 145–46.

4. Ofer, *Escaping the Holocaust*, pp. 162ff. According to documents uncovered in Soviet archives, Stalin had apparently given a secret order to sink neutral ships sailing from the Bosporus into the Black Sea to disrupt the delivery of chromium from Turkey to Germany. See Frantz and Collins, *Death on the Black Sea*, pp. 159 and 341.

5. Mihail Sebastian, *Journal, 1935–1944* (Chicago, 2000), pp. 476–47.

6. Hitler's New Year's speech to the German people was in fact dated December 31, 1941, but was published by the *VB* on January 1, 1942. See Adolf Hitler, *Hitler: Reden und Proklamationen, 1932–1945: Kommentiert von einem deutschen Zeitgenossen*, ed. Max Domarus, 4 vols. (Leonberg, 1987–88), part 2, vol. 4, pp. 1820, 1820n.

7. Adolf Hitler, *Monologe im Führer-Hauptquartier 1941–1944*, ed. Werner Jochmann and Heinrich Heim (Munich, 2000), pp. 228–29.

8. Hitler, *Reden*, pp. 1828–29. (Emphasis in the original.)

9. Kulka/Jäckel, *Die Juden*, p. 485.

10. Ibid., p. 486.

11. Chaim Aron Kaplan, *Scroll of Agony: The Warsaw Diary of Chaim A. Kaplan*, ed. Abraham I. Katsh (Bloomington, 1999), p. 297.

12. Hitler, *Reden*, p. 1844.

13. Karl Dürkefälden, *Schreiben, wie es wirklich war: Aufzeichnungen Karl Dürkefäldens aus den Jahren 1933–1945*, Herbert Obenaus and Sibylle Obenaus, eds. (Hannover, 1985), p. 108.

14. Ibid., pp. 107–8.

15. Joseph Goebbels, *Die Tagebücher von Joseph Goebbels: Sämtliche Fragmente*, ed. Elke Fröhlich (Munich, 1996), part 2, vol. 3, p. 104.

16. Ibid., pp. 320–21.

17. Ibid., part 2, vol. 3, p. 561.

18. Ibid., part 2, vol. 4, p. 184.

19. See Hitler, *Reden*, part 2, p. 1865.

20. Ibid., pp. 1865–69.

21. Goebbels, *Tagebücher*, part 2, vol. 4, p. 188.

22. Victor Klemperer, *I Will Bear Witness: A Diary of the Nazi Years, 1933–41* (New York, 1998), vol. 2, p. 45 (emphasis in original).

23. David Bankier, "The Use of Antisemitism in Nazi Wartime Propaganda," in *The Holocaust and History: The Known, the Unknown, the Disputed and the Reexamined*, ed. Michael Berenbaum and Abraham J. Peck (Bloomington, 1998), p. 45.

24. Ibid., pp. 45–46.

25. Ibid., p. 46.

26. Kulka/Jäckel, *Die Juden*, p. 489.

27. Ibid., p. 491.

28. Ibid., p. 494.

29. Martin Doerry, *My Wounded Heart: The Life of Lilli Jahn, 1900–1944* (London, 2004), pp. 95–96.

30. For the main details about the conference see Kurt Pätzold and Erika Schwarz, eds., *Tagesordnung Judenmord: Die Wannsee-Konferenz am 20. Januar 1942: Eine Dokumentation zur Organisation der "Endlösung."* (Berlin, 1992) See also Mark Roseman, *The Villa, the Lake, the Meeting: Wannsee and the Final Solution* (London and New York, 2002).

31. See Yehoshua Büchler, "A Preparatory Document for the Wannsee Conference," *Holocaust and Genocide Studies* 9, no. 1 (1995), pp. 121ff.

32. There is no indication, however, of Heydrich's wish to convey to the participants (and to their chiefs) that he, the newly appointed SS Obergruppenführer and acting *Reichsprotektor* was in fact the man whom the Führer had personally put in charge of the "Final Solution," independently of the SS Reichsführer. Had that been Heydrich's intention (and had Hitler indeed appointed him) the RSHA chief would probably have avoided indicating immediately at the outset that the ultimate executive authority in the matter was that of the SS Reichsführer. For this hypothesis see Eberhard Jäckel, "On the Purpose of the Wannsee Conference," in *Perspectives on the Holocaust*, ed. James S. Pacy and Alan P. Wertheimer (Boulder, CO, 1995), pp. 39ff.

33. In Heydrich's view, mixed breeds of the first degree were to be considered identical to Jews, when not married to full-blooded Germans with whom they had children; in the latter case they would be exempted from deportation. In order to solve once and for all the problem of the *Mischlinge*, mixed breeds of the first degree exempted from evacuation would be sterilized. Mixed breeds of the second degree were put on equal footing with Germans, except if they were "bastards" (that is, the offspring of parents both of whom were themselves *Mischlinge*), if their physical appearance

pointed to their Jewishness, or if an incriminating police record indicated that they felt and behaved as Jews.

The issue of mixed marriages followed. Heydrich emphasized the impact that decisions in this domain could have on German partners. In marriages between full Jews and Germans, the decision about the Jewish spouse's deportation depended on the existence of children. In childless marriages the Jewish spouse would be deported. In marriages between a Mischling of the first degree and a German, the mixed-breed partner would also be deported if the marriage was childless. If the couple had children (*Mischlinge* of the second degree), and if these children were put on an equal footing with Jews (in the three cases previously mentioned), the *Mischling* parent and the children would be deported. If the children were not identified with Jews (the rule), they would not be deported, nor would their parent, the mixed breed of the first degree.

In regard to marriages of *Mischlinge* of the first degree among themselves or with Jews, everybody, including the children, would be "evacuated." Finally, in the case of marriages of mixed breeds of the first degree and mixed breeds of the second degree, everybody would be "evacuated," as children in these unions tended to present a racially stronger influence of the Jewish blood than mixed breeds of the second degree (*"da etwaige Kinder rassenmässig in der Regel einen stärkeren Jüdischen Bluteinschlag aufweisen, als die Jüdischen Mischlinge 2. Grades"*).

34. For the full text of the conference see Pätzold and Schwarz, *Tagesordnung*, pp. 102–12.

35. Himmler, *Der Dienstkalender*, p. 355n.

36. For this Hitler order, see Richard Breitman, *Official Secrets: What the Nazis Planned, What the British and Americans Knew* (New York, 1998), p. 111.

37. Miroslav Kárný, Jaroslava Milotová, and Margarita Kárná, eds., *Deutsche Politik im "Protektorat Böhmen und Mähren" unter Reinhard Heydrick 1941–1942: Eine Dokumentation* (Berlin, 1997), p. 229. See also Himmler, *Der Dienstkalender*, p. 353n.

38. Himmler, *Der Dienstkalender*, p. 321.

39. Himmler to Glücks, 25.1.1942, *U.S. v. Flick: The Flick Case. Trials of War Criminals Before the Nuremberg Military Tribunals under Control Council Law no. 10, Nuremberg, October 1946–April 1949*, 15 vols., vol. 6 (Washington, DC: US. GPO, 1952), Nuremberg doc. NO-500, p. 365.

40. Quoted in Peter Longerich and Dieter Pohl, eds., *Die Ermordung der europäischen Juden* (Munich, 1989), p. 165ff. See also Peter Longerich, *Politik der Vernichtung: Eine Gesamtdarstellung der nationalsozialistischen Judenverfolgung* (Munich, 1998), p. 483.

41. Pätzold and Schwarz, *Tagesordnung*, pp. 118 and 118n.

42. Schlegelberger to Stuckart et al., 8 April 1942, Nuremberg doc. NG-2586-I; Hilberg, *The Destruction*, vol. 2, p. 440.

43. For a good summary see Beate Meyer, *"Jüdische Mischlinge": Rassenpolitik und Verfolgungserfahrung 1933–1945* (Hamburg, 1999), p. 99ff. The protocols of both meetings are reproduced in Nuremberg doc. NG-2586, *U.S. v. von Weizsaecker: The Ministries Case.* Trials of war criminals before the Nuremberg Military Tribunals, 15 vols., vol. 13 (Washington, D.C.: U.S. G.P.O., 1952), pp. 221–25. One of the exemptions

granted by Hitler led to a strange conflation between a mixed marriage and the measures deriving from the Eleventh Ordinance regarding the loss of citizenship and of all assets by German Jews "residing outside of the Reich." On September 16, 1942, the Propaganda Ministry intervened with the Ministry of the Interior in favor of the Jewish wife of one of Germany's most famous actors, Hans Moser. Moser had been authorized by "a decision at the highest level" (*allehöchster Entscheidung*) to pursue his activities without any hindrance. In the meantime, however, his wife had moved to Budapest and, as a consequence of the Eleventh Ordinance, had automatically lost her German citizenship (and passport); she had become "stateless." Moser was understandably distressed by this sudden blow. The Ministry of the Interior was asked to restore Mrs. Moser's citizenship (and passport). To support its demand, the Propaganda Ministry added the names of other actors who had also been allowed by "a decision at the highest level" to live and work in the Reich with their full-Jewish wives: Paul Henckels, Max Lorenz and Georg Alexander. See *Archives of the Holocaust,* vol. 20, pp. 118ff.

44. The protocol of the March 6 conference is quoted in Peter Longerich and Dieter Pohl, eds., *Die Ermordung der europäischen Juden: Eine umfassende Dokumentation des Holocaust 1941–1945* (Munich: Piper, 1989), pp. 167ff. For a discussion of the conference see Yaacov Lozowick, *Hitlers Bürokraten: Eichmann, seine willigen Vollstrecker und die Banalität des Bösen* (Zurich, 2000), pp. 130–31. At about the same time, Eichmann divided *IVB4* into sections a and b: IVB4a, in charge of the logistics of deportations, was headed by the transportation specialist Franz Novak, while section IVB4b, in charge of legal and technical matters, was under Friedrich Suhr (followed by Otto Hunsche). Rolf Günther faithfully served as Eichmann's deputy and an intense "esprit de corps" characterized the entire group of Eichmann's men. For this tightly knit group see Hans Safrian, *Die Eichmann-Männer* (Vienna, 1992); Lozowick, *Hitlers Bürokraten: Eichmann, seine willigen Vollstrecker und die Banalität des Bösen*; David Cesarani, *Becoming Eichmann: Rethinking the Life, Crimes, and Trial of a "Desk Murderer"* (New York, 2006), particularly pp. 126ff.

45. Wolf Grüner, "Zwangsarbeit," in Wolfgang Benz et al., *Enzyklopädie des Nationalsozialismus,* p. 814.

46. Quoted in Arno J. Mayer, *Why Did the Heavens Not Darken?: The "Final Solution" in History* (New York, 1988), p. 333.

47. Ibid, pp. 333–34.

48. Dawid Sierakowiak, *The Diary of Dawid Sierakowiak,* ed. Alan Adelson (New York, 1996), p. 148.

49. Christopher R. Browning, *Nazi Policy, Jewish Workers, German Killers* (Cambridge, 2000), pp. 71ff.

50. Ibid. p. 74.

51. Ibid., p. 75.

52. Ibid., p. 76.

53. Goebbels, *Tagebücher,* part 2, vol. 4, p. 350.

54. Ibid., p. 351.

55. Ibid., p. 355.

56. Ibid., p. 386.

57. Himmler, *Der Dienstkalender*, p. 437n86.

58. Goebbels, *Tagebücher*, part 2, vol. 4, p. 405.

59. Ibid., p. 406.

60. Ibid. A few days later, Goebbels noted that hundreds of Jewish hostages should be shot for each assassination attempt: "The more of this filth we eliminate, the better the security of the Reich will be." Ibid., p. 433.

61. Kurt Pätzold, "Lidice," in Wolfgang Benz, Hermann Graml, and Hermann Weiss, eds., *Enzyklopädie des Nationalsozialismus* (Stuttgart, 1997), p. 569.

62. For the interim period, see Michael Wildt, *Generation des Unbedingten: Das Führungskorps des Reichssicherheitshauptamtes* (Hamburg, 2002), pp. 681ff.

63. Himmler, *Der Dienstkalender*, pp. 448, 450, 451.

64. Heinrich Himmler, *Heinrich Himmler: Geheimreden, 1933 bis 1945, und andere Ansprachen*, ed. Bradley F. Smith and Agnes F. Peterson (Frankfurt am Main, 1974), p. 159. Himmler imitates Hitler's expressions about the extermination of the Jews ("and soon none will laugh anymore" as well as "wiping the slate clean").

65. Nuremberg doc. No-5574, reproduced in Tatiana Berenstein, ed., *Faschismus, Getto, Massenmord: Dokumentation über Ausrottung und Widerstand der Juden in Polen während des zweiten Weltkrieges* (East Berlin, 1961), p. 303.

66. The most detailed monograph on Theresienstadt remains H. G. Adler, *Theresienstadt, 1941–1945: Das Antlitz einer Zwangsgemeinschaft. Geschichte, Soziologie, Psychologie* (Tübingen, 1960). Although extremely detailed, Adler's study is considered highly biased in terms of personal assessments; on this issue see any number of essays in Miroslav Kárný, Vojtech Blodig, and Margita Kárná, eds., *Theresienstadt in der "Endlösung der Judenfrage"* (Prague, 1992).

67. All details on Edelstein are taken from Ruth Bondy, *"Elder of the Jews": Jakob Edelstein of Theresienstadt* (New York, 1989).

68. Ibid., pp. 159ff.

69. Ibid., pp. 208ff.

70. Ibid., p. 246.

71. Egon Redlich, *The Terezin Diary of Gonda Redlich*, ed. Saul S. Friedman (Lexington, KY, 1992), pp. 3ff.

72. Bondy, *"Elder of the Jews,"* p. 270.

73. Redlich, *The Terezin Diary of Gonda Redlich*, p. 5. Actually the nine men who were hanged had smuggled letters out of Terezin. See Eva Roubièkova, *We Are Alive and Life Goes On: A Theresienstadt Diary* (New York, 1998), p. 20; also Bondy, *"Elder of the Jews,"* pp. 260ff.

74. Redlich, *The Terezin Diary of Gonda Redlich*, p. 53.

75. Ibid.

76. Ibid., pp. 53 and 54 n. 26. See also Bondy, *"Elder of the Jews,"* pp. 300ff.

77. Bondy, *"Elder of the Jews,"* p. 301.

78. Ibid., p. 302.

79. Ibid., p. 61.

80. Ruth Kluger, *Still Alive: A Holocaust Girlhood Remembered* (New York, 2001), pp. 78–79.

81. Ibid. The 1942 film was a failure from the Nazi propaganda viewpoint, as the "ghetto" looked too close to reality. For a thoroughly researched article on the history of this first film, see Karel Margry, "Der Nazi-Film über Theresienstadt" in Miroslav Karny et al., *Theresienstadt in der "Endlosüng der Judenfrage"* (Prague, 1992), pp. 285ff.

82. This letter, among others, was brought to Marianne Ellenbogen by the owner of a truck dealership in Essen who knew both Ernst and Marianne. He had joined the SS and traveled frequently to Izbica. For the document and the context see Mark Roseman, *A Past in Hiding: Memory and Survival in Nazi Germany* (New York, 2001), pp. 179ff.

83. Ibid., p. 186.

84. Ibid., p. 188.

85. Ibid.

86. Ibid., p. 192.

87. Ibid.

88. Ibid., pp. 207ff.

89. Memo by Rauter, March 17, 1942, in Berenstein, *Faschismus, Getto, Massenmord.* pp. 269–70. Test gassings in which hundreds of Jews were exterminated had taken place from the end of February to mid-March. See Eugen Kogon, Hermann Langbein, and Adalbert Rückerl, eds., *Nazi Mass Murder: A Documentary History of the Use of Poison Gas* (New Haven, 1993), p. 109.

90. For the details see Yitzhak Arad, *Belzec, Sobibor, Treblinka: The Operation Reinhard Death Camps* (Bloomington, 1987), pp. 72ff; Kogon, Langbein, and Rückerl, *Nazi Mass Murder*; Dieter Pohl, *Von der "Judenpolitik" zum Judenmord: Der Distrikt Lublin des Generalgouvernements, 1939–1944* (Frankfurt am Main, 1993), pp. 113ff. It appears that Majdanek was included among the "Aktion Reinhardt" camps by the headquarters in Lublin. As for the spelling of Reinhard(t), both forms were used by Heydrich himself.

91. There has been some debate about the number of Jews exterminated in Belzec, until the discovery in the Russian archives of a message sent on January 11, 1943, by Hermann Hōfle (Globocnik's deportation specialist) to Franz Heim (at the RSHA in Kraków), which indicates the number mentioned above. See on this issue Peter Witte and Stephen Tyas, "A New Document on the Deportation and Murder of Jews during "Einsatz Reinhardt 1942," *Holocaust and Genocide Studies* 95 (2002), pp. 458ff. The document will be quoted in chapter 8.

92. Gitta Sereny, *Into That Darkness: From Mercy Killing to Mass Murder* (London, 1974), p. 111.

93. Ibid., p. 117.

94. Arad, *Belzec*, p. 80.

95. Zygmunt Klukowski, *Diary from the Years of Occupation, 1939–44*, ed. Andrew

Klukowski and Helen Klukowski May (Urbana, IL, 1993). Klukowski's diary raises some problems. One editor, Zygmunt's son, mentions that the full text, deposited at the library of the Catholic University in Lublin, has been cut by some 8 percent; moreover, in the collaborative effort with Zygmunt's grandson to translate the text into English, some changes in the wording were apparently made and short paragraphs "that were clearly related" were combined (Klukowski, *Diary*, p. xix). Some passages that were rephrased in the English translation offer, in the original, a very negative image of the behavior of the local Polish population; these passages will be quoted in part of the next note, and can be compared in the note with their translation by Jan T. Gross.

96. Ibid. Jan T. Gross's translation runs as follows: "All the scum are milling around, a lot of [peasants with] wagons came from the countryside and stood waiting the entire day for the moment when they could start looting. News keeps reaching us from all directions about the scandalous behavior of segments of the Polish population who rob emptied Jewish apartments. I am sure our little town will be no different." Quoted in Jan T. Gross, "A Tangled Web: Confronting Stereotypes Concerning Relations between Poles, Germans, Jews and Communists," in *The Politics of Retribution*, ed. István Deák, Jan T. Gross, and Tony Judt (Princeton, 2000). Klukowski was right. Many of the Jews of Sczebrzeszyn were murdered on the spot, on May 8, 1942. "The next morning," Klukowski noted, "behavior of a certain part of the Polish population left a lot to be desired. People were laughing, joking, many strolled to the Jewish quarter looking around for an opportunity to grab something from the deserted houses." Gross, "Tangled Web," p. 90.

97. In her day-by-day chronicle of the events in Auschwitz, Danuta Czech noted for February 15, 1942: "The first transport of Jews who have been arrested by the [Ge]stapo and destined for death in Auschwitz arrives from Beuthen. They are unloaded on the platform of the camp siding. They have to leave their bags on the platform. The standby squad takes charge of the deportees from the Stapo and leads them to the gas chamber in the camp crematorium. There they are killed with Zyklon B gas." Danuta Czech, *Auschwitz Chronicle, 1939–1945* (New York, 1990), p. 135.

98. Debórah Dwork and Robert Jan van Pelt, *Auschwitz* (New York, 2002), p. 301.

99. Ibid., pp. 302–3.

100. For the stagewise beginning of the second sweep from the end of 1941 on, see Raul Hilberg, *The Destruction of the European Jews*, 3 vols. (New Haven, Conn., 2003), vol. 1, pp. 382ff.

101. Nuremberg doc. PS-2174, pp. 72–75. Quoted in Dieter Pohl, "Schauplatz Ukraine," in *Darstellungen und Quellen zur Geschichte von Auschwitz Ausbeutung, Vernichtung, Öffentlichkeit: Neue Studien zur nationalsozialistischen Lagerpolitik*, ed. Norbert Frei, Sybille Steinbacher, and Bernd C. Wagner, vol. 4 (Munich, 2000), p. 155.

102. For a detailed overview see mainly Shmuel Spector, *The Holocaust of Volhynian Jews 1941–1944* (Jerusalem, 1990). Regarding the results of the "first sweep" and the extermination in Rovno, see pp. 113–15.

103. Pohl, "Schauplatz Ukraine," pp. 156–57.

104. For the function of these auxiliary forces see in particular Martin Dean, *Collaboration in the Holocaust. Crimes of the Local Police in Belorussia and the Ukraine, 1941–44* (New York, 2000).

105. Ibid., p. 96.

106. Pohl, "Schauplatz Ukraine," p. 158.

107. Ibid., pp. 159–61.

108. Jäger's report of February 9, 1942, is reproduced in Friedlander and Milton, eds., *Archives of the Holocaust,* vol. 22, doc. 82, p. 177.

109. Ibid., vol. 22, doc. 91, p. 196.

110. See the basic documentation in Helmut Heiber, "Aus den Akten des Gauleiters Kube," *Viertelsjahrhefte für Zeitgeschichte* 4 (1956), pp. 67ff.

111. International Military Tribunal, *Trial of the Major War Criminal Before the International Military Tribunal, Nuremberg, 14 November 1946–9 October 1946*, PS-3428, vol. 12, p. 67, quoted in Gerald Fleming, *Hitler and the Final Solution* (Berkeley, 1984), p. 118.

112. Ibid., p. 148.

113. For the response, see Longerich and Pohl, eds., *Die Ermordung,* pp. 355–56.

114. Ibid.

115. For the details of this operation, see the partly diverging interpretations in Christopher R. Browning, *Fateful Months: Essays on the Emergence of the Final Solution* (New York, 1985) and in Menachem Shelach, "Sajmiste—An Extermination Camp in Serbia," *Holocaust and Genocide Studies* 2, no. 2 (1987), pp. 243ff.

116. Shelach, "Sajmište," pp. 253–54. For the full text of Schäfer's telegram, see Nuremberg doc. 501-PS, U.S. Office of Chief of Counsel for the Prosecution of Axis Criminality, and International Military Tribunal, *Nazi Conspiracy and Aggression*, 8 vols. (Washington, DC, 1946), vol. 3, p. 418–19.

117. Shelach, "Sajmište," p. 254.

118. Berenstein, *Faschismus, Getto, Massenmord*, p. 278.

119. For a detailed history of the Bielskis, see mainly Nechama Tec, *Defiance: The Bielski Partisans* (New York, 1993).

120. Ibid.

121. About the situation in Minsk, see mainly Shalom Cholavsky, "The Judenrat in Minsk," in *Patterns of Jewish Leadership in Nazi Europe, 1933–1945.* Yisrael Gutman and Cynthia J. Haft, eds. (Jerusalem, 1979), pp. 120ff. See also Hersh Smolar, *The Minsk Ghetto: Soviet-Jewish Partisans Against the Nazis* (New York, 1989).

122. Ingo Müller, *Hitler's Justice: The Courts of the Third Reich* (Cambridge, MA, 1991), p. 114ff.

123. Nuremberg doc. NG-1012, quoted in John Mendelsohn and Donald S. Detwiler, eds., *The Holocaust: Selected Documents in Eighteen Volumes* (New York, 1982), vol. 13; John Mendelsohn, *The Judicial System and the Jews in Nazi Germany* (New York, 1982), p. 233.

124. Mendelsohn, *The Judicial System and the Jews in Nazi Germany*, pp. 240–41.

125. Ibid., p. 243.

126. See Jörg Wollenberg, ed., *The German Public and the Persecution of the Jews, 1933–1945* (Atlantic Highlands, NJ, 1996), p. 137.

127. Müller, *Hitler's Justice*, p. 114. See also Otto Dov Kulka and Eberhard Jäckel, *Die Juden in den geheimen NS-Stimmungsberichten 1933–1945* (Düsseldorf, 2004), p. 498.

128. Klemperer, *I Will Bear Witness: A Diary of the Nazi Years, 1942–45*, pp. 4–5.

129. Helmut Heiber, ed., *Akten der Partei-Kanzlei der NSDAP: Rekonstruktion eines verlorengegangenen Bestandes. Regesten*, vol. 1, part 2 (Munich, 1983), abs. no. 26106.

130. Joseph Walk, ed., *Das Sonderrecht für die Juden im NS-Staat: Eine Sammlung der gesetzlichen Massnahmen und Richtlinien, Inhalt und Bedeutung* (Heidelberg, 1981), p. 360.

131. Heiber, *Akten der Partei-Kanzlei der NSDAP*, vol. 1, part 2, abs. no. 26106.

132. Ibid.

133. Ibid., p. 366.

134. Peter Longerich, ed., *Akten der Partei-Kanzlei der NSDAP: Rekonstruktion eines verlorengegangenen Bestandes. Regesten.*, vol. 2, part 4 (Munich, 1992) abs. no. 42409.

135. Walk, ed., *Das Sonderrecht*, p. 368.

136. Klemperer, *I Will Bear Witness: A Diary of the Nazi Years, 1942–45*, p. 58.

137. Ibid., p. 52.

138. Wolf Gruner, *Judenverfolgung in Berlin 1933–1945: Eine Chronologie der Behördenmassnahmen in der Reichshauptstadt* (Berlin, 1996), p. 84.

139. Ibid.

140. *Akten der Parteikanzlei der NSDAP*, part 2, vol. 4, abs. no. 42900.

141. Gruner, *Judenverfolgung in Berlin*, p. 85.

142. Bormann's letter and Fiehler's answer are quoted in Ernst Piper, "National Socialist Cultural Policy and Its Beneficiaries: The Example of Munich," in *The German Public and the Persecution of the Jews, 1933–1945*, ed. Jörg Wollenberg (Atlantic Highlands, NJ, 1996), p. 110.

143. Klemperer, *I Will Bear Witness: A Diary of the Nazi Years, 1941–1945*, vol. 2, p. 8.

144. Ibid., p. 9.

145. Ibid., p. 28.

146. Hertha Feiner, *Before Deportation: Letters from a Mother to Her Daughters, January 1939–December 1942*, ed. Karl Heinz Jahnke (Evanston, IL, 1999), p. 102.

147. On this issue see in particular Beate Meyer, "Das unausweichliche Dilemma: Die Reichsvereinigung der Juden in Deutschland, die Deportationen und die untergetauchten Juden," in *Überleben im Untergrund: Hilfe für Juden in Deutschland*, ed. Beate Kosmala and Claudia Schopmann (Berlin, 2002), pp. 278ff.

148. Ibid., pp. 280–81.

149. Paul Sauer, ed., *Dokumente über die Verfolgung der jüdischen Bürger in Baden-Württemberg durch das nationalsozialistische Regime 1933–1945*, 2 vols. (Stuttgart: 1966), vol. 2, pp. 317–18.

150. Ibid., pp. 322–23.

151. Ibid.

152. Ruth Andreas-Friedrich and June Barrows Mussey, *Berlin Underground, 1938–1945* (New York, 1947), p. 77.

153. Ibid., p. 78.

154. For the events in Slovakia see mainly Livia Rothkirchen, "The Situation of the Jews in Slovakia between 1939 and 1945," *Jahrbuch für Antisemitismusforschung* 7 (1998), pp. 46ff. and particularly 51ff.

155. Michael Phayer, *The Catholic Church and the Holocaust, 1930–1965* (Bloomington, 2000), p. 88.

156. Ibid., p. 89.

157. Ibid.

158. Ibid., p. 90.

159. Ingrid Krüger-Bulcke and Hans Georg Lehmann, eds., *Akten zur deutschen auswärtigen Politik, 1918–1945*, Series E, *1941–1945* (Göttingen, 1974), vol. 3, pp. 65–66.

160. Ibid., p. 66 n. 1.

161. Yehuda Bauer, *Jews for Sale? Nazi-Jewish Negotiations, 1933–1945* (New Haven, 1994), pp. 62ff.

162. For the text of Dannecker's memorandum of June 15, see Serge Klarsfeld, *Vichy-Auschwitz: Le rôle de Vichy dans la solution finale de la question juive en France* (Paris, 1983), vol. 1, pp. 202–3.

163. Ibid., p. 70ff.

164. J. Presser, *Ashes in the Wind: The Destruction of Dutch Jewry* (Detroit, 1988), p. 92.

165. Ibid., pp. 94ff.

166. Ibid., pp. 98ff.

167. Ibid., pp. 100ff.

168. Etty Hillesum, *An Interrupted Life: The Diaries of Etty Hillesum, 1941–1943* (New York, 1983), p. 93.

169. Ibid., p. 107.

170. Ibid., p. 118.

171. Ibid., p. 122.

172. For the chronology of events in France and in the early summer of 1942 most of the relevant documents see mainly Klarsfeld, *Vichy-Auschwitz*, vol. 1 (Paris, 1983).

173. Ibid., vol. 1, p. 236.

174. Ibid., p. 237.

175. For the introduction of the star in Holland, see Bob Moore, *Victims and Survivors: The Nazi Persecution of the Jews in the Netherlands, 1940–1945* (London, 1997), p. 86ff. For France, see Michael R. Marrus and Robert O. Paxton, *Vichy France and the Jews* (New York, 1981), pp. 234ff.

176. Moore, *Victims and Survivors*, pp. 85–89.

177. Presser, *Ashes in the Wind*, pp. 124–26.

178. Michael R. Marrus and Robert O. Paxton, *Vichy et les juifs* (Paris, 1990), pp. 236–37.

179. Renée Poznanski, *Être juif en France pendant la Seconde Guerre mondiale* (Paris, 1994), p. 358.

180. Ibid.

181. Biélinky, *Journal*, p.191.

182. Ibid., p. 209.

183. Ibid., pp. 209–10.

184. Ibid., pp. 214ff.

185. Nuremberg doc. NG-183, *The Ministries Case*, p. 235.

186. Pierre Drieu la Rochelle, *Journal, 1939–1945*, ed. Julien Hervier (Paris, 1992), p. 302.

187. Lucien Rebatet, *Les Décombres* (Paris, 1942), pp. 568–69 (translated in David Carroll, *French Literary Fascism: Nationalism, Anti-Semitism, and the Ideology of Culture* [Princeton, 1995], p. 212).

188. Ibid., p. 605 (Carroll, *French Literary Fascism*, p. 211).

189. Quoted in Frédéric Vitoux, *Céline: A Biography* (New York, 1992), p. 378.

190. Quoted in Carroll, *French Literary Fascism*, p. 121.

191. Ibid., p. 275.

192. See in particular Robert Belot, "Lucien Rebatet, ou L'Antisémitisme comme Événement Littéraire," in *L'Antisémitisme de plume, 1940–1944: Études et documents*, ed. Pierre-André Taguieff (Paris, 1999), pp. 217ff. See also Robert Belot, *Lucien Rebatet: Un itinéraire fasciste* (Paris, 1994).

193. Pierre Assouline, *Gaston Gallimard: A Half-Century of French Publishing* (San Diego, 1988), p. 279.

194. Richard I. Cohen, *The Burden of Conscience: French Jewish Leadership During the Holocaust* (Bloomington, 1987), pp. 71ff, 116ff.

195. Raymond-Raoul Lambert, *Carnet d'un témoin: 1940–1943*, ed. Richard I. Cohen (Paris, 1985), p. 163. Much of what Lambert writes about the overall attitude of the Consistoire is true; the donations to "l'Amitié Chrétienne," however, were intended as financial support for Jewish children helped by the organization. See Simon Schwarzfuchs, *Aux Prises avec Vichy: Histoire politique des Juifs de France, 1940–1944* (Paris, 1998), p. 263.

196. Herman Kruk, *The Last Days of the Jerusalem of Lithuania: Chronicles from the Vilna Ghetto and the Camps, 1939–1944*, ed. Benjamin Harshav (New Haven, 2002), pp. 173–74.

197. The report written by G. Jaszunski, head of the cultural department of the council, is reproduced in Lucy S. Dawidowicz, ed., *A Holocaust Reader* (New York, 1976), pp. 208ff.

198. Avraham Tory, *Surviving the Holocaust: The Kovno Ghetto Diary*, ed. Martin Gilbert and Dina Porat (Cambridge, MA, 1990), p. 67.

199. Ibid.

200. Ibid., p. 72.

201. Quoted in Antony Polonsky, "Beyond Condemnation, Apologetics and Apologies: On the Complexity of Polish Behavior toward the Jews during the Second World War," in *Holocaust: Critical Concepts in Historical Studies*, vol. 5, ed. David Cesarani (New York, 2004), p. 46.

202. Ibid., p. 47.

203. Ibid.

204. Ibid.

205. Dawid Rubinowicz, *The Diary of Dawid Rubinowicz* (Edmonds, WA, 1982), p. 38.

206. Ibid., p. 43.

207. Ibid., pp. 85–87.

208. Alexandra Zapruder, *Salvaged Pages. Young Writers' Diaries of the Holocaust* (New Haven, 2002), pp. 322–23.

209. Ibid., p. 325.

210. Ibid., p. 327.

211. Ibid., p. 306.

212. Sierakowiak, *Diary*, p. 149.

213. Ibid., p. 151.

214. Introduction to Lucjan Dobroszycki, ed., *The Chronicle of the Lódz Ghetto, 1941–1944* (New Haven, 1984), p. xx.

215. Avraham Barkai, "Between East and West: Jews from Germany in the Lodz Ghetto," in *The Nazi Holocaust: Historical Articles on the Destruction of European Jews*, ed. Michael R. Marrus (Westport, CT, 1989), p. 418.

216. Ibid., p. 420.

217. Ibid., pp. 419ff.

218. Dobroszycki, *The Chronicle*, pp. 163–64.

219. Ibid., pp. 181–182.

220. Ibid., p. 185.

221. Ibid., pp. 193–94.

222. Berenstein, *Faschismus, Getto, Massenmord*, pp. 292–93.

223. Emanuel Ringelblum, *Notes from the Warsaw Ghetto: The Journal of Emanuel Ringelblum*, ed. Jacob Sloan (New York, 1974), p. 251.

224. Chaim Aron Kaplan, *Scroll of Agony: The Warsaw Diary of Chaim A. Kaplan*, ed. Abraham Isaac Katsh (New York, 1965), p. 237.

225. Adam Czerniaków, *The Warsaw Diary of Adam Czerniaków*, ed. Raul Hilberg, Stanislaw Staron, and Josef Kermisz (New York, 1979), p. 328 (at this level the annual mortality rate would have been 14 percent).

226. Ibid., p. 328.

227. Ibid., p. 330.

228. Ibid., p. 339.

229. Ibid.

230. Ibid., p. 342.

231. For the meeting, see Yisrael Gutman, *The Jews of Warsaw, 1939–1943: Ghetto,*

Underground, Revolt (Bloomington, 1982), pp. 168ff; Yitzhak Zuckerman, *A Surplus of Memory: Chronicle of the Warsaw Ghetto Uprising* (Berkeley, 1993), pp. 170ff; Daniel Blatman, *Notre liberté et la vôtre: Le mouvement ouvrier juif Bund en Pologne, 1939–1949* (Paris, 2002), pp. 130ff.

232. Gutman, *The Jews of Warsaw*, p. 168; Zuckerman, *A Surplus of Memory*, p. 174; Blatman, *Notre liberté et la vôtre*, p. 130.

233. One may also argue that the time had not yet come, as there was a collective responsibility for the Jewish population. On that important point see Ruta Sakowska, "Two Forms of Resistance in the Warsaw Ghetto—Two Functions of the Ringelblum Archives," *Yad Vashem Studies* 21 (1991), p. 217.

234. Gutman, *The Jews of Warsaw*, p. 169; Zuckerman, *A Surplus of Memory*, p. 174; Blatman, *Notre liberté et la vôtre*, p. 130.

235. For a history of the Bund in Poland during the war and immediate postwar years and for the Bundist view of a common front with the Zionists, see Blatman, *Notre liberté et la vôtre*, particularly pp. 129ff. In his memoirs Zuckerman describes the Bund's attitude as seen from the Zionist perspective. See Zuckerman, *A Surplus of Memory*, pp. 170ff.

236. About the publicity given to the Bund report in the British media, see Martin Gilbert, *Auschwitz and the Allies* (New York, 1981), pp. 42–43.

237. Laurel Leff, *Buried by the Times: The Holocaust and America's Most Important Newspaper* (New York, 2005), p. 139.

238. Czerniaków, *Warsaw Diary*, p. 343.

239. Note in Ibid., p. 344n. The killings took place during the night of the seventeenth to the eighteenth: Czerniakow noted them under the April 17 entry, usually, the April 18 date is referred to.

240. Note in ibid., p. 344 n.

241. Zuckerman, *A Surplus of Memory*, pp. 177ff.

242. See Zuckerman's indications about the rise and fall of the "Anti-Fascist Bloc" in the late spring of 1942. Ibid., pp. 180ff.

243. Hersch Wasser, "Daily Entries of Hersch Wasser," *Yad Vashem Studies* 15 (1983), pp. 271–72.

244. Almost every study or memoir about the Warsaw ghetto mentions Rubinstein. See in particular Jan Marek Gronski, *Life in Nazi-Occupied Warsaw. Three Ghetto Sketches* (1992), p. 192ff.

245. Yitzhak Perlis, "Final Chapter: Korczak in the Warsaw Ghetto," in *The Ghetto Diary*, ed. Janusz Korczak (New York, 1978), pp. 78ff.

246. Janusz Korczak, *Ghetto Diary*, ed. Aaron Zeitlin (New York, 1978), p. 192.

247. For details about Lewin see Antony Polonsky, introduction to his edition of Lewin's diary, Abraham Lewin, *A Cup of Tears: A Diary of the Warsaw Ghetto*, ed. Antony Polonsky (Oxford, 1988).

248. Ibid., p. 80.

249. Quoted in Ruta Sakowska, *Menschen im Ghetto: Die jüdische Bevölkerung im*

besetzten Warschau 1939–1943 (Osnabrück, 1999), p. 220. The author assumes that the message was well understood; this cannot be established.

250. Czerniaków, *Warsaw Diary*, pp. 376–77.

Chapter Seven: July 1942–March 1943

1. This report, titled "Observations about the 'Resettlement of Jews' in the General Government" (*IfZ*, Munich, doc. ED 81) is reproduced in Raul Hilberg, ed., *Documents of Destruction: Germany and Jewry, 1933–1945* (Chicago, 1971), pp. 208ff.

2. For the growing crisis and the unfolding military situation, see Ian Kershaw, *Hitler, 1936–45: Nemesis* (New York, 2000), pp. 526ff.

3. Ulrich von Hassell, *Die Hassell-Tagebücher 1938–1944: Aufzeichnungen vom Andern Deutschland*, ed. Klaus Peter Reiss (unter Mitarbeit) and Freiherr Friedrich Hiller von Gaertringen (Berlin, 1988), p. 330.

4. Adolf Hitler, *Hitler: Reden und Proklamationen, 1932–1945: Kommentiert von einem deutschen Zeitgenossen*, ed. Max Domarus, 4 vols., vol. 2, part 1 (Munich, 1965), p. 1920. For an analysis of these sadistic aspects of Hitler's "prophecy," see Philippe Burrin, *Ressentiment et Apocalypse. Essai sur l'antisemitisme nazi* (Paris, 2004), pp. 78ff.

5. Mihail Sebastian, *Journal, 1935–1944*, ed. Radu Ioanid (Chicago, 2000), p. 511.

6. Victor Klemperer, *I Will Bear Witness: A Diary of the Nazi Years, 1942–1945* (New York, 1998), p. 150.

7. Joseph Goebbels, *Die Tagebücher von Joseph Goebbels: Sämtliche Fragmente*, ed. Elke Fröhlich (Munich, 1996), part 2, vol. 6, pp. 445–46.

8. Ibid., vol. 5, p. 378.

9. Nuremberg doc. NO-205, in John Mendelsohn and Donald S. Detwiler, eds., *The Holocaust: Selected Documents in Eighteen Volumes* (New York, 1982), vol. 9, p. 173.

10. See Longerich and Pohl, *Die Ermordung*, p. 371–72.

11. Helmut Heiber, ed., *Akten der Partei-Kanzlei der NSDAP: Rekonstruktion eines verlorengegangenen Bestandes. Regesten.*, vol. 1, part 2 (München, 1983), abs. no. 26773.

12. Ibid., part 1, vol. 1, abs. no. 16019.

13. Ibid., part 1, vol. 2, abs. no. 26778. The pamphlet *Der Untermensch* (Berlin, 1942) was published by the SS Hauptamt.

14. Rudolf Höss, *Kommandant in Auschwitz: Autobiographische Aufzeichnungen.*, ed. Martin Broszat (Stuttgart, 1958), p. 207; Heinrich Himmler, *Der Dienstkalender Heinrich Himmlers 1941/42*, ed. Peter Witte et al. (Hamburg, 1999), p. 492 n. 70.

15. Höss, *Kommandant in Auschwitz*, p. 188. The order was brought to Höss by Paul Blobel, the former head of *Sonderkommando 4a* of *Einsatzgruppe C*, who in the meantime had been put in charge of *Aktion* 1005, the elimination of all traces of the murder operations, mainly by opening the mass graves and burning the bodies. See Shmuel Spector, "Aktion 1005—Effacing the Murder of Millions," *Holocaust and Genocide Studies* 5, no. 2 (1990), p. 159.

16. Höss, *Kommandant in Auschwitz*, p. 210.

17. Bob Moore, *Victims and Survivors: The Nazi Persecution of the Jews in the Netherlands, 1940–1945* (London, 1997), pp. 92–93.

18. Quoted in Peter Longerich and Dieter Pohl, eds., *Die Ermordung der europäischen Juden: Eine umfassende Dokumentation des Holocaust 1941–1945* (Munich, 1989), p. 258.

19. Guus Meershoek, "The Amsterdam Police and the Persecution of the Jews," in *Holocaust: Critical Concepts in Historical Studies*, ed. David Cesarani (New York, 2004), vol. 3, p. 547.

20. Gerhard Hirschfeld, *Nazi Rule and Dutch Collaboration: The Netherlands under German Occupation, 1940–1945* (Oxford, 1988), p. 175.

21. Mussert's party was more strongly represented in the police than in any other Dutch agency. Ibid., pp. 175ff.

22. Ibid., p. 178.

23. Johannes Houwink ten Cate, "Der Befehlshaber der Sipo und des SD in den besetzten niederländischen Gebieten und die Deportation der Juden 1942–1943," in *Die Bürokratie der Okkupation: Strukturen der Herrschaft und Verwaltung im besetzten Europa*, ed. Wolfgang Benz, Johannes Houwink ten Cate, and Gerhard Otto, *Nationalsozialistische Besatzungspolitik in Europa 1939–1945* (Berlin, 1998), vol. 4, p. 202.

24. Ibid., pp. 206ff.

25. Louis de Jong, *The Netherlands and Nazi Germany* (Cambridge, MA, 1990), p. 12.

26. Ibid., p. 13.

27. Quoted in J. Presser, *Ashes in the Wind: The Destruction of Dutch Jewry* (Detroit, 1988), p. 167.

28. Moore, *Victims and Survivors*, p. 96.

29. Etty Hillesum, *An Interrupted Life: The Diaries of Etty Hillesum, 1941–1943* (New York, 1983), p. 147.

30. Ibid., pp. 152–53.

31. Ibid., p. 166.

32. Ibid., p. 167.

33. Anne Frank, *The Diary of a Young Girl: The Definitive Edition*, ed. Otto Frank and Mirjam Pressler (New York, 1995), pp. 18ff. and 21.

34. Presser, *Ashes in the Wind*, pp. 152–53.

35. Ibid., pp. 154–55. Presser's sharp criticism of the council has itself been forcefully attacked. In regard to the August event for example, Presser does not mention that De Wolff, a student of his, saved Presser's wife from deportation on this occasion. About this and other aspects of Presser's account see Henriette Boas, "The Persecution and Destruction of Dutch Jewry, 1940–1945," *Yad Vashem Studies* 6 (1967). The highly emotional feuding about the behavior of the Jewish Council in Amsterdam and even more specifically about its two leaders Cohen and Assher (particularly Cohen) has been going on since the end of the war. See, for example, the attack on Cohen's main detractors De Jong, Isaak Kisch, and Presser and the favorable interpretation of his stewardship in Piet H. Schrijvers, "Truth Is the Daughter of Time: Prof. David Cohen as Seen

by Himself and by Others." In Chaja Brasz and Yosef Kaplan, eds. *Dutch Jews as Perceived by Themselves and by Others* (Leiden, 2001, pp. 355ff).

36. Ibid., pp. 40–41.

37. Ibid., p. 41.

38. Benjamin Leo Wessels, *Ben's Story: Holocaust Letters with Selections from the Dutch Underground Press*, ed. Kees W. Bolle (Carbondale, IL, 2001), p. 43. The stealing and mistreatment by the Wehrmacht unit stationed in Oostvoorne is confirmed in other letters.

39. Most of the details mentioned here are quoted from Louis de Jong, "The Netherlands and Auschwitz," *Yad Vashem Studies* 7 (1968), pp. 39ff.

40. Ibid., pp. 47–48.

41. Ibid., p. 50.

42. Bob Moore, *Victims and Survivors: The Nazi Persecution of the Jews in the Netherlands, 1940–1945* (London, 1997), p. 128.

43. Ingrid Krüger-Bulcke and Hans Georg Lehmann, eds., *Akten zur deutschen auswärtigen Politik, 1918–1945* (Göttingen, 1975), vol. 4, p. 328.

44. If Cohen knew of these clandestine activities and approved them, his role appears in a different light; the testimonies on this issue are contradictory.

45. See Debórah Dwork, *Children with a Star: Jewish Youth in Nazi Europe* (New Haven, 1991), pp. 45ff.

46. The number one thousand is mentioned in Werner Warmbrunn, "Netherlands," in Laqueur and Baumel, eds., *Holocaust Encyclopedia*, p. 440.

47. See in particular Bob Moore, "The Dutch Churches, Christians and the Rescue of Jews in the Netherlands," in *Dutch Jews*, ed. Chaya Brasz and Yosef Kaplan (Leiden, 2001), pp. 277ff; see also Bert Jan Flim, "Opportunities for the Jews to Hide from the Nazis, 1942–45," in ibid., pp. 289ff. Louis de Jong has estimated the number of Dutch families that hid Jews at one stage or another at approximately 25,000 (De Jong, *The Netherlands and Nazi Germany*, p. 21).

48. Quoted in Presser, *The Destruction*, p. 182.

49. Ibid., p. 183 (emphasis in original).

50. Ibid., p. 184 (emphasis in original).

51. Ibid.

52. Ibid., p. 183.

53. On the function of Vught, see in particular J. W. Griffioen and R. Zeller, "A Comparative Analysis of the Persecution of the Jews in the Netherlands and Belgium During the Second World War" (Amsterdam, 1998), p. 11.

54. For these statistics see Gerhard Hirschfeld, "Niederlande," in Wolfgang Benz, ed., *Dimension des Völkermords: Die Zahl der jüdischen Opfer des Nationalsozialismus* (Munich, 1991), p. 151.

55. Biélinky, *Journal*, pp. 232–33.

56. Robert Gildea, *Marianne in Chains: Everyday Life in the French Heartland under the German Occupation* (New York, 2003), pp. 259–60.

57. André Kaspi, *Les Juifs pendant l'occupation* (Paris, 1991), p. 222.

58. Renée Poznanski, *Être juif en France pendant la Seconde Guerre mondiale* (Paris, 1994), p. 385.

59. On July 15, Biélinky noted in his diary: "It appears that Jews and Jewesses aged eighteen to forty-five are going to be arrested and sent to forced labor in Germany." Jacques Biélinky, *Journal, 1940–1942: Un journaliste juif à Paris sous l'Occupation*, ed. Renée Poznanski (Paris, 1992), p. 233.

60. Kaspi, *Les Juifs pendant l'occupation*, p. 224.

61. Quoted in ibid., p. 226–27.

62. Poznanski, *Être juif*, p. 385.

63. Ibid., 386.

64. Ibid., p. 386.

65. Michael R. Marrus and Robert O. Paxton, *Vichy et les juifs* (Paris, 1990), p. 258.

66. Ibid., p. 260.

67. Ibid., pp. 260–61.

68. Biélinky, *Journal*, p. 236.

69. Michael R. Marrus and Robert O. Paxton, *Vichy et les juifs*, p. 255.

70. Serge Klarsfeld, *Vichy-Auschwitz: Le rôle de Vichy dans la solution finale de la question juive en France*, 2 vols. (Paris, 1983–85), vol. 1, p. 328.

71. Ibid., p. 330.

72. Georges Wellers, *De Drancy à Auschwitz* (Paris, 1946), pp. 55ff.

73. Klarsfeld, *Vichy-Auschwitz*, vol. 1, p. 355.

74. Richard I. Cohen, *The Burden of Conscience: French Jewish Leadership during the Holocaust* (Bloomington, 1987), p. 79.

75. Raymond-Raoul Lambert, *Carnet d'un témoin: 1940–1943*, ed. Richard I. Cohen (Paris, 1985), p. 180.

76. Ibid., p. 178.

77. Simon Schwarzfuchs, *Aux prises avec Vichy: Histoire politique des Juifs de France, 1940–1944* (Paris, 1998), pp. 253–56. For the text of a draft of July 28, see Klarsfeld, *Vichy-Auschwitz*, vol. 1, p. 295.

78. Cohen, Richard I. *The Burden of Conscience: French Jewish Leadership during the Holocaust* (Bloomington, 1987), pp. 80ff and 122ff.

79. Schwarzfuchs, *Aux Prises avec Vichy;* see also Richard I. Cohen, "Le Consistoire et L'UGIF—La Situation Trouble des Juifs Français Face à Vichy," *Revue d'Histoire de la Shoah: Le monde juif* 169 (2000), pp. 33ff.

80. Serge Klarsfeld, *Les transferts de juifs du camp de Rivesaltes et de la région de Montpellier vers le camp de Drancy en vue de leur déportation 10 août 1942–6 août 1944* (Paris, 1993), p. 31–32.

81. For some of the préfets' reports about reactions in their districts, see Klarsfeld, *Vichy-Auschwitz*, vol. 1, pp. 305ff.

82. Renée Poznanski, "Jews and non-Jews in France During World War II: A Daily Life Perspective," in *Lessons and Legacies V: The Holocaust and Justice*, ed. Ronald M. Smelser (Evanston, IL, 2002), p. 306.

83. Ibid.

84. Kaspi, *Les Juifs pendant l'occupation*, pp. 306–7. The main Catholic periodical of the Free French in London, *Volontaires pour la cité chrétienne,* hardly mentioned the persecution and extermination of the Jews at all. See Renée Bédarida, *Les Catholiques dans la guerre, 1939–1945: Entre Vichy et la Résistance* (Paris, 1998), p. 176.

85. The notes are published in Michèle Cointet, *L'Église Sous Vichy, 1940–1945: La rèpentance en question* (Paris, 1998), p. 224.

86. For part of the interpretation, see ibid. In part the reading of the notes is my own.

87. For the French original see Klarsfeld, *Vichy-Auschwitz,* vol. 1, p. 280. See also Cointet, *L'Église Sous Vichy, 1940–1945*, p. 225. Cardinal Suhard was known for his support of Vichy's policies even against the Jews. Thus he took disciplinary measures against two priests of his diocese who had counterfeited baptismal certificates to help Jews. See Bédarida, *Les Catholiques dans la guerre, 1939–1945: Entre Vichy et la Résistance*, p. 78.

88. Cointet, *L'Église Sous Vichy*, p. 266. For Valerio Valeri's letter to Maglione, where the expression is used, see Klarsfeld, *Vichy-Auschwitz*, vol. 1, p. 297

89. Schwarzfuchs, *Aux prises avec Vichy*, pp. 209–10.

90. About Chaillet's assistance to Jews, see mainly Renée Bédarida, *Pierre Chaillet: Témoin de la résistance spirituelle* (Paris, 1988).

91. Translated in Saul Friedländer, *Pius XII and the Third Reich: A Documentation* (New York, 1966), p. 115.

92. Cointet, *L'Église Sous Vichy*, pp. 234ff. A few days after the reading of the letter, the deputy attorney general of Toulouse questioned Saliège. The prelate declared that the parties had "indecently misused his letter." See the text of the interrogation in Eric Malo, "Le camp de Récébédou (Haute-Garonne)," *Le Monde Juif* 153 (1995), pp. 97–98.

93. For the assistance offered by Christian rescuers in France see, among numerous studies, Asher Cohen, *Persécutions et sauvetages: Juifs et Français sous l'Occupation et sous Vichy* (Paris, 1993).

94. Ibid., p. 430.

95. Ingrid Krüger-Bulcke and Hans Georg Lehmann, eds., *Akten zur deutschen auswärtigen Politik, 1918–1945. Series E, 1941–1945* (Göttingen, 1974), vol. 3, p. 125.

96. On the Catholic response in Belgium see Mark Van Den Wijngaert, "The Belgian Catholics and the Jews During the German Occupation, 1940–1944," in *Belgium and the Holocaust: Jews, Belgians, Germans*, ed. Dan Michman (Jerusalem, 1998), pp. 225ff.; see also Luc Dequeker, "Baptism and Conversion of Jews in Belgium," in *Belgium and the Holocaust: Jews, Belgians, Germans*, ed. Dan Michman (Jerusalem, 1998), pp. 235ff.

97. Griffioen and Zeller, "A Comparative Analysis of the Persecution of the Jews in the Netherlands and Belgium during the Second World War," p. 21.

98. On this specific aspect see Rudi von Doorslaer, "Jewish Immigration and Communism in Belgium, 1925–1939," in *Belgium and the Holocaust: Jews, Belgians, Germans*, ed. Dan Michman (Jerusalem, 1998), pp. 66n and 67ff.

99. Peter Longerich, ed., *Akten der Partei-Kanzlei der NSDAP: Rekonstruktion eines verlorengegangenen Bestandes. Regesten.*, vol. 2, part 4 (Munich, 1992), abs. no. 43548.

100. Ibid.

101. Ibid., abs. no. 43518.

102. Nuremberg doc. L-61, U.S. Office of Chief of Counsel for the Prosecution of Axis Criminality and International Military Tribunal, *Nazi Conspiracy and Aggression*, 8 vols. (Washington, DC, 1946), vol. 7, pp. 816–17 (emphasis in original).

103. Wolf Gruner, "Die Fabrik-Aktion und die Ereignisse in der Berliner Rosenstrasse: Fakten und Fiktionen um den 27. Februar 1943," *Jahrbuch fur Antisemitismusforschung* 11 (2002), p. 146. See now Wolf Gruner, *Widerstand in der Rosenstrasse. Die Fabrik-Aktion und die Verfolgung der Mischehen 1943* (Frankfurt am Main, 2005).

104. Ibid., pp. 148–49.

105. Ibid., pp. 152–54.

106. Ibid., pp. 160–64.

107. Ibid., pp. 167ff.

108. H. G. Adler, *Der verwaltete Mensch: Studien zur Deportation der Juden aus Deutschland* (Tübingen, 1974).

109. Rivka Elkin, "The Survival of the Jewish Hospital in Berlin, 1938–1945," *Leo Baeck Institute Year Book* 38 (1993), pp. 167ff.

110. Ibid., p. 177.

111. Ibid.

112. Nuremberg doc. PS-1472, U.S. Office of Chief of Counsel for the Prosecution of Axis Criminality and International Military Tribunal, *Nazi Conspiracy and Aggression*, vol. 4, p. 49.

113. Hertha Feiner, *Before Deportation: Letters from a Mother to Her Daughters, January 1939–December 1942*, ed. Karl Heinz Jahnke (Evanston, II 1999), pp. 27–28.

114. Jochen Klepper, *Unter dem Schatten Deiner Flügel? Aus den Tagebüchern der Jahre 1932–1942*, ed. Hildegard Klepper (Stuttgart, 1956), p. 1127.

115. Ibid., p. 1130.

116. Ibid., p. 1133.

117. Ibid.

118. Walter Manoschek, ed., *"Es gibt nur eines für das Judentum—Vernichtung": Das Judenbild in deutschen Soldatenbriefen 1939–1944* (Hamburg, 1997), p. 58.

119. Hans Frank, *Das Diensttagebuch des deutschen Generalgouverneurs in Polen 1939–1945*, ed. Werner Präg and Wolfgang Jacobmeyer (Stuttgart, 1975), pp. 508ff., translation in Wolfgang Scheffler, "The Forgotten Part of the "Final Solution": The Liquidation of the Ghettos," in *Simon Wiesenthal Center Annual* (Chappaqua, NY, 1985), p. 817.

120. Adam Czerniaków, *The Warsaw Diary of Adam Czerniaków: Prelude to Doom*, ed. Raul Hilberg, Stanislaw Staron, and Joseph Kermish (New York, 1979), pp. 382–83.

121. Ibid., p. 384.

122. Marcel Reich-Ranicki, *The Author of Himself: The Life of Marcel Reich-Ranicki* (London, 2001), p. 164.

123. Ibid., pp. 165–66. Höfle's orders and threats are quoted in Scheffler, "The Forgotten Part," p. 820.

124. Czerniaków, *Warsaw Diary*, p. 385.

125. Hilberg and Staron, "Introduction" to ibid., pp. 63–64. See also Jerzy Lewinski, "The Death of Adam Czerniaków and Janusz Korczak's Last Journey," *Polin: Studies in Polish Jewry* 7 (1992), pp. 224ff.

126. Chaim Aron Kaplan, *Scroll of Agony: The Warsaw Diary of Chaim A. Kaplan*, ed. Abraham Isaac Katsh (New York, 1965), pp. 324–25.

127. Ibid., pp. 208–9.

128. Chaim Aron Kaplan, *Scroll of Agony: The Warsaw Diary of Chaim A. Kaplan*, ed. Abraham I. Katsh (Bloomington, 1999), p. 391.

129. Yitzhak Perlis, "Final Chapter: Korczak in the Warsaw Ghetto," in Janusz Korczak, *The Ghetto Diary* (New York, 1978), pp. 40ff.

130. Korczak, Ibid., p. 143.

131. Gutman, *The Jews of Warsaw*, p. 147.

132. Janusz Korczak, *Tagebuch aus dem Warschauer Ghetto 1942* (Göttingen, 1992), p. 119.

133. Abraham Lewin, *A Cup of Tears: A Diary of the Warsaw Ghetto*, ed. Antony Polonsky (Oxford, 1988), p. 148. There have been many descriptions of this march, and quite a few "literary" embellishments were added to the bare facts, which certainly do not need any added pathos. For a detailed critique of some of these descriptions see Lewinksi, "The Death of Adam Czerniaków," pp. 224ff.

134. Kaplan, *Scroll of Agony*, p. 340.

135. Gutman, *The Jews of Warsaw*, p. 213.

136. Wilm Hosenfeld, "Extracts from the Diary of Captain Wilm Hosenfeld," in *The Pianist: The Extraordinary Story of One Man's Survival in Warsaw, 1939–45*, ed. Wladyslaw Szpilman (New York, 1999), p. 198. For a detailed account of Hosenfeld's attitude and activities, see Wilm Hosenfeld, *"Ich versuche jeden zu retten": Das Leben eines deutschen Offiziers in Briefen und Tagebüchern* (Munich, 2004).

137. Quoted in Ruta Sakowska, "Two Forms of Resistance in the Warsaw Ghetto: Two Functions of the Ringelblum Archives," *Yad Vashem Studies* 21 (1991), p. 215.

138. Yitzhak Arad, *Belzec, Sobibor, Treblinka: The Operation Reinhard Death Camps* (Bloomington, 1987), pp. 40–42.

139. Ibid., p. 87.

140. Ibid.

141. Arad, *Belzec*, pp. 87–88.

142. Gitta Sereny, *Into that Darkness: From Mercy Killing to Mass Murder* (London, 1974), p. 161.

143. Ibid., p. 157. Sereny shows that, apart from some errors in dates and some "tactical" changes in the sequence of events, Stangl's descriptions were amply confirmed during his trial and that of ten Treblinka guards in Düsseldorf in 1964. Among the documents produced at the 1964 trial, the diary of Hubert Pfoch, who traveled on the

same railway line in August 1942, confirmed the killings and the corpses lying along the tracks. Ibid., pp. 158–59.

144. Josef Zelkowicz, *In Those Terrible Days: Writings from the Lodz Ghetto*, ed. Michal Unger (Jerusalem, 2002), pp. 258–59.

145. Lucjan Dobroszycki, ed., *The Chronicle of the Lódz Ghetto, 1941–1944* (New Haven, 1984), pp. 250ff.

146. Dawid Sierakowiak, *The Diary of Dawid Sierakowiak: Five Notebooks from the Lódz Ghetto*, ed. Alan Adelson (New York, 1996), p. 214.

147. Ibid., pp. 219–20.

148. Zelkowicz, *In Those Terrible Days*, pp. 280–83.

149. Ibid., p. 280.

150. Dobroszycki, ed., *The Chronicle*, pp. 250–54.

151. Zelkowicz, *In Those Terrible Days*, pp. 259–60.

152. Thomas Sandkühler, *Endlösung in Galizien: Der Judenmord in Ostpolen und die Rettungsinitiativen von Berthold Beitz, 1941–1944* (Bonn, 1996), p. 221.

153. Philip Friedman, *Roads to Extinction: Essays on the Holocaust*, ed. Ada June Friedman (New York, 1980), p. 279.

154. Ibid., p. 280.

155. Ibid., p. 279.

156. Ibid., p. 317.

157. Jerzy Ficowski, *Regions of the Great Heresy: Bruno Schulz: A Biographical Portrait* (New York, 2003), p. 134.

158. Ibid., p. 136.

159. Ibid., p. 138.

160. Friedman, *Roads to Extinction*, pp. 365–66.

161. Ibid.

162. Isaac Rudashevski, *The Diary of the Vilna Ghetto, June 1941–April 1943*, ed. Percy Matenko (Tel Aviv, 1973), pp. 70–71.

163. Herman Kruk, *The Last Days of the Jerusalem of Lithuania: Chronicles from the Vilna Ghetto and the Camps, 1939–1944*, ed. Benjamin Harshav (New Haven, 2002), p. 389.

164. Yitzhak Arad, Yisrael Gutman, and Abraham Margaliot, eds., *Documents on the Holocaust: Selected Sources on the Destruction of the Jews of Germany and Austria, Poland, and the Soviet Union* (Jerusalem, 1981), p. 445.

165. Ibid., p. 446.

166. Kruk, *The Last Days of the Jerusalem of Lithuania*, pp. 421–22.

167. Frank, *The Diary of a Young Girl*, p. 53.

168. Ibid., p. 71.

169. Rudashevski, *The Diary of the Vilna Ghetto, June 1941–April 1943*, p. 66.

170. Etty Hillesum, *Letters from Westerbork* (New York, 1986), pp. 26–27.

171. Egon Redlich, *The Terezin Diary of Gonda Redlich*, ed. Saul S. Friedman (Lexington, KY, 1992), p. 50.

172. Biélinky, *Journal*, p. 245.

173. Ibid., p. 271.

174. Renée Poznanski, introduction to ibid., p. 11.

175. Lambert, *Carnet d'un témoin*, pp. 201–2.

176. Ibid.

177. Klemperer, *I Will Bear Witness: A Diary of the Nazi Years, 1942–1945*, p. 156.

178. Ibid., p. 157.

179. Quoted in Robert Moses Shapiro, "Diaries and Memoirs from the Lodz Ghetto in Yiddish and Hebrew," in *Holocaust Chronicles: Individualizing the Holocaust through Diaries and Other Contemporaneous Personal Accounts*, ed. Robert Moses Shapiro (Hoboken, NJ, 1999), p. 97 (the same lack of punctuation appears in the original Yiddish. Shapiro also quotes at some length from the diary of a survivor, Shlomo Frank, who died in Israel in 1966. Frank's recordings indicate precise knowledge about the fate of the Lodz deportees to Chelmno. However, it seems that the author thoroughly "improved" various editions of his notes, excising and adding parts, changing entry dates, etc.) See Ibid., pp. 101ff. Such editing makes Frank's diary historically unreliable.

180. Lewin, *A Cup of Tears*, p. 153.

181. Ibid., pp. 170–71.

182. Moses Flinker, *Young Moshe's Diary: The Spiritual Torment of a Jewish Boy in Nazi Europe*, ed. Shaul Esh and Geoffrey Wigoder (Jerusalem, 1971), pp. 25–26.

183. Ibid., p. 32.

184. Ibid., p. 37.

185. Ibid., pp. 42–43.

186. Ibid., pp. 58–59.

187. Ibid., pp. 69–70.

188. Ibid., p. 71.

189. Biélinky, *Journal*, pp. 254–55.

190. Sebastian, *Journal*, p. 509.

191. Klemperer, *I Will Bear Witness: A Diary of the Nazi Years, 1942–1945*, pp. 147–48.

192. Redlich, *The Terezin Diary of Gonda Redlich*, p. 72.

193. Gutman, *The Jews of Warsaw*, p. 212.

194. Peretz Opoczynski, "Warsaw Ghetto Chronicle—September 1942," in *To Live with Honor and Die with Honor! . . . : Selected Documents from the Warsaw Ghetto Underground Archives "O.S." ("Oneg Shabbat,")* ed. Joseph Kermish (Jerusalem, 1986), p. 109.

195. Lewin, *A Cup of Tears*, p. 184.

196. Avraham Tory, *Surviving the Holocaust: The Kovno Ghetto Diary*, ed. Martin Gilbert and Dina Porat (Cambridge, UK, 1990), pp. 133–36.

197. Kruk, *The Last Days of the Jerusalem of Lithuania*, pp. 360–61.

198. Rudashevski, *The Diary of the Vilna Ghetto*, pp. 56–57.

199. Dobroszycki, *The Chronicle*, p 258.

200. Oskar Rosenfeld, *In the Beginning Was the Ghetto: Notebooks from Lódz*, ed. Hanno Loewy (Evanston, IL, 2002), p. 134.

201. Haim Avni, "Spain" in Walter Laqueur and Judith Tydor Baumel, eds., *The Holocaust Encyclopedia* (New Haven, 2001), p. 602.

202. Independent Commission of Experts Switzerland—Second World War, *Switzerland, National Socialism and the Second World War* (Zurich, 2002), p. 134.

203. Ibid., p. 113.

204. Ibid., p. 114.

205. Ibid.

206. Ibid.

207. Paul A. Levine, "Attitudes and Action: Comparing the Responses of Mid-Level Bureaucrats to the Holocaust," in *Bystanders to the Holocaust: A Re-Evaluation*, ed. David Cesarani and Paul A. Levine (London, 2002), pp. 223ff.

208. For a detailed analysis of Swedish policy see Paul A. Levine, *From Indifference to Activism: Swedish Diplomacy and the Holocaust, 1938–1944* (Oppsala, 1998).

209. The only book in English on this issue is Hannu Rautkallio, *Finland and the Holocaust: The Rescue of Finland's Jews* (New York, 1987). Rautkallio's interpretations have been strongly questioned in William B. Cohen and Jorgen Svensson, "Finland and the Holocaust," *Holocaust and Genocide Studies* 9 (1995), pp. 70ff. The numbers mentioned are taken from Cohen and Svensson, "Finland," p. 71.

210. Rautkallio, *Finland and the Holocaust: The Rescue of Finland's Jews*, p. 166.

211. Cohen and Svensson, "Finland and the Holocaust," p. 76.

212. Ibid., p. 77.

213. Ingrid Krüger-Bulcke and Hans Georg Lehmann, *Akten zur deutschen auswärtigen Politik, 1918–1945, Ser. E*, vol. 3 (Göttingen, 1974), p. 526.

214. Radu Ioanid, "The Fate of Romanian Jews in Nazi Occupied Europe," in *The Destruction of Romanian and Ukrainian Jews during the Antonescu Era*, ed. Randolph L. Braham (Boulder, CO, 1997), p. 160ff.

215. Quoted in Peter Longerich, *Politik der Vernichtung: Eine Gesamtdarstellung der nationalsozialistischen Judenverfolgung* (Munich, 1998), pp. 522ff.

216. For the details see Radu Ioanid, *The Holocaust in Romania: The Destruction of Jews and Gypsies under the Antonescu Regime, 1940–1944* (Chicago, 2000), pp. 241ff.

217. Ibid., pp. 246–47.

218. Krüger-Bulcke and Lehmann, *ADAP: Ser. E,* vol. 5 (Göttingen 1978), p. 134.

219. Helmut Heiber, *Reichsführer! Briefe an und von Himmler* (Munich, 1970), p. 184.

220. Yehuda Bauer, *Jews for Sale? Nazi-Jewish Negotiations, 1933–1945* (New Haven, 1994), p. 149.

221. For these details see essentially Lorand Tilkovszky, "The Late Interwar Years and World War II," in *A History of Hungary*, ed. Peter F. Sugar et al. (Bloomington, 1994), pp. 348–49.

222. Krüger-Bulcke and Lehmann, *ADAP, Ser. E,* vol. 4 (Göttingen, 1975), pp. 24ff.

223. Ibid., p. 150.

224. Jonathan Steinberg, *All or Nothing: The Axis and the Holocaust, 1941–1943* (London, 1990), pp. 85–86.

225. Klarsfeld, *Vichy-Auschwitz,* vol. 2, pp. 13ff.

226. Ibid., pp. 16–17.

227. Ibid., p. 18.

228. Commissione per la pubblicazione dei documenti diplomatici, *I documenti diplomatici italiani. Nona serie: 1939–1943,* 10 vols. (Rome, 1954–90), quoted and translated in Susan Zuccotti, *Under His Very Windows: The Vatican and the Holocaust in Italy* (New Haven, 2000), pp. 108–9.

229. Per Ole Johansen, "Norway," in Laqueur and Baumel, *The Holocaust Encyclopedia,* p. 450.

230. Gutman, *The Jews of Warsaw,* pp. 253ff.

231. Quoted in Polonsky, "Condemnation, Apologetics," in David Cesarani, *Holocaust: Critical Concepts in Historical Studies,* vol. 5 (New York, 2004), pp. 59–60.

232. For the declaration of September 17, see Gutman, *The Jews of Warsaw,* pp. 253 and 257–58.

233. For the early Karski report see chapter 1, pp. 46–47.

234. See mainly David Engel, "The Western Allies and the Holocaust: Jan Karski's Mission to the West, 1942–1944," in *Holocaust and Genocide Studies* 5 (1990), pp. 363ff.

235. Ibid., p. 366.

236. Daniel Blatman, *Notre liberté et la vôtre: Le mouvement ouvrier juif Bund en Pologne, 1939–1949* (Paris, 2002), p. 195.

237. For a detailed analysis see David Engel, *In the Shadow of Auschwitz: The Polish Government-in-Exile and the Jews, 1939–1942* (Chapel Hill, NC, 1987), pp. 180ff.

238. On this issue the Western Allies stood on the side of the Soviet Union, almost from the outset. The Soviet demands were explicitly accepted at the Tehran conference in November 1943 and reconfirmed at Yalta in February 1945. For a spirited defense of the Polish positions see, among numerous other studies, Norman Davies, *Rising '44: The Battle for Warsaw* (London, 2003).

239. For this specific threat see Tuvia Friling, *Arrows in the Dark: David Ben-Gurion, the Yishuv Leadership, and Rescue Attempts during the Holocaust* (Madison, WI, 2005), vol. 1, p. 88.

240. On Kot's negotiations in Palestine see Shabtai Teveth, *Ben-Gurion and the Holocaust* (New York, 1996), pp. 35ff.; see also David Engel, "Soviet Jewry in the Thinking of the Yishuv Leadership 1939–1943," in *The Holocaust in the Soviet Union* ed. Lucjan Dobroszycki and Jeffrey S. Gurock, (Armonk, NY, 1993), pp. 111ff.

241. Friling, *Arrows in the Dark*; vol. 1, p. 64.

242. Porat, *The Blue and the Yellow Stars,* p. 259.

243. About Gerstein and his mission see Saul Friedländer, *Kurt Gerstein, The Ambiguity of Good* (New York, 1969) particularly pp. 100ff.

244. Ibid., pp. 109–10.

245. Ibid., pp. 117–19.

246. Ibid., pp. 122–26.

247. Ibid., pp. 128–29.

248. Ibid., p. vii.

249. For Vendel's report see Jozef Lewandowski, "Early Swedish Information about the Nazis' Mass Murder of the Jews," *Polin: Studies in Polish Jewry* (2000), vol. 13, pp. 113ff.

250. The translation of Vendel's report is based on Lewandowski's translation as well as on that of Steven Kublik. Kublik is the first historian to have published Vendel's report. See Steven Kublik, *The Stones Cry Out* (New York, 1987).

251. Lewandowski, "Early Swedish Information about the Nazis' Mass Murder of the Jews," p. 123.

252. For the Schulte mission and the Riegner telegram see mainly Gerhart M. Riegner, *Ne Jamais Désesperer: Soixante années au service du peuple juif et des droits de l'homme* (Paris, 1998), pp. 55ff; David S. Wyman, *The Abandonment of the Jews: America and the Holocaust, 1941–1945* (New York, 1998), pp. 42ff.; Martin Gilbert, *Auschwitz and the Allies: How the Allies Responded to the News of Hitler's Final Solution* (London, 1981), pp. 57ff. See also Walter Laqueur and Richard Breitman, *Breaking the Silence* (New York, 1986).

253. Jean-Claude Favez, *The Red Cross and the Holocaust* (Cambridge, U.K., 1999), pp. 39–41.

254. David S. Wyman, *The Abandonment of the Jews: America and the Holocaust, 1941–1945* (New York, 1998), p. 51.

255. Bernard Wasserstein, *Britain and the Jews of Europe, 1939–1945* (London, 1979), p. 172.

256. Either during the visit or in preparation for it, Roosevelt was handed a memorandum prepared by the World Jewish Congress that described the extermination in precise details and mentioned in particular Ozwiecim as one of the main killing centers. For early knowledge in London and Washington about the function of Auschwitz as a major extermination camp, see Barbara Rogers, "British Intelligence and the Holocaust," *Journal of Holocaust Education* 8, no. 1 (1999), pp. 89ff. and particularly 100.

257. Wyman, *The Abandonment of the Jews*, p. 72.

258. Wasserstein, *Britain and the Jews of Europe, 1939–1945*, p. 173.

259. Willi A. Boelcke, ed., *Wollt Ihr den totalen Krieg? Die geheimen Goebbels Konferenzen 1939–1943* (Herrsching, 1989), p. 313.

260. For Wise's information, see Henry L. Feingold, *The Politics of Rescue: The Roosevelt Administration and the Holocaust, 1938–1945* (New Brunswick, NJ, 1970), p. 170. See, moreover, Heinrich Himmler, *Der Dienstkalender Heinrich Himmlers 1941/42*, ed. Peter Witte et al. (Hamburg, 1999), p. 619, n. 43.

261. Heiber, *Reichsführer! Briefe an und von Himmler*, p. 169.

262. Friedländer, *Pius XII*, pp. 104ff. Strangely enough Bernardini's report has not been included in the volumes of documents published by the Vatican.

263. Pierre Blet, Angelo Martini, and Burkhart Schneider, eds., *Actes et documents du Saint Siège relatifs à la Seconde Guerre mondiale* (Vatican City, 1974), vol. 8, p. 453.

264. Ibid., p. 534 (quoted and translated in Zuccotti, *Under His Very Windows*, p. 102).

265. For most of the details, see Shimon Redlich, "Metropolitan Andrei Sheptys'kyi, Ukrainians and Jews During and After the Holocaust," in *Holocaust and Genocide Studies* 5, no. 1 (1990), pp. 39ff.

266. Blet, Martini, and Schneider, *Actes et documents du Saint Siège relatifs à la Seconde Guerre mondiale* (Vatican City, 1967), vol. 3, part 2, pp. 625 and 628. Excerpted and translated in Redlich, "Metropolitan Andrei Sheptys'kyi, Ukrainians and Jews During and After the Holocaust," pp. 45–46.

267. Friedländer, *Pius XII*, pp. 121–22.

268. Cable from Tittman to Hull, 10/10/1942 in ibid., pp. 123–24.

269. John Cornwell, *Hitler's Pope: The Secret History of Pius XII* (New York, 1999), pp. 290–91.

270. Ibid. About Maglione's answer, see also Friedländer, *Pius XII*, p. 125.

271. Friedländer, *Pius XII*, p. 131.

272. On these reactions, see Cornwell, *Hitler's Pope*, p. 293.

273. Goebbels, *Tagebücher*, part 2, vol. 6, p. 508.

274. For this anonymous report see Kulka/Jäckel, *Die Juden*, p. 511.

275. Martin Gilbert, *Auschwitz and the Allies* (New York, 1981), p. 105.

276. For this text, see Saul Friedländer, "History, Memory and the Historian: Dilemmas and Responsibilities," *New German Critique* 80 (Spring-Summer 2000), pp. 3–4.

Chapter Eight: March 1943–October 1943

1. Louise Jacobson and Nadia Kaluski-Jacobson, *Les Lettres de Louise Jacobson et de ses proches: Fresnes, Drancy, 1942–1943* (Paris, 1997), p. 141.

2. Ibid., pp. 41–42.

3. For a vivid description of the Battle of Kursk, see Michael Burleigh, *The Third Reich: A New History* (London, 2000), pp. 510–11.

4. For a good summary of these developments see Ian Kershaw, *Hitler, 1936–45: Nemesis* (New York, 2000), pp. 566ff. For a lively but obviously self-serving description of the intrigues that swirled at the highest reaches of the regime, particularly around the "Committee of Three" and other attempts at reorganization, see Albert Speer, *Inside the Third Reich: Memoirs* (New York, 1970), pp. 252ff.

5. For the translation of the speech excerpts and the reference to Körner's verse, see Jeremy Noakes and Geoffrey Pridham, eds., *Nazism, 1919–1945: A Documentary Reader*, vol. 4: *The German Home Front in World War II* (Exeter, UK, 1998), pp. 490ff.

6. Moses Flinker, *Young Moshe's Diary: The Spiritual Torment of a Jewish Boy in Nazi Europe*, ed. Shaul Esh and Geoffrey Wigoder (Jerusalem, 1971), pp. 78–79.

7. Mihail Sebastian, *Journal, 1935–1944* (Chicago, 2000), p. 546.

8. Victor Klemperer, *I Will Bear Witness: A Diary of the Nazi Years 1942–1945* (New York, 1999), p. 202.

9. Joseph Goebbels, *Die Tagebücher von Joseph Goebbels: Sämtliche Fragmente*, ed. Elke Fröhlich (Munich, 1996), part 2, vol. 7, p. 287.

10. Adolf Hitler, *Hitler: Reden und Proklamationen, 1932–1945: Kommentiert von einem deutschen Zeitgenossen*, ed. Max Domarus, 4 vols. (Leonberg, 1987–88), part 2, vol. 4, p. 2001.

11. Goebbels, *Tagebücher*, part 2, vol. 8, p. 119.

12. Ibid.

13. Ibid., p. 235.

14. Ibid., p. 261.

15. Ibid., pp. 287ff.

16. Ibid.

17. Ibid., pp. 287–88.

18. Ibid., pp. 288ff and 90.

19. Quoted and translated in Noakes and Pridham, eds., *Nazism*, vol. 4, p. 497.

20. Klemperer, *I Will Bear Witness: A Diary of the Nazi Years 1942–1945*, pp. 230–31.

21. Ibid., p. 234.

22. Ibid., pp. 235–36.

23. Kulka and Jäckel, *Die Juden*, p. 517.

24. Ibid.

25. Klemperer, *I Will Bear Witness: A Diary of the Nazi Years 1942–1945*, p. 304.

26. For ideological fanaticism in the RSHA, see mainly Michael Wildt, *Generation des Unbedingten: Das Führungskorps des Reichssicherheitshauptamtes* (Hamburg, 2002), and Yaacov Lozowick, *Hitlers Bürokraten: Eichmann, seine willigen Vollstrecker und die Banalität des Bösen* (Zurich, 2000); for the WVHA main figures see in particular Michael Thad Allen, *The Business of Genocide: The SS, Slave Labor and the Concentration Camps* (Chapel Hill, NC, 2002).

27. All the details about these documents (which were declassified by the British Public Record Office in 2001) are taken from Peter Witte and Stephen Tyas, "A New Document on the Deportation and Murder of Jews during 'Einsatz Reinhardt 1942,'" *Holocaust and Genocide Studies* 15, no. 3 (2001), pp. 468ff.

28. Ibid., p. 470.

29. Heinrich Himmler, *Der Dienstkalender Heinrich Himmlers 1941/42*, ed. Peter Witte et al. (Hamburg, 1999), p. 513 n. 32.

30. Witte and Tyas, "A New Document on the Deportation and Murder of Jews during 'Einsatz Reinhardt 1942,'" p. 476.

31. Helmut Heiber, *Reichsführer! Briefe an und von Himmler* (Munich, 1970), p. 183. Quoted and translated in Gerald Fleming, *Hitler and the Final Solution* (Berkeley, 1984), p. 136.

32. Fleming, *Hitler and the Final Solution*, p. 136.

33. Ibid., p. 137. See also Raul Hilberg, "Le bilan démographique du génocide," in *L'Allemagne nazie et le génocide juif: Colloque de l'École des Hautes Études en Sciences Sociales (EHESS)*, ed. École des hautes études en sciences sociales (Paris, 1985), pp. 265ff.

34. For the report and the estimate see the introduction to Wolfgang Benz, ed.,

Dimension des Völkermords: Die Zahl der jüdischen Opfer des Nationalsozialismus (Munich, 1991), p. 3.

35. For this argument see Hilberg, "Le bilan démographique du génocide," p. 265.

36. Raul Hilberg, *The Destruction of the European Jews* (New Haven, 1961), vol. 1, pp. 407–8.

37. Fleming, *Hitler and the Final Solution*, p. 138.

38. Nuremberg doc. 015-PS, U.S. Office of Chief of Counsel for the Prosecution of Axis Criminality and International Military Tribunal, *Nazi Conspiracy and Aggression*, 8 vols. (Washington, D.C., 1946), vol. 3, pp. 41–45.

39. Fleming, *Hitler and the Final Solution*, p. 139.

40. Ibid., p. 137.

41. Andreas Hillgruber, *Staatsmänner und Diplomaten bei Hitler: Vertrauliche Aufzeichnungen über Unterredungen mit Vertretern des Auslandes* (Frankfurt am Main, 1970), vol. 2, pp. 256–57.

42. Eugene Levai, *Black Book on the Martyrdom of Hungarian Jewry* (Zurich, 1948), p. 33.

43. Translated and excerpted in Raul Hilberg, *The Destruction of the European Jews*, vol. 2, pp. 877–78.

44. The most detailed survey of the events in Bulgaria remains Frederick B. Chary, *The Bulgarian Jews and the Final Solution, 1940–1944* (Pittsburgh, 1972).

45. Ingrid Krüger-Bulcke and Hans George Lehmann, eds., *Akten zur deutschen auswärtigen Politik, 1918–1945, Ser. E, 1941–1945* (Göttingen, 1978), vol. 5, p. 521.

46. Ibid., p. 538.

47. Livia Rothkirchen, "The Situation of the Jews in Slovakia between 1939 and 1945," *Jahrbuch für Antisemitismusforschung* 7 (1998).

48. For Ludin's report see Ingrid Krüger-Bulcke and Hans Georg Lehmann, *Aktien zur deutschen auswärtige Politik, 1918–1945, Ser. E, 1941–1945,* vol. 5 (Göttingen, 1978) pp. 581ff.

49. Hillgruber, *Staatsmänner*, vol. 2, p. 268. Hitler's unbridled obsession with all aspects of the Jewish question took on yet another weird aspect when he corrected Tiso about Lord Rothermere; according to the Nazi leader, Rothermere was not a Jew but had a Jewish mistress, Princess Hohenlohe, born Richter from Vienna. Ibid., p. 268.

50. *Trials of War Criminals Before the Nuremberg Military Tribunals*, 15 vols., vol. 13 *U.S. v. von Weizsaecker: The Ministries Case.* (Washington, DC, 1952), Nuremberg doc. Steengracht 64, pp. 300–301.

51. On the extermination of Croatian Jewry see mainly Menachem Shelach, ed., *Yugoslavia* (Jerusalem: 1990), pp. 137ff [Hebrew].

52. For the exact date of Wisliceny's and Brunner's arrival in Salonika, see Daniel Carpi, "Salonika during the Holocaust: A New Approach," in *The Last Ottoman Century and Beyond: The Jews in Turkey and the Balkans 1808–1945*, ed. Minna Rozen (Ramat-Aviv, 2002), p. 263n9.

53. Mark Mazower, *Salonica, City of Ghosts: Christians, Muslims and Jews, 1430–1950* (New York, 2004), pp. 402 and 411.

54. For the role played by Simonides and Altenburg, see in particular Andrew Apostolou, "The Exception of Salonika: Bystanders and Collaborators in Northern Greece," *Holocaust and Genocide Studies* 14, no. 2 (Fall 2000), pp. 179ff.

55. Mazower, *Salonica, City of Ghosts*, pp. 392ff. and 411.

56. Ibid., p. 405.

57. Ibid., pp. 392ff.

58. For a more nuanced view of Koretz's role, see Minna Rozen, "Jews and Greeks Remember Their Past: The Political Career of Tsevi Koretz (1933–43)," *Jewish Social Studies* 12, no. 1 (2005), pp. 111ff.

59. Ibid., p. 401.

60. Apostolou, "The Exception of Salonika," pp. 181ff.

61. Ibid., p. 183.

62. Carpi, "Salonika During the Holocaust: A New Approach," p. 271.

63. Ibid., p. 272.

64. Ingrid Krüger-Bulcke and Hans Georg Lehmann, *Aktien zur deutschen auswärtige Politik, 1918–1945, Ser. E, 1941–1945,* vol. 5 (Göttingen, 1978), pp. 731ff.

65. Mazower, *Salonica, City of Ghosts*, p. 407.

66. Ibid.

67. Ibid., pp. 397–99.

68. Henry Friedlander and Sybil Milton, eds., *Archives of the Holocaust: An International Collection of Selected Documents*, 22 vols. (New York, 1993), vol. 20, doc. 7, pp. 17–18. The "Da" appellation (Da 152) was generally used for deportation trains; it was most probably an abbreviation for "*Durchgangaussiedler-[Zug]*" ("evacuees' transit train"). See Götz Aly, *Im Tunnel: Das kurze Leben der Marion Samuel 1931–1943* (Frankfurt am Main, 2004), p. 137.

69. Raul Hilberg, *The Destruction of the European Jews,* 3 vols. (New Haven, Conn., 2003), vol. 2, pp. 424ff and particularly p. 429.

70. Quoted in Tatiana Berenstein, ed., *Faschismus, Getto, Massenmord: Dokumentation über Ausrottung und Widerstand der Juden in Polen während des zweiten Weltkrieges* (East Berlin, 1961), p. 321.

71. Adalbert Rückerl, ed., *NS-Prozesse. Nach 25 Jahren Strafverfolgung: Möglichkeiten, Grenzen, Ergebnisse* (Karlsruhe, 1971), p. 114 (quoted in Yitzhak Arad, *Belzec, Sobibor, Treblinka: The Operation Reinhard Death Camps* (Bloomington, IN, 1987), p. 51).

72. Alfred C. Mierzejewski, "A Public Enterprise in the Service of Mass Murder: The Deutsche Reichsbahn and the Holocaust," *Holocaust and Genocide Studies* 15, no. 1 (Spring 2001), p. 36.

73. Ibid.

74. Nuremberg doc. PS-3688 (quoted in Arad, *Belzec*, p. 52).

75. Berenstein, *Faschismus, Getto, Massenmord*, p. 346.

76. Friedlander and Milton, *Archives of the Holocaust*, vol. 20, doc. 8. Incidentally the matter received its formal closure on May 26. On that day the Regierungspräsident in Düsseldorf informed the Gestapo that all the assets of Elsa Sara Frankenberg, Julius

Israel Meier, and Augusta Sara Meier from Krefeld, who had committed suicide before their deportation to Izbica, had been credited to the Reich. The relevant ordinance was published in the *Deutsche Reichsanzeiger und Preussische Staatsanzeiger* no. 112 of May 15, 1942. Ibid., vol. 20, doc 10.

77. Quoted and translated in Arad, *Belzec*, p. 145.

78. Oskar Rosenfeld, *In the Beginning Was the Ghetto: Notebooks from Lódz*, ed. Hanno Loewy (Evanston, IL, 2002), pp. 11–12.

79. Primo Levi, *Survival in Auschwitz: The Nazi Assault on Humanity* (New York, 1958; reprint, 1996), p. 18.

80. Ibid.

81. Ruth Kluger, *Still Alive: A Holocaust Girlhood Remembered* (New York, 2001), pp. 91–92.

82. Christopher R. Browning, *Collected Memories: Holocaust History and Postwar Testimony* (Madison, WI, 2003), p. 75.

83. Ibid., p. 76.

84. Ibid., pp. 76–77.

85. Ibid., pp. 78ff.

86. Ibid., p. 81.

87. Yitzhak Arad, Yisrael Gutman, and Abraham Margaliot, eds., *Documents on the Holocaust: Selected Sources on the Destruction of the Jews of Germany and Austria, Poland, and the Soviet Union* (Jerusalem, 1981), pp. 287ff.

88. Ibid., p. 289–90.

89. For various aspects of these plans see Allen, *The Business of Genocide: The SS, Slave Labor and the Concentration Camps*, pp. 245ff.

90. Berenstein, *Faschismus, Getto, Massenmord*, pp. 354–55.

91. Ibid., p. 356.

92. Hans Frank, *Das Diensttagebuch des deutschen Generalgouverneurs in Polen 1939–1945*, ed. Werner Präg and Wolfgang Jacobmeyer (Stuttgart, 1975), pp. 681–82.

93. Each category of stolen goods demanded the issuing and implementing of precise rulings, mostly issued by the Finance Ministry for customs' use. See, among others, Michael MacQueen, "The Conversion of Looted Assets to Run the German War Machine," *Holocaust and Genocide Studies* 18, no. 1 (Spring 2004), p. 31.

94. Ibid., p. 30.

95. Ibid., p. 31.

96. For the Degussa involvement see now Peter Hayes, *From Cooperation to Complicity: Degussa in the Third Reich* (Cambridge, MA, 2004).

97. MacQueen, "The Conversion of Looted Assets to Run the German War Machine," pp. 34ff.

98. Nuremberg doc. NO-724, quoted in Rückerl, *NS-Prozesse*, pp. 109–11.

99. For these details see Bertrand Perz and Thomas Sandkühler, "Auschwitz und die 'Aktion Reinhard' 1942–1945: Judenmord und Raubpraxis in neuer Sicht," *Zeitschrift für Geschichtswissenschaft* 5, no. 26 (1999), p. 291.

100. Note included in Nuremberg doc. NG-3058, *The Ministries Case*, pp. 201–4.

Much of this booty must have found its way to the *Judenmärkte* (Jew markets) described in Frank Bajohr, *"Arisierung" in Hamburg: Die Verdrängung der jüdischen Unternehmer 1933–1945* (Hamburg, 1997), and particularly Bajohr, "The Beneficiaries of 'Aryanization': Hamburg as a Case Study," *Yad Vashem Studies* 26 (1998), pp. 198ff.

101. Filip Müller, *Eyewitness Auschwitz: Three Years in the Gas Chambers* (Chicago, 1999), p. 12.

102. For these specific details see Götz Aly, "Arisierung: Enteignung: Was geschah mit den Besitztümern der ermodeten Juden Europas? Zur Ökonomie der Nazis," *Die Zeit* 47 (2002), p. 47.

103. Berenstein, *Faschismus, Getto, Massenmord*, pp. 421–22.

104. Tatiana Berenstein, ed., *Faschismus, Getto, Massenmord: Dokumentation über Ausrottung und Widerstand der Juden in Polen während des zweiten Weltkrieges* (East Berlin, 1961), pp. 412–13.

105. Joseph Walk, ed., *Das Sonderrecht für die Juden im NS-Staat: Eine Sammlung der gesetzlichen Massnahmen und Richtlinien, Inhalt und Bedeutung* (Heidelberg, 1981), p. 399.

106. Perz and Sandkühler, "Auschwitz und die 'Aktion Reinhard' 1942–1945: Judenmord und Raubpraxis in neuer Sicht," p. 292.

107. See Raul Hilberg, "Auschwitz," in Laqueur and Baumel, *The Holocaust Encyclopedia* (New Haven, 2001), p. 37.

108. According to Wolfgang Sofsky's computation, the gassing capacity of Bunker I was 800 persons, of Bunker II: 1,200 persons, of crematoriums II, III, IV, and V, 3,000 persons each. See Wolfgang Sofsky, *The Order of Terror: The Concentration Camp* (Princeton, 1997), p. 263.

109. Allen, *The Business of Genocide*, p. 141.

110. Quoted in ibid. On Kammler see, moreover, Rainer Fröbe, "Hans Kammler, Technokrat der Vernichtung," in *Die SS: Elite unter dem Totenkopf: 30 Lebensläufe*, ed. Ronald M. Smelser and Enrico Syring (Paderborn, 2000), pp. 305ff. and particularly pp. 310ff.

111. Quoted in Eugen Kogon, Hermann Langbein, and Adalbert Rückerl, eds., *Nazi Mass Murder: A Documentary History of the Use of Poison Gas* (New Haven, 1993), pp. 157–58.

112. All the technical details about the functioning of the gas chamber in Crematorium II are taken from Jamie McCarthy, Daniel Keren, and Harry W. Mazal, "The Ruins of the Gas Chambers: A Forensic Investigation of Crematoriums at Auschwitz I and Auschwitz-Birkenau," *Holocaust and Genocide Studies* (2004), pp. 68ff.

113. Sybille Steinbacher, *Auschwitz: A History* (London, 2005), p. 99.

114. Hilberg, *The Destruction of the European Jews*, vol. 3, p. 946.

115. Levi, *Survival in Auschwitz*, pp. 19–20. Exactly 536 members of Levi's transport were immediately gassed. See Myriam Anissimov, *Primo Levi: Tragedy of an Optimist* (Woodstock, NY, 2000), p. 105.

116. Kluger, *Still Alive*, p. 94.

117. Quoted in Hermann Langbein, *People in Auschwitz* (Chapel Hill, NC, 2004), pp. 65–66.

118. Kogon, Langbein, and Rückerl, *Nazi Mass Murder*, p. 133.

119. Robert Jay Lifton and Amy Hackett, "Nazi Doctors," in *Anatomy of the Auschwitz Death Camp*, ed. Yisrael Gutman and Michael Berenbaum (Bloomington, 1994), p. 313. For an overview of the medical experiments in Auschwitz and in other camps, see, among a vast literature, Robert Jay Lifton, *The Nazi Doctors: Medical Killing and the Psychology of Genocide* (New York, 1986).

120. See for example Eugen Kogon, *Der SS-Staat: Das System der deutschen Konzentrationslager* (Frankfurt, 1964 [1946]), pp. 50–51, as well as almost all general studies about Auschwitz. Thus, see also Yisrael Gutman and Michael Berenbaum, *Anatomy of the Auschwitz Death Camp* (Bloomington, 1994), pp. 20, 312, 398, and others.

121. Hilberg, *The Destruction of the European Jews*, vol. 3, p. 984.

122. Ibid.

123. The process has often been described, also in the diaries of the *Sonderkommando* members. Here, the indications are mainly taken from Gideon Greif, *Wir weinten tränenlos. . . . Augenzeugenberichte der jüdischen "Sonderkommandos" in Auschwitz* (Cologne, 1995), pp. xxxivff.

124. This notorious diary is quoted here from Henry Friedlander, "Physicians as Killers in Nazi Germany: Hadamar, Treblinka, and Auschwitz," in *Medicine and Medical Ethics in Nazi Germany*, ed. Francis R. Nicosia and Jonathan Huener (New York, 2002), pp. 69–70.

125. Lifton and Hackett, "Nazi Doctors," p. 310.

126. Kogon, Langbein, and Rückerl, *Nazi Mass Murder*, p. 154.

127. Quoted in Danuta Czech, "The Auschwitz Prisoner Administration," in Yisrael Gutman and Michael Berenbaum. *Anatomy of the Auschwitz Death Camp* (Bloomington, 1994), p. 374. For the periodic liquidiation of members of the *Sonderkommando* see Greif, *Wir weinten tränenlos*, p. xxv.

128. The camp experience does not seem to have changed the violence of Polish anti-Semitism. Among a long list of examples, Langbein quotes a Polish woman inmate who declared that notwithstanding the horrible means utilized, the Jewish problem in Poland was being solved: "This may sound paradoxical," she concluded, "but we owe this to Hitler." See Langbein, *People in Auschwitz*, p. 75.

129. Yisrael Gutman, "Social Stratification in the Concentration Camps," in *The Nazi Concentration Camps: Structure and Aims, the Image of the Prisoner, the Jews in the Camps*, ed. Yisrael Gutman and Avital Saf (Jerusalem, 1984), p. 172.

130. Quoted in Langbein, *People in Auschwitz*, pp. 78–79.

131. See Danuta Czech, "The Auschwitz Prisoner Administration" in Yisrael Gutman and Michael Berenbaum, *Anatomy of the Auschwitz Death Camp* (Bloomington, 1994), pp. 363ff.

132. Peter Hayes, "Auschwitz, Capital of the Holocaust," *Holocaust and Genocide Studies* 17, no. 2 (2003), p. 330.

133. Walter Manoschek, ed., *"Es gibt nur eines für das Judentum—Vernichtung": Das Judenbild in deutschen Soldatenbriefen 1939–1944* (Hamburg, 1997), p. 63.

134. For the total number of SS personnel see Steinbacher, *Auschwitz: A History*, p. 40.

135. See for example Norbert Frei et al., ed., *Standort- und Kommandanturbefehle des Konzentrationslagers Auschwitz 1940–1945* (Munich, 2000), p. 472.

136. See in particular Gabriele Knapp, *Das Frauenorchester in Auschwitz: Musikalische Zwangsarbeit und ihre Bewältigung* (Hamburg, 1996).

137. Steinbacher, *Auschwitz, a History*, p. 42.

138. Sybille Steinbacher, *"Musterstadt" Auschwitz: Germanisierungspolitik und Judenmord in Ostoberschlesien* (Munich, 2000), p. 247

139. Rudolf Höss, *Kommandant in Auschwitz: Autobiographische Aufzeichnungen*, ed. Martin Broszat (Stuttgart, 1958), p. 190.

140. Elizabeth Harvey, *Women and the Nazi East: Agents and Witnesses of Germanization* (New Haven, 2003), p. 216.

141. Ibid., p. 216–17.

142. Peter Longerich, *"Davon haben wir nichts gewusst!": Die Deutschen und die Judenverfolgung 1933–1945* (München, 2006), p. 236–37.

143. Ibid., p. 237.

144. Quoted in Noakes and Pridham, *Nazism*, vol. 3, p. 614.

145. Hans Mommsen, "Der Widerstand gegen Hitler und die nationalsozialistische Jundenverfolgung," in *Alternative zu Hitler: Studien zur Geschichte des deutschen Widerstandes*, (Munich, 2000), pp. 396ff.

146. Helmuth James von Moltke, *Letters to Freya: 1939–1945*, ed. Beate Ruhm von Oppen (New York, 1990), p. 252.

147. For the details and the quotations, see Wolfgang Gerlach, *And the Witnesses Were Silent: The Confessing Church and the Persecution of the Jews*, ed. Victoria Barnett (Lincoln, NE, 2000), pp. 210 and 212ff.

148. Ibid., p. 213.

149. Ibid.

150. For the text of the leaflet see Inge Scholl, *The White Rose: Munich, 1942–1943* (Middletown, CT, 1983), p. 78.

151. SD-Aussenstelle Detmold, 31.7.42, Staatsarchiv Detmold, *Preußische Regierung Minden.* I thank Dr. Sybille Steinbacher for examination of this document.

152. Otto Dov Kulka and Eberhard Jäckel, *Die Juden in den geheimen NS-Stimmungsberichten 1933–1945* (Düsseldorf, 2004), p. 503.

153. Ibid., p. 527n2.

154. Ibid., p. 528.

155. Ibid., p. 529.

156. Michael Phayer, *The Catholic Church and the Holocaust, 1930–1965* (Bloomington, 2000), pp. 70–71.

157. Ibid., p. 71.

158. For the quotation see ibid., pp. 73–74.

159. Ibid., p. 75.

160. Ibid., p. 76.

161. For Pius XII's answer to Preysing enunciating the freedom left to the bishops, see Saul Friedländer, *Pius XII*, pp. 135ff.

162. Ibid.

163. For the full text of Wurm's letter, Richard Gutteridge, *Open Thy Mouth for the Dumb! The German Evangelical Church and the Jews 1879–1950* (Oxford, 1976), pp. 353ff.

164. Gerlach, *And the Witnesses Were Silent*, p. 204.

165. See Martin Doerry, *My Wounded Heart: The Life of Lilli Jahn, 1900–1944* (London, 2004), pp. 113ff.

166. Klemperer, *I Will Bear Witness: A Diary of the Nazi Years 1942–1945*, p. 278.

167. Ibid., p. 277.

168. Ibid., p. 295.

169. Cordelia Edvardson, *Gebranntes Kind sucht das Feuer* (Munich, 1989), pp. 58ff and 68.

170. Beate Meyer, "Gratwanderung zwischen Verantwortung und Verstrickung: Die Reichsvereinigung der Juden in Deutschland und die Jüdische Gemeinde zu Berlin 1938–1945," in *Juden in Berlin, 1938–1945*, ed. Beate Meyer and Hermann Simon (Berlin, 2000), pp. 323 and 325ff.

171. Edvardson, *Gebranntes Kind sucht das Feuer*, pp. 69ff.

172. Ibid., pp. 73–74.

173. Ibid., pp. 74–75.

174. Yisrael Gutman, *Resistance: The Warsaw Ghetto Uprising* (Boston, 1994), pp. 152ff.

175. Yisrael Gutman, *The Jews of Warsaw, 1939–1943: Ghetto, Underground, Revolt* (Bloomington, 1982), p. 272.

176. Abraham Lewin, *A Cup of Tears: A Diary of the Warsaw Ghetto*, ed. Antony Polonsky (Oxford, 1988), p. 186.

177. Ibid., p. 188.

178. Ibid., p. 203.

179. Ibid., p. 205.

180. Ibid., p. 225.

181. Ibid., p. 240.

182. Ibid., pp. 241–42.

183. These negotiations are described in detail in an abundant literature. For a useful and concise presentation see Shmuel Krakowski, *The War of the Doomed: Jewish Armed Resistance in Poland, 1942–1944* (New York, 1984), pp. 167–68.

184. Ibid., pp 168–69.

185. Antony Polonsky, introduction to Lewin, *A Cup of Tears*, p. 53.

186. Nuremberg doc. NO-2494, in Yitzhak Arad, Yisrael Gutman, and Abraham

Margaliot, eds., *Documents on the Holocaust: Selected Sources on the Destruction of the Jews of Germany and Austria, Poland, and the Soviet Union* (Jerusalem, 1981), p. 292.

187. Yitzhak Zuckerman, *A Surplus of Memory: Chronicle of the Warsaw Ghetto Uprising* (Berkeley, 1993), pp. 319–36.

188. Apart from the already mentioned studies on the Jews of Warsaw and on Jewish resistance (Gutman, *The Jews of Warsaw*; Gutman, *Resistance*; Krakowski, *The War of the Doomed*) and the memoirs of Zuckerman, *A Surplus of Memory*, I have used a number of widely known books, in particular Marek Edelman, *The Ghetto Fights* (1945; reprint, London, 1990); Kazik [Simha Rotem], *Memoirs of a Warsaw Ghetto Fighter* (New Haven, 1994).

189. About the Jewish armed underground in Kraków and the "Cyganeria" action, see Yael Peled, *Jewish Cracow, 1939–1943: Resistance, Underground, Struggle [Krakov ha-Yehudit, 1939–1943: Amidah, Mahteret, Ma'avak]* (Tel Aviv, 1993) (In Hebrew), particularly pp. 216ff.

190. Emanuel Ringelblum, "Little Stalingrad defends itself," in *To Live with Honor and Die with Honor! . . . : Selected Documents from the Warsaw Ghetto Underground Archives "O.S." ("Oneg Shabbath")* ed. Joseph Kermish (Jerusalem, 1986), pp. 599–600.

191. This topography of the early fighting is based on Moshe Arens, "The Warsaw Ghetto Revolt: The Narrative," p. 1.

192. See mainly Moshe Arens, "The Jewish Military Organization (ZZW) in the Warsaw Ghetto," *Holocaust and Genocide Studies* 19, no. 2 (Fall 2005), pp. 201ff.

193. Ibid.

194. "The Jewish Quarter of Warsaw Is No More!" Sybil Milton, ed., *The Stroop Report* (New York, 1979), May 24, 1943 entry.

195. U.S. Office of Chief of Counsel for the Prosecution of Axis Criminality and International Military Tribunal, *Nazi Conspiracy and Aggression*, pp. 726–27.

196. Goebbels, *Tagebücher*, part 2, vol. 8, p. 192. Regarding the "military reports," the minister was referring to the communiqués issued by Adolf Berman and Yitzhak Zuckerman on April 19, 20, and 21 and the subsequent ones issued in the name of the Coordinating Committee with the participation of Feiner from the Bund. The reports were passed on to the Polish underground, which broadcast some of them on its secret radio station.

197. Ibid., p. 343.

198. Frank, *Diensttagebuch*, p. 682.

199. Moltke, *Letters to Freya: 1939–1945*, p. 330.

200. Ulrich von Hassell, *Die Hassell-Tagebücher 1938–1944: Aufzeichnungen vom Andern Deutschland*, ed. Klaus Peter Reiss and Freiherr Friedrich Hiller von Gaertringen (Berlin, 1988), p. 365.

201. Helmut Heiber and David M. Glantz, eds., *Hitler and His Generals: Military Conferences 1942–1945: The First Complete Stenographic Record of the Military Situation Conferences, From Stalingrad to Berlin.* (London, 2002), p. 472.

202. Nuremberg doc. NO-2496.

203. Note by Heiber in Heiber and Glantz, *Hitler and His Generals,* pp. 993–94.

204. Klemperer, *I Will Bear Witness: A Diary of the Nazi Years, 1942–1945*, p. 234.

205. Oskar Rosenfeld, *Wozu noch Welt: Aufzeichnungen aus dem Ghetto Lodz*, ed. Hanno Loewy (Frankfurt am Main, 1994), p. 207.

206. Avraham Tory, *Surviving the Holocaust: The Kovno Ghetto Diary*, ed. Martin Gilbert and Dina Porat (Cambridge, UK, 1990), pp. 304–5.

207. Herman Kruk, *The Last Days of the Jerusalem of Lithuania: Chronicles from the Vilna Ghetto and the Camps, 1939–1944*, ed. Benjamin Harshav (New Haven, 2002), p. 520.

208. Ibid., p. 524.

209. David G. Roskies, "Landkentenish: Yiddish Belles Lettres in the Warsaw Ghetto," in *Holocaust Chronicles: Individualizing the Holocaust through Diaries and Other Contemporaneous Personal Accounts*, ed. Robert Moses Shapiro (Hoboken, NJ, 1999), pp. 20–21.

210. Alf Lüdtke, "The Appeal of Exterminating "Others": German Workers and the Limits of Resistance," in *Resistance Against the Third Reich, 1933–1990*, ed. Michael Geyer and John W. Boyer (Chicago, 1994), p. 72.

211. For the events in Białystok see Sara Bender, *Facing Death: The Jews of Białystok 1939–1943* (Tel Aviv, 1997) [Hebrew].

212. Berenstein, *Faschismus, Getto, Massenmord*, p. 449.

213. Bender, *Facing Death: The Jews of Białystok 1939–1943*, pp. 233ff.

214. Ibid., pp. 260ff.

215. Ibid., pp. 274ff.

216. Bernhard Chiari, *Alltag hinter der Front: Besatzung, Kollaboration und Widerstand in Weissrussland 1941–1944* (Düsseldorf, 1998), p. 240.

217. Kruk, *The Last Days of the Jerusalem of Lithuania*, p. 566.

218. Arad, Gutman, and Margaliot, *Documents on the Holocaust*, p. 450.

219. Isaac Rudashevski, *The Diary of the Vilna Ghetto, June 1941–April 1943*, ed. Percy Matenko (Tel Aviv, 1973), pp. 138–39.

220. Heiber, *Reichsführer! Briefe an und von Himmler*, p. 214.

221. For these debates see Dina Porat, *Beyond the Reaches of Our Souls: The Life and Times of Abba Kovner* (Tel Aviv, 2000), pp. 135ff [Hebrew].

222. Ibid.

223. Ibid., pp. 140ff.

224. Ibid., pp. 134ff.

225. See Harshav, introduction to Kruk, *The Last Days of the Jerusalem of Lithuania*, pp. xlviiiff.

226. Zelig Kalmanovitch, *Diary in the Vilna Ghetto* [Hebrew] (Tel Aviv, 1977), pp. 114ff.

227. Yitzhak Arad, *Ghetto in Flames: The Struggle and Destruction of the Jews in Vilna in the Holocaust* (Jerusalem, 1980), p. 425. Gens's leadership was not only praised by an eminent contemporary such as Kalmanovitch as against the FPO, but years later it received recognition from quite an unexpected side. Nathan Alterman was undoubtedly Israel's most prominent poet, the voice of "heroic" Zionism from the mid-1930s to

the late 1960s. He interrogated Kovner at great length about the history of the Vilna ghetto and, in the end, declared: "Had I been in the ghetto, I would have been on the side of the Judenrat." Tom Segev, *The Seventh Million: The Israelis and the Holocaust* (New York, 1993), p. 292.

228. Leni Yahil, *The Holocaust: The Fate of European Jewry, 1932–1945* (New York, 1990), pp. 466ff.

229. Porat, *Beyond the Reach of Our Souls*, pp. 155ff. According to historian Yehuda Bauer, various degrees of armed resistance took place in 24 ghettos in western and central Poland; moreover, there were sixty-three armed groups in the 110 ghettos and other Jewish concentrations in western Belorussia, and some forms of armed preparedness in another 30 ghettos. See Yehuda Bauer and Nili Keren, *A History of the Holocaust* (New York, 1982), p. 270.

230. Rudashevski, *The Diary of the Vilna Ghetto, June 1941–April 1943*, p. 140.

231. Ibid., p. 12.

232. Dawid Sierakowiak, *The Diary of Dawid Sierakowiak*, ed. Alan Adelson (New York, 1996), p. 268.

233. Alan Adelson's note, ibid.

234. For the text of the poem and Milosz's comment on it, see Jan Blonski, "The Poor Poles Look at the Ghetto," *Polin: Studies in Polish Jewry* 4 (1989), pp. 322–23.

235. Quoted in Michael Steinlauf, *Bondage to the Dead: Poland and the Memory of the Holocaust* (Syracuse, 1997), p. 32.

236. Marcel Reich-Ranicki, *The Author of Himself: The Life of Marcel Reich-Ranicki* (London, 2001), pp. 190ff. and 194.

237. Ibid.

238. Ibid., pp. 197ff.

239. Arad, *Belzec*, p. 348.

240. Jan T. Gross, "A Tangled Web: Confronting Stereotypes Concerning Relations between Poles, Germans, Jews and Communists," in *The Politics of Retribution*, ed. István Deák, Jan T. Gross, and Tony Judt (Princeton, 2000), p. 80 (emphasis in original).

241. Quoted in Shmuel Krakowski, "The Attitude of the Polish Underground to the Jewish Question during the Second World War," in *Contested Memories: Poles and Jews during the Holocaust and Its Aftermath*, ed. Joshua D. Zimmerman (New Brunswick, NJ, 2003), pp. 100–01.

242. Aryeh Klonicki and Malwina Klonicki, *The Diary of Adam's Father: The Diary of Aryeh Klonicki (Klonymus) and His Wife Malwina, With Letters Concerning the Fate of Their Child Adam* (Jerusalem, 1973), p. 25.

243. Ibid., pp. 31–32.

244. Ibid., p. 34.

245. Ibid., pp. 78–79. Klonicki's diary, written in Hebrew, was retrieved in 1948 from Franka's brother, Stanislaw Wanshik, by New York relatives of the author; a series of letters exchanged between the family in the United States and the Wanshiks was

appended to the published diary; it provides the details about the Klonickis' end and Adam's disappearance.

246. Karel C. Berkhoff, *Harvest of Despair: Life and Death in Ukraine under Nazi Rule* (Cambridge, MA, 2004), pp. 71ff.

247. Ibid., p. 73.

248. For a description of the anti-Jewish violence in the Ukraine in the last year of the war and later, see Amir Weiner, *Making Sense of War: The Second World War and the Fate of the Bolshevik Revolution* (Princeton, 2002), pp. 191ff.

249. In the Polish context of the summer of 1942, Kossak's declaration made a difference; yet the attitude towards the Jews that it expressed remained highly problematic. For a convincing analysis, see Jan Blonski, "Polish-Catholics and Catholic Poles: The Gospel, National Interest, Civic Solidarity, and the Destruction of the Warsaw Ghetto," *Yad Vashem Studies* 25 (1996), pp. 181ff.

250. All details and quotations are taken from Joseph Kermish, "The Activities of the Council for Aid to Jews ("*Zegota*") in Occupied Poland," in Yisrael Gutman and Efraim Zuroff, eds., *Rescue Attempts During the Holocaust.* (Jerusalem, 1977), pp. 367ff.

251. Ibid., p. 372.

252. Goebbels, *Tagebücher*, part 2, vol. 7, p. 454.

Chapter Nine: October 1943–March 1944

1. Saul Friedländer, *Kurt Gerstein, The Ambiguity of Good* (New York, 1969), pp. 201ff.

2. Ibid., p. 108.

3. For these strategic plans, see Gerhard L. Weinberg, *A World at Arms: A Global History of World War II* (Cambridge, England, 1994), pp. 656ff. and particularly pp. 665–66.

4. Albert Speer, *Inside the Third Reich: Memoirs* (New York, 1970), p. 299.

5. Tatiana Berenstein, ed., *Faschismus, Getto, Massenmord: Dokumentation über Ausrottung und Widerstand der Juden in Polen während des zweiten Weltkrieges* (East Berlin, 1961), p. 296.

6. The pamphlet appropriately opened with a Himmler quotation from 1935: "As long as there are human beings on earth, the fight between humans and subhumans will be a historical law and the fight led by the Jew against the nations belongs, as far back as we can see, to the natural course of life on our planet. One can safely arrive at the conclusion that this struggle for life and death is as much a law of nature as the fight of the plague germ against the healthy body." See Walter Hofer, ed., *Der Nationalsozialismus: Dokumente 1933–1945* (Frankfurt am Main, 1957), p. 280 (doc. 1576).

7. Berenstein, *Faschismus, Getto, Massenmord*, pp. 357–58.

8. Heinrich Himmler, *Heinrich Himmler: Geheimreden, 1933 bis 1945, und andere Ansprachen*, ed. Bradley F. Smith and Agnes F. Peterson (Frankfurt am Main, 1974), p. 169.

9. Ibid.

10. Ibid., pp. 201ff.

11. Joseph Goebbels, *Die Tagebücher von Joseph Goebbels*: ed. Elke Fröhlich (Munich, 1995), vol. 10, p. 72.

12. Nuremberg doc. PS-1919, *Nazi Conspiracy and Aggression*, vol. 4 (Washington, DC, 1946), pp. 563–64. The translation has been slightly amended.

13. Höss may have been treated with such care because of his close ties to Bormann. See Raul Hilberg, "Auschwitz and the Final Solution," in *Anatomy of the Auschwitz Death Camp*, ed. Yisrael Gutman and Michael Berenbaum (Bloomington, IN, 1994), p. 83.

14. On the entire episode see also Hermann Langbein, *People in Auschwitz* (Chapel Hill, NC, 2004), pp. 39–40.

15. Frank Dingel, "Waffen-SS," in *Enzyklopädie des Nationalsozialismus*, ed. Wolfgang Benz, Hermann Graml, and Hermann Weiss (Stuttgart, 1997), p. 792.

16. See, for example, Speer, *Inside the Third Reich: Memoirs*, p. 336.

17. Heinz Höhne, *Canaris* (Garden City, NY, 1979), pp. 487ff.

18. For these aspects, see Ulrich Herbert, *Best: Biographische Studien über Radikalismus, Weltanschauung und Vernunft, 1903–1989* (Bonn, 1996), p. 327.

19. Ibid., p. 330

20. Ibid., p. 332.

21. For the standard work on the Jews of Denmark during the Holocaust see Leni Yahil, *The Rescue of Danish Jewry: Test of a Democracy* (Philadelphia, 1969). Yahil's study can be usefully complemented by relevant chapters in Ulrich Herbert's biography of Werner Best and by Hans Kirchhoff, "Denmark: A Light in the Darkness of the Holocaust? A Reply to Gunnar S. Paulsson," in Cesarani, *Holocaust: Critical Concepts in Historical Studies*, vol. 5, pp. 128ff. As for Gunnar S. Paulsson, "The Bridge over the Øresund: The Historiography on the Expulsion of the Jews from Nazi-occupied Denmark" (in Cesarani, *Holocaust*, vol. 5, pp. 99ff), it is not always convincing, particularly in view of Herbert's study on Best.

22. Herbert, *Best*, p. 362ff.

23. Ibid., p. 366.

24. Ibid., p. 367.

25. Ibid., p. 368.

26. Ibid., p. 369.

27. About Best's attitude, see ibid. As for the participation of the Danes in the rescue operation, see Kirchhoff, "Denmark," in Walter Laqueur and Judith Tydor Baumel, eds., *The Holocaust Encyclopedia* (New Haven, 2001), p. 148.

28. Bob Moore, *Victims and Survivors: The Nazi Persecution of the Jews in the Netherlands, 1940–1945* (London, 1997), p. 104.

29. Ibid., p. 102.

30. For this summary see ibid., p. 125.

31. Philip Mechanicus, *Waiting for Death: A Diary* (London, 1968), p. 48.

32. Ibid., p. 49.

33. Ibid., p. 33.

34. Ibid., pp. 32–33.

35. Ibid., p. 76.

36. Etty Hillesum, *Letters from Westerbork* (New York, 1986), p. 97.

37. Ibid., p. 55–56.

38. Anne Frank, *The Diary of a Young Girl: The Definitive Edition*, ed. Otto Frank and Mirjam Pressler (New York, 1995), p. 187.

39. Herman Kruk, *The Last Days of the Jerusalem of Lithuania: Chronicles from the Vilna Ghetto and the Camps, 1939–1944*, ed. Benjamin Harshav (New Haven, 2002), p. 525.

40. Michael R. Marrus and Robert O. Paxton, *Vichy et les juifs* (Paris, 1990), pp. 325ff.

41. Serge Klarsfeld, *Vichy-Auschwitz: Le rôle de Vichy dans la solution finale de la question juive en France*, 2 vols. (Paris, 1983–85), vol. 2, p. 331.

42. Jacques Adler, "The Changing Attitude of the 'Bystanders' Toward the Jews in France, 1940–1943," in John Milfull, *Why Germany?: National Socialist Anti-semitism and the European Context* (Providence, RI, 1993), pp. 184ff.

43. Richard I. Cohen, *The Burden of Conscience: French Jewish Leadership during the Holocaust* (Bloomington, 1987), pp. 91–92.

44. Ibid., pp. 90–91.

45. Ibid., p. 97.

46. For the clandestine efforts, see Jacques Adler, *The Jews of Paris and the Final Solution: Communal Response and Internal Conflicts, 1940–1944* (New York, 1987), pp. 154ff.; Cohen, *The Burden of Conscience*, pp. 96–97.

47. Klarsfeld, *Vichy-Auschwitz*, vol. 2, p. 124.

48. Ibid.

49. André Kaspi, *Les Juifs pendant l'occupation* (Paris, 1991), pp. 294ff.

50. Ibid., p. 298.

51. Ibid.

52. Klarsfeld, *Vichy-Auschwitz*, vol. 2, pp. 124–25.

53. Raymond-Raoul Lambert, *Carnet d'un témoin: 1940–1943*, ed. Richard I. Cohen (Paris, 1985), pp. 233–34.

54. Ibid., pp. 235–36.

55. Ibid., p. 238.

56. Simon Schwarzfuchs, *Aux Prises avec Vichy: Histoire politique des Juifs de France, 1940–1944* (Paris, 1998), pp. 304–6.

57. Aharon Weiss, "Jewish Leadership in Occupied Poland—Postures and Attitudes," *Yad Vashem Studies* 12 (1977), pp. 363–64.

58. Dan Diner, "Historical Understanding and Counterrationality: The Judenrat as Epistemological Vantage," in *Probing the Limits of Representation: Nazism and the "Final Solution,"* ed. Saul Friedländer (Cambridge, MA, 1992), pp. 128ff.

59. Quoted in Yitzhak Arad, *Belzec, Sobibor, Treblinka: The Operation Reinhard Death Camps* (Bloomington, 1987), p. 276.

60. For these details, see mainly ibid., pp. 282ff.

61. Ibid., pp. 290ff.

62. Gitta Sereny, *Into That Darkness: From Mercy Killing to Mass Murder* (London, 1974), pp. 239–40.

63. Arad, *Belzec*, p. 298.

64. Ibid., p. 297.

65. Jacob Wiernik became one of the main witnesses in Claude Lanzman's film *Shoah.*

66. For the preparations of the uprising in Sobibor see Arad, *Belzec*, pp. 299ff. and mainly 306ff.

67. For the events of October 14, 1943, see ibid., pp. 322ff.

68. On the basis of the "SD decodes" and other sources, Richard Breitman reached the conclusion that Himmler's order to Kappler was issued on September 24 or possibly a few days earlier. See Richard Breitman, "New Sources on the Holocaust in Italy," *Holocaust and Genocide Studies* 16, no. 3 (Winter 2002), pp. 403–4.

69. For these details see mainly Robert Katz, *The Battle for Rome: The Germans, the Allies, the Partisans and the Pope, September 1943–June 1944* (New York, 2003), pp. 61ff.

70. Breitman, "New Sources on the Holocaust in Italy," p. 404.

71. Katz, *The Battle for Rome*, pp. 63ff.

72. Stanislao G. Pugliese, "Bloodless Torture: The Books of the Roman Ghetto Under the Nazi Occupation," in *The Holocaust and the Book: Destruction and Preservation*, ed. Jonathan Rose (Amherst, MA, 2001), p. 52.

73. Ibid., p. 53.

74. Ibid.

75. Katz, *The Battle for Rome: The Germans, the Allies, the Partisans and the Pope, September 1943–June 1944*, p. 77; Breitman, "New Sources on the Holocaust in Italy," pp. 405–6.

76. Breitman, "New Sources on the Holocaust in Italy," p. 407.

77. For the sequence of the events see Daniel Carpi, "Italy," in Laqueur and Baumel, eds., *The Holocaust Encyclopedia*, pp. 336–39.

78. Ingrid Krüger-Bulcke and Hans Georg Lehmann, eds., *Akten zur deutschen auswärtigen Politik, 1918–1945, Ser. E, 1941–1945* (Göttingen, 1969), vol. 7, p. 31.

79. Ibid., p. 31 n. 2.

80. Katz, *The Battle for Rome: The Germans, the Allies, the Partisans and the Pope, September 1943–June 1944*, pp. 78ff.

81. Pierre Blet, Angelo Martini, and Burkhart Schneider, eds., *Actes et documents du Saint Siège relatifs à la Seconde Guerre mondiale* (Vatican City, 1975), vol. 9, pp. 505–6.

82. According to some historians, one of the German diplomats, Gerhard Gumpert, dictated the letter to Hudal. See for example Katz, *The Battle for Rome*, pp. 106ff.

83. For the text of Weizsäcker's cable see Saul Friedländer, *Pius XII and the Third Reich: A Documentation* (New York, 1966), p. 207.

84. Ibid., p. 208.

85. Krüger-Bulcke and Lehmann, *ADAP, Ser. E,* vol. 7, pp. 130–31.

86. Ibid., vol. 5, p. 97.

87. Goebbels, *Tagebücher*, part 2, vol. 7, p. 295.

88. Ibid., p. 465.

89. Ibid., p. 569.

90. *ADAP*, *Ser. E*, vol. 6 (Göttingen, 1979), pp. 232–33.

91. Saul Friedländer, *Pius XII*, p. 190.

92. Ibid., pp. 191–192.

93. Krüger-Bulcke and Lehmann, *ADAP*, Series E, vol. 6 (Göttingen, 1979), pp. 584–86.

94. Goebbels, *Tagebücher*, part 2, vol. 9, pp. 264–65.

95. Ibid., part 2, vol. 10, p. 104.

96. Michael Phayer, *The Catholic Church and the Holocaust, 1930–1965* (Bloomington, 2000), pp. 100–101.

97. For the text of the address entitled "Grandezza dolori e speranze del popolo Polacco" see Blet, Martini, and Schneider, *Actes et documents du Saint Siège relatifs à la Seconde Guerre mondiale*, vol. 3, part 2, pp. 801–2. For a discussion of Pius XII's attitude to the Polish issue and for the translation of the quotes from his speech of May 31, 1943, see Robert S. Wistrich, "The Vatican Documents and the Holocaust: A Personal Report," *Polin: Studies in Polish Jewry* 15 (2002), pp. 426ff. and particularly 429.

98. See for example, among many other such interventions, the nuncio's protest to Weizsäcker about the fate of Polish priests, on September 20, 1940, and the Holy Office's Declaration of early December 1940 concerning euthanasia, in Friedländer, *Pius XII*, pp. 63 and 66.

99. Father Pierre Blet's study on the pope's policies and decisions during World War II is unconvincing, notwithstanding the fact that Blet, as one of the three editors of the Vatican documents, had full access to Vatican archives. Blet's core argument regarding Pius's silence in the face of the deportation and extermination of the Jews of Europe is that of ignorance about the ultimate fate of the victims ("As long as the war lasted, the fate of the deportees was shrouded in obscurity."). Yet, Blet stated, "Pius XII never used this continuous shadow regarding an unknown destination as an excuse for abandoning those who were being persecuted. On the contrary, he employed all the means at his disposal to save them. As much as possible he took care to limit what he said in public, expecting nothing worthwhile to come out of this. He did not speak, but he took action." Pierre Blet, *Pius XII and the Second World War: According to the Archives of the Vatican* (New York, 1999), p. 167.

100. For the text, see Friedländer, *Pius XII*, p. 143.

101. For the emphasis on Poland see the comments added to the mention of the address in Blet, Martini, and Schneider, *Actes et documents du Saint Siège relatifs à la Seconde Guerre mondiale*, vol. 9, p. 327.

102. Quoted in Friedländer, *Pius XII*, p. 143.

103. Letter from Preysing to Pius XII, March 6, 1943, quoted in Burkhart Schneider, Pierre Blet, and Angelo Martini, eds., *Die Briefe Pius XII. an die deutschen Bischöfe 1939–1944* (Mainz, 1966), p. 239n1.

104. Quoted in Friedländer, *Pius XII*, p. 139.

105. Ibid. (emphasis added).

106. For this argument, see most recently John Cornwell, *Hitler's Pope: The Secret History of Pius XII* (New York, 1999), pp. 295–97.

107. Pius's special affection for the German people and his love for German culture have often been recognized. The way he chose at times to express his feelings was neither subtle nor diplomatic. Thus, at the end of October 1941, as the German attack on Moscow was still in full swing, the pope gave a private audience to Goebbels's sister Maria, on a visit to Rome, and asked her to transmit his personal blessing to the propaganda minister. Goebbels noted the event with highly sarcastic comments in his diary entry of October 26. See Joseph Goebbels, *Die Tagebücher von Joseph Goebbels*, ed. Elke Fröhlich (Munich, 1998), part 2, vol. 2, p. 185.

108. Friedländer, *Pius XII*, pp. 141–42.

109. Susan Zuccotti, *Under His Very Windows: The Vatican and the Holocaust in Italy* (New Haven, 2000), p. 307.

110. Ibid., pp. 307–8.

111. Ibid., p. 208.

112. Regarding Vatican policy toward Croatia, see Carlo Falconi, *The Silence of Pius XII* (London, 1970), which remains the most thorough study on this issue; see, also, Menachem Shelach, "The Catholic Church in Croatia, the Vatican and the Murder of the Croatian Jews," *Holocaust and Genocide Studies* 4, no. 3 (1989), pp. 323ff.

113. According to historian Giovanni Miccoli, Pius XII was essentially guided by the rule of necessary neutrality (formulated by Benedict XV during World War I) in a war opposing "post-Christian" nation-states over which the pope had no authority but that included Catholics fighting on each side. Miccoli himself considers this attitude as highly problematic in the face of Nazi atrocities and interprets Pius's position as attributing to the war itself the responsibility of all evils. For this thesis, see mainly Giovanni Miccoli, *Les Dilemmes et les silences de Pie XII. Vatican, Seconde Guerre mondiale et Shoah* (Bruxelles, 2005), pp. 425ff. This interpretation would be convincing if the Vatican had not taken such a resolute, albeit non-public, position against the Soviet Union.

114. Tittmann to Hull, October 19, 1943, *FRUS*, 1943, vol. 2 (Europe), Washington, p. 950.

115. Quoted in Kenneth C. Barnes, "Dietrich Bonhoeffer and Hitler's Persecution of the Jews," in *Betrayal: German Churches and the Holocaust*, ed. Robert P. Ericksen and Susannah Heschel (Minneapolis, 1999), pp. 125–26.

116. Ibid., p. 126.

117. Ludwig Volk, ed., *Akten deutscher Bischöfe über die Lage der Kirche, 1933–1945*, 6 vols., vol. 6: *1943–1945* (Mainz, 1985), p. 310.

118. Ibid., p. 480.

119. See the document discovered in the French archives and published by Alberto Melloni in *Corriere della Sera*, on December 28, 2004. The authenticity of the document is unquestionable. I am grateful to Carlo Ginzburg and to Michael R. Marrus for having drawn my attention to this document and to various aspects of the controversy sur-

rounding it. For a thorough discussion of the Vatican's stance, see Michael R. Marrus, "Le Vatican er les orphelins juifs de la Shoah," *L'Histoire* 307 (March 2006), pp. 75–85.

120. Cordelia Edvardson, *Gebranntes Kind sucht das Feuer* (Munich, 1989), pp. 81ff.

121. Ruth Kluger, *Still Alive: A Holocaust Girlhood Remembered* (New York, 2001), pp. 104ff. and 107–08.

122. Ibid., p. 107.

123. Ruth Bondy, *"Elder of the Jews": Jakob Edelstein of Theresienstadt* (New York, 1989), pp. 386ff.

124. Egon Redlich, *The Terezin Diary of Gonda Redlich*, ed. Saul S. Friedman (Lexington, KY, 1992), p. 129.

125. Jean-Claude Favez, *The Red Cross and the Holocaust* (Cambridge, 1999), p. 41.

126. Otto Dov Kulka, "Ghetto in an Annihilation Camp: Jewish Social History in the Holocaust Period and its Ultimate Limits," in Yisrael Gutman and Avital Saf, eds., *The Nazi Concentration Camps* (Jerusalem: 1984), p. 328.

127. See, among others, Nili Keren, "The Family Camp," in Yisrael Gutman and Michael Berenbaum, *Anatomy of the Auschwitz Death Camp* (Bloomington, 1994), pp. 428ff.

128. Ibid., p. 436.

129. Ibid., p. 440.

130. For details on the diarists see Nathan Cohen, "Diaries of the Sonderkommando," in *Anatomy of the Auschwitz Death Camp*, ed. Yisrael Gutman and Michael Berenbaum (Bloomington, 1994), pp. 592ff.

131. Ibid., p. 523.

132. Zalman Gradowski, "The Czech Transport," quoted in David G. Roskies, *The Literature of Destruction: Jewish Responses to Catastrophe* (Philadelphia, 1988), pp. 562–63.

133. Ibid., p. 563.

134. Roskies, "The Great Lament" in *The Literature of Destruction*, p. 518.

135. Gradowski, "The Czech Transport," in ibid., pp. 563–64.

136. Krüger-Bulcke and Lehmann, *ADAP*, Series E, vol. 8 (Göttingen, 1979), pp. 153–54.

137. For a typical camp of this category, see Felicja Karay, *Death Comes in Yellow: Skarzysko-Kamienna Slave Labor Camp* (Amsterdam, 1996).

138. Krüger-Bulcke and Lehmann, *ADAP*, Series E, vol. 5 (Göttingen, 1978), pp. 326–27.

139. Eberhard Kolb, "Bergen-Belsen, 1943–1945," in Yisrael Gutman and Avital Saf, *The Nazi Concentration Camps: Structure and Aims, the Image of the Prisoner, the Jews in the Camps* (Jerusalem, 1984), p. 335.

140. Ibid., pp. 336–37.

141. Martin Gilbert, introduction to Avraham Tory, *Surviving the Holocaust: The Kovno Ghetto Diary*, ed. Martin Gilbert and Dina Porat (Cambridge, UK, 1990).

142. Avraham Tory, *Surviving the Holocaust: The Kovno Ghetto Diary*, ed. Martin Gilbert and Dina Porat (Cambridge, 1990), pp. 508ff.

143. Gilbert, Introduction to ibid., pp. xxiii and xxiv.

144. Ibid., pp. 506–7.

145. See on this issue, Lucjan Dobroszycki, ed., *The Chronicle of the Lódz Ghetto, 1941–1944* (New Haven, 1984), pp. lx and lxi.

146. Ibid., p. lxii.

147. Ibid., pp. 422–23.

148. For these cultural aspects see also Gila Flam, "Das kulturelle Leben im Getto Lodz," in *"Wer zum Leben, wer zum Tod . . ." Strategien jüdischen überlebens im Ghetto*, ed. Doron Kiesel et al. (Frankfurt, 1992), p. 92.

149. Dobroszycki, *The Chronicle.*, p. 413.

150. Ibid., p. 470–71.

151. Helmut Heiber, *Reichsführer! Briefe an und von Himmler* (Munich, 1970), p. 120.

152. Ibid., p. 213.

153. Ibid., pp. 246–47.

154. Ibid., pp. 175–76. Rumor had it that Richard Wagner was the illegitimate son of the Jewish actor Ludwig Geyer.

155. Warren Paul Green, "The Nazi Racial Policy Towards the Karaites," *Soviet Jewish Affairs* 8, no. 2 (1978), p. 40.

156. Ibid., p. 38.

157. Philip Friedman, *Roads to Extinction: Essays on the Holocaust*, ed. Ada June Friedman (New York, 1980), p. 155.

158. Green, "The Nazi Racial Policy Towards the Karaites," p. 40.

159. Ibid.

160. Friedman, *Roads to Extinction*, pp. 164–65.

161. Green, "The Nazi Racial Policy Towards the Karaites," pp. 38–39.

162. For details on the activities of "Amt VII," see Jürgen Matthäus, "Weltanschauliche Forschung und Auswärtung. Aus den Akten des Amtes VII im Reichssicherheitshauptamt," *Jahrbuch für Antisemitismusforschung* 5 (1996), pp. 287ff., and Lutz Hachmeister, *Der Gegnerforscher,* pp. 212ff.

163. See Wolfgang Behringer, "Der Abwickler," in *Himmlers Hexenkartothek: Das Interesse des Nationalsozialismus an der Hexenverfolgung*, ed. Sönke Lorenz et al. (Bielefeld, 2000), pp. 121ff.

164. Jürgen Matthäus, "Weltanschauliche Forschung und Auswärtung. Aus den Akten des Amtes VII im Reichssicherheitshauptamt," *Jahrbuch für Antisemitismusforschung* 5 (1996), p. 288.

165. Ibid., p. 289.

166. For many of the details see David E. Fishman, "Embers Plucked from the Fire: The Rescue of Jewish Cultural Treasures in Vilna," in *The Holocaust and the Book: Destruction and Preservation*, ed. Jonathan Rose (Amherst, MA, 2001), pp. 68ff.

167. Kruk, *The Last Days of the Jerusalem of Lithuania*, p. 311.

168. Fishman, "Embers," p. 69.

169. Ibid.

170. Kruk, *The Last Days of the Jerusalem of Lithuania*, p. 408.

171. On the book rescue operation, see mainly Fishman, "Embers," pp. 70ff. See also Dina Abramowicz, *Guardians of a Tragic Heritage: Reminiscences and Observations of an Eyewitness* (New York, 1999).

172. Kruk, *The Last Days of the Jerusalem of Lithuania*, p. 578.

173. For the memorandum, see Kurt Pätzold, ed., *Verfolgung, Vertreibung, Vernichtung: Dokumente des faschistischen Antisemitismus 1933 bis 1942* (Frankfurt am Main, 1984), pp. 341–42.

174. For the entire issue, see the painstaking research in Michael H. Kater, *Das "Ahnenerbe" der SS 1935–1945: Ein Beitrag zur Kulturpolitik des Dritten Reiches* (Stuttgart, 2001), pp. 245ff.

175. Ibid., p. 249.

176. Ibid. The inclusion of "Innerasiaten" may indicate that Schäfer was somehow informed of the project.

177. Ibid.

178. Ibid., p. 250.

179. Ibid., pp. 254–55.

180. On this issue see, most recently, Dirk Rupnow, " 'Ihr müsst sein, auch wenn ihr nicht mehr seid': The Jewish Central Museum in Prague and Historical Memory in the Third Reich," *Holocaust and Genocide Studies* 16, no. 1 (2002), pp. 23ff. On this puzzling issue, see also Jan Björn Potthast, *Das Jüdische Zentralmuseum der SS in Prag: Gegnerfoschung und Völkermord im Nationalsozialismus* (Frankfurt, 2002).

181. Rupnow, " 'Ihr müsst sein, auch wenn ihr nicht mehr seid,' " p. 29.

182. Ibid., p. 35.

183. For the quotation, see Ariel Hurwitz, "The Struggle Over the Creation of the War Refugee Board (WRB)," *Holocaust and Genocide Studies* 6 (1991), p. 19.

184. On Bergson see mainly David S. Wyman and Rafael Medoff, *A Race Against Death: Peter Bergson, America, and the Holocaust* (New York, 2002).

185. Ibid., p. 211.

186. Quoted in Gulie Ne'eman Arad, *America, Its Jews, and the Rise of Nazism* (Bloomington, 2000), pp. 220ff.

187. Ibid.

188. Long claimed that since 1933, 580,000 Jewish refugees had entered the United States; it soon became known that the real number was 210,732. See Hurwitz, "The Struggle Over the Creation of the War Refugee Board (WRB)," p. 20.

189. Henry L. Feingold, *Bearing Witness: How America and Its Jews Responded to the Holocaust* (Syracuse, 1995), pp. 83–84.

190. Dina Porat, *The Blue and the Yellow Stars of David: The Zionist Leadership in Palestine and the Holocaust, 1939–1945* (Cambridge, MA, 1990), pp. 62–63.

191. Ibid., p. 78.

192. Ibid., p. 79.

193. Ibid., pp. 82ff. and 86.

194. Blatman, *Notre Liberté*, p. 195.

195. Ibid., p. 198–99.

196. Quoted in Yitzhak Arad, Yisrael Gutman, and Abraham Margaliot, eds., *Documents on the Holocaust: Selected Sources on the Destruction of the Jews of Germany and Austria, Poland, and the Soviet Union* (Jerusalem, 1981), pp. 324ff.

197. Blatman, *Notre Liberté*, p. 199.

198. Etty Hillesum, *An Interrupted Life: The Diaries of Etty Hillesum, 1941–1943* (New York, 1983), pp. 220ff.

199. Hillesum, *Letters from Westerbork*, p. 146.

200. Hillesum, *An Interrupted Life*, p. xiii.

Chapter Ten: March 1944–May 1945

1. Translated in Serge Klarsfeld, *Vichy-Auschwitz: Le rôle de Vichy dans la solution finale de la question juive en France*, 2 vols. (Paris, 1983–85), vol. 2, p. 382.

2. Ibid., p. 161.

3. Ingrid Krüger-Bulcke and Hans Georg Lehmann, eds., *Akten zur deutschen auswärtigen Politik, 1918–1945, Ser. E, 1941–1945*, (Göttingen, 1979), vol. 3, p. 338.

4. Joseph Goebbels, *Die Tagebücher von Joseph Goebbels*, ed. Elke Fröhlich (Munich, 1995), part 2, vol. 12, p. 202.

5. This correlation does incidentally confirm the probable link between the first major military crisis, in December 1941, and the Nazi leader's final decision to exterminate all the Jews of Europe.

6. Thousands of full-time guidance officers and tens of thousands of part time NSFO lecturers or writers certainly contributed to the intense anti-Semitism so pervasive in the Wehrmacht to the very end. The indoctrination was particularly apparent in a flood of publications issued by the OKW that must have reached soldiers and officers in their hundreds of thousands (probably in their millions). Thus, for example, "Der Jude als Weltparasit" (The Jew as Global Parasite) was issued as number 7 in the series of *Richthefte des Oberkommandos der Wehrmacht* (guidance publications of the OKW), in 1944. See Nuremberg doc. NO-5722.

7. Heinrich Himmler, *Heinrich Himmler: Geheimreden, 1933 bis 1945, und andere Ansprachen*, ed. Bradley F. Smith and Agnes F. Peterson (Frankfurt am Main, 1974), p. 203.

8. For the full text, see Hans-Heinrich Wilhelm, "Hitlers Ansprache vor Generalen und Offizieren am 26 Mai, 1944," *Militärgeschichliche Mitteilungen* 2 (1976), pp. 123–70, here p. 136.

9. The quote was excerpted and translated in Ian Kershaw, *Hitler, 1936–45: Nemesis* (New York, 2000), pp. 636–37.

10. Krüger-Bulcke and Lehmann, *ADAP, Ser. E,* vol. 7, pp. 526ff and in particular 534.

11. Andreas Hillgruber, *Staatsmänner und Diplomaten bei Hitler: Vertrauliche Aufzeichnungen über Unterredungen mit Vertretern des Auslandes,* vol. 2 (Frankfurt am Main, 1970), p. 439.

12. Ibid.

13. Ibid., pp. 389ff.

14. Krüger-Bulcke and Lehmann, *ADAP*, Series E, vol. 7, pp. 396–97.

15. Philip Mechanicus, *Waiting for Death: A Diary* (London, 1968), p. 255.

16. Ibid.

17. Ibid.

18. Ibid., p. 256.

19. Presser, introduction to ibid.

20. For the postcard see Benjamin Leo Wessels, *Ben's Story: Holocaust Letters with Selections from the Dutch Underground Press*, ed. Kees W. Bolle (Carbondale, IL, 2001); for the date of Ben's death, see ibid., p. 9.

21. Anne Frank, *The Diary of a Young Girl: The Definitive Edition*, ed. Otto Frank and Mirjam Pressler (New York, 1995), p. 257.

22. Ibid.

23. Ibid.

24. Ibid., pp. 297–98.

25. Ibid., p. 298.

26. Ibid.

27. Moses Flinker, *Young Moshe's Diary: The Spiritual Torment of a Jewish Boy in Nazi Europe*, ed. Shaul Esh and Geoffrey Wigoder (Jerusalem, 1971), pp. 7–8.

28. Krüger-Bulcke and Lehmann, *ADAP*, Series E, vol. 7, p. 102.

29. For this ultimate surge of French collaborationism, see Philippe Burrin, *France Under the Germans: Collaboration and Compromise* (New York, 1996), pp. 448ff. and particularly 451.

30. Quoted in Renée Poznanski, *Jews in France during World War II* (Waltham, MA, 2001), p. 445.

31. Renée Poznanski, "The Jews of France and the Statutes on Jews, 1940–1941," *Yad Vashem Studies* 22 (1992), p. 462.

32. Ibid., p. 463.

33. Jacques Adler, *The Jews of Paris and the Final Solution: Communal Response and Internal Conflicts, 1940–1944* (New York, 1987), p. 159.

34. Ibid., p. 159.

35. Klarsfeld, *Vichy-Auschwitz*, vol. 2, p. 390.

36. Krüger-Bulcke and Lehmann, *ADAP, Ser. E,* vol. 7, p. 218.

37. Susan Zuccotti, *Under His Very Windows: The Vatican and the Holocaust in Italy* (New Haven, 2000), pp. 267–68. At times the Jews who attempted to flee to Switzerland were turned back by the Swiss and, at times, turned over to Germans by Italian collaborators in the border towns. The Germans did not shy away from executing the betrayed Jews on the spot. In some cases they also burned the corpses on the spot to erase all traces. See, for example, Alexander Stille, *Benevolence and Betrayal: Five Italian Jewish families under Fascism* (New York, 1993), p. 89.

38. Stille, *Benevolence and Betrayal*, p. 161.

39. Mark Mazower, *Inside Hitler's Greece: The Experience of Occupation, 1941–44* (New Haven, 1993), p. 252.

40. For these details see Götz Aly, "Die Deportation der Juden von Rhodos nach

Auschwitz," *Mittelweg 36: Zeitschrift des Hamburger Instituts für Sozialforschung* 12 (2003), pp. 83ff. Aly's argument about the "economic importance" of the booty seized from the Jews of Rhodes and Kos is unconvincing: The booty could have been seized without deporting these Jews to their death. For the further significance of this particular deportation, see also Walter Laqueur, "Auschwitz," in Michael J. Neufeld and Michael Berenbaum, eds., *The Bombing of Auschwitz: Should the Allies Have Attempted It?* (New York, 2000), pp. 189–90.

41. Berlin was well informed of the Hungarian intentions to change sides and, moreover, Hungary's raw material reserves were considered vital for the pursuit of the war. On this aspect see Christian Gerlach and Götz Aly, *Das Letzte Kapitel: Realpolitik, Ideologie und der Mord an den ungarischen Juden, 1944/1945* (Stuttgart, 2002), p. 97.

42. Goebbels, *Tagebücher*, part 2, vol. 11, 1994, pp. 397–98.

43. About the concentration and deportation from the provinces, see Randolph L. Braham, *The Politics of Genocide: The Holocaust in Hungary*, vol. 2, pp. 595ff. Farther on, both the 1981 original two-volume edition of Braham's *The Politics of Genocide* and the 2001 abridged edition will be used. The original edition is identifiable by the use of the volume number.

44. See Yehuda Bauer, *Jews for Sale? Nazi-Jewish Negotiations, 1933–1945* (New Haven, 1994), p. 157.

45. For various arguments of the controversy, see Rudolf Vrba, "Die missachtete Warnung: Betrachtungen über den Auschwitz-Bericht von 1944," in *Vierteljahrshefte für Zeitgeschichte*, vol. 44 (1996), pp. 1–24; and Yehuda Bauer, "Anmerkungen zum 'Auschwitz-Bericht' von Rudolf Vrba," in *Vierteljahrshefte für Zeitgeschichte*, vol. 2 (1997), pp. 292ff.

46. For this statement see Braham, *The Politics of Genocide*, vol. 2, p. 705.

47. See in particular Randolph L. Braham, "The Role of the Jewish Council in Hungary: A Tentative Assessment," *Yad Vashem Studies* 10 (1974), pp. 69ff. See also Braham, *The Politics of Genocide*, p. 84.

48. Both groups of Orthodox Jews and Zionist youth groups used escape over the borders as the main avenue to safety. Between 7,000 and 8,000 Jews may have succeeded in escaping Hungary to Yugoslavia, Slovakia and mainly Romania between March and September 1944. Fighting in these areas put an end to the escapes. For these details see Robert Rozett, "Jewish and Hungarian Armed Resistance in Hungary," *Yad Vashem Studies* 19 (1988), p. 270. Bauer mentions the much lower number of 4,000 to 4,500. Bauer, *Jews for Sale? Nazi-Jewish Negotiations, 1933–1945*, p. 160.

49. Braham, *The Politics of Genocide*, p. 84.

50. See Eleanore Lappin, "The Death Marches of Hungarian Jews Through Austria in the Spring of 1945," *Yad Vashem Studies* 28 (2000), p. 203.

51. For the excerpting and translating of Broad's statement, see Jeremy Noakes and Geoffrey Pridham, eds., *Nazism, 1919–1945: A Documentary Reader*, vol. 3: *Foreign Policy, War and Racial Extermination* (Exeter, UK, 1998), p. 592.

52. Paul Steinberg, *Speak You Also: A Survivor's Reckoning* (New York, 2000), pp. 97–98.

53. Rudolf Höss, *Kommandant in Auschwitz: Autobiographische Aufzeichnungen.*, ed. Martin Broszat (Stuttgart, 1958), p. 152.

54. Primo Levi, *Survival in Auschwitz: The Nazi Assault on Humanity* (1958, reprint, New York, 1996), p. 132.

55. Ibid., pp. 134–35.

56. Braham, *The Politics of Genocide*, p. 161.

57. Hillgruber, *Staatsmänner*, vol. 2, pp. 463–64.

58. Braham, *The Politics of Genocide*, p. 161.

59. For Horthy's vacillation during these weeks, see Randolph L. Braham, *The Politics of Genocide: The Holocaust in Hungary*, 2 vols. (New York, 1981), vol. 2, pp. 743ff.

60. See the exchange of documents about these late deportations in Jenö Lévai, *Eichmann in Hungary: Documents* (Budapest, 1961), pp. 128ff.

61. Nuremberg doc. NG-2263.

62. Randolph L. Braham, "Hungarian Jews," in *Anatomy of the Auschwitz Death Camp*, ed. Yisrael Gutman and Michael Berenbaum (Bloomington, 1994), p. 466.

63. Leni Yahil, *The Holocaust: The Fate of European Jewry, 1932–1945* (New York, 1990), p. 640.

64. First published in Eugene Levai, *Black Book on the Martyrdom of Hungarian Jewry* (Zurich, 1948), p. 232.

65. Braham, *The Politics of Genocide*, p. 240.

66. Michael Phayer, *The Catholic Church and the Holocaust, 1930–1965* (Bloomington, 2000), p. 90; Randolph L. Braham, "The Christian Churches of Hungary and the Holocaust," *Yad Vashem Studies 29* (2001), pp. 248–49.

67. Braham, "The Christian Churches of Hungary and the Holocaust," pp. 250ff.

68. Quoted in ibid., p. 264.

69. Phayer, *The Catholic Church*, p. 109.

70. Ibid., p. 106.

71. Quoted in Braham, "The Christian Churches of Hungary and the Holocaust," pp. 258–59.

72. For the details of these contacts, see Bauer, *Jews for Sale? Nazi-Jewish Negotiations, 1933–1945*, pp. 163ff.

73. Krüger-Bulcke and Lehmann, *ADAP*, Series E, vol. 7, p. 602.

74. Bauer mentions these arguments but appears inclined to believe that already at that time Himmler was interested in putting out genuine feelers to the West. Despite some circumstantial evidence regarding various contacts apparently initiated by the Reichsführer, the very course of the deportations from Hungary would seem massive evidence to the contrary. See Bauer, *Jews for Sale? Nazi-Jewish Negotiations, 1933–1945*, pp. 168ff.

75. Tuvia Friling, *Arrows in the Dark: David Ben-Gurion, the Yishuv Leadership, and Rescue Attempts during the Holocaust* (Madison, WI, 2005), vol. 2, pp. 7ff.

76. According to Brand's postwar declarations, Eichmann offered to liberate one hundred thousand Jews! See Bauer, *Jews for Sale? Nazi-Jewish Negotiations, 1933–1945*, p. 174.

77. Martin Gilbert, *Auschwitz and the Allies* (New York, 1981), p. 227.

78. Braham, *The Politics of Genocide*, p. 208.

79. Quoted in Tom Segev, *The Seventh Million: The Israelis and the Holocaust* (New York, 1993), p. 113.

80. Krüger-Bulcke and Lehmann, *ADAP, Ser. E,* vol. 3, p. 194.

81. Ibid., p. 222.

82. Richard Breitman, "Nazi Jewish Policy in 1944," in *Genocide and Rescue: The Holocaust in Hungary 1944*, ed. David Cesarani (New York, 1997), p. 78.

83. Helmut Heiber, *Reichsführer! Briefe an und von Himmler* (München, 1970), p. 276.

84. Bauer, *Jews for Sale? Nazi-Jewish Negotiations, 1933–1945*, pp. 196ff.

85. A sensational trial in Israel in the 1950s brought up grave accusations against Kastner and led to his assassination in Tel Aviv. A second trial before Israel's Supreme Court rehabilitated him posthumously. The core of the public issue focused on Kastner's choice of whom to include among the train's passengers.

86. Jean-Claude Favez and Geneviève Billeter, *Une Mission impossible?: Le CICR, les déportations et les camps de concentration Nazis* (Lausanne, Switzerland, 1988), p. 331. (These details are included only in the original French edition.)

87. Ibid., p. 332.

88. On this well-known deal, see in particular Raul Hilberg, *The Destruction of the European Jews*, 3 vols. (New Haven, CT, 2003) vol. 2, pp. 886–87.

89. Quoted in Neufeld and Berenbaum, eds., *The Bombing of Auschwitz: Should the Allies Have Attempted It?*, p. 250.

90. Weissmandel's letter is quoted in Lucy S. Dawidowicz, ed., *A Holocaust Reader* (New York, 1976), p. 321ff.

91. Neufeld and Berenbaum, eds., *The Bombing of Auschwitz: Should the Allies Have Attempted It?*, p. 256.

92. Ibid., pp. 258, 259.

93. Ibid.

94. Gilbert, *Auschwitz and the Allies*, p. 285.

95. Sybille Steinbacher, *Auschwitz: A History* (London, 2005), p. 109.

96. Zygmunt Klukowski, *Diary from the Years of Occupation, 1939–44*, ed. Andrew Klukowski and Helen Klukowski May (Urbana, IL, 1993), pp. 344–45.

97. Ibid., p. 345.

98. Ibid.

99. Ibid., p. 346.

100. For a powerful rendering of the Polish uprising see Norman Davies, *Rising '44: The Battle for Warsaw* (London, 2003); see also a balanced account of responsibilities East and West in Max Hastings, *Armageddon: The Battle for Germany, 1944–1945* (London, 2004), pp. 99ff.

101. Anonymous diarist quoted and excerpted in Alexandra Zapruder, *Salvaged Pages. Young Writers' Diaries of the Holocaust* (New Haven, 2002), pp. 368–96.

102. Lucjan Dobroszycki, ed., *The Chronicle of the Lódz Ghetto, 1941–1944* (New Haven, 1984), p. lxii. Sonderkommando Bothmann reactivated Chelmno in April 1944.

103. Oskar Rosenfeld, *In the Beginning Was the Ghetto: Notebooks from Lódz*, ed. Hanno Loewy (Evanston, IL, 2002), p. 281.

104. Ibid., p. 312.

105. Quoted in Zapruder, *Salvaged Pages*, pp. 393–94.

106. Introduction, Dobroszycki, *The Chronicle*, p. lxv.

107. Ibid.

108. For the statistics, see Antony Polonsky, "Beyond Condemnation, Apologetics and Apologies: On the Complexity of Polish Behavior Toward the Jews During the Second World War," in David Cesarani, ed., *Holocaust: Critical Concepts in Historical Studies*, 6 vols. (New York, 2004), p. 31.

109. For details and numbers, see mainly Dov Levin, "July 1944—The Crucial Month for the Remnants of Lithuanian Jewry," in *The Nazi Holocaust: Historical Articles on the Destruction of European Jews*, ed. Michael Marrus (Westport, CT, 1989), pp. 447ff.

110. Ibid., pp. 458–59.

111. Herman Kruk, *The Last Days of the Jerusalem of Lithuania: Chronicles from the Vilna Ghetto and the Camps, 1939–1944*, ed. Benjamin Harshav (New Haven, CT, 2002), p. 703.

112. Ibid.

113. Ibid., p. 704.

114. Ibid.

115. Ibid., p. 705.

116. Stephen G. Fritz, " 'We Are Trying to Change the Face of the World': Ideology and Motivation in the Wehrmacht on the Eastern Front: The View from Below." *Journal of the Military History* 60, A (Oct. 1996).

117. Walter Manoschek, ed., *"Es gibt nur eines für das Judentum—Vernichtung": Das Judenbild in deutschen Soldatenbriefen 1939–1944* (Hamburg, 1997), p. 73.

118. Quoted and translated in Noakes and Pridham, *Nazism*, vol. 4, pp. 632–33.

119. Manoschek, *"Es gibt nur eines für das Judentum—Vernichtung,"* p. 75.

120. Hillgruber, *Staatsmänner*, vol. 2, p. 494.

121. Ruth Bondy, *"Elder of the Jews": Jakob Edelstein of Theresienstadt* (New York, 1989), pp. 396ff. and 441–42.

122. Ibid., p. 446.

123. On Murmelstein see Jonny Moser, "Dr. Benjamin Murmelstein, ein ewig Beschuldigter?," in *Theresienstadt in der "Endlösung der Judenfrage,"* ed. Miroslav Kárný, Vojtech Blodig, and Margita Kárná (Prague, 1992), pp. 88ff.

124. See in particular Karel Margry, "Der Nazi-Film über Theresienstadt," Ibid., pp. 285ff.

125. Vojtěch Blodig, "Die letzte Phase den Entwicklung des Ghettos Theresienstadt," Ibid, p. 274.

126. See Egon Redlich, *The Terezin Diary of Gonda Redlich*, ed. Saul S. Friedman (Lexington, KY, 1992), p. 160 n. 19.

127. Aaron Kramer, "Creation in a Death Camp," in *Theatrical Performance During the Holocaust: Texts, Documents, Memoirs*, ed. Rebecca Rovit and Alvin Goldfarb (Baltimore, 1999), pp. 181–83. See also David Bloch, "Versteckte Bedeutungen: Symbole in der Musik von Theresienstadt," in *Theresienstadt in der "Endlösung der Judenfrage,"* ed. Miroslav Kárný, Vojtech Blodig, and Margita Kárná (Prague, 1992), p. 142.

128. For these estimates, see Hilberg, *The Destruction of the European Jews*, vol. 2, p. 455.

129. Redlich, *The Terezin Diary of Gonda Redlich*, p. 161.

130. Saul S. Friedman, introduction to ibid., p. xiv.

131. Martin Doerry, *My Wounded Heart: The Life of Lilli Jahn, 1900–1944* (London, 2004), pp. 250ff.

132. Livia Rothkirchen, "Slovakia" in Walter Laqueur and Judith Tydor Baumel, eds., *The Holocaust Encyclopedia* (New Haven, CT, 2001), p. 600.

133. Livia Rothkirchen, "The Situation of the Jews in Slovakia between 1939 and 1945," *Jahrbuch für Antisemitismusforschung* 7 (1998), p. 63.

134. John F. Morley, *Vatican Diplomacy and the Jews during the Holocaust, 1939–1943* (New York, 1980), pp. 73ff.

135. Braham, *The Politics of Genocide*, p. 184.

136. Quoted in Krisztián Ungváry, *The Siege of Budapest: One Hundred Days in World War II* (New Haven, CT, 2005), p. 289.

137. Ibid.

138. Ibid., p. 293.

139. Ibid., p. 294.

140. Krüger-Bulcke and Lehmann, *ADAP*, Series E, vol. 8, p. 509.

141. Ungváry, *The Siege of Budapest*, pp. 298–99.

142. Ibid., p. 300.

143. Many of the forged papers had been produced and distributed by Zionist youth groups. See Rozett, "Jewish and Hungarian Armed Resistance in Hungary," p. 272.

144. For the numbers mentioned see Ungváry, *The Siege of Budapest*, p. 293. About Carl Lutz, see Alexander Grossman, *Nur das Gewissen, Carl Lutz und seine Budapester Aktion: Geschichte und Porträt* (Wald, 1986); regarding Friedrich Born's role, see mainly Arieh Ben-Tov, *Facing the Holocaust in Budapest: The International Committee of the Red Cross and the Jews in Hungary, 1943–1945* (Geneva, 1988). There are several publications about Wallenberg's activities; See in particular Leni Yahil, "Raoul Wallenberg: His Mission and his Activities in Hungary," *Yad Vashem Studies* 15 (1983), pp. 7–54. For details about less well known helpers such as Giorgio Perlasca, see Ungváry, *The Siege of Budapest*, p. 294. Ben-Tov's study about the ICRC also gives his due to the delegate who preceded Born and was recalled because of his insistence on intervening for

the Jews of Hungary: Jean de Bavier; it offers a harsh assessment of the Geneva organization.

145. Quoted in Ungváry, *The Siege of Budapest*, p. 302.

146. Ibid.

147. Most of the details that follow and the translation of Radnóti's poem are quoted from Zsuzsanna Ozsváth, *In the Footsteps of Orpheus: The Life and Times of Miklós Radnóti* (Bloomington, 2000), pp. 212ff. About this early death march see the personal testimony of Zalman Teichman as published in Nathan Eck, "The March of Death from Serbia to Hungary (September 1944) and the Slaughter of Cservenka," *Yad Vashem Studies* 2 (1958), pp. 255ff.

148. Ozsváth, *In the Footsteps of Orpheus*, pp. 217ff.

149. Quoted in Hastings, *Armageddon: The Battle for Germany, 1944–1945*, pp. 211–12.

150. Christian Gerlach and Götz Aly, *Das letzte Kapitel: Der Mord an den ungarischen Juden* (Munich, 2002), p. 97.

151. Adolf Hitler, *Monologe im Führer-Hauptquartier 1941–1944*, ed. Werner Jochmann and Heinrich Heim (Munich, 2000), pp. 412–13.

152. Adolf Hitler, *Hitler: Reden und Proklamationen, 1932–1945: Kommentiert von einem deutschen Zeitgenossen*, ed. Max Domarus, 4 vols. (Leonberg, 1987–88), vol. 4, p. 2185.

153. Ibid., pp. 2195ff.

154. Ibid., p. 2204.

155. Ibid., p. 2206.

156. Ibid.

157. Joseph Goebbels, *Die Tagebücher von Joseph Goebbels: Sämtliche Fragmente*, ed. Elke Fröhlich (Munich, 1998–), part 2, vol. 15, p. 82.

158. Ibid., p. 316.

159. Nuremberg doc. R-124. *Nazi Conspiracy and Aggression*, vol. 8 (Washington, DC, 1946), p. 189.

160. André Sellier, *The History of the Dora Camp* (Chicago, 2003), pp. 120–21.

161. See mainly Eleanor Lappin, "The Death Marches of Hungarian Jews through Austria in the Spring of 1945," *Yad Vashem Studies* 28 (2000).

162. Edit Raim, "Zwangsarbeit und Vernichtung im letzten Kriegsjahr," in *Theresienstadt in der "Endlösung der Judenfrage,"* ed. Miroslav Kárný, Vojtěch Blodig, and Margita Kaŕná (Prague, 1992), p. 262.

163. Ibid.

164. Breitman, "Nazi Jewish Policy", pp. 84ff.

165. Ibid.

166. For details about the Swedish initiatives, see Bauer, *Jews for Sale? Nazi-Jewish Negotiations, 1933–1945*, pp. 243ff.

167. Daniel Blatman, "The Death Marches, January–May 1945: Who Was Responsible for What?," *Yad Vashem Studies* 28 (2000), p. 169.

168. Höss, *Kommandant in Auschwitz*, p. 170.

169. Blatman, "The Death Marches," p. 173.

170. Höss, *Kommandant in Auschwitz*, pp. 169–70.

171. Steinberg, *Speak You Also: A Survivor's Reckoning*, pp. 140–41.

172. Gudrun Schwarz, *Eine Frau an seiner Seite: Ehefrauen in der "SS-Sippengemeinschaft"* (Frankfurt, 1997), p. 7.

173. Blatman, "The Death Marches," p. 178.

174. Ibid., pp. 189–90.

175. Ibid., p. 191.

176. Levi, *Survival in Auschwitz: The Nazi Assault on Humanity*, p. 171.

177. Ruth Kluger, *Still Alive: A Holocaust Girlhood Remembered* (New York, 2001), pp. 113ff. and 128ff.

178. Cordelia Edvardson, *Gebranntes Kind sucht das Feuer* (Munich, 1989), pp. 100ff.

179. Filip Müller, *Eyewitness Auschwitz: Three Years in the Gas Chambers* (Chicago, 1999), pp. 166ff.

180. Ibid., p. 171.

181. Sybil Milton, "Deportations," in *1945: The Year of Liberation* (Washington, DC, 1995), p. 90.

182. Ibid. (Reproduced from Marlene P. Hiller, ed., *Stuttgart im Zweiten Weltkrieg: Katalog* [Gerlinger, 1989].), p. 181.

183. Victor Klemperer, *I Will Bear Witness: A Diary of the Nazi Years, 1942–1945* (New York, 1998), p. 404.

184. Robert Gellately, *Backing Hitler: Consent and Coercion in Nazi Germany* (Oxford, 2001), pp. 253–54.

185. Otto Dov Kulka and Eberhard Jäckel, *Die Juden in den geheimen NS-Stimmungsberichten 1933–1945* (Düsseldorf, 2004), p. 546.

186. Ibid., p. 547.

187. Quoted in Hastings, *Armageddon*, p. 435.

188. Otto Dov Kulka, "The German Population and the Jews: State of Research and New Perspectives," in *Probing the Depths of German Antisemitism: German Society and the Persecution of the Jews, 1933–1941*, ed. David Bankier (New York, 2000), p. 279.

189. See in particular Gellately, *Backing Hitler*, and Marlis G. Steinert, *Hitler's War and the Germans: Public Mood and Attitude during the Second World War*, ed. Thomas E. J. de Witt (Athens, OH, 1977).

190. Goebbels, *Tagebücher*, part 2, vol. 15, p. 586.

191. Ibid., pp. 654–55.

192. Ibid.

193. Hitler, *Reden*, pp. 2223–2224.

194. All details about this notorious murder operation are taken from Günther Schwarberg, *The Murders at Bullenhuser Damm* (Bloomington, 1984).

195. Ibid., p. 22.

196. Ibid., pp. 37–41 (excerpted in U.S. Holocaust Museum, ed., *1945*, pp. 88–89).

197. Martin Broszat, "Soziale Motivation und Führer-Bindung des Nationalsozialismus," *Vierteljahrshefte für Zeitgeschichte* 18 (1970).

198. Jeffrey Herf, *Reactionary Modernism: Technology, Culture, and Politics in Weimar and the Third Reich* (New York, 1986).

199. See mainly Norbert Frei, *1945 und Wir: das Dritte Reich im Bewusstsein der Deutschen* (Munich, 2005).

200. Hitler, *Reden*, p. 2226.

201. Ibid.

202. Ibid., p. 2250.

203. Klaus Schölder, *A Requiem for Hitler: And Other New Perspectives on the German Church Struggle* (London, 1989), p. 166.

204. Klemperer, *I Will Bear Witness: A Diary of the Nazi Years, 1942–1945*, p. 435.

205. Notwithstanding various computations, an exact estimate of the number of victims of the Holocaust is not possible. For detailed statistical analyses see Raul Hilberg, *The Destruction of the European Jews*, vol. 3, pp. 1301ff (whose estimate of 5,100,000 is on the low side) and Wolfgang Benz, ed., *Dimension des Völkermords: Die Zahl der jüdischen Opfer des Nationalsozialismus* (Munich, 1991), p. 17, whose minimal estimate reached 5,290,000 and who also calculated a maximum of just above 6,000,000 victims.

206. The places indicated are those where the diaries were mostly written; at times I chose the diarists' places of origin.

207. For these additional diarists, see Alexandra Zapruder, *Salvaged Pages* (New Haven, 2002); Robert Moses Shapiro, "Diaries and Memoirs from the Lodz Ghetto in Yiddish and Hebrew," in *Holocaust Chronicles: Individualizing the Holocaust through Diaries and Other Contemporaneous Personal Accounts*, ed. Robert Moses Shapiro (Hoboken, NJ, 1999); and Alexandra Garbarini, *Numbered Days: Diaries and the Holocaust* (New Haven, 2006).

Bibliography

Given its nature, this volume is essentially based on published documents and monographs. The only exception has been the systematic use of documents from the Archives of the NSDAP (*Akten der Parteikanzlei der NSDAP*). These documents are listed as abstracts in a series of volumes indicated below and have been retrieved on microfiches, generally available in major libraries. Here the microfiches come from the collection of the Young Research Library at UCLA.

Published Pre-1945 Documents

Foreign Relations of the United States. Washington, D.C.

German Propaganda Archive CAS Department—Calvin College, 2004. Available from www.calvin.edu/academic/cas/gpa/goeb18.htm.

Akten der Parteikanzlei der NSDAP (abstracts). Part 1, vols. 1 and 2, edited by Helmut Heiber. Munich, 1983. Part 2, vols. 3 and 4, edited by Peter Longerich. Munich, 1992.

U.S. v. Pohl: The Pohl Case. Trials of war criminals before the Nuremberg Military Tribunals under Control Council law no. 10, Nuremberg, October 1946–April, 1949. 15 vols. Vol. 5. Washington, DC, 1951.

U.S. v. Brandt: The Medical Case. Trials of war criminals before the Nuremberg Military Tribunals under Control Council law no. 10, Nuremberg, October 1946–April, 1949. 15 vols. Vol. 1. Washington, DC, 1951.

U.S. v. Flick: The Flick Case. Trials of war criminals before the Nuremberg Military Tribunals under Control Council law no. 10, Nuremberg, October 1946–April, 1949. 15 vols. Vol. 6. Washington, DC, 1952.

U.S. v. von Weizsaecker: The Ministries Case. Trials of war criminals before the Nuremberg Military Tribunals. 15 vols. Vol. 13. Washington, DC, 1952.

I documenti diplomatici italiani. Nona serie: 1939–1943. 10 vols. Rome, edited by Commissione per la pubblicazione dei documenti diplomatici, 1954–1990.

Documents on German Foreign Policy. Series D, 1937–1945. Washington, DC, 1956.

Akten zur deutschen auswärtigen Politik, 1918–1945. Ser. E: 1941–1945.

Göttingen, edited by Ingrid Krüger-Bulcke and Hans Georg Lehmann., 1969.

Arad, Yitzhak, Yisrael Gutman and Abraham Margaliot, eds. *Documents on the Holocaust: Selected Sources on the Destruction of the Jews of Germany and Austria, Poland, and the Soviet Union.* Jerusalem, 1981.

Benz, Wolfgang, Konrad Kwiet and Jürgen Matthäus. *Einsatz im "Reichskommissariat Ostland": Dokumente zum Völkermord im Baltikum und in Weissrussland, 1941–1944.* Berlin, 1998.

Berenstein, Tatiana, ed. *Faschismus, Getto, Massenmord: Dokumentation über Ausrottung und Widerstand der Juden in Polen während des zweiten Weltkrieges.* Berlin (East), 1961.

Blet, Pierre, Angelo Martini, and Burkhart Schneider, eds. *Actes et documents du Saint Siège relatifs à la Seconde Guerre mondiale. Volume 8: Le Saint Siège et les Victimes de la Guerre, Janvier 1941–Décembre 1942.* Vatican City, 1968.

Boberach, Heinz, ed. *Berichte des SD und der Gestapo über Kirchen und Kirchenvolk in Deutschland 1934–1944.* Mainz, 1971.

———, ed. *Meldungen aus dem Reich, 1938–1945: Die geheimen Lageberichte des Sicherheitsdienstes der SS.* 17 vols. Herrsching, 1984.

Boelcke, Willi A., ed. *Wollt Ihr den totalen Krieg? Die geheimen Goebbels Konferenzen 1939–1943.* Herrsching, 1989.

Büchler, Yehoshua. "A Preparatory Document for the Wannsee Conference." *Holocaust and Genocide Studies* 9 no. 1 (1995).

Dawidowicz, Lucy S., ed. *A Holocaust Reader.* New York, 1976.

Eichmann, Adolf. *The Trial of Adolf Eichmann: Record of Proceedings in the District Court of Jerusalem.* 9 vols. Jerusalem, 1992.

Frei, Norbert, ed. *Standort- und Kommandanturbefehle des Konzentrationslagers Auschwitz 1940–1945.* Munich, 2000.

Friedlander, Henry and Sybil Milton, eds. *Archives of the Holocaust: An International Collection of Selected Documents.* 22 vols. New York, 1989.

Heiber, Helmut. "Aus den Akten des Gauleiters Kube." *Viertelsjahrhefte für Zeitgeschichte.* 4 (1956).

Hilberg, Raul, ed. *Documents of Destruction: Germany and Jewry, 1933–1945.* Chicago, 1971.

International Military Tribunal. *Trial of the Major War Criminals Before the International Military Tribunal, Nuremberg, 14 November 1945–1 October 1946.* 42 vols. New York, 1971.

Kaden, Helma, Ludwig Nestler, Kurt Frotscher, Sonja Kleinschmidt and Brigitte Wölk, eds. *Dokumente des Verbrechens: Aus Akten des Dritten Reiches, 1933–1945*. Berlin, 1993.

Kárný, Miroslav, Jaroslava Milotová and Margita Kárná, eds. *Deutsche Politik im "Protektorat Böhmen und Mähren" unter Reinhard Heydrich 1941–1942: Eine Dokumentation*. Nationalsozialistische Besatzungspolitik in Europa 1939–1945, Vol. 2. Berlin, 1997.

Klarsfeld, Serge, ed. *Die Endlösung der Judenfrage in Frankreich: Deutsche Dokumente 1941–1944*. Paris, 1977.

Klee, Ernst, Willi Dressen and Volker Riess, eds. *"The Good Old Days": The Holocaust as Seen by Its Perpetrators and Bystanders*. New York, 1991.

Kogon, Eugen, Hermann Langbein and Adalbert Rückerl, eds. *Nazi Mass Murder: A Documentary History of the Use of Poison Gas*. New Haven, 1993.

Krausnick, Helmut, ed. "Denkschrift Himmlers über die Behandlung der Fremdvölkischen im Osten." *Vierteljahrshefte für Zeitgeschichte* 5, no. 2 (1957).

Kulka, Otto Dov and Eberhard Jäckel. *Die Juden in den geheimen NS-Stimmungsberichten 1933–1945*. Düsseldorf, 2004.

Levai, Eugene. *Black Book on the Martyrdom of Hungarian Jewry*. Zurich, 1948.

Lévai, Jenö. *Eichmann in Hungary: Documents*. Budapest, 1961.

Longerich, Peter and Dieter Pohl, eds. *Die Ermordung der europäischen Juden: Eine umfassende Dokumentation des Holocaust 1941–1945*. Munich, 1989.

Mendelsohn, John, and Donald S. Detwiler, eds. *The Holocaust: Selected Documents in Eighteen Volumes*. New York, 1982.

Milton, Sybil, ed. *The Stroop Report*. New York, 1979.

Milton, Sybil, and Frederick D. Bogin, eds. *Archives of the Holocaust*. Vol. 10, Parts 1 and 2. New York, 1995.

Noakes, Jeremy, and Geoffrey Pridham, eds. *Nazism, 1919–1945: A Documentary Reader. Volume 3: Foreign Policy, War and Racial Extermination*. Exeter, UK, 1998.

Pätzold, Kurt, ed. *Verfolgung, Vertreibung, Vernichtung: Dokumente des faschistischen Antisemitismus 1933 bis 1942*. Frankfurt am Main, 1984.

Pätzold, Kurt and Erika Schwarz, eds. *Tagesordnung Judenmord: Die*

Wannsee-Konferenz am 20. Januar 1942: Eine Dokumentation zur Organisation der "Endlösung." Berlin, 1992.

Peck, Abraham J., ed. *Archives of the Holocaust.* Vol. 8. New York, 1990.

Poliakov, Léon and Josef Wulf. *Das Dritte Reich und seine Denker. Dokumente.* Berlin, 1959.

Sauer, Paul, ed. *Dokumente über die Verfolgung der jüdischen Bürger in Baden-Württemberg durch das nationalsozialistische Regime 1933–1945.* 2 vols. Stuttgart, 1966.

Schneider, Burkhart, Pierre Blet, and Angelo Martini, eds. *Die Briefe Pius' XII. an die deutschen Bischöfe 1939–1944.* Mainz, 1966.

U.S. Office of Chief of Counsel for the Prosecution of Axis Criminality and International Military Tribunal. *Nazi Conspiracy and Aggression.* 8 vols. Washington, DC, 1946.

Volk, Ludwig, ed. *Akten Kardinal Michael von Faulhaber.* Vol. 2: *1935–1945.* Mainz, 1978.

———. *Akten deutscher Bischöfe über die Lage der Kirche, 1933–1945.* 6 vols. Vol. 5 (1940–1942). Mainz, 1983.

———. *Akten deutscher Bischöfe über die Lage der Kirche, 1933–1945.* 6 vols. Vol. 6 (1943–1945). Mainz, 1985.

Walk, Joseph, ed. *Das Sonderrecht für die Juden im NS-Staat: Eine Sammlung der gesetzlichen Massnahmen und Richtlinien, Inhalt und Bedeutung.* Heidelberg, 1981.

Witte, Peter and Stephen Tyas. "A New Document on the Deportation and Murder of Jews during "Einsatz Reinhardt 1942"." *Holocaust and Genocide Studies* 15, no. 3 (2001).

Wulf, Josef, ed. *Literatur und Dichtung im Dritten Reich: Eine Dokumentation.* Gütersloh, 1963.

———, ed. *Presse und Funk im Dritten Reich: Eine Dokumentation.* Gütersloh, 1964.

———, ed. *Theater und Film im Dritten Reich: Eine Dokumentation.* Frankfurt am Main, 1989.

Wyman, David S., ed. *America and the Holocaust: A Thirteen-Volume Set Documenting the Editor's Book The Abandonment of the Jews.* 13 vols. New York, 1989–1991.

Speeches, Letters, Diaries and Other Pre-1945 Literature

"Das Kriegsziel Roosevelts und der Juden: Völlige Ausrottung des deutschen Volkes. Ungeheuriges jüdisches Vernichtungsprogram nach den Richtlinien Roosevelts." *Völkischer Beobachter*, July 24, 1941.

"Roosevelt, Hauptwerkzeug der jüdischen Freimaurerei." *Völkischer Beobachter*, July 23, 1941.

Adelson, Alan and Robert Lapides, eds. *Lodz Ghetto: Inside a Community Under Siege*. New York, 1989.

Andreas-Friedrich, Ruth and June Barrows Mussey. *Berlin Underground, 1938–1945*. New York, 1947.

Benjamin, Walter. *Briefe*. Edited by Gershom Scholem and Theodor Adorno. Vol. 2. Frankfurt, 1978.

Benz, Wolfgang. *Patriot und Paria: Das Leben des Erwin Goldmann zwischen Judentum und Nationalsozialismus: eine Dokumentation*. Berlin, 1997.

Berg, Mary. *Warsaw Ghetto, A Diary*. Edited by Sh. L. Shnayderman. New York, 1945.

Biélinky, Jacques. *Journal, 1940–1942: Un journaliste juif à Paris sous l'Occupation*. Edited by Renée Poznanski. Paris, 1992.

Buchbender, Ortwin and Reinhold Sterz, eds. *Das Andere Gesicht des Krieges. Deutsche Feldpostbriefe 1939–1945*. Munich, 1982.

Ciano, Galeazzo. *Diary 1937–1943: The Complete Unabridged Diaries of Count Galeazzo Ciano, Italian Minister for Foreign Affairs, 1936–1943*. London, 2002.

Cohn, Willy. *Als Jude in Breslau 1941*. Edited by Joseph Walk. Gerlingen, 1984.

Czerniaków, Adam. *The Warsaw Diary of Adam Czerniaków*. Edited by Raul Hilberg, Stanislaw Staron and Josef Kermisz. New York, 1979.

Dietrich, Otto. *Auf den Strassen des Sieges: Erlebnisse mit dem Führer in Polen: Ein Gemeinschaftsbuch*. Munich, 1939.

Dobroszycki, Lucjan, ed. *The Chronicle of the Lódz Ghetto, 1941–1944*. New Haven, 1984.

Drieu La Rochelle, Pierre. *Journal, 1939–1945*. Edited by Julien Hervier. Paris, 1992.

Dürkefälden, Karl. *Schreiben, wie es wirklich war . . . : Aufzeichnungen Karl*

Dürkefäldens aus den Jahren 1933–1945. Edited by Herbert Obenaus and Sibylle Obenaus. Hannover, 1985.

Eiber, Ludwig. "...'Ein bischen die Wahrheit': Briefe eines Bremer Kaufmanns von seinem Einsatz beim Reserve-Polizeibataillon 105 in der Sowjetunion 1941," *1999: Zeitschrift für Sozialgeschichte des 20. und 21. Jahrhunderts* 6, no. 1 (1991).

Fabre-Luce, Alfred. *Journal de la France 1939–1944*. Vol. 1. Geneva, 1946.

Feiner, Hertha. *Before Deportation: Letters from a Mother to Her Daughters, January 1939–December 1942*. Edited by Karl Heinz Jahnke. Evanston, 1999.

Feuchtwanger, Lion. *The Devil in France, My Encounter with Him in the Summer of 1940*. New York, 1941.

Flinker, Moses. *Young Moshe's Diary: The Spiritual Torment of a Jewish Boy in Nazi Europe*. Edited by Shaul Esh and Geoffrey Wigoder. Jerusalem, 1971.

Frank, Anne. *The Diary of a Young Girl: The Definitive Edition*. Edited by Otto Frank and Mirjam Pressler. New York, 1995.

Frank, Hans. *Das Diensttagebuch des deutschen Generalgouverneurs in Polen 1939–1945*. Edited by Werner Präg and Wolfgang Jacobmeyer. Stuttgart, 1975.

Galen, Bischof Clemens August Graf von. *Akten, Briefe und Predigten*. Edited by Peter Löffler. Vol. 2 (1939–1946). Mainz, 1988.

Goebbels, Joseph. *Das eherne Herz: Reden und Aufsätze aus den Jahren 1941/42*. Edited by Moritz Augustus Konstantin von Schirmeister. Munich, 1943.

———. *Die Zeit ohne Beispiel: Reden und Aufsätze aus den Jahren 1939/40/41*. Munich, 1941.

———. *Die Tagebücher von Joseph Goebbels*. Edited by Elke Fröhlich. Munich, 1998.

Groscurth, Helmuth. *Tagebücher eines Abwehroffiziers 1938–1940: Mit weiteren Dokumenten zur Militäropposition gegen Hitler*. Edited by Helmut Krausnick and Harold C. Deutsch. Stuttgart, 1970.

Guéhenno, Jean. *Journal des années noires, 1940–1944*. Paris, 1947.

Halder, Franz. *Kriegstagebuch: Tägliche Aufzeichnungen des Chefs des Generalstabes des Heeres, 1939–1942*. Edited by Hans Adolf Jacobsen. Stuttgart, 1962–1964.

Hassell, Ulrich von. *Die Hassell-Tagebücher 1938–1944: Aufzeichnungen vom Andern Deutschland.* Edited by Klaus Peter Reiss and Freiherr Friedrich Hiller von Gaertringen. Berlin, 1988.

Heiber, Helmut. *Reichsführer! Briefe an und von Himmler.* Munich, 1970.

Hillesum, Etty. *An Interrupted Life: The Diaries of Etty Hillesum, 1941–1943.* New York, 1983.

———. *Letters from Westerbork.* New York, 1986.

Himmler, Heinrich. *Der Dienstkalender Heinrich Himmlers 1941/42.* Edited by Peter Witte et al. Hamburg, 1999.

———. *Heinrich Himmler: Geheimreden, 1933 bis 1945, und andere Ansprachen.* Edited by Bradley F. Smith and Agnes F. Peterson. Frankfurt am Main, 1974.

Hitler, Adolf. *Hitler and His Generals: Military Conferences 1942–1945: The First Complete Stenographic Record of the Military Situation Conferences, From Stalingrad to Berlin.* Edited by Helmut Heiber and David M. Glantz. London, 2002.

———. *Hitler: Reden und Proklamationen, 1932–1945: Kommentiert von einem deutschen Zeitgenossen.* Edited by Max Domarus. 4 vols. Leonberg, 1987–1988.

———. *Hitler's Second Book: The Unpublished Sequel to Mein Kampf.* Edited by Gerhard L. Weinberg. New York, 2003.

———. *Hitler's Table Talk, 1941–1944.* Edited by H. R. Trevor-Roper. London, 1953.

———. *Hitlers Tischgespräche im Führerhauptquartier 1941–1942.* Edited by Henry Picker. Stuttgart, 1965.

———. *Monologe im Führer-Hauptquartier 1941–1944.* Edited by Werner Jochmann and Heinrich Heim. Hamburg, 1980.

———. *Staatsmänner und Diplomaten bei Hitler: Vertrauliche Aufzeichnungen über Unterredungen mit Vertretern des Auslandes.* Edited by Andreas Hillgruber. 2 vols. Frankfurt am Main, 1967–1970.

Hosenfeld, Wilm. "Extracts from the Diary of Captain Wilm Hosenfeld." In Wladyslaw Szpilman, *The Pianist: The Extraordinary Story of One Man's Survival in Warsaw, 1939–45.* New York, 1999.

Huberband, Shimon. "The Destruction of the Synagogues in Lodz." In *Lodz Ghetto. Inside a Community under Siege,* edited by Alan Adelson and Robert Lapides. New York, 1983.

———. "Kiddush Hashem: Jewish Religious and Cultural Life in Poland during the Holocaust." Edited by Jeffrey S. Gurock and Robert S. Hirt. New York, 1987.

Jacobson, Louise and Nadia Kaluski-Jacobson. *Les Lettres de Louise Jacobson et de ses proches: Fresnes, Drancy, 1942–1943*. Paris, 1997.

Kalmanovitch, Zelig. *Diary in the Vilna Ghetto* [in Hebrew]. Tel Aviv, 1977.

Kaplan, Chaim Aron. *Scroll of Agony: The Warsaw Diary of Chaim A. Kaplan*. Edited by Abraham I. Katsh. Bloomington, 1999.

Kermish, Joseph, ed. *To Live with Honor and Die with Honor! . . . : Selected Documents from the Warsaw Ghetto Underground Archives "O.S." ("Oneg Shabbath")*. Jerusalem, 1986.

Klemperer, Victor. *I Will Bear Witness: A Diary of the Nazi Years, 1933–41*. New York, 1998.

———. *I Will Bear Witness: A Diary of the Nazi Years 1942–1945*. New York, 1999.

Klepper, Jochen. *Unter dem Schatten Deiner Flügel. Aus den Tagebüchern der Jahre 1932–1942*. Edited by Hildegard Klepper. Stuttgart, 1956.

Klonicki, Aryeh and Malwina Klonicki. *The Diary of Adam's Father: The Diary of Aryeh Klonicki (Klonymus) and His Wife Malwina, With Letters Concerning the Fate of Their Child Adam*. Jerusalem, 1973.

Klukowski, Zygmunt. *Diary from the Years of Occupation, 1939–44*. Edited by Andrew Klukowski and Helen Klukowski May. Urbana, IL, 1993.

Korczak, Janusz. *Ghetto Diary*. Edited by Aaron Zeitlin. New York, 1978.

———. *Tagebuch aus dem Warschauer Ghetto 1942*. Gottingen, 1992.

Kruk, Herman. *The Last Days of the Jerusalem of Lithuania: Chronicles from the Vilna Ghetto and the Camps, 1939–1944*. Edited by Benjamin Harshav. New Haven, 2002.

Lambert, Raymond-Raoul. *Carnet d'un témoin: 1940–1943*. Edited by Richard I. Cohen. Paris, 1985.

Langer, Lawrence L., ed. *Art from the Ashes: A Holocaust Anthology*. New York, 1995.

Lewin, Abraham. *A Cup of Tears: A Diary of the Warsaw Ghetto*. Edited by Antony Polonsky. Oxford, 1988.

Löffler, Klara. *Aufgehoben: Soldatenbriefe aus dem Zweiten Weltkrieg*. Bamberg, 1992.

Manoschek, Walter, ed. *"Es gibt nur eines für das Judentum—Vernichtung": Das Judenbild in deutschen Soldatenbriefen 1939–1944*. Hamburg, 1997.

Mechanicus, Philip. *Waiting for Death: A Diary*. London, 1968.

Moltke, Helmuth James von. *Letters to Freya: 1939–1945*. Edited by Beate Ruhm von Oppen. New York, 1990.

Mounier, Emmanuel. "A Letter from France." *The Commonweal*, October 25, 1940.

Perechodnik, Calel. *Am I a Murderer?: Testament of a Jewish Ghetto Policeman*. Edited by Frank Fox. Boulder, CO, 1996.

Rebatet, Lucien. *Les Décombres*. Paris, 1942.

Redlich, Egon. *The Terezin Diary of Gonda Redlich*. Edited by Saul S. Friedman. Lexington, KY, 1992.

Ringelblum, Emanuel. *Notes from the Warsaw Ghetto: The Journal of Emanuel Ringelblum*. Edited by Jacob Sloan. New York, 1974.

Rosenberg, Alfred. *Das politische Tagebuch Alfred Rosenbergs, 1934/35 und 1939/40*. Edited by Hans Günther Seraphim. Munich, 1964.

Rosenfeld, Oskar. *In the Beginning Was the Ghetto: Notebooks from Lódz*. Edited by Hanno Loewy. Evanston, IL, 2002.

Rubinowicz, Dawid. *The Diary of Dawid Rubinowicz*. Edmonds, WA, 1982.

Rudashevski, Isaac. *The Diary of the Vilna Ghetto, June 1941–April 1943*. Edited by Percy Matenko. Tel Aviv, 1973.

Sebastian, Mihail. *Journal, 1935–1944*. Chicago, 2000.

Seidman, Hillel. *The Warsaw Ghetto Diaries*. Southfield, 1997.

Shirer, William L. *Berlin Diary: The Journal of a Foreign Correspondent, 1934–1941*. Boston, 1988 (1941).

Sierakowiak, Dawid. *The Diary of Dawid Sierakowiak*. Edited by Alan Adelson. New York, 1996.

SS-Hauptamt. *Der Untermensch*. Berlin, 1942.

Tory, Avraham. *Surviving the Holocaust: The Kovno Ghetto Diary*. Edited by Martin Gilbert and Dina Porat. Cambridge, 1990.

Wasser, Hersh. "Daily Entries of Hersh Wasser." *Yad Vashem Studies* 15 (1983).

Wessels, Benjamin Leo. *Ben's Story: Holocaust Letters with Selections from the Dutch Underground Press*. Edited by Kees W. Bolle. Carbondale, 2001.

Zapruder, Alexandra. *Salvaged Pages. Young Writers' Diaries of the Holocaust*. New Haven, 2002.

Zariz, Ruth, ed. *Mikhtave halutsim mi-Polin ha-kevushah, 1940–1944. [Letters of Halutzim from Occupied Poland, 1940–1944]*. Ramat Ef'al, 1994.

Zelkowicz, Jozef. *In Those Terrible Days: Writings from the Lodz Ghetto*. Edited by Michal Unger. Jerusalem, 2002.

Post-1945 Memoirs and Studies

Abella, Irving M. and Harold Martin Troper. *None Is Too Many: Canada and the Jews of Europe, 1933–1948*. Toronto, 1982.

Abramowicz, Dina. *Guardians of a Tragic Heritage: Reminiscences and Observations of an Eyewitness*. New York, 1999.

Adam, Uwe Dietrich. *Judenpolitik im Dritten Reich*. Düsseldorf, 1972.

Adler, H. G. *Theresienstadt, 1941–1945: Das Antlitz einer Zwangsgemeinschaft. Geschichte, Soziologie, Psychologie*. Tübingen, 1960.

———. *Der verwaltete Mensch: Studien zur Deportation der Juden aus Deutschland*. Tübingen, 1974.

Adler, Jacques. *The Jews of Paris and the Final Solution: Communal Response and Internal Conflicts, 1940–1944*. New York, 1987.

Adler-Rudel, Salomon. *Jüdische Selbsthilfe unter dem Naziregime 1933–1939, im Spiegel der Berichte der Reichsvertretung der Juden in Deutschland*. Tübingen, 1974.

Ahren, Yizhak, Stig Hornshøj-Møller and Christoph B. Melchers. *Der ewige Jude: Wie Goebbels hetzte: Untersuchungen zum nationalsozialistischen Propagandafilm*. Aachen, 1990.

Alfonso, Rui. "Le 'Wallenberg Portugais': Aristides de Sousa Mendes." *Revue d'Histoire de la Shoah. Le monde juif* 165 (1999).

Allen, Michael Thad. *The Business of Genocide: The SS, Slave Labor and the Concentration Camps*. Chapel Hill, 2002.

———. "The Devil in the Details: The Gas Chambers of Birkenau, October 1941." *Holocaust and Genocide Studies* 16, no. 2 (2002).

Almog, Shmuel. "Alfred Nossig: A Reappraisal." *Studies in Zionism* 7 (1983).

Altschuler, Mordechai. *Soviet Jewry on the Eve of the Holocaust: A Social and Demographic Profile*. Jerusalem, 1998.

Aly, Götz, ed. *Aktion T4, 1939–1945: Die "Euthanasie"—Zentrale in der Tiergartenstrasse 4*. Berlin, 1987.

———, and Susanne Heim. *Architects of Annihilation: Auschwitz and the Logic of Destruction*. Princeton, NJ, 2002.

———. "Arisierung. Enteignung: Was geschah mit den Besitztumern der ermodeten Juden Europas? Zur Ökonomie der Nazis." *Die Zeit* 47 (2002).

———, Peter Chroust, and Christian Pross, eds. *Cleansing the Fatherland: Nazi Medicine and Racial Hygiene*. Baltimore, 1994.

———. "Die Deportation der Juden von Rhodos nach Auschwitz." *Mittelweg 36: Zeitschrift des Hamburger Instituts für Sozialforschung* 12 (2003).

———. *'Final Solution': Nazi Population Policy and the Murder of the European Jews*. New York, 1999.

———. *Hitlers Volksstaat: Raub, Rassenkrieg und nationaler Sozialismus*. Frankfurt, 2005.

———. *Im Tunnel: Das kurze Leben der Marion Samuel 1931–1943*. Frankfurt am Main, 2004.

———. " 'Jewish Resettlement': Reflections on the Political Prehistory of the Holocaust." In *National Socialist Extermination Policies: Contemporary German Perspectives and Controversies*, edited by Ulrich Herbert. New York, 2000.

———. *Macht-Geist-Wahn: Kontinuitäten deutschen Denkens*. Berlin, 1997.

———. "Theodor Schieder, Werner Conze oder die Vorstufen der physischen Vernichtung." In *Deutsche Historiker im Nationalsozialismus*, edited by Winfried Schulze and Otto Gerhard Oexle. Frankfurt, 1999.

Ancel, Jean. "The 'Christian' Regimes of Romania and the Jews, 1940–1942." *Holocaust and Genocide Studies* 7, no. 1 (1993).

———. "The Romanian Way of Solving the Jewish Problem in Bessarabia and Bukovina, June-July 1941." *Yad Vashem Studies* 19 (1988).

Angrick, Andrej. *Besatzungspolitik und Massenmord. Die Einsatzgruppe D in der Südlichen Sowjetunion 1941–1943*. Hamburg, 2003.

Anissimov, Myriam. *Primo Levi: Tragedy of an Optimist*. Woodstock, NY, 2000.

Apostolou, Andrew. "The Exception of Salonika: Bystanders and Collaborators in Northern Greece." *Holocaust and Genocide Studies* 14, no. 2 (Fall 2000).

Arad, Yitzhak. *Belzec, Sobibor, Treblinka: The Operation Reinhard Death Camps*. Bloomington, 1987.

———. *Ghetto in Flames: The Struggle and Destruction of the Jews in Vilna in the Holocaust*. Jerusalem, 1980.

———. "Plunder of Jewish Property in the Nazi Occupied Areas of the Soviet Union." *Yad Vashem Studies* 29 (2001).

Arendt, Hannah. *Eichmann in Jerusalem. A Report on the Banality of Evil.* New York, 1963.

———. *The Jew as Pariah: Jewish Identity and Politics in the Modern Age.* Edited by Ron H. Feldman. New York, 1978.

Arens, Moshe. "The Jewish Military Organization (ZZW) in the Warsaw Ghetto." *Holocaust and Genocide Studies* 19, no. 2 (2005).

———. "The Warsaw Ghetto Revolt: The Narrative." Unpublished Manuscript.

Arndt, Ino and Heinz Boberach. "Deutsches Reich." In *Dimension des Völkermords: Die Zahl der jüdischen Opfer des Nationalsozialismus*, edited by Wolfgang Benz. Munich, 1991.

Aronson, Shlomo. *Hitler, the Allies and the Jews.* Cambridge, UK, 2004.

Aschheim, Steven E. *Brothers and Strangers: The East European Jew in German and German Jewish Consciousness, 1800–1923.* Madison, 1982.

Assouline, Pierre. *Gaston Gallimard: A Half-Century of French Publishing.* San Diego, 1988.

Avni, Haim. *Spain, the Jews, and Franco.* Philadelphia, 1982.

Ayalon, Moshe. "Jewish Life in Breslau, 1938–1941." *Leo Baeck Institute Yearbook.* (1996).

Azéma, Jean-Pierre. *De Munich à la Libération.* Paris, 1979.

Bajohr, Frank. *"Arisierung" in Hamburg: Die Verdrängung der jüdischen Unternehmer 1933–1945.* Hamburg, 1997.

———. "The Beneficiaries of "Aryanization": Hamburg as a Case Study." *Yad Vashem Studies* 26 (1998).

———. *Parvenüs und Profiteure: Korruption in der NS-Zeit.* Frankfurt am Main, 2001.

Bankier, David. *The Germans and the Final Solution: Public Opinion under Nazism.* Oxford, 1992.

———, ed. *Probing the Depths of German Antisemitism: German Society and the Persecution of the Jews, 1933–1941.* New York, 2000.

———. "The Use of Antisemitism in Nazi Wartime Propaganda." In *The Holocaust and History: The Known, the Unknown, the Disputed and the Reexamined*, edited by Michael Berenbaum and Abraham J. Peck. Bloomington, 1998.

Barkai, Avraham. "Between East and West: Jews from Germany in the Lodz Ghetto." In *The Nazi Holocaust: Historical Articles on the Destruction of European Jews*, edited by Michael R. Marrus. Westport, CT, 1989.

———. *From Boycott to Annihilation: The Economic Struggle of German Jews, 1933–1943*. Hanover, NH, 1989.

Barnes, Kenneth C. "Dietrich Bonhoeffer and Hitler's Persecution of the Jews." In *Betrayal: German Churches and the Holocaust*, edited by Robert P. Ericksen and Susannah Heschel. Minneapolis, 1999.

Bartoszewski, Wladislaw. "The Martyrdom And Struggle of the Jews in Warsaw Under German Occupation 1939–1943." In *The Jews in Warsaw. A History*, edited by Wladislaw T. Bartoszewski and Antony Polonsky. Oxford, 1991.

Bartov, Omer. "The Conduct of War: Soldiers and the Barbarization of Warfare." In *Resistance against the Third Reich, 1933–1990*, edited by Michael Geyer and John W. Boyer. Chicago, 1994.

———. *Hitler's Army: Soldiers, Nazis, and War in the Third Reich*. New York, 1991.

Baudot, Marcel. "Les Mouvements de Résistance devant la persécution des juifs." In *La France et la question juive: 1940–1944*, edited by Georges Wellers, André Kaspi and Serge Klarsfeld. Paris, 1981.

Bauer, Yehuda. *American Jewry and the Holocaust: The American Jewish Joint Distribution Committee, 1939–1945*. Detroit, 1981.

———. "Anmerkungen zum 'Auschwitz-Bericht' von Rudolf Vrba." *Vierteljahrshefte für Zeitgeschichte* 2 (1997).

———. *Jews for Sale? Nazi-Jewish Negotiations, 1933–1945*. New Haven, 1994.

———. *Rethinking the Holocaust*. New Haven, 2001.

Bauer, Yehuda, and Nili Keren. *A History of the Holocaust*. New York, 1982.

Bauman, Zygmunt. *Modernity and the Holocaust*. New Haven, 2001.

Baumann, Ursula. "Suizid im Dritten Reich—Facetten eines Themas." In *Geschichte und Emanzipation*, edited by Reinhard Rürup, Michael Grüttner, Rüdiger Hachtmann and Heinz-Gerhard Haupt. Frankfurt am Main, 1999.

Bazyler, Michael J. *Holocaust Justice: The Battle for Restitution in America's Courts*. New York, 2003.

Bédarida, François, and Renée Bédarida. "La Persécution des Juifs." In

La France des années noires, 2 vols, vol. 2: De l'occupation à la libération, edited by Jean-Pierre Azéma and François Bédarida. Paris, 1993.

Bédarida, Renée. *Les Catholiques dans la guerre, 1939–1945: Entre Vichy et la Résistance*. Paris, 1998.

———. *Pierre Chaillet: témoin de la résistance spirituelle*. Paris, 1988.

Behringer, Wolfgang. "Der Abwickler." In *Himmlers Hexenkartothek: Das Interesse des Nationalsozialismus an der Hexenverfolgung*, edited by Sönke Lorenz et. al. Bielefeld, 2000.

Beinfeld, Solon. "The Cultural Life of the Vilna Ghetto." *Simon Wiesenthal Center Yearbook*. 1 (1984).

———. "Health Care in the Vilna Ghetto." *Holocaust and Genocide Studies* 12, no. 1 (1998).

Belot, Robert. "Lucien Rebatet, ou L'Antisémitisme comme événement littéraire." In *L'Antisémitisme de plume, 1940–1944: Études et documents*, edited by Pierre-André Taguieff. Paris, 1999.

———. *Lucien Rebatet: Un itinéraire fasciste*. Paris, 1994.

Ben-Sasson, Havi. "Christians in the Ghetto: All Saints' Church, Birth of the Holy Virgin Mary Church, and the Jews of the Warsaw Ghetto." *Yad Vashem Studies* 31 (2003).

Ben-Tov, Arieh. *Facing the Holocaust in Budapest: The International Committee of the Red Cross and the Jews in Hungary, 1943–1945*. Geneva, 1988.

Bender, Sara. *Facing Death: The Jews of Bialystok 1939–1943*. Tel Aviv, 1997.

Benz, Wolfgang. ed. *Dimension des Völkermords: Die Zahl der jüdischen Opfer des Nationalsozialismus*. Munich, 1991.

———, "Judenvernichtung aus Notwehr? Die Legenden um Theodore N. Kaufman." *Vierteljahrshefte für Zeitgeschichte* 29 (1981).

———. "The Persecution and Extermination of the Jews in German Consciousness." In *Why Germany?: National Socialist Anti-Semitism and the European Context*, edited by John Milfull. Providence, RI, 1993.

Benz, Wolfgang, Hermann Graml, and Hermann Weiss, eds. *Enzyklopädie des Nationalsozialismus*. Stuttgart, 1997.

Berend, Ivan T. *Decades of Crisis: Central and Eastern Europe before World War II*. Berkeley, 1998.

Berg, A. Scott. *Lindbergh*. New York, 1998.

Bergen, Doris L. "Catholics, Protestants and Christian Antisemitism in

Nazi Germany." In *Holocaust: Critical Concepts in Historical Studies*, edited by David Cesarani. New York, 2004.

———. *Twisted Cross: The German Christian Movement in the Third Reich*. Chapel Hill, 1996.

Berkhoff, Karel C. *Harvest of Despair: Life and Death in Ukraine under Nazi Rule*. Cambridge, MA, 2004.

Billig, Joseph. *L'Institut d'étude des questions Juives*. Paris, 1974.

Birn, Ruth Bettina. *Die höheren SS- und Polizeiführer: Himmlers Vertreter im Reich und in den besetzten Gebieten*. Düsseldorf, 1986.

Birnbaum, Pierre. *Anti-semitism in France: A Political History from Léon Blum to the Present*. Oxford, 1992.

———. *Prier pour l'État: Les juifs, l'alliance royale et la démocratie*. Paris, 2005.

Black, Peter R. *Ernst Kaltenbrunner: Ideological Soldier of the Third Reich*. Princeton, 1984.

———. "Rehearsal for 'Reinhard'? Odilo Globocnik and the Lublin *Selbstschutz*." *Central European History* 25, no. 2 (1992).

Blasius, Rainer. "Bis in die Rolle gefärbt: Zwei Tagungen zum Einfluβ von Hans Rothfels auf die deutsche Zeitgeschichtsschreibung." *Frankfurter Allgemeine Zeitung*, July 19, 2003.

Blatman, Daniel. "The Death Marches, January-May 1945: Who Was Responsible for What?" *Yad Vashem Studies* 28 (2000).

———. *Notre liberté et la vôtre: Le mouvement ouvrier juif Bund en Pologne, 1939–1949*. Paris, 2002.

Blet, Pierre, *Pius XII and the Second World War*. New York, 1999.

Bloch, David. "Versteckte Bedeutungen: Symbole in der Musik von Theresienstadt." In *Theresienstadt in der "Endlösung der Judenfrage,"* edited by Miroslav Kárný, Vojtěch Blodig and Margita Kárná. Praha, 1992.

Blom, J. C. H. "The Persecution of the Jews in the Netherlands: A Comparative Western European Perspective." *European History Quarterly* 19, no. 3 (July 1989).

Blonski, Jan. "Polish-Catholics and Catholic Poles: The Gospel, National Interest, Civic Solidarity, and the Destruction of the Warsaw Ghetto." *Yad Vashem Studies* 25 (1996).

———. "The Poor Poles Look at the Ghetto." *Polin. Studies in Polish Jewry* 4 (1989).

Boas, Henriette. "The Persecution and Destruction of Dutch Jewry, 1940–1945." *Yad Vashem Studies* 6 (1967).

Bodo, Béla. "The Role of Antisemitism in the Expulsion of Non-Aryan Students, 1933–1945." *Yad Vashem Studies* 30 (2002).

Boll, Bernd. "Zloczow, July 1941: The Wehrmacht and the Beginning of the Holocaust in Galicia: From a Criticism of Photographs to a Revision of the Past." In *Crimes of War: Guilt and Denial in the Twentieth Century*, edited by Omer Bartov, Atina Grossmann and Mary Nolan. New York, 2002.

Bondy, Ruth. *"Elder of the Jews": Jakob Edelstein of Theresienstadt*. New York, 1989.

Botz, Gerhard. *Wohnungspolitik und Judendeportation in Wien 1938 bis 1945: Zur Funktion des Antisemitismus als Ersatz nationalsozialistischer Sozialpolitik*. Vienna, 1975.

Bourgeois, Daniel. *Business helvétique et Troisième Reich: Milieux d'affaires, politique étrangère, antisémitisme*. Lausanne, 1998.

Böhler, Jochen. *Auftakt zum Vernichtungskrieg. Die Wehrmacht in Polen 1939*. Frankfurt, 2006.

Braham, Randolph L. "The Christian Churches of Hungary and the Holocaust." *Yad Vashem Studies* 29 (2001).

———. "The Holocaust in Hungary: A Retrospective Analysis." In *Genocide and Rescue: The Holocaust in Hungary 1944*, edited by David Cesarani. Oxford, 1997.

———. "Hungarian Jews." In *Anatomy of the Auschwitz Death Camp*, edited by Yisrael Gutman and Michael Berenbaum. Bloomington, IN, 1994.

———. *The Politics of Genocide: The Holocaust in Hungary*. 2 vols. New York, 1981.

———. *The Politics of Genocide: The Holocaust in Hungary* [abridged edition]. Detroit, 2000.

———. "The Role of the Jewish Council in Hungary: A Tentative Assessment." *Yad Vashem Studies* 10 (1974).

Brayard, Florent. *La "Solution finale de la question juive": La Technique, le temps et les categories de la decision*. Paris, 2004.

Brechenmacher, Thomas. "Teufelspakt, Selbsterhaltung, universale Mission? Leitlinien und Spielräume der Diplomatie des Heiligen Stuhls gegenüber dem nationalsozialistischen Deutschland (1933–1939) im

Lichte neu zugänglicher vatikanischer Akten." *Historische Zeitschrift* 280, no. 3 (2005).

Breitman, Richard. *The Architect of Genocide: Himmler and the Final Solution*. New York, 1991.

———. "A Deal with the Nazi Dictatorship? Himmler's Alleged Peace Emissaries in Autumn 1943." *Journal of Contemporary History* 30, no. 3 (July 1995).

———. "Nazi Jewish Policy in 1944." In *Genocide and Rescue: The Holocaust in Hungary 1944*, edited by David Cesarani. New York, 1997.

———. "New Sources on the Holocaust in Italy." *Holocaust and Genocide Studies* 16, no. 3 (Winter 2002).

———. *Official Secrets: What the Nazis Planned, What the British and Americans Knew*. New York, 1998.

Breitman, Richard, and Alan M. Kraut. *American Refugee Policy and European Jewry, 1933–1945*. Bloomington, 1987.

Broszat, Martin. *Nationalsozialistische Polenpolitik 1939–1945*. Frankfurt am Main and Hamburg, 1965.

———. "Soziale Motivation und Führer-Bindung des Nationalsozialismus." *Vierteljahrshefte für Zeitgeschichte* 18 (1970).

Browning, Christopher R. *Collected Memories: Holocaust History and Postwar Testimony*. Madison, WI, 2003.

———. *Fateful Months: Essays on the Emergence of the Final Solution*. New York, 1985.

———. *The Final Solution and the German Foreign Office: A Study of Referat D III of Abteilung Deutschland, 1940–43*. New York, 1978.

———. *Nazi Policy, Jewish Workers, German Killers*. Cambridge, 2000.

———. *Ordinary Men: Reserve Police Battalion 101 and the Final Solution in Poland*. New York, 1992.

———. *The Path to Genocide: Essays on Launching the Final Solution*. Cambridge, 1992.

———. "The Wehrmacht in Serbia Revisited." In *Crimes of War: Guilt and Denial in the Twentieth Century*, edited by Omer Bartov, Atina Grossmann and Mary Nolan. New York, 2002.

Browning, Christopher R., and Yisrael Gutman. "The Reports of a Jewish 'Informer' in the Warsaw Ghetto—Selected Documents." *Yad Vashem Studies* 17 (1986).

———, and Jürgen Matthäus. *The Origins of the Final Solution: The Evo-*

lution of Nazi Jewish Policy, September 1939–March 1942. Lincoln, NE, 2004.

Buchbender, Ortwin. *Das tönende Erz. Deutsche Propaganda gegen die Rote Armee in Zweiten Weltkrieg*. Stuttgart, 1978.

Buchheim, Hans and et al. *Anatomie des SS-Staates*. 2 vols, 1965.

Burleigh, Michael. *Death and Deliverance: "Euthanasia" in Germany c. 1900–1945*. Cambridge, 1994.

———. *Germany Turns Eastwards: A Study of Ostforschung in the Third Reich*. Cambridge, UK, 1988.

———. *The Third Reich: A New History*. London, 2000.

Burrin, Philippe. *La Dérive fasciste: Doriot, Déat, Bergery, 1933–1945*. Paris, 1986.

———. *France under the Germans: Collaboration and Compromise*. New York, 1996.

———. *Hitler and the Jews: The Genesis of the Holocaust*. London, 1994.

———. *Hitler und die Juden: Die Entscheidung für den Völkermord*. Frankfurt am Main, 1993.

———. *Ressentiment et Apocalypse. Essai sur l'antisemitisme nazi*. Paris, 2004.

Büchler, Yehoshua. "Kommandostab Reichsführer SS: Himmler's Personal Murder Brigades in 1941." *Holocaust and Genocide Studies* 1 (1986).

Büttner, Ursula. " 'The Jewish Problem Becomes a Christian Problem:' German Protestants and the Persecution of the Jews in the Third Reich." In *Probing the Depths of German Antisemitism: German Society and the Persecution of the Jews, 1933–1941*, edited by David Bankier. New York, 2000.

Carpi, Daniel. "Salonika during the Holocaust: A New Approach to Some Episodes in the History of the Jews in Salonika during the Holocaust—Memory, Myth, and Documentation." In *The Last Ottoman Century and Beyond: The Jews in Turkey and the Balkans 1808–1945*, edited by Minna Rozen. Ramat-Aviv, 2002.

Carroll, David. *French Literary Fascism: Nationalism, Anti-Semitism, and the Ideology of Culture*. Princeton, 1995.

Carroll, James. *Constantine's Sword: The Church and the Jews: A History*. Boston, 2001.

Cesarani, David. *Becoming Eichmann: Rethinking the Life, Crimes, and Trial of a "Desk Murderer."* New York, 2006.

———. *The Final Solution: Origins and Implementation*. New York, 1994.

———, ed. *Holocaust: Critical Concepts in Historical Studies*. 6 vols. New York, 2004.

Cesarani, David, and Paul A. Levine, eds. *Bystanders to the Holocaust: A Re-Evaluation*. London, 2002.

Chary, Frederick B. *The Bulgarian Jews and the Final Solution, 1940–1944*. Pittsburgh, 1972.

Chiari, Bernhard. *Alltag hinter der Front: Besatzung, Kollaboration und Widerstand in Weissrussland 1941–1944*. Düsseldorf, 1998.

Cholavsky, Shalom. "The German Jews in the Minsk Ghetto." *Yad Vashem Studies* 17 (1986).

———. "The Judenrat in Minsk." In *Patterns of Jewish Leadership in Nazi Europe, 1933–1945*, edited by Yisrael Gutman and Cynthia J. Haft. Jerusalem, 1979.

Cochavi, Yehoyakim. " "The Hostile Alliance": The Relationship Between the Reichsvereinigung of Jews in Germany and the Regime." *Yad Vashem Studies* 22 (1992).

Cohen, Asher. *Persécutions et sauvetages: Juifs et Français sous l'Occupation et sous Vichy*. Paris, 1993.

Cohen, Nathan. "Diaries of the Sonderkommando." In *Anatomy of the Auschwitz Death Camp*, edited by Yisrael Gutman and Michael Berenbaum. Bloomington, 1994.

Cohen, Raya. "The Lost Honor of Bystanders? The Case of Jewish Emmissaries in Switzerland." In *Bystanders to the Holocaust: A Re-Evaluation*, edited by David Cesarani and Paul A. Levine. London, 2002.

Cohen, Richard I. *The Burden of Conscience: French Jewish Leadership during the Holocaust*. Bloomington, IN, 1987.

———. "Le Consistoire et L'UGIF—La situation trouble des juifs français face à Vichy." *Revue d'Histoire de la Shoah. Le monde juif* 169 (2000).

Cohen, William B., and Jorgen Svensson. "Finland and the Holocaust." In *Holocaust and Genocide Studies* 9 (1995).

Cointet, Michèle. *L'Église Sous Vichy, 1940–1945. La repentance en question*. Paris, 1998.

Connelly, John. "The Use of Volksgemeinschaft: Letters to the NSDAP Kreisleitung Eisenach 1939–1940." *The Journal of Modern History* 68, no. 4 (1996).

Conway, John S. *The Nazi Persecution of the Churches, 1933–45*. New York, 1968.

Cornwell, John. *Hitler's Pope: The Secret History of Pius XII*. New York, 1999.

Culbert, David. "The Impact of Anti-Semitic Film Propaganda on German Audiences: *Jew Süss* and *The Wandering Jew* (1940)." In *Art, Culture, and Media under the Third Reich*, edited by Richard A. Etlin. Chicago, 2002.

Czech, Danuta. *Auschwitz Chronicle, 1939–1945*. New York, 1990.

———. "Entstehungsgeschichte des KL Auschwitz, Aufbau und Ausbauperiode." In *Auschwitz: Nationalsozialistisches Vernichtungslager*, edited by Franciszek Piper and Teresa Swiebocka. Oswiecim, 1997.

———. *Kalendarium der Ereignisse im Konzentrationslager Auschwitz-Birkenau 1939–1945*. Reinbek bei Hamburg, 1989.

Davies, Norman. *God's Playground: A History of Poland*. Vol. 2. New York, 1984.

———. *Rising '44: The Battle for Warsaw*. London, 2003.

Dawidowicz, Lucy S. *The War Against the Jews, 1933–1945*. Toronto, 1986.

Deák, Istvan, Jan T. Gross, and Tony Judt. *The Politics of Retribution in Europe: World War II and its Aftermath*. Princeton, NJ, 2000.

Dean, Martin. *Collaboration in the Holocaust. Crimes of the Local Police in Belorussia and the Ukraine, 1941–44*. New York, 2000.

———. "The Development and Implementation of Nazi Denaturalization and Confiscation Policy up to the Eleventh Decree to the Reich Citizenship Law." *Holocaust and Genocide Studies* 16, no. 2 (2002).

Deichmann, Ute. *Biologen unter Hitler: Porträt einer Wissenschaft im NS-Staat*. Frankfurt am Main, 1995.

Delacor, Regina M. "Auslieferung auf Verlangen: Der deutsch-französische Waffenstillstandsvertrag 1940 und das Schicksal der sozialdemokratischen Exilpolitiker Rudolf Breitscheid und Rudolf Hilferding." *Vierteljahrshefte für Zeitgeschichte* 30 (1999).

———. "From Potential Friends to Potential Enemies: The Internment of 'Hostile Foreigners' in France at the Beginning of the Second World War." *Journal of Contemporary History* 35, no. 3 (2000).

Delpech, François. "L'Episcopat et la persecution des juifs et des étrangers." In *Églises et chrétiens dans la IIe Guerre mondiale: La France*, edited by Xavier de Montclos. Lyon, 1982.

Dequeker, Luc. "Baptism and Conversion of Jews in Belgium." In *Belgium and the Holocaust: Jews, Belgians, Germans,* edited by Dan Michman. Jerusalem, 1998.

Dieckmann, Christoph. "Der Krieg und die Ermordung der litauischen Juden." In *Nationalsozialistische Vernichtungspolitik, 1939–1945: Neue Forschungen und Kontroversen*, edited by Ulrich Herbert. Frankfurt am Main, 1998.

Diner, Dan. "Historical Understanding and Counterrationality: The Judenrat as Epistemological Vantage." In *Probing the Limits of Representation: Nazism and the "Final Solution,"* edited by Saul Friedländer. Cambridge, MA, 1992.

Dingel, Frank. "Waffen-SS." In *Enzyklopädie des Nationalsozialismus*, edited by Wolfgang Benz, Hermann Graml and Hermann Weiss. Stuttgart, 1997.

Dobroszycki, Lucjan and Jeffrey S. Gurock. *The Holocaust in the Soviet Union: Studies and Sources on the Destruction of the Jews in Nazi-occupied Territories of the USSR, 1941–1945.* Armonk, NY, 1993.

Doerry, Martin. *My Wounded Heart: The Life of Lilli Jahn, 1900–1944.* London, 2004.

Doorslaer, Rudi van. "Jewish Immigration and Communism in Belgium, 1925–1939." In *Belgium and the Holocaust: Jews, Belgians, Germans,* edited by Dan Michman. Jerusalem, 1998.

Döscher, Hans-Jürgen. *Das Auswärtige Amt im Dritten Reich: Diplomatie im Schatten der "Endlösung."* Berlin, 1987.

Dubnov-Erlich, Sophie. *The Life and World of S.M. Dubnov. Diaspora Nationalism and Jewish History.* New York, 1991.

Duffy, Peter. *The Bielski Brothers: The True Story of Three Men Who Defied the Nazis, Saved 1,200 Jews, and Built a Village in the Forest.* New York, 2003.

Dülffer, Jost. *Nazi Germany, 1933–1945: Faith and Annihilation.* New York, 1996.

Dwork, Debórah. *Children With a Star: Jewish Youth in Nazi Europe.* New Haven, 1991.

Dwork, Debórah and Robert Jan van Pelt. *Auschwitz, 1270 to the Present.* New York, 1996.

Eck, Nathan. "The March of Death from Serbia to Hungary (September 1944) and the Slaughter of Cservenka." *Yad Vashem Studies*. 2 (1958).

Eckel, Jan. *Hans Rothfels. Eine intellektuelle Biographie im 20. Jahrhundert*. Göttingen, 2005.

Edelman, Marek. *The Ghetto Fights*. London, 1990 [1945].

Edvardson, Cordelia. *Gebranntes Kind sucht das Feuer*. Munich, 1989.

Eichmann, Adolf. *Ich, Adolf Eichmann*. Edited by R. Aschenauer. Leoni am Starnberger See, 1980.

Elkin, Rivka. "The Survival of the Jewish Hospital in Berlin, 1938–1945." *Leo Baeck Institute Yearbook*. 38 (1993).

Engel, David. "An Early Account of Polish Jewry under Nazi and Soviet Occupation Presented to the Polish Government-In-Exile, February 1940." *Jewish Social Studies* 45 (1983).

———. *Facing a Holocaust: The Polish Government-in-Exile and the Jews, 1945–1945* 1993.

———. *In the Shadow of Auschwitz: The Polish Government-in-Exile and the Jews, 1939–1942*. Chapel Hill, 1987.

———. "Lwów, 1918: The Transmutation of a Symbol and its Legacy in the Holocaust." In *Contested Memories: Poles and Jews during the Holocaust and Its Aftermath*, edited by Joshua D. Zimmerman. New Brunswick, 2003.

———. "The Western Allies and the Holocaust: Jan Karski's Mission to the West, 1942–1944." *Holocaust and Genocide Studies* (1990)

Eshkoli, Hava. "Destruction Becomes Creation": The Theological Reaction of National Religious Zionism in Palestine to the Holocaust." *Holocaust and Genocide Studies* 17, no. 3 (2003).

Ettinger, Shmuel. "Jews and Non-Jews in Eastern and Central Europe between the World Wars: An Outline." In *Jews and Non-Jews in Eastern Europe, 1918–1945*, edited by Bela Vago and George L. Mosse. New York, 1974.

Ezergailis, Andrew. *The Holocaust in Latvia, 1941–1944: The Missing Center*. Riga, Washington, DC, 1996.

Fahlbusch, Michael. *Wissenschaft im Dienst nationalsozialistischer Politik. Die "Volksdeutschen Forschungsgemeinschaften" von 1931–1945*. Wiesbaden, 1999.

Falconi, Carlo. *The Silence of Pius XII*. London, 1970.

Fass, Moshe. "Theatrical Activities in the Polish Ghettos during the Years 1939–1942." In *Theatrical Performance during the Holocaust:*

Texts, Documents, Memoirs, edited by Rebecca Rovit and Alvin Goldfarb. Baltimore, 1999.

Fatal-Knaani, Tikva. "The Jews of Pinsk, 1939–1943: Through the Prism of New Documentation." *Yad Vashem Studies* 29 (2001).

Favez, Jean-Claude. *The Red Cross and the Holocaust*. Cambridge, 1999.

Favez, Jean-Claude, and Geneviève Billeter. *Une Mission impossible?: le CICR, les déportations et les camps de concentration Nazis*. Lausanne Switzerland, 1988.

Feingold, Henry L. *Bearing Witness: How America and Its Jews Responded to the Holocaust*. Syracuse, 1995.

———. *The Politics of Rescue: The Roosevelt Administration and the Holocaust, 1938–1945*. New Brunswick, NJ, 1970.

Feld, Bernard T. "Einstein and the Politics of Nuclear Weapons." In *Albert Einstein, Historical and Cultural Perspectives*, edited by Gerald James Holton and Yehuda Elkana. Princeton, 1982.

Feliciano, Hector. *The Lost Museum: The Nazi Conspiracy to Steal the World's Greatest Works of Art*. New York, 1997.

Fest, Joachim C. *Plotting Hitler's Death: The Story of the German Resistance*. New York, 1996.

Ficowski, Jerzy. *Regions of the Great Heresy. Bruno Schulz: A Biographical Portrait*. New York, 2003.

Fink, Carole. *Marc Bloch: A Life in History*. Cambridge, 1989.

Fischer, Fritz. *Germany's Aims in the First World War*. New York, 1967.

Fischer-Galati, Stephen. "The Legacy of Anti-Semitism." In *The Tragedy of Romanian Jewry*, edited by Randolph L. Braham. New York, 1994.

Fishman, David E. "Embers Plucked from the Fire: The Rescue of Jewish Cultural Treasures in Vilna." In *The Holocaust and the Book: Destruction and Preservation*, edited by Jonathan Rose. Amherst, 2001.

Flam, Gila. "Das kulturelle Leben im Getto Lodz." In *"Wer zum Leben, wer zum Tod . . ." Strategien jüdischen überlebens im Ghetto*, edited by Doron Kiesel et al., eds. Frankfurt, 1992.

Fleming, Gerald. *Hitler and the Final Solution*. Berkeley, 1984.

Flim, Bert Jan. "Opportunities for the Jews to Hide from the Nazis, 1942–45." In *Dutch Jews as Perceived by Themselves and by Others: Proceedings of the Eighth International Symposium on the History of the Jews in the Netherlands*, edited by Chaya Brasz and Yosef Kaplan. Leiden, 2001.

Förster, Jürgen. "Operation Barbarossa as a War of Conquest and Annihilation." In *Germany and the Second World War, Volume 4: The Attack on the Soviet Union*, edited by Horst Boog and et al. Oxford, 1998.

———. "The Wehrmacht and the War of Extermination Against the Soviet Union." *Yad Vashem Studies* 14 (1981).

Frankel, Jonathan. "Empire tsariste et Union Sovietique." In *Les juifs et le XXe siècle: Dictionnaire critique*, edited by Elie Barnavi and Saul Friedländer. Paris, 2000.

Frei, Norbert. *1945 und Wir: das Dritte Reich im Bewusstsein der Deutschen*. Munich, 2005.

Frei, Norbert, and Johannes Schmitz. *Journalismus im Dritten Reich*. Munich, 1989.

Freund, Florian, Bertrand Perz, and Karl Stuhlpfarrer. "Das Ghetto in Litzmannstadt (Lodz)." In *Unser einziger Weg ist Arbeit [Unzer eyntsiger veg iz arbayt]*, edited by Hanno Loewy and Gerhard Schoenberner. Vienna, 1990.

Freund, Elisabeth. "Waiting." In *Hitler's Exiles: Personal Stories of the Flight from Nazi Germany to America*, edited by Mark M. Anderson. New York, 1998.

Friedlander, Henry. "Darkness and Dawn in 1945: The Nazis, the Allies, and the Survivors." United States Holocaust Memorial Museum (ed.), *1945: The Year of Liberation*. (1995).

———. "The Deportation of the German Jews: Post-War German Trials of Nazi Criminals." In *Year Book of the Leo Baeck Institute*. London, 1984.

———. *The Origins of Nazi Genocide: From Euthanasia to the Final Solution*. Chapel Hill, 1995.

———. "Physicians as Killers in Nazi Germany. Hadamar, Treblinka, and Auschwitz." In *Medicine and Medical Ethics in Nazi Germany*, edited by Francis R. Nicosia and Jonathan Huener. New York, 2002.

Friedländer, Saul. "History, Memory and the Historian: Dilemmas and Responsibilities." *New German Critique* 80 (2000).

———. *Kurt Gerstein, The Ambiguity of Good*. New York, 1969.

———. *Nazi Germany and the Jews, Volume I: The Years of Persecution, 1933–1939*. New York, 1997.

———. *Pius XII and the Third Reich: A Documentation*. New York, 1966.
———. *Prelude to Downfall: Hitler and the United States, 1939–41*. New York, 1967.
———, ed. *Probing the Limits of Representation: Nazism and the "Final Solution"*. Cambridge, MA, 1992.
———. "The Wehrmacht, German Society, and the Knowledge of the Mass Extermination of the Jews." In *Crimes of War: Guilt and Denial in the Twentieth Century*, edited by Omer Bartov, Atina Grossmann and Mary Nolan. New York, 2002.
Friedman, Philip. *Roads to Extinction: Essays on the Holocaust*. Edited by Ada June Friedman. New York, 1980.
Friling, Tuvia. *Arrows In the Dark: David Ben-Gurion, the Yishuv Leadership, and Rescue Attempts during the Holocaust*. Madison, WI, 2005.
———. "Nazi-Jewish Negotiations in Istanbul in Mid-1944." *Holocaust and Genocide Studies* 13, no. 3 (1999).
Fritz, Stephen G. " "We are trying . . . to change the face of the world": Ideology and Motivation in the Wehrmacht on the Eastern Front: The View from Below." *The Journal of Military History* 60, no. 4 (1996).
Fröbe, Rainer. "Hans Kammler, Technocrat der Vernichtung." In *Die SS : Elite unter dem Totenkopf : 30 Lebensläufe*, edited by Ronald M. Smelser and Enrico Syring. Paderborn, 2000.
Fry, Varian. *Surrender on Demand*. New York, 1945.
Garbarini, Alexandra. *Numbered Days: Diaries and the Holocaust*. New Haven, 2006.
Gassert, Philipp. *Amerika im Dritten Reich: Ideologie, Propaganda und Volksmeinung 1933–1945*. Stuttgart, 1997.
Gelber, Yoav. "Zionist Policy and the Fate of European Jewry (1939–1942)." *Yad Vashem Studies* 13 (1979).
Gellately, Robert. *The Gestapo and German Society: Enforcing Racial Policy, 1933–1945*. Oxford, 1991.
———. *Backing Hitler: Consent and Coercion in Nazi Germany*. Oxford, 2001.
Gerlach, Christian. "Failure of Plans for an SS Extermination Camp in Mogilev, Belorussia." *Holocaust and Genocide Studies* 7, no. 1 (1997).
———. "German Economic Interests, Occupation Policy, and the Murder of the Jews in Belorussia 1941/43." In *National Socialist Extermi-*

nation Policies: Contemporary German Perspectives and Controversies, edited by Ulrich Herbert. New York, 2000.

———. "Hitlergegner bei der Heeresgruppe Mitte und die "verbrecherische Befehle"." In *NS-Verbrechen und der militärische Widerstand gegen Hitler*, edited by Gerd R. Uberschär. Darmstadt, 2000.

———. *Kalkulierte Morde: Die deutsche Wirtschafts- und Vernichtungspolitik in Weissrussland 1941 bis 1944*. Hamburg, 1999.

———. *Krieg, Ernährung, Völkermord: Forschungen zur deutschen Vernichtungspolitik im Zweiten Weltkrieg*. Hamburg, 1998.

———. "Männer des 20 Juli und der Krieg gegen die Sowjetunion." In *Vernichtungskrieg : Verbrechen der Wehrmacht 1941–1944*, edited by Hannes Heer and Klaus Naumann. Hamburg, 1995.

———. "Militärische "Versorgungszwänge", Besatzungspolitik und Massenverbrechen: Die Rolle des Generalquartiermeister des Heeres und seiner Dienststellen im Krieg gegen die Sowjetunion." In *Ausbeutung, Vernichtung, Offentlichkeit*, edited by Norbert Frei et al. Munich, 2000.

———. *Die Wannsee-Konferenz, das Schicksal der deutschen Juden und Hitlers politische Grundsatzentscheidung, alle Juden Europas zu ermorden*. Hamburg, 1997.

Gerlach, Christian, and Götz Aly. *Das letzte Kapitel. Der Mord an den ungarischen Juden*. Munich, 2002.

Gerlach, Wolfgang. *And the Witnesses Were Silent: The Confessing Church and the Persecution of the Jews*. Edited by Victoria Barnett. Lincoln, 2000.

Geyer, Michael and John W. Boyer. *Resistance against the Third Reich, 1933–1990*. Chicago, 1994.

Gilbert, Martin. *Auschwitz and the Allies*. New York, 1981.

Gildea, Robert. *Marianne in Chains: Everyday Life in the French Heartland under the German Occupation*. New York, 2003.

Goldhagen, Daniel Jonah. *Hitler's Willing Executioners: Ordinary Germans and the Holocaust*. New York, 1996.

Goodstein, Laurie. "New Look at Pius XII's Views of Nazis." *The New York Times*, August 31, 2003.

Gorodetsky, Gabriel. *Grand Delusion: Stalin and the German Invasion of Russia*. New Haven, 1999.

Goshen, Seev. "Eichmann und die Nisko-Aktion im Oktober 1939. Eine Fallstudie zur NS-Judenpolitik in der letzten Epoche vor der "Endlösung.'"" *Vierteljahrshefte für Zeitgeschichte* 29 (1981).

———. "Nisko- Ein Ausnahmefall unter der Judenlagern der SS." *Vierteljahrshefte für Zeitgeschichte* 40 (1992).

Gotovitch, José. "Resistance Movements and the "Jewish Question"." In *Belgium and the Holocaust: Jews, Belgians, Germans*, edited by Dan Michman. Jerusalem, 1998.

Green, Warren Paul. "The Nazi Racial Policy Towards the Karaites." *Soviet Jewish Affairs* 8, no. 2 (1978).

Greif, Gideon. *Wir weinten tränenlos . . . Augenzeugenberichte der jüdischen "Sonderkommandos" in Auschwitz*. Cologne, 1995.

Griech-Polelle, Beth. "Image of a Churchman-Resister: Bishop von Galen, the Euthanasia Project and the Sermons of Summer 1941." *Journal of Contemporary History* 36, no. 1 (2001).

Griffioen, J. W., and R. Zeller. *A Comparative Analysis of the Persecution of the Jews in the Netherlands and Belgium during the Second World War.* Amsterdam, 1998.

Gronski, Jan Marek. "Life in Nazi-Occupied Warsaw: Three Ghetto Sketches." In *Polin: Studies in Polish Jewry* 7 (1992).

Gross, Jan T. *Neighbors: The Destruction of the Jewish Community in Jedwabne, Poland.* Princeton, 2001.

———. "A Tangled Web: Confronting Stereotypes Concerning Relations between Poles, Germans, Jews and Communists." In *The Politics of Retribution*, edited by István Deák, Jan T. Gross and Tony Judt. Princeton, 2000.

Grossman, Alexander. *Nur das Gewissen, Carl Lutz und seine Budapester Aktion: Geschichte und Porträt.* Wald, 1986.

Gruner, Wolf. "Die Fabrik-Aktion und die Ereignisse in der Berliner Rosenstrasse: Fakten und Fiktionen um den 27. Februar 1943." *Jahrbuch fur Antisemitismusforschung* 11 (2002).

———. *Judenverfolgung in Berlin 1933–1945: Eine Chronologie der Behördenmassnahmen in der Reichshauptstadt*. Berlin, 1996.

———. "Poverty and Persecution: The Reichsvereinigung, the Jewish Population, and Anti-Jewish Policy in the Nazi State, 1939–1945." *Yad Vashem Studies* 27 (1999).

———. "Public Welfare and the German Jews under National Socialism." In *Probing the Depths of German Antisemitism: German Society and the Persecution of the Jews, 1933–1941*, edited by David Bankier. New York, 2000.

———. *Widerstand in der Rosenstrasse. Die Fabrik-Aktion und die Verfolgung der Mischehen 1943*. Frankfurt, 2005.

Grynberg, Anne. *Les Camps de la honte: Les internés juifs des camps français, 1939–1944*. Paris, 1991.

———. "1939–1940: L'Internement en temps de guerre. Les politiques de la France et de la Grande-Bretagne." *Vingtième Siècle. Revue d'Histoire*. April-June. (1997).

Gutman, Yisrael. "Debate." In *Patterns of Jewish Leadership in Nazi Europe, 1933–1945*, edited by Cynthia J. Haft and Yisrael Gutman. Jerusalem, 1979.

———, ed. *Encyclopedia of the Holocaust*. New York, 1990.

———. *The Jews of Warsaw, 1939–1943: Ghetto, Underground, Revolt.* Bloomington, 1982.

———. "Polish Antisemitism Between the Wars: An Overview." In *The Jews of Poland Between Two World Wars*, edited by Yisrael Gutman, Ezra Mendelsohn, Jehuda Reinharz and Chone Shmeruk. Hanover, NH, 1989.

———. *Resistance: The Warsaw Ghetto Uprising*. Boston, 1994.

———. "Social Stratification in the Concentration Camps." In *The Nazi Concentration Camps: Structure and Aims, the Image of the Prisoner, the Jews in the Camps*, edited by Yisrael Gutman and Avital Saf. Jerusalem, 1984.

———. "Zionist Youth." In *Zionist Youth Movements during the Shoah*, edited by Asher Cohen and Yehoyakim Cochavi. New York, 1995.

Gutman, Yisrael, and Michael Berenbaum. *Anatomy of the Auschwitz Death Camp*. Bloomington, 1994.

Gutman, Yisrael, and Cynthia J. Haft. *Patterns of Jewish Leadership in Nazi Europe, 1933–1945*. Jerusalem, 1979.

Gutman, Yisrael, and Shmuel Krakowski. *Unequal Victims: Poles and Jews during World War Two*. New York, 1986.

Gutman, Yisrael, and Avital Saf, eds. *The Nazi Concentration Camps.* Jerusalem, 1984.

Gutman, Yisrael, and Efraim Zuroff, eds. *Rescue Attempts During the Holocaust*. Jerusalem, 1977.

Gutteridge, Richard. *Open Thy Mouth for the Dumb! The German Evangelical Church and the Jews 1879–1950*. Oxford, 1976.

Haar, Ingo. *Historiker im Nationalsozialismus. Deutsche Geschichtswissenschaft und der "Volkstumskampf" im Osten*. Göttingen, 2002.

Hachmeister, Lutz. *Der Gegnerforscher: Die Karriere des SS-Führers Franz Alfred Six*. Munich, 1998.

Hagen, William W. "Before the "Final Solution": Toward a Comparative Analysis of Political Anti-Semitism in Interwar Germany and Poland." *The Journal of Modern History* 68, no. 2 (1996).

Hampicke, Evelyn and Hanno Loewy. "Juden ohne Maske: Vorläufige Bemerkungen zur Geschichte eines Kompilationsfilms." In *"Beseitigung des jüdischen Einflusses . . . ": Antisemitische Forschung, Eliten und Karrieren im Nationalsozialismus*, edited by Fritz Bauer Institut. Frankfurt, 1999.

Hartglas, Apolinary. "How Did Czerniakow Become Head of the Warsaw Judenrat?" *Yad Vashem Bulletin* 15 (1964).

Harvey, Elizabeth. *Women and the Nazi East: Agents and Witnesses of Germanization*. New Haven, 2003.

Hastings, Max. *Armaggedon: The Battle for Germany, 1944–1945*. London, 2004.

Hayes, Peter. "Auschwitz, Capital of the Holocaust." *Holocaust and Genocide Studies* 17, no. 2 (2003).

———. "The Degussa AG and the Holocaust." In *Lessons and Legacies: The Holocaust and Justice*, vol. 5, edited by Peter Hayes. Evanston, IL, 1991.

———. *From Cooperation to Complicity: Degussa in the Third Reich*. Cambridge, UK 2004.

———. *Industry and Ideology: IG Farben in the Nazi Era*. New York, 1987.

Heiber, Helmut. *Walter Frank und sein Reichsinstitut für Geschichte des neuen Deutschlands*. Stuttgart, 1966.

Herbert, Ulrich. *Best: Biographische Studien über Radikalismus, Weltanschauung und Vernunft, 1903–1989*. Bonn, 1996.

———. "Die deutsche Militärverwaltung in Paris und die Deportation der französischen Juden." In *Von der Aufgabe der Freiheit: Politische Verantwortung und bürgerliche Gesellschaft im 19. und 20. Jahrhundert: Festschrift für Hans Mommsen zum 5. November 1995*, edited by Christian Jansen, Lutz Niethammer and Bernd Weisbrod. Berlin, 1995.

———, ed. *National Socialist Extermination Policies: Contemporary German Perspectives and Controversies*. New York, 2000.

Herf, Jeffrey. *The Jewish Enemy: Nazi Propaganda during World War II and the Holocaust*. Cambridge, MA, 2006.

———. "The 'Jewish War': Goebbels and the Antisemitic Campaign of the Nazi Propaganda Ministry." *Holocaust and Genocide Studies* 19, no. 1 (2005).

———. *Reactionary Modernism: Technology, Culture, and Politics in Weimar and the Third Reich*. New York, 1986.

Heschel, Susannah. "Deutsche Theologen für Hitler. Walter Grundmann und das Eisenacher Institut zur Erforschung und Beseitigung des Jüdischen Einflusses auf das deutsche kirchliche Leben." In *"Beseitigung des jüdischen Einflusses—": Antisemitische Forschung, Eliten und Karrieren im Nationalsozialismus*, edited by Fritz Bauer Institut. Frankfurt, 1999.

———. *Transforming Jesus from Jew to Aryan: Protestant Theologians in Nazi Germany*. Tucson, AZ, 1995.

Hilberg, Raul. "Auschwitz and the Final Solution." In *Anatomy of the Auschwitz Death Camp*, edited by Yisrael Gutman and Michael Berenbaum. Bloomington, 1994.

———. "Le bilan demographique du génocide." In *L'Allemagne nazie et le génocide juif: Colloque de l'École des Hautes Études en Sciences Sociales (EHESS)*, edited by École des hautes études en sciences sociales. Paris, 1985.

———. *The Destruction of the European Jews*. 3 vols. New Haven, CT, 2003.

———. "German Railroads/Jewish Souls." In *The Nazi Holocaust: Historical Articles on the Destruction of European Jews*, edited by Michael Robert Marrus. Westport, 1989.

———. *Perpetrators, Victims, Bystanders: The Jewish Catastrophe, 1933–1945*. New York, 1992.

———. *Sources of Holocaust Research. An Analysis*. Chicago, 2001.

Hiller, Marlene P., ed. *Stuttgart im Zweiten Weltkrieg: Katalog einer Ausstellung des Projekts Stuttgart im Zweiten Weltkrieg vom 1.9.1989 bis 22.7.1990.* Gerlingen, 1989.

Hirschfeld, Gerhard. *Nazi Rule and Dutch Collaboration: The Netherlands under German Occupation, 1940–1945*. Oxford, 1988.

———. "Die Universität Leyden unter dem Nationalsozialismus." In *Universitäten im nationalsozialistisch beherrschten Europa*, edited by Dieter Langewiesche. Göttingen, 1997.

Hoensch, Jörg K. "Slovakia: "One God, One People, One Party!" The Development, Aim and Failure of Political Catholicism." In *Catholics, the State, and the European Radical Right, 1919–1945*, edited by Richard J. Wolff and Jörg K. Hoensch. Highland Lakes, NJ, 1987.

Hoffmann, Hilmar. *Und die Fahne führt uns in die Ewigkeit: Propaganda im NS-Film*. Frankfurt am Main, 1988.

Hoffmann, Stanley. "Collaborationism in France during World War II." *Journal of Modern History* 40 (1968).

Höhne, Heinz. *Canaris*. Garden City, NY, 1979.

Hollstein, Dorothea. *"Jud Süss" und die Deutschen: Antisemitische Vorurteile im nationalsozialistischen Spielfilm*. Frankfurt am Main, 1983 (1971).

Horwitz, Gordon J. *In the Shadow of Death: Living Outside the Gates of Mauthausen*. New York, 1990.

Hosenfeld, Wilm. *"Ich versuche jeden zu retten." Das Leben eines deutschen Offiziers in Briefen und Tagebüchern*. Munich, 2004.

Höss, Rudolf. *Kommandant in Auschwitz: Autobiographische Aufzeichnungen*. Edited by Martin Broszat. Stuttgart, 1958.

Houwink ten Cate, Johannes. "Der Befehlshaber der Sipo und des SD in den besetzten niederländischen Gebieten und die Deportation der Juden 1942–1943." In *Die Bürokratie der Okkupation: Strukturen der Herrschaft und Verwaltung im besetzten Europa*, edited by Wolfgang Benz, Johannes Houwink ten Cate and Gerhard Otto. Berlin, 1998.

Hurwitz, Ariel. "The Struggle Over the Creation of the War Refugee Board (WRB)." *Holocaust and Genocide Studies* 6 (1991).

Hürter, Johannes. "Auf dem Weg zur Militäropposition. Tresckow, Gersdorff, der Vernichtungskrieg und der Judenmord. Neue Dokumente über das Verhältnis der Heeresgruppe Mitte zur Einsatzgruppe B im Jahr 1941." *Vierteljahrshefte für Zeitgeschichte* 3 (2004).

Hürter, Johannes, and Hans Woller. *Hans Rothfels und die deutsche Zeitgeschichte*. Munich, 2005.

Hyman, Paula. *From Dreyfus to Vichy: The Remaking of French Jewry, 1906–1939*. New York, 1979.

———. *The Jews of Modern France*. Berkeley, 1998.

Independent Commission of Experts Switzerland—Second World War. *Switzerland, National Socialism and the Second World War*. Zurich, 2002.

International Commission on the Holocaust in Romania. *Final Report of the International Commission on the Holocaust in Romania. Presented to Romanian President Ion Iliescu. November 11, 2004.* Available from http://www.ushmm.org/research/center/presentations/programs/presentations/2005-03-10/pdf/english/chapter_03.pdf.

Ioanid, Radu. "The Antonescu Era." In *The Tragedy of Romanian Jewry*, edited by Randolph L. Braham. New York, 1994.

———. "The Fate of Romanian Jews in Nazi Occupied Europe." In *The Destruction of Romanian and Ukrainian Jews during the Antonescu Era*, edited by Randolph L. Braham. Boulder, CO, 1997.

———. *The Holocaust in Romania: The Destruction of Jews and Gypsies under the Antonescu Regime, 1940–1944*. Chicago, 2000.

Jäckel, Eberhard. "On the Purpose of the Wannsee Conference." In *Perspectives on the Holocaust*, edited by James S. Pacy and Alan P. Wertheimer. Boulder, CO, 1995.

———. "Zur Politik des Heiligen Stuhls im Zweiten Weltkrieg." *Geschichte in Wissenschaft und Unterricht* 15 (1964).

James, Harold. *Die Deutsche Bank und die "Arisierung."* Munich, 2001.

Jansen, Christian and Arno Weckbecker. *Der "Volksdeutsche Selbstschutz" in Polen, 1939/40*. Munich, 1992.

Johnson, Eric A. *Nazi Terror: The Gestapo, Jews, and Ordinary Germans*. New York, 1999.

Johnson, Eric A., and Karl-Heinz Reuband. *What We Knew: Terror, Mass Murder and Everyday Life in Nazi Germany: An Oral History*. Cambridge, MA, 2005.

Jong, Louis de. "Jews and Non-Jews in Nazi Occupied Holland." In *The Nazi Holocaust: Historical Articles on the Destruction of European Jews*, edited by Michael R. Marrus. Westport, 1989.

———. "The Netherlands and Auschwitz." *Yad Vashem Studies*. 7 (1968).

———. *The Netherlands and Nazi Germany*. Cambridge, MA, 1990.

Kaplan, Marion A. *Between Dignity and Despair: Jewish Life in Nazi Germany*. New York, 1998.

Karay, Felicja. *Death Comes in Yellow: Skarzysko-Kamienna Slave Labor Camp*. Amsterdam, 1996.

Kárný, Miroslav, Vojtěch Blodig and Margita Kárná, eds. *Theresienstadt in der "Endlösung der Judenfrage."* Prague, 1992.

Kaspi, André. *Les Juifs pendant l'occupation*. Paris, 1991.

Kassow, Samuel David. "Vilna and Warsaw, Two Ghetto Diaries: Herman Kruk and Emanuel Ringelblum." In *Holocaust Chronicles: Individualiz-*

ing the Holocaust through Diaries and Other Contemporaneous Personal Accounts, edited by Robert Moses Shapiro. Hoboken, NJ, 1999.

Kater, Michael H. *Das "Ahnenerbe" der SS 1935–1945: Ein Beitrag zur Kulturpolitik des Dritten Reiches*. Stuttgart, 2001.

———. *The Twisted Muse: Musicians and Their Music in the Third Reich*. New York, 1997.

Katz, Robert. *The Battle for Rome: The Germans, the Allies, the Partisans and the Pope, September 1943–June 1944*. New York, 2003.

Kazik [Simha Rotem]. *Memoirs of a Warsaw Ghetto Fighter*. New Haven, CT, 1994.

Kennedy, David M. *Freedom from Fear: The American People in Depression and War, 1929–1945*. New York, 1999.

Kent, Peter C. "A Tale of Two Popes: Pius XI, Pius XII and the Rome-Berlin Axis." *Journal of Contemporary History* 23, no. 4 (1988).

Keren, Daniel, Jamie McCarthy and Harry W. Mazal. "The Ruins of the Gas Chambers: A Forensic Investigation of Crematoriums at Auschwitz I and Auschwitz-Birkenau." *Holocaust and Genocide Studies* 18, no. 1 (2004).

Kermish, Yosef. "The Judenrat in Warsaw." In *Patterns of Jewish Leadership in Nazi Europe, 1933–1945*, edited by Yisrael Gutman and Cynthia J. Haft. Jerusalem, 1979.

Kershaw, Ian. *Hitler, 1889–1936: Hubris*. London, 1998.

———. *Hitler, 1936–45: Nemesis*. New York, 2000.

Kertzer, David I. *The Popes Against the Jews: The Vatican's Role in the Rise of Modern Anti-Semitism*. New York, 2001.

Kingreen, Monica. "Raubzüge einer Stadtverwaltung: Frankfurt am Main und die Aneignung "Jüdischen Besitzes"." *Beiträge zur Geschichte des Nationalsozialismus* 17 (2001).

Kirchhoff, Hans. "Denmark: A Light in the Darkness of the Holocaust? A Reply to Gunnar S. Paulsson," in Cesarani, David, ed. *Holocaust: Critical Concepts*. New York, 2004.

Klarsfeld, Serge. *Les transferts de juifs du camp de Rivesaltes et de la région de Montpellier vers le camp de Drancy en vue de leur déportation 10 août 1942–6 août 1944*. Paris, 1993.

———. *Vichy-Auschwitz: Le rôle de Vichy dans la solution finale de la question juive en France*. 2 vols. Paris, 1983–1985.

Klawitter, Nils. "Nationalsozialistischer Führungsoffizier." In *Enzyk-*

lopädie des Nationalsozialismus, edited by Wolfgang Benz et. al. Stuttgart, 1997.

Klee, Ernst. *"Euthanasie" im NS-Staat: Die "Vernichtung lebensunwerten Lebens"*. Frankfurt am Main, 1983.

———. *Die SA Jesu Christi: Die Kirchen im Banne Hitlers*. Frankfurt am Main, 1989.

Klein, Anne. "Conscience, Conflict and Politics: The Rescue of Political Refugees from Southern France to the United States, 1940–1942." In *Year Book of the Leo Baeck Institute*. London, 1998.

Klein, Peter, ed. *Die Einsatzgruppen in der besetzen Sowjetunion 1941/42*. Berlin, 1997.

Klink, Ernst. "The Conduct of Operations: 1. The Army and the Navy." In *The Attack on the Soviet Union*, edited by Horst Boog et. al. Oxford, 1998.

Klinken, Gert van. "Dutch Jews as Perceived by Dutch Protestants, 1860–1960." In *Dutch Jews As Perceived by Themselves and by Others*, edited by Chaya Brasz and Yosef Kaplan. Leiden, 2001.

Kluger, Ruth. *Still Alive: A Holocaust Girlhood Remembered*. New York, 2001.

Knapp, Gabriele. *Das Frauenorchester in Auschwitz: Musikalische Zwangsarbeit und ihre Bewältigung*. Hamburg, 1996.

Koblik, Steven. *The Stones Cry Out*. New York, 1987.

Koestler, Arthur. *Scum of the Earth*. New York, 1947.

Kogon, Eugen. *Der SS-Staat: Das System der deutschen Konzentrationslager*. Frankfurt, 1964 [1946].

Kolb, Eberhard. *Bergen-Belsen: vom "Aufenthaltslager" zum Konzentrationslager, 1943–1945*. Göttingen, 1996.

Krakowski, Shmuel. "The Attitude of the Polish Underground to the Jewish Question during the Second World War." In *Contested Memories: Poles and Jews during the Holocaust and Its Aftermath*, edited by Joshua D. Zimmerman. New Brunswick, 2003.

———. *The War of the Doomed: Jewish Armed Resistance in Poland, 1942–1944*. New York, 1984.

Kramer, Aaron. "Creation in a Death Camp." In *Theatrical Performance during the Holocaust: Texts, Documents, Memoirs*, edited by Rebecca Rovit and Alvin Goldfarb. Baltimore, 1999.

Krausnick, Helmut. "Hitler und die Morde in Polen." *Vierteljahrshefte für Zeitgeschichte* 11 (1963).

Krausnick, Helmut, and Hans-Heinrich Wilhelm. *Die Truppe des Weltanschauungskrieges: Die Einsatzgruppen der Sicherheitspolizei und des SD, 1938–1942*. Stuttgart, 1981.

Kulka, O. D. "The German Population and the Jews: State of Research and New Perspectives." In *Probing the Depths of German Antisemitism: German Society and the Persecution of the Jews, 1933–1941*, edited by David Bankier. New York, 2000.

———. "The Reichsvereinigung and the Fate of German Jews, 1938/9–1943." In *Die Juden im nationalsozialistichen Deutschland*, edited by Arnold Paucker. Tubigen, 1986.

———. "The Reichsvereinigung of the Jews in Germany" (1938/9–1943)." In *Patterns of Jewish Leadership in Nazi Europe, 1933–1945*, edited by Cynthia J. Haft and Yisrael Gutman. Jerusalem, 1979.

Kushner, Tony. *The Persistence of Prejudice: Antisemitism in British Society During the Second World War*. Manchester, 1989.

Kwiet, Konrad. "Erziehung zum Mord: Zwei Beispiele zur Kontinuität der deutschen 'Endlösung der Judenfrage.' " In *Geschichte und Emanzipation*, edited by Michael Grüttner et al. Frankfurt, 1999.

———. "Nach dem Pogrom: Stufen der Ausgrenzung." In *Die Juden in Deutschland, 1933–1945: Leben unter nazionalsozialistischer Herrschaft*, edited by Wolfgang Benz. Munich, 1988.

———. "Rehearsing for Murder: The Beginning of the Final Solution in Lithuania in June 1941." *Holocaust and Genocide Studies* 12, no. 1 (1998).

———. "The Ultimate Refuge: Suicide in the Jewish Community under the Nazis." In *Year Book of the Leo Baeck Institute*. London, 1984.

Laborie, Pierre. "The Jewish Statutes in Vichy France and Public Opinion." *Yad Vashem Studies* 22 (1992).

Lambauer, Barbara. "Opportunistischer Antisemitismus. Der deutscher Botschafter Otto Abetz und die Judenverfolgung in Frankreich." *Vierteljahrshefte für Zeitgeschichte* 2 (2005).

Landau-Czajka, Anna. "The Jewish Question in Poland: Views Expressed in the Catholic Press between the Two World Wars." *Polin. Studies in Polish Jewry* 11 (1998).

Langbein, Hermann. "The Auschwitz Underground." In *Anatomy of the Auschwitz Death Camp*, edited by Yisrael Gutman and Michael Berenbaum. Bloomington, 1994.

———. *People in Auschwitz*. Chapel Hill, 2004.

Lappin, Eleanore. "The Death Marches of Hungarian Jews Through Austria in the Spring of 1945." *Yad Vashem Studies* 28 (2000).

Laqueur, Tom. "The Sound of Voices Intoning Names." *London Review of Books* June 5, 1997.

Laqueur, Walter. *The Terrible Secret: An Investigation into the Suppression of Information about Hitler's "Final Solution."* London, 1980.

———. "Three Witnesses: The Legacy of Viktor Klemperer, Willy Cohn and Richard Koch." *Holocaust and Genocide Studies* 10, no. 3 (1996).

Laqueur, Walter, and Judith Tydor Baumel, eds. *The Holocaust Encyclopedia*. New Haven, 2001.

Laqueur, Walter, and Richard Breitman. *Breaking the Silence*. New York, 1986.

Large, David Clay. *And the World Closed Its Doors: The Story of One Family Abandoned to the Holocaust*. New York, 2003.

Leff, Laurel. *Buried by The Times. The Holocaust and America's Most Important Newspaper*. New York, 2005.

Lerchenmueller, Joachim. "Die "SD-mässige" Bearbeitung der Geschichtswissenschaft." In *Nachrichtendienst, politische Elite, Mordeinheit: Der Sicherheitsdienst des Reichsführers SS*, edited by Michael Wildt. Hamburg, 2003.

Levi, Erik. *Music in the Third Reich*. New York, 1994.

Levi, Primo. *Survival in Auschwitz: The Nazi Assault on Humanity*. New York, 1996 [1958].

Levin, Dov. "The Jews in the Soviet Lithuanian Establishment, 1940–1941." *Soviet Jewish Affairs* 10, no. 2 (1980).

———. "July 1944—The Crucial Month for the Remnants of Lithuanian Jewry." In *The Nazi Holocaust: Historical Articles on the Destruction of European Jews*, edited by Michael Marrus. Westport, 1989.

———. "The Sovietization of the Baltics and the Jews, 1940–1941." *Soviet Jewish Affairs* 21, no. 1 (1991).

Levine, Hillel. *In Search of Sugihara: The Elusive Japanese Diplomat Who Risked His Life to Rescue 10,000 Jews from the Holocaust*. New York, 1996.

Levine, Paul A. "Attitudes and Action: Comparing the Responses of Mid-Level Bureaucrats to the Holocaust." In *Bystanders to the Holo-*

caust: A Re-Evaluation, edited by David Cesarani and Paul A. Levine. London, 2002.

———. *From Indifference to Activism: Swedish Diplomacy and the Holocaust, 1938–1944*. Uppsala, 1996.

Lewandowski, Jozef. "Early Swedish Information about the Nazis' Mass Murder of the Jews." *Polin. Studies in Polish Jewry* 13 (2000).

Lewinski, Jerzy. "The Death of Adam Czerniakow and Janusz Korczak's Last Journey." *Polin. Studies in Polish Jewry* 7 (1992).

Lewy, Guenter. *The Catholic Church and Nazi Germany*. New York, 1964.

———. *The Nazi Persecution of the Gypsies*. New York, 2000.

Lifton, Robert Jay. *The Nazi Doctors: Medical Killing and the Psychology of Genocide*. New York, 1986.

Lifton, Robert Jay, and Amy Hackett. "Nazi Doctors." In *Anatomy of the Auschwitz Death Camp*, edited by Yisrael Gutman and Michael Berenbaum. Bloomington, 1994.

Lipstadt, Deborah E. *Beyond Belief: The American Press and the Coming of the Holocaust, 1933–1945*. New York, 1986.

London, Louise. *Whitehall and the Jews 1933–1948: British Immigration Policy, Jewish Refugees and the Holocaust*. Cambridge, UK, 2000.

Longerich, Peter. *Politik der Vernichtung: Eine Gesamtdarstellung der nationalsozialistischen Judenverfolgung*. Munich, 1998.

———. *The Unwritten Order: Hitler's Role in the Final Solution*. Charleston, SC, 2003.

Lottman, Herbert R. *La Rive gauche: Du Front populaire à la guerre froide*. Paris, 1981.

Lower, Wendy. *Nazi Empire-Building and the Holocaust in Ukraine*. Chapel Hill, 2005.

Lozowick, Yaacov. "Documentation: 'Judenspediteur,' Deportation Train." *Holocaust and Genocide Studies* 6, no. 3 (1991).

———. *Hitlers Bürokraten: Eichmann, seine willigen Vollstrecker und die Banalität des Bösen*. Zurich, 2000.

———. "Malice in Action." *Yad Vashem Bulletin* 27 (1999).

———. "Rollbahn Mord: The Early Activities of Einsatzgruppe C." *Holocaust and Genocide Studies* 2 (1987).

Lüdtke, Alf. "The Appeal of Exterminating "Others": German Workers and the Limits of Resistance." In *Resistance Against the Third Reich, 1933–1990*, edited by Michael Geyer and John W. Boyer. Chicago, 1994.

Luebke, David Martin and Sybil Milton. "Locating the Victim: An Overview of Census-Taking, Tabulation Technology, and Persecution in Nazi Germany." *IEEE Annals of the History of Computing* 16, no. 3 (1994).

Lukacs, John. *The Duel: Hitler vs. Churchill: 10 May–31 July 1940.* Oxford, 1992.

MacQueen, Michael. "The Context of Mass Destruction: Agents and Prerequisites of the Holocaust in Lithuania." *Holocaust and Genocide Studies* 12 (1998).

———. "The Conversion of Looted Assets to Run the German War Machine." *Holocaust and Genocide Studies* 18, no. 1 (2004).

———. "Massenvernichtung im Kontext: Täter und Voraussetzungen des Holocaust in Litauen." In *Judenmord in Litauen*, edited by Wolfgang Benz and Marion Neiss. Berlin, 1999.

Macrakis, Kristie. *Surviving the Swastika: Scientific Research in Nazi Germany.* New York, 1993.

Madajczyk, Czeslaw. *Die Deutsche Besatzungspolitik in Polen (1939–45).* Wiesbaden, 1967.

Magocsi, Robert. *A History of the Ukraine.* Seattle, 1996.

Malinowski, Stephan. "Vom blauen zum reinen Blut. Antisemitische Adelskritik und adliger Antisemitismus, 1871–1944." *Jahrbuch für Antisemitismusforschung* 12 (2003).

Mallmann, Klaus-Michael. "Der qualitative Sprung im Vernichtungsprozess. Das Massaker von Kamenetz-Podolsk Ende August 1941." *Jahrbuch fur Antisemitismusforschung* 10 (2001).

Mallmann, Klaus-Michael, and Bogdan Musial. *Genesis des Genozids. Polen 1939–1941.* Darmstadt, 2004.

Malo, Eric. "Le camp de Récébédou (Haute-Garonne)." *Le Monde Juif* 153 (January–April 1995).

Manoschek, Walter. "The Extermination of the Jews in Serbia." In *National Socialist Extermination Policies: Contemporary German Perspectives and Controversies*, edited by Ulrich Herbert. New York, 2000.

———. *"Serbien ist judenfrei": Militärische Besatzungspolitik und Judenvernichtung in Serbien 1941/42.* Munich, 1993.

Marrus, Michael R. "Le Vatican et les orphelins juifs de la shoah." *L'Histoire.* 307 (2006).

Marrus, Michael R., and Robert O. Paxton. *Vichy France and the Jews*. New York, 1981.

Matthäus, Jürgen. "Ausbildungsziel Judenmord? Zum Stellenwert der "weltanschaulichen Erziehung" von SS und Polizei im Rahmen der 'Endlösung.'" *Zeitschrift für Geschichtswissenschaft* 47 (1999).

———. "Jenseits der Grenze: Die ersten Massenerschiessungen von Juden in Litauen (Juni–August 1941)." *Zeitschrift für Geschichtswissenschaft* 2 (1996).

———. "Weltanschauliche Forschung und Auswärtung. Aus den Akten des Amtes VII im Reichssicherheitshauptamt." *Jahrbuch für Antisemitismusforschung* 5 (1996).

Matthaüs, Jürgen, Konrad Kwiet, Jürgen Förster, and Richard Breitman. *Ausbildung Judenmord? "Weltanschauliche Erziehung" von SS, Polizei, und Waffen-SS im Rahmen der "Endlösung."* Frankfurt, 2003.

Mayer, Arno J. *Why Did the Heavens not Darken?: The "Final Solution" in History*. New York, 1988.

Mayeur, Jean-Marie. "Les Églises devant la Persécution des Juifs en France." In *La France et la question juive: 1940–1944*, edited by Georges Wellers, André Kaspi and Serge Klarsfeld. Paris, 1981.

Mazower, Mark. *Inside Hitler's Greece: The Experience of Occupation, 1941–44*. New Haven, 1993.

———. *Salonica, City of Ghosts: Christians, Muslims and Jews, 1430–1950*. New York, 2004.

McCarthy, Jamie, Daniel Keren and Harry W. Mazal. "The Ruins of the Gas Chambers: A Forensic Investigation of Crematoriums at Auschwitz I and Auschwitz-Birkenau." *Holocaust and Genocide Studies* 8 (2004).

Meershoek, Guus. "The Amsterdam Police and the Persecution of the Jews." In *Holocaust: Critical Concepts in Historical Studies*, edited by David Cesarani. New York, 2004.

Mendelsohn, Ezra. *The Jews of East Central Europe Between the World Wars*. Bloomington, 1983.

Messerschmidt, Manfred. *Die Wehrmacht im NS-Staat: Zeit der Indoktrination*. Hamburg, 1969.

———. "The Wehrmacht and the Volksgemeinschaft." *Journal of Contemporary History* 18, no. 4 (1983).

Meurant, Jacques. *La Presse et l'opinion de la Suisse romande face à l'Europe en guerre, 1939–1941*. Neuchâtel, 1976.

Meyer, Ahlrich. *Täter im Verhör. Die Endlösung der Judenfrage in Frankreich 1940–1944*. Darmstadt, 2005.

Meyer, Beate. "Das unausweichliche Dilemma: Die Reichsvereinigung der Juden in Deutschland, die Deportationen und die untergetauchten Juden." In *Überleben im Untergrund: Hilfe für Juden in Deutschland*, edited by Beate Kosmala and Claudia Schopmann. Berlin, 2002.

———. "Gratwanderung zwischen Verantwortung und Verstrickung: Die Reichsvereinigung der Juden in Deutschland und die Jüdische Gemeinde zu Berlin 1938–1945." In *Juden in Berlin, 1938–1945*, edited by Beate Meyer and Hermann Simon. Berlin, 2000.

———. *"Jüdische Mischlinge": Rassenpolitik und Verfolgungserfahrung 1933–1945*. Hamburg, 1999.

Meyer, Winfried. *Unternehmen Sieben: eine Rettungsaktion für vom Holocaust Bedrohte aus dem Amt Ausland/Abwehr im Oberkommando der Wehrmacht*. Frankfurt am Main, 1993.

Miccoli, Giovanni. *Les Dilemmes et les silences de Pie XII. Vatican, Seconde Guerre mondiale et Shoah*. Bruxelles, 2005.

Michlic-Coren, Joanna. "Battling Against the Odds: Culture, Education and the Jewish Intelligentsia in the Warsaw Ghetto, 1940–1942." *East European Jewish Affairs* 27, no. 2 (1997).

Michman, Dan, ed. *Belgium and the Holocaust: Jews, Belgians, Germans*. Jerusalem, 1998.

———. *Holocaust Historiography: A Jewish Perspective*. London, 2003.

Michman, Joseph. "The Controversial Stand of the Joodse Raad in the Netherlands: Lodewijk E. Visser's Struggle." *Yad Vashem Studies* 10 (1974).

Mierzejewski, Alfred C. "A Public Enterprise in the Service of Mass Murder: The Deutsche Reichsbahn and the Holocaust." *Holocaust and Genocide Studies* 15, no. 1 (2001).

Milfull, John. *Why Germany?: National Socialist Anti-semitism and the European Context*. Providence, 1993.

Milgram, Avraham. "Portugal, the Consuls and the Jewish Refugees, 1938–1941." *Yad Vashem Studies* 37 (1999).

Milton, Sybil. "Deportations." In *1945: The Year of Liberation*, edited by

The United States Holocaust Memorial Museum. Washington, DC, 1995.

Milton, Sybil, and Genya Markon. "Photography and the Holocaust." *History of Photography* 23, no. 4 (1999).

Moeller, Felix. *Der Filmminister: Goebbels und der Film im Dritten Reich*. Berlin, 1998.

Moll, Martin. "Die Abteilung Wehrmachtpropaganda im Oberkommando der Wehrmacht." *Beiträge zur Geschichte des Nationalsozialismus* 17 (2001).

Mommsen, Hans. *Auschwitz, 17. Juli 1942: Der Weg zur europäischen "Endlösung der Judenfrage."* Munich, 2002.

———. "The Realization of the Unthinkable." In *From Weimar to Auschwitz*. Princeton, 1991.

———. "Der Widerstand gegen Hitler und die nationalsozialistische Judenverfolgung." In *Alternative zu Hitler: Studien zur Geschichte des deutschen Widerstandes*. Munich, 2000.

Moore, Bob. "The Dutch Churches, Christians and the Rescue of Jews in the Netherlands." In *Dutch Jews*, edited by Chaya Brasz and Yosef Kaplan. Leiden, 2001.

———. *Victims and Survivors: The Nazi Persecution of the Jews in the Netherlands, 1940–1945*. London, 1997.

Morley, John F. *Vatican Diplomacy and the Jews during the Holocaust, 1939–1943*. New York, 1980.

Moser, Jonny. "Dr. Benjamin Murmelstein, ein ewig Beschuldigter?" In *Theresienstadt in der "Endlösung der Judenfrage"*, edited by Miroslav Kárný, Vojtěch Blodig and Margita Kárná. Prague, 1992.

Müller, Filip. *Eyewitness Auschwitz: Three Years in the Gas Chambers*. Chicago, 1999.

Müller, Ingo. *Hitler's Justice: The Courts of the Third Reich*. Cambridge, 1991.

Müller, Melissa. *Anne Frank: The Biography*. New York, 1998.

Müller, Rolf-Dieter. "From Economic Alliance to a War of Colonial Exploitation." In *Germany and the Second World War*, edited by Horst Boog et al. Oxford, 1998.

———. *Hitlers Ostkrieg und die deutsche Siedlungspolitik: Die Zusammenarbeit von Wehrmacht, Wirtschaft und SS*. Frankfurt am Main, 1991.

München, Stadtarchiv, ed. *"... verzogen, unbekannt wohin": Die erste Deportation von Münchner Juden im November 1941*. Zürich, 2000.

Musial, Bogdan. "Das Schlachtfeld zweier totalitären Systems. Polen unter deutscher und sowjetischer Herrschaft 1939–1941." In *Genesis des Genozids. Polen 1939–1941*, edited by Klaus-Michael Mallmann and Bogdan Musial. Darmstadt, 2004.

Nadelhaft, Erica. "Resistance through Education: Polish Zionist Youth Movements in Warsaw, 1939–1941." *Polin. Studies in Polish Jewry* 9 (1996).

Ne'eman Arad, Gulie. *America, Its Jews, and the Rise of Nazism*. Bloomington, 2000.

Neufeld, Michael J. and Michael Berenbaum, eds. *The Bombing of Auschwitz: Should the Allies Have Attempted It?* New York, 2000.

Niewyk, Donald L., ed. *Fresh Wounds: Early Narratives of Holocaust Survival*. Chapel Hill, 1998.

Noakes, Jeremy. "The Development of Nazi Policy Towards the German-Jewish 'Mischlinge' 1933–1945." In *Holocaust*, vol. 1, edited by David Cesarani. London, 2004.

Ofer, Dalia. *Escaping the Holocaust: Illegal Immigration to the Land of Israel, 1939–1944*. New York, 1990.

Overy, R. J. *War and Economy in the Third Reich*. New York, 1994.

Ozsváth, Zsuzsanna. *In the Footsteps of Orpheus: The Life and Times of Miklós Radnóti*. Bloomington, 2000.

Papen, Patricia von. "Schützenhilfe nationalsozialistischer Judenpolitik: Die Judenforschung des Reichsinstituts für Geschichte des neuen Deutschlands, 1935–1945." In *"Beseitigung des jüdischen Einflusses ...": Antisemitische Forschung, Eliten und Karrieren im Nationalsozialismus*, edited by Fritz Bauer Institut. Frankfurt, 1999.

Passelecq, Georges and Bernard Suchecky. *L'Encyclique cachée de Pie XI: Une occasion manquée de l'Église face à l'antisémitisme*. Paris, 1995.

Paucker, Arnold and Konrad Kwiet. "Jewish Leadership and Jewish Resistance." In *Probing the Depths of German Antisemitism: German Society and the Persecution of the Jews, 1933–1941*, edited by David Bankier. New York, 2000.

Paulsson, Gunnar S. "The Bridge over the Øresund: The Historiography on the Expulsion of the Jews from Nazi-occupied Denmark." In Cesarani, David, ed. *Holocaust: Critical Concepts*. New York, 2004.

Paxton, Robert O. *Vichy France: Old Guard and New Order, 1940–1944*. New York, 2001.

Payne, Stanley G. *A History of Fascism, 1914–1945*. Madison, 1995.

Peled, Yael. *Jewish Cracow, 1939–1943. Resistance, Underground, Struggle. [Krakov ha-Yehudit, 1939–1943. Amidah, Mahteret, Ma'avak]*. Tel Aviv, 1993.

Perlis, Yitzhak. "Final Chapter: Korczak in the Warsaw Ghetto." In Janusz Korczak, *The Ghetto Diary*. New York, 1978.

Perz, Bertrand and Thomas Sandkühler. "Auschwitz und die 'Aktion Reinhard' 1942–1945. Judenmord und Raubpraxis in neuer Sicht." *Zeitschrift für Geschichtswissenschaft* 5, no. 26 (1999).

Peschanski, Denis. "The Statutes on Jews October 3, 1940 and June 2, 1941." *Yad Vashem Studies* 22 (1992).

———. *Vichy, 1940–1944: contrôle et exclusion*. Bruxelles, 1997.

Petropoulos, Jonathan. *Art as Politics in the Third Reich*. Chapel Hill, 1996.

Peukert, Detlev. "The Genesis of the "Final Solution" from the Spirit of Science." In *Reevaluating the Third Reich*, edited by Thomas Childers and Jane Caplan. New York, 1993.

Phayer, Michael. *The Catholic Church and the Holocaust, 1930–1965*. Bloomington, 2000.

Pietrow-Ennker, Bianka. "Die Sowjetunion in der Propaganda des Dritten Reiches: Das Beispiel der Wochenschau." *Militärgeschichtliche Mitteilungen* 46, no. 2 (1989).

Piper, Ernst. "National Socialist Cultural Policy and Its Beneficiaries: The Example of Munich." In *The German Public and the Persecution of the Jews, 1933–1945*, edited by Jörg Wollenberg. Atlantic Highlands, NJ, 1996.

Pohl, Dieter. "Hans Krüger and the Murder of the Jews in the Stanisławów Region (Galicia)." *Yad Vashem Studies* 26 (1998).

———. "The Murder of the Jews in the General Government." In *National Socialist Extermination Policies: Contemporary German Perspectives and Controversies*, edited by Ulrich Herbert. New York, 2000.

———. *Nationalsozialistische Judenverfolgung in Ostgalizien 1941–1944: Organisation und Durchführung eines staatlichen Massenverbrechens*. Munich, 1996.

———. "Schauplatz Ukraine: Der Massenmord an den Juden im Militärveraltungsgebiet und im Reichskommissariat 1941–1943." In *Ausbeutung, Vernichtung, Öffentlichkeit: Neue Studien zur nationalsozial-*

istischen Lagerpolitik, edited by Norbert Frei, Sybille Steinbacher and Bernd C. Wagner. Munich, 2000.

———. *Von der "Judenpolitik" zum Judenmord: Der Distrikt Lublin des Generalgouvernements, 1939–1944*. Frankfurt am Main, 1993.

Pollmann, Viktoria. *Untermieter im Christlichen Haus: Die Kirche und die "jüdische Frage" anhand der Bistumspredigte der Metropolie Krakau 1926–1935*. Wiesbaden, 2001.

Polonsky, Antony. "Beyond Condemnation, Apologetics and Apologies: On the Complexity of Polish Behavior toward the Jews during the Second World War." In *Holocaust: Critical Concepts in Historical Studies, vol. 2*, edited by David Cesarani. New York, 2004.

———. "A Failed Pogrom: The Demonstrations in Lwow, June 1929." In *The Jews of Poland Between Two World Wars*, edited by Yisrael Gutman, Ezra Mendelsohn, Jehuda Reinharz, and Chone Shmeruk. Hanover, NH, 1989.

Polonsky, Antony, and Norman Davies, eds. *Jews in Eastern Poland and the USSR, 1939–46*. New York, 1991.

Polonsky, Antony, and Joanna B. Michlic, eds. *The Neighbors Respond: The Controversy over the Jedwabne Massacre in Poland*. Princeton, 2004.

Porat, Dina. *Beyond the Reaches of Our Souls: The Life and Times of Abba Kovner*. Tel Aviv, 2000.

———. *The Blue and the Yellow Stars of David: The Zionist Leadership in Palestine and the Holocaust, 1939–1945*. Cambridge, MA, 1990.

———. "The Legend of the Struggle of the Jews from the Third Reich in the Ninth Fort near Kovno, 1941–1942." *Tel Aviver Jahrbuch für deutsche Geschichte* 20 (1991).

———. "The Transnistria Affair and the Rescue Policy of the Zionist Leadership in Palestine, 1942–1943." In *The Nazi Holocaust: Historical Articles on the Destruction of European Jews*, edited by Michael Marrus. Westport, 1989.

———. "The Vilna Proclamation of January 1, 1942 in Historical Perspective." *Yad Vashem Studies* 24 (1996).

———. "Zionist Pioneering Youth Movements in Poland and Their Attitude to Erets Israel during the Holocaust." *Polin. Studies in Polish Jewry* 9 (1996).

Porter, Brian. "Making a Space for Antisemitism: The Catholic Hierarchy and the Jews in the Early Twentieth Century." *Polin: Studies in Polish Jewry* 16 (2003).

Potthast, Jan Björn. *Das Jüdische Zentralmuseum der SS in Prag. Gegnerforschung und Völkermord im Nationalsozialismus*. Frankfurt, 2002.

Poznanski, Renée. "Jews and non-Jews in France during World War II: A Daily Life Perspective." In *Lessons and Legacies V: The Holocaust and Justice*, edited by Ronald M. Smelser. Evanston, IL, 2002.

———. *Jews in France during World War II*. Waltham, MA, 2001.

———. "The Jews of France and the Statutes on Jews, 1940–1941." *Yad Vashem Studies* 22 (1992).

Presser, Jacob. *Ashes in the Wind: The Destruction of Dutch Jewry*. Detroit, 1988.

———. "Introduction." In Philip Mechanicus, *Waiting for Death: A Diary*. London, 1968.

Przyrembel, Alexandra and Jörg Schönert, eds. *Jud Süss. Hofjude, literarische Figur, antisemitisches Zerrbild*. Frankfurt am Main, 2006.

Raim, Edit. "Zwangsarbeit und Vernichtung im letzten Kriegsjahr." In *Theresienstadt in der "Endlösung der Judenfrage"*, edited by Miroslav Kárný, Vojtěch Blodig, and Margita Kárná. Prague, 1992.

Rajsfus, Maurice. *Drancy: Un camp de concentration très ordinaire, 1941–1944*. Paris, 1996.

Raphael, Lutz. "Die Pariser Universität unter deutscher Besatzung 1940–1944." In *Universitäten im nationalsozialistisch beherrschten Europa*, edited by Dieter Langewiesche. Göttingen, 1997.

Rautkallio, Hannu. *Finland and the Holocaust: The Rescue of Finland's Jews*. New York, 1987.

Redlich, Shimon. "Metropolitan Andrei Sheptys'kyi, Ukrainians and Jews During and After the Holocaust." *Holocaust and Genocide Studies* 5 (1990).

———. *Propaganda and Nationalism in Wartime Russia: The Jewish Antifascist Committee in the USSR, 1941–1948*. Boulder, CO, 1982.

———. *Together and Apart in Brzezany: Poles, Jews, and Ukrainians, 1919–1945*. Bloomington, 2002.

Reich-Ranicki, Marcel. *The Author of Himself: The Life of Marcel Reich-Ranicki*. London, 2001.

Rémond, René. *Le "Fichier juif."* Paris, 1996.

Rentschler, Eric. *The Ministry of Illusion: Nazi Cinema and Its Afterlife.* Cambridge, MA 1996.

Reymes, Nicolas. "Le pillage des bibliothèques appartenant à des juifs pendant l'Occupation." *Revue d'Histoire de la Shoah. Le monde juif* 168 (2000).

Riegner, Gerhart M. *Ne Jamais Désesperer: Soixante années au service du peuple juif et des droits de l'homme.* Paris, 1998.

Rigg, Bryan Mark. *Hitler's Jewish Soldiers: The Untold Story of Nazi Racial Laws and Men of Jewish Descent in the German Military.* Lawrence, 2002.

———. *Rescued from the Reich: How One of Hitler's Soldiers Saved the Lubavitcher Rebbe.* New Haven, 2004.

Rogers, Barbara. "British Intelligence and the Holocaust." *The Journal of Holocaust Education* 8, no. 1 (1999).

Röhm, Eberhard and Jörg Thierfelder. *Juden, Christen, Deutsche, 1933–1945.* 3 vols. Stuttgart, 1990.

Rose, Norman. *Chaim Weizmann: A Biography.* New York, 1986.

Roseman, Mark. *A Past in Hiding: Memory and Survival in Nazi Germany.* New York, 2001.

———. *The Villa, the Lake, the Meeting: Wannsee and the Final Solution.* London; New York, 2002.

Rosenkötter, Bernhard. *Treuhandpolitik. Die "Haupttreuhandstelle Ost" und der Raub polnischen Vermögens, 1939–1945.* Essen, 2003.

Roskies, David G. "Landkentenish: Yiddish Belles Lettres in the Warsaw Ghetto." In *Holocaust Chronicles: Individualizing the Holocaust through Diaries and Other Contemporaneous Personal Accounts*, edited by Robert Moses Shapiro. Hoboken, NJ, 1999.

———. *The Literature of Destruction: Jewish Responses to Catastrophe.* Philadelphia, 1988.

Rossino, Alexander B. "Destructive Impulses: German Soldiers and the Conquest of Poland." *Holocaust and Genocide Studies* 7, no. 3 (1997).

———. *Hitler Strikes Poland: Blitzkrieg, Ideology and Atrocity.* Lawrence, KS, 2003.

———. "Polish 'Neighbors' and German Invaders: Anti-Jewish Violence in the Bialystok District during the Opening Weeks of Operation Barbarossa." *Polin: Studies in Polish Jewry* 16 (2003).

Rössler, Mechtild, Sabine Schleiermacher and Cordula Tollmien, eds. *Der "Generalplan Ost": Hauptlinien der nationalsozialistischen Planungs- und Vernichtungspolitik*. Berlin, 1993.

Rother, Bernd. "Franco und die deutsche Judenverfolgung." *Vierteljahrshefte für Zeitgeschichte* 46, no. 2 (1998).

———. *Spanien und der Holocaust*. Tübingen, 2001.

Rothkirchen, Livia. "The 'Final Solution' in Its Last Stages." In *The Nazi Holocaust: Historical Articles on the Destruction of European Jews*, edited by Michael Marrus. Westport, CT, 1989.

———. "The Protectorate Government and the "Jewish Question," 1939–1941." *Yad Vashem Studies* 27 (1999).

———. "The Situation of the Jews in Slovakia between 1939 and 1945." *Jahrbuch für Antisemitismusforschung* 7 (1998).

Rozen, Minna. "Jews and Greeks Remember Their Past: The Political Career of Tsevi Koretz (1933–43)." *Jewish Social Studies* 12, no. 1 (2005).

———. *The Last Ottoman Century and Beyond: The Jews in Turkey and the Balkans 1808–1945*. Ramat-Aviv, 2002.

Rozett, Robert. "Jewish and Hungarian Armed Resistance in Hungary." *Yad Vashem Studies* 19 (1988).

Rubenstein, Joshua. *Tangled Loyalties: The Life and Times of Ilya Ehrenburg*. New York, 1996.

Rückerl, Adalbert, ed. *NS-Prozesse. Nach 25 Jahren Strafverfolgung: Möglichkeiten, Grenzen, Ergebnisse*. Karlsruhe, 1971.

Rupnow, Dirk. " 'Ihr müsst sein, auch wenn ihr nicht mehr seid': The Jewish Central Museum in Prague and Historical Memory in the Third Reich." *Holocaust and Genocide Studies* 16, no. 1 (2002).

Saerens, Lieven. "Antwerp's Attitude Toward the Jews from 1918 to 1940 and Its Implications for the Period of Occupation." In *Belgium and the Holocaust: Jews, Belgians, Germans*, edited by Dan Michman. Jerusalem, 1998.

Safrian, Hans. *Die Eichmann-Männer*. Vienna, 1992.

Sakowska, Ruta. *Menschen im Ghetto: die jüdische Bevölkerung im besetzten Warschau 1939–1943*. Osnabrück, 1999.

———. "Two Forms of Resistance in the Warsaw Ghetto: Two Functions of the Ringelblum Archives." *Yad Vashem Studies* 21 (1991).

Salemink, Theo. "Strangers in a Strange Country: Catholic Views of

Jews in the Netherlands, 1918–1945." In *Dutch Jews As Perceived by Themselves and by Others*, edited by Chaya Brasz and Yosef Kaplan. Leiden, 2001.

Sandkühler, Thomas. "Anti-Jewish Policy and the Murder of the Jews in the District of Galicia 1941/1942." In *National Socialist Extermination Policies: Contemporary German Perspectives and Controversies*, edited by Ulrich Herbert. New York, 2000.

———. *"Endlösung" in Galizien. Der Judenmord in Ostpolen und die Rettungsinitiativen von Berthold Beitz, 1941–1944*. Bonn, 1996.

Sattler, Friederike. "Der Handelstrust West in den Niederlanden." In *Die Expansion der Dresdner Bank in Europa*, edited by Harald Wixforth. Munich, 2006.

Sauer, Paul. "Otto Hirsch (1885–1941): Director of the Reichsvertretung." In *Year Book of the Leo Baeck Institute*, 1987.

Scheffler, Wolfgang. "The Forgotten Part of the 'Final Solution': The Liquidation of the Ghettos." In *Simon Wiesenthal Center Annual 2*. Chappaqua, 1985.

Schiefelbein, Dieter. "Das Institut zur Erforschung der Judenfrage Frankfurt am Main." In *"Beseitigung des jüdischen Einflusses . . . ": Antisemitische Forschung, Eliten und Karrieren im Nationalsozialismus*, edited by Fritz Bauer Institut. Frankfurt, 1999.

Scholl, Inge. *The White Rose: Munich, 1942–1943*. Middletown, CT, 1983.

Schölder, Klaus. *A Requiem for Hitler and Other New Perspectives on the German Church Struggle*. London, 1989.

Schöttler, Peter, ed. *Geschichtsschreibung als Legitimationswissenschaft 1918–1945*. Frankfurt, 1997.

Schulte, Erik. *Zwangsarbeit und Vernichtung: Das Wirtschaftsimperium Oswald Pohls und das SS-Wirtschafts- und Verwaltungshauptamt*. Paderborn, 2001.

Schulze, Winfried and Otto Gerhard Oexle. *Deutsche Historiker im Nationalsozialismus*. Frankfurt, 1999.

Schwarberg, Günther. *The Murders at Bullenhuser Damm: The SS Doctor and the Children*. Bloomington, 1984.

Schwarz, Gudrun. *Eine Frau an seiner Seite: Ehefrauen in der "SS-Sippengemeinschaft."* Frankfurt, 1997.

Schwarzfuchs, Simon. *Aux Prises avec Vichy: Histoire politique des Juifs de France, 1940–1944*. Paris, 1998.

Segev, Tom. *The Seventh Million: The Israelis and the Holocaust*. New York, 1993.

Sellier, André. *The History of the Dora Camp*. Chicago, 2003.

Sereny, Gitta. *Into that Darkness: From Mercy Killing to Mass Murder*. London, 1974.

Shapiro, Paul A. "The Jews of Chisinău (Kishinev): Romanian Reoccupation, Ghettoisation, Deportation." In *The Destruction of Romanian and Ukrainian Jews during the Antonescu Era*, edited by Randolph L. Braham. Boulder, CO, 1997.

Shapiro, Robert Moses. "Diaries and Memoirs from the Lodz Ghetto in Yiddish and Hebrew." In *Holocaust Chronicles: Individualizing the Holocaust through Diaries and Other Contemporaneous Personal Accounts*, edited by Robert Moses Shapiro. Hoboken, NJ, 1999.

Shelach, Menachem. "The Catholic Church in Croatia, the Vatican and the Murder of the Croatian Jews." *Holocaust and Genocide Studies* 4, no. 3 (1989).

———. "Jasenovac." In *Encyclopedia of the Holocaust*, edited by Yisrael Gutman. New York, 1990.

———. "Sajmiste—An Extermination Camp in Serbia." *Holocaust and Genocide Studies* 2, no. 2 (1987).

———, ed. *Yugoslavia*. Jerusalem, 1990.

Sijes, B. A. "The Position of the Jews during the German Occupation of the Netherlands: Some Observations." In *The Nazi Holocaust: Historical Articles on the Destruction of European Jews*, edited by Michael Robert Marrus. Westport, 1989.

Singer, Claude. *Le Juif Süss et la propagande Nazie: L'Histoire confisquée*. Paris, 2003.

———. *Vichy, l'université et les juifs: Les silences et la mémoire*. Paris, 1992.

Slezkine, Yuri. *The Jewish Century*. Princeton, 2004.

Smelser, Ronald M., ed. *Lessons and Legacies V: The Holocaust and Justice*. Evanston, IL, 2002.

Smelser, Ronald M. *Robert Ley: Hitler's Labor Front Leader*. New York, 1988.

Smelser, Ronald M., and Enrico Syring. *Die SS: Elite unter dem Totenkopf: 30 Lebensläufe*. Paderborn, 2000.

Smolar, Hersh. *The Minsk Ghetto: Soviet-Jewish Partisans Against the Nazis*. New York, 1989.

Sofsky, Wolfgang. *The Order of Terror: The Concentration Camp*. Princeton, NJ, 1997.

Spector, Shmuel. "Aktion 1005—Effacing the Murder of Millions." *Holocaust and Genocide Studies* 5, no. 2 (1990).

———. *The Holocaust of Volhynian Jews 1941–1944*. Jerusalem, 1990.

Speer, Albert. *Inside the Third Reich: Memoirs*. New York, 1970.

Stargardt, Nicholas. *Witnesses of War: Children's Lives under the Nazis*. London, 2005.

Steinbacher, Sybille. *Auschwitz: A History*. London, 2005.

———. "In the Shadow of Auschwitz: The Murder of the Jews of East Upper Silesia." In *The Holocaust,* vol. 2, edited by David Cesarani. New York, 2004.

———. *"Musterstadt" Auschwitz: Germanisierungspolitik und Judenmord in Ostoberschlesien*. Munich, 2000.

Steinberg, Jonathan. *All or Nothing: The Axis and the Holocaust, 1941–1943*. London, 1990.

Steinberg, Lucien and Jean Marie Fitère. *Les Allemands en France: 1940–1944*. Paris, 1980.

Steinberg, Maxime. "The *Judenpolitik* in Belgium within the West European Context: Comparative Observations." In *Belgium and the Holocaust: Jews, Belgians, Germans*, edited by Dan Michman. Jerusalem, 1998.

———. *La Persecution des Juifs en Belgique (1940–1945)*. Brussels, 2004.

Steinberg, Paul. *Speak You Also: A Survivor's Reckoning*. New York, 2000.

Steinert, Marlis G. *Hitler's War and the Germans: Public Mood and Attitude during the Second World War*. Athens, 1977.

Steinlauf, Michael. *Bondage to the Dead: Poland and the Memory of the Holocaust*. Syracuse, NY, 1997.

Sternhell, Zeev. *La Droite Révolutionnaire: 1885–1914: Les Origines françaises du fascisme*. Paris, 1978.

———. *Neither Right nor Left: Fascist Ideology in France*. Berkeley, 1986.

Stille, Alexander. *Benevolence and Betrayal: Five Italian Jewish Families under Fascism*. New York, 1993.

Streim, Alfred. "Zur Eröffnung des allgemeinen Judenvernichtungsbefehls gegenüber den Einsatzgruppen." In *Der Mord an den Juden im Zweiten Weltkrieg: Entschlussbildung und Verwirklichung*, edited by Eberhard Jäckel and Jürgen Rohwer. Stuttgart, 1985.

Streit, Christian. *Keine Kameraden. Die Wehrmacht und die Sowjetischen Kriegsfangenen 1941–1945*. Stuttgart, 1978.

Szobar, Patricia. "Telling Sexual Stories in the Nazi Courts of Law: Race Defilement in Germany, 1933–1945." *Journal of the History of Sexuality* 11, no. 1–2 (2002).

Szpilman, Władysław. *The Pianist: The Extraordinary True Story of One Man's Survival in Warsaw, 1939–1945*. New York, 1999.

Tec, Nechama. *Defiance: The Bielski Partisans*. New York, 1993.

Tec, Nechama, and Daniel Weiss. "The Heroine of Minsk: Eight Photographs of an Execution." *History of Photography*. Winter. (1999).

Tegel, Susan. " 'The Demonic Effect': Veit Harlan's Use of Jewish Extras in *Jud Süss." Holocaust and Genocide Studies* 14, no. 2 (2000).

———. "The Politics of Censorship: Britain's 'Jew Süss' (1934) in London, New York and Vienna." *Historical Journal of Film, Radio and Television* 15, no. 2 (1995).

Teveth, Shabtai. *Ben-Gurion and the Holocaust*. New York, 1996.

Tilkovszky, Loránd. "The Late Interwar Years and World War II." In *A History of Hungary*, edited by Peter F. Sugar et al. Bloomington, 1994.

Tönsmeyer, Tatjana. *Das Dritte Reich und die Slowakei 1939–1945: Politischer Alltag zwischen Kooperation und Eigensinn*. Paderborn, 2003.

Trunk, Isaiah. *Jewish Responses to Nazi Persecution: Collective and Individual Behavior in extremis*. New York, 1979.

———. *Judenrat: The Jewish Councils in Eastern Europe under Nazi Occupation*. New York, 1972.

Tucker, Robert C. *Stalin in Power: The Revolution from Above, 1928–1941*. New York, 1992.

Ultee, Wout, Frank von Tubergen, and Ruud Luigkx. "The Unwholesome Theme of Suicide: Forgotten Statistics of Attempted Suicides in Amsterdam and Jewish Suicides in the Netherlands for 1936–1943." In *Dutch Jews As Perceived by Themselves and by Others,* edited by Chaya Brasz and Yosef Kaplan. Leiden, 2001.

Ungváry, Krisztián. *The Siege of Budapest: One Hundred Days in World War II*. New Haven, 2005.

Uziel, Daniel. "Wehrmacht Propaganda Troops and the Jews." *Yad Vashem Studies* 29 (2001).

Verdès-Leroux, Jeannine. *Refus et violences: politique et littérature à l'extrême droite des années trente aux retombées de la Libération*. Paris, 1996.

Verheyde, Philippe. "L'aryanisation economique: Le cas des grandes entreprises." *Revue d'Histoire de la Shoah. Le monde juif* 168 (2000).

Vital, David. *A People Apart: A Political History of the Jews in Europe, 1789–1939*. Oxford, 2001.

Vitoux, Frédéric. *Céline: A Biography*. New York, 1992.

Volovici, Leon. *Nationalist Ideology and Antisemitism: The Case of Romanian Intellectuals in the 1930s*. Oxford, 1991.

Vrba, Rudolf. "Die missachtete Warnung." *Vierteljahrshefte für Zeitgeschichte* 1 (1996).

Wapinski, Roman. "The Endecja and the Jewish Question." *Polin. Studies in Polish Jewry* 12 (1999).

Wasser, Bruno. "Die 'Germanisierung' im Distrikt Lublin als Generalprobe und erste Realisierungsphase des 'Generalplans Ost.'" *Der "Generalplan Ost": Hauptlinien der nationalsozialistischen Planungs- und Vernichtungspolitik.* Berlin, 1993.

Wasserstein, Bernard. *Britain and the Jews of Europe, 1939–1945*. London, 1979.

———. "Polish Influences on British Policy Regarding Jewish Rescue Efforts in Poland 1939–1945." *Polin. Studies in Polish Jewry* 11 (1998).

Weber, Eugen. *Action Française: Royalism and Reaction in Twentieth Century France*. Stanford, 1962.

Weinberg, Gerhard L. *A World at Arms: A Global History of World War II*. Cambridge, UK, 1994.

Weiner, Amir. *Making Sense of War: The Second World War and the Fate of the Bolshevik Revolution*. Princeton, 2002.

Weinreich, Max. *Hitler's Professors: The Part of Scholarship in Germany's Crimes against the Jewish People*. New York, 1946.

Weiss, Aharon. "Jewish Leadership in Occupied Poland—Postures and Attitudes." *Yad Vashem Studies* 12 (1977).

———. "Zionist Youth Movements in Poland during the German Occupation." In *Zionist Youth Movements during the Shoah*, edited by Asher Cohen and Yehoyakim Cochavi. New York, 1995.

Weiss, Yfaat. "The 'Emigration Effort' or 'Repatriation.'" In *Probing the Depths of German Antisemitism: German Society and the Persecution of the Jews, 1933–1941*, edited by David Bankier. New York, 2000.

Wellers, Georges. *De Drancy à Auschwitz*. Paris, 1946.

White, Elizabeth B. "Majdanek: Cornerstone of Himmler's SS Empire in the East." *Simon Wiesenthal Center Yearbook* 7 (1990).

Wierzbicki, Marek. "Die polnisch-jüdischen Beziehungen unter sowjetischer Herrschaft. Zur Wahrnehmung gesellschaftlicher Realität im Westlichen Weissrussland 1939–1941." In *Genesis des Genozids. Polen 1939–1941*, edited by Klaus-Michael Mallmann and Bogdan Musial. Darmstadt, 2004.

Wijngaert, Mark van den. "The Belgian Catholics and the Jews During the German Occupation, 1940–1944." In *Belgium and the Holocaust: Jews, Belgians, Germans*, edited by Dan Michman. Jerusalem, 1998.

Wildt, Michael. *Generation des Unbedingten: Das Führungskorps des Reichssicherheitshauptamtes*. Hamburg, 2002.

Wistrich, Robert S. "The Vatican Documents and the Holocaust: A Personal Report." *Polin. Studies in Polish Jewry* 15 (2002).

Witte, Peter. "Two Decisions Concerning the "Final Solution to the Jewish Question": Deportations to Lodz and Mass Murder in Chelmno." *Holocaust and Genocide Studies* 9, no. 3 (1995).

Wollenberg, Jörg, ed. *The German Public and the Persecution of the Jews, 1933–1945*. Atlantic Highlands, NJ, 1996.

Wyman, David S. *The Abandonment of the Jews: America and the Holocaust, 1941–1945*. New York, 1998.

Wyman, David S., and Rafael Medoff. *A Race Against Death: Peter Bergson, America, and the Holocaust*. New York, 2002.

Yahil, Leni. *The Holocaust: The Fate of European Jewry, 1932–1945*. New York, 1990.

———. "Raoul Wallenberg: His Mission and his Activities in Hungary." *Yad Vashem Studies* 15 (1983).

———. *The Rescue of Danish Jewry: Test of a Democracy*. Philadelphia, 1969.

Zeugin, Bettina and Thomas Sandkühler. *Die Schweiz und die deutschen Lösegelderpressungen in den besetzten Niederlanden: Vermögensentziehung, Freikauf, Austausch 1940–1945: Beitrag zur Forschung*. Edited by

Independent Commission of Experts Switzerland–World War II. Zurich, 2001.

Zuccotti, Susan. "The Italian Racial Laws, 1938–1943: A Reevaluation." In *Studies in Contemporary Jewry, vol. XIII: The Fate of European Jews, 1939–1945, Continuity or Contingency?*, edited by Jonathan Frankel. Oxford, 1997.

———. *Under His Very Windows: The Vatican and the Holocaust in Italy.* New Haven, 2000.

Zuckerman, Yitzhak. *A Surplus of Memory: Chronicle of the Warsaw Ghetto Uprising*. Berkeley, 1993.

Zuroff, Efraim. "Rescue Via the Far East: The Attempt to Save Polish Rabbis and Yeshivah Students, 1939–1941." *Simon Wiesenthal Center Annual* 1 (1984).

Index